A CONCISE HISTORY

OF THE

COMMON LAW

ENGLAND: BUTTERWORTH & CO. (PUBLISHERS) LTD.
                 LONDON: 88 Kingsway, W.C.2
AUSTRALIA: BUTTERWORTH & CO. (AUSTRALIA) LTD.
                 SYDNEY: 20 Loftus Street
                 MELBOURNE: 473 Bourke Street
                 BRISBANE: 240 Queen Street
CANADA: BUTTERWORTH & CO. (CANADA) LTD.
                 TORONTO: 1367 Danforth Avenue, 6
NEW ZEALAND: BUTTERWORTH & CO. (NEW ZEALAND) LTD.
                 WELLINGTON: 49/51 Ballance Street
                 AUCKLAND: 35 High Street
SOUTH AFRICA: BUTTERWORTH & CO. (SOUTH AFRICA) LTD.
                 DURBAN: 33/35 Beach Grove
U.S.A.:   BUTTERWORTH INC.
                 WASHINGTON, D.C.: 7300 Pearl Street, 20014

A CONCISE HISTORY

OF THE

COMMON LAW

By

THEODORE F. T. PLUCKNETT

Fellow of the British Academy

Professor of Legal History in the University of London

FIFTH EDITION

LONDON

BUTTERWORTH & CO. (PUBLISHERS) LTD.

1956

1929
First Edition
Lawyers' Cooperative Publishing Company
Rochester, New York, U.S.A.

1936
Second Edition
Lawyers' Cooperative Publishing Company
Rochester, New York, U.S.A.
Butterworth & Co. (Publishers) Ltd.
London

1940
Third Edition
Butterworth & Co. (Publishers) Ltd.
London

1948
Fourth Edition
Butterworth & Co. (Publishers) Ltd.
London

1956
Fifth Edition

Butterworth & Co. (Publishers) Ltd.
London
Little, Brown and Company
Boston, Massachusetts, U.S.A.

MADE AND PRINTED IN GREAT BRITAIN
BY THE CHAPEL RIVER PRESS,
ANDOVER, HANTS

PREFACE TO THE FIFTH EDITION

THE decision of the publishers to reprint this work in a larger type will have made it easier for the reader to use it, I hope; it has also made it possible to effect a good deal of revision. No new subjects have been added, however, for the object of the work has always been to treat only a limited number of topics, but with sufficient detail to make them intelligible. This has made it necessary to place the history of English law in its setting of canon, civil, and general European law in order to show the intellectual influences which have moulded our own system. Comparison with other legal systems is therefore essential to the method here pursued. The point of view adopted throughout is that of a historian who surveys the law from the outside, as it were, and contributes both comparison and criticism to the historical study contained in the following pages.

Besides a few additions (which are distributed fairly evenly through the book), there have been numerous revisions, occasionally rearrangements (especially in dealing with the jury), and sometimes a more ample explanation of difficult points.

The general plan of the work remains unchanged. The first half of the book is an historical introduction to the study of law, and stress has therefore been placed upon those conditions in political, economic, social and religious thought which have contributed to its formation. As the readers for whom this part is designed will generally be first-year undergraduates, it seemed prudent to assume that their previous knowledge of history would be by no means extensive; hence the distinctly elementary note of the first eighty pages.

The courts, the profession, and such general factors in legal development as legislation and the principle of precedent, are subjects which deserve close attention at the introductory stage, for they are the foundation of much that follows. It would, no doubt, be possible to state the essential facts in a very condensed form by using an encyclopaedic style, but such a treatment is not very helpful to beginners. Enough illustrative material has therefore been used to give, I hope, some of the spirit and atmosphere in which the common law system grew up.

The place of legal history in the law school curriculum is still a matter of debate. It may be remarked, however, that if law is a difficult study to the beginner, the history of the law, with its different outlook and unfamiliar concepts, is apt to be more difficult still. This book has therefore been planned on the principle that the first part, " A General Survey of Legal History," is as much legal history as a first-year student can be expected to master, in view of the fact that he is embarking upon a subject for which his earlier studies have given him little preparation.

At a later stage he can embark upon legal history in more detail, either as a separate subject, or as part of the study of substantive law.

The second half of the book, therefore, consists of introductions to the history of a few of the main divisions of the law. Other topics, indeed, might have been added, but only at the risk of defeating the object of the book, which is to convey a sense of historical development, and not to serve as a work of reference. The mere recital of historical data is not enough, and so a limited field, treated with careful exposition, seemed more likely to interest those who are just embarking upon their legal education, than a more comprehensive (and therefore less intimate) treatment of a larger field. The increase of size in this edition is very slight, and is attributable principally to the amplification of expository passages, and not to the introduction of new subjects for treatment.

Everyone who is interested in the history of the law is under an immense debt to the writings of Pollock, Maitland and Holdsworth in England, and of Holmes, Thayer and Ames in America. Were it not for the thirteen masterly volumes of the Vinerian Professor, neither this nor any other short history of English law could be written with any degree of confidence. The stately series of the Selden Society's publications has provided a rich harvest of original materials which adds immensely to the vividness of legal history whenever teachers and students make use of them. The even longer series of many of our county historical societies afford rich illustration of our legal history, and the grateful thanks of legal historians are due to these bodies, and especially to the enlightened bands of subscribers who make it possible to continue the work of publication, even in these inauspicious days. The footnotes to this history have been designed to place illustrative cases and statutes easily within the reach of readers. The Council of the Selden Society have kindly allowed me to reproduce a lengthy extract from one of their publications, and I hope that readers will be tempted to explore these and the other sources cited.

It should be explained that the text and pagination of this fifth edition correspond entirely, both in the English issue by Messrs. Butterworth, and in the American issue by Messrs. Little, Brown and Company.

My thanks are due once again to many friends who have discussed legal history and its teaching with me in a very helpful way, and to many English and American teachers who used the earlier editions and were kind enough to send me valuable suggestions. I am once again particularly grateful to Professor H. A. Hollond of Cambridge and Professor A. D. Hargreaves of Birmingham for their learned criticisms and interest, to Mr. K. Howard Drake for the Index, and to Messrs. Butterworth for their constant and sympathetic care in the production of this volume, and in the preparation of the Tables.

T. F. T. P.

LONDON SCHOOL OF ECONOMICS,
    July, 1956.

CONTENTS

BOOK ONE

A GENERAL SURVEY OF LEGAL HISTORY

PART I

THE CROWN AND THE STATE

PART II

THE COURTS AND THE PROFESSION

PART III

SOME FACTORS IN LEGAL HISTORY

BOOK TWO

SPECIAL PART

PART I

PROCEDURE

PART II

CRIME AND TORT

PART III

REAL PROPERTY

PART IV

CONTRACT

PART V

EQUITY

PART VI

SUCCESSION

INDEX

TABLE OF MEDIAEVAL CASES

TABLE OF MODERN CASES

N.B. The report references, which appeared in this table in earlier editions, will be found incorporated in the footnotes in the text.

TABLE OF LAWS AND STATUTES

BOOK ONE

A GENERAL SURVEY OF
LEGAL HISTORY

PART 1

THE CROWN AND THE STATE

SUMMARY

A GENERAL SURVEY OF LEGAL HISTORY

Legal history is a story which cannot be begun at the beginning. However remote the date at which we start, it will always be necessary to admit that much of the still remoter past that lies behind it will have to be considered as directly bearing upon the later history. Moreover, the further back we push our investigations, the scantier become our sources, and the more controversial and doubtful their interpretation. The comparatively short period of recorded history based upon documents soon leads us back to the immensely long ages of which we know nothing save through the methods of the archaeologist. Into this enormous field of pre-history we shall not venture, although from time to time it will be necessary to refer to it when the problems of history raise immediate questions of pre-history. Indeed, even the relatively brief span of written history is too complex and too diverse for treatment here. The age which saw the first beginnings of English history, witnessed also the decline of Roman law which had run a course of a thousand years, making priceless contributions to civilisation. But behind the Roman system were others still more ancient—Greek, Semitic, Assyrian, Egyptian—all with long histories of absorbing interest.[1] These remoter systems are all being studied with great skill by many modern experts, and the list of them is still growing. Recent researches, for example, have brought to light much material on the law of the Hittites, who were little more than a name to us a generation ago.

THE ROMAN EMPIRE

For the purposes of this concise history we can begin with the advent of Christianity. Itself the culmination of several centuries of religious and ethical thinking in Judaea, it entered a world which was dominated by legal and political ideas which were in turn the result of centuries of political and juristic experience. Rome had reached the peak of its greatness. An Empire which spread over the entire civilised world, and which owed so much to the ideas of law and of government, seemed to be almost a revelation of the divine mission of the State. Government was the sacred destiny of the Roman people. To others might be left the vocations of art, of literature, of science; the Roman's part was to rule the nations, to impose the Roman peace and respect for law upon the

---

[1] See the remarkable *Panorama of the World's Legal Systems*, by Dean Wigmore where brief descriptions of most of them are given.

3

barbarian, sparing the submissive with statesmanlike tolerance, and crushing resistance with ruthless force. This immense Empire had been acquired through the energy of Roman armies, and preserved by the diligence of Roman administrators, but the time came when both services betrayed their master. Generals indulged in the game of making and deposing emperors; provincial governors exploited their subjects, a hierarchy of functionaries grew up such as China possessed, and as part of the system of taxation imposed upon the people, a similar system of caste from which escape was almost impossible. In the meantime, a steady infiltration of barbarian blood changed the character, the culture, and finally the language of the ruling classes.[1] By slow and almost imperceptible degrees the ties that bound together the Roman Empire dissolved, and the mysterious and complicated fall of Rome became complete.

" The two greatest problems in history, how to account for the rise of Rome, and how to account for her fall, never have been, perhaps never will be, thoroughly solved."[2]

THE RISE OF CHRISTIANITY

While imperial Rome was slowly declining, Christianity was entering on a period of remarkable growth. At first it was hardly noticed among the numerous new cults which were fashionable importations from the Near East, some of which were extremely popular. After being ignored, it was later persecuted, then under the great Constantine it was at last tolerated (324). So far, the established " Hellenistic " religion had been considered as an official department, and its priests as civil servants. Attempts had been made to incorporate with it the religions of Isis, Mithras, Christ, and others, on a similar footing, combining all the known gods in one vast polytheism, whose cult was to be maintained and controlled by the State. It was soon evident, however, that Christianity would not accept this inferior position. Although some things were Caesar's, others were God's, and from this fundamental conflict arose the problem of Church and State, which has lasted from Constantine's day to our own. The controversy took a variety of forms in the course of the succeeding sixteen centuries. Stated in its broadest and most general terms, it means that many earnest thinkers find it impossible to accept the State as the highest form of human society, and that they recognise some situations in which they would feel bound to obey some other duty than that imposed by the State. On the continent it lay at the root of the long conflict between the Empire and the papacy; in England it took such varied forms as the conflict with Thomas Becket, the discussion in Bracton as to the real

[1] For an admirable short account, see Sir Paul Vinogradoff in chapter xix of the *Cambridge Mediaeval History*, vol. i.

[2] J. S. Reid in *Cambridge Mediaeval History*, i. 24 ff., 54.

position of the King (who is subject, he says, to God " and the law "), the Puritan revolution—and may even be traced in the American constitutions, for the modern attempts to curb the power of the State by means of constitutional limitations are the result of the same distrust of the State as was expressed in former days in the conflict between religion and the secular power. It was also during the reign of Constantine that the great Council of Nicaea was held (325), attended by almost three hundred bishops from all parts of the world. Besides settling many fundamental matters of doctrine, this council gave an imposing demonstration of the world-wide organisation of the Church, and from this point onwards that organisation grew increasingly effective, and the Church became more and more a world power. As a result, the Empire had to admit the presence first of a potent ally, and soon of a vigorous rival.

" The Nicene canons are the earliest code that can be called canon law of the whole Church, and at least in the West they enjoyed something like the same finality in the realm of discipline that the Nicene Creed enjoyed in the realm of doctrine."[1]

Indeed, while the organisation of the Empire was slowly breaking down, that of the Church was steadily growing, with the result that the Church soon offered a career comparable to, if not better than, that afforded by the State to men of ability who felt called to public life.[2] Some specialised in the study of theology; others took up the work of creating the great body of canon law which for a long time was to perpetuate the old Roman ideal of universal law. With all this, the growth of the power of the episcopate, and particularly of the papacy, was to give a new aspect to the ancient city of Rome, and slowly, but certainly, the Empire ruled from Rome was being replaced for many purposes by Christendom ruled by the papacy.

[1] C. H. Turner in *Cambridge Mediaeval History*, i. 179.
[2] Pollock and Maitland, *History of English Law*, i. 4.

THE ANGLO-SAXON PERIOD: RACES AND RELIGION

THE COMING OF THE ROMANS

While this was happening at the heart of the Empire, many of the outskirts were witnessing a process such as went on in Britain. The conquest of Gaul inevitably drew the attention of Roman generals to Britain, whose population had intimate ties of race, language and sympathy with the Gauls. At times the Britons seem to have sent assistance to their Celtic kinsmen on the continent, and so attracted the wrath of Rome. Finally in A.D. 43 the systematic conquest of the island was begun by Agricola, and for the next three and a half centuries Britain was under Roman rule. The character of this occupation cannot be better described than in the words of Haverfield, the scholar who has shed most light on this difficult and obscure period:

> " From the standpoint alike of the ancient Roman statesman and of the modern Roman historian, the military posts and their garrisons formed the dominant element in Britain. But they have left little permanent mark on the civilisation and character of the island. The ruins of their forts and fortresses are on our hill-sides. But, Roman as they were, their garrisons did little to spread Roman culture here. Outside their walls, each of them had a small or large settlement of womenfolk, traders, perhaps also of time-expired soldiers wishful to end their days where they had served. But hardly any of these settlements grew up into towns. York may form an exception. . . . Nor do the garrisons appear greatly to have affected the racial character of the Romano-British population."[1]

Britain was prosperous for a time. Then towards the middle of the fourth century troubles began; invasions from the north by the Picts and along the east coast by the Saxons grew more and more serious, until

> " finally, the Great Raid of Barbarians who crossed the Rhine on the winter's night which divided 406 from 407, and the subsequent barbarian attack on Rome itself, cut Britain off from the Mediterranean. The so-called ' departure of the Romans ' speedily followed. This departure did not mean any great departure

[1] F. J. Haverfield in *Cambridge Mediaeval History,* i. 370. See especially R. G. Collingwood and J. N. L. Myres, *Roman Britain* (the *Oxford History of England*).

of persons, Roman or other, from the island. It meant that the central government in Italy now ceased to send out the usual governors and other high officials and to organise the supply of troops. No one went: some persons failed to come."[1]

It is significant that sites which have been thoroughly explored fail to reveal Roman coins of later date than the opening years of the fifth century.[2] Before these invaders, towns were abandoned; Roman speech and boundaries vanished: only the massive foundations of the roads survived. The Britons retired to the hills of Wales and Scotland and there resumed their Celtic culture and speech, and became, in the fulness of time, one of the springs of mediaeval art and learning.

THE ENGLISH CONQUEST

Of the three tribes who constituted the bulk of the invaders, two—the Angles and the Saxons—are hardly distinguishable either in language or customs, both coming, moreover, from the narrow neck of land which now separates Denmark from the mainland. From the end of the third century the Saxons appear in history as raiders and pirates, although the Angles, on the other hand, drop back into obscurity (as far as Roman writers are concerned) ever since Tacitus mentioned them in the beginning of the second century until the sixth century, when we read of them in England. They have left a mass of epic poetry, however, which gives some idea of the life their chieftains led; indeed, the similarities of this literature with that of Norway, Sweden and Germany suggest an international culture covering Northern Europe. The material remains of these tribes while still on the mainland, which have been unearthed, show a high degree of perfection in weaving, and that " the warriors of the period were armed in a manner not substantially improved upon for many centuries afterwards ". Many of their swords bear the marks of Roman manufacturers. They had also a Runic alphabet of their own devising, which long remained in use. Of their religion little is known with certainty; Woden, Thunor and Frig have given us the names of Wednesday, Thursday and Friday, but the surviving legends are too late to tell us much about early English culture and history. As early as the Bronze Age they had been familiar with the plough.[3] The invaders must not be regarded as complete savages, therefore. Of the Jutes much less is known. They were the dominant settlers in Kent and it is significant that the early Kentish laws have marked peculiarities of social structure, although the language differs but slightly. It is certainly curious how Kent from the beginning and all through the middle ages preserved peculiar local variants, but it must not be assumed too confidently that all this necessarily relates to an original difference in the Jutish invaders. The geographical position of Kent at the gateway of

[1] F. J. Haverfield, *op. cit.* 379.

[2] *Ibid.*, 381. (The latest date seems to be about 420.)

[3] F. M. G. Beck in *Cambridge Mediaeval History*, i. 384–386.

England has in fact given it an exceptional position in the religious, military and commercial, as well as in the legal, history of the country, but this position was won after, rather than before, the Conquest.[1]

The invasion and settlement of the country by these tribes occupies about two centuries (roughly from 400 to 600). In the end, a number of different kingdoms were established—at least ten of them are known with certainty to have existed at various dates—and for the next two centuries the main themes are the spread of Christianity and the growth of unity in place of these warring kingdoms. It is true that the later years of the Roman occupation had seen the first introduction of Christianity into the island, and that an important and vigorous church had been organised, but the English invaders crushed the British Christians and maintained their own ancient mythology. England therefore had to be converted anew, and the year 597 was a momentous one, for the arrival of St Augustine established contact between the English tribesmen and the Roman Church which was now (under St Gregory I, " the Great ") definitely entering upon its mediaeval task of establishing one supreme spiritual authority in Europe. Gregory " was a Roman of the Romans, nurtured on traditions of Rome's imperial greatness, cherishing the memories of pacification and justice, of control and protection ".[2]

THE ADVENT OF CHRISTIANITY

The results of the re-introduction of Christianity were of the highest importance. The existing tribal organisation must have seemed weak and inefficient to the missionaries coming from such well-organised States as existed on the continent, and very soon we see the results of their teaching in the enhanced value placed upon the monarchy, and in the tendency towards larger national units. After long years of warfare the petty tribal units were replaced by a few large kingdoms ruled and administered by kings who watched European methods. Soon, too, they learned the Roman art of taxation, which consisted in dividing the land into units of equal assessment instead of equal area (calling them in English " hides ").[3] Again, the advent of the clergy meant the introduction of a new class into English society, and so a new law of status had to be devised for their protection. Consequently laws were made, and, " in the Roman style ",[4] were written down. It is possible that legislation was occasionally effected upon other subjects as well. And finally, the Church brought with it moral ideas which were to revolutionise English law. Christianity had inherited from Judaism an

[1] See the very interesting suggestions in Pollock and Maitland, i. 186; and the monograph of J. E. A. Jolliffe, *Pre-Feudal England and the Jutes* (1933).

[2] W. H. Hutton in *Cambridge Mediaeval History*, ii. 251.

[3] The word " hide " was already used to denote the normal holding necessary for the maintenance of a family. See especially, F. M. Stenton, *Anglo-Saxon England*, 276, 638.

[4] Bede, *Historia Ecclesiastica*, ii. 5.

outlook upon moral questions which was strictly individualistic. The salvation of each separate soul was dependent upon the actions of the individual. This contrasted strongly with the custom of the English tribes which looked less to the individual than to the family group of which the individual formed a part. Necessarily such a system had little place for an individualistic sense of morals, for the group, although it was subjected to legal liability, can hardly be credited with moral intention in the sense that an individual can. With the spread of Christianity all this slowly changed. First, responsibility for actions gradually shifted from the whole group to the particular individual who did the act; and then the Church (and later the law) will judge that act, if necessary, from the point of view of the intention of the party who committed it.

ENGLAND AND THE DANES

The Anglo-Saxon period is very long, and a great deal of development took place in it.[1] Beginning for practical purposes about 597 (the landing of St Augustine) we have a continuous stream of legal sources which are definitely Anglo-Saxon in character down to the Norman Conquest in 1066 and even later.[2] There are treatises dating about the year 1118 which are still typically Anglo-Saxon in content and outlook.[3] We may therefore place the limits of this period roughly and in round figures between 600 and 1100, a period of five hundred years. The length of this age can be realised by remembering that five hundred years is the interval between Bracton and Blackstone, between Chaucer and Kipling, and between the battles of Agincourt and the Marne. In so long a period we must omit details. The one fact of capital importance besides the growing unification of England, is the coming of the Norsemen and Danes, for it has left definite traces upon our history. The very word " law " is not English but Norse.

Scandinavia was peopled by tribes who were as astute in trade as they were fierce in war. The discoveries of English coins in the islands of the Baltic, together with Arabian coins from Bagdad and Samarcand (which had reached the Baltic through Russia), are witness to the distant foreign commence of the Norse. During the ninth century, for reasons unknown, the Norse became unusually active on the sea, and a series of

---

[1] For a short but authoritative account of Anglo-Saxon life and institutions, see D. Whitelock, *The Beginnings of English Society* (Penguin Books, 1952). She has also collected and translated the most important of the sources in *English Historical Documents* (ed. D. C. Douglas, 1955), vol. i.

[2] The Anglo-Saxon laws have been edited on a monumental scale by Felix Liebermann, *Die Gesetze der Angelsachsen* (1903–1916). A very serviceable text with English translations and notes is given by F. L. Attenborough, *Laws of the Earliest English Kings* (Cambridge, 1922), and A. J. Robertson, *Laws of the Kings of England from Edmund to Henry I* (Cambridge, 1925). There are extracts in W. Stubbs, *Select Charters of English Constitutional History* (9th edn., Oxford 1913).

[3] See below, pp. 15, 255–256.

maritime raids resulted in the colonisation of Iceland, parts of Ireland and Scotland, the Orkneys, Shetlands, Hebrides, and portions of Northern France (thenceforward to be known as Normandy). A Scandinavian tribe of " Rus " gave its name (although not its language) to Russia, while a few even penetrated to the Mediterranean. In England, after fierce fighting, they succeeded in retaining from King Alfred almost the whole eastern half of the kingdom (879), and more than a century after his death a Danish dynasty united under a single ruler—the great King Cnut (1016–1035)—England, Norway and Denmark. Cnut's laws were long popular in England, and in after years men looked back with respect to his reign, trying to revive his legislation. The Danes left a permanent mark on that part of the country where they had longest ruled. They independently developed a sort of grand jury, of which we shall speak later; they arrived earlier than the rest of the country at the stage where land could be freely bought and sold; they had a marked tendency to form clubs and guilds; their peasantry were less subject to the lords; borough institutions seem to have flourished peculiarly under their rule.[1]

The death of Cnut and the division of his Empire brings us to the accession of St Edward the Confessor (1043–1066), who throughout the middle ages was the national hero of the English when they resented Norman influence. (Hence it is that a large body of " Laws of Edward the Confessor " was forged as a patriotic weapon against the Norman dynasty.) In fact, the antithesis was false, and the spread of foreign culture in England increased immensely during his reign, which in some respects seems a sort of peaceful Norman conquest. The disputed succession on his death brought William the Conqueror in 1066 and Norman arms finished what Norman civilisation had already begun.

[1] Vinogradoff, *English Society in the Eleventh Century*, 4–11; Corbett in *Cambridge Mediaeval History*, iii. 401; J. E. G. de Montmorency, *Danish Influence on English Law and Character*, Law Quarterly Review, xl. 324–343; F. M. Stenton, *The Danes in England*, History, v. 173–177; R. H. C. Davis, *East Anglia and the Danelaw*, Transactions of the Royal Historical Society (1955), 23.

CHAPTER 2

THE CONQUEST TO HENRY II :
THE BEGINNINGS OF ADMINISTRATION

The greatest result of the Norman Conquest was the introduction of precise and orderly methods into the government and law of England. The Norse invaders who had settled in Normandy had made it in a century and a half (911–1066) the best-ruled state in Europe, and the gifts for strong administration and for orderly accounting and finance which had been displayed in the duchy were to have fuller opportunities in the conquered kingdom. William the Bastard had been Duke of Normandy since 1035, and by 1047 (when he was twenty) the turbulent barons were beginning to feel his strength. Nearly twenty years of hard work in Normandy preceded the expedition to England, and in that interval William had imposed some sort of discipline upon his baronage, and had finally made peace with the Church (after a long quarrel) through the help of Lanfranc, whom he afterwards made Archbishop of Canterbury. Personally a devout Christian, he yet insisted that the Church should keep the place which he assigned to it, and in fact he secured an effective control over its policy, notably in appointments to the higher dignities. Then, too, he had developed a remarkably good financial organisation, the " Chamber " (*camera*), and although the duchy revenues were not particularly large, yet there was clearly the machinery ready to collect revenue energetically and to control its disposition.

THE CONQUEST AND " DOMESDAY BOOK "

Such was the position of Duke William when he undertook the desperate adventure of invading England by transporting 5,000 men and 2,500 horses across the Channel, an astonishing performance in those days. The Battle of Hastings (1066) and the death of King Harold quickly settled him upon the throne of his new kingdom. Reforms began at once. The casual " treasure " of the Anglo-Saxon kings was reorganised as an Exchequer on business lines, and was used to keep a firm hold upon the sheriffs and local government generally. As for the Church, he continued the Norman attitude of strengthening the Church internally, enriching it and maintaining its discipline (newly reformed by the great Pope Gregory VII), although at the same time restricting its political power. This strongly contrasted with the pre-conquest state of things when the bishops sat in all the courts and mingled ecclesiastical and secular business. William, by an ordinance,[1] insisted that the bishops should not transact ecclesiastical business in the hundred courts, but should hold their own Courts Christian for the purpose; and from that day to this the Church has maintained its separate system of courts administering canon law. Church and State which had been inextricably connected in the Anglo-Saxon age henceforth were strictly separate, a policy which happened to coincide with the Church's own ambitions as well as with William's. His last years were absorbed in the great survey of the kingdom which is known as *Domesday Book*. The original two volumes together with the chest constructed for their preservation are still in the Public Record Office in London, where *Domesday Book* holds an honoured place as the oldest public record. Indeed, during the middle ages it was so respected that it was called simply " the record ", so great was its authority. The land was described county by county, village by village, the owners and their subtenants were listed and their holdings valued, even the farm stock was recorded, with a view to settling clearly the rights of the Crown and the taxable resources of the country. In several cases a few precious lines will summarise the customs of a county or city, and so give us an insight into the local law in force.[2] Most valuable information can be extracted from it as to the state of freedom or serfdom in different parts of the country, and it is possible that the strict insistence of the Exchequer officials upon the letter of *Domesday Book*, and their refusal to allow it to be questioned, was the beginning of the notion of " record " as a technical thing. From this one book the idea of certain officially compiled documents being beyond question seems to have spread to the rolls of the Exchequer, and thence to the rolls of the courts of law. If this conjecture is true, then " Records " must be regarded as financial in origin, and only later becoming judicial.[3]

---

[1] The ordinance expressly refers only to the hundred, and it would seem from *Leges Henrici Primi*, vii. 3 (reprinted in Stubbs, *Select Charters*), that the bishops continued to administer canon law in the county court as late as the reign of Henry I. This seems to be the last we hear of such a practice, however. (But see Stenton, *English Feudalism*, 108.)

[2] Some of them are reprinted in Stubbs' *Charters*. For brief general accounts, see D. C. Douglas, *The Domesday Survey*, History (1936), xxi. 249 and V. H. Galbraith, *Studies in the Public Records*, 89–121.

[3] For an extreme development of this theory see the introduction by H. G. Richardson to the *Memoranda Roll of 1 John* (Pipe Roll Society, 1943). On the origin of the idea of " record ", see S. E. Thorne, *Notes on courts of record in England*, West Virginia Law Quarterly, xl. 347 ff., and *Courts of record and Sir Edward Coke*, University of Toronto Law Journal, ii. 24; Esmein, *La Chose jugée*, Revue historique de Droit français et étranger (1887), 545; Julius Goebel, introduction to John Henry Smith, *Appeals to the Privy Council*, xxvi ff.

Another effect of *Domesday Book* was to assert the chain of feudal relationships and to assure the overlordship of the Crown. Thus the title of every piece of land in England could be expressed in the formula that A holds it of his feudal lord B, who holds of C, who holds of —— the King. This insistence of the Norman and succeeding kings that they were the undisputed lords, direct or indirect, of every piece of land in the country is of the gravest importance, for it provided a sure foundation for the growth in later times of the common law. For this and many other reasons too technical to mention here, it has been said that " If English history is to be understood, the law of *Domesday Book* must be mastered ".[1] This opportunity of systematising the land situation enabled the Conqueror to make England the most perfectly organised feudal state in Europe, and in this sense we may say that we are indebted to him for the feudal system. But he refused to allow the great barons whose tenure intervened between him and their sub-tenants to turn their position to political advantage, and one of his last acts was to assemble a great meeting (1086) at Salisbury where came all his counsellors " and all the land-owning men of property that there were all over England, whosesoever men they were, and all bowed down to him and became his men, and swore oaths of fealty to him that they would be faithful to him against all men "[2]—even against their immediate lords. In this way William tried to prevent the feudal anarchy and private war against which he had struggled for so many years in Normandy.[3]

His work, then, was pre-eminently that of systematisation. A few great reforms there were, but his greatest contribution was the Norman spirit of clever administration and orderly government, and his own stern enforcement of royal rights. Upon this basis was the common law to be built in later days. In other respects he was content to continue the old English laws and customs, expressing his policy in a brief but stately charter which is still preserved by the City of London:[4]

" King William greets in friendly wise William the bishop and Gosfrith the portreeve, and all the burgesses in London, both French and English. I let you wit that I will that you two be worthy of all the laws that you were worthy of in King Edward's day. And I will that every child be his father's heir after his father's day,[5] and I will not endure that any man offer any wrong to you. God keep you."

[1] Maitland, *Domesday Book and Beyond*, 3.

[2] *Anglo-Saxon Chronicle*, cited in Stubbs, *Select Charters*.

[3] The attempt by G. B. Adams, *Origin of the English Constitution*, 186–187, to minimise the importance of the oath is not convincing; William's motive in summoning so extraordinary an assembly seems undeniable. Cf. F. M. Stenton, *First Century of English Feudalism* (Oxford, 1932), 111–113, 137; D. C. Douglas, *Feudal Documents from the Abbey of Bury St. Edmunds* (Oxford, 1932), xcix–c, c, n. 1; H. A. Cronne, in History, xix. 248. In 1136 King Stephen spared certain rebels as they had not sworn fealty to him, but were the men of Baldwin of Redvers, Pollock and Maitland, i. 505 n. 5.

[4] Stubbs, *Select Charters*. The Conqueror's work is well summarised by Corbett in *Cambridge Mediaeval History*, v. 496, 505–520.

[5] A. Ballard, *British Borough Charters*, 74, suggests that this is a promise to abandon the claim to a forfeiture upon intestacy (as to which, see below, p. 726).

Of William II (Rufus) there is little to say except that he rashly provoked a feud with the Church, in consequence of which Archbishop Anselm suffered years of exile and " by his firmness set up a new standard of independence for the English clergy, and made the opening move in the struggle between Church and State in England ".[1] At the same time, the efficient central administration was employed under the direction of the king's principal minister, Ranulf Flambard, in converting the incidents of feudal tenure into engines of financial oppression.

CHURCH AND STATE

With the reign of Henry I (1100–1135) we come to a more important period of legal history. His first act was very significant. Just as the Conqueror had made the short promise of good government to London which we have just quoted, so his son Henry I issued a formal Charter in 1100 promising to stop the oppressive practices which his brother Rufus had introduced; then he chose as his queen Edith, who was a representative of the old English royal house, and so conciliated the English. His principal trouble (apart from a baronial revolt which was soon quelled) came from the Church which was growing anxious at the rapid rise of powerful monarchies which were apt to use the Church for political ends. Soon the issue became definite and Europe-wide in the form of the " Investiture Contest ". The Conqueror had compelled the cathedrals to elect his nominees as bishops and had himself delivered to them the emblems of spiritual as well as of temporal authority. Gregory VII as early as 1075 prohibited lay investiture, holding that the Church was independent of the State, and that no temporal ruler could confer ecclesiastical authority. A long struggle followed which on the continent took the form of the spectacular struggle between the Empire and the papacy. In England Henry I and Archbishop Anselm were subject to the moderating influence of the great canon lawyer Ivo of Chartres who devised a compromise in 1107; the King resigned his claim to invest bishops with the ring and staff (the emblems of their spiritual authority), while Anselm agreed that cathedral chapters should come to the King's chapel and elect bishops in his presence—thus leaving room for a reasonable amount of royal influence. This wise settlement was extended to all Europe only after much bitter strife in 1122.

The conflict is one of the central facts in mediaeval history, for it shows a clear-cut issue upon which a saintly man of Anselm's type would unhesitatingly decide that he had higher duties than those which he owed to the Crown. The Concordat of Worms of 1122 did not permanently end the dispute, which soon revived upon slightly different ground; indeed, in its most general sense the quarrel is likely to last as long as government itself. It has had important results upon the political

[1] Corbett in *Cambridge Mediaeval History*, v. 526.

theory of the State, some of the greatest minds of the middle ages having devoted their powers to the examination of the nature of kingship, the authority of law, and the limits which ought to be put upon the power of temporal rulers. Jurisprudence to-day bears the traces of these great events, in the course of which the State was criticised in terms of the highest ideal of government which then existed, that of the universal Church.[1]

HENRY I's REFORMS

The rest of the reign is occupied with the peaceful activities of the Justiciar, Roger, Bishop of Salisbury, a Norman from Caen, who like so many of his race had something of the efficiency expert in his blood. Official tradition long respected him for his organisation of the Exchequer on strict business lines, and to him we owe the series of " Great Rolls of the Pipe ". The earliest in existence is dated 1130 and contains important legal as well as financial information. Some of the earlier rolls must be lost; but with a few gaps there is an almost complete series of Pipe Rolls from 1156 down to 1832—a remarkable sign of the permanence of Roger's work. In this reign, therefore, we may place the elaboration of an efficient governmental organisation at Westminster. In local government Henry I was equally active; eleven untrustworthy sheriffs were dismissed in 1129; justiciars were sent on circuit to look after the pleas of the Crown (and they soon usurped for their master immense jurisdiction by asserting that any matter which concerned the King's peace could be treated as a plea of the Crown), while it is clear that the Norman sheriffs were still administering in the county what was essentially Anglo-Saxon law, for we have some curious treatises (written between 1113 and 1118) which are attempts to state that old law in language that the Normans could understand.[2] This in fact is the justification for the statement we have already made to the effect that the period of Anglo-Saxon law extended later than the Norman Conquest, and at least as late as the year 1100 or thereabouts. We therefore see that in the reign of Henry I the law was substantially Anglo-Saxon and administered by the sheriffs locally according to ancient custom (which was certainly not the same all over the country). As yet there was very little that could be called " common law ". So far

---

[1] For the political history of the investiture contest see Brooke in *Cambridge Mediaeval History*, v. 51–111; for the theory see a brief account in Dunning, *History of Political Theories, Ancient and Mediaeval*, 161–188, Sabine, *History of Political Theory*, 224 ff, McIlwain, *Growth of Political Thought in the West*, 203–318 (whose treatment will be of special interest from the legal point of view), and more fully, Carlyle, *Mediaeval Political Theory*, iv. 49–164. The Church's view is expounded in detail in Walter Ullmann, *Medieval Papalism* (1949) and *The Growth of Papal Government in the Middle Ages* (1955). See also the brilliant lectures of A. L. Smith, *Church and State in the Middle Ages*. An important contribution to the study of early canon law in England has been made by Z. N. Brooke, *The English Church and the Papacy from the Conquest to the reign of John* (Cambridge, 1931).

[2] See below, p. 256.

there was only a great administrative machine well on the way towards a complete domination of the realm. From this great machine there will develop the future common law.[1] Only in Sicily was such efficient administration to be found, and there too it was the work of Norman invaders.[2]

Henry's death was a great loss to the nation:

> " then there was tribulation soon in the land, for every man that could forthwith robbed another. . . . A good man he was and there was great awe of him. No man durst misdo against another in his time. He made peace for man and beast. Whoso bare his burden of gold and silver, no man durst say him aught but good."[3]

The reign of King Stephen (1135–1154) is frequently called " the Anarchy ", so great were the disorders which filled it attendant upon the disputed title to the Crown. The machine which Henry I had perfected needed a firm hand to run it, and Stephen was content to let things drift. Art and letters, indeed, flourished, and Vacarius came to Oxford to teach Roman law and to write a less expensive text-book for poor English law students,[4] but from the point of view of Norman efficiency the reign was disappointing: still,

> " to those who do not place order above everything and who realise how oppressive Henry's government was becoming in spite of its legality, it must always remain a moot question whether Stephen's reign was such a total set-back as the ecclesiastical writers of the day would have us believe ".[5]

HENRY II's EMPIRE

With his successor, Henry II, we come to one of the most critical epochs in the history of the common law. By inheritance or by marriage he had acquired the rulership of England, Normandy, Aquitaine and Anjou, and like many of his barons divided his time between England and the continent. This close connection with France was to have important results for English law as we shall see later. Whatever the lessons of Anglo-Norman public administration, the revival of learning now in progress may have brought broader views and more generous ideals. Stubbs has made the attractive suggestion that perhaps the rapid growth of the universities

" conduced to the maintenance in the educated class of an ideal of free government,

[1] For Henry I, see in general Corbett in *Cambridge Mediaeval History*, v. 527–541, and A. L. Poole, *Domesday Book to Magna Carta*.

[2] For Sicily, see Chalandon, *ibid.*, 203–206.

[3] *Anglo-Saxon Chronicle*, in Stubbs, *Select Charters*. The same principle of the king's peace dying with him haunted the books long after: Y.BB. Edward II (Selden Society), xx. 159 no. 71 (no date).

[4] This book, the *Liber Pauperum*, has been edited for the Selden Society (vol. xliv) by Professor de Zulueta, who has re-examined the evidence and reached the conclusion that " to doubt whether Vacarius ever taught at Oxford is to doubt against the evidence ".

[5] Corbett in *Cambridge Mediaeval History*, v. 552.

drawn from ancient Greek and Roman history, which, although never likely to be realised in detail, tended to make tyranny such as that of William Rufus impossible."[1]

It must never be forgotten that the general standard of learning and culture of a nation has a large part in determining its law and polity.

CONSTITUTIONS OF CLARENDON

The reign opens (1154) with the confirmation of Henry I's Charter of 1100, and with the great conflict between the King and Archbishop Becket. The separation of the ecclesiastical courts by William the Conqueror had had unexpected results, for in the succeeding hundred years the Church had developed a large mass of canon law and claimed wide jurisdiction. This law Becket determined to apply rigorously. Henry was equally determined to impose his own lay law (which also had recently been considerably enlarged in content and strengthened administratively).[2] Many people were amenable in criminal matters to both jurisdictions, and Becket proclaimed that such people should not be tried twice—in other words, they should be tried but once, and that in the Church courts. Then certain things also were subject to both jurisdictions—Church lands, and the rights of ecclesiastical patronage (called advowsons). Finally, at a council in 1164 all the magnates of the realm " recognised " (the word is borrowed from the " recognition " or verdict of a jury) a list of customs which they declared were the practice of the reign of Henry I.

This statement, called the Constitutions of Clarendon, Henry II proposed as the basis of a compromise.[3] Some of these provisions repeat practices dating from the reign of William I, such as in requiring the King's permission before a tenant-in-chief can be excommunicated, or an appeal carried from the Church courts in England to Rome (cc. 7, 8, 10). Chapter 13 introduces the striking rule that a lord shall be held responsible by the King if his servants do wrong to a bishop. All litigation concerning advowsons is to be in the King's court (c. 1), and so also cases involving the Church's lands unless they be held in free alms (a tenure comporting no earthly services, and peculiar to Church property), but the fact of free alms or lay tenure is to be decided in the King's court—which had been the rule in Normandy as well (c. 9). Chapter 15 contains the highly important rule that no plea of debt shall be withdrawn from the King's jurisdiction on the grounds that the debt was accompanied by an oath or pledge of faith—spiritual censures may be imposed for breach of faith, but the civil jurisdiction over debt is not to be thereby ousted. This clause was not an unmixed benefit, for although the State thereby appropriated to itself a large jurisdiction

[1] Stubbs, *Select Charters* (Sketch of the Reign of Henry II).

[2] See *The English Church and the Papacy*, by Z. N. Brooke (Cambridge, 1931); R. Foreville, *L'Église et la royauté sous Henri II* (Paris, 1943); and for a different view, A. L. Poole, *Domesday Book to Magna Carta*, 197 ff.

[3] The text is in Stubbs, *Charters*

over contract, nevertheless the law of the Church in this field was rapidly becoming more modern, more equitable and less formalistic. She had long punished breach of faith as a crime, and was soon to extend the idea and proclaim in addition the enforceability in law of promises (opinions to this effect appear first in 1212).[1]

Finally, it was declared by chapter 3 that clerks (that is to say, all who were in major or minor orders) when under accusation of crime should first answer in the King's court, and then be remitted for trial by the bishop, and if he convicted, then they were to be returned to the lay court for punishment, for Henry insisted that degradation (the severest penalty the Church could inflict) was too mild for felonies. Last of all, Henry objected to laymen being tried in ecclesiastical courts, even for canonical offences, merely upon informations. So he offered the bishops the aid of a sheriff's jury of presentment if the Church could find no other means of getting a public accuser.[2]

This compromise on the basis of old customs was effective, except as to the punishment of convicted clerks. On this point Henry had to yield after the murder of Becket in 1170, and thenceforward " benefit of clergy " eventually began to operate as a sort of first offender's law, for it was the later rule that the culprit escaped punishment for the first offence only on proving his clergy.

THE EXCHEQUER

After the dramatic murder of Becket the interest turns to the rapid development of the administration under Henry II's officials. The Treasury was under Nigel, Bishop of Ely (a nephew of Henry I's Justiciar, Roger, Bishop of Salisbury), who further elaborated its constitution and procedure. Finally, having bought the office of Treasurer he conferred it upon his son, Richard fitz Nigel, Bishop of London, who wrote an extremely detailed account of the working of the Exchequer called the *Dialogue of the Exchequer* (1177–1179).[3]

The last ten years of the reign are dominated by Ranulf de Glanvill, the Justiciar. A competent general, diplomatist and judge, although an unscrupulous sheriff (he was twice removed from office), his name was attached to the first treatise upon the common law. The date is soon after 1187 and Glanvill's nephew, Hubert Walter, has been suggested as possibly its author. It is a short, simple book, for the common law was neither very extensive nor very complicated. But for all that, it

---

[1] Spies, *L'Observation des simples conventions en droit canonique* (1928), 40 ff.

[2] See Maitland, *History of English Law*, i. 151–152, Haskins, *Norman Institutions,* 219, 329 ff., and Plucknett, *The Medieval Bailiff* (1954), 11–13.

[3] Text in the first eight editions of Stubbs, *Charters*, and in a critical edition by Hughes, Crump and Johnson (Oxford, 1902; revised, with translation by Charles Johnson, Edinburgh, 1950). Poole, *Exchequer in the Twelfth Century* (Oxford, 1912), is a full commentary. A manuscript was known to Coke, who cites it (Co. Lit. 58, 68 *b*) as " Ockam ". Cf. W. O. Hassall, *Catalogue of the Library of Sir Edward Coke,* no. 308.

set the style of legal literature for many centuries to come, for the author of Glanvill invented the method of writing law in the form of a commentary upon the different writs.[1]

THE PLACE OF HENRY II

There are many other great events of this reign which we shall describe more fully in later chapters of this book. The extension of the system of itinerant justices; the growing definition of the courts of law; the widespread use of the jury; the establishment of the petty assizes[2] as speedy methods of trying cases of recent dispossession of land; the Assize of Clarendon (1166) remodelling criminal procedure and systematising the presenting or grand jury;[3] the Assize of Northampton (1176) which strengthened the claims of an heir to land against the feudal lord; the Assize of Arms (1181) which reorganised the local defence and police measures—these are only the greatest of the many reforms of Henry II's reign. In the words of Bishop Stubbs:

" Henry II was far more than an inventor of legal forms or of the machinery of taxation. He was one of the greatest politicians of his time; a man of such wide influence, great estates, and numerous connections, that the whole of the foreign relations of England during the middle ages may be traced directly and distinctly to the results of his alliances and his enmities. He was regarded by the Emperor Frederick, by the Kings of Spain and Sicily, by the rising republics of Lombardy, by the half-savage dynasts of Norway, and by the fainting realm of Palestine as a friend and patron to be secured at any cost. He refused the crowns of Jerusalem and Sicily; he refused to recognise the anti-pope at a moment when the whole influence of the papacy was being employed to embarrass and distress him. His career is full of romantic episodes, and of really great physical exploits.

" Yet the consent of the historians of the time makes him, first and foremost, a legislator and administrator. Ralph Niger, his enemy, tells how year after year he wore out men's patience with his annual assizes; how he set up an upstart nobility; how he abolished the ancient laws, set aside charters, overthrew municipalities, thirsted for gold, overwhelmed all society with his scutages, his recognitions, and such like. Ralph de Diceto explains how necessary a constant adaptation and readjustment of means was to secure in any degree the pure administration of justice, and lauds the promptness with which he discarded unsatisfactory measures to make way for new experiments. William of Newburgh and Peter of Blois praise him for the very measures that Ralph Niger condemns; his exactions were far less than those of his successors; he was most careful of the public peace; he bore the sword for the punishment of evil doers, but to the peace of the good; he conserved the rights and liberties of the churches; he never imposed any heavy tax on either England or his continental estates, or grieved the Church with undue exactions; his legal activity was especially meritorious after the storm of anarchy which preceded. In every description of his character the same features recur, whether as matters of laudation or of abuse."[4]

[1] Glanvill has been edited with a wealth of valuable notes by Professor G. E. Woodbine (Yale University Press, 1932). See further, p. 256 below.

[2] For the different meanings of the word *assize*, see below, p. 112.

[3] For a translation and comments, see below, pp. 112-113.

[4] Stubbs, *Constitutional History*, § 147. Many of the original sources are collected and translated in *English Historical Documents*, ed. D. C. Douglas, vol. ii. (1954).

CHAPTER 3

THE GREAT CHARTERS:
LAW SEPARATES FROM ADMINISTRATION

Henry II was followed successively by his sons Richard I (1189–1199) and John (1199–1216), and his grandson Henry III (1216–1272). During these reigns every sort of strain was placed upon the administration and upon the infant common law. It is a great tribute to his work that they both survived. Richard was absent from the realm for almost the whole of his ten years' reign; John was involved in disastrous war abroad, civil war at home, insurrection, invasion and interdict. Henry III was a child of nine at his accession, with only his mother's bracelet for a crown, and yet a few great-hearted nobles, encouraged by the paternal interest of Pope Honorius III, spared the land most of the troubles which usually attended a minority in those days. And soon, by the middle of Henry's reign, one of his judges, Henry de Bracton, was already preparing material for an immense and detailed treatise on the common law beside which the little book of Glanvill would seem a mere pamphlet, and he tells us that the best cases are those in the earlier years of the reign—so flourishing was the law even in those troubled times. The secret is surely to be found in the permanence of the administration established by the Norman kings, which withstood all these shocks, grew, prospered, and finally (as every administration must) became the parent of new law, and of new legal machinery.

THE POSITION OF THE CROWN

Then, too, the Crown through all these disasters survived the attempts of certain interests which would have reduced its power to ineffectual limits; on the other hand, the opposite tendency of the Crown to use the powerful machinery of government to institute a tyranny was likewise frustrated. And so, on a broad view, both the oppressions and the rebellions of the period appear as efforts to find and maintain the just mean between private liberty and public order, while through it all, steadily and constantly, proceeds the growth of better and more expert judicial institutions, and the development of more and more rules of law, and their organisation into a coherent legal system which already was beginning to separate from the purely administrative machinery of the realm. By the time we reach the second half of Henry III's reign the judiciary is already distinct from the administration and can stand aside while the national leaders in arms assert the necessity of imposing restraint upon the speed and the direction of so dangerous an engine; while very soon, Parliament will appear with this as one of its main duties.

THE IDEAS OF HUBERT WALTER

Of all the threads which run through this period, many of them highly important, we shall here follow only one—the struggle for the charters. The absence of Richard I had shown that it was possible for the machinery to work without a king to direct it, provided that there was a trusty minister to take his place. The great Archbishop Hubert Walter took this rôle, and assisted by the great council of magnates ruled well, retaining his power into the next reign. The brilliant outburst of literature, art, law and general culture which marked the close of the twelfth century was accompanied by the development of an idea of government of which Hubert Walter[1] was the embodiment.

"King John, in fact, felt with much truth that he was not his own master so long as his great minister was alive. Hubert Walter held the view, natural in an ecclesiastical statesman, that the kingship was an office invested with solemn duties. Royal power must be inseparable from the law. And the Archbishop's prestige was so great that a word from him on the interpretation of the law could set aside the opinion of the King and his advisers."[2]

His successor, Stephen Langton, whom Pope Innocent III forced John to accept, was of the same school, holding that "loyalty was devotion, not to a man, but to a system of law and order which he believed to be a reflection of the law and order of the universe".[3] Conflict was inevitable between such statesmen and John, whose life had been spent in constant turbulence, intrigue and treachery, with complete indifference to "those principles of harmony in life and nature which underlay all the current belief in justice and responsibility".[4] The rapid growth of the central administration and the development of the courts of law (which we shall consider in more detail later[5]) was only equalled by the growth of local government, of boroughs, of trade both internal and foreign, and the close co-operation of central and local authorities. Litigation, negotiations, compromises, definitions of official power, the statement of precise limits to all sorts of jurisdictions public and

[1] Remember that it may be his hand which is concealed beneath the name of Glanvill in the first book of the common law. Above, p. 18.

[2] Powicke in *Cambridge Mediaeval History*, vi. 218.

[3] *Ibid.*, 219. There is an admirable discussion of the mediaeval view of law by C. H. McIlwain, *The Growth of Political Thought in the West* (New York, 1932).

[4] *Ibid.*, 220; this chapter is full of insight into the mediaeval conception of law.

[5] Below, pp. 139 *et seq.*

private, organisation between groups of towns and the elaboration of machinery for holding international representative chapters in certain religious bodies—these are all signs of the spirit of legal order which filled the opening years of the thirteenth century. It is from this standpoint that the events leading to *Magna Carta* must be considered.

JOHN AND THE POPE

John's troubles opened with Innocent III's refusal to permit his candidate to become Archbishop of Canterbury, the Pope substituting his own much better choice, Stephen Langton.[1] The Great Interdict followed, to which John replied by confiscating Church property. The political thought on both sides of the struggle is clear. John regarded bishops as higher civil servants, and looked back to the old days when Church and State in England were mingled, the papacy weak, and the Church subservient to the Crown. Hence he was able to strike the attitude of a patriot against foreign meddling. Langton started by assuming the separate sphere of Church and State, attacked the shifty details of John's recent conduct, and proclaimed that John's vassals were not bound to him after he himself had broken faith with the King of Kings, arguing " as an exponent of feudal custom in the light of those high principles of law to which all human law should conform ".[2] The conflict was thus one of fundamental principle. John poured out money in Europe to buy support, and built up an imposing coalition against the Pope's ally, King Philip Augustus of France. Then, in his customary sudden manner, he abandoned all his plans, submitted to Rome and did homage to the Pope's legate. The next year his allies were ruined in one of the most important battles of the middle ages (Bouvines, 1214). It was now time to reckon with the discontent aroused by the reckless oppression to which John had resorted during the Interdict. Archbishop Langton undertook to force the King to make amends, and produced the old Charter of Henry I as the basis of what was normal and just, adding a long list of more recent grievances. London opened its gates to the barons, and soon after the fifteenth day of June, 1215, John had to put his seal to the Great Charter.[3]

THE GREAT CHARTER

This is a long document of sixty chapters and represents the extreme form of the baronial demands. The next ten years saw the progressive shortening of the Charter by omitting much that was temporary, by

[1] There is now available an excellent biography of this great statesman: F. M. Powicke, *Stephen Langton* (Oxford, 1928).

[2] Powicke in *Cambridge Mediaeval History*, vi. 234.

[3] See A. J. Collins, *The Documents of the Great Charter of 1215*, Proceedings of the British Academy, xxxiv. 233 ff. for a minute and illuminating discussion. The texts of the charters of 1215, 1216, 1217 and 1225 are all printed in Stubbs, *Select Charters*.

putting the important clauses concerning the forests into a separate document (called the Charter of the Forest), and by pruning the excesses of the victorious barons. John obtained a bull from his new over-lord, the Pope, annulling the charter.[1] Indeed, some of its provisions were much too extreme, particularly the last, which erected a commission of twenty-five barons with power to enforce the Charter by coercing the King. The Great Charter of 1215 was therefore actually law for only about nine weeks. The King died shortly after (1216).

The council who ruled in the name of the infant Henry III re-issued the charter in 1216 (this time with papal assent) very much modified in favour of the Crown, with a promise to re-open the question when the French invasion, undertaken at the will of the rebel barons, had been defeated. This promise they fulfilled in 1217 on the occasion of the treaty whereby Prince Louis withdrew, and this, the third, Great Charter contains " numerous, important, and minute " changes whose general tendency was again in favour of the Crown. It was felt that the boy King ought not to suffer for his father's sins, and that the difficult period of a minority was no time to weaken the central government; in any case, it was a committee of nobles who actually ruled in Henry's name and any limitation on his power would only make their task of governing the harder. Hence the successive compromises of 1216 and 1217. At length, in 1225, Henry III came of age and issued the fourth Great Charter which differed from the third in slight details only. This is the document which is still law (except in so far as it has been repealed) and is cited by the old authors as the charter or statute of the ninth year of Henry III. It was not enrolled until many years later when, in 1297, it was put on the statute roll (word for word, except one slight slip), and so is also sometimes cited as the statute *Confirmatio Cartarum* of 25 Edward I.[2] On numerous later occasions during the middle ages it was solemnly confirmed and from that day to this has been held in the deepest respect both in England and in America. After all these revisions *Magna Carta* as it now stands on the statute books of common law jurisdictions is a sober, practical, and highly technical document. A complete understanding of all its provisions would require a whole volume upon numerous aspects of mediaeval law and administration; for our present purpose the following summary will suffice.[3]

CONSTITUTIONAL PROVISIONS.

" First, we have granted to God, and by this our present charter have confirmed for us and our heirs for ever, that the English Church shall be free and shall have

[1] The legal aspect of Innocent III's action is discussed by G. B. Adams in *Magna Carta Commemoration Essays*, 26–45 (reprinted in his *Council and Courts in Anglo-Norman England*, 353–372).

[2] On the absence of early enrolments of the Great Charter see V. H. Galbraith, *Studies in the Public Records*, 139 ff.

[3] The traditional views are expressed in Coke's commentary in the *Second Institute*; the modern learning is in McKechnie, *Magna Carta* (2nd edn.).

all her rights and liberties, whole and inviolable. We have also given and granted to all the freemen of our realm, for us and our heirs for ever, these liberties underwritten, to have and to hold to them and their heirs, of us and our heirs for ever " (Chapter 1; note the formulas of a conveyance of real property which are here used).

" The City of London shall have all her old liberties and customs. And moreover we will and grant that all other cities, boroughs, towns . . . and ports shall have all their liberties and free customs " (Chapter 9).

" No freeman shall be taken or imprisoned, or disseised of his free tenement, liberties or free customs, or outlawed or exiled or in any wise destroyed, nor will we go upon him, nor will we send upon him, unless by the lawful judgment of his peers, or by the law of the land. To none will we sell, deny, or delay right or justice " (Chapter 29). These words have provoked centuries of discussion. Originally, it seems, " the law of the land " covered all the usual modes of trial, whether it be by indictment, petty jury, appeal or compurgation. " Trial by peers ", on the other hand, was undoubtedly an importation from continental feudal law, and was the solemn trial of a vassal by his fellow-vassals in the court of their lord.[1] It has always been rather rare, and is apt to have a political aspect. King John himself was tried by his peers in the court of King Philip of France who was his overlord in respect of the lands held by John in France. In certain cases an English peer could claim to be tried by members of the House of Lords, either in Parliament or in the Court of the Lord High Steward. As time went on the phrase was given a newer and wider meaning. We find for example that a knight accused of felony will claim successfully a jury composed of knights.[2] Later still the notion will get abroad that " trial by peers " means trial by jury, which it certainly did not at the time when the charter was first made.

The Regulation of Feudal Incidents.

The numerous feudal incidents of relief, wardship, marriage, and the rights of widows, were regularised to prevent the oppression which had grown up during the reign of King John. These reforms applied also to the relations between the barons and their undertenants, and form the basis of a great deal of feudal law (Chapters 2–6, 10).

Restraints on the Prerogative.

" The writ called *praecipe* shall not be used in the future to deprive any lord of his court "[3] (Chapter 24). Purveyance and the forfeiture of lands for felony were likewise regulated (Chapters 19, 21, 22).

The Regulation of the Courts.

" Common pleas shall not follow our court but shall be held in some certain place " (Chapter 11). The taking of the assizes was ordered for regular terms every year and was to be in the proper counties. Sheriffs was forbidden to hold pleas of the Crown. The County Court was also regulated and ordered to be held not more than once a month (Chapters 11–14, 17, 28, 35).

The Law of Land.

The rights of widows were protected and landowners were forbidden to alienate so much of their land that the lord of the fee suffered detriment; and finally, collusive gifts to the Church (which were frequently made in order to evade feudal service) were forbidden (Chapters 7, 32, 36).

---

[1] Powicke in *Magna Carta Commemoration Essays*, 96–121.

[2] Y.B. 30 & 31 Edward I (Rolls Series), 531.

[3] As to this, see below, p. 357.

TRADE AND COMMERCE.

The sureties of the King's debtors were not to be liable until after the default of the principal debtor, and were to have the lands of the debtor until they were satisfied for what they had paid for him. There was to be one system of weights and measures throughout the land, and foreign merchants were to be allowed free entry except in war-time, their treatment depending upon the treatment of English merchants abroad (Chapters 8, 25, 30).

From this it will be seen that the provisions of the Great Charter which became permanent were those of a practical nature, while the revolutionary machinery invented by the barons to supersede the Crown was quickly dropped as unworkable and contrary to the current of English history.

The Great Charter was by no means unique in European history. Many kings and nobles about this time were granting charters to their tenants and subjects, and their general character was not dissimilar even in different countries. It has even been suggested that Spanish influence can be traced in our own Charter.[1] In 1222 Hungary obtained a very similar charter.[2] The difference between the English Charter and these other documents lies not in its contents but in the use made of it in subsequent history. The Charter gradually grew bigger than the mere feudal details which it contained and came to be a symbol of successful opposition to the Crown which had resulted in a negotiated peace representing a reasonable compromise. As time went on, therefore, the Charter became more and more a myth, but nevertheless a very powerful one, and in the seventeenth century all the forces of liberalism rallied around it. The great commentary upon it by Sir Edward Coke in the beginning of his Second Institute became the classical statement of constitutional principles in the seventeenth century, and was immensely influential in England, America and, later still, in many other countries as well.[3] To explode the " myth " of the Greater Charter is indeed to get back to its original historical meaning, but for all that, the myth has been much more important than the reality, and there is still something to be said for the statement that " the whole of English constitutional history is a commentary upon the Great Charter ".[4]

Its immediate result, apart from the reforms contained in it, was to familiarise people with the idea that by means of a written document

[1] Altamira in *Magna Carta Commemoration Essays,* 227–243.

[2] It is translated in Sayous, *Histoire générale des Hongrois* (1900), 116–121.

[3] See Hazeltine, *The Influence of Magna Carta on American Constitutional Development (Magna Carta Commemoration Essays),* 180–226; also in Columbia Law Review, xvii. (1917).

[4] For the " myth " and the historical interpretations, see A. L. Cross, *An Unpopular Seventeenth-century View of Magna Carta,* in American Historical Review, xxix. 74 (1923), and F Jenks, *The Myth of Magna Carta,* in Independent Review, vi. 260 (1904). The posthumous history of the charter has been traced in two works by Faith Thompson, *The First Century of Magna Carta* (1925), and *Magna Carta, its role in the making of the English Constitution, 1300–1629* (1948).

it was possible to make notable changes in the law.   Within the period of ten years, four successive charters had made numerous changes in law and procedure.   Was not this an indication that many other difficult questions might be settled in a similar manner?   And as a matter of fact we soon find a stream of legislation beginning to appear, which we shall describe later.

THE BARONS' WARS

The rest of the reign of Henry III is notable chiefly for the revolt of the barons in 1258, which repeats the main outlines of the revolt against King John.   The results also were similar.   A revolutionary organisation was set up by the barons with the idea of reducing the Crown to complete powerlessness; and this, like the previous attempt in 1215, had soon to be abandoned.   But in this later struggle the barons had been dependent to a considerable extent upon the assistance of smaller landowners who also had to be satisfied by a measure of reform.   Recent work on this period has shown how largely it was concerned with legal problems, and to lawyers there are two especial reasons for studying the baronial revolt with care.   First, it was the age of Bracton,[1] who ceased to revise his great treatise just as the crisis approached; and secondly, it was the one occasion in English history when the laity carried out *vi et armis* an important and complicated programme of law reform.   Its full significance can hardly yet be appreciated, but recent research has already shown that the development of the forms of action, and especially trespass, during this period is of importance,[2] that the working of the law of seisin was also the cause of difficulty,[3] and that the abuse of the lord's right of extra-judicial distress—" the beginning of all wars," as Simon de Montfort called it[4]—was a problem of great urgency.   Many of the reforms the victorious barons effected were continued a'ter the fall of Simon de Montfort and became the Statute of Marlborough, 1267.   Even before his accession Prince Edward took part in this post-war period of reconstruction, and the Statute of Marlborough is therefore really a part of the great programme of law reform which was carried out in the reign of Edward I.

[1] Of Bracton we shall speak later, pp. 258 ff.

[2] This suggestion was made by E. F. Jacob, *Studies in the Period of Baronial Reform* (1925), xii, 108 ff., 115.

[3] Plucknett, *Statutes and their Interpretation* (1922), 100.   The whole period is admirably discussed in R. F. Treharne, *The Baronial Plan of Reform* (1932), and Sir Maurice Powicke, *Henry III and the Lord Edward* (1947).

[4] C. Bémont, *Simon de Montfort* (ed. E. F. Jacob), 77.

CHAPTER 4

EDWARD I TO RICHARD II:
STATUTES AND SOCIAL REVOLUTION

We now come to a period of steady growth in the common law covering just over a century and a quarter (1272–1399). The reign of Edward I is marked by one of the greatest outbursts of reforming legislation in English history until the nineteenth century.[1] The first Statute of Westminster (1275) made numerous changes in procedure, many of them designed to protect the subject against the King's officers, for the evidence collected by the commission of inquiry set up in the previous year had revealed a good deal of oppression.[2] The statute may be regarded in some ways as being a sort of supplement to the Great Charter, which was now fifty years old. The Statute of Gloucester (1278) made important amendments to the law of land, especially on the subjects of waste, curtesy and dower. The next year the great Statute of Mortmain did something to check the feudal losses which resulted when land was given to churches, monasteries and corporate bodies, by completely forbidding all amortisation.[3] In 1284 we have a remarkable statute re-stating the fundamentals of the common law for the information of sheriffs who were engaged in applying English law to the newly conquered land of Wales. This statute is so long that it almost amounts to a short treatise on the state of the law in 1284; its practical interest to historians is therefore considerable, for it contains information which is difficult to find elsewhere.

---

[1] See generally, Plucknett, *Legislation of Edward I* (1949).

[2] H. M. Cam, *Studies in the Hundred Rolls*, 36.

[3] By a " secret of law " (Co. Lit. 99) the crown dispensed with the statute; see Wood-Legh, *Church Life under Edward III*, 60 ff.

WESTMINSTER THE SECOND

The next year (1285) saw an astonishing series of epoch-making statutes. Of these the first was the second Statute of Westminster, which leaves hardly a single department of the law untouched. Of its fifty chapters, the first is the famous *De Donis* of which we shall have much to say later on, for it lies at the foundation of the idea of legal estates in land. Among many others are the following important provisions. The common mode of fraudulently conveying land by allowing judgment to go by default in a collusive action brought for the purpose was checked (c. 4).[1] The rights of joint-tenants and reversioners were given more prompt protection in such cases, and it was enacted that this device should not bar a widow's claim to dower. By chapter 11 a very stringent process was created for the action of account. In its origin it dealt with the relationship of the lord of a manor to his bailiff or estate manager, but as history proceeds it becomes a commercial as well as a feudal action, and the regular remedy lying between partners. The statute imposes imprisonment as soon as an accountant is found in default, and this penalty can be inflicted by the lord's auditors without the intervention of a court. Equally drastic is the penalty upon the sheriff or gaoler if such a prisoner escapes, for in such a case the gaoler shall be liable to the lord in the same sum as the accountant was. This perhaps is a reflection of the insecurity of mediaeval prisons, which were by no means so massive as is sometimes thought. Chapter 18 established the writ of *elegit* whereby a judgment creditor could, as an alternative to the old *fieri facias*, elect to take all the debtor's chattels and to hold half of his lands until the debt be levied out of the chattels and the rent.

THE STATUTE AND SIMILAR CASES

Chapter 24 contains the famous provision that—

" whensoever from henceforth it shall happen in the Chancery that there is to be found a writ in one case, but not in another case although involving the same law and requiring the same remedy, the clerks of the Chancery shall agree in framing a writ, or else they shall adjourn the plaintiffs to the next Parliament, or else they shall write down the points upon which they cannot agree and refer them to the next Parliament, and so a writ shall be framed by the consent of the learned in the law; to the end that the court from henceforth shall no longer fail those who seek justice."

Here indeed is laid down a regular procedure for the steady expansion of the law by the enlargement of the available writs in certain narrowly defined circumstances. Its primary object was to authorise the extension of remedies which already existed between parties, so that they would become available between the heirs (or successors in office) of those who would primarily have been entitled to use them. It is clear that the

[1] This device was invented in order to convey the property of a married woman against her will, and to enable life tenants to defeat reversions, *etc.*

Chancery clerks did not regard this statute as giving them wide powers of creating new forms of action, for where we find the chapter invoked at all (and it is not very often) it is used with great caution. The only serious extension of the law as a result of the statute was the creation of the writ of entry *in consimili casu*.[1] In fact, the large part assigned to Parliament in the chapter shows that it was the general feeling that matters of legislative importance ought to be handled there. In the fourteenth century, moreover, parliamentary proceedings were often extremely informal, and are by no means always recorded on the rolls; consequently it is most likely that these statutory powers were exercised, if at all, by the little group of administrators and lawyers who formed the kernel of the fourteenth-century Parliaments. Very soon, however, the statute rolls seem regularly to contain express declarations in legislative form as to the extension of old writs to new cases, and it may well be that the form of a statute was chosen because the publicity attaching to it made the reform more quickly effective.[2]

BILLS OF EXCEPTIONS

Chapter 31 relates that it sometimes happens that parties who allege an exception which the court overrules have difficulty when they attempt to test the lawfulness of the decision by a writ of error, because the court may not have enrolled the unsuccessful exception. The higher court is therefore unable to pass upon the matter because it is not on the record before them. To remedy this, the statute allows such exceptions to be written down in a " bill " to which the trial judge must affix his seal. If the exception is not enrolled, then the " bill of exceptions " is to be sufficient record for proceedings in error. The chapter shows that the roll is still under the absolute control of the court, which can include or exclude matters in its discretion; it is not surprising that judges said many hard things against the new " bill of exceptions " and more than once flatly refused to seal them.[3]

THE NISI PRIUS SYSTEM

Chapter 30 regulated the new system of *nisi prius* justices, who become more important in practice as a result of many succeeding statutes amending the system in details. In this way it became less necessary for juries from remote parts of the country to undertake the slow and costly journey to Westminster.

In the same year the Statute of Winchester established a system of police by compelling citizens to possess armour according to their means

---

[1] Below, p. 362.

[2] For the modern theory that the action of case is based upon this statute, see below, pp. 372–373, and compare pp. 163–164.

[3] Plucknett, *Statutes and their Interpretation* (1922), 67; *Bridgman* v. *Holt* (1693) Shower, P.C. 111 is a late example of this attitude.

for the defence of the peace. Then the Statute of Merchants (also of 1285) established a system of recording debts and of making land liable to execution, which lasted down to the eighteenth century with some modifications.[1]   In 1290 we find the great Statute *Quia Emptores* which has been rightly called one of the pillars of real property law.

The burden of foreign war and the Crown's growing need for money provoked a good deal of unrest, and finally, as the price of a heavy grant of taxes, the King had to confirm the Charters. It was on this occasion (1297) that the Great Charter was first enrolled among the public archives.

EDWARD I AND FEUDALISM

There is one general aspect of Edward I's legislation which has especial interest. This is the belief of many historians, expressed in several different forms, that there was something anti-feudal in his policies.[2] We have already mentioned the fact that the Statute of Marlborough was passed under his influence and is historically part of the great mass of legislation passed in Edward I's reign, and so we shall consider it together with the statutes of Westminster the first and second, and especially the statute of *Quia Emptores*. Of the Statute of Marlborough Maitland wrote that " in many respects it marks the end of feudalism ",[3] and of Edward's legislation as a whole Stubbs wrote that it endeavoured to eliminate the doctrine of tenure from political life.[4]   These two statements, sometimes repeated in less guarded language by other historians, deserve more minute examination than can be accorded them at the present moment, but a few general observations can be made.

It would indeed be a remarkable tribute to the intellectual powers of Edward I if it could be shown that he set his face against the whole pattern of contemporary society as it existed throughout civilised Europe. The demand for a new social structure is common enough in our own day because we have numerous examples, both contemporary and in the history of the last two generations, of revolutionary attempts to remodel society on the lines of military and economic dictatorships, communes, soviets and the like. But it is hard to imagine a statesman of the year 1300 suggesting an alternative to the social structures over which three such legal-minded monarchs as Edward I, Philip the Fair and Boniface VIII presided.

If Edward's legislation is examined, it will be seen that its general tendency is not to weaken, but to strengthen, the position of feudal lords. Lords must have been grateful for two statutes which gave

---

[1] The earlier Statute of Acton Burnell (1283) was much less stringent; for details, see Plucknett, *Legislation of Edward I*, 140–148.

[2] For what follows, see Plucknett, *Legislation of Edward I* (1949), 21–23, 157.

[3] Maitland, *Equity and Forms of Action*, 336. Cf. Pollock and Maitland, i. 209, on Bracton's attitude towards the Church and baronage.

[4] Stubbs, *Constitutional History*, § 179.

them immense power over their bailiffs;[1] the feudal rights of wardship and marriage were protected by new civil and criminal procedures;[2] the default of tenants in paying services (which at this moment left the lord in a very weak position) was for the future visited with the forfeiture of the tenement;[3] and lords were also given extended powers of appropriating commons.[4] Most striking of all, Edward I risked a bitter quarrel with the Church over mortmain in order to prevent lords losing their feudal incidents when land passed to ecclesiastical bodies,[5] and *Quia Emptores* itself was designed in order to preserve those same rights of wardship, marriage, relief and escheat.[6] Continued sub-infeudation would probably have introduced such chaos into the system of tenures that these incidents would have eventually been evaded almost universally, but *Quia Emptores* perpetuated them. Edward I certainly did a great deal for the feudal lord. But he was not prepared to tolerate abuses, and he was equally active in assuring to tenants their rights. Many great statutes defined the law of distress and replevin,[7] and the action of mesne (which protected a sub-tenant when his lord defaulted in services to the lord above) was made more practicable.[8] There seems no escape from the conclusion that this legislation assumed the reasonableness and desirability of the feudal structure, and deliberately strengthened it. The fact that all the incidents of military tenure survived until the sixteenth century, and that the persons interested in them were to enjoy them for an additional century (thanks to the statute of uses), is all testimony to the soundness of the legal structure of feudalism as Edward I left it. His policy in fact was based on that simple and straightforward idea of " justice " which was taken as an axiom in the middle ages—the rendering to every man his own. Edward assured to the tenant the peaceful enjoyment of his lands with the same impartial justice as he confirmed to the lord the fruits of his seignory.

EDWARD II AND THE ORDINANCES

The troubles which began in the reign of Edward I became chronic under his son, Edward II (1307–1327), and once again an attempt was made by a series of " Ordinances " (1311) to put the Crown under the domination of a group of barons.[9] For a time they were successful, but in the end a counter-revolution repealed the Ordinances by the

[1] Marlborough, c. 23; Westminster II, c. 11; above, p. 28.
[2] Marlborough, c. 7; Westminster II, cc. 16, 35.
[3] Gloucester, c. 4; Westminster II, cc. 21, 41.
[4] Westminster II, c. 46.
[5] *De Religiosis*, 7 Edw. I.
[6] 18 Edw. I; see below, p. 541.
[7] Marlborough, cc. 1, 2, 4, 9, 15; Westminster I, cc. 16, 35; Westminster II, c. 2.
[8] Westminster II, c. 9.
[9] The Ordinances are printed in *Rot. Parl.*, i. 281.

famous Statute of York (1322). This Statute contains the important declaration that matters relating to the estate of the King and the country must be agreed upon by the prelates, earls, barons and commons in parliament. It has been very persuasively argued[1] that this statute already shows a feeling that matters which would now be called " constitutional " ought to be reserved for very special deliberation in a parliament which contained commons as well as lords. In any case,

" it is not too much to say that one result of the reign of Edward II was the establishment of the practice of regarding only those parliaments as true parliaments which contained representatives of the commons".[2]

EDWARD III: THE BLACK DEATH

The tragic ending of the reign and the mysterious death of the unfortunate Edward bring us to the reign of his son, Edward III (1327–1377), and a period of fifty years of uneasy tension. Once again we find the Charters solemnly confirmed in 1352. The middle of his reign was marked by a series of fearful calamities which have left their mark upon society and the law. The nation was already weakened by a succession of famines when the arrival of the Black Death (1348–1349) from the East wrought a revolution in social and economic conditions. The terrible mortality from this plague completely disorganised the manorial system, which had hitherto depended upon a plentiful supply of labour born and bred within the manor. The plague accelerated and intensified forces which were already at work, and the result was a very serious depletion of the labour supply. The population of the manor was no longer sufficient to work the lord's estates. Consequently lords began to compete among themselves for such free labour as was available. This tempted servile inhabitants of manors to leave their holdings and become hired labourers. So keen was the competition that a series of ordinances and statutes beginning in 1349 regulated for the first time the relationships between master and servant, and provided machinery for the establishment of scales of wages above which any payment would be unlawful.[3] This system depended largely for its operation upon the "justices of labourers " (later justices of the peace), and remained in force as late as the eighteenth century.

RICHARD II: THE PEASANTS' REVOLT

The situation culminated in the next reign in the Revolt of the Peasants of 1381. Into the long controversy over the causes and character of this rising we cannot enter at this moment, but very briefly stated, the history of the revolt may be summarised like this. In the first place, it is clear that the old theory which saw the cause of the revolt in a

[1] By G. T. Lapsley in English Historical Review, xxviii. 118–124, and in his Crown, Community and Parliament, 253 ff.; cf. C. H. McIlwain, Political Thought in the West, 377–378; G. L. Haskins, The Statute of York (1935).

[2] T. F. Tout, Place of Edward II (Manchester, 1914), 151.

[3] B. H. Putnam, The Statute of Laborers (1908).

supposed attempt by landlords to reimpose the conditions of serfdom after having first abandoned them is no longer tenable. It seems rather that in this, as in many other revolts, the motive of the movement was not so much a blank despair as a certain hopefulness. It is not in the depth of the night that social revolutions occur, but with the first gleam of dawn. The economic results of the Black Death had already brought a considerable improvement in the lot of the agricultural labourer, and it was the disappointment that this improvement had not been spread more equally among the masses, or proceeded more rapidly, that provoked the impatient peasants to rebellion. The insurgents were mainly those who had not yet been able to establish their position as free labourers, and their hatred was principally directed against the lawyers and the stewards who kept manorial records. Wherever possible the rebels destroyed the manorial rolls which contained the legal evidence of their servitude. The parochial clergy seem to have viewed the movement with considerable sympathy, although the higher ecclesiastics were markedly indifferent. It is now clear, moreover, that the ideas of the early reformer Wyclif played very little part in the movement, although it is certainly true that there were active agitators who were preaching a somewhat crude form of communism. Several independent risings occurred in different parts of the country, and one body of rebels was welcomed by the mass of the Londoners who were at odds with the mayor. A serious massacre took place in the streets of the city, and the rebels beheaded John Cavendish,[1] Chief Justice of the King's Bench, the Archbishop of Canterbury and the Lord Treasurer.

It is very difficult to find any clear results of the revolt. Indeed, the latest opinion tends to lay stress upon the ineffectiveness of the whole movement. It was one of the very few occasions in English history when a definitely social, as distinct from a political, revolution, was proposed, and its failure was immediate and complete. Fortunately, the natural movement towards the emancipation of villeins, which had long been in progress, continued as before the revolt, and during the following century a great silent revolution slowly took place. The majority of the populace who had been serfs gradually acquired economic independence. Lords of manors who could no longer find servile labour, either leased their lands to free labourers (or to labourers who were soon to become free), or else tacitly conceded to their peasants the benefits of ownership in their holdings. This latter process is truly remarkable, and deserves close attention from students of legal history. Through the machinery of custom, which was always a powerful influence for experiment or change in the middle ages, the rightless villein slowly acquired customary property rights in the land he worked. For a long time the common law refused to recognise this process, and it was

---

[1] Cavendish was in fact entitled to the gratitude rather than the enmity of the peasants, for tradition ascribes to him an important decision in their favour: Y.B. 13 Richard II (Ames Foundation, ed. Plucknett), 123–124.

to the courts of equity that the customary tenant, or copyholder as he was later called, looked first for protection.[1]   In the early seventeenth century Sir Edward Coke took up the cause of the copyholders, and finally extended to them the protection of the common law courts. In this way those sweeping and violent social revolutions which occurred in Switzerland and France were avoided in English history through the slow adaptation of the law to new social conditions, no doubt assisted by the lack of a precise definition of property, while the willingness to tolerate for a time a few anomalies helped to accomplish by peaceful means the great task of transforming the ancient serfdom into a class of free workers.

Throughout this period we find the steady growth of the legal profession and the development of a remarkable series of law reports called " Year Books " which we shall describe later.   Then, too, Parliament becomes more definite in its composition and gradually takes its place as the ultimate court in the land, as a national legislature, and as a representative body which could give voice to the feelings of the nation when the ministers of the Crown incurred its dissatisfaction.

Richard II (1377–1399) is one of the most picturesque and puzzling figures in English history.[2]   The troubles in his reign (apart from the Peasants' Revolt) were ultimately of a dynastic character, turning upon the conflicting claims of the Houses of York and Lancaster to succeed. Richard's tactless policies gave an opportunity to the House of Lancaster to steal a march upon the Yorkists, and the result was the deposition, and soon the mysterious death, of Richard II in 1399.

[1] For a summary of the legal problem see Y.B. 13 Richard II (Ames Foundation), xxxii–xliii.

[2] Professor Tout has given a noteworthy history of the reign from a novel standpoint in his *Chapters in Administrative History*, vols. iv. and v.   A later survey is by A. Steel, *Richard II* (1941).

CHAPTER 5

THE FIFTEENTH CENTURY :
THE PROBLEM OF ENFORCEMENT

Henry IV, who began the line of Lancaster in 1399, together with his descendants, Henry V and Henry VI, were all under the same disability, that is to say, kings by a doubtful title. They were therefore dependent to a large extent upon the series of family alliances and political factions which had placed them upon the throne, and in consequence we have what has been called the " Lancastrian experiment ". The experiment seems to have consisted in associating a fairly large body of nobles with the daily business of government, and so the chief characteristic of the fifteenth century is the important place occupied by the Council.

THE IMPORTANCE OF THE COUNCIL

" Practically the first public utterance of the new dynasty was its founder's pledge to be governed by the counsel of the ' Sages and Ancients of the Realm ', and when, three-quarters of a century later, the line had ended in violence and exile, the last echo of its departed polity was heard in Fortescue's plea for more ' counsel '. Time after time, Parliament prayed for ' sufficient counsel ', and as often did Henry IV inform them of the names of his advisers and swear them to be upright and true; later, in the troublous times of his grandson, it is still the Council which was the storm centre, the Council's dissensions which raged round the child King's throne, and the Council's collapse, which eventually wrought his ruin. To appreciate how intimately the fortunes of the Council were bound up with those of the nation itself, it is well to consider how widely its ramifications spread throughout the body-politic; Parliament, Chancery, Exchequer, law courts—all these still remained so closely connected with the parent body, as represented by the group of men nearest the King, that it is difficult to determine at what period, and to what extent, one should regard them as separate institutions. This interpenetration of the various government departments by the Council can be regarded as the administrative aspect of the growing political supremacy of the Crown. For centuries the Crown was steadily gathering strength and building up a political unity out of the discordant elements of feudalism. One King was to be felt at work throughout the realm, and as the task grew heavier, it was one Council which ensured the smooth working of the various organs of the administration. As a result, the fifteenth century possessed as highly centralised a constitution as one could expect to find, considering that communications—the nerves of a bureaucracy —were still so tardy; such machinery as did exist, however, was to a striking degree amenable to Council influences, and at times subject to Council control."[1]

For a time the system worked; while the novelty of it lasted, the barons appeared fairly regularly at the Council table and busied themselves with the daily work of government. But it could not last very long. To lords who were used to power and longed for more, the tiresome routine of a government office was irksome, and as the fifteenth century proceeds we note the increasing difficulty of assembling any number of lords. With their defection the machinery of government was bound either to collapse completely or else to fall into the hands of a group of minor officials. Finally a way was found whereby the regular business of administration was left to professional clerks and household officials, while the lords trusted to their influence in Parliament and the Great Council to be able to supervise the general progress of events. But even this proved too much for the barons. Sooner or later it was unavoidable that they should be divided into the two camps of Lancaster and York, and the Wars of the Roses were an inevitable result; and so the mediaeval baronage finally destroyed itself.

THE LANCASTRIAN CONSTITUTION

To the historians and political antiquaries of the seventeenth century the records of the Lancastrian period were a rich mine of precedents for parliamentary procedure, and their interpretation of the history of the fifteenth century was decisive during the period of the Great Rebellion. To the leaders of the opposition to Charles I, the Parliaments of Henry IV and his successors seemed just the same in composition, in powers and in constitutional spirit as the Parliaments of their own day. Just as the " myth " of the Great Charter is more significant than the Charter itself, so the seventeenth-century interpretation of Lancastrian history has had more practical effect than the actual events would warrant.[2] But to an historian who would examine the constitution under the Lancastrian kings and free his mind from the theories which were current in the reigns of James I and Charles I the picture seems rather different. The institutions were there and we can read about them in language which looks strangely modern, but, nevertheless, the spirit within them is still feudal. It was characteristic of the middle ages that the law of land and the property ideas connected with it should take the place and serve the purpose of what is now called constitutional or public law. It is perfectly clear that this was still the case under the Lancastrians.

[1] Plucknett, *The Place of the Council in the Fifteenth Century* (Transactions of the Royal Historical Society, 1918), 163.

[2] See, for example, J. E. Neale, *Free Speech in Parliament* (Tudor Studies presented to A. F. Pollard), 257–286.

PROPERTY AND PUBLIC LAW

When great public questions arose, as happened more than once, they were discussed in terms of feudal property. Indeed, since this paragraph was first written, a distinguished mediaevalist has expressed this attitude in words which deserve careful thought:

" If I were asked which of the famous maxims into which the political thought of the world has at times been compressed is the one which on the whole best comprises the living political conceptions of the later middle ages, my choice, I imagine, would be rather unexpected, and not in all cases accepted, but it is one which my study of this period makes me willing to defend. It is the aphorism from Seneca's *De Beneficiis*, ' Ad reges enim potestas omnium pertinet: ad singulos, proprietas '—to kings belongs authority over all: to private persons property."[1]

Nor were the middle ages alone in looking to the idea of property for their principal protection, for it lies at the root of much American constitutional law: the peculiarity lay rather in the fact that the elaborate doctrines of property law were themselves used as a sort of constitutional law. It was not until we reach the reign of Edward IV that we find the first examples of reasoning which are truly and essentially modern upon such questions.[2]

THE ENFORCEMENT PROBLEM

The same thing is true of local conditions. The barons who hoped to establish their domination over the Crown were carrying out the same policy in the sphere of local politics. Large masses of evidence[3] bear witness to the extent to which local government was demoralised through the influence of the great landowners. Trial by jury collapsed utterly;[4] parliamentary elections either represented the will of the local magnate or took the form of small battles; the administration of law both at Westminster and in the country was seriously hampered by the breakdown of local machinery and widespread corruption. The lawyers did all they could under the circumstances. They elaborated the law patiently and skilfully. A succession of judges of marked ability were making decisions of great importance, but it was on the administrative and political side that the common law became ineffectual.

[1] McIlwain, *Political Thought in the West* (1932), 394.

[2] The cases upon which these conclusions are based will be found discussed in Plucknett *The Lancastrian Constitution* (Tudor Studies presented to A. F. Pollard), 161–181. For much additional material, see S. B. Chrimes, *English Constitutional Ideas in the Fifteenth Century* (1936).

[3] Much will be found in the introductions to Fortescue, *Governance of England* (ed. Plummer) and to *The Paston Letters* (ed. Gairdner).

[4] The Abbot of Battle in 1475 secured a special procedure for selecting a jury in a case he had brought against the Archbishop of Canterbury, since the sheriff of Kent was the primate's steward, and the four coroners were either his tenants and " within his distress ", or else " had robes of him " (*i.e.* wore his livery).—Y.B. 15 Edw. IV, Pasch. no. 4 (f. 24). A less powerful litigant at this date would be unlikely to obtain such a concession. The extensive liberties of the Archbishop had made it difficult to get juries for some centuries: cf. a case of 1277 printed in *Casus Placitorum, &c.* (Selden Society, vol. 69), 92–96.

THE YORKISTS

By the time the Wars of the Roses were over the baronial ranks on both sides had been seriously depleted. In fact the baronage, as a political class, had destroyed itself and there remained only the Crown, weakened indeed, but still ready at a suitable moment to resume the great tradition of re-establishing orderly government. With the exile of Henry VI (1461) and the accession of the Yorkist, Edward IV, the work of reconstruction begins. New instruments and new methods begin to appear. The Court of Chancery becomes much more prominent and fills gaps where the common law had been too timid or too weak to attempt reform. The Court of Star Chamber was at this time nothing more nor less than the Council, and it struggled manfully to enforce order in cases where the normal criminal law was hopelessly inadequate. In all this the mainspring was necessarily the Crown, and so we find that the nation turned to the monarchy with a sigh of relief after sixty years of baronial anarchy. This brings us to what has been called the " new monarchy ", which will eventually culminate in the popular nationalist dictatorship of the great Tudor monarchs, especially Henry VIII and Elizabeth.

CHAPTER 6

THE TUDORS:
RENAISSANCE, REFORMATION AND RECEPTION

The house of Tudor came to the throne with the accession of Henry VII after the battle of Bosworth in 1485, and ruled England during one of its most brilliant periods, the sixteenth century, until the death of Queen Elizabeth in 1603. It was the golden age of literature, beginning with Sir Thomas More and ending with Bacon and Shakespeare; an age, too, of heroic adventure when the seamen ranged the ocean in search of new continents, and planted distant colonies whose future they could never have guessed. But besides the remote new worlds which adventurers had discovered, there was something like a new world in old Europe too. A wave of new ideas was remaking the intellectual life of Italy and France, Germany and England, and these ideas are usually grouped together by historians under the three headings of the Renaissance, the Reformation and the Reception. The movement begins with the revival of classical studies, and especially of Greek. Sometimes this resulted in a sort of new paganism; instead of the frigid logic of Aristotle which had dominated the middle ages, attention turned to the genial romance of Plato, and to the poets. More occasionally the movement took a distinctly religious form, and the tragic lives of Pico, Politian and Savonarola illustrate the beauty of Christianity lived in the light of classical humanism. In England the movement is represented best by Sir Thomas More, Chancellor, historian and romantic philosopher, who combined a platonic fancy for Utopias with a steadfast devotion to traditional Catholicism which cost him his life in 1534. Erasmus also was influential in England, where he lived for some time as Professor of Greek at Cambridge. As with every great intellectual movement, the Renaissance had profound effects upon the conception of law.

THE MEDIAEVAL ACHIEVEMENT

The mediaeval man has never succeeded in ridding himself of his reputation for lawless behaviour. It is possible, no doubt, to overestimate the amount of disorder that existed, but nevertheless the fact remains that violence is a conspicuous element in almost any mediaeval chronicle. Born amid the ruins of the Roman peace, the early days of the middle ages witnessed the successive failures of several attempts to restore some semblance of authority; and this confusion was further confounded by persistent invasions. Feudalism was the compromise finally reached, and although it made wide concessions to the military idea, nevertheless in the end it accomplished the difficult task of subjecting armed force to the rule of law. Naturally progress was quicker in some places than in others, but everywhere at least a lip service was paid to the idea of law, and as the middle ages proceed it becomes more and more evident that law was winning. Religion had an important rôle in this development and contributed the valuable conception of Jehovah as a law-giver and law-enforcer—a conception derived from Judaism. Out of all the confusion and disaster of the middle ages there arose the unanimous cry for law, which should be divine in its origin, supreme in its authority, rendering justly to every man his due. Of the many intellectual systems devised in the middle ages, there was one which proved to be a practical as well as an intellectual answer to some of the most urgent of life's problems, and that was law, law which was directly based upon the divine attribute of justice.

It might have been that the idea of law was no more than a despairing refuge in an impossible Utopia, devised by minds frightened by the evils around them. But Utopias belong to modern history; the mediaeval man was above all a man of action, and out of the night of the dark ages he began to build the fabric of law. To him the rule of law was not only a worthy achievement of the spirit, but also a great active crusade, and the greatest of all the crusades, because it alone survived its defeats.

THE RENAISSANCE AND THE STATE

Such is the subject matter of legal history in the middle ages where we can follow the rise and progress of law and the rule of law. When we come to Machiavelli we reach the spirit of the Renaissance, and begin to find law itself questioned, for his distinction between public and private morality is essentially the same heresy as to divide the substance of the Godhead; a double standard introduces a sort of polytheism utterly repugnant to mediaeval thought. And true enough, there soon came the State, as a sort of anti-Christ, to wage war with the idea of law. The issue of this conflict is perhaps still uncertain, but mediaeval thought is to-day fighting hard for the cause of law against the amoral, irresponsible State. It was mediaevalists in England, armed with Bracton and the Year Books, who ended Stuart statecraft, and the Constitution of the United States was written by men who had *Magna Carta* and Coke upon Littleton before their eyes. Could anything be more mediaeval than the idea of due process, or the insertion in an instrument of government of a contract clause? *Pacta sunt servanda*,[1] it seems to say, with the real mediaeval accent. It was Machiavelli himself who gave us the word " state " and filled it with the content which we now associate with it.[2] Instead of the mediaeval dominion based upon divine right and subject to law, we have the modern State based upon force and independent of morality. And so, where many a mediaeval thinker would ultimately identify law with the will of God, in modern times it will be regarded as the will of the State.

THE REFORMATION

The second aspect of this intellectual revival is the Reformation. The study of Greek led scholars to examine the New Testament in the original tongue, and soon they began to interpret it in the light of private judgment instead of following traditional custom. This abandonment of custom is highly significant of the change from mediaeval to modern times. The attempt to reconstruct Christianity from the New Testament and the earliest fathers meant a denial of over a thousand years' growth and development in Christianity, based upon custom. This denial of the validity of theological development operating through custom and slowly shifting tradition had its parallel in legal history. Custom tends to be depreciated more and more by the State, until finally the legal restrictions within which it is confined eliminate it as one of the major sources of law. In other words, the State and the central organs of government, the courts and the legislature, are becoming the sole source of law.

The quarrel of Henry VIII with the papacy was for a time purely mediaeval in its character. Many a king and noble had been involved in similar matrimonial tangles and had incurred the displeasure of the Holy See. There was even mediaeval precedent for the confiscation of monastic property and the limitation of appeals to the papal court, but the modern spirit appears when the quarrel is carried a step further, and the doctrinal basis of Catholicism is questioned. With the reign of Edward VI the Reformation is definitely accepted as a political weapon against Rome, and (after a short reaction under Mary) the early years of Elizabeth made it the permanent basis of English political and religious life.

THE REFORMATION AND THE LAW

This attack upon the foundation of the Church was bound to undermine the mediaeval State as well. Church and State had frequently

---

[1] " Pacts should be kept " (motto of Edward I).

[2] For the history of the word, see Dowdall, *The Word " State "*, Law Quarterly Review, xxxix. 98, and Plucknett, *Words*, Cornell Law Quarterly, xiv. 263–273.

quarrelled during the middle ages, but it was the very intimacy which existed between them that provoked dissension. They were not two different powers, but merely two aspects of the one divine mission of ruling the souls and bodies of men by law. Law in the theological sense, and law as the lawyer knew it, were both based upon the same foundation—the will of God as expressed through authority (whether ecclesiastical or royal), tradition and custom. To attack the authority of the Church was therefore to attack the whole mediaeval system of law. Just as the Reformers went behind traditional Christianity to the historical sources, so there was a movement to go behind traditional law and seek for its origins. A striking example of this is the growth of two schools of Roman law, the first of which was content with Roman law as it was modified by mediaeval custom, while the second insisted upon a return to the strict letter of the classical texts.

The attack upon the traditional basis of mediaeval Christianity had its counterpart in political theory. It soon became evident that as a result of the Reformation, religion was no longer to be universally admitted as the basis of civil government. The foundations of religion had been shaken, and were differently interpreted in different countries and by different thinkers. As substitutes, various theories were proposed. In a number of them " the people " were brought into the reckoning, and attempts were made to base the theory of government upon the idea that kings existed for the convenience of their subjects, instead of (as in the middle ages) both king and people working together for the glory of God. An early form of this idea is to be found in the controversies during the sixteenth century upon the question (at that time very topical) whether a bad king could be properly assassinated by his outraged subjects. Later still it was proposed that kings, that is to say, the State, and all the forces of government, including law, are based upon a contractual relationship between ruler and subject. Some were prepared to assert this as an historical fact; to others the contract was merely to be presumed from existing circumstances.

THE REFORMATION AND THE CONSTITUTION

This secularisation of law had its effects upon the constitution. In England, as in several other States, government fell into the hands of the professional administrator, and " reasons of State " placed in his hands an extremely wide, over-riding discretion. In England this took the form of the dominance of the Council under all the Tudor sovereigns, and in the rise to importance of the office of Secretary of State. As long as Queen Elizabeth lived she was generally able to maintain this novel supremacy of the administration above the old feudal legalism, which was timidly asserted from time to time by the common lawyers. Only in her very last years did she suffer an occasional reverse. In general terms the conflict between the Council and the courts, between administration and law, is the theme of sixteenth- and also of seventeenth-century history, and its origins are clearly to be traced back to the Reformation and the resulting disorganisation of mediaeval political thought. During all this period the typical common lawyer was generally on the conservative side. He still pored over mediaeval books, he practised in mediaeval courts, and was often suspected of being secretly an adherent of the old religion. There was, therefore, a tendency to look outside of the legal profession for men to fill administrative posts, and it was to the civilians that Henry VIII turned when he was founding or reorganising such administrative courts as the Privy Council, the Star Chamber, the Court of Requests, the Court of High Commission, the Council of the North, the Council of Wales, and the rest.

Attendant upon the Reformation came the Church settlement. It is a striking feature of Henry VIII's reign that he was able to use Parliament itself as a convenient machinery for effecting the complicated settlement. The results were momentous. Parliament thereby acquired the experience of carrying out measures which were in fact revolutionary. In one statute it declared that the supreme head of the Church was not the Pope, but Henry; in another it confiscated enormous quantities of property which had been held by the Church for centuries undisputed; in another even so sacred a thing as Christian doctrine was restated by Parliament in the Statute of Six Articles; soon it was to establish a prayer-book to replace the age-old formularies hitherto in use. When in later years the powers of the modern State came to be analysed, Parliament held a very large place in the scheme of things. Those who maintained the omnipotence of Parliament found their most striking illustrations in the acts which carried out the Reformation in England. Henry VIII has been well described as the " great architect of Parliament ".[1]

THE RECEPTION

And, finally, we come to the movement known as the Reception.[2] This was a widespread tendency in various countries of Europe to receive the classical Roman law in place of the mediaeval customary law which had only been partially Romanised, if at all. The legal scholars of the day had taken anew to the study of the books of Justinian, ignoring the thousand years of history which had introduced serious modifications in adapting Roman law to current conditions. The same problem arose in England. Traditional Christianity as represented by the mediaeval Catholic Church was replaced by a system which to its adherents seemed simpler, more reasonable and more in accord with ancient history. Ought not a similar reform to be carried out in the sphere of law? Ought not the mediaeval common law which was inexpressible in any decent

[1] Pollard, *Evolution of Parliament* (2nd edn.), 126.

[2] As to this see Maitland's famous lecture *English Law and the Renaissance* (reprinted in *Select Essays in Anglo-American Legal History*, i. 168–208), and the remarks below, p. 299.

language, French, Latin or English, to be replaced by the pure and ancient doctrine of the Digest? This question was seriously considered. Reginald Pole, cardinal and last of the Yorkist line, who stood equally good chances of becoming King of England or Pope, had committed himself to the idea. Henry VIII was well aware of the merits of the civilians, and founded the still existing Regius Professorships at Oxford and Cambridge for the propagation of their learning. As administrators and as judges in the prerogative courts their influence was paramount. They also maintained an ancient feud with the canonists and the papacy. But against the courts of common law they stood little chance of success. The close organisation of the profession and the numerous vested interests which it contained, the strong tradition of its educational system centring in the Inns of Court, and the practical impossibility of superseding the courts by a newer system, had the result of entrenching the common lawyers within the tangles of their feudal learning, which, moreover, had become the basis of every family fortune in the land. We venture to suggest that once again the common law stood impregnable upon the foundations laid by Henry II. It was he who gave the common law its firm grip upon the land, and for the future the more elaborate the land law became and the more subtly it contrived to entangle both present and future generations in the maze of real-property law, the more impossible it became for the landed classes to contemplate any interference with the system which assured to them and their children the complicated benefits of inheritance. In Germany, France and Scotland the Reception was accomplished with varying degrees of thoroughness; but not in England. Nevertheless the common law for a time had to maintain a stubborn defence, and for the first time in its history it made a definite alliance with the members of the House of Commons, who were equally willing to accept the aid of the lawyers. In this way were laid the foundations of the coalition between the House of Commons and the common law which was to dominate English history during the seventeenth century.

The Tudor period had its own social problem. The transition from serfdom to copyhold was nearly complete, but nevertheless there was considerable economic distress, and from the later years of Queen Elizabeth proceeds a stream of legislation dealing with unemployment and the relief of paupers, while the mediaeval machinery for the fixing of wages was kept in steady operation and even enlarged. Then, too, we find English writers for the first time taking an interest in such topics as international law and in the international aspects of commercial and maritime law, of which we shall speak later.

TUDOR LEGISLATION

Finally some words must be said on the extremely important legislation of the Tudor sovereigns. The reign of Henry VIII saw an outburst of legislation which is almost comparable to that of Edward I. The great statutes which carried out the Reformation have already been mentioned, and their importance exceeds even their position as the foundation of the Church of England, for they were astonishing examples of the almost limitless powers assumed by Parliament. Besides this, a good deal of legislation was concerned with treason, illustrating the growth of the idea of the State and the inadequacy of merely mediaeval law for its protection against the new dangers which its own activities had aroused.[1] Of the rest of Henry VIII's legislation we must mention the Statute of Proclamations (1539). Although soon repealed it is nevertheless highly significant. The old view that this statute constituted a sort of *Lex Regia* conferring upon the Crown the power of wide legislation without the concurrence of Parliament has been abandoned.[2] The growing complication of government had brought the proclamation into prominence for the first time as a useful means of supplementing statute law on points of detail, and of carrying out those processes which to-day are effected by administrative bodies with powers delegated from the legislature. The latest and best opinion is that

" the existing law was obscure and the inconvenience of this obscurity was not likely to be overlooked by a King who was remarkable for his political prescience. Henry VIII's Statute of Proclamations was an extremely able attempt by King and Parliament to deal finally with the problem in a manner which should commend itself to the public opinion of the day."[3]

The statute provided that in cases of emergency the King and Council may issue proclamations which shall have the force of an act of Parliament. They were to be published in a manner prescribed by the act, and offenders against them were to be tried by a board of councillors named in the act, constituting, as it seems, a special tribunal for the enforcement of proclamations.[4] This device is certainly in accord with Henry VIII's general policy of erecting special courts for special business, instead of enlarging the jurisdiction of the old common law courts. The second section of the statute contains carefully drawn safeguards to prevent proclamations being used in an oppressive manner; the principles of the common law, existing acts of Parliament, and property rights were put beyond the reach of proclamations. Moreover, it is equally clear that the use made of these powers by Henry VIII and his Council was moderate and reasonable; there is no evidence that the King hoped by means of proclamations to establish an absolutism or to supersede the legitimate activities of Parliament. The immediate occasion for the act was the refusal of the judges to give effect to certain

[1] See the admirable study by Andrew Amos, *The Statutes of the Reformation Parliament* (1859).

[2] See Tanner, *Tudor Constitutional Documents*, 530, and more at large, E. R. Adair, *The Statute of Proclamations*, English Historical Review, xxxii. 34–46, whose extreme scepticism is rather difficult to justify.

[3] Holdsworth, *History of English Law*, iv. 102.

[4] See below, pp. 182–183. They were to sit in the Star Chamber.

proclamations by which, as an emergency measure, the government had attempted to control dealings in corn at a moment of scarcity.[1] There is nothing in the numerous proclamations which have come down to us which would suggest that the act was accompanied by any serious change in their contents or their numbers, nor did the repeal of the act in 1547 prevent the constant use of proclamations by Queen Elizabeth. There is much to be said for the view put forward by Sir Cecil Carr, who suggests that its principal effect was of a more subtle order. It is one of those acts which, by conferring on the Crown powers which it already possessed, made it seem that those powers were really the gift of Parliament. Under the guise of strengthening the prerogative, it therefore really weakened it when, in after years, the implications of the act were judged from a different standpoint.[2] If this is so, then an interesting parallel is to be found in the unexpected results drawn from the famous Star Chamber Act of 1487.

The two other great statutes of this reign, the Statute of Uses and the Statute of Wills, must be considered more at length in discussing the history of real property.[3] Here it will be sufficient to mention them and to premise that their policy was dictated by deep political causes and required a good deal of bargaining between the Crown and different classes of society. At the basis of them lies the grave movement of agrarian unrest which was to produce several insurrections under Henry VIII and Edward VI.

THE CLOSE OF THE TUDOR AGE

With the reign of Queen Elizabeth (1558–1603), and especially the second half of it, we come to a sort of uneasy peace. The Reformation is an accomplished fact; the various attacks upon the position of the Crown, whether from domestic pretenders or from foreign foes, had definitely failed; the deposition of Queen Elizabeth by papal bull and the attempt to execute it by foreign invasion had likewise failed; the defeat of the Spanish Armada (1588) had given to England security upon the sea, and henceforward there was to be no serious question of foreign interference with her domestic politics—at least openly. In the sphere of law there is a similar feeling of problems having been settled or at least shelved; the common law courts begin to revive; the momentous legislation of Henry VIII is being absorbed; a new generation of lawyers brings fresh life to the old system, and a sincere attempt is made to stretch the common law to the measure of the growing needs of the nation. Parliament, although less frequently summoned, was settling its sphere of activity within the enlarged boundaries which Henry VIII's

---

[1] See the very able discussion of this and other matters of law and politics under Henry VIII in *Letters of Stephen Gardiner* (ed. Muller), 391.

[2] C. T. Carr, *Delegated Legislation*, 52.

[3] Below, pp. 585 ff.

reign had assigned to it.   The House of Commons was growing steadily more important; it attracted men of great ability and was establishing close contact with the administrative side of the government.   It is during this period that officials, secretaries of state, and members of the Privy Council begin to appear explaining and defending their policy before the Commons and acting as a *liaison* between the government and the governed.   Although the Tudor age at first sight seems to end upon a quiet note, nevertheless there are indications that a loyal and devoted respect for the great Queen had a great deal to do in preventing the Commons from insisting too pointedly upon matters where they differed from the Crown.   The extraordinary knowledge of human nature which Queen Elizabeth possessed, together with her admitted ability and prestige, had enabled her to prevent the raising of difficult questions; upon the first signs of trouble a motherly scolding was usually effective in reducing the House of Commons to respectful silence and even apologies.   In the meantime the House developed a considerable degree of control over its own procedure, and discipline over its members. The constant enlargement of " parliamentary privilege " helped a great deal in establishing a spirit of united self-consciousness in the House, and the precedents themselves stood in good stead in the succeeding troubles with the Stuarts.   In short, the quiet closing days of Queen Elizabeth's reign were in fact a period of armed peace, interrupted, it is true, by a few significant incidents, during which both Crown and Parliament were quietly strengthening themselves for a conflict which both of them seemed to apprehend.   It must never be forgotten that the Tudor monarchs were wise enough and strong enough to use Parliament as an implement of their policy, but that the success of this method depended upon the monarch commanding the personal devotion of the Commons, both by reason of a policy which was at least to some degree popular, and of the certainty that the Crown really did stand for the good of the realm.   When the Commons begin to doubt whether the King is more concerned for his own or the nation's interest, then this working alliance between Crown and Parliament will cease.   There is no longer any question of a feudal nobility stepping into the breach; if the Crown cannot govern to the satisfaction of the nation, then the House of Commons will be compelled to undertake the government itself.   This brings us to the Stuart age.

CHAPTER 7

THE STUARTS:
STRUGGLE FOR THE SUPREMACY OF LAW

Much new light has been thrown upon the history of the seventeenth century, and large masses of new documents have become available since Hallam wrote his classical *Constitutional History* over a century ago.[1]

POLITICAL SPECULATION

The seventeenth century was an age when conscious and deliberate political theory entered the arena of practical politics. At the same time there were undoubtedly important economic factors which played a large part in the conflict. Religion also added endless complications to an already baffling situation. Elizabeth held the reins of Church and State, but the Church itself had been based upon a denial of tradition and authority; the Church consequently had no answer to fresh denials, save to shelter behind the throne. To an extraordinary extent public thought was turning to various forms of sectarianism, and speculation very frequently took the form of theological controversy. The theory of the State was less developed. The age of the Tudors and of the

[1] See the references below, p. 52 n. 1. The 4th, 5th and 6th volumes of Holdsworth's *History* supersede previous histories of the Tudor and Stuart periods on the legal aspects of the struggle. More general studies are by K. Pickthorn, *Tudor Government* (2 vols., 1934); J. E. Neale, *Elizabeth* (1934), *The Elizabethan House of Commons* (1949), and *Elizabeth I and her Parliaments* (1953); G. R. Elton, *Tudor Revolution in Government* (1953).

Reformation had for the moment carried practice far ahead of political theory, and the pressing business of administration had overshadowed the more sober business of law. The great names in the age of Elizabeth are not those of lawyers or of judges, but of councillors and secretaries. Against the administrative State there was bound to be a reaction, especially when the nation began to doubt the wisdom of the policies pursued. The spirit of theological questioning was to be extended to the State, and so the uncertainty of the foundations of religion, and the breakdown of the old theories of ecclesiastical authority in the established church, resulted inevitably in the bewilderment of those who sought for the foundations of the State as well. In the end, attempts were made to use the few remnants of mediaeval thinking. The Crown naturally turned to the doctrine of the divine right of Kings, but interpreted it in a narrow sense which a mediaeval philosopher would hardly have recognised. In this way the old doctrine of the divine origin of civil government became restricted to a particular form of government, that is to say, a monarchy, and to a particular section of that form, the King himself. In opposition to all this, the revival of the common law brought back a view which more nearly represented the mediaeval attitude. This view was drawn to a large extent from the pages of our greatest mediaeval lawyer, Bracton, whose celebrated work on the laws of England was first printed in 1569 and again in 1640. In this book Sir Edward Coke and other common lawyers found the simple mediaeval doctrine of the supremacy of law. In an alleged altercation between James I and the great Chief Justice the issue was clearly expressed: James, by his prerogative, claimed to be above the law by divine right, and to this Coke replied by quoting the memorable words of Bracton: " The King is subject not to men, but to God and the law."[1] In other words, Coke was prepared to revive the age-old dogma that law, divine in its origin and sanction, is the basis upon which civil society is built, and that this law is supreme above King and people equally. The theory of the divine right of Kings, on the other hand, ascribed this religious character to one branch only of the machinery of government, the King. Soon it became evident that there was danger of the latter doctrine combining with the newer notions of the State (resembling somewhat the theories of irresponsibility which a later age was to produce), to create thereby a sort of " Leviathan "—to use the later term of Hobbes. Regarded in this light, the conflict of theory between Crown

[1] Coke's version of the incident in *Prohibitions del Roy*, 12 Rep. 63 (and in Tanner, *Constitutional Documents of James I*, 186–187) has been examined by R. G. Usher in English Historical Review, xviii. 664–675, who suggests 1608 as the date, and shows that a violent scene did occur during which Coke expressed some such doctrine as that in the text above, " after which, his Majestie . . . looking and speaking fiercely with bended fist offering to strike him, which the lord Coke perceiving, fell flatt on all fower ". It is not so certain that Coke actually quoted Bracton (though he may have done). All the evidence indicates that Coke argued long and sufficiently effectively to put James into a frenzy in consequence of which the King lost his dignity and Coke his nerve.

and Parliament is one between the mediaeval view of a paramount divine law, supreme over every aspect of government, and an attempt to transfer this divine sanction to a monarch who is also to embody the State in the more modern aspect of the word. From this point of view, Parliament represents the conservative side and the Crown the side of innovation. From another angle, however, the positions might appear to be reversed. When it came to the details of the actual powers which the Crown had exercised in the past independently of parliamentary control, it was a plausible argument for the Crown to insist that it was, in fact, basing its position upon mediaeval precedent. This was particularly true on various matters of indirect taxation which the middle ages had left in great obscurity. In asserting control over these matters, the House of Commons laid itself open to historical arguments of considerable force, which would have been stronger still if the Crown had been able to secure the services of antiquaries as learned and zealous as those of the parliamentary party. Even so, when it came to the judicial interpretation of mediaeval precedents, the courts more than once had to find for the Crown—and we are at perfect liberty to assert that the judges who made these decisions reached them honestly and properly upon the historical evidence available to them, although they often spoilt the effect by gratuitously introducing a good deal of dogma on divine right. The historians of a later age, imbued with partisan spirit, have certainly exaggerated their wholesale accusations of subserviency against the Stuart judges. From this point of view, therefore, it is the Crown which seems conservative and Parliament the innovator. However, the Commons were fortunate in possessing several antiquaries of truly prodigious learning; William Prynne, for example, had read enormous quantities of mediaeval rolls. Sources which are voluminous even in modern reprints and abstracts, Prynne could quote at great length from the original manuscripts, which he had studied by candlelight in the dank vaults of the Tower. Only those who have had to spend many hours with mediaeval records can appreciate the immensity of his labours. As we have already mentioned, the ambiguous rolls of the fifteenth-century Parliaments were a particularly rich mine for the opposition, being easily susceptible of interpretations in their favour.

THE SUPREMACY OF THE COMMON LAW

From what has just been said it will be clear that the frank acceptance of the principle that current problems were to be settled upon the basis of antiquarian research might work both ways, and in fact the very honesty with which it was followed has had the effect of making some judges give inconsistent decisions. At times, Sir Edward Coke seems to be a champion of prerogative, although at other times he is one of the most intrepid of parliamentarians. He must not be blamed too much for these inconsistencies[1] which were really implicit in the whole of the parliamentarian argument. He himself seems aware of this weakness, and to remedy it he fell back with great ingenuity upon a position which he skilfully developed, and which has had immense influence, especially in America:

" Urged by a presentiment of the coming conflict of Crown and Parliament, he felt the necessity of curbing the rising arrogance of both, and looked back upon his country's legal history to find the means. This instinctive appeal to history for guidance was characteristic, and the choice of a legal rather than any other solution was amply justified by the remarkable continuity and stability of English law during the vicissitudes of the seventeenth century. His attitude is aptly expressed in one of his own picturesque phrases. ' Let us now peruse our ancient authors,' he wrote, ' for out of the old fields must come the new corne.' So it was in this spirit that he laboured at the ancient patrimony of his profession, those short, thick folios of black-letter *Year Books*, and from their forbidding mass of obsolescent technicalities raised a harvest of political theory which was destined to be the food of far-distant states to which he had never given a thought.

" The solution which Coke found was in the idea of a fundamental law which limited Crown and Parliament indifferently. What that law was, its nature and its contents, were questions as difficult as they were insistent—and, as subsequent events showed, capable of surprising solutions. The nearest we find to an explicit definition of this fundamental law is the assertion of the paramount law of ' reason '. For the rest, the common lawyer's ' reason ' is left in as much uncertainty as he himself ascribed to the Chancellor's equity. Moreover, Coke was prepared to advance mediaeval precedent for his theory, and in so doing has drawn upon his head the criticisms of later investigators. Just as these criticisms are, from the point of view of modern scholarship, it is only fair to the Chief Justice to insist that his view of history was not ours, and that it is only by the standard of his own day that a true evaluation of his learning and intellectual honesty can be formed. Although it must be confessed that even then he cannot be found altogether faultless, yet it is believed that a sufficient explanation will be found to establish his *bona fides*. His doctrine is certainly based largely upon mediaeval precedents and the extent to which they justify it is an interesting subject for investigation. But if we reach a different estimate from his of the *Year Book* authority for his dogma, this must not be taken as necessarily involving a severe censure of Coke. He himself has told us that though the fields are old, the corn is new."[2]

This doctrine was first proclaimed by Sir Edward Coke in his judgment in *Dr. Bonham's Case* (1610),[3] and for nearly a century afterwards the idea that the common law could be regarded as a fundamental law seemed attractive to certain minds. The Crown viewed the new theory with alarm, and Coke was ordered by the government to explain his doctrine and to " correct " his reports.

[1] For further remarks on this topic, see below, pp. 242–245.

[2] Plucknett, *Bonham's Case and Judicial Review*, Harvard Law Review, xl. 30; cf. Mackay, *Parliamentary Sovereignty or the Supremacy of the Law*, Michigan Law Review, xxii. 215–247. L. B. Boudin, *Lord Coke and the American doctrine of judicial power*, New York University Law Review, vi. 233–246, suggests that Coke later dropped the idea, and S. E. Thorne, *Dr. Bonham's Case*, Law Quarterly Review, liv. 543 that he had never held it. The latest survey is J. W. Gough, *Fundamental Law in English Constitutional History* (1955).

[3] 8 Rep. 114.

THE GROWTH OF THE CONFLICT

A solution so simple as this frank return to the mediaeval idea of law could hardly have a chance amid the riot of party passion which was soon aroused. In this place we shall be content with only a very brief summary of the stirring events which occupy the reigns of James I and Charles I.[1] To begin with, we have a long series of precedents on the subject of parliamentary privilege such as *Shirley's Case* (1604),[2] and *Darnel's* or the *Five Knights' Case* (1627).[3] The powers of Parliament were further asserted in impeaching unpopular ministers. Worse still, the procedure by bill of attainder was revived. Then again a long constitutional conflict arose over matters of taxation. The obscurities of this subject during the middle ages had never been thoroughly cleared up, and there was a good deal of justifiable doubt as to the powers of the Crown in this respect. *Bate's Case* or the *Case of Impositions* (1606)[4] decided that the Crown without the concurrence of Parliament could increase the rate of customs duties. A variety of other expedients were devised for raising money, such as the revival of the forest dues and the demand for ship-money. This latter was contested in *Hampden's Case* (1637),[5] which also was decided in favour of the Crown. It is noteworthy that previous to the trial the King called upon the judges to give him an extrajudicial opinion upon the questions at issue. Their answers were in favour of the Crown and were ordered to be read publicly in the Star Chamber and enrolled in all the courts of Westminster. In the midst of this conflict Sir Edward Coke was compelled to take a side, and finally became one of the leaders of the parliamentary party. The crisis came in 1616 when the *Case of Commendams*[6] raised some technical points of ecclesiastical law and the validity of a royal grant *in commendam*. Coke's dissenting opinion in this case immediately brought about his dismissal from office. Events steadily moved to a climax. The House of Commons defended its privileges fiercely and claimed complete freedom from royal interference for its debates and its members. At the same

---

[1] Further details are to be found in the classical work of Hallam, *Constitutional History of England* (1827), of which there are many editions, including one in the handy " Everyman's Library "; the standard work is S. R. Gardiner, *History of England* (10 vols., 1883) covering the years 1603–1642. A very careful discussion of the legal aspects of the period will be found in Holdsworth, vi. 1–302. Valuable and easily accessible collections of documents are Prothero, *Select Statutes and other Constitutional Documents, 1558–1625* (4th edn., Oxford, 1913); Gardiner, *Constitutional Documents of the Puritan Revolution, 1625–1660* (3rd edn., Oxford, 1906); and Tanner, *Constitutional Documents of the Reign of James I* (Cambridge, 1930).

[2] Fully discussed by Prothero in English Historical Review, viii. 735; documents in Tanner, 302–317, and Prothero, 320–325; *Commons' Journals*, i. 149.

[3] 3 S.T. 1; extracts in Gardiner, 57.

[4] 2 S.T. 371; extracts in Tanner, 337–345, and Prothero, 340–355; commentary by Derek Hall in Law Quarterly Review, lxix. 200.

[5] 3 S.T. 825; extracts and other documents in Gardiner, 105–124.

[6] Reported as *Colt and Glover* v. *Bishop of Coventry*, Hobart, 140. A *commendam* is a papal (later, royal) permission allowing a bishop to hold a benefice at the same time as his bishopric; see Gibson, *Codex Juris Ecclesiastici* (1761), 912, 1528.

time the House was assuming control over every source of revenue and was deliberately using the power of the purse in an attempt to compel the Crown to dismiss ministers, and to pursue policies at the dictates of the Commons. It is this claim which makes the history of the seventeenth century so totally different from that of preceding ages, save, perhaps, the superficial resemblances in some respects which are to be found in the fifteenth century, while the Lancastrian monarchy was extraordinarily weak. Finally, the Commons embodied their demands in the Petition of Right[1] (1628) which contained a long list of grievances. Rehearsing a number of statutes and several provisions of the Great Charter, the Commons declared that arbitrary imprisonment is unlawful and that a Privy Council warrant setting forth the King's special command shall be no sufficient return to a writ of *habeas corpus*. The unreasonable billeting of soldiers and the trial of civilians by martial law were likewise denounced.

THE CHURCH IN POLITICS

From 1629 to 1640, Charles I contrived to rule without calling a Parliament. Grievances were steadily accumulating. The Church of England (unwisely led by Archbishop Laud) was suffering more and more from the spread of dissent, and it was inevitable that the Church and the Crown should make common cause against those who combined a dislike for the establishment with anti-royalist principles. The laws already existing against nonconformists were enforced with great harshness by those courts which were most amenable to royal influence— the Star Chamber and the Court of High Commission. Consequently, the conflict was still more embittered by the introduction of a religious feud. Finally the Church question was to be the ruin of Charles. He rashly undertook to impose Anglicanism in Scotland upon a people whose religious fanaticism even exceeded his own. A war was the immediate result and then came inevitably the summoning first of the short Parliament (1640), and then of the long Parliament (1640–1660). By this time, Parliament was master of the situation. The Earl of Strafford and Archbishop Laud were attained and put to death. Shipmoney was abolished; so also were the Courts of Star Chamber and High Commission, and a statute was passed to prevent a dissolution without Parliament's own consent. The Church and the universities were both attacked, and Charles replied by impeaching before the House of Lords five members of the Commons, a proceeding which the Commons claimed was their sole privilege. The House vigorously defended its members, and when the King in person came to order their arrest, the word " privilege " was uttered loud enough for him to hear. From this date (1642) the Civil War became inevitable. All sense of moderation was lost and in 1649 a revolutionary tribunal condemned and executed

---

[1] Text in Stubbs, *Charters*, Appendix, and in Gardiner, *Constitutional Documents*.

the King.   From 1649 to 1660 various forms of government were devised which are of great interest as early examples of the erection of ready-made constitutions.   Most important of all was the Instrument of Government, a document which purported to be a fundamental constitution which was to be unchangeable save by particularly complicated machinery.   This document, therefore, may be properly regarded as a prototype of the written fundamental constitution, as it is known to American public law.[1]

THE COURTS DURING THE INTERREGNUM

Although Sir Edward Coke had found it impossible to avoid taking a vigorous part in national politics, his successor, Chief Justice Hobart, succeeded in winning the confidence both of the royalists and the parliamentarians.   In fact, the courts were well served during the period of the Commonwealth; Henry Rolle became Chief Justice of the " Upper Bench ", while Sir Matthew Hale sat in the Court of Common Pleas during the Commonwealth and won royal favour after the Restoration. It is interesting to note that a good many anticipations of modern legal reforms were proposed during this period although it is hardly necessary to say that most of these premature advances ceased at the Restoration. Among them we may mention the settlement of the jurisdiction of the various courts in order to prevent the scandalous competition between them.   Chancery, which had been bitterly attacked by Sir Edward Coke, undertook to reform itself; ecclesiastical jurisdiction had already been abolished.   The growth of overseas commerce provoked the reorganisation of the admiralty courts, while district courts for small claims were proposed.   Legal education was revived in the Inns of Court and legal records were for a time in English.   A good deal of thought was given to a projected codification of the law, and a system of registering titles to land was likewise proposed.   As early as 1648 an essayist suggested that there should be only two legal estates, fee simple and for life, abolishing the entail entirely.   Rather less creditable was the proposal to restrict the equity of redemption to very narrow limits;[2] it is difficult to resist the conclusion that this project emanated from the military and financial interests who were deeply engaged in speculative, and sometimes corrupt, operations in land.[3]   The eleven short years of Republican rule were too much filled with war and high politics and religious dissension for these proposals to reach any very practical result, and the restoration of

---

[1] See E. Jenks, *Constitutional Experiments of the Commonwealth* (1890); text in Gardiner, *Constitutional Documents*.   Cf. similar instruments of even earlier date in the New World, *e.g.* Fundamental Orders of Connecticut (1639), New Haven (1639), and the earliest, the *Mayflower* compact (1620), brief extracts of which are in MacDonald, *Documentary Source Book of American History*.

[2] R. W. Turner, *Equity of Redemption*, 30.

[3] H. E. Chesney, *The Transference of Lands in England, 1640-1660* (Transactions of the Royal Historical Society, 1932), 181-210.

Charles II, in 1660, automatically restored the state of affairs as it existed at the eve of the civil war.[1]

REFORMS AT THE RESTORATION

The movement had its results, however, for Charles II's reign was in fact a period of legal reform. At the very commencement tenure in chivalry was abolished. This abolition of a great deal of mediaeval law relating to such subjects as wardship, marriage and military tenure was counterbalanced, however, by an increase in complexity in other departments of the law of real property. There may be a certain amount of truth in the suggestion that has several times been made, that periods of civil disturbance have been frequently accompanied by the development of new devices by the conveyancers with a view to tying up property in land so as to put it, as far as possible, beyond the reach of such political accidents as forfeiture and improvident management. Thus the fifteenth-century landowners seem to have resorted to the use as a protection—which the legislature soon defeated, however—against the frequent forfeitures of legal estates attendant upon the Wars of the Roses. So in the seventeenth century the widespread confiscations of royalists' properties[2] during the period of the Commonwealth was accompanied by numerous developments in the art of conveyancing which from this date onward reached an astonishing degree of technicality.

THE STATUTE OF FRAUDS

The reign of Charles II saw the enactment of the Statute of Frauds (1677). This statute has been so constantly before the courts from that day to this, and has been adopted in so many jurisdictions, that a few words must be said as to its origin and policy. There exist a number of drafts and projects of legislation which illustrate quite clearly the problem involved.[3] A detailed examination of these drafts confirms the claim of Lord Nottingham to the principal share in its authorship, although a number of additions and improvements came from other hands. Like every piece of legislation it must be judged from the standpoint of the place it held in the legal system as it then existed. If, in the course of the centuries, conditions have so changed that a piece of old legislation no longer conduces to justice, then the blame for the situation must obviously lie not upon the original authors of the statute but upon the legislatures of to-day. The lawyers of the seventeenth century had the courage to meet a serious situation by deliberate legislation, and

---

[1] See Robinson, *Anticipations under the Commonwealth of Changes in the Law* (Select Essays in Anglo-American Legal History, i. 467–491). For the Commonwealth practice of giving new trials when verdicts were unsatisfactory (an innovation at that date) see below, p. 135.

[2] And, also, the improvidence of many royalists in selling or mortgaging their lands to finance the civil war, and to pay fines.

[3] They are fully discussed in Holdsworth, vi. 379–397.

we can do no less. If the statute has proved in some respects unsatisfactory under modern conditions, then the remedy lies in our own hands. We shall therefore examine for a moment the position which the statute occupied in the environment wherein its makers placed it.

To begin with, it must be remembered that jury trial in 1677 was still essentially mediaeval.[1] The modern device of ordering a new trial when the verdict is clearly against the weight of the evidence was in its infancy. Again, at this date the law had barely begun to acquire experience in the handling of parole evidence; such rules as did exist were ancient and obstructive, for parties to the action, their husbands, and wives, and all other persons interested in the outcome of the litigation were incompetent as witnesses. It is obvious, therefore, that the law was faced with two alternatives in 1677: either the whole law of evidence as it then existed would have to be scrapped and replaced by a hastily improvised system upon modern lines, or else parties who desired legal protection for their transactions must be compelled to take the precaution of embodying them in documents whose contents and authenticity were easily ascertainable. The first alternative in point of fact hardly existed; it has taken two centuries of hard experience to develop the law of evidence thus far, and a great deal still remains to be done. It was only reasonable, therefore, that the profession, guided by Lord Nottingham,[2] should have adopted the second policy; and from what has just been said it will surely be clear that under the circumstances they followed the only practicable path.

As far as these provisions refer to transactions concerning land there has been less serious cause for complaint. It is in matters of trade and commerce where business habits have always been to a large extent informal, that the principal difficulties have arisen. But there is surely some force in the argument that there should be, in common prudence, some impersonal evidence available when serious matters are at stake. " To be fair to its framers, we should, I think, remember three things ", writes Sir William Holdsworth. " Firstly, the law of contract was as yet young; it had been developed wholly by decided cases; and it had very few rules as to the characteristics and incidents of particular contracts. It follows that the framers of the statute were legislating on a branch of the law which was not fully developed, and on a topic which had not before been a subject of legislation."

If a legal system is to depend upon legislation to any extent at all for its readjustment to newer needs, then the principle of legislation must be frankly admitted in its entirety, and the profession must be prepared to undertake a constant and sustained task of securing legislation again and again in order to enable the law to keep pace with the march of events. It is clearly illogical to impose legislation at long intervals, restricting the courts to the comparatively humble work of interpreting the letter, and

[1] This can be seen from *Bushel's Case* (1670) below, p. 134.
[2] At this moment he was Lord Finch.

then, when confusion results, to blame the legislature of two hundred years ago.[1]

THE *HABEAS CORPUS* ACT

The period from 1660 to the Revolution of 1689 is, however, more remarkable for its contributions to public than to private law. The one other great legal reform of the reign of Charles II was the passing of the *Habeas Corpus* Act[2] in 1679. The writ of *habeas corpus* has played such a large part in the struggle for liberty that a short history of it must be given here.[3] Like a good many other common law writs, its history can be traced back to the early age when legal procedure and administrative methods were still not distinguished, and, together with the other prerogative writs of *mandamus, certiorari* and the rest,[4] its ultimate origin is in a simple command from the Crown to one of its officials. In the reign of Edward I there were several varieties of *habeas corpus* serving different purposes, such as to secure the appearance of a defendant or of jurymen. Gradually the courts acquired the habit of issuing the writ in order to bring before them persons who had been committed by inferior jurisdictions—particularly the courts of cities and local franchises. The motive of this policy seems to have been to enlarge the powers of the Courts of Westminster at the expense of local tribunals, and the result was not infrequently confusion and injustice. Parties were even allowed to use this process when they had been committed by judgment of local courts for debt so as to obtain their release and to defraud their creditors. It is not surprising, therefore, to find a steady stream of legislation restricting the scope of *habeas corpus*.

At the end of the fifteenth century the common law courts had nothing more to fear from local jurisdictions. A new antagonist appeared in the form of Chancery, followed soon after by the Courts of Requests and Star Chamber. The writ of *habeas corpus* was now turned against this larger game. The common law courts were indignant when Chancery committed parties for suing at common law after they had been enjoined, and Chief Justice Huse proposed to release such prisoners by means of *habeas corpus* (1482).[5] The Courts of Admiralty and High Commission were similarly attacked, but it was in the seventeenth century that *habeas corpus* fought its greatest battle. The Crown had established the right of imprisoning without trial upon a warrant signed by the Secretary of State and a few Privy Councillors, alleging " her Majesty's special commandment ".[6] Against so serious a claim

[1] Section 4 of the Statute of Frauds was repealed by 2 & 3 Eliz. II, c. 34 (1954).

[2] Text in Stubbs, *Select Charters*, Appendix, and C. Grant Robertson, *Select Statutes*.

[3] For details see Holdsworth, ix. 108–125, x. 658–672.

[4] See generally, E. Jenks, *The Prerogative Writs in English Law*, Yale Law Journal, xxxii. 523, and S. A. de Smith, *The Prerogative Writs*, Cambridge Law Journal, xi. 40.

[5] Y.B. 22 Edw. IV, Michs. 21.

[6] So it seemed from the " Rules in Anderson ": Holdsworth, v. 495, x. 661, Taswell-Langmead, *Constitutional History of England* (10th edn.), 347.

of State absolutism *habeas corpus* became in the words of Selden " the highest remedy in law for any man that is imprisoned ".

Throughout the Stuart period *habeas corpus* was steadily used and improved by the courts of common law. But procedural difficulties stood in the way. *Darnel's Case*[1] had shown doubts; the special command of the King was nevertheless there held to be a sufficient return, and this rule was only abolished by the Petition of Right.[2] There were also doubts as to which courts were competent to issue it. Many of these defects were remedied in the *Habeas Corpus* Act[3] of 1679, which after much discussion finally passed the House of Lords—and then only owing to a mistake in the counting of the votes, so the story goes. By this act any judge during term or vacation must issue the writ unless the prisoner is obviously committed by lawful means. Prisoners are not to be imprisoned beyond the realm, and the writ is to run in all privileged places. Later legislation at various dates introduced still further improvements. Some striking examples of its use in more modern times are *Sommersett's Case*,[4] where a writ of *habeas corpus* released a negro slave from confinement in a ship on the Thames, on the ground that an allegation of slavery was not a sufficient return. In 1798 the writ was used to ensure a trial at common law of a prisoner, Wolfe Tone, who had been condemned by a court-martial.[5]

THE STOP OF THE EXCHEQUER

There is one other incident in the reign of Charles II which must be mentioned, for it introduces us to a more modern element in law and society. Merchants and tradesmen who had the means frequently made loans as a subsidiary to their normal business. The scriveners (professional writers of " court-hand " who engrossed legal documents) were particularly associated with this business in the reign of Elizabeth, but after the Civil War and under the Restoration it was the goldsmiths who became most prominent. Moreover, these goldsmiths invented a few variations which really turned the old casual money-lending into professional banking. They accepted deposits from customers, at first merely for storage in their vaults, but soon in the more modern sense of deposits against which they issued notes.[6] Already in Charles II's reign, such deposits could be drawn upon by the customer's cheque. The goldsmiths became financiers, discounted bills, and also purchased tallies (receipts for money lent to the Exchequer). These tallies were

---

[1] 3 S.T. 1 (1627).

[2] 3 Charles I, c. 1, s. 5 (1628).

[3] 31 Charles II, c. 2. See David Ogg, *England in the Reign of Charles II*, ii. 510–512.

[4] 20 S.T. 1; E. Fiddes, *Lord Mansfield and the Sommersett Case*, Law Quarterly Review, i. 499.

[5] 27 S.T. 614.

[6] See Professor Tawney's long and illuminating introduction to his edition of Sir Thomas Wilson's *Discourse upon Usury*, and R. D. Richards, *Early History of Banking in England*, 37 ff. (1929); below, p. 68.

sometimes sold direct to the goldsmiths by the Exchequer,[1] thus serving as the machinery whereby the government raised short-term loans, and in 1672 the Government found itself unable to meet them when they became due. This crisis was called the " Stop of the Exchequer " and had serious results for the goldsmiths and their depositors. Recent research suggests that the King's motives may have been less fraudulent than the Whig historians asserted, and that the resulting ruin has been grossly exaggerated.[2] Here we are concerned only with the more general significance of the rise of banking and public finance with the need for new legal principles to govern them, and with the great *Bankers' Case*[3] growing out the stop of the exchequer which settled the constitutional question of the right to bring a petition of right.

RESTORATION OF CHURCH AND PREROGATIVE

The reign of Charles II saw the re-establishment in a harsher form of the Church of England, and the short reign of James II witnessed a rapid crisis. The determination of that monarch to pursue a religious policy which was contrary to that solemnly laid down by Parliament in a long series of statutes was the immediate cause of his fall. It may have been that his project of complete toleration for Roman Catholics as well as Dissenters was intrinsically an advance upon the partisanship of the Church as represented in Parliament. But it is impossible to discuss the merits of the policy when the methods of its promotion were so drastic and so completely contrary to the spirit of contemporary institutions. James II claimed that by his prerogative he could dispense individual cases from the operation of a statute; more than that, he even endeavoured to suspend entirely the operation of certain of the religious laws. Upon this clear issue the conflict was fought out. After an ineffective show of military force James II retired to France, William III of Holland was invited by Parliament to become joint ruler with his wife, Mary II, James's daughter, and so " the great and glorious revolution " was accomplished. The terms of the settlement were embodied in the last great constitutional documents in English history, the Bill of Rights (1689) and the Act of Settlement (1701).

THE BILL OF RIGHTS

The principal portions of the Bill of Rights[4] are as follows:

" That the pretended power of suspending of laws, or the execution of laws, by regall authority, without consent of Parlyament is illegall.

[1] Tallies, being in wood, were often accompanied by written " orders for repayment " whose importance is described by R. D. Richards, *op. cit.* 58 ff.

[2] R. D. Richards, *The Stop of the Exchequer*, in Economic History (supplement to the Economic Journal), ii. 45–62.

[3] 14 S.T. 1 (1690–1700); the case is fully discussed in Holdsworth, ix. 32–39.

[4] 1 William & Mary, sess. 2, c. 2 (1689).

" That the pretended power of dispensing with laws, or the execution of laws, by regall authoritie, as it hath beene assumed and exercised of late, is illegall.

" That the commission for erecting the late Court of Commissioners for Ecclesiasticall Causes, and all other commissions and courts of like nature, are illegall and pernicious.

" That levying money for or to the use of the Crowne by pretence of prerogative, without grant of Parlyament for longer time or in other manner than the same is or shall be granted, is illegall.

" That it is the right of the subject to petition the King, and all commitments and prosecutions for such petitioning are illegall.

" That the raising or keeping a standing army within the kingdome in time of peace, unless it be with consent of Parlyament, is against law.

" That the subjects which are Protestants may have arms for their defence suitable to their conditions, and as allowed by law.

" That elections of members of Parlyament ought to be free.

" That the freedome of speech, and debates or proceedings in Parlyament, ought not to be impeached or questioned in any court or place out of Parlyament.

" That excessive baile ought not to be required nor excessive fines imposed; nor cruell and unusuall punishment inflicted.

" That jurors ought to be duely impannelled and returned, and jurors which passe upon men in trialls for high treason ought to be freeholders.

" That all grants and promises of fines and forfeitures of particular persons before conviction, are illegal and void.

" And that for redresse of all grievances, and for the amending, strengthening, and preserveing of the lawes, Parlyament ought to be held frequently.

" And they doe claime, demand, and insist upon all and singular the premisses, as their undoubted rights and liberties; and that noe declarations, judgments, doeings or proceedings, to the prejudice of the people in any of the said premisses, ought in anywise to be drawne hereafter into consequence or example."

THE ACT OF SETTLEMENT

After the death of Queen Mary (1694), William III ruled alone, until he in turn was succeeded by her sister, Anne (1702–1714), who was therefore the last of the reigning Stuarts; in order to secure the succession, the Act of Settlement was passed in 1701 which not only limited the descent of the Crown (in accordance with which the present royal family reigns) but also added a few constitutional provisions supplementary to those of the Bill of Rights. It required the monarch to be in communion with the Church of England, and not to leave the country without parliamentary consent—an irksome provision which was soon repealed. Membership of the Privy Council and of Parliament was limited to British subjects of British parentage. It was likewise provided " that no person who has an office or place of profit under the King, or receives a pension from the Crown, shall be capable of serving as a member of the House of Commons ". This attempt to limit the Crown's influence in Parliament was subsequently amended[1] in order to permit ministers of the Crown to sit in the House of Commons by allowing them to seek re-election after their appointment to a salaried office. Such was the practice until 1926, when the need for

[1] By a long line of statutes too numerous to detail here.

re-election was abolished. Another chapter provided that judges should hold office during good behaviour at fixed salaries, and that they should only be removable by His Majesty upon an address of both Houses of Parliament; the complete independence of the bench was therefore permanently established.

REVOLUTIONS AND POLITICAL THEORY

The changes and chances of seventeenth-century politics had produced a great number of varying theories concerning the State and the nature of government. In the beginning of the century divine right was ranged against a parliamentarianism which looked to the middle ages for its justification. The period of the Commonwealth accustomed people to see a succession of different forms of government set up and then deliberately pulled down. The lesson was clear: the people had in their hands the power and the right to set up forms of government according to their fancy. A large number of political thinkers of different schools took up this idea, and were prepared to treat existing governments as if they had been the deliberate product of popular action. It merely remained to ascertain exactly what policy the people had proposed to pursue when they did this. We consequently find many different suggestions as to the form which this original contract, as they regarded it, received. The seventeenth century and much of the eighteenth were occupied in searching for forms of contract which should afford a reasonable justification for political society, either as it existed, or as the philosopher thought it ought to exist.

THOMAS HOBBES

Out of this welter of speculation only a few names can be mentioned here. Undoubtedly the most remarkable of them was Thomas Hobbes, whose greatest work, *The Leviathan*,[1] appeared in 1651. Unlike almost all of his contemporaries, he entirely rejected the study of history as having any bearing on political science; instead, he pinned his faith to " geometry, which is the only science that it hath hitherto pleased God to bestow on mankind "—words which have a strangely familiar sound in these latter days. His outlook was entirely materialistic. All knowledge is derived through the senses; every idea is the result of an effect produced upon an organ of sense by the motion of an external object; felicity means success in getting what one wants. Were it not for civil government, life would consist of the ruthless competition of unmoral men for desirable things, and would be " solitary, poor, nasty, brutish and short ". It is only the tremendous power of the State which protects the natural man against himself and his fellows, and from this power are derived the ideas of justice and property—for in the pre-civil

[1] *The Leviathan* has been edited with an illuminating introduction by Michael Oakeshott (Oxford: Blackwell).

State " that only is a man's that he can get, and for so long as he can keep it ". Where other thinkers had conceived of society as involving a contract between ruler and subject, Hobbes devised a completely different scheme. According to his view, helpless and miserable mankind made a contract, every man with another, to submit to a ruler whom they all clothed with authority to govern them. This ruler was no party to the contract and is therefore bound by no limitations. Consequently it is impossible to talk about a sovereign having broken his contract with the nation (which was a common argument in the seventeenth century), for no such contract existed. Nor is there any justification for resistance to the sovereign. We seem to see in these theories a deep impatience with the turmoils of the Stuart period. Neither the antiquarianism of Parliament nor the mysticism of divine right had any meaning to the dry, penetrating, but narrow mind of Hobbes. The troubles of the Commonwealth, deeply involved as they were with religion, are reflected in his treatment of the Church. His own position seems to be that of a deist. He recommends that there be but one Church in a State, and that under the absolute control of the sovereign leviathan; he even asserts that the sovereign necessarily has full authority to preach, baptise and administer the sacraments, and that the clergy only perform these functions by delegation from the State, whose will is the source of both temporal and spiritual law. It is only natural that a century which was so animated by sincere religious dissension should either neglect or revile a thinker at once so original and so cynical.[1]

JOHN LOCKE AND THE REVOLUTION

If Hobbes represents the desperate longing for an omnipotent peaceful State which was natural in the midst of the darkest hours of the seventeenth century, it is in John Locke (1632–1704) that we find, after the storm had passed, a quiet summary of achievement full of the spirit of compromise. In the nineteenth century when it seemed that the leviathan had indeed come to life, Hobbes was to receive due recognition, but in the eighteenth century it was rather John Locke's influence which was paramount, for it was he who discovered a reasonable philosophical basis for the whole of seventeenth-century history, and more particularly for the Revolution of 1689. John Locke learned from history something that Hobbes refused to consider. He made a great plea for religious toleration and embodied it in the " Fundamental Constitution " of Carolina, which he drafted in 1669 on the invitation of the proprietors of the province, and his example was to be improved by William Penn in his form of government for Pennsylvania. It is to John Locke that we owe a reasonable theory of limited monarchy which

[1] It is worth noting that Sir Frederick Pollock writes: " I have learned much from Hobbes, and hold acquaintance with his work at first hand indispensable for all English-speaking men who give any serious consideration to the theoretical part of either politics or law " (*First Book of Jurisprudence*, vii).

was to become the creed of the Whig party.   Locke's view of the contract was much less extreme than that of Hobbes.   In his thought every individual conveys to society as a whole his right of executing the law of nature; all other natural rights he retains.   Locke, therefore, brings us back to the old idea that the powers of the State are limited to certain purposes.   It is his discussion of the mode in which those powers are exercised which has the greatest interest at the present day.   His theory of reserved natural rights leaves a large place for religious toleration, while the limitations he places upon the State are more in accordance with history than is the absolute leviathan which Hobbes conceived.   Where Hobbes had considered law to be the command of the State, Locke returned to the notion of natural law—a conception which was easily reconciled with the mediaeval view of law as the will of God.   Where Hobbes had made law the tool of the State, Locke regarded it as the guardian of liberty.

Locke declared that the legislature is the supreme power in the State, and from this he deduced certain maxims of constitutional practice which, in fact, were the historical settlement reached at the end of the seventeenth century.   And so beginning from general philosophical and theoretical considerations, Locke proceeds to give a philosophical defence of such very practical measures as the Bill of Rights, the Act of Settlement, parliamentary control over taxation, and the whole machinery of limited monarchy.

It seems that Locke was the first modern theorist to propound a doctrine of the separation of powers.   He observed that legislation is (or in his day was) an intermittent function, while the executive, on the other hand, must never cease its activity.   Consequently, the two are better assigned to different bodies, which, he observes, is almost universally the practice—and here we seem to see an example of that comparative study of institutions which had been prominent in England ever since the days of Fortescue, Sir Thomas Smith and others.   In his discussion of the relations between the legislature and the executive, Locke very clearly is thinking of current politics although his treatment is confined to scrupulously general terms.   How close this theory was to current practical politics can be seen where he urges the separation of legislature from executive; this object would have been achieved through the passage we have just quoted from the Act of Settlement excluding ministers from the House of Commons, which was passed only four years before the death of Locke.[1]   Locke's suggestions on the separation of powers were obviously derived from his observation of contemporary English practice; indeed, the easy way in which he seems to take the situation for granted is an indication that he felt it too obvious to need very detailed theoretical treatment.   It is only a century later that his work will be used as a basis for a rediscovery by the great philosopher Montesquieu of a general theoretical doctrine

[1] Above, p. 60.

of the separation of powers such as Aristotle and Marsiglio had suggested in ancient and mediaeval times.

John Locke, therefore, may be regarded as expressing to a peculiar degree the compromise and settlement which the nation had reached when the expulsion of the Stuarts and the accession of William III had enabled political passions to die down. His summary of the results of the great conflict remained for many years the justification on philosophical grounds of the compromise which practical politics had reached, and with his work the tumultuous drama of the seventeenth century fittingly ends on a quiet and hopeful note.[1]

[1] Locke's theories have been aptly summarised in the following words: " It was a theory of a state of nature that was not altogether bad, and its transformation into a civil state that was not altogether good, by a contract that was not very precise in its terms or very clear in its sanction. It embodied, moreover, a conception of sovereignty of the people without too much of either sovereignty or people; of the law of nature that involved no clear definition of either law or nature; of natural rights, but not too many of them; and of a separation of powers that was not too much of a separation. It concluded, finally, with a doctrine as to the right of revolution that left no guaranty whatever for the permanence of the rather loose-jointed structure which the rest of the theory had built up. Yet this illogical, incoherent system of political philosophy was excellently adapted to the constitutional system which England needed at that time and which the Whigs actually put and kept in operation. It was a good, respectable, common-sense view of the features of political life that impressed a philosophical observer; it was strong in the individual parts, if not in their correlation, and it was far better adapted to make an impression on thinking Englishmen than were the more logical systems of Hobbes and Spinoza " (Dunning, *History of Political Theories: Luther to Montesquieu*, 367–368).

CHAPTER 8

THE EIGHTEENTH CENTURY: INDUSTRIAL REVOLUTION

AGRICULTURE

The eighteenth century is the great dividing line in English economic development between mediaeval and modern times. The central point in its history is usually referred to as the industrial revolution, which was rather, in point of fact, a long and slow process which began to accelerate towards the middle of the century. Its results were to change the face of England completely; its mode of life, its source of wealth, even its colonial possessions were all radically changed as an outcome of this movement. So far the structure of the nation had been essentially mediaeval; so, too, had been its law. If we are to seek the fundamental notes of this mediaeval policy we shall find that they were based upon the fact that the normal occupation of the bulk of the inhabitants was agriculture. The great source of wealth was the land, and such capitalism as existed looked mainly to the land for its profits. The social structure of society was built upon this idea. The legal aspect of all this is clearly visible. Land was the principal form of wealth, and therefore the principal source of power, and the law had to take account of this situation. First of all the King's Court assumed complete control over the land—and thereby over the landowners. The law of land was rapidly developed to an astonishing degree, and every means was adopted of protecting landed property to the fullest extent. It was only natural that the land should therefore be the symbol of economic and social permanence, and that efforts should be made to perpetuate the social system founded upon it.

Even in the middle ages, however, there were the beginnings of other forms of wealth, and as time proceeds commerce takes an increasing place in national life. Nevertheless for a long time it was the policy of the law to separate the two; it is curious to observe that merchants very nearly became an estate of the realm and occasionally we find what looks like a parliament of merchants;[1] there was a chance that in England as in some other countries there might have grown up a House of Merchants in Parliament. The separation of commerce from the normal occupation of the nation was further emphasised by the fact that the merchants had their own organisation and their own law.[2] It is only as a result of many centuries of history culminating in the industrial revolution that these barriers were broken down; it is familiar knowledge that such bodies of mercantile law as those relating to bankruptcy and negotiable instruments for a long time pertained exclusively to merchants; indeed, a separate organisation was set up to supervise the affairs of insolvent debtors who were not merchants and therefore outside of the law of bankruptcy. It was only as late as 1690 that the law considered the possibility of a non-merchant being a party to a bill of exchange.[3]

MERCHANTS AND FINANCE

Although the middle ages were so predominantly agricultural, it is still possible and indeed very necessary to trace in them the beginnings of commerce. In English history two commodities are of particular significance, wool and wine. Wool-growing was the great source of England's position in international politics during the middle ages. The wool which was grown in England was exported to Flanders, and there in the great Flemish fairs it was distributed throughout Europe. England's monopoly of wool was so effective that the Crown could afford to leavy heavy taxes upon its export, and upon occasion could bring powerful pressure to bear on foreign nations by diverting the wool trade from one port to another, or even by suspending it altogether. Financially, the wool trade was conducted on a capitalistic basis. In its early days, the leaders of the industry were the Cistercian monks whose mode of life was to build their abbeys in remote places among the hills and occupy themselves with sheep farming. As for the smaller growers of wool, it seems that arrangements were made to buy up their crops in advance, the sale being effected through the assistance of foreign capital. It is significant that credit took the form principally of advanced payments to the growers for future delivery.[4] Middlemen were a prominent feature of the trade and behind them stood great foreign capitalists.

---

[1] For a list of these " Assemblies of Merchants ", see *Interim Report of the Committee on House of Commons Personnel and Politics* (1932, Cmd. 4130), 109. More than a score of such assemblies were summoned in the forty years between 1316 and 1356.

[2] It had long been recognised, however, that a merchant was not excluded from using common law remedies when they were available: Y.B. 21 & 22 Edward I (Rolls Series), 456–458 (1294).

[3] *Witherley* v. *Sarsfield* (1690), Show. 125.

[4] M. Postan, *Credit in Mediaeval Trade*, Economic History Review, i. 234–261 (with which compare Bulletin of the Institute of Historical Research, v. 176–178). For an interesting indenture date 12 Sept. 1478, for the sale of wool to be delivered by 2 Feb. 1479, the purchaser paying £81 : 17s. down, and a further £58 : 3s. on delivery, see *Supplementary Stoner Letters* (ed. Kingsford), 12 (in Camden Miscellany, xiii).

The same was true of the important import trade in wine. It is obvious that we have here complicated relationships involving very important interests, and we may be certain that the result must have been the development of a good deal of commercial law. It is typical of the middle ages, however, that this law should be not the law of the land but the law of a particular class of people, developed through their custom and enforced through their own organisation. As for the capitalists whom we have mentioned, their place becomes increasingly important through the middle ages. In England a large part was played by the Jews until they were expelled by Edward I. Their place was then taken by various groups of bankers from the cities of northern Italy—the financial centre of London is still called Lombard Street. A considerable place too was occupied by certain religious orders whose international organisation was a convenient machinery ready-made for large-scale banking.[1] Their considerable wealth also enabled them at one time to undertake capitalistic operations (although by the close of the middle ages many monasteries were in financial difficulties as a result of heavy royal and papal taxation). Indeed, this tendency of large religious organisations being deeply involved in finance persisted into modern times; in more than one country the principal cause for the expulsion of the Jesuits in the eighteenth and nineteenth centuries was a fear of their financial activities.

As for manufacturers, development was at first most rapid in Flanders where English wool was made up on a large scale. It was to Edward III that credit is largely due for the establishment of the textile industry in England. His Queen was Flemish, and it may be her connection with Flanders which led him to invite some Flemish weavers to settle in England.[2] Nevertheless, the English textile industry was still purely domestic, that is to say, carried on in the home of the worker, and not in a factory.

THE INDUSTRIAL REVOLUTION

The transition from this state of things to conditions which are familiar to-day was effected principally in the eighteenth century. Wool-growing had increased enormously and was conducted on a very large scale. This became possible through the great enclosure movements of the sixteenth and eighteenth centuries whereby a great deal of common land, together with land which once had been arable, was turned over to sheep farming. Besides this great change from crop-raising to sheep-rearing (which was the cause incidentally of a great deal of unemployment and agrarian unrest), the textile industry also underwent a great change. The already existing tendency for a number of textile workers to become dependent upon one employer was immensely increased by

[1] R. Génestal, *Le Rôle des monastères comme établissements de crédit.*

[2] For earlier efforts in the same direction, see Cunningham, *Growth of English Industry and Commerce*, i. 648.

the introduction of machinery, and here we reach the greatest single cause of the industrial revolution. By means of machinery more work could be done at less expense and with less labour. Soon it became clear that the price also was reduced, and the great movement began whereby trade gathered an ever-increasing momentum. The more there was produced the more the demand increased, and in the end the manufacturers were able to some extent to set the pace of industrial development. The introduction of water power, and very soon afterwards of steam power, gave England a tremendous advantage, for ample supplies of coal were easily accessible. Consequently the industrial revolution pursued a much more rapid course in England than in the rest of Europe.

LEGAL CONSEQUENCES

The task which faced the law was to meet these new requirements. Land was no longer to be its principal concern; other forms of wealth were demanding protection. As the growth of machinery proceeded, the cost of equipping a factory became considerable and usually exceeded the resources of a single manufacturer. Various forms of co-operative effort had been inherited from the middle ages which had long been familiar, at least on the continent, where there was a developed law of partnership in several varieties. Such forms of joint enterprise in seventeenth-century England were usually employed in colonial expansion or distant foreign trade. The law had now to consider some means of placing these advantages within the reach of smaller men who did not require the elaborate organisation of such bodies as the East India Company, or the Bank of England. It was also a growing necessity that banking should be developed, and out of the practice of the London goldsmiths who would receive deposits and issue against them interest-bearing notes,[1] there arose, first of all, the Bank of England (1691), and soon a large number of private banks in different parts of the country. The law had, therefore, to consider all the complicated relationships which were being created through the machinery of credit and joint enterprise. It is to the eighteenth century, therefore, that we must look for the rise of most of the law which is of a distinctly modern character, that is to say, of personal property in general (and especially of stock, shares and the like), of companies and their stock, partnerships, of negotiable instruments, contract, bankruptcy, and master and servant. In effecting these developments the eighteenth century achieved the transition from mediaeval to modern times.

Politics had its part in the history of this development. The fall of James II had been due, in some measure at least, to the fact that the City of London and the financial interests thoroughly distrusted his policy. Although his opponents were, of course, drawn largely from

---

[1] See Richards, *Early English Banking Schemes*, Journal of Economic and Business History (1928), i. 36–76. See p. 58 above.

the nobility, nevertheless City interests played a considerable part. One of the most significant results of the Revolution of 1689 was the foundation of the Bank of England, which was designed primarily to finance the French War, the founders lending a considerable sum of money to the government and using this government debt as part of their capital. In consequence the bank was closely connected with the Revolution settlement; it was generally felt through the country that any restoration of the Stuarts would imperil the bank, and as the bank's activities grew wider the country was less and less inclined to take this risk. The Whig party had, therefore, a marked commercial character, while the Tories were still apt to be representative of the landed interest.

The legal consequences of the industrial revolution were effected, partly through legislation, but more largely through the development of case law, and a little group of judges who were far-sighted enough to divine the direction in which events were moving were able quietly and without commotion to perform the great work of taking over the existing mercantile law and custom, and incorporating it into the law of the land. Of this we shall speak more in treating of the history of the law merchant.

One other great result of the industrial revolution has been to produce a new internationalism. Internal commerce in many different nations was to develop along parallel lines, and the basis of the new commercial law was in every case to be the old custom of merchants, and one of the features of this custom had been its growing international character. There was, therefore, a tendency for commercial law in different countries to proceed broadly upon parallel lines. Local diversities there were inevitably; they had been even more serious in the middle ages. But in spite of this some general features remained constant. At the same time international trade was taking a much greater place. More and more commodities passed from country to country and an increasing number of merchants were engaged in foreign business. This also emphasised the tendency for commercial problems to be considered from an international standpoint. The movement is one of the most striking features of our own day; international trade and finance are having their effect upon commercial law, and the time seems not far distant when commercial law will regain its mediaeval aspect of internationalism. This progressive feature of our eighteenth-century law is admirably shown in the life of Lord Mansfield,[1] who tried to treat some of the ancient portions of the common law in the same liberal spirit as the newer commercial law which he was so instrumental in developing.

His contemporary, Sir William Blackstone,[2] although an admirer of Mansfield, and at times a critic of the law as it then existed, was not a reformer by temperament, and his *Commentaries* (1776) then, as now, leave the impression of almost indiscriminate praise for the great bulk

[1] For Mansfield, see below, p. 248.
[2] For Blackstone. see below, p. 285.

of the old law which the courts had been accustomed to administer. The law of real property, notably, was undergoing immense elaboration with results which were by no means satisfactory. If the landed interests were to retain their dominant place in national affairs, then agriculture would have to compete with the newer forms of commercialism. Great improvements were made during the eighteenth century in scientific farming, and agriculture made rapid strides as a source of wealth. The effective output, both in crops and herds, was increased and improved enormously, until it became clear that agriculture afforded opportunities for commercial enterprise. This development, however, could only be achieved by considerable capital outlay upon improvement, and was seriously hampered by the law of real property. Land could not take its place in a commercial scheme of things as long as it was so difficult to deal with it. The seventeenth- and eighteenth-century lawyers had developed elaborate methods of placing land beyond the control of the tenant in possession, and when they tried to retrace their steps in an endeavour to give the great landlord powers to charge and to sell, their remedies were equally cumbersome, uncertain and expensive. It is not until the close of the eighteenth century that any substantial progress was made towards providing a simpler law of land, and to this day the process is still going on.

At the same time there was a movement, not fully effective until the early years of the nineteenth century, for radically reforming the whole of the procedural side of law.

MONTESQUIEU

The most tremendous event in the eighteenth century was the French Revolution with which it closed, and a few words must be said here of its implications in legal and political science. These can best be illustrated by considering two great thinkers, Montesquieu who just preceded it, and Burke who was contemporary with it. In 1748 Montesquieu published his *Esprit des Lois*, which, like his earlier essays, was an attempt to give a political interpretation to history. The sources he used were Roman and more particularly English history. He classified the different forms of government and assigned to each its characteristic principle: thus despotism depends upon fear, monarchy upon honour, aristocracy upon moderation, and democracy upon virtue (in the Roman sense of the word). The corruption and fall of a government whereby it changes into another form he attributes to the corruption of its fundamental principle; but as long as the principle remains fairly pure he sees little to choose between the different possible forms. The really vicious situation is when institutions which are fitted for one principle of government are still forced to work although that principle has been replaced by another. Montesquieu tells us little about sovereignty, although he has a good deal to say about liberty. He regards liberty as best assured by the supremacy of law rather than of men, and to achieve this the best way, in his opinion, was the separation of powers. This part of his work is greatly indebted to John Locke. The aspect which he develops at most length is not the mere administrative convenience of specialising the functions of government, but rather the constitutional safeguards which result when each power operates as a check upon the others. It is this system of " checks and balances " which Montesquieu regards as particularly important, and as the secret of constitutional monarchy in England. It was he who had the romantic notion that English constitutionalism was directly derived from the ancient Germans of Tacitus.[1] "*Ce beau système a été trouvé dans les bois.*" He even went so far as to develop a theory of the influence of geography upon politics. He is essentially modern in the emphasis which he places upon legislation, but it is his theory of the separation of powers and his insistence upon its value as affording constitutional safeguards which are most important for our purposes, for he was read by influential men in America and has had a marked influence upon constitutional development in that country.

EDMUND BURKE

Into the causes and character of the French Revolution we cannot enter; but some of its results upon English political thought may well be mentioned. The greatest political thinker at this time in England was Edmund Burke, and anyone who wishes to have a summary of English political wisdom by an experienced statesman who could adopt a philosophical attitude without losing touch with practical events must read the writings and speeches of Burke. They are likely to remain for a long time an authoritative statement of the results which had been achieved by parliamentary government in the seventeenth and eighteenth centuries. At the present day his words are constantly upon the lips of the best English statesmen. His thought is characterised by its intimate contact with practical politics; rarely does he allow a theory to divert his attention from the practical problems of everyday government. A noteworthy portion of his work is in answer to Rousseau and to the theories of the rights of man. With a natural tendency to admire aristocracy, he felt that an extreme democracy as suggested by some theorists contained great dangers, and insisted that it was hazardous to abandon those sentiments for aristocracy which in his day seemed natural to mankind. He observes that a democracy is not affected by the fear which besets a monarch; when shameless acts are done the moral responsibility vanishes when spread among numerous persons, while the alleged liberty of a democracy is more often a delusion. The horrors with which the Revolution began made an increasing impression upon Burke as upon his countrymen, and had the practical effect of delaying reform for over a generation. Typical measures of this period were the Treasonable

[1] These famous chapters from the *Germania* of Tacitus will be found in Stubbs, *Charters.*

Practices Act[1] and the Seditious Meetings Act[2] of 1795, the suspension of the *Habeas Corpus* Act on several occasions, and the imposition of heavy stamp duties with the object of checking the circulation of cheap newspapers.   Numerous State trials took place.[3]   Even purely private law fell under the influence of the extreme conservative reaction of which Lord Ellenborough was the personification in the King's Bench (1802–1818) and Lord Eldon in Chancery (1801–1806, 1807–1827).   To this result Burke largely contributed, nor must he be blamed overmuch for his caution at a moment when the wildest theories were being proclaimed in all seriousness.   His speeches on America[4] are the best expression of his philosophy, for they were made before the French Revolution came to strike terror throughout the rest of Europe.   There in particular the political realism of Burke is apparent; he almost alone of British statesmen at the moment was prepared to face the facts, and having done so, to advocate a frank acknowledgment of the situation as it actually existed. He poured ridicule upon the government for their weak attempts to compel recognition of a principle which had no relation to the existing state of affairs; he was the embodiment of the spirit of compromise, and appreciated fully the fact that situations slowly change, and that the change must be recognised frankly.   He was prepared to state that the American colonies had entered upon the stage of adult political life, and to counsel the government to treat them accordingly.   Perhaps the most interesting passages in his speeches on America are those where he shows that the demands of the colonists were the very same which Englishmen at home had made in a more heroic age, and where he stresses the deep respect for legality which characterised English political development, urging that this very spirit lay at the root of the American case.

[1] 36 Geo. III, c. 7.

[2] 36 Geo. III, c. 8.

[3] Many details will be found in T. Erskine May, *Constitutional History of England* (ed. Francis Holland, 1912), chapters ix–xiv.

[4] There are numerous cheap editions of Burke's principal speeches and books.

CHAPTER 9

THE NINETEENTH CENTURY: LIBERALISM AND REFORM

The Need for Reform – – – – – – – – – – – 73
Jeremy Bentham – – – – – – – – – – – 73
Concluding Remarks – – – – – – – – – – 75

At length, the end of the Napoleonic war brought some relief from the political tension, and a wave of constitutional and legal reform swept away many ancient institutions which had long survived their usefulness.

THE NEED FOR REFORM

The state of the law at the beginning of the nineteenth century has been thus described by an eminent legal historian:

" Heart-breaking delays and ruinous costs were the lot of suitors. Justice was dilatory, expensive, uncertain, and remote. To the rich it was a costly lottery: to the poor a denial of right, or certain ruin. The class who profited most by its dark mysteries were the lawyers themselves. A suitor might be reduced to beggary or madness, but his advisers revelled in the chicane and artifice of a lifelong suit and grew rich. Out of a multiplicity of forms and processes arose numberless fees and well-paid offices. Many subordinate functionaries, holding sinecure or superfluous appointments, enjoyed greater emoluments than the judges of the court; and upon the luckless suitors, again, fell the charge of these egregious establishments. If complaints were made, they were repelled as the promptings of ignorance: if amendments of the law were proposed, they were resisted as innovations. To question the perfection of English jurisprudence was to doubt the wisdom of our ancestors . . . a political heresy which could expect no toleration."[1]

The romantic fancy which led Blackstone to tolerate such a system, comparing it to a picturesque old Gothic castle,[2] could hardly survive the shocks of war, and a very different point of view ushered in the great reform movement.

JEREMY BENTHAM

The prophet of the new era was Jeremy Bentham[3] (1748–1832). At Oxford, Bentham had heard Blackstone lecture, and deemed his matter unsound: as a young law student he had listened with admiration to the judgments of Lord Mansfield. The publication of Blackstone's *Commentaries* (1776) stirred him to fierce criticism expressed in his *Fragment on Government* (1776), and he abandoned the professional study of

[1] Sir Thomas Erskine May, *Constitutional History*, ii. 384.
[2] 3 Comm. 268; cf. 4 Comm. 442 (both passages in Pound and Plucknett, *Readings*, 235–237).
[3] For a very full discussion of Bentham, see Holdsworth, xiii. 41–133.

73

law in order to devote himself to the basic principles upon which law rests. *The Principles of Morals and Legislation* (1789) proclaimed that there should be constant, radical legislation as the mainspring of law, and it should be directed to the end of securing the greatest happiness of the greatest number. His faith in acts of Parliament was perhaps a little overstated: the century since his death has revealed some of the limitations in written constitutions and legislative enactments, but nevertheless, the main position still stands—rules and institutions must henceforth submit to the test of utility and be judged by their fruits, and where reform is necessary, it must be effected in most instances by deliberate, planned legislation. Besides providing a theoretical basis for criticising the law and the constitution, he also entered into detailed and vigorous discussion of practical details, as in *The Rationale of Judicial Evidence*. He was a firm believer in codes and ever ready to offer advice. In 1811 he offered to codify the law of the United States. The offer was not accepted, and even Pennsylvania, which for a moment seemed tempted by it, finally yielded to the professional interests of the lawyers. Nevertheless Bentham's influence has been enormous, and has become much more diffused than his writings. Many people act on his principles who have never read a word that he wrote—and a great deal of what he wrote is barely readable, so tortuous did his style become. It has well been said that

> " his doctrines have become so far part of the common thought of the time that there is hardly an educated man who does not accept as too clear for argument truths which were invisible till Bentham pointed them out."[1]

Even some of the strange new words he invented have become familiar, *e.g.* " international ", " utilitarian " and " codification ".

From Bentham's day to our own a long line of measures has approached nearer and nearer to his idea of " utility ", reducing law from the position of semi-religious mysticism to that of a practical branch of the business of government with expediency as its guiding principle. At the head of this movement comes the great Reform Act of 1832, which brought Parliament into direct contact with public opinion— and thereby subjected law, too, to the pressure of the same force. Three years later the Municipal Corporations Act, 1835, abolished those curious and venerable monuments of the middle ages and substituted a uniform pattern of town government. It would be hard to imagine a more spectacular break with the past than these two statutes. They were accompanied by scores of others which abolished the accumulated survivals of centuries. On the procedural side came the Uniformity of Process Act, 1832, and the Civil Procedure Act of 1833 which buried a great deal of subtle learning and abolished some hoary antiquities, such as wager of law. A group of statutes from 1827 to 1837 made numerous changes in the criminal law and greatly reduced the number of capital

---

[1] T. E. Holland in the *Encyclopaedia Britannica* (11th edn.), *s.v.* " Bentham ".

offences. This in fact was the one subject on which the eighteenth century had legislated incessantly and vigorously. Statutory interference with the penal law was therefore no novelty; the real change was in the spirit. Sir Rober Peel and Lord Brougham were the promoters of these reforms for which Sir Samuel Romilly and Sir James Mackintosh had long struggled in the face of bitter opposition, and Peel in particular made the capital contribution of setting up a professional police force,[1] thus rendering the criminal law less savage but more certain in its operation. In the law of property no less far-reaching reforms were made; one single year (1833) saw the Fines and Recoveries Act, the Administration of Estates Act and the Inheritance Act.[2]

CONCLUDING REMARKS

The end of this chapter therefore brings us from the old world to the new, from the ruins of the Roman Empire to a crisis in another empire thirteen centuries later. We have seen the gradual formation of the English State under the Anglo-Saxon kings, which later was transformed by the Norman genius and furnished with the first necessity of government—a financial administration. Developing within that administration we have seen the germs in the reign of Henry II of the common law, while under his sons we begin to find the claim that law and administration had now come to the parting of the ways, and the text of the Great Charter lays down the principle of the supremacy of law. Besides this internal limitation upon a powerful monarchy, we also see the Church using considerable influence in politics, and its rôle expressed in the terms of a general formula that although the State, like the Church, may enjoy divine sanction (or at least divine tolerance), nevertheless religion is superior to politics. It is clearly asserted that there are things which kings cannot do, and in the middle ages there was a papacy powerful enough in many cases to punish monarchs who transgressed. We have seen, too, the growing weakness of law in the fifteenth century and the rise in the sixteenth of administrative bodies using semi-legal forms, which alone were adequate to meet the crisis under the Yorkists and early Tudors. When this movement had gone too far, the Stuart dynasty was to suffer for its failure to adapt itself to new conditions—although it is typical of English development that the really innovating party found its main support in history, and even in

---

[1] Of the earlier pioneers in criminal reform, one of the most interesting is the great novelist Henry Fielding, the first stipendiary magistrate to sit at Bow Street. See B. M. Jones, *Henry Fielding, Novelist and Magistrate* (London, 1933). Abundant material is collected in L. Radzinowicz, *History of English Criminal Law*, vol. i (1948).

[2] For the period of reform, see A. V. Dicey, *Law and Public Opinion in England* (1905); Sir Arthur Underhill, *Changes in the English Law of Real Property* (*Select Essays in Anglo-American Legal History*, iii. 673). The novels of Charles Dickens are a fair picture of the unreformed state of the law; see the entertaining lectures of Sir William Holdsworth, *Dickens as a Legal Historian* (Yale University Press, 1928).

antiquarianism. With the Commonwealth there came a period unique in English history and its failure was as conspicuous. The Revolution completed the work of the Rebellion and expressed its results in a form more nearly legitimate. The strange, but fascinating, theories of Hobbes gave way to the reasonableness of Locke, and when a century later the French Revolution issued a challenge to all established governments, it was Burke who found an answer which served England and America equally well. That answer was an appeal to history, to experience, and to the traditional English habit of compromise and cautious reform—to what Montesquieu might have called the spirit of the common law.

The French Revolution, the long and weary war, and the fearful distress that followed the peace, came near to bringing disaster. Contemporaries felt themselves on the brink of revolution and civil war, and if this last catastrophe was averted it may perhaps have been because the party of privilege and conservatism was so clearly founded on sentiment rather than on political theory. There was no clash of philosophies as there had been in the seventeenth century. Even Benthamism, in spite of the formidable array of logic, ethics and jurisprudence which decorated it, was at bottom as sound common sense as it was dubious philosophy. Benthamism triumphed in spite of its technical apparatus and became merged in the practical good sense of the commercial middle class, avoiding the mysticism of the State as well as the mysticism of the rights of man, just as at the present moment it seems that the political thought which is derived from the common law will again stand aside from the corresponding mysticisms of our own day.

PART 2

THE COURTS AND THE PROFESSION

SUMMARY

THE COURTS AND THE PROFESSION

We now come to the history of the law courts and the legal profession. Few matters are more obscure than the early history of our courts, especially of the inferior or local jurisdictions.

THE DIFFERENT SORTS OF COURT

Compared with the courts of Westminster the local tribunals of the county and the hundred are centuries more ancient, and have a past stretching back to pre-Conquest days. Into the great questions of the ultimate origin of the county and the hundred courts, which in the opinion of some writers extends back into Teutonic pre-history, it would be impossible to enter without examining a great deal of technical controversy. Questions equally grave and controversial also obscure the history of those jurisdictions which are commonly called feudal— jurisdictions which competed with, and in one or two cases supplanted, the older institutions. Last of all there came the royal power and the erection of a hierarchy of courts acting in the King's name, and applying the common law, which in the end superseded all the other jurisdictions. We therefore have, roughly speaking, three main types of courts: the oldest is the communal system represented principally by the county and the hundred; next we have the feudal or seignorial tribunals, of which the court leet is the best-known example; while finally we have the royal courts at Westminster gradually overshadowing all the rest. Within each of these classes there exists the utmost variety, and the further back we trace the history of these courts the more difficult it becomes to make a general statement which shall be approximately true about any of them. The Anglo-Saxon age in particular shows us countless examples of local variance, although it is significant that soon after the Norman Conquest faint signs of order begin to appear.

The remarks that follow, therefore, are only very general observations which will have to be taken subject to a good deal of modification if they are to be fitted into any particular case. Very broadly speaking the threefold division which we have indicated comprises three different classes of courts, each with its own separate type of history; but it is an essential part of that history that each type existed side by side with the others, and therefore was constantly influenced by them. The communal courts are characterised by a territorial jurisdiction coinciding with some administrative district within whose limits their authority extends. The seignorial courts are less definitely territorial in their character; there are occasions when their jurisdiction seems rather to depend upon a personal relationship between lord and tenant. This statement, however, is subject to some reservations since a purely personal jurisdiction of a lord over particular men is very apt, during the middle ages, to become gradually transformed into a jurisdiction over the land of those men. A jurisdiction which was originally personal will therefore become in time territorial, and it is characteristic of this process that such a territory often is of extremely irregular outline; indeed, it is quite common to find that there will be small islands of one jurisdiction scattered at some distance away from the main body. The most plausible explanation of this seems to be that these outlying portions were originally the property of a tenant under a personal jurisdiction, and that in the course of time this personal jurisdiction became territorial.[1] Still further confusion between the two types is caused by the constant tendency for old communal jurisdictions (especially the smaller ones) to fall under the domination of some great man and to become in the end his private " franchise ".

ROYAL JURISDICTIONS

Both of these classes of courts, however, differ fundamentally from the third class, the royal jurisdiction. Both of the former were in flourishing condition and apparently equal to the requirements of the nation before the Crown began to intervene. One thing at least is very clear, namely, that the royal courts were intruders upon ground which had been occupied for centuries by older jurisdictions, and that the authority of these older jurisdictions was original and in no way derived from the Crown. This undoubted historical fact begins to be obscured by legal theory in the twelfth, and still more in the thirteenth centuries. By that date the royal courts at Westminster were in a period of active expansion and were prepared to make wide claims on their own behalf and on that of the King. Already, between 1109 and 1111, Henry I had spoken of " my counties and hundreds ",[2] and a century and a half later Bracton lays down a general principle that strictly speaking the King is the proper judge for all temporal causes, and that it is only the great mass of business that has compelled him to delegate judicial power to a number of judges, sheriffs, bailiffs and ministers.[3] About the year 1256, therefore, a royal justice like Bracton is already considering the Crown as the sole fountain of justice. A generation later another royal official, whom we only know under the disguise of " Fleta ", presses this doctrine to its extreme limit.[4] In an extraordinary chapter Fle a

---

[1] This occurs both with hundreds and counties; Pollock and Maitland, i 532, 557

[2] Hn. com. i, in A. J. Robertson, Laws of the English Kings, 287.

[3] Bracton, f. 107.

[4] For Fleta see below, p. 265.

discusses all the courts of the land, and introduces each one of them with the significant formula that " the King has his court. . . ." Although *Fleta* may have known the historical falseness of this, nevertheless he insists that the King now has his court not only in Parliament, the King's Bench, the Common Pleas and the Exchequer, but also in the county, in boroughs, in hundreds, and in manors, even although he has no judge there, the decisions being made by suitors. With *Fleta*, therefore (about the year 1290), we come to the complete dogma that all judicial power is derived from the Crown.

Clearly it is only the fact of the Norman Conquest, seconded by the organisation of the Norman kings, that enabled England to be so centralised as this. In the course of two hundred years not only had the central courts at Westminster been erected and furnished with royal law and procedure where previously there had been little or none, but in addition the idea of royal supremacy and of the centralisation of justice had so firmly taken root that it was possible to assert that all judicial power, whether it be in royal courts, seignorial courts or the ancient communal courts, was exercised by delegation from the Crown. From this point onwards the character of the local courts was gradually being transformed in order to make them fit in with this theory. In the end, they were either to be abolished or virtually superseded by new institutions which would be in fact as well as in theory created by the Crown.

THE CROWN AND THE JURY

The ultimate supremacy of the central courts of the Crown was only achieved slowly. There was little direct attack, save perhaps a few words in the Statute of Gloucester (1278), c. 8, and the important rule in the Statute of Marlborough (1267), c. 20;[1] for the most part, the change was effected by peaceful penetration and skilful competition in offering better remedies, notably, trial by jury. The points of contact between central and local courts thus become particularly significant. On the one hand, there is the Crown's determined endeavour to tame the sheriff; on the other, there is the Crown's use of the jury. It had long been the practice for royal emissaries to summon juries when the central government wished to make contact with the men of the county, hundred or vill. When, in later times, the jury was given the new function of trying issues of fact reached in litigation, the Crown claimed to have the monopoly of what had now become a desirable procedure, and thereby achieved an overwhelming superiority over those jurisdictions whose powers did not extend that far.

Such, then, is the general trend of institutional history in the course of a thousand years. It now remains to consider in a little more detail

[1] For these two statutes see below, p. 93.

the rise and fall of local institutions, and their gradual subjection to the central authority.   First of all we shall treat of the communal courts; secondly, of seignorial jurisdiction and its relations with them;   then of the Crown's contact with the local courts, and of the jury which grew up at that point of contact;   and finally, of the royal courts at Westminster which were destined to overshadow and destroy both the seignorial and communal courts.

CHAPTER 1

THE COMMUNAL COURTS

THE VILL OR TOWNSHIP

Beginning at the very bottom of the scale, the lowest institution we find is the vill or township.[1] It is moreover the most complicated and obscure. Its history was possibly different in different parts of the country and is extremely difficult to disentangle from that of certain other institutions—the ecclesiastical unit of the parish, the social unit of the village, and the economic unit of the manor, which are all the subject of learned controversy. It would seem as if the typical vill (if one can use the term of an institution which varied so greatly) would have looked something like this. There will be a little group of houses, sometimes in a cluster, and sometimes ranged along an ancient road. Nearby there will be the parish church, and in many cases there will be the hall or mansion of the lord of the manor, if it so happens that the vill coincides with a manor, which may or may not be the case; sometimes a manor consists of several vills; on the other hand, a vill may contain several manors. Surrounding it there will be two, or more usually three, large fields. Each of these fields will be divided into a large number of long, narrow strips of about half an acre each, and every household in the village will own a greater or less number of these strips scattered irregularly through the fields. This system of scattered strips is very ancient and lasted long after the middle ages. It has been suggested that the method was imported by the Anglo-Saxons and was not native to England. The prehistoric field seems to have been a small

[1] Maitland suggested that it would be a convenient practice to use " vill " to mean the territory, and " township " to mean the inhabitants; Pollock and Maitland, i. 563.

83

irregular plot; the Celtic field which replaced it in England was apt to be oblong owing to the necessities of ploughing. It seems also to have been a peculiarity of Celtic agriculture to prefer hills or elevated ground, while the Saxons introduced valley settlements. The Saxons, moreover, were accustomed to use the large team of eight[1] oxen to draw their ploughs; this, of course, gave more power, but made turning more cumbersome. Consequently it became necessary to plough a much longer furrow in order to secure the advantage of the larger team, and hence the long narrow strips—but why they were scattered, has long been debated. It was never easy to believe that an egalitarian dogma was applied regardless of efficiency and convenience; more probably, those who co-operated in each day's ploughing took a share each, as the work proceeded from day to day.[2] It is not uncommon for fields in England at the present day still to bear traces of these arrangements; on the hillside Celtic divisions may still be found represented by the banks caused by constantly ploughing the same plot, while lower in the valleys the long, narrow strips of the mediaeval field may be discerned. Photographs from an aeroplane are particularly useful in revealing these features.[3]

THE VILL IN AGRICULTURE

The one bond which holds the vill together is a system of communal agriculture. The machinery necessary was expensive, for the plough of eight oxen was often beyond the means of any individual villager, and so we find that the vill co-operated in the performance of a good many of the more difficult operations of farming. Besides this, after harvest the fields were thrown open and all the villagers turned their cattle into them, as well as on to the field which for that year was remaining fallow (for the general system was to have two or three fields one of which was left fallow each year).

From what has just been said it will be obvious that there were many features of the agricultural life of the vill which would need regulation, and in spite of Maitland's doubts it seems now fairly clear that there was a moot in the vill which ordered its economic life, made bylaws and enforced their observance. It is tempting to regard the numerous "halimotes" of which we have evidence as being survivals of the earlier vill moot. To the eyes of some historians the co-operative element in the village community appears so strong that they describe it as an agrarian communism; but at this point we again touch upon a difficult and controversial subject upon which we can here say no more

[1] Historical doubts have been expressed by H. G. Richardson, *The Medieval Plough Team*, History, xxvi. 287 ff., who argues for a normal team of four. A working team of eight oxen, however, is clearly indicated in *Pleas before the King* (Selden Society, vol. 68), ii. no. 273 (1201).

[2] C. S. Orwin, *Open Fields* (Oxford, 1938); Economic Hist. Rev., viii. 125.

[3] See some remarkable photographs in E. C. Curwen, *Air-Photography and Economic History the Evolution of the Corn-Field* (Economic History Society).

than that it is almost as difficult to prove a true agrarian communism as it is to find the modern notion of individual private property in land. There has been a great deal of conjecture as to the probable character of the primitive village community, and much of it has removed the question from the realm of history into that of speculative pre-history.[1]

Whatever its origin, the mediaeval village community was dissolved in the sixteenth and eighteenth centuries as a result of the great enclosure movements promoted by landowners with two distinct objects—first, to abandon the old system of strips,[2] re-survey the land and allot to each holder a compact area instead of his scattered strips, and also to enclose portions of the common land and restrict them to private use, generally of the lord of the manor.

THE VILL AND LOCAL GOVERNMENT

Besides this powerful economic bond which produced a unity from within, as time went on there came constant pressure from without which tended to the same result. Especially after the Conquest and down to the middle of the thirteenth century, the vill was being constantly used by the central authorities as the lowest unit of local government. As the Crown interfered more and more with local questions, so we find more and more reference in public documents to the vill, first one and then another duty being thrust upon it. The middle ages were fond of the very rough-and-ready, but effective, method of imposing a duty upon a group of people and holding them jointly and severally bound to perform it; any arrangement for apportioning the burden among the individual members of the group was their private concern, the Crown refusing to take any notice or to give any assistance to the process. At the close of the twelfth century the Crusades caused a good deal of taxation. The method by which it was assessed was simple; each county was assigned a quota proportionate to its estimated wealth (this estimate is the technical meaning of the word *taxatio*); the county then divided this quota in a similar manner among the hundreds and the vills, and so a vill would be responsible for raising a particular sum of money—no doubt by negotiation among its members, although often under the eye of royal taxers.

[1] Vinogradoff, *Growth of the Manor* (1911), 194, 273 (but see Pollock and Maitland, i. 567, and Maitland, *Collected Papers*, ii. 363–364). For by-laws, cf. Vinogradoff, *op. cit.* 185–189, and the Littleport rolls mentioned below, p. 98. Sir Paul Vinogradoff's article " Village Communities " in the *Encyclopaedia Britannica* (11th edn.) is a good introduction to the literature of the subject. The works of Maitland, *Domesday Book and Beyond* and *Township and Borough*, and the writings of Seebohm and Vinogradoff, treat it more technically. The *Cambridge Economic History*, vol. i., contains a general survey of English and European agrarian history during the middle ages. Of especial legal interest is H. M. Cam, *The Community of the vill*, Mediaeval Studies presented to Rose Graham (1950), 1–14.

[2] The lord's land also might frequently lie in scattered strips, mingled with those of his tenants. Both economic and legal aspects are discussed in W. H. R. Curtler, *Enclosure and Redistribution of our Land* (Oxford, 1938).

THE VILL AND CRIMINAL LAW

The vill is most remarkable, however, for its place in the system of police and criminal procedure.

"It ought to attend the court held by the Justices in Eyre. It ought to attend the sheriff's turn. It ought to attend the hundred and county courts whenever it has any crime to present. It must come at the coroner's call to make inquest when a dead man's body is found. It is bound to see that all its members who ought to be in frankpledge are in frankpledge. In some parts of the country the township is itself a frankpledge, a tithing . . . and in this case it is responsible for the production of any of its members who is accused of crime. Apart from this, it was bound to arrest malefactors; at all events if a person was slain within its boundaries during the daytime and the slayer was not arrested, it was liable to an amercement. . . . Again, from of old it was the duty of the township to raise the hue and cry and follow the trail of stolen cattle. . . . Moreover, it was the common practice to commit prisoners to the charge of the *villata*, and then if the prisoners escaped the *villata* was amerced. So if a malefactor took sanctuary, the neighbouring townships had to watch the church and prevent his escape. Most of these liabilities can be traced back into the reign of Henry II."[1]

The thirteenth-century statutes systematised the police powers of the vill; watchmen were to be kept throughout the night and the assize of arms enforced; in 1252 constables were to be appointed, and in 1253 vills were ordered to provide at their own cost the necessary weapons, while, as we have already said, the Statute of Winchester in 1285 consolidated these previous enactments for the rest of the middle ages. The vill was further under heavy obligations in the maintenance of roads and bridges and the cleansing and repairing of river-banks. From all this it will be clear that the vill could hardly escape being many times amerced, and it seems that the inhabitants were jointly and severally liable to find the money.

Finally, the vill had very important duties in the system of presentments. When a crime occurred within the vill it was the duty of the reeve and the four best men to report it to the hundred court and if possible to produce the guilty party, while on numerous occasions the King's Justices would summon the vill where a crime was committed (together with four or more neighbouring vills, all appearing by their reeve and four best men) to pass upon the guilt or innocence of a prisoner accused of crime.

In the later middle ages the vill ceased to be of general legal importance. From the administrative point of view it was gradually replaced by the parish with which in fact it frequently coincided, and ever since Elizabeth's poor law the parish has tended to become a unit of civil taxation.[2] Rules of pleading, however, continued to insist upon places being assigned to a particular vill, and so the vill for centuries

---

[1] Pollock and Maitland, i. 564–565.

[2] The parish first appears in this connection in the poor law of 1536 (27 Hen. VIII, c. 25; extracts in Tanner, *Tudor Documents*, 479–481); the acts of Elizabeth I may be seen in Prothero, *Documents*, 96–105.

survived as a troublesome anachronism. To make matters worse, the boundaries of vills were uncertain, and a good many places were definitely not in any vill at all.[1] At length it was enacted that the specification of the county should be enough.[2]

THE EARLY HUNDRED

The term " hundred " occurs in various parts of Europe as an administrative unit, and great controversy has arisen as to its ultimate origin. Tacitus tells us of Germans organised by groups of hundreds; five centuries later the Frankish kings legislated on the " hundred " as a criminal jurisdiction (595); and the English hundred appears nearly four centuries later still (between 946 and 961). Tempting as it is to see some connection between these phenomena, the hazardous nature of such a speculation is emphasised by modern historians. One recent theory[3] would stress the efforts made in the tenth century to enforce order by means of voluntary associations, such as London had set up.[4] The members undertook police duties, and the Crown gave them a share in the property of convicted criminals, and powers to find out informally whether suspects were guilty. From this gild it was a short step to the ordinance ascribed to Edgar on the holding of the hundred.[5] The principal change was to substitute regular judicial procedure and trial by ordeal for the gild's informal inquiry. While that theory takes note of the documents, as they have come down to us, it is difficult to resist the suggestion that the hundred must be a good deal older than the texts mentioned. Sometimes a connection can be traced between a hundred and the tax assessment of 100 hides, and it may be that our texts show not the origin, but the re-modelling of an already ancient institution.

King Edgar commanded that the hundred should meet every four weeks; thieves are to be pursued and judgment executed upon them; contempt of the hundred's decisions is punished by a fine and on the fourth offence by outlawry; in following the trail of stolen cattle one hundred may call upon another to assist; the hundred is ordered to establish fixed terms at which parties are to appear; fines were payable to it by those who disobeyed its commands, and half the property of convicted thieves also went to the hundred. The laws of Cnut (made between 1027 and 1034)[6] show even more clearly how important the

---

[1] Examples in Y.B. 1 Hen. VI (ed. Williams, Selden Society, vol. 50), 49, 114.

[2] 16 & 17 Car. II, c. 8 (1664).

[3] J. E. A. Jolliffe, *Constitutional History* (1937), 116–120. See, however, the review by H. M. Cam in English Historical Review, liv. 485, and F. M. Stenton, *Anglo-Saxon England*, 295; and see the *Calendar of Plea and Memoranda Rolls, 1413–1437* (ed. A. H. Thomas), xxxi. ff. for the problem of the London wards.

[4] vi Aethelstan. (The date is between 925 and 946.)

[5] i Edgar. (Between 946 and 961.)

[6] ii Canute 17, 19, 20.

hundred was in Anglo-Saxon England. No distress was to be levied until the remedies available in the hundred had been exhausted: every freeman over twelve years of age was to be in a hundred; no one was to appeal to the King unless he was unable to get justice in the hundred; and until the famous ordinance[1] of William the Conqueror, the bishop used the hundred to transact ecclesiastical business.

When we get to the Conquest the hundred is treated by the Norman administrators as the most convenient of the smaller units of government. The *Dialogue of the Exchequer* tells us[2] of the rule long observed in that court as a result of the numerous assassinations of Normans, presumably by Englishmen. In order to check this it was ordained that every hundred wherein a Norman was found slain by an unknown hand should be liable to a very heavy murder fine. As time went on the hundred was allowed to relieve itself of the fine by proving that the dead man was not a Norman but an Englishman, but in the end the races had become so mingled that it was impossible to maintain this procedure of " presentment of Englishry " and the murder fine was abolished by Edward III. The principle of making the hundred liable in respect of undetected crimes was not abandoned, however, and the Statute of Winchester (1285) lays down a general rule that the whole of the hundred where a robbery was done shall be answerable for it unless they can produce the offender.[3] For the next five hundred years Parliament constantly increased the civil liability of the hundred for crimes committed within its borders, especially by rioters, until in 1827 a long list of such statutes was repealed,[4] and the hundred's liability was restricted to damage done by rioters;[5] later still the burden was placed on the county or borough rate-payers by the Riot (Damages) Act, 1886.

All this will serve to illustrate the varied aspects of mediaeval institutions, for besides this police and administrative side of the hundred, its judicial powers continued, although their decline came rather earlier. By the Assize of Clarendon (1166)[6] it had been ordained that in every county and in every hundred the twelve most lawful men of each hundred and the four most lawful men of each vill should be sworn to present any man who was suspected of serious crime either to the King's Justice or to the sheriff. If the hundred or the vill had been successful in

---

[1] Wl. ep. (*c.* 1072); above, p. 12.

[2] I. 10. A passage in *Hic Intimatur*, 3, seems to suggest that at first it was the lord who was responsible; if so, we have one more example of a lord shifting a liability from his own shoulders to those of his hundred. This change already appears in *Leis Willelme* 22 (a compilation made between 1090 and 1135). For another instance see below, p. 97. See the note in A. J. Robertson, *Laws of the Kings of England*, Cambridge, 1925, 362–363; below, p. 445.

[3] When Henry III in 1253 tried, unsuccessfully, to introduce this rule, it was denounced as a novelty from Savoy; it had certainly been recently enacted in Provence. See Pollock and Maitland, i. 181.

[4] 7 & 8 Geo. IV, c. 27.

[5] 7 & 8 Geo. IV, c. 31.

[6] The text is in Stubbs, *Select Charters*; for an extract, see below, pp. 112–113.

capturing a suspect, they were to deliver him over, accompanied by two lawful men " to bear the record of the county or the hundred "—in other words to state verbally the circumstances under which the prisoner was captured.   In 1234 a royal ordinance[1] declared that hundred courts had been held too frequently and that rich and poor had been equally oppressed thereby;   it was therefore ordained that they should meet every three weeks instead of once a fortnight as heretofore—it may be observed in passing that this is not the only complaint we hear during the middle ages of too many courts and too much justice;   earlier still Henry II admitted that the country had suffered grievously " by reason of the multitude of justices, for they were eighteen in number ", reducing their number to five (1178).[2]

THE LATER HUNDRED

The hundred court (or, as it was more usually called, " the hundred " simply) was under the presidency of an official called the hundred man or the reeve, but his importance rapidly declined, for the hundred lost the independence which it seems to have had originally.   On the one hand, many hundreds fell into the power of the sheriffs, and when the sheriffs in turn have been subjected to the Crown, those hundreds will become the king's hundreds.   In the Norman period sheriffs frequently purchased their counties, and sublet the hundreds—a sure way of encouraging extortion.   On the other hand, many hundreds fell into the hands of neighbouring landowners either by royal grants of varying extent, by purchase from the sheriffs, or by usurpation.   By the reign of Edward I more than half were in private hands.[3]   As in all the communal courts, the judgment proceeded from the whole body of people who constituted the court, and in the case of the hundred these people (" suitors " as they were called) seem to have been usually quite small landowners, and it soon became the practice for the obligation of attending the court to be restricted to the owners of particular pieces of land—another peculiarity which is common in the middle ages.

THE SHERIFF'S TOURN: COURTS LEET

We have already mentioned the success of the sheriff in securing control over the hundred by appointing one of his underlings as bailiff of it;   his influence was further increased by means of the " sheriff's tourn ".   Twice a year every hundred held an especially full meeting which was attended by the sheriff or his deputy, at which there came to meet him the reeve and the four best men of each vill in the hundred to undergo a searching examination at his hands.   They had to lay

[1] *Statutes of the Realm*, i. 118.

[2] As to this, see below, p. 148.

[3] See the map in H. M. Cam, *The Hundred and the Hundred Rolls* (London, 1930), and *ibid.*, 180 ff., for the civil jurisdiction of some hundreds (the origin of which is obscure).

before him their suspicions upon the members of their community; those suspected of grave matters were arrested by the sheriff and held for the King's Justice, while less serious offenders were amerced by the sheriff. For the purposes of these specially important meetings twelve freeholders were appointed to revise the presentments by the vills.[1] Upon the occasion of the sheriff's tourn a thorough investigation was always made of the condition of the frankpledges, of which we shall speak later. By the close of the middle ages the hundred was reduced to insignificance, and the tourn lost its powers to the Justices of the Peace.[2] Those hundreds which fell into private hands lasted longer, for their profits were sufficient to interest their owners, especially those who had the valued privilege of holding " courts leet " to replace the sheriff's tourn. We shall return to the leet in the following chapter when dealing with seignorial jurisdictions.

THE COUNTY COURT

We now come to the county court, or " county " as it was more simply called, for it must be remembered that in the early Norman period administration and adjudication were still not separated, and there was hardly need for the word " court "—even when the word does occur it does not necessarily bear the modern meaning of an organ of justice. The shire is the most ancient of English institutions. Many of the individual counties are directly descended from the ancient Anglo-Saxon kingdoms of the age when the land was divided into numerous petty realms. In such cases as this the shire moot was the direct representative of the national assembly of a once independent kingdom, and for a time was presided over by an alderman, who was sometimes a member of the ancient royal family. It seems that some other counties, however, are of later origin and were deliberately erected as units of provincial government in imitation of the place which the ancient county now occupied in a united England. The history of the county falls into two periods; in the first the Crown is endeavouring to secure complete control over the county organisation; in the second, that control having been acquired, we see the steady decline of the county in practical importance.[3] The original jurisdiction of the county was once limitless both in kind and in degree. The county was the greater and more solemn body, but it was not " superior " to the hundred in the modern sense of the word: decisions of the hundred, for example, were not subject to review in the county, and the county, like the hundred, was a court of first instance. In Anglo-Saxon times the shire-moot was an impressive assembly of all the greatest people of the shire who met in order to transact all the functions of government. There are surviving charters which testify to the fact that some of that business was judicial,

[1] See below, p. 108 n. 1.
[2] 1 Edward IV, c. 2 ; *Select Cases in Council* (Selden Society, vol. 35), lxxxvii.
[3] Below, p. 102.

but both before and after the conquest all sorts of administrative duties were performed in the shire or county, as well as those more distinctly judicial functions which entitle it to be described as a court.[1]

The county came to exercise two jurisdictions, and the method appropriate to each is well worth study, for it illustrates the difference between ancient courts and modern ones.

THE SUITORS IN THE COUNTY COURT

Taking first the more ancient aspect of the county, we find that its constitution and procedure resembled those of the hundred and other ancient courts both in England and on the continent. According to the classical theory, it was composed not of judges but suitors who sometimes bear the significant name of " Doomsmen ".[2] They were not lawyers, nor even officials, but merely lay persons who by custom were bound to attend. In theory the court ought to consist of all the great men of the county, and representatives of the lesser folk from the vills and towns, in a great assembly which almost looks like a county parliament. But attendance at courts (like attendance at parliaments) was a costly and troublesome burden rather than a political or social privilege, and so those who could succeeded in avoiding it. Sometimes they asserted the principle that if they sent a steward or a few villagers their duty was done; stewards certainly became conspicuous in the county court—" they swayed the judgements, and the rest followed like sheep ".[3] Sometimes lords enfeoffed a tenant whose service was to consist in doing the suit;[4] in 1236 they procured a statute[5] allowing all freemen to do suit by attorney. In the end, suit of court was frequently a burden attached to particular pieces of land. The common result of all these devices was to substitute for the great men of the county a body of lesser suitors whose dignity and numbers were alike bound to decline with the passage of the centuries.[6] We may associate this withdrawal of the magnates from the county court with the demands which the Crown began to make upon them for attendance at the king's own

[1] There is no evidence of shire courts before the reign of Edgar (Tait, *Medieval English Borough*, 35) when the shire reasserted its supremacy (Jolliffe, *Constitutional History*, 126).

[2] The word is rare, but perhaps authentic; in Latin a suitor is a *sectator* or a *judicator*, while a judge (in the modern sense) is a *justiciarius*. The word *judex* is generally used only of judges in ecclesiastical courts, or by ecclesiastical writers. (There are difficulties in the theory of " Doomsmen " which cannot be examined here.)

[3] *Fleta*, II, 67.

[4] For a villein who held by such a service in 1221 see *Eyre Rolls of Gloucestershire &c.* (Selden Society, vol. 59), no. 227.

[5] Statute of Merton (20 Hen. III), c. 10. For the bishop in the county court, see above, p. 12 n. 1. The bishop of Bath bought exemption from shires and hundreds: *Pipe Roll II John* (Pipe Roll Society), 97, and exemption from suit seems to have meant exemption from amercements: *Close Rolls (1227–31)*, 31, 315; *(1247–51)*, 267.

[6] For some attractive speculations on the later fate of the county suitors, see G. T. Lapsley, *Buzones*, in English Historical Review, xlvii. at 565–566.

court, and it must be remembered that many landowners had property in different counties and that personal suit to all the county courts would be practically impossible.

Over the body of suitors presided the sheriff, but he, too, was not a judge. He spoke for the court and acted as the chairman of the meeting, but decisions were reached by the suitors, the sheriff's part being merely to announce them. So Hengham explained that if a false judgment was given in the county it is the county and not the sheriff who will be punished, for the suitors gave the judgment,[1] which was normally upon matters of procedure, summons default, etc. As we shall see later on, there was as yet no need for a judge or a jury to decide which party had proved his case, for this was ascertained by the purely mechanical means of ordeal, battle or compurgation. It was, however, necessary to decide which of the parties was to have the privilege of undertaking proof by these means, and here the suitors must often have exercised a truly judicial function.

THE SHERIFF AS JUDGE: VISCONTIAL WRITS

To this jurisdiction whereby the county court administered justice, was added another jurisdiction exercised by the sheriff in the county court in virtue of a royal writ addressed to him, beginning with the word *iusticies*, " do justice upon " the defendant " so that rightly and without delay he render " to the plaintiff, *e.g.* a debt which he owes. The old view that these writs of *justicies* were an attempt to revive the county so as to relieve congestion at Westminster is no longer tenable, for it is now known that our earliest registers of writs contain many such writs, and that the more familiar forms returnable at Westminster are a later development. Certain other writs were also " viscontial ", giving the sheriff jurisdiction, although not drawn in the form *justicies*. The implication seems clearly that down to the middle of the thirteenth century a large part of the nation's litigation was in the county court.[2] In this type of proceeding the sheriff was a judge in the modern sense, and the county court was merely the occasion upon which he exercised his jurisdiction. So complicated a situation could only result in confusion, and in fact it is very difficult to disentangle the two branches; *Fleta*[3] was able to assert the existence of the difference, but after his day the boundaries became obscured (partly as the result of legislation), until the classical doctrine as described by Coke[4] makes the suitors judges of the court in almost all cases. Thus was fulfilled the ancient policy of the

---

[1] *Hengham Magna* (ed. Dunham), 13–14.

[2] This is the main theme of the late G. J. Turner's introduction to *Brevia Placitata* (Selden Society, vol. 66).

[3] *Fleta*, ii. 43 (p. 94) and ii. 53 (p. 115); cf. Pollock and Maitland, ii. 577.

[4] *Jentleman's Case*, 6 Rep. 11 (1583); the stages have been described by Professor Thorne, *Courts of Record in England*, West Virginia Law Quarterly, xl. at 355.

crown in reducing the judicial importance of the sheriff at every possible opportunity.

THE DECLINE OF THE COUNTY

In early times there seems to have been no limit to the jurisdiction of the county court; civil and criminal cases, pleas common and royal, were alike within its power. The Crown (and apparently the public also) so thoroughly distrusted the sheriffs, however, that constant reductions of their jurisdiction were made. Henry II's criminal reforms were briefly confirmed by Magna Carta[1] which removed pleas of the Crown from the sheriff (and the county). When later on it was found that criminal justice would have to be decentralised, it is significant that the old powers of the sheriff were not restored to him, but a new jurisdiction was set up in the justices of the peace. On the civil side another principle at least as old as Henry II made it unnecessary for a man to answer an action for land unless it was brought by the king's writ.[2] The statute of Marlborough reserved all writs of false judgment for the king's court[3] and so the county was prevented from becoming a court of review over the lesser local jurisdictions. No trespass alleging *contra pacem regis* could be tried in the county, for it was technically a plea of the Crown;[4] and no trespass, debt or detinue could be brought where more than forty shillings were involved—a rule which is stated in the reign of Edward I, although its origin is uncertain.[5] It came to be held (as we have seen) that the suitors were still the judges, even in actions brought under a writ with the *justicies* clause, a collection of archaic rules and procedure had to be observed, with the result that *justicies* could not compete with another reform more in accordance with the trend of legal development— that is to say, the system of trials at *nisi prius*.[6]

The county was never a " court of record " in the eyes of the superior courts at Westminster,[7] and its rolls (when rolls were kept) were not

[1] *Magna Carta* (1215), c. 24; (1225), c. 17.

[2] See below, pp. 156 n. 2; 357.

[3] Statute of Marlborough, 52 Hen. III (1267), c. 20. This principle is as old as *Leges Henrici Primi*, x. 1; see Plucknett, *Legislation of Edward I*, 24–25 (this rule limited seignorial courts also). Below, p. 156 n. 2.

[4] For a full statement of the rule, see *Brevia Placitata* (Selden Society, vol. 66), lxiv n. 1; but a breach of " the peace of God and the sheriff " was within the county's jurisdiction. Allegations of wounds, imprisonment and *vi et armis* made it a plea of the Crown.

[5] As to this, see Pollock and Maitland, i. 553. The Statute of Gloucester (1278), c. 8, enacted that the royal courts should not entertain claims for less than 40*s.*; this apparently was regarded as implying that the county should not hear cases involving more than 40*s.* *Fleta* and *Britton* both mention this limit.

[6] Below, p. 616.

[7] Except for outlawry proceedings. On the county see W. A. Morris, *The Early English County Court* (1926), and Plucknett, *New Light on the Old County Court*, Harvard Law Review, xlii. 639–675, xliii. 1083–1118. For a careful and critical review of this controversy, see Lapsley, *The County Record and Roll of the County in the Thirteenth Century*, Law Quarterly Review, li. 299–325.

admissible in evidence on the same basis as " solemn " records; instead, when a plea was removed from the county to the Court of Common Pleas, four knights came up to Westminster and recounted what had happened—and on some occasions we even find them ready to wage battle by a champion in support of the truth of their unwritten " record ".[1]

[1] *Bracton's Note Book*, 243 (1227); cf. below, p. 122.

CHAPTER 2

SEIGNORIAL JURISDICTION

Besides all this there is the second aspect of the courts we have just described, namely, the effect upon them of the local territorial magnate. Here we come to an extremely obscure and difficult subject. The sources of the authority of a great lord or baron can usually be traced with some confidence, but the rise of numerous petty lordships all over the country and their effect upon the existing communal organisation are matters of greater complexity.[1] It is even difficult to classify the different sorts of power which a local lord could exercise at various times. In some cases the lord's jurisdiction was personal; in others it was territorial; and in many cases it is impossible to draw the line. On the one hand we have the development of the manor, and, closely connected with it, of the view of frankpledge; on the other it is clear that in many cases the whole organisation of the hundred court fell into private hands, and it is even fairly common to find that besides owning the hundred court the lord will even exclude the sheriff entirely, and instead of the sheriff's turn the lord's steward will hold a " court leet ".

THE MANOR

The manor as it existed in its typical form in the England of the thirteenth century is the product of a large number of different lines of development, some of them of very ancient date, which gradually converged to form one institution. One of its most striking features is the fact that all the tenants hold dependently of the lord of the manor. The origins of this may perhaps be sought in the tendency of small landowners to commend themselves and their land to some local magnate who seemed more likely to give them protection during such troubled times as the Danish invasions and the fairly constant wars between petty kingdoms. The weakness of the central power, too, undoubtedly promoted the growth of small local jurisdictions which were ready to undertake the task of repressing crime and organising military defence. This process was very probably hastened by the heavy burden of taxation.

[1] The difficulty is not confined to England: compare Chanteux, *Moyennes et basses justices*, in Travaux de la semaine d'histoire du droit normand (1938), 283.

In many parts of the world, even to-day, it has been found necessary to curb the activities of the capitalist who takes advantage of a small landowner who is unable to meet his taxes. In pre-Conquest days no such limits were ever thought of, and it is extremely probable that a great deal of free land was converted into land dependently held under the pressure of taxation. This did not mean that the poor owner was dispossessed; the change was principally to burden him with services in money, labour or products payable regularly, in return for which the lord took upon himself the public burdens of the property. In this connection it is essential to remember that taxation in the middle ages did not usually recur at regular intervals; the small man who had little economic reserve might therefore have to meet sudden liabilities quite beyond his means, although if those liabilities had been evenly spread over a length of years they would have been much less burdensome.

These dependent tenants were, it seems, originally freemen; there is no evidence of any extensive number of slaves or bondmen in early Anglo-Saxon England. In the course of time, however, the burdens upon these tenants steadily increased; more and more labour becomes due, and the increasing arbitrariness of its exaction will emphasise the baseness of the tenure. By the time we get to *Domesday Book* the development of serfdom has rapidly proceeded. On many manors it seems to be completed; on others a few faint traces of freedom still remain, and this is particularly so on the vast but scattered estates of the Crown. Throughout the middle ages these " sokemen of the ancient demesne " will be accounted as slightly higher than the villeins, and centuries later we shall find ambitious bondmen having lawyers search *Domesday Book* for them in the hope that it may turn out that their manor once formed part of the ancient demesne of the Crown.

In the majority of cases, however, these once free tenants became servile. Besides this lordship over land there was a good deal of personal jurisdiction. There are various origins for this also. Doubts have recently been cast upon Maitland's view that the Anglo-Saxon " *sac* and *soc* " included the right to hold a petty court, to compel tenants to attend it, and to take profits from it.[1] In those cases where a manor contained freemen as well, there may have operated the universal feudal principle that every lord can hold a court for his free tenants. Where the whole area of an ancient village community had fallen into the power of a lord it was natural that he should supervise the whole business of arranging the agricultural economy of the inhabitants, for, in spite of all the feudal superstructure which the common law has erected, the foundation of the later manor is often an ancient village community.

---

[1] See, especially, F. E. Harmer, *Anglo-Saxon Writs* (1952), and cf. Julius Goebel, *Felony and Misdemeanour*, i. 364 ff., 374; *contra* Maitland, *Domesday Book*, 80 ff. and Jolliffe, *Constitutional History*, 70. In 1414 the burgesses of Liverpool claimed that the words *sac* and *soc* are interpreted to mean a free court, " as it is declared of record in the exchequer ": *Rot. Parl.*, iv. 55 no. 2.

FRANKPLEDGE

To all this must be added the system of frankpledge which later became typical of a good many manors. Its history can be clearly traced back to the Anglo-Saxon period where we find the institution of fri-borh. "Borh" is the root which we have in the modern word "borrow", and seems to have the significance of security or surety. Its general feature is the provision for every person of some other persons who shall be borh or security that whatever moneys have to be paid will be forthcoming, and that if necessary the party can be produced in court. A master was always borh for his servants; members of a family might be borh for one another; or gilds might be formed whose members undertook to be borh for their brethren. To all this must be added the obscure institution of the tithing whose root signifi-cance is a group of ten men, naturally suggesting some intimate relation-ship with the hundred. Eventually the tithing became a territorial division with a tendency to coincide with the vill or township, and the tithing-man, its head, became the village constable. Cnut required his subjects to be in tithing and in borh as well,[1] and regular means were established for ascertaining that every person (who was not of some substance) was duly enrolled in tithing and in borh. This machinery was operated by the sheriff through the hundred court. At the time of the Conquest it seems that lords were able to shift their responsibility of being borh for their tenants on to the tenants themselves;[2] this change was not very difficult, especially where the lord either owned or controlled the hundred court which had the duty of working the tithing system. The result was known to the Norman lawyers as frankpledge, and lords who owned hundred courts might also have the additional right (which normally belonged to the sheriff), of verifying the proper enrolment of every tenant in a frankpledge. This was called "view of frankpledge".[3]

Under seignorial influences, then, we have seen the vill gradually falling under the control of the lord of the manor, save only for a few important police duties which the Crown imposed upon the vill direct, and even here it may be that the lord found ways of taking a profit. The institution next above the vill, the hundred, likewise fell into private hands in numerous cases, and in many instances the lord of a hundred could exclude the sheriff from his tourn in that particular hundred and hold it himself as a "court leet". In later times, legal theory attributed to many manors three different courts—court leet, court baron, court customary. Even when the theory was current law, there were practical

---

[1] II Cnut, 20.

[2] Cf. p. 88 n. 2 above.

[3] For all this see W. A. Morris, *The Frankpledge System*. "There were endless variations in the division of labour and the division of profits between the private views of frankpledge and the tourn in any hundred": H. M. Cam, *The Hundred and the Hundred Rolls*, 127.

difficulties in separating the three jurisdictions[1] and during the middle ages there was little attempt to draw fine distinctions. The leet was the most distinctive, with its view of frankpledge: for the rest, a general and wide jurisdiction was exercised without regard for speculative difficulties.

A MANORIAL COURT AT WORK

An interesting example of a manorial court (with a court leet held, as usual, twice a year) is to be found at Littleport near Ely, and a few extracts from its rolls[2] will give a good idea of the vigour and usefulness of such courts, and explain, incidentally, why some boroughs found it useful to acquire from the Crown a grant of leet jurisdiction. As an example of its most solemn form of procedure we may take what looks very much like an original writ[3] addressed by the lord of the court (the bishop of Ely) to his steward in 1316: but more typical of its usual activities are the numerous cases of petty offences, principally larcenies, which are punished by banishment[4] and offences against the by-laws relating to the agricultural arrangements of the village—and like most mediaeval communities there was a strong protectionist policy which even went so far as to fine persons who " exported " eggs " to the great destruction " of the people.[5] Two men incurred a fine for having " falsely, maliciously and in contempt of the lord, defamed his court by saying that no one can obtain justice there ".[6] Civil cases illustrate the wide variety of remedy obtainable in the court. A seller who warranted two ewes as sound has to pay fine and damages when they turned out to be diseased,[7] and the owner of a dog has to pay for the damage it does:[8] Rose called Ralph a thief, and Ralph called her a whore, and so both are fined, and since the trespass done to Ralph exceeds the trespass done to Rose she must pay him damages of twelve pence for the difference.[9] Slandering a man's goods so that he lost a sale is visited with fine and damages.[10] Beatrice, who should have made a shirt for Agnes, has to pay one penny damages for failing to do so, and in at least two cases of contracts to do work, the court ordered the defaulter to be distrained until he did it—remarkable examples of specific performance.[11] These and many other entries show how vigorous and flexible was this

[1] See the warning given in Bacon, *Abridgement* (ed. 1832), ii. 534.

[2] Portions of these rolls are printed by Maitland in *The Court Baron* (Selden Society, vol. 4); the following references are to the pages of that edition.

[3] *Op. cit.*, 121–122.

[4] *Ibid.*, 123.

[5] *Ibid.*, 126.

[6] *Ibid.*, 127.

[7] *Ibid.*, 128.

[8] *Ibid.*, 131. (No *scienter* is alleged as a rule.)

[9] *Ibid.*, 133.

[10] *Ibid.*, 136.

[11] *Ibid.*, 115.

manorial law in the period around the year 1300, when it is certain that the common law administered by the king's courts at Westminster gave no remedy for the breach of simple contracts, nor for such torts as slander.

In these cases it will be seen that prosecutions are on the presentment of a jury. In manors which had not received (or had not assumed) this royal right, it was the bailiff who prosecuted.[1]

The efficiency of the manorial form of government is attested to a remarkable degree in the history of Manchester. This rich and flourishing community was a manor belonging to the Mosley family, who purchased the manorial rights in 1596 and continued to enjoy them until 1845, when the municipality (created in 1838) bought them for £200,000.

" The lord of the manor had the right to tax and toll all articles brought for sale into the market of the town. But, though the inhabitants were thus to a large extent taxed for the benefit of one individual, they had a far greater amount of local self-government than might have been supposed, and the court leet, which was then the governing body of the town, had, though in a rudimentary form, nearly all the powers now possessed by municipal corporations."[2]

COUNTIES, PALATINATES, HONOURS

When we come to the county, however, we find that seignorial influence was less easy to assert. In one or two cases the office of sheriff became hereditary in a great family, but this advantage was soon destroyed by the strictness with which hereditary sheriffs, like all other sheriffs, had to account to the Exchequer. Even the appointment of an earl did not have the effect of putting the county into private hands; the county was still administered by a royal sheriff accountable to the Crown, the earl only receiving the third penny. A few counties became palatine, that is to say, exempt, or almost so, from royal jurisdiction (Chester, Lancaster and Durham); for this there were definite military reasons, as these border counties had to be kept almost continuously on a war footing as a defence against the Welsh and Scotch. The processes which we have seen at work in the township and the hundred, the Crown refused to tolerate in the county; and so the county became the basis of royal power in local government.

Generally speaking, therefore, private persons did not enjoy any jurisdiction higher than that of a hundred court with court leet. The result was inevitably to simplify the task of the Crown in effecting and maintaining the unity of the country, and, in the end, to facilitate the rise of the common law into its present position of complete and unrivalled primacy. At one moment, however, it seemed that things might have been otherwise. Even before the Conquest there were some very extensive private jurisdictions, and after the Conquest they continued to exist in a more feudalised form, very frequently being styled

[1] Plucknett, *The Mediaeval Bailiff*, 9–13.
[2] Article " Manchester " in *Encyclopaedia Britannica* (1911), 548.

" Honours ". The honour was governed by a court which consisted of the barons who held land of it, and the procedure and jurisdiction of the court resembled closely that of the King's own court. A few good examples[1] of cases in honorial courts in the middle of the twelfth century show how important questions of property could be litigated, and sometimes settled by means of final concords, in the court of an honour without the necessity of invoking royal justice or its machinery.[2]

The decline of such jurisdictions is an important factor in our legal history. Some survived late because they were held by churches, but many vanished through escheat or forfeiture, or were broken up through descent to heiresses. There seems to have been little direct attack upon them at any date, though they must all have felt in time the competition of the royal courts with which they had concurrent jurisdiction principally in matters of real property.

We have therefore traced, very briefly, the characteristics of the old communal jurisdictions, together with their partial subjection to the growing forces of seignorial jurisdiction. The only place where these forces were checked was in the county, and their antagonist there was the Norman monarchy. We now come, therefore, to the consideration of the power of the Crown over the more ancient local jurisdictions.

[1] They are printed and discussed by Stenton, *English Feudalism*, 46–55.

[2] Described below, pp. 613–614.

THE CROWN AND LOCAL COURTS

The unification of England by the Anglo-Saxon kings raised the problem of local institutions. It can hardly be said that they solved it, for throughout the Anglo-Saxon period government was local rather than royal—indeed, the idea of national institutions centring in the Crown is Norman rather than Anglo-Saxon.[1]

THE RISE OF THE SHERIFF

For all that, the Anglo-Saxon Crown did begin a policy of establishing connections with local institutions, and, as far as circumstances permitted, of exercising some sort of control over them. The shire or county, as we have said, frequently represented an ancient petty kingdom, and its titular head, the alderman, represented the ancient royal family. It is clear, therefore, that the alderman might be expected to uphold local institutions against any attempt at centralisation. This, in fact, seems to have been the case, and the situation was soon met by placing beside him a new official, the King's reeve, who was answerable to the national King and not to the alderman. The duties of the king's reeve seem to have been very miscellaneous, including both administration and judicial business.[2] It was inevitable that as time went on the King's reeve should grow in importance at the expense of the alderman, and that finally he should take the alderman's place and become the principal officer of the shire under the name of " sheriff " or " shire reeve ". The complaints of his extortion and oppression are constant in the later Anglo-Saxon age, and it is clear that the Crown had some difficulty in maintaining control over its own sheriffs. After the Conquest there was a tendency to regard the English sheriff as the equivalent of the Norman *vicomte* and to develop the office upon those lines. The Norman kings steadily resisted this; they were strong enough to control even the very powerful sheriffs of the late eleventh century, and to use their local influence in the interest of the Crown. They therefore did not hesitate to appoint as sheriffs men of considerable importance.

[1] Jolliffe, *Constitutional History*, 107–138, rates highly the Anglo-Saxon Crown's success.
[2] *Ibid.*, 112.

After a long period of political struggle, the Crown finally adopted the policy of limiting the sheriff's tenure to one year, and of choosing him from the upper middle class of landowners.

The principal factor in controlling the sheriff was the annual accounting at the Exchequer. The severity of the exchequer's dealings with sheriffs is a remarkable testimony to the power of the Crown, and observers noted with grim satisfaction that their local tyrant entered the exchequer, shaking in his shoes.[1] Nor did a sheriff's troubles cease with his term of office—or even at his death, for the exchequer process remorselessly pursued his heirs for arrears of his account.[2] Such ruthlessness left the sheriff no alternative to amassing as big a surplus as possible in order to meet these contingencies. Unusual situations were met, however, by extraordinary means, and more than once large numbers of sheriffs were summarily deposed, while Henry II's reign has left us some illuminating documents concerning his Inquest of Sheriffs—a general inquiry into the misdeeds of those officers.[3] It is not an infrequent occurrence to find a wholesale removal from office of other ministers too, even judges—a famous example was when Edward I removed all the judges—for in the middle ages, as now, the enforcement of political morality was apt to be spasmodic rather than continuous. Into the political history of the sheriff's office we cannot now enter.[4] For our purpose the important aspects are the effect of these devices upon judicial institutions.

At the time of the Norman Conquest the sheriff, as the King's representative, enjoyed a good deal of judicial power, which caused the Crown considerable anxiety, for there was no effective means of controlling him, except the somewhat desperate remedy of discharging him when popular unrest grew too strong. In the Norman age a number of attempts were made to find some check upon his powers as a royal judge. Sometimes the Crown appointed a permanent justiciar to sit in the county; the office of coroner was developed in order to serve as a check upon the sheriff; by the Great Charter it was finally declared that no sheriff should for the future hold pleas of the Crown. This definitive solution robbed the sheriff of a great deal of his ancient power, but it only became workable because the Crown had been steadily developing other means for disposing of Crown pleas.

ITINERANT JUSTICES

In the first place, recourse was had to an ancient device whereby the Crown sent out travelling officials who should inquire into the

[1] See the passage relating to the year 1121 printed in J. H. Round, *Commune of London*, 123, from an unpublished manuscript in the College of Arms.

[2] H. M. Cam, *The Hundred and the Hundred Rolls*, 63–64, where the heir of a sheriff settled his ancestor's official debts to the Crown some seventy-five years after they were incurred.

[3] Printed in Stubbs, *Select Charters*.

[4] It has been explored in W. A. Morris, *The Mediaeval English Sheriff*.

conduct of local officers and hold the royal court in the localities they visited. Sometimes their commission was general; at others they were specially delegated for the trial of some particular action or class of actions. We thus have numerous references to royal commissioners sitting in the county court for the transaction of some particularly important business. Henry II systematised some early experiments of his grandfather Henry I, and sent travelling justices on several occasions through the realm.

In the thirteenth and fourteenth centuries these justices sometimes received the very ample civil, criminal and administrative jurisdiction which modern historians call the General Eyre,[1] and their session in the county court was an impressive demonstration of the royal power over all sorts and conditions of men, from the baronial owners of great franchises and the sheriffs down to the meanest villein. A thorough investigation took place of all the judicial and administrative business which had arisen in the county since the last eyre. The sheriff's records (and those of his predecessors) were checked from those of the coroners; oral presentments of long-past occurrences were checked from the rolls, and the slightest discrepancy entailed a fine. Presenting juries were empanelled and provided with a list of " chapters of the eyre " reminding them of over a hundred matters of which they were to inquire. Besides its administrative powers and criminal jurisdiction, the justices in eyre also had the jurisdiction of the court of common pleas and so all civil business affecting the county was also theirs, for the entry of the eyre into a county automatically transferred to it all pleas then in progress concerning the county before the court of common pleas. Indeed, this was inevitable on those occasions when all the justices of the common pleas were commissioned to travel in eyre, for then the court of common pleas at Westminster ceased to sit.[2] By the opening of the fourteenth century the general eyre had become something of an anachronism, albeit a source of great financial profit to the Crown and correspondingly oppressive to the subject. A rule was established that an eyre should not visit a county within seven years of a previous eyre,[3] and several times the commons petitioned against them. It is believed that eyres ceased to be commissioned after the middle of the fourteenth century.[4]

The eyre was too ponderous and too intermittent a machine to deal

---

[1] See more on the eyre, below, pp. 144ff.

[2] But matters before the king's bench and exchequer were unaffected: Holdsworth, i. 267.

[3] For the origins of the rule, see R. F. Treharne, *Baronial Plan of Reform*, 398–406. For a chronological list of eyres, see H. M. Cam, *Studies in the Hundred Rolls*, 104–113.

[4] Later commissions were sometimes countermanded when suitable financial offers were made to the government; the threat of an eyre thus became an effectual means of blackmail: B. H. Putnam, *Proceedings before the Justices of the Peace* (Ames Foundation), xlvi–xlvii. The original sources of the *Eyre of Kent (1313–1314)*, which are particularly full, have been printed in three volumes by the Selden Society, and form the basis of a little book by W. C. Bolland, *The General Eyre* (Cambridge, 1922).

with the ever-present problem of bringing royal justice to the shires. For practical purposes the Crown relied on a variety of travelling justices (some of whom were not professional lawyers) with limited commissions. Thus Magna Carta provided for frequent justices to take the assizes of novel disseisin and mort d'ancestor;[1] frequent commissions were issued to " deliver the gaols ", *i.e.* to try the prisoners; a single case, or a group of cases, might be tried before special justices of oyer and terminer; and in the middle of the fourteenth century it looked as if the King's bench might become a sort of eyre court, for it was frequently sent on hasty tour through several counties.[2]

The process was carried even further. Just as the King's justices in eyre went around the country sitting in each county court, as it were, for the transaction of all sorts of business and a general inquiry into abuses, so the sheriff himself travelled around his county sitting in each hundred court twice a year. Here he acted strictly as a royal deputy, serving merely as a *liaison* between the central authority and local institutions, for since the Great Charter he could no longer " hold " pleas of the Crown, but only " keep " them, that is to say, guard the prisoners and make memoranda of the circumstances, which were to be laid before the king's commissioners at their next visitation; and by the time of Bracton and *Fleta* it came to be the accepted theory that not only the sheriff's turn, but also its equivalent, the " court leet ", are royal courts held in virtue of a presumed delegation of power from the Crown. In short, the Crown, for most practical purposes, is the fountain of justice.

THE REMOVAL OF PLEAS

The royal supremacy was asserted in yet other ways. Early in the twelfth century it was already a principle that " false judgment " (*i.e.* proceedings to review a judgment in an inferior court) was a royal plea, and over a century later it was embodied in a statute.[3] Hence a judgment of a county court could be examined in the court of common pleas by means of a writ of *recordari facias loquelam*, and a judgment in a seignorial court by the very similar *accedas ad curiam*.[4] Nor was it necessary to await judgment before invoking the royal jurisdiction, for a plea pending in a seignorial court could be removed into the county court by a procedure called *tolt*, and from the county into the common pleas by a writ of *pone*.

[1] Magna Carta (1215), c. 18, amended (1217), c. 13 and (1225) c. 12. For the professionalisation of the commission of assize about the year 1242, see C. A. F. Meekings, *Alan de Wassand*, in Yorkshire Archaeological Journal, xxxviii. 469

[2] The motive was partly financial; see the detailed study in B. H. Putnam, *Proceedings before Justices of the Peace*, lvii ff., and cf. E. L. G. Stones, *Sir Geoffrey le Scrope*, in English Historical Review, lxix. i.

[3] For references see p. 156 n. 2 and p. 388 below.

[4] And error could go from the eyre to the common pleas: *Bracton's Note Book*, no. 1412.

THE RESULTS OF CENTRALISATION

The removal of pleas of the Crown from the sheriff, accompanied by the transfer of that jurisdiction to the Justices in Eyre and to other commissioners or travelling justices as the Eyre became obsolete, and the centralisation of pleas concerning land in the hands of royal justices sitting by royal writ, mark the permanent subjection of the county and all its officers to the Crown. A unitary state was no doubt an advantage in the middle ages when so many nations were divided into feudal sub-divisions; but the cost was heavy. The very fact of several bodies of law and custom existing in one nation sometimes had fruitful results for legal science. In France the multiplicity of jurisdictions led to a comparative study of legal rules which was a valuable incentive to criticism and improvement, just as in America to-day the numerous state systems invite and indeed compel a critical appraisal of their respective merits. In England, on the other hand, our too early unification left the common law without an effective competitor, and bred up a profession which was only just sufficiently aware of the existence of other systems to glory in its isolation. That state of mind is not altogether past, and its results are indelible.

A more specific consequence of the dominance of Westminster is the fact that England had to wait until 1846 for a co-ordinated system of local courts. The Crown's incurable fear of the sheriff is largely responsible for this. How great an opportunity was missed can be seen by looking at the vigorous and useful institution of the sheriff in Scotland, where the office was allowed to develop along natural lines.[1]

---

[1] Compare the article " Sheriff " in the *Encyclopedia of Social Sciences*.

THE JURY

It is in this complicated interplay of royal and local institutions that the origins of the jury are to be sought; so we can now appropriately turn from the study of the vill and the hundred to the growth of the system of presentment which was so prominent a part of their constitution, and to the later transformation of that system into a method of trial as well as accusation. At the same time, the county's loss of effective jurisdiction over pleas of land was intimately connected with the rise of the royal writ, and this will be almost synonymous with the use of an assize or a jury of twelve. The criminal jury, therefore, can be treated here because it grew out of the natural expression of the vill and the hundred; but the civil jury in the old real actions was based (as we shall see) upon a somewhat different, though related, idea, which only came to an end with the abolition of real actions. The modern civil jury, it must be remembered, is descended from the old criminal jury through the action of trespass, which was at first partly criminal and later entirely civil in its character.

The discussion may well open with Maitland's definition of the jury: a jury is a body of neighbours summoned by a public officer to answer questions upon oath.[1] It will be seen that there is nothing in this definition which restricts the jury to judicial proceedings; on the contrary, the definition deliberately makes room for the fact that the jury, like so many institutions, was an administrative device which only later became confined to courts of law.

The story is complicated because several different lines of development were being pursued simultaneously, and so it is particularly necessary to have the outlines clearly in mind while the details of this chapter are being studied. The subject will be dealt with in the following order:

1. Early prototypes of the jury;
2. The jury for royal administrative inquiry;
3. The jury for the trial of property cases;
4. The jury for royal criminal inquiry;
5. Ancient modes of trial;
6. The jury as a new mode of trial;
7. Post-mediaeval problems.

1. Early prototypes of the jury

SUPPOSED ANGLO-SAXON ORIGINS

Ever since the seventeenth century when juries began to express sentiments against the government, there has been a tendency for the jury to become, at least in popular thought, a safeguard of political liberty. It is only natural, therefore, that its history should have been idealised and traced back for patriotic reasons to the supposed golden age of Anglo-Saxon institutions. Various theories have been proposed.

[1] Pollock and Maitland, i. 117.

According to one the jury is descended from the doomsmen who find the judgment and declare the law and custom in the ancient communal courts. This explanation, however, is by no means satisfactory, for the doomsmen did not find facts (for which there was other machinery available) but declared the law which applied to a state of facts which had already been established. A second suggestion would seek the origin of the jury in the compurgators, of whom we shall speak later; this is open to the objection that the compurgators were summoned by a party and not by a public officer, and could not be compelled to act unless they cared to.

ENGLISH AND SCANDINAVIAN JURIES

A third and more plausible suggestion would see an origin of the jury in a remarkable passage in the laws of King Ethelred promulgated at Wantage, which probably dates from about the year 997.[1] It is this:

> " And that a gemot be held in every wapontake; and the xii senior thegns go out, and the reeve with them, and swear on the relic that is given them in hand, that they will accuse no innocent man, nor conceal any guilty one. . . ."

It cannot be denied that we have here a remarkable anticipation of the Assize of Clarendon which later was to establish as a regular procedure the presentment of suspected criminals by the hundred. There are one or two other traces in various parts of Scandinavia which may point in the same direction, and by the fourteenth century Sweden certainly had a developed system of presenting juries, and indeed had also created a trial jury (called the *Nämnd*) both in civil and criminal proceedings.[2] The origin and the growth of the *nämnd* seem to be quite independent of the corresponding institutions in England, and in fact it is not unprecedented to find that two different systems independently come to substantially the same conclusion; but when the historian sees the similarity of the conclusions he must beware of assuming that they are the result of direct contact, unless that contact can be proved by independent evidence. It may well be that this passage in the laws of Ethelred, enacted with a view to the Scandinavian institutions prevailing in that portion of England which had been occupied by the Danes, represents an independent tendency of Scandinavian law. Moreover, before we are entitled to see here an origin of the jury, it will be necessary to establish continuity between the Law of Wantage and the jury as it existed after the Norman Conquest. This it is impossible to do, and here is the second lesson for those who would undertake historical

---

[1] The translation here given is from Stubbs, *Select Charters*. (For another version see A. J. Robertson, *Laws of the Kings of England*, 65, 319–320.) For comments see Holdsworth, i. 12 n. 10 (who identifies the twelve thegns with the twelve freemen of the hundred mentioned above, p. 90), and Vinogradoff, *English Society in the Eleventh Century*, 6. The hundred in the Danish part of England was called a wapontake.

[2] For a description of the *nämnd*, see A. Engelmann (ed. R. W. Millar), *History of Continental Civil Procedure* 225–232.

investigation.   The appearance of a principle or institution in one age, followed by the appearance of the same or a similar institution at a considerably later age, must not lead one to suppose that the later is derived from the earlier.   Before this conclusion would be justified further evidence of continuity must be adduced; in the case now before us there is a gap of nearly two hundred years between the Wantage enactment and the next appearance of the presenting jury.   Until that gap has been filled by showing continuity between the Anglo-Danish institution and the jury which is continuous from Anglo-Norman times, it would be unsafe to look to Ethelred's law for the origin of the grand jury.[1]

2.   The jury for royal administrative inquiry

FRANKISH JURIES

The history of the jury has now been settled by the famous researches of Brunner,[2] supplemented by those of Haskins,[3] who from newly discovered evidence partly filled the gap which Brunner had to admit. This history certainly goes back to the early ninth century, when we find the Emperor Louis the Pious, son and successor of Charlemagne, ordering in 829 that for the future the royal rights shall not be ascertained through the production of witnesses, but by the sworn statement of the best and most credible people of the district.[4]   It seems that the government had little faith in the production of witnesses by parties who were disputing its claims; such testimony, it was felt, was sure to be interested.   Instead, the Emperor undertook to compel the most considerable people of the county to declare upon oath what the customary royal rights were, and it may very well be that this method was more likely to produce the truth than the voluntary testimony of witnesses supporting their friends against the government.   If we put ourselves for a moment in the place of a contemporary, we might imagine that there would be some grumbling at superseding an ancient institution of witness proof by the high-handed proceeding of compelling people selected by the government to speak on oath, whether they wished to or not.   It might have seemed, perhaps, that the administration had usurped dangerous powers and was settling disputes in its own favour by unorthodox methods.   To such an objection, if ever it were raised, history has given an answer: in the

[1] For an attempt in this direction, see N. D. Hurnard, *The Jury of Presentment and the Assize of Clarendon*, English Historical Review (1941), lvi. 374–410. For differing views, see Sir Frank Stenton, *Anglo-Saxon England*, 502–504, and A. L. Poole, *Domesday to Magna Carta*, 397–398. It may be mentioned here that the significance of the very obscure synodal jury used in the Church's criminal procedure is proper to this inquiry. See a few references in Taswell-Langmead, *English Constitutional History* (ed. Plucknett), 86.

[2] H. Brunner, *Entstehung der Schwurgerichte* (Berlin, 1872). For a criticism of Brunner, see Ernst Mayer, *Geschworenengericht* (1916).

[3] C. H. Haskins, *Norman Institutions* (Harvard University Press, 1918).

[4] *Monumenta Germaniae Historica, Capitularia*, ii. no. 188, translated in Pound and Plucknett, *Readings*, 141.

course of a thousand years this drastic administrative machine has been transplanted to an unknown continent, where by a strange twist of history it has become the constitutional bulwark of the public against the executive.

It has been suggested that Louis the Pious did not invent this, and that there was some precedent for the device as early as a law of Valentinian I (369), but the argument here is not quite so convincing—at least to Romanists, who are rather loath to admit the paternity of the jury. But from Louis the Pious onwards the evidence is clear enough, until the failure of the line of Charlemagne, when we come to a very obscure period—the darkest moment of the dark ages—and it was here that Brunner had to admit that there was a gap in his evidence.

3. *The jury for the trial of property cases*

NORMAN JURIES AND ASSIZES

This gap has been filled to some extent (though not entirely) by the discoveries of Professor Haskins, who has accepted Brunner's theory that the institution was carried over from the crumbling empire of the Carolingians to the new duchy of Normandy, and that the dukes used it there in much the same way as the emperors had before them.[1]

At first the jury had been used by the government only as a particularly drastic means of establishing its own rights. This indicates some dissatisfaction with existing methods of proof, and it is clear that this dissatisfaction was shared by litigants as well, for the next stage in the history shows us private persons seeking as a favour from the duke or the King the privilege of having their rights ascertained by means of an " inquisition ", as the institution was then called. In other words, the jury of administrative inquiry was on the point of becoming a jury of trial in civil procedure. Some lords, both lay and ecclesiastical, even went so far as to introduce the jury into their private courts without royal or ducal permission (as far as we can see). The crown therefore was in peril of losing its monopoly of jury trial, although it retained and developed the natural advantage of finding it easier to compel the attendance of jurors than did most other lords.

Henry I while he was duke of Normandy occasionally bestowed the privilege of trial by inquisition (or jury) upon a favoured church, such as Bayeux;[2] Duke Geoffrey[3] carried the process a step further and

---

[1] Michel de Boüard, *De la Neustrie carolingienne à la Normandie féodale: continuité ou discontinuité?* Bulletin of the Institute of Historical Research, xxviii. 1, argues persuasively against Carolingian survivals, and for Norman originality.

[2] For a similar concession by William I in England, see Bigelow, *Placita Anglo-Normannica*, 33 (translated in Pound and Plucknett, *Readings*, 141–142).

[3] From 1145 to 1150 (for the former date see Haskins, 130, and also *Normannia*, i. 223–224). Geoffrey was also count of Anjou, and the question of priority between Anjou and Normandy in the development of the jury is still open: see Chartrou, *L'Anjou de 1109 à 1151* (Paris, 1928), 156, and cf. Halphen. *Institutions judiciaires angevines*, Revue d'Anjou (n.s.), xlvi. 372 ff.

by means of an enactment, called an assize, made trial by inquisition the
general method for all important litigation of a civil character.

INQUISITIONS IN ENGLAND

Very soon after the Norman Conquest the inquisition appears in
England as an administrative device for obtaining all sorts of information
useful to the government from an unwilling populace. The officers of
William the Conqueror were told to—

> " enquire by the oath of the sheriff and of all the barons and of their Frenchmen,
> and of all the hundred, of the priest, of the reeve, and of six villeins of every vill,
> what is the name of the manor, who held it in the time of King Edward, who
> now, how many hides, how many ploughs,—how many men, how many villeins . . .
> how much it was worth and how much now; and all this at three times, the time
> of King Edward, the time when King William gave it, and now "—[1]

and the answers were collected in *Domesday Book*. The Constitutions
of Clarendon, which settled the controversy of Church and State in 1164,
recount that—[2]

> " This record or recognition was made in the year 1164 in the presence of the
> King concerning a part of the customs and liberties of his ancestors which ought to
> be held and observed in the realm. And by reason of the dissensions and discords
> which have arisen between the clergy and the King's justices and barons concerning
> his dignities and customs, this recognition was made before the archbishop and
> bishops and clergy, and the earls, barons and nobles of the realm."

Here we have the principle of the inquisition used to ascertain even
such vague matters as the customary political relations between Church
and State.

ASSIZES IN ENGLAND

Henry II, when he became King of England, adopted the same
policy as his father Geoffrey, and by a series of enactments, likewise
called assizes, threw open trial by inquisition to the whole public, who
could choose between half a dozen different procedures, according to
the nature of their cases. Thus, the Constitutions of Clarendon, c. 9,
in 1164 allowed a recognition or inquest to determine whether particular
land was held by ecclesiastical or lay tenure.[3] Two years later another
assembly at Clarendon seems to have established the assize of novel
disseisin.[4] In 1176 *mort d'ancestor* was created,[5] and probably in 1179
came the most striking extension of inquest trial[6] when it was allowed

[1] Text in Stubbs, *Select Charters*.

[2] *Ibid.*

[3] Translated in Pound and Plucknett, *Readings*, 74. Cf. Thorne, *The Assize Utrum*,
Columbia Law Review, xxxiii. 428.

[4] Pollock and Maitland, i. 145.

[5] Assize of Northampton, c. 4 (text in Stubbs, *Charters*).

[6] This date is suggested by J. H. Round in English Historical Review, xxxi. 268-269.

as a matter of course (at the option of the defendant) to replace battle in the most solemn of all actions, the writ of right.

From this time onwards the word " assize " takes several new meanings; it began by signifying a solemn session of a council or a court, and soon came to mean an enactment made at such a meeting; among the most important of these assizes were those establishing trial by inquisition, and so it soon became customary to describe the inquisition of twelve men as an assize, while the various procedures leading up to this form of trial (which we should now call forms of action) were likewise called assizes. Finally, travelling justices were established in the thirteenth century in order to try these assizes more speedily, and these justices were naturally called justices of assize, and their sessions in the provinces were called the assizes.

All of this history (with the exception of the Law of Wantage) has therefore been concerned with the use of the inquisition as a means of trying royal rights, and later, by royal favour, the rights of litigants who have been fortunate enough to acquire the privilege, and finally its extension to everybody who makes use of certain procedures called assizes—whose nature we shall discuss more fully in treating of the forms of action. Nothing, so far, has been said of the jury in criminal trials, and to this aspect of the question we must now turn.

4. The jury for royal criminal inquiry

CRIMINAL LAW: THE GRAND JURY

A great deal of information of value to the King could be obtained by compelling the inhabitants of a small community to answer questions, to inform against evil-doers, to disclose mysterious crimes, and to tell of their suspicions. Here we come to royal rights which are not matters of property or custom, but rather possible sources of jurisdiction, and therefore of profit. An inquisition, vill by vill, had established the enormous tax-return called *Domesday Book*, but the inquiry into crime and criminals was also a matter of deep concern to the Crown, not merely as a matter of public policy but also as a source of revenue, for criminal jurisdiction with its fines and forfeitures was always lucrative.

By this means the transition was effected, and in the Assize of Clarendon (1166) we find the establishment of a definite system of inquisitions as part of the machinery of criminal justice which have come down to our own day[1] as " grand juries ".

> " *Chapter I*
>
> " First the aforesaid King Henry established by the counsel of all his barons for the maintenance of peace and justice, that inquiry shall be made in every county and in every hundred by the twelve most lawful men of the hundred and by the

[1] The grand jury has been abolished (except in very few cases) in England, Administration of Justice (Miscellaneous Provisions) Act, 1933.

four most lawful men of every vill, upon oath that they shall speak the truth, whether in their hundred or vill there be any man who is accused or believed to be a robber, murderer, thief, or a receiver of robbers, murderers or thieves since the King's accession. And this the justices and sheriffs shall enquire before themselves.

"Chapter II

" And he who shall be found, by the oath of the aforesaid, accused or believed to be a robber, murderer, thief, or a receiver of such since the King's accession shall be taken and put to the ordeal of water and made to swear that he was no robber, murderer, thief, or receiver of such up to the value of five shillings, as far as he knows, since the King's accession. . . .

"Chapter IV

" And when a robber, murderer, thief or receiver of such is captured as a result of the oath, the sheriff shall send to the nearest justice (if there are no justices shortly visiting the county wherein he was captured) by an intelligent man saying that he has captured so many men. And the justices shall reply telling the sheriff where the prisoners are to be brought before them. And the sheriff shall bring them before the justices together with two lawful men from the hundred and the vill where they were captured to bring the record of the county and the hundred as to why they were captured; and there they shall make their law before the justices.

"Chapter XII

" And if anyone is captured in possession of stolen or robbed goods and is of bad repute and can produce no testimony of public purchase nor a warrantor of title he shall not make his law. And if the goods were not publicly acquired he shall go to the water because they were found in his possession.

"Chapter XIV

" The lord King also wishes that those who make their law and clear themselves shall, nevertheless, forswear the King's land if they are of bad renown and publicly and evilly reputed by the testimony of many lawful men, and cross the sea within eight days unless detained by the weather, and with the first favourable wind they shall cross the sea and never come back to England save by the King's permission, and shall be outlawed, and if they come back shall be captured as outlaws."[1]

5.   Ancient modes of trial

THE ORDEALS

An attentive study of this document will show the difficulties which confronted the government in the administration of criminal justice. The presenting jury from every hundred would very soon provide the royal officers with a goodly number of suspicious characters. But suspicion is not proof, and the presentment by the hundred, like its modern descendant, indictment by grand jury, is merely an accusation and not a conviction. Having found the suspects, how is the question of their guilt or innocence to be determined? The document we have just quoted mentions two methods, " making one's law " and " going to the water ". We must now for a moment describe these and one or

---

[1] Stubbs, *Charters*; the Constitutions of 1164 had already told juries to present sinners to the bishop. Above, pp. 18, 109 n. 1.

two other methods of trial then in use, for it was the limitations and uncertainties of the ancient methods which led to the development of the modern petty jury.

The most ancient of these was the ordeal, which took a variety of different forms. Its origin must date from before the introduction of Christianity, but the practice was so deep-rooted that the Church, in this as in other cases, felt bound to adopt it. In consequence we find the ordeal surrounded by Christian ceremonies which must, no doubt, have added considerably to its moral effectiveness—and perhaps even to its practical value as a psychological test of truth-telling. Of the several forms of ordeal in use the ordeal of hot iron was that most common for freemen. It was administered at the most solemn moment of the Mass; a special ritual was prescribed in the old service books telling us how the heated iron was to be carried by the accused over a distance of nine feet; then—

" the hand was sealed and kept under seal for three nights and afterwards the bandages removed. If it is clean, God be praised; but if unhealthy matter is found where the iron was held he shall be deemed guilty and unclean."[1]

Another variant was the ordeal of boiling water, where the accused had to plunge his hand into a bowl of boiling water and take out a stone; his guilt or innocence was ascertained by inspecting his hand after three days. The ordeal of cold water was more often applied to the unfree. The accused was solemnly exhorted by the priest during Mass to confess his guilt if he were guilty; if he persisted in maintaining his innocence then—

" let the hands of the accused be bound together under the bent knees after the manner of a man who is playing the game of *Champ-estroit*. Then he shall be bound around the loins with a rope strong enough to hold him; and in the rope will be made a knot at the distance of the length of his hair; and so he shall be let down gently into the water so as not to make a splash. If he sinks down to the knot he shall be drawn up saved; otherwise let him be adjudged a guilty man by the spectators."[2]

Still another variety of ordeal was that of the cursed morsel, which was used only for the trial of clergy. This consisted in making the accused swallow a piece of food in which was concealed a feather or such like; if he was successful, he was innocent, but if he choked he was guilty. Although the Church adopted the ordeals which it found in use among the populace, some of the more critical clergy had misgivings. Then also there was obviously the possibility of the priest manipulating the ordeal, and Peter the Chanter, a celebrated theologian of the university of Paris (*ob.* 1197), suggests that he had some sort of moral responsibility

---

[1] This and other forms are translated in Sayre, *Cases on Criminal Law*, 28–32, from Liebermann, *Gesetze*. See generally, Lea, *Superstition and Force*, and much illustrative material in A. L. Poole, *Obligations of Society*, 82 ff.

[2] For a contemporary picture, see Sayre, 29.

for the rightness of the result.[1] Its abolition was rendered all the more difficult by the system of fees which grew up around it—always a powerful obstruction in the way of reform. A particular church, like St. Peter's, Northampton, might have a monopoly of the proceedings;[2] elsewhere, the archdeacon might be entitled to dues—as at Coventry where he received thirty pence for each ordeal.[3]

In the great majority of cases the ordeal was the accused's mode of defence; yet on rare occasions we may find a prosecutor offering to undergo an ordeal himself in proof of his accusation,[4] and in two cases of 1202 the accused was given the choice of bearing the iron himself or of letting the accuser do it—and naturally elected the latter procedure.[5] Countless varieties of ordeal are still in use in different parts of the world among primitive tribes.[6]

WAGER OF LAW

The " wager of law " which we have just mentioned, although still essentially an ordeal, contained features which give the impression that its principle was rather more rational. The party who was called upon to make his law had to find a number of people, twelve or some other number fixed by the court according to circumstances, and then take a solemn oath that he was innocent. His companions, or " compurgators " as they were called, then swore that the oath which he had taken was clean.[7] In other words, the court calls upon the accused to produce a specified number of people (occasionally from a particular class or even from the names on a given list) who are prepared to swear that in their opinion his oath is trustworthy. They do not swear to the facts of the case, but merely to their judgment that the accused is a credible person. Wager of law, therefore, reduces itself to a character test; in the earlier period when there were strong religious sanctions surrounding the oath it is clear that a disreputable person would have difficulty in finding compurgators. Cases of failure to make one's law do occur from time to time in the records.[8] The Church used it considerably under the title of " Canonical Purgation " in circumstances

---

[1] Migne, *Patrologiae Latinae Cursus*, ccv. 230–1.

[2] F. M. Stenton, *Acta Episcoporum*, Cambridge Historical Journal, iii. 12 (date before 1166).

[3] Pope Alexander III (1159–1181) relates, and condemns, the practice: c. 3, X. 5. 37; Maitland, *Domesday Book and Beyond*, 282.

[4] D. M. Knowles, *The case of St. William of York* (1154), Cambridge Historical Journal, v. 175.

[5] Lady Stenton, *Lincolnshire Assize Roll* (Lincoln Record Society, vol. 22), nos. 595, 843; A. L. Poole, *Obligations of Society*, 82.

[6] Cf. M. M. Kovalevskii, *Coutume contemporaine: droit ossétien* (1893); Patetta, *Le Ordalie* (1890); E. Jobbé-Duval, *Les Idées primitives dans la Bretagne contemporaine* (1920).

[7] There is a long discussion in *City of London* v. *Wood* (1701), 12 Mod. 669, showing the extent to which it had been rationalised by that date.

[8] See for example *The Court Baron* (Selden Society), 123. Maitland, *ibid.*, 17, argues that compurgation was difficult to perform.

where other modes of proof were impossible, and long after the Reformation it survived in ecclesiastical courts. Opinion as to its value seems always to have been divided. The passage we have quoted from the Assize of Clarendon[1] makes it clear that the Crown had little respect for it, at least as a defence to criminal charges. On the other hand, certain towns, and notably the city of London, stubbornly retained compurgation as a defence to charges even of felony. They seem to have regarded it as a valuable privilege, which is surely not without significance, for business interests, then as now, must have had the firm enforcement of criminal law often in mind. It should perhaps be noted that the privilege was restricted to actual members of the city and was not extended indiscriminately to all the inhabitants. The " great law " of London must have been a severe test. City officials chose the compurgators, eighteen east of Walbrook and eighteen west of Walbrook, subject to challenges by the accused; if the charge was homicide, the failure of any one of the thirty-six compurgators would be enough to send the accused to the gallows.[2]

In civil matters, however, there are signs that it had a place; contemporaries seem to have regarded it as superior in some cases to witness proof.[3] The citizens of London as late as 1364 obtained a statute preserving their right to wage law as a defence to debts which were claimed on the evidence of a merchant's books—it is significant that a mercantile community should consider compurgation successfully performed as more weighty evidence than a merchant's accounts.[4] In the actions of debt and detinue wager of law as a defence lasted until the nineteenth century. The courts in such cases endeavoured to substitute jury trial as far as possible, both by developing alternative actions and by strictly defining those few cases in which it lay. It was not finally abolished until 1833.[5]

TRIAL BY BATTLE

The Normans introduced trial by battle—unless, indeed, " trial by battle may well have been known in the Danelaw throughout the tenth century ".[6] In civil cases it was not fought between the parties themselves, but between their respective champions. The ancient formula

---

[1] Above, p. 113.

[2] See *Borough Customs* (Selden Society), i. 38.

[3] Esmein, *Histoire du droit français* (ed. Génestal), 91, 92. Parties might voluntarily accept this mode of proof, Y.B. 16 Edward III (Rolls Series), ii. 118.

[4] Statute 38 Edw. III, stat. 1, c. 5. (Compare *Plymouth Colonial Records*, ix. 49.) Leicester seems to have had difficulties with wager of law (*Borough Customs*, i. 164). In the Exchequer, jury trial was replaced by wager of law at the petition of the Commons in 1376, *Rot. Parl.*, ii. 337 no. 92. See below, p. 160.

[5] Civil Procedure Act, 1833 (3 & 4 Will. IV, c. 42), sec. 13.

[6] Pollock and Maitland, i. 39 n. 5. The standard work is G. Neilson, *Trial by Combat*; cf. H. C. Lea, *Superstition and Force*, chap. ii. Much illuminating material is discussed in V. H. Galbraith, *Death of a Champion*, Studies presented to F. M. Powicke, 283. Cf. C. de Smedt's two articles on the *Duel judiciaire* in *Etudes* of 15 Nov. 1894 and 15 Jan. 1895.

suggests that the champion was originally a witness who was also a tenant bound by homage to defend his lord's title, and that a judicial duel between contradictory witnesses was allowed to decide the rights of the parties. The champion's regular oath (which soon became a matter of mere form)[1] stated that his father on his deathbed had informed him that the plaintiff had the right which was then in dispute, and charged him to maintain that right with all his power. We have already mentioned that when the county court recorded its proceedings for the purpose of review by the Court of Common Pleas, a party might dispute the accuracy of the record and compel the county to defend it by battle. We very soon find from the rolls that there was a professional band of champions who undertook business all over the country; courts would arrange the dates of battle so that the champions could fit in their engagements conveniently. Some very great landowners, such as the larger monasteries, were so constantly involved in litigation that they maintained their own full-time champions. The names of these champions constantly appear on the rolls, and we sometimes hear of a champion's " master " or manager,[2] and of a champion who abandoned his client because the other side offered him a premium.[3] It is therefore not surprising that a bishop should have regarded a champion as unsuitable for holding a rectory.[4] But in criminal cases battle was a much more serious affair. It lay when a private person brought a criminal charge against another, and was fought by the accuser and accused in person. It was deadly; if the defeated defendant was not already slain in the battle he was immediately hanged on the gallows which stood ready. As it only lay in these private proceedings (called " appeals of felony ") there was no question of trial by battle where the accused had been indicted or where the Crown was a party.[5]

A curious incident in 1774 throws light upon the perverse uses to which history can be put, especially by those who have given but little thought to it. Events in Boston decided the English Government to improve the administration of justice in Massachusetts by means of a bill which *inter alia* abolished battle on appeals of murder. This proposal roused opposition in England from those who affected to regard trial by battle as a great pillar of the constitution, and in the end it was withdrawn on the more liberal grounds that parliament ought not to restrain

[1] " Concerning the oath of champions, forasmuch as the demandant's champion is frequently prejured in swearing that he or his father saw the seisin of his lord (or the lord's ancestor) and that his father ordered him to defend it, it is provided that henceforth the champion of the demandant shall not be compelled to swear to this; but the oath shall be retained in all other respects."—Westminster I, c. 41 (1275). Personal battle by a tenant is very rare; *Bracton's Note Book*, no. 980.

[2] *Bracton's Note Book*, no. 185. For a deed retaining a champion at the annual fee of 6s. 8d. by the bishop of Hereford (1276), see *Swinfield's Household Expenses* (Camden Society, o.s. 39), 201

[3] *Bracton's Note Book*, no. 1038.

[4] *Ibid.*, no. 1416; see also Round, *Family Origins*, 117 ff.

[5] But see Sir Maurice Powicke in *Magna Carta Commemoration Essays* (ed. H. E. Malden), 100 n. 1; Hoveden, *Chronica* (Rolls Series), iv. 176.

the liberties of the colonies.[1]   A last attempt to bring an appeal of murder in 1819 was frustrated by a hasty act abolishing appeals and also trial by battle in real actions.[2]

These, then, were the methods of proof available to the justices when confronted by the crowd of suspects brought before them through the presentment of the juries of the hundreds and vills.[3]   As for those whose guilt was beyond question, no difficulty arose. They had already been dealt with by very summary methods (which can hardly be called a trial) immediately upon their capture.[4]

It will be seen that there was very little choice. A criminal could be tried by battle only at the suit of a private prosecutor, and not at suit of the Crown; as for compurgation, the Assize of Clarendon tells us that a successful defence by this means was not very convincing, and even imposes punishment upon those who thereby clear themselves, if they are of bad character generally. Only the ordeal remained, and this was no doubt the general method of trial at the end of the twelfth century—tempered perhaps by the discretion of the justices, who may have allowed their private judgment upon the guilt or innocence of the accused to overrule the result of the ordeal if it turned out obviously unsatisfactory.

ABOLITION OF THE ORDEAL

The opposition within the Church to trial by ordeal[5] which dates from the days of Agobard, bishop of Lyons (*d.* 840), was particularly constant at Rome. Remoter provinces, however, were faced by a more primitive populace. Regino of Prüm (*c.* 906) admitted the ordeal into his work on canon law, and so did Burchard of Worms later still (1008–12), who was so dismayed at the prevalence of perjury, that the ordeal seemed to him preferable to the oath as a mode of trial.[6] A century later still, in 1116, Ypres received a charter abolishing both ordeals and trial by battle.[7] It was yet another century before reform reached England when Innocent III in the Fourth Lateran Council (1215) forbade clergy from performing any religious ceremonies in connection with ordeals. This, of course, robbed the ordeal of all religious sanction,

---

[1] *Parliamentary History*, xvii. 1291.

[2] 59 Geo. III. c. 46. And see *Ashford* v. *Thornton*, 1 Barn. & Ald. 405.

[3] For full contemporary descriptions of these archaic modes of trial, see Pound and Plucknett, *Readings*, 134–141; English Historical Review, xvi. 730.

[4] Below, p. 427.

[5] See H. C. Lea, *Superstition and Force*; S. Grelewski, *La Réaction contre les ordalies en France* E. Vacandard, *L'Église et les ordalies* (in his *Études de critique et d'histoire religieuse* (1905), i. 191 ff) Agobard had also attacked trial by battle, but it survived since there were no ecclesiastical ceremonies which were essential to it.

[6] P. Fournier and G. Le Bras, *Collections canoniques*, i. 409–10.

[7] F. L. Ganshof, *Droit urbain en Flandre*, Revue d'Histoire du Droit, xix. 388; cf. St. Omer (1227), *ibid.*, 403.

and to all intents and purposes abolished it as a regular means of trial (although it seems that in some localities it still persisted with the connivance of disobedient clergy). Henry III's government immediately recognised the decree, and appreciated the extremely difficult position which it created, for the only remaining method of trying suspected criminals had been forbidden by the Church. A writ to the Justices in Eyre was therefore issued in 1219 giving temporary instructions how to proceed until further order was taken. It reads as follows:

" The King to his beloved and faithful . . . Justices Itinerant . . . greeting: Because it was in doubt and not definitely settled before the beginning of your eyre, with what trial those are to be judged who are accused of robbery, murder, arson, and similar crimes, since the trial by fire and water (the ordeal) has been prohibited by the Roman Church, it has been provided by our Council that, at present, in this eyre of yours, it shall be done thus with those accused of excesses of this kind; to wit, that those who are accused of the aforesaid greater crimes, and of whom suspicion is held that they are guilty of that whereof they are accused, of whom also, in case they were permitted to abjure the realm, there would still be suspicion that afterwards they would do evil, they shall be kept in our prison and safeguarded, yet so that they do not incur danger of life or limb on our account. But those who are accused of medium crimes, and to whom would be assigned the ordeal by fire or water if it had not been prohibited, and of whom, if they should abjure the realm there would be no suspicion of their doing evil afterwards, they may abjure our realm. But those who are accused of lesser crimes, and of whom there would be no suspicion of evil, let them find safe and sure pledges of fidelity and of keeping our peace, and then they may be released in our land. . . . We have left to your discretion the observance of this aforesaid order . . . according to your own discretion and conscience."[1]

From this writ it will be seen that the justices were to be guided entirely by suspicion, and were to reach their conclusions as to the reasonableness of that suspicion solely from their own discretion. A rough scale was recommended whereby those suspected of greater crimes were to be imprisoned instead of suffering judgment of life or limb (as would have been the case if they could have been regularly convicted); those suspected of medium crimes were to be banished; lesser crimes were leniently treated, the suspect being simply bound over. This was only meant to be temporary, and obviously could be nothing more, for the whole compromise was based upon the fallacy that a half-proof of guilt was equivalent to a proof of half-guilt. The Crown, however, seems never to have given any further guidance to its justices, at least as far as the available sources show. The Church had abolished the one lawful means of trial, and the only suggestion which the Crown had made was a false and unworkable compromise.

The problem was therefore left to be solved in a way typical of English law—the justices were to make such experiments as they saw fit and gradually feel their way towards a solution.

[1] The text is printed by Wells, *Origin of the Petty Jury*, Law Quarterly Review, xxx. 97 ff.; *Patent Rolls, 1216–1225*, 186.

6. *The jury as a new mode of trial*

EVOLUTION OF THE PETTY JURY

Various devices which they tried have been traced with some success through the rolls. Even before the crisis of 1219 occasional cases are to be found of the presentment juries giving what has been called a " medial judgment ", that is to say, declaring what ordeal ought to be assigned. Again, a jury might be summoned to declare whether an appeal was brought " maliciously out of hate and spite " (*de odio et atia*). This issue was very frequently introduced by appellees who had purchased this concession from the Crown, and in fact came to be really conclusive as to the main question. It was, moreover, a first step in the direction of a criminal trial by jury, for after some years of hesitation it was realised that if a jury could by its verdict declare that an appeal was brought maliciously, there was no valid reason why it should not answer the straight question whether the prisoner was guilty or innocent.[1] We soon find that this last step was taken. It must be remembered that all these proceedings took place in the course of eyres in the early years of the thirteenth century, when that institution was in its most vigorous period. On such an occasion the King's justices had before them a very considerable number of jurors making presentments from vills and hundreds, from boroughs and the county itself. A presentment would be made by the representatives of one of these vills or hundreds,[2] and in order to get a final verdict on the guilt or innocence of the prisoner the justices hit upon the device of associating with the presenting jury the juries of the four neighbouring vills; " afforced " in this way, the larger body then proceeded to answer the question whether the prisoner was guilty of the crime ior which he had been indicted.

At first the judges exercised a good deal of discretion in making up the trial jury;[3] at times they did not even trouble to add any further jurors at all, but merely inquired of the presenting jury whether the prisoner was guilty. At other times we find a very large body of jurors associated together as a trial jury—in one case we even find a jury of eighty-four persons. It seems, however, that in the early stages such a large body of jurors did not sit together, but was examined unit by unit, the verdict of the representatives from each of the different communities being taken separately. From the numerous verdicts so obtained (sometimes contradictory[4] and sometimes expressed in terms of hesitation)

---

[1] For an early example, see *Eyre Rolls of Gloucestershire, Warwickshire and Staffordshire* (ed. D. M. Stenton, Selden Society, vol. 59), no. 751.

[2] Frequently both; the vill would present to the hundred, and the hundred presented in the county.

[3] Lady Stenton discusses several cases in *Eyre Rolls* (Selden Society, vol. 53), pp. lxviii-lxxi.

[4] For a case in 1221 where a jury was contradicted by the vills and amerced, see *Eyre Rolls* (Selden Society, vol. 59), no. 822.

the court formed its own conclusion and proceeded to judgment accordingly. Nor can we always say that these composite juries are giving verdicts in the modern sense of the word, for at times they merely provide the court with material upon which the court itself bases its finding of guilty or not guilty.

AN EXAMPLE OF THE NEW CRIMINAL PROCEDURE

In order to illustrate the old and the new procedures the following case is translated in full, since it contains numerous points of interest. It occured in 1220 immediately after the writ mentioned above. Since Henry III was under age there was no court of king's bench in regular session; hence, although it was a criminal case, it seems to have been heard in the court of common pleas upon a writ of false judgment which enabled royal courts to review the judgments of seignorial courts, although at a later stage of the proceedings the king's council (representing the king's bench during the minority) took part in forming the decision. The text from the plea roll is printed in Maitland's *Select Pleas of the Crown* (Selden Society), no. 192.[1]

" Philip the son of Hervy, Robert the son of Humphrey, Henry the son of Andrew, and William the son of Richard, being four free men of the court of the Earl of Brittany in Cheshunt, and summoned to make record of a battle waged[2] in his court between Hamo of More, appellant, and Elias Piggun, appellee, concerning a stolen horse for which Hamo appeals, come and record that:

" Hamo de la Mare complained in the Earl's court that Philip le King stole his mare in his common pasture wickedly, feloniously and in larceny in the peace of God and in the peace of his lord the Earl; and this he offered to prove by his body as the court shall award for one hour of the day.

" And Philip came and defended the wickedness, the felony and the larceny, and said that he had a warrantor thereof, that is to say, one Edward, and that he would produce him at the hour; and a day was given him to produce Edward. After making three essoins,[3] Philip himself came and produced Edward his warrantor, and Edward entered into the warranty of the mare.

" And when Hamo saw Edward seised of the mare, he spoke the same words against him as before, adding that he knew no other thief than this Edward whom he saw seised and who warranted the mare; and he offered to prove against him by his body.

" And Edward denied everything, word by word, and vouched Elias Piggun to warranty, whom he produced with him. And Elias took the mare and entered into warranty, and said that he sold the mare as his own chattel to Edward.

" When Hamo saw this Elias seised of the mare, he spoke against him saying he knew no other thief than this Elias whom he saw seised and who warranted against him, and that wickedly and in larceny and in the peace of God and the Earl he stole that mare (as before), and this he offered to prove against him, as the court should award, by his body.

" And Elias defended everything word by word, and offered to act against Hamo concerning that mare as his own chattel, as the court shall award.

[1] Bracton, f. 151 *b*; *Eyre Rolls* (Selden Society, vol. 56), xvii; cf. *Bracton's Note Book*, no. 824.

[2] Not fought; " to wage " is to give security.

[3] Lawful excuses for not appearing.

" It was awarded that Elias should give gage for defending himself, and Hamo gage to deraign.

" And Hamo says that in part they record well, and in another part too little, for when Elias was vouched to warranty and warranted the mare to Edward, he challenged him, Elias, as being a hired champion whom Edward brought in to become warrantor in return for money, whereof he produced sufficient suit; and that this is true, he offers to prove by one who heard and another who saw; and if this is not enough, he offers our lord the king one mark to have an inquest, for he says that he could not get this allowed him although he asked it.

" And the said four men on behalf of the Earl's court say that the record is as they have recorded, and not as Hamo says; and they offer to deraign that it is as they say by the body of a certain free man of the court, or otherwise as the King's court shall consider; or to defend that it is not as Hamo says, as the King's court shall consider.

" And Elias being asked where he got that mare, says that she was given to him before the war [*i.e.* before 1215] together with some pigs at Cardiff in Wales by a man to whom he gave fencing lessons, that he had her for six weeks and brought her from Wales to this part of the country, and that he sold her to Edward for three shillings and a penny outside Waltham Cross. But he produces no suit of that sale, and admits that he and Edward were alone. So says Edward, and Edward also says that he had the mare for five years.

" Hamo says that the mare was foaled to him and that he still has her mother, and that she was stolen at Easter in [1219] the third year of king Henry, and of this he has sufficient suit.

" Elias being asked how he identifies the mare after so long a time, says by a mark, that is, by a slit in the ear.

" Eight men of the vill of Cheshunt and as many from the vill of Waltham, of Wormley and of Enfield are summoned to certify the justices.   Thomas of Muleton, Peter of Nereford and the four knights with the record are pledges for having Elias Piggun on [7 March, 1220] Monday before mid-Lent. A day is given them to hear their judgement on Monday before mid-Lent when they are to come unarmed. On which day they came, and Elias is committed to the Fleet gaol by the king's council. Hamo's pledges to prosecute are William the Tanner of London, and John del Hale.

" The eight men of Waltham being sworn say upon their oath that according to their belief (for all the countryside say so) the mare was foaled to Hamo, was taken in the common of Cheshunt, and was found by Hamo in the plough of Philip le King, and that Edward gave her in marriage with his daughter to this Philip; and that after this plea was begun in the court of Cheshunt, Philip handed over the mare to Elias Picon the warrantor so that he could safely swear; and they say that in no other way was the mare Elias' nor did he bring her into this part of the country. They further say that the mare worked in Philip's plough for two years, so they think; and they rather think that Edward took her from the pasture by mistake and ignorance and not otherwise.

" The eight men of Cheshunt being sworn, say that they do not know whether she was foaled to Hamo, and rather think that she was not; they are sure that Edward gave her in marriage to Philip as aforesaid, but they do not think that Elias ever sold her to Edward; but they are sure that Elias said before all the parish of Cheshunt that he did this for God's sake, and asked all men to pray for him as truly as true it was that he did this for God's sake and not for money; and so they rather think that he did this for God's sake and not for any other reason. They have not heard anything about the marriage portion of Edward's daughter.

" The eight men of Wormley being sworn say that they do not know whether she was foaled to Hamo or not; but they are sure that Edward gave her with his daughter in marriage to Philip, and they believe that Edward bought her, but they do not know from whom; they do not believe that Elias ever sold her to Edward.

" The eight men of Enfield say upon their oath that they believe that the mare was Hamo's and foaled to him, for everybody says so, and that Edward gave her as a marriage portion as said above; they are sure that Elias never sold her to Edward, but that he did this for money—for ten marks as they believe, of which he had five and five are owing to him; and some of them say that they think he did this so as to have Edward's daughter in marriage as well as the money.

" By the king's council: the Earl of Brittany shall regain his court as regards Hamo and Edward, who have licence to compromise; and let Elias have his judgement in the king's court. It is awarded that he lose his foot; and be it known that the king's council is dealing with him leniently for by law he deserved a greater punishment."

It would be difficult to find one case which illustrated more points of mediaeval law than this one. Note the words of felony, and the vouching to warranty in the court below, and the way in which the appellee and his warrantors successively take seisin of the mare while the appellant recites his accusation; the method of recording pleas in courts which do not themselves bear record, and the possibility of verifying the record by battle;[1] note also that Hamo offers the King one mark (13s. 4d.) to have an inquest, as alternative to the ancient production of one witness who heard and another who saw. The king's court did not stand on technicalities. The issue of the truth or otherwise of the record brought from the court below is not even considered, and Pateshull (for it was Bracton's hero who was on the bench[2]) went straight to the points at issue—the ownership of the mare and the fraud of Elias.

Hamo had purchased the privilege of having his charges investigated by a jury, and the roll shows us four juries of eight summoned from the four neighbouring vills. The proceedings, however, were singularly unlike a modern jury trial. It is true that the parties themselves were examined, but it was before the juries were summoned. The juries did not sit together, but returned four separate (and conflicting) reports— we can hardly call them verdicts. They say that they are sure of some things; others they " rather think " are true; some other statements they believe because " everybody says so ". They were not asked, and did not say, whether anyone was guilty or innocent. Nor were they witnesses, for none of them claimed to have direct knowledge of the happenings which they relate.

Such a proceeding can only be described as an inquisition. The court examined the parties, and examined thirty-two jurors, and upon the evidence so obtained, itself decided upon the guilt of Elias. If this system had become permanently established, we should have had a regular inquisitorial procedure, such as that described on the continent by Beaumanoir,[3] with a judge deciding questions of fact as well as law,

---

[1] An averment was allowed by 1 Edw. III, stat. 1, c. 4 (1327); cf. Y.B. 11-2 Edward III (Rolls Series), 326 (1337).

[2] Cf. below, p. 235.

[3] Beaumanoir, c. 40 (ed. Salmon, 1899), §§ 1224-1260. The work was written in the years about 1283.

and examining parties and groups of local representatives whose function was not to state facts, nor to decide the question of guilt or innocence, but merely to retail the gossip of the countryside. Before the writ of 1219 the accused would have gone to his ordeal: but now the court finds him guilty on the unsworn statements of the parties, and on the juries' sworn returns.[1]

TRIALS ON INDICTMENT

This was a logical development in cases of appeal, where the substitution of an inquest for battle or ordeal was frequently obtained. The case of indictment, however, presents a somewhat different situation, for the countryside has already spoken once. At times we find justices in eyre acting in a high-handed manner. Thus in 1221, in Warwickshire, they had before them Thomas de la Hethe, who was presented by the grand jury as an associate of a notorious felon named Howe Golightly; but Thomas refused to put himself on the country. Notwithstanding his refusal, the court declined to permit him any sort of ordeal, but realising the gravity of the situation they empanelled an impressive jury of twenty-four knights. The knights said he was guilty, and he was therefore hanged.[2] Even a villein who refused jury trial might have this panel of twenty-four knights.[3]

So large and distinguished a trial jury clearly shows the court's apprehension at compulsorily depriving a man of his right to trial by ordeal; but sometimes the situation was not so difficult. In this same year, 1221, an indictment found that the carcase of a stolen cow had been discovered in William's shed. William did not claim any particular sort of trial, but said that the thing was put there by his lord who hoped that William would be convicted and so the lord get his land as an escheat for felony. The serjeant who arrested William stated that the lord's wife had arranged for his arrest. In such a case the court simply asked the indictors for more information, and they related the whole story and so William was acquitted by the court, and the lord committed to gaol.[4]

In the case the court quickly detected the plot and merely needed confirmation. But what of cases of real doubt? It was these which caused the gravest difficulty after the abolition of the ordeals. Courts were naturally afraid to compel jury trial, and yet there seemed little else to do. If the case arose in a general eyre where a thousand or more jurymen and officials were present, it would be fairly easy to assemble a large collection of jurors (as was done by Pateshull in trying Elias),

[1] The same general result followed in Normandy: *Summa de legibus Normanniae* (ed. Tardif), LXXVI. 2.

[2] Maitland, *Select Pleas of the Crown*, no. 157; also in *Eyre Rolls* (Selden Society, vol. 59), no. 767 and in 2 Hale, P.C. 322.

[3] *Eyre Rolls* (Selden Society, vol. 59), no. 728.

[4] Maitland, *Select Pleas of the Crown*, no. 170.

question them, and pronounce the prisoner guilty or not as a result. But if the proceedings were upon gaol delivery, for example, before non-professional judges with limited jurisdiction, that plan was less feasible. In most cases prisoners were persuaded to put themselves (more or less voluntarily) upon a jury. If they did not, there seemed no alternative but to keep them in prison, for if they were not convicted, they were still not acquitted.

THE INSCRUTABLE JURY

Under such circumstances, a jury was just a newer sort of ordeal. The judges, after the brief period of hesitation already mentioned, cease to play the part of inquisitors and no longer undertake to examine it or weigh its report; the jury states a simple verdict of guilty or not guilty and the court accepts it, as unquestioningly as it used to accept the pronouncements of the hot iron or the cold water. Since it is taken by consent there is no need to look too closely at the method by which the verdict was reached. At first, the jury was no more regarded as " rational " than the ordeals which it replaced, and just as one did not question the judgments of God as shown by the ordeal, so the verdict of a jury was equally inscrutable. It is but slowly that the jury was rationalised and regarded as a judicial body.

JURY TRIAL BECOMES COMPULSORY

The Crown did not feel too confident, however; the petty jury in criminal trials was a makeshift expedient and an innovation. Under the old law a prisoner could undoubtedly have been compelled to submit to the ordeal and to abide by any construction which the justices might place upon the outcome of it; but was it reasonable to compel a man to submit to trial by jury? Even the Crown felt that this was unreasonable, and it soon became customary to put the astonishing question to the prisoner whether he consented to trial by jury. If he refused to say the necessary words and " put himself upon the country " it seemed as though nothing further could be done. If such a prisoner could have spoken the language of modern constitutional law he would very likely have raised a doubt whether trial by jury in criminal cases was " due process of law ", for the time-honoured methods of trial were the ordeals, and the petty jury was a new-found device of very recent origin. Put in a quandary by a prisoner's refusal to plead, a court could only exercise its discretion by adopting one or another of several high-handed courses. Sometimes, as we have already noted, it would cast the responsibility on a larger jury of twenty-four knights; alternatively, it might allow the prisoner to abjure the realm, even for homicide,[1] while for lesser charges a prisoner could purchase (for 20s.) the privilege of merely finding sureties.[2]

[1] As in 1221, *Eyre Rolls* (Selden Society, vol. 59), no. 877.

[2] *Ibid.*, no. 1239.

Towards the close of the century the Crown felt strong enough to impose jury trial by sheer force, and the Statute of Westminster I, c. 12 (1275), provided—

" that notorious felons who are openly of evil fame and who refuse to put themselves upon inquests of felony at the suit of the King[1] before his justices, shall be remanded to a hard and strong prison as befits those who refuse to abide by the common law of the land; but this is not to be understood of persons who are taken upon light suspicion."

This statute begins with a threat and concludes with an argument; could there be any better indication of the government's difficulty in imposing trial by jury? It is surely noteworthy that in 1275 it was found expedient to declare by statute that the petty jury was now " the common law of the land " even if the rigours of that common law were to be confined to " notorious felons ". Conservatives perhaps found comfort in the proviso that jury trial or its painful alternative was not to extend to those whose reputation was not too bad. As is well known, the words " prison forte et dure " by some unaccountable means became transformed into " peine forte et dure ", and finally into a form of torture which, by the sixteenth century, took the barbarous form of placing the accused between two boards and piling weights upon him until he accepted trial by jury or expired. Felons whose guilt was obvious sometimes heroically chose to die in this manner rather than plead, be convicted and hanged, for a prisoner who died under peine forte et dure had never been tried and never convicted, and consequently his goods and chattels could not be forfeited to the Crown. It was abolished in 1772.[2]

RATIONALISATION OF JURY TRIAL

By the middle of the thirteenth century, moreover, the justices had finally chosen the simpler procedure. Instead of taking separate verdicts from numerous vills and hundreds, they selected a petty jury of twelve from among the numerous jurors present in court, and took the verdict of these twelve. It regularly happened that at least some of these twelve had also been members of the presenting jury, for it must be remembered that the whole principle of jury trial was to get information useful to the Crown from those people most likely to have it—the principle of the ancient inquisition. It is at this point that we first find signs of a rational approach to jury trial. The indictors were under some pressure to

[1] But one appealed (which is not at the suit of the king) of robbery, who stands mute of malice, as found by an inquest, will be hanged as undefended: Y.B. 21 Edward III, Pasch. no. 26 (1347). In Normandy if a married woman was appealed, her husband could, but need not, defend her by battle; if he did not, she could be imprisoned until she accepted jury trial: R. Génestal, La femme mariée, [1930] Revue historique de droit français, 480.

[2] By 12 Geo. III, c. 20, which substituted a conviction; by 7 & 8 Geo. IV, c. 28 (1827), a plea of not guilty was to be entered. See Thayer, Preliminary Treatise on Evidence, 74; Stephen, History of Criminal Law, i. 297–300. The year books generally call it " penance ". Cf. A. Esmein, History of Continental Criminal Procedure, 94 ff.

maintain their accusation and a subsequent acquittal occasionally landed the indictors themselves in prison.[1]   It is therefore clear that a prisoner could not expect a disinterested verdict from a petty jury consisting wholly or   partly of indictors.   Those with sufficient court influence could obtain certain procedural favours.   Thus, Prince Edward (afterwards Edward II) sent a letter in 1305 to Brabazon, J., on behalf of one of his friends who was indicted for murder, asking that he be tried by a fresh jury on which none of the indicting jurors were present.[2]   We sometimes find prisoners challenging petty jurors on the ground that they had sat on the grand jury—a challenge which shows that the petty jury is now regarded (by prisoners at least) as no longer representative of the countryside, but as a truly judicial body which should be free from fear and interest.   Such challenges were unsuccessful.   As late as 1341 the court refused to allow a petty juryman to be challenged on the ground that he had been a member of the presenting jury: " if the indictors be not there it is not good for the King ", it was said.[3]   The commons in parliament protested against the practice in 1341 and again in 1345,[4] but not until 1352 did a statute allow challenge to be made on this ground.[5]

THE JURY AS REPRESENTATIVES

From this it will be seen that in its origin the jury is of a representative character; the basis of its composition in the early days, when its structure was determined by the vill or the hundred, was clearly the intention to make it representative of the community.   Its object was either to present the suspicions of the countryside, or, in the case of a petty jury, to express its final opinion.   Consequently, the jury as a whole must come from the county concerned, and some at least of them from the hundred where the fact lay.[6]   In civil cases these requirements were much modified by legislation,[7] and finally abolished in 1705.[8]   They applied also to criminal cases, but by Lord Hale's time it was no longer

[1] Y.B. 30 & 31 Edward I, 522 (1302); s.c. *Eyre of Kent*, i. 112.   Until 1 Edward III, stat. 2, c. 11, persons indicted and then acquitted could take proceedings in church courts against the grand jurymen for defamation (cf. p. 428 below).   For a civil action of conspiracy against indictors see G. O. Sayles, *Cases in King's Bench* (Selden Society), i. 76 (1281).   So unwilling were indictors to present in view of this peril that the Crown in 1304 forbad the use of actions for conspiracy against them: *Calendar of Chancery Warrants*, i. 241–242 (cf. Y.B. 32 & 33 Edward I, 462).   The same result was reached on principle (the warrant being unknown then) in *Floyd* v. *Barker* (1607), 12 Co. 23.   Much new material is furnished in Sayles, *op. cit.*, iii. intro. liv ff.

[2] *Letters of Prince Edward* (ed. Hilda Johnstone, for the Roxburghe Club, 1931), 37.

[3] Y.B. 14–15 Edward III, 260, 261.

[4] *Rot. Parl.*, ii. 128 no. 14, 134 no. 67, 140 no. 30.

[5] 25 Edward III, stat. 5, c. 3.

[6] Y.B. 48 Edward III, Michs. no. 17 (1374).

[7] 35 Hen. VIII, c. 6 (1544);   27 Eliz. I, c. 6 (1585);   21 James I, c. 13 (1624);   16 & 17 Charles II, c. 8 (1664).

[8] 4 Anne, c. 16.

the practice to challenge a jury for lack of hundredors,[1] as long as it came from the proper county.

The county requirement was less tractable, for procedure could only be conducted through a sheriff. Problems abounded, moreover. By some ancient oversight there were roads, bays, creeks and harbours in England, as late as 1816,[2] which were not in any county; felonies committed there (like those on the high seas) could not be tried by jury until 1536 when a statute gave the crown power to appoint a county by commission.[3] Further, in 1549 a statute explained that if A wounded B in one county, and B died in another, then A could not be tried, because a jury of the first county will know nothing of the death, and the jury of the second county will know nothing of the wounding.[4] Likewise, a felon in one county may be hanged, but his accessory who received him in another cannot be tried because a jury there will not know of the conviction.[5]

The representative idea of the jury was wearing very thin now that some of its consequences were being abrogated by the acts of 1536, 1549 and others.[6] Survivals lasted into the nineteenth century: pickpockets in stage-coaches could be tried in any county along the route only after 1826,[7] and the completely rational view of jury trial finally triumphed in 1856 when a trial could be moved to the Central Criminal Court if it was feared that a local jury would not be impartial.[8] Its character was certainly not that of witnesses;[9] it was indeed expected to speak of its own knowledge, but that does not necessarily mean that its knowledge must be as strictly first-hand as that of a modern witness. There is no trace of a requirement that jurymen should themselves have witnessed the events in question. Indeed, that would often be impossible, especially in property cases—such as occurred in 1222 when a jury had to find the terms of a verbal lease made in 1170.[10] Bracton has introduced some confusion at this point. He was writing a very big book and had a tendency to fill in the gaps of native English law from other sources, and so there is always difficulty in distinguishing between Bracton as the expositor of contemporary practice and Bracton the

---

[1] Hale, *History of Pleas of the Crown*, 272.

[2] 53 Geo. III, c. 100.

[3] 28 Hen. VIII, c. 15.

[4] For analogous complications see *State* v. *Hall*, 114 N.C. 909 (North Carolina, 1894).

[5] 2 & 3 Edw. VI, c. 24, which abolished both rules.

[6] Such as 35 Hen. VIII, c. 2 (1544), which made treason committed abroad triable by the king's bench and a jury of the county where it was sitting.

[7] 7 Geo. IV, c. 64.

[8] 19 Vict., c. 16.

[9] Cf. below, p. 433.

[10] *Eyre Rolls* (Selden Society, vol. 59), no. 1477. In 1312 a jury was called to say whether the chapter of Winchester cathedral assented to an alienation made before 1238: Y.BB. Edward II (Selden Society), x. 40–41.

idealiser and scholar of foreign learning. In one passage[1] he gives us a list of challenges which can be used against jurymen, and seems to have imported the exceptions against witnesses which were available in canon law, and used them as challenges against jurors.[2] However this may be, he is surely describing contemporary practice faithfully when he shows us how the justices will help the jury to express an uncertain verdict in more satisfactory form, adding:

" If the jurors are altogether ignorant about the fact and know nothing concerning the truth, let there be associated with them others who do know the truth. But if even thus the truth cannot be known, then it will be requisite to speak from belief and conscience at least."

Clearly, therefore, the jury spoke as representative of the countryside rather than as a body of witnesses.

EARLY OPINION ABOUT THE JURY

Bracton seems to be fairly satisfied with the jury as an institution, but other writers of almost the same date confirm the impression conveyed by the statute which we have just quoted. The *Mirror of Justices*, which was a vigorous criticism of the administration of the law written about 1290, contains a violent attack on the jury.[3] In those parts of France also, where the jury for a time took root, there were protests against it as oppressive.[4]

From the reign of Edward I onwards the function of the jury was slowly being judicially defined; questions of law began to be separated from questions of fact,[5] and gradually unanimity was required—although for some time there were doubts whether a verdict by eleven jurors was not sufficient, in which case the twelfth might be committed to prison.[6]

In 1468 Fortescue gives us a picture of jury trial which is to all intents and purposes in modern form. By this date he is able to regard the jury as a body of impartial men who come into court with an open mind; instead of finding the verdict out of their own knowledge of the events, the parties or their counsel in open court present their evidence

---

[1] Bracton, f. 186; translatedi n Pound and Plucknett, *Readings*, 149–154.   (Cf. Y.B. 20–21 Edward I, 170–172, and *Reniger* v. *Fogossa*, Plowd. 12.)

[2] For a very interesting draft list of challenges in a case of *c*. 1293, see N. Denholm-Young, *Seignorial Administration*, 117–118.

[3] *Mirror of Justices* (Selden Society, vol. 7), bk. V, ch. I, §§ 19, 35, 77, 126, 134, 136 (*Readings*, 154).

[4] See the French political song, in Leroux de Lincy, *Recueil de chants historiques*, i. 218 (translated in *Readings*, 154).

[5] For an interesting early case, see Y.B. 21 & 22 Edward I, 273 (*Readings*, 155); see further, pp. 417–418 below.

[6] 29 Ass. 4; 41 Ass. 11 (*Readings*, 155, 156); Sayles, *King's Bench* (Selden Society), ii. 90; Winfield *History of Conspiracy*, 196.

to the jury, and witnesses are examined upon oath.[1]   A century later, Sir Thomas Smith gives a vivid account of a jury trial and shows not only the examination but also the cross-examination of witnesses in the presence of the judge, the parties, their counsel and the jury.[2]   Although this was becoming the practice, relics of the older order survived, and we have the perennial spectacle of trouble caused by casual reform which did not make a clean sweep of the past.   Just as Fortescue harked back to an obsolete conception of the jury in saying that a man who volunteered to give evidence would be punished for maintenance (for he ought to have waited until the jury went to his house in the country to ask him what he knew[3]), so too, while Sir Thomas Smith was describing the jury as a purely judicial body, and statute was compelling the attendance of witnesses,[4] jurors were still allowed to use their own knowledge in reaching a verdict,[5] and might reach a verdict although no witnesses and no evidence had been produced.[6]

THE EARLY HISTORY SUMMARISED

From one common origin, therefore, we have derived several varieties of jury.   On the criminal side the royal inquisition became the grand jury for presenting criminals, and when the older forms of trial ceased to function then a trial jury for indicted prisoners was assembled from the indictors and the neighbouring vills: simultaneously, many appellees avoided trial by battle by purchasing from the crown the privilege of a jury, and so we get the trial jury for felonies.   On the civil side the royal inquisition became available to private litigants for the trial of right to real property, and the petty assizes, with the " grand assize ", were clearly the model for jury trial in writs of entry and other real actions.   Somewhere between these two lines of development there lies the action of trespass.   According to one view it derives from the appeals of felony; others trace it to the petty assizes.   However that may be, jury trial almost immediately became normal in trespass, both for the trial of misdemeanours and of torts.   In the end, trespass and its derivatives supplanted the old real actions (and also the old personal actions of debt, detinue, etc.) with the result that all the civil trial juries now in use

[1] Fortescue, *De Laudibus Legum Anglie* (*c.* 1468), chaps. 25, 26 (translated and edited by S. B. Chrimes).   In 1277 a party got the court's permission to show his title deeds to the jury, *Casus Placitorum* (Selden Society), 94;   and in 1312 counsel addressed a civil jury: Y.BB. Edward II (Selden Society), xi. 20.

[2] Smith, *De Republica Anglorum* (ed. Alston), 94–103.   For some intriguing glimpses of " evidence " to a jury, see Y.B. 27 Henry VIII, Michs. no. 3, f. 24 (1535).

[3] Y.B. 28 Henry VI, Pasch. no. 1.   Thayer, *On Evidence*, 124 ff., shows clearly how trial procedure was hampered through the danger of witnesses incurring the penalties of conspiracy and maintenance.

[4] 5 Eliz. I, c. 9 (1563).

[5] " Some of the jurors knew this to be true "—*Reniger* v. *Fogossa* (1550), Plowden, 5.

[6] *Ibid.,* 12.   For the growth of the modern jury-trial with witnesses see below, p. 433.

descend directly from the jury in trespass, as likewise the juries for the trial of misdemeanours.

7. Post-mediaeval problems

THE REVIEW OF VERDICTS

Even as Fortescue wrote, however, jury trial, both civil and criminal, had already entered upon its decline, and there were numerous complaints of the corruption and partiality of jurors. The heavy expense falling on jurors was evidently a problem. Jurors attending the eyre at Bedford in 1330 seem to have been paid out of a county rate levied for the purpose.[1] Whether this was done elsewhere, and for other occasions, is not known. Wealthy litigants certainly seem to have felt it proper (perhaps even prudent) to contribute fairly handsomely to the expenses of jurors—and jurors had themselves to pay fees in an eyre.[2] Surviving household accounts show that litigants incurred considerable expense in the matter of jurors,[3] and it is obvious that the line between legitimate contributions to the expenses of a costly journey, and corrupt practices, was difficult to draw. It therefore became more and more necessary to devise means for reversing verdicts.

The only ancient method available was by attaint.[4] This consisted in summoning a jury of twenty-four, and the proceedings were not merely a reconsideration of the facts in dispute, but also a criminal trial of the first jury for perjury. This was only logical at a time when every jury spoke out of its own knowledge of the facts involved in the case. Their function was to tell upon oath the facts which they knew; it was not their duty to act as impartial judges of evidence produced before them. If such jurymen returned a verdict which was demonstrably false, and in spite of their own better knowledge of the facts, then it was obvious that they had committed perjury and deserved the punishment provided for attainted juries:

> "All of the first jury shall be committed to the King's prison, their goods shall be confiscated, their possessions seized into the King's hands, their habitations and houses shall be pulled down, their woodland shall be felled, their meadows shall be plowed up and they themselves forever thenceforward be esteemed in the eye of the law infamous."[5]

[1] *Rolls from the office of the sheriff of Beds. and Bucks., 1332–1334*, ed. G. H. Fowler (Quarto Memoirs of the Bedfordshire Historical Record Society, vol. 3), 79, § 64.

[2] *Fleta*, i. 19.

[3] N. Denholm-Young, *Seignorial Administration*, 113 ff., for the thirteenth century. For the eighteenth century, an attorney's diary in the Salt Library, Stafford, records on 6 and 7 Feb. 1710 over £200 "spent on the jury". (Information from S. A. H. Burne, Esq.)

[4] There was also a procedure called "Certification" which called upon members of a petty assize to come back and elucidate an obscure verdict: Fitzherbert, *New Natura Brevium*, 181A, Panel *v.* Moor (1556), Plowd. 91. It was occasionally used to accuse the assize of a false oath: *Bracton's Note Book*, no. 63 (1219).

[5] Fortescue, *De Laudibus*, cap. xxvi; cf. Bracton, f. 292 *b*.

Attaint first appears as a remedy against the false verdicts given by members of the " assizes " in actions of novel disseisin, mort d'ancestor and the like. In these actions the defendant had always been compelled to accept trial by assize, and so it was but reasonable that he should have a means of punishing untruthful jurors. In writs of right, on the other hand, it was the demandant who might be compelled (at the tenant's choice) to submit to the " grand assize ". Here, too, the writ of attaint could be brought.[1] In other cases, however, both civil and criminal, it was possible to argue that the parties had voluntarily (in form at least) put themselves upon a jury, and that since they had chosen this form of trial they were not entitled to any relief if it turned out unsatisfactorily. Attaint was extended by statute first to one action and then to another, and finally in 1361 to every action tried by jury;[2] but never to criminal trials. In London, local legislation wisely reduced the penalty upon attaint.[3] But as for the common law, Queen Elizabeth's Secretary of State, Sir Thomas Smith, wrote in 1565:[4]

> " Attaints be verie seldome put in use, partly because the gentlemen will not meete to slaunder and deface the honest yeomen their neighbours, so that of a long time they had rather paie a mean fine than to appeare and make the enquest. And in the meane time they will intreat so much as in them lyeth the parties to come to some composition and agreement among themselves, as lightly they do, except either the corruption of the enquest be too evident, or the one partie is too obstinate and headstrong. And if the gentlemen do appeare, gladlyer they will confirme the first sentence, for the causes which I have saide, than go against it. But if the corruption be too much evident, they will not sticke to attaint the first enquest: yet after the gentlemen have attainted the yeomen, if before the sentence be given by the Judge (which ordinarily for a time is differred) the parties be agreed, or one of them be dead, the attaint ceaseth."

As the character of the jury slowly changed, the logic of the action of attaint became less apparent. As the middle ages proceed the custom grows of assisting the jury by producing evidence in court in their presence. From quite an early date the witnesses named in a deed, if still living, were summoned to sit with the jury (and it became a rule that if they did so, then the jury was immune from attaint);[5] but gradually, first in one case and then in another, it became customary to examine other witnesses in the presence of the jury. As a result the jury speaks less and less out of its own knowledge and becomes instead a judge of

---

[1] Glanvill (ed. Woodbine) II. 19, and the notes thereon. By the time of Bracton, attaint no longer lay against a grand assize.

[2] 34 Edw. III, c. 7; in 1532 the statute 23 Hen. VIII, c. 3 (in Pound and Plucknett, *Readings*, 160–163), extended the penalties of attaint to a party who relied on a false verdict. (Note that this statute refers to the jury of twenty-four as the " grand jury "; this confusing usage is exceptional.)

[3] Thayer, *On Evidence*, 151.

[4] *De Republica Anglorum* (ed. Alston), 111; first published in 1583. For an attaint in 1568 see L. Hotson, *Justice Shallow*, 160–161.

[5] Y.B. 20–21 Edward I, 110.

the evidence placed before it. The situation in respect to attaint thus becomes very different. A jury may return an erroneous verdict as a result of inadequate or inaccurate evidence, or a misunderstanding of the true import of the evidence adduced; but such an error of judgment in making a wrong deduction from evidence which may have been conflicting, insufficient or improperly presented is surely not sufficient reason for the severe penalty provided in the old action of attaint. It is no longer a question (at least in many cases) of deliberate perjury, but only of a more or less excusable error of judgment. It is only natural to find, therefore, that the action of attaint falls into disuse, as the quotation from Sir Thomas Smith has shown. This, however, did not help the situation. The more the jury becomes a judge of facts which parties attempt to prove before them, the more room there is for honest mistake, more especially as there is practically no trace of a law of evidence at this period. In short, there was an increasing need of some machinery for revising the verdicts of petty juries—more especially in civil actions, which always received in the middle ages more careful attention than criminal matters. Occasionally we find an appeal to Parliament where even an attainting jury was alleged to be prejudiced.[1]

THE PUNISHMENT OF OBSTINATE JURORS

In the sixteenth century examples are to be found of various prerogative courts undertaking to punish jurymen who found verdicts manifestly against the evidence.[2] In an age when political trials were becoming more frequent, it became a serious matter that verdicts could be set aside and jurors punished in courts which were really a disguised form of the Council. In Crompton's treatise on the jurisdiction of courts (1594) we read:

"Note that the London jury which acquitted Sir Nicholas Throckmorton, Knight, about the first year of Queen Mary, of high treason, was called into the Star Chamber in October, 1544 (*sic*), forasmuch as the matter was held to have been sufficiently proved against him; and eight of them were there fined in grea sums, at least five hundred pounds each, and remanded back to prison to dwell there until further order were taken for their punishment. The other four were released, because they submitted and confessed that they had offended in not considering the truth of the matter.

"See also eleven jurymen who acquitted one Hodie of felony before Sir Roger Manwood, Chief Baron, on circuit in Somersetshire, against obvious evidence, were fined in the Star Chamber and made to wear papers in Westminster Hall about 1580; and I saw them.

"Note that one G. wrote a letter to a juryman who was about to sit on a case

---

[1] *Paston Letters* (1904), ii. 231. There is much interesting matter on the legal history of jurors' misconduct in Winfield, *History of Conspiracy*, 175–199.

[2] Statute authorised the Council in the Marches to punish Welsh jurors: 26 Hen. VIII, c. 4 (1534), and the courts of law recognised the similar jurisdiction of the English Council: 2 Hawkins, P.C., c. 22, s. 20; Winfield, *op. cit.*, 196.

between Lane and O. D., requesting him to follow his conscience according to the evidence; he was fined here twenty pounds because it was not his business, about 1585. Note this, that one ought not to meddle with any matter pending in suit which is not one's own business."[1]

Throckmorton's prominent share in Wyatt's rebellion put his guilt beyond the slightest question, but he was a protestant hero to the Londoners, and the jury's verdict was purely political. From now onwards the jury enters on a new phase of its history, and for the next three centuries it will exercise its power of veto on the use of the criminal law against political offenders who have succeeded in obtaining popular sympathy.

BUSHEL'S CASE

A very famous case on this matter was *Bushel's Case*[2] in 1670, where Chief Justice Vaughan in his judgment defined the position and duties of the jury. Although he retained the ancient view that a jury may depend upon its own knowledge, yet he gave a larger place to their independence. He insisted upon the ancient law; in his opinion the jury was not bound to follow the direction of the court, for the very good reason that if they returned a wrong verdict it was the jurors who were punished by attaint, and not the judge who directed it. Every jury sat with the shadow of attaint overhanging it, and this was ample sanction. Acting, therefore, under so great a peril, the jury must be left completely free from directions by the bench and from any subsequent punishment in Star Chamber or elsewhere, with the sole exception of the ancient proceeding of attaint. In other words, there was just enough of the doctrine of attaint left to enable the court to say that there was adequate means of dealing with a dishonest jury, and therefore of declaring in general terms the jury's right to independence. The judgment of Vaughan was very ingenious in its combination of antiquarianism and logic. Under the circumstances these were no doubt proper weapons in the defence of juries against political interference. But Vaughan knew, as well as everybody else, that for practical purposes attaint was obsolete, and that his judgment therefore amounted to a declaration of the irresponsibility of the jury. However useful this might have been in certain types of political trial, it was obvious that it worked hardship in private litigation. The courts were well aware of this, and were already at work even before *Bushel's Case* in search of some means of setting aside obviously unsatisfactory verdicts.

[1] Crompton, *Authoritie et jurisdiction des Courts*, f. 32 *b*. His date " 1544 " is an obvious slip for 1554, when in fact the trial took place. It is fully reported in Holinshed, *Chronicles*, under that date, but his account of the jury's imprisonment states that the fines were £220 on five jurors and £60 on three others.

[2] Vaughan, 135; it was returned to a *habeas corpus* that Bushel was one of a jury which acquitted William Penn of unlawful assembly against full and manifest evidence, wherefore Bushel had been committed to prison.

NEW TRIALS

They began to devise rules under which a new trial could be ordered.[1] The mediaeval law on the subject of new trials was not very promising. The only early grounds which they admitted were misconduct of the jurymen, such as eating and drinking before returning their verdict, and even then the verdict was not necessarily set aside.[2] Where damages or costs awarded by a jury were manifestly too high or too low, the court would sometimes fix its own figure, in the fifteenth and sixteenth centuries, without ordering a new trial or a new inquiry of damages.[3]

The amount of discretion which jurors might exercise varied with the form of action. Thus in an action on the case in 1615 to recover damages which by covenant had been fixed at a certain rate, a jury saw fit to award only about half the sum due. Coke declared that " there may be divers reasons why in equity they ought not to give so much damage as this amount, for it seems here that the jurors are chancellors " in the matter of assessing damages, and entitled to use an uncontrolled discretion. He agreed, however, that if it had been an action of debt the plaintiff would have recovered in full.[4] During the Commonwealth, there was the striking case of *Wood* v. *Gunston* in 1655, when the Upper Bench allowed a motion for a new trial when a jury had awarded unreasonably high damages in an action for slander (once again, an action on the case), against the direction of the court.[5] There was certainly no authority for this; a Commonwealth precedent of course carried little weight after the Restoration, and it was a long time before juries lost their arbitrary power over damages.[6]

For a time the courts took refuge in the distinction between trials at *nisi prius* and trials at bar; the former being regarded as less solemn, the verdicts were liable to be set aside; but Lord Holt in *Argent* v. *Darrell* (1700)[7] while admitting that new trials were often granted after verdicts at *nisi prius*, declared that " there never was a new trial after a trial at bar in ejectment ". By 1757 Lord Mansfield was able to say in *Bright* v. *Eynon*[8] that new trials were frequently granted, although there

---

[1] On new trials, see E. Jenks, *According to the Evidence* (in Cambridge Legal Essays), 197 ff.

[2] See 1 Dyer, 37 b, and 2 Dyer, 218 a (in Pound and Plucknett, *Readings*, 160).

[3] G. T. Washington, *Damages in Contract at Common Law*, Law Quarterly Review, xlvii 354–359 (1931). Printed records show judges doing this as early as Edward I: Sayles, *King's Bench* (Selden Society), ii. cxi.

[4] *Hixt* v. *Goats*, 1 Rolle, 257. Note that the " equitable " element which Lord Mansfield stressed in actions on the case is already attracting attention. For an early example, see *Brevia Placitata*, 207–208.

[5] Style, 466.

[6] See the first edition (New York, 1847) of Theodore Sedgwick, *Damages*, 201–202, in Pound and Plucknett, *Readings*, 168.

[7] Salk. 648; Thayer, *On Evidence*, 171. There was a special reason for this, since a plaintiff could bring a new ejectment.

[8] 1 Burr. 390; he explained that equity would relieve against unjust verdicts by ordering a new trial at law, and that common law courts felt bound to follow this lead.

is no trace of it in the books, because the old reports do not give any account of decisions upon motions. This fortunate omission no doubt assisted matters greatly, and it soon became easy to believe that the practice of granting new trials was established.[1] Thus was a revolutionary reform quietly effected without leaving many traces in the books; as we have seen, the work was half done by 1700, and declared to be complete in 1757. It need hardly be said that all through mediaeval times down to our own day, a jury was always at liberty to find a special verdict by stating the facts (often at great length and drafted by counsel as an agreed statement of facts) as it found them, and leaving it to the court to determine whether this verdict was in law a determination for the plaintiff or the defendant.

From all this it is clear (in spite of Vaughan's judgment in *Bushel's Case*) that for practical purposes the jury depended very largely, if not entirely, upon the evidence placed before it in court. This was certainly true of the seventeenth century and probably true of a large part of the sixteenth century. The further question when jurors were excluded from using their own sources of information, is more difficult to answer. An indirect solution has been attempted, but the result is not conclusive.[2] Even within the last hundred years expressions are to be found suggesting that, at least in criminal cases, a jury was entitled to make use of its (by now, very exiguous) " general knowledge ".[3] However, the survival of a theory is not always reconcilable with contemporary facts, and the principle of *Bushel's Case* was no doubt felt to be politically desirable without necessarily endorsing all of Vaughan's reasoning—which even for his own day may have seemed (like some of his other views) somewhat artificial.

Juries, in fact, came to rely on evidence offered by parties, and it was this circumstance which made necessary the development of a law of evidence; this will be discussed at a later stage.[4]

CONSTITUTIONAL POSITION OF THE JURY

We have now traced in brief the history of local institutions in their judicial aspect, together with the points of contact between them and the central government. It is at these points of contact that we first find signs of the development of the jury. For quite a long time the machinery of the jury was the regular means of communication between royal officials and the local public. Nor was this merely in judicial affairs; administration, police and fiscal matters, were all likely to be conducted through some form or other of the jury. From these beginnings as an

---

[1] Note that the lack of reported decisions on a point is sometimes an advantage.

[2] Jenks, *According to the Evidence*, in Cambridge Legal Essays (1926), 191–201. Cf. Winfield, *History of Conspiracy*, 185.

[3] *R.* v. *Rosser* (1836), 7 C. & P. 649.

[4] Below, p. 436.

administrative machine for extorting truth on any matter of royal concern
from a reluctant countryside, the jury soon acquired a representative
character.   This idea of the jury representing the public of a particular
locality had enormous consequences in an age when representative institutions were rapidly developing.[1] From the presenting jury of the
hundred and the county it was a short step to the House of Commons
in its most primitive aspect, which at first consisted of representatives
from such local communities as the county and the borough, all sitting
together at the King's summons to hear and to do what he should command.   An early meeting of Parliament must have resembled to some
extent an enormous eyre; all the lords and notables of the land together
with representatives from the local communities met together in the
presence of the King or his justices for the transaction of all sorts of
business, judicial, administrative and fiscal.   The seventeenth-century
pamphleteers had some grounds for regarding the Commons as the
" Grand Inquest of the Nation ".[2]

As for the jury, this representative aspect served as the foundation
for its later irresponsibility, which in turn created a situation of exceptional difficulty.   On the one hand, ancient history and current convenience both insisted upon the necessity of the jury's independence; a
representative institution, be it a jury, a parliament or a congress, must
necessarily have certain immunities if it is to do its duty, and within
the broad limits set by the writ of attaint, juries were independent.
On the other hand, slowly changing practice was altering the character
of the jury by transforming it into a judge of facts; in this aspect of
its work irresponsibility was out of place.   The decisions of the judges
themselves on matters of law were subject to proceedings in error;
why, then, should the decisions of a jury on matters of fact be completely irreversible? Both functions were essentially the same, that is to
say, an exercise of judgment, as Vaughan was keen enough to see in
Bushel's Case.   It was inevitable therefore that the practice should arise
of setting aside verdicts for erroneous conclusions as to facts, in the same
way as decisions upon law could be reversed if they were erroneous.
As far as purely private litigation is concerned, this was inevitable and
entirely desirable.

The division between law and fact upset some of those ancient
forms of the common law which had survived from an earlier age.   The
ordeals of fire or water or battle resulted in a decision of the general
issue whether the accused was guilty or not guilty; no separation of
law from fact could be imposed upon the judgment of God.   The
verdict of the jury necessarily occupied the same position.   In time it
became clear that the general issue in criminal pleadings could only be

---

[1] For an excellent historical sketch of the idea of representation, see M. V. Clarke, *Medieval
Representation* (1936), especially ch. xiii.

[2] But things went too far when the Commons were said to " indict " when they started an
impeachment.

retained if some preliminary device were employed to separate the law from the facts. This became all the more necessary as the law—for example, of larceny—hardened into a logical, but technical dogma.[1] The device adopted was for the judge to direct the jury, explaining to them what facts would constitute the crime laid in the indictment. In the light of this exposition the jury continued to give its general verdict. Some difficulty arose, however, in trials of a political character, for here the jury retained its old representative character to a marked degree, and there has been a natural feeling that here if anywhere the jury's independence ought to be most jealously guarded. A remarkable illustration of the feeling that a jury is likely to be more independent (or at least more representative of national feeling) than a judge is to be seen in Fox's Libel Act[2] of 1792, which reduced the position of the bench in libel cases (which were frequently apt to have a political character) to a minimum by allowing the jury not only to find the facts but also to declare whether those facts in law amounted to a libel.[3]

[1] A very similar situation arose in property cases when the jury was asked to say whether there had been a disseisin—a proposition even more technical and artificial than the law of larceny.

[2] 32 Geo. III, c. 60.

[3] Below, p. 500.

THE ORIGINS OF THE CENTRAL COURTS

So far we have discussed the local courts, both communal and seignorial, and the contacts which took place between them and the royal authority, and particularly the most important of these contacts, the jury. It now remains to sketch the rise of the central courts at Westminster.

THE ROYAL HOUSEHOLD

During the Anglo-Saxon age there was nothing which could be described as a central royal court of law, although there were certainly central royal institutions. Their formation is the product of two elements, the one being the royal household and the other the national assembly. It is to the royal household that we must look for the origins of the administrative machinery of the Anglo-Saxon monarchy. The principal household officers inevitably acquired political influence and took a part in public affairs. Similarly the group of clergy attached to the King's chapel naturally formed the nucleus of a secretariat which in time will be called the Chancery. It was only natural that the King should surround himself with men whose advice he valued, frequently placing them in high positions in the household. The household therefore consisted not merely of the King's domestic servants but also of men of an official class whose assistance was useful in the daily task of government.[1] When there was added to them the body of King's

---

[1] See the account in J. E. A. Jolliffe, *Constitutional History*, 130 ff.

clerks there was all that was required for the day-to-day business of government. This system of household government survived long after the Anglo-Saxon times. The Norman kings systematised it; in the thirteenth century portions of it became separated from the household, and in the fourteenth century developed into independent offices of State closely resembling the modern civil service. But this machinery was still controlled by the household, and bitter constitutional struggles were constantly occurring as the nobility at large endeavoured to curb the activities of the household officials. The Exchequer, for example, at a very early date, had achieved a completely independent existence, and yet to the end of the fifteenth century the effective control of finance was in the hands of the household, working through the offices of the Wardrobe and the Chamber. So, too, the Chancery very soon became an independent office for the management of the Great Seal, and yet its policies were controlled either by the Council working through the Privy Seal office, or else by an inner group of household officials (especially the chamberlain of the household) working through the office of the Signet.[1] The effective power wielded by the holders of the signet can be seen by the rapid rise to importance of the Secretary who was its official custodian. In the sixteenth century he becomes a " Secretary of State ", and at the present day English secretaries of state are created by the delivery of the signets, which are handed to them by the King himself as symbols of their office. The household, therefore, is not merely the original germ of our central institutions, but has continued all through the middle ages to occupy a central position of effective political control, even over those departments of state which in former times had separated from it.

THE NATIONAL ASSEMBLY

The second element in the growth of these institutions may be described as that of the national assembly. The household was adequate enough for the ordinary daily business, but from time to time questions arose which required the advice of a larger number of people representing more varied interests. The effective political public for a long time coincided with the small class of great nobles and great ecclesiastics. Matters of grave importance would naturally be discussed at a somewhat large meeting of the most notable men of the nation. There is no need to apply precise terms and definitions to such assemblies, or to seek for exact rules as to their competence. Still less is it appropriate to ask questions as to what matters must be done with the concurrence of such an assembly and what matters could be done without it. There was nothing in the Anglo-Saxon age, or for a long time afterwards, which could be described as a body of public law. Conferring with the magnates

[1] The struggle for the seals is described in Plucknett, *Place of the Council in the Fifteenth Century*, Transactions of the Royal Historical Society, 1918, pp. 176–183.

of the realm was not a legal necessity, but a dictate of political prudence. It was only natural that the Crown should take counsel upon grave matters with those magnates whose co-operation was necessary if a policy was to be carried out. When we speak, therefore, of the national assembly under the Anglo-Saxon kings—" Witan " as they called it—we must not expect to describe its composition and powers as if it were a modern congress or parliament. There were some persons who certainly expected to be summoned when important matters were on the table; the position of others was less definite and varied with circumstances; but in any case it would be misleading to speak of anyone having a right to attend. On the contrary, for many centuries attendance at assemblies and Parliaments was a burden rather than a privilege, and people considered themselves lucky if they could obtain the royal privilege of not being summoned to Parliaments. The national assembly, therefore, was not a body of fixed composition or definite powers. Sometimes it seems hardly larger than the household itself, while at others we find a very imposing array of nobles and prelates.

THE RESULT OF THE CONQUEST

It is after the Norman Conquest that these institutions take a more definite form. The household continues to be the real political centre, and beside it, or perhaps within it, there develops a small council consisting of clerks and minor officials who are continually at hand for the transaction of daily business. The national assembly, on the other hand, begins to take a different complexion. It was one of the main features of feudalism that a lord could demand counsel from his tenants, and that those tenants were legally bound to attend their lord upon demand and to sit as a court in order to give him advice, to pass legal judgment upon fellow tenants, and to grant financial and moral support to the lord. The old national assembly therefore became a court with comparatively definite powers, and a well-defined obligation of attendance. For the time being it is true that its business was principally what we may describe as feudal. But in the eleventh and twelfth centuries feudal matters were of first-rate importance. Feudal custom regulated the position of the Crown with respect to the great nobles, and therefore supplied the place of a body of public law. The King's Court, therefore, is not merely the Anglo-Saxon consultative assembly, but also a body entrusted with the power of applying such constitutional law as then existed.

It was also a peculiarity of feudalism that these matters of public law— the prerogative of the Crown, the rights and duties of the baronage, the means of extraordinary taxation and so on—were intimately connected with land. From this it resulted, first, that the King's Court had to pay special attention to the law of land upon which these public rights and duties were based, and secondly, that these matters of essentially public law came to be regarded from the point of view of private property law. Political rights and privileges, the powers of particular officers and the like were treated as if they were land—or at least incorporeal hereditaments, which mediaeval law hardly distinguished from land. In this way there grew up the habit of regarding political and constitutional rights as sharing the specially sacred character of private property. As long as the common law controlled political thought, this attitude of mind persisted. No doubt there were grave disadvantages in the feudal view which treated governmental powers as private property—for one thing, they were apt to be regarded as private resources to be exploited to the limit; yet, on the other hand, the English constitution and the common law itself owed a good deal of their stability and continuity to the fact that all the sanctity which attached to private property could be invoked to protect the liberty of the subject. It is only when the modern theory of the State appears after the Reformation and the Renaissance that this point of view is theoretically attacked. This does not mean to say, of course, that the Crown never violated the rights of private liberty and property; as we shall see, more than once encroachments were made upon privileges which were the property rights of local magnates. Nevertheless, the theory was universally admitted, and in times of stress played an important rôle. As late as the fifteenth century many important questions of public law, such as the relations of Crown and Parliament, the theory of taxation, and so on, were discussed entirely from the point of view of a real property lawyer.[1] All this, therefore, was the direct result of the feudal character of the King's Court as it appears after the Conquest.

THE MEANING OF THE WORD " COURT "

Before we discuss further the character and development of the King's Court (which historians usually refer to by its old Latin style of the *Curia Regis*) it may be well to examine the various meanings of the word " court " or " *curia* ". The original sense of the word is the rectangular open space around which the mediaeval house was built; the usual plan was that of a hollow square of buildings, the inside space of which was called the court. The colleges at Oxford and Cambridge are all built upon this plan, which was originally that of the ordinary dwelling-house, and in Cambridge their interior spaces are still called courts. The next development is to extend the word " court " to the house itself, and many famous houses in England are still called courts—Hampton Court, for example. Then the word " court " can also be used of the household and personal attendants of a king or great noble. Upon certain festivals during the year kings and nobles were accustomed to gather around them a particularly large company, and this event, too, becomes known as a court; the word will serve furthermore to designate the persons who

[1] See above, p. 37.

were present on such an occasion. At Christmas and Easter the Anglo-Norman kings held courts of this character. The word was also applied to those assemblies at which attendance was compulsory as a feudal duty, and thence by a natural transition to any assembly for the purpose of transacting important public business; the Bank of England is governed by a court, and the Commonwealth of Massachusetts by a General Court. Finally, the word " court " is particularly used of such assemblies when they are engaged in judicial business. In mediaeval usage the word " court " may bear any of these different meanings singly or in combination, and if mediaeval institutions are to be understood properly it must be remembered that a court might be at the same time legislative, judicial, deliberative, and even festive.

It was all the more easy to combine these different functions in one body because early courts were very different from modern ones. The central figure of a court to-day is the judge, but, as we shall see later,[1] it required some time before English law developed this office. Feudal courts seem generally to have consisted not of judges but of a number of " suitors " with whom rested the decision. The lord of the court indeed presided in person or more usually by his steward, but the president was in no sense a judge as the word is understood to-day. Under the Norman kings, we have descriptions of trials where it plainly appears that the king himself demanded of his barons in the court to pronounce a judgment.[2] His lords, as we have seen, had courts of their own. Like the royal courts, these seignorial courts could sometimes take a political appearance, and from time to time we find lords holding assemblies of tenants like little parliaments in order to obtain grants of money.[3] The House of Lords when sitting as a criminal court preserved, at least in theory, this old conception of a court of many suitors who are judges, irrespective of their being professional lawyers, and exactly reproduced an old feudal court of barons who are judges, while the presiding officer (the steward of the lord—in this case the King's Lord High Steward) is merely chairman.[4]

THE ANGLO-NORMAN *CURIA REGIS*

The court of the Anglo-Norman kings consisted, therefore, of the Anglo-Saxon Witan, which was essentially deliberative in character, radically transformed by the infusion of Norman ideas. There is a long and somewhat fruitless discussion as to whether the Norman *Curia Regis* is or is not the same institution as the Anglo-Saxon Witan; in this form the question can hardly be answered. It seems rather to have been the fact that the formless and indefinite Witan was so

[1] Below, p. 232.
[2] See the cases cited in Pollock and Maitland, i. 109 n.
[3] *Bracton's Note Book*, no. 1146.
[4] Below, pp. 203, 232

thoroughly transformed by the Norman kings that it is purely a matter of fancy whether one describes the product as a new institution or as a modification of the old one.

There are cases to be found where the Witan, under the Anglo-Saxon kings, exercised quasi-judicial functions; it is perfectly clear, however, that the Witan did not entertain the ambition of becoming a national court. The whole spirit of Anglo-Saxon law made for the maintenance of local institutions, and more than once we find laws prohibiting parties to appeal to the King unless there has been a grave default of justice in the regular courts. When judicial matters do appear before the King and the Witan they are apt to be treated as political disputes requiring a political solution by negotiation, compromise, and royal mediation rather than a strictly judicial treatment. With the Norman Conquest we begin to find the transformation of the deliberative Witan into the judicial court. The transformation was, of course, slow, and even after the conquest there are proceedings in the King's Court of the more ancient type. Still, the feudal idea of a court of tenants-in-chief was sufficient to supply the model of a supreme royal court, and it was from that model that the judicial system of the common law later developed.

THE TRAVELLING COURT: JUSTICES IN EYRE

It was a feature of mediaeval life that the King and his court were constantly travelling through the length and breadth of the kingdom, and that in the course of these journeys a general supervision would be effected over the conduct of royal officers, the working of local institutions, the collection of revenue and the redress of grievances. It was only natural that the idea should be extended, and that kings should send out some trusted officer to conduct similar progresses through the country for the same general purposes. Charlemagne in the early ninth century had developed a regular system of such *missi dominici*,[1] and very soon after the Conquest, as we have already seen,[2] a similar device is found in England. At the head of this travelling group of officials were the Justiciars—and it must be remembered that their title does not imply that their duties were primarily judicial, but merely that they were the direct personal representatives of the King.[3] The King's Court was thus enabled to be in several places at once; besides the principal body, which was always in the presence of the King himself, there might be several groups of officials touring the country as Justices in Eyre, as they soon came to be called. In this way the custom and practice of the King's Court was made more familiar by being spread

---

[1] They are described by G. Seeliger in *Cambridge Mediaeval History*, ii. 682 ff.

[2] Above, pp. 101–104.

[3] On the spread of the office throughout Europe, and doubts on its Norman origin, see Madame J. Devieké-Navakas, *L'Expansion du justiciarius sicilien*, in Atti del Convegno Internazionale di Studi Fredericiani (Palermo, 1950), 481 ff.

over the country, and by being brought into contact with local institutions. During the reign of Henry II these Eyres are very frequent, and Bracton and his successors treat them as a separate judicial jurisdiction.[1] The experiment was so successful that Philip Augustus soon set up a similar system in France.[2] There can be no doubt that there was much important legislation effected (which is now largely lost) by means of instructions to the justices as they set out upon their Eyre.

Their jurisdiction varied; in the early years of Henry III they might be commissioned " ad omnia placita ", and then their impressive " general eyre " (as Maitland called it[3]) became in effect the court of common pleas on circuit, instead of at Westminster. These justices with their " roll of secrets " and their " book of death "[4] undoubtedly struck terror into the country,[5] but as their organisation became more refined they became more and more an engine of oppression. Technical errors in legal and administrative procedure, slight inaccuracies in matters of detail were made the excuse for fines upon the whole vill or county. In the thirteenth century Eyres were frequent[6] and the financial yield considerable: in 1227 a judge reckoned a profit of 40 marks a day for the king, and in 1301 Edward I " caused justice to be done on malefactors " in order to recoup the expenses of twenty years of war, and thereby " amassed great treasure ".[7] In the early fourteenth century we have a full report of an Eyre which visited Kent in 1313 from which every detail of its work can be traced.[8] Already protests against general Eyres appear in Parliament and after the middle of the century Eyres ceased to be commissioned. For a time it seemed as if the new device of constant tours by the King's Bench from the middle of the fourteenth century onwards might serve the same purposes as an eyre,[9] but in the end it was seen that they were in fact no longer necessary, for (as we shall see in

[1] Bracton, f. 105 b; *Fleta* II. 2; *Britton*, I, 1.

[2] Ralf de Diceto, *Opera Historica* (ed. Stubbs, Rolls Series), ii. 7–8; C. V. Langlois, *Doléances recuellies par les enquêteurs de saint Louis*, Revue Historique, xcii. 1 (who observes that by 1226 they had ceased to wander, and became resident *baillis*); C. Petit-Dutaillis, *Monarchie féodale*, 206–207.

[3] Maitland, *Bracton's Note Book*, i: 54.

[4] Maitland, *Select Pleas of the Crown* (Selden Society), no. 91; Lady Stenton, *Eyre Rolls* (Selden Society, 53), xvii–xviii; they also had the common pleas roll with them: C. A. F. Meekings in English Historical Review, lxv. 500.

[5] In 1233 the men of Cornwall fled to the woods for fear of the justices; Pollock and Maitland, i. 202.

[6] For a list see H. M. Cam, *Studies in the Hundred Rolls*, 109. For the rule that a county ought not to be visited by an Eyre more than once in seven years, see Treharne, *Baronial Plan of Reform, 1258–1263*, 398–406.

[7] *Royal Letters* (ed. Shirley, Rolls Series), i. no. 350 (1227); *Croniques de London* (ed. G. J. Aungier, Camden Society), 28–29.

[8] *Eyre of Kent* (Selden Society) 3 vols. There are similar reports (still unprinted) for the eyres of London (1321) and of Derby, Nottingham, Northampton and Bedford (1330–1331). For a lively and popular account of an Eyre see Bolland, *The General Eyre* (Cambridge, 1922).

[9] B. H. Putnam, *Proceedings before Justices of the Peace* (Ames Foundation), lvii ff.

the next chapter) newer means were being developed which put local institutions under an even more effective control, while the rise of parliamentary taxation provided a more satisfactory source of revenue.

THE LINES OF SEPARATION

The King's Court, however, still remained constantly at work in his presence, and the development of the jurisdiction of the Eyre did not seriously diminish the powers exercisable in the King's Court proper. It soon became evident, however, that convenience required a certain amount of specialisation within the *Curia Regis*.[1] It is curious to remark, however, that the divisions were not made along strictly functional lines; in the end a rough allocation of duties was made whereby finance went to the Exchequer, legislation to Parliament, judicature to the courts and executive duties to the Council, but this classification of powers was never very strictly carried out. Parliament and Exchequer both had considerable judicial business. The courts did a certain amount of administrative work, and the Council had a large share in judicature as well as in legislation. The development of these different bodies, therefore, was not dictated primarily by any idea of the classification, and still less of the separation, of powers. It seems rather that the growth of these new institutions was determined along lines of administrative procedure. Types of business of frequent occurrence would necessarily encourage the development of a routine, which would enable subordinate officials (if properly instructed in a well-planned procedure) to do the work in a regular, though somewhat mechanical way. The bulk of their duties consisted in following a preordained mode of practice, and it is only in exceptional cases that they would find it necessary to invoke the discretion of the whole of the King's Court. We therefore find very soon the development of certain courses of administrative practice, and around these practices there naturally gathered a group of officials who were skilled in the conduct of them. It is such a group of officials, adept in a particular body of procedural rules, which forms the first beginnings of new departments or institutions. The reason for their existence and the key to their activities is therefore a body of administrative procedure rather than a theoretical analysis of the powers of government. In the course of time a number of such procedures appear, gather around them a little group of officials, and finally give rise to new institutions.

THE OLDEST OFF-SHOOT: THE EXCHEQUER

The first of these was the Exchequer, which represents the oldest routine of government. Its beginnings had been primitive.

---

[1] The similar developments in France furnish instructive parallels: see G. Viard, *La Cour au commencement du XIV*e. *siècle*, Bibliothèque de l'École des Chartes, lxxvii. 74 and *La Cour et ses " parlements "*, *ibid.*, lxxix. 60.

" Edward the Confessor kept his treasure in his bedroom so that the thief, who aspired to rob the national treasury, had to wait until the king took an after dinner nap before he could venture into the royal chamber, and extract from the king's treasure chest some portion of its precious contents."[1]

Within a century there was a well-organised department, and in the reign of Henry II the Exchequer, with its formal departmental seal, had become the first separate government department in Europe.[2] About the year 1179 it was possible to write a very substantial treatise upon Exchequer procedure.[3] That procedure was primarily designed to do the King's book-keeping and to watch his financial interests, but it was inevitable that many other matters should also arise. In the Exchequer twice a year all the great officials of the realm sat together to supervise the whole of the financial machinery. At its head sat the Justiciar, and when that office became extinct he was replaced by the Treasurer; the Chancellor also attended and brought with him some of his clerks who issued process " from the Chancery in the Exchequer ". At the close of the twelfth century the Chancellor's office had become so important in other directions that for the future he is only represented in the Exchequer by a deputy, the Chancellor of the Exchequer. With such a great array of high officials at the solemn meeting of the Exchequer, it was natural that any great difficulty could be immediately settled, for the highest authorities in the land were sitting around the table. In this way, a good deal of important government business of a general character was apt to take place on the occasion of a great Exchequer meeting, especially at Michaelmas term, when besides all the high officials there were also in attendance all the sheriffs who were present for the examination of their accounts.

In the first of these administrative routines, therefore, we see that a variety of functions were performed whose single bond of union was the fact that they arose in the course of one procedure, that of the Exchequer.

THE NEXT OFF-SHOOT: THE COURT OF COMMON PLEAS

We have already mentioned the very numerous Eyres which took place during Henry II's reign. Indeed the popular complaint was that there were too many of them, and in 1178 we find a remarkable passage in a chronicler[4] which tells us that—

[1] Tout, *Place of Edward II*, 44; but the incident must not be misunderstood. See the important comments in V. H. Galbraith, *Studies in the Public Records*, 43 ff.

[2] Tout, *op. cit.*, 45.

[3] See above, p. 18. See the passages from it in Stubbs, *Select Charters*, the description in R. L. Poole, *The Exchequer in the Twelfth Century*, the text and translation edited by Crump, Hughes and Johnson (Edinburgh, 1955).

[4] Stubbs, *Select Charters*.

" While he was staying in England, the King enquired whether the justices whom he had set up in England had treated the people fairly; and when he learned that the country and the people were much aggrieved by the number of justices (for there were eighteen of them), by the advice of the wise men of his realm he chose five only, two clergy and three laymen, all of his personal household, and decreed that these five should hear all the complaints of the realm, and do right, and not depart from the King's court but remain there to hear the people's complaints. And if any question should arise among them which they could not solve, they were to bring it up in the royal hearing for determination according to the pleasure of the King and the wiser men of the realm."

The current interpretation of this passage, first suggested by Maitland and later modified by Pike and Adams, is that in 1178 Henry II by a deliberate act established a new court, which in later times became known as the Court of Common Pleas. Adams[1] insists that the powers of this court, like those of its descendant, the later Court of Common Pleas, were strictly limited, and that it was expressly debarred from exercising that wide discretion which was the privilege of the *Curia Regis*. The " limitations ", however, were not of the sort we would associate to-day with the expression " limited jurisdiction ". As Holdsworth points out, in criticising Adams' view, the new court in fact entertained every sort of business (including occasional pleas of the crown).[2] The situation seems best described as the effective, but informal, subordination of the new justices to the king and his court of " wiser " men, rather than limitation to a precise list of powers. Its foundation was suggested by the experience of the Justices in Eyre, and was designed to render available all the time the judicial advantages of the intermittent or occasional Eyre, while, on the other hand, the high-handed action of certain of those justices was to be prevented by subjecting the new court to the supervision of the king's council and by confining it within the limits of a procedure which was soon to become comparatively strict. The result was to give the public access to royal justice which was no longer mingled with the financial functions of the Eyre. The fact that this body of judges was erected as a separate court[3] was not allowed to stand in the way of practical convenience, however, and if for any reason it became desirable to move a case backwards and forwards between the newly erected court and the body which met around the king himself, then there was nothing to prevent such a course. This event of 1178 must not be regarded as a sudden creation of a new court by an act of legislation, but rather as the culmination of a number of earlier experiments,[4] which all had the general characteristic of subjecting the

[1] Adams, *Council and Courts in Anglo-Norman England*, 214 ff.; *Origin of the English Constitution*, 136–143.

[2] Holdsworth, i. 51 n. 6 (p. 52).

[3] Its oldest title is simply " the Bench "; it was only later, when its jurisdiction had become even more limited in practice, that it was informally referred to as the Court of Common Pleas. Holdsworth, *oc. cit.*

[4] This point is emphasised in the very valuable introduction by G. O. Sayles, *Select Cases in King's Bench* (Selden Society), i, intro. xx–xxv.

itinerant justices to the limitations set out in their commissions or instructions.[1]

Maitland discerned signs in the middle of the twelfth century of an old oral and traditional formalism,[2] which by the end of the century has developed into a written and authoritative formalism—the writ-system of the common law which Glanvill described in some detail; and, as Professor Baldwin remarks, such limitations are appropriate to the new body of 1178, and not to the *Curia Regis* itself.

> " It must be understood that the so-called formulaic and restrictive procedure began, and could begin, only in the courts held by the royal commissioners—that is, first by the itinerant justices and then the central court established on similar lines."[3]

It was a notable feature of the new arrangement of 1178 that the justices were to remain with the King; that necessarily meant perpetual perambulation. On the other hand, the " chief court ", *capitalis curia*, whose practice is the subject of Glanvill's treatise (written soon after 1187), seems fairly fixed at Westminster. Professor Sayles expresses a doubt whether the five justices of 1178 are indeed the same institution as that which Glanvill described, and suggests that the latter may be " a different creation ". It may be; there were indeed many " creations ". The difficulty largely disappears when one remembers that these " creations " were casual, temporary expedients, with no similarity to a " creation " of a court by a modern act of parliament. The repetition of these expedients slowly resulted in an institution, and its settlement at Westminster naturally resulted from Henry II's absence abroad, which made it impossible to stay with the king and at the same time to hear the complaints of the realm. A generation later *Magna Carta* was to fix the Court of Common Pleas permanently at Westminster.[4] The second administrative routine to become an institution is therefore largely a judicial one, and, after a period of experiment in the Eyres, it finally developed into the Court of Common Pleas, or " The Bench " as the older books call it.

THE COURT OF KING'S BENCH

The five justices who at first constituted the new court were expressly subordinated to the magnates and wiser men to whom difficult cases

---

[1] The Assize of Northampton (1176), c. 7, is an example.

[2] *History of the Register of Writs*, Harvard Law Review, iii. 97; *Collected Papers*, ii. 110; *Select Essays in Anglo-American Legal History*, ii. 560–561.

[3] Baldwin, *The King's Council*, 49.

[4] *Magna Carta* (1215), c. 17; (1225), c. 11. The charter in fact only required the court to sit in " some certain place ", but in practice that place was nearly always Westminster. Exceptions were in the thirteenth century when the common pleas judges were all away on Eyre, and in the fourteenth when the seat of government moved to York when there was war with Scotland. King's Bench, on the other hand, was constantly moving until well into the fifteenth century: B. H. Putnam, *Justices of the Peace* (Ames Foundation), 29.

were to be referred. For some years the highest law court consisted, therefore, of these greater and wiser men who were in constant attendance upon the King. It is a frequent recurrence in all this judicial and constitutional history that the group of advisers in the immediate presence of the King should exercise in his name a wide discretion, and that these powers should in no way be diminished by the successive developments of the Exchequer and the Court of Common Pleas. Just as the Exchequer had formed round the financial routine, and the Court of Common Pleas was to grow up with the common law forms of action, so the constant occupation of the King's immediate advisers with matters referred to them from the Common Pleas, and also with matters particularly touching the King, gave rise to a new body of procedure, and soon to a new court—the Court of King's Bench, or, in its full mediaeval title, " The Justices assigned for the holding of Pleas before the King himself ".[1] Normally, such pleas would have been heard literally " before the King himself ", but that was impossible with an absentee King such as Richard I. The court *coram rege* appears under John, but vanishes when he goes to the continent. The minority of Henry III again made it impossible to speak of pleas *coram rege*, but by this time the need for such a jurisdiction was so great that it was determined by way of compromise to hold some pleas *coram consilio*, the rest being deferred until the King should come of age. Hence in its early days it is often impossible to distinguish these judicial proceedings before the King (*Coram Rege*) from proceedings before the Council, and the early rolls of the court sometimes contain miscellaneous acts of the Council. The procedures around which it finally developed were the correction of error in the Common Pleas, and the trial of those pleas of the Crown which were of exceptional concern to the King.[2]

There are rolls still in existence, bearing the proceedings of both branches of the *Curia Regis*, beginning in the year 1194; a separate series of common plea rolls (technically called *de banco* rolls) begins in the year 1234, and in 1237 a defendant in a plea *coram rege* is found objecting that the case ought to have been brought in the common pleas.[3]

THE CONNECTION BETWEEN KING'S BENCH AND THE COUNCIL

For a long time it was a striking feature of the court before the King himself (*Coram Rege*) that it was closely associated with the Council. Many magnates might attend its solemn sessions; for less important business a small group of officials was sufficient. Although the two procedures

---

[1] Remember that old books, in speaking of " The Bench ", always mean the Court of Common Pleas, and not the King's Bench.

[2] The above is a necessarily simplified version of a complicated and obscure story; for details see Sayles, *King's Bench* (Selden Society), i, intro. xxii ff.

[3] *Bracton's Note Book*, no. 1220. The exception failed, since although it was a plea of land yet the King was demandant.

which we have mentioned very soon appear (jurisdiction in error from the Common Pleas, and the trial of the more important pleas in which the Crown was concerned), they are for a long time mingled with the political and administrative duties of the Council. In the end, these two procedures were both entrusted to a small group of professional justices who were specially commissioned " to hold pleas before the King himself ". In other words, the King's Bench becomes a separate institution, early in the reign of Edward I. For long after that date, l owever, there still remained a close connection between the King's Bench and the parent body. Just as in earlier times a piece of private litigation in the King's Bench, which raised a difficult point as to whether trial by battle lay or not, was adjourned " because there were not enough members of the King's Council present ",[1] so " the recurrence of pleas before the King and his council, *Coram Rege et consilio suo*, in this manner, can hardly be said to be discontinued until the reign of Edward III ".[2] In the reign of Edward I, therefore, although the King's Bench had its own establishment, working its own procedure, and may therefore be regarded as a separate institution, there nevertheless existed a good deal of intimate contact both then and later between it and the Council.

COUNCIL AND PARLIAMENT

In the thirteenth century this central group of officials and advisers who remained constantly in the King's presence was described by a variety of names; a chronicler will usually call it " the Council "; a law-writer such as Bracton, who is mainly interested in its judicial duties, will call it the King's Court or *Curia Regis*. As for those occasional meetings when this body is enlarged by the addition of numerous magnates, the chroniclers will usually call them a " colloquy ", and such is at first the usual official term. In common speech, however, such meetings were often referred to as " parliaments ". For a time this word was popular rather than official; it could be used of any sort of conference or meeting; even a disorderly assembly could be called a parliament, and in 1267 Henry III forbade the assembly of parliaments or other meetings in breach of the peace. In early days, therefore, the word " parliament " does not mean an institution but an event.[3] Any unusually large meeting of the King's Council will be popularly described as a parliament. A variety of influences began to work in the direction of giving more definite shape to these occasional parliaments. As time goes on, the King's Bench will become as closely confined within the

[1] Baldwin, *The King's Council*, 53. Cf. Sayles, *King's Bench*, ii, intro. lxv ff.

[2] Baldwin, *op. cit.*, 64. This need not mean the " substantial identity " of the two bodies, but merely that separate institutions were still capable of intimate collaboration upon occasion. In the king's absence or minority the court *coram rege* could only be held *coram consilio*, as we have already seen.

[3] H. G. Richardson, *The Origins of Parliament*, Transactions of the Royal Historical Society, 4th series, xi. 137.

common law forms of procedure as the Court of Common Pleas itself, and it will be necessary to provide some other means for the exercise of equity and discretion and for the handling of cases which fall outside of those limits.   This task naturally fell to the Council, whose mission during a great part of the middle ages was to act as an extraordinary court of unlimited jurisdiction, both original and appellate.

These discretionary powers of the Council covered a wide variety of subjects.   Some could be settled at the discretion of skilled official councillors, while others demanded the attention of a larger body of magnates;   and so their work naturally falls into two groups—matters which could be handled by the Council continually attending the King, and matters upon which they preferred to take the advice of the magnates at large.   An important discussion, whether of judicial matters or political might equally be called a parliament, whether it actually took place in the smaller Council or in the larger assembly surrounding it.

With the reign of Edward I we find a new series of rolls appear for the first time, and these are the Parliament Rolls.[1]   Much of the business on the early Parliament Rolls is of a judicial character, although not all of it is in the forms of the common law.   By this time the King's Bench had lost much of its early discretionary power and contented itself with working the common law system of writs and its own particular procedure;   it was therefore Parliament which now undertook to wield some of the discretionary powers which the King's Bench had resigned—and herein we see the origin of the appellate jurisdiction of the House of Lords.   Indeed, in the fourteenth century a case might move backwards and forwards between the King's Bench, the Council and a Parliament of the Council with the greatest ease.[2]   The judges of the King's Bench were in frequent attendance, both at the continual Council and at Parliaments.   But besides this common law business, the Council was continually receiving a large number of petitions from individuals, churches, cities, counties and others, which were of the utmost variety.   Some simply prayed for relief which was already to be had in the regular law courts;   others, if the Council approved them, were transferred to the law courts, and the Council's endorsement served to supply any lack of jurisdiction which might otherwise have prevented them from giving a remedy;   others merely demanded favours which the administration might grant or withhold, while others might raise very difficult questions upon which the Council would wish to take the advice of the magnates of the realm.   Those petitions which the Council did not deal with

[1] See the classical discussion in Maitland, *Memoranda de Parliamento*, lxxix–lxxxi (largely reprinted in Maitland, *Selected Papers*, ed. H. D. Hazeltine, G. Lapsley and P. H. Winfield), with which cf. H. G. Richardson in Bulletin of the Institute of Historical Research, vi. 129, Plucknett, in *English Government at Work, 1327–1336* (ed. J. F. Willard), i. 90 ff., and J. G. Edwards, *Justice in Early English Parliaments,* Bulletin of the Institute of Historical Research, xxvii. 35 (1954).

[2] A famous example is *Staunton* v. *Staunton* (1341), Y.B. 13 & 14 Edward III (Rolls Series), xxxvii–xliv; Y.B. 14 & 15 Edward III (Rolls Series), 288–300.

alone were held over until one of the Parliaments, which were frequently
held.

THE ADDITION OF THE COMMONS

At the same time a remarkable development was taking place which
was to modify profoundly the political aspect of Parliament. The
strong, centralised monarchy of the thirteenth century was never tired
of devising means for keeping in closer contact with local institutions.
The annual visits of the sheriffs to the Exchequer and the frequent visits
of Justices in Eyre to the various counties were still not enough; what
the Crown particularly desired was an independent check upon the
activities of its local officers, and a means of treating directly with the
people. Various experiments were therefore made in the course of the
thirteenth century with this end in view. They were in fact simply an
extension of machinery which had existed for many years. It was a
familiar occurrence for every hundred, vill and borough to send representatives to the county court, where a general investigation would be
made into local government and apparently even a vote of taxes might
occasionally be made.[1] Nothing was more simple than to extend this
time-honoured system to the whole nation. Just as hundreds and vills
appeared by representatives in the county court (more especially when the
King's Justices in Eyre were present) so it was possible to call upon the
county courts (together with the more important boroughs) to send
representatives to meet the King himself when he and his Council were
holding a Parliament.[2] Such representatives later on brought with them
numerous grievances, which they laid before the Council in the form of
petitions, and this accounts for a large number of petitions which appear
upon the Parliament Rolls—to say nothing of many more which were
never enrolled at all. By Edward I's reign, therefore, a Parliament of
the Council may consist of a number of elements. There may be a greater
or less number of magnates and prelates; there may or may not be a
collection of representatives of the various communities of the land (who
will afterwards be called the Commons, or in French *Communes*); at the
same time it was customary for the lower clergy also to be represented by
proctors, and these (together with the prelates, who are also summoned
to the parliament) will form the later convocation. But in the centre
of all this, controlling and directing all the proceedings, is the King's
Council. It is the King's Council which is the motive force in the
Parliament; the lords, the commons and the clergy merely attend to
answer the Council's questions, to advise it upon points referred to them,
and to present humble petitions for the redress of their grievances. It

[1] Pollock and Maitland, i. 555.

[2] The details of this process belong to constitutional rather than to legal history. Early
experiments were made from 1213 onwards; Parliaments which some modern historians have
called " Model " were held in 1275 and 1295. See Adams, *Constitutional History of England*;
Pollard, *Evolution of Parliament*; Pasquet, *Origins of the House of Commons*, and Taswell-Langmead,
Constitutional History (ed. Plucknett), 143–167.

required a powerful monarchy to organise such an institution. It is a constant observation in the middle ages that it is only the strongest kings who can compel their subjects, be they lords or commons, to give them advice, to attend their courts, and to take part in the work of government. Centuries later Parliament will become an instrument, first in the hands of the lords and later of the commons, which can be turned against the King himself and his Council. But this is far in the future; Parliament was not intended to play that rôle when it first took rise. In its earliest days it was a sign of royal strength and not of royal weakness, and this can be seen from the fact that the weaker kings had great difficulty in collecting a Parliament at all.

The future of Parliament may be political, but its origin was legal and administrative. In its origin and throughout the middle ages it deserved its later title of the " High Court of Parliament "—and in this expression it must be remembered that the word " court " must be taken in the broadest mediaeval sense.

We have insisted that the real centre of Parliament in the middle ages was the King's Council. *Fleta* expresses this idea when he says that " the king has his court in his council in his parliaments ",[1] and even as late as the fifteenth century it is abundantly clear that the Council was still the moving force in Parliament; even at so late a date a chronicler will speak of a " Parliament of the Council ", and we constantly find official documents which say that " the King by the advice of his Council in Parliament " has taken certain action. Even at the present day the brilliant ceremonial with which the King opens Parliament bears witness to this fact. The proceedings take place in the House of Lords. The King on his throne is surrounded by the councillors standing on the steps of the throne; immediately in front are the judges (and in former times the law officers of the Crown); this little group of the King and his councillors and judges (who anciently were active members of his Council) is the core of the Parliament. At a greater distance are assembled the peers of the realm and the prelates, and so we see *Fleta's* phrase visually expressed, " the King is in his Council in his Parliament ". Right at the bottom of the room is a bar, and outside of the bar are the latest additions to the constitution of Parliament, the Commons. They are always standing—the older pictures show them kneeling—and at their head is the Speaker. He derives his title from the fact that of all the Commons present the Speaker alone has the right of raising his voice in the Parliament. To safeguard both himself and the Commons in case he should speak erroneously on their behalf, he made a sort of protestation or petition at the opening of parliament. At first it is only

---

[1] " For the king has his court in his council in his parliaments, in the presence of the prelates, earls, barons, nobles and other experienced men, where doubtful judgements are decided, and new remedies are established as new wrongs arise, and where justice is done to everyone according to his deserts ": *Fleta*, lib. ii. c. 2, § 1. Cf. Maitland, *Memoranda de Parliamento*, lxxix–lxxxix.

a prayer that he may have permission to correct his mistakes if he should make any; later, in the reign of Henry VIII, he became more bold, and prayed for the allowance of the Commons' privileges.[1] This ceremonial faithfully reproduces the appearance of a Parliament of the early fourteenth century. Whatever deliberations the Commons or Lords may make among themselves are merely their private concern; the proceedings in Parliament take place when the Council is present, attended by the lords, and in those proceedings the Council plays a dominant part.

With the close of the middle ages the position of the judges in Parliament becomes less important. They attend upon ceremonial occasions, and give advice when called upon by the Crown or by the lords, but no longer take a regular part in its general business except for the purpose of handling certain types of petition, and soon this too becomes obsolete.

THE JUDICIAL SYSTEM UNDER EDWARD I

And so by the reign of Edward I we have all the elements, save one,[2] of the present judicial system of England. There was the Bench, or Court of Common Pleas, where the common law forms of action were developed and where the bulk of the important litigation of the country took place (with the exception of the smaller matters which went before the local courts). Then there was the King's Bench which had a jurisdiction in error from the Common Pleas, and an original jurisdiction over the pleas of the Crown of unusual importance; it was the proper place for state trials and for matters which closely concern the King. Above the King's Bench, and working in close harmony with it, was the King's Council, ready to supply from the reserves of royal discretion at its command any defects of jurisdiction which might occur in the lower courts, and to take the advice of a Parliament, if necessary, to resolve their doubts and remove their difficulties. In the Council, in Parliament, and to some extent in the King's Bench, there was, therefore, an ample source of equity, discretion and extraordinary power to meet any emergency.   At the same time the King's financial interests were controlled by the Court of Exchequer, and difficult legal questions could be informally discussed in the Exchequer or in Council by a full meeting of all the available legal talent. As for the ordinary criminal jurisdiction, there were many local authorities with summary powers, which were supplemented by numerous visits of commissioners of gaol delivery (who delivered the gaols of prisoners committed for trial), and commissioners of *oyer* and *terminer*, who had wide powers of holding pleas of the Crown. Both these classes of commission were in constant use and their activities were recorded upon hundreds of rolls. At the same time certain types of common plea concerning land, called " assizes "

[1] See Neale, *The Commons' Privilege of Free Speech* (in Tudor Studies presented to A. F. Pollard, 257–286).

[2] Chancery was not yet a court of equity.

which were of very frequent occurrence were also heard locally by travelling commissioners of assize, who only reserved points of special difficulty for discussion at Westminster in the Court of Common Pleas. All these were in existence in Edward I's reign.

FACTORS IN THE GROWTH OF THE COMMON LAW

At this point, moreover, it is well to remember the striking passage in Maitland's *Constitutional History* where he indicates six principles which combined to increase the jurisdiction of the royal courts. They are briefly these:[1]

(1) Under the Norman kings the Crown by its writ of right supplied the real or imaginary defects of justice in the feudal courts.

(2) Under Henry II it was established that no man need answer for his freehold without a royal writ unless he cared to.[2]

(3) Henry II also ordained that a defendant in certain pleas of land in the King's Court could have jury trial (grand assize) instead of battle if he chose.

(4) The possessory assizes established by Henry II deliberately ignored the feudal courts and by their swiftness immediately became very popular.

(5) The idea of contempt was used very effectively. The King would issue a writ ordering a subject to do right and justice, and if he refused, he was guilty of contempt of the King's writ. The defendant in a writ of debt, for example, not only denies his liability, but also denies tort and force in resisting the King's command.

(6) The idea of the King's peace was not only the basis of criminal jurisdiction, but could also be used to enlarge the civil jurisdiction of the King's Court. This was effected through the action of trespass, which although criminal in form was constantly becoming more and more a civil action.

---

[1] Maitland, *Constitutional History*, 111–114.

[2] The rule is stated to be customary by Glanvill, xii. 25 (on which see Woodbine's note; Adams, *Origin of the English Constitution*, 97 ff. finds it difficult to accept, and would explain it away as too " anti-feudal ". More recently Lady Stenton, in *Cambridge Mediaeval History*, v. 586, has traced the rule back to Henry I). In 1202 the royal judges based a decision on the rule (*Earliest Northamptonshire Assize Rolls*, ed. Stenton, 782). Half a century later, however, it was the insurgent barons themselves who first put the rule in statutory form in 1259, Provisions of Westminster, c. 18, re-enacted in the Statute of Marlborough (1267), c. 22. Cf. Plucknett, *Legislation of Edward I*, 25–29.

Closely connected with it, is the parallel principle that false judgment is a plea of the crown, *i.e.* the review of a feudal court's decisions can only be had in the king's court, and not in any superior feudal court. This too is early twelfth century (*Leges Henrici Primi*, x. 1) and reappears in the Provisions of Westminster, c. 16, and the Statute of Marlborough, c. 20. In short, even in the hey-day of feudalism there were rules which at first sight seem " anti-feudal " to us, although to contemporaries they doubtless seemed natural enough.

CHAPTER 6

THE ELABORATION OF THE JUDICIAL SYSTEM: 1307-1509

The last chapter has briefly told the beginning of a long story. When once the superior courts had come into existence there still remained the question whether they would continue upon the course which they had begun.

THE POSITION OF THE COURTS

Their subsequent history will show that much was to happen which would have astonished the statesmen of Henry II and Edward I. For example, a great characteristic of the early judicial system was its flexibility. Cases could move from court to court as occasion required: the lines of division between the different jurisdictions were not insurmountable; the King was in constant contact, through the council, with the judges, and his intervention was often to the advancement of justice, although at times no doubt it might be used by a weak monarch for personal ends. The judges themselves, closely co-operating with the council, exercised a good deal of discretion, and in many cases tempered law with equitable considerations. As the centuries passed, however, many changes came about. The courts gained some degree of independence of the Crown, but in doing so lost their discretionary powers. Their procedure became rigid and mechanical, unchangeable save by parliamentary statute Reform, if it came at all, came from without.

THE ISOLATION OF THE JUDGES

We have already noticed the close connection which once existed between the courts and the council, and indeed with the King himself. The result, while it lasted, was that the judges normally exercised a considerable amount of discretion, particularly in procedural matters. It must not be rashly assumed that the further back we go the more rigid was the law. On the contrary, investigation has shown the wide discretion which was allowed to the courts both in the twelfth and thirteenth centuries.[1] It is not until the middle of the fourteenth century that this discretion begins to disappear. A great step in this development was the solemn enactment of the Statute of Northampton[2] in 1328 which declared that no royal command under the Great or the Smaller Seal shall disturb the course of the common law, and that if such a command is issued, the judges shall ignore it. Slowly but steadily the judges ventured to enforce the plain words of this important act,[3] and so to assume the detached position which is typical of most modern judiciaries.

The remarkable political crisis[4] of 1340 took matters a stage further by showing the unseemliness of treating judges as though they were politicians, and about the years 1340 to 1350 we find several expressions from the bench and bar which seem to indicate that the position of the courts is changing. In cases where we know that discretion was once exercised we now find it refused. Instead of bending the rules of procedure to the broad requirements of justice, we find the courts declaring that "we will not and cannot change ancient usages "; "statutes are to be taken strictly "; an innocent man might lie indefinitely in prison, or a creditor might be deprived of his remedy through the manipulation of procedural rules, and all the court will say is that "we can do nothing without a statute ".[5] In short, the judges attempted to cast upon parliament the responsibility for future legal reform.

Similarly, there were difficult cases where the judges could not make up their minds—to the great delay of litigants. Already, in theory, *Fleta* had attributed to parliament the duty of resolving judicial doubts,[6] and in 1311 the Ordinances, c. 29, required the termination of such cases in parliament—instances occur of the ordinance being applied.[7]

In the next reign Parliament passed a curious statute in 1340 giving powers to commissioners (evidently non-lawyers) to decide cases which had been delayed because the judges found them too difficult.[8] So

---

[1] Hazeltine, *Judicial Discretion in English Procedure* (Festschrift Otto Gierke), 1055; *Early English Equity* (Essays in Legal History, ed. Vinogradoff), 262.

[2] 2 Edw. III, c. 8. While the Ordinances (1311) c. 32 were in effect, their prohibition of royal interference with litigation was sometimes enforced, as in Y.BB. Edward II (Selden Society), xxii. 315. Three centuries later attempts were made to use royal letters of privy seal to enable infants to suffer common recoveries: Holdsworth, iii. 518.

[3] For some cases on this statute, see Plucknett, *Statutes and their Interpretation*, 142–143.

[4] Below, p. 240.

[5] Plucknett, *op. cit.*, 121–127.

[6] *Fleta*, ii. c. 2 § 1.

[7] Y.BB. Edward II (Selden Society), x. 171 (1311).

[8] 14 Edw. III, stat. 1, c. 5. The commission was to one prelate, two earls and two barons; the judges were to be re-sworn, to refresh their memories. Cf. Hemmant, *Cases in Exchequer Chamber* (Selden Society), i. intro. xlv. For attempts in 1348 to make the statute work, see *Rot. Parl.*, ii. 172 no. 60, 195 no. 82 and 222 no. 64.

public an expression of distrust in the judiciary could only have the effect of making the benches retire still more strictly into the seclusion of their courts and the technicalities of their procedure. Moreover, if the five could not agree, the lords at large undertook to settle the matter—and from this date the lords assert their ascendancy, and treat the judges (and the councillors) as merely assistants in their house.[1]

The common law is therefore beginning to retire to a definite and limited field, resigns its flexibility and declines to be drawn into attempts to remove its own defects: that will henceforth be the province of Parliament. Later still, when Parliament fails to keep pace with the needs of litigants, it will be the Chancellor who will take up the task. This loss is compensated to some extent by the growing independence of the judges. Less and less often do we find them at the council board or giving effect to royal commands from the bench.

COMPETITION BETWEEN COURTS

The formulary system, which once had been a labour-saving device, developed into the system of forms of action which finally stunted and crippled the common law to such an extent that an entirely new system or prerogative courts of equity was needed. Even within the common law itself, the formulaic system was recognised as mischievous, for the common law courts began to compete with one another for business, piling fiction upon fiction in an endeavour to escape from the heavy burden of their history. Most strange of all, the common law courts found themselves champions of the popular cause against the Crown in the seventeenth century, although just a century before they had been loudly condemned by the public for their weakness, their slowness and their costliness.

The Restoration opened a long period of comparative quiescence during which the common law courts remained unchanged until the nineteenth century, thanks to the restoration of equity, which alone made tolerable so archaic a system.

THE EXCHEQUER OF PLEAS

Perhaps the earliest example of competition between common law courts comes from the Exchequer. We have already mentioned the rise of this institution as an accounting organisation, and as an assembly of high officials who combined the audit of the royal accounts with the discussion of related problems as they arose.[2] The development of a law court out of this purely administrative procedure can be clearly traced in the various series of rolls produced in the Exchequer.[3] In

---

[1] Hemmant, *loc. cit.* At this moment, moreover, the judges cease generally to be sworn of the council: J. F. Baldwin, *The King's Council*, 76.

[2] Above, p. 147.

[3] The history is traced in detail in Sir Hilary Jenkinson's introduction to *Select Cases in the Exchequer of Pleas* (Selden Society). Cf. Baldwin, *King's Council*, ch. ix.

its early days the Exchequer kept but one roll, the great roll of the pipe which contained detailed accounts. In the course of business there arose many matters which could not be immediately settled, and so such matters were removed from the pipe roll and reserved for further consideration, being entered on a new series of Memoranda Rolls created for the purpose. There are hints of such rolls under Henry II;[1] they are known to have existed under Richard I, and one has survived for the first year of John (1199–1200).[2] Some of the matters on these rolls called for judicial treatment, and so in time we find a further specialisation in the rolls. In 1220 we have a separate roll of pleas concerning the King's Jews,[3] and in 1236 we have the first roll of the Exchequer of Pleas.[4] The revenue department had become a revenue court. This court, moreover, was essentially a common law court; it used the common law procedure, although in a more stringent form, and apart from revenue cases which formed the bulk of its work, it did useful service in permitting subjects to bring proceedings against officials (especially sheriffs) who had acted irregularly. Such a court was likely to win public sympathy, and although its rolls are not very bulky it seems to have been active.

In 1300 we find a statutory provision that no common pleas shall be heard in the Exchequer,[5] and this is the first great attempt by one common law court to prevent another from competing with it. The Exchequer was in a position to offer substantial advantages to plaintiffs who resorted to it, since Exchequer process extended to Wales and the palatinates (where king's bench and common pleas had no jurisdiction)[6], simple contract debts could be recovered from executors,[7] and wager of law did not lie. This latter rule raised protests in some quarters, and in 1376 wager of law was authorised by parliament (save where the King was party) in the Exchequer, on the ground that jury trial was to the great damage of the people and the impoverishment of the jurors, and caused much delay.[8]

There were several grounds upon which the Exchequer could hear " common pleas "—meaning thereby non-revenue cases. In the first place, the officials of the Exchequer and their servants were privileged: as plaintiffs they could compel their adversaries to answer in the Exchequer court, and as defendants they could refuse to answer save in the Exchequer. Secondly, merchants are frequent litigants in the

---

[1] *Dialogus de Scaccario*, lib. ii. c. 15.

[2] *Memoranda Roll, 1 John* (ed. H. G. Richardson, Pipe Roll Society, 1943).

[3] Printed in *Select Pleas of the Jewish Exchequer* (ed. Hilary Jenkinson, Selden Society).

[4] Printed in *Select Cases in the Exchequer of Pleas* (ed. Hilary Jenkinson, Selden Society).

[5] *Articuli super Cartas* (28 Edw. I), c. 4. (For some earlier such restrictions, see Holdsworth, i. 235.) Contrast Westminster II, c. 11 (below, p. 449).

[6] P. Burton, *Exchequer Practice*, i. 105, ii. 474. *Process into Wales*, Vaughan 395 is a long historical note on the subject.

[7] Cf. below, pp. 647, 741.

[8] *Rot. Parl.*, ii. 337 no. 92.

Exchequer,[1] and in some cases at least, the affairs of merchants, friars and other favoured persons were treated there because the King had so ordered.[2] Furthermore, parties could voluntarily enrol recognisances of debt in the Exchequer records, and if they did so, then any resulting litigation would take place in the Exchequer. Then, too, many decedents died in debt to the Crown, with the result that executors and administrators were constantly before the court. Finally, any Crown debtor could invoke the Crown's very effective machinery against his own debtors, by means of the allegation that by their remissness he was less able to discharge his own debt to the King. This principle is as old as the *Dialogue of the Exchequer*.[3] The earliest cases show the King as co-plaintiff with his debtor against the debtor's debtor;[4] forms vary somewhat, but when the action succeeded, the debt was paid to the Exchequer and not to the plaintiff. There is no trace of the famous writ of *Quominus* under Henry III or Edward I,[5] and the first example so far known is said to be in 1326.[6]

According to Blackstone[7] the allegation of indebtedness to the King contained in the writ of *Quominus* was treated in his day as a fiction; curiously enough Coke and Hale are silent on this development, and so is Burton (writing in 1791). It is impossible to say when this fiction began.[8]

THE EXCHEQUER CHAMBER, 1357

There was one issue, however, upon which the Exchequer won a clear victory. The Court of King's Bench, which from its earliest days had jurisdiction in error from the Court of Common Pleas, in 1338 claimed the right to hear errors from the Court of Exchequer. To this the barons strongly objected and showed from their records that the only jurisdiction in error above them was in the King, who might issue a special commission *ad hoc*. It was becoming evident, however, that

---

[1] Jenkinson, *Exchequer of Pleas* (Selden Society), xcix.

[2] For the text of a " writ of aid " in 1336, see A. Beardwood, *Alien Merchants*, 110. For some earlier examples, see J. C. Davies, *Baronial Opposition to Edward II*, 549 no. 9, 551 no. 14.

[3] *Dialogus de Scaccario*, lib. II, c. 16.

[4] Jenkinson, *op. cit.*, c–ci, who remarks that the practice " is strongly reminiscent of the crown's attitude in the matter of Jewish debts ".

[5] Jenkinson, *loc. cit.* The phrase does occur, however, in writs of distress about 1230, apparently unconnected with judicial proceedings: H. Wurzel, *Origin of Quo Minus*, in Yale Law Journal, xlix. 45.

[6] P. Burton, *Exchequer Practice*, i. 105 (reading 20 Edw. II instead of Burton's impossible date of " 22 Edw. II ").

[7] Blackstone, *Commentaries*, iii. 286.

[8] The allegation was traversable in early times: Jenkinson, *loc. cit.* The statement in Holdsworth i. 240 that the fiction existed in 1345 seems unsupported by the case mentioned: Y.B. 20 Edw. III, i. 16-20. The Exchequer promised not to take jurisdiction by regarding parties as fictitiously the servants of exchequer officials: Ordinances (1311), c. 25, and Exchequer Rules (1323), c. 1 (H. Hall, *Red Book of the Exchequer* (Rolls Series), iii. 848). See generally, H. Wurzel, *Origin of Quo Minus*, Yale Law Journal, xlix. 39.

this traditional method was unsatisfactory, and the commons in parliament in 1348 urged the claims of the King's Bench, but the king would only agree to a commission of errors, composed of the Chancellor, Treasurer and two Justices.[1] Eventually, in 1357, a statute[2] erected a new court to hear errors in the Exchequer, which was to sit in " any council room nigh the exchequer "—hence its name, " Exchequer Chamber ". It was composed of two great officers of state, the Chancellor and the Treasurer, who alone were the judges, but they could call upon the justices of the common law courts as assessors, and could put questions to the barons of the Exchequer. Such a system was clearly unworkable, for as a matter of practical politics it was rarely possible to get two such great men together at any stated date. The commons again prayed for legislation which would give the King's Bench the right to hear error from the Exchequer, but in vain.[3] The barons stood on their statute and let their court decline rather than submit to the King's Bench. Three hundred years later attempts were still being made to render this old statutory court more useful in an age when the Chancellor was too busy and when there was frequently no Treasurer at all.[4]

THE EXCHEQUER CHAMBER FOR DEBATE

At all times judges of the common law courts have discussed important and difficult cases in meetings consisting of all the judges of both Benches, and sometimes the Lord Chancellor and the barons of the Exchequer.[5] Sometimes the Council is also mentioned, and the judgment proceeded from this impressive assembly as a whole.[6] The several benches might sit together on other occasions to debate legal points referred to them by the Crown. At the beginning of the fifteenth century such meetings were often in the " Exchequer Chamber " and the courts slowly developed the practice of themselves referring difficult cases to the Exchequer chamber. On such occasions a decision was reached by the judges and serjeants together,[7] but the judgment was formally pronounced in the

---

[1] *Rot. Parl.*, ii. 168 no. 26; they renewed their petition without result in the next parliament: *ibid.*, 203 no. 25.

[2] 31 Edw. III, stat. 1, c. 12 (1357). For the texts of documents in the controversy, see Y.B. 14 Edward III, xvii ff., and cf. Baldwin, *The King's Council*, 233.

[3] *Rot. Parl.*, iii. 24 no. 105.

[4] Below, p. 171.

[5] For such a meeting as early as 1324, see C. Johnson, *The Exchequer Chamber under Edward II*, English Historical Review, xxi. 726–727. For an earlier and clearer case, see Y.BB. Edward II (Selden Society), xxiv. 8 (1319).

[6] See examples in Sayles, *King's Bench*, i. 148 (1285) and further examples, *ibid.*, ii, intro, lxvii n. 9.

[7] Indeed, in 1478, although all the justices of both benches had concurred on a point, yet it was referred to the Exchequer Chamber where " all the justices *and the serjeants* " reconsidered it; 18 Edw. IV, Pasch. 18, Trin. 8. See Hemmant, *Select Cases in the Exchequer Chamber* (Selden Society), ii. intro. xvi; the choice of the Exchequer as the meeting-place is simply due to the fact that the Exchequer had ample office accommodation.

court where the case originated. Moreover, an argument in the Exchequer chamber could take place only at the instance of the judges hearing the case; it could not be demanded by either party. There might be less formal meetings at Serjeants' Inn, where the judges and serjeants lodged together during term time, and obviously such talks are simply the usual professional conversation of men engaged in a common task; they are not in any sense the proceedings of a court.

The system had merits which unfortunately were not conserved. While it lasted it did much to take the place of a system of appellate courts. Instead of burdening litigants with the expense and delay of taking a case through several courts, in each of which a few judges gave perhaps hurried decisions, under this system the case went at once for discussion by all the judges of all the courts sitting together in order to reach a definitive ruling, which very naturally was accepted with the greatest respect as settling the point.

KING'S BENCH AND TRESPASS

Defeated in its attempt to assert a jurisdiction in error over the Exchequer, the King's Bench next engaged in a conflict with the Court of Common Pleas. Although the King's Bench had always tried aggravated trespasses, and those where royal interests were involved, yet the ordinary run of trespass cases had always been in the Common Pleas. In 1372 the commons complained that the clerks of the King's Bench (apparently by arrangement with the Chancery) had contrived to prevent writs of trespass being made returnable in the Common Pleas, and procured them to be directed instead to the King's Bench. This caused hardship, as men of wealth already had to keep standing attorneys in the Common Pleas for their general affairs, and the King's Bench was still a perambulating body. The reply to the complaint seems to indicate that once again the King's Bench was defeated.[1]

THE COMMON LAW SIDE OF CHANCERY

We have said nothing so far of the Chancery.[2] Its functions were in fact almost entirely secretarial in its early days, and it is not until about 1307 that we can say that it has become an independent office free from household control.[3] Indeed, " office " was thought to be the most suitable word for the Chancery, as we can see from *Fleta* (*c.* 1290) who refrains from using the word " court " in this connection.[4]

[1] *Rot. Parl.*, ii. 311 no. 21.

[2] On the difficult point of origins, see V. H. Galbraith, *Public Records*, 36 ff.; F. E. Harmer, *Anglo-Saxon Writs*, 57 ff.

[3] Tout, *Place of Edward II*, 60; *Collected Papers*, ii. 143; Sayles, *Household of the Chancery*, Scottish Historical Review, xxv. 109.

[4] *Fleta*, ii. 13; cf. Pollock and Maitland, i. 193-197. As late as 1339 the common law side of Chancery was open to the objection of being merely an " office ": Y.B. 12 & 13 Edward III (Rolls Series), 98.

The Chancellor was often the King's principal adviser in political matters, but his staff was a highly specialised body of clerks. The duties of many of them were partly mechanical—copies of all important documents which passed the Great Seal were prepared upon the voluminous rolls which survive in thousands in the Public Records Office. They had also the duty of drafting and writing the original writs which were so vital to the conduct of litigation. In the early thirteenth century it would seem that they had a part to play in the formation of the common law, for it was they who sanctioned the numerous variants upon traditional forms which applicants urged them to make, and thus indirectly extended the scope of the common law. Such powers, however, were peculiar to the early formative period of the century. By its close it was already well established that the issue of a writ from the Chancery was no guarantee that the writ was valid at common law, for the judges asserted their right to quash writs which they considered unsuitable. Hence the real control over the issue of writs soon passed to the common law courts, for it was they who had the last word in sustaining or quashing the writs brought before them in litigation. The Chancery therefore exerted little influence over the creation of new writs after the thirteenth century, and the "register of writs" never became an official Chancery collection.[1] It soon becomes evident that the parties themselves, or their legal advisers, draft the writs they desire, get them engrossed and sealed in the Chancery, and then support them by such arguments as they can when the time comes to plead them in the common law courts. One thing seems certain, and that is that the business of issuing writs was not the origin of either the common law or the equity jurisdiction of the Chancellor.[2]

Of much greater importance were the powers connected with the feudal rights of the Crown. When a tenant-in-chief died, a writ issued from Chancery to inquire by means of a jury into the lands of the late tenant and to ascertain the Crown's rights to primer seisin, relief, the wardship of his heir if an infant, and to arrange for the dower (and sometimes the re-marriage) of his widow. Interested parties could intervene, and so a good deal of litigation arose under the head of "traverses of offices", as these proceedings were called. Similarly, when the Crown made grants of lands or offices by letters patent, persons whose rights were affected could bring proceedings to repeal them.[3]

[1] Plucknett, *Case and the Statute of Westminster II*, Columbia Law Review, xxxi. at 792 ff. For the text of the statute, see above, p. 28. For valuable light on how writs were obtained, see Sayles, *King's Bench*, ii, intro. lxxxvi.

[2] The oft-repeated statement that these clerks were always civilians or canonists seems to have originated in nothing more substantial than a guess by the seventeenth-century civilian Dr Duck, *Use and Authority of the Civil Law* (p. xxix of the 1724 translation). This may have been the case, however, in the reign of Elizabeth (Spence, *Equity Jurisdiction*, i. 363 e). Cf. Maitland, *English Law and the Renaissance*, 85–86, and *Register of Writs*, Select Essays in Anglo-American Legal History, ii. 558.

[3] The matter is well debated in Y.B. 16 Edward III, i. 108.

It also had important jurisdiction in petitions of right and *monstrans de droit*. The judges were so frequently engaged upon business of this sort in the Chancery that the Commons complained in Parliament that the courts of common law suffered considerable delays.[1] These powers, which are in frequent use from the reign of Edward III onwards, are clearly derived from the administrative functions of the office, and can be compared with those of the common law side of the Exchequer with which they were in some cases concurrent. It is a difficult question how far the common law jurisdiction was an origin of the equitable jurisdiction, which may have had, in the main, a different history.[2]

THE NEED FOR DE-CENTRALISATION

The " impoverishment of the jurors " and the " ruin of the country " by jury trial was a real problem. When Henry II instituted the petty assizes he seems to have made the requirement that as far as possible the assize of twelve should meet in the county where the land lay—in the county where the assizemen resided. With the use of the jury in the Court of Common Pleas a similar requirement soon arose for the jury to come from the county where the cause of action lay. While the judges of the Bench were continually touring with the King, there was a fair chance of juries being taken in or near their own counties, but with the tendency for the Bench to stay in one place it was becoming more and more necessary for the jury to come to the court, instead of the court travelling about and taking the juries locally. The Great Charter[3] settled the most pressing part of the question by enacting that most of the assizes (which were then the most frequently used of the common law actions) must be taken in the county where the land lay, and as the assizemen had to be neighbours from that same county, they did not have to travel very far. Hence the Crown sent commissioners at regular intervals to take the assizes in the counties.

THE *NISI PRIUS* SYSTEM

As for the Bench in the reign of King John, it was sufficiently important for the Charter to enact that it should no longer travel but sit permanently in some fixed place. This was perhaps convenient for suitors, but as the business of the court increased it was a grave hardship to bring jurors from the remoter parts of England to Westminster; indeed, in many cases it was utterly impossible. The solution of the problem was all the more difficult now that the Common Pleas (and for

[1] *Rot. Parl.*, iii. 474 no. 95 (1401).

[2] See below, pp. 180 ff. and the important and original paper by A D. Hargreaves, *Equity and the Latin side of Chancery*, Law Quarterly Review, lxviii. 481. Pike had taken a somewhat similar view: Y.B. 12 & 13 Edward III, intro., cv–cxi.

[3] Magna Carta (1215), c. 18; (1225), c. 12.

that matter, the Exchequer) were fixed at Westminster.[1] The verbal altercation which resulted in the formulation of irrevocable pleadings had to take place (at this date) in court before the judges, who supervised the process and helped the parties to reach a suitable issue. Once the issue was reached, however, it was a simple business to put the issue to the jury and record their verdict. This second process, it was realised, need not take place at Westminster. As early as 1196 parties were given a day at Westminster " *nisi justiciarii interim veniant* " in Norfolk,[2] and in the early years of Henry III justices in eyre would sometimes order juries to be taken locally (instead of before themselves) in order to save trouble to all concerned,[3] and would likewise order the verdicts of locally taken inquests to be returned if necessary to Westminster.[4] This separation of fact-finding from the rest of legal procedure gave the solution to the problem, and so legislation beginning with Edward I in the Statute of Westminster II, c. 30 (1285) slowly built up the system of *nisi prius*, whereby actions which began at Westminster in the Court of Common Pleas, when once they had been pleaded to an issue, could be continued by taking the jury's verdict in the county before justices of *nisi prius*, instead of compelling the jurymen to undertake a costly journey to Westminster as had formerly been the case. The rise of this system had the result that a great deal of jury work took place in the country and not in Westminster; such proceedings were rarely reported, for the compilers of the Year Books were most concerned with what went on at Westminster Hall, and so the whole procedure of putting evidence before a jury, charging it and taking its verdict is an obscure matter, for neither the reporters nor the rolls give us very much information.[5] Of these two sources the rolls are perhaps the more promising for the early history of the law of evidence.

The commissioners of assize need not be justices (although they were frequently serjeants, and local knights had to sit with them); the commissioners of *nisi prius*, on the other hand, had to be sworn justices. At the same time, it was a frequent practice to issue special commissions from time to time to justices and others authorising them to hear and determine (*oyer* and *terminer*) all pleas arising in a particular county, or all pleas of a particular type—sometimes to hear and determine one case of special importance. Furthermore, commissions of gaol delivery were a frequent necessity in order to try the persons indicted before various authorities. As a matter of obvious convenience these commissions were eventually issued to the same commissioners. Justices

---

[1] Magna Carta (1215), c. 17; (1225), c. 11.

[2] *Curia Regis Rolls,* vii. 332.

[3] *Eyre Rolls of Gloucestershire, &c.* (Selden Society, vol. 59), nos. 715, 1184; cf. Lady Stenton's introduction, lvi ff. Both cases were in 1221.

[4] *Ibid.,* no. 1458 (the date is 1222).

[5] The problem is fully discussed in Turner's introduction to Y.BB. Edward II (Selden Society), ix.

had to be sent at stated intervals to take *nisi prius* trials; the same justices
could also take the assizes, and it was convenient to give them *oyer* and
terminer and gaol delivery[1] powers as well. Hence there arose the
circuit system whereby the justices of the superior courts made regular
tours of the country and thus brought the courts of Westminster into
direct contact with local needs. To complete their powers, it was
customary to make the judges of assize justices of the peace in the counties
they visited.

JUSTICES OF THE PEACE

Besides these travelling commissions, both new and old, which were
sent through the country from Westminster, there developed a different
type of commission composed of local gentry who were assigned first to
keep the peace, and afterwards to be justices of the peace. From the
end of the twelfth century local knights and gentry, often described as
" keepers of the peace ", were occasionally called upon to co-operate
with the sheriff in enforcing law.[2] Their duties were principally of an
administrative and police character. The Statute of Winchester (1285)
laid down the rudiments of a scheme for maintaining order, but created
no machinery for carrying it out. It thus became the practice to set up
commissioners under varying titles to enforce the statute. From the
beginning of Edward III's reign a stream of legislation begins to enlarge
their powers. Nor were their powers entirely statutory, for the Crown
frequently increased or diminished the powers of keepers of the peace
merely by changes in the terms of their commission, and regardless of the
state of the statutory law existing at the moment.[3] As before, they were
to receive prisoners and to produce them to the justices of gaol delivery—
and here it seems that the Crown showed some distrust of the sheriff
who ordinarily would have performed these duties; indeed, the justices
of gaol delivery were given authority in 1330 to punish the sheriff if he
abused his powers of releasing prisoners upon bail.[4] Very soon the
keepers of the peace were allowed not only to keep prisoners, but to
try them; in 1344 it was enacted " that two or three of the best people
of each county should be assigned as guardians of the peace by the
King's commission ", and that these keepers should be associated with

---

[1] The exact power conferred by each of these commissions has never been exactly determined, and a convenient theory was propounded that it was unnecessary to distinguish
between the different commissions. The principal statutes are *De finibus Levatis*, 27 Edw. I,
c. 3 (1299); 2 Edw. III, c. 2 (1328); 4 Edw. III, c. 2 (1330).

[2] An order of 1195 in Stubbs, *Select Charters*, 257–258, is generally cited in this connection
as foreshadowing the " conservators " or " keepers " of the peace. It has been suggested
that developments in London influenced government policy: A. H. Thomas, *Plea and Memoranda Rolls, 1323–1364*, xi. ff. In the north and west of England an ancient system survived
which long served instead of justices of the peace in those parts: R. Stewart-Brown, *The
Serjeants of the Peace* (1936).

[3] On this and other matters in this paragraph, see the massive study by B. H. Putnam,
Proceedings before Justices of the Peace (Ames Foundation, 1938).

[4] 4 Edw. III, c. 2.

lawyers in a commission of oyer and terminer for the trial and punishment of felonies and trespasses against the peace.[1] There was some hesitation about entrusting wide powers to the keepers of the peace, and legislative policy fluctuated;[2] but the keepers (now called " justices ") by themselves, without the association of professional lawyers with them, exercised judicial powers regularly from 1368 onwards.[3]

Meanwhile, in 1349 came the Black Death, and in 1351 began the Statutes of Labourers, which attempted to regulate the disorganised labour market. This labour legislation set up elaborate machinery for fixing prices and wages and enforcing labour contracts, and established " justices of labourers " for the difficult task of enforcing it. Shortly afterwards the keepers of the peace and the justices of the labourers were merged into one commission with the new title of " justices of the peace ",[4] which first appears officially in 1361. For the rest of the middle ages, and indeed ever since, hardly a Parliament passed without adding some new duty to the work of the justices of the peace. At first they received salaries payable out of the fines which they inflicted, but as time went on the change in the value of money made their wage too small to be worth collecting; it has now long been obsolete.[5] They were and generally still are laymen and not lawyers,[6] but it must be remembered that during the middle ages the average landowner had a fairly good knowledge of elementary law; what further technical assistance they needed was supplied by the clerk of the peace who served as a professional clerk to the justices. The clerk of the justices was frequently appointed also to the office of clerk of the Crown, the duties of which were to act as a permanent local secretary to the travelling justices who came down from Westminster to hold the pleas of the Crown. The clerk of the peace was technically the deputy appointed by the *Custos Rotulorum*, a mysterious official of whose history very little is known.[7]

The justices of the peace, like most other mediaeval bodies, held two sorts of meetings, large and small. The large meetings held four times a year are called quarter sessions. In the fourteenth century they must have looked something like the older Eyre, although on a smaller scale. Grand juries were charged, made presentments, and the persons so

---

[1] 18 Edw. III, stat. 2, c. 2.

[2] Details in B. H. Putnam, Transactions of the Royal Historical Society (1929), 19 ff.

[3] 42 Edw. III, c. 6. The keepers frequently received powers of trial by commissions of 1350 and onwards (Putnam, *op. cit.*, 43), and in 1361 by 34 Edw. III, c. 1, they were given powers of trial by statute (in Lodge and Thornton, *Constitutional Documents*, 331–332); nevertheless trial powers were withheld in commissions issued in 1364 (Putnam, *op. cit.*, 46), in spite of the statute.

[4] Putnam, *Proceedings before Justices of the Peace* (Ames Foundation, 1938), and Transactions of the Royal Historical Society (1929), 19–48.

[5] By the eighteenth century a system of fees had come into existence, apparently without authority, and a " trading justice " could do very well out of his office: J. F. Stephen, *History of Criminal Law*, i. 230.

[6] The chairman and deputy chairman of quarter sessions are generally lawyers of standing.

[7] See Putnam, *Early Treatises on Justices of the Peace*, 102–104.

indicted were forthwith tried. Until the eighteenth century, quarter sessions tried capital cases, which after that date they reserved for the Justices of Assize. Quarter sessions also possessed an appellate jurisdiction from petty sessions. Petty sessions on the other hand consisted of two or more justices acting in the most informal manner for minor business and the lesser offences entrusted to them for summary trial without a jury, by virtue of numerous statutes in Tudor times and later.[1] Both quarter and petty sessions were ultimately subject to the Court of King's Bench, which by a writ of *certiorari* could remove and review their proceedings.

THE FATE OF THE LOCAL COURTS

The establishment of the justices of the peace marks the end of the practical importance of the old communal jurisdictions which we described in chapter I. Even in boroughs, where such jurisdictions as the court leet survived longest, the competition of the justices of the peace was severe, and ultimately successful. Whether the justices of the peace were deliberately designed to take the place of the local jurisdictions, which had already declined, or whether, on the other hand, they were part of a conscious policy whereby the Crown attempted to supplant local jurisdictions (dependent as they usually were upon the sheriff), it is impossible to say; there may be some truth in both views.[2] It is certainly significant that the justices of the peace were fairly closely supervised by the central courts and ultimately by the Council; in this way they became not merely the local representatives of the royal jurisdiction, but also to a large extent the administrative and political agents of the King and Council. During the later Stuart period the government tried to exploit to the utmost the political influence of the justices of the peace.

This state of affairs, however, is not to be found in the fourteenth century when the institution was for the first time rapidly developing; in the critical reign of Edward III it is beyond doubt that the demand for the expansion of powers of justices of the peace came from the commons in parliament, and that the opposition to the demand came from the council and the Crown lawyers. It is presumably the Tudors who inaugurated the new policy of making the justices of the peace their instruments in local government.

Politics apart, the justices of the peace were a notable essay in decentralisation in criminal jurisdiction, and the development of the *nisi prius* system contributed to the same result in matters of civil litigation. The justices from Westminster came down into the county, bringing with them the advantages of metropolitan law administered in every county town. The problem of over-centralisation created at the end of the twelfth century was thus satisfactorily solved—at least for a moment.

[1] The earliest is 11 Hen. VII, c. 3. Much material is collected by Frankfurter and Corcoran, *Petty Federal Offenses and Trial by Jury*, Harvard Law Review xxxix. 917 at 924 ff.

[2] See the suggestions by Miss Putnam, *Proceedings* (Ames Foundation), xxxvi.

CHAPTER 7

THE TUDORS AND THE COMMON LAW COURTS

As the last chapter has shown, the fourteenth and fifteenth centuries were devoted to consolidating the monopoly enjoyed by the common law courts. In criminal justice alone did they allow developments to take place outside the system, and no doubt the reason was that the profession as a whole was not particularly interested in this arduous and unremunerative branch of law. The justices of the peace were therefore given a fairly free hand at the instance of the House of Commons, which seems to have felt in a dim sort of way that here was a field in which local self-government could be developed.[1]

The next chapter will discuss the darker side of this picture, and the emergency measures which the prerogative courts resorted to in restoring tranquillity after the Wars of the Roses. But although (as that chapter will show) the great contribution of the Tudors lay in the field of prerogative courts, nevertheless they did carry out some notable reforms in the common law courts as well.

THE COURT OF EXCHEQUER

We have already noticed the growth of the Exchequer of Plea, and its pretensions to become more than a purely revenue court.[2] During the middle ages it seems to have held common pleas from time to times but certainly not in any great number. During the sixteenth century it is said to have claimed a general jurisdiction over many sorts of common pleas by means of the fiction that one of the parties was a Crown debtor,[3] and this claim was admitted. For a long time the judges of the

---

[1] This point is well made by Professor Putnam in Transactions of the Royal Historical Society (1929), 47.

[2] Above, p. 159.

[3] The famous writ of *Quominus* is described in Holdsworth, i. 240; cf. above, p. 161.

court (technically called Barons[1]) had been lawyers (although not necessarily serjeants). The history of this has never been explored, but it is clear that, by means unknown, the barons of the exchequer steadily raised their position until, in 1579, Queen Elizabeth, in making a new appointment, expressly gave the new baron an equal status with the judges of the other common law courts, and for the future the barons of the Exchequer shared with the justices of the King's Bench and the Common Pleas the duties of going on circuit. Henceforth there were to be three common law courts of first instance.

THE EXCHEQUER CHAMBER, 1585

Late in the reign of Elizabeth still further confusion[2] was created by the erection of yet a third court in the Exchequer chamber. The Court of King's Bench had succeeded in acquiring a good deal of jurisdiction which once was peculiar to the Court of Common Pleas, and so acted as a court of first instance in these matters. If such actions had been brought in the Common Pleas, error would have lain to the King's Bench; but when they were now brought in the King's Bench in the first instance, error lay only to Parliament. Here the difficulty arose. Parliaments were originally held several times a year; Elizabeth summoned but ten in a reign of forty-five years, and so for long periods there was no court in existence which could hear the errors of the King's Bench. To meet this situation two statutes[3] erected a new court to hear errors from the King's Bench. This court was to consist of all the judges of the other two common law courts—the Common Pleas, and those Barons of the Exchequer who were also serjeants—sitting together in the Exchequer chamber, and at least six were necessary before judgment could be given. Their decision was subject to further proceedings in error in Parliament, and the second statute explained that a party could still go directly from King's Bench to Parliament if he chose.[4] There was thus the disadvantage of an intermediate court of appeal, together with the anomaly that the use of that court was optional. A still further defect was that it was very difficult to assemble six of the justices and barons. The statutory body was not a court with fixed meetings every term, but a special assembly which might or might not meet—and it seems to have depended upon the influence of the litigants whether it met or not. If it did not meet at the date to which the case had been adjourned,

---

[1] They are described as barons as early as the *Dialogus de Scaccario*, i. 7. Bracton, f. 116 *b*, observes that earls and barons must be amerced by their peers, and that the barons of the exchequer are their peers for this purpose.

[2] Cf. pp. 161–162 above.

[3] 27 Eliz. c. 8 (1585) amended by 31 Eliz. c. 1 (1589); both will be found in Tanner, *Tudor Constitutional Documents*, 343–346.

[4] Cases which were brought to the King's Bench on error from other courts were reviewable only in Parliament, and not in the new court; likewise proceedings to which the Crown was a party,

then the record was discontinued. True, the second statute remedied this by saying that the absence of the judges shall not discontinue the process, but no effective means were ever provided for getting the court together within a reasonable period.

The same inadequate concession was made in respect of the other Exchequer chamber body to hear errors from the Exchequer of Pleas,[1] and with the same disappointing results.

THE KING'S BENCH

The fact that these special arrangements had to be made for the review of judgments given in the King's Bench will show that that court was enjoying unusually good business during the sixteenth century. The preamble to the earlier of the two statutes cited explains that the new court shall hear writs of error brought on " actions or suits of debt, detinue, covenant, account, action on the case, *ejectione firmæ*, and trespass " in the King's Bench. These seven actions properly belonged to the Court of Common Pleas. Trespass (and *ejectione firmæ* resembled trespass) seems also to have been part of the original jurisdiction of the King's Bench, but during the middle ages the only trespasses usually brought in the King's Bench were those of unusual violence or importance.[2] Most of this jurisdiction, therefore, had been acquired at a later period, and by somewhat devious means.

We have already mentioned the conflict of the King's Bench with the Exchequer and with the Common Pleas in the fourteenth century;[3] in the fifteenth century a second effort brought the King's Bench once more into competition, if not into conflict, with the Common Pleas. The device employed in order to acquire the wide jurisdiction mentioned in Elizabeth's statute[4] of 1585 was fairly commonly used in the reign of Henry VI and was in constant use throughout the Tudor period. A bill of Middlesex made the defendant actually or fictitiously a prisoner in the custody of the marshall of the court's marshalsea. This done, the court could entertain any sort of action against him since he was already within the jurisdiction of the court—a principle, moreover, which most courts professed. In such cases the proceedings were by bill instead of by original writ. Before the end of the century means were found[5] whereby the defendant could be really arrested if he would not voluntarily admit that he was technically in the custody of the

---

[1] Above, p. 162. By 16 Car. II, c. 2 (1664) the presence of the two chief justices sufficed to continue the process, but judgment had to be by the Treasurer and Chancellor; by 19 & 20 Car. II, c. 9 (1668) a Lord Keeper could give judgment when there was no Treasurer or Chancellor.

[2] Above, p. 163.

[3] Above, pp. 160–162.

[4] Above, p. 171.

[5] The details are discussed in Reeves, *History of English Law* (1869), ii. 602; for a summary see Holdsworth, i. 219 ff.; below, p. 387.

marshall, and so the new procedure served as the complete equivalent of an original writ.   Throughout the sixteenth century the court enjoyed this usurped jurisdiction, with curious results.   The competition between King's Bench and Common Pleas was sometimes not merely a matter of offering procedural advantages, but sometimes even in offering better substantive law.   Thus in at least one matter, which we shall refer to later,[1] the two courts deliberately competed by offering two different rules of law for litigants to choose from, and in the end it was the more enlightened rule which prevailed.

PREROGATIVE WRITS

There is another aspect of the King's Bench during this period which deserves attention, and that is the growth of the " prerogative " writs.   The history of *mandamus*, *certiorari*, prohibition and some other similar writs is still unwritten,[2] but it is clear that they first become important during the Tudor period, and that they were a proper development of the jurisdiction of the King's Bench, for that court had long been close to the Council in the exercise of royal discretion in judicial matters.   The writs themselves seem to have been originally mere administrative orders from superior officials to their subordinates telling them to do something, to give some information, or the like. Clearly, the King's Bench was making a great contribution to public law when it adapted these writs to legal purposes, and assumed the task of directing them as occasion required to various departments of central and local government.   When one considers the enormous activity of the King's Council under the Tudors, it is a little surprising that the Council should have allowed the court to handle the prerogative writs, for it seems just as likely that the Council itself should have undertaken to supervise local officers by its own purely administrative machinery. If it had done so it is clear that our constitutional law would have been very different.

THE TUDORS AND LOCAL COURTS

In spite of their centralising policy, the Tudors realised that there was a proper place and function for the older local jurisdictions and so they attempted to prevent their continuing decline.   To this end an act[3] was passed in 1601 which is a striking example of the unforeseen effects of legislation.   It was enacted that in certain personal actions a

---

[1] See below, p. 644.

[2] S. A. de Smith, *The Preroga   Writs*, Cambridge Law Journal, xi. 40 (1951) is the best historical introduction to the whole group.   The history of *habeas corpus* has been studied in full, however; see Jenks, *The Prerogative Writs in English Law*, Yale Law Journal, xxxii. 523, and *The Story of Habeas Corpus*, Law Quarterly Review, xviii. 64–77 (reprinted in *Select Essays in Anglo-American Legal History*, ii. 531–548); and the extended treatment given in Holdsworth, ix. 108–125, x. 658–672; above, p. 57.

[3] 43 Eliz. c. 6 (1601).

successful plaintiff shall not recover more costs than damages, if the justices certify that the damages are less than forty shillings.   The object of the act was to exclude small cases from the courts at Westminster, where costs were out of all proportion to the issues at stake. The statute operated not on the verdict but on the judges' certificate. Evasion of the act became general,[1] and in many cases judges were loath to grant a certificate which would deprive a successful plaintiff of his costs.   Full use of it was not made until the middle of the eighteenth century, but in the meantime other statutes[2] continued its policy, notably in actions of slander.[3]   This legislation failed entirely in its object of reviving the local courts and excluding small cases from the central courts, but it did have the curious result of distinguishing arbitrarily between trespass (which was within the statute) and case (which was outside of the statute) as remedies for personal injuries.   It thus became perilous to bring trespass on a battery if there was a possibility of getting a verdict of only nominal damages.   Such actions are therefore generally framed in case for negligence.[4]

THE TUDOR FINANCIAL COURTS

These courts have never been studied in detail and so little is known of them apart from the statutes creating them.   If they were to be investigated, however, it might appear that the Tudors were not so prejudiced against the common law as is often supposed.   It is perfectly true, as we shall see, that the Tudors developed the prerogative and equitable jurisdictions to a remarkable degree, but the creation of the financial courts seems to show that they were equally appreciative of common law forms, and were ready to use them on suitable occasions. Beside Chancery, Star Chamber and the Court of Requests, we must in fairness place those predominantly common law courts which were equally the creation of the Tudors, the Courts of Augmentations, First Fruits, Wards, Liveries (later combined with the Court of Wards), and Surveyors.[5]

The Court of Augmentations was erected by statute[6] in 1536 partly as a department of audit, partly as an estate office, and partly as a franchise court (modelled in part on the chamber of the duchy of Lancaster[7]) to deal with the vast quantity of lands confiscated from the monasteries upon their suppression.   Then, in 1540, the Court of First Fruits and

[1] Bacon, *Abridgement*, Costs B; Holdsworth, i. 74 n. 7.

[2] 22 & 23 Car. II. c. 9, s. 136 (1670); below, p. 461.

[3] 21 James I, c. 16 (1624); below, p. 495.

[4] Below, pp. 461–462; this resulted from the act of 1670.

[5] So, too, the Court of the Common Weal, below, p. 183.

[6] 27 Hen. VIII, c. 27.

[7] On the Court of Duchy Chamber, see Holdsworth, i. 116 and R. Somerville, *The Duchy of Lancaster Council and Court of Duchy Chamber*, Transactions of the Royal Historical Society (1941), 159.

Tenths was erected[1] to manage sundry payments hitherto made to the popes, and recently transferred to the Crown.

In the same year, the Court of Wards was similarly constituted to manage the ancient feudal revenues of the Crown, and especially to enforce the rights of wardship and marriage,[2] in 1540. As Coke[3] observed, an office in that court was partly " ministerial " and partly judicial, so that the exercise of administrative as well as judicial powers by the same institution is particularly remarkable. In the next year a Court of Surveyors was established to manage other portions of the royal estates.[4] It is noteworthy that these bodies were primarily administrative departments for the management on business lines of a vast quantity of property, but they were given judicial powers which were very likely to be used when the Crown itself was a party. From this point of view they resembled the old Exchequer, and it has been suggested that the example of the Exchequer practice was the inspiration for certain provisions which facilitated claims in these courts by subjects against the Crown.[5] As courts they were not oppressive (although no doubt feudalism in itself gave rise to hardships). It is interesting to note that when the rights of the subject in litigation against the Crown were thoroughly examined in *Pawlett* v. *Attorney-General*[6] and later in the *Bankers' Case*[7] the practice of the Exchequer and the Court of Augmentations was discussed.[8]

A curious point arose later in the reign when Henry VIII by letters patent dissolved and re-founded the Court of Augmentations and abolished the Court of Surveyors, although they had been created by statute. Under Edward VI doubts arose as to the propriety of this, and so an act was passed which grudgingly condoned this use of the prerogative.[9] Queen Mary attempted (unsuccessfully) the still more curious feat of dissolving the Court of Augmentations, and (the next day) uniting it with the Exchequer.[10]

---

[1] 32 Hen. VIII, c. 45.

[2] 32 Hen. VIII, c. 46. By 33 Hen. VIII, c. 22, it became the Court of Wards and Liveries. Its history is admirably told in H. E. Bell, *History and Records of the Court of Wards and Liveries* (1953).

[3] *Auditor Curle's Case*, 11 Rep. 2 b.

[4] 33 Hen. VIII, c. 39. In establishing this court, Henry VIII seems to have been developing the curious office of " Surveyor of the King's Prerogative " which his father created in 1508; *Calendar of Patent Rolls, 1494–1509*, 591.

[5] Holdsworth, ix. 35.

[6] Hardres, 465 (1668).

[7] 14 S.T. 1 (1690–1700).

[8] A few extracts from the many statutes erecting and modifying these courts can be seen in Tanner, *Tudor Constitutional Documents*; for a general account of them, it is still necessary to consult Reeves, iii. 293–300. They are entitled to be called common law courts, although they were organised on the plan of Chancery, for it was from the common law side of Chancery and the revenue side of the Exchequer that they drew their inspiration.

[9] 7 Edw. VI, c. 3 (1553).

[10] Reeves, *History of the English Law* (ed. Finlayson), iii. 296–297.

CHAPTER 8

THE RISE OF THE PREROGATIVE COURTS

The previous chapter has told only half the story of Tudor reform in the sphere of law, for besides the common law courts the Tudors also inherited a group of institutions which modern historians describe as prerogative courts. The ancient common law courts had been consecrated by the centuries; the Tudor financial courts had been solemnly established by parliamentary statutes; but the courts to be considered in this chapter could claim neither antiquity nor legislative sanction. Some of them had grown up imperceptibly in various departments of government or around some officer of state; others were erected by royal commission. There was nothing irregular or " unconstitutional " in this, and the legitimacy of these institutions was undoubted. We have already seen, even in the fourteenth century, that the powers of Justices of the Peace owed as much to their royal commissions as to the statutes of Parliament.

The principal characteristic of prerogative courts, apart from their peculiar origins, was that they did not use the ancient system of common law writs, forms of action, or procedure. Instead, they used various forms of bill or petition between party and party, while crown proceedings could be begun by information, citation and like. The fundamental limitation on their jurisdiction came from the common law rule that a man could not lose his land, save by a royal (which was interpreted as a common-law) writ.   Legal estates in real property were thus beyond their reach.[1]   It likewise followed that prerogative courts could not try treason or felony, for the forfeiture or escheat of land would be involved. During the Tudor age these courts nevertheless elaborated important bodies of law such as equity in the Chancery, maritime and commercial law in the Admiralty[2] and Court of Requests, libel and slander and much criminal law in the Star Chamber, and so on.

THE NEED FOR NEWER INSTITUTIONS

We have frequently insisted that the common law was essentially the law of land.   The implications of this fact were very far-reaching. Its procedure was designed to reach people who owned land, and consequently was directed principally against the land rather than the person. The King's Court was at first concerned with the king's tenants and their feudal rights and duties, and such people could be most surely reached through their feudal holdings.   When the common law of the King's Court was becoming the common law of the country, it had to deal with very different problems.   Other heads of law besides real property had to be developed, and litigants of the newer type were not always landowners of any consequence, although they may have had other forms of wealth.   The old procedure was not always effective in these cases.   The common law procedure was generally patient and long-suffering, for it well knew that the tenant's land at least could not be removed from its jurisdiction.   It knew also that haste was practically undesirable, for agriculture was an exacting pursuit which made it impossible for a landowner to leave his estate at a moment's notice. Relics of this still persist, for the long vacation of the courts and universities was once necessary to permit bench, bar and litigants to reap and garner their crops and plough their lands.   Fixed terms, widely spaced, were designed to enable court work to fit in with agricultural work.[3]

With the growing complication of society, law had to deal with people who could not be reached quickly, if at all, by means of a procedure directed against land—with people, that is to say, who could not be identified with certain acres.   Similarly, there were matters which could best be settled by securing the prompt personal attendance of parties, and by giving them direct personal commands to act or to desist in certain matters.   The common law rarely achieved anything so logically direct as this action *in personam*, simply because its main pre-occupation was real property, and in that particular subject it was as convenient to reach a man by attacking his land, as later admiralty found it useful to reach a man by attacking his ship.

[1] This did not prevent Chancery from adjudicating upon uses, or the Council in Star Chamber from awarding possession.

[2] For the Admiralty courts, see below, pp. 660 ff.

[3] Plucknett, *Legal Chronology*, in Handbook of Dates, ed. C. R. Cheney.

Again, the common law was slow to admit the evidence of parties and witnesses. There was in fact little need for such evidence in the early days of the common law, for its main concern was with records and documents (to which it attached exaggerated importance) or else with such publicly notorious facts as seisin, which were better proved by a jury than by the interested statements of parties or their friends. For minor matters where no deeds were used compurgation was good enough. Here again, the development of law beyond the confines of real property made it desirable to collect evidence, especially from the parties themselves. How useful this could be was apparent from the success with which the canonists were using written depositions.

If any further reason for using such a method were needed, it could be found by observing the decline of the jury. Especially in the fifteenth century there are complaints that juries were packed, bribed, intimidated, partial and difficult to obtain within any reasonable space of time. Distrust of juries is an important factor in the early popularity of equity courts.

Finally, there were those who favoured as a remedy to all this the direct business methods of the administrator. They felt that there were cases which could not be satisfactorily handled by the common law with its writs, its delays, its pleadings, its limited resources in the finding of facts and the awarding of judgment, and its weakness in the face of disorder and corruption. The abandonment of court forms and the substitution of executive methods, moreover, brought with it other consequences. Some of the substantive rules of the common law, defensible enough when considered purely from a technical point of view, seemed unjust to the unlearned who had to suffer from them, and so we need not be surprised that there grew up a desire for more equitable rules as well as more effective procedure.

THE COUNCIL AND PETITIONS

Persons who desired such extraordinary relief addressed themselves to the King and his Council. As the ultimate source of jurisdiction the King had long been accustomed to receive complaints from persons who alleged that they were unable, in law or in fact, to obtain redress in the usual courts. It has been suggested[1] that Edward I was glad to encourage these approaches, but was compelled by their numbers, and by the need of checking the handling of them by his subordinates, to insist that they be presented in writing, as petitions. In doing this, he was following papal practice, and like the popes, soon found it necessary to devise a procedure by which the easy cases were dispatched to the departments and dealt with by officials, while difficult matters came before him and the Council, in order to prevent the work of Parliament

[1] L. Ehrlich, *Proceedings against the Crown*, 95.

being obstructed by their number.[1] It soon became normal for large panels of "receivers" and "triers" of petitions to be set up at the beginning of every parliament. When Parliaments were less frequent, it seems that these applications (which continued to increase rapidly during the later fourteenth century), finally constituted a large and steady charge upon the Council's time.

Just as one part of the local enforcement problem was attacked by setting up the new institution of justices of the peace for local matters, so the deficiencies of the central courts were being supplied by the King's Council. For a time, Parliament had occasionally served as a court of royal discretion,[2] but by the middle of the fourteenth century Parliament itself had become an institution which to some extent could be regarded as separate from the Council.[3] The Council nevertheless remained in its ancient position of a small group of officials, household officers, clerks and advisers, continually attendant upon the King, and therefore exercising in his name that residuum of discretion and equity which was inseparable from the royal person. As Parliament became more settled in its powers, petitioners who sought extraordinary relief addressed themselves to the Council; and in any case, even if their petitions had been presented in Parliament, it was most likely that it would be the Council which actually passed upon them.

Indeed, a variety of addresses occur in the petitions of the middle and later fourteenth century. Sometimes they are sent to the King, sometimes to the Council or the Parliament, and sometimes to the Chancellor or some household official. In any case it was the Council which generally took action, irrespective of the address upon the petition. The administrative and political duties of the Council were already exceedingly heavy, and the mass of petitions which streamed in every day immensely increased its task. Then, too, besides petitions, the Council itself would sometimes initiate proceedings of a semi-judicial character by calling upon some local magnate who was too powerful to be reached by the ordinary courts, to appear before the Council under the penalty (*sub poena*) of a sum of money to answer for his misdeeds—which were

---

[1] Cf. the ordinance of 1280, *ibid.*, 235. For similar situations in Sicily and Hungary, see *ibid.*, 92 ff. The popes, in turn, could find some basic principles, already settled by Roman emperors from Diocletian onwards, conveniently assembled in Cod. i. 19: A. de Boüard, *Diplomatique française et pontificale*, i. 67.

[2] Occasionally, relief of a sort which would later be described as " equitable " was given in Parliament when the parties were important personages. Thus, relief against a specialty was granted in 1327 (*Cal. Close Rolls, 1327–1330*, 47); in 1366 a petition for a decree of specific performance was referred by Parliament to the Chancellor, justices and others; the Council finally compelled the defendant to convey (*Cal. Close Rolls, 1364–1368*, 237); and in 1421 Parliament heard a suit for, and decreed, the performance of certain uses (*Rot. Parl.*, iv. 151–153). On the other hand, the word " equity " may be used without any technical implication whatever, as in *Rot. Parl.*, ii. 181 no. 23 (1348); cf. " this high court of Parlement, that ministreth all justice and equitee ", *Rot. Parl.*, v. 240 no. 28 (1454).

[3] In Ireland, on the other hand, it has been suggested that the Irish Chancellor had no original equity jurisdiction but merely acted as the delegate of Parliament in any particular case: H. G. Richardson and G. O. Sayles, *The Irish Parliament in the Middle Ages*, 219.

usually some form of oppression or disorder. The Council therefore found itself burdened with a growing mass of semi-judicial business; some of it could be transferred to the courts of common law, but some of it had to be considered by the Council itself, either because unusual relief was necessary, or because the parties were too influential to be amenable to the ordinary process of the courts. The problem arose of how to deal with this business. The same solution was found as in previous cases. A routine was established and officials were assigned for its working, only in this case an already existing institution, the Chancery, was used to carry out these new duties.

THE ORIGIN OF CHANCERY JURISDICTION

A variety of theories have been proposed to account for the origins of Chancery jurisdiction, but the general trend has been to establish an old theory first put forward by Palgrave.[1] According to this view the Chancellor's jurisdiction was not by virtue of his office; still less had it anything to do with his supposed position of keeper of the King's conscience.[2] At a later date, it is true, Chancery became a court of conscience, with a jurisprudence deliberately based upon that idea, but that was a later development and will not account for the earliest period of Chancery history. It now seems clear that the Chancellor's position was originally that of an informal delegate of the Council.[3] Overburdened with work of every description, the Council delegated particular matters to the Chancellor, who of all the officials was the one who was most constantly in attendance. Moreover, the Chancellor already had a well-organised office staff which had long been familiar with the judicial work arising on the common law side of Chancery,[4] and for a long time had exercised the power of issuing writs both judicial and administrative to all the King's officials, central and local. The Chancellor, therefore, commanded the machinery which sooner or later would have to be set in motion in order to give redress to the petitioners, and so nothing could be simpler than for the Council to transmit the

[1] Palgrave, *Original Authority of the King's Council* (1834); Baldwin, *The King's Council* (1913), 236–261.

[2] Sir Christopher Hatton in 1587 seems the first to have described himself, rhetorically, as keeper of his Sovereign's conscience; Spence, *Equitable Jurisdiction*, i. 406, 414. *Rot Parl.*, i. 74 *b* (1292) is possibly unique in deciding a highly political trespass case in Parliament " ex premeditato judicio consciencie domini regis ". The still wilder legend that the Chancellor was the King's confessor is easily refuted, as lists of confessors have been compiled—and they were not Chancellors (*The Antiquary*, xxii. 114, 159, 202; *Home Counties Magazine*, 1910). Kings' confessors rarely appear in public affairs, although Richard II's was impeached (*Rot. Parl.*, iii. 241 *a*), and Henry IV's confessor was removed in Parliament: *Rot. Parl.*, iii. 525 no. 16.

[3] As late as 1641 Lord Keeper Finch could assert that an order of the council was in itself adequate ground for making a decree in chancery: Holdsworth, v. 257.

[4] Cf. above, p. 165 n. 2, for the view that the Chancellor's equity originated in the common-law jurisdiction of his court. Under either view, the common-lawyers seem significantly prominent in the creative days of early equity.

petitions addressed to it to the Chancellor, sometimes (but not always) endorsing them with a brief instruction what to do.   Both on the common law and on the equity sides the Chancellors frequently called upon the judges of the common law courts to sit in Chancery, and it may well be the case that a good deal of genuine collaboration took place in the great task of creating the system of equity.

THE ORIGIN OF THE STAR CHAMBER

It was only natural that petitions concerning civil matters should be treated in this way.   Many petitions, however, raised questions of a criminal character.   As we pass through the fifteenth century, disorder and oppression by local magnates constantly becomes more common; petitioners are continually complaining of the lawlessness of their great neighbours, and it is perfectly evident that the courts of common law were helpless in face of this situation.   Their procedure was too slow and too mild; juries and sometimes judges were intimidated by large forces of retainers who constituted the private armies of unruly subjects. With such grave matters the Council alone was powerful enough to deal. Peremptory commands to appear before the Council were the only effective procedure.   Consequently the Council retained control of these graver matters in its own hands.   The Council's original jurisdiction, therefore, shows signs of dividing into two portions, most of its civil jurisdiction being exercised in its name by the Chancellor, while the rest, together with its criminal powers, was exercised at the Council board.

When, finally, the House of Lancaster had fallen and the Yorkist, Edward IV, had established himself upon the throne, important changes took place in the Council.   As far as we can judge (the affair is somewhat mysterious) what happened was this:[1] the Council lost the power of controlling the administration which it had exercised so rashly under the Lancastrian kings.   Edward IV retained in his own hands the control of the State machinery, which he operated through officials responsible to him alone.   The Council's attempt to become the supreme power in the State failed with the fall of the House of Lancaster.   The evidence which survives of the Council's activity under Edward IV is very scanty indeed; yet on the other hand we know that the Council was a very large body.   It would seem that Edward IV deliberately confined its activities to the sort of business we have mentioned, namely, the handling of petitions, especially when those petitions raised questions of public order, and the administration of criminal law.   Of the many rooms which the Council used in the fifteenth century its favourite seems to have been the Star Chamber, and from the reign of Edward IV onwards it seems that the Council is steadily turning into the Court of Star Chamber.

[1] Plucknett, *The Place of the Council in the Fifteenth Century*, Transactions of the Royal Historical Society (1918), 186–188.   But see Bayne, *Cases in the Council of Henry VII*, ed. W. H. Dunham (Selden Society), intro. xxiv for another view.   See below, p. 182 n. 3.

Not until the reign of Henry VIII do we find the deliberative and executive functions of the old Council revive. But by this time the old Council had become the Court of Star Chamber with a large and regular judicial business. Henry VIII, therefore, had to create a new institution, the Privy Council. When the Court of Star Chamber was abolished in 1641, the old mediaeval Council at last came to an end, and there only remained Henry VIII's recent invention, the Privy Council.

A word must be said of the famous act of 1487.[1] Old writers took it as the statutory origin of the Court of Star Chamber, principally on the strength of a marginal title on the statute roll which reads "*pro camera stellata*". So firm was this belief that when the court was abolished in 1641 the act of 1487 was repealed. It has now been shown that this act has no connection with the Star Chamber, and that the marginal title is an addition in a later handwriting. The act's principal effect was to emphasise the separation between the civil jurisdiction of the Chancery and the criminal jurisdiction of the Council, for it called upon the principal officers of State[2] to exercise wide powers for the repression of serious crime—and it is certain that they had already exercised these powers for many years. In short, the act was one more public threat by the government, which proclaimed its intention of vigorously enforcing the law by a summary procedure in the Council.[3]

Nevertheless, as far as the reign of Henry VII is concerned,

"the most striking characteristic of the court was its moderation. It was surely the mildest-mannered tribunal that ever sentenced a criminal, considerate in its procedure, gentle in its punishments, and failing altogether to live up to the reputation of ruthlessness that the Star Chamber has enjoyed since the seventeenth century."[4]

STAR CHAMBER AND STATUTE LAW

The tradition which associated the Star Chamber with the act of 1487 has some significance, however, for it emphasises the importance of the problem of enforcing statute law. The fifteenth-century government tried to check the growth of disorder and corruption by enacting heavy penalties against persons guilty of these offences. But statutes are unavailing without enforcement, and they had little effect until the Council

---

[1] 3 Hen. VII, c. 1 (reprinted in Tanner, *Tudor Constitutional Documents*, 258); Baldwin, *The King's Council*, 438–442; Bulletin of the Institute of Historical Research, iii. 115 and plate II; Pollard, *Council, Star Chamber and Privy Council under the Tudors*, English Historical Review, xxxvii. 516; C. H. Williams, *The So-called Star Chamber Act*, History, xv. 129.

[2] For some other powers which it was proposed to confer upon the same group of officers see Holdsworth, iv. 458 n. 6; the Statute of Proclamations set up substantially the same group in 1539 (31 Hen. VIII, c. 8; reprinted in Tanner, *Tudor Constitutional Documents*, 532). Above, p. 45.

[3] The late C. G. Bayne left a volume of *Select Cases in the Council of Henry VII*, with a valuable introduction on the early history of the Star Chamber and the act of 1487. It is being prepared for publication in the Selden Society's series by Professor W. H. Dunham, Jr.

[4] C. G. Bayne, *op. cit.*, clxxii.

and the Star Chamber took the matter in hand. It thus came about that the Star Chamber was largely concerned with the summary enforcement of legislation. Simultaneously, attempts were made from time to time to provide special courts for the enforcement of particular groups of statutes. The act of 1487 is an example of this policy, and the similarity of the means and the end may well account for the rise of the opinion that the act was the origin of the court, instead of both being independent attempts to enforce the same body of statute law.

Indeed, it was becoming a common opinion that drastic legislation can only be effectively enforced by courts erected *ad hoc*, and untrammelled by the ancient common law traditions. An early example is a statute of 1362 which contains the following remarkable, but little-known provision:

> " Item, if any man feels himself grieved contrary to any of the articles above written or any others contained in divers statutes, if he will come into the chancery (or someone on his behalf) and make his complaint, he shall now have a remedy there by force of the said articles and statutes without suing anywhere else to have redress."[1]

If the provisions of this and similar acts had been consistently followed, the Chancery would have become a court for the application of statute law, and particularly that of a constitutional, international or commercial character. The act of 1487, as we have seen, set up a special body to deal with statute law of a criminal character, and this was amended in 1529.[2] In 1535 or 1536 it was proposed to empower the group mentioned in the act of 1487 to hear charges of corruption against certain public officials,[3] and still more interesting is a bill of about the same date which would have set up a court of " conservators of the common weal " to enforce all statutes passed since 1485.[4] Of the greatest examples of this tendency, the financial courts of Henry VIII, we have already spoken: one other, the Court of High Commission, will be mentioned later.

The connection of the Star Chamber with the numerous statutory offences created during the fifteenth and sixteenth centuries was carried a step further when, under the Tudors and Stuarts, it undertook to enforce royal proclamations. The legal questions involved belong to constitutional history, where they had much to do with the growing unpopularity of the court, which was considerably augmented by a

---

[1] 36 Edw. III, stat. 1, c. 9; cf. 20 Edw. III, c. 6 (1346), on sheriffs; 27 Edw. III, st. 1, c. 1 (1353), provisors; 37 Edw. III, c. 18 (1363), on informations; 38 Edw. III, st. 2, c. 2 (1364), provisors; 15 Rich. II. c. 12 (1391); below, p. 186 n. 5.

[2] 21 Hen. VIII, c. 20 (in Tanner, *Tudor Constitutional Documents*, 259).

[3] Draft bill printed in Holdsworth, iv. 584 (9).

[4] *Letters and Papers of Henry VIII*, vii. 1611 (4) printed in full in Plucknett, *Some proposed legislation of Henry VIII*, Transactions of the Royal Historical Society (1936), 119. In 1495 Parliament gave wide powers to justices of the peace to try all statutory offences less than felony (11 Hen. VII, c. 3). See below, p. 438.

further development whereby the Star Chamber assumed legislative powers by making " decrees ".[1]

THE COURT OF REQUESTS

Numerous courts were founded upon the model of the Council. Many of them have faint beginnings in the reign of Henry VII or even earlier, but it is to Henry VIII and Elizabeth that they owe the bulk of their power. We have already mentioned the Council and the Star Chamber; there were many more besides. The Court of Requests first appears in 1483[2] and was modelled to some extent on the *Chambre des Requêtes*, a similar institution in France. The next we hear of it is in 1485 when a bill to abolish it was introduced into parliament and passed the commons, but got no further.[3] Under Henry VII it was, in effect, a committee of the Council for the hearing of poor men's causes and matters relating to the King's servants. Sometimes it appears in two divisions, one in the White Hall at Westminster and the other travelling with the King. Its jurisdiction was mainly civil, although at times it entertained matters of a criminal character, such as grave disorder, forgery, etc., and for some time the court seems to have been genuinely popular. Its head was the Lord Privy Seal, and assisting him were a number of masters of requests, two of whom deserve to be remembered for their contributions to legal literature: Christopher St. Germain, and Sir Julius Caesar. Its organisation closely followed that of the Chancery. Its procedure was at first intended to be informal, but the abuses to which this led compelled the court to follow the Chancery system of having bills drawn and signed by counsel. In the end it passed from an extreme of informality to the opposite extreme of technicality when it had adopted the summary procedure of the civil law—which was far from summary according to modern ideas. No doubt the example of Chancery was influential here, as also in its claims to administer equity. Later in Elizabeth's reign the presence of civilians in the Court of Requests led that court to exercise a wide Admiralty jurisdiction, including mercantile as well as maritime and prize jurisdiction.[4]

COURTS OF THE MARCHES

Exercising concurrent jurisdiction with the Council and the Star Chamber were two other courts, the Council of Wales and the Council

---

[1] One of them is printed in Tanner, *Tudor Constitutional Documents*, 279.

[2] For this date, see A. F. Pollard, *The Council under the Tudors*, English Historical Review, xxxvii, at p. 344.

[3] A. F. Pollard, *The Growth of the Court of Requests*, English Historical Review, lvi. 300. The whole matter is re-examined by C. G. Bayne in the introduction to the work mentioned, above, p. 182 n. 3.

[4] See the examples collected in Holdsworth, v. 139 n. 7. For an admiralty judge who would have found it convenient to be a master of requests in 1588, see Lord Eustace Percy, *Privy Council under the Tudors*, 49.

of the North. These remarkable bodies combined with the utmost facility the political business of governing Wales and the North (where there was considerable unrest at this time) with such judicial duties as seemed to them expedient. They controlled local government within their area, and acted as courts of equity and of extraordinary criminal jurisdiction.

ROYAL CHURCH COURTS

The Reformation statutes necessitated the creation of yet more special courts to enforce their provisions and carry out their policy. Appeals which once went from the archbishop to the pope were reserved by a statute of 1534 to the King, who was to follow the papal practice of commissioning delegates to hear them.[1] Hence there was created the High Court of Delegates. The judges were not permanent but nominated *ad hoc* for each case, and, as they were paid latterly but a guinea a day, only very junior men would consent to act, and so the court enjoyed very little esteem.[2] Its powers are now exercised by the Judicial Committee of the Privy Council.

The Act of Supremacy[3] conferred upon the Crown the whole remaining jurisdiction of the pope, and to exercise this immense and vague authority commissions were issued from time to time, which finally became stabilised in their content, and the persons empowered to act by them became known as the Court of High Commission.[4] It consisted mainly of bishops and devoted itself largely to the criminal side of the ex-papal jurisdiction. Its proceedings were later likened (with some justice) to those of the continental inquisitions, so severely did it search for ecclesiastical offenders.[5]

EQUITY SIDE OF THE EXCHEQUER

In 1415 the Commons believed that John of Waltham, who died in 1395, had invented the writ *sub poena* in the reign of Richard II (1377–1399), and complained of its use in the Exchequer as well as in the Chancery.[6] This seems to be the first reference, faint and doubtful as it is, to a court of equity in the Exchequer in the modern sense. Its history is by far the most obscure of all the English jurisdictions, and all that seems known of it is that it acted as a court of equity, duplicating to

[1] 25 Hen. VIII, c. 19 (partly in Tanner, *Tudor Constitutional Documents*, 22–25).

[2] Holdsworth, i. 605.

[3] 26 Hen. VIII, c. 1 (1534); in Tanner, *Tudor Constitutional Documents*, 47.

[4] Specimens of the commissions will be found in Tanner, *op. cit.*, 367 ff.

[5] Its oath *ex officio*, against which there was great outcry, could be matched in the Star Chamber; see the letters in Tanner, *op. cit.*, 373–374, and M. M. Maguire, *The oath " ex officio "* in *Essays in honor of C. H. McIlwain* (1936), 199.

[6] *Rot. Parl.*, iv. 84 (46).

some extent the Chancery during the seventeenth and eighteenth centuries,[1] and indeed down to 1842 when its jurisdiction was transferred to the Chancery.

EQUITY IN SEIGNORIAL COURTS

A remarkable and illuminating parallel to the development of equity beside the common law courts of the Crown is to be found in the history of certain great seignorial estates, especially those of the abbey of St Albans, many of whose archives have survived. The abbot had courts in the several manors, and also a central court which supervised the estates as a whole. These may be called his " common law " jurisdictions. Already in 1308, however, we find that the abbot had a council,[2] and in 1338 we find that council legislating on the rules of succession governing the abbey's tenants,[3] and towards the end of the century this council had a civilian and canonical element: in 1381 the insurgent villeins chased away the doctors of both laws, saying that they would not henceforth submit to the civil or the canon law.[4] The movement and the antipathy towards it were not confined to St Albans, for a few years later a royal statute recited

" the grievous complaint of the commons made in full parliament for that many of the king's subjects are made to come before the councils of divers lords and ladies, to answer there concerning their freeholds and many other things real and personal which ought to be conducted according to the law of the land; against the estate of our lord the king and his crown, and in defeasance of the common law."[5]

The need for newer institutions was therefore felt both in royal and in seignorial judicial systems, and in both it was the conciliar form which was tried. Moreover, in both systems there was a tendency to

[1] Blackstone, *Commentaries*, iii. 45–46. It is suggested by Emyr Gwynne Jones, *Exchequer Proceedings (Equity)*, (University of Wales, Board of Celtic Studies: History and Law Series, no. 4), (1939) that the equity side grew out of the common law jurisdiction of the court. A similar thesis has been put forward (with reference to chancery) by L. O. Pike, intro. to Y.B. 12 & 13 Edward III (Rolls Series), cvi–cxi. See, however, G. O. Sayles, *Select Cases in King's Bench*, ii. intro. lix who would find equity in the Exchequer under Edward I, and Alice Beardwood, *Alien Merchants in England*, 107, who suggests that there were equity cases in the Exchequer under Edward III. Neither seems convincing. Holdsworth i. 241 is noncommittal.

[2] Levett, *The Courts of St. Albans*, Transactions of the Royal Historical Society (1924), 62. Cf. Page, *Crowland Abbey* (1934), 45–49.

[3] Levett, *loc. cit.*, 66; and in *Mélanges Lot*, 431.

[4] *Ibid.*, 63; cf. Plucknett, Year Book 13 Richard II (Ames Foundation), xlii and Economic History Review, ii. 332. The suggestion that such councils, unconnected with tenure, do not appear while feudalism was at its height (Levett, in *Mélanges offerts à F. Lot*) was questioned by D. C. Douglas, *Feudal Documents from Bury St. Edmunds* (1932), cxlix–cl, and it is now known that an instance occurs as early as 1140 (Stenton, *English Feudalism*, 73). Valuable references are collected in Hilda Johnstone, *The Queen's Household* (in J. F. Willard and W. A. Morris, *English Government at Work*, i. 292 n. 2) and N. Denholm-Young, *Seignorial Administration*, 26–30.

[5] 15 Rich. II, c. 12 (1391), which appoints the Chancellor to enforce it (cf. above, p. 183); by 16 Rich. II, c. 2 (1393) such lords and ladies were to be fined twenty pounds.

turn to civilians and canonists. In England, the seignorial council of civilians had much less influence than on the continent, where the influence of civilians is said to have done much to depress the position of the peasantry and to prevent their gradual rise in status.[1] The growth of copyhold and its recognition as a " customary " freehold in England had the result of gradually and almost imperceptibly enfranchising the villeins, but this would hardly have been possible if the civilians had succeeded in imposing their distrust of custom.[2]

RELATIONS OF THE OLD COURTS TO THE NEW

In the middle ages, as now, the appearance of new institutions, making light of the solemnities of dogma and procedure which were dear to practitioners before the older courts, aroused some fear and more resentment. Then, as now, conservatives were persuaded that the constitution (or the common law) was in danger, and the first impulse was not to reform the old, but to attack the new order of courts.

The rolls of the mediaeval English parliaments contain numerous petitions and acts directed against the Council and the Chancery. The promise of justice in the Great Charter[3] was regarded as a declaration that the common law courts, and they alone, had jurisdiction over the lives, persons and property of Englishmen. In 1331 its provisions were pointedly re-enacted;[4] in 1352 it was again recited and the King had to promise that the Council would not proceed without indictment or common law process on an original writ;[5] although this was confirmed several times, we find in 1363 another attempt to enforce this construction of the charter—the Council must take security from complainants, and even then proceed only by common law.[6] In 1368 the Commons once more tried to insist upon indictment or original writ as the sole foundation for legal proceedings.[7] All these statutes denouncing the council were obviously ineffective, despite the show of assent given to them by the Crown. In 1389 the Chancellor is coupled with the Council in a petition to which Richard II only replied with a saving of the royal prerogative.[8] The tide was on the turn. A statute of 1394 tried a different policy by allowing the Chancellor to award damages to a defendant when the plaintiff's suit appeared founded upon false-

---

[1] Maitland, *English Law and the Renaissance*, 23, 83 (Select Essays in Anglo-American Legal History, i. 195). This was, in fact, the result of the reception in Scotland according to H. Goudy in English Historical Review, xvii. 359.

[2] Below, pp. 310–312.

[3] Magna Carta (1215), c. 39; (1225), c. 29.

[4] 5 Edw. III, c. 9.

[5] *Rot. Parl.*, iii. 239 (19); 25 Edw. III, stat. 5, c. 4.

[6] 37 Edw. III, c. 18.

[7] 42 Edw. III, c. 3.

[8] *Rot. Parl.*, iii. 267 (33); the Commons would have fined the Chancellor £100 for each offence. Cf. below, p. 684 n. 1.

hood,[1] but the fall of Richard II brought back the older type of remonstrance. In 1415 the writ *sub poena* was denounced as a subtlety invented in the previous reign by John Waltham, and the examination of parties and witnesses without lawyers and without records and the use of civil and canon law forms were again vigorously denounced. The petition was bluntly rejected by the King.[2] Another in 1421 which alleged that a *sub poena* was not " due process " was likewise refused.[3] Clearly the Council and the Chancery were now solidly established. Indeed, for the future, legislation took the opposite course of increasing the powers of the Chancellor and the Council by a series of acts[4] of which the act *pro camera stellata*[5] is only one example.

The petition of 1389 was therefore the first to which the Crown ventured a refusal, and that of 1394 begins a line of statutes which accept and even enlarge the jurisdiction of the Chancellor and Council. We may therefore conclude that during the fifteenth century the Commons were gradually reconciling themselves to the existence of a jurisdiction which the country at large seems to have welcomed, and their protests can be largely ascribed to the professional common lawyers who largely directed its proceedings.

COMMON LAW AND EQUITY IN THE FIFTEENTH CENTURY

Whatever the bar may have thought about the problem, the common law judges seem to have been prepared to work with the Chancery in a spirit of co-operation. They were constantly in consultation with the Council and the Chancellor, both for the statutory purposes already mentioned, and also to assist him when called upon in the exercise of his equitable jurisdiction. The frequent conferences in the Exchequer chamber for discussing difficult cases afforded yet one more opportunity of contact. There is therefore no further questioning of the powers of the Chancellor or the Council, but instead we find an endeavour to define the limits of the two jurisdictions.[6] In this there was naturally some conflict, especially as Chancery already enjoined parties from pursuing common law remedies, and the common law courts sometimes talked about prohibiting suitors from going into equity, and at least once threatened to release by *habeas corpus* one who had been committed by the

[1] 17 Rich. II, c. 6; confirmed by 15 Hen. VI, c. 4 (1437).

[2] *Rot. Parl.*, iv. 84; the writ is older than Waltham. Indeed, it is found even in common law procedure; see Y.B. 30–31 Edw. I, 195 (Rolls Series).

[3] *Rot. Parl.*, iv. 156.

[4] 2 Hen. V, stat. 1, c. 9 (1414), confirmed by 8 Hen. VI, c. 14 (1429); 31 Hen. VI. c. 2 (1453); 33 Hen. VI, c. 1 (1455).

[5] 3 Hen. VII, c. 1 (1487); above, p. 182.

[6] For examples of early bills in Chancery, see especially *Select Cases in Chancery* (Selden Society); for an early specimen see Pound and Plucknett, *Readings*, 195–196. The relations of common law and equity are further discussed below, p. 193.

Chancellor for contempt.[1]   However, occasional outbursts of ill-feeling such as this contrast with the general atmosphere, which seems to have been one of mutual tolerance.   Indeed, in 1464 the Court of Common Pleas was once given the chance of recognising an equitable estate, with the reasoning that " the law of chancery is the common law of the land ". This golden opportunity was lost,[2] and so we had to wait four hundred years for the fusion of law and equity.

EQUITY UNDER THE TUDORS

The sixteenth century shows us Council government at its best. The courts of Star Chamber, Requests and High Commission collaborated in the most intimate manner with the Privy Council in the task of government.   All the troubles brought about by religious dissension, economic distress, foreign wars and domestic sedition were handled courageously and effectively by the newer institutions.   Nowhere will be found so striking a contrast with the inadequacy of the Lancastrian age.   No doubt there was some ruthlessness: legal and constitutional barriers had to yield when the State was believed to be in danger—and it certainly was on more than one occasion.   The Privy Council itself exercised a jurisdiction more vague even than that of its offshoots, and all the conciliar courts inflicted " unusual " and sometimes picturesque punishments when occasion demanded.   Torture was not unknown to its procedure: sedition, defamation, heresy, unlicensed printing, play-acting, perjury, riot—all these might be visited with fine and imprisonment, while all sorts of mercantile disputes (especially those involving aliens), domestic disputes and private litigation of all sorts flowed in an ever-growing stream through the Council chamber, in spite of all attempts to divert it to other courts of law or equity.[3]

By the middle of the sixteenth century the Court of Chancery had a great deal of business and a large and complicated establishment.   In theory it remained, almost to the end, one court with a single judge, the Chancellor himself, but the legal work alone, without considering the political duties attached to the office, was very heavy and devices had to be found for lightening the burden.   Minor matters were left to the Masters in Chancery, while the Master of the Rolls was coming into prominence as an assistant, and sometimes as a deputy, to the Chancellor.[4]

[1] (1482), Y.B. 22 Edward IV, Mich. no. 21, f. 37   translated in Pound and Plucknett, *Readings*, 197–198).

[2] *Anon.*, Y.B. 4 Edward IV, Pasch. 9 (translated in Digby, *History of the Law of Real Property* (5th edn., 1897), 338–340: extracts in Pound and Plucknett, *Readings*, 196–197).

[3] See the Council orders printed in Tanner, *Tudor Constitutional Documents*, 242–245; for an excellent brief account see Lord Eustace Percy, *The Privy Council under the Tudors* (Oxford, 1907), and longer discussions by C. G. Bayne and others in introductions to the relevant volumes of the Selden Society.

[4] Some details will be found in Spence, *Equitable Jurisdiction*, i. 360–362.

The tolerably good relations which we have seen existing in the fifteenth century between common law courts and Chancery were interrupted during the chancellorship of Cardinal Wolsey (1515–1529). The list of charges against the Cardinal[1] accuse him of misusing injunctions as well as publicly insulting common law judges. The fact that harmony once again reigned under his successor, Sir Thomas More, would seem to indicate that the fault lay as much with Wolsey's character as with his policy. More, trained as a common lawyer, even suggested to the judges that they should adopt equitable principles and so render injunctions unnecessary.[2] He at least seems to have thought this a practicable solution, but again the judges replied with a *non possumus*. The one hopeful sign was that there was no distinction of a common law bar from a Chancery bar; as Bacon was able to remark much later, many of the common law judges had either sat as commissioners in Chancery, or had practised there earlier in their careers. Not until the accession of James I did discord reappear.

[1] Printed in 4 *Inst*. 89–95: Coke's statement that Wolsey was indicted for trying to subvert the common law (2 *Inst*. 626; 3 *Inst*. 208) was based upon a careless confusion of documents; Holdsworth, iv. 257.

[2] More details will be found in Holdsworth, v. 223.

CHAPTER 9

PREROGATIVE, EQUITY AND LAW UNDER THE STUARTS

Many different movements contributed to the great crisis which dominates the Stuart period, and not all of them can be considered here. Economic movements enhanced the cost of government, although the revenue of the Crown was much less elastic. A fiscal crisis was therefore an important factor, bringing in its train difficult problems of law when the Crown attempted to adapt mediaeval machinery to the needs of a modern State. Hence there was a long struggle over benevolences, forced loans, impositions, feudal dues, ship-money[1] and the like, in which both Crown and Parliament appealed to the practice of the middle ages. Resistance naturally centred in the House of Commons where the financial crisis took the form of a constitutional crisis, and where several cases asserting parliamentary privileges expressed the high pretensions of the parliamentary party—advised, of course, by common lawyers.

To this must be added all the bitterness aroused by violent religious controversy. In its extreme form this might even go so far as to advocate social or communistic revolution, while at the opposite pole was the combination of " divine right " in political theory and " high church " doctrines in theology.

THE COURTS AND THE CRISIS

Of the general aspects of this complicated situation we have already spoken;[2] in this chapter we are especially concerned with the position of the courts during the struggle. There is little difficulty in understanding why the Court of High Commission should incur the hatred of Puritans whom it punished for their non-conformity to the established Church and for their vigorous attacks upon its doctrine and ritual. So, too, the Star Chamber dealt heavily with political offences, especially political and seditious libels, and sometimes inflicted forms of mutilation

---

[1] For a discussion of ship-scot, see F. E. Harmer, *Ang o-Saxon Writs* (1952), 266 ff., 483.

[2] Above, pp. 48–53.

unknown to the common law. " But nothing was done by the Stuarts by way of fine and corporal punishment ", observes Dr Tanner,[1] " that had not been already done under the Tudors. The later unpopularity of the court was due to a change in the popular point of view, and not in the action of the court." It is this change which is our concern in this chapter, for it took the form of a denial of the Star Chamber's legal right to exist. Why should the common lawyers of the seventeenth century deny the legality of the Star Chamber and, indeed, of the Chancery as well?

A certain amount of factiousness must be admitted. The common law had little power against the newer sorts of offences which modern governments have to deal with—sedition, libel and the like. To hamper the Star Chamber would therefore remove many restraints from the opposition. Professional jealousy was not involved to so obvious an extent as is sometimes thought. The common law judges often sat, and were indeed the most permanent element in the composition of the Star Chamber. The bar was not restricted to any peculiar body. In affairs of state, however, the judges may well have felt that other influences than their own were at work. The historical doubts professed by the common lawyers as to its legality rested partly on the old mediaeval protests in Parliament against the jurisdiction of the Council and Chancery,[2] and partly on the alleged statutory origin of the court in the act *pro camera stellata*,[3] the scope of which was constantly being exceeded in Star Chamber practice. The former argument was attractive, no doubt, but only the absence of an historical conscience can account for the use made of the latter: Coke and other contemporary scholars[4] knew perfectly well that it was specious.

Perhaps the greatest blow to the court came from its friends rather than its enemies. King James attended in person on several occasions, and the spectacle of the sovereign sitting for five days and giving judgment in a libel action must have compelled a sharp division of opinion.[5] To some it must have seemed a heavy blow to the idea of an independent judiciary which was just emerging; to others it would naturally appear as a triumph of the principle of personal monarchy, and monarchists indulged in fantastic flights of mysticism as they acclaimed the Star Chamber,[6] not for its usefulness, but for its embodiment (in their view) of the principle of personal monarchy.

---

[1] Tanner, *Tudor Constitutional Documents*, 256–257. Cf. the comparison between the government's action after Perkin Warbeck's rebellion (1498) and Essex's conspiracy (1601) in Bayne, *Council of Henry VII*, clxxiv.

[2] Above, pp. 187–188.

[3] Above, p. 182.

[4] See the views of Smith, *De Republica Anglorum*; Lambarde, *Archeion*; Bacon; and Coke's 4th *Institute* collected in Tanner, *Tudor Constitutional Documents*, 284–294.

[5] The incident is recounted by Hudson in *Collectanea Juridica*, ii. 8 (reprinted in Tanner, *Constitutional Documents of James I*, 142).

[6] Cf. Bacon's letter to the King, printed in Tanner, *op. cit.*, 141.

As we have seen, in its foundation the Star Chamber was not based upon any such theory or practice, but its defenders chose to support it upon this ground, and in so doing they took an issue upon which they eventually failed—and failed without having tried the real merits of the Star Chamber as a judicial institution.

Both the manner and the time of the Star Chamber's fall was therefore determined by the fatal support of royalist partisans.[1] The meeting of the Long Parliament in November 1640 sealed its doom. Parliament first established anew the claims of Parliament to be summoned frequently, then declared its absolute control over taxation, and then, in 1641, abolished the Star Chamber, the analogous Council courts of the North and of Wales, and the Court of High Commission.[2] They are almost the last legitimate acts to be passed by King, Lords and Commons until the Restoration nineteen years later.

The act did not mention the Court or Requests, which in fact continued to sit until the outbreak of the civil war. At the restoration, masters of requests were appointed, but it was clearly felt impolitic for them to exercise judicial functions. The court was therefore not really revived after the interruption in 1642.

THE COMMON LAWYERS AND CHANCERY

Chancery presented a more difficult problem, and the struggle was longer—and ended differently. By the time of Coke the jurisdiction of Chancery and the principles of equity were already sufficiently well known for opponents of the system to feel that they would have to discuss the relative merits of common law and equity. A purely historical argument was rather hazardous, for the old mediaeval attacks on Chancery had been followed by many statutes which recognised the jurisdiction. The machinery of injunctions and prohibitions was certainly admirably adapted to the creation of friction between courts of law and equity, and the personality of Coke was sufficient to make a delicate situation an impossible one. Open conflict was all the more inevitable since here, too, the extreme royalists asserted that Chancery was a prerogative court—and gave to the word " prerogative " the full meaning of the word as they conceived it.

This was hardly true. The recently published decisions of Lord Bacon show that the court was already transacting a large mass of useful business along fairly settled lines, and that whatever arbitrary element there may once have been in equity, was now to a large extent eliminated. The wild speculation of many royalists to the effect that the Court of Chancery and the system of equity were dependent upon a personal prerogative of the monarch threw the whole legal system of the country

---

[1] The story is told by H. E. I. Phillips, *The Last Years of the Court of Star Chamber*, Transactions of the Royal Historical Society (1939), 103 ff.

[2] 16 Car. I, cc. 10, 11 (1641).

into the political arena. The common lawyers, whenever they touched upon the substance of the controversy, had to take up the difficult position that specific performance was unjust, that the injunction against enforcing a judgment obtained by fraud was reprehensible, and a number of other equally doubtful theses. Indeed, the case which precipitated the conflict forced the common lawyers to take the defence and sustain the operations of an arrant swindler. In 1616 James I personally adjudicated between the two jurisdictions and decided in favour of the Chancery, thereby showing that he was " judge over all his judges ", and Bacon hailed the vindication of the Chancery as the court of the King's " absolute power ".

CHANCERY AND ABSOLUTE POWER

Bacon's words certainly have a sinister sound.[1] And yet there was good mediaeval authority for them—and here again we must remark that Bacon's knowledge of the Year Books was quite as extensive as Coke's, and his use of them more accurate. In the letter where he alludes to " absolute power " in Chancery he must surely have been thinking of this passage in the Year Book of 1469:[2]

> " In chancery, it was remarked by the chancellor that a man will not be prejudiced by mispleading or defects of form, but only by the truth of the matter; we have to judge according to conscience and not according to pleadings.[3] Thus if a man supposes in his bill that another has done him wrong and the defendant says nothing, still the plaintiff will not recover if it comes to our knowledge that the defendant did him no wrong. There are two sorts of power and process, to wit, ordinary power and absolute power: the ordinary is where a certain order is observed, as in positive law; but the law of nature has no ' certain order ' but resorts to whatever means there are whereby the truth may be known; such process is therefore said to be ' absolute '. . . ."

In this passage the words " absolute power " simply mean that Chancery has not yet tied itself and its suitors by the burdensome rule that matters not denied in pleading must be taken as admitted. Hence the Chancellor will consider the whole mass of facts before him whether they have been elicited in the ordinary course of pleading or otherwise. His power is therefore " absolute " because it is not confined to matters properly pleaded.

The words " absolute power " are there in the Year Book, and yet there is a world of difference between their meaning in 1469 and the

[1] Bacon's letter using the term is conveniently accessible in Campbell's *Lives of the Chancellors*, chap. 50. (It may be said that this entertaining work did a great deal to arouse interest in legal history at a moment when the only works available on the subject were Hale's unfinished study and the highly technical pages of Reeves. Its tone of gossip makes it irresistible reading, and like all good gossip, it is richly spiced with malice. It is valuable, in spite of some inaccuracies and harsh judgments, because many original sources are printed in it, sometimes from private papers; it also contains useful matter on professional organisation in the eighteenth century.)

[2] Y.B. 9 Edward IV, Trin. 9.

[3] Cf. Walter Ullmann, *The Medieval Idea of Law*, 127.

use Bacon made of them in 1616.   The whole incident is typical of the subtle complications introduced into the controversy by the slow change in sense of political terms—one might almost say by the tone in which they were uttered.   The word " absolute " is particularly interesting from its use by Sir Thomas Smith late in the reign of Elizabeth.[1]

THE SURVIVAL OF CHANCERY

James' decision, taken by itself, is no explanation for the survival of equity.   As the country drifted nearer to civil war one would naturally expect to find the question reopened.   Why, for example, was not the matter raised again in 1641 when the Star Chamber was abolished?

The abolition of a criminal court like the Star Chamber is very easy, and if ever it is wanted again, it is equally easy to erect a substitute—as was done under the Commonwealth when there were political prisoners to be tried.   But the abolition of a civil court such as Chancery is quite a different matter.   It is clear that equitable relief was necessary, and was valued; when debates took place upon the fate of Chancery it was an unanswerable argument to show the numerous sorts of fraud which equity would relieve but which the common law would almost seem designed to promote.   Then, too, there were rapidly increasing property interests whose protection rested solely in Chancery.   If Chancery were abolished, indescribable confusion would result, for the common law courts showed no inclination to take over the law of trusts.   The question of abolishing Chancery was several times mooted,[2] but in the end it took the more practical form of reforming its procedure and reducing its delays.   As we shall see, however, the feeling against equity was to cross the ocean and leave its mark on American history too.

THE PREROGATIVE AND ADMINISTRATIVE LAW

An attractive suggestion has been made connecting the theory of prerogative in this period with the notion of administrative law. Gardiner, and later Dicey, remarked that the Tudor and Stuart monarchy bore a striking likeness both in theory and in practice to that of France.

" A lawyer, who regards the matter from an exclusively legal point of view, is tempted to assert that the real subject in dispute between statesmen such as Bacon and Wentworth on the one hand, and Coke or Eliot on the other, was whether a strong administration of the continental type should, or should not, be permanently established in England.   Bacon and men like him no doubt underrated the risk that an increase in the power of the Crown should lead to the establishment of despotism.   But advocates of the prerogative did not (it may be supposed) intend to sacrifice the liberties or invade the ordinary private rights of citizens; they were struck with the evils flowing from the conservative legalism of Coke, and with the necessity for enabling the Crown as head of the nation to cope with the selfishness

[1] The word " absolute " is discussed with great insight and originality by McIlwain, *Political Thought in the West* (1932), 364 ff.

[2] These discussions are dealt with in Holdsworth, i. 463–464.

of powerful individuals and classes. They wished, in short, to give the government the sort of rights conferred on a foreign executive by the principles of administrative law. Hence for each feature of French *droit administratif* one may find some curious analogy either in the claims put forward or in the institutions favoured by the Crown lawyers of the seventeenth century."[1]

These theories of the royal power found their natural expression in the Council and the Court of Star Chamber, which may indeed be compared with the Council of State (*Conseil d'État*) which crowns the system of administrative courts in France. It is further suggested that the old writ *de non procedendo rege inconsulto* was used to attain part of this purpose.[2]

" The working of this writ, if Bacon had obtained his object, would have been to some extent analogous to that provision which has been found in so many French constitutions, according to which no agent of the goverment can be summoned before a tribunal for acts done in the exercise of his office without a preliminary authorisation by the Council of State."[3]

There is much to be said for this view. Some extremely interesting references collected by Sir William Holdsworth show how active the Council and Star Chamber were in upholding royal and local officials and in protecting them from vexatious proceedings at law, at the same time protecting the public from the abuse of official powers.[4] This policy was not altogether new, however, in the Tudor and Stuart period, for precedents can be found for it in the middle ages, especially in the activities of the Court of Exchequer, which was particularly solicitous in matters involving royal sheriffs and bailiffs.[5] The writ which Gardiner mentions in the passage last quoted is in fact a regular feature of mediaeval common law procedure, and Bacon's argument in moving for the writ is an admirable example of the combination of old law and new theory. The high prerogative doctrine with which he opens soon gives way to more solid arguments based on numerous Year Book precedents, which together made his case unanswerable. The startling theory has therefore obscured the fact that the writ *rege inconsulto* was simply the time-honoured procedure which allowed the Crown to intervene when two subjects were litigating about property to which the Crown had a title.

The position may be summarised thus. Many of the claims of the Crown lawyers were perfectly defensible on established common law

---

[1] Dicey, *Law of the Constitution* (8th edn.), 365–366. For a suggestion in 1325 that a royal treasurer could not be sued while he was in office, see *Chronicles of Edward I and Edward II* (ed. Stubbs, Rolls Series), ii. 283, and cf. *Rot. Parl. Inediti*, 134, and the comments of J. G. Edwards, " Justice in early English Par iaments ", Bulletin of the Institute of Historical Research, xxvii. 35 at 46 n. 4.

[2] Bacon's argument, as Attorney-General, in support of this writ will be found in *Collectanea Juridica*, i. 168–213, and in his *Works* (ed. Spedding), vii. 681–725. For some early precedents for the writ, see Bulletin of the Institute of Historical Research, vi. 79 n. 5.

[3] Gardiner, *History of England*, iii. 7 n. 2, cited by Dicey, *loc. cit.*

[4] Holdsworth, iv. 87–88.

[5] See *Select Cases in the Exchequer of Pleas* (ed. Jenkinson and Formoy, Selden Society).

principles; but the antagonism of contemporaries (and the confusion of later historians) was created by the claims that these rights were the result of " absolute " or " prerogative " powers in the monarch, when in fact they were nothing of the sort. The result of this mistaken policy was therefore to arouse opposition to many Crown practices which would never have been attacked had it not been for this attempt to regard them as extra-legal when in sober fact they were really legal. As for the " administrative " practice of Tudor and Stuart governments, there were undoubtedly some striking innovations, especially in the direction of injunctions by the Council against suing officials at common law. But even here the mediaeval principle that officials had privileges to the courts to which they were responsible will account for much, and the practice of the Exchequer relieving subjects against the oppression of royal officers must also be regarded as evidence that " administrative " principles were no novelty in the sixteenth and seventeenth centuries.

THE COMMON LAW, SOLE AND SUPREME

The conflict with the Star Chamber and the Court of Chancery was not the only aspect of the crisis, for the common lawyers had formed the grandiose plan of making their system sole and supreme over all persons and causes.

Against Chancery they had suffered a defeat which was well deserved; their own justice was an inferior product to that of the chancellors. Against the Star Chamber and High Commission they won a victory which, on the balance, we may regard as fortunate, although here again it must be admitted that the common law criminal procedure was behind that of the Star Chamber, which did at least allow the accused to give evidence in his defence. The struggle with other rivals must now be briefly mentioned.

There was a network of ecclesiastical courts covering England which played a large part in the lives of the ordinary folk. Archdeacons, bishops, archbishops, deans and an immense variety of peculiar and anomalous jurisdictions dispensed criminal and civil justice based on canon law. For five centuries there had been a steady growth of common law restrictions upon their activities, some based upon tradition, others on statute. Writs of prohibition to ecclesiastical judges and parties were a common feature of mediaeval law and continued after the Reformation. The courts of the Church ceased to be a serious rival to the common law, and were permitted to retain their anomalous probate jurisdiction and their more natural matrimonial jurisdiction until the middle of the nineteenth century.

Admiralty courts presented a different situation.[1] During the reign of Elizabeth they had maintained a fairly equal struggle with the common

---

[1] See Holdsworth, i. 548–568; cf. below, p. 663.

law courts, and in 1575 a conference resulted in a compromise. Coke, in 1606, renewed the struggle and declared that the alleged compromise of 1575 never existed. Here again the crippling of a court with established civil jurisdiction (important parts of it even being statutory) at once raised serious prospects. Foreign merchants properly protested that the common law offered them no such remedies in commercial causes as were available in Admiralty. Another conference followed in 1632 and again Admiralty jurisdiction was vindicated. The critical year 1641 saw another unsuccessful attack on the Admiralty, but slowly the common law courts usurped its jurisdiction over general commercial law and so were able to argue the Admiralty's proper province was the remaining purely maritime business. Here at least the common lawyers did provide a substitute in their own system for the services formerly rendered by their vanquished rival. One cannot help being tempted to wonder what the course of English law would have been if they had adopted the same policy in their struggle with Chancery. If the common law had recognised trusts, and had allowed equitable defences to actions on specialties (then a much agitated question), they might have succeeded in abolishing Chancery and uniting law and equity.

In the event, however, the common law chose to cling to its traditional views of legal estates and the sacramental character of seals, and in so doing they made the continuance of Chancery essential.

CHAPTER 10

PARLIAMENT AND THE PRIVY COUNCIL

The seventeenth and eighteenth centuries saw little change in the judicial system after the Restoration. The year 1660 was reckoned the twelfth year of the reign of Charles II, which theoretically began with the execution of Charles I. The stormy period of the Interregnum was erased as far as possible from legal memory. Its clumsy efforts at reform, the institutions which it created and the legislation it passed were swept away, and the strand of legal history was joined up again at the place where it had been broken. The authentic line of statutes came to an end even earlier, for after 16 Charles I, c. 37 (1642) no further acts were passed in the legitimate fashion by King, Lords and Commons. All editions of the statutes contain a gap between that date and the Restoration, and the legislation of the Interregnum must be sought in many scattered places. Not until 1911 were these relics collected into one single work.[1] So too with reports; the meagre pages of Style, Hardres and Siderfin are only just enough to show that the common law courts struggled on under the able leadership of Chief Justice Rolle and Sir Matthew Hale.

FROM THE RESTORATION TO THE REFORM ACT

The century and three-quarters which followed 1660 are a period of rising prosperity, at least for the governing class, ending in a serious decline after the Napoleonic wars. Only the pinch of adversity was needed to destroy the contentment of the eighteenth century with its

---

[1] *Acts and Ordinances of the Interregnum, 1642–1660* (ed. Firth and Rait, 3 vols., 1911).

institutions. Its legislation is voluminous, but largely devoted to matters of detail which only acquire significance as precursors of the more sweeping reforms of the nineteenth century. Their importance is, however, none the less for that. There was in fact a slow, steady trend towards amelioration where practicable, but the limits of practicability were unhappily narrow, and the inertia of vested interests was immense. The fate of Lord Mansfield's efforts admirably illustrates the difficulty of reform when all the forces of traditional learning were arrayed against it.

Some progress was made, however, by the efforts of those country gentry who bore the burden of local adjudication and administration as justices of the peace. Their labours have been well described in words which deserve quotation :[1]

> " Parliament lacked the guidance of a central authority with broad and bold vision. On the other hand it was composed of those who were wrestling with the immediate problems and who could suggest workable expedients for tackling present difficulties. The result was a flood of statutes carrying out minor amendments in the old law and, in the second half of our period, establishing new *ad hoc* bodies to deal with special problems in particular areas. These policies of piecemeal amendment and sectional reconstruction went some way towards meeting the more pressing needs of the moment by adapting the law to changing circumstances and grafting modern devices on to the main stock of mediaeval institutions. In the process, however, confusion became more confounded. . . ."

These words are as true of general legal history during this period as they are of local government. They are significant for their confirmation of the view that the eighteenth century ought not to be dismissed (as too often it is) as a period of complete stagnation, and also for their indication of the class from which the larger reforms were to come in the fullness of time—from the middle class which required sound institutions in tune with its moderate liberalism, and satisfying its sense of the practical. A small and very powerful legal profession guarded the central courts against any such meddling, and so these efforts were confined to local jurisdictions and minor criminal and administrative matters.

THE JURISDICTION OF PARLIAMENT

At the other end of the scale, however, slow changes were taking place whose effects are still with us.

The earliest description of the judicial powers of Parliament which has come down to us in the famous passage in *Fleta*, where we are told that—[2]

> " the king has his court in his council in his parliaments, in the presence of prelates, earls, barons, nobles and other experienced men, where doubts concerning judgments are resolved, new remedies are provided for newly arisen wrongs, and justice is done to everyone according to his deserts."

[1] Dowdell, *Hundred Years of Quarter Sessions, 1660–1760* (Cambridge, 1932), 191.
[2] *Fleta*, ii. 2, § 1.

In the light of other evidence this passage must be interpreted as meaning that the jurisdiction of Parliament was essentially extraordinary, that it was both original and appellate, and that it was both civil and criminal.   How often these powers were used during the middle ages it is difficult to determine.   The earliest parliamentary rolls describe themselves as " plea rolls " and do in fact contain a large proportion of judicial business; on the other hand it is well known that these rolls are by no means exhaustive, and that Parliament actually transacted an unascertainably large quantity of business of all sorts which has left no trace on the rolls—even where rolls are extant, and in many cases they have disappeared.

The separation of the Court of King's Bench[1] relieved Parliament of a good deal of its judicial business, with the result that it became more and more a legislature and a political organ of national government. Its judicial powers were therefore less frequently invoked, and its civil jurisdiction was principally concerned with proceedings in error from the King's Bench.   Still further discouragement to litigants proposing to appeal to Parliament was due to the growing infrequency of its sessions, already marked in the fifteenth century and still more conspicuous in the sixteenth.   Error in Parliament was never a very frequent proceeding, and in form it remained for centuries a matter of grace rather than of course, for a petition to the King was a necessary preliminary.[2]   The assent to the petition was held to be the authority upon which the errors were heard.

SCOTLAND AND IRELAND

The territorial extension of this jurisdiction has fluctuated from time to time.   During the middle ages there are precedents showing that error lay from the Irish courts to the Parliament at Westminster, but doubts were raised early in the eighteenth century with the result that a statute[3] declared that error lay from Irish courts to the English, and not to the Irish, Parliament.   This has remained the position (with the exception of the period 1783–1800) until the present century.   Error from Scottish courts lay to the Parliament of Great Britain since the Act of Union.[4]

APPEALS FROM THE COURTS OF EQUITY

Parliament was a common law court, and it was some time before it concerned itself with equity.[5]   Hence it was said in 1459 that Parliament

---

[1] See above, pp. 149–151.

[2] The lords resolved " that a writ of error is not a writ of grace, but of right, and ought not to be denied to the subject "—*Lords' Journals*, 17 February 1704–1705; Sir Matthew Hale, *Jurisdiction of the Lords' House*, 145 (writing between 1674 and 1676) was not in a position to be so positive.   See Francis Hargrave's preface to Hale, pp. cxcix–ccii, and below, p. 213.

[3] 6 Geo. I, c. 5 (1719).

[4] 6 Anne, c. 11 (1707).   For Scotland and Ireland, see Holdsworth, xi. 4–35.

[5] For occasional examples of original equitable jurisdiction exercised in Parliament, see above, p. 179 n. 2.

could hear error from the common law side of Chancery but not from the equity side.[1]   In the early seventeenth century several attempts were made to persuade the Lords to assume this jurisdiction, but they declined to do so.   After the Restoration the Lords began to hear appeals, and very slowly the controversy over their right to do so died away.

THE POSITION OF THE COMMONS

It is a common practice to refer to this jurisdiction as being in the House of Lords.   It is they in fact who exercise it, but the historical character of the jurisdiction shows that we are dealing with Parliament in its mediaeval sense rather than with one of the houses—which is a post-mediaeval notion.   There is very slight authority to show that the Commons ever joined in the exercise of the civil jurisdiction of Parliament, and in 1400 they actually petitioned for a declaration[2] that they were relieved of this business " except in cases when it pleases the King of his special grace to show them the said judgments ".   This last phrase is a sufficient explanation of the few instances where the Commons are associated with appellate proceedings.

ERROR IN THE COUNCIL

It is an interesting illustration of the close connection between Parliament and Council to note that we do occasionally find the Council engaged in proceedings in error.[3]   The point is neatly put in a case in 1366 where we find that one party sued to Parliament, with the result, however, that the proceedings in error thus initiated were heard in the Council, which reversed the Common Pleas; " but the justices took no notice of the reversal before the council, because that is not the place where judgments can be reversed ".[4]   In other words, proceedings in error are common law proceedings, and must take place in the common law court of Parliament, since no common law jurisdiction in error remains in the Council after the separation of Parliament.

THE AUTHORITY OF HOUSE OF LORDS DECISIONS

The House of Lords was singularly slow in acquiring the present authority for its decisions.   The principle of precedent should logically have taken account of the Lords as the final civil court as soon as that position was in fact attained, but historically it did not.   The fundamental reason, no doubt, is that the Lords were not fitted for the great place they had assumed, and in the seventeenth and eighteenth centuries

[1] Y.B. 37 Henry VI, Hil. 3.
[2] *Rot. Parl.*, iii. 427.
[3] Baldwin, *The King's Council*, 57, 232–235, 334–338; *Rot. Parl.*, ii. 154 no. 40 (1344).
[4] Y.B. 39 Edward III, f. 14 (bastardy).

their decisions received little respect. All peers were entitled to vote, and there is evidence to show that votes were cast on considerations of family alliance and personal friendship rather than of legal doctrine—which can hardly have interested unprofessional laymen.[1] It is significant that no serious attempt was made to report the house's decisions until comparatively recent times. Shower's reports (1698), although designed to be helpful to the nobility, were actually voted a breach of the privilege which both houses claimed to prevent the reporting of their proceedings. In 1762 a text writer who introduced some House of Lords cases was threatened with similar action. Consequently, lawyers were not only unwilling, but also unable, to pay any serious attention to decisions of the Lords until authorised reporting was begun just about a hundred years ago, and it required the Judicature Act to establish the place of the Lords at the head of the hierarchy of courts and to reform its personnel so as to give its decisions the great authority which they now enjoy.

CRIMINAL JURISDICTION OVER PEERS

Like all mediaeval courts, Parliament had a special, and in some matters an exclusive, jurisdiction over its members. The Commons specially valued their famous " privileges " which belong to constitutional history; the Lords concentrated on the idea that they were members of a superior court and ought not to be tried for serious crimes in courts which they regarded as inferior. This notion was much reinforced by the growth of the conception of peerage, and so the trial of peers by their peers—a principle conveniently embodied in the Great Charter—became the distinctive badge of their order. Into the details of this curious history there is no need to enter, for it is singularly obscure, and in any case only concerns a very small class of persons. In one respect it presents a unique problem, for it is the only topic in English legal history where a Year Book has been charged with being a forgery.[2]

The most significant element in the trial of peers by the House of Lords is one to which we shall refer later[3]—namely, the fact that the Lords sit in their ancient character as a seignorial court of vassals or suitors, each one of whom is a judge, the presiding officer being the lord's steward—in this case, the Lord High Steward of England. If Parliament is not in session, the trial takes place before the Lord High Steward, who will then hold the entirely different position of a true judge, and the

---

[1] See generally, A. S. Turberville, *House of Lords in the Eighteenth Century*, and *The House of Lords as a Court of Law, 1784–1837*, in Law Quarterly Review, lii. 189–219.

[2] Y.B. 1 Henry IV, 1. These matters are discussed in L. W. Vernon Harcourt, *His Grace the Steward and Trial of Peers* (1907), and L. O. Pike, *Constitutional History of the House of Lords* (1894). Suspicion has also attached to Y.B. 1 Henry VII, Michs. no. 3 (as to which see A. F. Pollard, *Henry VII*, ii. 10 and M. Hemmant, *Cases in Exchequer Chamber* (Selden Society 51) 185). For a case which has been tampered with, see Y.BB. Edward II (Selden Society) xxiv. 83 and the intro. lxxv ff.

[3] Below, pp. 232–233.

Lords will be merely a jury from whom a unanimous verdict must be given. The use of either procedure was naturally rare,[1] although by no means obsolete; it was abolished in 1948.[2]

THE LORDS AND IMPEACHMENT

Impeachment is another aspect of mediaeval courts which has become part of the constitution of Parliament.[3]　Once again the Lords sit as the suitors of a seignorial court under the presidency of the Lord High Steward (or the Chancellor if the charges are only of misdemeanours); the decision therefore will rest with the Lords and will be given by a majority. The Commons, however, initiate the proceedings by making their accusation, much as if they were the presenting jury in a court leet, save only that they take a more active part and through their " managers " conduct an elaborate prosecution. The procedure is not so very old, for it first appears as late as 1376, and throughout its history has been confined to political prosecutions, frequently of royal ministers. It was, however, quite independent of the Crown, which had no part in the proceedings. No instances appear under the Yorkists or the Tudors, but many examples occur under the Stuarts and in the eighteenth century; the last was in 1805. In America impeachment still exists, where it is a formal exception to the principle of the separation of powers, inherited from English practice, and preserved in the Federal and State constitutions.

APPEALS OF TREASON

Still another aspect of seignorial courts was introduced for a short while into Parliament, and that was the " appeal " or private accusation of treason or felony determinable by combat between the appellant and the appellee. Appeals were common in seignorial and county courts, and were sometimes brought in the King's Bench, but the only examples in Parliament come from the reign of Richard II when they seemed to afford a welcome opportunity for baronial factions to fight spectacular judicial combats under the presidency of the King himself. As things turned out, no battles were fought, and the novelty of such proceedings in Parliament is shown by the doubts as to the proper procedure. At first it was thought that civil law might govern,[4] and it was popularly believed that such proceedings were actually carried out

---

[1] R. v. Russell, [1901] A.C. 446 and Proceedings on the Trial of Lord De Clifford, 12 Dec., 1935 (Stationery Office, 1936) are the last examples.

[2] Criminal Justice Act (1948).

[3] See Plucknett, Origin of Impeachment, Transactions of the Royal Historical Society (1942), 47, and Impeachment of 1376, Transactions (1951), 153; cf. ibid. (1952), 159, (1953), 145.

[4] Rot. Parl., iii. 236. The notion that civil law might be helpful in State trials long persisted: as late as 1710, when Dr Sacheverel was impeached, he was assigned as counsel by the House of Lords civilians as well as common lawyers.

under civil law rules.[1] At the beginning of the next reign a statute[2] was passed saying that appeals were henceforth to be governed by the ancient law of the land and were not to be brought in Parliament. A curious exception in the statute allows appeals of crimes done outside the realm to be brought in the Court of the Constable and Marshal, which later on was certainly governed by the civil law.

BILLS OF ATTAINDER

These bills are examples of King, Lords and Commons concurring in a criminal sentence whose sole justification, at least under the Stuarts, lay in reasons of state and political expediency. They began during the Wars of the Roses and were employed both under the Tudors and Stuarts, but more rarely in the eighteenth century, the last being in 1798. In some cases counsel were allowed to conduct the defence, but it has always been clear that a bill of attainder may be lawfully passed without any opportunity for defence being given. The procedure has therefore been very unpopular with Whig historians.

There was originally some reason other than mere vindictiveness for bills of attainder, since there was no common law means of trying a criminal in his absence. Attainders were therefore often used against persons who had taken refuge abroad. The effect of the attainder was much the same as that of the outlawry of the accused by the old common law process (which had become highly technical and uncertain). Even at common law one who had fled for felony would lose his chattels to the King and his lands would escheat to the lord, and his blood would be " corrupted ". The effect of an attainder was almost the same, save that the lands would go to the Crown instead of to the lord. The real abuse of attainders was their use against prisoners who were within the jurisdiction of the common law courts, and who therefore could have been lawfully tried.[3]

THE JURISDICTION OF THE PRIVY COUNCIL

So far this chapter has been concerned with the ultimate and extraordinary jurisdiction which passed from the mediaeval council to Parliament, and we have seen that such jurisdiction was, in principle, common law jurisdiction. The common law, however, during the middle ages was limited, and there was a fair amount of business outside its scope. Clergy and foreign merchants, for example, in practice looked to canon law and to the powers of the council to uphold their treaty privileges,

[1] *English Chronicle* (ed. J. S. Davies, Camden Soc., vol. 64), 131.

[2] 1 Hen. IV, c. 19 (1399).

[3] It began under Henry VIII; Coke, *Fourth Institute*, 37; J. R. Tanner, *Tudor Documents*, 423. Thomas Cromwell invented this abuse, and very properly was the first to suffer by it. For the origins and early history, see Plucknett, in Transactions of the Royal Historical Society (1953), 145.

while there was also the important territorial limitation which confined the common law to the body of an English county.

Now, as we have seen, the mediaeval council at the close of the fifteenth century became almost entirely judicial under its new style of the Star Chamber. Its advisory and executive functions passed to the newer and smaller body which Henry VIII organised as the " Privy Council ", and it is to this institution that much of the jurisdiction outside the common law eventually passed.[1]

In the seventeenth century the acts of the Privy Council show it engaged in a large mass of legal and judicial work in which it was constantly helped by the law officers of the Crown. In the reign of James I it almost seems as if the Council had come to occupy the position of its mediaeval forerunner, but after the Restoration this business would seem to have declined, and for the future it was particularly concerned with complaints—one may also say appeals—concerning the decisions of courts in the Channel Islands, the American colonies, and courts in India. The right of the Council to enjoy this jurisdiction may have been sound in constitutional theory and practice, but its remoteness in distance and in spirit from many of the disputes brought before it made its task difficult, while it was constantly reduced to impotence by the sturdy provincialism of courts which declined to recognise its authority. Like the House of Lords, the Privy Council in its judicial aspect is virtually a creation of the nineteenth century.

---

[1] Already under Henry VII the crown had a " council learned in the law " for advice on legal matters, feudal and others: R. Somerville, *The King's Council Learned in the Law*, English Historical Review, liv. 427; H. E. Bell, *Court of Wards and Liveries*, 4–5, 10, 12; C. G. Bayne, *Cases in Council* (Selden Society), xxv ff.

CHAPTER 11

THE COURTS IN THE NINETEENTH CENTURY

The nineteenth century is occupied almost continuously with changes in the judicial system, many of them individually of slight extent, and in the earlier half uncertain of their ultimate aim. In the middle of the century the experience obtained was sufficiently definite to make it clear that a policy of detailed readjustment was inadequate, and so the more thorough policy of the judicature acts eventually triumphed.

LOCAL COURTS OF REQUESTS

Reference has already been made to the high degree of centralisation which was reached by the common law at an early date. On the criminal side, the jurisdiction of the justices of the peace in quarter sessions and of the justices of assize provided an adequate remedy. Civil proceedings were not so well served, however, and with the decline of the local communal and seignorial courts (to some extent, at least, due to the interference of the central courts) the situation became serious. The eighteenth century attacked this problem in its own characteristic fashion. Communities which felt a special need for newer judicial organs secured special acts of Parliament, and in this way there came into existence a number of "courts of requests". They are interesting in many ways, notably because they embodied several legal heresies which did not become orthodox until a century or more later, such as a summary procedure without juries, and the examination of the parties themselves; nor did they form a part of the judicial system, for no appeal lay from them to the central courts.[1]

[1] See Winder, *The Courts of Requests*, Law Quarterly Review lii. 369.

THE REFORMED COUNTY COURTS

The ancient county courts had seriously declined, although a few were more active than others. In any case, they had inherited many centuries of obscure technicalities which made them quite inadequate for the need of the new communities growing up as a result of the industrial revolution. A significant attempt to reform one of them was made in 1750 by an act[1] which allowed the county clerk of the sheriff of Middlesex and the suitors of the county court to sit for small claims in the various hundreds in turn. It is clear that the effect of the act is not to create a new court, but to allow the clerk and suitors of the county to adopt a summary procedure for small claims and to sit in various parts of the county for that purpose. Decisions were reached by the clerk (a barrister) and the suitors together.

THE MODERN COUNTY COURTS

A somewhat similar procedure was finally adopted and applied to all the counties of England. An " act for the recovery of small debts and demands " (now generally referred to as the County Courts Act, 1846) made such radical changes that it is regarded by most writers as instituting a completely new set of courts.[2] In point of fact the act takes careful precautions to make it clear that its innovations are all grafted on the ancient stock of the old county court. The fruitful idea of the Middlesex experiment in sending an officer of the old county court to tour the county for small-claim business under a summary procedure was now developed. The eighteenth-century courts of requests and courts of conscience (as they were sometimes called) were by the statute now deemed to be " branches " of the county court. Paid judges, who must be barristers of standing, were to hold, in the name of the county, courts for small claims, each judge having a group of counties within his circuit.

The novelty therefore consisted in the appearance of many new " branches " of the ancient county court for small claims. The old court was left untouched with its unlimited jurisdiction (if a writ of *justicies* had been brought), and is still the only place where outlawry could be pronounced. The act of 1846 confined the branches to distinctly small business, but they flourished so exceedingly that their jurisdiction has been steadily increased; in 1888 a consolidating act[3] was passed, but the flood of new powers continued to flow, and at the

---

[1] 23 Geo. II, c. 33. For a rather different view of this act see Holdsworth, i. 191. An early attempt to set up a " court of conscience " in Middlesex appears in *Commons' Journals*, 17 December 1680. The erection of the " manor of Dunkerton " in 1721 was an eccentric way of solving the same problem in a rural area of Ireland: J. L. Sanford and M. Townsend, *Great Governing Fami ies of England*, ii. 144.

[2] 9 & 10 Vict., c. 95.

[3] 51 & 52 Vict., c. 43.

present moment they are the most important courts in the country for the ordinary run of business. The luxuriant branches have completely overlaid the venerable stock on which they were grafted.

THE STATE OF THE SUPERIOR COURTS

The reform of the central courts was a much more difficult enterprise, for one of the greatest causes of trouble consisted in their clerical staffs. Any reform in their procedure would inevitably involve the abolition of some lucrative sinecure or at least the reduction of its emoluments. These offices constituted valuable patronage for the government or the judges (who were still paid by fees and casual profits), and their incumbents were not removable. The expense of this fantastic system fell upon litigants, who received services from these officers by no means commensurate with the fees they paid. The biting sarcasms of Dickens are amply justified by the evidence given before the several commissions which investigated the machinery of the courts of law and equity.[1]

THE REFORM OF CHANCERY

The Chancery had long suffered from the fact that it was in practice as well as in theory a one-judge court. As its work increased the first expedient adopted was to delegate formal and detailed business to subordinate officers, whose work was to be supervised by the Chancellor.

In the middle ages the Chancellor had at his disposition a college or community of clerks the most important of whom acquired the title of Masters in Chancery. Their duties were very miscellaneous, but with the growth of the equitable jurisdiction of the Chancellor they became more and more specialised in assisting him in its exercise. The chief of the masters, known as the Master of the Rolls, in particular was sometimes called upon to take the place of a Chancellor who could not be spared from political and state duties. By the opening of the seventeenth century the Master of the Rolls was the constant assistant of the Chancellor in his judicial work, and a good deal of controversy as to his exact position took place.[2] A century later a statute[3] did something, but not much, to settle a question which historical research was unable to elucidate. The old feud prevented the office of Master of the Rolls being as useful as it might have been.

In 1813 the enormous arrears in Chancery accumulated under Lord Eldon provoked the appointment of a Vice-Chancellor, but as his acts were reviewable by the Chancellor the net result was still more delay

---

[1] See the interesting and illuminating lectures of Sir William Holdsworth, *Dickens as a Legal Historian* (New Haven, 1928).

[2] From 1596 to 1603, however, Sir Thomas Egerton was both Master of the Rolls and Lord Keeper.

[3] 3 George II, c. 30 (1730).

and increased arrears. Persisting in this policy, however, the Master of the Rolls was authorised to sit as a regular court in 1833 under the same restrictions—and with the same results, in spite of the fact that in 1831 a new system of courts was erected to take over Chancery's bankruptcy business. This reduction of work was soon nullified by the transfer to Chancery of the equity jurisdiction of the Exchequer in 1841, and so two more Vice-Chancellors had to be appointed.[1]

Then another policy was tried. It was now evident that even the appeals from subordinate equity judges were more than one Chancellor could dispatch, and so in 1851 two Lords Justices (a new title) were constituted, with the Master of the Rolls, as Court of Appeal in Chancery, intermediate between the courts of the Vice-Chancellors and Master of the Rolls, who all sat singly as judges of first instance, and the Lord Chancellor himself.

THE COURTS OF COMMON LAW

Here the situation was somewhat different. The competition between the King's Bench, Common Pleas and Exchequer which we have already mentioned resulted in these three courts having co-ordinate jurisdiction in many common classes of cases, although the differences of procedure between them were numerous and troublesome. The main problem was the complicated system of jurisdiction in error, for King's Bench heard errors of the Common Pleas, and the Exchequer Chamber those of the Exchequer; a differently constituted Exchequer Chamber might hear errors from the King's Bench, or they might go to Parliament, and still a third Exchequer Chamber was a court of discussion. The common characteristic of all the Exchequer Chambers was their delay and expense. In 1830, therefore, this tangle of jurisdictions was simplified by abolishing the jurisdiction in error of the King's Bench, leaving it a court of first instance. The statutory Exchequer Chambers were amalgamated into one court with the same name consisting of all the judges of all three courts, it being provided that an appeal from any one court should be heard by the judges of the other two courts.[2] The ultimate jurisdiction in error of Parliament was left untouched.

Thus while the Chancery was given an appeal court of Lords Justices in 1851, the common law courts were left since 1830 with a court of error consisting entirely of trial judges.

THE RELATIONS OF LAW AND EQUITY

The more harmonious relations between law and equity during the eighteenth century resulted in each system becoming closely involved

[1] 5 Vict., c. 5 (1841).
[2] 11 Geo. IV & 1 Will. IV, c. 70.

in the working of the other.   Chancery would send issues to be tried by a jury in a common law court, and would get the opinion of the judges on points of common law; litigants in the common law courts on the other hand would have recourse to Chancery in order to obtain discovery and other like advantages.

A symptom of this new atmosphere is the gradual introduction into common law courts of procedures and doctrines which were originally the peculiar province of Chancery.   Sometimes this was the result of statute, but at times a bold decision was sufficient.   The process appears early in the eighteenth century and is continuous down to the Judicature Acts, and its significance lies in the fact that the revolution effected by those acts was the culmination of a tendency which had long been at work.   Thus a statute of 1706 allowed certain equitable defences to be pleaded in common law actions upon bonds under seal;[1] and a decision of 1789 allowed a party in a common law court to plead a deed which had been lost or destroyed without producing it.[2]

This tendency was carried very much further by the Common Law Procedure Act, 1854, which required Chancery to find its own law without sending to a common law court for a judicial opinion, and to hear oral evidence and to use a jury; common law courts on the other hand were empowered to grant injunctions, to compel discovery and to admit a variety of equitable defences.

Year after year new acts made further changes in the system of procedure along these lines, and it soon became evident that the reforms, although useful, were creating an enormous body of detailed statute law with the inevitable multiplication of anomalies as defects in the acts became apparent.   The mere fact that cases outside the acts began to look like anomalies helped forward the movement for a simpler and more radical remedy.[3]

THE JUDICATURE ACTS

Lord Selborne drafted and piloted through Parliament the Judicature Act of 1873.   By it all the old central courts were abolished and replaced by a Supreme Court of Judicature, which consisted of a High Court of Justice and a Court of Appeal.   To the High Court was transferred the jurisdiction of all the courts of common law and of equity, and of the courts of divorce, probate, bankruptcy and Admiralty.   To the Court of Appeal was transferred the jurisdiction of the Court of Appeal in Chancery and of the Court of Exchequer Chamber.   There was thus one court of appeal and one court of first instance.   Moreover, there was only one

[1] 4 & 5 Anne, c. 3.

[2] *Read* v. *Brookman*, 3 Term Rep. 151; for numerous other examples, see Ames, *Lectures on Legal History*, 104–115.

[3] For the corresponding movement abroad, see J. H. Beale, *Equity in America*, Cambridge Law Journal, i. 21.

appeal, for the 1873 act abolished the appellate jurisdiction of Parliament, but in spite of Lord Selborne's efforts an amending act in 1875 restored it, and thus retained the double appeal. As we have seen, the Court of Appeal in Chancery consisted of special Lords Justices of Appeal, but the Exchequer Chamber consisted of the judges of first instance of the common courts; both principles were retained under the Judicature Acts. The Court of Appeal was to consist of Lords Justices of Appeal, but the Chancellor could call upon any judge of the High Court to sit in the Court of Appeal, and this possibility is still open, although it is not often used.

The High Court at first sat in five divisions (Chancery, Queen's Bench, Common Pleas, Exchequer, Probate, Divorce and Admiralty—the last three topics being kept together because they were until now the concern of a special branch of the profession organised as Doctors' Commons). In 1881 all the common law divisions were amalgamated into one King's Bench Division. These divisions are not separate jurisdictions but merely administrative devices to bring particular types of business before judges who are particularly familiar with them. The creation of the " commercial list " is an example of the flexibility of this system.

Finally, there is the important provision which effected the fusion of law and equity.[1] It is often stated that this fusion was the work of the judicature acts—which of course is perfectly true. But there would also be a good deal of truth in the converse proposition that the fusion of law and equity which had already taken place to some extent (as we have seen) was itself the cause of the judicature acts, for the synthesis of the two into one body of law could only operate effectively through a unified court.

THE APPELLATE JURISDICTION ACT

Owing to the retention of the double appeal, it became necessary to reform the constitution of the ultimate court. This was done in 1876 by the Appellate Jurisdiction Act which authorised the appointment of Lords of Appeal in Ordinary who were to be lords of Parliament for life and whose presence was required when the House of Lords was engaged on judicial business.

The appellate jurisdiction exercised by the Privy Council in the eighteenth century from colonial tribunals has already been mentioned; to this an act of 1832 added appellate jurisdiction over ecclesiastical courts in England, and the Appellate Jurisdiction Act of 1876 provided for the new Lords of Appeal in Ordinary sitting both in the Lords and in the judicial committee of the Privy Council, thus affording a valuable link between the two bodies.

---

[1] A similar course had already been adopted in the constitution of the State of New York in 1846. Cf. J. H. Beale, *Equity in America*, Cambridge Law Journal, i. 21.

CRIMINAL JURISDICTION

Criminal law was the slowest to change. For centuries it was an unwritten axiom that a criminal trial could not be reviewed. The solemnity of jury trial was so great that it was hardly thinkable that a verdict could be set aside for any reason; and if a jury's view of the facts was final, the court's view of the law was almost equally decisive. A writ of error might be brought, but as the Crown prosecuted and had also the duty of issuing this writ, it followed that error could only be brought where the Crown itself was disposed to admit that the trial was unsatisfactory. A bold decision of 1705 held that the writ of error *must* be issued[1]—at least in cases of misdemeanour. Such a procedure was very capricious, at the best, for the record in which error had to be found was a highly artificial document, bearing little relation to the material points of the trial. Rather more promising was the growth of a practice of granting new trials—but again only in cases of misdemeanour.

Hence trial judges, realising how little chance there was of revising their decisions, resorted to the practice of reserving difficult cases for informal discussion among their colleagues at Serjeants' Inn. At last, official sanction was given to this procedure by the creation in 1848 of the Court for Crown Cases Reserved. The result was not to add any new means of reviewing criminal cases, which remained exactly as before the act. Nothing was done, for example, to extend to felonies the facilities for review, meagre as they were, which existed in respect of misdemeanours.

COURT OF CRIMINAL APPEAL

Only in 1907 did a sensational case arouse public interest in a matter which Sir James Stephen and a Royal Commission had long ago considered as crying for reform.

The writ of error and the Court for Crown Cases Reserved were abolished and appeals involving law or fact were allowed to a newly erected Court of Criminal Appeal. In exceptional cases a further appeal was permitted to the House of Lords.

THE PROFESSION AND REFORM

The above outline contains the barest essentials of the great movement of institutional reform in the nineteenth century. Large and important subjects have not been treated here, and reference should be made to Sir William Holdsworth's *History* for such matters as ecclesiastical, bankruptcy and Admiralty jurisdictions which were the subjects of numerous changes during this period.

[1] *Paty's Case*, 1 Salk. 504. Cf. above, p. 201 n. 2.

A word may be said about the attitude of lawyers as a profession to the bewildering mass of legislation which swept over them.   A recent article[1] has suggested (on the strength of general and professional newspapers published during the period) that the legal profession was wholly obstructionist in the nineteenth century.   This is surely an exaggeration. No judgment of a profession can be fair which omits to mention its accredited leaders, whose energy and vision have always to contend with conservatism and obstructionism among sections of their followers. To correct the impression it will be enough to refer to a few among many great lawyers who devoted their abilities to the cause of reform— to Cairns, Selborne, Blackburn, Bramwell and many others.[2]

[1] E. R. Sunderland, *The English Struggle for Procedural Reform* (1926), Harvard Law Review, xxxix. 725.

[2] See, for example, *Select Essays in Anglo-American Legal History*, i. 533, where Lord Bowen names others, many of whom are now provided with memoirs or biographies.

CHAPTER 12

THE LEGAL PROFESSION

It is very difficult to say at what date professional lawyers first appear in the common law system. We could hardly expect to find them until there was a settled jurisdiction with regular courts; and, as we have seen, it took some time before these elementary conditions were reached. In this, as in many other matters, it is necessary to consider the local and the central courts separately if the discussion is to be put in the right perspective.

In the ancient local communal courts there was often some specialisation along legal lines, but those lines did not at all correspond to the present organisation of the profession. Certain legal functions became attached to certain pieces of land (eventually becoming hereditary like the land), but they were apparently judicial functions. We constantly find that attendance at courts is " real " and an incident of tenure; we even find some tenants holding by the services of advising the court, or of taking part in its sessions, when particularly difficult questions are under discussion, thereby sharing the peril of being amerced if a mistake occurred. But we hardly find any trace of lawyers who make a living by giving advice to actual or prospective litigants. The only trials in the Anglo-Saxon age which we can follow in any detail are important cases involving high ecclesiastical dignitaries, and yet even they seem to conduct their cases in person. There is no convincing evidence of a legal profession in the Anglo-Saxon period.[1]

[1] The portion of Herman Cohen's *History of the English Bar* (London, 1929) dealing with the Anglo-Saxon and Norman ages collects every available scrap of evidence.

THE ADVOCATUS

Even the word " advocate " is obscure in its early meaning. While the normal use of it to denote one who presents a litigant's case in court for him is certainly old, yet it is often difficult to distinguish whether in any given case it may not mean that special protector whom churches and laymen sought in the dark ages, whose rights over laymen became a feudal seignory, and over churches the later *advocatio* or advowson.

NARRATORS AND ATTORNEYS

As for the central courts, for some time it seems that there were no professional advocates. Proceedings were informal, and at times (as Maitland remarked) hardly distinguishable from a family quarrel. The parties themselves presented their case as best they could before the King, who was attended by such nobles, clergy and trusted advisers as happened to be at court at the moment.

The growth of the King's intervention, measured by the extension of the use of royal writs, had the effect that the hearings were now more commonly delegated to a group of courtiers (who in time became a regular bench), and inevitably, as soon as business was entrusted to deputies, it became necessary to confine them within a routine, a strict procedure, a set of forms and a system of pleading. These in turn necessitated the growth of a legal profession, for the public could hardly be expected to understand the newly invented office machinery of the King's Court.

Under Henry II it is already apparent from Glanvill's treatise that parties can appear in person or by substitute, and this " *responsalis* " seems already to be particularly concerned with the procedural steps of the case—the appearances, defaults, essoins and the like. Such a person may be a friend, a relative or (as often happened in the petty assizes) a bailiff. Early in the next century a fuller type of representation becomes general, and so in the time of Bracton we read much of the " attorney ", who had already proved more useful than the " *responsalis* ".[1] The attorney is appointed by the party in court, under elaborate safeguards, and has power to bind his principal. His appearance or default is equivalent to that of his master; he has power to commit his master to a particular plea. Such a lawyer needs great integrity and diligence, although perhaps no great powers of intellect or learning other than procedural.

The attorney was a great convenience to wealthy landowners who were constantly involved in litigation and found it troublesome to appear personally, as also to ecclesiastical bodies and others, but law was becoming so complicated that the public needed further assistance of a

[1] For the intricate distinction at different dates between *responsales* and attorneys, see Holdsworth, ii. 316; Herman Cohen, *History of the English Bar*, 128; Glanvill (ed. Woodbine), 262; Plucknett, *The Mediaeval Bailiff*, 15.

different kind. Already in Henry III's reign there are signs of a new type of professional lawyer. A plaintiff no longer felt confident that he could even tell his tale in court without making slips, while, as for the latter proceedings, they would certainly be even more tricky. So he would resort to an experienced *narrator* (or *conteur* as they put it in French), who told the tale for him. Very soon the *narratores* become a regular profession, and later still their exploits form the subject of the Year Books. On the other hand, they figure but little on the plea rolls, which are more concerned with the attorney, whose acts are binding on his principal.

It is somewhat difficult to say precisely when these two functions become the province of professional lawyers. When more plea rolls are printed it will be easy to trace the attorneys, for their names often appear in the pleadings and also in separate rolls of attorneys.[1] The constant recurrence of the same names will show the existence of a profession, but at present there are few thirteenth-century plea rolls in print. The *narratores* are more elusive and the existing lists are conjectural—and even imaginative—for the earlier period.[2] It would seem that the habit of enrolling certain details in the levying of fines (which are the source of our knowledge that certain persons were *narratores*) only began towards the close of the thirteenth century;[3] failing this information, the reign of Henry III is necessarily represented only by casual scattered references.[4]

In the present state of our knowledge it therefore seems safe to say that there certainly were professional *narratores* and attorneys during the reign of Edward I, and that possibly these professions already existed under Henry III.

THE WRIT OF 1292 AND LEGAL EDUCATION

An inevitable result of the development of a professional element of this kind was the tendency to perpetuate itself by a system of legal education, and it is in this connection that we first find official recognition of the new state of affairs. In 1292 a royal writ was sent to Meetingham, C.J., and his fellows of the Common Bench, in these terms:

" Concerning attorneys and learners (' apprentices ') the lord King enjoined Mettingham and his fellows to provide and ordain at their discretion a certain number, from every county, of the better, worthier and more promising students

---

[1] John de Hotoft in 1307 received pensions and payments as the " attorney and councillor " of many magnates, but denied that he was thereby a conspirator: Sayles, *King's Bench* (Selden Society), II. cxxxv.

[2] For example, the list prefixed to Pulling, *Order of the Coif*.

[3] The procedure is explained by G. J. Turner in Y.BB. Edward II (Selden Society), IV. xv; compare Pike in Y.BB. 16 Edward III, II. xi, and 20 Edward III, II. xii.

[4] Collected by Herman Cohen, *History of the Bar*, 172 ff.

. . . , and that those so chosen should follow the court and take part in its business; and no others."[1]

This brief order was evidently the result of mature reflection, for it is enrolled on the Parliament roll. The interpretation of it is not so easy. Mr Cohen's attempt[2] to simplify it by treating the word " attorneys " as an interpolation is not supported by the original roll, which is accurately printed. On the other hand, his suggestion that at this time the apprentice might, and sometimes did, act as attorney is supported by evidence,[3] and the writ would indicate that both professions began with a common education.

It will be seen that this writ did not touch the existing pleaders, but merely made arrangements for perpetuating the profession by putting aspirants under the control of the court. The use of the word " apprentice " suggests that the student was attached to a practising lawyer whom he assisted in minor matters in return for instruction—such was the general nature of the apprenticeship system in the middle ages. On this point there is little light; but we soon find that the apprentices have a special enclosure, humorously called the " crib ",[4] from which they could follow the proceedings in court. It is also clear that some of them were no tyros either; they will criticise the serjeants on occasion, and the earlier Year Books occasionally think it worth while to record " what was said in the crib ". The provisions of the writ that attorneys should be classified by counties were certainly put into effect, for such mediaeval evidence as exists shows that each county had its group of attorneys who confined their activities to business arising within their county. Whether this means that the attorney's usual place of business was in the country with a town agent, or in town with a country agent, does not appear; but one of these arrangements must be presumed from the nature of the attorney's duties.

The most remarkable features of the writ, however, are its policy of putting legal education under the direction of the court, and its promise to successful students of a monopoly of practice. The attorneys' branch was henceforth a closed profession,[5] reserved for those who had been educated to it, and admitted to it, in the official course. The fact that the writ applies to apprentices in general most probably means that it

---

[1] *Rot. Parl.,* i. 84. Long afterwards, substantially the same provisions were imposed by statute 4 Henry IV, c. 18 (1402), and in 1455 the judges were consulted on a petition to reduce the number of attorneys in Norfolk from 80 to 6 only: *Rot. Parl.,* v. 326 no. 57.

[2] Herman Cohen, *History of the Bar,* 283.

[3] Cohen, *op. cit.,* 283.

[4] Y.BB. Edward II (Selden Society), ii. xvi, iv. xli.

[5] In so far as it was exercised for reward. Unprofessional attorneys constantly appear, *e.g.* husband for wife, bailiff for lord. Clerks of the courts often acted as attorneys for members of the public: G. O. Sayles, *Select Cases in King's Bench,* i, xcviii, H. G. Richardson in Transactions of the Royal Historical Society (1932), 66–68, T. W. Simons in University of Colorado Studies, xxii. 381–396.

had a similar effect on the position of the *narratores*, although here the evidence is a little less clear.

Was this writ the beginning of legal education in England? Here we must distinguish. Even in the darkest age a few tags of legal learning persisted as part of the conventional study of grammar and rhetoric; the establishments of successive archbishops of Canterbury were an effective, if informal, school of law in the twelfth century; at Oxford there was already something like a law school in the middle of the century. The first we hear of law schools in London is that they were closed by royal edict[1] in 1234, but, like the other instances of law teaching just mentioned, they can hardly have been schools of English law. London may have been in a peculiar position with regard to lawyers, for there were many courts there, or near by—royal, civic and ecclesiastical. In 1259 the writ abolishing law schools was followed by a royal grant that parties should not be compelled to retain counsel in small matters.[2] Then came a reaction. In 1280 we read that the complaint is now that lawyers are not sufficiently educated—which is not at all surprising. The city authorities therefore refuse audience except to those whom they have admitted as knowing their work " reasonably well "; they further divide the profession into three branches, counters, attorneys and essoiners, each being confined to his special function.[3] There is no evidence to suggest that the London bar and the Westminster bar had anything in common, but it is significant that both of them were in need of regulation and education almost at the same time.

Even manorial courts were being invaded by hired lawyers, and the tendency caused some alarm;[4] the King himself shared this suspicion of professional pleaders, and in 1297 excluded them from the exchequer.[5]

EDUCATION IN COURT

The alternative to this system of education in court would have been education at the universities. That would have given a very different complexion to English law. Students would have learned either the civil law or the canon law, very frequently both; and would have learnt it from a cosmopolitan literature of texts and text-books. Such teaching would necessarily have been dogmatic and doctrinal, seeking principles common to many lands rather than the actual practice of any of them. If advocates trained in such schools had ever been admitted to the English bar during the middle ages, some sort of reception would have been inevitable. It must not be assumed that a reception then or later would necessarily have been a disaster—in the field of private law it

---

[1] *Close Rolls* (1234–1237), 26–27. For comments, see H. G. Richardson, *Azo, Drogheda and Bracton*, English Historical Review, lix. 40.

[2] *Liber de Antiquis Legibus*, 42–43.

[3] *Liber Custumarum*, i. 280.

[4] Maitland, *Select Pleas in Manorial Courts*, 136.

[5] Text in G. O. Sayles, *Select Cases in King's Bench*, I, cv. n. 3.

might even have accelerated our progress considerably. The danger, if any there was, would lie rather in the adoption of Romanistic political theory which so frequently accompanied a reception of Romanesque law. Disaster or blessing, it is quite clear that the course of English legal history would have been very different if Edward I had looked to the universities instead of to the crowd of students haunting his courts at Westminster for the future generation of lawyers. This momentous decision had a significance which extended further even than the legal profession, as Maitland has pointed out in words which deserve quotation and reflection:

> " No, the clergy were not the only learned men in England, the only cultivated men, the only men of ideas. Vigorous intellectual effort was to be found outside the monasteries and universities. These lawyers are worldly men, not men of the sterile caste; they marry and found families, some of which become as noble as any in the land; but they are in their way learned, cultivated men, linguists, logicians, tenacious disputants, true lovers of the nice case and the moot-point. They are gregarious, clubable men, grouping themselves in hospices which become schools of law, multiplying manuscripts, arguing, learning and teaching, the great mediators between life and logic, a reasoning, reasonable element in the English nation."[1]

THE LAW AN OPEN PROFESSION

It is but natural that leading lawyers should begin to form marriage alliances, with the result that families arose with well-marked professional characteristics; the same thing happened among the nobility, the gentry, the merchants, and for a time even in the church.[2] Nevertheless, " Edward I would not, like his uncle Frederick II, have closed the high offices of the law to all but the legal families, and so turned the class, as Frederick did the knightly class, into a caste."[3] Nor did seats in the king's court become hereditary or vendible, as in the French *parlements*. As a result, the law together with the church constituted the two main avenues to fame and fortune which were open to men of outstanding ability, however obscure their origin.

NARRATORS BECOME SERJEANTS

The quiet and patient labours of the attorneys have assuredly not been without their influence on the law, but it was the more spectacular career of the newer branch that is most evident in the literature of our legal history. The *narratores* whose nimble fencing at the bar of the court became so essential to the success of an action at law must have seemed to the public, as well as to the students, the embodiment of all those qualities which are appreciated by lovers of intellectual combat. When the common law was still young and just setting out to extend its jurisdiction and enlarge its store of doctrine, a career at the bar must

---

[1] Y.BB. Edward II (Selden Society), i. lxxxi.

[2] See the examples in R. Foreville, *L'Église et la royauté* (Paris, 1943), 393.

[3] Stubbs, *Constitutional History* (1875), ii. 189–190.

have been intensely exciting, and profoundly important for the development of the law. For some centuries they continued to be called, on certain occasions, by their old name of *narratores*, but in general use this term gave way to the title " serjeant-at-law ".[1] The tempting coincidence that serjeanty was a tenure, that lawyers got " fees ", and did fealty to their " lords ",[2] need not prove that serjeants were feudally provided with lands, although the word serjeant does seem to imply a rather more permanent relationship of employment than is usually the case with the ordinary litigant and his counsel. Indeed, even the word " counsel " suggests membership of a " council " such as great nobles retained during the middle ages to guide them in the management of their affairs.[3]

The word " serjeant " not only excludes merely casual engagement, but also lays stress on the employer. A serjeant is the *serviens* of someone, and it is a difficult problem to determine of whom. The Statute of Westminster I in 1275 speaks of " serjeant counters ", but the form serjeant-at-law as a settled title (and not merely as a description) is hardly earlier than 1310, and as it occurs at that date in a writ[4] from the King commanding William Herle to " take the state and degree of serjeant at law " it has been argued that a serjeant was so called because he was the King's serjeant. " The *servientes* begin and end as *servientes regis*; other people employ them and *regis* is dropped." The fact that the Crown as early as 1310 (if we can trust to Coke's memory) began to appoint " serjeants " just at the moment when the word becomes commonly associated with lawyers, lends a good deal of support to this theory. On the other hand, there is the difficulty of explaining how it was that serjeant became co-terminous with narrator: can it be that the Crown retained the whole bar?[5] In the fifteenth century we have only serjeants and apprentices, with no intermediate grade;[6] what then had become of the *narratores*? If we are not bound to hold that all serjeants were the King's serjeants,[7] then it is easier to account for the change as merely a change of style.

[1] " Serjeant-counter " is a transitional form; Cohen, *Origins of the English Bar,* Law Quarterly Review, xxxi. 61–65.

[2] *Brevia Placitata* (Selden Society), 135, explains that clerks, counters, champions or serjeants may do fealty or homage but are not thereby necessarily bound to do suit of court.

[3] See above, p. 217 n. 1.

[4] The text is known only from 10 Rep. xxxix; see the discussion of the whole matter by Herman Cohen, *History of the English Bar,* 185 ff.

[5] In 1321 " evil councillors " abetted Edward II in retaining the *élite* of the serjeants, so that good counsel could not be had against the crown: B. Wilkinson in English Historical Review, lxiii. 20; *Chronicles of Edward I and Edward II* (ed. Stubbs, Rolls Series), ii. 62–64.

[6] So too under Richard II; *Rot. Parl.,* iii. 58, 101, which are referred to more fully below, p. 224.

[7] Some of the serjeants were specially distinguished above their fellows as " King's serjeants " (Y.B. 20 & 21 Edward I, 442, and Y.B. 21 & 22 Edward I, 222, are possibly early examples from 1293; Geoffrey Scrope and Herle in 1321 had fees as King's serjeants: Herman Cohen, *History of the English Bar,* 287); if all serjeants ever were the King's, then this would show that the fact had been forgotten.

THE WORK OF THE SERJEANTS

The functions of the serjeant are easily distinguished from those of the attorney. The arguments, the clever altercations which at this period seem to be conducted *ex tempore* (later they will be committed to writing with great particularity as written pleadings), the offering of exceptions and answering them, the groping through masses of doubtful facts and uncertain law in search for a safe point on which to take issue, the arguments upon the inevitable faults in process, and upon the legal consequences of an ascertained state of facts—all this is the highly skilled work of the serjeants. To it they brought various gifts, sound legal learning above all, supported by quick wit, resource and ingenuity—sometimes even a clever fallacy may be tried; but the bench consists of men who have already passed by the bar, and from the Year Books it is clear that the court was not easily fooled, and good-naturedly it would sometimes remind a serjeant so. Once when an extra subtle point was raised, the court was unimpressed; the judge remembered that he himself had once resorted to it while at the bar taking a case for which there was nothing better to be said.[1] The court constantly declined to be lured into discussions too far removed from the question judicially before it; it would sometimes close a discussion where it suspected that the apprentices had manufactured a difficult case for the sake of enjoying the arguments upon it.[2] Even a *bona fide* case involving difficult questions would be adjourned term after term until the parties found a compromise, rather than allow the court to be enticed out of its depth. The proceedings were therefore as practical as contemporaries could make them; no unnecessary pedantry or cleverness, and above all no oratory. Nowhere during the middle ages do we find a trace of rhetoric in the English courts. True to their administrative origin, they kept themselves in a strictly business attitude. It is only after the Renaissance that we find the bad old classical tradition of Greece and Rome which turned lawsuits into an oratorical contest appearing in England.

The earliest Year Books show us the serjeants conducting these altercations (which later are so carefully arranged by counsel in written pleadings) orally in court, and apparently with little previous knowledge of what lay behind them or of which way they would turn. It seems that there was always room for surprise, and that each side did its utmost to conceal the facts from the other side. From this it will be seen that a successful serjeant depended upon quick thinking in order to understand his own case and his opponent's, for it would seem that hardly any work was done on a case before it came into court. It is not surprising, therefore, that the group of serjeants practising in the last years of Edward I was small, very busy and amazingly clever. As we shall later see, the

[1] Y.B. 15 Edward III (Rolls Series), 390.
[2] Y.B. 33–35 Edward I (Rolls Series), 64.

Year Books of this period are full of admiration for the brilliant serjeants whose feats of intellect are there recounted, and the modern reader can entirely share that feeling; from 1290 to 1310 there was a very brilliant bar in England.

As we have seen, the early serjeant was rather in the dark about his case until he had wrung a few admissions from his adversary. Consequently, what a serjeant said might or might not correspond to the facts of the case. Those facts are in the knowledge of the party but not of his serjeant, unless he has seen fit to enlighten him. So when there is a chance that an alleged state of facts may be material to the decision of the case, the serjeant has to " get himself avowed ", that is to say, procure a confirmation or denial by the party or his attorney of the statement made by the serjeant. The party therefore has the advantage of a second thought before he finally commits himself to the line of action proposed by the serjeant.

The serjeants from the beginning held a high place in the legal world; we soon find Parliament referring hard questions to the serjeants as well as to the judges, and quite early in the fourteenth century the Crown adopts the policy of recruiting the bench from the outstanding men at the bar. Wherever this policy has been thoroughly adopted, the result is a remarkable relationship of goodwill and understanding between judge and barrister, which permits of real co-operation in the administration of justice. A spirit of hostility or distrust between bench and bar, on the other hand, inevitably adds to the length of proceedings, without improving the quality of the product.

LATER HISTORY OF THE SERJEANTS

In the course of the fourteenth century the serjeants consolidated their position, becoming a close guild in complete control of the legal profession. Within their fraternity are united the bench and the leaders of the bar; the junior practitioners (who have developed out of the old class of apprentices) are outside the guild but under its supervision, and so too is the whole system of legal education. By the close of the fourteenth century the judges are all members of the order of serjeants, and serjeants alone can be heard in the principal court, that of Common Pleas. Their dignity increased with their emoluments, which must have been enormous; they ranked as knights and surrounded themselves with elaborate and costly ceremonial. The creation of a serjeant obliged him to provide a feast comparable to a king's coronation, to distribute liveries and gold rings in profusion, and to maintain the proceedings for seven days. Their numbers were always low, as can be seen by the fact that every serjeant had his own pillar in St. Paul's Cathedral which served him as office and consultation room.[1] The fact that apprentices

---

[1] Sed quære: Herman Cohen, History of the Bar, 490 n.

were able to sustain these heavy charges and to become serjeants indicates that they too did not labour without reward. In the middle ages counsel conferred directly with their clients, and contracts for fees were enforceable in law. The serjeant's dress varied considerably at different dates, the most constant element being the coif, a close-fitting cap of white silk or linen fastened under the chin; hence the term " order of the coif " for the guild of serjeants. For the rest, they used on solemn occasions a long robe with short cape and hood which was party-coloured, the left side and the right being of different colours. In later times they wore on ordinary occasions a red robe (somewhat like the present judges' scarlet robes, but without the fur), and later still, black. All these (like academic and most other robes) were derived from what used to be the ordinary civilian dress in the middle ages. No part of English judicial costume is of ecclesiastical origin, as is sometimes erroneously stated.[1] In 1877 the order was dissolved, Serjeants' Inn sold, and the proceeds divided among the surviving members.

APPRENTICES, BARRISTERS AND INNS

When the writ of 1292 speaks of " apprentices " it is clear that it means literally learners; but it is equally clear less than a century later that the term has ceased to be appropriate and that its meaning has radically changed. In the assessments for Richard II's poll-tax of 1379 " every serjeant and great apprentice of the law " is taxed at the same rate as a baron, " other apprentices following the law " pay only half, and " all the other apprentices of less estate " one sixth.[2] Great apprentices are therefore as wealthy as serjeants, barons and aldermen of London. Similarly, when a commission to inquire into the possibility of legal reforms was appointed in Parliament in 1381 its composition was fixed at eight members—two justices, two serjeants and four lawful apprentices.[3] These apprentices were therefore men of eminence in their profession, competent to give the government useful technical advice, and some of them were of sufficient substance to be taxed on the highest scale of the profession, on a par with the bulk of the nobility.

Another curious anomaly. When Fortescue wrote in the fifteenth century he likened the serjeants to the doctors in the universities. There was indeed an external resemblance, perhaps the result of deliberate imitation. The red robe, the coif (equivalent to the doctor's hat), the costly feast on taking the degree, the requirement of having delivered two readings—are all closely parallel to university traditions. But in essentials there was a grave difference. The degree of doctor entitled one to teach, but the degree of serjeant was actually a disqualification.

---

[1] See the admirable article " Robes " in the *Encyclopaedia Britannica* (11th edition).

[2] *Rot. Parl.*, iii. 58. (This list will repay study; it is a most interesting outline of the structure of English society in the time of Chaucer.)

[3] *Rot. Parl.*, iii. 101.

If the doctors of the common law did not teach, however, the " students " did, and so we have the curious fact of legal education being conducted by apprentices.[1]

Their life centred in the Inns of Court, which, like a university, provided for their general education and common life. Here they studied law and many other things—history, music and dancing, for example—and this full and fashionable education made the Inns a great resort for the youth of wealthy and noble families, even although they had no intention of practising law. In the beginning of the seventeenth century it was in the Middle Temple Hall, before the Queen and a fashionable audience, that Shakespeare's play *Twelfth Night* was first performed. There were more than a dozen such inns, and during the fourteenth century the apprentices changed their quarters many times, leasing first one inn, then another. In exactly the same way came into existence some of the halls at Oxford and Cambridge. It may be that these groups of apprentices formed round some senior master who headed their community and directed their studies, while the bench approved the arrangement and permitted the master to choose those whom he considered fit for call. The largest of these inns were Lincoln's Inn, Gray's Inn, the Middle Temple and the Inner Temple, but their early history is largely conjectural. Of the numerous smaller inns (which have not survived), even less is known with certainty. In time, the inns acquired a roughly uniform type of constitution; the benchers formed a governing body somewhat similar to the fellows of a college at Oxford or Cambridge, while the readers conducted an elaborate system of legal instruction. It was from among the readers that the serjeants were chosen. Next below the readers came the utter (or outer) barristers,[2] who were the most notable rank among the apprentices and were privileged to argue in the mock trials or moots[3] which were staged for the instruction of the students. Below them were the inner barristers, who soon are known simply as " students ". There were also some professional attorneys, until in the later middle ages they were excluded from the Inns of Court. As numbers grew, subsidiary inns were formed subject to one or the other of the four great inns, and these were called Inns of Chancery;[4] finally these Inns of Chancery were reserved for attorneys and solicitors only.

[1] By way of digression it may be noted that law students abroad were notable for their independence. At Bologna they reversed the usual order of things, and instead of that university being ruled by the masters, it was ruled by the students, who imposed a very strict discipline upon the professors. Our own apprentices required the resignation from the inn of those members who became serjeants.

[2] The word first occurs in 24 Henry VIII, c. 13, s. 3 (1533)—Herman Cohen in Law Quarterly Review, xlvi. 405–406.

[3] The importance of these moot cases may be judged from the fact that they sometimes appear in the old reports: see an example in Pound and Plucknett, *Readings*, 130.

[4] For these, see Tout, *Collected Papers*, ii. 143 ff.

SEVENTEENTH-CENTURY CHANGES

Coming to the seventeenth century, we find that numerous developments took place. The class of attorneys rapidly grew. The barrister now looked upon the attorney as a superior sort of clerk; this was justifiable, for the attorneys were now regarded as technically part of the clerical staff of the courts. For this reason, the attorneys were the more likely to be in contact with the client, receiving his instructions and only consulting a barrister when difficulties arose. Attorneys therefore did the bulk of the more straightforward conveyancing and drafting of pleadings, while the barristers acted as consulting experts. In this way, the attorney was actually the client of the barrister, rather than the layman who had first engaged the attorney. The barrister asserted a social superiority by declining to sue for his fees (the rule appears in 1629–1630), although attorneys continued to do so. In the meanwhile, many students of the Inns of Court specialised in pleading and conveyancing, and practised as members of new sub-divisions of the legal profession as " pleaders ", " equity draftsmen " and " conveyancers ". There was no need for such men to be called to the bar, and as a rule they were not. They were therefore described as " practitioners under the bar "; generally they were members of an Inn of Court, however, and therefore subject to the inn's professional discipline. The attorneys, on the other hand, being thrust out of the Inns of Court in the middle of the sixteenth century,[1] were in a difficult position, until about 1729 we find that a " Society of Gentlemen Practicers in the Courts of Law and Equity " was established for their government and protection, together with the solicitors.

SOLICITORS, PLEADERS AND CONVEYANCERS

The courts of equity—Chancery, Star Chamber, Court of Requests —were differently organised. The permanent clerical establishment of each of these courts undertook the duties of attorneys, and so professional attorneys had no place there. Still, there remained numerous duties of a quasi-legal character which had to be done, and litigants soon found it convenient to have a sort of law agent who would set the complicated machinery in motion by engaging and conferring with the various branches of the profession as occasion required, and doing other duties, sometimes of a legal and sometimes of a business character. These were the " solicitors ". When they first appear in the fifteenth century they seem more business agents than lawyers, but by the seventeenth century they have won a place beside the attorneys and a recognised standing, especially as practising in courts of equity.

During the eighteenth century these various branches continued to exist side by side. An act of 1729, subsequently renewed, imposed

---

[1] H. H. L. Bellot, *Exclusion of Attorneys from the Inns of Court*, Law Quarterly Review, xxvi. 137.

regulations upon attorneys and solicitors, and formed the basis of future development.[1] At the same time the act imposed rather heavy taxation upon these practitioners. By the nineteenth century, the solicitors gained a definite lead over the other branches of the profession, and although there were still a few conveyancers and pleaders licensed to practise, the profession for all ordinary purposes in England now consists of two branches only, barristers and solicitors.

Sir Frederick Pollock has made an interesting suggestion that the development of the profession in the eighteenth century had been influenced by the fact that Roman Catholics were prevented by the Test Act[2] from practising at the bar. Instead of becoming barristers, therefore, Roman Catholics who took to the law practised as pleaders and particularly as conveyancers. A famous example is Charles Butler, and the last of a distinguished line of Catholic conveyancers was H. W. Challis, who died in 1898. Sir Frederick concludes:

" Whether their real property doctrine was at all coloured by scholastic methods, I do not know. The probable influence of the Schoolmen on mediaeval pleading has often been pointed out. In fact my late friend Mr. H. W. Challis, the most acute of recent real property lawyers and second to none in learning, was a disciple of Cardinal Newman's for some years. So there would seem to be some subtle affinity."[3]

Even at the present day the scale of costs to which solicitors are entitled is complicated and archaic, bearing striking witness to the fact that in origin the solicitors were more concerned with running errands and doing clerical work than with advising clients on general legal problems. By modern statutes solicitors have acquired the right of audience in the inferior courts.

NOTARIES AND SCRIVENERS

Of the other branches of the legal profession below the bar the only one which survives is that of the notary, which in England is of slight importance, except for foreign and ecclesiastical matters. In 1884 it was stated that there were only forty-eight notaries in England.[4]

The scriveners were originally scribes, but soon undertook to draft for the public the commoner sorts of deeds—especially bonds. They often acted as intermediaries between borrowers and lenders, and themselves earned an unsavoury reputation as merciless usurers. For a moment the scriveners seemed likely to become professional conveyancers, but the other branches of the profession withstood them, and

[1] 2 Geo. II, c. 23.

[2] 25 Charles II, c. 2.

[3] [1926] Journal of the Society of Public Teachers of Law, 38; with which compare Law Quarterly Review, xiv. 219.

[4] Christian, *Short History of Solicitors*, 226.

eventually they turned to the more lucrative, if less learned, parts of their traditional work.[1]

THE LATER BARRISTERS

A few words must now be said upon the later developments which took place among the barristers. The exclusive right of audience which the serjeants enjoyed in the Court of Common Pleas was one of the causes of the attempts made by other courts, especially King's Bench and Exchequer, to enlarge their jurisdiction so that matters originally cognisable in the Common Pleas could be determined in these other courts without resort to the expensive services of a serjeant.[2] These attempts were highly successful and upon their success was built the development of the barristers' position.

LAW OFFICERS OF THE CROWN

Far from being merely an " apprentice ", the barrister had now ample opportunities for practice in courts of equity and common law, and the Crown itself began to offer dignified offices to barristers just as in earlier times certain serjeants, called King's serjeants, had enjoyed a pre-eminence in their order.   Two of these offices—those of Solicitor- and Attorney-General—are of special importance, and something must be said of their history.

All through the middle ages the Crown employed a considerable number of attorneys to represent it in the various courts, and in 1461 we find the appearance of a " solicitor " as well.   It is clear that these officials performed the same duties for the King as they would have done for private clients, with the sole difference that the Crown could give them much more business, and so the royal solicitors and attorneys had greater opportunities for making profits.   In the course of the fifteenth century these numerous attorneys were replaced by a single attorney (later called the attorney-general) who had the right to appoint deputies;   he therefore became something like a permanent official with a staff of assistants.   But even so, it was a long time before the attorney-generalship came to be filled by men of any eminence.   Until the middle of the sixteenth century promotion to the bench was the exclusive privilege of the serjeants, who considered the offices of solicitor- and attorney-general beneath the dignity of their order.   When these offices became too important to be held by mere solicitors and attorneys, it was therefore the barristers and not the serjeants who aspired to them. Moreover, after the middle of the sixteenth century we find with in-creasing frequency that attorneys-general are promoted directly to the

---

[1] H. C. Gutteridge, *The Profession of Notaries*, in Cambridge Legal Essays (1926).   There is much material concerning scriveners and money-lending in R. H. Tawney's edition of Wilson's *Discourse upon Usury*.

[2] However, serjeants did at times appear in other courts than the Common Pleas.

chancellorship or to the chief justiceship of one of the benches (a practice which is still generally followed), thus leaving the serjeants with only a puisne judgeship in view.[1] As long as the order of the coif lasted, however, membership of it was still a technical requirement for a seat on the bench of a common-law court, and so an attorney-general who was promoted chief justice of either bench was simultaneously created serjeant in order to qualify for it.

From 1530 we find the custom established of appointing the King's solicitor to succeed the King's attorney upon a vacancy in the latter office, and this is still the general practice at the present day. These two officers soon began to extend their functions and acquired the position of general legal advisers to the government; in Elizabeth's reign we already find her solicitors elected members to the House of Commons (or else summoned to the House of Lords—occasionally both) in order to explain and defend the government's legal policy before the House. For a long time, however, the House of Commons declined to allow the attorney-general to be a member, fearing that the influence of the Crown in the House would thereby be enhanced to a dangerous degree. Objections gradually ceased after the Restoration, and after the Revolution the attorney-general was regularly elected a member of the House of Commons, but his summons to the House of Lords had become a mere formality.

The rapid rise in importance of these officers is largely due to the fact that the mediaeval King's serjeant was no longer big enough to cope with sixteenth-century conditions. The rise of new courts and the extension of the jurisdiction of old ones had far outgrown the limits within which the serjeant cared to act, and his ancient monopoly was now in fact an irksome restriction. Indeed, the position of the law had changed considerably under the Tudors. Justice was no longer the exclusive concern of judges and serjeants, assisted by the humble attorney. It was now an affair of state requiring constant attention from the Crown, which was viewing with some anxiety the activities of its courts. The Reformation settlement brought with it numerous questions which had to be settled in the courts—questions of land titles arising out of the dissolution of the monasteries, questions of criminal law created by the insecurity of the dynasty, and still more difficult questions of constitutional law due to the inadequacy of the mediaeval financial system. All these problems needed a newer point of view than that of the serjeants complacently resting on their monopoly. As we have already noticed, there was a chance of the Crown turning to the civilians for exponents of a newer technique of law and government; but in the end a sort of compromise was worked out. The attorney- and solicitor-general served as links between the executive and the legal system, and the practice of promoting the attorney-general to the

---

[1] If a serjeant became attorney- or solicitor-general, his appointment as serjeant was revoked (as in the case of Sir John Popham in 1579).

highest judicial offices ensured the presence on the bench of men who had not merely a legal training such as that of the serjeants, but also experience of government gained in the inner circle of politics. In this way the law was brought once more into vital contact with the world of affairs and politics. That contact was necessary if the law was to continue as a growing system, but the dangers were of the gravest, as the history of the Stuart judiciary will show.

A single attorney-general and solicitor-general were, of course, unable to deal with the mass of business created by the sixteenth-century State, and it therefore became necessary for them to secure a more or less permanent staff of assistants. We therefore find the rise at the same time of the class of " King's Counsel Learned in the Law ". These were barristers upon whose services the Crown had a prior claim, and their duties were largely to assist the attorney-general and solicitor-general when called upon. They ranked next below the serjeants in Elizabeth's reign and already had regular precedence and seats in Parliament upon the woolsacks. It was Bacon who did a great deal to define the position of the King's Counsel and secured for them a life fee. By the close of the eighteenth century, however, the tendency was to regard the title of King's Counsel as merely a mark of distinction with purely nominal duties.[1]

DEPARTMENTAL LEGAL STAFFS

The eighteenth century saw the creation of numerous commissions and boards for the conduct of national administration, and they naturally looked ultimately to the law officers of the Crown for their legal assistance. For ordinary matters, however, they soon felt the need of the exclusive services of a legal staff of their own, and so we find them appointing solicitors to assist them. The oldest and most important of these is the Treasury Solicitor, whose office dates from about 1655. He often acted for other departments besides the Treasury,[2] and by statute other similar offices have been amalgamated with his; thus he became Director of Public Prosecutions for a time,[3] and is still King's Proctor.

[1] There are still numerous important details which in England differentiate the K.C. from his fellow barristers.

[2] Holdsworth, xii. 11.

[3] By the Prosecution of Offences Act (1884) until the offices were separated by the Prosecution of Offences Act (1908).

CHAPTER 13

THE GROWTH OF THE JUDICIARY

Amid all these changes, one thing remained constant, and that was the immense influence exercised by the judges, which was all the greater in view of the fact that before reaching the bench they had already achieved distinction at the bar, either as serjeants or barristers and King's Counsel, and in some cases had been solicitor- or attorney-general. From one point of view quite a good deal of the history of the common law could be written in the form of a chronological series of biographies of the leading judges. Except in the case of the comparatively small number of judges, such as Coke, whose life is a part of the general politics of the day, the actual biographical details are of little importance. Most legal careers run upon a regular pattern: student days, the call to the bar, the growth of practice, the tenure of public offices and the rise to the bench—all these follow in regular course in the lives of most of the great judges, and there is no point in trying to remember all these details. It is much more important to try to ascertain the peculiar gifts and qualities of each judge, and the incidents in his career which contributed to the formation of his character and mental outlook. In the light of all this it would become possible to evaluate his contributions to the law; but unfortunately not all of the judges have been blessed with biographers of sympathy and imagination

The present chapter will be devoted to biographical sketches of the principal common law judges; the Chancellors will be similarly treated when we deal with the history of equity.

THE OFFICE OF JUDGE

In the first place, however, there is the difficult problem of the evolution of the office of judge. Our earliest courts, according to the prevailing opinion, consisted of suitors who constituted the court and rendered its judgments. This tradition, developed in the communal courts, was continued by the feudal courts, whose suitors were bound by the condition of their tenure to render this " service " to their lords.[1] In important matters the lord himself might preside, but more generally it was his steward who " held " the court. We have also seen that even the King's court was at first of this nature;[2] how then did the more modern type of court consisting of a judge come to supplant the ancient system?

This transformation took place late in the twelfth century and appeared first in the King's courts. The details seem to be no longer recoverable, for that period has left but scanty records; all the same, it may be possible to suggest what happened by studying first the repetition of the process which took place much later in the history of the House of Lords. The ancient *curia regis*, consisting of household officers, officials of state, lawyers, prelates and nobles, has survived as the House of Lords with singularly little formal change in spite of its adaptation to more modern conditions. Of ceremonial survivals we have already spoken, but even more striking than these is the continued function of the House of Lords as a court of law. Its original jurisdiction was still exercisable in the ancient manner—that is to say, the House sat as a court consisting of suitors, every member of which took part in forming the judgment of the court, irrespective of his qualifications as a lawyer. The trial of peers and impeachments were of this character. It is indeed a curious reflection that the ancient conception of a court of suitors should have lasted, not merely as a historical survival in the House of Lords, but also as a fairly frequent procedure in cases of impeachment in America, although Europe began to abandon it in the twelfth century.

The jurisdiction of the House in error is partly an outcome of the

---

[1] For some details throwing light on this obscure but important transition, see Ganshof, *Origines des cours féodales* in [1928] Revue historique de droit, 644–665, and cf. Maitland, *Select Pleas in Manorial Courts*, 105; J. Goebel, in J. H. Smith, *Appeals to the Privy Council*, xl ff.; Vinogradoff, in *Magna Carta Essays* (ed. H. E. Malden), 87–88. In some places it was only the decisions of the suitors which became *res judicata*, and not those of the presiding bailiff, whose decisions were not true judgments: Beaumanoir, *Coutumes de Beauvaisis*, art. 31; Vinogradoff, *Roman Law in Mediaeval Europe* (ed. de Zulueta), 95. See too the interesting suggestion that this process may have begun before the Conquest: J. E. A. Jolliffe, *Constitutional History*, 112–113. For Bracton and the Romanists, cf. F. Schulz, *A new approach to Bracton*, Seminar, ii. 45.

[2] Above, p. 143.

fact that Parliament is the ultimate court, and partly of the fact that
the King himself is there surrounded by all the talent of the realm to
resolve difficulties and to supervise all the organs of government, both
judicial and administrative. For centuries there has been a natural
antipathy between the public and the functionary, between the baron
and the official. It is but natural, therefore, that there should be some
question whether the judicial powers of Parliament should be exercised
by the lords or by the councillors. Once again the older principle
prevailed, and the whole House maintained its ancient constitution as a
court of suitors. And so it remains to-day in theory. Certain modifications have been introduced, however. Before the Act of 1876 the House
frequently consulted the judges, and generally (though not always)
accepted their opinion. Lay peers ceased to vote upon appeals[1] in 1844,
and in 1876 the Appellate Jurisdiction Act required the presence of certain
law lords when appeals were heard. That act did not exclude lay lords
from participating, and it was as late as 1883 that a lay lord's vote was
for the first time held void.[2]

The nineteenth century was probably repeating unconsciously what
had been going on in the twelfth. There were several factors in that
history. First, there was the powerful example of the ecclesiastical
courts which consisted of judges—generally, in this period, single judges.
Then there was the strong trend towards administrative forms which
had already transformed certain sessions of the *curia regis* into the highly
professional Exchequer. The success of that institution must certainly
have strengthened the tendency towards professionalism in the King's
Court. Then there was the similar success of the judicial eyres. These
were at first no doubt regarded as meetings of county courts presided over
by royal commissioners,[3] but the county itself so often fell under the
displeasure of the commissioners that there can be no doubt that the eyre
soon became in substance a court held before judges rather than before
suitors.

Again, suit of court, whether of local courts or of the King's own
court, was an expensive burden, and agricultural pursuits do not leave
much time for distant travel and prolonged absences. In many county
and seignorial courts[4] the statutory permission for suitors to attend by
attorney must have compelled the steward to assume truly judicial functions if the courts were to meet with the accustomed frequency. Indeed,
the reluctance of people to admit themselves suitors might lead the court's
owner to appoint judges to serve in their place. Thus the burgesses

---

[1] Holdsworth, i. 376–377, citing *Re Lord Kinross*, [1905] A.C. 468, at 476. Cf. Mr Megarry's
note in the Law Quarterly Review, lxv. 22 ff.

[2] It is probable that the same process on a much smaller scale was going on in the Middlesex
County Court as a consequence of eighteenth-century legislation; see above, p. 208.

[3] See above, p. 103.

[4] Statute of Merton (1237), c. 10. Royal writs might still be necessary: Denholm-Young,
Collected Papers, 160.

of Bury St Edmunds and the abbot's council affirm that there is no question of suitors there, but that the abbot by his letters patent appoints judges to hear and determine suits.[1] In the King's Court the rapid increase of business would have needed almost permanent assemblies of barons for its dispatch if the old system was to endure.   The solution was found in 1178 in the establishment of the five whom we have already mentioned;[2] at first perhaps they acted as a sort of sub-committee of the whole *curia*,[3] but the mass of business before them, and their success in handling it, must very soon have established them as true judges of a court of the new model.

Even this device only brought temporary relief; there was still constant recourse to the parent body—the King himself in his court, and there too the process was repeated when justices were " assigned to hear pleas before the king himself ".   Once again, the result was a new bench of judges, and again it was possible to explain the anomaly by regarding them as a committee of the *curia regis*.   In Parliament itself, as we have just seen, the process was slowest, being only completed within the last few generations.   In logic the distinction between judges and suitors is perfectly clear, but in practice it is probable that the novelty of the new benches was obscured by the fact that they were regarded as deputies for the larger *curia*.   As we have already seen, the connection between the judges and the council in Parliament was at one time very real.[4]

With the establishment of the Court of Common Pleas, the decisive step was taken: the future of the common law was put into the hands of judges.[5] Everything will therefore depend on the mode of selection of these judges, and the position assigned to them.

THE APPOINTMENT OF JUDGES

Several possibilities were open, but in the later years of the twelfth century there was little room for hesitation.   The judges were drawn from the small group of royal clerks who constituted the nascent civil

[1] *Select Cases in King's Bench* (Selden Society), ii. 3–5 (1290).

[2] Above, p. 148.

[3] Vinogradoff, *Roman Law in Mediaeval Europe* (ed. de Zulueta), 95, 105, remarks on the use of the idea of custom, both in Bracton and in Beaumanoir, to avoid the difficulty which was felt as to the power of a single judge to lay down the law.

[4] Above, p. 151.

[5] N. Denholm-Young, *Collected Papers* (1946), 150, produces a highly interesting argument that the " paper constitution of 1244 " really belongs to 1238, and that its object was to check the professionalising of the courts (typified by Raleigh) by reverting to ideas of peerage (*i.e.* a court of barons as suitors of the *curia regis*).   It is difficult to follow Mr Denholm-Young, however, in thinking that Raleigh had any sympathies with this policy.   The famous *addicio* in Bracton, f. 34, expresses the same sort of high baronial claim, but the view of H. Kantorowicz, *Bractonian Problems* (1942), 49 ff., that the *addicio* is genuinely Bracton's, has been subjected to rigorous criticism by G. Lapsley, English Historical Review (1947), 1.   This restoration of Maitland's view that the *addicio* is spurious restores to Bracton his reputation for lawyerly professionalism, and makes it easy to suppose that his master Raleigh held similar views.

service. Their names are in many cases unknown, but their work was well done in the great tradition of Norman administration. At their head was often a justiciar who seemed to his contemporaries second only to the King in power and dignity. His duties, military, civil and judicial, were the product of the unseparated powers of the King himself. The justiciar is best regarded as a prime minister when the King was present, and as a viceroy when he was abroad. In the twelfth century, therefore, it is impossible to distinguish the lawyer from the statesman and the politician; men such as Glanvill and Becket, Lanfranc and Hubert Walter, must have had considerable influence upon legal development, but still we can hardly describe them as lawyers, or judges.

PATESHULL AND RALEIGH

In the early years of the thirteenth century it is easier to recognise the beginning of the modern judiciary in the great judges, Pateshull and Raleigh, whose judgments were the inspiration of our first great law writer, Bracton. Martin de Pateshull[1] was Archdeacon of Norfolk and Dean of St. Paul's; he became a Justice of the Bench in 1217 and was constantly employed upon judicial Eyres. So active was he that one of the clerks, on behalf of himself and his colleague Raleigh, complained to the Justiciar of the way in which Martin worked his colleagues from sunrise to sundown. When he died in 1229 he had gained the reputation (at least with Bracton) of being the finest lawyer in England. More than sixty years after his death, litigants asked that Pateshull's rolls be searched for precedents, so highly were his judgments esteemed.[2]

William de Raleigh was rector of Bratton Fleming in Devon, which was perhaps the birthplace of Bracton himself. In any case, one Odo de Bratton was his vicar. Raleigh began his legal career as clerk to the great Pateshull (and it is quite possible that young Henry de Bracton began in his turn as Raleigh's clerk[3]). In 1228 he became a Justice of the Bench and in 1234 treasurer of Exeter Cathedral—of which Bracton was later to become Chancellor. In 1238 he was bishop-elect of Winchester but did not gain possession until 1244 owing to opposition from a rival candidate promoted by the King. He died in 1250. He seems to have been one of the most important promoters of the Statute of Merton, from which we learn that he strongly supported the barons in their refusal to " change the laws of England " by adopting the canon law rule of legitimation by subsequent marriage. A cleric who held high ecclesiastic preferment could therefore take an independent view, and reconcile his orders with a nationalist outlook; because a man

[1] For his career, see D. M. Stenton, *Eyre Rolls of Lincs. and Worcs.* (Selden Society), vol. liii, xvii ff.; C. A. F. Meekings, *Martin Pateshull and William Raleigh*, Bulletin of the Institute of Historical Research, xxvi. 157 ff.; *Six Letters concerning the Eyres of 1226–8*, English Historical Review, lxv. 492; Maitland, *Gloucester Pleas of the Crown*, xii.

[2] *Rot. Parl.*, i. 66 *b*.

[3] D. M. Stenton, *op. cit.*, xx.

was a cleric it did not necessarily mean that he would favour the canon over the common law.

CLERICAL JUDGES AND THE CIVIL SERVICE

These thirteenth-century judges, like most of the clerks and officials, were technically " clergy ". This does not imply that they undertook parochial or diocesan duties; as a rule they were not priests nor even deacons, but had received one of the lowest orders. But however low their orders, they were still able, lawfully or unlawfully, to hold rich benefices, receiving the emoluments and appointing deputies to carry out the pastoral duties. This was a regular way of making provision for civil servants in the middle ages, for the Church was rich and the King comparatively poor. Salaries were indeed attached to many offices, but they were small and payment of them was irregular. The judges frequently had to complain that their salaries were several years in arrear. Moreover, the fact that many judges in this period were clerics must not be taken as evidence that they were also canonists. Canon law, like theology and philosophy, was one of the Church's great contributions to civilisation, but it must not be supposed that every clerk in minor orders was a canonist, any more than that he was a theologian—or a saint. Many ways of advancement were open to an able and ambitious cleric—theology, canon law, ecclesiastical politics, diplomacy, finance, the royal civil service, and as part of the last-named, service in the royal courts of law. But it is unsafe to say that any mediaeval cleric was a canonist unless there is some direct evidence; it certainly cannot be presumed. In any case, we already find at the middle of the century a few knights on the bench, and at the close the proportion of lay judges steadily increases.

JUDGES AND THE LEGAL PROFESSION

During most of the thirteenth century, therefore, the bench was part of the civil service. Moreover, this same period saw the rise of a group of practitioners before the King's courts which was small, active, learned and (like the court itself) centralised. Although the material traces of their organisation come from a later date, we can hardly escape the conclusion that this group of expert pleaders was united by something like a professional spirit, its members being in constant and intimate contact with one another, and drawn together by their common interest in the law and procedure of the King's Court. In such a state of affairs there must arise the question of the relations between bench and bar. Not only is there the purely formal relationship to be settled, but there is the even more fundamental psychological attitude of bench and bar to be considered. When the same half-dozen judges are constantly being addressed by the same score or so of practitioners, these two small groups cannot help influencing each other.

The practitioners will be constantly comparing the decisions of the court, taking notes of them, and endeavouring to reduce them to consistent principles. However much the bench might be tempted to handle cases in the spirit of administrative discretion, the small, vigilant body of pleaders with long memories and ready tongues are there to protest that decisions ought to be consistent and that settled courses of practice ought not to be disturbed. Much depended upon the personality of the judges, and some of the earlier members of Henry III's bench were men of outstanding ability, as we have just seen. As we approach the great political crisis of the middle years of the century, however, it is clear that the situation has changed. Both Bracton and the baronial opposition openly accused the judges of ignorance and corruption—charges which were brought against other branches of the civil service as well.

Officialdom was under a cloud, and the result was momentous. If the old system had persisted, and if the judges had continued to be members of the civil service, with different careers from the bar, we should have had in England (and probably in America too) something like the system prevailing in several continental countries to-day. According to this system, the young lawyer has to decide very early in his career whether he will go to the bar or to the bench. Naturally, these two careers attract different types of men. At the bar the competition is severe, progress slow, but success brings considerable wealth and great social and political influence. Brilliant and adventurous men are attracted by a career at the bar. A candidate who elects for the bench has very different prospects. He has a salary instead of prospective profits, certainty instead of a gamble. His first post is in a petty court in the provinces; like other functionaries, satisfactory service will bring him advancement from lower to higher courts, from distant towns to the metropolis. The mentality which such a career attracts is very different from that of the advocate, and the result is that bench and bar are divided by differences of interest and training.

The movement away from the civil service element in the administration of justice at the end of the thirteenth century led to an experiment in a different direction. Instead of recruiting judges from the ranks of officialdom, recourse was had to the bar. Even here there were at least two possibilities. Among the canonists at this moment the pope had become not only the ultimate court of appeal, but also a court of first instance as well. Litigants went direct to the highest tribunal of the Church. In practice this meant that the pope appointed delegates to hear the case, and these delegates were appointed *ad hoc* from among eminent practitioners. We did in fact have this same system in England some centuries later in admiralty and in ecclesiastical causes. Under such an arrangement there were no permanent professional judges, but simply a bar whose members might be advocates at one moment and judges-delegate at another. Dickens has given a vivid picture of the red-robed doctors of law who practised under this system in England, just as the canonists and civilians did in the middle ages. There are traces that in some cases at least we might have adopted this arrangement. It was in fact a common practice for the King to appoint special commissioners to hear particular cases which had been brought to his attention. Criminal matters could be heard by special commissions of oyer and terminer consisting partly of notable laymen and partly of professional lawyers. This system did not become general in England, however, and the principal reason must be that the hierarchy of courts one above the other had become too well established to be disturbed in favour of a method which implied that all jurisdiction was exercisable by the King. Such a theory would only fit English facts if it was qualified by the reservation that portions of this jurisdiction had been permanently delegated to the courts and that there could be no question of revoking the powers granted to the King's Bench and Common Pleas.

JUDGES DRAWN FROM THE SERJEANTS

Hence the only remaining way of combining the permanent courts with the legal profession was to choose the permanent judges from among the serjeants (who for the moment were the branch of the profession which mattered most).[1] The system has persisted, with very little modification, to the present day both in England and in all jurisdiction where the common law prevails. Its great characteristic is the intimate connection between bench and bar. In the middle ages this was emphasised by the fact that the serjeants during term time lived together in their inns and discussed their cases informally together simply as serjeants, without distinction between those on the bench and those at the bar. Even with the rise of newer branches of the profession, the decline of the serjeants and the rise of the attorney- and solicitor-general, the same fundamental situation remained. The judges had passed through the same career as the bar; they had achieved success in the same keen competition, and were therefore generally the equals of the best men at the bar; their point of view and their conception of law were derived from their experience as advocates instead of being the product of a different career under civil service conditions. Moreover, the judges were men who had passed a large portion of their lives in the world of practical affairs and had won success there. And finally, the common experience and training unite bench and bar in an understanding of each other which is difficult to attain when their professional lives are

---

[1] The first attempt at a list of English judges is W. Dugdale, *Origines Juridiciales* (1666). E. Faoss, *Judges of England* (9 vols., 1848–64) and *Biographica Juridica* (1870) must be supplemented by the lists by Maitland in *Bracton's Note Book*, by T. F. Tout in his *Edward II*, and by G. O. Sayles in his *King's Bench* (Selden Society). Cf. the valuable lists in R. Somerville, *The Duchy of Lancaster* (1953) and C. A. F. Meekings, *Justices of the Jews*, Bulletin of the Institute of Historical Research, xxviii. 173. The *Chancellors* and *Chief Justices* of Lord Campbell, Atlay's *Chancellors*, and F. E. Ball. *The Judges in Ireland* are well known.

spent in different careers. This co-operation between bench and bar is of the utmost importance for the working of the common law system.

THE SCANDAL OF 1289

The thirteenth century has one other distinguished English judge, Henry de Bracton; his eminence rests so much upon his writings, however, that we speak of him in detail in discussing his book; and so with the closing years of the century, we come to the age of Edward I. Here we find the one great judicial scandal of English history (1289). Charges of corruption were investigated by a special commission headed by the Chancellor, Burnell.[1] Lurid accusations of all sorts of crimes, from sorcery and murder downwards, were brought against various officials as well as the judges, and it is clear that the civil service came out worse than the judicial service. The Chief Justice of the Common Pleas fled the country; the Chief Justice of the King's Bench, the famous Ralf de Hengham, was found guilty of tampering with a record—later tradition says that he did it out of charity for a poor man—and paid a very heavy fine. Short afterwards, however, he was restored to favour and made Chief Justice of the Common Pleas. Tradition has it that the fine was used to build a clock tower at Westminster which remained until 1715. Like Bracton before him, he became Chancellor of Exeter Cathedral. At least once in Parliament he withstood the King to his face in the cause of justice.[2] And, as we shall mention later, he took a prominent share in drafting Edward's legislation, notably the statute De Donis.

LAY JUDGES: BEREFORD

Most of the judges so far had been ecclesiastics, but from Edward II onwards the proportion of clergy on the bench tends to decline. The connection with the civil service is still close, and we find cases where the bench is used as a sort of honourable retirement for a civil servant.[3] We also begin to find, however, that the law becomes a profession and a career. There is a tendency to promote serjeants from the bar to the bench—the first seems to have been Lawrence[4] de Brok, who became a judge early in 1268—and so we finally arrive at the period of professional justices who had a long training at the bar as preparation for their high office.

[1] The history and the documents are printed in Tout and Johnstone, State Trials of Edward I.

[2] Y.BB. Edward II (Selden Society), iii. 196. See, in general, Vinogradoff's article on him in Essays presented to Tout, 189 (reprinted, with mutilations, in Vinogradoff's Collected Papers, i. 245), and the life prefixed by W. H. Dunham to his edition of Hengham's works.

[3] John Benstede, for example, after a long career as Keeper of the Wardrobe became a Justice of the Common Pleas in 1309.

[4] Not Thomas, as Holdsworth, ii. 229.

William de Bereford is a typical example of the new professional justice.[1] Bereford became distinguished in the service of Edward I; yet it is remarkable to notice that immediately Edward II came to the throne he was well known to be an intimate friend of the notorious favourite, Piers Gaveston. Indeed, he remained so constant to Gaveston that the baronial opposition demanded his banishment from the kingdom as one of the four men who had given the King evil counsel. At this critical moment his fortunes took a sudden and mysterious turn; instead of being banished, he was shortly afterwards promoted to succeed Hengham as Chief Justice of the Common Pleas (1309), and almost immediately the opposition adopted a formal vote of confidence in the new Chief Justice. By what feat of diplomacy this happy result was accomplished we are not told, but it is clear that the adroit Chief Justice enjoyed the fruits of his dexterity for the rest of his life. As a lawyer he stands out clearly among his fellows, and the Year Books of Edward II owe their peculiar flavour very largely to Bereford's presence. His character appears most vividly even after a lapse of six hundred years; his quick temper, his anti-clericalism, his refusal to allow formalities and even statutes to stand in the way of substantial justice, appear constantly. On many points his views were highly original and it is not uncommon to find him in a very select minority. He was certainly one of the greatest and one of the most influential judges of mediaeval England. Although his career was almost entirely devoted to the law, like other judges he was occasionally employed upon diplomatic missions.

JUDGES AND POLITICS IN THE FOURTEENTH CENTURY

The political adventures of Bereford can be matched by others during the fourteenth century, which all go to prove that the bench in this period was still part of the government, if not of the civil service. Thus in 1340 a financial crisis compelled Edward III to suspend his war with France. Returning unexpectedly to England, the King dismissed the Chancellor, the Treasurer, many clerks in their offices, Stonor, C.J., C.P., Shardelow, Sharshull and Willoughby, JJ., together with a number of financiers. An attempt to prove charges of corruption against them failed, for no accusers of consequence came forward, and it is clear that the incident was really an attempt by the King to dismiss with ignominy a ministry which he thought had betrayed him. A serious political crisis was the result, and in the end the judges were restored. It was vigorously maintained that these men were not responsible for the King's difficulties, but no one suggested that judges, as such, were or ought to be outside of politics.[2]

---

[1] For his life, see Bolland, *Chief Justice Bereford* (Cambridge, 1924).

[2] Cf. p. 158 above. The fact that in 1341–1345, 1371–1372, and 1372–1377 the chancellorship was held by common law judges is one further proof that they were eligible for a purely political office.

To be independent of national politics was easier than to be independent of local connections, and entanglements of the latter sort were frequent. There is clear evidence that great monasteries (which, like great businesses of our own day, were constantly engaged in litigation) paid regular retaining fees to royal judges[1]—and of course numerous gratuities to all grades of officials.[2]

A rather different and much more serious conflict occurred in the next reign. In 1386 a parliamentary commission was set up with powers which virtually superseded the normal functions of the King. Richard II formed a court party with Tresillian, C.J., K.B., at its head, and then called the other judges to Nottingham in August 1387 to pronounce on the legality of the commission. It seems clearly implied in this tactic that the judges were sufficiently outside party politics for their support— apparently impartially accorded on a point of law—to be valuable to the King. They declared that the commission was invalid and traitorous. The opposition, however, appealed the King's friends of treason and Tresillian, C.J., was hanged. The judges who gave the opinion at Nottingham were impeached and banished; they were Belknap, C.J., C.P., Fulthorp, Holt, Burgh, JJ., and the chief baron.[3]

THE WARS OF THE ROSES

With the beginning of the fifteenth century we come to one justice who has achieved a fame in legend, Sir William Gascoign. Of him is told the famous story that the young Prince, afterwards Henry V, was charged before the Chief Justice and even offered violence to the court, whereupon Gascoign committed him to prison for contempt. The opinion of authorities is divided upon the authenticity of this story, the latest of them being content to present the authorities and to leave the question open.[4] Of the two other outstanding judges in the fifteenth century, Littleton and Fortescue, we shall say more in the next chapter.

More important are the growing number of cases where the judges asserted the rule of law in the face of attempts to introduce royal influence into their courts, while it is abundantly clear that they had learnt the lessons of Richard's reign. During the manifold changes of the fifteenth century, the judges quietly stood aside from the clash of party, with the result that successive changes of dynasty left the bench unaffected. Fortescue alone took any part in those struggles, and after long years of exile finally abandoned the attempt to combine dynastic attachments with judicial office. Not until 1553 do we again find judges removed

---

[1] G. Sayles, *Medieval Judges as Legal Consultants*, Law Quarterly Review, lvi. 247. The statute 8 Richard II, c. 3 (suspended by 9 Richard II, c. 1), represents the mediaeval point of view.

[2] N. Denholm-Young, *Seignorial Administration*, 116.

[3] The most recent interpretations of these events will be found in Tout, *Chapters in English Administrative History*, iii. 323–495, iv. 1–68, and in A. Steel, *Richard II*.

[4] Fox, *Contempt of Court*, 52, 53.

for political or (since the Reformation) religious reasons. On Mary's accession Cholmeley and Montague, C.JJ., and Hales, J., were dismissed,[1] but Elizabeth made no changes on the bench when she restored Protestantism in 1558.

THE TUDORS AND THE JUDGES

The final separation of the Privy Council from the Star Chamber was a salutary development, for it kept the judiciary distinct from the executive. From 1540 onwards Henry VIII had no judges in his Privy Council. Edward VI and Mary put the Chief Justices on the Privy Council, but Elizabeth excluded them for some forty years. Only at the end of her reign was Popham, C.J., sworn of the Privy Council, in 1599. Thus the intimate connection of Star Chamber and Privy Council once again began,[2] and was rapidly intensified under the earlier Stuarts, with disastrous results.

Meanwhile, the old practice of lawyers seeking election to Parliament meant that many judges had had some parliamentary experience, as part of the normal career of an ambitious lawyer. Some of them went even further, and in the sixteenth century many Speakers of the House of Commons were promoted to the judicial bench—and the Speakership was then an important political position.

THE STRUGGLES OF COKE AND BACON

The sixteenth century, although rich in legal changes, presents us no particularly striking figures in the law until its close when in the last years of Elizabeth we find the rise of Sir Edward Coke.[3] Born in 1552, he proceeded in due course to Trinity College, Cambridge, and in his later years became High Steward of the University. He entered the Inner Temple and was called to the bar in 1578. Owing to the influence of Burghley he rapidly rose in public office, became Recorder of London in 1591, Solicitor-General in 1592, Speaker of the House of Commons in 1593, and Attorney-General in 1594. By 1601 he had made an enormous fortune, and entertained Queen Elizabeth in his house with great magnificence. In 1600 he began the publication of his Reports. In this early stage of his career, distinguished by his astonishingly rapid rise in the law and in politics (for it must be remembered that in his day a Speaker of the House of Commons was something like a modern Leader of the House), it is only natural that he should be full of enthusiasm for the Tudor conception of the State as

---

[1] Hales committed suicide, whence *Bp. of Chichester* v. *Webb*, Dyer, 108, and *Hales* v. *Petit* (1562), Plowden, 253; cf. Shakespeare, *Hamlet*, Act V, scene 1.

[2] Pollard, in English Historical Review, xxxviii. 59–60.

[3] For a full and entertaining biography, see Lyon and Block, *Edward Coke, Oracle of the Law* (Houghton Mifflin, 1929); his library catalogue, ed. W. O. Hassall, with a preface by S. E. Thorne, is no. 12 of the Yale Law Library Publications.

expressed by Queen Elizabeth. Full of patriotism and national pride, Coke shared the feelings of others of his contemporaries who exalted the idea of the State, and displayed a violent hatred of Roman Catholics and political prisoners. Even contemporaries sometimes felt that he exaggerated a little, while his prosecution of Raleigh overstepped all bounds and was conspicuous among the State trials even at this period for its brutality. However, it must be remembered that Elizabeth's reign had often been seriously threatened by a combination of foreign and domestic intrigue, and Coke, as a member of the Government, was well aware of these public dangers. During this period of his career he was naturally a firm supporter of the royal prerogative.

COKE AS CHIEF JUSTICE

The peaceful accession of James I in 1603 must have surprised many contemporaries, for there had been widespread anxiety in Elizabeth's later years concerning the future after her decease. For a few years all went well. James seemed firmly seated on the throne and constantly proclaimed his adherence to the Tudor idea of government. In 1606 Coke became Chief Justice of the Common Pleas, and therefore high priest of the common law, for whose mysteries he had an almost superstitious reverence. As so often happened in mediaeval times (and Coke's mind was essentially mediaeval), the attainment of a high office brought a change in his character and outlook. Just as the soldier and courtier, Thomas Becket, became transformed into a churchman of the sternest school on becoming Archbishop of Canterbury, so Coke, once the upholder of prerogative, discovered a new point of view from the bench at Westminster. Perhaps it was a tendency of his character to idealise whatever position he happened to be in; as a Crown lawyer he magnified the prerogative; as the head of the common law system he exalted law to almost mystical heights. This meant a complete revision of his attitude towards the Crown, and there can be no doubt that many capable minds besides Coke, who were content to trust the Crown under Elizabeth, were equally likely to distrust it under James, whose previous record in Scotland was not reassuring. Coke now transferred to the common law, of which he had become the oracle, that supremacy and pre-eminence which he had ascribed to the Crown while he was Attorney-General. A line of decisions, of which *Bonham's Case* was a notable example, contained his new teaching.[1] From this time onwards he never lost an opportunity of declaring against the prerogative. His first quarrel was with the ecclesiastical courts, and especially the Court of High Commission. The prerogative was soon involved in this dispute, and Coke quoted Bracton's famous words that " the King is subject to God and the law " (that is to say, according to his enemies' interpretation, to Chief Justice Coke and the Court of Common Pleas), while in the *Case of Proclamations*

[1] His views are discussed above, pp. 50–51.

(1610) Coke found yet another opportunity of attacking the prerogative. So far Coke had contrived to maintain his personal popularity. The Prince, afterwards Charles I, enjoyed his company because " he so mixed mirth with wisdom ", and the youthful enthusiasm which runs through all his writings, and his undoubted sincerity, still further contributed to his popularity, while according to the fashion of the times he was fond of splendid attire, " delighting in good clothes, well worn, and being wont to say that the outward neatness of our bodies might be a monitor of purity to our souls ". Consequently, although he gave constant cause of annoyance to the King, yet for a long time the court party was prepared to tolerate him. Indeed, Coke's position as the champion of the supremacy of the common law was extremely strong, for it certainly represented public feeling based upon centuries of mediaeval thought which had always looked to law rather than to the State. Proposals were soon made that Coke should be removed to some other sphere of activity, finance for example, in which he was reputed to be skilled, and finally, on the advice of Bacon, who was now entering upon a career of open rivalry with Coke, the latter was promoted to the less important but more dignified position of Chief Justice of the King's Bench (1613).

BACON AS CHANCELLOR

The contrast between Coke and Bacon was as great as could possibly be imagined. As a scientist and a philosopher Bacon was laying the foundations of the modern scientific method, which to Coke was completely incomprehensible and only evoked satirical couplets. Bacon was a whole-hearted supporter of the Crown, and perhaps thought that Coke might be brought back to his early views if he were given one more change of office. But by this time Coke had decided not to change again. From the King's Bench, Coke issued writs of prohibition to the Court of Chancery, thus opening a general attack upon equity. Coke, whose domestic affairs (in which Bacon also was involved) grew steadily more disastrous, now endeavoured to use his daughter, a child of fourteen, to consolidate his position at court by marrying her to the brother of the reigning favourite, Lord Buckingham. Lady Coke objected and the girl eloped, and Bacon no doubt enjoyed the opportunity of filing an information against Coke in the Star Chamber. At the same time Coke was at last dismissed from office in 1616. From 1617 to 1621 Bacon held the Great Seal and the two protagonists were now fairly ranged one against the other. Coke now entered Parliament and began the third epoch of his career as leader of the parliamentary opposition (1621). This time he got his revenge upon Bacon, for he was one of the managers of his impeachment, and from now onwards he was prominent in all the activities of the opposition. In 1622 he was put in the Tower for several months and his papers confiscated.

In 1625 James I was succeeded by his son, Charles I, and Coke was soon identified with the opposition's policy of restricting supplies. The next year he was nominated sheriff (which was a compulsory office and conveniently disqualified the holder from sitting in Parliament, as he himself had once decided from the bench). These last years of his life (he was now seventy-seven) he devoted to preparing his manuscripts for the press. In 1628 he was again returned to Parliament, receiving the striking distinction of election in two different counties. By this time the Crown had attempted a variety of methods for obtaining money, and after much discussion in the Commons, Coke's suggestion of presenting a Petition of Right was adopted, to which Charles in the end had to give his assent. This was beyond doubt the crown of Coke's career. After six years of retirement he died in 1634, and immediately his manuscripts (including his will, upon which he had spent many years of learned care) were seized and, it would seem, destroyed. Of his political theory we have already spoken,[1] and of his writings something will be said in the next chapter. His general influence upon the course of English law was to maintain continuity between modern and mediaeval times, and this achievement had vices as well as virtues. But, most important of all, he preserved the fabric of the common law, and in his judgments began the tendency towards bringing it into harmony with more modern needs. It is unfortunate that his mediaeval foundation made it necessary to advance by way of increasing complexity instead of simplification. Yet even here Coke's mediaeval learning had such an air of finality about it that further recourse to mediaeval law was not so necessary, and it became more and more the tendency to take Coke's word on matters of Year Book learning.

THE RESTORATION: HOLT

Of Chief Justice Hale, and of John Selden (who never held legal office), we shall speak more at length in describing legal literature; and so we pass to the Restoration,[2] which saw the rise to prominence of Sir John Holt. His father was a serjeant and Recorder of Reading. His student days at Oxford were no doubt lively, and tradition has it that he was the only member of his set who did not end on the gallows. At the age of ten his name was already put upon the books of Gray's Inn and at twenty-one he was called to the bar (1663). It was only after some ten years that Holt became prominent. In 1679 he defended Lord Danby in his impeachment; he was also counsel for Lord Russell and appeared for the East India Company in support of the royal grant of monopoly. In 1686 he became Recorder of London, was knighted and became a King's serjeant, but he soon resigned the recordership rather than pass sentence of death upon a soldier who had deserted the

---

[1] Above, p. 50.

[2] See now, A. F. Havighurst, *The Judiciary and Politics in the reign of Charles II,* Law Quarterly Review, lxvi. 62, 229, and *James II and the twelve Men in Scarlet, ibid.,* lxix. 522.

Army in time of peace. When James II left the kingdom, Sir John Holt took a prominent part in finding a formula which would express the revolution in terms of constitutional law. He was immediately appointed Lord Chief Justice of the King's Bench, where many notable cases came before him, for by this time the King's Bench had become more important than the Common Pleas. Holt declined the Great Seal under the excuse that he was not an equity lawyer. He retired from the bench in 1710 and died shortly after. In politics he gave mortal offence to James II by resigning the recordership, and so he naturally maintained the revolution settlement which he had helped to formulate. As an advocate his early training under Hale had made him a sound lawyer with a contempt for trickery, while as a judge he restored the credit of the bench after the evil days of Charles II and James II. In the field of constitutional law he resisted innovation on all sides; if he took a firm stand against the excesses of martial law, he was also ready to defend the dispensing power of the Crown, and resisted an extreme claim of privilege by the House of Lords, which for a moment proposed to commit the Chief Justice for contempt. In the Aylesbury Election Case (*Ashby* v. *White*[1]) Holt held that although the plaintiff had suffered no loss in consequence of the constables' refusing to allow him to vote, yet he had a good cause of action on the principle that every right has a remedy—and this in spite of some pretention by the House of Commons to make it a question of privilege. In the *Bankers' Case*[2] he and his fellow justices held that a petition of right lay against the Crown for damages on breach of contract. It is interesting to note that he several times anticipated Lord Mansfield's decision in *Summersett's Case*, holding that one could not be a slave on English soil.[3] In another case he laid down the rule that land which is colonised by English settlers is thereby subject to English law, while land which is conquered retains its own laws until further order.[4] In private law he laid the foundation of modern commercial law. Coke had already stated the claim of the common law courts to entertain mercantile cases, but a great practical advance was made when Holt adopted the policy of deciding such cases in the light of mercantile custom instead of by the strict rules of the common law, which were, indeed, entirely unsuitable as a basis of commercial law. Like Lord Mansfield after him, he readily accepted evidence of mercantile custom and consulted merchants freely upon the matter. He tells us that once when he had to decide whether a bill could be accepted after it was due he invited all the eminent merchants in London to discuss the matter with him.[5] He has also given us an early decision upon an employer's liability

---

[1] 2 Ld. Raym. 938 (1703).

[2] 14 S.T. 1 (1700).

[3] *Smith* v. *Brown* (1705), 2 Salk. 666; *Chamberlain* v. *Harvey* (1667), 1 Ld. Raym. 146.

[4] *Blankard* v. *Galdy* (1693), 2 Salk. 411; *Smith* v. *Brown*, 2 Salk. 666.

[5] *Mutford* v. *Walcot* (1700), 1 Ld. Raym. 574.

for the acts of his servants done in the course of their employment.[1]
He dissented, however, from a decision that the Postmaster-General
was not liable for packets lost in the post.[2]   Another of his decisions
on master and servant has a less modern sound:

> " If a master gives correction to his servant it ought to be with the proper
> instrument, as a cudgel, etc.   And then if by accident a blow gives death this
> would be but manslaughter.   The same law of a schoolmaster.   But a sword is
> not a proper instrument for correction."[3]

Unlike most of his predecessors he was willing to favour the action of
slander.   The most famous of all his decisions is, of course, *Coggs* v.
Bernard (1703),[4] which is an elaborate treatment of the general principles
of the law of bailments, based upon a Romanesque passage in Bracton.
As Lord Birkenhead has observed, " throughout all branches of law
one may still cite judgments delivered by Holt ".[5]   As a criminal judge
he had enormous influence in changing the tone of the courts.   In
trials for treason he atoned for the legal disabilities under which prisoners
were then placed by treating them with great patience and indulgence;
he even allowed Lord Preston to address the jury in his defence after his
own summing up, and he discontinued the practice of bringing prisoners
into court in chains.   It was an old theory that prisoners tried for felony
needed no counsel, for the judge was their defender; Holt lived up to
the letter of the rule.   As Sir Richard Steele wrote in the *Tatler*:

> " Wherever he was judge he never forgot that he was also counsel.   The
> criminal before him was always sure he stood before his country, and, in a sort,
> the parent of it.   The prisoner knew that though his spirit was broken with guilt
> and incapable of language to defend itself, all would be gathered from him which
> could conduce to his safety; and that his judge would wrest no law to destroy
> him, nor conceal any that would save him."[6]

One notable piece of legislation associated with him was the Statute 3
& 4 Anne, c. 8, which made promissory notes negotiable, for when the
point was raised before him in a case Lord Holt would not venture to
make so great a departure.[7]   He therefore felt compelled as the law
then stood to hold that notes were not negotiable, using his influence
with the legislature to make the necessary reform.

Holt's career at the bar coincides with the darkest page in the history
of the English judiciary.   The most notorious examples are Scroggs
and Jeffreys, both men of ability but unscrupulous in any matter which
involved politics: many others were men of undistinguished attainments

---

[1] *Tuberville* v. *Stampe* (1697), 1 Ld. Raym. 264.

[2] *Lane* v. *Cotton* (1701), 1 Ld. Raym. 646.

[3] *R.* v. *Keite* (1697), 1 Ld. Raym. 138.

[4] 2 Ld. Raym. 909; for some extracts, see Pound and Plucknett, *Readings*, 593–601.

[5] Birkenhead, *Fourteen English Judges*, 116.

[6] Quoted in Holdsworth, vi. 519.

[7] *Clerke* v. *Martin* (1702), 2 Ld. Raym. 757.   It is discussed in J. M. Holden, *History of Negotiable Instruments in English Law*, 77 ff.

whose names are unknown outside of biographical dictionaries, their appointment being solely due to their pliability. Many who showed signs of resistance to the wishes of the court party were removed— Pemberton was twice dismissed; Bertie, Wilde and Dolben are others who were removed for political reasons. So high did political passions run that even Parliament, after the revolution of 1688, followed the example of the Stuarts and went so far as to imprison ex-judges whose decisions years before had limited the vast privilege claimed for either house.

AFTER THE ACT OF SETTLEMENT

We have already mentioned this act which restored the tenure of judges *quamdiu se bene gesserint* as it generally had been until Charles II and James II had made appointments *durante bene placito*. It did not take the bench entirely out of politics: that would be impossible, and perhaps undesirable. As far as English conditions are concerned, parliamentary experience may even be useful and broadening to a lawyer who might otherwise become too far removed from the world of affairs. Once on the bench, however, judges no longer are expected to take part in political affairs. For more than a century no Chief Justice has been a member of the Cabinet:[1] and although the Chancellor goes out with his party, and while in office is a member of the Cabinet, there are nevertheless conventional limits to his political activities—to say nothing of physical limits due to the multifarious nature of his duties.

MANSFIELD

Mansfield is, in fact, an example of a judge who remained in active politics while on the bench.

William Murray, first Earl of Mansfield, was the fourth son of Lord Stormont, a Scotch peer of distinguished lineage but slender fortune. He was educated at Oxford, being intended first for the Church, but a friend afterwards assisted him in preparing for the law. His family were staunch Jacobites and all through his career his enemies were ready to reproach him, no doubt unjustly, with only a half-hearted devotion to the House of Hanover. At Oxford and soon afterwards, Murray made the acquaintance of the principal wits of the time, including the poet Alexander Pope, before whom and a looking-glass he practised eloquence. His reputation as a man of culture was so high that even Dr Johnson (who had a deep-rooted prejudice against Scots) was bound to admit that one could do a lot with a Scot if he were caught young enough. The most significant event in his career at Oxford was his winning a prize for Latin verse against William Pitt, afterwards Earl of

---

[1] Ellenborough was the last in 1806; unless, indeed, the remarkable career of Lord Reading during the 1914–18 war is treated also as an exception.

Chatham, for here began a bitter rivalry which lasted all their lives. Being a Scotchman, Murray was soon able to acquire a good deal of Scotch business, both legal and political. As early as 1733 he argued a Scotch case before the House of Lords. In 1742 he became Solicitor-General, entered the House of Commons, and immediately became the most brilliant defender of the government in the House, withstanding single-handedly the fierce attacks of Pitt. In spite of his supposed Jacobite sympathies he prosecuted the Jacobite lords who had been concerned with the Rebellion of 1745. Notwithstanding Pitt's incessant attacks, Murray continued his successful defence of the government; in 1754 he became Attorney-General, but in 1756 he insisted upon leaving the House of Commons to become Lord Chief Justice of the King's Bench, and was created Baron Mansfield. In the House of Lords he continued to take an active part in politics. He opposed the repeal of the Stamp Act by Lord Rockingham, taking on this and some other constitutional questions a somewhat narrow view. On the bench he inevitably incurred some unpopularity in connection with the cases in which Wilkes was involved, and was bitterly assailed by the anonymous Junius. His rulings in several libel actions, to the effect that the jury had no right to pass upon anything except the facts of authorship and publication, increased his unpopularity, although there is little doubt that his view of the law was correct until the passing of Fox's Libel Act.[1] On the other hand, in 1771 he decided the famous *Summersett's Case* in favour of a slave. In 1774 he decided that the Crown had no right to legislate for conquered countries merely by prerogative in such a way as to contravene the usual principles of constitutional law. In 1776 he received an earldom, and soon took less part in politics. In 1778 when it was known that he supported a bill which would have relieved Roman Catholics his house was burnt in the course of the Gordon riots. Lord Chatham, who had followed him in the Lords, died in 1778, and Mansfield absented himself from the funeral and refused to join in the acts of mourning for his late rival. In 1784 he himself retired from politics, and in 1788 resigned from the bench to devote the rest of his days to society and letters. In 1793, at the age of eighty-nine, he died and was buried in Westminster Abbey.

As an orator in Parliament he was second only to Pitt, with whose thunderous style Mansfield's own quiet and elegant manner was in striking contrast. At the bar the same gift enabled him to present his case and his arguments with winning lucidity. On the bench he acquired a reputation for complete impartiality, long patience and a profound understanding of legal problems. To these advantages he added the study of somewhat unusual subjects for lawyers of his day. His old master Denison had taught him special pleading and conveyancing on black-letter lines, but at the same time Mansfield felt more attracted by the cosmopolitan learning of Bracton, and under his influence was

[1] Below, p. 500.

drawn (like Holt before him) to a study of Roman law and of the French commercial *ordonnance* which at that moment was the best body of mercantile law in existence. His interest in commerce was deep; a generation before it was fashionable he had adopted free trade principles, and among his many claims to fame his commercial decisions are perhaps the most imposing. It is impossible here to enumerate all the really important decisions which Mansfield made, and we must be content with reproducing two somewhat differing estimates of his work. In one of them Sir William Holdsworth examines Mansfield's place in the legal controversies of his time:

> " Lord Mansfield was a Scotchman by birth, but he was educated at Westminster and Oxford, and he was a barrister of Lincoln's Inn. He had kept up some connection with Scotland and Scotch law, so that both his birth and his education, as well as the qualities of his mind, tended to make him a jurist learned in Roman and continental law as well as in English law. The breadth of his learning prevented him from attaining that accurate knowledge of the development of common law rules which could only come to an English lawyer who had devoted the largest part of his time to the study of its complex technicalities. He approached the common law from the viewpoint of a student of the broad principles of jurisprudence, not from the viewpoint of a student of the evolution of its rules. These qualities of his mind fitted him admirably for the work of creating and settling the law merchant, which in England was in a backward and unsettled state. They enabled him also to rationalise and liberalise other branches of the common law, notably quasi-contract and estoppel, by an infusion of broad and equitable principles. But, naturally, the continued exercise of these qualities tended to make him think that he could settle on rational principles all the branches of the common law. This was a mistake. The principles of some of the older branches of that law were too well settled to be thus reformed. The ground was covered by authority; and the authorities could be understood aright only by lawyers who had studied their history and development. An attempt to rationalise these branches of the common law by the help of pure reason and foreign analogies could not succeed, because the principles founded on this basis could be proved to be contrary to ascertained principles of the common law. Thus Lord Mansfield's attempts to recast the doctrine of consideration, to restate the rule in *Shelley's Case*, and to make the court of King's Bench a court of equity as well as a court of law met the same fate as [his] attempt to extend the doctrine of disseisin at election."[1]

In the other, Lord Birkenhead setting aside those things which Mansfield failed to achieve, estimates his place in legal development in these words:[2]

> " It was first and foremost his work in developing and explaining the commercial law that has ensured him a foremost place among English judges. His practice was to try such cases at the Guildhall with a jury. The panel was chosen with great care from among the merchants of the city, to whom there was no greater source of pride than to become " Lord Mansfield's jurymen ". He invited them to dine with him frequently, and enquired minutely into the practice of

[1] Holdsworth, vii. 44, 45. There is now a full treatment of Mansfield and his colleagues in Holdsworth, xii. 464–560, and C. H. S. Fifoot's *Lord Mansfield* is a learned and entertaining biography.

[2] Birkenhead, *Fourteen English Judges*, 186. Compare the words of Lord Campbell, quoted in Pound and Plucknett, *Readings*, 223–226.

reputable merchants, in return explaining to them with the greatest care the principles of law.   When a case arose which involved a point of principle or some novel practice, he was accustomed to take their verdict subject to a case for the opinion of the full court.   He was aware that such a practice might cause undue delays, and was therefore careful to draw the case at once and see that it was signed by counsel, before calling on another case.   He made it an invariable condition that the case was set down for argument in the first four days of the next law term. In this way he examined, restated, or created the whole of the law of merchants. His long career and deserved reputation have somewhat obscured the work of his predecessors, especially Holt, who in many instances will be found to have decided the same point the same way.   No judge can be a complete innovator.   He is one of a long procession of fellow workers, and undue prominence given to one may obscure the merits of another.   Nevertheless, Holt could not have done Mansfield's work.   He lived too soon, but he did noble work on the foundations of which Mansfield built the commanding fabric of our commercial law.   The law relating to shipping, commercial transactions, and insurance was practically remade by Mansfield, who never lost sight of the fact that international commerce requires the law of each country to be based on the same principles; the practice of honesty and fair dealing among prudent and honourable merchants.   Coke captured the law merchant for the common law; Holt retained it; Mansfield formally incorporated it into our system."

PROFESSIONAL LITERATURE

" Legal precepts and legal institutions are far from being all with which we have to do. Indeed, in the everyday administration of justice, along with legal precepts, the traditional art of the lawyer's craft—the traditional mode of selecting, developing, and applying the received legal materials, the traditional technique of finding the grounds of decision in those materials and of developing them into a judgment—is a factor of no less importance. That art, and a certain body of received ideals as to the end of law and what legal precepts should be in view thereof, are in truth much more enduring than legal precepts. They give unity and continuity to legal development. They make the lawyers of to-day conscious of kinship with the lawyers of the sixteenth century, and even with the great lawyers of the middle ages, and give us a sense of continuity from the Year Books to the present, which would have little warrant if we looked only at institutions and at legal precepts. They give unity to the law of English-speaking peoples throughout the world. For, diverse as the social, economic, political, and physical conditions may be, diverse as legislation may be, far as statute or judicial decision may have departed from the common legal materials of the seventeenth century, and divergent as the paths of departure may be, the lawyers in England, the United States, Canada, and Australia feel that they live under what is essentially one legal system, and each knows at once how to make use of the other's law. An American lawyer uses recent English or Canadian or Australian decisions with entire assurance because they are made to be used as he knows how to use them. The American legislator knows, as it were instinctively, how to adapt English or Canadian or Australian legislation because it has been drawn to be used as he knows how to use it. The traditional art of applying it, and of developing it into grounds of decision of particular controversies, is familiar to him. On the other hand, when the American lawyer seeks to use the legal materials of the Roman law or of the modern Roman-law world, he proceeds blunderingly and with a certain consciousness of helplessness. For these materials took shape for a wholly different technique. The traditional art of developing grounds of decision from them and applying them is very different from our own, and they are adapted to that technique. Ours is a technique of utilizing recorded judicial experience. The civilian's is a technique of finding his grounds of decision in written texts. Even when we have written texts, as in American constitutional law, we proceed at once to look at them through the spectacles of the common law, and our method is not one of development of the text but of development of judicially found grounds of decision which, if they began in the text, have since led an independent existence."[1]

The words we have just quoted clearly define the point of view from which historical sources are best studied. It is, of course, necessary that the would-be legal historian should know what sources are available and should understand their value and their use. But the study of the sources of legal history has a wider and more general significance. Besides being the sources which the modern historian uses in reconstructing the past, these sources were also the tools in daily use by ancient lawyers. It was by the constant use of the reports, registers, pamphlets and other works which we shall mention that the lawyers of former days gained their living, and, as in every other human creation, the peculiarities of the tools employed have left a permanent mark upon the finished product. A system of law therefore is largely influenced by the technical methods used by the lawyers in going about their daily business. When faced with a difficult case, the advocates and the judges have to undertake research in order to find what law will govern it. The method which they pursue, the character of the books and sources which they use, and the attitude of mind with which they approach them, all have their influence upon the shaping of the law, and upon their conception of law itself. Even in our own day the enterprise of law publishers in reporting and making available thousands upon thousands of cases every year is showing signs of influencing the modern conception of law in America. First there is an heroic attempt to keep pace with the mass of material pouring from the presses, which is soon followed by an

---

[1] Pound, Introduction to Winfield, *Chief Sources of English Legal History*, xiii, xiv.

inevitable reaction, and a change in attitude towards case law. It is, of course, perfectly true that to some extent legal literature is the product of the professional point of view; but it is even more important to observe that a particular type of legal literature when it has come into constant and widespread use exerts very considerable influence upon legal thought. By the words " legal thought ", moreover, we do not merely mean the deliberate reflections of the specialist in jurisprudence; such speculations are occasionally influential, but quite frequently they do not extend outside of academic circles. A more important part of legal thought is the half-conscious formation of ideas which is bound to go on in the mind of every active practitioner. It was the same in the middle ages. If we are to understand the point of view of the founders of the common law these questions

> " must be approached from the point of view of the royal judge and the pleader. The one was a hard-worked and underpaid official, the other a busy professional man intent on winning cases and learning the practical wisdom of the courts. Neither class was in any sense of an academical turn of mind, and theories as such seem to have played little part in their thinking. Yet with such men one often finds that an unexpressed, half-conscious notion or prejudice is extremely influential, and, indeed, it is mainly to such factors as this that one must look for an explanation of the attitude of court and pleaders."[1]

It is only natural that it should be more difficult to catch the turn of thought of people whose thoughts are only half expressed, than it is to follow the argument of a jurist who is deliberately expounding his speculations. In the former case we have to search for the thought as well as we can among the daily practical affairs of the old lawyers; in the latter we have merely to read attentively a carefully written exposition. Yet, as everybody knows, the ideas which most powerfully influence conduct in every department of life are not the ideas of a systematic philosophy deliberately held, but rather the vague notions and unconscious prejudices, habits of mind, and so forth, of which we are for the most part unaware. Such notions are partly the cause, but more frequently the effect, of the legal literature which one habitually uses, and the principal object of this chapter will be to trace the relationship of the law to professional literature from this point of view.

THE ANGLO-SAXON AGE

If we begin with the Anglo-Saxon period we shall find a fair number of sources for legal history, but very few of these are what we would call professional literature. As we have seen, it is hardly possible to speak of a legal profession in the Anglo-Saxon period. The sources which have survived are for the most part formal documents. The laws, or the declarations of law, made by the Anglo-Saxon kings, have survived in considerable numbers and have been published in an edition

---

[1] Plucknett, *Statutes and Their Interpretation in the Fourteenth Century*, 7.

which is a monument of patient learning and keen textual criticism.[1]
In the matter of form hardly anything can be deduced save a general
similarity in method (or lack of method) with various continental collections.[2] Perhaps the one great difference—namely, that the Anglo-
Saxon laws are written in English while the continental collections are
in Latin instead of in the vernacular—is more obvious than important;
the spirit in both cases seems the same. In the case of the charters, on
the other hand, matters of form are more illuminating. It was the
object of the charters in most cases to make bookland, and for this
purpose they used forms and expressions which can definitely be traced
to the continent. This constitutes one of the main arguments used by
Sir Paul Vinogradoff in establishing Roman influence upon Anglo-
Saxon law.[3] To this extent no doubt the forms of the Anglo-Saxon
charters indicate the direction in which Anglo-Saxon thought was
searching for a professional technique. It seems, moreover, that these
documents were not drafted in the Royal Chancery (at least until comparatively late) but were prepared by the recipient, who presented them
to the donor in the hope that he would execute them. There is, therefore,
a good deal of room for the exercise of fancy in their construction.
Many of them bear a distinctly literary character; elegance, latinity and
rhetoric all enter into the Anglo-Saxon charter.

Those slight productions which might be called legal treatises coming
from the Anglo-Saxon age are few and short.[4] In form they consist
of the brief statement of a few rules, usually matters of detail which
might be apt, otherwise, to slip from the memory.

ANGLO-NORMAN LEGAL LITERATURE

It is not until the Norman age has made some progress that we
begin to find a definitely professional literature in the modern sense of
the term.

In the middle of the reign of Henry I, between the years 1113 and
1118, we get the first outburst of legal writing in England. A little
group of treatises attempted to state the old Anglo-Saxon law in a
form suitable for the Norman age. Several of these treatises are closely
connected, and may perhaps come from the same hand. Most important of them is the *Leges Henrici Primi*. It seems to have obtained
this title because it commences with the coronation charter of Henry I;

---

[1] Liebermann, *Die Gesetze der Angelsachsen*. Many of these texts are now available in the
less costly (and very serviceable) editions by F. L. Attenborough, *Laws of the Earliest English
Kings* (Cambridge, 1922), and A. J. Robertson, *Laws of the Kings of England from Edmund to
Henry I* (Cambridge, 1925).

[2] They are briefly described in Pollock and Maitland, i. 6–13, and Holdsworth, ii. 18–34.

[3] See his *Romanistische Einflüsse im angelsächsischen Recht: Das Buchland*, in his Collected
Papers, i. 168–191, and for an authoritative introduction, F. M. Stenton, *Latin Charters of the
Anglo-Saxon Period* (1955).

[4] They are printed by Liebermann.

the rest of the book, in fact, is drawn mainly from the Anglo-Saxon laws, with some references to civil, canon and Frankish law. The author suffered under the disability of writing a very bad Latin style and his meaning is often far from clear: but in spite of all his limitations Maitland insists " that he was engaged on an utterly new task; he was writing a legal text book, a text book of law that was neither Roman nor canon law. To have thought that a law book ought to be written was no small feat in 1118 ". The legal situation in Henry I's reign was largely also a political question, and a remarkable trace of the political and racial controversy which must have been going on is to be found in a book called the *Laws of Edward the Confessor*. The anti-Norman element in England naturally looked back to the days of the Confessor as the Golden Age of English law, and the author, or rather forger, of this text, endeavoured to show the good old law which in his opinion ought to prevail. He is a staunch upholder of West Saxon institutions and of the Church; his principal antipathy is for the Danes. Unfortunately Coke and all the older historians took this book seriously, and so a good deal of legend came to pass as history.

HENRY II: GLANVILL'S TREATISE

Two generations later we come to another outburst of legal writing. The *Dialogue of the Exchequer* we have already mentioned;[1] at almost the same date we find another treatise which is more exclusively concerned with law. This book goes by the name of *Glanvill*.[2] It is highly significant that in or about the year 1187 it should have been possible to write two separate treatises, one about administration, and the other about law; already these two subjects have their separate spheres. There is no reason to believe that Ranulph de Glanvill wrote this book, although he may have inspired Hubert Walter to compose it; the manuscripts merely say that it was composed in the time of Glanvill. The high importance of this work lies in the fact that it settled the method of legal writing for many centuries to come. This method consists in giving a specimen form of writ current in the King's Court and adding to it a commentary. In Glanvill's day the writs were not very numerous and the law attached to them was not very complicated. The King's Court was as yet young and its jurisdiction was not very extensive. Besides the law of land and the feudal incidents attached to it, there was not very much to be said, nor was it felt desirable to extend the jurisdiction of the King's Court to other matters. Glanvill's treatise, therefore, is not very long or very difficult. The contrast between *Glanvill* and the *Leges Henrici Primi* is very marked. The author of the older book

---

[1] Above, pp. 18, 147.

[2] Edited by Woodbine, *Glanvill: De Legibus* (1932). This edition has been criticised by R. W. Southern, English Historical Review, lxv. 81, and by H. G. Richardson, Juridical Review, lxvii. 155. A new edition is in preparation.

is overcome by the confusion of competing systems of law, none of which alone was adequate. Even in England he had to recognise three territorial laws, the Dane Law, the Law of Mercia and the Law of Wessex, but in order to make sense out of them he had to appeal to Roman, canon and Frankish law. When we come to Glanvill everything is beautifully simple. He is only concerned with the law of the King's Court and with cases which originated there; all the tangled masses of local custom which certainly were still in force he completely ignores; most of the surviving traces of pre-Conquest law are likewise absent from his work. He is, in fact, the first exponent of the new common law which in the course of the centuries was to supersede the ancient legal institutions of the land. Already we can see the main features of that common law in Glanvill's book: it is royal, flowing from the King's Court; it is common, for local variations receive very little sympathy; it is strongly procedural, being based upon writs and expressed in the form of a commentary upon them.

Manuscripts of Glanvill continued to be copied as a useful book for the next hundred years—even after Bracton's much larger (but much more costly and difficult) treatise was available. Attempts to re-edit Glanvill seem never to have got beyond the stage of private experiments which did not reach the general public[1]—at least, in England: in Scotland, however, a much revised version of Glanvill became influential under the title of its opening words, *Regiam Maiestatem*.[2]

THE BEGINNINGS OF THE PUBLIC RECORDS

We find at the opening of the thirteenth century several very imposing series of public records consisting of the rolls of the several courts and administrative departments.[3] These are highly important as sources for legal history, but it is only very much later that they become in any sense a product of the profession. The steps by which this took place seem never to have been fully explored. In their early days, no doubt, these rolls of the King's Courts were prepared by royal officials for strictly practical purposes.[4] They are hasty, rapidly written, full of slips and interlineations. There is an air of informality about them which seems to show that they were taken down in court as cases proceeded, and never revised. If, however, we look at a plea roll of the fourteenth century or later a great change has taken place. Pleadings

[1] Maitland, *Glanvill Revised*, Collected Papers, ii. 266; N. Denholm-Young, *Robert Carpenter and the Provisions of Westminster*, Collected Papers (1946), 96; Richardson, *Glanvill Continued*, Law Quarterly Review, liv. 381.

[2] Prefixed to the Record Commission's edition of the Scottish statutes. There is now a new edition of *Regiam Maiestatem* by Lord Cooper (Stair Society). See also H. G. Richardson *Roman Law in the Regiam Majestatem*, Juridical Review, lxvii. 155.

[3] See V. H. Galbraith, *Introduction to the Use of the Public Records* (Oxford, 1934).

[4] Changes in the appearance of legal records can be traced through the plates in C. Johnson and C. H. Jenkinson, *English Court Hand*, and C. H. Jenkinson, *Later Court Hands*.

are set forth in formal language and written in a large set hand. Subsidiary notes are commonly made in very hasty writing, but the formal record always appears in precise phrases and careful writing. At some time or another the responsibility for drafting these records seems to have shifted. In the earlier rolls it is clear that the clerk recorded any matter of interest to the Crown, and this without consulting the parties, who very probably did not have access to the rolls. By the time we reach the classical age of the common law, it seems to have become the practice for the lawyers engaged upon a case to settle the pleadings and the form in which they should appear upon the plea roll. From this point, therefore, the enrolment is not merely an administrative document for the confidential use of the royal officials, but a document drawn by lawyers in accordance with the learning of their art, and therefore a form of professional literature.[1]

Besides the pleadings themselves the writ has also undergone a somewhat similar development. In the early Norman age a party who was fortunate enough to obtain a royal writ against his adversary was probably uncertain of the form which that writ would take. In substance it was merely a command from the King to a sheriff in connection with the matter, and might contain any orders which the King thought appropriate. Gradually a few forms became more and more commonly in use, and it was obviously convenient that the public as well as the clerical staff of the Chancery should know the more common forms available. And so we find collections of forms of writs, at first very small, and later growing to formidable dimensions. With the writs, as with the pleadings, the responsibility for drafting them gradually shifts from the royal officials to the legal profession at large, and so they too pass from the category of administrative documents into that of professional literature. It is impossible to be certain that this change is completed until we reach the sixteenth century, but it may well be that its beginnings go back several centuries.

Such, then, is the general character of the development of legal forms in the earlier period. The preparation of documents which was once the private concern of the King's officials, gradually passed from the administration to the legal profession, who exercised it subject to criticism by the courts. As we shall soon see, even the treatises owe a great deal to this process.

HENRY III: BRACTON

Two generations after Glanvill's book we come to " the flower and crown of English jurisprudence "—Bracton. Of Bracton's life we know a good deal of insignificant detail; of the really important matters in his career we have very little information. He seems to be of Devonshire origin and held a great deal of preferment in the

---

[1] On the relationship between the roll and the pleadings, and the growth of professional influence over the enrolment, see below, p. 402.

Church, finally becoming Chancellor of Exeter Cathedral. He spent many years in the royal service, principally as a Judge of Assize, constantly visiting his own county of Devonshire in that capacity.[1] He seems never to have sat in the Court of Common Pleas although for a short time he was a Justice in Eyre and of the King's Bench. Although he was constantly in the government's service we find little trace of his taking a side during the Barons' War. It is, in fact, impossible to regard him as a partisan, for he served both the barons and the King.[2] It has been suggested that we have here an early example of the sound judicial policy of remaining absolutely neutral in times of political strife. His great book was never finished, for he seems to have stopped working upon it in 1256; the civil war which soon followed may well have prevented further study.[3]

The work consists of two distinct portions. The first quarter is a somewhat lengthy introduction; the rest is a series of separate treatises upon the various forms of action. The second and main portion of his work is based on the original plan of Glanvill, that is to say, each form of action is treated separately in the form of a commentary upon the appropriate writ. But Bracton does a good deal more than use Glanvill's plan and merely bring his matter up to date by the inclusion of vast masses of new law developed since Glanvill's day. He made, in fact, two capital contributions of his own to the art of legal writing.

BRACTON'S USE OF CASES

First of all, besides studying the form of the original writs, he also procured, for his own private use, complete transcripts of the pleadings in selected cases, and even referred to the cases in the course of his treatise. This great innovation gives to his work in several places a curiously modern air, for like modern law writers he sometimes praises and sometimes criticises his cases. At the beginning of his book he explains, however, that the contemporary bench is not distinguished by ability or learning, and that his treatise is, to some extent, a protest against modern tendencies. He endeavours to set forth the sound principles laid down by those whom he calls " his masters " who were on the bench nearly a generation ago; hence it is that his cases are on the average about twenty years older than his book. Of really recent

---

[1] This practice was prudently forbidden by later statutes: *Rot. Parl.*, ii. 334 no. 75 (1376), 8 Ric. II, c. 2 (1384) and others.

[2] For Bracton's life, see Maitland, *Bracton's Note Book*, i. 13 ff.; J. H. Round, *Bractoniana*, English Historical Review, xxvi. 586; D. M. Stenton, *Eyre Rolls for Lincs. and Worcs.* (Selden Society, vol. 53), xv ff. and the references below, p. 262 n. 1.

[3] Maitland, *Bracton's Note Book*, i. 34–45. Holdsworth, *History of English Law*, ii. 236–237 (stated more emphatically in his *Makers of English Law*, 16–17), assigns a date *c.* 1240 and H. Kantorowicz, *Bractonian Problems* (1941), argues for " before 1239 ". Both dates seem quite impossible. Maitland's demonstration (*Bracton's Note Book*, i. 40) that Bracton was at work on the book in 1254 is reinforced by the observation of H. M. Cam, *Studies in the Hundred Rolls*, 23, 89, that Bracton used the 1254 version of the chapters of the eyre.

cases he used very few. It must not, therefore, be assumed that we have in Bracton the modern conception of case law. He never gives us any discussion of the authority of cases and clearly would not understand the modern implications of *stare decisis*. Indeed, his cases are carefully selected because they illustrate what he believes the law ought to be, and not because they have any binding authority; he freely admits that at the present moment decisions are apt to be on different lines. Bracton's use of cases, therefore, is not based upon their authority as sources of law, but upon his personal respect for the judges who decided them, and his belief that they raise and discuss questions upon lines which he considers sound.[1] Although it is true that the use of cases as a source of law in the modern sense was still far in the future, nevertheless Bracton's use of cases is very significant. He accustomed lawyers of the thirteenth and early fourteenth centuries to read and to discuss the cases which he put in his book, and this was a great step towards the modern point of view. It may be that Bracton's priority in this matter can be regarded as established. He is certainly very soon followed by little treatises or pamphlets which also contain transcripts of records, but unlike Bracton these later little treatises have either suppressed the names of the parties or have contented themselves with an imaginary rather than an actual record. As for Bracton, it was only his official position and his legal connections which enabled him to obtain access to the rolls of the King's Courts. The ordinary lawyer at this time would certainly not have been able to spend years of study upon these official and confidential documents.

BRACTON'S *NOTE BOOK*

It is still possible to trace the stages of Bracton's work, for a *Note Book* was discovered by Sir Paul Vinogradoff and edited by Maitland which contains his transcripts of some two thousand cases from the plea rolls. Most of those plea rolls still survive and in their margins are still to be seen the pencil directions which Bracton wrote for his copyist.[2] It may be that Bracton's work was never completed in consequence of an order which we know he received demanding the instant return of all plea rolls in his possession. Even for a judge such as Bracton access to cases on the plea rolls was therefore difficult, and there is no possibility of any system of case law developing when the cases are inaccessible to the profession. We may conjecture, however, that Bracton's use of cases was favourably received by the profession; the small tracts we have just mentioned which contain either records of cases or drafts of imaginary records bear witness to this fact. It may well be that Bracton's discussion of cases so impressed lawyers at the

---

[1] See pp. 342–345 below.

[2] For facsimiles of some of the markings and of a page of the *Note Book*, see D. M. Stenton, *Eyre Rolls of Lincs. and Worcs.* (Selden Society, vol. 53), whose introduction is very illuminating.

time that there was a real demand for case material, especially after Bracton's treatise began to grow old. Such a demand might have been met in a variety of ways; on the continent it was not unusual for a clerk of the courts to prepare a collection of interesting cases from the documents in his custody, but in England a different policy was adopted. It is, perhaps not too fanciful to suggest that Bracton's use of cases gave the first impetus towards the preparation of the Year Books.

BRACTON'S ROMANISM

The second contribution which Bracton made was to overspread the technicalities of the English courts with a broad cosmopolitan learning. His use of foreign material, and especially of Roman law, may well be compared with the Romanism of such treatises as the *Leges Henrici Primi* of a hundred and forty years before, and with the few passages where Glanvill also drew upon Roman sources. There has been a great deal of controversy as to the extent and the character of Bracton's Romanism. To some he has seemed so completely Roman that he must be denied a place in the literature of English law;[1] Sir Henry Maine regarded him as something like an inexplicable fraud in passing off sheer Romanism as English law.[2] Maitland believed that the extent of Bracton's Romanism was not considerable and that his knowledge of Roman law was neither accurate nor deep.[3] To all this Sir Paul Vinogradoff replied that Bracton's Roman law must not be tested by the Digest but by the somewhat Romanised customs in force on the continent, and that judged from this standpoint Maitland's charges of mishandling Roman law break down, for Bracton was using Roman law in the popular form in which it was then current, rather than in the academic purity of the Digest.[4] We may probably assume, therefore, that when Bracton used foreign law he had a fairly good idea of what he was about.

It is interesting to note the places where Bracton's Romanism occurs. It is most apparent in the earlier portion of his work, which consists very largely of general considerations serving as an introduction to the subject.[5] The identification of these Romanesque passages and the discussion of their significance are by no means easy, and a good deal of controversy has resulted. This has been rekindled by the brilliant and provocative little book of H. Kantorowicz, *Bractonian Problems* (Glasgow, 1941), suggesting that the blunders in the text are not due to

---

[1] Thus David Hoüard, *Les Coutumes anglo-normandes* (1776).

[2] Maine, *Ancient Law*, chap. iv (1861).

[3] Maitland, *Bracton and Azo* (Selden Society, 1895), where he pursued further the discovery of Carl Güterbock, *Bracton* (1861; tr. by Brinton Coxe, 1866), that Bracton had frequently used the *Summa* of Azo (written before 1211).

[4] Vinogradoff, *Collected Papers*, i. 237 (from Yale Law Journal, xxxii. 751; 1923). Cf. Woodbine, *The Roman Element in Bracton*, Yale Law Journal, xxxi. 827 (1922).

[5] Summarised in Holdsworth, ii. 271–282.

Bracton but to an anonymous redactor who prepared his manuscript for circulation. Several scholars have lately enlarged the list of Roman and Canon writers to whom Bracton's indebtedness can be proved, and thus the general problem of Bracton's foreign learning, its quality, and the use he made of it, is very much an open question. In the meantime, a valuable but very technical mass of research is being published.[1] As Sir William Holdsworth has observed:

> " We cannot say that all Bracton's law is English in substance, that the influence of Roman law is merely formal. No doubt there is a body of thoroughly English rules; and Bracton differs at very many points from the Roman texts. But it is clear that he has used Roman terms, Roman maxims, and Roman doctrines to construct upon native foundations a reasonable system out of comparatively meagre authorities. Even when he is dealing with purely English portions of his treatise, and discoursing upon the Assizes, the writs of entry, or the writ of right, Roman illustrations and phrases naturally recur to him. And it is clear that his study of Roman law has led him to discuss problems which, when he wrote, were very far from any actual case argued in the royal courts. Thus he deals with *accessio, specificatio,* and, *confusio*; and ' where ', says Maitland, ' in all our countless volumes of reports shall we find any decisions about some questions that Azo has suggested to Bracton? ' Similarly he deals with many questions relating to obligation and contract, fraud and negligence, about which the common law had as yet no rules. In dealing with these matters he necessarily uses Roman terms and borrows Roman rules. It is, as we shall see, because his treatise has given to English law at least one authority upon many matters which were outside the routine of the practising lawyer of the thirteenth century that his influence upon the history of English law has been so great. That his treatise deals with such matters is due to the Roman law which it contains."[2]

BRACTON'S INFLUENCE

Bracton's influence has varied greatly from century to century. In his own day it must have been high, for numerous copies of his book are still extant and many more must have perished. This does not mean that there was any tendency to follow Bracton's doctrine—even on points which were still open. As an example, we may mention a point in the law of descent in which Bracton, *Fleta* and *Britton* all agreed

---

[1] It consists at present of the following items. Woodbine has reviewed Kantorowicz in Yale Law Journal, lii. 428 (1943); C. H. McIlwain, *The Problem of the Bracton Text*, Harvard Law Review, lvii. 220 (1943); F. Schulz, *Critical Studies on Bracton's Treatise*, Law Quarterly Review, lix. 172 (1943); H. G. Richardson, *Azo, Drogheda, and Bracton*, English Historical Review, lix. 22 (1944); F. Schulz, *A New Approach to Bracton*, Seminar (annual supplement of The Jurist), ii. 41 (1944); H. G. Richardson, *Tancred, Raymond and Bracton*, English Historical Review, lix. 376 (1944); F. Schulz, *Bracton and Raymond de Penafort*, Law Quarterly Review, lxi. 286 (1945); F. Schulz, *Bracton on Kingship*, English Historical Review, lx. 136 (1945); F. Schulz, *Bracton as a Computist*, Traditio, iii. 265 (1946); Gaines Post, *A Romano-canonical maxim, " quod omnes tangit "*, in *Bracton*, Traditio, iv. 197 (1946); G. Lapsley, *Bracton and the authorship of the " Addicio de cartis "*, English Historical Review, lxii. 1 (1947); H. G. Richardson, *Studies in Bracton*, Traditio, vi. 61 (1948); C. A. F. Meekings, *Martin Pateshull and William Rayleigh*, Bulletin of the Institute of Historical Research, xxvi. 157 (1953); C. A. F. Meekings, *Henry de Bracton, Canon of Wells*, Somerset and Dorset Notes and Queries, xxvi. 141 (1953), and H. G. Richardson, *Roman Law in the Regiam Majestatem*, Juridical Review, lxvii. 155 (1955).

[2] Holdsworth, ii. 286.

(with Glanvill) in a somewhat speculative proposition. Maitland[1] firmly rejected them all, and an unprinted Year Book has just come to light, showing that the courts also rejected that doctrine.[2] As we shall see later, Bracton is also firmly in favour of admitting the half-blood to inherit, but here again the courts declined to follow him.[3] After a century his work became less popular. At first it suffered the usual fate of every successful book in the middle ages, that is to say, various writers prepared epitomes of it or revised it, but after 1350 or thereabout his popularity waned. The broad view and wide learning of Bracton gave way before the less genial science of procedure. For a time the common law devoted itself to the development of a rigid and rather needlessly complicated system, which demanded a close study of formidable masses of detail. It was only centuries later that the printing press was to establish Bracton's position in English legal literature. The first edition, 1569, is a stately volume, perhaps the best printed law book we have ever had, and it came at a time when mediaeval learning was needed. The steady growth of the powers of the Crown and the tendency towards State absolutism acting through the person of the monarch were inevitable after the Reformation. It is curious to mark the contrast between two books which appeared very close together, Bracton in 1569, and Smith, *De Republica Anglorum*, in 1583. In the latter, Elizabeth's Secretary of State, Sir Thomas Smith, set forth the truly fearful powers of the Crown in Parliament, which can make and unmake law, change rights and possessions of private men, legitimate bastards, establish religions, condemn or absolve (by its attainders, etc.) whomsoever the Prince will. Smith was no friend of tyranny, but he clearly enjoyed enumerating in an imposing list the powers of the Tudor State. In Bracton, on the other hand, the emphasis was not upon power but upon responsibility; the King was subject to God, to the law, and (according to a doubtful but much-quoted passage) to his feudal court. Here was an antidote to that State absolutism which the later Tudors and the Stuarts attempted. This was the immediate effect of the publication of Bracton, but it was not the effect which the anonymous editor intended. To him Bracton had different merits to which he called attention in his interesting preface. He observes that even the best of our books are none too good, while the rest are but an *indigesta confusio*, and so commends to students the treatise of Bracton with its laudable imitation of the Roman clarity and order. In fact, the first edition of Bracton is part of the Romanising movement of the reign of Elizabeth, when there were several eminent civilians in the public service. English law, however, was still too mediaeval to feel the force of such an argument. Not until Holt's time was Bracton read because he was Roman; in the meantime, he was read because he was mediaeval, and so it is not surprising

---

[1] Pollock and Maitland, ii. 301 n. 1.

[2] Y.BB. Edw. II (Selden Society), x. xlv, 276.

[3] Below, pp. 719–722.

that when the political storm grew darker Coke eagerly seized upon
Bracton as a powerful weapon, and a second edition was published
in the heat of the conflict of 1640.[1]

Bracton's influence was to extend to private law in the course of
the eighteenth century. The passage we have already quoted from
Professor Holdsworth indicates the reason. The time had come when
the speculative questions which Bracton had raised turned up in actual
practice. In looking for authority, attention turned to Bracton and
there were found Bracton's own suggestions. But these suggestions
were mostly drawn from the Roman legal literature, which was the
only place in his day where such " academic " matters were to be
found; and so the guidance which was found in Bracton's treatise was
really Roman law. Thus, in the famous case of *Coggs* v. *Bernard*,[2] Lord
Holt made great use of Roman passages in Bracton (whom he praised
highly) and thereby brought our law of bailments into line with that of
the Roman law. Similarly, in the seventeenth and eighteenth centuries,
passages of Bracton were much used in settling the law of easements,[3]
which so far had been obscured by procedural considerations.

BRACTONISM AND PARLIAMENTARISM

This curious history of Bracton's tardy influence on the law moved
Maitland to the notable reflection that the rise of parliamentary supremacy
had its disadvantages as well as its benefits. The decline of Bracton's
influence in the middle of the fourteenth century coincides with Parliament's first assertions of its powers; already it had come to be the
principal, if not the only, legislative body, and the dominant interest
in it was that of the common lawyers. The common lawyers were
rapidly becoming a narrow profession, moreover, and the Crown adopted
the fateful practice of appointing judges from among the leading practitioners at the bar. Bench, bar and Parliament, therefore, were alike
under the influence of the conservative, professionalised lawyer, to
whom the complexities and technicalities of the law were a peculiar and
valuable learning. What is more, these very men also acquired control
of legal education as well. The inevitable result was the disappearance
of a liberal outlook upon law, and the loss of contact with other systems.
The speculative parts of Bracton's treatise must have seemed unpractical
and academic; instead of this broad learning they turned to the narrow
and tangled studies of procedure and pleading. It was the common
lawyers who were mainly instrumental in making parliamentary
supremacy a fact, but, as Maitland has said, " the supremacy of Parliament

---

[1] The third edition by Twiss in six volumes is most unreliable; the fourth, by Professor
Woodbine, is now complete, and is the only one based upon a collation of most of the manuscripts. The strictures of H. Kantorowicz, *Bractonian Problems*, are for the most part un-
warranted. A reprint with a translation is contemplated.

[2] (1703), 2 Ld. Raym. 909.

[3] See Holdsworth, vii. 323 ff.

may have been worth the price paid for it; none the less, the price was high ".[1] The price consisted in the extreme centralisation of justice, the decline of old local institutions, the subjection of custom to the common law, the growth of immense quantities of technicality, opposition to reform, and the rejection of the broader and more liberal attitude towards law which showed so clearly in Bracton. It was very appropriate that when some of the mediaeval deficiencies of the common law were at length supplied, Bracton should have played a noteworthy part, albeit four or five centuries after his death.

BRACTON'S IMITATORS

Some curious things happened to Bracton's book. Several smaller treatises were based upon it, but the longest and most important of them were *Fleta* and *Britton*. *Fleta* was written in Latin, and although based largely upon Bracton, contains some new matter; we have already mentioned his original and illuminating treatment of the courts of law, and the significant formula which he uses in describing them.[2] This is the portion of *Fleta's* work which is of most general importance. The rest is mainly an attempt to modernise Bracton in view of the legislation of Edward I. There has been much speculation on the identity of the author;[3] a recent study has made out a persuasive case for ascribing it to Matthew Cheker (or de Scaccario).[4] It was printed by Selden in 1647 from the unique manuscript now in the British Museum—the work obviously never reached the legal public. A new edition for the Selden Society is in course of publication.

Britton is a rather different book. It is written in French and is of almost exactly the same date as *Fleta* (1290–1292). The remarkable thing about *Britton* is that it is in the form of a code and purports to be issued by royal authority. It is not impossible that the idea of codifying English law had been entertained by Edward I. That monarch had done something of the sort in the Statute of Wales to which we have already referred, and in 1305 contemplated doing the same for Scotland;[5] certainly if a code was contemplated the great book of Bracton was an obvious model to which to turn. As Professor Winfield has observed, it is time that *Britton's* pretensions were investigated; it is hardly likely that such a claim would have been made if there had been no foundation for it whatever.[6] In any case, *Britton* enjoyed a great popularity for

---

[1] Maitland, *Bracton's Note Book*, i. 7.

[2] Above, p. 154.

[3] Borris M. Komar, *Two Claims to Fleta's Honors*, West Virginia Law Quarterly (1924), xxx. 167.

[4] N. Denholm-Young, *Collected Papers*, 68–85 (from English Historical Review, 1943, 1944).

[5] Palgrave, *Parliamentary Writs*, i. 161.

[6] Winfield, *Chief Sources of English Legal History*, 264. It must, however, be remembered that a similar claim was made, without any foundation, for the *Établissements de Saint Louis* (ed. Paul Viollet, 4 vols., 1881–1886). There it was an apocryphal prologue which made the claim; in *Britton* the claim is made constantly throughout the book.

· many centuries, and was soon put into print. *Fleta*, on the other hand, was hardly a success, probably because common lawyers, as time went on, read Latin with less ease, and so naturally turned to the familiar French of *Britton*. Its authorship is still more obscure than *Fleta's*. It is only some of the manuscripts which call the work *Britton*, and the significance of that word is far from clear; it was long taken to mean that John le Breton, bishop of Hereford, was the author. Most scholars have agreed with F. M. Nichols, the editor of the admirable Oxford edition (1865), that there is no evidence to support that ascription.[1]

Still a third treatise from this period is the *Summa* of Gilbert de Thornton, C.J. For many centuries the text of this work was lost, but a manuscript recently discovered has been acquired by the Harvard Law Library.[2]

THE MINOR TREATISES

Just at this moment (the earlier portion of Edward I's reign[3]) we come to the new style of literature which was eventually to supplant the Bractonian tradition. It consists of a number of little treatises on writs, declarations, and other procedural matters, sometimes interspersed with a number of cases which may be either narrated at some length, or merely represented by extracts from the pleadings. The proportions in which these various elements occur vary considerably; it has been well observed:

> " It was a period in which men were groping for forms of expressing the law. They did not quite know what ought to go into a law book, or how the matter should be distributed, or whether portions of it had better be left for incorporation in some other book, or what the title of the book should be. On all these points the period was one of experiment. In a later era cases will go to one book, writs to another, pleadings to yet another; abridgments of cases will be separated from reports of them, and land law and pleas of the Crown will be dignified with separate monographs. . . . And so in the dawn of our legal literature we can see men treading in the uncertain light, first in one direction, and then in another. Some thought that the right path was report *plus* pleading *plus* note *plus* institutional instruction, some that a combination of any three or two of these would suffice."[4]

Indeed, this very hesitation as to the form which legal literature should take shows how completely practitioners were turning their backs upon the Bractonian tradition. It may perhaps be conjectured that these little treatises we are discussing are intimately connected with the beginnings of legal education. It was a momentous decision when

[1] G. J. Turner, *Brevia Placitata*, xxiv, argues in support of le Breton's claim; and for some connection between le Breton and the *Brevia Placitata*.

[2] See *Selden's Dissertatio ad Fletam* (ed. Ogg); Woodbine, *The Summa of Gilbert de Thornton*, Law Quarterly Review, xxv. 44; Plucknett, *The Harvard Manuscript of Thornton's Summa*, Harvard Law Review, li. 1038; Thorne, *Thornton's Summa de Legibus*, Univ. of Toronto Law Journal, vii. 1. The manuscript is being edited for the Ames Foundation by Professor Thorne.

[3] Work now in progress will possibly put some of these compositions back a few years into the close of Henry III's reign.

[4] Winfield, *Chief Sources of English Legal History*, 161–162, 170.

that important function was left entirely in the hands of the practitioners themselves, and carried out, it would seem, by allowing students to attend the courts and to rely for an explanation of what they heard there upon conversation which crossed the dinner table in the lawyers' inns, assisted perhaps by some of these little treatises. " The common lawyers were self-educated, so to speak ",[1] and an examination of this class of text seems to show that they compiled as best they could their own text-books.[2]

There is one other work which defies classification, and almost baffles description. The *Mirror of Justices* was written about the year 1290, at the moment when *Britton*, *Fleta* and Thornton were bending their energies towards the serious task of rewriting English law. Andrew Horn, the presumptive author of the *Mirror*, adds one more mystery (and a very entertaining one) to the mysterious outburst of activity which marks that moment. Andrew Horn was chamberlain of London, and so had the custody of the civic archives, in the reign of Edward II. He did useful work in collecting city records, and wrote a valuable chronicle. All this is perfectly sober, but the *Mirror* is certainly the most fantastic work in our legal literature. The author knew some of the Anglo-Saxon laws (and fabricated many more), and was well acquainted with canon law. His method is to give a description of contemporary law, freely criticised in the light of a golden age, which he places in the reign of King Alfred, of whose legal work he tells a great many wild stories. In some places he seems acute and earnest; in others he must be joking. That the sober and learned city chamberlain should have produced, even in his youth, such a puzzling mixture of sense and nonsense is hardly credible, yet his authorship seems on other grounds to be probable. The work never circulated during the middle ages, but in the sixteenth century, when antiquaries were looking for material on Anglo-Saxon law, the *Mirror* came to light, and was treated as solemn history by Coke and others. It was printed in 1642 and several times afterwards,[3] and no one seems to have suspected its veracity until John Reeves[4] expressed doubts in 1787. Meanwhile it introduced a good deal of legend into our legal history.[5]

[1] Plucknett, *Place of the Legal Profession in the History of English Law*, Law Quarterly Review, xlviii. 328 at 339.

[2] G. E. Woodbine, *Four Thirteenth Century Law Tracts* (1910), has edited those called *Fet Asaver*, *Judicium Essoniorum*, *Modus Componendi Brevia* and *Excepciones ad Cassandum Brevia*. W. H. Dunham, *Hengham's Summae* (1932) is followed by an edition of *Casus Placitorum* (Selden Society) and by G. J. Turner, *Brevia Placitata* (Selden Society); an edition of *Novae Narrationes* is in preparation for the Selden Society by Dr Shanks.

[3] It was edited, with an introduction by Maitland, for the Selden Society in 1893.

[4] Reeves (ed. Finlason), ii. 232–238. Finlason in his note to the 1869 edition is eager, as always, to contradict Reeves, and so maintains that the *Mirror* is a first-rate authority. It is generally safe for beginners to neglect all Finlason's notes, unless they deal with Year Book cases; in the latter field Finlason is worthy of attention.

[5] The latest contribution to this entertaining puzzle (mentioning no names, however) comes from H. G. Reuschlein, *Who Wrote the Mirror of Justice?*, Law Quarterly Review, lviii. 265; N. Denholm-Young, *Collected Papers*, 79, n. 1, hints darkly at some connection with *Fleta*.

THE ORIGIN OF THE YEAR BOOKS

It has been suggested by Professor Winfield with a good deal of reason that the Year Books may have begun in the following way. It would seem that a treatise upon procedure, then as now, needed constant revision if it was to retain its usefulness. It is only natural that the owner of one of these little compendiums should annotate it in the light of recent cases.[1] This becomes abundantly clear when one examines the group of treatises, represented by *Brevia Placitata* and *Casus Placitorum*, which stand closest to the Year Books. Those treatises consist of the French oral forms which the serjeant must address to the court. While there is a good deal of verbal rigidity at any particular date, nevertheless there was a constant process of change over a period of years, such as one would expect in a procedure which was still fundamentally oral, rather than written. The source of such changes and novelties as lawyers would feel it essential to know, is therefore to be sought in the words uttered by the leaders of the profession in court. They must be listened to diligently, and noted faithfully—in a word, reported. The treatises themselves give the forms in common use; it will be the function of the reports to tell of the novelties, the modifications to meet particular cases, and the discussions which soon arose as to whether some particular form of words was good or bad. A practitioner who set out to modernise his legal knowledge might do it either by watching proceedings in court or by consultation with lawyers who would give him access to the notes[2] of their pleadings. In this way some of the illustrations would be French reports, while others might be Latin forms. In the end it must have occurred to several minds at once that such reports need not necessarily be interspersed through one of these treatises, and that a small separate collection could be made consisting only of cases. As a result the treatises will assume a more definite form, while the fluctuating case material will become a separate class of literature. It will be a matter of individual taste whether the compiler keeps his cases as they come (*i.e.* in a chronological collection) or whether he rearranges them under a rough classification of actions and subject headings (thus resembling the later abridgments). This leaves the treatises free to take a more permanent and stable shape, and it is certainly a fact that after the early years of the fourteenth century these treatises can be identified with fair certainty, although in their earliest form no two manuscripts agree, and it is extremely difficult to say with confidence whether one has two manuscripts of the same treatise or two different treatises.[3]

---

[1] " Possibly the embryo of the Year Books lies in some treatise which is not primarily a report at all."—Winfield, *op. cit.,* 169.

[2] Some such hypothesis must be admitted, for it is clear that (*a*) formal written pleadings were not yet in use; (*b*) that the plea rolls were not yet accessible to the profession, even in such extreme cases as when private rights could be established from them. Lambert, *Les Year Books,* 20 n. 1.

[3] Winfield, *op. cit.,* 271.

CHANGES IN THE YEAR BOOKS

Our earliest Year Books, therefore, seem to be subsidiary to these little manuals of procedure, and this theory is confirmed by the fact that the matters which they recount are mainly concerned with the details of process and pleading. But one of the most puzzling features of the history of the Year Books is the constant change in their character and outlook; the combination of causes which produced them in the first place was very different from the circumstances which made for their continuance; indeed several periods can be discerned during which the Year Books seem to have fulfilled distinctly different functions. Having originated early in the reign of Edward I, by the time we come to his son and successor, Edward II, the Year Books have already taken another aspect. In the first place the number of manuscripts still surviving of the years of Edward II is very great—much greater than for Edward I— and the relationship between them very complex. They seem to fall into numerous small groups, and yet even these groupings at the end of a year or even of a term are dissolved and new associations formed. The differences between them are enormous, and there must have been a large number of persons independently reporting cases. At the same time their character changes somewhat; their outlook becomes broader and the reports are much more thorough. A large amount of the material which they contain is hardly strictly necessary for professional purposes. Long and rambling conversations are reported at great length. A large amount of irrelevant material is carefully recorded. There seems to be a definite interest in the personalities of judges and serjeants. If the object of the Year Books still remained what it was in the reign of Edward I, it would surely have been unnecessary to report so many cases or to report them so fully. One cannot avoid the feeling that the anonymous authors of these Year Books took a great delight in the work of compiling them, whatever the technical object was which they had in view. In an endeavour to explain the peculiarities of the manuscripts Mr G. J. Turner has developed what he has called the " pamphlet theory ". According to this hypothesis the Year Books first circulated in the form of small pamphlets containing comparatively few cases. As these pamphlets passed from hand to hand, the material they contained was recopied into volumes such as those which now survive. These secondary compilations usually contain several terms together, and are clearly based upon a number of different temporary texts assembled by chance in the hands of their compilers. Mr Turner's theory therefore goes a long way towards explaining both the divergences of the existing texts and the absence at the present day of anything which can be justly regarded as an original Year Book.[1]

We may well predicate the existence of such pamphlets as a pre-

---

[1] It may be supposed that the originals were not preserved when they were superseded by larger volumes—cf. the modern " advance sheets " of reports.

liminary to the final stage of compilation of the Year Books; but even
the pamphlet is not the ultimate original. Over fifty years ago Maitland[1] gave thought to this problem, and noted that the very first stage
must have been a single slip of parchment, from which only a later stage
could produce a pamphlet. Such a slip would be small, scribbled and
unfit for permanent preservation, and would bear one case (or a few
short cases) at most. It was the good fortune of Professor W. H.
Dunham to clinch the argument by discovering, and printing, two such
slips.[2] After the creation of rough notes in the form of loose slips,
the compilation of a more or less continuous volume is clearly the next
stage, and it may be that such a volume has been identified by Professor
Collas.[3]

In the reign of Edward II—

" there were frequently found to be two, three, four, or even more versions of one
case, so different that collation was impossible, and each of these versions might
be represented (with minor variants) by several manuscripts. It is this abundance
and diversity of material which has put such a heavy load upon the heroic editors
of Edward II's Year Books. Behind it all we seem to catch glimpses of a big and
busy profession in a state of almost feverish activity; reports were taken independently by many hands, then borrowed, copied, collated, and annotated; in an age
when great judges were discussing momentous matters, their words were awaited
with eagerness by the quick-witted serjeants who practised before them. It is
impossible to miss the note of admiration for the heroes of the bench and bar
which runs through the reports, and the almost excited interest which follows the
success or failure of some clever attempt by counsel to maintain a difficult position
when called upon to do so. To contemporary readers who were perfectly familiar
with the rules of the game these early Year Books must have read something like
vivid newspaper reports of a highly intellectual sport, where even irrelevancies—
the quip, the jest, the neat quotation—all have a natural part. Legal science no
doubt was their ultimate aim, but they are so full of the joy of forensic battle that
one is inclined to look upon them as allied to literature rather than to the cold,
impersonal law report of the present day. Throughout the Year Books of Edward II
there breathes a spirit of keenness, of combativeness and restlessness which makes
them the gayest of law books."[4]

In fact we venture to suggest that the Year Books of Edward II
resemble not so much the modern law report as a professional newspaper
which combines matters of technical interest with the lighter side of
professional life. They represent not merely the legal learning of the
time of Edward II, but also its high spirits and its professional feeling—
even bits of gossip and anecdotes; perhaps, too, its teaching methods.[5]
In consequence of this broadening of the field covered by the Year
Books, they incline towards a much greater variety of matter. Although

---

[1] Y.BB. Edward II (Selden Society), II. xc.

[2] *Casus Placitorum* (Selden Society), xlix ff., xc.

[3] See his note on MS. Faustina C. vi in Y.BB. of Edward II (Selden Society), xxIII, xxv–xxix.

[4] Plucknett, Y.B. 13 Richard II, xiii, xiv.

[5] The occurrence of questions and answers in the Year Books has already been noted:
Year Books of Edward II (Selden Society), xxIx, lxv–lxvii.

the proper conduct of mesne process is still an essential part of a lawyer's business, the Year Books no longer confine themselves to technicalities of this sort. Similarly, the proper forms of declarations and pleadings, and ingenious methods of putting some facts into issue, or of keeping others in the background, do not exhaust the possibilities of pleading. Matters of substantive law are raised and argued and reported as occasion requires. In the Year Books of Edward II a very prominent place is occupied by the recent legislation of Edward I; hardly any branch of law in daily use had been left unchanged by the great statutes with which the thirteenth century concludes, and the Year Books of Edward II are deeply concerned with the questions which those statutes raised. They are constantly discussing the relationship between the " old " law and the " new ", and it may very well be that the remarkably increased production of Year Books in Edward II's reign was stimulated by this critical situation. A good deal of the common law had to be revised in view of this remarkable outburst of legislation.

Of the reign of Edward III less can be said at present, for comparatively few of his Year Books have been edited with the same thoroughness as those of Edward II. One of the great puzzles of his reign is the *Liber Assisarum* or *Book of Assizes*.[1] During the first half of his reign the situation still seems comparable to that under Edward II. It would appear that manuscripts are still numerous and their divergences considerable. Although in many cases the reports are as full and journalistic, so to speak, as under his father, there is, we believe, a tendency to make them less verbose and more businesslike. More than this can hardly be said in the present state of our knowledge.

THE LATER YEAR BOOKS

With the reign of Richard II we enter upon a new era in the history of the Year Books. The following remarks are based upon a study of the manuscripts of the thirteenth year:

" With this atmosphere [of Edward II's reign] the years of Richard II are in the strongest contrast. The high spirits of the youthful common law are now replaced by a slightly solemn application to business; clearly, we are settling down. Or, to change the metaphor, the somewhat rough and tumble sport of the early years of the century has become a ' national institution ' at its close, and with the usual result. The reflection of this change can be seen clearly in the textual apparatus to the pages that follow, for we find that our manuscripts are united by a surprising unanimity on all but the slightest details. All our texts are well within the limits of collatability. They are all clear, well reported, succinct and practical. There

[1] See the chatty description in Bolland, *The Book of Assizes*, Cambridge Law Journal, ii. 192, and Putnam, *Sharshull and the Codes*, University of Toronto Law Journal, v. 251 at 269 ff. who associates it with Sharshull's clerks. Both seem unaware of the statutes 27 Edw. I, c. 3, 2 Edw. III, c. 3, and 4 Edw. III, c. 2, which confer criminal powers on justices of assize, and so account for the criminal cases in the *Liber Assisarum*, and A. W. Reed, *Early Tudor Drama*, 206. Cf. H. S. Bennett, *English Readers*, 82, 85, for the esteemed " Quadragesms " or Year Books of 40–50 Edward III.

are no irrelevancies to distract attention from the main interest—for there is abundant interest here, although of a different kind. In the Year Books of Edward II, it is very common to find 'uncollatable reports' and their origin is simple enough to discover. In prolonged argument, it is inevitable that the same proposition should be repeated several times in slightly differing forms; and all the more so when the discussion has been adjourned to 'another day', as the books put it. Consequently, if several people are independently reporting the debate, it is very likely that they will not all select the same from among the alternative forms of that particular argument. Their reports, though in substance consistent, will very likely be uncollatable. Now in the reign of Richard II we still find, both in the reports and in the rolls, instances of debates being adjourned from one day to another, where the point is difficult, as well as some debates which are reported at considerable length. And yet all our manuscripts are easily collatable. In the exchange of oral argument, all our manuscripts give us the same portions of the discussion, even the same repetitions; never do we find in the 13th year any ground for thinking that there was another version before us, or accessible to the surviving manuscript writers. The conclusion is irresistible: there was but one report—perhaps only one reporter."[1]

Further than this we cannot go, for the Year Books of the fifteenth century have not yet been re-edited, and so the condition of the manuscripts is not known with certainty. Our own impression is that the manuscripts are few and closely related, and that they are represented with tolerable accuracy by the old printed versions.[2] As for their contents, the cases reported are apt to be fewer and better chosen (judged from the standpoint, of course, of the modern report). The fifteenth-century Year Books are less vivacious than those of Edward II, but on the other hand the material they contain is of more uniform quality, in many cases consisting of full-dress debates by many judges of really important legal questions. Yet even here it sometimes happens that the reader will receive a shock in finding out that what he at first thought was a formal argument in court turns out to be, on fuller examination, a supper-table discussion among the judges and serjeants. Indeed, for a long time it seems to have been the custom to continue court discussions after court hours in Serjeants' Inn, for it is a significant feature of the English system that the judges and serjeants lodged together during term time. There thus existed the closest intimacy between bench and bar.

THE OBJECT OF THE YEAR BOOKS

One thing at least is clear. The Year Books did not exist for the same reason as the modern law report. They were not intended to be collections of precedents whose authority should be binding in later cases. This is clear from examining the manuscripts; from the style of the handwriting it is obvious that the manuscripts were written within a

---

[1] Plucknett, Y.B. 13 Richard II, xiv (Ames Foundation), xv.

[2] Since the above was written the Selden Society has published Y.BB. 1 Henry VI and 10 Edward IV, edited by Professors C. H. Williams and N. Neilson respectively; both volumes confirm the view expressed in the text above. In the case of the later Year Books, the early printed editions may present a better text than the surviving manuscripts.

few years of the cases they contained. Older cases which might have been authoritative according to modern ideas were no longer interesting. It is common to find a fifteenth-century manuscript which contains a long range of statutes covering two centuries or more; but a Year Book manuscript rarely covers more than a few years, and those years are not very far removed from the date of the handwriting. Even with the invention of printing it was comparatively recent cases which were first put into print, although it is significant that by 1520 a few, at least, of the Year Books of Edward III had been printed; by the time we reach the reign of Queen Mary, however (1553–1558), it was possible to make up a tolerably complete series of Year Books from the middle of Edward III's reign onwards. This is surely a token of a change of attitude toward the Year Books. While the Year Books are in the journalistic stage it is only the recent numbers which are of interest; but when the principle of case law begins to be understood, then even old cases may turn out to be of practical importance, and consequently a longer range of reports is desirable.

Much still remains to be done in the study of the Year Books, for generalisations based upon one reign cannot with confidence be used of other periods. Extending as they do from *c.* 1260 (these earliest proto-Year Books, however, still remain partly in manuscript unpublished) down to 1535, it is only natural that they should reflect the changes in thought and legal outlook which took place in the course of two and a half centuries, and it is essential, if good work is to be done, to resist the temptation of treating all the Year Books as if they were simultaneously produced by the same causes and for the same purpose.

THE ABRIDGMENTS

After this long digression in tracing the series of the Year Books from mediaeval to modern times, we must now return to the thirteenth and fourteenth centuries. Very intimately connected with the Year Books are the Abridgments.[1] Just as the character of the Year Books fluctuated, so their relationship to the Abridgments was by no means always the same. The very earliest Year Books known to us in one or two cases do in fact take the form of what we should now call an abridgment.[2] This form consists in the arrangement of the cases according to subject matter, and it may be that our earliest Year Books appeared in this form before they assumed the more familiar shape of a chronological arrangement independent of subject. Having once abandoned a subject arrangement, it seems soon to have been felt that owing to the growing bulk of the Year Books (and perhaps also owing to the growing importance placed upon them) there should be some

[1] Winfield, *Chief Sources*, 200 ff.
[2] Cf. p. 268 above.

easy means of access provided. It became a universal custom to place a word or two in the margin indicating the form of action or other principal matter, and this seems to have led to the practice of arranging abstracts of Year-Book cases in a subject classification. Occasionally we find that the so-called Abridgment gives in fact the full text of the case, but more generally we find condensed reports. These Abridgments have the same characteristic as the Year-Book manuscripts themselves— the period of years they cover is comparatively short. It seems rather likely that the preparation of Abridgments was always closely connected with teaching methods. This is undoubtedly true in the sixteenth and seventeenth centuries, when it seems to have been the regular practice for law students to buy an enormous folio volume completely blank; having headed the pages in an engrossing hand with the titles under which the matter was to be distributed, the student then proceeded to read selected Year Books or the early reporters and place abstracts of the cases under the appropriate headings. This was no doubt an effective discipline but it was certainly laborious; many of these seventeenth-century commonplace books have come down to us in almost their original condition, that is to say, almost completely blank. It may be possible that the fourteenth- and fifteenth-century Abridgments were also originally of the nature of students' exercises. In time, no doubt, Abridgments were found to have other uses, and this seems to be indicated by the fact that lawyers were apt to collect old Abridgments, take them to pieces and reassemble them in one large alphabet.[1] Examples of this are to be found towards the close of the fifteenth century, and it is tolerably certain that the Abridgments printed in the sixteenth century had a similar origin. No other hypothesis would explain the curious arrangement of the cases within each title of the works of Statham and Fitzherbert.

The first Abridgment to get into print[2] is traditionally known as Statham, although there is no indication in the book or elsewhere of its authorship. It was printed in France for the English publisher Pynson about 1490 or 1495, and besides being a rare and costly book is also a beautiful piece of printing. As with all the earlier Abridgments the arrangement of the cases within the titles is curious, and seems only explicable by supposing that it was based on a composite volume which had been made up from the fragments of earlier Abridgments.[3]

Very soon, however, Statham was practically superseded by a very much larger work, the later editions of which claim to be " the grand

---

[1] Such is a manuscript in the Harvard Law Library (Dunn, 41) described in Harvard Law Review, lix. 408.

[2] For the printed editions, see J. D. Cowley, *Bibliography of Abridgments* (Selden Society, 1932).

[3] See Cowley, *op. cit.*, xxix ff., who argues for *c.* 1488 as the date of printing. For Nicholas Statham see C. C. Williams, *Note on Statham's Abridgment*, West Virginia Law Quarterly, xlvi. 233–245. The translation by M. C. Klingelsmith (2 vols., Boston, 1915) is inadequate.

Abridgment collected by the Right Reverend Judge Sir Anthony Fitz-herbert ". The earliest edition (1516)[1] does not bear Fitzherbert's name or any other indication of alleged authorship. Fitzherbert's name first appears in the edition of 1565. All the same, the authorship is well attested, for in 1514 John Rastell announced in print that he was at work on this immense undertaking, and that Serjeant Anthony Fitzherbert was the author; Fitzherbert himself died in 1538. In Fitz-herbert, as in Statham, the cases are grouped in a peculiar manner and the conclusion is irresistible that his book too was a product of the scissors-and-paste method. However, while Statham is a fairly small book, Fitzherbert's is in three large folio volumes (subsequently com-pressed by means of small print to one short, thick folio). Fitzherbert's book immediately became extremely popular. It has even been suggested that for practical purposes people rarely went behind him to the Year Books. It seems to be a fact that most of the Year Book cases of any consequence are to be found in Fitzherbert's Abridgment, being repre-sented there by fairly long extracts and sometimes by a full text. The convenience of having a large mass of case material within the covers of one book is obvious, and it seems that for a long time Fitzherbert served the purpose of a large selection of the most important cases in the Year Books. It is clear that he had access to some very choice material. The very earliest known Year Books are represented in his collection, and are not to be found elsewhere. Occasionally he gives us a better text than is to be found elsewhere. Most remarkable of all, Fitzherbert knew and used that memorable collection of cases which Bracton made for his own private use; it was only the discovery and the publication of Bracton's *Note Book* in 1887 which revealed the source whence Fitzherbert derived his cases from the reign of Henry III. So, too, Fitzherbert has numerous cases from the reign of Richard II which still remain un-printed anywhere else.

Citation of Fitzherbert's Abridgment was facilitated by a new device. The cases are numbered consecutively throughout each title, the titles themselves being in a rough alphabetical arrangement. So famous was the book that it was cited without its author's name; hence a reference to *Briefe 949* is understood to mean the case bearing that number in the title *Briefe* of Fitzherbert's Abridgment. Any other Abridgment would have to be cited by name. From the constant use and hard study which were bestowed upon Fitzherbert's Abridgment, it is clear that in the sixteenth century lawyers had a practical interest in a volume of cases ranging over three hundred years; the later editions of Fitzherbert, printed by Richard Tottell, contain mechanical improvements enabling it to be used as a quick means of access to the Year Books themselves. This was effected by giving a reference to the page of the printed Year Book (which were now to be had in convenient uniform volumes—printed by Richard Tottell) in the margin of the Abridgment. At the

[1] As to this date see Winfield, *Chief Sources*, 225, and Cowell, *Bibliography*, xlv–xlvi.

same time Tottell's editions of the Year Books contain cross references to the Abridgment.[1]

In January 1574 Tottell brought out another massive collection, attributed to the late Chief Justice Sir Robert Brooke, of the Court of Common Pleas.[2] This had the advantage of including cases of Henry VIII, which of course were not in Fitzherbert, and he also mingled extracts from various treatises with his cases. To make room for this new material, he abridged the cases much more drastically than his predecessor. He also used many more title headings.

Numerous other Abridgments followed in a continuous stream down to the encyclopaedias and digests of our own day.[3]

THE REGISTER OF WRITS

It now remains to mention in brief the history of the Register of Writs.[4] We have already referred to the importance with the writ attained in the English legal system, and it is only natural that collections should be made of those forms most generally in use. No light whatever has been thrown upon the authorship of the Register. As it was the privilege of Chancery to issue original writs, one would naturally expect to find official collections of forms prepared by the office for its own use. This, however, seems hardly the case. Individual clerks in the Chancery may well have compiled registers for their own personal use, but there seems no trace of any officially compiled, and therefore authoritative, text. There may have been a Register in the reign of Henry II, which lay under Glanvill's eyes as he wrote. Coke actually owned a register which he said was as old as Henry II—but that may have been his collector's enthusiasm.[5] The great bulk of the surviving manuscripts come from private hands—either monasteries or practitioners being the usual owners. Of the numerous manuscripts which have survived hardly any two exactly correspond, for the Register of Writs is an extremely variable and shifting collection. On the other hand, there was a certain amount of official sanction for it, for the government sent a copy of a Register to the authorities in Ireland[6] in 1227, while an

---

[1] Cf. Plucknett, *Bibliography and Legal History*, Papers of the Bibliographical Society of America, xxvi. 128, 139; S. E. Thorne, *Fitzherbert's Abridgment*, Law Library Journal, xxix. 59.

[2] Alleged earlier editions in 1568 and 1570 are not supported by any evidence: Cowley, *op. cit.*, xlix.

[3] See the elaborate *Bibliography of Abridgments* edited by J. D. Cowley for the Selden Society (1932), and the valuable chapter in Winfield, *Chief Sources*.

[4] *Registrum Omnium Brevium*. There are four editions between 1531 and 1687. A new edition is being prepared for the Selden Society.

[5] *Webb's Case* (1608), 8 Rep. 47b.

[6] The monks of St Augustine's, Canterbury, got a copy of it, before it was sent, which has survived: Maitland, *Collected Papers*, ii. 110; cf. Richardson, *Glanvill Continued*, Law Quarterly Review, liv. 382 ff., and G. J. Turner, *Brevia Placitata*, xlvi.

apparently official copy for use in Chester[1] is also still surviving. In 1279 we hear of an " ancient register " of the Channel Islands[2] (whose law was more Norman than English), while in 1288 the King's Bench quashed the writ in an assize of darrein presentment originating in Carmarthen, because it did not conform to " the king's register of writs used in his chancery there ".[3] Most of what we know concerning the history of the Register has been set forth by Maitland in his famous articles in the Harvard Law Review,[4] and it must be confessed that he raised a good many more problems than he solved. It was characteristic of mediaeval administration that the compilation of collections of forms (which nowadays would often be done officially) was then left to the enterprise of anyone who cared to undertake it, and consequently the results of such effort were at best only semi-official.

LITTLETON'S TENURES

The whole of the fourteenth century is therefore occupied with the development of the Year Books, the Register, and the procedural tracts. There is no trace of any attempt to write an extended work comparable to the treatise of Bracton. So, too, in the fifteenth century until we reach the remarkable book of Littleton. Littleton filled several local offices in Worcestershire and became reader in the Inner Temple; in 1453 he became serjeant, and in 1455 he rode the northern circuit as Judge of Assize. Just as it is impossible to detect Bracton's sympathies in the Barons' War, so we have no indication of Littleton taking sides during the Wars of the Roses. In 1466 he became a judge of the Courts of Commons Pleas and in 1475 he was made a knight. He died in 1481 and was buried in Worcester Cathedral.[5]

His treatise *Of Tenures* is the first great English law book since Bracton. By Littleton's day the law of real property had become quite complicated, and he displays a superb mastery in arranging and reducing a difficult mass of law to an orderly and logical system. His work consisted of a discussion in order of the various estates possible in his day; this occupies the first book. The second treats of the incidents of tenure, while the third deals with co-ownership and various special doctrines connected with real property. Throughout the work his expression is singularly lucid, and never is substantive law obscured by

---

[1] Public Record Office, Chester 38/13. Earl Ranulf gave a register to the men of Chester, which the domesmen there regarded as authoritative: Pollock and Maitland, i. 551 citing *Placitorum Abbreviatio*, 268–269 (s.c. Sayles, *King's Bench*, i. 42, at 43).

[2] J. H. Le Patourel, *Mediaeval Administration of the Channel Islands*, 97.

[3] Sayles, *King's Bench*, i. 172, no. 115. The Statute of Wales (1284) is to some extent an annotated register of writs, but it does not contain darrein presentment.

[4] Harvard Law Review, iii. 97, 167, 212; reprinted in *Select Essays in Anglo-American Legal History*, ii. 549–596, and in his *Collected Papers*.

[5] The fullest life of Littleton is Eugene Wambaugh's introduction to his translation of the *Tenures*.

procedure. To some extent Littleton was anticipated by a little treatise of the reign of Edward III which is now generally called the *Old Tenures*. This little book, however, will not bear comparison with Littleton, although he was modest enough to pretend that his work was merely an expansion of the older treatise. Although Littleton does not very often mention cases, it is perfectly obvious that cases have played a large part in settling the law as he lays it down. The great characteristic of his work is its value as a text-book; for three hundred years it was the usual introduction read by students of real property law. It very early found its way into print, and won the admiration of Coke, who declared that it was the most perfect work in any human science. Coke composed a commentary upon it (forming the first part of his *Institutes*) which is extremely discursive, but full of valuable information.

THE WORKS OF FORTESCUE

Contemporary with Littleton was Sir John Fortescue. He studied law at Lincoln's Inn, became serjeant in 1430, and Chief Justice of the King's Bench in 1442. Unlike Littleton, however, he became involved in politics, joining the Lancastrian party and going into exile in France with the Queen. It was apparently during this time that he was given the title of Chancellor, for he seems never to have exercised the office in England. After the failure of the short restoration of Henry VI in 1471, Fortescue recognised that the Lancastrian cause was irretrievably lost, and so he submitted to Edward IV, was pardoned, and made a member of the Council. We hear nothing of him after the year 1477. His was truly a remarkable mind. Both he and Littleton lived in an age when the common law developed a strong liking for technicality for its own sake. Littleton mastered this by sheer power of analysis, while Fortescue arrived at a similar mastery through a different experience. The wretched years of exile which he passed in danger and poverty had enabled him to study the working of foreign systems. His treatise *In Praise of the Laws of England*[1] was written in 1470 or 1471 for the instruction of the young Prince Edward, in order to teach him the character of the limited monarchy which he was fated never to exercise. Cast in the form of a dialogue between Fortescue and the Prince, the book is mainly concerned with a comparative study of English and French government. It is therefore an early example of the comparative method in politics. In describing England he gives us our earliest account of the Inns of Court and of the legal profession, while he explains in simple words some of the fundamental ideas of the common law. As Sir William Holdsworth observes: " It is probably the first legal book which was avowedly written to instruct a layman in the elements of law. The consequent lucidity of its style together with the unique character of the

---

[1] The best edition, with translation, is S. B. Chrimes, *Sir John Fortescue De Laudibus Legum Anglie* (Cambridge, 1942).

information it contains explains why it has always been among lawyers the most popular of Fortescue's works."[1] He wrote one work in English under the title *The Governance of England*.[2] In this treatise he endeavours to discover the real causes of the collapse of Lancastrian government, and here we see how deeply Fortescue had thought upon the evils of his time. Fortescue throughout his works shows a passionate devotion to the idea of limited monarchy; time after time he denounces tyranny and such oppressive devices as the judicial use of torture which were currently used in contemporary France. Like many people who have to live abroad, he found it difficult to resist the tendency to idealise his own country; even the French language as it was spoken in France seemed to him rude and corrupt when compared with the French of the Year Books.

DOCTOR AND STUDENT

The effect of the new learning upon English law is clearly seen in the work of Christopher St Germain (1460–1540). He was a barrister of the Inner Temple who had a remarkable knowledge of legal philosophy and canon law[3] which he used as the basis of his criticism of the common law in two *Dialogues between a Doctor of Divinity and a Student of the Common Law*. The first was apparently published in 1523 (in Latin) and the second in English in 1530, the whole being revised and translated in 1532.[4] This work is very important for the history of English legal thought and particularly for the ideas which underlie equity. According to St Germain, the philosophical justification for equity was to be found in the canon law which had long accepted the principle that the circumstances of human life are so infinitely various that it is impossible to make a general rule which will cover them all. Equity in some form or other is therefore a necessity if injustice is to be prevented. No amount of ingenuity can devise a system which will do justice by rule, for life is bigger than any generalisation that can be made about it. And so discretion based upon conscience is bound to enter into any legal system which is at all adequate. The principle of equity St Germain declared to be conscience, and this was a typical conception of moral theology and canon law. As Sir William Holdsworth has observed, these *Dialogues* appeared at a critical moment. As the result of the impending Reformation the long line of ecclesiastical chancellors was soon to end, and if the fundamental notions upon which they had acted were not to be forgotten, then some such book as this was a prime necessity. It had all the success which St Germain could have wished. The new

[1] Holdsworth, ii. 570.

[2] Ed. Plummer (Oxford, 1885).

[3] The greater part of his voluminous output, however, was purely theological.

[4] It is the text of the 1532 edition which is frequently reprinted. It differs considerably from those of 1528 and 1530. No copy of the 1523 edition is now extant. A critical edition for the Selden Society is in preparation.

school of lay chancellors learned from it the ancient doctrine of conscience, and so they were able to continue the work of their predecessors
in the same spirit.   The *Dialogues* were followed by a small controversial
literature which bears witness to the deep effect St Germain's book
produced upon the public mind.

THE REPORTERS

The appearance of *Doctor and Student* coincides with the end of the
Year Books, which ceased to be compiled after 1535.   Their place was
taken by something which was at first not so very different, namely,
the early reporters.   These almost always appear under the name of
some distinguished lawyer or judge, with the implication that he was
in some way concerned with their composition.   As a matter of fact
many of the named reports have little visible connection with the distinguished lawyer whose authority is invoked on their behalf.   While
some of them were deliberately made in an attempt to provide a complete
report of striking cases, others seem to be extremely informal notes
which were no doubt intelligible to the author of them, but give very
little light to a modern reader.   A number of such reports were published after their authors' death, sometimes, it would seem, under un-
ethical circumstances.   There is, therefore, every possible variety of
report, good, bad and indifferent, and in using them it is well to have
at hand some such book as Wallace, *The Reporters* (fourth edition, 1882),
where the characteristics and traditional reputation of each volume are
carefully discussed.[1]

One of the first of these reports, that of Dyer, runs from 1537 to
1582 and immediately achieved a high reputation.   Plowden duplicated
most of this period (1550–1580) in a volume of very fine reports, which
immediately became highly authoritative.   It is significant that Plowden's
book, although actually consisting of reports, is entitled *Commentaries*.

Coke, the most famous of all the reporters, covers the years 1572 to
1616, and was so highly considered by the profession that his work is
cited simply as *The Reports*.[2]   Their method is far from ideal, but their
influence has been tremendous.   Coke seems to have set himself no less
a task than that of stating in systematic and historical form the principles
of English law as they arose in litigation before him.   Each case, therefore, contains a thorough summary of all authority upon it down to his
own day.   However bewildering this must have been to the practising

---

[1] Wallace ends at 1776.   His work has been continued by Sir J. C. Fox, *Handbook of
English Law Reports*, of which Part I (House of Lords, Privy Council and Chancery) appeared
in 1913.   A useful rapid survey by Van Vechten Veeder will be found in *Select Essays in
Anglo-American Legal History*, ii. 123–154.

[2] For a discussion and comparison of the reporting methods of Plowden and Coke, see
Plucknett, *The Genesis of Coke's Reports*, Cornell Law Quarterly, xxvii. 190–213 (1942).   Since
that article was written, the Harvard Law Library has announced its acquisition of a unique
copy of Plowden's Part II dated 1579.   Until then the 1585 edition was thought to be the
first: R. B. Anderson, *Supplement to Beale's Bibliography* (Ames Foundation, 1943), p. 16 (R 485 a).

lawyer, to the historian it constitutes one of the main merits of Coke's *Reports*; by far the easiest way of finding mediaeval authority on a point is to begin with a case in Coke's *Reports*—and in fact it is almost always possible to find a case in point among his thirteen volumes. Even in Coke's day, however, the modern attitude towards case law had hardly been completely accepted. In his hands a law report takes the form of a somewhat rambling disquisition upon the case in question. He frequently gives the pleadings, but less often does he tell us the arguments. As for the decision, it is often impossible to distinguish the remarks of the judge (where it was not Coke himself) from the comments of the reporter. There was no clear boundary in his mind between what a case said and what he thought it ought to say, between the reasons which actually prompted the decision, and the elaborate commentary which he could easily weave around any question. A case in Coke's *Reports*, therefore, is an uncertain mingling of genuine report, commentary, criticism, elementary instruction, and recondite legal history. The whole is dominated by Coke's personality, and derives its authority from him. All the miscellaneous elements which appear in his *Reports* are apt to acquire a fairly uniform authority; even if a particular passage is in fact Coke's comment, and not part of the case he purports to have reported, it is none the worse for that; anything that Coke wrote, be it case or comment, was received with the highest respect.

The reporters who succeed Coke are much lesser men. Although they do not intrude their own opinions into their books to the extent that he did, they are for other reasons still very unsatisfactory. Their reports are frequently short and inaccurate, and sometimes unintelligible. Matters are not helped by the fact that one case is commonly reported by three or four reporters, for they are often equally bad. The poorness of the reports after Coke until the middle of the eighteenth century makes the legal history of that period a difficult study.

Burrow's *Reports* (1756–1772) introduced a new standard.[1] At last we find a clear discrimination between facts, arguments and decision, and from his day onwards the necessary qualities of a good law report were understood, although sometimes they were not always reached. By the close of the eighteenth century judges adopted the practice of looking over the draft reports of their decisions, and in this way certain reporters were regarded as " authorised ". This was the first step towards the establishment of the official series of Law Reports in 1865.

THE LATER TREATISES: COKE

Besides the works we have mentioned, there were during the sixteenth and seventeenth centuries a good many treatises of less importance, such as those dealing with the jurisdiction of courts, the authority of justices of the peace, local courts and jurisdictions, and the like. As

[1] For Burrow and his successors, see Holdsworth, xii. 110.

we approach the middle of the seventeenth century, we once again find an attempt to deal with English law comprehensively, such as had not been made since the days of Bracton. The form which it now took in Sir Edward Coke's hands, however, was peculiar and deeply significant of the historical development of English law.[1] Of his *Reports* we have already spoken. They were in fact only one of the methods whereby he hoped to restate English law. His other attempts were all of them based upon one or another of the various forms through which the common law had developed. In the *Reports* he embodied the bulk of English law in the form of decisions, or comments upon decisions. In his *First Institute* (1628) he covered much the same ground by the slightly different method of a comment upon Littleton's *Tenures*. In his *Second Institute* (1642) he did it all again by means of a commentary upon the principal statutes. The *Third Institute* (1644) is a treatise on criminal law, taking the pleas of the Crown in order, while the *Fourth Institute* (1644) is a description of the jurisdiction and history of the courts.

Coke seems to have established his reputation by sheer weight of learning. Any criticism was immediately met by an overpowering broadside of citations to the Year Books. His attitude towards English law was largely mediaeval; he saw in the law the great controlling factor in social life by which Crown and Parliament were equally governed. But outside of the common law he never ventured. The cosmopolitan learning of his predecessors, such as Bracton or Fortescue, meant no more to him than did the wide culture of Bacon or Selden. The whole of his intellectual equipment was to be found in the Year Books.[2] We have already mentioned that the reprinting of the early Year Books indicates some sort of interest in the older English law. Coke in particular would cite authorities from them on any proposition from any century in English legal history. This does not mean, of course, that Coke was a professed historian; on the contrary, all his ancient learning was meant to be of immediate practical value. Then again, although he was so devoted to the remoter past of English law, he was nevertheless of a progressive turn of mind, and there is really little trace of any marked conservatism in his judgments. The great value of his *Reports*, in fact, lies in this, that although they summarise mediaeval authority upon a point, yet in many cases they also lay the foundations of a modern doctrine.[3] In short Coke was essentially progressive in spite of his antiquarian bent. He is therefore a curious combination of an apparent conservatism based upon a superstitious reverence for black-letter, and a

[1] See Holdsworth, *Elizabethan Age in English Legal History*, Iowa Law Review, xii. 321–335; *Influence of Coke on the Development of English Law*, in Essays in Legal History (Oxford, 1913), 297–311; Holdsworth, v. 425–493.

[2] To judge, at least, from his writings. The humanist side of his character can be seen in his autograph *Catalogue* of his extensive library at Holkham, ed. W. O. Hassall, with a preface by Samuel E. Thorne, 1950.

[3] For the mode of their compilation see Plucknett, *The genesis of Coke's Reports*, Cornell Law Quarterly, xxvii. 190–213.

truly progressive and constructive outlook upon current legal questions.

Indeed, his principal limitations came less from his antiquarian learning than from his professional feeling as a common lawyer. This is particularly the case with his attacks upon the Court of Chancery; from reading Coke's writings one would hardly suspect that there was already a flourishing system of equity. It must be confessed that there are very few literary graces to be found in his writings. His statements are usually terse but overburdened with allusions and citations, while the arrangement of his matter is often careless. He also had a very curious habit of using passably good Latin maxims which usually had an air of antiquity about them, in spite of the fact that he himself invented them. This is a small detail, but it shows how easily Coke's mind would run upon mediaeval lines. In Maitland's pointed words, " we were having a little Renaissance of our own: or a Gothic revival if you please ".[1]

Indeed, Coke's great mission was to reconcile the mediaeval and the modern. The rapid growth of the law in the sixteenth century had taken place in an environment of unfamiliar ideas. The Reformation and the Renaissance seemed to constitute a serious break with the past. Coke's great contemporary, Bacon, expressed a fear that English law was being uprooted and losing its contact with the experience of former ages. Bacon likewise admitted that it was Coke who checked this tendency, and restored a continuity in spirit and method between his own age and the period before the Reformation. The value of such a work can hardly be overestimated. For a moment it had been uncertain how far the common law would survive either in substance or in its traditional technique. Many proposals were in the air, some for a codification of the common law, others for a resort to a somewhat formless equity. If either of these had succeeded, English law would have developed a different set of tools, new methods of handling them, and, in consequence, a very different spirit. It was the influence of Coke, assisted by the political conditions of the Stuart conflict, which prevented all this. The momentous alliance of Parliament with the common lawyers made a clear issue between tradition, common law and the mediaeval view on one hand, and, on the other, the newer ideas of statecraft, absolutism and a supreme royal equity. In fighting out this issue, the work of Coke was of very great value to the parliamentarian side.

He was one of the few men who had thoroughly mastered the forbidding mass of the Year Books, and so deep was his erudition that most people were inclined to take his word for almost any proposition. There was almost immediately a tendency not to go behind Coke. The old authorities which he cited would continue to be cited; those which he omitted would never be dug up. Consequently the seventeenth century was apt to see the mediaeval authorities only through Coke's eyes. This was a distinct practical advantage. If every lawyer had gone to the Year Books for himself and read them as uncritically as Coke did, it

[1] Maitland, *English Law and the Renaissance*, 29.

might well have turned out that his idea of the continuity of English law would have broken down. As it happened, lawyers voluntarily resigned to him their private judgment of the Year Books, and so by a careful selection of material Coke was enabled to conceal the inconsistencies and difficulties which were inherent in his position. In fact, there is truth in the paradox that it was Coke, the greatest exponent of Year Book learning, who killed the study of Year Books in England; his knowledge of them was so complete, and he used it with so great authority, that contemporaries immediately recognised that to go behind Coke's apparatus was simply to seek for confusion and doubt. In fact, from Coke's day onward lawyers rarely ventured to look at the Year Books unless they had first assured themselves of Coke's guidance, and made up their minds to reach Coke's conclusions.

There is, of course, another side to the picture. The triumph of Coke's view in many cases meant the triumph of doctrines which were already nearly obsolete in his own day. At the same time the opposition of Coke and his party to the jurisdictions of equity and admiralty retarded very considerably development in those directions. Their insistence that all courts should be common law courts, when as a matter of fact there was no adequate common law on several important topics, eliminated the foreign influences which were normally active in courts with a commercial jurisdiction. It is therefore not unfair to say that Coke's influence made for the establishment of a supreme common law, and for the abolition or severe restriction of all other forms of law in the country. His triumph therefore introduced a certain narrowness and conservatism which stood in the way of reform. Indeed, it was not until the early nineteenth century that we began to make reforms which had actually been demanded in Coke's own day by his great rival Bacon.

SELDEN: PRYNNE: HALE

The other legal writing of Coke's day is either of a strictly practical character, or concerned with legal history. Of the latter type there are several notable examples in the seventeenth century. One of the greatest of English historical scholars was John Selden (1584–1654) who had a deep and broad learning of many legal systems, English, Roman and Jewish.[1] His *Table Talk* (re-edited by Sir Frederick Pollock) contains his brief and weighty opinions on many important subjects, and has long been a great classic among lawyers.

William Prynne[2] (1600–1669) was an historian of extraordinary learning with a great familiarity with public records of every class. It is his extensive quotations from rolls which are still unpublished

---

[1] See Hazeltine, *Se den as a Legal Historian*, Harvard Law Review, xxiv. 105–118, 205–219; the introduction to *Ioannis Seldeni ad Fletam Dissertatio* (ed. Ogg), Cambridge, 1925, and Herzog, *Selden and Jewish Law*, Journal of Comparative Legislation, xiii. 236–245.

[2] See the entertaining study by E. W. Kirby, *William Prynne* (1931).

which make his works valuable even to-day; to contemporaries, how-ever, he was chiefly known as a very violent, but brilliant, controversialist.

Sir Matthew Hale (1609–1676) was one of the most remarkable characters of the seventeenth century. After short experiences in the Church and the Army, he finally took to the law, and rapidly rose in the profession. He defended Archbishop Laud and others whom Parliament attacked, but was only a moderate royalist. On the execu-tion of Charles I he accepted the Commonwealth, and in 1654 he became Judge of the Common Pleas. At the same time he worked for the Restoration; when it was accomplished he became Chief Baron, and in 1671 Chief Justice of the King's Bench. He died in 1676. He had a remarkable and winning personality and soon achieved enormous influence through his learning and his honesty. A valuable collection of his books and manuscripts (including several Year Book manu-scripts) is now in the library of Lincoln's Inn. He wrote a *History of the Common Law*, or rather a sketch of a proposed history, which has considerable merit besides being the first general history of English law. His history of the *Jurisdiction of the Lords' House* is still a very sound piece of work, and all the more remarkable in view of the fierce controversy on the subject then prevailing. His most important work, however, was his *History of the Pleas of the Crown*, which from that day to this has enjoyed a very high reputation. His works (which also included theological and scientific studies) were almost all published only after his death. In one of them, not published until 1787, he described certain wharves as " affected with a public interest ", and this conception was adopted with fruitful results in application to modern conditions.[1]

BLACKSTONE

It is not until the middle of the next century that we come to a legal writer with a broad outlook. There had been a growing class, it is true, of text-book writers upon various branches of the law, but they are all overshadowed by the mastery with which Sir William Blackstone (1723–1780) drew a general picture in his *Commentaries* of the whole of English law. He was an Oxford scholar of varied accomplishments. Among his unpublished works are a treatise on architecture and many verses. He was also a Shakespearean scholar of some ability. Dividing his time between the bar and the University, he was slow to establish a professional position. In 1758 he was made the first Vinerian professor, the chair having been founded by Charles Viner with the copyright of his *Abridgment* as an endowment. Even before 1758 Blackstone had given regular lectures at Oxford, and these were eventually printed in 1765 under the title of *Commentaries on the Laws of England*, having first been

[1] See Macalister, *Hale and Business affected with a Public Interest*, Harvard Law Review, xliii. 759–791; Hamilton, *Affectation with Public Interest*, Yale Law Journal, xxxix. 1089–1112.

very much pirated. He became a Member of Parliament and in 1770 became Judge of the Common Pleas, an office which he almost immediately exchanged for a seat in the King's Bench, moving back to the Common Pleas six months later. His judicial career was distinguished. During the latter part of his life he became an advocate of prison reform and secured some legislation in that direction. It was not, however, until forty years later that prison reform became a matter of practical politics. His *Reports* were published the year after his death.

A word must be said concerning the *Commentaries*. " Twice in the history of English law has an Englishman had the motive, the courage, the power, to write a great, readable, reasonable book about English law as a whole." First it was Bracton, and five hundred years later Blackstone. Blackstone always had a literary inclination, and his career resembles much more that of a professor of law in America than that of the usual legal practitioner of his own time and country. It was not common in his day for intending lawyers to seek high University honours, and it was still more unusual to reach the bench without spending many years in active practice. His great skill consisted in affording a reasonable explanation for the state of English law as it then existed. Some portions he explained on logical grounds, others from history. His history was not very profound, for like so many practising lawyers of that time (and later), he expected little more in history than a plausibility at first sight. Our law came from the middle ages, of which Lord Bolingbroke said that " some indulgence may be had to a temperate curiosity in the review of them, but to be learned about them is a ridiculous affectation in any man who means to be useful to the present age ". Blackstone was therefore in harmony with the thought of his age when he regarded our legal history as an object of " temperate curiosity " rather than of exact scholarship. His equipment in jurisprudence was also somewhat slender, but his freedom from excessive learning was an actual merit; he found explanations which seemed adequate, clear, and above all interesting, and the one object he kept constantly before him was to maintain a variety of interest throughout his book. The point of view here involved is of great importance. We have said that Blackstone was the first Vinerian professor, in fact the very first Professor of English Law, and this in itself is highly significant. The common law became a subject of University study by people who did not necessarily intend to become lawyers.

Blackstone's lectures and *Commentaries* are therefore an attempt to explain and justify the common law in the eyes of the laity. He recognised that the law is not merely the concern of a small and exclusive profession, but a matter of broad public importance which is the proper interest of every educated man. Not only were the *Commentaries* an attractive piece of literature; they were on the whole remarkably sound law. If we contrast his work with that of Coke we can see in Blackstone the completion of the process which Coke initiated. It is abundantly clear that the transition which Coke tried to effect from mediaeval to modern law was successful, for in Blackstone we see the final product—a united and coherent body of common law. The fact that such a large mass of legal detail was made available in one work, in an interesting and easily mastered form, made Blackstone's work particularly useful in eighteenth-century America. The *Commentaries* had a tremendous sale there, for not only did they contain some very useful matter on public law, but also served as the principal means of the colonists' information as to the state of English law in general. It was a happy coincidence that Blackstone had addressed himself to the interested layman, who, although he might be a justice of the peace and a prominent figure in local government, was nevertheless not a trained lawyer, for this was the very type of person who used Blackstone's *Commentaries* in America, where the legal profession was either viewed with disfavour or deliberately eliminated.

The reputations of great lawyers sometimes undergo curious changes. Thus Lord Mansfield, whom many contemporaries regarded as a backstairs courtier, intent on destroying political freedom, is now thought of solely as a daring reformer. So, too, Blackstone, who enthusiastically took up Mansfield's ideas,[1] has come to be treated as " complacent ". Much of Bentham's savage attack still haunts us—even though we do not read Bentham in the original—and causes us to forget that quite an interesting list could be compiled of suggestions for law reform scattered through Blackstone's work.[2]

Blackstone was also deeply interested in the problems of legal education, but his efforts had more influence in America than in England. The Vinerian Professorship (1758) long remained unique in England, although Sir George Downing (who died in 1749) had already provided in his will for the eventual foundation of Downing College, Cambridge, to which a chair of English law was to be attached; this intention was finally carried out in 1800. In America it inspired the foundation of several chairs which did not survive the eighteenth century; one, however, established under the will of Isaac Royall (*d.* 1781) came into existence in 1815, was annexed to Harvard Law School and has continued ever since. Another was the Dane Professorship at the Harvard Law School, whose first occupant, Joseph Story (1829), wrote many famous treatises, while Dane himself, like Viner, had compiled an Abridgment.[3] The modern form of legal education as it exists in America, and has been more recently developed in England, is really a fulfilment of Blackstone's wishes.

[1] Holdsworth, *Blackstone and Equity*, Harvard Law Review, xliii. 1.

[2] Holdsworth, *Aspects of Blackstone and his Commentaries*, Cambridge Law Journal, iv. 261 and 274. Cf. Dicey, *Blackstone's Commentaries*, National Review, liv. 413; reprinted in Cambridge Law Journal, iv. 286; and below, p. 622. Blackstone's life and work are fully discussed in Holdsworth, xii. 702–737.

[3] The MS. is at Harvard; it was printed in 9 volumes, 1823–1829.

BLACKSTONE'S SUCCESSORS

The imposing scale of Blackstone's work, covering the whole field of law, deeply impressed his contemporaries and succeeding generations. In America his volumes did particularly valuable service at a critical moment, and it is not surprising that the commentary became accepted as the ideal form of legal literature. Inspired by Blackstone's book, young James Kent resolved to study law, and eventually after laying anew the foundations of American equity, he followed the master's example by publishing his lectures at Columbia in the form of *Commentaries on American Law*, which first appeared in 1826—sixty years after Blackstone's.

In England, too, the Blackstonian tradition was strong. Numerous editions were published, but the radical reforms of the early nineteenth century necessitated so much revision that Serjeant H. J. Stephen deemed it better to produce his *New Commentaries on the Laws of England, partly founded on Blackstone*, the first edition of which appeared in 1841. The book quickly became a standard students' work and has remained so ever since: the twentieth edition appeared in 1938.

THE RISE OF THE MODERN TEXT-BOOK

The eighteenth century therefore brought to a high state of development two main types of law book, the comprehensive abridgment and the general commentary. The one was technical and strictly procedural in its outlook, the other broad and general. The future lay largely with a third type of literature which only just began to appear in Blackstone's age. This was the text-book upon some compact and coherent portion of the law, treated systematically, based upon principle, and often transcending merely procedural divisions. The tendency towards this newer type of literature is discernible in several quarters. Thus the ancient type of formularies accompanied by glosses occasionally produced books like Sheppard's *Touchstone of Common Assurances* (1641), but for a really scientific study of land law we must look either to Charles Fearne's *Essay on Contingent Remainders and Executory Devises* (1772) or to the studies of comparative jurists such as Sir Martin Wright's *Introduction to the Law of Tenures* (1730). A parallel development took place in the abridgments. Although they remained alphabetical, the internal arrangement within each title steadily tended to become more logical and systematic, the whole work therefore looking rather like a collection of treatises arranged in alphabetical order of titles. Thus many short but excellent treatises by Chief Baron Gilbert, who died in 1726, were embodied by Matthew Bacon in his *Abridgement* which was published in 1736. And finally, certain outlying portions of law were receiving a systematic literature of their own. Thus the old books of useful information for merchants were in time succeeded by such purely legal text-books as Bayley on *Bills of Exchange* (1789) and Park on *Marine Insurances* (1787).

One of the earliest texts on a common law subject is Sir William Jones, *Essay on the Law of Bailments* (1781) where history, analysis and comparative law are applied with great learning.[1] But works of this sort are still very rare in the eighteenth century. Possibly one of the most powerful influences making for the new style of legal literature came from America. While Kent at Columbia embraced the Blackstonian tradition, his contemporary, Joseph Story at Harvard, preferred the newer type of legal writing, and although he called his books " commentaries " they were in fact detailed and critical treatments of particular branches of law—in other words, text-books. In rapid succession he published commentaries on *Bailments* (1832, a significant subject to begin the series, for he gave high praise to Jones' pioneer essay), *The Constitution* (1833), *Conflict of Laws* (1834), *Equity Jurisprudence* (1836), *Equity Pleadings* (1838), *Agency* (1839) *Partnership* (1841), *Bills of Exchange* (1843), and *Promissory Notes* (1845). In these works Story used English and civilian learning to illustrate American law. Several of these books immediately appeared in English editions and became very influential. From that date onwards the steady stream of texts became the principal form of legal literature, but it was only made possible by the decline in the importance of procedure and pleading. It represents in fact the triumph of substance over form.

[1] See S. G. Vesey-FitzGerald, *Sir William Jones, the Jurist*, Bulletin of the School of Oriental and African Studies, xi. 807, who observes that this treatise is centred on *Coggs* v. *Bernard*, just as J. D. Mayne's *Damages* is centred on *Hadley* v. *Baxendale*.

PART 3

SOME FACTORS
IN LEGAL HISTORY

SUMMARY

SOME FACTORS IN LEGAL HISTORY

In Part I of this general survey we have placed the law in its environment of national life as a whole. We have seen its early dependence on the crown, its gradual separation from royal administration, and its final assumption of an independent position in the state, as a result of its victory in the conflict of the seventeenth century.

In Part II we have watched the development of the institutions through which the law has worked, some of them ancient and communal, others a little more recent and feudal, and still others of even later date whose origin was due to the crown. With the passage of time these royal courts supersede all the rest, and begin to be regarded as a judicial system which ought to be, and finally was, taken apart and reassembled in logical fashion as an organisation for the speedy and convenient administration of justice. There has been in fact a steady growth of the conception of law as distinct from its machinery; the idea of jurisdiction with its implications of monopoly and profit to courts, their owners, and their practitioners, has yielded to the newer feeling that institutions are valuable only so far as they fulfil useful functions.

We now come to a third part, where a brief examination of some of the more imponderable factors in legal history must be made. Leaving aside the visible institutions into which lawyers were organised, we must consider the thought which animated them, and first of all certain external forces such as civil and canon law. After that we shall discuss custom, legislation and precedent from the same point of view.

CHAPTER 1

THE CIVIL LAW OF ROME

THE BARBARIANS AND ROMAN LAW

For twenty-five centuries Roman law has had a continuous history of which only a relatively small portion lay in the middle ages or influenced English legal development. Into this complicated story we cannot enter. As Vinogradoff said, " The story I am about to tell is, in a sense, a ghost story. It treats of a second life of Roman law after the demise of the body in which it first saw the light."[1]   At the moment when it begins to concern us the classical Roman law had already entered upon its decline. With the fall of the Roman Empire the once universal system of Roman law depended for its continued existence upon custom, and it was largely in the form of custom that it continued to be applied during the middle ages. With the establishment of the new Teutonic kingdoms in the fifth century this aspect of Roman law was conspicuous; the problems raised by the clash of races were solved by a system of personal laws whereby each individual was subject to the law peculiar to his race—a system which still obtains in several parts of the world where numerous different races and religions are in close contact, as in Palestine. The barbarian kings, therefore, were put to the trouble of finding out the principal rules of this personal Roman law to which many of their subjects were entitled, and a number of texts from about the year 500 embody the results. Farther east, Roman law retained to some extent its imperial character and in 438 portions of it were codified by the Emperor Theodosius. In the west, however, Roman law suffered the common fate of personal laws and rapidly degenerated in quality and diminished in quantity—at least from the point of view of a classicist. It was inevitable that there should be cross influences; Roman law was modified as a result of neighbouring customs, while on the other hand

[1] Vinogradoff, Roman Law in Mediaeval Europe (2nd edn.), 13.

294

originally Germanic customs underwent a certain degree of Romanisation.[1]

ROMAN LAW IN THE MIDDLE AGES

All through the middle ages, therefore, there were two aspects of
Roman law. First there was that of the pure academic doctrine which
was from time to time revived through the learning of scholars; but
in contrast with it there was the customary Roman law which had grown
up in numberless communities all over Europe, and which had been
modified in infinite variety according to local needs. Between these
two aspects of Roman law there was not infrequently open conflict, for
scholars naturally wished to restore the orthodox doctrine of classical
times, and were apt to be impatient when less learned lawyers persisted
in retaining the practical working-day law of their local communities.
By this time there was no practical question of academic Roman law
being imperially enforced—the Holy Roman Empire itself bore little
resemblance to the Roman Empire of the classical Roman law. The
struggle between these two views of Roman law took place principally
in the universities, and may be roughly described as an attempt made
from time to time by certain law schools to influence practice. It may
very well be that the great mediaeval Romanists took too academical a
view of the situation, and some of their attempts to restore classical law
were ill-advised. Nevertheless it was they who accomplished the great
feat of the middle ages in preserving classical law for many centuries
during which it remained of ideal rather than practical value, until such
time as society had sufficiently developed in thought and economic
structure to be able to appreciate and make full and wise use of its ancient
inheritance; while the more practical school of Bartolus and his followers
had already made of it a body of living, growing law. It was the
Romanists who maintained through the middle ages a scientific attitude
towards law, and even in those cases where we find a scientific approach
to bodies of non-Roman law it is, in fact, usually due to the example of
the Romanists. Our own Glanvill and Bracton are eminent examples.

THE RECOVERY OF JUSTINIAN'S BOOKS

Until the close of the eleventh century, Western Europe had relied
principally upon the Theodosian code and abridgments of it for an
official text of Roman law, in the light of which it developed its various
local Roman customs. Early in the twelfth century the great *Corpus
Juris Civilis* of Justinian, which came a century later[2] than that of Theodosius, began to be studied in Italy, where it took a natural part in the

---

[1] To contrast " Germanic " and " Roman " law is therefore an over-simplification; see
the important study of Ernst Levy, *West Roman Vulgar Law* (1951) and my review in *Traditio*,
viii. 446.

[2] It came into force in 534.

great revival then going on in various branches of culture, assisted no doubt by the new material prosperity of the Italian cities. Justinian's books were much larger and much more thorough in their return to classical Roman law than the code of Theodosius. In Constantinople there were greater facilities both in books, in tradition, and in spirit for an antiquarian revival—for to some extent this was the nature of Justinian's work; the jurists whose opinions figure most frequently in the *Digest* were as remote from his day as Coke is from ours. To the professors of the Law School of Bologna the books of Justinian came as a new revelation. At their head was the great Irnerius (*d.* 1135) and around him were his pupils, including the famous " Four Doctors ", Bulgarus, Martinus, Ugo, and Jacobus. Hardly less distinguished were Azo, from whom Bracton learned a great deal, and Vacarius, who travelled from Italy to the distant University of Oxford.[1] There soon arose a school of glossators whose commentaries upon the books of Justinian were finally summarised in the thirteenth century into one great gloss by Accursius (1182–1260), whose son, Francis, visited the court of Edward I, attended a Parliament, and saw the enactment of a statute.[2] This academic movement in the end went too far; the refinements and subtleties of the doctors were too much for the common people who insisted upon retaining their imperfectly Romanised customs. A reaction therefore occurred, and Bartolus (1314–1357), frankly recognising the place which local custom actually held, and the difficulties created by local custom and local legislation (of which there was a good deal), applied himself to the study of the problems of statute law and conflict of laws[3] which were constantly arising in Italy in the course of inter-city commerce.[4]

CUJAS AT BOURGES

The next great revival of Roman law was in the sixteenth century, and began in the tiny University of Bourges which sprang into fame on account of its illustrious teacher Cujas (1522–1590). The origin of the movement was in the Renaissance, and its object was pure scholarship, aiming at the restoration of classical Roman law and good Latin instead of the mingled custom and graceless language of the Bartolists. In the field of jurisprudence and legal history the School of Bourges exerted immense power, but practice was less amenable to university

---

[1] The evidence is re-examined by Professor de Zulueta in his edition of Vacarius' *Liber Pauperum*, xvi (Selden Society).

[2] The Statute of Bigamists (Statutes of the Realm, i. 42); see also Stubbs, *Constitutional History* (1875), ii. 107 n. 2.

[3] For a translation of some of his remarks, see Beale, *Bartolus on the Conflict of Laws*.

[4] General introductions to this enormous field of study can be found in Hazeltine's chapter in the *Cambridge Mediaeval History*, vol. v; R. L. Poole, *Illustrations of Medieval Thought* (2nd edn., 1932); C. N. S. Woolf, *Bartolus of Sassoferrato* (1913); W. Ullmann, *The Medieval View of Law* (1946), which has a well-chosen bibliography.

influence. This was fortunate on the whole, for however valuable the study of philosophy and legal history might be to the formation of a science of law, there was nothing to be gained by denying the experience of over a thousand years of legal development. As one example, the civilians introduced mischief in the sixteenth century when they attacked the transferability of debts, as then universally practised by mercantile custom, on the ground that it conflicted with the law laid down a thousand years earlier in the books of Justinian.[1]

ROMAN LAW IN ENGLAND

It now remains to indicate very briefly the principal points of contact between English and Roman law. As we have already remarked,[2] Roman influence begins in England with the coming of Christianity, and its specific influence upon Anglo-Saxon legal doctrine can be traced principally in the law relating to bookland. After the Conquest, England became once again a part of the European system, and Glanvill's treatise shows some familiarity with the Roman texts. No doubt one of the principal links between English law and Italy was Lanfranc. In the eleventh century he had taught in the Law School of Pavia; then he went to Normandy, founded the school at Bec, and became the chief adviser of Duke William, who brought him to England and made him Archbishop of Canterbury; this must have made him a very powerful source of foreign influence—it has been observed that *Domesday Book* itself is written in an Italian style of handwriting. Lanfranc's foundation at Bec influenced England for a long time; from Bec there came Anselm who precipitated the Investiture Contest in England; after him came another archbishop, Theobald, in whose household Thomas Becket had been trained, and who brought Vacarius to England.[3]

When we come to the reign of Henry II we find even more direct influences at work.[4] By this time we have to reckon not only with Roman law, but also with canon law, which was partly a Romanisation of the Church's customs, and partly an attempt to adapt Roman law to Christian and mediaeval use. It may be that Glanvill's treatise was in imitation of some of the little books of canonical procedure which became frequent at this time,[5] while Vinogradoff has suggested that there is significance in the fact that William Longchamp, Justiciar to Richard I, had written a short treatise on canonical procedure in which he urged the advisability of establishing definite formulae of actions. It may be that this treatise had some influence in causing Glanvill to

---

[1] Holdsworth, viii. 122, 123.

[2] Above, p. 8; below, p. 511.

[3] Holdsworth, ii. 147; cf. *ibid.*, 133–137.

[4] Holdsworth, ii. 202–206.

[5] They are described in Professor Hazeltine's introduction to *Radulfi de Hengham Summae* (ed. Dunham).

[6] Edited by Caillemer, *Le droit civil dans les provinces anglo-normandes.*

insist upon the importance of the original writ and to plan his book as a commentary upon writs and forms of action.[1] Already the canon law rules on the competence of witnesses were borrowed by Glanvill, who used them as challenges to jurors. Glanvill also took pains to point out that when the King's Court uses the Latin word *dos* it does not mean the dowry of Roman law, but the completely different dower of English law, while at the same time he observes that there are differences between the English and the Roman law of legitimacy. He even gives us the different forms of contract known to Roman law, but immediately observes that the King's Court takes no notice of them. It seems clear that Glanvill anticipates that his readers will have some knowledge of Roman law, but it is equally significant that he frequently has to warn them against being misled by superficial resemblances. As we shall see later on, the principle of the assize of *novel disseisin* was deliberately borrowed from canon law, which developed it from Roman models.

When we come to Bracton, as we have already seen,[2] the problem of Roman influence, first upon Bracton himself, and secondly upon English law (these two different problems must always be carefully distinguished), raised many complicated questions. With the close of the age of Bracton the most influential period of Roman law in England comes to an end until we reach the sixteenth century, when it was raised in somewhat different forms. All the same, it is now clear that many monasteries in England were well equipped with books on Roman law,[3] and its influence never entirely ceased. Some of our forms of action are definitely of Roman or canonical origin (such as *novel disseisin* and *cessavit*), while even our statutes may import Roman devices, such as double and treble damages. The distinction between private and public law was a discovery of the Romanists, and some parts of our public law— the idea of treason (even in Anglo-Saxon times) and the conduct of state trials—were in danger of being romanised.[4] On the other hand, the queer legend that Roman law survived in English towns has long been exploded.[5]

ENGLAND AND THE RECEPTION

On the continent there was the great movement called the Reception, when many courts, from the Imperial Chamber in Germany down to petty lordships and cities, abandoned their traditional law and adopted instead the civil law, generally in a Bartolist form. This resulted from a mingling of many motives, some legal and constitutional, others

[1] Vinogradoff, *Roman Law in Mediaeval Europe* (ed. F. de Zulueta), 100.

[2] Above, pp. 261–263.

[3] Senior, *Roman Law MSS. in England*, Law Quarterly Review, xlvii. 337.

[4] Above, p. 204. For a fuller discussion, see Plucknett, *The Relations between Roman Law and English Common Law*, Univ. Toronto Law Journal, iii. 24.

[5] Hart, *Roman Law and the Custom of London*, Law Quarterly Review, xlvi. 49

political, religious and economic. The Reception on the continent had its echo in England, and Maitland even went so far as to suggest that during the reign of Henry VIII the common law itself was in danger from the civilians. This view is certainly somewhat exaggerated.[1] However high a view Henry VIII may have taken of his position, it is clear that he regarded it as based upon the common law, and although with some difficulty he succeeded in managing his Parliaments, he was well aware of the important position Parliament now occupied as a national legislature and of the decisive influence which the common lawyers exercised in it. This combination of common law and Parliament made any substantial legal changes very difficult—as witness the events leading to the Statute of Uses.[2] But, as Sir William Holdsworth remarks, although the continued existence of the common law was never in serious danger, yet its supremacy as the one and only legal system in England was vigorously challenged. The Councils and Star Chamber, the Courts of Requests and of Admiralty, made a high bid for jurisdiction over the whole of commercial law and portions of criminal law, and threatened to develop a constitutional law of their own. Chancery, too, became infected with the same spirit. During the middle ages equity was not regarded as being altogether outside of the common law system, still less as essentially hostile to it, but at the beginning of the seventeenth century Chancery was regarded by the Stuarts as one of the prerogative courts, and there was a danger that the common law would be challenged by a rival civilian system developed in Chancery as well as in the prerogative courts. This situation was well understood at the time, and produced a controversial literature which intelligently attacked the problem. In such a state of feeling there was no room for direct Roman influence upon English law. Indirectly, however, there was still opportunity for contact. As we have already observed, Bracton had looked very far ahead in several parts of his treatise. Questions then unsettled, fields of law with which the common law courts in his day refused to be concerned, he explored, taking Roman law as his guide. In the sixteenth century when lawyers were searching for help in expanding the common law, they turned to the pages of Bracton. His book was printed for the first time in 1569; his imitator, *Britton*, had already been printed about 1534; and readers of both these works came into contact with Bracton's Romanism, which they found already adapted, more or less, to common law needs.

LATER ROMAN INFLUENCES

Under the later Stuarts, civilians were particularly active, and the Dutch wars kept the Admiralty busy. As in the middle ages, they

---

[1] Maitland, *English Law and the Renaissance* (reprinted in *Select Essays in Anglo-American Legal History*, i. 168–207); the criticisms that follow are set forth in more detail in Holdsworth, iv. 253–262.

[2] See below, pp. 584 ff.

continued to be regarded as the experts in legal theory and legislative policy; thus they were much consulted when the Statute of Frauds[1] was being drafted, and it was said by Jekyll, M.R., that " the Statute of Distributions[2] was penned by a civilian, and except in some few particular instances mentioned in the statute, is to be governed and construed by the civil law ".[3]

It is since the Restoration and during the early and middle eighteenth century that Roman law once again exercised noteworthy influence upon English legal doctrine, and here too Bracton is the key to the situation. It is worth noting that a new edition was brought out in 1640. Lord Holt presided over the King's Bench from 1689 until 1710, and although he was in no sense a profound Romanist, yet he had been a careful student of Bracton, and through his decisions some of the academic speculations of Bracton became living common law.[4] A generation later Lord Mansfield carried on the work. The law of his native country, Scotland, had undergone the Reception and had thereby been considerably Romanised, but, as with Holt, it was his reading of Bracton as a student which turned his mind definitely to a study of Roman law at first hand.[5]

All through the eighteenth century English lawyers were reading Continental works on natural law and jurisprudence, while English scholars were themselves producing comparative studies of their own and foreign systems. Particularly interesting to them were the works of Pothier which circulated widely in England and America, both in the original French and in translation. A study of the books bought by old libraries, and of books translated for the publishers, will show that men like Holt and Mansfield were not lonely geniuses, but outstanding examples of the spirit of legal inquiry which was abroad during this supposedly " stagnant " century.

Even at the present day English courts upon occasion will refer to Roman law in something like Bracton's spirit in rare cases where the native law gives no guidance.[6]

---

[1] 29 Charles II, c. 3 (1677).

[2] 22 & 23 Charles II, c. 10 (1670).

[3] W. H. D. Winder, *Sir Joseph Jekyll*, Law Quarterly Review, lvii. 512 at 535.

[4] See above, pp. 247, 264.

[5] Above, pp. 249–250.

[6] See Oliver, *Roman Law in Modern Cases in English Courts* (Cambridge Legal Essays), 243.

CHAPTER 2

THE CANON LAW OF THE CHURCH

We have already casually referred to the growth of Church organisation which accompanied the decline of the Roman Empire.[1] For a
time it seemed as though the Church was the only body which could
carry on the ancient tradition of universal law. The sources, both
official and unofficial, for ecclesiastical law, grew steadily in quantity
and variety and at last proved overwhelming, not only in their bulk
but also in the difficulty of assigning to each its proper value and sometimes even of determining its authenticity.

THE EARLY COLLECTIONS

The forces of feudalism had compelled the Church as well as the
State to decentralise, and the result was a large mass of local ecclesiastical
law. When the worst days were passed and the Church began to
reorganise itself on the basis of the papal monarchy, it was a prime
necessity to bring some sort of order into ecclesiastical law. In the
eleventh century systematic research was undertaken in order to find
authorities in canon law which were ancient and universally recognised;
libraries were searched, and it has been plausibly suggested that the
discovery of the Florentine manuscript of Justinian's *Digest* may have
been one of the results. Even so, the mass even of admissible material
was enormous and its interpretation particularly difficult. A number
of scholars attempted to collect the more important texts, to reconcile
them with one another, and to unite them in one coherent commentary.
One of the more successful of these attempts was that of Ivo of Chartres,
whose *Decretum* appeared about 1095.[2] Ivo developed a distinction

[1] Above, pp. 4–5.

[2] For the sources and literature of both civil and canon law see Hazeltine, *Roman and
Canon Law in the Middle Ages*, in Cambridge Mediaeval History, v. 697–764. For very valuable
accounts of their general influence, see Meynial, *Roman Law*, and Le Bras, *Canon Law*, both in
Crump and Jacob, *Legacy of the Middle Ages*.

which assisted considerably in reconciling the discordant mass of material which lay before him. Some rules, in his opinion, were fundamental, and must be preserved at all costs; others were more local, particular, or accidental, and although there might be reasons for their validity in particular cases, they must not be regarded as limitations upon fundamental rules of law. With this sensible notion a great deal could be done, for although it allowed plenty of room to legitimate exceptions, it nevertheless kept its eye firmly fixed upon broad principle.

THE DECRETUM OF GRATIAN

At the same time the study of civil law based upon the newly discovered texts of Justinian was likewise flourishing, and all through the middle ages the canonists and the civilians were at odds. The two systems tended more and more to separate: the civilians looked to antiquity and were often tempted to become mere theorists or antiquaries, while the canonists were more concerned in adapting Roman law with great freedom to contemporary conditions, and in replacing its paganism by a Christian spirit. The civilians, too, were apt to take the side of the Emperor against the Pope. The study of civil law was forbidden to monks in 1180 and to priests in 1219; Henry III in 1234 ordered the sheriffs of London to close the schools of civil law. These measures were ineffective in suppressing the study of civil law, but they succeeded in establishing the right of the canonists to develop their law in accordance with current needs as they understood them, without being bound by ancient authority. The systematisation of canon law was carried still further by the great work of Gratian whose *Decretum* appeared very soon after 1140. Its general character is admirably expressed by the title which he gave it, " *The Concordance of Discordant Canons* ". So well did Gratian do his work that his results were accepted as being virtually final, and although his *Decretum* was unofficial and never received legislative force, yet in practice it was treated with great respect, and indeed has taken an undisputed place as the first portion of the *Corpus Juris Canonici*. It is also highly significant that just at this moment the famous Peter Lombard was publishing his *Sentences* which attempted something like the same task for theology; the appearance of these two books, the *Decretum* and the *Sentences*, marks the definite separation of canon law from theology.

THE CORPUS JURIS CANONICI

The papacy became increasingly active and a series of great councils added considerably to the body of universal canon law; thus the Third Lateran Council of 1179 established a system of cathedral schools and severely punished usury; the Fourth Lateran Council (1215) forbade clergy to take part in judicial ordeals,[1] and passed seventy chapters of

[1] See above, p. 118.

reforming canons. The Pope also legislated by means of decretal letters which decided particular law cases and at the same time laid down general rules of law. Many unofficial collections of these *Decretals* were made, and at length an official compilation was published in 1234 with statutory authority by Gregory IX. The texts in this collection were arranged in five books, and when in 1298 another collection of those *Decretals* which were issued since 1234 became necessary, it was published as a sixth book and is therefore called *The Sext*. The last few pages are of interest to common and equity lawyers, for they contain a collection of maxims some of which became well known in the English courts. The *Decretum* of Gratian, the *Decretals* of Gregory IX, the *Sext*, and a few smaller collections, form the *Corpus Juris Canonici*.[1] At the same time there arose a host of commentators, text-book writers and experts on procedure who have left us an immense literature.

THE SPIRIT OF THE CANON LAW

Throughout all this period the canonists were constantly endeavouring to make their system correspond as closely as possible with the ideal of Christian conduct, and to reduce to a minimum the divergence between law and morals.[2] A great danger was that—

" the purpose of the law might be defeated, either by malicious use of the powers it conferred or by artful evasion of the restrictions set by it on individual rights. Canonists and civilians were at one in forbidding acts of unfair competition, exercise of rights with the object of injuring another, . . . and acts in deceit of the law. Finally, since the law could not make provisions for every hypothetical case, the door was always open to custom. The danger of unauthorized rules was met by the canonists in this way: they declared custom to be binding only when it is reasonable, *i.e.* when it is in accordance with the principles of the Church, and with the assumed intention of the legislator, and when it has been in use for a sufficient length of time (*legitime praescripta*). The decision as to the presence of these qualifications lay with the judge. If proved to satisfy these requirements, a customary rule might, at least from the time of Gregory IX, supersede statutory law. Thus the old rigidity of the civil law was opposed the equity of the canon law, exemplified in the intelligent, loyal, and benevolent interpretation and application of its rules. A system which allowed so much freedom to the legislator and which was tempered by so judicious a method of interpretation could and ought to possess great logical consistency, and it is this which gives its most striking feature to the law of the Church."[3]

THE SCOPE OF CANON LAW

Although a great deal of the Church's law was naturally concerned with its world-wide organisation, the powers and duties of the various

[1] An excellent short introduction is F. Cimetier, *Les Sources du droit ecclésiastique* (Paris, 1930).

[2] A brief account of the Church's view of law will be found in Sertillanges, *La philosophie des lois* (Paris, 1946).

[3] Le Bras *Canon Law* (in Crump and Jacob, *Legacy of the Middle Ages*), 328, 329.

ranks of clergy, and the spiritual discipline of churchmen, regular, secular and lay, nevertheless a great deal of it did affect the daily life of the laity in a variety of ways, and in the end exerted profound influence upon the development of national laws. The most important, no doubt, is the law of marriage, which is of fundamental importance in every society. In the law of wills the Church succeeded in greatly simplifying the civil law on the subject, while it also influenced the law of intestate succession. On this latter subject the views of the Church were singularly modern, for she opposed the feudal notions which excluded women from the inheritance of land, and urged that land and chattels should descend along similar lines. As we shall see later, the Church also took up the idea of protecting possession as such, and developed a series of possessory remedies. Although the theory of possession and ownership was no part of the English law of land, yet the canonical idea was easily adapted and a recent disseisin was protected by Henry II's Assize in the same way as a recent dispossession in canon law. In connection with the theory of possession the Church also modified the Roman law of prescription by insisting that good faith was absolutely necessary not only at the commencement but all through the period upon which the prescription was founded. " The civil law punished the negligence of the owner who did not possess; the canon law reproved the sin of one who sought to prescribe without good faith."[1]

In the field of contract the Church's contribution was most notable, for here again the Christian conception of good faith was employed to great effect. As many of the greatest fairs and their courts were owned by churches, there was ample opportunity to free the law of contract from formalism, and finally the canonists declared, in spite of the Roman maxim *ex nudo pacto actio non oritur*, that a simple promise was enforceable. It must have needed a great deal of courage to reach this position when against it was all the authority of Roman law and the custom and practice of most of the other systems of secular law.[2]

ECONOMIC VIEWS OF THE CANONISTS

The Church also attempted—and here she was, for the time being, less successful—to impose her view upon economic life. The attempts to suppress usury are well known; they are in fact part of a general theory of wages and profits which looked with favour upon the products of labour while it regarded as suspect the profits of speculation, banking, and finance. Acting from the same point of view, the Church discountenanced the fluctuations in wages and prices caused by the law of supply and demand, and attempted to maintain fixed standards of

---

[1] Le Bras, *op. cit.*, 351.

[2] A useful collection of material is available in Spies, *Observation des simples conventions en droit canonique* (Paris, 1928).

value. On the other hand, the liberal and equitable view which the canon lawyers took of contract considerably aided the development of commerce in other directions, for it did not confine contract within the limits of the civil law of a remote age; insurance and the assignability and negotiability of debts are striking examples of matters which the canonists developed on the basis of good faith, but which the civilians refused to touch. Similarly the canonists developed a summary procedure which was widely copied by other systems (defined in the famous decretal *Saepe* in 1306), and here again the canonists broke with formalism in an earnest attempt to do speedy and substantial justice.[1]

THE CHURCH AND CRIME

In the field of criminal law the Church also made a notable contribution by insisting that crime should be treated from the point of view of sin, and consequently the theories of the moral theologians concerning the place of intention in sin became part of the law of crime. Mediaeval punishments were frequently cruel, and in many cases capital, but the Church introduced the idea of imprisonment in an endeavour to bring the offender to repentance through solitary contemplation. As part of her criminal procedure she adopted and modified the civilian criminal procedure, and here again a great deal of formalism was abandoned and much was left to the discretion of the judge in examining witnesses and weighing their evidence. Even after the Reformation had struck a seemingly heavy blow at the canon law, its influence was still powerful, for the Bartolists had been glad to embody in their system of civil law a good many ideas drawn from the canonists, and so the Reception was often as much a reception of canon as of civil law.

THE CANONISTS' CONTRIBUTION

During the middle ages the Church was the one body which exercised universal jurisdiction, and which therefore could act as a bond of union between the divergent forces of the day, and the unity which she achieved has had lasting results upon law. As it has been admirably expressed by Professor Le Bras:

" The ideas of good faith and equity which underlay the canonist theory of contracts still influence the legislators of to-day, and those shrewd conceptions of the just price and a just wage are more vital than any system that has been practically applied, because they express our permanent ideal. Thus the present is linked to the distant centuries of Innocent III and Gregory VII; and indeed even to those more distant, for many of the ideas which bore fruit in the classic age were the heritage of past civilizations. The care of the poor and the oppressed which was characteristic of Judaism, the Roman love of order and authority, the Greek conceptions of political economy and formal logic, the enthusiasm and scrupulousness

---

[1] For the text and some comments see Engelmann (ed. Millar), *History of Continental Civil Procedure*, 495.

of the Celts, which were shown more particularly in their penitential system,—all these conquests of the human mind, which seemed to her in accordance with her fundamental principles,—went to the enrichment of the Church's law, and were assimilated to her own doctrine after such modification and correction as was required to bring them into harmony with her own point of view. It is indeed the highest moral tradition of the West and of the Mediterranean peoples which has been gathered up and handed down to us in the classic law of the Church."[1]

[1] *Legacy of the Middle Ages*, 361.

CUSTOM

The conditions of society, and men's attitude towards them, are slowly but constantly changing, and the law must do its best to keep in harmony with contemporary life and thought. The law, too, must therefore change, and one of the most instructive aspects of legal history is the study of the various means which have served to bring about the necessary revision of the legal fabric.

THE FLEXIBILITY OF CUSTOM

The modern age of legislation by means of laws deliberately set up and expressed in certain authoritative texts covers but a very small period of legal history. Preceding it the principal element in most legal systems was custom. There were, of course, other factors as well in many cases. In canon law, for example, there were authoritative texts from the Bible and elsewhere, and most systems had at least a few examples to show of deliberate legislation. But the great mass of the law into which these exceptional elements had to be fitted was custom. Our earliest Anglo-Saxon " laws " are modifications of detail and obviously assume that the legal fabric is essentially customary. The communal courts which survived into historical times, especially the hundred and the county, were customary in their origin, and declared customary law whose sanction was derived from custom. But the remarkable feature of custom was its flexibility and adaptability. In modern times we hear a lot too much of the phrase " immemorial custom ". In so far as this phrase implies that custom is or ought to be immemorially old it is historically inaccurate. In an age when custom was an active living factor in the development of society, there was much less insistence upon actual or fictitious antiquity. If we want the view of a lawyer who knew from experience what custom was, we can turn to Azo (*d.* 1230), whose works were held in high respect by our own Bracton. " A custom can be called *long* ", he says, " if it was introduced within ten or twenty years, *very long* if it dates from thirty years, and *ancient* if it dates from forty years."[1]

The middle ages seem to show us bodies of custom of every description, developing and adapting themselves to constantly changing conditions. We can see the first beginnings of a custom and trace its rise and modification; we can even see it deliberately imported from one place to another; it is a common sight to see a group of townspeople examine the customs of more advanced communities, choose the one they like best, and adopt it *en bloc* as their own. Indeed nothing is more evident than that custom in the middle ages could be made and changed, bought and sold, developing rapidly because it proceeded from the people, expressed their legal thought, and regulated their civil, commercial and family life. The custom of a mediaeval community may well have been much more intimately a product of the work and thought of those who lived by it, than is a modern statute enacted by a legislature whose contact with the public at large is only occasional.

FEUDAL CUSTOM

With the progress of history, therefore, we see the constant growth of new custom, which is the natural method of making provision for new communities and the more modern needs of old ones. Just as the communal courts declared the custom of those who were subject to them, so we find that the newer feudal courts developed and declared the custom governing the feudal relationship. Feudalism was a rearrangement of society upon a military rather than a capitalistic basis, designed to meet a grave emergency created by external invasion and the fall of the central authority. This rearrangement was effected and maintained by the development of new bodies of custom governing novel situations. In short, feudalism is a very striking example of the radical changes in society which can be effected by the rapid modification of custom. This flexibility of custom enabled society in the tenth and eleventh centuries to reorganise itself with much greater ease and responsiveness to changing conditions, than if all this had to be done by drafting and adopting explicit legislation. Later still, the decline of feudalism was likewise effected by changes in custom; the growth of heritability in feudal fiefs, the strict limitation of feudal services, the development of the supremacy of the Crown, were all in effect the recognition by shifting custom that the spirit had departed from feudalism.

With the decline of feudalism came the growth of the royal authority, and this at first took the form of customary modifications in the relation-

---

[1] Wehrlé, *De la coutume dans le droit canonique,* 139–140. Cf. " twice makes a custom " P. de Fontaines (*c.* 1259), *Conseil à un ami,* 492.

ship between the Crown and its vassals. By this time society was developing so rapidly that changes in custom had to be made with unusual precision; conflicts of interests sometimes resulted in rebellion or civil war, which in turn produced drastic changes in custom by a new method—legislation. Typical of such incidents are the events leading to *Magna Carta*, and from that date onwards it becomes steadily more clear that the growing supremacy of the Crown will bring with it national legislation, and that this national legislation will be in the end compelled to destroy custom in self-defence. Such in the broadest outline is the history and ultimate fate of custom.

During the middle ages, however, the conflict was still undecided; until the rise of the modern state and modern ideas of sovereignty, custom still had a large if diminishing place in our legal history.

CONSTITUTIONAL CUSTOM

Feudal custom includes the relationship of Crown and nobles until the moment when this body of custom separates and becomes, first, the law of the prerogative, and then later still combines with the custom of the King's High Court of Parliament to form modern constitutional law. Indeed, those changing " conventions of the constitution ", which needed all Dicey's ingenuity to reconcile them with nineteenth-century jurisprudence,[1] are just such a body of living, growing custom as existed in the middle ages. The King's other courts rapidly produced a body of custom—the contrast between Glanvill's tiny treatise and Bracton's heavy folio shows how much custom could be developed in two generations—which is the basis of the common law. Very soon there is a substantial quantity of legislation, but nevertheless that legislation always assumes that it will be construed in the light of the whole body of customary law. In striking witness to this we have the curious phenomenon of some statutes gradually being assimilated into the common law; *Magna Carta* very soon became in theory as well as in practice part of the common law, and so did other statutes.[2] Indeed, when English common law was being adopted in America there was sometimes a question as to how far certain statutes were to be regarded as inseparable from the customary common law.

THE ATTITUDE OF THE CANONISTS

Exactly parallel to the growth of national unity in England was the development of the primacy of the papacy. The same problems were involved; a large number of scattered communities had developed masses of ecclesiastical custom, and if Christianity was to maintain itself

---

[1] Dicey, *Law of the Constitution*, 1885; 8th edn., 1915.
[2] Plucknett, *Statutes and Their Interpretation*, 134.

against the disruptive forces of feudalism the papal monarchy was a political necessity. That monarchy itself grew up largely through the operation of custom, and when its dominance was practically assured, its position was defined in dogmatic form. Then came the problem of the relationship between the Holy See and numerous bodies of local ecclesiastical custom which still survived, and which under newer conditions hampered the work of the papacy. To this situation many canonists devoted careful thought, and the result of their speculations was to provide a philosophical basis in justification of papal policy.[1] It was the canonists who (building on the foundation of Roman law) devised a rational basis for a general attack upon custom. As the papal monarchy became more centralised, the canonists were laying down what was in effect the modern doctrine, and from them the common lawyers were to learn some very useful rules whereby custom could be subjected to the national sovereign.

MANORIAL CUSTOM

The attack upon custom which had already begun in England before the close of the middle ages did not proceed with equal force; some types of custom for a long time were hardly affected. Beginning at the bottom we have that complicated economic unit, the manor, whose rural economy and social structure were almost entirely a matter of custom. Within the manor there proceeded a dramatic struggle between various groups of custom which has had the profoundest effects upon society. It is clear that the condition of the tenants of a manor is in fact the condition of the bulk of the population, and the changing social and legal condition of the peasant is an important part of the history of the modern working class. Originally free, or nearly so, the growth of feudal custom depressed the inhabitants of the manor to the position of serfs, and this change took place partly by the manorial courts developing and declaring local custom, and partly by the royal courts developing and declaring customary common law. The rapid rise to supremacy of the Court of Common Pleas had the practical effect that property in land was ultimately whatever the Court of Common Pleas should adjudge. Now, after a moment of hesitation, the Court of Common Pleas decided that it could not be bothered with the affairs of peasants. To say that the peasant's property rights could not be defended in the Court of Common Pleas was almost immediately recognised as equivalent to saying that he had no property rights at all. This was the accepted theory from the beginning of the fourteenth century onwards; Westminster Hall expressed it in the form of the dogma that the freehold in a villein's lands was in the lord.

---

[1] See in general, Lambert, *La Fonction du droit civil comparé*, i. 103–208; Wehrlé, *De la coutume dans le droit canonique*.

THE RISE OF COPYHOLD

Then came the Black Death, and with it the economic revolution of the middle of the fourteenth century. This crisis emphasised tendencies which had already appeared long before the plague—tendencies which took the characteristic form of the growth of new custom. There grew up in the manors of tolerant lords the custom of allowing villeins to succeed by hereditary right to their ancestors' holdings. They were permitted to buy and sell servile land; in some cases the lord's manorial court would entertain litigation between villeins, using all the forms of Westminster Hall with their technical allegations of " fee and right which ought to descend " and so on. The only difference was that the villeins' claims always concluded with the words " according to the custom of the manor ".

CHANGING CUSTOM AND SOCIAL REVOLUTION

By this means the villeins of many manors acquired all the benefits of common law ownership through the machinery of the custom of the manor. Many landlords, however, were shrewd enough to detect this tendency, and to take steps to prevent the growth of a custom. The courts of common law refused to recognise such a revolutionary custom; according to their reasoning the freehold was in the lord, and they refused to admit that the custom of the manor could have any effect upon the lord's position in the Court of Common Pleas. Indeed, if this custom had been immediately recognised the effect would have been most startling, but in point of fact recognition came so late that public opinion was already thoroughly familiar with its implications. In this great work Coke played a prominent and honourable part,[1] and a line of his decisions at the close of the sixteenth century finally established the principle that the customary interests of a villein in his lands under the custom of the manor could be recognised and defended in the Court of Common Pleas.

" The fate of the erstwhile villein is, therefore, linked with some of the momentous movements in our legal history, but this is not the place to pursue the discussion further. A thorough history of copyhold would occupy a very important position in the social and legal history of England. Here we shall make but one more observation, and that will be to remark upon the strange ebb and flow of property rights which the history of copyhold reveals. In the early days of Henry III, when Pateshull and Raleigh were judges, the villein was almost protected, even in the royal courts. Perhaps it would be more accurate to say, as Maitland has suggested, that he had hardly yet been entirely excluded from royal justice. But in any case the evil day was not far off, and soon the dogma takes shape which will deprive the villein of his property. Within two centuries the tide begins to turn. Custom will be recognised by the courts of equity and they will begin the sober task of ' receiving rather than reforming ' manorial custom. Lords of manors,

[1] He wrote an admirably lucid little book on copyhold (as such customary tenure was later called).

who for two centuries have been assured by the common lawyers that they own the freehold in their tenants' copyhold and customary lands ('freehold' being now a word of great power), are informed that they are only 'instruments of the custom'. Finally, even the common law courts will be drawn into the stream and allow the copyholder to bring ejectment as if he were a freeholder. In all this, moreover, a great part will be played by the illustrious Coke, who in other respects proved such a champion of conservative and propertied interests against innovation. And thus the heirs and successors in title of the fourteenth century villein are once again restored to their property rights. There are surely few movements in legal history so curious as this silent shifting of property back and forth. One need only glance at the corresponding processes in France and Russia to realise the gravity of this social revolution, which in England was effected without an insurrection, without legislation, and almost without deliberate thought."[1]

THE REACTION AGAINST CUSTOM

By this time the Court of Common Pleas had grown a little bit afraid of this powerful force of custom. It became necessary to impose limits and to do something to check social changes carried out solely through custom. They were content to allow at least some of the villeins to achieve property rights under the new name of copyholders, but in order to prevent a too rapid transference of property rights from lords to copyholders, they confined the operation of the new doctrine to those cases where the custom was, or seemed to be, immemorially old. This was a new device and an effective one whenever the law courts wished to limit the operation of a custom; it was easy to say that the antiquity of a custom would have to be proved right back to the time of legal memory (3rd September, 1189, so too the date of limitation of the writ of right).[2] Such a distinction was completely false; nothing is more certain than that there was no copyhold anywhere in the year 1189; but the doctrine served as a means of checking any further rapid growth of customary tenures, and in its practical effect it retarded, without completely stopping, the movement. When we get to this doctrine of immemorially old custom it is obvious that we are in modern and not mediaeval times.[3] The whole idea is as artificial as the date of limitation which it set, and it is clear that in the sixteenth century, when this doctrine first appears, custom had largely ceased to be a familiar notion to the common lawyers, who regarded it henceforth as a troublesome and perhaps a dangerous anomaly which must be confined as strictly as possible within harmless limits. This idea is nowhere better exemplified than in the famous *Case of Tanistry*[4] when the common law tests of

---

[1] Plucknett, Y.B. 13 Richard II, Introduction, pp. xlii, xliii.

[2] This is the date of limitation fixed in 1275 (Westminster I, c. 39) for writs of right. It was also the limit in Normandy: *Summa de Legibus*, cxi. 13 and *Arresta Communia* (ed. Perrot), p. 33 n. 2. Its transference to custom was helped by the fact that in 1290 it was enacted that the user of franchises ever since that date would be an answer to a writ of *quo warranto*; st. 18 Edw. I. Below, p. 719.

[3] Littleton, s. 170, states the rule but with doubt and disapproval; Coke is more positive, Co. Lit., *in loc.*

[4] *Case of Tanistry* (1608), Dav. 28.

custom were used to break up the social organisation of the Irish nobility, the case becoming a leading authority upon the law of custom.

An almost equally remarkable product of customary law occurred upon the Continent among the lesser free landowners down to the early thirteenth century. As the result of the coincidence of a number of different customs and practices, there developed the famous custom of community property between husband and wife, a system which obtains in most continental countries and in some parts of America.[1]

THE EXTENT OF CUSTOM IN ENGLAND

Many of the counties in England had customs of their own, some of them well known (like the recently abolished gavelkind), others much more obscure.[2] Then, too, in England there were numerous customs of cities and towns which throw an extraordinary light upon law and society in the middle ages. The common law was the custom of the King's Court, and an outgrowth of feudal conditions which applied particularly to the larger landowners; for the upper classes of society its rules were no doubt appropriate, but it is only in the local custom of numerous cities, towns and villages that we can see how different the life of the ordinary people was. In these customs, for example, we find that the position of the married woman was very different from that which the common law assigned her, the complete merging of personality being obviously out of harmony with bourgeois habits. Local customs frequently keep the woman's property free from her husband's control, accord her liberty of contract (which was denied at common law), and even allow her to trade separately upon her own account. The extent of these local customs is hardly known. Many custumals have survived,[3] but many others have not. Indeed, it was typical of customary law that there was no need for it to be written down, and there can be no doubt that many communities had notable bodies of custom without ever possessing a written custumal. By the merest chance an example of this recently came to light. In defence to an action of account in 1389, it was pleaded that by the custom of the little village of Selby in Yorkshire a husband was not liable for the

---

[1] This is the most recent suggestion made by Lemaire, *Les Origines de la communauté de biens entre époux*, Revue historique de droit (1928), 584–645. Even in England we had customs which might have grown into a system of community (*e.g.* Leis Willelme, c. 27) had not the Crown insisted on so extensive a right of forfeiture (*Rot. Parl.*, ii. 8 (13), 11). Cf. Maitland, *Collected Papers*, ii. 289. Similarly, we find a wife making a will (with her husband's assent, it was said) of half the goods of her and her husband—a practice which in some places largely contributed to the growth of the idea of marital community: Y.BB. Edward II (Selden Society), x. 243 (1311).

[2] For a list of county customs, see N. Neilson in Harvard Law Review, xxxviii. 483–484.

[3] For the boroughs, their provisions have been arranged according to subject matter in one *corpus* by Mary Bateson, *Borough Customs* (2 vols. Selden Society). Borough charters have been similarly treated by Ballard and Tait. For royal charters empowering boroughs to ordain, amend and add fresh customs, see A. K. Kiralfy, *Action on the Case*, 236.

commitments of his wife incurred in the course of her separate trading.[1] There is no extant custumal of Selby, and apart from this case no other indication is known of Selby possessing a body of customary law. Only the accident which raised the point in the Court of Common Pleas has enabled us to learn this important fact, which is a strong warning to bear constantly in mind that the common law, even so late as 1389, did not extend to all persons and places, and that there was an incalculably large mass of customary law involving very different principles in numerous different communities of which we only know a fraction.

THE CUSTOM OF MERCHANTS

Of these local customs, those which were developed in particular places where fairs and large mercantile interests existed naturally acquired strong mercantile characteristics. In this way we come to the growth of a body of mercantile law which was commonly called the law merchant. It seems to have grown out of strictly local custom, and all through its history local variations are conspicuous. Inevitably, however, there grew up forces which made for greater uniformity, and in the end, as we have seen, what used to be the custom of numerous towns and fairs became the unified custom of a particular class, that of the merchants.

On examining the vast mass of customary law of which we still have surviving evidence, we get the impression of great activity in countless small communities, which are constantly endeavouring to regulate their life by developing approved courses of conduct which can be imposed and enforced upon the recalcitrant in the name of custom. The great variety of customary provisions, and the eagerness with which new communities compared different bodies of custom in order to choose the one best suited to their needs, seem to show that we must not neglect custom if we would find initiative, experiment and new thought in mediaeval law. An examination of our earlier statutes will show that many of them adopt into the common law principles which had been developed already in some one or another custumal, and this confirms the impression that the common lawyers themselves in the formative period of their profession were glad to look to local custom and to choose from it those principles and devices which, having been tried, had been found satisfactory, and to extend them to the nation at large by enacting them as statute law.[2]

[1] Plucknett, Y.B. 13 Richard II (Ames Foundation), 80, and Introduction, xlvi.

[2] See the recent suggestive article by Schechter, *Popular Law and Common Law*, Columbia Law Review, xxviii. 269–299.

CHAPTER 4

LEGISLATION

At the present day the most powerful instrument for legal change
in the hands of the State is legislation. Every modern nation possesses
one or more legislatures—in America, over four dozen—which are all
extremely active. Immense quantities of statute law are produced every
session; a great deal of it, no doubt, is concerned with problems of
administration and police, but nevertheless at the present day it can
no longer be denied that legislation has a large place in modern legal
systems. Few topics in legal history are more interesting than the rise
and progress of legislation, the development of special bodies for the
purpose of making statute law, and the attitude of the law courts in
applying and interpreting the results of their labours.

IS LEGISLATION A ROMAN TRADITION?

Professor Jenks has developed the interesting thesis that legislation was only known to the middle ages through Roman law. According to this view true legislation is the product of Roman ideas; if these ideas are present, then legislation must be regarded as a conscious imitation of Roman practices; if these ideas are absent then we find likewise an absence of true legislation. The early Germanic laws under this theory are not really legislative, but only official memoranda of tribal custom. When, however, the barbarians had settled down within the old Roman Empire, and had become familiar with its political ideas, we begin to find the appearance of express legislation. Indeed, Professor Jenks would go so far as to say that

> " just as a party of savages will disport themselves in the garments of a shipwrecked crew, so the Merovingian and Carolingian kings and officials deck themselves with the titles, the prerogatives, the documents of the imperial State. No doubt the wisest of them, such as Charles the Great, had a deliberate policy in so doing. But the majority of them seem to have been swayed simply by vanity, or ambition, or admiration."[1]

One of the most striking functions of the Roman Emperor was his power to legislate, and the Carolingians likewise produced a considerable body of legislative acts called " capitularies ". These instruments are partly administrative, being substantially instructions to royal officials, but some of them are beyond doubt truly legislative, and openly profess to introduce new law. It is perfectly clear that they were an important element in the machinery of government throughout the ninth century. With the fall of the Carolingian Empire at the close of that century, the Roman imperial idea suffered an eclipse. The tenth and eleventh centuries are the periods during which central authority completely failed, and was replaced by the extremely decentralised form of government which we call feudalism.

> " If we leave England out of sight there is an almost unbroken silence in the history of Teutonic law during the tenth and eleventh centuries. The Roman Empire, real and fictitious, is dead, and with it the idea of legislation, if not of law. When the idea revives again in the prospering France of the thirteenth century, we find the legist asserting the royal power of legislation in maxims which are simply translations of the texts of Roman law. ' That which pleases him (the King) to do must be held for law ', says Beaumanoir. A century later Boutillier is careful to explain that the King may make laws ' because he is Emperor in his realm '. "[2]

It is a difficult question to decide how far this theory can be applied to the special facts of English history. Dr Jenks insists that the Anglo-Saxon laws are really declarations of custom, and do not become truly

---

[1] Jenks, *Law and Politics in the Middle Ages* (2nd edn.), 17.

[2] Jenks, *op. cit.,* 21. Fritz Kern, *Kingship and Law* (1914; tr. S. B. Chrimes, 1939) contains many brilliant, but hazardous, generalisations which it is impossible to deal with here. For a reading of English history in the light of Kern's theories, see Geoffrey Barraclough, *Legislation in Medieval England*, Law Quarterly Review, lvi. 75. Somewhat similar views had already been expressed by C. H. McIlwain, *High Court of Parliament* (1910).

legislative until the reign of Egbert, who had visited the court of Charles the Great, and there learnt the imperial idea. However, if this theory is to be applied to English legal history at all, we shall have to start earlier than Egbert. The very first Anglo-Saxon law we possess, two hundred years before his day, contains matter which surely must be legislative—it is largely concerned with making provision for a completely new class of society, namely, the clergy, which previous to this date had not existed. Here, then, was a piece of radical legislation. If we are to find imperial influence in this, it is to the Church rather than to the Empire directly that it must be ascribed, and there is no doubt that the early Christian missionaries to England deliberately adopted the policy of magnifying the kingly office. In fact, whatever is ultimate origin may be, we find a fairly constant stream of legislation from the very beginning of authentic Anglo-Saxon legal history about the year 600 continuously down to the present day. Of course, at some periods this legislation was more important than in others; for quite long stretches of time we find only comparatively trivial matters, but nevertheless, when radical legislation became necessary, there were the power and the machinery to effect it.

LEGISLATION AND FEUDALISM

An alternative theory would regard legislation as an inseparable element in adjudication. Thus, those lords in France who had rights of justice, inevitably developed legislative powers as well.[1] The result is worth noting, for it shows what the common law escaped. In France, every feudatory legislated for his own demesne, but as a necessary result, it followed that an overlord, and even the King, could not legislate for the demesnes of his under-tenants for they were under the jurisdiction of their immediate lord. Hence even the Crown could only legislate for the royal domains and not for the country at large. When national legislation was needed, the Crown would hold a solemn court of vassals and endeavour to persuade them to adopt what we may call, on the American pattern, a " uniform law ". If they agreed, the bargain was embodied in an oath by the vassals to legislate along particular lines. If this practice had continued, France would have had in the end a legislature of King and lords somewhat like the English, although attained by a different line of historical development. It so happened that things went otherwise; where most of the barons agreed, those in the majority would take an oath promising to compel the rest by force to legislate in accordance with the wishes of the greater number.[2] Only later did the reception of Romanist maxims make the Crown sole legislator, to the exclusion of the feudatories.

[1] Declareuil, *Histoire générale du droit français* (1925), 213–214. The very interesting theory of Goebel, *Felony and Misdemeanour*, i. 229 n. 80, is attractive.

[2] Declareuil, 795–796.

EARLY LEGISLATION IN ENGLAND

In England the Crown was stronger, and although there may have been local legislation occasionally,[1] and even feudal legislation,[2] there was never much doubt that royal statutes were binding throughout the land.[3]

Needless to say, legislative methods have changed in the course of thirteen hundred years. Under the Anglo-Saxon kings there was no part of the government which could be described as a legislature. It is impossible in the present state of our knowledge to ascertain the relative influence upon legislation of the King, the clergy, the nobles and the King's more intimate advisers. It may very well be that the Anglo-Saxon assemblies which were frequently associated with legislation were modelled upon ecclesiastical councils—indeed, it is sometimes impossible to distinguish a royal Witan from a Church council.

The Norman Conquest made little change in the general attitude toward legislation, save to enhance the position of the Crown, assisted by a small, intimate and informal Council. Legislation still continued, and William the Conqueror effected several important changes; he abolished the death penalty for certain offences, and penal slavery,[4] and made radical changes in the constitution of the hundred court.[5] If we find no legislation under his second son and successor William II, we soon find that his third son, Henry I, did something towards resuming the practice. In 1100 he issued a Charter of Liberties,[6] and from that time forward the Charter becomes a frequent form of legislation. Large portions of this Charter, no doubt, consist of a withdrawal of certain oppressive claims by the Crown which were of doubtful legality; other parts, however, seem definitely to establish new rules in the place of old ones; various feudal dues, for example, instead of being arbitrary, were reduced to " reasonable " limits, and this was clearly a change in the law; moreover, the Charter concludes with a grant of the law as it was under Edward the Confessor, " together with those revisions which my father [William the Conqueror] made by the advice of his barons ". In short, Henry I maintains the legislative changes which William the Conqueror

---

[1] Examples of county legislation come from Kent in 1259 (E. F. Jacobs, *Baronial Reform*, 351–352) and Chester in 1260 (R. Stewart-Brown, *Chester County Court Rolls*, 5–6); borough bye-laws are very common; we hear of manorial statutes in 1234 (*Bracton's Note Book*, no. 842), and there is much material in the thirteenth century (W. O. Ault, *Some Early Village Bye-laws*, English Historical Review, xlv. 208; G. C. Homans, *English Villagers*); the text of a late example in 1756 has survived (Vinogradoff, *Collected Papers*, i. 138–148, 286–296).

[2] An example from St Albans is mentioned, p. 186 above.

[3] The city of London sometimes claimed that general statutes would not derogate from the city's franchise. Cf. *Rot. Parl. Inediti*, 128 (5); Sayles, *King's Bench*, iii. p. xxxix; Y.B. 19 Henry VI, ff. 64–65 (Pasch. no. 1), *per* Fortescue. For a similar claim by ancient demesne, see Plucknett, *Statutes and their Interpretation*, 64.

[4] *Hic Intimatur*, c. 10 (in Stubbs, *Select Charters*, 8th edn., 83–85).

[5] Above, p. 12.

[6] Above, p. 14.

made in Anglo-Saxon law. He also restored capital punishment in those cases where it had been abolished.[1] A recently discovered charter of the reign of Stephen (1135–1154) refers to a " *statutum decretum* " which established the rule that where there is no son, daughters will inherit by spindles. It is interesting to have proof that this rule is older than the great age of reform under Henry II, but it is even more remarkable to find it expressly attributed to legislation.[2]

It is when we come to the reign of Henry II that we find the first great outburst of legislation. The forms which it took were various. Instead of the ancient and solemn charter we find more frequently the assize, but in most cases the text is no longer extant and as a rule we have to depend upon chroniclers for our information. Thus we have the Assize of Clarendon in 1166 which was made with the assent of all the prelates and barons of England, and is in form an expression of the King's will. Several assizes during his reign established new forms of trial by inquisition or jury, and established new forms of action in the law of real property. At the same time what professed to be ancient custom was ascertained and declared by the remarkable procedure of an inquisition consisting of all the " prelates, nobles and ancients of the realm " in the Constitutions of Clarendon (1164).[3] Under his sons Richard I and John we have only the Great Charter of 1215, which, although largely declaratory of ancient custom, was still in other respects legislative, in several cases substituting new rules for old. During the next ten years the Charter was three times revised and much of the first Charter was abrogated—and it must be remembered that the repeal of existing law is just as much legislation as the introduction of new law.

During the long reign of Henry III legislation becomes steadily more frequent. A good deal of it is already known, but it is certain that there is still more awaiting discovery on the voluminous rolls in the Public Record Office.[4] The charter still continues to be a form for the most solemn type of legislation, but others also occur. Brief and informal instructions to Justices in Eyre were a particularly convenient method for introducing new rules and practices into the law. In 1236 we find the Provisions of Merton, which all the old collections of statutes agree in treating as the earliest English statute.[5] There is, of course, no real basis for this tradition; there are other documents upon the public records of an earlier date which can be regarded as legislation with equal justice. The Provisions (or Statute) of Merton long remained

---

[1] Pollock and Maitland, ii. 461.

[2] Stenton, *English Feudalism*, 37–40.

[3] Summarised above, pp. 17–18.

[4] Valuable references are in Pollock and Maitland, i. 189 n. 4; cf. one such example translated above, p. 119.

[5] The current text is composite: Maitland, *Bracton's Note Book*, i. 104 ff.; G. J. Turner, *Some Thirteenth Century Statutes*, Law Magazine and Review, 4th ser., xxii. 245–250; Woodbine, *Statute of Merton*, Law Quarterly Review, xxvi. 151; Holdsworth, ii. 221; Powicke, *Henry III* (1947), ii. 769.

important, particularly in matters of commons, for which it was invoked
as late as the eighteenth century. In the middle of Henry III's reign
a revolutionary body of barons established a special machinery for the
purpose of legislation, and the Provisions of Westminster (1259) were
the result; and when finally the revolution came to an end, most of the
Provisions of Westminster were re-enacted in a more regular form in
the great Statute of Marlborough (1267).[1] Indeed the Statute of Marlborough really belongs to the great group of legislative acts which took
place in the next reign, for there are only eight years between it and
Edward I's Statute of Westminster I in 1275.

EARLY LEGISLATIVE FORMS

This brings us to the greatest outburst of legislation in England
during the middle ages; it was only equalled in extent and importance
by that of the first half of the nineteenth century.[2] It will therefore
be well at this point to examine very briefly the available forms and
methods of legislation existing in the reign of Edward I. The forms,
to begin with, were extremely varied. We have already mentioned the
form of the charter, and it must be remembered that the charter is really a
conveyance, and that the various charters of liberty which we have
mentioned are drawn in identically the same form as a conveyance of
real property. The Great Charter of 1215, for example, announces
that " we have granted and by this present charter confirmed for us and
our heirs forever " the following liberties, " to have and to hold to all
the freemen of the realm and their heirs, of us and our heirs "—which is
exactly the form which would be used in a grant of lands. The Provisions of Merton which we have already mentioned similarly use the
word " grant ", although here we find that the grant is embodied in a
form which becomes more frequent henceforward—the provision. They
begin thus:

> " It is provided in the King's Court on Wednesday[3] after the feast of St. Vincent
> in the twentieth year of the reign of King Henry, the son of King John, at Merton
> in the presence of the Archbishop of Canterbury and the other bishops and the
> greater part of the earls and barons of England there present for the coronation of
> the said King and of Eleanor, the Queen (for which purpose they were summoned),
> after discussion of the common good of the realm upon the articles underwritten:
> wherefore it was provided and granted . . ."

Here we clearly see a form which is half-way between the charter
which technically moved from the King alone, and the later statute
which was made in Parliament. The Statute of Marlborough (1267)
is in a rather peculiar form, and this may perhaps be attributed to the

[1] For its significance, see above, p. 26.

[2] The general nature of Edward I's legislation has been described above, pp. 27–31.

[3] 23 January 1236.

presence of several distinguished foreigners. It bears the title " Provisions made at Marlborough in the presence of King Henry, and Richard, King of the Romans, and of Edward, eldest son of the said King Henry, and of the Lord Ottobon, then papal legate in England ", and begins with a short preamble.

All these documents were in Latin; the First Statute of Westminster (1275) is somewhat unusual in being in French. It also adopts a French word for legislative acts, *établissement*, which is reminiscent of the legislative acts of Louis IX bearing the same name. The Statute of Gloucester three years later (1278) is also in French and claims to have been " established and ordained ", the King himself " providing " for the amendment of his realm with the concurrence of the most discreet persons in the Kingdom, both great and small. The Statute of Mortmain (1279), on the other hand, which is in every way as important as the preceding, is simply in the form of an administrative instruction addressed to the Justices of the Bench. The Statutes of Merchants[1] (1283 and 1285) are in French and recount that " the King by himself and his Council " had ordained and established the matters following; the Statute of Westminster II (1285), however, is in Latin and sets the form for subsequent statutes, although for a long time deviations are not uncommon. We now find that " the Lord King in his Parliament at Westminster after Easter on the thirteenth year of his reign caused to be recited the many oppressions and defects of the laws, with a view to supplementing the statutes made at Gloucester, and published these statutes following ". Here we get a form which is clearly and consciously legislative. The Statute of Winchester, however, in the same year, professes to be nothing more than the command of the King alone, no Parliament and not even a Council being mentioned.

THE COUNCIL'S SHARE IN LEGISLATION

So far it is clear that these legislative acts ran in the name of the King and very probably were initiated by him or by his most intimate councillors; there is as yet no necessary connection between legislation and Parliament. In the reign of Edward I we find some extremely important legislation which seems to have emanated from the King in Council alone, or at most from a Council in Parliament, for we find no mention of the Commons; so, too, with the Statute of Westminster II and many others. On the other hand, some of his statutes profess to have been made " by the advice of the barons, earls, magnates, great men and other nobles, and of the commons of the realm in Parliament " (Statute of Carlisle, 1307).[2] There is, however, no legal difference

---

[1] The earlier is sometimes called the Statute of Acton Burnel.

[2] As finally published in 1307, the enacting clause thus omits to recite the assent of the bishops; but when first brought before parliament in 1305 the bishops are said to have assented: Maitland, *Memoranda de Parliamento*, li, 314.

whatever in the effect or authority of statutes produced in these different ways. As far as we can see, a statute in the reign of Edward I simply means something established by royal authority; whether it is established by the King in Council, or in a Parliament of nobles, or in a Parliament of nobles and commons as well, is completely immaterial. It is equally immaterial what form the statute takes, whether it be a charter, or a statute enrolled and proclaimed, or merely an administrative expression of the royal will notified to the judicial authorities by means of a letter close (which at this period was a species of interdepartmental correspondence). In short, while we are in the reign of Edward I we feel the typical mediaeval atmosphere, which was, above all, intensely practical. The great concern of the government was to govern, and if in the course of its duties legislation became necessary, then it was effected simply and quickly without any complications or formalities. Even after parliamentary legislation had begun to appear, we still find that the Council exercised a preponderant influence and that among the councillors were frequently to be found the judges, for it is only natural in so practical an age that the Council should call upon the judges to draft legislation, and such in fact was the case.

These variations, both in form and method—

" seem to be the direct result of what was then the novelty of enacted law, which as yet had not become a regular product of the routine of government. This conclusion can be confirmed by an examination of the circumstances under which some of the most famous of our early statutes were passed. Several will be seen to have resulted from what would be described to-day as ' direct action '. The barons in arms dictated *Magna Carta*, and a military crisis eighty-two years later put it on the statute roll. The Provisions of Westminster originated in what Stubbs called a ' provisional government ', and it was only as part of the pacification following the Barons' War that they became incorporated in the Statute of Marlborough. The ' New Ordinances ' of 5 Edward II were likewise the product of a revolutionary movement. One statute—that of Bigamists, c. 5—is an interpretation of a papal constitution."[1]

As Professor Winfield remarks:

" The enactment may resemble a grant of lands, a proclamation of successful revolutionaries, a treaty of peace dictated by conquerors, a bargain between two contractors, or a writ to the judges, precisely as it originated in a gift of the King, a fight against the King, an agreement with the King, or an order by the King."[2]

STATUTES AND ORDINANCES

At various times we find a distinction drawn between statutes and ordinances. Down to the middle of the fourteenth century the words are used interchangeably, and it is only in the latter part of the century that some sort of distinction begins to appear. It seems to take the line of discriminating between those acts which received the consent of the King, the Lords and the Commons, and those in which one of

[1] Plucknett, *Statutes and Their Interpretation*, 9.
[2] Winfield, *Chief Sources of English Legal History*, 72, 73.

these consents was absent.[1] As we have seen, in the fourteenth century legislation was none the worse for being extra-parliamentary; as a late example it may be observed that the Ordinance of Labourers (1349) was constantly applied in every respect as if it had been a parliamentary statute, although it had no parliamentary authority until it was included in a general confirmation of all labour legislation nearly thirty years later.[2] Indeed it may be that this tardy grant of parliamentary sanction is an early case of doubts first appearing as to the validity of non-parliamentary legislation. A much later example of the confirmation by Parliament of legislation by Crown alone, has already been mentioned in connection with the court of augmentations.[3] For the rest, ordinances have played a very small part in English public law, if we are to except the thirteenth- and early fourteenth-century examples, which, moreover, as we have seen, were not distinguished from statutes by contemporaries.

PARLIAMENTARY LEGISLATION

As we pass through the fourteenth century, parliamentary legislation becomes more and more general. Not only does the King use Parliaments for the purpose of giving authority to his own decrees, the Parliament merely ratifying decisions which have really been reached by the Council, but we also find that Parliament will request the Crown to legislate upon some particular matter. At first we find general complaints put into the form of a petition, either by particular members, or outsiders and local bodies. Next, come petitions by the whole Commons. Such petitions will state grievances and pray for a remedy. When the Parliament is over, the Council will consider these requests at its leisure, and if it thinks legislation is necessary it will prepare it according to its discretion and publish it as a statute with parliamentary authority. As the Commons grow more powerful politically they express increasing dissatisfaction at the working of this method. Sometimes the government failed to act at all upon a petition; at other times we find the Commons complaining that although they had petitioned for one thing, the Council had legislated along different lines, of which they did not approve. Henry V promised that " from henceforth nothing be enacted to the petitions of his Commons that be contrary to their asking whereby they should be bound without their assent ", but even after a statute had been passed, the Crown sometimes assumed wide powers of altering or suspending it.[4]

In the fifteenth century, however, we find the beginnings of a new

---

[1] Plucknett, *Statutes and Their Interpretation*, 32–34; Holdsworth, *Sources and Literature of English Law*, 48. A slightly different view is taken by Richardson and Sayles, *Early Statutes*, Law Quarterly Review, l. 556 ff.

[2] Putnam, *Enforcement of the Statutes of Labourers*, 179.

[3] Above, p. 175.

[4] Examples are given by Richardson and Sayles, Law Quarterly Review, l. 549 ff., 562, who suggest that such action was not so irregular as historians have generally thought.

system which had in fact first been used for government business.[1] This consisted of presenting a bill which contained the exact form of words which it was proposed to enact. Even at this late date, however, there were occasional doubts whether the consent of the Commons was always necessary. When we get to this stage we can rightly regard Parliament as being a legislature. In the fifteenth century it also becomes the regular practice for statutes to be written in English, instead of in French as in the fourteenth century, or Latin in the thirteenth.

TUDOR LEGISLATION

As we enter the Tudor period we begin to see clear traces of modern parliamentary procedure, the system of three readings and so on. In mere bulk, the change is striking, for the thirty-eight years of Henry VIII's reign (although half of them passed without a parliamentary session) produced a volume of statutes equal to the combined output of the previous two and a half centuries. In part, at least, this may be attributed to the verbosity of Henry himself, or his draftsmen. Another cause may be found in the newer view of what a statute should be; the brief indications in an easy—almost conversational—style which sufficed under Edward I had to be accompanied by a wide discretion in their interpretation by the courts. The newer view restricted the courts much more narrowly to the text of the statute, and so that text had to be more artificially drawn, and if all the possible repercussions of the new statute were to be foreseen and provided for, the text necessarily became long, full of enumerations, exceptions, provisions, saving clauses and the like. The Tudor period, moreover, is the great age of the preamble. We may well see in this an involuntary tribute to the growing importance of public opinion. Statutes were not only proclaimed, as in the middle ages, but were now printed and published through the press. Henry VIII was quick to see the advantage of prefixing to his most drastic acts a vigorous polemical defence of their policy, which has been aptly compared to " a leading article in a government newspaper " as the nearest modern equivalent.

Parliament also began to act in a more independent spirit. While it is doubtless true that Henry contrived to secure parliaments which were in general sympathy with his policies, nevertheless even they would balk at some of his proposals. Several government bills on the vital subject of uses, for example, were thrown out before the famous statute was finally passed.

If much of the more notorious legislation of the Tudors was purely political and social, there was still a great deal which made considerable changes (and generally improvements) in the law. Uses, wills, charities, conveyancing, bankruptcy, commercial law and criminal law are all conspicuous in Tudor legislation.

[1] As to this, see Taswell-Langmead, *Constitutional History* (ed. Plucknett), 210–211. Cf. p. 333 below.

Not only did legislation become more detailed, but it also flowed at a more rapid pace. Parliament having once taken up a subject was apt to return to it again and again, piling act upon act, sometimes with confusing results. From time to time it therefore became necessary to clarify a complicated mass of related statutes, and as early as 1563 we get an example of the typically modern device, the consolidating act, which " digested and reduced into one sole law and statute " the substance of many statutes of artificers which it repealed.[1] Another modern feature which appears under Elizabeth is the grant of statutory powers to all and sundry for the performance of things which so far had to be done by special powers obtained *ad hoc* from the Crown. Thus in 1597 all persons were allowed to erect and even to incorporate various charitable foundations by the simple machinery of a deed enrolled in chancery.[2] Nearly a century before this, we find an early example of delegated legislation[3] under Henry VII; the practice received more conspicuous employment in the next reign, when the statute of proclamations[4] and the act for the succession were striking examples.[5]

It is in this period, moreover, that we find the regulation of commercial and professional life transferred from the old gild and ecclesiastical authorities to the Crown. The result is a flood of " social " legislation far in excess of any to be found in the middle ages, and this necessitated a theory to support it. Coke, with his unfailing patter of Latin apophthegms, enshrined the new view of the field of legislation in words with the required antique sound. " The king ", said he,[6] " is a mixed person, the physician of the realm, the father of the country, the husband of the kingdom to which he is wedded with a ring at his coronation ". In speaking of Henry VIII's foundation of the Royal College of Physicians, which replaced the Church in supervising the medical profession, Walmesley, J., linked up the new paternalism with the old feudal wardship:[7]

" It is the office of a king to survey his subjects, and he is a physician to cure their maladies, and to remove leprosies amongst them, and also to remove all fumes and smells which may offend or be prejudicial to their health, as it appears by the several writs in these several cases provided, and so if a man be not right in his wits, the king is to have the protection and government of him."

[1] 5 Eliz., c. 4.

[2] 39 Eliz., c. 5 (made perpetual, 21 Jac. I, c. 1, § 2). Nothing could be more modern than a general corporation statute, but it will be noticed that Elizabeth's act ends with an interpretation clause which looks quite mediaeval: " such construction shall be made upon this act as shall be most beneficial . . . for the . . . poor, and for repressing and avoiding all acts and devices to be invented or put in ure [use] contrary to the true meaning of this act ".

[3] 19 Hen. VII, c. 28 (1504).

[4] 31 Hen. VIII, c. 8 (1539).

[5] 28 Hen. VIII, c. 7 (1536). Others are 37 Hen. VIII, c. 12, and 2 & 3 Philip and Mary, c. 4, s. 19.

[6] *Magdalen College Case* (1615), 11 Rep. 70. Cf. " rex enim omnes artes censetur habere in scrinio pectoris sui "—*Bonham's Case* (1610), 8 Rep. 116 *b*. Similar words were applied to mediaeval popes.

[7] *Bonham's Case* (1610), 2 Brownl. 260.

THE CITATION OF STATUTES

One of the methods of citation of statutes was exactly the same as that used by the civil and canon lawyers, and consisted of calling each statute by the first words. In a few cases this practice has survived; we still speak of the Statutes *De Donis* and *Quia Emptores*, and in the fourteenth century there were many more. As parliaments became more frequent, statutes were cited according to the place where the Parliament sat; we therefore have the Statutes of Gloucester, York, Northampton, etc., and numerous Statutes of Westminster. With the growth of statute law it became necessary to have a more precise system, and by the close of the fourteenth century statutes are cited by date (that is, by the regnal year). The Statute of Westminster II, therefore, may also be cited as Statute 13 Edward I. Gradually, although not always, the legislation of one Parliament was published all together in one document, which will therefore contain a number of unrelated matters. For convenience such a long document is divided into chapters; the numbering of the chapters is common in fourteenth-century manuscripts although we do not find it on the rolls; and so citations will take the form of the regnal year followed by the number of the chapter. Occasionally we find more than one of these long statutes in a single year, and the modern printers have made a practice of numbering these as separate statutes. Unfortunately there was no uniformity among the many different editions of the older statutes, and indeed no official reprints at all, until the publication of the *Statutes of the Realm* between 1810 and 1825 in nine immense folio volumes. At the present day, citations of statutes earlier than 1713 (at which date the *Statutes of the Realm* end) are usually made according to the regnal years and numberings in this edition, which moreover has received a certain amount of parliamentary sanction.[1] Although the citation of a statute consists of a date, that date may need adjustment if the historical date of the statute is to be ascertained,[2] and the *Statutes of the Realm* lays traps for the unwary by retaining the old practice of beginning the year of grace on 25 March instead of 1 January. In the eighteenth century the citation of statutes became more complicated, for Parliaments lasted longer and their sessions overlapped the regnal years. If the whole of a session falls within one year there is no difficulty, but if it overlaps, all of its acts are described as of both years.

" To take a concrete case, let us see how the system is working at the present moment. King George V came to the throne on May 6th, 1910. After the 1924 general election a new Parliament began in November, 1924, that is to say in the fifteenth regnal year of His Majesty. Any acts passed in March or April of 1925

---

[1] Interpretation Act, 1889. For a survey of the older editions of statutes, see Winfield, *Chief Sources of English Legal History*, 84–95.

[2] See Plucknett, *Legal Chronology*, in Handbook of Dates for students of English History (ed. C. R. Cheney: Royal Historical Society, 1945).

are consequently referred to as being of the regnal year ' 15 Geo. 5 '. Parliaments being mortal, it is not safe to assume in April of 1925 that the session will endure until the sixteenth regnal year. But, as soon as the session has got past the date of May 6th, it has spread itself over two regnal years; therefore acts passed in June or July of 1925 must be referred to as of ' 15 & 16 Geo. 5 '. Indeed it seems to be the better opinion that even the acts passed before May 6th and hitherto labelled by the single year (15 Geo. 5) should at this stage attract to themselves the second year and thereafter be cited by reference to the two regnal years (15 & 16)."[1]

THE AUTHENTICITY OF STATUTES

So much then for the forms and methods of legislation. We must now consider the authority and the interpretation of these documents. As for their authority we find very little question. Indeed, there seems a curious tendency to extend statutory authority to a variety of documents, some of them of very questionable origin. An important case as recorded upon the Parliament rolls in the course of time will acquire the reputation and name of the Statute of Waste.[2] A few useful extracts from Bracton will also be referred to during the middle ages as statutes.[3] The term " statute ", therefore, is a decidedly inclusive one, and it is not often that we find a reputed statute questioned. Occasionally we find suspicions expressed because a particular document has not been sealed— the meaning of which is far from clear.[4] Sometimes a very cautious litigant who is relying upon a recent statute will go to the trouble of having an official copy authenticated under the Great Seal, and of bringing it into court. On such occasions it would seem that the court took the precaution of enrolling the statute in question as part of the pleadings. Indeed, it is extremely curious that there was more difficulty in pleading a very recent statute than an old one. The courts seem to have felt a certain reluctance when faced with the problem of applying a statute for the first time. Moreover, it would have been quite difficult in the fourteenth century to decide whether a particular text was a statute, and, if so, what exactly its words were. From the Year Books it would seem that the bench did not always have a copy of the statutes at hand. On those occasions when the bench did examine a copy of the statutes, the Year Books are careful to report the precise words as they were read; more than that, it is not unusual to find statutes even then seriously misquoted. In at least one case everybody concerned seems to have been unaware that a certain statute had been repealed. It is therefore not surprising that there have grown up certain legends as to the operation and effect of particular statutes which have no historical basis.[5]

[1] Carr, " Citation of Statutes " in *Cambridge Legal Essays*, 72.

[2] Plucknett, *Statutes and Their Interpretation*, 23.

[3] The early printers greatly increased the list of pseudo-statutes in their endeavours to bring out ever bigger and more complete collections.

[4] See now, Richardson and Sayles, *Early Statutes*, in Quarterly Review, l. 548.

[5] References will be found in Plucknett, *op. cit.* Even in Coke's day, the problem of proving a statute might be difficult; *The Prince's Case* (1606), 8 Rep. 1.

THE COMMENCEMENT OF STATUTES

Late in the reign of Edward III there is a case[1] which shows that several characteristics of statutes, as they remained for centuries, were already being settled. The Crown was prosecuting the Bishop of Chichester under one of the statutes of premunire, and the defence raised some interesting points. The statute was very recent, and it was objected that it had not been proclaimed in the counties; to this Thorpe, C.J., replied: " although proclamation was not made in the county, everyone is now bound to know what is done in Parliament, for as soon as Parliament has concluded a matter, the law holds that every person has knowledge of it, for the Parliament represents the body of all the realm, and so proclamation is unnecessary for the statute has already become effective ". A further objection seems to suggest that the Commons had not assented to the statute in question; to this Thorpe, C.J., replied, rather mysteriously, " when all the lords are assembled they can make an ordinance, and it shall be held for a statute ". Whatever the last cryptic sentence may mean (and it may relate to peculiar circumstances attaching to that statute),[2] it is clear that statutes were already regarded as operative as soon as made, and not from the date of publication. Later ages added a refinement by regarding a statute as operative from the first day of the session in which it was made—which in effect might antedate it by several weeks or even months.[3] In doing this they were probably imitating the analogous rules of the law courts, whose judgments dated from the first day of term. The Statute of Frauds[4] abolished the rule as to judgments, but the rule as to statutes was not reformed until 1793 when it was enacted that they should take effect from the date of the royal assent unless otherwise provided.[5]

THE PROBLEM OF INTERPRETATION

Until late in the middle ages, lawyers tried to avoid facing the problem of interpretation. Indeed, even the word connoted in their minds fraud or evasion. Nor was the division of labour into law-making and law-interpreting generally accepted in fourteenth-century thought; the canonists, for example, had a maxim that interpretation properly belonged to the power that ordained, which alone could authoritatively

---

[1] R. v. Bishop of Chichester (1365), Y.B. 39 Edward III, f. 7.

[2] 38 Edw. III, stat. 2; they have been noticed by Richardson and Sayles, Law Quarterly Review, l. 559; cf. Plucknett, Statutes and their Interpretation, 34, 143.

[3] The rule is settled in Partridge v. Strange and Croker (1553), Plowd. 77; Maitland, Collected Papers, iii. 195, must have overlooked this case, for he there suggested that the rule may have been unknown in 1559; for its history, in England and America, see Kent, Commentaries, i. 454 ff.

[4] 29 Car. II, c. 3 (1677), ss. 14–16.

[5] 33 Geo. III, c. 13 (1793).

interpret its own acts.[1] The civilians were of the same mind: *ejus est interpretari cujus est condere*.[2] There was a possibility that the common law might accept this principle, which the best legal opinion seemed to approve. Early in the reign of Henry III dispute arose on the interpretation of the great charter between certain sheriffs and the inhabitants of their shires; the King therefore called the disputants before him to clear the matter up.[3] The same procedure was followed eight years later, when the greater part of the bishops, earls and barons, by their common counsel, placed an interpretation upon c. 35 of the great charter, which the King then published by letters close.[4] Nor was this merely a royalist theory, for a quarter of a century later, when Henry III was at the mercy of his barons, they wrote in his name a warning to the Bishop of Durham in these terms—

"in view of the fact that the interpretation of laws and customs belongs to us and our nobles, and none other, we of the counsel of our nobles forbid you, as you would desire to use those royal liberties which you pretend are yours, to put any interpretation on them contrary to the laws and customs current in our realm."[5]

Edward I frequently put the principle into practice; the King and his justices published an extra-judicial "exposition" of the Statute of Gloucester[6] in 1278, and in 1281 the King in Council made a "correction" in the same statute.[7]

The common law courts themselves acknowledged the principle of appealing to the legislator when faced with difficulties of interpretation. In 1303 Hengham, C.J., cut short a discussion of the statutory procedure of *elegit* by saying: "this statute was put before the king and his council, who accorded that when the debtor came with the debt ready, his lands should be restored to him; so will you take your money?"[8] Even as late as 1366 Thorpe, C.J., recalled that there had been a discussion before him on the interpretation of a statute, "and Sir Hugh Green, C.J., K.B., and I went together to the council where there were a good two dozen bishops and earls, and asked those who made the statute what it meant". The archbishop told them what the statute meant, after remarking (with some justification) that the judges' question was rather a silly one.[9]

---

[1] *Unde jus prodit, interpretatio quoque procedat*: c. 31, X. 5, 39. The canonists restricted the doctrine somewhat; Lyndewoode, *Provinciale* (ed. 1679), 246 *declarandum*.

[2] Bartholomaeus de Saliceto on C. 1. 14. 12. Compare Bracton, f. 106: *est enim eius interpretari cuius est concedere* (of fines levied in the king's court), and f. 34 (of the king's charters). See generally, H. Kantorowicz and W. W. Buckland, *Studies in the Glossators*, 192, and W. Ullmann, *Medieval Idea of Law*, 112 ff.

[3] Stubbs, *Select Charters* (1905), 357. The date was 1226.

[4] *Statutes of the Realm*, i. 118.

[5] *Close Rolls* (1256–1259), 489.

[6] Exposition of the Statute of Gloucester, *Statutes of the Realm*, i. 50.

[7] *Ibid.*, 52.

[8] Y.B. 30 & 31 Edward I (Rolls Series), 441.

[9] Y.B. 40 Edward III, f. 34 b.

Practice, however, was setting the other way, and after this date interpretation was relinquished to the courts.   The inherent reasonableness of the principle that the legislator was the best interpreter was still, however, admitted by those who gave thought to the problem.   For example, a tract attributed to Lord Ellesmere[1] maintains that it would be more reasonable for statutes to be interpreted by Parliament which made them than by the courts.   More recently, Lord Nottingham in an early case on the Statute of Frauds reports himself thus:[2]

> " I said that I had some reason to know the meaning of this law for it had its first rise from me who brought in the bill into the Lords' House, though it afterwards received some additions and improvements from the judges and the civilians."

Such would appear to be the attitude of some continental systems at the present day,[3] but the common law courts have completely reversed their policy since the days of Nottingham.   No greater contrast to his words just quoted could be imagined than this statement of Lord Halsbury:[4]

> " I have more than once had occasion to say that in construing a statute I believe the worst person to construe it is the person who is responsible for its drafting.   He is very much disposed to confuse what he intended to do with the effect of the language which in fact has been employed. . . .   I was largely responsible for the language in which this enactment is conveyed, and for that reason, and for that reason only, I have not written a judgement myself."

With the growth of international legislation this divergence of view has already created difficulty.[5]

THE JUDICIAL INTERPRETATION OF STATUTES

If we had completely adopted the principle that the lawgiver was the only competent interpreter, we should have had to erect a chamber or council specially devoted to the work as legislation grew in bulk and complexity.   This in fact is the solution which the canonists reached in the end,[6] and the tendency which we have already noticed for the enforcement of statute law to be entrusted to special bodies[7] is perhaps a symptom of the same trend in the common law.

The principal reason, however, for the triumph of the present system in the common law may be sought in the history of Parliament.   While

---

[1] " It is *magis congruum* that Acts of Parliament should be corrected by the pen that drew them, than to be dashed to pieces by the opinion of a Law Judge " [Egerton], *Observations on Coke's Reports*, ii.

[2] *Ash* v. *Abdy* (1678), 3 Swans. 664.

[3] Gutteridge, *Comparative View of the Interpretation of Statute Law*, Tulane Law Review, viii. 10.

[4] *Hilder* v. *Dexter*, [1902[A.C. 474 at 477.

[5] See the literature mentioned by Professor H. C. Gutteridge, above n. 3.

[6] In 1564 Pope Pius IV created a special congregation of cardinals to whom Pius V shortly afterwards gave the exclusive power of interpreting the decrees of the Council of Trent.

[7] Above, p. 183.

legislation was the work of a very small group of judges and councillors in close contact with the King, recourse to the same small group was easy when an interpretation was desired. The rise of Parliament and its increasing participation in the task of law-making created a very different situation. We have already noted the proposition that things settled by Parliament cannot be altered save by Parliament. Now Parliament served well as a legislature and as a political assembly, but its sessions were too irregular and its activities too much engaged in other directions to allow it to become a permanent organ for the interpretation of statutes. Declaratory acts represent the best that Parliament could be expected to do under such circumstances. In the meantime, there was the important fact that the legislature and the judiciary did actually have a common membership in the thirteenth century, and so nothing was more natural than to allow the judges considerable latitude in the reign of Edward I and even of his son, for they were intimately connected with the group which in fact drew up the statutes.

EARLY FREEDOM OF INTERPRETATION

It must also be remembered that the earlier mediaeval statute had very little in common with modern legislation. It was possible to handle these enactments with an easy unconcern as to their authenticity and precise content, and obviously there was no trace of the modern notion that every letter of the statute may be significant. Nor did the judges have difficulty in deciding what the real intention of an act was. The famous Chief Justice Hengham, for example, settled a difficult question in these words, " We agreed in Parliament that the wife if not named in the writ should not be received ",[1] and when counsel suggested an interpretation of another statute, Hengham again had an authoritative answer. " Do not gloss the statute," he said, " for we know better than you; we made it."[2] In short, the court was well aware of the intention of a statute because the judges had had the biggest share in making it, and consequently there was little difficulty; the law-maker was simply explaining his own policies. A little later we find the next stage. The great Hengham had gone, but his successors remembered his words. When counsel suggested a particular construction of a statute, Sharshulle, J., replied that when he was at the bar he had used the same argument, and Herle, J., had informed him that Hengham, who had made the statute, read it another way.[3] Again, in a remarkable case involving the Statute De Donis, Chief Justice Bereford used these words:

" He that made the statute meant to bind the issue in fee tail, as well as the feoffees, until the tail had reached the fourth degree, and it was only through

[1] Y.B. 32 & 33 Edward I (Rolls Series), 429.

[2] Y.B. 33 & 35 Edward I (Rolls Series), 82. As a litigant remarked in an Irish case of 1290, " no one ought to gloss the king's statute ": Sayles, King's Bench, ii. 76.

[3] Y.B. 15 Edward III (Rolls Series), 388–394.

negligence that he omitted to insert express words to that effect in the statute; therefore we shall not abate this writ."

In short there is a tradition among the judges as to the intention of the principal statutes.[1] Finally, as we approach the middle of the fourteenth century, the judges have separated from the Council to such an extent that they treat legislation as the product of an alien body, of which they know nothing save from the words of the statute itself, and from that wording alone can they infer its intention—and with the rise of this idea we reach the modern point of view.

CHARACTERISTICS OF FREE INTERPRETATION

This impression is confirmed when we examine the way in which statutes were interpreted in the fourteenth century. Sometimes their wording is strictly applied; sometimes it is stretched very considerably; sometimes the court finds it necessary to restrict the operation of a statute which was too widely drawn; on other occasions the court simply refuses to obey the statute at all. But in this connection two points must be emphasised.

" First, the courts undoubtedly did disregard statutes when they thought fit, and secondly, they expressed no principle of jurisprudence or political theory which would serve as an explanation—still less as a reason—for their attitude. . . . If reasons of however great technicality made it desirable to neglect some words of a statute, then they were quietly set aside, but in doing so neither counsel nor judges enquired into the nature of statutes and legislation, the sovereignty of Parliament, the supremacy of the common law, the functions of the judicature, and all the other questions which the modern mind finds so absorbingly interesting. . . . We shall be getting nearest the truth, it seems, when we remember that the fourteenth century was in urgent need of good law, firmly enforced, for then we shall understand that the judges' great pre-occupation was to apply the best law they knew as courageously as they could, and that our modern difficulties, whether political or juridical, to them would have seemed, if not unintelligible, at least irrelevant and pedantic."[2]

THE LIMITATION OF JUDICIAL DISCRETION

In the middle of the fourteenth century this free and easy attitude begins to disappear. We are beginning to find statements in the Year Books that statutes ought to be interpreted strictly, while in other matters, too, the bench is less confident in using its ancient powers of discretion. By 1340 or thereabout the Court of Common Pleas had developed an elaborate procedure which required considerable technical skill to work. More than that, the intimacy between the Council and the judges which had been such a feature of Edward I's reign had almost ceased. As a result the judges no longer felt themselves in the position of councillors whose nearness to the King enabled them to exercise the

[1] Y.BB. Edward II (Selden Society), xi. 176–177.

[2] Plucknett, *Statutes and Their Interpretation*, 70.

wise royal discretion which, as we have seen, was the privilege of the King's closest advisers. Instead, the Court of Common Pleas regards itself as a government department whose function is to carry out its duties along prescribed lines. At about this time, therefore, we find such statements as that of Hilary, J., that " we will not and cannot change ancient usages ",[1] and " statutes are to be interpreted strictly ",[2] while at the same date we see the earliest distinctions drawn between strict law and equity.[3] Then, too, it is highly significant that the Chancery begins to appear, in the early years of Richard II, as a court exercising the Council's discretion.[4] Towards the middle of the fourteenth century, therefore, the judges begin to interpret statutes strictly. No longer are they to be regarded as merely suggestions of policy within whose broad limits the court can exercise a wide discretion. Instead they are regarded as texts[5] which are to be applied exactly as they stand, and so we find the beginnings of a radical separation into two functions: the first legislates and establishes a text, and the second adjudicates and interprets the text. This separation was momentous for English history, for more than anything else it promoted the isolation of the law courts and the judges, enabling them to develop an independent position and to act as checks upon the executive and as critics of the legislature. This became all the more significant since the legislature inevitably became a political body controlling the executive; the courts now stood outside of both. The extent to which the courts were conscious of this special position is clear from their endeavours to prevent any tribunal except the superior common law courts from exercising the function of interpreting statutes. Ecclesiastical courts were to be resolutely barred, and the admiralty was attacked; even Chancery was expected to send to a common law court when the high mystery of interpretation had to be performed.[6]

A TECHNIQUE OF INTERPRETATION

As we pass through the fifteenth century to the sixteenth and the age of Coke, we find the courts applying themselves with great diligence to the task of interpreting statutes, which to this day is one of the most difficult functions which a judge has to perform. Shorn of their powers

[1] Y.B. 16 Edward III (Rolls Series), i. 90 (1342).

[2] Y.B. 17 Edward III (Rolls Series), 142 (1343); Y.B. 17 & 18 Edward III (Rolls Series), 446; Y.B. 18 Edward III (Rolls Series), 131.

[3] Y.B. 17 Edward III (Rolls Series), 370 (1343).

[4] Baldwin, *Select Cases before the King's Council* (Selden Society), xxiv.

[5] The practice of basing statutes upon common petitions naturally directs attention to the written text, but it is the adoption of the bill procedure (above, p. 324) which finally compels parliament, the courts and the public to scrutinise the *ipsissima verba* of a statute.

[6] The movement was not successful, although traces of it have survived. Its abandonment may be due to its inconsistency with a more important principle, viz. that statutes are binding even in ecclesiastical matters. See *Articuli Cleri*, c. 20 (1605) in 2 Inst. 599 ff.; March, N. C., 90, No. 148 (1640); *Gould* v. *Gapper* (1804), 5 East, 345.

of openly exercising discretion, the common law judges took refuge in logic. Attempts were made to devise rules whereby the grammatical structure of a sentence, combined with a general consideration of the nature of the act, could be used as a guide to the interpretation of the text in question. Some statutes confirmed or amended previous law; others removed abuses; some commanded things to be done, while others prohibited certain actions; some statutes conferred benefits and others were penal. Combined with these general considerations a statute might be drawn in affirmative or negative terms, and out of all this the courts elaborated a system of great complexity.[1]

THE EQUITY OF THE STATUTE

As a result of this development, there was a multiplicity of rules available for the interpretation of any particular statute. So great was their variety, and so diverse were the rules, that almost any conclusion might be reached, simply by selecting the appropriate rule. The real problem therefore receded farther back than ever, and the power of the courts to construe or misconstrue legislation was unimpaired, and indeed increased.

This became obvious by the reign of Elizabeth, and many lawyers, notably Plowden, gloried in the liberty which the courts enjoyed in playing fast and loose with statutes. " The judges who were our predecessors have sometimes expounded the words quite contrary to the text, and sometimes have taken things by equity contrary to the text in order to make them agree with reason and equity ",[2] said Bromley, C.J., in 1554. Rules of construction which produced such striking results were clearly inadequate as an explanation of this situation, and so, when a general theoretical justification was needed, lawyers turned to the convenient word " equity ".

The " equity " of the chancellor and the " equity " of a statute have nothing in common; their nature is different, and their origins are different. The equity of the chancellor is a native growth (although, of course, some of its doctrines may have felt foreign influences); the equity of the statute, however, seems to be a continental notion imported to explain the situation which had grown up in England. Blackstone was looking in the right quarter when he sought a definition of equity in Grotius' remark that equity was " the correction of that wherein the law (by reason of its universality) is deficient ".[3] When the courts

[1] See the outline in Blackstone, *Commentaries*, i. 59–61, 85–91, and Kent, *Commentaries*, i. 454–468 (both reproduced in Pound and Plucknett, *Readings*, 40–42, 252–269). There is an elaborate discussion of interpretation by a divided court in Y.B. 4 Edward IV, Pasch. no. 4 and no. 19.

[2] *Fulmerston* v. *Steward* (1554), Plowd. 109.

[3] Blackstone, *Commentaries*, i. 61. See in general, Loyd, *The Equity of the Statute*, in Univ. Pennsylvania Law Review, lviii. 76; Thorne, *The Equity of a Statute*, Illinois Law Review, xxxi. 202–217, and Thorne, introduction to [Egerton], *Discourse on Statutes*.

therefore spoke of the equity of a statute they meant only that adjustment of detail which is necessary when applying a general rule to a specific case. Obviously it might sometimes amount to subordinate legislation by the courts, and such work had to be done by the courts if it was not done by the legislature or its deputy.

INADMISSIBILITY OF EXTERNAL EVIDENCE

At some time in the middle of the eighteenth century our courts came to the curious conclusion that a statute can only be construed in the light of strictly professional learning. It was permissible to consider what the law was before the statute, what " mischief " the statute was meant to remedy, and what the statute actually said; it was not permissible to refer to the debates in Parliament for light on what the statute meant, nor to the changes which were made in the original bill before it became an act.

The exclusion of parliamentary debates could have been justified, one would have thought, on the ground that there was no official reporting of those debates, and that the reports which did circulate were highly imaginative (as Dr Johnson, himself a reporter, confessed) and actually unlawful, for the House of Commons regarded them as breaches of privilege;[1] but this reason for the rule does not seem to have been put forward. The more formal history of amendments, changes in title, and the like, could be traced in the journals of the House, however, and those journals were accessible; but they too were inadmissible.[2] The rule appears first, it seems, in the long judgment of Willes, J., on the interpretation of the Copyright Act of 1709:

" The sense and meaning of an act of parliament must be collected from what it says when passed into a law, and not from the history of changes it underwent in the house where it took its rise. That history is not known to the other house, or to the sovereign."[3]

No authority is cited for this proposition, which rests solely on the reason which follows. As a statement of fact it seems questionable, for there was a great deal of discussion and agitation accompanying the act, and the Houses must have been aware of the views expressed. More interesting is the tacit denial that there is such a thing as the " intention of the legislature " on the ground that the King, Lords and Commons are independent of one another and so cannot have an intention. The rule was not strengthened by the fact that its author immediately abandoned it, and discussed at some length the change in the bill's title during its passage in the House of Commons.[4]

---

[1] Cf. the treatment of appeal cases in the House of Lords, above, pp. 202–203.

[2] Such material may be sometimes used now: see *Re C., an Infant*, [1937] All E.R. 783 at 787

[3] *Millar* v. *Taylor* (1769), 4 Burr. 2303 at 2332. Cf. Thorne, in Speculum, xi. 457.

[4] In *Entick* v. *Carrington* (1765) 19 S.T. 1030, Lord Camden used the Commons' Journals to elucidate the statute 16 Charles I, c. 10.

The most remarkable extension of the principle was that made by Chief Baron Pollock (again giving no reason) when he refused to admit the report of the real property commissioners as elucidating the legislation based upon it.[1] Here we have another aspect of the common law rules of statutory interpretation which is at variance with the practice of other systems, which regard *travaux préparatoires* as particularly valuable aids to interpretation. The principle has made interpretation a difficult and uncertain operation in our own system, and " may have very unfortunate repercussions " in the growing field of international co-operation in legal matters.[2] The interpretation of the codes in India raises the question in a very acute form and has led an eminent authority on that system to urge that—

> " the function of the court [in interpretation] is primarily not to expound legal principles but to consider the effect of evidence. The enquiry what was in the mind of the Mother of Parliaments when passing a particular statute does not differ generically from the enquiry what was in the mind of any other old lady when she made her last will and testament," [3]

and to make the attractive speculation that the English rule has some connection with the Whigs' mysticism of Parliament.

STATUTES AND FUNDAMENTAL LAW

One more question remains for consideration. From time to time the theory has been propounded that a statute might actually be invalid because it contravened some fundamental principle or law. It has indeed been suggested that this was, in fact, mediaeval theory and practice.[4] This position, however, becomes difficult to maintain after a detailed examination of the authorities. Of course, there is no doubt that the mediaeval mind would never think of postulating the absolute sovereignty of Parliament or State. The whole scheme of things in the middle ages was based upon the assumption that municipal law derived its force from divine law; but we do not find in mediaeval English cases any decisions which clearly hold that a statute is void because it contravenes some fundamental principle. On the contrary, the Year Books constantly assert in express terms that statutes were making new law and abrogating old law, and their consciousness of the fact of radical legislation is therefore apparent. A similar claim has

---

[1] *Salkeld* v. *Johnson* (1848), 2 Exch. 256 at 273. Cf. the useful note on this point in Law Quarterly Review, lv. 488–490.

[2] Gutteridge (*supra*, p. 330 n. 3), 20; cf. H. A. Smith, *Interpretation in English and Continental Law*, J. Soc. Comparative Legislation (1927), 153.

[3] S. Vesey-FitzGerald, *The Interpretation of Codes in British India*, Madras Law Journal, lxviii. 67 at 69.

[4] McIlwain, *High Court of Parliament* (1910); McIlwain, *Magna Carta and Common Law* (Magna Carta Commemoration Essays); McIlwain, *American Revolution* (1924). For criticisms see Plucknett, *Statutes and Their Interpretation*, 26–31; Plucknett, *Bonham's Case and Judicial Review* (Harvard Law Review, xl. 30–70); Holdsworth, *Sources and Literature*, 41–43; Allen, *Law in the Making*, 250–257; Thorne, *Bonham's Case* (Law Quarterly Review, liv. 543).

been made in favour of *Magna Carta*, but here again it is clear that *Magna Carta* itself has been amended and in part repealed, even during the middle ages. A practical limitation upon the legislature was of course the competing jurisdiction of the Church, and it was universally admitted during the middle ages that an act of Parliament could not operate within the sphere of the Church—a restriction in every way analogous to the inability of Parliament to legislate for a foreign country, for Church and State were two independent sovereign powers, each supreme within its own sphere, in just the same way as two nations exercise sovereignty within their respective frontiers.

It is in the early seventeenth century that the idea of a fundamental law begins to appear for the first time as a practical principle in the law courts under the influence of Coke. As we have already remarked,[1] he hoped to subject both Crown and Parliament to a paramount common law, and for a time we find some decisions[2] which accept this theory. In the eighteenth century, however, the principle was slowly abandoned— not so much because the mediaeval authority for it adduced by Coke is unconvincing as because subsequent events had proved that there were no legal limitations upon the powers of Parliament. The establishment of the Reformation settlement and of new forms of religion, changes in the succession to the Crown, and extremely radical legislation (much of it in the reign of Henry VIII), finally convinced lawyers, in their own picturesque phrase, that Parliament could do anything except make a man a woman.[3] The last great judge to accept the principle wholeheartedly was Holt, who regarded it as part of a judge's daily work to " construe and expound acts of Parliament, and adjudge them to be void ".[4] If the theory disappeared in England[5] it bore fruit elsewhere, and the close attention with which Coke's writings were read in America had something to do with preparing the way for the system of judicial review as it exists in that country.

THE NON-OBSERVANCE OF STATUTES

On the continent there was some speculation during the middle ages as to whether a law could become inoperative through long-continued desuetude. In England, however, the idea of prescription and the acquisition or loss of rights merely by the lapse of a particular

[1] Above, p. 51.

[2] *Bonham's Case* (1610), 8 Rep. 118; *City of London* v. *Wood* (1701), 12 Mod. 669 (both in Pound and Plucknett, *Readings*, 33, 34). Some new material has been collected by C. F. Mullett, *Fundamental Law and the American Constitution* (1933), and for a critical examination of the whole question, see now J. W. Gough, *Fundamental Law in English Constitutional History* (1955).

[3] It was easier to make a woman a man: 1 Mary, sess. 3, c. 1, s. 3.

[4] *R.* v. *Earl of Banbury* (1695), Skin. 517, 527.

[5] The later stages of the doctrine can be seen in *Day* v. *Savadge* (1614), Hob. 85; *City of London* v. *Wood* (1701), 12 Mod. 669; *Duchess of Hamilton's Case* (1712), 10 Mod. 115; *Lee* v. *Bude & Torrington Junction Ry.* (1871), L.R., 6 C.P. 576.

length of time found little favour. Moreover, statutes were definitely pronouncements of the Crown, and the royal prerogative included the maxim that "time does not run against the King". There was consequently no room for any theory that statutes might become obsolete.[1]

We did have a theory, however, which was much more curious, and which permitted a great deal of discretion to the judiciary in the enforcement of statutes. According to this view, a court was not bound to apply a statute if it could be shown that the statute had never been enforced. If this is strictly construed as a legal principle, it is difficult to escape the conclusion that the judiciary had a veto upon acts of Parliament. It seems likely that by this means the courts regained with one hand the power they lost with the other in abandoning the rule in *Bonham's Case*. Nor must it be supposed that we are dealing with an isolated vagary of judicial speculation. On the contrary, there is a long line of examples of its use extending over a period of more than five centuries, although there was certainly no attempt made to explore the theoretical implications or the principle.

As early as 1287 we find the first example, in a case in the county court of Chester.[2] The demandant in this case brought a writ founded on the Statute of Gloucester (1278), but the tenant pleaded that no such writ had ever before issued from the Chancery. The demandant then put himself on the statute: "the lord King in his statutes issued at Gloucester established that an action by a writ of entry was available for the heir of the woman in the case proposed". To this the tenant rejoined "that although the statute is as the tenant has alleged, nevertheless no such writ of entry has so far issued out of the chancery, and so he prays judgment". The court agreed, and quashed the writ.

In 1345 when a defendant pleaded a statute, Thorpe, J., observed that "some people noid that statute to be of no value as against the King, for it was never put into operation". Scot, C.J., agreed and told the defendant to say something else.[3] The point was raised again in 1409 in a case on the Statute of Provisors of 1351, but seems not to have been argued.[4] It is almost certainly the existence of this rule which prompted litigants who wished to rely on a very recent statute to get a special writ from the Crown directed to the judges, which ordered them to apply the statute, the text of which was annexed. Such a writ, and the text of the statute, would be embodied in the pleadings of the case on

---

[1] [Egerton] *Discourse upon Statutes* (ed. Thorne), 165–166, refuses to admit that a statute can become obsolete, but has to confess that it may be " enfeebled " by passage of time. The statute 1 Henry V, c. 1, gave great difficulty in the seventeenth and eighteenth centuries when it was never observed; see the curious arguments in R. H. Peckwell, *Reports of Elections*, I. i. 53 ff. (Owing to the privilege of the House, the law courts were not confronted with this particular puzzle.)

[2] *Chester County Court Rolls*, ed. R. Stewart-Brown (Chetham Society), 75–76.

[3] *R.* v. *Bishop of Lincoln* (1345), Y.B. 19 Edward III (Rolls Series), 170.

[4] *R.* v. *Bishop of St. Davids* (1409), Y.B. 11 Henry IV, ff. 7, 39 b. In 1464 the matter was put in doubt: Y.B. 4 Edward IV, Pasch. 4.

the roll.[1] The notion reappears late in the fifteenth century in the honoured pages of Littleton and concerns no less a statute than *Magna Carta* itself, and the Statute of Merton, c. 6, which re-enacted it. " It seems to some," says Littleton, " that no action can be brought upon this statute, for it has never been seen or heard that any action has been brought." Coke had obvious difficulty in glossing this passage:

" Hereby it appeareth how safe it is to be guided by judicial precedents. . . . And as usage is a good interpreter of the laws, so non-usage (where there is no example) is a great intendment that the law will not bear it. . . . Not that an act of Parliament by non-user can be antiquated or lose his force, but that it may be expounded or declared how the act is to be understood."[2]

If Littleton's words seem to imply that he personally doubts the rule, Coke's gloss clearly shows how difficult it was to defend it. In 1712 an act which had been passed only seven years before was set aside on the grounds of continuous non-user.[3] Nearly a century after Coke the principle was swept aside by Lord Holt, who declared in general terms that if statute gives a right, the common law will give a remedy.[4] Another liberal judge, Pratt, C.J., when the old principle was urged upon him,[5] declared that he hoped he would never hear such an objection again, after *Ashby* v. *White*.

That ought to have been the end of the matter, but even emphatic declarations by two great chief justices were unavailing, and we still find statutes being nullified on the ground that they had never been enforced. A statute of 1702 had been flatly disobeyed ever since it was enacted, and so Kenyon, C.J., dared not upset the settled law in 1795.[6] A few years earlier a statute of James I met the same fate at his hands;[7] this time Buller and Grose, JJ., concurred with him in explaining that this did not mean that a statute could be repealed by non-user! It is clear that the courts adopted this principle to frustrate legislation which they considered undesirable. It is particularly interesting to see Park, J., in another case taking refuge in the rule in order to nullify a statute which enabled a party to be examined on oath. This was " repugnant to common right " within the rule in *Bonham's Case*, which he quoted at length. Coke's doctrine of fundamental common law was too heroic by now (the date was 1823), so he based his decision on a line of cases which had ignored the act.[8]

---

[1] For such a case, see Y.B. 13 Richard II (ed. Plucknett), 161 (1390).

[2] Littleton, s. 108; Co. Litt. 81 b; cf. Glanville, J., in *Corbet's Case* (1600), 1 Rep. 88, and Choke, J., on the statute 15 Hen. VI, c. 3, in *R.* v. *London* (1465), Long Quinto, ff. 33–34.

[3] *R.* v. *Bailiffs and Burgesses of Bewdley* (1712), 1 Peere Wms. 207 at 223 *per* Parker, C.J.

[4] *Ashby* v. *White* (1703), 2 Ld. Raym. 938 at 944, 946, 957.

[5] *Chapman* v. *Pickersgill* (1762), 2 Wilson 146.

[6] *R.* v. *Inhabitants of Cumberland* (1795), 6 Term Rep. 194, 195, 197.

[7] *Leigh* v. *Kent* (1789), 3 Term Rep. 362.

[8] *Stewart* v. *Lawton* (1823), 1 Bing. 374.

INTERPRETATION, PAST AND PRESENT

These cases must not be regarded as curiosities, and in studying them we have not left the highway of history to explore a mere by-path. Legislation is such an important factor in legal development that its rise and progress and the development of the attitude of the courts towards it, must receive careful attention in any discussion of the common law system. There is, moreover, the additional interest provided by the fact that the common law has developed a different theory and a different technique of handling statutes from that prevailing in other systems. A glance at the long lines of statutes extending through seven centuries and numerous volumes is apt to obscure the differences between the present attitude and that of other periods. The interpretation of statutes has passed through several stages, and it is not without interest to compare its history with that of the interpretation of deeds. Written deeds, like written statutes, were not essential in our earlier history. The King could legislate, and the subject could enfeoff, without parchment, ink or wax. Even when a written text was drawn up, it was merely evidence, and by no means the best evidence, of what had been done. We therefore find that the wording of a statute is not at first taken very seriously. Copies used by the profession were only approximately accurate; even government departments and the courts were no better off; the recording of statutes in the national archives was by no means regular.

Interpretation in this early period could not be precise. There was no sacrosanct text, but only a traditional one whose meaning was restricted to a general policy, details being left to be filled in as required by the legislator, or by the council, or the courts. So too with deeds. It was possible to say that the actual transaction took place at the livery of seisin—an oral proceeding—and if the deed contradicted the words used in the livery, then the livery prevailed.

As government and law develop, they become mechanised. Print and paper form a vast machine for the government of the nation. In the search for precision, oral livery of seisin, and oral or informal legislation, have to be abandoned, and deeds and statutes are treated with more respect. It is important to realise how long this process took in the case of statutes. The courts professed at times to have a great respect for the letter of the statutes and invented a maze of rules for their construction on grammatical lines. But they did not surrender their will absolutely to the legislator. There were limits, they asserted, sometimes defiantly, but later in veiled language. Until little more than a hundred years ago the courts were able, overtly or covertly, to exercise considerable discretion in dealing with statutes, and it is only in the last two or three generations that they have accepted the theory of their absolute submission to the word and the letter of the legislature. It may be doubted, however, whether the acceptance of the principle of literal interpretation brings us nearer to the enforcement of the intention of the legislature. The courts are excluded from using evidence which any historian or scientific investigator would regard as highly valuable, especially in the modern age when statutes introduce changes of social policy, and not merely of technical procedure.[1]

[1] Some recent work on the subject is reviewed in Plucknett, *L'Interprétation des lois*, in *Introduction à l'étude du droit comparé, Recueil Lambert*, i. 434–449. The more recent history of the notion is well worked out in the later chapters of J. W. Gough, *Fundamental Law* (Oxford, 1955).

THE PRINCIPLE OF PRECEDENT

The common law in its ultimate origin was merely the custom of the King's courts; the regular routine which they developed in the administration of justice became settled and known, and therefore served as the basis upon which people could forecast with some certainty the future decisions of the courts. The growth of such a custom depends to some extent upon the habit of following precedents, although it is more than likely that this development took place quite unconsciously. From earliest times, therefore, the royal courts have always had some sort of regard for previous decisions, although at first, no doubt, this was based upon a desire to save trouble. There was no need to consider a question *de novo* if it had recently been decided; and the whole principle underlying the Court of Common Pleas, which, as we have seen, was a court of limited and delegated jurisdiction, must have encouraged it to develop a routine in handling its business. This does not mean that there was anything in the twelfth century even faintly resembling the modern principle of precedent; there was merely a tendency to establish a procedure, and perhaps to adopt a few substantive principles which, taken together, constituted the custom of the court.

BRACTON'S USE OF PLEA ROLLS

The Court of Common Pleas was about eighty years old when Bracton was engaged upon his treatise, and as every historian has observed, that treatise is distinguished by its extensive use of cases. Some consideration must therefore be given to the use which Bracton made of the material which he collected in his famous *Note Book*. The very first page of Bracton's treatise throws remarkable light upon his point of view. He asserts that the present bench is much inferior to its predecessors; foolish and ignorant judges, who have mounted the judgment-seat before they have learnt the law, have corrupted its doctrine; they decide cases by fancy rather than by rule. And so Bracton, using words which would sound presumptuous in any lesser man, announces his intention of instructing the younger generation in the principles of the law by writing this treatise, which he solemnly commends to perpetual memory. Bracton's book, therefore, is an attempt to bring back the law to its ancient principles, and the attempt is made by one whose official position was no doubt impressive, but who was still more conscious of his own intellectual powers and of his mission in restoring the law. In this same sentence he tells us that he looks largely to the decisions of a previous generation of upright judges together with their private opinions—and the two thick volumes of his *Note Book* justify his claim that he collected them diligently and laboriously. His intention, therefore, is to use cases. But it must be observed that whatever use he made of these cases was necessarily peculiar to himself. He alone of all the lawyers in England sought and obtained access to the plea rolls; he used the originals, and there were no copies until he made one for his own convenience, containing the cases which he selected.[1] None of his contemporaries attempted such a thing. Bracton clearly was the only lawyer of his day who chose to exert a good deal of court influence in order to obtain the loan of numerous plea rolls, and who was ready to devote immense pains and labour in searching hundredweights of manuscript and having his discoveries copied in a very substantial volume. Clearly, then, we have no right to assume that Bracton's use of case law was any part of contemporary legal thought. On the contrary, it is clear that he was undertaking research into the present and former condition of the law by a novel method which he had devised, namely, the search of plea rolls, which was a new discovery in his day. Any use of cases on Bracton's lines by the profession at large, or even by the bench alone, would have been manifestly impossible. The plea rolls are immense in number and there was and still is no guide to their contents; they have to be read straight through from beginning to end without any assistance from indexes or head-notes.

BRACTON'S USE OF CASES

Bracton, therefore, had discovered a new instrument of research, and owing to his fortunate official position he was enabled to use it. If we examine the use which he actually made of the cases he discovered, it will be clear at once that he was not actuated by any of the modern ideas of case law. Many of the cases he uses are quite old, and he admits that many of them are not law to-day. But the whole of his argument is that his contemporaries have perverted the law, and that the recent cases are bad ones, while the old cases were good—intrinsically

---

[1] It was edited and printed as *Bracton's Note Book*, ed. Maitland, 1887. Above, p. 260. (See *Casus et Judicia* (printed in *Casus Placitorum*, ed. Dunham, Selden Society. vol. 69) for an attempt to abstract plea-roll cases).

good, that is to say, as embodying sound principle. In other words, Bracton has no hesitation in using cases which we should call out of date or overruled, in order to maintain that the law ought to be something different from what it is. From this it is clear that the whole of Bracton's position would fall if decisions, as such, were in any modern sense a source of law. Under any such theory if decisions were authoritative a choice would have to be made between contradictory decisions, and so a theory of case law would have to be devised. It is the very absence of such a theory which enabled Bracton to carry out his plan, and that plan seems to have been to state in logical order a series of legal propositions, and then to illustrate their working from cases. Bracton first states his principles and then adduces his cases as historical evidence of the accuracy of his statements. This is a vastly different method from taking the cases first and deducing rules of law from them. Bracton's whole purpose is to reconstruct, and, if possible, to revive the law of nearly a generation ago; he would put the clock back and restore the court's custom as it used to be in its best period, and it is as evidence of that custom that he uses his cases. In Bracton's hands a case may illustrate a legal principle, and the enrolment may be historical proof that that principle was once applied, but the case is not in itself a source of law.[1]

BRACTON'S INFLUENCE ON CASE LAW

This does not mean that Bracton's novel method of studying law was without effect; we have already suggested that his use of cases may have interested his contemporaries and the succeeding generation, and it may be that it prompted other lawyers to collect records of cases when they had the opportunity.[2] Indirectly, therefore, Bracton's influence may have something to do with the rise of the Year Books. The plea rolls of Edward I show that litigants would cite older cases.[3] Access to the plea rolls was still almost impossible to obtain, and so, instead, reports were circulated of discussions in court as the next best thing—and with the growth of scientific pleading these reports were superior for practical purposes to the plain transcript of the record which Bracton used, for the reports give the discussions and the reasons for the matters which appeared upon the record. Of the Year Books we have already spoken; they cover several centuries and copies are fairly numerous; but were they used for the same purposes as a modern law report? There seems no doubt that they were not. There are quite frequent cases in the Year Books where we find judges or counsel mentioning previous decisions. They seem generally to quote from memory;

---

[1] T. E. Lewis, *History of Judicial Precedent*, Law Quarterly Review, xlvi. 212, suggests that it was.

[2] Above, pp. 260–261.

[3] Sayles, *King's Bench*, ii, cviii, iii, xxx.

sometimes they give us the names of the parties, but not always. Occasionally such a citation is answered by a denial that the situation is the same; more rarely it will be retorted that the case cited is bad law; a little more frequently the court will indicate that whatever the older case may say, the court does not intend to apply that principle.[1] In short, the citation of a case in point may perhaps be persuasive enough for counsel to think it worth while, but it is certainly not in the least degree binding.

THE YEAR BOOKS AND PRECEDENT

And yet, on the other hand, when a novel or important point is raised, the court is fully conscious that its decisions may start a stream of other decisions in a particular direction. In 1274 there was a remarkable test case between the Queen of Germany and the Earl of Cornwall on the law of dower in which the queen spoke " for the common benefit of other ladies seeking dower in the future "[2] and a generation later, in an early Year Book we find counsel reminding the bench " that the judgment to be given by you will be hereafter an authority in every *quare non admisit* in England ",[3] but, as Professor Winfield remarks,—

" this contention does not go beyond insisting that the judges are expected to keep the law unchanged *in pari materia*. It falls very far short of arguing that in later cases on writs of *quare non admisit* this case will be cited to them and that they will have to follow it."[4]

This is clearly in accord with the opinion of the best legal theory of the Middle Ages; in 1315 Bereford, C. J., quoted from Bracton the well-known adage that *non exemplis, set racionibus adjudicandum est*.[5]

Still, it would be rash to say that there was no conscious judicial legislation in the Year Book period; in 1305 Hengham ordered a party to use a particular procedure, adding " and consider this henceforth as a general rule ".[6] In 1310 Chief Justice Bereford observed that " by a decision on this avowry we shall make a law throughout all the land ".[7] He certainly did not mean that the Year Book report of this case would be quoted as authoritative in later cases, for we are still clearly in the

---

[1] Numerous examples will be found in Winfield, *Chief Sources*, 149–152; Allen, *Law in the Making*, 126–136; and T. E. Lewis, *History of Judicial Precedent*, Law Quarterly Review, xlvi. 207, 341, xlvii. 411, xlviii. 230. It is not always easy to distinguish citations in the report from subsequent annotations by later readers which have by now become part of the text—or even may have corrupted the text: cf. Y.BB. Edward II (Selden Society), xxiv. lxxxiii ff.

[2] *Casus Placitorum* (Selden Society), 61.

[3] Y.B. 32 & 33 Edward I (Rolls Series), 32.

[4] Winfield, *Chief Sources*, 149.

[5] Y.BB. Edward II (Selden Society), xvii. 118; the maxim comes from Cod. 7.45.13.

[6] Y.B. 33 & 35 Edward I (Rolls Series), 6. Note that five years later Bereford adjudged the contrary of Hengham's " general rule ": Y.BB. Edward II (Selden Society), iii. 91–92.

[7] Y.BB. Edward II (Selden Society), iv. 161. (For the history of which this case was a part, see Plucknett, *Legislation of Edward I*, 63 ff.) These examples suggest a comparison with the *Attiremens et Jugiés d'Eschequiers*, ed. Génestal and Tardif (Caen, 1921) of Normandy.

period when the common law was primarily the custom of the King's Court; the decision of an important point after due deliberation added one more element to the mass of custom which the King's Court applied—and, as we have already seen, the remarkable feature about custom was the ease with which it grew up and the facility with which it could be changed. Even such striking words as those we have just quoted cannot be properly interpreted as evidence of the existence of a system of case law. Even in the later Year Books down to the fifteenth century the same observation holds true; the Year Books themselves (of which there were a goodly number by this time) were not regarded as collections of authoritative or binding decisions. The nearest resemblance to such a notion is to be found in some remarkable words of Chief Justice Prisot in 1454. In spite of three large folios of discussion Prisot maintained that the matter was clear:

> " If we have to pay attention to the opinions of one or two judges which are contradictory to many other judgments by many honourable judges in the opposite sense, it would be a strange situation, considering that those judges who adjudged the matter in ancient times were nearer to the making of the statute than we are, and had more knowledge of it. . . . And moreover if this plea were now adjudged bad, as you maintain, it would assuredly be a bad example to the young apprentices who study the Year Books, for they would never have confidence in their books if now we were to adjudge the contrary of what has been so often adjudged in the books."[1]

Clearly there is the faint beginning of a more modern spirit in these words; the Chief Justice is seeking the contemporaneous exposition of the statute in question and maintains that there is a balance of authority in favour of his view. His objection to going against that authority is that it would be " strange "—a common expression in the Year Books for " inconsistent ". He would strike a balance between " some opinion of some judge or two " and many judgments by several honourable judges; but even then the result is not the discovery of an authentic binding precedent.[2] The thought of a decision against such a weight of authority shocks him chiefly because it will confuse law students and shake their confidence in their books; which perhaps is another way of saying that even a mere student in reading the case would detect its inconsistency with established principle, and would perhaps hardly credit what he read. This is possibly the meaning of some other passages in the Year Books where the court finds it salutary to look at a proposition from the point of view of the law student; Bereford explained his decisions " for the sake of the young men who are present ", and down to the eighteenth century judges in court would bear in mind the fact that a judgment might be expanded into a lecture for the law students who were present.[3] Clearly, students studied their law in court and also in

[1] Y.B. 33 Henry VI, Michs. 17, fo. 41.

[2] It resembles much more closely the weighing of authorities in Roman and canon law.

[3] " Lord Mansfield delivered the opinion of the court, having first desired Mr Hussey to state the case for the sake of the students " (R. v. *Peters* (1758), 1 Burr. 568).

the Year Books, and as late as 1454 an awkward decision in the Year Books will be criticised (as we have seen) because it is confusing to students. But the most significant part of Prisot's remarks lies in the fact that he regards even the decisions of many honourable judges as only persuasive; neither he nor the other lawyers who argued the case regarded themselves as bound by any of the decisions mentioned.[1]

CUSTOM AND PRECEDENT DISTINGUISHED

An important point to remember is that one case constitutes a precedent; several cases serve as evidence of a custom. In the Year Book period cases are used only as evidence of the existence of a custom of the court. It is the custom which governs the decision, not the case or cases cited as proof of the custom. Nor does it appear that a court would follow a case where it felt the result would be mischievous. The distinction is clearly seen when mediaeval practice is contrasted with that of our own day; at the present time it is possible for a judge to explain that his decision works substantial injustice, and is questionable on principle, but he is bound by a particular case. This is a typical example of the working of the principle of precedent. Such things are not to be found in the Year Books, however. A single case was not a binding authority, but a well-established custom (proved by a more or less casual citing of cases) was undoubtedly regarded as strongly persuasive.

EXCHEQUER CHAMBER CASES

We have already mentioned the constitution of the court of discussion which was held in the Exchequer Chamber.[2] Decisions given by this imposing array of judges enjoyed exceptional prestige. In the popular speech of the sixteenth century a " chequer chamber case " means any difficult matter which needs mature deliberation and authoritative decision.[3] The judges themselves shared this respect for the decisions reached by all the benches assembled. A striking example of this is an incident in 1483 when the chamber reached a decision on a case originating in the court of common pleas by a majority. When the chief justice of the common pleas gave judgment, he explained that he disagreed with the decision of the chamber, but was bound to adopt the view of the majority.[4]

This, no doubt, was merely the application of the majority principle, but the extension of it to other situations was almost inevitable. If the decision of the chamber bound the judges who took part in it,

---

[1] On the citation of decisions in colonial America, see Joseph Henry Smith, *Appeals to the Privy Council from the American Plantations*, 464 n. 2.

[2] Above, p. 162.

[3] See the passages in Dr Hemmant's introduction to *Select Cases in Exchequer Chamber* (Selden Society, vol. 51), xiv, on which this paragraph is largely based. Cf. Y.B. 19 Edward III (Rolls Series), 140.

[4] Y.B. 1 Richard III, Michs. no. 2 (at the end).

there would soon follow the question whether it might not bind judges who were trying subsequent cases involving principles which the chamber had previously settled.

In the sixteenth century this actually took place, and in the seventeenth it was settled that a decision of the Exchequer Chamber was a binding precedent. Coke asserted that a resolution of all the judges was almost as high as a statute,[1] Bacon urged that even the chancellor would yield to the opinion of all the judges;[2] in 1602 a decision of the chamber was referred to as " the resolution of all the judges of England " which was " to be a precedent for all subsequent cases ",[3] and in 1686 Herbert, C.J., announced it as " a known rule that after any point of law has been solemnly settled in the Exchequer Chamber by all the judges, we never suffer it to be disputed or drawn in question again ".[4]

Here we find for the first time the principle that a single case may be a binding precedent, but such high authority attaches only to decisions of the Exchequer Chamber; it does not apply to decisions of either bench, nor to those of the House of Lords.

THE AGE OF THE REPORTERS

When we come to the sixteenth century we get a little nearer the modern point of view, although even such a reporter as Dyer thought it worth while to report what the judge said privately and what was said in mock trials in Lincoln's Inn.[5] If he uses the word " precedent " in 1557 (which Sir Carleton Allen thinks is the first occurrence of the word) it is merely to tell us that in spite of two " precedents " the court adjudged the contrary.[6] At about the same time there is a passage in Plowden wherein it is stated " that the records of every court are the most effectual proofs of the law in relation to the things treated of in the same court ";[7] but the examples which he gives are all matters of criminal law, and it is well known that the Crown frequently had its records searched where royal interests were involved—as they were in matters of treason and felony. There is no indication that in Plowden's day anyone save a Crown lawyer would usually be allowed to search Plea Rolls for precedents.

As for cases (apart from records) the continuance of the mediaeval attitude is clearly shown by the remark of Wray, C.J., and Gawdy, J., in 1587: " as he who is a bastard born hath no cousin, so every case imports suspicion of its legitimation, unless it has another case which shall be as a cousin-german, to support and prove it ".[8] It is when we

---

[1] 2 Inst. 618, *Articuli Cleri.*

[2] Argument in *Calvin's Case* (1608), *Works* (ed. Spedding), vii. 642.

[3] *Slade* v. *Morley* (1602), Yelv. 21.

[4] *Godden* v. *Hales* (1686), 11 S.T. 1254.

[5] 1 Dyer, 14, 111.

[6] *Anon.*, Dyer, 148 b.

[7] *The Case of Mines*, Plowd. 310, at 320 (1567).

[8] *Walker's Case* (1587), 3 Rep. 23.

come to the time of Coke that we find the citation of precedents particularly common, and the theme of his discourse is still that " two or three precedents " cannot prevail against a long *catena* of older authority.[1]

After the Restoration we find a few rules judicially laid down to govern their use. In 1670 Chief Justice Vaughan distinguished *dicta* from those parts of the judgment which form an integral part of it, although he admits that if a judge believes a previous case in another court to be erroneous he is not bound to follow it.[2] A hundred years later Blackstone was not able to add very much to this.[3] A considerable amount of material from the reporters during this period has been collected, and seems to indicate that although more attention was given to cases, yet the fundamental attitude towards them had not changed. Printing and the later abridgments obviously made it possible to assemble a large number of citations, and so an increase in the number of cases cited is easily explained. Their very number is significant: under a developed system of precedents one case is as good as a dozen if it clearly covers the point, and at the present day citations are consequently few and to the point. The eighteenth century, however, still seems tempted to find safety in numbers, and to regard the function of citations to be merely that of proving a settled policy or practice.

As Sir William Holdsworth has pointed out,[4] there were circumstances under which the courts considered themselves free from any obligation to follow precedents. If following them would lead to " inconvenient " results, then it was arguable that the precedents did not represent the true state of the law—a specious argument typical of Coke's mentality. Another possibility was to blame the reporter for cases one did not like (a device often used by Mansfield, who loved to contrast principle with precedent[5]), while the fact that there were then several common law courts with concurrent jurisdiction enabled some picking and choosing to take place, it being recognised that the decisions of one of these courts did not bind the others.

The growth of precedent in chancery is remarkable for the speed with which it supplanted the original basis of equity. Conscience, *ratio*, was yielding to cases, *exempla*, already in the seventeenth century, possibly because chancery was very sensitive to the taunts of common lawyers. The use of cases in chancery therefore resembled closely the practice of the common law courts.[6]

THE ESTABLISHMENT OF THE STRICT THEORY

While these reservations were possible, the modern strict theory

---

[1] *Slade's Case* (1596), 4 Rep. 91, contains Coke's views on the use of cases. For a criticism of the principle in 1649 see Holdsworth, vi. 414.

[2] *Bole* v. *Horton* (1670), Vaughan, 360, 382; cf. *Edgecomb* v. *Dee* (1670), Vaughan, 89 at 93.

[3] Bl. Commentaries, i. 69–72.

[4] Holdsworth, *Case Law*, Law Quarterly Review, l. 180–195, reprinted in his *Essays in Legal History*, 147.

[5] Fifoot, *Lord Mansfield*, 198–229.

[6] See W. H. D. Winder, *Precedent in Equity*, Law Quarterly Review, lvii. 245.

could not be established. It is to the nineteenth century that we must look for the final stages in the erection of the present system.[1] We have already noticed how little attention was paid to decisions in the House of Lords.[2] That tribunal began to take a prominent part in the elaboration of private law when it undertook to upset the reforming efforts of Lord Mansfield, and it may be suspected that the overruling of some of his most famous judgments did much to attract the attention of legal conservatives to the House.[3] But even as late as the days of Baron Parke, less than a hundred years ago, it was possible for that very learned judge to ignore decisions of the House of Lords;[4] while Exchequer and Queen's Bench held different views on the same point as late as 1842.[5]

The nineteenth century produced the changes which were necessary for the establishment of the rigid and symmetrical theory as it exists to-day. The exclusion of lay lords from judicial functions in the House of Lords, together with the addition of professional lords of appeal in ordinary, left that house a much stronger body than ever before. The organisation of one court of appeal instead of many had a similar result in the middle rank of the hierarchy,[6] while the unification of the high court cleared away the possibilities of choice which existed as long as there were uncoordinated courts of King's Bench, Common Pleas and Exchequer. Even law reporting is now standardised and semi-official.

Nowhere is the difference between the eighteenth century and the nineteenth century attitude more clearly seen than in the treatment of custom. We have already insisted on the flexibility of a living custom, and when Lord Mansfield incorporated the custom of merchants into the common law, it was a living flexible custom, responding to the growth and change of mercantile habits. It is so still, but if perchance a court has given a decision on a point of that custom, it loses for ever its flexibility and is fixed by the rule of precedent at the point where the court touched it.[7] The custom of the court itself now undergoes the same sort of change, and the custom of the common law is in some danger of losing its old adaptability. If judicial decision is a source of law, it would not be inappropriate to describe it in this connection as a *source pétrifiante*.

---

[1] Goodhart, *Case Law*, Law Quarterly Review, l. 196–200; *contra*, Holdsworth, xii. 146, Law Quarterly Review, l. 180, and *Essays in Legal History*, 147.

[2] Above, p. 220; cf. below, p. 591 n. 2.

[3] Thus the House of Lords in *Rann* v. *Hughes* (1778), 4 Bro. P.C. 27; 7 Term Rep. 350, overruled Mansfield's view of consideration expressed in *Pillans* v. *Van Mierop* (1765), 3 Burr. 1663.

[4] Lord Hanworth, *Life of Chief Baron Pollock*, 198.

[5] When the Queen's Bench in *Fuller* v. *Wilson*, 3 Q.B. 58, differed from the Exchequer of Pleas in *Cornfoot* v. *Fowke* (1840), 6 M. & W. 358, on the fundamental nature of deceit.

[6] It is still possible for the court of appeal to differ from the court of criminal appeal. See Jenks, *Short History of English Law* (1934), 419, 420.

[7] Cf. Lord Chorley, *Conflict of Law and Commerce*, Law Quarterly Review, xlviii. 51 at 63.

BOOK TWO

SPECIAL PART

PART 1

PROCEDURE

SUMMARY

CHAPTER 1

THE FORMS OF ACTION

The forms of action are in themselves a proof that the King's Court
only intended to intervene occasionally in the disputes of his subjects.
It was no doubt possible to argue with perfect justice that the country
was well provided with competent courts for all ordinary purposes,
and that the King's Court was only concerned with matters of state
and matters of special difficulty which could not be otherwise determined. A few classes of cases with which the King's Court concerned
itself were therefore most naturally treated along formulary lines. They
constituted one or two of the several routines of government which the
administration had developed, and in order to handle them more easily
it was a simple device to standardise the forms which were used. As
long as this condition of things lasted a formulary procedure was clearly

an advantage, and for a while it may have limited the activities of the administration and prevented them from overstepping the proper boundaries of their jurisdiction.

THE RELATION OF WRIT AND REMEDY

Whenever it became necessary to enlarge the scope of the King's Court, the change could be effected simply by the invention of a new set of forms, and so the early development of the jurisdiction of the King's Court very closely resembles the enlargement of the sphere of an administrative body by means of the invention of new administrative routines. Once the habit was formed, future development for a long time seemed simple. Glanvill had described a royal court which had very little interest in enlarging its jurisdiction beyond certain matters. Two generations later Bracton described this same court and shows us how greatly it had elaborated its machinery; indeed, Bracton was even ready to contemplate an indefinite expansion of the common law in virtue of which the King's Court was to administer a law as rich in its variety and as wide in its extent as the Roman law itself. The means whereby such a prodigious expansion was to be effected (and indeed had already been begun) was the invention of new forms of action; many new forms were invented by Bracton's hero Raleigh, and Bracton had no hesitation in saying that there will be as many forms of action as there are causes of action. " There ought to be a remedy for every wrong; if some new wrong be perpetrated then a new writ may be invented to meet it."[1] This was a bold programme. It contemplated special sets of forms through which the King's Court would exercise general jurisdiction and afford a remedy for every wrong. One would expect that so ambitious a scheme would emanate from some great monarch such as Henry II, and in truth he may have taken the first steps in that direction; but it was under the comparatively weak rule of Henry III that the greatest progress was made—and here we have a striking example of the way in which organisations such as the King's Court and Council could do effective and even constructive work although their nominal head was undistinguished. The secret seems to lie in a little group of lawyers whom we can only see, at this distance of time, in the appreciative pages of Bracton. As Maitland has observed, this formulary system is distinctively English,—

" but it is also, in a certain sense, very Roman. While the other nations of Western Europe were beginning to adopt as their own the ultimate results of Roman legal history, England was unconsciously reproducing that history; it was developing a formulary system which in the ages that were coming would be the strongest bulwark against Romanism and sever our English law from all her sisters."[2]

[1] Bracton, f. 413 b.

[2] Pollock and Maitland, ii. 558; at first the system was not exclusively English, for it also existed in Normandy.

THE BEGINNINGS OF ROYAL INTERVENTION

It was, of course, civil business—common pleas—which was most susceptible of this treatment; pleas of the Crown, which at this time were mainly criminal, had already been provided with a different machinery necessarily based upon the system of local government. Of these civil pleas, then, those which first received the attention of the King's Court were pleas of land. Reasons of state demanded that the Crown through its court should have a firm control of the land; the common law, therefore, was first the law of land before it could become the law of *the* land. But here, too, it was possible to argue that the existing local jurisdictions, communal and seignorial, were numerous enough and competent enough to administer real property law. In a sense this was true. Each landowner could litigate concerning his land in the court of his feudal lord; if, as often happened, it was part of the dispute who was the feudal lord (such as when A claims to hold a piece of land of X while his adversary B claims to hold it of Y), then recourse was had to the lord who had feudal jurisdiction over both X and Y, and in this way such litigation would very likely come before the court of the King himself. Again, it may be that there were practical difficulties; the feudal court may be weak or partial, and then, too, recourse will be had to a higher court. Frequently it seems that a writ from the King will facilitate matters in seignorial courts, and the Crown at an early date would issue sharp admonitions commanding feudal lords to do immediate justice or else to explain their action in the King's Court. Such intervention was at first of a political or administrative character. The King used his influence, sometimes in the form of a threat, to set his vassal's judicial machinery in motion. For this there was Anglo-Saxon precedent,[1] and the early Anglo-Norman writ is undoubtedly continuous with the Anglo-Saxon writ (and here it must be remembered that the word " writ ", in Latin *breve*, means nothing more than a formal letter of a business character; it does no necessarily imply either a court or court procedure).[2]

THE NATURE OF THE EARLIEST WRITS

Some of the earliest of our writs, therefore, are not, strictly speaking, documents directly instituting litigation. They are in form administrative commands to an alleged wrongdoer or to some inferior jurisdiction to do justice in a particular matter in such wise that the King shall no more hear complaints concerning it; disobedience of this writ will be punished in the King's Court unless a satisfactory explanation can be given. A writ of right, for example, may be in various forms. It may command the feudal lord of two contestants to do justice between them;[3]

---

[1] W. H. Stevenson, *Yorkshire Surveys*, English Historical Review, xxvii. 4.

[2] See now the important work of Miss F. E. Harmer, *Anglo-Saxon Writs*.

[3] This is the writ of right *de recto*.

but the Crown deliberately encroached upon seignorial jurisdiction when it devised a new variant which is called the writ of right *praecipe quod reddat*, which soon became the most usual form. This writ completely ignores the feudal lord and is directed to the sheriff of the county where the land lies; he is instructed to command the defendant to render to the plaintiff the land which he claims, justly and without delay, and if he fails to do so the sheriff is to summon him before the King or his justices to show cause, and the sheriff is to return the original writ together with the names of the summoners who witnessed its service. By the time we get to this form it is clear that we have only a slight disguise for a writ virtually initiating litigation in the King's Court in complete disregard of the lawful rights—property rights as they then were—of the feudal lords. The writ of right *praecipe quod reddat*, therefore, has its beginning in somewhat discreditable circumstances; the Crown, by these writs, deprived feudal lords of their rightful jurisdiction.[1] Thus it was that the insurgent barons extorted from King John a promise in the Great Charter[2] that henceforward the writ called *praecipe* should not issue in such wise that a lord lost his court; though retained in all succeeding charters, this clause had little effect. The feudal court of freeholders was already declining; many lords voluntarily waived their rights in particular cases.[3] Those who wished to assert their jurisdiction when it was imperilled by a *praecipe*, could obtain a writ for that purpose.[4] As law became complicated, both lords and their tenants were disposed to avoid the responsibility of having to try writs of right,[5] and so there was little serious opposition when, in the early years of Henry III, the Crown invented a variety of other writs in the form *praecipe quod reddat*— notably the very popular writs of entry.

Whatever its form, the original writ was not the assertion of the jurisdiction of the court, but rather a royal commission conferring on the judges the power to try the matters contained in it. For every case a separate *ad hoc* authority was thus conferred, and Bracton naturally compared the jurisdiction of the common pleas to that of papal judges delegate.[6] The results of this situation upon pleading will be considered later.[7]

---

[1] The procedure (including the dilatory writ *de pace*) peculiar to a writ *de recto* (described by Richardson in Law Quarterly Review, liv. 387) must have made *praecipe quod reddat* much more popular. For an alternative speculation on this point, see Lady Stenton's introduction to *Pipe Roll of 6 John* (Pipe Roll Society, N.S. xviii), xxx ff.

[2] Magna Carta (1215), c. 34; (1216), c. 27; (1217), c. 30; (1225), c. 24. Cf. Miss N. D. Hurnard, in *Essays presented to F. M. Powicke*, 157–179.

[3] Hence a variety of writs of right with the clause *quia dominus remisit curiam suam*.

[4] *De non intromittendo*. Even without getting that writ, a lord might intervene orally, and " pray his court ": *Eyre of Kent* (Selden Society), ii. 86–7. But if the lord took no steps, the parties to the action could not raise the matter. Y.B. 30 & 31 Edward I (Rolls Series), 233–234.

[5] Not infrequently, tenants held by the services of attending the lord's court " when a writ of right is to be tried, or a thief is to be hanged ".

[6] Bracton, f. 108. Cf. Y.BB. Edward II (Selden Series), xxii. 31–32, *per* Bereford, C.J.

[7] Below, p. 408.

NEW WRITS UNDER HENRY II

At the same time it became an established principle that no freeman need answer for his land without a royal writ unless he chose. This rule is well known in the reign of Henry II and may date from the reign of Henry I.[1] Its effect was drastic; any defendant if he chose could have real property cases removed from seignorial courts into the King's Court. The steps were (1) a procedure called *tolt* which removed a plea from a seignorial court to the county court, and (2) a writ of *pone* which moved it from the county into the common pleas.[2] On the accession of Henry II, therefore, the operation of this principle, combined with the growing practice of issuing the writ of right called *praecipe*, had already given to the King's Court the basis of a very wide jurisdiction over land. Henry II improved the occasion by devising some new forms of action which again deliberately attacked the position of the lords. He modified the proceedings on a writ of right by allowing the defendant (or, more technically, the " tenant ") to choose if he wished trial by a Grand Assize, which was a jury of twelve knights, instead of trial by battle. The principle of recognition, or jury trial, was further extended by Henry II in the establishment of the petty assizes.[3] These were all modelled on the general principle that a person who had recently been evicted from the quiet enjoyment of his land was entitled to be restored.

PETTY ASSIZES, SEISIN AND POSSESSION

Bracton set the fashion of regarding these actions as definitely designed for the protection of possession as distinct from ownership, but it has recently been objected with a good deal of force that Bracton's use of these Roman terms " ownership " and " possession " does not accurately fit contemporary English law. Into this question we cannot enter in any detail, but it is clear that the petty assizes (which Maitland and Holdsworth, following Bracton, call " possessory assizes ") were based upon more than one consideration. " Disseisin ", as such wrongful ejection was technically called, was viewed partly as a crime, and so a defendant who was found guilty would be fined and occasionally imprisoned.[4] The maintenance of peace and order was, therefore, one element in the petty assizes; but there was also a strong element of tort, for the plaintiff very soon recovered damages; at the same time it was a thoroughly real action, giving recovery of the land. In short,

[1] Above p. 156.

[2] The technicalities are discussed by G. J. Turner in *Brevia Placitata* (Selden Society), lxiii, lxxxvi. If the plea had been by plaint instead of writ, then it had to be recorded before removal into a royal court.

[3] The assize of fresh force existed in the city of London before 1166. See the references by Dr A. H. Thomas in his edition of *Plea and Memoranda Rolls, 1323-1364*, 141 n. 1; Mary Bateson, in English Historical Review, xvii. 708 (from B.M. Add. 14252).

[4] There is an example in Y.B. 21 & 22 Edward I (Rolls Series), 276.

these assizes were designed to protect " seisin ", which was a conception peculiar to the middle ages; it is an enjoyment of property based upon title, and is not essentially distinguishable from right. In other words, the sharp distinction between property and possession made in Roman law did not obtain in English law; seisin is not the Roman possession, and right is not the Roman ownership.[1] Both of these conceptions are represented in English law only by seisin, and it was the essence of the conception of seisin that some seisins might be better than others. The most solemn action in real property law, the writ of right, merely ascertained whether the demandant or the tenant had the better right (without prejudice to third parties), by investigating which of them claimed on the older and better seisin.

NATURE AND ORIGIN OF NOVEL DISSEISIN

Although the writ of right would answer the serious question of the relative merits of the two titles according to the antiquity of the seisin from which they were derived, there seemed room for the invention of forms of action of more limited scope. If A unjustly and without a judgment disseised B of his free tenement, then it seemed reasonable that B should be restored to the enjoyment of his property upon satisfactory proof, first, that he was in quiet enjoyment (that is to say, seised), and secondly, that A had turned him out. There was surely no need in a situation such as this, which in fact was usually brought about by acts of violence, to compel B, merely because he had been wrongfully evicted, to make out a title good enough and old enough to sustain a writ of right, and to compel him, if A so elects, to wage battle on it. It seems that we get at this point a trace of the influence of the canon law. The tenant (*i.e.* defendant in a real action) had marked advantages over the demandant (plaintiff); he could interpose almost interminable delays, and even when the case finally came to be argued the demandant had to sustain a heavy burden of proof. Hence, one who had been disseised and attempted to recover by a writ of right was at a great disadvantage.[2]

This problem of preventing a disseisor, *spoliator*, from acquiring procedural advantages from his own tort, was not local to England, nor peculiar to the twelfth century. The solution was in fact ancient. It consisted in the requirement that the *spoliatus* should be restored at once to his possession, and that he be not called upon to defend his title while he is out of possession. From the *Sentences of Paul*,[3] early in the third century, the idea passed to the Theodosian Code (A.D. 319).[4]

---

[1] Joüon des Longrais, *Le Conception anglaise de la saisine* (whose views we have summarised in Harvard Law Review, xl. 921–925) and *La Portée politique des réformes d'Henry II*, [1936] Revue historique de droit, 540.

[2] Cf. the comment and references of F. Barlow, *Letters of Arnulf of Lisieux*, lxv, for the corresponding position in canon law.

[3] *Sententiae Pauli* (ed. P. Krueger), i. 7.

[4] *Codex Theodosianus* (ed. Mommsen), ix. 10. 3.

It appears in the False Decretals of the mid-ninth century,[1] and thence passed to our own *Leges Henrici Primi*[2] and a little later to the *Decretum* of Gratian.[3] The False Decretals which announced this principle also appear in the collection of canon law which Lanfranc[4] introduced into England. The general principle had therefore long been common knowledge, and both the Conqueror and Henry I forbad the disturbance of the *status quo* until their court had pronounced on the rights of the dispute. In other words, novel disseisin was designed to redress the situation created by one party who had had recourse to self-help.

Such a policy is so obvious, that it is hardly necessary to look to canon law for its origin.[5] The famous *actio spolii* in which the canonists finally enshrined their ancient principle seems actually later in date to the assize of novel disseisin.[6] It is also to be remembered that " it is said that German Law without foreign help " went a good deal of the way towards novel disseisin.[7]

Henry II's new action, the assize of *novel disseisin*, worked on these lines. One who had been ejected from his land was first of all to be restored. When he has been restored, and not until then, the rights and the wrongs of the case can be brought into question. If the ejector wished to raise questions of title he could then proceed later on as demandant in a writ of right.[8] Henceforth he could not pursue his claim by the too-simple device of forcibily ejecting the tenant in seisin, thereby compelling him to assume the difficult rôle of a demandant in a writ of right. In its earliest form the assize of *novel disseisin* was thus subsidiary and preliminary to a writ of right. It was only natural, however, once the assize had passed, that the parties should in many cases be content with its verdict, and therefore the petty assize becomes a complete form of action and not merely a subsidiary to the writ of right. This idea was so attractive that Henry II applied it to several different situations, and by the end of his reign there were three petty assizes all fashioned on the same model. There can be very little doubt that one of his strongest motives was the desire to treat disseisin as an offence which should be cognisable solely in the royal courts. In France the

---

[1] *Decretales Pseudo-Isidorianae* (ed. Hinschius), 18, 108–109, etc. (full list of references in Joüon des Longrais, *La Portée politique des réformes d'Henry II*, [1936] Revue historique de droit, 548 n. 1).

[2] In *Gesetze der Angelsachsen* (ed. Liebermann), v. 3; xxix. 2; liii. 3–6; lxi. 20.

[3] cc. 1–6, C. 2, q. 2; and also in C. 3, q. 1.

[4] Z. N. Brooke, *English Church and the Papacy*, 57 ff.; references are given by Joüon des Longrais, *loc. cit.*, 548 n. 3.

[5] This very sensible suggestion is from Joüon des Longrais, *loc. cit.*, 550.

[6] Richardson and Sayles, *Procedure without Writ* (Selden Society, vol. 60), cxxix ff.

[7] Pollock and Maitland, ii. 47. On possession and seisin in this connection, see Ernst Levy, *West Roman Vulgar Law: The Law of Property*, 96 ff., and on possessory remedies, *ibid.*, 243.

[8] The date of its establishment seems to be 1166; Maitland, *Equity and Forms of Action*, 339. Thus in 1218 a plaintiff (who was in under a tortious feoffment) succeeded in novel disseisin against the true owner (who had disseised him) " who may pursue in another way if he wants to ": *Eyre Rolls* (Selden Society, vol. 53), no. 38.

same policy was pursued, in spite of protests from lords who found that their jurisdiction suffered serious prejudice thereby.[1]

SCOPE OF THE PETTY ASSIZES

In the case of the assize of *novel disseisin* the original writ was directed to the sheriff of the county where the lands lay, commanding him, if the plaintiff gave security for prosecuting, to summon twelve free and lawful men who should view the lands in dispute and be ready to recognise before the King's justices whether the defendant had unjustly and without a judgment disseised the plaintiff of his free tenement since the period of limitation. In the assize of *mort d'ancestor* set up in 1176 by the Assize of Northampton,[2] the assize of twelve is to recognise whether the plaintiff's ancestor died seised[3] in his demesne as of fee of the tenements in dispute, whether he died since the period of limitation, and whether the demandant is his next heir. The assize of *darrein presentment* applied the principle of *novel disseisin* to the difficult case of advowsons, and called upon the assize to say whether the plaintiff was the last patron in time of peace who presented a parson to the church in dispute.[4] If so, he was seised, and is therefore entitled to present again. All three of these petty assizes ignored the court of the feudal lord; the assize of *mort d'ancestor* seems to have been definitely directed against the lords, for the defendant was frequently a feudal lord who refused to admit the heir of his deceased tenant to succeed him, and this assize therefore played a large part in the final establishment of the hereditary principle. A fourth assize called *utrum* also began as a preliminary proceeding in order to ascertain whether litigious land fell under the jurisdiction of the Church or the Crown, but in course of time the decision in this preliminary question became in effect a decision upon the principal question.[5]

THE ASSIZES SUPPLEMENTED

By the time we come to the reign of Henry III we find the beginnings of the *Register of Writs*; the forms of action are numerous enough to be collected in a formulary. Some new actions were invented about 1237 expressly to supply the place of gaps in the assize of *mort d'ancestor*; originally the only ancestor from whom one could claim was father, mother, brother, sister, uncle or aunt. Special actions which were not

[1] Joüon des Longrais, *La Saisine*, 52 n. 1.

[2] In Stubbs, *Charters*. For an example as early as 1157, see Joüon des Longrais, *op. cit.*, 50 n. 1.

[3] This was essential. The only instance of success where the ancestor did not die seised is in *Eyre Rolls* (Selden Society, vol. 59), no. 474 (1221), where the court frustrated a lord's attempt to evade a possible assize by disseising the ancestor just before he died—a bold piece of equity. The word " ancestor " included only father, mother, brother, sister, uncle and aunt.

[4] Cf. J. W. Gray, *The Jus Praesentandi*, English Historical Review, lxvii. 481.

[5] See above, p. 17

assizes, but variants of the writ of right, were now provided for claims based upon the seisin of grandfather (*aiel*) and great-grandfather (*besaiel*) and from " cousins ", which in law means all other relations (*cosinage*).[1] " Great-great-grandfather by the use of the Chancery is called cousin."[2]

THE WRITS OF ENTRY

By this time, however, it is abundantly clear that the King's Court began to dream of something like a general jurisdiction over land without the slightest reference to the existing feudal courts.

We have seen that the petty assizes were based on the allegation that the tenant had obtained the land recently and wrongfully. The next step is to be seen in the writ of gage (which was another *praecipe*) demanding restitution of land which the tenant held lawfully at first, although later this title failed. In the case of the writ of gage it was alleged that the plaintiff made over his land to the defendant as security for a debt, and that since he is now ready to pay the debt the defendant has no more right to the land, but must restore it. The result was the pattern for a new and important group of writs called writs of entry.[3] Like the writ of gage, they expressly alleged that the tenant only had entry into the land by a particular means which is set forth, thereby acquiring only a defective title. As time goes on a great variety of writs of entry is devised. At first the writ recounts all the hands through which the land has passed since the original defect, although there were limits placed upon the number of changes (whether alienations or descents) which could be alleged; finally, by statute demandants were allowed to say that the tenant had no entry save after (*post*) a particular defective title; dealings in the land subsequent to that event and leading down to the entry of the tenant no longer need be specified in the writ.[4] Of these numerous varieties of writs of entry it will only be necessary to say that they all ignore the lord's court and begin with the formula *praecipe quod reddat*. They were common in the time of Bracton,[5] and the fact that it is impossible to say whether they are possessory or proprietary[6] is only proof that these terms imported by Bracton really did not fit contemporary English law.

---

[1] *Bracton's Note Book*, no. 1215.

[2] Y.B. 19 Edward III (Rolls Series), 332. There was a long tussle between the courts and the Chancery over this; the Chancery won: Y.B. 20 & 21 Edward I (Rolls Series), 228, Y.BB. Edward II (Selden Series), x. xxxix, 95, xii. xl, 107.

[3] For all this, see G. E. Woodbine, *Curia Regis Rolls*, Yale Law Journal, xxxix. 509. Another element was the tender of a demi-mark, in writs of right, for permission to take a specially narrow issue: D. M. Stenton, *Pipe Roll of 6 John* (Pipe Roll Society, N.S. xviii), xxxj.

[4] Statute of Marlborough, c. 29 (1267); Pollock and Maitland, ii. 71; Plucknett, *Statutes and their Interpretation*, 80.

[5] For an early example, see *Select Civil Pleas* (Selden Society), no. 59 (1200).

[6] Maitland, *Equity and Forms of Action*, 338, 340. Cf. Maitland's note to *Bracton's Note Book*, no. 1215.

In one or two cases they supplement the assize of *novel disseisin*. That assize only lay between the disseisor and the disseisee. If in the meantime the disseisor had died and his heir entered by descent, the assize did not lie against the heir. So in 1205 a writ of entry *sur disseisin* was established to cover this case. If, on the other hand, the disseisee died, the assize again was not available to his heir, and so the writ of entry called " *de quibus* " or " entry in the nature of an assize " filled the gap.[1] Other varieties were entry *ad terminum qui praeterit*, which lay to recover lands against one who held them originally for a term of years, which term had expired.[2] An action which was very common during the middle ages was entry *cui in vita*, which lay for a widow to recover lands which were her own property, but which had been alienated by her husband, since she during his lifetime could not prevent his dealing with her property. If, however, the wife predeceases her husband, her heir can recover such lands by a writ of entry *sur cui in vita*. It frequently happened that a doweress wrongfully alienated her dower, and by a writ of entry " at common law " the reversioner could recover such lands only after her death. By statute, however, it was enacted that if a doweress alienated her dower the reversioner might obtain immediate entry (virtually a forfeiture) by a writ to be devised in the Chancery;[3] this was called entry *in casu proviso*. But it did not apply to alienations by other life tenants, and so, after a famous incident between Chief Justice Bereford and the Chancery officials,[4] a writ of entry *in consimili casu* was devised for use by reversioners and remaindermen against the alienees of tenants for life, and by the curtesy, immediately after such an alienation.

THE EARLIEST FORMS OF PERSONAL ACTIONS: DEBT

In one or two rare cases the King's Court was prepared to intervene in matters which did not involve land, although the forms which it used were almost identical. The writ of debt, for example, was in the same form as the *praecipe quod reddat*, and at first looks very much as if it were a real action; as Maitland remarks, " We are tempted to say that Debt is a ' real action ', that the vast gulf which to our minds divides the ' give me what I own ' and ' give me what I am owed ' has not yet become

---

[1] There are useful references in Powicke, *Henry III*, i. 400 n. 3.

[2] As land could be gaged either in fee or for a term of years, there is a close connection between the writs of gage and entry *ad terminum*; gage thus became the ancestor of the writs of entry. Maitland, *op. cit.*, 333.

[3] Statute of Gloucester, c. 7 (1278); a right of entry was given by 11 Hen. VII, c. 20.

[4] Bereford's words " Blessed be he who made that statute [Westminster II, c. 24]. Make the writ and we will maintain it " occur in only one manuscript and concern the remainderman's rights (Y.BB. Edward II (Selden Society), iii. 19); the same MS. tells a similar story in another case where alienations by other particular tenants and the reversioner's recovery are involved, *ibid.*, 108–109.

apparent ".[1]   There is fairly old authority for the theory that a contract consists of " mutual grants "—a view which seems to be merely a deduction from the consensual character of the sale of chattels in the later common law.[2]   Such reasoning, however, is really a sixteenth-century phenomenon; it is not to be found in the early days of the action of debt. Still more modern is the belief that because many actions for land beginning with a writ in the form *praecipe quod reddat* are real actions, therefore all actions so commenced are real actions, and among them the action of debt.   There are no historical grounds for this view.   Twelfth-century lawyers in the King's Court were not given to metaphysical speculation, but were just practical administrators who saw a need for enforcing some of the commoner types of debt in the King's Court. They propounded no theory of obligation; they said nothing about mutual grants, consent, consideration or any other theory of contract. All they did was to establish a procedure for compelling debtors to pay their obvious dues.   It so happened that original writs at this critical moment were framed on a uniform pattern:[3] the King tells the sheriff to order the defendant to do what he ought to do, and if he does not, then to summon him to the King's Court.   The only significance attaching to the words *praecipe quod reddat* is their indication of the date of origin of the writ, and its nature as a " demand " rather than a " complaint "; it is only the oldest actions which are cast in this form.   The numerous writs *praecipe quod permittat* may be proprietary or possessory according to circumstances.   As we shall see, later forms of action are based on a different model.

The writ of debt existed already in Glanvill's day, and follows precisely the same form as the writ of right and was available for a number of purposes.   It could always be brought upon " obligations ", that is to say, debts acknowledged by deed under seal, and in such cases the establishment of the genuineness of the deed was conclusive.   Where there was no deed under seal, debt could still be used to recover a loan, to collect the rent due upon a lease, the price upon a sale, and, later on, to enforce various statutory penalties.   The action of debt, therefore, was fairly comprehensive, but as time went by the defects of the action became more apparent.   In the first place, trial was by compurgation

---

[1] Maitland, *Equity and Forms of Action*, 332.   Note the veiled doubt, characteristically expressed in Maitland's words (he was more positive in Pollock and Maitland, ii. 205).   The theory is reduced to an absurdity when it is argued (as has been done) that the action of debt is designed to recover the identical coins lent.   *Praecipe quod reddat* is the current blank form for writs in the twelfth and very early thirteenth centuries.   It seems to recall the solemn demand for restitution which was a necessary preliminary to litigation before the Conquest, only now it is the King's sheriff who makes it.   Cf. Ine, 9; Canute II, 19; *Leges Henrici Primi*, 51, 3; Bateson, *Borough Customs* (Selden Society), i. 89.   But see the curious bond in Pollock and Maitland, ii. 193, n. 3.

[2] *Edgecomb* v. *Dee* (1670), Vaughan 89 at 101.

[3] The only important exception is the group of assizes; *novel disseisin* begins by reciting a complaint, *questus est nobis* . . .; *mort d'ancestor* is merely a summons.

(wager of law)[1], and as the middle ages proceed this was felt to be increasingly irrational; although decisions substituted trial by jury in a number of cases, the place left for compurgation still remained considerable.   And secondly, as with all the oldest groups of actions, a particularly complicated system of pleading grew up around it.   As a result, from the beginning of the fifteenth century we see a tendency to avoid using the writ of debt and to make other forms of action serve its purpose.

DETINUE

The action of detinue was very similar, and it is evident that the two actions were originally one.   Glanvill describes but one action, which covers the field later divided between debt and detinue.   The form of writ he gives is that of debt, the demand being for a sum of money, but he goes on to say that the " debt " may be demanded for various reasons, such as a loan of money, the price on a sale, the loan of a chattel, a letting to hire or a deposit.   The writ was also available for a creditor against a surety on the default of the principal debtor.   In his discussion of it, Glanvill speaks simply of " debt " and the writ is designed to secure to the plaintiff his *debitum*, his due, whether it be money or chattels. Even in the Year Books we sometimes find it expressed as " duty ". The basic idea of the action, therefore, is not confined to contract, or tort, or property concepts, but is simply the enforcement of what is " due ".

Superficially, then, it might seem that Glanvill's undifferentiated action of debt-detinue will enforce any sort of obligation, but as with several other of our writs, the form is in broader terms than the practical scope of the action.   In spite of a few sweeping words, Glanvill's real meaning is to be found in the enumeration of situations in which the writ can be used.   In the course of the succeeding half-century these are classified into two groups, one of which we have already described as the province of debt, while the remainder are allocated to detinue with a slight modification in the terms of the writ.   A broad distinction grew up which treated detinue as the particular remedy of a bailor against his bailee—*i.e.* where the defendant acquired the chattel with the plaintiff's consent.   If the defendant had acquired the chattel by violating the plaintiff's possession, however, the remedy was obviously trespass *de bonis asportatis*.   A third situation was that classified by later lawyers as trover; here there was some hesitation.[2]

In their subsequent history, debt becomes an important factor in the history of the contract, while detinue contributes much to the development of the rules of personal property law.   It is also worth remembering that a frequent use of detinue was to obtain possession of charters, on the principle that one who was entitled to land was thereby entitled to bring detinue for the deeds relating to it.   Cases of detinue of charters,

---

[1] Except when a sealed deed was the basis of the demand; below, p. 633 n. 3.
[2] For this, see below, p. 375.

therefore, may contain important discussions of the law of real property.[1]

ACCOUNT

The action of account is particularly interesting and its history deserves more investigation than it has yet received. It appears on the plea rolls from 1200 onwards. In form it is a *praecipe quod reddat*, and is based on the existence of a duty to render a " reasonable account ".[2] Originally it was used between a lord of a manor and his bailiff in order to compel the latter to account for the profits of the manor. The word " bailiff ", however, gradually shifted its meaning, and by the end of the fourteenth century account could be used against certain types of bailees who had to be described as " bailiffs ", although this allegation was not traversable.[3] This transition was assisted, no doubt, by the fact that quite early in its career the action of account could also be used between partners; when commercial matters appear in the Year Books, it is usually in actions of account.

Account could also be brought against one who had received money to the use of the plaintiff. Here (as with the bailiff), the earlier law only concerned itself with the " common receiver " who was authorised to act as such for a period of time.[4] Soon, a casual receiver, like a casual bailee, came within the action.

COVENANT

The action of covenant appears soon after the time of Glanvill, and is stated in some of the earlier sources to have very wide scope over contractual matters. The Statute of Wales in 1284 informs us that land or chattels may be demanded by the writ of covenant according to circumstances; " and forasmuch as contracts in covenants are infinite in their variety, it is impossible to mention each one in particular, but judgment is to be done according to the nature of each covenant and according to the statements and denials of the parties ". It would therefore seem that covenant almost became a general contractual action. In local jurisdictions it remained so until comparatively late. In the county court we find it used as late as 1333 to obtain damages for breach of a covenant to use care in handling a borrowed fishing boat.[5] In the

---

[1] And consequently, a doweress could not demand dower unless she handed over her late husband's charters: Y.B. 41 Edward III, Pasch. no. 9.

[2] Cf. Pollock and Maitland, ii. 221, citing Langdell, *Equity Jurisdiction*, 75; Ames, *Lectures in Legal History*, 116; Plucknett, *The Mediaeval Bailiff*, 22 ff.; *Curia Regis Rolls*, i. 191, 249; iv. 64, 145.

[3] See the details in Plucknett, *Words*, Cornell Law Quarterly, xiv. 263, 270.

[4] Y.BB. Edward II (Selden Series), xxii. 264. Unless appointed by the creditor, the receiver's acquittance did not discharge the debt: *ibid.*, xxiv. 84 (1319) and Intro., p. lxxxvi. Cf. Y.B. 5 Edward III, Michs. no. 104 (1331).

[5] Plucknett, *New Light on the Old County Court*, Harvard Law Review, xlii. 666, citing Morris, *Early English County Court*, 185.

King's Court it is mostly a covenant concerning land, apparently,[1] and very often the writ seems brought merely in order to proceed to a fine, or final concord, which already was a popular conveyancing device. It had one other function—a minor one—and that was to afford a modicum of protection to lessees against their lords. Like the other writs we have mentioned, it was on the ancient pattern, slightly modified: *praecipe quod teneat conventionem*. It ceased to be of much importance after the reign of Edward I, when the rule became established that covenant would only lie on a deed under seal.

THE NEW PATTERN OF WRIT

So far, the writs we have considered have been either summary, like the petty assizes, or else based on a single pattern, that of the *praecipe quod reddat*, and as we have seen, this same pattern is used whether the action is real or personal.

At the end of the twelfth century a new formula appears, and many of the newer actions are commenced with writs of the new model. Instead of the archaic demand for restitution which was the essence of the *praecipe quod reddat*, we have a much more modern form which begins immediately with an order to summon the defendant (if the plaintiff has given security to prosecute) to come before the justices to show why he had done a particular act. The change is partly one of arrangement, for even a *praecipe quod reddat* concludes with a summons to show why the defendant has not made restitution; the new model begins with the summons, and the defendant is called on to explain his action, instead of his inaction as in the *praecipe quod reddat*. If the old model emphasises the failure to do what is due, the new one rests on a positive misdeed. This misdeed, moreover, is frequently described in the writ as being a breach of the peace.

THE ACTION OF TRESPASS

The summons *ostensurus quare*, to show why the defendant did something to the damage of the plaintiff and the breach of the King's peace, was a momentous development, for it gave us the action of trespass. The breach of the peace, however, was not always alleged, and there are numerous examples of summonses to show why the defendant had done something which damaged the plaintiff where the phrase does not occur.

In accordance with a constant tendency, the commonest cases give rise to well-settled forms. Thus we get distinct varieties of trespass for assault, imprisonment, for taking away chattels, and for unlawfully entering upon land, and by 1249 we get a trespass case enrolled in what seems already a settled form. By the thirty-fifth year of Henry III (1250–1251) payments for writs of trespass become numerous on the

---

[1] Subject to exceptions and qualifications: C. H. S. Fifoot, *History and Sources of the Common Law: Tort and Contract*, 255–256.

Fine Rolls.[1] Besides these, however, it is important to remember that in the early years of the thirteenth century there were numerous unclassified cases where defendants were summoned to show why they had caused damage to the plaintiff, with or without a breach of the peace, and with or without the allegation that the act was done *vi et armis*, with force and arms.[2]

Trespass is therefore one variety of the great class of writs which call upon the defendant to come before the justices *ostensurus quare*, to show why he caused damage to the plaintiff. We may note that the allegation of a breach of the peace is not necessarily present, and that the King's Court takes jurisdiction over these cases, therefore, on broader grounds than a mere technical breach of royal peace. It is, however, quite clear that if a breach of the King's peace is mentioned, no court save the King's Court dare proceed. The great importance of trespass and its related *quare* actions is abundantly clear, but it is a great misfortune that Bracton, whose official career coincides with its formative period, did not live to write upon it the systematic treatise which he had planned.[3]

At first sight it seems strange that trespass begins to appear in the King's Court only in the middle of the thirteenth century, and does not become common there until the middle of the fourteenth century. There is nevertheless good reason. The King's Court was interested in land, in the first instance, for feudal reasons only; and it was interested in trespasses for criminal reasons only. Hence it was the felonies and indictable trespasses (later called misdemeanours) which received attention at Westminster. From the point of view of litigants, trespasses usually involved much less valuable stakes than real-property cases, and so it was much more difficult to persuade juries to trudge across the country to give their verdicts in the King's Court. The issues would almost always be trivial in comparison with the trouble and expense. Trespass could not become a common action in royal courts until means were found to try it locally. In the late thirteenth century the baronial governments made extended use of judicial eyres; early in the fourteenth century the invention of the *nisi prius* system allowed juries to try issues reached at Westminster without going out of their counties. It is just at those moments that we find the action of trespass making sudden advances in the King's Court.[4]

THE ACTION OF REPLEVIN

The continuous history of trespass to the person, to goods and to land stands out clearly from among the scores of *quare* actions in use at

[1] The enrolment is on J.I. 1/1177 m. 1 d. This reference, and figures relating to the Fine Rolls, were kindly communicated by Mr. C. A. F. Meekings of the Public Record Office.

[2] See the long and varied assortment of *quare* actions (brought in 1200 and shortly afterwards) listed in the index of *Select Civil Pleas* (Selden Society), 107–108.

[3] Bracton, f. 164.

[4] Cf. below, p. 371 n. 1.

the beginning of the thirteenth century. But what became of the others? Some of them vanished, to be revived later under somewhat different circumstances; but many in their turn crystallised into distinct forms of action. This happened to *quare ejecit* (as we shall see later) which became an important remedy for lessees.

Still another became the action of replevin, and one of the most valued defences of the feudal tenant against his lord. In the thirteenth century this was often a *quare* action, calling on the defendant to show why he took cattle in distress and kept them in spite of the owner's offer of gage and pledge. The final form of the proceedings was greatly modified,[1] for the Crown realised the urgent necessity of moderating this powerful relic of self-help which still survived, as distress, in daily use.

The action of replevin was greatly used in the middle ages in circumstances such as these. When a lord distrained his tenant to perform services and the tenant desired to dispute his liability to do them, he could recover possession of the chattels distrained by giving security to the sheriff for maintaining his contention in a law court. The procedure was then for the tenant to declare that his beasts were taken, to which the lord might reply by denying that he took them, or else (and this was almost universally the case) by admitting the distress and disclosing the reasons—such as services and rents in arrear, homage not performed, relief unpaid, etc. This is technically called an " avowry ", and in this form of action a great number of questions relating to the feudal relationship could be conveniently raised. If the lord's case is proved, judgment is given that he shall " have the return "; that, is the chattels which he originally distrained and which the sheriff restored to the tenant are given back to the lord by judgment of the court to hold again as a distress. In early times, if the question of the ownership of the chattels was raised in replevin, it was determined by interlocutory proceedings called *de proprietate probanda*. In the early fourteenth century the convenience of the action of replevin led to determined attempts to make it serve the purpose of certain other actions, and these attempts were nearly successful; in the fifteenth century we have this distinction drawn by Chief Justice Newton: " If you have taken my beasts, it is in my choice to sue replevin (which proves property in me), or to sue a writ of trespass (which proves the property in him who took them); and so it is in my will to waive the property or not ".[2] By this time it was settled doctrine that even a thief acquired property in the stolen goods. We therefore have here in the choice between replevin and trespass a curious parallel to the doctrine of disseisin at election in real property law. In England replevin was generally restricted to its proper field of

---

[1] The early history of replevin is somewhat obscure; for the *quare* form of replevin see *Bracton's Note Book* (ed. Maitland), no. 157. There is much material on the procedure and pleading of replevin in F. A. Enever, *History of the Law of Distress* (1931).

[2] Y.B. 19 Henry VI, 65 (Pasch. 5), cited in Ames, *Lectures on Legal History*, 69, 70. See the discussion by Bordwell, *Property in chattels*, Harvard Law Review, xxix. 374.

testing the legality of a distress, but in America it was frequently used instead of detinue.

THE ORIGIN OF TRESPASS

There has been much controversy over the origin of trespass. The question is certainly one of the greatest importance, for the later history of trespass has grown so wide as to cover the largest part of the field of law. This is not the place to undertake a fresh investigation into a very debatable subject, but some reference to it is unavoidable.

According to one theory the action of trespass developed from the old appeal.[1] According to this view the changes which took place were as follows: the appeal of larceny (like the appeals of murder, mayhem or other felony) was in very truth a " form of action " for criminal matters. The injured party pursued the trail, caught the criminal and then formally charged him with the crime; if he denied his guilt, the action concluded with trial by battle; if the plaintiff was successful he recovered the stolen property, and if he had not already slain the thief in battle he was expected to hang him. Gradually, means were found for substituting jury trial upon the appellee's allegation that the appeal was only brought by hate and spite (*de odio et atia*). Technically a side issue tried by jury, in fact it went to the root of the case.[2] If trespass developed from the appeal, then the changes must have been these: first, where the stolen goods were no longer forthcoming, or would have gone to the king,[3] the plaintiff in trespass is now able to recover their money value from the defendant; this seems to have been impossible by the appeal. Secondly, words of felony must be omitted; this was already optional in an appeal, which could thus be changed from a criminal into a civil action.[4] This, it is suggested, naturally led to the idea of trespass.

Another theory would regard the action of trespass as having its origin in the assize of *novel disseisin*.[5] The assize only gave recovery of the land; it was always uncertain whether chattels which had been on the land (most commonly crops) could be recovered—if they had been consumed, at first there was to remedy. Hence the assize of *novel disseisin* was modified so as to give damages representing the value of those chattels removed in the course of the disseisin whose restoration was impossible. And so in this way, too, the element of damages in trespass

---

[1] Holmes, *The Common Law*, 3, 4, 101, 102; Ames, *op. cit.*, 56–61. For an example of an " appeal ", see above, p. 121.

[2] Numerous examples are collected by Elsa de Haas, *Antiquities of Bail*, 118 ff.

[3] See below, p. 452.

[4] Bracton describes this form as an action *de re adirata*. It came very near to being a real action for those chattels which the demandant had lost involuntarily (it did not lie if the chattels had been bailed; in that case, detinue alone would serve).

[5] Woodbine, *Origins of the Action of Trespass*, Yale Law Journal, xxxiii. 799–816, xxxiv. 343–370.

has been accounted for, although Woodbine insists that the idea of damages was borrowed from Roman law.

A third theory suggests that " Roman law was a solvent acting upon the appeal of larceny, from which the action of trespass by almost insensible stages separated itself ".[1]

THE PROBLEM RESTATED

These theories were framed with special reference to trespass for taking away chattels, but, as we have suggested, the problem is much wider than that. The origin of trespass *de bonis asportatis* is part of the larger question of the origin of all the actions which were directed against a defendant who had done damage to a plaintiff. The original writ in all these cases is in the same form *ostensurus quare*, and the origin of that form is the real root of the matter. If we may be so rash as to confound the confusion by offering yet another theory, it would be to suggest that in this, as in other matters, the King's Court was adopting methods already in use in the local courts. From local customs which are still extant we can trace the gradual change (which in fact was not a very great or fundamental one) between the Anglo-Saxon *bot* and the later damages.[2] The idea of damages, therefore, has no necessary connection with trespass as a form of action, being indeed much older, and there is no doubt that there was forms in use in the local courts whereby these damages could be obtained. If this would explain the nature of the remedy, it still remains to determine the origin of the form which the royal courts adopted. In the writs of trespass there is a constant formula. The King orders the sheriff to summon the defendant (or else to take pledges for his appearance) to show in the King's Court why (*ostensurus quare*) he did certain things. In the enrolment of such cases upon the plea rolls the recital of the writ is immediately followed by the words " whereof A. B. (the plaintiff) complains that . . . (*unde queritur quod . . .*) ". It may be that in these words we have a clue to the origin of the form through which the royal courts gave remedy by damages. The origin of *quare* actions in the King's Court lies near the year 1200, but many writs were granted at first only as a matter of favour. Even the writ of debt might be purchased at the cost of a champertous bargain to give the Crown a large percentage of the sum recovered.

A complaint might be pursued by means of a writ,[3] and, indeed, Bracton constantly refers to novel disseisin as a *querela*. The writ does in fact use the phrase *questus est nobis . . .* to introduce the crucial words

---

[1] Richardson and Sayles, *Procedure without Writ under Henry III* (Selden Society, vol. 60), cxvi.

[2] A clear example of damages in Anglo-Saxon law occurs in Ine, 42, and the twelfth-century custumal of Preston shows the old *bot* changing to damages including costs and expenses: *Borough Customs* (Selden Society), i. 30–31 .

[3] Bracton, f. 179; cf. below, p. 394.

alleging the disseissin.   But it is clear that a writ was not always necessary, and that many complaints were dealt with without an original writ.

We may well suspect that the earlier summonses to show *quare* were granted only of grace, but the political crisis in the middle of the thirteenth century coincided significantly with the final settlement of the form of trespass, and no doubt contributed largely to its popularity.   In the course of the inquiries into abuses by royal officials which then took place, great use was made of a vague procedure of complaint (*querela*). In these circumstances anyone could complain of the oppressions of public ministers, and the enrolment of these complaints is curiously similar to that of an action of trespass.[1]   It is not without significance that in France, too, the Crown was developing machinery whereby such complaints could be heard.[2]   According to this hypothesis the procedure of complaint against public officials was extended to complaints against any wrongdoers in general, and this, combined with the already existing idea of damages in local jurisdictions, as well as the existing practice of the summons to a royal court *ostensurus quare*, would give us all the elements of trespass.   However, no final settlement of these controversies is possible until more plea rolls of the earlier thirteenth century are available in print.

REMOTER ORIGINS

We have spoken of trespass as a newer type of remedy in the King's Court, appearing at a slightly later date than the *praecipe quod reddat* type; but the first appearance of trespass on the rolls is by no means the actual beginning of the remedy.   The King's Court was a newcomer among much older institutions, and although it did invent some things (such as the petty assizes) it borrowed many more, and among these borrowings, the complaint, or *querela*, must be numbered.   Moreover, even the Crown's first venture into the field of general adjudication was likewise no new invention.   There was litigation for land long before the King's Court threw open its doors to litigants, and we have reason to believe that the writ of right also was derived from the older but unwritten procedure of the ancient courts of the shire and hundred.

The two main types of action in the King's Court may both be traced back therefore to the age before the common law.   In that age England still lived under a customary law which can be conveniently described as " Germanic ", and which was matched in many other European countries with similar customs; " in all probability neither

---

[1] For discussion of the *quare* group of actions and of the *querela* see Jacob, *Baronial Rebellion and Reform*, 65; Adams, *Council and Courts*, 348; Treharne, *The Baronial Plan of Reform*, i. 147, and Woodbine in Yale Law Journal, xxxiv. 349–356.   The volume of *Proceedings without Writ under Henry III*, edited by Mr. Richardson and Dr. Sayles (Selden Society, 1941), constitutes a large collection of material on the history of trespass for that very reason.   Many of the cases come from eyre rolls, and very few from common pleas rolls (cf. above, p. 367).

[2] Joüon des Longrais, *La Saisine*, 52 n. 1.

the victors nor the vanquished on the field of Hastings knew any one legal formula or legal formality that was not well known throughout many lands ".[1] Now this old Germanic custom had two main types of procedure. One was a demand for a thing or the enforcement of a due; the other was a complaint against a wrong. The former looked forward to specific relief; the latter to compensation, *bot* or some similar form of settlement.[2] Here, then, we already have the prototypes of the two great groups of actions, the demand becoming the writ of right, and the complaint the action of trespass.

TRESPASS AND CASE

We must now examine these complaints. They are extremely varied, but those most persistently recurring will naturally turn into settled forms. The assizes of novel disseisin and nuisance (beginning *Quaestus est nobis*) separated under Henry II.[3] In the thirteenth century the Crown will show a special interest in complaints of wrongs done *vi et armis* and *contra pacem*; in the days of Bracton, these complaints will involve outlawry,[4] and will become familiar with their recurrent allegations of assault and battery, asportation of chattels, and breach of close. These also become separate actions. So too did *quare ejecit infra terminum*, about 1235.[5] At first, the King's Court concentrated upon these real or supposed breaches of the peace, and only occasionally troubled itself with other complaints. Local courts, however, preserved the undivided field of tort; in such courts " trespass was a rough equivalent of our modern tort in general; under it were included many wrongs (such as defamation) that the royal courts were later to reserve for the action of case. It was not limited to direct wrongs."[6]

As forms became settled, it was evident that writs of trespass for assault, breach of close, and asportation were practically common form; the others were an unclassified mass of instances where the writ had to be specially drafted so as to include a good deal of narrative matter. Such writs were said to be " upon the case "—an expression constantly used of writs (and also of pleadings) which set out particular circumstances in unusual detail.[7] In some (but not all) of these cases, the narrative was prefaced by an important preamble introduced by *cum*. This may recite the " custom of the realm " (as against innkeepers), or it may recite one of scores of statutes, the breach of which caused loss to the plaintiff; later still, it will recite the *assumpsit* which played so large a part in the history of contract. The ancient formula *summone* A.

[1] Pollock and Maitland, ii. 558.
[2] *Ibid.*, 571; Maitland, however, did not connect the old complaint with trespass.
[3] The recital of a complaint does not appear in *mort d'ancestor* or *darrein presentment*.
[4] Below, p. 385; Bracton, f. 441.
[5] Below, p. 571.
[6] Glanville Williams, *Liability for Animals*, 128.
[7] See the passages cited in Maitland, *Register of Writs*, Harvard Law Review, iii. 104 n. 1.

ostensurus quare . . . is thus immensely expanded (and complicated) by inserting the lengthy clause *cum* . . . immediately after *quare*.

This orderly development in the science of diplomatic took many years to accomplish.   At the same time legal habits were growing up which attached certain forms to certain circumstances, and often hardened into law without much regard for formal propriety.   Many anomalies were created, particularly in the use, or omission, of the words *vi et armis* and *contra pacem*.   It was always necessary to distinguish trespass from case, because the defendant could be arrested or outlawed in trespass, but not in case (until 1504);   but the line came to be drawn without close reference to the form of the writ, or to the nature of the complaint. Trespass and case are clearly distinguished as early as 1368,[1] but for a long time every situation had to be considered separately in order to decide (*a*) whether the remedy was to be in the nature of trespass or case, and (*b*) in either event, what the form of the writ should be.

There seems to be no foundation for the belief that the action of case has any connection with the *Consimili casu* clause of the Statute of Westminster II, c. 24 (1285).[2]

THE RISE OF EJECTMENT

Another special form of trespass is *de ejectione firmae*.   This lies for a lessee against anyone[3] who ejects him, and at first gives him damages, although not the recovery of his term.   This writ is therefore the termor's equivalent for the freeholder's *quare clausum fregit*.   The distinction between them is nevertheless clear: the freeholder speaks of the breach of " his close ", but the lessee uses no such proprietary language; instead, the writ recites the lease to the plaintiff of the premises, and his ejection from his term (*firma sua*).[4]   At the end of the fifteenth century it would seem the courts finally decided to allow the lessee to recover his term as well by this writ,[5] and soon afterwards this great change enabled it

---

[1] Y.B. 42 Edward III, f. 11, no. 13 (below, p. 481), where the question whether process was by *capias* was discussed.   For another example, see Y.B. 13 Richard II (Ames Foundation), 104 (1390).

[2] Maitland, *Equity and Forms of Action*, 345, 346, states the old view, but with obvious hesitation.   For a discussion of this see Plucknett, *Case and the Statute of Westminster II*, Columbia Law Review, xxxi. 778, and the comments of Sir William Holdsworth in Law Quarterly Review, xlvii. 334;   P. A. Landon, Law Quarterly Review, lii. 63 (and cf. *ibid.*, 220);   Dix, *Origins of Trespass on the Case*, Yale Law Journal, xlvi. 1142;   Kiralfy, *The Action on the Case* (1951).

[3] There was already an older action *quare ejecit infra terminum* (ascribed to Raleigh, *c.* 1235) whose usefulness was very limited as it only lay between rival lessees who both claimed to hold from the same lessor.   It is notable that Bracton, f. 220, gives two forms of it, one is a *praecipe quod reddat*, and the other is a summons *ostensurus quare*.   For more as to the termor's remedies see below, pp. 570–574.

[4] Pollock and Maitland seem confused on this;   the writ is printed in Maitland's *Forms of Action*.

[5] See the data in Maitland, *Forms of Action*, 350, which represents the state of the printed sources.   An unpublished case of 1389 (De Banco Roll, Michs. 13 Ric. II, roll ccclxxxvii) already shows recovery of the term.

to be used instead of most of the old forms of real action. When two parties wished to try the title to a piece of land, one of them leased it to an imaginary person (John Doe), and the other similarly leased to another (William Styles). One lessee ejects the other (this will be all fiction), and in order to try the rights of the rival lessees the court has to enter into the question of the rights of the lessors. This procedure was known as *ejectment*, and after the close of the middle ages was the principal method of trying title to land. The nominal plaintiff in such actions was the fictitious John Doe on the demise of the real plaintiff; and so an action which to-day would be called *A* v. *B* used to be described as *Doe d. A* (that is, *Doe* on the demise of *A*) v. *B*. The fictitious William Styles was usually replaced by his lessor, for in the earlier proceedings the plaintiff's solicitor writes a letter to the defendant in the name of " your loving friend, William Styles ", asking the defendant to defend Styles's interest. This development took place in the seventeenth century, but it was not until late in the eighteenth that a judgment in ejectment became really definitive. Until then, a persistent but unsuccessful plaintiff could start a new action as often as he liked. Useful as it was, ejectment did not entirely supersede the old real actions. In 1852 the fictitious John Doe was abolished by statute, and in 1875 this, together with all other forms of action, was abolished.

ASSUMPSIT: TROVER

We have already mentioned[1] that the preamble introduced into *quare* writs by the word *cum* may allege that the defendant undertook (*assumpsit*) to do something. This is a development of the highest importance, and it will be discussed in due course.[2]

Another (and the latest) of these clauses contains the allegation of trover, and deals with situations which involve neither bailment nor a trespassory taking. In Bracton's day the appeal of larceny could be converted into an action *de re adirata* by omitting the words of felony. By this means a chattel could be recovered against a finder.[3] Proceedings of that sort were typical of manorial courts, but an obscure note in a Year Book[4] suggests that in 1294 detinue could be brought against a finder. Cases on stray cattle are not quite in point, for the franchise of estray had rules of its own, but detinue against the finder of charters seems to have been possible in 1389.[5] But charters, like strays, have peculiar features, and these actions deal principally with executors who

---

[1] Above, pp. 372–373.

[2] More will be said of assumpsit in discussing the history of tort and contract; below pp. 481 ff., 637 ff.

[3] But indirectly; if the finder refuses in court to restore the chattel as an *adirata*, then the plaintiff counts afresh, this time with words of felony: Bracton, f. 150 b.

[4] Y.B. 21 & 22 Edward I (Rolls Series), 466–468. It is said there that the trial is by wager of law by the plaintiff (*not* by the defendant).

[5] Y.B. 13 Richard II (Ames Foundation), 56.

withhold the heir's title deeds which came into their hands (*devenerunt ad manus*) with the ancestor's chattels. In 1455 Littleton explained the "new-found haliday" which consisted in counting upon a finding (*invencio*) instead of the traditional *devenerunt*.[1]

The preoccupation of detinue with the two special cases of estrays and title-deeds persisted, and the general problem of recovering chattels which had neither been stolen nor bailed was only solved when a new start was made by inventing a new preamble to be inserted in the writ *ostensurus quare*. This preamble alleged that the plaintiff casually lost possession of the chattel, that the defendant found it, refused to restore it, and converted it to his own use. This development of case for trover and conversion had begun by 1510.[2] Just as forms of *assumpsit* replaced debt, so in the seventeenth century trover[3] replaced detinue.

By the end of the seventeenth century, therefore, the great bulk of the litigation of the kingdom was conducted through the various forms of action which had developed from trespass, and this remained the case until the nineteenth century, when first of all the real actions, and finally, in 1875, all remaining forms of action, were abolished by statute and replaced by a single uniform writ of summons upon which the plaintiff endorses his statement of claim. At that moment, the change was purely procedural, but it has undoubtedly affected the development of substantive law by freeing it from the mediaeval classification imposed by the old forms of action, and permitting broad general concepts (such as liability in tort) to aid in the development of a field which was formerly subdivided on lines which were traditional rather than rational.

ACTIONS REAL AND PERSONAL

As long as the forms of action were living things, this was the only classification which really fitted them. The writs *praecipe quod reddat* had a system of procedure and pleading quite different from that applicable to those which summoned the defendant to show why (*quare*) he had damaged the plaintiff.

The study of Roman law, especially in the pages of Bracton, introduced much confusion. Instead of this Germanic classification based on the nature of relief sought, the Roman classification was based upon the nature of the right asserted, and Bracton attempted to apply this classification to the existing English material. In the Romanesque introduction to his treatise he regards the assize of novel disseisin as a personal action because it is based upon tort, and because the procedure in it is directed against the person of the disseisor and not against the land,[4]

---

[1] Y.B. Trin. 33 Henry VI, no. 12, ff. 26–27; Pollock and Maitland, ii. 175 (criticised by Ames, *Lectures*, 82 n. 4).

[2] *Intrationum excellentissimus Liber* (1510, *i.e.* 1511), f. 22 and f. 71; cited in Ames, *Lectures*, 83.

[3] In America replevin was more often used in place of detinue; in England the scope of replevin was practically restricted to distress.

[4] Bracton, f. 103 b–104.

but when he comes to the detailed discussion of English law he changes his mind and says that novel disseisin is a real action because the judgment is for the restitution of a *res*, a specific piece of land.[1]　This latter decision brings him nearer to the old Germanic notion than to the Roman, but still it is not quite the same thing.　The difference appears when the action of detinue is considered.　On the old Germanic plan detinue belongs exactly where we find it, in the *praecipe quod reddat* group, because it is a demand for something which is the demandant's right or due.　Bracton discusses the nature of detinue in a well-known passage,[2] and asks whether it is a real action since the writ demands the restitution of a specific chattel.　He concludes that it is not a real action because in practice the defendant can elect between restoring the chattel or paying its price.

This was the test which was finally adopted in England: an action is real if it compels the specific restitution of the *res*.　Littleton adopts the rule[3] and since his day it has become current.　The words " real" and " personal " in later ages came to be applied (or misapplied) in a very curious fashion to property.　It became customary to call land " real property " while chattels were " personal property ", apparently because land could be recovered specifically in a real action, but chattels could only be made the subject of an action for damages.[4]　This usage becomes common in the late seventeenth century, after the time of Coke.[5]　The use of these distinguishing terms is not, of course, the origin of the distinction between the two different types of property; the differences between them are much older and deeper than these unhappy attempts to apply Roman terminology to English law, and will be mentioned later.

ACTIO PERSONALIS MORITUR CUM PERSONA

Our remarks about this famous brocard can happily take the form of an obituary notice.　Although of mediaeval origin,[6] the maxim owes its currency to Coke and is thus one of those *fioretti* which the faithful Ashe collected in his *Fasciculus Florum: or, a Handfull of Flowers* (1618). When Coke propounded it, the maxim certainly did not correspond with the state of the law of the reign of James I.　There may have been a time, however, when such words as these would have summed up the situation with rough accuracy; rather curiously, however, the maxim certainly did not then exist.

---

[1] Bracton, f. 159 b, which may be contrasted with f. 161 b.

[2] *Ibid.*, f. 102 b.

[3] Littleton, *Tenures*, s. 508.

[4] A few exceptional cases show the specific recovery of chattels in trespass: Sayles, *King's Bench*, i. 178–179 (1289) and ii. 16–17 (1290).

[5] See the *New English Dictionary* (ed. Murray), *s.vv.*　It occurs first in 1441; E. F. Jacob, *Chichele's Register*, II. 593.

[6] III Æthelred 14 (*c.* 997); Y.B. 18 Edward IV, Michs., no. 17; Winfield, *Death as affecting liability in tort*, Columbia Law Review, xxix. 239 at 244.

Even as early as Glanvill, however, the heir is liable for his ancestor's debts,[1] and in Bracton we are told that an heir can enforce his ancestor's credits.[2] It would almost seem as if this were a twelfth-century innovation made with the deliberate intention of competing with the Church; if so, its success was bought at the cost of some inconvenience, and only in the reign of Edward I[3] did the common law courts allow executors to appear before them in their representative capacity. This therefore did away with the cumbrous machinery of making the heir party to the litigation although the chattels were in the hands of the executors. Without legislation, therefore, the courts granted actions of debt by and against executors, and before the death of Edward I *Fleta* was able to say that the heir was not liable unless under a deed which expressly bound him.[4] Statute soon afterwards gave executors an action of account.[5]

A certain amount of provision had therefore been made by the end of Edward I's reign for the survival of personal actions, especially those of a contractual nature. Even so, serious limitations affected them; where the testator could have waged his law as a defence, the executors escaped liability, for they could not wage law in their testator's name. Hence cases of this sort (and they were common) had to wait for equitable relief, which only came late in the fifteenth century.[6]

Actions of tort had a curious history. Trespass certainly died with the person, until the first tentative inroad upon the simplicity of the rule was made in 1267, when abbots were allowed to sue upon trespasses done to their predecessors during the Barons' War.[7] Sixty years later, the civil wars of the reign of Edward II resulted in the defeat of the Despenser faction, the deposition of Edward II and the accession of Edward III. The victorious Mortimer party secured a statute to the effect that the executors of those who were slain " in the said quarrel " should have an action in respect of the goods and chattels of their testators,

---

[1] Glanvill, vii. 8.

[2] Bracton, f. 407 b.

[3] This is the conjecture of Pollock and Maitland, ii. 347.

[4] *Fleta*, ii. 62. 10. Nevertheless, the plaintiff does not describe himself in the writ as " heir ": Y.BB. Edward II (Selden Society), xxiv. 129, with which cf. *ibid.*, xxiii. 28. According to the later law, this liability only attached if the heir had inherited from the ancestor, but his liability was not limited to the value of the inheritance (Y.B. 40 Edward III, 15); a petition in Parliament to that effect was denied (*Rot. Parl.*, ii. 240–241). Such cases are rare (*Davy* v. *Pepys* (1573), Plowd. 441).

[5] Westminster II, c. 23 (1285). It may be that the statutory change was the earlier, and that the courts merely extended its policy.

[6] Ames, *Lectures in Legal History*, 95 n. 5. When the attitude of Chancery was well established, this sort of case was again brought in the common law courts, and the defendant executors refrained from abating the writ by insisting on a specialty. Their theoretical right to do so remained (as to this, see p. 703 below). After all, executors should care for their testator's soul by paying his just debts: *Edgecomb* v. *Dee* (1670), Vaughan, 89 at 93. Below, p. 647.

[7] Statute of Marlborough, 52 Henry III, c. 28. See also Westminster II, c. 35 (1285), for another aspect of the matter.

if they had been members of the party.[1] That was in 1327, and for the moment was merely an example of politicians, flushed by victory, sweeping aside established rules of law for their personal benefit. It did not rest there, however, for the reform seemed so beneficial that it was extended in 1330 to the world at large by the enactment that executors for the future shall have an action for damages against those who had taken the chattels of their testators during their lifetime.[2] From these two beginnings the law by devious paths gradually abandoned portions of the principle that personal actions died with the person, but progress was much faster in the field of contract than of tort. The replacement of the old actions of debt and detinue by assumpsit and trover brought further complications by confusing the two lines of mediaeval development.[3] In our own day the ravages of the automobile have completed the work begun by the feud of the Despensers and the Mortimers. The Chancellor, Lord Sankey, referred the rule to the Law Revision Committee over which Lord Hanworth then presided, and their recommendation[4] to abolish the rule (except in cases of defamation and seduction) has now been carried out.[5]

[1] 1 Edw. III, stat. 1, c. 3 (1327). The solecisms in this chapter suggest that the text originated with laymen rather than with lawyers.

[2] 4 Edw. III, c. 7 (1330).

[3] Details will be found in Holdsworth, iii. 576 ff.; cf. Goudy, " Two Ancient Brocards " in *Essays in Legal History* (ed. Vinogradoff), 215–229; Vinogradoff, *Collected Papers*, i 240.

[4] Law Revision Committee, *First Interim Report*, 1934 (Cd. 4540).

[5] Law Reform (Miscellaneous Provisions) Act, 1934.

CIVIL PROCEDURE

It is universally observed that in old legal systems the place of procedure is especially prominent. In general, this is true. In repeating that statement, however, it should be added that procedure is by no means negligible even in modern law, and that if the observation is to be valuable, we must search for the reasons for its position in early law and in modern law respectively.

Superficially, our oldest sources speak mostly of procedural matters—especially the best sources. An orderly discussion of writs such as we find in Glanvill is more illuminating to the reader than the heroic (though hopeless) attempt of Bracton in the earlier part of his book to state the law in terms of general principles. To a historian, it is the practical detail of old sources which gives him his richest material. If historians prefer the precise detail of the plea rolls and Year Books to the obscure generalities of Bracton's first hundred folios, it is because they are seeking the old law in action, rather than old law in theory. We may well believe that old lawyers themselves felt the same. The details of process and the practical side of pleading were as vital to them as recent cases or new statutes are to-day.

THE SLOWNESS OF OLD PROCEDURE

There is, however, a real difference between the place of procedure in the thirteenth and the twentieth centuries. Old procedure had to grow as it could. Much of it was ancient and traditional, but the very fact that it was not written in authoritative codes of rules left room for modification. Old procedure is therefore full of uncertainties, as a glance at any Year Book will show. Then, too, it has to contend with many difficulties which modern mechanical progress has eliminated. Most of the people whom it touched could neither read nor write, and so were easily victimised by dishonest officials. It could not rely on upright sheriffs, and sheriffs' underlings were a by-word in the middle ages. Considering their difficulties, the middle ages achieved remarkably good communications, but at their best, those communications were apt to be slow and uncertain. Their system of sending out writs into the country, and the sheriff returning them with an endorsement, was based on sound principles of business routine, and it is now clear that these writs and returns were filed, and could be handled with comparative speed.[1] But however good the system at the centre, there was always the peril of delay, mistake and fraud in the country. Procedure therefore had to be slow,[2] allowing for accidents, taking an irrevocable step only after abundant precautions, and providing means for correcting blunders as it went along.

PROCEDURE AS A CONSTITUTIONAL SAFEGUARD

This slow and cautious procedure was therefore regarded as a valuable safeguard by litigants. Where modern public opinion would insist upon a trial which was substantially fair, the mediaeval public looked rather at the procedure and inquired whether all the steps in it were properly carried out.[3] As a result, there is ample material for a history of mediaeval procedure, in the sense of process, for it was carefully recorded and widely studied, but very little light upon what actually went on before the eyes of a jury.

Procedure, considered as a safeguard, played a large part in constitutional struggles. Arbitrary action by the Crown or its officials

---

[1] See Sir Hilary Jenkinson's introduction to *Select Cases in the Exchequer of Pleas* (Selden Society); J. Conway Davies, in *Bulletin of the Institute of Historical Research*, xxvi. 125, xxvii. 1.

[2] Cf. Hengham (ed. Dunham), 16, 17.

[3] Cf. the demand in 1368 that no legal proceedings should be begun, except by indictment or original writ; above, p. 187.

necessarily involved a breach of procedural rules sooner or later. In 1215 the barons at Runnymede appealed to procedure as the only effective protection for their persons and property, and nearly two centuries earlier the same principle had been formulated in an edict of the Emperor Conrad II (1037) for the Holy Roman Empire. It is represented to this day in the due process clauses in the federal and state constitutions of America.

PROCEDURE AND SUBSTANTIVE LAW

The previous chapter has described the rise of the original writs and the forms of action which they initiated, and it will already be apparent that substantive law was discussed in terms of procedure. The rights of the parties will be expressed in the form of writs and pleading: the plaintiff in given circumstances can bring a particular writ, but if he does, the defendant in certain other circumstances may use a particular plea. Gradually there will come slight modifications as cases a little outside the ambit of the traditional forms are brought in, either by construction or by a modification of the forms. The result is a change in substantive law, but the machinery of the change, and its technical expression, will be in the rules about writs and pleadings.

THE SEPARATION OF LAW AND PROCEDURE

One of the most significant themes in the study of legal history is the growth of the power to think of law apart from its procedure. This power naturally can only develop when civilisation has reached a mature stage. It is essentially the statement of the results which have emerged from long and extensive experiment. Roman law, at the end of its long history, had reached this stage, and the results it obtained served in the middle ages as a valuable body of principles for the guidance of the younger national laws. In England, as elsewhere, premature attempts were made to express law in abstract terms by separating its principles from its practice. As we have already noticed, the failure of these attempts is clear evidence that the law was not yet strong enough to stand alone, for obscurity rather than clarity was the outcome. Glanvill is lucidly written wherever the author deals with writs, and it is only when he endeavours to generalise that he becomes obscure. Bracton's first hundred and seven folios have caused endless discussion and are little use as a historical source unless their statements can be verified from the mass of valuable detail which fortunately forms the bulk of his treatise. Littleton, however, wrote at a time when it was just becoming possible to state some general propositions about real property; but the statute of uses soon robbed real property law of any trace of clarity, and thenceforward no attempt was made to write a text-book (apart from beginners' manuals) on general lines.

Inspiration finally came, once again, from abroad. The middle of the eighteenth century is distinguished by the interest English lawyers took in French and Dutch works, and under this stimulus they attempted to think in terms of substantive law rather than merely of procedure. Mansfield on the bench set the example, and Blackstone at Oxford improved upon it by achieving the astonishing feat of writing his commentaries. At this time it is difficult to appreciate the daring of Blackstone. It can best be realised by looking at Viner's *Abridgement* which then held the place of honour in legal literature. To abandon all the time-honoured titles from " Abatement " to " Withernam " and replace them by a logical and analytical scheme required great courage and great skill. Blackstone had both, and in his pages we find the first comprehensive attempt to state (as far as was then possible) the whole of English law in the form of substantive rules.

The procedure was still there, however; in actual fact, the law was still entangled in it, and Blackstone's venture could be plausibly dismissed by conservatives as a mere literary device. In the course of the succeeding century the great revolution took place. With the abolition of forms of action and the unification of courts and procedure, it became possible for law to flow more freely and to escape the confinement of the old procedural categories. Only then did it become possible to consider the law in practice as being the application of substantive, rather than procedural, rules.

PROCEDURE IN MODERN TIMES

The separation affected procedure as well. Its position was more lowly henceforth, but its functions were more clearly defined, and its details could be more freely modelled in order to fulfil its objects. In the middle ages the rights of a party were the right to enjoy certain procedures, just as in the United States the citizen has a constitutional right to due process. In the newer order the place of procedure is purely ancillary—a means to an end. There is consequently growing up a science of procedure, based on an analysis of its functions, and a search for the quickest, cheapest and most reliable methods of organising the practical side of the law. Much experiment is going on, both in England and America.[1]

Confining our attention, for the moment, to contested litigation, any system of procedure must contain first of all a means whereby the plaintiff sets the machine in motion. Next the defendant must be notified and brought into court. Then we come to one of the most difficult problems—the discovery of the precise nature of the dispute between them, and its termination by judgment. In the more advanced systems there will have to be means of reviewing the first decision, and

---

[1] Much material is analysed by R. W. Millar, *The Formative Principles of Civil Procedure*, Illinois Law Review, xviii. 1, 94, 150 (reprinted as *prolegomena* to his translation of A. Englemann and others, *History of Continental Civil Procedure*, 1927).

in all systems there will have to be some method for enforcing whatever ultimate decision is reached.

Bearing in mind these general remarks on the history of procedure, we may now turn to an examination of some of its characteristics.

THE INITIATION OF PROCEEDINGS

A good many relics of Anglo-Saxon procedure are preserved in mediaeval borough customs; thus we find that in the time of Glanvill, Whitby had this custom:[1]

> "If any complaint (*querimonia*) should arise between burgesses, the plaintiff ought to demand thrice at the defendant's house that he should do him right and whatever law requires; and if at the third demand satisfaction is refused, let him at length make a reasonable complaint to the justice of the town."

The object of the provision was to prevent matters coming into court before it was clear that private negotiations had been tried and had failed. Several legal systems at the present day pursue the same end by a regular procedure of "conciliation" which is a necessary stage before litigation proper.

As we have already observed,[2] the King's Court adopted a similar principle in the writs *praecipe quod reddat*, the main difference being that the sheriff, instead of the party, made the demand for restitution.

SELF-HELP: DISTRESS

In some circumstances a party could do much more than merely demand his right. The ancient procedure of distress enabled him to take security from one who owed him services or rent arising out of freehold or leasehold tenure. There were rules, both of common law and statute, which prescribed the method. The distress must be made within the lord's fee, and not on the King's highway. Cattle were most usually taken, but plough beasts and certain essential implements of agriculture were privileged. If the tenant offered gage and pledge to contest the lord's claim, then the cattle had to be restored pending an action of replevin. Throughout the middle ages the lord had no right to dispose of the things taken. They were merely security and the property remained in the tenant; if the lord misused the chattel he became guilty of trespass—and some thought, of felony. The right of distress was immensely enlarged when a statute of 1690 gave the distrainor power to sell the distress.[3]

SECURING THE DEFENDANT'S APPEARANCE

If private endeavours failed, the next step was to get the defendant into court. The coercive power of the State generally has no difficulty

---

[1] *Borough Customs* (ed. Bateson, Selden Society), i. 89.

[2] Above, p. 363 n. 1.

[3] 2 William & Mary, session 1, c. 5.

in doing this under modern conditions, but early law found it immensely difficult. It first resorted to long and patient persuasion, in the hope that the adversary would promise to come into court. Appearance, in fact, was contractual—one of the earliest contracts which the law undertook to enforce.[1] Slowly, however, the State assumed coercive powers and undertook to compel appearance, but even when this was accomplished the forms were still relics of the earlier method. Instead of the party voluntarily giving gages and finding friends who would be his pledges, the sheriff is sent to take them, and if they are not forthcoming he will in the end seize the recalcitrant one's property as a security for his appearance.

In the King's Court we find a compromise between the old oral procedure and the newer machinery of written documents. The plaintiff began the proceedings by purchasing an original writ suited to his case. We find little more trace of the actual requirement of previous demands for right, although formal words long survived in the declaration on writs of debt saying that " the defendant though often requested has not paid the said sum to the plaintiff, but has so far refused, and still refuses ". If the older writs require the sheriff to urge the defendant to do right, the more modern type, represented by novel disseisin and trespass, begins at once with an order to summon.

Most original writs were not " served "; they went to the sheriff, and he carried out the order through machinery which looks very old. He appointed two " good summoners " (and at first they were certainly not officials) who went to the party and summoned him. In Glanvill's day they had to come to court in order to testify whether they had properly summoned the defendant.[2] Thrice was the party summoned, and if he had not yet appeared, process issued to take his land. This oral summons was a weak point, and disputes whether summons had been duly made were frequent. The early stringent proof of summons by the testimony of the summoners was soon relaxed, and it became general to allow wager of law—an easy " proof " of non-summons—as a means of " curing a default ".

Instead of merely failing to appear, the defendant might send certain excuses called " essoins ". A number of " essoiners " were sent to explain that the party was sick, abroad, on the King's service, cut off by a flood, a broken bridge, and so forth. These secured delays of varying length, and in early times were verified. The court would send four knights to see whether the party was actually in bed. As one was entitled to an essoin if one had previously appeared, it was possible to spin out a long series of appearances and essoins. Worse still, in certain actions, especially debt, it was necessary to have all the co-defendants in court together. This might never happen if they arranged to cast

[1] Holdsworth, ii. 83.
[2] Glanvill, i. 7.

essoins in turn. This practice of "fourcher" was particularly favoured by executors, until it was stopped by statute.[1]

The distinction already noted[2] between "demands" and "complaints" was extended to the procedure. Upon writs of *praecipe quod reddat* the process consisted of a long series of distresses directed against the tenant's land; upon writs *ostensurus quare* the process was a series of summonses, attachments, and possibly arrest (*capias*) and even outlawry.

OUTLAWRY IN CIVIL PROCESS

The dreadful penalty of outlawry was originally the last resort of criminal law. In the time of Bracton, however, it makes its appearance in civil procedure, and it is not surprising that the first form of action to involve outlawry was trespass. Further extensions of outlawry were made by statute to actions of account[3] in 1285, debt, detinue and replevin[4] in 1352, and to actions of case[5] in 1504. Necessarily, this procedural outlawry had to be in a much mitigated form, and so what was once equivalent to a death sentence was shorn of such terrors as peril of life, corruption of blood and escheat of lands;[6] the insurgent peasants demanded its abolition, both in civil and criminal proceedings, but without success; down to 1870 it still involved forfeiture of chattels.[7] Moreover, the use of outlawry was hedged about with procedural precautions which left many chances of getting it reversed upon a writ of error.

JUDGMENT BY DEFAULT

The common law was reluctant to give judgment by default. The principle of the petty assizes, however, made it necessary, and so we find that, as part of the very summary procedure of the assize of novel disseisin, the twelve recognitors were summoned at the same time as the defendant; if the defendant persistently defaulted, then the verdict of the assize would be taken even in his absence, and judgment given. In other real actions judgment could be given against a tenant who had exhausted his liberal allowance of defaults. A tenant who lost by default was not for ever barred, but could regain his land if he succeeded in a writ " of a higher nature "; thus, if he had lost by default

---

[1] Fourcher was forbidden between parceners and joint-tenants in 1275 (Westminster I, c 43), and between husband and wife in 1278 (Gloucester, c. 10); since 1335 actions of debt against executors were to proceed against whichever one appeared first (9 Edw. III, stat. 1, c. 3); a petition for such legislation is printed in Sayles, *King's Bench*, iii. p. cxix. Fourcher in account survived: Y.BB. Edward II (Selden Society), xxii. 115.

[2] Above, p. 372.

[3] Westminster II, c. 11.

[4] 25 Edw. III, stat. 5, c. 17.

[5] 19 Hen. VII, c. 9.

[6] See the discussion in Y.B. 3 Edward III, Michs. no. 19 (1329).

[7] Forfeiture Act, 1870 (33 & 34 Vict., c. 23).

in an assize he could still recover (if his title was sufficient) in a writ of entry, or if he had lost by default in a writ of entry, he could resort to a writ of right. Even in a writ of right, a judgment by default will not bar a future writ of right except in certain circumstances.[1]

In personal actions the situation was rather different. The subject matter of the dispute was not indestructible like land, and there was the additional factor of the rights of the Crown. Especially in trespass, there was the idea that people ought to be punished for their torts as well as making reparation, and where the Crown and a subject were in competition, the issue was inevitable. Bracton indeed had argued that debts and damages ought to be levied from a defaulter's personal property, but (as Maitland remarked) it took six hundred years for his view to prevail.[2] There was a time when something of the sort could be done in actions of debt,[3] but the experiment was abandoned and the common law clung to the principle that no judgment should be given in personal actions against an absent defendant. The Crown did, indeed, pursue him with rigorous process, but the resulting attachments and forfeitures only benefited the Crown and not the party.

THE NEW CONVENTIONAL PROCEDURE

In the course of the seventeenth century the courts and the profession combined to evolve a remarkable reform in procedure. This revolution —it was nothing less—was effected by a series of fictions, and had for its object nothing less than the abandonment of the old system of original writs.

We have already noticed the fact that the common law courts were often rivals for business, and this rivalry was no doubt the main motive of these reforms, for their primary object was not so much the relief of litigants as the attraction of business from one court into another.

PROCEEDINGS BY BILL

It had long been a principle with the mediaeval courts that proceedings could be taken by bill, without further preliminaries, against an officer of the court or against a person who for any reason was already within the jurisdiction of the court; particularly, the King's Bench would hear bills based upon causes of action arising in the county where the court happened at the time to be sitting.[4] The exploitation of this rule had far-

---

[1] See the discussion in Bracton. f. 367.

[2] Pollock and Maitland, ii. 595; Uniformity of Process Act, 1832 (2 Will. IV, c. 39).

[3] *Bracton's Note Book*, no. 900 (1224).

[4] In the fourteenth century it moved frequently. Cf. below, p. 470. H. G. Richardson and G. O. Sayles, *Proceedings without Writ: Henry III* (Selden Society), have assembled material showing an even greater use of bills than that mentioned in the text. The interpretation of this material is difficult, and cannot be attempted here. The frequency of bills of trespass is evident from statutes of 1331 (5 Edw. III, c. 7) and 1354 (28 Edw. III, c. 8).

reaching results. In the middle of the fifteenth century the King's Bench allowed a real or fictitious bill of Middlesex to be proffered against a person, supposing him to have committed within that county (where the court had by now settled down) a trespass with force and arms. This was within the court's normal jurisdiction, and if the defendant surrendered and was committed or bailed he was sufficiently within the court's jurisdiction to be put to answer any other bill proffered against him while in custody. If the defendant did not come in, process called *latitat* issued, and eventually he might find himself in contempt. An ingenious but complicated system of bail gave some reality to the proceedings, but the Court of Common Pleas procured a statute in 1661 which rendered the device ineffective by enacting that arrest and bail could only be had if the process disclosed the true cause of action.[1]

The bill of Middlesex only alleged a fictitious trespass, and so was useless after the statute, until the King's Bench took the simple course of adding to the fictitious trespass (which gave it jurisdiction) a clause *ac etiam*, " and moreover ", which set out the real cause of action. The King's Bench therefore regained the use of this device to capture business (but not real actions) from the Common Pleas. Retaliation followed when the Common Pleas used its ancient writ of trespass *quare clausum fregit* with an *ac etiam* clause containing other matter, which enabled it to compete with King's Bench.

In both cases the commencement of the proceedings was a document whose contents were completely fictitious, and in practice neither the bill of Middlesex nor the writ of trespass *quare clausum fregit* was issued. Process therefore began immediately with the *latitat* (in the King's Bench) or with the *capias* (in the Common Pleas).[2]

In the eighteenth century this omission was extended to trespass actions which did not have a fictitious origin, with the result that most actions, apart from the older real actions, began with a *capias* instead of an original writ. By such devious means the courts achieved a considerable measure of reform, which paved the way for the more thorough simplification effected in 1832.[3]

The proceedings between appearance and judgment will be described in the next chapter in so far as they are pleadings; modes of trial and the *nisi prius* system have already been described.

APPELLATE PROCEEDINGS

The hierarchy of ecclesiastical courts—archdeacon, bishop, archbishop, pope—gave English lawyers their first sight of appeals being carried from court to court. Within the limits of their own system they

[1] 13 Car. II, st. 2, c. 2.

[2] On some surviving manuscript criticisms of these developments, see Faith Thompson, *Magna Carta . . . 1300-1629*, 201-202.

[3] Uniformity of Process Act, 1832 (2 Will. IV, c. 39).

copied it, at least in externals. Bracton likened the King to the Pope, and, like the Pope, the King could call into his court cases which were in progress in inferior tribunals. By means of *tolt* a plea could be removed from a seignorial court into the county, and by a writ of *pone* it could be thence transferred to the Common Pleas. It is interesting to observe that by 1294 these were merely paper proceedings, so to speak, and that such a case did not in fact come before the county court on its way to Westminster.[1]

If a plea in the local court had proceeded to judgment, it could be reviewed only in the King's Court. There was thus no possibility of pleas moving up through a hierarchy of feudal courts, for as early as the reign of Henry I the principle was formulated that " false judgment is a royal plea ".[2] The proceedings in the local courts were oral, and so they had to be committed to writing before the King's Court could examine them. A writ of *recordari facias loquelam* in the form of an *accedas ad curiam* ordered the sheriff to go to the court of a lord and cause its proceedings in the case to be recorded; this record was then brought into the King's Court by four suitors of the court below—or four knights if the case came from the county court. If one of the parties disputed the accuracy of the record, battle might be waged. The record being settled, the King's Court would hear the objections to it and act accordingly; it might even continue the remaining stages of the case itself, for the error below will amost certainly have been a procedural one.[3]

The expression " false judgment " is not one which any prudent person would apply to the decision of a royal court. The proper expression will be " error on the record " if the acts of the Common Pleas are to be reviewed, and the procedure will be a writ of error to move the record (or rather, a copy of it) into the King's Bench,[4] and thence maybe to Parliament.[5] Like false judgment, the writ of error will only secure a review of whatever appears on the record of the court below. This will be largely concerned with matters of procedure, although implicit in them there may well be a question of substantive law. Questions of fact, however, were definitely outside the operation of a writ of error.[6]

---

[1] Y.B. 21 & 22 Edward I (Rolls Series), 452. See generally, F. L. Ganshof, *Faussement de Jugement* (Bulletin de la Commission royale des anciennes lois de Belgique, XIV. ii) 1935, and Julius Goebel, " The Matrix of Empire ", in J. H. Smith, *Appeals to the Privy Council*, 1950

[2] Plucknett, *Legislation of Edward I*, 24–25.

[3] An example of this procedure has been given above, p. 121.

[4] For the earliest writ of error in the King's Bench from the Common Pleas, see *Bracton's Note Book*, no. 1166 (dated 1236).

[5] In 1376 Parliament refused to hear error in the Common Pleas, *Rot. Parl.*, ii. 330 (48); the procedure is explained in Y.B. 1 Henry VII, 19, and Y.B. 14 & 15 Edward III (Rolls Series), 364.

[6] The writs of error *coram nobis* and *coram vobis* are only apparent exceptions to this principle See the note in Harvard Law Review, xxxvii. 744.

FINAL PROCESS

The successful demandant in a real action obtained a writ directed to the sheriff, who was thereby authorised to put him into seisin.[1]

The final process in personal actions, however, was not so simple a matter. The plaintiff had judgment for a sum of money as a debt, or damages, or both. Different possibilities have been open to such creditors at different epochs of our legal history. Obviously there are three principal types of execution to be considered, which may be directed against the defendant's person, his chattels, and his land respectively.

Personal slavery in satisfaction of debts is an ancient institution and undoubtedly formed part of Anglo-Saxon law,[2] as also of old German law.[3] It disappeared, however, after the Conquest, with the result that for a time our law did not issue process against the person of a judgment debtor. Its reappearance is largely statutory. The King could always use it for Crown debts, but in 1285 masters, without judicial proceedings of any sort, were authorised by statute—one of the most drastic enactments in our history—to commit to gaol servants and bailiffs whose accounts were in arrears.[4]

Meanwhile, the statutes of merchants (to be mentioned later) gave similarly stringent execution against the persons of merchants, who, it must be remembered, were a well-defined class or estate, subject to peculiar rules of law, and against such others as had expressly placed themselves within the terms of the statutes. " Common persons " could not be imprisoned for debt until after 1352, when the initial process of actions of debt was assimilated to that of account.[5] In terms the statute only dealt with mesne process, but by this time there was a common law rule that if a defendant could be imprisoned on mesne process, then he could also be imprisoned on final process; indirectly, therefore, the result was to introduce imprisonment for debt.[6] The rule in question no doubt derived from trespass *vi et armis* to which it originally applied. Imprisonment was not extended to actions on the case until 1504.[7] It seems early to have been established that if the plaintiff takes a *capias ad satisfaciendum* he must abandon all other modes of execution, and so (as a general rule) cannot proceed against the defendant's property if once he has proceeded against his person.

---

[1] To enter without the sheriff is disseisin: Y.B. 20–21 Edward I, 52; Sayles, *King's Bench* II. 98 (but see the denial by Bereford in Y.BB. Edward II (Selden Society), xxii. 104).

[2] Pollock and Maitland, ii. 596.

[3] Tacitus, *Germania*, c. 24.

[4] Westminster II, c. 11 (1285). Cf. Plucknett, *The Medieval Bailiff*, 22 ff.

[5] 25 Edw. III, st. 5, c. 17 (1352).

[6] Y.B. 40 Edward III, 25, pl. 28 (1366). If, however, the defendant appeared before the mesne process had got as far as the *capias ad respondendum*, then he was not liable to a *capias ad satisfaciendum*: Y.B. 49 Edward III, 2, pl. 5 (1375), which doubts whether outlawry was possible after judgment.

[7] 19 Henry VII, c. 9 (1504).

It is not surprising, then, that the majority of creditors saw more chances of satisfaction by proceeding against the debtor's property. Down to the reign of Edward I only the debtor's chattels could be reached by the two common law writs available. Of these, *fieri facias* authorised the sheriff to " cause " the sum due " to be made up " from the debtor's goods and chattels; *levari facias* went a little further and allowed it to be levied out of the produce of his land as it became available. This included crops, rents and the like, and leases,[1] all of which the sheriff could take and realise.

These writs of execution were only available upon judgments in the King's courts. In local courts " of wapontakes, hundreds, and courts of barons " it was only possible to distrain the defendant. This caused him harm, but it did no good to the creditor; a petition in 1348 that such distresses might be sold in order to satisfy the judgment was rejected.[2] This archaic procedure must have had much to do with the decline of the local courts.

STATUTORY PROCESS OF ELEGIT

We have already hinted that dealings with, and through the medium of, the sheriff were not always entirely satisfactory in the middle ages. The levying of judgment debts could no doubt be done quicker and cheaper by the creditor himself than by the ancient machinery of the county executive. It took the common law some time to get over its repugnance to putting a creditor in possession of a debtor's lands, and the restrictions on alienation may also have proved an obstacle. However, as early as 1215 the first step in this direction was taken. The Great Charter enacted that if a surety had discharged his principal's debt to the Crown, then the surety could be put into possession of the principal's lands, to hold them until he had levied the debt from the issues.[3] The courts themselves made one more effort in this direction, in a situation which has already been mentioned,[4] but a general procedure allowing the creditor to reach the proceeds of land without the intervention of the sheriff only appears in 1285. By the Statute of Westminster the Second,

" When a debt has been recovered, or acknowledged, or damages awarded in the king's court, it shall henceforth lie in the election of the plaintiff to sue a writ to the sheriff ordering that he cause to be made (*fieri facias*) out of the lands and chattels; or, that the sheriff deliver to him all the chattels of the debtor (except cattle and beasts of the plough) and one half of his land (according to a reasonable

---

[1] Leases could also be sold under *fi. fa.*

[2] *Rot. Parl.*, ii. 167 no. 21.

[3] Magna Carta (1215), c. 9; (1225), c. 8.

[4] Above, p. 377 n. 4; where the heir was expressly made liable for the debt by his ancestor's deed, then the heir's land was delivered to the creditor; otherwise execution would be impossible, for the testator's goods go to the executors. *Fleta* ii. 62, 10; *Davy* v. *Pepys* (1573), Plowd. 441 (cf. *Harbert's Case* (1584), 3 Rep. 12 b); Jews already had such a remedy by the Statute of Jewry, 3 Edw. I.

price or extent) until the debt shall have been levied. And if he is ejected from the tenement let him recover by novel disseisin. . . ."[1]

The alternative procedure here provided was called *elegit* because the writ recites that the creditor " has chosen " it instead of *fieri facias*. A jury was summoned to make the " extent " or valuation of the land, and to fix a fair price for the chattels. The concluding clause of the statute is interesting, for it contemplates the creditor entering into possession of the lands, and protects him by novel disseisin, although it would clearly be anomalous to describe him as " seised "; we have here, therefore, an early example of a statutory estate which will not fit into the common law system of seisin.[2] Leases held by the debtor were also in an anomalous position, for the sheriff might deliver them to be sold by the creditor as " chattels " or he might extend them as " lands ", in which case the creditor merely takes over the remainder of the lease from the debtor.

DEBTS OF RECORD

So far, this chapter has been concerned with contentious litigation. Many persons, however, desired to obtain the benefits of a judgment without the hazards and delays of a long process; particularly, lenders wished to have judgment entered at the moment the loan was contracted, and thus avoid the difficulties of getting the debtor into court, and also the further risks of meeting a defence of wager of law, of depending on the appearance of witnesses, or the risk of losing a bond under seal— for if it were lost or defaced, the action was extinguished. Prudent lenders in the early thirteenth century almost always solved these difficulties by bringing an action of debt and pursuing it as far as judgment against their prospective debtors—" and we may be pretty certain that in many cases no money has been advanced until a judgment has been given for its repayment ".[3] Many actions, collusive no doubt, did not proceed to judgment, but concluded with a compromise which was recorded on the plea rolls, often with a covenant that the sheriff may levy the debt if it is defaulted. Still other cases are to be found on the close rolls of Chancery. These were not judicial records, but merely copies of State correspondence for official reference, but on the backs of the rolls numerous private deeds are to be found, generally concerned with debts. Private debts might also be acknowledged in the Exchequer.

The principal advantage of these measures was the ease with which

---

[1] Westminster II, c. 18; the reference in the statute to " lands " in connection with *fi. fa.* is curious. It possibly means those devisable burgages in towns which the law regarded more as chattels than lands (as in the Statute of Acton Burnell); cf. also p. 390 n. 1 above. Cf. Plucknett, *Legislation of Edward I*, 148 ff.

[2] It soon became customary to describe the tenant by *elegit* as " seised ".

[3] Pollock and Maitland, ii. 203.

the debt could be proved from documents which were kept in official custody with great care. Moreover, such a recognisance enrolled in a court of record operated immediately as a charge upon the debtor's lands. Upon default *fieri facias* or *elegit* could be had.[1] The Statute of Westminster the Second enacted that matters enrolled by the chancellor or judges, whether they concern land or debts, ought not to admit of further pleading, and that the plaintiff at any time within a year of the record may henceforth have a writ of execution upon them; if more than a year has elapsed, he may have a *scire facias* calling on the defendant to show cause why execution should not be issued.[2]

STATUTES MERCHANT

The class of merchants were particularly interested in procedures of this sort, and at this same moment were procuring legislation especially adapted to their requirements. Speed, ease of proof and drastic execution were the principles which they incorporated into the traditional deed enrolled and the recognisance. In 1283 the Statute of Acton Burnell made special provision for the enrolment of mercantile debts in the principal towns, where the mayor was to keep a roll, and a clerk appointed by the Crown was to enter upon it the details of recognisances; the clerk was also to draw a deed and give it to the creditor, sealed with the debtor's seal and his own official seal. Upon default, the mayor was to order the sale of the debtor's chattels and devisable burgage lands; if there were none within the jurisdiction, the Lord Chancellor was to make suitable process. If the debtor had no such property he was to be imprisoned, the creditor providing him bread and water only.[3]

Defects in the working of the statute soon became apparent, and there was talk of " malice and delay ". The matter was therefore taken up again two years later and the result was the great Statute of Merchants of 1285.[4] The details of enrolment and sealing were changed so as to leave less room for fraud by the local officials, but the greatest change was in the execution allowed. The process was to begin with the imprisonment of the debtor, instead of using imprisonment as a last resort. There was to be no escaping this; if the gaoler did not accept the prisoner he (or failing him, the owner of the gaol) became liable for the debt. During the first three months the debtor was to have facilities

---

[1] Y.BB. Edward II (Selden Society), xxii. 96 (1317), was an ingenious fraud to evade the statute; the court stated the nature of a recognisance in its judgment enrolled, *ibid.*, 110.

[2] Westminster II, c. 45 (1285). For *scire facias* awarded against an infant heir, see Y.BB. Edward II (Selden Society), xxii. 238–241 (1318); for the charge falling upon after-acquired land, *ibid.*, 244. There seem no grounds for the suggestion in Y.B. 12 & 13 Edward III (Rolls Series), cvii, that there is anything " equitable " about *scire facias*.

[3] Statute of Acton Burnell, 11 Edw. I (1283). This was a much more thorough system than the one devised in France a few years earlier and summarised by Beaumanoir, § 52; cf. Barré, *L'Ordonnance de Philippe le Hardi*, Bibliothèque de l'École des Chartes, xcvi. 5.

[4] For the differences between the statutes of 1283 and 1285, see Plucknett, *Legislation of Edward I*, 138 ff.

for selling not only his chattels but also his land. If the debt had not been settled within those three months, the chattels were delivered to the creditor for sale and all the land (not merely half as by *elegit*) was to be held by the creditor, who was to be " seised " of it until the debt was levied from the issues. A very peculiar feature of the statute is that it makes all lands held at the time of the recognisance liable to execution, even if they had since been alienated.[1]

The object was clearly to circumvent the prejudice against compulsorily stripping a debtor of his land by selling it. The statute did not venture to do this, but the drastic process of immediate close imprisonment was evidently meant to compel the debtor to sell. A clause was necessary to declare that such sales should be valid, no doubt because at common law a deed made in prison could generally be avoided.

Recognisances entered into in accordance with this act were called shortly " statutes ", and a creditor who was in under the act was called a " tenant by statute merchant ". It remained the principal form of security during the middle ages, and even for centuries afterwards it was in very general use.

STATUTES STAPLE

Similar machinery was set up in every staple town by Edward III in 1353 for the special convenience of the members of those particular communities of merchants.[2] The law and the forms were the same as for statutes merchant, the only difference being that the officials who took the recognisances were the staple officers, and that (at first) the recognisances were practically confined to operations in the " staple " commodities of wool, leather, etc.

In later times both statutes merchant and statutes staple were used by non-merchants.

AUDITA QUERELA

The principle behind all these devices was that no defence could be possible to a recognisance made under these forms. No provision therefore was made for pleadings or defences by the debtor.

It soon became clear that the legislature had been too optimistic in this respect. The resources of mediaeval fraud and forgery were considerable, and the complication of the land law introduced many nice points in the execution of " statutes ". We therefore find that the necessary procedure finally appears, taking the form of the writ *audita*

---

[1] Statute of Merchants, 13 Edw. I (1285). For material illustrating the use of statutes merchant and staple in both mediaeval and modern times see *Select Cases in Law Merchant* (ed. Hall, Selden Society), vols. ii and iii; A. Beardwood, *Bishop Langton's use of statute merchant recognisances,* Medievalia et Humanistica, ix. 54; E. E. Rich, *Staple Court Books of Bristol.*

[2] Statute of Staples, 27 Edw. III (1353).

querela.[1]   It issued out of Chancery and was directed to the judges of the King's Bench or Common Pleas, ordering them to do speedy justice to the debtor, after having heard his complaint (*audita querela*) and the reasons of the parties.   There is good ground for believing that this writ was first authorised by Parliament in 1336 as a remedy in these circumstances.[2]

The scope of the writ was, in general, to permit the defendant to raise matters which in ordinary cases he could have raised by way of plea in common law actions.   It replaced the action of deceit and the writ of error to a large extent in matters arising under the statutes of merchants and staple, and later in the middle ages was used as a general remedy for those who had been the victims of the forgery or fraudulent manipulation of any type of procedure and records.[3]   It may be added that the defences available do not seem to extend beyond the common law's traditional relief against the abuse of legal procedure, and that there seems to be no ground for regarding *audita querela* as being particularly " equitable " in its nature.[4]   It seems that the words of Stonor, C.J., " I tell you plainly that *audita querela* is given rather by equity than by common law ",[5] simply mean that the writ allows the debtor to plead common law defences, although the statutes deliberately deprived him of that opportunity.

PREROGATIVE WRITS

The writs mentioned here and in the last chapter have been essential parts in the conduct of litigation; but the primary function of a writ was merely to convey the King's commands to his officers and servants, of whatever nature those commands might be.[6]   The *Register of Writs* shows in fact a large variety of writs whose nature was administrative rather than judicial.   Some of these writs acquired the name of " prerogative writs " in the seventeenth and eighteenth centuries.[7]   A few of them have been the subject of special study.[8]   At the present time, writs on administrative matters are of importance in local government matters,

---

[1] Of the " complaint " as a procedure we have already spoken.   Those complaints which could be immediately dealt with were brought into court (as we have seen) sometimes by an assize of novel disseisin, which Bracton f. 179 and elsewhere constantly calls a *querela*, and sometimes by a summons *ostensurus quare . . . unde queritur* (above, pp. 370, 371).   Those which required preliminary investigation were often dealt with by writs reciting *ex gravi querela* or *audita querela*: examples in Sayles, *King's Bench*, iii. 11, and in intro. p. lxiv. n. 3.   Indeed, there was a marked trespassory element (including damages) in *audita querela*: Y.BB. Richard II (Ames Foundation), v. 147–149 (1388).

[2] See the statement made in 1344: Y.B. 18 Edward III (Rolls Series), 308.   Cf. Plucknett, *Legislation of Edward I*, 145.

[3] See the fifteenth-century example, in Rastell's *Entries*.

[4] Y.B. 20 Edward III (Rolls Series), i. 92–94 (1346), is a good example.

[5] Y.B. 17 Edward III (Rolls Series), 370 (1343); cf. Holdsworth, ii. 344, 593.

[6] F. E. Harmer, *Anglo-Saxon Writs*, 1 ff.

[7] S. A. de Smith, *Prerogative Writs*, Cambridge Law Journal, xi. 40.

[8] E. Jenks, *Story of the Habeas Corpus*, Law Quarterly Review, xviii. 64.

mandamus and *certiorari* for example; in the middle ages prohibition played an important part in the conflict of church and state,[1] and could be used against the admiralty and local courts as well.[2] Occasionally it happened that the constant issue of prohibitions would result in the creation of a new form of action.[3]

THE ISSUE OF WRITS

The precise functions of chancery in the drafting and issuing of writs leave room for controversy.[4] The ambiguity of the word " writ " is a source of trouble, for it has led some historians to regard restrictions upon the issue of " writs " by the council's authorisation as if they were restrictions upon its supposed power to create new writs for judicial use,[5] and the efforts of Bracton and *Fleta* to explain the procedure are hardly successful. The statute *in consimili casu* of 1285 shows that chancery had important functions,[6] and a famous year book passage shows how those functions were carried out.[7] It was confessedly the aim of the writ-system to cover the whole field of law,[8] and the responsibility of chancery in controlling so vast a movement was of the gravest—in effect it threatened to be the supreme legislator of the common law. But one great check was maintained over its activities: the common law courts could, and did, quash writs of which they disapproved.[9] The ultimate decision to quash or to sustain a novel writ therefore lay with the common law judges.

Royal justice was so good that it could overcome the inherent defect that the issue of writs was almost a monopoly of the chancery—a distant and peripatetic office. Certain prudent concessions had, indeed, been made—plaints could be brought in local courts, and even in the King's Court,[10] and on the occasion of a general eyre some original writs could be got from the court (as judicial writs regularly could[11]). Some alleviation could thus be brought lest the writ-system become impossibly

---

[1] Norma Adams, *The Writ of Prohibition to Court Christian,* Minnesota Law Review, xx. 272; G. B. Flahiff, *The use of prohibitions by clerics against ecclesiastical courts in England,* Mediaeval Studies (Pontifical Institute of Mediaeval Studies, Toronto), iii. 101, *The Writ of prohibition in the thirteenth century, ibid.,* vi. 261, vii. 229.

[2] Above, pp. 197–198.

[3] Below, p. 570 (waste); so also *Contra formam feofamenti* and champerty (Plucknett, *Statutes and their Interpretation,* 9–10).

[4] The references given above, p. 373 n. 2, all deal with the matter.

[5] Provisions of Oxford (in Stubbs, *Charters*).

[6] Westminster II, c. 24.

[7] Y.BB. Edward II (Selden Society), iii. 19, 108–109; above, p. 362 n. 4.

[8] Cf. above, p. 354.

[9] Bracton, f. 414 b.

[10] Above, pp. 370 ff.

[11] Y.BB. 30 & 31 Edward I (Rolls Series). 124; *Rot. Parl.,* i. 154 no. 5, ii. 229 no. 25; *Brevia Placitata* (Selden Society), xlvi ff.

difficult, but the erection of local branches of the chancery never took place.[1]

NINETEENTH-CENTURY REFORMS

There have been two main lines of procedure, therefore, the one concerned with contested litigation, and the other with uncontested forms in which the proceedings consisted of final process issuing out of records upon which the parties had voluntarily enrolled their obligations. Parties who had not taken the preliminary precautions of entering into recognisances had perforce to go through all the forms of contested litigation, but as early as Coke's day this was made less formidable by the practice of the profession.[2] It had already become impossible, and indeed unnecessary, to pronounce judgment in open court upon the thousands of cases in which there was actually no defence. In such circumstances, where the functions of the court were purely ministerial, the attorneys carried on the proceedings between themselves, making up the record and procuring its enrolment, even going so far as to enter judgment in multitudes of cases which had never been mentioned in court. Of course, the record, if erroneous, was liable to be quashed if the defendant brought a writ of error, but the careful copying of approved forms out of the current books of practice (of which there was a great number) was almost always a sufficient precaution. The way was therefore well prepared for the still speedier and easier summary judgment which we owe to nineteenth-century statute law.

The conventional procedure of the seventeenth and eighteenth centuries likewise achieved a very large measure of reform which made the work of the legislature much simpler, for it constituted a substantial advance towards uniformity of process by its extended use of the *capias* in initiating all sorts of actions.[3]

METHODS OF REFORM

It is not without interest to notice the different methods of law reform which are illustrated by various episodes in the history of procedure (and for that matter, of other branches of the law as well). If a rule, a procedure or an institution is working unsatisfactorily, there are several courses from which to choose. The simplest is to abolish it and substitute something better. It is natural that so straightforward a remedy should only be employed when there are men with vigour and courage to carry it out. It is apt to be characteristic of the great moments of the

---

[1] G. O. Sayles, *Local Chanceries*, Bulletin of the Institute of Historical Research, xiv. 69.

[2] Holdsworth, ix. 259.

[3] The history of the successive reforms made by the legislature in the nineteenth century involves a formidable mass of detail; the main changes have been skilfully extracted by Professor Jenks in chapter xix of his *Short History of English Law* (4th ed. enlarged, 1934).

common law, therefore, rather than of those less heroic times when the system is in repose. The last years of the thirteenth century may be rightly regarded as the golden age of the common law, and it was a moment when some things were being abolished by statute (especially in the field of procedure) and other new things were being established. It is not a little curious that the most conservative minds, looking back to a distant golden age, are apt to light upon a period which was distressing to the conservatives who lived in it; " new king, new laws, new judges, new masters " is the lament of a Year Book in reporting a case decided by Chief Justice Bereford, who is the brightest figure in the brightest period of the Year Books.[1]

A less drastic policy is to diminish the importance of the offending member without excising it. The long line of statutes of jeofail is an example. These statutes adopted the policy of enacting that certain minute slips in enrolling should not for the future invalidate the record.[2] They began with slips of spelling, and proceeded by cautious stages to defects slightly less trivial. The result was disastrous. By excusing some slips, the others were by implication rendered still more grave, with the inevitable result that pleadings as a whole became still more dependent upon minute accuracy for their effect than they were before.

A third policy was to neutralise the wrong done at one point by introducing a new mechanism to counteract the old. This is surely the most tempting, and the most fallacious, of all. It is also the most frequent, for the courts must make their own reforms if the legislature will not, but the courts cannot (as a rule) abolish anything. Their efforts are therefore confined to providing safeguards against other legal rules. We thus get as a result an increase in the bulk of the law, for the old subsists with the new, and an increase in its complexity because the question of the relationship between the old and the new is bound to arise. Nor is this situation confined to judicial legislation, for even the statutes of Edward I raised the question by their failure to complete their work by abolishing unsatisfactory law. One of the most notorious examples, however, is the law of outlawry. Its traditional machinery was slow, but crushing. When it was felt that it was too severe, reform took the shape, not of modifying the nature of mesne process, but of insisting upon extraordinary accuracy in every detail of the outlawry procedure.[3] This terrible engine was fitted with prodigious brakes, therefore, and so its energy, which might have been usefully applied, was carefully neutralised. The result frequently was that when it ought to have moved it did not, while at other times it might unexpectedly get out of control. The law of outlawry thus became

---

[1] Y.BB. Edward II (Selden Society), xi. 87.

[2] They begin with 14 Edw. III, st. 1, c. 6 (1340), when the record was still beyond the reach of the parties. Later these statutes benefited attorneys and counsel who drew pleadings.

[3] Cf. the statute of additions, 1 Hen. V, c. 5 (1413), explained in Reeves, *History of English Law*, ii. 520 n. Below, p. 429.

notoriously tricky and ineffective.[1] Another example we shall find later in the history of defamation. Early in the seventeenth century the courts felt that the law of slander was unsatisfactory because a great many persons invoked its protection. Such reasoning is not very promising, and the remedy devised was worthy of it—the courts insisted upon a fantastically strict observance of pleading and other technicalities. The greatest of all examples is of course the history of the conventional and fictitious procedure which we have just related, while nearly as remarkable is the development of vast masses of law dealing with " falsifying recoveries ", " counterpleas of voucher " and similar matters in real property law, where one procedure is piled on another in the hope that the last will counteract the defects of the earlier ones.

---

[1] The great severity of the criminal law in general likewise produced the " safeguard" of minutely technical indictments and definitions of various crimes.

PLEADING

In the well-known words of Littleton[1] in his advice to his son, " it is one of the most honourable, laudable, and profitable things in our law to have the science of well pleading in actions real and personal; and therefore I counsel thee especially to employ thy courage and care to learn this ". Care and courage were indeed necessary to master the science of pleading as it flourished in the seventeenth and eighteenth centuries, though we may perhaps think that the pleading of Littleton's day was sufficiently accurate and commendably free from the later subtleties which finally compelled its abandonment. Littleton's words had the fortunate result of prompting Coke to write in his most concise style a little manual of the elements of pleading which is a useful introduction to the subject.[2]

THE ORIGINS OF PLEADING

It is clear that the origins of pleadings were oral altercations between the parties which took place in court. They were not preliminaries, nor were they part of process, but a distinct stage—indeed, the central stage—

[1] Littleton, *Tenures*, s. 534.
[2] Co. Lit. 303–304 b.

of the litigants' progress. It may be conjectured that in their earlier form they consisted entirely of sworn statements, and so were part of the machinery for adducing proof. Thus in debt, the plaintiff swears:[1]

" In the name of the living God, as I money demand, so have I lack of that which *N* promised me when I mine to him sold."

To this the defendant replies:

" In the name of the living God, I owe not to *N* sceatt nor shilling nor penny nor penny's worth; but I have discharged to him all that I owed him, so far as our verbal contracts were at first."

These forms therefore serve a double purpose: first, they make clear the nature of the dispute between the parties, and secondly, they contribute towards the proof. Upon a consideration of these pleadings, as we may call them, the court awarded the benefit of making the final proof by compurgation or ordeal.

For the period between the Conquest and the appearance of the first plea rolls the evidence is somewhat scanty and especially difficult to interpret. Changes undoubtedly took place, and the formulae, which are often described as rigid and invariable, suffered considerable modification. The position of the courts was strengthened, and so pleadings were expressly addressed to the court; the oath, on the other hand, is either eliminated or postponed to a later stage, and so the new type of pleading concludes with an offer to prove it, instead of opening with an oath. The steps in this development are obscure, but when we reach the thirteenth century, forms are once again well settled, both in local and royal courts, and specimens of them are easily available in contemporary treatises. Considering the relative activity of the royal and the communal courts during this period, it seems reasonable to conclude that the change took place in the hundreds and counties, and that when the King's Court needed forms, it simply adopted those in common use.

THE LANGUAGE OF PLEADINGS

Two further changes took place—the introduction of French as the language of the courts at the time of the Conquest, and then its replacement by English in 1362,[2] without substantially changing the forms, however. We thus find counts (*i.e.* tales, *contes*, or declarations) in such forms as this:

" This sheweth unto you Walter of Ferlang by his attorney, who is here, that Richard Bremel, who is there by his attorney, wrongfully deforces him of the manor of Folham with the appurtenances, a messuage . . . (*long enumeration of parcels*) . . .; and wrongfully for this, that they are his right and heritage of which one *A* his ancestor was seised in his demesne as of fee and of right in time of peace in the time of king Richard, cousin of the king who now is (whom God preserve),

---

[1] Oaths, 10 (Liebermann, *Gesetze*, i. 398).

[2] 36 Edw. III, c. 15; the rolls continued in Latin until 1731: 4 Geo. II, c. 26.

taking the esplees,[1] as in homage, rents, rolls . . . (*enumerated*); and from *A* the right descended . . . (*all descents traced down to*) Walter who now demands. And that such is the right of Walter, he has suit and good proof."[2]

The example from which the above is abbreviated is particularly long, as it was drawn for teaching purposes and contains every imaginable complication. The outline, however, is clear. The whole count is addressed to the court, and the demandant " who is here " solemnly claiming lands from the tenant " who is there " reminds one of the ancient demand of right, and of the necessity of both parties being present. The statement of the demandant's title drawn from an ancestor who took " esplees " looks more modern, although the claim that the lands are " his right and heritage " preserves, perhaps, one of the older and vaguer forms. The " suit " is the group of friends who are prepared to assert that the demand is just;[3] as late as the reign of Edward III we find examples of the suit, or *secta*, being demanded,[4] and *Magna Carta* confirmed the principle that no one should be forced to answer a bare demand unsupported by suit.[5]

The example just given is a count or declaration on a writ of right. The plea or defence would run as follows:

"*X* who is here, denies (*defende*) tort and force and the right of *Y* who is there, entirely and completely (*tut attrenche*) and the seisin of his ancestor called *N* of whose seisin he has counted as of fee and of right, to wit, of a messuage . . . (*long enumeration of parcels as before*) . . .; and he is ready to deny it by the body of one *J* his free man who is here ready to deny it by his body, or by anything that this court may award that he ought; and if any evil betide this same *J* (which God forbid), he is ready to deny it by another who ought to and can."

The demandant then replies that " wrongfully he denies etc.", repeats the title and descent as in his count, and offers to substantiate (technically " deraign ") his right by his own free man, and so the " mise," or issue, is joined.

PLEADINGS AND THE PLEA ROLL

It is essential to remember that these forms are oral, and that they were oral in their origin. It is only later that they became written, and it is clear that the change was brought about by the influence of the enrolling practice of the King's Court. This is a peculiarity of the

[1] Esplees (*expleta*) are the various profits and dealings with the land which are visible indications that the owner was in continued and peaceful possession.

[2] This and the following example are translated from *Novae Narrationes*, which are being re-edited for the Selden Society by Dr. Elsie Shanks. For a demandant to offer battle, is an early and rare anomaly. The example in *Select Civil Pleas* (Selden Society), no. 76 (1201), may be compared with the prosecutor's offer in the criminal case mentioned above, p. 115.

[3] For a case in 1222 where the suit was examined, but knew nothing of the matter save by hearsay, see *Eyre Rolls* (Selden Society, vol. 59), no. 1477.

[4] Y.B. 17 & 18 Edward III (Rolls Series), 72 (1343).

[5] Magna Carta (1215), c. 38; amended (1217), c. 34, and (1225), c. 28. For the possible ecclesiastical origin of the rule see Henry II's edict of 1159 in Haskins, *Norman Institutions*, 329, and Plucknett, *The Medieval Bailiff*, 12 ff.

English system of " records ", and one of its features is the absence of any serious influence of canon law, whose method of pleading was different, and only adopted as a finished system in several other countries.

If we look at the earlier plea rolls, we shall find that they are brief and informal. Their object is merely to serve as memoranda of the proceedings for official use. They were not for the use of the parties, and the parties had no control whatever over the form in which their case was enrolled. The pleadings which we have set out above will be represented on the roll merely by a word or two, and that in a simple narrative form. Thus an action on a writ of right is briefly enrolled like this:

> " *T* demands two hides of land in Battersea and Wandsworth against *R* as his right and inheritance, whereof *A* his father was seised as of fee and right the day and year in which King Henry I died, taking esplees to the value of five shillings and more. Richard comes and denies his right and puts himself on the grand assize as to which of them has the greater right to that land. . . ."[1]

It will be seen that the record is merely a brief narrative of the proceedings which sweeps aside the forms of the pleadings and confines itself to their substance.

The next stage is the result of the establishment of a permanent and numerous organisation of enrolling clerks. The entries become much longer, and tend to become settled in their wording; what is still more important, they bear a fixed relationship to the oral forms which were used in court. By the early years of Henry III the change is complete and the forms remain substantially the same for the next six hundred years. The distinctive features of the final form of English enrolment can be seen by contrasting it with a continental roll, such as we find in Normandy. The Norman roll seems to compare most easily with the older type of English enrolment such as we have just described it. It is narrative, and ignores the forms used by the parties in an effort to state the substance in as few words as possible.[2]

THE CLASSICAL PLEA ROLL

The contrast of this with what we may call the classical style of English enrolment is unmistakable. Examples are easily found in *Bracton's Note Book*, in the notes from the records printed by the editors of the Selden Society's edition of the Year Books, in many old reporters who reproduce pleadings, notably Plowden and Coke, and above all, in the *Books of Entries* which consist of choice specimens of enrolments, collected for the use of pleaders in the days when pleadings were settled by the parties out of court, and merely copied on to the rolls.[3]

The new model begins with a reference to the original writ and the

---

[1] *Select Civil Pleas* (ed. Maitland, Selden Society), no. 17.

[2] For an almost unique fragment of Norman judicial enrolment, see *Plaids de la Sergenterie de Mortemer* (ed. Génestal), Caen, 1924.

[3] Below, pp. 405–406; Winfield, *Chief Sources*, 303 ff.

state of the process: " B is summoned " (or " attached " as the case may be) " to answer A in a plea that he render him " money (or chattels). Then comes a novelty: " whereof he says " (or in trespass " complains ") that—and here follows the substance of the count. The old oral count is therefore directly represented for the first time on the roll. It soon becomes clear that this carefully recorded Latin declaration on the roll is sharing the importance of the old French *conte* which was orally delivered in court. As we shall see, it became even more important at the close of the middle ages.

A slight, but significant, innovation is the fact that the rolls of the new model commence a new paragraph for the defendant's plea, the plaintiff's replication, and so on. The result is greater clarity from the point of view of the reader, but ultimately much more important consequences followed.

In the first place, there was undoubtedly a deliberate attempt to put on the roll all the essential details, and not merely the general substance of the parties' allegations. Hence it will be increasingly possible to decide a case merely from the enrolment, now that the roll contains all that is necessary for that purpose.[1]

Secondly, lawyers will be driven to the conclusion that what really matters henceforth is not so much what they say (as under the old system), as what the clerks write on the roll.[2] This led to two different results. On the one hand, lawyers could free themselves from the old bonds of the spoken forms and indulge in tentative pleadings and arguments, trusting that nothing will be recorded until the informal altercation has finished, and the parties have reached definite positions—the early Year Books are in consequence full of instances of counsel " licking their plea into shape " (as Maitland put it[3]) in open court. This was clearly an advance from the old system where the oral forms were binding. On the other hand, there are plenty of cases (and even statutes[4]) which testify to the great uneasiness felt by lawyers about the roll, for they could not get access to it, and could only guess what was on it.[5] Their new freedom was thus limited by the fear of the mysterious roll, and they could not expect every judge to be as kindly as the one who warned counsel " mind what you say, for henceforth we shall record ".

Thirdly, it would seem that for a time the lead passed from the hands

---

[1] " The aforesaid record having been read and more fully understood " is a common preamble to judgments. Contrast *Bracton's Note Book*, no. 1383, where judgment is based on " count counted, and plea pleaded ".

[2] This is already apparent in *Fet Asaver* (ed. Woodbine), 85–86.

[3] In the introduction to Y.BB. Edward II (Selden Society), III. lxx.

[4] Westminster II, c. 31, as to which see Plucknett, *Statutes and their Interpretation*, 67–68, 140; cf. below, p. 406 n. 2.

[5] An appeal to the roll might reveal a disagreeable surprise, but for a time it was possible to invoke the " record " (*i.e.* official memory) of the judges to supplement a defective roll: Y.BB. Edward II (Selden Society), x. p. xxviii; xi. p. 139. For this distinction between roll and record, see S. E. Thorne, *Courts of Record*, West Virginia Law Quarterly, xl. 347, 352.

of the bar to those of the clerks.   The future of pleading, and the settlement of its forms, became a matter for the people who drew up the rolls;
in later times they were a distinct body of officials, headed by the pro-
thonotaries, and under the control of the courts, but their early history
is unknown.   What is still more serious, we do not know what was their
relationship to the bar on the one hand, or to the general body of royal
clerks on the other.   Some light is now to be had on the relationships
between chancery clerks and law students,[1] and a stage in the " inns of
chancery " was normal for lawyers in the later middle ages, but how far
there was contact, openly or secretly, between lawyers and court clerks
is not yet known.   For a moment, in the troubled years of Edward II,
the office of chief clerk in the common pleas was a political issue,[2] and
at least once a chief clerk and keeper of the rolls of the common pleas
was raised to the bench.[3]

Fourthly, as with almost every question which touches the general
development of the law in this period, we must consider the matter from
the point of view of Bracton's treatise.   We have already spoken of
Bracton's use of cases, and it now remains to insist that those cases were
in fact enrolments.   The examples he gave, and his discussion of " exceptions "—that is to say, defences—must have some bearing on the present
subject.   Was the plea roll in his day already such a vital document that
a real understanding of the law depended upon understanding it?   If so,
Bracton's book must have been a welcome revelation of the form which
the old oral pleadings might take when the clerks enrolled them, and the
eager study of Bracton's book is easily explained.   Or, was it the accident
that Bracton had plea rolls at hand, and so used them, which first directed
attention to enrolling practice, and so enhanced its importance?   In
short, was Bracton's use of plea rolls the result or the cause of their
importance as pleadings?   To these questions there is no answer at
present, but an appreciation of the Bractonian problem will be very
helpful, we believe, in putting the common law system of pleading into
its historical perspective.

THE PROFESSION AND THE PLEA ROLLS

Although lawyers had a glimpse, thanks to Bracton, of what the plea
rolls might contain, those rolls in theory were closed to them, and in
practice were not subject to their control.   An awkward situation,
undoubtedly, and what informal arrangements made it workable, we
shall perhaps never know.   The Year Books very occasionally note the

---

[1] Tout, " The Household of the Chancery ", in his *Col ected Papers*, ii. 143.

[2] Tout, *Place of Edward II in English History*, 369; and again under Richard II in the case
of Thomas Haxey, for which see Taswell-Langmead, *Constitutional History* (ed. Plucknett),
195–196, 217.   (It is now known that Haxey was also the abbot of Selby's proctor in the parliament of 1397: *Register of Henry Chichele*, ii. 657.)

[3] John Bacon was chief clerk from 1292 until 1313 when he became a justice of the common
pleas: Tout, *Edward II*, 372.

clerks of the court as joining in the forensic conversation, and sometimes we read a note of what the clerk told the compiler. This sort of evidence may be just enough to suggest that the bar contrived to win the favours of the clerks by some means or other. It is certainly clear from the fourteenth-century Year Books that counsel no longer directed their attention solely to the oral words; on the contrary, it is plain that their great concern was to get some things on the record, and to keep other things off. Pleading was therefore the art of saying things in court in such a way as to produce a particular result on the roll,[1] it being well understood that judgment would be on the basis of the enrolled pleadings, and not of the oral pleadings which in the course of the hearing might be advanced, withdrawn, modified—or just forgotten.

Granted that the enrolling clerks were in cordial relations with the bar, the system worked remarkably well. It demanded great learning and still greater skill from the serjeants, for they were in effect settling the pleadings in the heat of battle and in the presence of the adversary. On the other hand, there was the substantial advantage that the court joined in the discussion, which thus sometimes became a round-table conference of judges and counsel who joined in trying to find a way of pleading a case which would bring out the real points. We thus find in these cases a discussion of the legal effect of many proposed pleas which in the end were abandoned—which of course explains why the Year Books give us so much matter which is not matter of decision from the modern point of view. Later ages concur in regarding the age of Edward III as the golden age of common law pleading, and the Year Books 40–50 Edward III as being the best place to study it; hence the renown of this volume (familiarly called *Quadragesms*) as a text for the students of later centuries.[2] The fifteenth century saw the beginning of a decline which became marked in the sixteenth; at the beginning of the seventeenth century Coke lamented the change, but his decisions actually accelerated it, and after the Restoration pleading became so subtle that a special branch of the profession grew up to guard its mysteries from the profane.

PAPER PLEADINGS

In the early days of its decline, a remarkable change took place. On the institutional side, it may be regarded as ultimately a victory of the bar over the clerks of court. We have already suggested that the root of the trouble was the gradual shift of emphasis from the spoken plea to the written enrolment, and the resulting anxiety of the bar as to what was put on the roll. We have also suggested that although there was occasional friction, yet in general the bar and the clerks contrived to

---

[1] *Hengham Magna* (ed. Dunham) frequently illustrates the steps in procedure by showing how they are recorded on the roll.

[2] They were " greatly bosted and noted of some students ", said Redman; his views and those of other early law printers are related in H. S. Bennett, *English Books and Readers*, 85.

work together in tolerably good relations   This relationship between the bar and the clerks took the form of the clerks acting as attorneys for litigants.   This inevitably established contact between the clerks on the one hand, and the litigants (and their advisers) on the other.   The situation was known to be dangerous, as affording opportunities for frauds of various sorts;[1] but from the reign of Edward I it seems established as a permanent feature.   The early fears that the system put too much power in the hands of the clerks had died down as the fifteenth century proceeded.

Then a change took place: instead of leaving it to the clerks to enrol a case in accordance with their own ideas of the way it was pleaded, the legal profession provided the clerks with drafts of the entries they desired to have, and so the clerks, in general, had nothing to do but to copy the drafts provided by the litigants' advisers on to the roll.   By this means the lawyers secured absolute control of what was written on the rolls, and were for ever relieved of the fear that the roll might contain unpleasant surprises—as, in the past, it sometimes did.[2]

On the obscure steps by which this revolution was effected, we have some valuable material collected by Reeves and Holdsworth.[3]   It seems that the first stage was reached when in the fourteenth century permission was gained (under certain circumstances) to amend the roll.[4]   This established professional contact between the bar and the clerks.   The second stage is marked by the entry of the clerks of court into competition with the outside branches of the profession.   There thus existed in the later fifteenth century two modes of proceeding: either counsel might be instructed to plead in a particular fashion, or the clerks of the court would be asked to draw pleadings on paper which were brought before the court by the parties (or their attorneys, perhaps) but certainly without counsel.   The original motive of this departure may have been to plead simple cases, or undefended cases,[5] without the expense of engaging a serjeant.   Finally it became possible for the attorneys, with or without the advice of counsel, to draft the pleadings by exchanging papers, as far as an issue or a demurrer.   In the case of an issue, the whole would be enrolled so as to serve as the record for the trial; in the case of a demurrer, the argument in court would take place on the basis of pleadings which had been settled out of court.

[1] For protests under Edward II, see Sayles, *King's Bench*, i. pp. lxxxvi n. 5, cxliv; under Richard II, *Rot. Parl.*, iii. 306 no. 28; under Henry IV, *Rot. Parl.*, iii. 642 no. 63, with the attorneys' indignant reply, *ibid.*, 666 no. 49. The problem was not peculiar to the benches: T. W. Simons, *Chancery and Exchequer Clerks as Attorneys*, University of Colorado Studies, xxii, 381–396.

[2] See the complaints in Parliament (1393), *Rot. Parl.*, iii. 306 no. 28. For the recording of arguments, as distinct from pleadings, cf. Sayles, *King's Bench*, ii. p. ci, and Margaret Hastings, *Common Pleas*, 189.

[3] Reeves, ii. 619; Holdsworth, iii. 639.

[4] Above, p. 397 n. 2.

[5] Actions of debt whose main object was to get one entry of judgment on the rolls seem to have been common.

More than this it is impossible to say without indulging in speculation.[1] The questions which arise, however, may be mentioned here, for
they will indicate the importance of the change. For example, were
pleadings drawn out of court at first for simple cases, or for difficult
cases? It might seem natural that straightforward cases would be the
first in which parties would dispense with counsel and allow the clerk
or attorneys to make up a record concluding to a common issue for a
jury. If this is so, it would no longer be necessary to see in the new
system the result of the growing complexity of pleading.[2] The reverse
might even be possible, for it is easier to introduce subtleties in documents
drawn at leisure, than in impromptu debate. It must certainly have been
less costly in simple cases to have written pleadings, than to have serjeants
to plead orally.

THE CONTINUITY OF PLEADING

However these questions may be answered in the light of future
research, the main outlines given above can be regarded as established.
Their principal significance is the continuity of common law pleading
from the beginning to the end, in spite of changes of practice. From
the Anglo-Saxon sworn demand and defence, through the Anglo-
Norman *conte* and *plee*, to the Latin entry on the plea roll, the line is
unbroken.[3] The plea roll, however, came to be distinctive of English
procedure, and it was inevitable that the main problem should centre
round it. The roll underwent the attraction of the oral forms, and
strove to represent them in its own idiom. But the more accurate and
skilful the roll became, the more necessary it was for the legal profession
to control the entries that were put upon it, and when they won that
victory, it was a victory for the methods (based on oral tradition) of the
old *serjeant-conteur* against the newer rationalism of ink and parchment.[4]
As Sir William Holdsworth has remarked, the sixteenth century was a
time when the canonical system of procedure—which was very much
written—seemed to some a tempting novelty. In Chancery and Star
Chamber it had some influence, but the plea roll protected the courts of
common law from so drastic an innovation, and the drawing of pleadings
out of court perhaps seemed to most lawyers a sufficient concession to
the idea of trial by paper. So the old counts, pleas, replications, rejoinders

---

[1] Interesting questions are raised by the presence of " bills " among exchequer archives
which have every appearance of being written pleas; for examples, see *Select Cases in the
Exchequer of Pleas* (ed. Jenkinson, Selden Society), cxxix. They occur as early as 1343. Many
of the *Select Bills in Eyre* (ed. Bolland, Selden Society), at an even earlier date, closely resemble
written pleadings. On bills generally, see above, pp. 386–387.

[2] But see Holdsworth, iii. 641.

[3] Cf. Guilhiermoz, *La Persistance du caractère oral dans la procédure civile fran aise*, [1889] Revue
historique du droit, 61.

[4] For an illuminating comparison between the two principles, see Sir Maurice Amos,
A Day in Court at Home and Abroad, Cambridge Law Journal, ii. 340–349.

and the rest, with the accompanying issues and demurrers, continued in use, and, consequently, the substantive law which was implicit in them.

THE ORIGINAL WRIT

Pleadings begin with the original writ, and from the earliest days of the common law the writ assumed a position of great importance. Unlike the civilian and canonical procedure, the course of the common law started with a statement of the nature of the claim which was largely common form, prepared in the royal chancery and not by the plaintiff's advisers. The fact that the writ was a royal writ made it for a time, at least, a formidable and rather cumbersome piece of machinery. On the one hand, it was regarded as the source of the jurisdiction of the court. The Court of Common Pleas was historically, and in legal theory, a court of delegates whose authority was not general, but derived from an *ad hoc* commission separately given for every individual case. Hence the court had no powers beyond those conferred by the original writ and could not go beyond the four corners of that document. It will not be surprising, therefore, that there should have been so rigid a boundary between the different forms of action, although we may expect the exercise of some ingenuity in the endeavour to make the system more elastic. On the other hand, this vital document remained for some years beyond the control of the parties: they had to take the writ ready-made, whether it quite fitted their case or not. Throughout the middle ages, therefore, the writ was largely a conventional document which generally throws little light on the real nature of the case. It is to the count that we must look for further information, and the very insufficiency of the writ must have compelled the continuance of the older system of the solemn declaration orally delivered in court.

The original writ, therefore, did not become anything like so informative as a *libellus*, for the good reason that it was drawn primarily in a public office and not by the plaintiff. Such a situation could not last if the use of the common law was to spread, and so we find traces of successful endeavours by the profession to influence the contents of the original writ. We have, in fact, in the thirteenth century, an anticipation of the problem we have already mentioned as arising late in the fifteenth century—the problem of the relationship between the legal profession and the clerical establishments of the State. Just as pleaders at the end of the middle ages succeeded in controlling what was entered upon the rolls of the courts, so in the thirteenth century they tried to influence the drafting of writs in the chancery. We find about the years 1285–1307 a little treatise which already has the suggestive title of *Modus Componendi Brevia*, " the way to compose writs ",[1] and certain forms of action (such as writs of entry) clearly show that the parties themselves must have had considerable influence in drafting them. When this becomes possible,

---

[1] Edited by G. E. Woodbine, *Four Thirteenth-Century Law Tracts*, 143–162.

the attitude of the court towards these documents had to be modified. The great seal, no doubt, was there, but it was no longer possible to suppose that the document represented in all its details a direct command in considered terms by the Crown. The courts will therefore have to scrutinise the writ closely, and countless cases in the Year Books show that writs could be " abated " if their contents erred too much on the side of originality.

EXCEPTIONS

At the same time, there were certain old rules which disabled persons from being litigants; an outlaw is not entitled to be heard, neither is an outlaw from the Church, in other words, an excommunicate. Persons under age were often under a temporary disability. Here, then, was a fairly large assortment of " dilatory exceptions ", and Bracton's treatise completed the tendency, already apparent, to fix the order in which they should be used. If they were unsuccessful, the court w uld order the defendant to " plead over " or to " say something else ", w hereupon the proceedings get nearer the merits of the case.

The pleading not only explores the law of the case; it al o serves to introduce new facts. As we have seen, the original writ cc ntains the barest statement of the nature of the claim; the count amp ifies this statement to some extent, but it is still mainly concerned with su, porting the writ, for any variance between the writ and the count will be a serious matter.

The defendant may take an exception to the writ, and urge that under the circumstances some different writ ought to be used (and if he does so, the plaintiff will call upon him to " give us a better writ "). It sometimes happened, however, that in doing so the defendant came near to saying that the plaintiff had no remedy by this or any other writ. The plaintiff may then point out that " that is an exception to the action ". Usually the defendant became cautious at this point, and took care to withdraw from the general question so as to take up a defence based upon the particular circumstances of the case. In simple cases this often took the form of traversing some essential statement in the writ or the count. Thus, if *A.* alleges that *B.* disseised him of his free tenement (novel disseisin), *B.* may say that *A.* was never seised, and so could not be disseised, or that the tenement is not " free " (because, perhaps, it is in villeinage, or a term of years); some writs, such as the writs of entry, contain so many statements of fact that most defences will involve a denial of one of them.

The defence may rest upon facts which are not even hinted at in the writ or the count. Various methods were available for bringing such new facts into the discussion. The defendant may " confess and avoid ", admitting the plaintiff's statements, but alleging other matters which will rob them of their importance. Or he may introduce new material followed by the clause *absque hoc* (on the roll), *sans ceo que* (in the oral plea), in which he formally denies the plaintiff's allegations. This is called a

" special traverse " and the plaintiff (as a rule) must answer the special or new matter so introduced.

RULES OF PLEADING

From the middle of the fourteenth century onwards there is an increasing rigidity of the rules of pleading; within limits this was all to the good. It clearly made for convenience when pleaders were excluded from " pleading evidence " and were driven to plead the fact itself, and not other facts which might or might not establish it. Rigidity had other effects, however, when it was combined with the fact that these pleadings were inscribed upon a public record. Under this rule it was impossible to deny facts which had been admitted in a previous case. Now as all facts not denied expressly were held to have been admitted, great caution was necessary. Hence we find long clauses *protestando* that the defendant does not admit numerous facts which the strict rules of pleading pr vented him from denying in the ordinary way.

There we e masses of rules[1] to produce particularity, balanced by other rules against surplusage, and rules tolerating general pleadings where the ecord would otherwise be too long. Pleadings should not be argum ntative; thus to an action on a bond to warrant lands, the defendan cannot merely say that the plaintiff has had peaceful enjoyment, but oug it to plead that he has warranted and that the plaintiff has not been d maged.[2] Nor must pleadings be double. One point must be selected and will be sufficient to decide the case; the rest can be eliminated as vexatious. This was an admirable principle, but in practice the rule against duplicity was difficult to apply, and in 1706 a statute[3] allowed double pleas by leave of the court. Another vice of pleading was " departure ", and was analogous to duplicity save that the several matters were not in the same plea but in successive ones; thus if the plaintiff has counted on an action at common law, he cannot turn it into an action on a statute in his replication. Among the most curious of rules are those concerning " negatives pregnant with an affirmative "; Reeves has pointed out that this is the converse case of an " argumentative " plea, which is in fact an affirmative pregnant with a negative.[4] Thus where a gift by deed is alleged, the reply that " he did not give by the deed " is bad (for the negative is pregnant with the affirmative that he gave by parole).

CERTAIN PLEAS IN REAL ACTIONS

Real actions were generally more complicated than personal ones, not only because they were older, but also because many persons were

---

[1] Just before the reforms of the nineteenth century there appeared two masterly works on the old system, Stephen, *On Pleading* (1824), and Chitty, *Treatise on Pleading* (1809). A very useful introduction to these larger works is Ralph Sutton, *Personal Actions at Common Law* (1929).

[2] For another example, see Y.BB. Edward II (Selden Society), x. 220.

[3] 4 & 5 Anne, c. 3.

[4] Reeves, *History of English Law*, ii. 627.

often concerned with the same piece of land. There was an old rule that all joint-tenants must be made defendants (or " tenants ") in a real action. Much use was made of it (by hasty feoffments to a friend who re-enfeoffed the tenant jointly with others) to obtain delays. Statutes finally stopped this manœuvre.[1] A further means of delay, sometimes necessary, but not always so, was the demand for the " view ".[2] If this is granted, an elaborate inspection of the land is made in order to identify precisely the property in dispute. Such an identification was not always easy when it consisted of scattered strips in open fields.

There were other pleas which had for their effect the joinder or substitution of new parties to the action. The need for such a procedure was largely the result of the old rule that a demandant must bring his writ against the person who is seised; this may be a tenant for life, and if so, the tenant for life may defend the action. He ought to " pray aid " of the reversioner, however, and if he does so, the reversioner will be summoned by the court and undertake the defence. Many tenants for life, acting in collusion with demandants, allowed judgment to be given against themselves by default, thus alienating the land and leaving the reversioner no remedy save a writ of right. It was therefore enacted that if a particular tenant is about to lose land by default, the reversioner may come any time before judgment and pray to be received to defend his right.[3] This is called " receipt " in the old books and both aid-prayer and receipt are illustrated by thousands of cases. An understanding of the main principles of these two pleas is necessary, for discussions upon them contain very illuminating material on the nature of estates.

Finally, there is voucher to warranty.[4] Deeds frequently contained a clause whereby the grantor binds himself and his heirs to warrant the grantee and his heirs;[5] besides this, every lord owed warranty to his freehold tenant who has done homage, and the tenant in fee who has created entailed estates owes warranty to the tenants in tail by statute.[6] Many tenants in real actions therefore " vouched to warranty " and numerous pleas might ensue. The demandant might urge that the tenant could not vouch at all, and the vouchee when he came might urge that he was not bound to warrant. The subject, already complicated, was rendered still more so by the misuse of vouchers for purposes of fraud or delay, with the result that several statutes established special

---

[1] Statute *de conjunctim feoffatis*, 34 Edw. I (1306).

[2] Much restricted by Westminster II, c. 48 (1285).

[3] Westminster II, c. 3 (1285), gives receipt for the reversioner on the default of tenant in dower, by curtesy, in tail or for life. Conversely, a termor could be received on the default of his lessor by Gloucester, c. 11 (1278). Cf. p. 555 below.

[4] The difference between aid-prayer and voucher is discussed in Y.B. 21 & 22 Edward I (Rolls Series), 468.

[5] More rarely, the grantor might bind, not himself or his heirs, but particular lands, to fulfil the warranty: Y.B. 21 & 22 Edward I (Rolls Series), 492.

[6] Statute of Bigamists, 4 Edw. I, c. 6 (1276).

procedures in certain cases.[1]   If the voucher was allowed and the vouchee
defaulted or lost by judgment, the demandant had judgment against the
tenant, but the tenant had judgment against the vouchee which entitled
him to recover from him lands of equal value.   If a voucher to warranty
failed, then there was usually nothing lost but time, and the case proceeded.

COLOUR

Of all the curiosities of pleading, colour is the strangest; its history
is worth examining, however, for it illustrates several important themes.
In the early days of the assize of novel disseisin there was need for a
summary action which would repress resort to self-help in disputes as to
land.   The assize therefore gave remedy to one who had been ejected
from land, irrespective of the lack of title in the disseisee or the presence
of title in the disseisor.   Whatever the rights or wrongs of the parties,
they must not resort to force.   Hence in novel disseisin the demandant
need not make out any title, save the fact that he had been seised and
disseised.

With the progress of time this action, with its attractive rapidity,
came to be used for trying questions of title as well as questions of seisin,
and so both parties took to the practice of pleading title.   A frequent
situation was one where *A.*, claiming land by a particular title against *B.*,
ejected *B.*   *B.* then in turn ejected *A.*, and *A.* brought the assize.

This situation was so common that it left its mark on the history of
pleading.   Under the old system the only course for *B.* in answer to the
assize would be to say (if he could) that *A.* was never seised, or that *B.*
never disseised him.   Under the newer system, however, he was allowed
to set out his own title and to plead that *A.* had entered under a certain
pretence of title which was in fact bad, and that *B.* ejected him.   Cases in
Bracton's Note Book seem to be half-way between these two systems.   The
new mode of pleading may therefore be regarded as a product of the
early fourteenth century.   The principal advantage was this: under the
old system such a plea would be treated as amounting to the general issue,
and so the case would go to the jury; under the new rules, the plea was
regarded as raising a matter of law which might confuse the " *lay gents* "
who were on the jury, and so it was reserved for the court.   As time goes
on, it is regarded as more and more desirable to leave for the court as
matters of law many things which in older days were sent to the jury
under the general issue.   The defective title which the defendant attributes
to the plaintiff is called " colour ", and in the earlier cases it seems that
it really did represent the facts.[2]   It soon became the practice, however,

[1] Westminster I, c. 40 (1275); statute *de vocatis ad warrantiam*, 20 Edw. I (1292); 14 Edw. III,
stat. 1, c. 18 (1340).

[2] This conclusion follows from the fact that in the fourteenth century the allegations made
as " colour " could be traversed, *e.g.* Y.B. 11 Richard II (ed. Thornley, Ames Foundation),
268–278.

to give feigned colour of a purely fictitious character; this raised a
fictitious question of law not amounting to the general issue, and served
as an excuse for leaving the whole case to the court—including, of
course, the real question of law which under the old system would
have been treated as merely an argumentative denial of the points of
the assize.

The history of trespass was very similar to that of the assize of novel
disseisin; both began as actions founded on tort, with a strong criminal
element, and both became in the course of time actions for the trial of
right to land or chattels respectively.   The same line of reasoning which
led to the use of " colour " in novel disseisin (and in its equivalent, entry
in the nature of an assize) led also to its use in trespass.   By 1440 we find
a little treatise on the subject in the Year Books[1] which seems to imply
that the system was in full use at that date.

THE DEMURRER

The object of pleadings is to explore the law and the facts of a case
by means of the assertions and denials of the parties until an issue has
been reached.   If it is an issue of fact, then the parties will have ascertained
a material fact which one asserts and the other denies in terms so precise
that a jury will have no difficulty in hearing evidence on the matter and
finding the truth of it.   If it is an issue of law, the parties will have
admitted the relevant facts, leaving it to the court to decide whether the
law applicable to them is as the plaintiff or as the defendant maintained.
This is called a " demurrer " because one of the parties has pleaded that
he is entitled to succeed on the facts admitted by the other, and is willing
to rest (*demourer*) at that point.   If his opponent does the same, then the
demurrer is joined, the pleadings are at an end, and the court hears the
arguments on the point of law, and decides it.

This appeal by both parties to the court's " consideration " on a point
of law is very common in the thirteenth century as an answer to dilatory
pleas—questions of view, age, aid, voucher, and the like.   It is only
later that we find the main question of a case raised in a demurrer, and
so as a means of concluding the pleadings we must regard the demurrer
as a fourteenth-century device.   The demurrer was frequently used to
draw attention to trifling defects in form in the pleadings, which could
thus be amended by consent, and with all the more ease when the pleadings were oral.   They might be insisted upon, however, and then the
case would have to be decided upon very technical points.

Several kinds of demurrer are distinguished, one of which may be
mentioned here.   Juries could often be persuaded to bring in special
verdicts (sometimes drafted by counsel) without, however, giving a
verdict for either party; the facts so found would be generally complicated and of such a nature that points of law were raised which the

[1] Y.B. 19 Henry VI, 21, pl. 42.

court would have to decide. But a jury was always at liberty to give a general verdict if so inclined, and so pleaders took steps to secure the advantages of a special verdict without its delay by means of a demurrer to the evidence. The evidence (documentary or parole) is thereby admitted to be true, but the question of its legal implications is referred to the court.[1]

In post-mediaeval times the demurrer required a good deal of regulation by statute. In 1540 a statute enacted that a number of highly technical flaws in the pleadings would be " cured by verdict " (as old books put it).[2] In 1585 an important act commanded judges who gave judgment upon demurrers to decide " according to the very right of the cause and matter in law " without regard to various technical defects in the pleadings, unless those defects were specifically mentioned in the demurrer.[3] In consequence of this act a sharp distinction was drawn between special demurrers which alleged a particular defect in the pleadings (which the court therefore had to adjudge), and general demurrers in which case the court's judgment was based upon a consideration of the record as a whole. A much more radical inroad upon the principles of common-law pleading was made in 1705 when a statute allowed defendants, by leave of the court to plead multiple defences[4]—a provision which the bench interpreted with considerable strictness.

THE GENERAL ISSUE

When the plaintiff has counted, the defendant can choose between two courses: he can make a special plea, or he can at once conclude the pleadings by taking the general issue. The latter course was the one most frequently taken in the earlier times of the common law, and always remained a valuable alternative, for by it the endless complexities and pitfalls of special pleading were avoided. It is very significant that when great trading companies were set up by Act of Parliament, they frequently procured a clause in their act empowering them to plead the general issue at all times, putting in their special matter as evidence;[5] occasionally the same privilege was accorded to natural persons as against the Crown.[6]

---

[1] The admissibility of evidence could not be tested in this way, but by bill of exceptions, which was analogous to a writ of error. Above, p. 29. As Thayer, *Evidence*, 121, points out, in many cases the " evidence " demurred to is not the testimony of witnesses but the statements of fact made by counsel. " A demurrer upon evidence goes to the law upon the matter, and not to the truth of the fact "—*Newis* v. *Lark* (1571) Plowd. 410; the pleadings of this case are a good example.

[2] 32 Hen. VIII, c. 30. It is entertaining to find that such great experts as Rickhill, J., and Serjeant Brenchesley, litigating in their own court, had their writ abated, even after a jury had found a verdict in their favour: Y.B. 2 Henry IV, Michs. no. 48, p. 11 (1400).

[3] 27 Eliz., c. 5.

[4] 4 & 5 Anne, c. 3.

[5] For example, the act incorporating conservators of Bedford Level, 15 Car. II, c. 17, s. 15 (1663), and certain insurance companies by 11 Geo. I, c. 30, s. 43 (1724).

[6] For example, in answer to informations for intrusion, 21 James I, c. 14 (1624).

Legislation of the Commonwealth had moved in that direction, and had been confirmed at the Restoration.[1] The origin of the general issue is therefore to be found in the age when special pleading was little used, and consequently when the general issue was employed for most ordinary purposes. The scope of the general issue is therefore unexpectedly wide, and in order to understand old cases it is necessary to know what matters could be proved by evidence to a jury which was trying a general issue.

The two pleadings with which this chapter opened are illustrations of the count in a writ of right, followed by a plea of the general issue (which, in writs of right, was called the " mise ")[2]—that is, the issue of the better right. In formedon, the general issue was *ne dona pas*; in debt on a specialty, *non est factum* (and on this issue the plaintiff is put to the proof of the whole of his declaration, while the defendant may show that the deed is void or obtained by fraud, but matters making it only voidable must be specially pleaded);[3] in debt on a simple contract, *nil debet*, which denies the existence of the debt and permits the defendant to prove performance, release or other matter in discharge of the action;[4] *non assumpsit* similarly denies the existence of the contract, either in fact or in law. Thus matters of capacity, duress, want of consideration, the statute of frauds, payment, may all be proved under this general issue.[5] In trespass and case, the general issue is not guilty. This plea in trespass denies the plaintiff's property in the chattels (just as it denies his title in ejectment) and also puts the alleged acts in issue.[6]

THE HILARY RULES, 1834

It will be seen that the general issue relieved the pleader, at least, of most of his difficulties. Those difficulties, however, were apt to reappear at the trial. The scope of the general issue was often wide, and by it the defendant not only forced the plaintiff to prove the whole of his case, but could also compel him to come prepared to answer any or all of several defences. The trial was therefore a costly and difficult matter, possibly involving large masses of evidence on a large number of points which might, or might not, turn out to be necessary. There seems to have been no way of compelling a defendant to disclose more precisely what part of the plaintiff's case he proposed to attack, nor which of the defences possible he proposed to raise. General pleading, as well as special pleading, therefore had its defects.

---

[1] *Acts and Ordinances*, ii. 455–456 (1650); 12 Charles II, c. 3, s. 4 (1660).

[2] Compare the " mise of Amiens " whereby Henry III and the baronial opposition submitted themselves to the arbitration of St Louis, in 1264.

[3] Chitty, *On Pleading* (1831), i. 519.

[4] *Ibid.*, 517.

[5] *Ibid.*, 511.

[6] Bacon, *Abridgement*, vii. 704.

Just about a hundred years ago, the whole question came up for discussion, and the Civil Procedure Act of 1833 delegated to the judges the power to draw up a new set of rules; this they did, and the new scheme, because it came into force in Hilary Term, 1834, was called " the Hilary Rules ". The policy of the scheme was to strike a balance between the extreme precision of special pleading and the extreme vagueness of the general issue. On the one hand, they limited the general issue to the actual meaning of the words used—thus the general issue of *non assumpsit* was to mean henceforth just what it said, " the defendant did not undertake ", and was no longer available if the defence rested on matters of contractual capacity, discharge, voidance and the like. These matters must for the future be specially pleaded.

The policy was the right one; a plaintiff ought to be told as clearly as possible what defence he will have to meet, and to be informed what facts the defence admits, and what facts it disputes. In principle, there could be little objection to requiring a defendant to plead specially, and the attempt to make such expressions as *non assumpsit, non est factum*, and others, mean exactly what they said and not something entirely different, surely deserves commendation. The failure of the Hilary Rules, in spite of these merits, lay in their insistence on special pleading as it was understood late in the eighteenth century. That parties should plead precisely, and clarify as far as possible the issues between them, is one thing; that their endeavours to do so should be judged by the extremely artificial standards of the old system, was quite another. Unfortunately, the result of the rules was to extend the necessity of conforming to that system to a great many cases which heretofore had not been encumbered with it. It is not surprising that substantive law felt the effects of this change.[1] The vagueness of the general issue permitted a certain flexibility in the law which Lord Mansfield, for one, had taken advantage of. Now that special pleading was required in such cases, this vagueness had to yield before statements so precise that subtle changes which had taken place in substantive law were forced into light, and found to be inconsistent with older authorities which now became of great importance. Hence the doctrine of consideration hardened along seventeenth-century lines, and the distinction between different forms of action was emphasised anew, although in the preceding century it had become of less vital importance.

The Hilary Rules only aggravated the situation, and it remained for the various Common Law Procedure Acts of 1854 and onwards to prune the luxuriant growth of pleading, and finally for the Judicature Acts to substitute a new system[2] which, in the view of some, leans to the other extreme of laxity.

---

[1] This matter has been discussed by Sir William Holdsworth, *The New Rules of Pleading of the Hilary Term, 1834*, Cambridge Law Journal, i. 261–278.

[2] The County Courts Act (9 & 10 Victoria, c. 95), s. 76, seems to have been a preliminary experiment in this direction.

LAW AND FACT

Gradually there is a growing recognition in English law of the distinction between law and fact.[1] It is so familiar as to seem obvious to modern English lawyers, yet there was a time when it did not exist, and the distinction, even when it was recognised, was not always drawn at the same point. If we look back to the days of the ordeal we find that the ordeal or the oath decided the whole case, and the case had not yet been analysed into its components of law and fact. Even the early common law retained the same attitude. In the writ of right the question at issue is whether the demandant or the tenant has the greater right to the land, and this issue was decided one way or the other by the outcome of the battle. Even if trial were by the grand assize, the members of the assize find for the demandant or the tenant without any discussion whether this is in consequence of a particular state of facts, or of a particular rule of law.

Even the jury system, therefore, existed for a while without forcing lawyers to recognise this distinction. The growth of formalism soon gave opportunities, however, for judgment to be given without a verdict —defects in writs, inconsistencies between writs and pleadings, reliance by a party upon a previous judgment—all these are common grounds of judgment in the earliest years of the thirteenth century. It thus became apparent that there were matters (generally preliminary matters) which might put an end to a case before the question of right or wrong had been formulated. Litigants who betake themselves to matters of this sort are generally raising what we should call matters of law. The commonest examples are those where a party rests his case upon the default of his opponent; as the law of process grew more elaborate, extremely difficult points of law were involved, as every reader of the year books knows.

Jurors as well as parties felt that some things were fact and others were law, and the assize of novel disseisin constantly forced it upon their attention. As early as 1202 an assize said " we will speak the truth of the matter, and having heard it, let the justices judge ".[2] Half a century later (in discussing novel disseisin) Bracton[3] declared that " truth is to be had from the juror, justice and judgement from the judge ". In the next line he had to admit, however, that the verdict of an assize is often upon law as well as facts. By 1285 statute[4] is clearly distinguishing law from fact by enacting that jurors shall not be compelled to say whether there has been a disseisin, so long as they tell the facts. In other words, seisin is no longer an obvious fact but an obscure legal technicality. This

---

[1] See generally Thayer, *Evidence*, 183 ff.; Pollock and Maitland, ii. 629; above, p. 129 n. 5.

[2] *Select Civil Pleas* (Selden Society), 179.

[3] Bracton, f. 186 b. Cf. Y.B. 30 & 31 Edward I (Rolls Series), 16.

[4] Westminster, II, c. 30; Y.B. 20 & 21 Edward I (Rolls Series), 10, shows that the statute did not remove all the difficulties felt by jurors. In 1348 the commons prayed for general permission for jurors to " tell the truth if they want to " in all cases, as well as in novel disseisin, but the petition was rejected: *Rot. Parl.*, ii. 203 no. 22.

change was possibly the most potent single factor in forcing the distinction between law and fact, and as time went on litigants devised means of raising questions of law, which earlier times had treated as questions of fact. Hence the frequency of special verdicts and of colour. From the assizes these devices spread to writs of entry and finally to trespass.

As early as 1329 a jury found a special verdict of *se defendendo* to an indictment of homicide.[1]

When commercial cases came into the common law courts, law and fact were often left indiscriminately to the jury until the time of Lord Mansfield,[2] and the same sort of thing happened in Admiralty; in both cases the development of clear principles upon which merchants could base their dealings was prevented.[3]

---

[1] Fitzherbert, *Corone*, 284.

[2] As Buller, J., observed in *Lickbarrow* v. *Mason* (1787) 2 T.R. 73.

[3] Holdsworth, *Makers of English Law*, 168 n. 1, 220–221.

PART 2
CRIME AND TORT

SUMMARY

420

CRIME AND TORT

The distinction between criminal and civil law has been a commonplace with English lawyers for over seven hundred years. Glanvill began his treatise with the remark that " some pleas are criminal, and some are civil ".[1] Already, then, the distinction in practice is of a procedural nature; Glanvill has simplified the question to a distinction between criminal proceedings and civil proceedings. What, then, are criminal proceedings? This question is confused by the existence of another distinction which nearly corresponds with it, but not entirely. This is the division of pleas into pleas of the Crown, and common pleas.

PLEAS OF THE CROWN

The older text-books to which we look for information on criminal law almost universally bear the title " pleas of the Crown "; thus Staunford (1557), Coke's third *Institute* (1644), Hale, and a host of others throughout the eighteenth century. Now the test of a plea of the Crown is purely historical, and although many of them would be classed as criminal under any system of classification, others owe their position there to historical accidents.

The antithesis to pleas of the Crown is " common pleas ", and most of the matters dealt with in the Court of Common Pleas are obviously civil.[2] In the main they are concerned with adjusting the rights and relationships between private parties, but all through these proceedings the Crown is apt to step in and exact fines and amercements which, in some cases at least, are clearly punitive. In the words of Sir James FitzJames Stephen:

> " Fines were paid on every imaginable occasion . . . at every stage of every sort of legal proceeding, and for every description of official default, irregularity, or impropriety. In short, the practice of fining was so prevalent that if punishment is taken as the test of a criminal offence, and fines are regarded as a form of punishment, it is almost impossible to say where the criminal law in early times began or ended. . . . It is impossible practically to draw the line between what was paid by way of fees and what was paid by way of penal fines."[3]

We are therefore faced with an impossible task if we are required to

---

[1] Glanvill, i. 1.

[2] But see below, p. 422 n. 1.

[3] Stephen, *History of Criminal Law*, ii. 198; he has neglected the technical distinction between fine and amercement, however; see Fox, *Contempt of Court*, 118 ff.

state the limits of criminal law as it was understood in early times. Glanvill's distinction was good enough as the first arresting phrase of a treatise, but it bore little relation to the state of the law in his time.   In this matter, as in others, there are two practical considerations which override formal and analytical distinctions.   First, the middle ages were more intent on doing what had to be done than on classifying the ways of doing it.   If some things which we regard as criminal could be dealt with more effectively under the forms of civil litigation, then they became common pleas.   If other things, which now seem indubitably civil, could only be effectively dealt with under criminal forms, then they became pleas of the Crown.   Indeed, we shall find, even in the Tudor period, that the Court of Star Chamber developed the law of libel without regard for any distinction between crime and tort.   It would be hopeless to attempt any classification in the face of these facts, and a modern history of criminal law is therefore bound to be a history of those matters which now are considered criminal, irrespective of whether they were in the middle ages common pleas or pleas of the Crown.   Secondly, the financial element has been even stronger in criminal matters than in others during the middle ages.   Jurisdiction over felonies and lesser offences was a steady source of revenue consisting partly of fines and amercements, and partly of forfeitures and dues of Court.   To establish that a particular proceeding is a plea of the Crown may mean that it was (in modern estimation) a serious crime, but it may also mean that it is merely a plea cognisable in the King's Court and not elsewhere.   The only contemporary significance all this had was that the King took the profits instead of some local franchise holder.   When it is said that the breach of the King's peace is a plea of the Crown, it does not mean that the whole field of trespass, in which this allegation is generally made, is part of the criminal law; it simply means that the plaintiff wants to sue in the King's Court, and the King's Court has devised a convenient technicality for inviting him to do so.   When the case comes to be pleaded, we shall find that the so-called plea of the Crown will be enrolled on the records of the Court of Common Pleas—although, for that matter, even down to the reign of Edward I cases which are purely criminal are said to appear occasionally on the rolls of the Court of Common Pleas.[1]

CRIME AND TORT

The modern distinction between crime and tort is therefore one of those classifications which it is futile to press upon mediaeval law.   This has long been recognised.   Maitland[2] observed that the criminal law, at the time of the Conquest, was also the law of torts; it is just as reasonable to put it the other way round (as one writer[3] has done) and to say that

[1] Pollock and Maitland, i. 199 n. 1.   There is the important possibility of early rolls being wrongly classified.

[2] *Ibid.*, ii. 449.

[3] Jeudwine, *Tort, Crime and Police*, 83.

the early period shows a progression from tort to crime, instead of from crime to tort. Trespass undoubtedly was more punitive, more criminal, in its early days than at the end of the middle ages, and so we can say that tort has grown out of crime. On the other hand, Anglo-Saxon proceedings consequent upon a murder, maiming, theft or serious outrage had little to do with the Crown and were conducted entirely by the party aggrieved; they might result in a punishment, but their principal element was undoubtedly compensation or restitution. Their main characteristic was thus analogous to that of a modern action in tort. Later on, the Crown took a much larger part in such proceedings, and so it is quite plausible to argue that the original stem was mainly tort, and that crime branched off from it. The imposition of a modern classification upon mediaeval facts thus leaves us with the inevitable result—a barren choice between two epigrams.[1]

THE NATURE OF CRIMINAL LAW

Once the distinction was established, criminal law was set aside as separate from other branches of law, and its distinctive nature was recognised as involving special rules. Examples are the " common-law misdemeanours " which English law has viewed with deep suspicion, the principle that statutes setting penalties should not do so retrospectively,[2] and the principle commonly expressed in the maxim, *nulla poena sine lege*.[3]

[1] See generally, Winfield, *Province of the Law of Tort*, 190 ff. In 1292 the king's bench regarded a " civil " action as one which tried proprietary rights as distinct from an *actio iniuriarum* (Sayles, *King's Bench*, ii. 134), although in another case in the same term it held that an action was civil and not criminal because it laid damages, notwithstanding the fact that the crown was plaintiff (*ibid.*, 136). Then, too, an assize of novel disseisin may contain talk of robbery: *Eyre Rolls* (Selden Society, vol. lix), no. 232 (1221).

[2] This rule could be transgressed unwittingly when a statute imposing penalties acquired an artificial date and so became in fact retrospective. On the ascription of fictitious dates to statutes, see Plucknett, *Legal Chronology* (Handbook of Dates, ed. C. R. Cheney), Sir Cecil Carr, *The Citation of Statutes* (Cambridge Legal Essays) and *Calendar-Year Statutes*, Law Quarterly Review, lvi. 459.

[3] On this, see Ernst Levy, *West Roman Vulgar Law*, 103; Jerome Hall, *Nulla Poena sine Lege*, Yale Law Journal, xlvii. 165; Marc Ancel, in Annales de l'Institut de Droit comparé de l'Université de Paris, ii. 245-272; Paul Weidenbaum, *Liberal Thought and Undefined Crimes*, Journal of Comparative Legislation [1937], 91. A few further references are in Alipio Silveira, *Interpretación de las Leyes* 17

CHAPTER 1

CRIMINAL PROCEDURE

In very general terms, the history of criminal procedure seems to follow this course. First, it is almost entirely in the hands of the injured party and his opponent, and takes place in local courts. Then the influence of the Crown makes itself felt, beginning with a cautious list of pleas of the Crown. There is for a long while no question of the Crown actually trying such cases—all it can hope for at first is a share of the proceeds. The second stage is when the Crown sets up machinery to discover hidden crimes. Many must have escaped altogether by reason of the unwillingness of anyone to bring an " appeal ", and this results in a loss of possible revenue to the King (to say nothing of the encouragement to criminals). The Crown henceforth will have a mass of crimes presented by grand juries, and will have to devise measures for trying them. Rapid development is therefore found in the various trial commissions, and the rise of the justices of the peace added materially to the resources of the Crown both in discovering crimes and in trying criminals. Thirdly, the existence of this elaborate machinery will permit the enlargement of the list of crimes since there are now numerous institutions capable of dealing with them. Many statutory felonies will be created, and many offences less than felony will be made cognisable by justices of the peace; this last development will be at the expense of those local jurisdictions which so far had dealt with them, and will also include some matters for which so far only trespass (in substance now a civil remedy) had been available.

ANGLO-SAXON CRIMINAL LAW

As we have already remarked, the Anglo-Saxon period is long[1] and yet it is difficult to trace clear development over those five centuries for which we have written remains.

It is tempting at first to make a neat plan of the progress from warfare —the feud between the two kin of the criminal and the injured—to money compensation. One would expect the early laws to say more about fighting, and the later ones more about payment.[2] The sources, however, do not align themselves so easily as this. Our earliest laws (Ethelbert's) are mainly tariffs of payment; our later ones say much about feuds. In the middle of the tenth century Edmund is still laying down rules for the feud,[3] and Canute is still legislating on it just before the Conquest.[4] It is not easy, therefore, to establish an orderly progression, and it seems more probable that several stages of development were in fact existing side by side. Indeed, half a century after the Conquest we read this:

> " If anyone kill another in revenge, or self-defence, let him not take any of the goods of the slain, neither his horse nor his helmet, nor his sword nor his money; but in the customary way let him lay out the body of the slain, his head to the west and feet to the east, upon his shield, if he has it. And let him drive in his spear [into the ground], and place round it his arms and tether to it his horse. Then let him go to the nearest vill and declare it to the first one he meets, and to him who has *soc* (jurisdiction over the place); thus he may have proof and defend himself against the slain's kin and friends."[5]

The avenger is thus something in the nature of an executioner, save that the trial of the slain takes place *post mortem* as part of the defence of the avenger.[6] Quite early, however, it became possible to " buy off the spear" if one preferred not to "bear it ". An offer of *wergeld* will therefore prevent the avenger doing justice himself, and in criminal as well as civil matters, no action ought to be taken until a formal demand for satisfaction has been made and proved ineffectual. The laws of Alfred are very explicit on the matter:

> " We also decree that a man who knows his adversary to be sitting at home, shall not fight him before he has asked for satisfaction.
> " If he has power to surround his adversary and besiege him, let him watch him

---

[1] Above, p. 9.

[2] Cf. the remark that, in compositions, it is the Christian rather than the Germanic spirit which is at work: Fustel de Coulanges, *La monarchie franque*, 483.

[3] II Edmund, 1. 7 (941–946).

[4] I Canute, 5 a (2 b). The date is 1020.

[5] *Leges Henrici Primi*, 83 (6).

[6] Similarly, the kinsman of a convicted thief could secure his posthumous rehabilitation by himself undergoing the ordeal; if this was successful, the remains of the deceased were exhumed and reinterred in consecrated ground: III Aethelred, 7 (*c.* 997). For late survivals in a civilised community, see C. Petit-Dutaillis, *Droit de vengeance dans les Pays-Bas au quinzième siècle* (Paris, 1908).

seven days without attacking him if he stays in. If after seven days he will surrender and give up his weapons, he shall guard him unhurt thirty days, and tell his kin and friends. . . .

"If he cannot besiege him, let him go to the alderman and ask help; if the alderman will not help, let him go to the king before attacking his adversary."[1]

We have here at least one element of legal procedure—delay. These intervals are obviously designed so that the offender may be put into touch with his family and friends with a view to settling the matter by paying (or promising to pay) the composition.

An even more striking fact is that so large a part of Anglo-Saxon criminal law had to be expressed in terms of money.

"*Wer* . . . is the value set on a man's life, increasing with his rank. For many purposes it could be a burden as well as a benefit; the amount of a man's own *wer* was often the measure of the fine to be paid for his offences against public order. *Wite* is the usual word for a penal fine payable to the king or to some other public authority. *Bot* . . . is a more general word, including compensation of any kind. Some of the gravest offences, especially against the king and his peace, are said to be *botleas*, 'bootless'; that is, the offender is not entitled to redeem himself at all, and is at the king's mercy."[2]

PLEAS OF THE CROWN

Gradually we hear of state-sanctioned punishments. Perhaps the injured party or his representatives will carry out the sentence, but the significance of the change lies principally in the fact that some of the greatest offences are now corporally punished and are not " emendable " with money save only by the King's very special grace. In the reign of Canute we get the first explicit lists of royal pleas—and it is significant there are are different lists for Wessex, Mercia and the Danelaw.[3] In Domesday Book[4] we find differing lists for various counties, and even for various towns, while some of the greater sees and abbeys had received even these royal rights by grant from the Crown. Typical pleas of the Crown are *foresteal* (murderous assault from an ambush), breach of the King's peace (in general, only if the peace had been granted under the royal seal), and *hamsocn* (violent breaking into a house). In some places larceny was a royal plea, but not generally. Glanvill gives us a short list[5] which is the basis for the common law of future centuries: treason, concealment of treasure trove, breach of peace, homicide, arson, robbery, rape and the counterfeiting of the King's seal or coinage. Larceny is omitted, as being only a plea of the sheriff.

By Glanvill's day the old scheme of *wer* and *wite* had vanished, leaving very few traces. If all the payments were exacted (and as Maitland has

[1] Alfred, 42.

[2] Pollock and Maitland, i. 48.

[3] II Canute, 12–15.

[4] Details in Pollock and Maitland, ii. 454–457 (but cf. Goebel, *Felony and Misdemeanour,* 402 ff.).

[5] Glanvill, i. 2.

calculated, the bill may be long and complicated) it is hardly imaginable that any ordinary person could pay it. The value of money changed, and the Normans reckoned by a shilling of twelve pence instead of the old English shilling of four or five pence. The Normans, moreover, with their memories of the duke's " pleas of the sword ", may have given a much more precise meaning to the old conception of pleas of the Crown.[1] Henceforward, the pleas of the Crown will be not merely pleas in which the Crown takes a particular pecuniary interest, but offences which were held to be committed against the Crown; the avenger will thus be the Crown as well as the injured party or his kin. These two ideas, one old and one new, make two alternative procedures necessary; and such in fact we find to be the case.

THE OLD PROCEDURE

The old procedure is of two sorts. The first dealt with the criminal taken in the act, and for him there was short shrift. Many local custumals[2] relate the various deaths assigned to the hand-having and back-bearing thief. In the Anglo-Saxon age there was the possibility (at least in theory) of a thief redeeming his life by paying a sum equal to his own *wer*.

When the theft was not manifest, some sort of procedure was felt to be necessary. Its general features are the summons of the accused by the accuser; when both are present, the accuser makes a solemn fore-oath in support of his charge, and to exclude frivolous or malicious accusations. In some cases it might be supported by oath-helpers. Then the accused as solemnly denied the charge upon oath, and the court proceeded to the " medial " judgment which was generally to the effect that the defendant should " clear himself " by one of the ordeals. This sort of procedure long survived in those places which preserved ancient customs unaffected by the common law, such as London and various boroughs.

The Norman Conquest brought one great innovation—trial by battle; the sworn accusation and the sworn defence were transformed by introducing the charge of " felony " (a Norman and feudal conception), and the battle served as the ordeal. Soon the difficulties of conflict of laws were overcome[3] and the mingling of races proceeded so far that, if the old procedure were invoked, it was generally the " appeal ", as it came to be called, and not the ordeal (save in some localities). The common law therefore accepted the old procedure into its system in the form of the appeal only.[4]

[1] For pleas of the sword, and Norman criminal law in general, there is a convenient summary in Le Foyer, *Exposé du droit pénal normand au XIII° siècle* (Paris, 1931). Cf. Ernest Perrot, *Les Cas royaux* (Paris, 1910).

[2] *Borough Customs* (ed. Bateson, Selden Society), vol. i; Law Quarterly Review, lv. 182.

[3] The rules, as between English and Norman, were settled in *Willelmes asetnysse* (in Robertson, *Laws of the English Kings*, 233).

[4] Cf. above, p. 121. Appeals of breach of the peace occur occasionally. For valuable details see Sayles, *King's Bench*, ii. p. lxxxi. For appeals of trespass in local courts tried by wager of law, see *Court Baron* (Selden Society), 76.

The appeal was in common use throughout the middle ages in county and other local courts. Even in the King's Bench appeals were allowed,[1] and appeals of treason were a particularly bizarre form of state trial. The " lords appellant " in the reign of Richard II are not the only nor the first examples. Robert de Montfort appealed, and convicted, Henry of Essex of treason in 1163,[2] and there was a curious case in the Court of the Constable of England in 1453 when Lialton appealed Norris of treason. The Court assigned counsel to each party (trainers, armourers and painters), gave them equipment, and the King ordered " a convenient skaffold for us to have the sight of the said battaill ", and more curious still, the Crown bore all the costs and treated the alleged traitor with the same consideration as the appellant.[3]

Appeals survived particularly as a means whereby the relatives of a murdered person could still harass one who had been tried and acquitted. Spencer Cooper (a future Chancellor's brother, and himself a future judge) was appealed after being acquitted of murder, but the process was quashed;[4] the last case was *Ashford* v. *Thornton*, in consequence of which appeals of felony were hastily abolished.[5]

THE NEW PROCEDURE

Of the proceedings of the judicial and administrative Eyres of the earlier twelfth century, we have little detailed knowledge. It is only towards the end of that century that our knowledge becomes precise. The Assize of Clarendon (1166) set up machinery for discovering alleged criminals by means of the jury of inquest—the grand jury of modern times.[6] This measure can hardly be explained save by assuming that the old procedure of private accusation had failed to give satisfaction. The King evidently hoped to hear of many criminals through the grand juries who would have escaped prosecution by private parties. Communal accusation is thus added to private accusation as an alternative procedure. The assize did much more than this, however, for it laid down the principle that persons indicted could be tried by the King alone, and that the forfeitures were his only. The indictment procedure therefore superseded all local jurisdictions both in the matter of trial and

---

[1] For an appeal of mayhem in the King's Bench when the appellant had judgment for damages, see *Attorney-General* v. *Hunston* (1488), Bayne, *Cases in Council of Henry VII* (Selden Society), 62, 64–67.

[2] Jocelyn de Brakelonde, *Chronica* (Camden Society, vol. xiii), 51–52; Henry had said, in battle, that the king was dead. Cf. *Select Pleas of the Crown* (Selden Society, vol. i), no. 115 (1214) for the felony of announcing the king's death (which spread despondency and alarm). Numerous appeals of treason are listed in L. W. Vernon Harcourt, *His Grace the Steward*, 349 n. 1.

[3] *Proceedings and Ordinances of the Privy Council* (ed. Nicolas), vi. 129 ff.

[4] *R.* v. *Toler* (1700), Ld. Raym. 555.

[5] (1819), 1 B. & Ald., 405; 59 Geo. III, c. 46. On the relation of acquittals on appeal and the suit of the crown, see 3 Hen. VII, c. 1, and Blackstone, *Commentaries*, iv. 335.

[6] Text in Stubbs, *Charters*; translated above, pp. 112–113.

of profits. From this time onwards it thus became very necessary for the Crown to maintain a regular succession of travelling justices to " deliver the gaols " of those who had been committed to prison on indictment.

LATER DEVELOPMENT OF INDICTMENT

These indictments were at first taken before royal justices and sheriffs. The next great enlargement of the procedure was in the growth of the powers of justices of the peace, whose early history has become known only recently.[1] In the reign of Edward II they were given powers of taking indictments, in addition to their older functions. Once again there must have been a sudden increase in the number of indicted persons awaiting trial. Justices of gaol delivery had therefore to be commissioned with more frequency; it was out of the question to send justices from the superior courts, and so, even in Edward II's reign, we find that commissions of gaol delivery were issued to small groups of experienced and trustworthy justices of the peace. The next reign saw the logical development of this; the justices were allowed to try indicted persons themselves, and without the issue of separate commissions, although not for all offences. Commissions of gaol delivery continued to issue, although the work of the commissioners was much lightened by the activity of justices acting under their enlarged commissions.

The early fourteenth-century indictment was as simple a document as later ones were complex. There were no formalities, but merely the date, list of jurors, and brief statements that A stole an ox, B burgled a house, C slew a man, and so on. The " fear of God ", the " instigation of the devil " and the rest of the horrific jargon of the classical forms seems not to be mediaeval. Too much simplicity gave room for abuse, in fact, and statutes were needed to protect the indictment from being " embezzled ",[2] and to ascertain the precise person accused by describing his station in life—a clause known as the " addition "[3] and productive of much technicality later on, when indictments fell into the hands of the special pleaders, who had further to use the greatest precision in setting out every element of the crime charged.

INFORMATIONS

The principle of private initiation was not lost; indeed, the strength of that principle is characteristic of the common law. Anyone who

---

[1] Putnam, *Proceedings before Justices of the Peace* (Ames Foundation); *Kent Keepers of the Peace* (ed. Putnam, Kent Archaeological Society).

[2] 1 Edw. III, st. 2, c. 17 (1327); 8 Hen. VI, c. 12 (1429). These acts dealt with removing a genuine indictment from the file; whether the placing of a false indictment upon the file is criminal, is entertainingly discussed in a star chamber case: Y.B. 2 Richard III, Michs. no. 22, ff. 9–11.

[3] 1 Hen. V, c. 5 (1413). The common law writ *De Idemptitate Nominis* for the relief of those whose property had been seized in error was quite inadequate; see the complaints in *Rot. Parl.*, ii. 277 no. 20 (1363).

cared to could procure an indictment and carry on the necessary proceedings—and if the statute book is to be believed, many indictments were in fact procured out of hate and spite. On the other hand, a grand jury could ignore a bill as it saw fit. The Crown had not yet gone very far in the direction of initiating criminal proceedings; at most it had made it reasonably easy for a private person to do so. From Edward I onwards, the Crown occasionally used " informations " to put a man on his trial for treason, felony or misdemeanour, and thus at last the Crown found ways of directly initiating a criminal proceeding.[1] The Star Chamber (and later on, statutes) allowed private persons as well as the law officers of the Crown to put in informations. It was the use of informations by the Council and Star Chamber, coupled with their lack of jurisdiction over felonies, that probably gave rise to the newer rule that informations lie only for offences less than felony. They became involved in the political and constitutional struggle of the seventeenth century, and strong efforts were made to get them adjudged illegal. These attempts failed, and informations, properly pruned by statute, received a settled position in criminal procedure.[2]

PROCESS AND OUTLAWRY

Criminal as well as civil procedure is to some extent the result of standardising and formalising natural impulses. The criminal caught in the act is thus summarily dispatched after a brief altercation before a local court or bailiff. When a crime has been discovered the natural thing to do is to call for help and pursue the trail of the criminal. This is regularised as " hue and cry " and neglect to raise it is a serious matter; even if the diligence of the hue and cry does not result in a capture, the whole vill will be amerced; so too it is a serious offence to raise the hue and cry without justification. The neighbours ought to turn out with their weapons (specified in the Statute of Winchester[3]) and go from vill to vill. The criminal who is caught as the result of hot pursuit will be dealt with summarily as just described.

If an appeal was begun against an absent person, the preliminaries to outlawry began (and it took five successive county courts to complete the process). If an absent person has been indicted, the sheriff ought to arrest him, but it generally happened that arrest was impossible, and so once again the long procedure of outlawry began.[4] The result of

---

[1] Pollock and Maitland, ii. 662, but the examples there given must be compared with others *contra*. In 1290 it was held that the king's suit could only be taken on an indictment, an appeal, or if the prisoner was found with the mainour, Sayles, *King's Bench*, ii. 26 (with which compare the protest, *ibid.*, 131).

[2] Their history will be found in Holdsworth, ix. 236–245. Many acts made provision to rewards to informers. The crown might also use exceptional procedure, *e.g.* when James I turned detective: *Sanchar's Case* (1612), 9 Rep. 114 at 120 *b*.

[3] 13 Edw. I (1285).

[4] It is very rare for a criminal jury to pass in the absence of the accused; see, however, Sayles, *King's Bench* (Selden Society), i. 102 (1282).

outlawry on criminal process is, in effect, a conviction; the outlaw is " attained " and forfeits his chattels, while his free land (after the King's " year, day and waste ") will escheat. If captured, the outlaw could be hanged merely upon proof of the outlawry having been made.[1] Anyone could capture him and kill him if he resisted. It needed a resolution of the judges in 1328 to save his life against anyone who took a fancy to kill him,[2] and the forfeiture for outlawry was still preserved by the Forfeiture Act of 1870.

SANCTUARY

It quite frequently happened that in the meantime the accused had fled to a sanctuary. In general, this would be a local church or monastery; once there, the accused had the right to " call for the coroner ", confess to him, and abjure the realm within forty days. The coroner assigned the nearest port, and the criminal was allowed safe conduct thither, and had to take the first available passage abroad.[3] Under Henry VIII he was also branded in order to facilitate his identification if ever he returned— which would make him liable to be hanged as a felon.[4] Flight to certain great liberties, such as the palatinates, the liberties of St. Martin le Grand, of Westminster, and others, afforded much greater protection. In these places the King's process did not run, in consequence of a " mixture of law and custom, grant and prescription, forgery and usurpation " which makes the history, as well as the legal foundation, of these greater sanctuaries very obscure.[5] In such favoured places even the coroner could not enter, and the sanctuaryman was completely immune. The lords of these places enforced discipline, registered their new subjects and took an oath of fealty from them. The houses of Lancaster, York and Tudor struggled hard against these anomalies. Henry VIII abolished many, and substituted eight " cities of refuge ".[6] Acts of Parliament availed but little, and many sanctuaries whose legal existence (if any) had been cut short, continued to flourish—like " Alsatia "—merely by virtue of gangster organisation and the absence of official police.

EXAMINATION

The old books make little reference to the examination of accused persons pending their trial, and in ordinary cases there was probably

[1] *Eyre Rolls* (Selden Society, vol. lix), no. 1005 (1221).

[2] Y.B. 2 Edward III, Hil. no. 17; 27 Ass. 41; but see also Bracton, f. 134.

[3] Bracton, f. 135–136, remarks that abjuration (in other circumstances) is as old as the Assize of Clarendon (1166).

[4] 21 Hen. VIII, c. 2 (1529).

[5] Thornley, " Destruction of Sanctuary ", in *Tudor Studies presented to A. F. Pollard*, 182–207. See generally, N. M. Trenholme, *The Right of Sanctuary in England* (University of Missouri Studies, vol. 1 no. 5), 1903. For the very similar " avowrymen " of Cheshire, see R. Stewart-Brown, *Avowries of Cheshire*, English Historical Review, xxix. 41.

[6] 32 Hen. VIII, c. 12 (1540); Numbers, xxxv. 6; they were abandoned under Edward VI (Thornley, *loc. cit.*).

none; in cases of political or social importance, however, there are indications that prisoners were examined, and occasionally tortured. Coke's attitude towards the matter throws a curious light upon his own and his age's point of view. In the preliminaries to the trial of Edmund Peacham for treason, the prisoner had been examined under torture by Bacon (then Attorney-General), who communicated the results to Chief Justice Coke, who would normally have tried the case. Coke properly protested, and Peacham was therefore tried by the Chief Baron. That was in 1614. The very next year, however, Coke himself did much of the investigation and collecting of evidence against the Earl of Somerset, whom he then proceeded to try for murder.

For lesser folk there was a statutory procedure of examination by justices of the peace. From quite early times, a coroner had the duty of making inquiries in certain cases, both by his jury and by examining on oath persons who could give information. In 1554 a statute[1] required him to commit to writing the results of his investigation, and at the same time extended the principle to justices of the peace. They were therefore empowered to examine prisoners and those who proceeded against them, and to write down the material portions of what they said for use subsequently at the trial. Stated in this way, it would appear that the act intended to introduce a reform of great importance into criminal procedure. It did effect an important reform, but apparently by accident, for the motive of the enactment was, it seems, to prevent collusion between justices and criminals;[2] it was alleged that justices were much too easy in bailing suspects and so the act required them to write down the statements of the prosecutor, the prisoner and the witnesses before bailing them—evidently to prevent a matter being stifled at its inception, and to prevent abuse of the power of admitting to bail. The next year another act[3] extended the procedure to cases where the prisoner was not bailed but committed, and soon it became apparent that an important novelty had been introduced, albeit obliquely, into criminal procedure.

These examinations were purely ministerial, and need not be taken in the presence of other parties. The effect was to turn the justice of the peace into something between a detective and a *juge d'instruction*. The creation of a professional police force in 1829 and succeeding years relieved the magistrates of the duty of investigation, and so it was possible to change the character of their preliminary examination; in 1848 Sir John Jervis' Act[4] required that witnesses should be examined in the prisoner's presence, and should be liable to cross-examination by him. The accused was permitted by the act to call witnesses who were to be

---

[1] 1 & 2 Phil. & Mar., c. 13 (1554). On the defendant's examination, see Bayne's introduction to *Cases in Council of Henry VII* (Selden Society), xciv ff.

[2] This is discussed by Sir James Stephen, *History of Criminal Law*, i. 219, 236–238.

[3] 2 & 3 Phil. & Mar., c. 10 (1555).

[4] 11 & 12 Vict., c. 42 (1848).

treated in the same way, and was entitled to have copies of the depositions. If the proceedings raise a " strong or probable presumption of guilt " in the minds of the magistrates, they are to commit or bail him for trial. The magisterial inquiry has thus become, in form at least, although not in substance, a judicial proceeding.

TRIAL BY JURY

Of arraignment and the prisoner's plea, and the imposition of jury trial sanctioned by the *peine forte et dure*, we have already spoken.[1] Of the old procedure by " appeal " we have likewise given an example.[2] It is now time to consider the proceedings on the occasion of a jury trial.

There is not much light on this subject in the mediaeval sources. The information they give us is generally concerned with state trials and there is the obvious difficulty of deciding how far they represented normal practice. There are rules about the challenging of jurors which Bracton lays down in rather general terms[3]—rules which he seems to have derived from the canonist rules which disqualified witnesses on the ground of relationship, interest, etc. Bracton also recommends the discreet justice to examine the jury rigorously on the grounds upon which their verdict is based.[4] By means unknown the rule arose, sometime between Bracton and Fortescue, that the prisoner could challenge up to thirty-five jurors peremptorily.[5] Here it is well to notice the difficulty which Sir James Stephen feels;[6] if the jurors were witnesses (as he believed), how strange it is that a prisoner can peremptorily exclude up to thirty-five of them. The answer clearly is, that jurors never were witnesses but were rather representatives, as we have seen. Challenges were freely used in the middle ages, both in civil and criminal cases, and leave their mark on the record in the words " the jury being elected, *tried* and sworn say upon their oaths that . . ." A juryman who was excluded from the jury might yet be competent as a witness to inform the jury.[7] Indictors, as we have seen, were removable by challenge from a petty jury since 1352.[8] The number of peremptory challenges in trials of petty treason and felony (but not high treason) was reduced from thirty-five to twenty in 1531.[9]

Fortescue says little of criminal trials, save the wide powers of challenging jurors, both peremptorily and for cause; he leads us to

[1] Above, p. 125.

[2] Above, p. 121.

[3] Bracton, f. 143 b.

[4] *Ibid.*, f. 143.

[5] Fortescue, *De Laudibus*, c. 27.

[6] *History of Criminal Law*, i. 301–302.

[7] Thayer, *On Evidence*, 124, where the method of " trying " a challenge to a juryman is described.

[8] Above, p. 127.

[9] 22 Hen. VIII, c. 14.

conclude that the proceedings in the presence of the jury are analogous to those on the trial of civil issues—the swearing of witnesses, their examination and so forth.

A century after Fortescue, we have a fairly full description of a criminal trial by Sir Thomas Smith.[1] He tells us of the arrangement of the court room, the criers, the proclamations and the impanelling of the jury. The case opens with the justice who committed the prisoner bringing into court the depositions taken under the act of Philip and Mary, which are read—from which it will be seen that they already serve the new purpose (for which they were not designed originally) of serving as evidence. The prosecutor, the constable and the witnesses are then sworn, give their evidence, and seem to engage in a lively altercation with the prisoner which lasts until " the judge hath heard them say enough ". He then charges the jury, although Smith does not distinctly say that he sums up. They then proceed to the next case, and by the time two or three more cases have been heard, the jury will protest that their memory is sufficiently taxed, and will ask to retire to consider their verdicts.

The main features of the Elizabethan criminal trial have been admirably summarised by Sir James Stephen in these words:

" (1) The prisoner was kept in confinement more or less secret till his trial, and could not prepare for his defence. He was examined and his examination was taken down.

" (2) He had no notice beforehand of the evidence against him, and was compelled to defend himself as well as he could when the evidence, written or oral, was produced on his trial. He had no counsel either before or at the trial.

" (3) At the trial there were no rules of evidence, as we understand the expression. The witnesses were not necessarily (to say the very least) confronted with the prisoner, nor were the originals of documents required to be produced.

" (4) The confessions of accomplices were not only admitted against each other, but were regarded as specially cogent evidence.

" (5) It does not appear that the prisoner was allowed to call witnesses on his own behalf; but it matters little whether he did or not, as he had no means of ascertaining what evidence they would give, or of procuring their attendance. In later times they were not examined on oath, if they were called."[2]

These remarks seem a fair summary, save perhaps that it ought to be mentioned that bail was granted freely, and so there was some opportunity for preparing a defence in such a case.

REPRESENTATION BY COUNSEL

It was a very ancient principle that no counsel was allowed to persons charged with treason or felony against the Crown; counsel were allowed in an appeal as this was brought by a private person and not by the Crown. A slight relaxation was made in the late fifteenth century when

---

[1] *De Republica Anglorum* (ed. Alston), 94 ff.

[2] Stephen, *History of Criminal Law*, i. 350.

it became general to allow counsel to argue points of law,[1] which at that time were generally objections to the indictment. The origin of the rule seems to have been the fact that counsel was hardly necessary. As we have seen, in Bracton's day the court took charge of the proceedings, and viewed indictors, prosecutors, jury and prisoner with impartial distrust. There was little that required expert knowledge until indictments became technical documents, and when that point was reached, counsel for arguing them was allowed almost at once. When the use of witnesses was more clearly understood, and a technique of examining them developed, the situation was again materially altered, and the prisoner was at a disadvantage in attempting to cross-examine when the case for the prosecution was sprung upon him, and his own defence still unprepared. This time the law did not bring its own corrective, and made little attempt for a long time to meet the changed circumstances.

From 1640 to the Revolution there are unmistakable signs that public and also professional opinion was dissatisfied with the existing trial practice in criminal cases, and the Revolution was quickly followed by reforms.[2] In 1696 momentous changes were made in trials for treason. The accused was allowed counsel, a copy of the indictment, and to bring witnesses on oath,[3] but not until 1837 was counsel allowed in cases of felony.[4]

WITNESSES

From the earliest days of the jury, witnesses were used, although by differing procedures. At first the jurors themselves might have first-hand knowledge of the facts, or they might obtain that knowledge by private inquiry. It was later possible to bring witnesses to give testimony before the jury, but they did so at some risk. As late as 1450 it was considered normal for the jurors to go to a man's house and ask him what he knows about a matter, but if he goes to the jury, it is maintenance.[5] Honest witnesses were therefore reluctant, although in Chancery proceedings a useful method was devised by summoning them by *sub poena*, which enabled them to testify without fear.[6] At common law witnesses were not compellable, and no process issued against them. In civil proceedings counsel were so closely identified with their principals, and so great an obligation rested on them to tell the truth, that the allegations of counsel seem to have been treated as evidence.[7] Even Coke was moved to say that the evidence of witnesses to the jury is no part of a criminal trial, for trial is by jury, not by witnesses. The jury was indeed

---

[1] Authorities are cited in Holdsworth, v. 192.

[2] Stephen, *op. cit.*, i. 357 ff.; Holdsworth, ix. 230–235.

[3] 7 & 8 Will. III, c. 3 (1696).

[4] 6 & 7 Will. IV, c. 114.

[5] Y.B. 28 Henry VI, Pasch. 1 (1450).

[6] Thayer, *Evidence*, 129.

[7] Thayer, *Evidence*, 120, 133; Holdsworth, iii. 638.

inscrutable, and trial by witnesses had been distrusted for some five hundred years in Coke's day.[1]

Nevertheless, the importance of witnesses steadily grew in spite of this tendency to what must have been already mere archaism. A great landmark is Elizabeth's statute[2] which established a process to compel the attendance of witnesses and made perjury by them a crime. This act seems only to touch civil proceedings, but as we have already noted, witnesses could be bound over to appear under the second act of Philip and Mary,[3] to testify against the prisoner, and so the Crown could compel its own witnesses.

A curious sign of the new spirit appears when courts began to allow prisoners to produce witnesses, although refusing to let them be sworn. A greater advance is to be found in an act of Elizabeth creating a new offence of " embezzling " arms from royal arsenals. This act concludes by allowing a person charged under it " to make any lawful proof that he can, by lawful witness or otherwise " for his defence.[4] So too under an act of 1606 making certain felonies done by Englishmen in Scotland triable in England, prisoners are allowed to produce witnesses, who shall be sworn, for their defence.[5] The same privilege was allowed on trials for treason in 1696, and in 1702 the legislature finally extended the principle generally by enacting that in treason and felony the defence may bring witnesses and have them sworn.[6]

EVIDENCE

The oldest portions of our law of evidence are concerned with the deed under seal, which for a long time was the only type of evidence to which it paid any regard, and which it has always treated with special respect. Somewhat analogous to this were the transaction-witnesses of Anglo-Saxon law, who had a somewhat similar function in criminal law. Just as the deed was a solemn evidence of civil obligation, so the transaction witnesses were pre-ordained evidence which could be used if need be as a defence to an accusation of theft. This type of evidence was in constant use during the middle ages, and combined neatly with the desire of lords to restrict buying and selling as far as possible to markets and such-like public occasions when the lord got his market-dues and the parties obtained the protection of publicity in their dealings.

Evidence given by witnesses to a jury, as we have seen, was for a long time an informal adjunct to legal proceedings rather than part of

[1] 3 Inst. 26–27; Nemo de capitalibus placitis testimonio convincatur—*Leges Henri Primi*, xxxi. 5.

[2] 5 Eliz., c. 9 (1563).

[3] 2 & 3 Phil. & Mar., c. 10 (1555).

[4] 31 Eliz., c. 4 (1589).

[5] 4 Jac. I, c. 4, s. 26.

[6] 1 Anne, stat. 2, c. 9 (1702). See now S. Rezneck, *The Statute of 1696*, Journal of Modern History, ii. 5–26.

their essence. It is not surprising, therefore, that there was hardly any law governing its admissibility—evidence of previous convictions, for example, was admitted without comment.[1] An old phrase alleging of two witnesses that one heard and the other saw occasionally appears, and in treason cases there was the statutory rule requiring two witnesses.[2] This was perhaps of foreign origin, and English law did not adopt the general principle of merely counting witnesses.

The prisoner himself could not give evidence.[3] The statements he made in court as he conducted his defence were not made upon oath, and the questioning he underwent in court in the sixteenth century based upon the magistrates' examination, though often searching, did not result in sworn evidence by him. Moreover, the examination itself was inadmissible if it were made upon oath, for an oath was regarded as involving some degree of compulsion. Questioning prisoners at the trial fell out of use at the Revolution, but prisoners were still allowed to make statements in the course of the trial, and when they had counsel, such statements were often made on their behalf.[4] In 1848 the magistrates' examination was, by statute,[5] to be preceded by the warning that it might be used in evidence, and that the prisoner need not make a statement unless he so wished. As a result, prisoners could not now be questioned either before or at the trial. Such a state of affairs, as Sir James Stephen observed,[6] did not necessarily work injustice if the defence was carefully prepared and skilfully conducted; but in practice most prisoners could not afford an elaborate defence, and for them the system often meant disaster. It was felt that expense and time could be saved if prisoners could give evidence on oath, and that this was the only practicable course in many cases if the real defence was to be elicited at all. A series of acts during the nineteenth century sponsored by Lord Denman and Lord Brougham enlarged the class of competent witnesses in civil cases, but not until 1898 were accused persons made competent (but not compellable) witnesses at their trial.[7] Compulsory examination on oath has never been applied to prisoners except in the Star Chamber and the Court of High Commission.[8]

---

[1] See the narrative of a case of 1542 related by G. R. Elton, *Informing for Profit*, Cambridge Historical Journal, xi. 149 at 159.

[2] 5 & 6 Edw. VI, c. 11 (1552); 7 & 8 Will. III, c. 3 (1696). For the history of the idea, see Holdsworth, ix. 203 ff.

[3] In the Anglo-Saxon period (and later still by local customs) an accused person might sometimes obtain acquittal by swearing an oath that he was innocent; such an oath is, of course, in the nature of an ordeal, and does not support evidence of any sort.

[4] Stephen, *History of Criminal Law*, i. 440 ff.

[5] 11 & 12 Vict., c. 42 (1848).

[6] Stephen, *op. cit.*, i. 444.

[7] 61 & 62 Vict., c. 36 (1898).

[8] On this, and on the privilege against self-incrimination, see Bayne's introduction to *Select Cases in Council of Henry VII* (Selden Society), xciii ff., and E. M. Morgan, *The Privilege against Self-Incrimination*, Minnesota Law Review, xxxiv. 1–45.

BURDEN OF PROOF

Rules of evidence and procedure (and especially those which are now obsolete and so outside our personal observation) cannot be judged apart from their actual working, and when that practical aspect of them is investigated, the result may be surprising. For example, the rule that the burden of proof lies upon the prosecution is now considered as a valuable safeguard for the accused. As at present administered, this is true, but it has not always been so. In times past a corollary was drawn from it to the effect that as the prosecution had the burden of proof the defence need do nothing;[1] hence the defence could not call witnesses nor engage counsel. Both were superfluous, for if the Crown proved its case, that was an end of the matter; if it did not, the failure would be apparent in spite of the silence of the defence.

On the other hand, the canonical system, as applied in the eighteenth century to clergy, and to laymen who had been tried under the Church's criminal jurisdiction, adopted the principle that it is for the accused to prove his innocence. This sounds harsh to modern ears, but the logical implication was drawn that since the accused bore a burden of proof he was entitled to call witnesses for his defence. The prosecution, having a merely passive rôle, could call none.[2] Acquittals consequently followed with monotonous regularity.

SUMMARY TRIAL

Very gradually the legislature ventured to make some offences triable " upon examination " by justices of the peace, that is to say, without a jury. This was a serious break with common law tradition at several points. An early experiment in this direction was made in the reign of Henry V, when justices of the peace were empowered to examine both masters and labourers who had transgressed the statutes of labourers " and thereupon to punish them upon their confession as if they had been convicted by inquest ".[3] It would seem that, if they did not confess, the justices could not proceed further without a jury. A statute of Henry VII apparently extended this power of trial on information by the Crown without jury to all statutory offences less than felony.[4] This statute was repealed[5] at the accession of Henry VIII, but new statutes

---

[1] For the lengths to which this logic was pressed in Scotland, see Stephen, *History of Criminal Law*, i. 352.

[2] The procedure is described in Stephen, *op. cit.*, i. 460; it consisted of an exculpatory oath by the accused, twelve compurgatory oaths, evidence for the accused, and a verdict by a jury. It is interesting to observe that centuries earlier, an accused who was " put to his purgation " with so many oath-helpers could " redeem the purgation " and so settle the matter by a money payment; Pollock and Maitland, ii. 538 n. 5. So, too, in civil matters a canonical plaintiff could prove his debt by witnesses, although in common law the defendant could make his defence by compurgation; *ibid.*, ii. 347 n.1.

[3] 2 Hen. V, stat. 1, c. 4 (1414); 8 Hen. VI, c. 4.

[4] 11 Hen. VII, c. 3 (1495). Cf. above, p. 183.

[5] 1 Hen. VIII, c. 6 (1510).

were made embodying the principle, and became very common under the Restoration, dealing with a vast number of petty offences. By 1776 a leading practice book devoted nearly two thousand pages to the offences triable by this procedure. Gradually it became customary for such statutes to grant an appeal to quarter sessions, but in the vast majority of cases there was no appeal.[1]

BENEFIT OF CLERGY

This ancient and curious privilege dates from the twelfth century.[2] Judging from the Anglo-Saxon laws, clergy were generally amenable to the same jurisdictions as laymen, although they had preferential treatment in the matter of proofs and penalties. The problem of competing jurisdictions became evident after the conquest. The Norman kings asserted the principle that clergy who also had a lay capacity (as earls and feudal tenants) could be tried by the King in respect of their misdeeds committed in their lay capacity. The Constitutions of Clarendon (1164), coming immediately in the midst of the conflict between Henry II and Becket, profess to perpetuate the practice of Henry I's reign—a " criminous clerk " was to be charged in the King's Court, tried by the Church and degraded if guilty, and returned to the King's Court for punishment as a layman. The murder of Becket produced such a psychological revulsion, however, that the Crown made no further attempt to enforce the Constitutions of Clarendon, and surrendered criminous clerks unconditionally to the Church.

That was the high-water mark of ecclesiastical privilege; the rest of the history is the story of its slow decline. There seems no sign in Bracton of that decline, but soon after his day it becomes apparent. Clergy were always charged in the first place before the secular court, and many of them immediately claimed their clergy; others, however, preferred to take their chance with a jury, and only demanded their clergy if the verdict was against them. The royal courts clearly preferred this latter course, and eventually came to insist upon it; even if clergy were claimed immediately upon arraignment, the lay court would proceed to a verdict before relinquishing them as " clerks convict ". In the meantime the convict's property is taken into the King's hand to abide the event in the Church Court. By 1352 the clergy are complaining that clerks have been hanged by judgment of secular courts, and the Crown admitted that things had moved too fast, and promised that " clerks convict " of petty treason or felony should be handed over, the Church in return promising to imprison them and punish them duly.[3] By this time, moreover, the usual test of clerical status was ability to read,

---

[1] See a full discussion by Frankfurter and Corcoran in Harvard Law Review, xxxix.

[2] See Gabel, *Benefit of Clergy in England in the later Middle Ages*; Stephen, *History of Criminal Law*, i. 459 ff.; Holdsworth, iii. 294 ff. For additional references, see A. L. Poole, *Domesday Book to Magna Carta*, 218 n. 4.

[3] Statute *Pro Clero*, 25 Edw. III, stat. 3, c. 4 (1352, not 1350 as generally stated).

although for a time some regard was paid to the prisoner's dress and tonsure. Once in the ecclesiastical court, various modes of trial were in theory possible, but in practice it was almost universally compurgation, or " canonical purgation " as it was technically called. With the decline in estimation for this form of trial a serious situation arose, for acquittals were much too frequent, the trial becoming little more than a formality. Even if the clerk failed in his purgation, there was considerably difficulty in preventing him from escaping out of the bishop's prison.

The whole affair thus became highly artificial, and queer results some-time followed. Thus, a married man could have the benefit (for clerks in the lowest orders were not excluded from marriage). But a bigamist lost his clergy, and a bigamist was a man who had (*a*) married twice, or (*b*) married a widow. Thus a married man's life may depend on whether his wife was a virgin when he married her, and the Court can " find that out straight away from a jury ".[1]

In 1376 a curious petition in parliament observed that bigamists were now numerous, " by reason of diverse pestilences ", having married twice, or having married widows. Others had avoided this perilous condition by not re-marrying after their first wife's death, but were living in sin. They suggest that benefit of clergy should not be lost in such circumstances. To this touching appeal by bigamists who evidently anticipated that they would some day commit felony, the crown replied with a short refusal.[2]

In 1490 it was enacted that a clerk convict should be branded,[3] for it had become a rule that the benefit could only be used once; this would make enforcement of the rule easy. The Reformation would at first sight seem to have been a convenient moment for abolishing so trouble-some a relic of Rome, but in fact policy fluctuated. It was actually extended in 1547 to bigamists, and to peers of the realm whether they could read or not,[4] and peers were excused the branding, too; it was further extended partially in 1624, and completely in 1692, to women.[5] In 1707 all the world were admitted, by the abolition of the reading test, or " neck verse ".[6]

As a matter of fact, all this means that the nature of benefit of clergy had undergone a radical change. In 1576 it was enacted that clerks convict should no longer be handed over to the ordinary, but should be forthwith discharged, and so the last connection of the benefit with either Church or clergy was severed, but the same act authorised one year's imprisonment before discharge, at the discretion of the court.[7]

[1] Y.B. 30 & 31 Edward I (Rolls Series), 530.

[2] *Rot. Parl.,* iii. 333 no. 63.

[3] 4 Hen. VII, c. 13 (1490, not 1487 as generally stated; *Rot. Parl.,* vi. 426, 437).

[4] 1 Edw. VI, c. 12, ss. 16, 14.

[5] 21 Jac. I, c. 6 (1624, not 1622 as usually stated); 3 Will. & Mar., c. 9 (1691).

[6] 6 Anne, c. 9 (1707, not 1705 as generally stated).

[7] 18 Eliz., c. 7 (1576). Stephen, *History of Criminal Law,* i. 360, is in error in stating that the act abolished canonical purgation.

Even before the Reformation, Parliament had ventured to enact that petty treason should no longer be clergyable (perhaps justifying its boldness on the ground that it was the statute *de clero*[1] which had made it so). After the Reformation a long line of statutes made murder, piracy, highway robbery, rape, burglary and a host of other crimes non-clergyable. The result was important. The gap between felony and misdemeanour was much too large, and by using the benefit of clergy Parliament was able to make some crimes capital for a first offence (non-clergyable) and others capital only for a second felony (clergyable). Thus a rough classification of crimes into more than the two mediaeval categories became possible. This process was carried further by developing the policy of the Act of 1576, and condemning persons convicted of clergyable larceny to transportation for seven years. Thus the survival of clergy greatly modified the harshness of the penal law and permitted the growth of a graduated scale of punishment.

Benefit of clergy was abolished in 1827, but its ghost continued to haunt the law until less than a hundred years ago.[2]

[1] 25 Edw. III, stat. 6, c. 4.

[2] " When benefit of clergy was abolished in 1827 by 7 & 8 Geo. IV, c. 28, the Act [of Edw. VI extending it to peers] was overlooked, and on the occasion of Lord Cardigan's trial in 1841 it was doubted whether, if he were convicted, he would not be entitled to the benefit of it, notwithstanding the Act of 1827. The question was finally set at rest by 4 & 5 Vict., c. 22 " (1841): Stephen, *History of Criminal Law*, i. 462.

CHAPTER 2

THE FELONIES

Even in Anglo-Saxon times, as we have seen, the Crown began to establish a list of pleas over which it had particular rights. Some of these became, after the Conquest, felonies. Not all of them, however; the breach of the King's peace, for example, became steadily less serious as the peace became further extended. As a serious crime it was confined to the days when the peace was given (as it was also in France) by a solemn diploma under the royal seal.

Felony is a feudal conception particularly applying to the breach of the fidelity and loyalty which should accompany the feudal relationship which has been consecrated by homage. Its characteristic punishment is therefore loss of tenement—escheat. On the continent felony was often confined to this class of crime, but in England, by means unknown, there came " a deep change in thought and feeling. All the hatred and contempt which are behind the word *felon* are enlisted against the criminal, murderer, robber, thief, without reference to any breach of the bond of homage and fealty ".[1] The transition may have been helped by the fact that already in Anglo-Saxon law there were crimes which put their author at the absolute mercy of the King, their property, limb and life. The King's " great forfeiture " may thus have caused these crimes to be equated with true felony which resembled it. In any case, this extension of the meaning of felony must have been welcome to lords, for it was they who reaped the harvest of escheats (subject always to the King's wasting the tenement for a year and a day).

The list of felonies during the middle ages was always short, and the definitions of the crimes within the list were generally narrow; they

[1] 1 P. & M., 304.

442

almost always were subject to benefit of clergy, and could always be prosecuted by appeal. Indeed, the appeal is distinctly an appeal of felony, and at least one crime, mayhem, was a felony if prosecuted by an appeal, although it was not a felony upon indictment.[1]

TREASON

The history of treason in the middle ages is as distinctive as the nature of the offence. It is one of the very few crimes which were defined by statute during that period; and it is one of the equally few crimes whose scope was extended by " construction ". Unlike treason, the mediaeval felony was (generally speaking) neither statutory nor constructive.[2]

High Treason was never clergyable, and more than one prelate has paid the penalty; for a time, however, there were certain sanctuaries which claimed the extraordinary privilege of protecting traitors. The definition of treason before the statute was certainly wide, including the murder of royal messengers, and apparently even highway robbery. Such extensions fell heavily on lords who lost their escheats (for these offences were capital felonies even if they were not treason). The matter was therefore raised in Parliament with the result that the famous statute of treasons in 1352 laid down a definition, coupled with the proviso that any further definitions in doubtful cases shall be made in Parliament. The statute makes treason to consist in[3]—

" compassing or imagining the death of the king, his consort, or his eldest son;
violating his consort, or eldest unmarried daughter, or the wife of his eldest son;
levying war against the king in his realm, or adhering to his enemies in his realm, giving them aid and comfort in the realm or elsewhere;
forging the great seal or the coinage, and knowingly importing or uttering false coin;
slaying the treasurer, chancellor or judges while sitting in court; "

all of which involved forfeiture of land and goods to the Crown. The statute further defined " another sort of treason " (which was generally called petty treason) as being—

" the slaying of a master by his servant;
the slaying of a husband by his wife;
the slaying of a prelate by his subject, secular or religious."

These were to involve escheat, and not forfeiture, of lands. Then follows the provision for the parliamentary declaration of treason in future cases not covered by the act, and a declaration that riding armed,

[1] From 1275–1285 rape was in a similar position.

[2] Conspiracy was defined by statute, 33 Edw. I (but not as a felony); for the few and unimportant statutory felonies created during the middle ages, see Stephen, *History of Criminal Law*, ii. 206–207.

[3] 25 Edw. III, st. 5, c. 2. Cf. B. M. Putnam, *Chief Justice Shareshull*, University of Toronto Law Journal, v. 265.

robbery, kidnapping for ransom and the like are not treason, and a rescission of recent judgments to the contrary, with the restoration of the forfeitures already exacted by the Crown to the lords of the fee as escheats. The motives of the statute are patently to prevent the loss of escheats by treating felonies of certain sorts as treason. This is made perfectly clear, moreover, in the petition which led to the statute.[1] There is no trace of political theory in the act.

It is impossible to enter here into the large number of judicial and statutory changes which took place in the ensuing five centuries of history. Many times of unrest produced statutory extensions which were repealed when quiet was restored, but all through the succeeding ages it has been felt that treason should, wherever possible, rest solely on the act of 1352. A few of these later statutes have become permanent or are otherwise remarkable. Thus there is the famous act declaring that service with a *de facto* king shall not be treason to the King *de jure*,[2] and the act requiring two witnesses of the overt act or acts alleged in the indictment.[3]

The act of 1352 may itself have hampered the orderly growth of the law relating to offences against public security by including so few of them in the definition of treason, making no provision for the lesser (but still serious) crimes. It remained for the Star Chamber and the Legislature to introduce some order into a tangled and dangerous mass of law by separating from treason such crimes as riot, sedition, espionage, incitement to mutiny, and the like. Similarly, the petty treasons were reduced to ordinary murder in 1828 (9 Geo. IV, c. 31).

MURDRUM

Murder is the product of many different lines of development. Slaying wilfully or accidentally had the same consequences in Anglo-Saxon law—the offender must bear the feud, or else he must provide the sum of money amounting to the dead man's *wer*. Even before the conquest, however, deliberately planned assassinations came to be distinguished and put into the list of Crown pleas as *forsteal*. The original sense of this word was lying in wait to ambush the victim. After the conquest this is expressed in various terms in French and Latin, but frequently takes the form of *assault purpensé*, or *assultus premeditatus*. In time this yields before *malitia excogitata*, and so introduces us to the very troublesome word " malice ".[4] Numerous pardons for accidental slayings explain that the offence was not done of malice aforethought, but on the positive side the word was used very vaguely; it seems impossible to maintain that it signified spite or hate, or indeed any

---

[1] *Rot. Parl.*, ii. 166 no. 15 (1348).

[2] 11 Hen. VII, c. 1 (1495).

[3] 7 & 8 Will. III, c. 3 (1696).

[4] Malice aforethought is occasionally alleged in actions of trespass: Sayles *King's Bench*, i. 66 (1280).

definite allegation of intention. It is best regarded as a traditional form which only occasionally coincided with the natural meaning of the word. The Anglo-Saxon *forsteal*, like much else of the older legal language, survived only in local courts, and like its surroundings gradually sank to a petty significance. Forsteal thus became " forstall ", an offence which consisted in intercepting sellers on the way to a market and attempting to raise prices artificially.

The word " murder " has also had a devious history. Its original sense is the particularly heinous crime of secret slaying. After the conquest it was observed that Normans were frequently found dead under mysterious circumstances, and so William I enacted that if anyone were found slain and the slayer were not caught, then the hundred should pay a fine; this fine is a *murdrum*.[1] The practice soon grew up of taking inquests and if it were presented that the dead man was English, then the fine was not due. In 1267 it was enacted that accidental deaths should not give rise to *murdrum*,[2] and finally in 1340 presentment of Englishry and *murdrum* were abolished.[3] Henceforth the word slowly tends to get linked up with " malice aforethought " and so we get the classical formulae describing the crime of murder.

Suicide (especially if it were done to avoid capture) involved for-feiture of chattels, and so it was argued backwards that it was a felony.

MURDER AND MANSLAUGHTER

In the thirteenth century misadventure and self-defence were still recognised, not so much as defences to a charge of homicide as circum-stances entitling one to a pardon; but if these defences were not involved, there was but one other case, and that was homicide. Whatever might be urged in mitigation of this offence could only be urged before the King as part of an appeal for pardon; it could not be considered by a court of law.[4] It is important to remember that the prerogative of mercy was the only point at which our mediaeval criminal law was at all flexible; hence pardons were issued with liberality for all sorts of felonies throughout the middle ages and long afterwards, and it is in the history of pardons, therefore, that the gradual growth of a classification of homicides is to be sought. A beginning was made in 1328 when a statute called in general terms, for restraint in issuing pardons,[5] and in

[1] *Leis Willelme*, 22; Yntema, *Lex Murdrorum*, Harvard Law Review, xxxvi. 146–179. By custom, *murdrum* was not due in some counties, *e.g.* Cornwall (Y.B. 30 & 31 Edward I (Rolls Series), 240), and Kent (*ibid.*, xl).

[2] 52 Hen. III, c. 25; Prov. Westm. (1259), c. 22; Treharne, i. 173 n. 2.

[3] 14 Edw. III, stat. 1, c. 4.

[4] By the Statute of Gloucester, 6 Edw. I, c. 9 (1278), it was enacted that there should be no need in the future to get a special writ from chancery authorising an inquest, but trial judges at gaol delivery should ask the jury if the homicide was accidental or in self-defence; " then the justices shall inform the king, and the king shall give him grace, if he pleases ".

[5] 2 Edw. III, c. 2. For the effectiveness of this statute to restrain the royal prerogative see Sayles, *King's Bench*, iii. p. xli.

1390 the Commons secured a statute which recognised certain pardons as issuing from the Chancery as a matter of course (no doubt cases of self-defence or misadventure); with these the statute contrasts pardons for " murders done in await, assault, or malice prepense ". In such cases pardons were subjected to almost impossible conditions.[1] The pardoning power in other cases was not touched, and so the Crown retained its normal powers and procedure for pardoning homicide, except cases of what we may call wilful murder. The distinction becomes clearer in the Tudor reigns when benefit of clergy was being redistributed among the various crimes. Thus, James Grame wilfully murdered his master, Richard Tracy, on 9th February 1497 and then pleaded his clergy. An indignant Parliament was determined that he should hang, and so attainted him, and abolished clergy for his and all like cases of prepensed murder in petty treason.[2] A number of such statutes followed in the reign of Henry VIII, and one of them[3] uses (probably for the first time) the words " wilful murder "; from that date it is clear that the statutes have, in effect, divided the old felony of homicide into two separate crimes, " wilful murder of malice aforethought " which was not clergy-able and therefore capital, and on the other hand, those homicides which were neither in self-defence, nor by misadventure. Some such division was obviously necessary, but unfortunately the boundary was generally sought in glossing the ancient formula " malice ". " Manslaughter ", as it came to be called, exercised the analytical skill of writers on pleas of the Crown for a century and more before very much order could be introduced, and even now serious questions as to the import of " malice " in murder have been raised.[4]

LARCENY

Few headings in criminal law have had so interesting a history as larceny. Its earliest form is naturally determined by the circumstances of agricultural life, and so the scope of larceny has gradually developed from the original type of cattle theft. We have already seen that the procedure derived from Anglo-Saxon times and remodelled as the appeal of larceny was merely a standardisation of the normal steps which would be taken upon the discovery of a theft of cattle—the hue and cry, the pursuit of the trail, and so on to summary judgment. One old distinction died away. This was the difference between manifest and secret theft. In Anglo-Saxon England, as in many early systems, the manifest thief fared much worse than the one whose guilt was only established after a

[1] 13 Rich. II, stat. 2, c. 1 (1390).

[2] 12 Hen. VII, c. 7 (1497).

[3] 23 Hen. VIII, c. 1 (1532).

[4] *Woolmington* v. *Director of Public Prosecutions*, [1935] A.C. 462, contains an elaborate history of certain aspects of " malice ". Marowe, *De Pace* (1503) in Putnam, *Early Treatises*, 378, speaks of manslaughter. Cf. Plucknett, " Commentary " in Putnam, *Justices of the Peace* (Ames Foundation), cxlvii ff.

lapse of time.   No reasons seem to be evident for the rule in England,[1] but some savages are said to adopt it as a special condemnation for those who are not merely thieves, but incompetent thieves.   The distinction between grand and petty larceny is also ancient, although the explanation by a glossator of Britton that a man can steal enough to keep himself from starvation for a week without committing a major crime seems more modern than the rule; perhaps the gloss is under canonical influence, for the Church would not condemn a famished man for stealing bread.[2]

Bracton adopts the Roman definition of theft,[3] but there has been some doubt whether contemporary English (or Norman) law really did look for an *animus furandi*, " intent to steal ".   There are dicta by judges, statements by text-writers, and even miracles, attesting the rule that a man who takes another's chattel, even without intent to steal, may be held guilty of theft.[4]   The burden of all of them is that a lord who distrains will get into trouble if his conduct is not scrupulously correct. That lesson had to be taught (and it has been learnt), but there seems no actual case where a distrainor who sold the goods was hanged.   It would almost seem that these are stories told from the bench to assembled landlords and that the gruesome ending was merely *in terrorem*.   Their ultimate basis, however, lies in the impossibility of expecting a jury to ascertain a person's state of mind.[5]

The list of things which can or cannot be the subject of larceny has varied, and for centuries after the reigns of the Norman kings became steadily more absurd and confused.   Wild animals were easily excluded, unless they were game on a private estate; deeds could be stolen under King John but not under Edward IV;   Coke without any authority extended this exception to all choses in action and so it became a rule of the common law that the theft of a bank-note was not larceny.   One judge even suggested that the theft of diamonds was not larceny because their value was dependent largely upon fancy.   So, too, peacocks and sporting dogs were luxury articles without economic value.   A huge mass of legislation has tackled all these points separately and with little reference to related points.   Often the rules of benefit of clergy were employed in order to introduce some sort of gradation in larcenies and their punishment.[6]

---

[1] For some speculations and analogies, see Pollock and Maitland, ii. 497; as Le Foyer remarks (*Droit pénal normand*, 135) the story of the Spartan boy who stole a fox (told by Plutarch, L*y*curgus) gives the ancient point of view.

[2] Britton, i. 56; Le Foyer, 133 n. 1.

[3] Bracton omits " lucri faciendi gratia veli psius rei vel etiam usus eius possessionisve "; these points are discussed in Stephen, *History of Criminal Law*, iii. 131 ff.

[4] The story told by a judge is in Y.B. 33 & 35 Edward I (Rolls Series) 503; the text-writer's views are in Britton, i. 116, 138; the miracle is described in Stephen, i. 79.

[5] The averment of a man's deceitful intention presented insuperable difficulties: Y.BB. 12 & 13 Edward III (Rolls Series), 83 (1339); " the thought of man shall not be tried, for the devil himself knoweth not the thought of man "—Brian, C.J., in Y.B. 7 Edward IV, Pasch. no. 2, f. 2 (1467).   Cf. the comment " — words that might well be the motto for the early history of criminal law ": Pollock and Maitland, ii. 474–475.

[6] Abundant references will be found in Stephen, iii. 142–149.

QUASI-THEFT

The nature of larceny is expressed in the old charge that the thief
" stole, took, and carried away ". This is clearly an old form derived
from the simplest type of stealing, and was made the basis of the theory
that larceny is a violation of possession. It covered the great majority
of cases likely to arise in simple agricultural communities, but as society
became more complex and newer forms of economic relationships
became frequent, many sorts of crime escaped the old definition of
larceny. Not until the reign of Henry VIII do we find much effort
made to include them, and not until the eighteenth century is the legislation on the subject very extensive. Both in Normandy and in England
there is some mention, even in the middle ages, of " quasi-theft ", and
in Normandy it is clear that the conception was capable of filling many
of the gaps in the old law of larceny. It included the use of false weights,
measures and coins; concealment of wreck and treasure trove; refusal
to replevy a distress; the use of forged bonds; usury; and removing
boundary marks.[1]

Bracton occasionally uses the expression quasi-theft, but his list is
not so extensive as it was in Normandy, for treasure trove and the use
of false coins might involve a charge of high treason, and coinage offences
soon became statutory felonies as well; weights and measures were
governed by their own assize and were best dealt with (although that
best was imperfect) locally;[2] withernam became a serious offence, but
separated from larceny owing to the need for special procedure; and the
use of forged deeds in court (but not elsewhere) seems to have been
dealt with summarily by the court which had been deceived.[3] Bracton
does use the idea of quasi-theft in connection with treasure trove,[4] and
more curiously still, in an argument that robbery is also larceny.[5] The
Mirror of Justices would have it that a great many sorts of fraud and
dishonesty were (or ought to be) larceny,[6] but it is plain that they were
not. Usury (a quasi-theft in Normandy) was left to the Church in
England.

How, then, were the gaps in the law of larceny supplied in practice
during the middle ages in England? We suggest that the action of
account will give the clue. This action was available against bailiffs
and also against receivers of money or goods to the use of their masters;

[1] Le Foyer, *Droit pénal normand*, 149 ff.

[2] The control of weights and measures appears in the Anglo-Saxon laws, and in legislation
during the next thousand years. For difficulties of enforcement see J. H. Thomas, *Town
Government in the Sixteenth Century*, 69, 83.

[3] A petition that the forgery of private seals and their apposition to deeds should be
punishable with life imprisonment upon indictment was rejected in 1371: *Rot. Parl.,* ii. 308
no. 45. A forged warrant of arrest in 1497 cost only a fine of 6s. 8d. in the king's bench:
Bayne, *Council of Henry VII*, cliv n. 1.

[4] Bracton, f. 119 b.

[5] *Ibid.,* f. 150 b.

[6] *Mirror of Justices* (ed. Whittaker, Selden Society), 25–28.

it was also used commonly between partners and joint traders of various sorts, so that a great many business relationships fell within its scope. The statutory process upon it was remarkable, and indeed unique. Persons entitled to an account from " servants, bailiffs, chamberlains and all manner of receivers " were allowed to appoint auditors, and if the accountant was in arrear, the auditors could commit the accountant to prison. There he was to lie until the account was discharged; if it was disputed and the accountant " could find friends " the matter could be reviewed in the court of exchequer.[1] This drastic procedure whereby imprisonment could be ordered without a court or trial, at the discretion of purely private persons (whom Coke[2] later had to call, nevertheless, judges of record), must have provided speedy sanctions against those who were later subject to the statutes on embezzlement and kindred offences.[3]

BREAKING BULK

Account, however, had its limitations and occasions arose when criminal sanctions were deemed necessary. An early example is to be seen in the curious case of breaking bulk.[4] The facts were that a carrier entrusted with merchandise to be transported to Southampton broke open a bale and misappropriated the contents. There was much argument first in the Star Chamber and then in the Exchequer Chamber whether this was felony. A majority of the judges finally held that it was, influenced no doubt by the fact that the owner of the goods was a foreign merchant who took his stand upon his treaty rights and the law of nature. In short, it was politically expedient to punish the carrier for larceny, but the devious reasoning by which this was accomplished was a native product of some antiquity;[5] it left its mark for centuries to come on the law of larceny.

STATUTORY CRIMES IN THE NATURE OF LARCENY

From the breaking bulk case it is clear that the great defect in the common law of larceny was the rule that larceny was a violation of possession; this, coupled with the rule that a bailee has possession[6] permitted a great many fraudulent misappropriations to pass unpunished.

---

[1] Westminster II, c. 11 (1285). The less drastic remedy of *Monstravit de Compoto* given by the Statute of Marlborough, c. 23 (1267), was virtually suspended by the council early in the reign of Edward III: Sayles, *King's Bench*, iii. p. cxix, app. *l*.

[2] 2 Inst. 380.

[3] Long before the statute it seems to have been the practice, rightly or wrongly, for a lord to imprison in his own house a defaulting accountant: *Eyre Rolls* (Selden Society, vol. lix), no. 978 (1221). The point of the statute is that it requires the accountant to be confined in the royal gaol instead of in the lord's private prison.

[4] Y.B. 13 Edw. IV, Pasch. 5 (1473). Cf. Glanvill, x. 13.

[5] The idea of " breaking bulk " occurs in a detinue case of 1315 Y.BB. Edward II (Selden Society), xvii. 136.

[6] Thus it was not larceny for a bailee to sell the chattel: *Calendar of Patent Rolls, 1266–1272*, 537.

The exception of cases where bulk had been broken depended on accident, and so the legislature was finally moved to intervene.

It began with the case of servants entrusted with their master's goods who leave their employment, taking the goods with them, or who " embezzle " them while in service; an act of 1529 made this felony if the goods were of the value of forty shillings or more, but it excluded from its penalty persons under eighteen years of age, and apprentices.[1] The statute therefore confirmed a tendency already apparent in case law[2] to distinguish possession from " charge " (the control which servants have over their masters' goods, which charge did not amount to possession, with the result that misappropriation was a violation of the master's possession and so larceny). The use of the word " embezzle " in this and several later statutes dealing with theft from arsenals and government departments does not correspond with the present definition; it later gave way to the word " purloin " which commonly appears in statutes dealing with thefts from factories—and it is typical that separate trades procured legislation covering their own machinery and operations instead of a general enactment about theft. There was, for a long time, therefore, not merely the law of theft, but various bodies of law of theft from weaving sheds, spinning mills, iron works and the like, which were not uniform.

" Embezzlement " in its modern form appears in the statute law in 1799 which reached " servants or clerks " who embezzle effects received in the course of their employment;[3] in 1812 it was necessary to extend this to brokers, bankers, attorneys and other agents who were neither servants nor clerks;[4] the frauds of factors were made criminal in 1827[5] and in 1857 trustees and bailees were reached.[6]

Most of these statutes were the immediate result of some unusually disturbing decision of the courts, and as a rule went little further than reversing that particular decision. The sum total was a frightfully complicated mass of law containing many artificial distinctions which made the work of a prosecution especially difficult, for it was often impossible to say which of several minutely differing crimes might eventually appear from the evidence. Indictments therefore became immensely long and technical documents as they endeavoured to provide for all eventualities.

Successive Larceny Acts of 1827,[7] 1861,[8] and 1916,[9] consolidated this

[1] 21 Hen. VIII, c. 7 (1529). This seems to be the earliest statute to put young offenders in a special category.

[2] The fluctuating authorities are collected in Holdsworth, iii. 364.

[3] 39 Geo. III, c. 85.

[4] 52 Geo. III, c. 63.

[5] 7 & 8 Geo. IV, c. 29, s. 51.

[6] 20 & 21 Vict., c. 54.

[7] 7 & 8 Geo. IV, c. 29.

[8] 24 & 25 Vict., c. 96.

[9] 6 & 7 Geo. V, c. 50.

vast mass of statutory exceptions to the common law, but did not provide a definition of larceny, as Sir James Stephen remarks.

OTHER COMMON LAW FELONIES

Every one of the common law felonies pursued its separate history with little reference to the others. Robbery gradually approached larceny, and blackmailing became a constructive robbery (and constructive felonies were rare) before it was made criminal by statute.[1] Burglary had some curious statutory adventures, especially when it was accompanied by putting inmates of a house in fear.[2] Rape, like several other crimes, could be made the subject of an appeal of felony, in which case it was variously punished, sometimes with mutilation, rarely with death. If no appeal was brought the crown could prosecute, and then the penalty was fine and imprisonment, and the offence seems in practice to have been dealt with rather leniently until 1275 when a statute prescribed two years' imprisonment—one of the first statutes to prescribe a fixed term.[3] Ten years later another statute brought a drastic change of policy by making rape a capital felony both on appeal and on indictment.[4]

The Larceny Act, 1861, was one of a group of consolidating acts passed in that year which repealed and consolidated the results of hundreds of statutes. Criminal law is very largely statutory, and periodical revision is essential where large numbers of acts dealing with comparatively minute sections of a subject are constantly being passed. A larger scheme was soon proposed. The application of English law in suitable circumstances in India made it desirable to " restate " it (to use a modern expression) in a form clear and compact enough to be intelligible in a distant and very different land. An Indian Penal Code was drafted by Lord Macaulay and a quarter of a century later was enacted as law in 1860. In 1878 a draft Criminal Code, drawn by Sir James Fitzjames Stephen, was introduced into Parliament, but subsequently referred to a royal commission. It was not proceeded with, but from time to time large topics of criminal law and procedure have been codified, and recodified, in the course of the last two generations.

THE RECOVERY OF STOLEN GOODS

As long as the appeal of larceny was in common use, the appellant recovered the goods if his appeal was successful—recovery being, in

---

[1] Extortion by letter was made criminal by statutes of 1722 (9 Geo. I, c. 22) and onwards; the actual extortion of money by only verbal threats was held a constructive robbery in *R.* v. *Jones* (1776), 1 Leach, 139; threatening with intent to extort became a statutory felony in 1823 (4 Geo. IV, c. 54).

[2] Cf. Plucknett, " Commentary " in Putnam, *Justices of the Peace* (Ames Foundation), cxlii, ff. for the relations of burglary and house-breaking.

[3] Westminster I, c. 13; cf. c. 20.

[4] Westminster II, c. 34. On these changes, see Pollock and Maitland, ii. 490–491.

fact, one of the main objects of the procedure. Indictment was felt to constitute a rather different situation. The discovery of the thief was to the credit of the grand jury, not of the loser; the accuser was the Crown, not the loser. Even an appeal might be quashed if it had not been brought with considerable diligence, and if none were brought at all, it was felt that the owner ought to lose his claim.

The felon forfeited his chattels to the King, and if the stolen goods were among them, they too went to him, unless by a prompt and successful appeal the owner had recovered them.[1] If the thief had been convicted after indictment then clearly the owner's remissness had extinguished his claim. From this followed the plausible (but not strictly accurate) deduction that a thief acquires property in the goods.[2] This seems to have been the law in the early fourteenth century and it remained law until it was enacted in 1529 that a writ of restitution should issue after conviction on indictment in the same way as it issued after conviction by appeal.[3]

There was, however, another aspect of the appeal. It could be brought against anyone found in possession of the goods, and a successful appellant could recover his chattels in this way from one who was not a thief; in other words, purchase in good faith would serve as a defence of the purchaser's neck, but it would not give him title against the owner. Our earliest plea rolls are quite clear on the point. There was in early times a tendency to treat secret sales as in themselves suspicious, and so this defence is often one of purchase in market overt. Towards the end of the middle ages, there was a tendency for the privilege of market overt to be enlarged, and to allow a *bona fide* purchaser in market overt even to acquire title in stolen goods, but this development was checked by decisions that the statutory writ of restitution would lie even against such a purchaser.[4]

RECEIVING STOLEN GOODS

There was clearly a strong popular feeling that receiving stolen goods ought to be a felony, but it took some centuries before the legislature finally accepted that view. As an appeal of felony could be brought against any possessor, it seemed to suggest that he could be properly regarded as a felon, and it was certain that the receiver of a felon (although

---

[1] For rules on the recovery of stolen goods, see the notes in Y.BB. Edward II, xxiv. 92 (c. 1319). Kindly suitors who improperly restored stolen goods to their owner might get into trouble: *Eyre of Kent* (Selden Society), i. 80 (1313). Even if taken with the maynor, the thief forfeited everything to the king: Joyce Godber, *Supervisors of the Peace*, Bedfordshire Historical Record Society, 65 no. G.2: the fact that he was acquitted at the king's suit would not save the forfeiture—*ibid.*, 67 no. G.7.

[2] See the exposition in Pollock and Maitland, ii. 166 n. 2. At common law (but not in the Cinque Ports) the thief also forfeited goods of which he was bailee; below, p. 474.

[3] 21 Hen. VIII, c. 11. Long before the statute, there may have been some similar writ—see the cryptic remarks of Bereford, C.J., in Y.BB. Edward II (Selden Society), xxiv. 116 (1319).

[4] Holdsworth, v. 110–111; *Case of Market Overt*, 5 Rep. 83 *b* (1596).

not of the goods) could be hanged as an accessory. When this is coupled with the fact that stolen goods generally ended up as forfeit to the Crown, it will be seen that receiving stolen goods looked very much like a felony. In the twelfth century the possessor of stolen goods, if of ill-fame, was sent to the ordeal;[1] in 1219 the receivers of a thief (but not of the stolen goods?) were hanged in circumstances which brought an amercement upon the judges;[2] in 1221 some receivers abjured and others were hanged;[3] late in the century a formula book treats " receiving larcenously " as a plea of the Crown.[4] We read of an appeal of receiving stolen goods in 1291,[5] and the hundred court of Maidstone certainly hanged a woman in 1300 for receiving stolen goods, the only objection raised when the justices in eyre went into the matter twelve years later being that she had received the goods in one hundred, but was convicted in another.[6] As late as 1358 a man was indicted for receiving, and tried for the offence on the assumption that it was a felony.[7]

In the middle of the fourteenth century, however, the superior courts adopted a policy of strictly defining the various crimes, and even restricted the already narrow scope of larceny. Hence we find in 1351 and 1353 that appeals of receiving stolen goods are no longer admissible.[8] There was uncertainty under Elizabeth,[9] and eventually parliament began to move, and made receivers of stolen goods accessories[10] (those who received the thief himself were of course accessories at common law). This step did not advance matters very much, for even accessories had many chances of escape, especially in the rule that they could not be tried until their principal had been convicted.[11] In the next century this line was abandoned and receiving was made an independent misdemeanour[12] in 1707 and an independent felony[13] in 1827.

ATTEMPTS

It was tempting to " take the will for the deed " and to punish attempts as if they had been successfully accomplished, but the temptation

[1] Assize of Clarendon, c. 12 (1166); above, p. 113.

[2] *Bracton's Note Book*, no. 67.

[3] Maitland, *Select Pleas of the Crown* (Selden Society), no. 169; s.c. *Eyre Rolls* (Selden Society, vol. 59), no. 1241.

[4] *Court Baron* (Selden Society), 64.

[5] Sayles, *King's Bench*, i. 70 (1280); ii. 53 (1291). Cf. below, p. 684 n. 1.

[6] *Eyre of Kent*, I. 88.

[7] Putnam, *Justices of the Peace* (Ames Foundation), 55.

[8] Y.B. 25 Edw. III, Pasch. 2; cf. 27 Ass. 69 (1353).

[9] See the notes to [Ellesmere], *Discourse on Statutes* (ed. S. E. Thorne), 116.

[10] 3 Will. & Mar., c. 9 (1691).

[11] This rule seems to have been non-existent in 1221: *Eyre Rolls* (Selden Society, vol. lix), no. 832, but well-established by 1253: Richardson and Sayles, *Proceedings without Writ* (Selden Society, vol. lx), 31–32.

[12] 6 Anne, c. 31.

[13] 7 & 8 Geo. IV, c. 29.

had to be resisted; our mediaeval common law was ill-equipped as yet for investigating a prisoner's state of mind, and Bereford was not alone in his distrust of the tendency.[1]

[1] For a story told by Bereford, see Y.BB. Edward II (Selden Society), xi, pp. xxix–xxx. See Ullmann, *Medieval Theory of Criminal Attempts*, Revue d'Histoire du Droit, xvii. 17–81, F. B. Sayre, *Criminal Attempts*, Harvard Law Review, xli. 821–859; Plucknett, commentary in Putman, *Proceedings before Justices of the Peace* (Ames Foundation), cliii.

CHAPTER 3

MISDEMEANOURS, TRESPASS AND TORT

Anglo-Saxon law knew neither felony or misdemeanour. In so far as it classified crimes at all, it was into " emendable " and " botless " crimes, and the latter became in most cases the felonies of later law. Even after the Conquest the idea of botless crimes still flourished, and the Norman kings sometimes enacted that a particular offence would be visited with the King's " full forfeiture ", and so the heavy penalty of loss of chattels might be inflicted for crimes which fell far short of felony. Henry I had to abandon this, and in his coronation charter promised what seems to be a return to the Anglo-Saxon system of pre-appointed fines or *wite*.[1] From the rolls of Henry III, however, it is clear that the King's courts once again used a wide discretion, this time in committing offenders to prison, with the understanding that the imprisonment would normally be commuted to a fine.

Fines were so common, however, even in civil proceedings, that they could not be regarded as typical of misdemeanour, and in fact criminal law was (apart from statute) practically confined to the felonies. This becomes all the clearer when it is remembered that most of the characteristics of criminal proceedings did not attach to misdemeanours. Thus they were not subject to benefit of clergy, nor to attaint of blood and its accompaniments, escheat and forfeiture; nor did the Crown use its oppressive power of forbidding counsel and sworn witnesses to the accused; on the other hand, the accused did not have the protection afforded him in felony trials of peremptory challenges to the jury. All this seems to indicate that the Crown regarded prosecutions for misdemeanours as being more akin to civil litigation than to trials for felony. It is not surprising, therefore, that misdemeanour and tort together occupy a large field where it is impossible in many cases to assign to each its severalty.

---

[1] Charter of Henry I (1100) c. 8 (in Stubbs, *Select Charters*).

TORT IN THE THIRTEENTH CENTURY

An examination of the early plea rolls indicates that there was a very wide field of tort in the reigns of John and Henry III.[1] As these are cases in the King's Court it is natural that most of them are concerned with torts to property, and especially to feudal interests, but nevertheless there is a large variety of them. The form is almost universally a summons or attachment to show *quare*, why, the defendant had damaged the plaintiff—in other words, the form which soon became typical of trespass. Some of these torts were litigated through the form of an assize, such as the assize of nuisance, but others continued in later years as trespass (for example, impleading a person wrongfully in Court Christian) or case. Early in the thirteenth century this type of action is much more common than the more familiar forms of trespass *de clauso fracto, de bonis asportatis*, and assault.

MISDEMEANOUR IN THE THIRTEENTH CENTURY

At this moment it would seem that a great deal of minor crime was dealt with in the local courts. The King's Court was not interested in that sort of work, and even when royal justices went on tour, they seem mainly concerned with real property matters and felony only, as may be seen from an examination of Lady Stenton's recent volumes of *Eyre Rolls* published by the Selden Society.

Late in the century several changes take place. The writs *quare* were extended to cases which would now be described as trespass; some of these new cases were independent of feudal rights and overlapped the old criminal law. Thus mayhem, which was a felony if the injured party proceeded by appeal, now became a trespass if he preferred to bring his writ. It must always be understood, however, that at this date the action of trespass (as distinct from the wider group of *quare* actions) had a criminal element which was sufficient to allow such a shifting of mayhem to seem reasonable, and that the word trespass was sufficiently vague and wide for Bracton to say that all felonies were trespasses, but all trespasses were not felonies.[2] The familar *quare* formula thus began a new branch with the addition of the words *contra pacem* which were characteristic of the new complaints of assault, breach of close and asportation of chattels. It is a significant illustration of Bracton's dictum, that only certain varieties of *quare* action acquired the name of " trespass ", and that those varieties used the allegation of *contra pacem*, and covered situations which might be considered with equal plausibility as crime or tort. The investigations made by the baronial reformers[3] show clearly that there was much oppression and injustice which the local jurisdictions failed to

[1] See the indexes of actions in *Select Civil Pleas* (ed. Maitland), and *Bracton's Note Book* (ed. Maitland).

[2] Bracton, .119 b.

[3] Above, p. 371.

check, and it seems extremely likely that the King's Court deliberately extended its *quare* actions so that they should cover these non-felonious " trespasses " of which Bracton spoke. The expedient was successful. It brought about the decline of the local courts and extended the work of the King's Court, but it made a symmetrical scheme of either crime or tort impossible, for those trespasses in breach of the peace (which might well resemble misdemeanours) soon partook of the civil nature of the other *quare* actions, and so became finally torts.

The second change during this period was the creation of several statutory trespasses or " actions on the statute " as the old books classify them. For example, in 1275 a statutory writ of trespass against poachers[1] gave punitive damages to the plaintiff, an arbitrary fine to the king, and three years' imprisonment for the defendant; another statutory writ of trespass[2] might involve even imprisonment for life as a " punishment ". The same procedure therefore gave a civil remedy to the plaintiff as well as punishment for the misdemeanour of the defendant.

MISDEMEANOURS AND INDICTMENT

Until recently, the only conclusion possible from the available evidence was that our mediaeval criminal law consisted of (*a*) the felonies, and (*b*) the few statutory misdemeanours of the sort just mentioned. Clearly this was much too meagre even for the needs of fourteenth-century England and the problem of discovering how the deficiency was supplied became very difficult. The solution suggested was that much of the law of misdemeanour was missing entirely, and that its place was taken by the civil action of trespass, which by this time was undoubtedly of considerable scope and importance. Tort had therefore taken over a great deal of the field of criminal law, and the civil aspect of trespass had ousted the criminal aspect.[3]

So difficult a hypothesis is now no longer necessary. It is now known from the Fine Rolls that by 1250 the action of trespass was rapidly getting common, and from the Trailbaston Rolls that at the death of Edward I petty larceny could be punished by imprisonment at the rate of a week for every penny stolen (three days for a halfpenny).[4] Moreover, thanks to the fascinating volume of *Proceedings before Justices of the Peace* recently edited for the Ames Foundation by Professor Putnam, it is now abundantly clear that the justices of the peace handled an enormous quantity of business, and that trespasses in great variety were indicted before them. Consequently there is no longer need to suppose that the civil aspect of trespass had overshadowed the criminal: on the contrary,

---

[1] Westminster I, c. 20.

[2] Westminster II, c. 35.

[3] Pollock and Maitland, ii. 522; Holdsworth, iii. 318, 370; Winfield, *Province of the Law of Tort*, 191.

[4] I am indebted for these results to Mr. C. A. F. Meekings and Mr. A. W. Mabbs both of the Public Record Office.

the indictable trespass is now known to have been the common and normal way of dealing with offences less than felony from the reign of Edward II onwards. The fact that the vast majority of these indictments were found and tried locally, and so appeared but rarely in the Year Books, resulted in their existence being unknown until the records of the justices of the peace were discovered and printed.

From the material now available it would seem that most matters which would support an action of trespass could also be laid in an indictment as constituting a misdemeanour,[1] although as early as the reign of Edward I it was recognised that an action for damages, on the other hand, was a civil action.[2] Moreover, matters which constituted a felony could be regarded alternatively as constituting a misdemeanour. Bracton had stated this long ago, and the new documents show that this was more than a piece of academic analysis, for the indictments bear him out, and in fact carry on the story down to the time of Marowe who wrote in 1503: " although a man has taken my goods feloniously, I can if I please treat that felony as a mere trespass, and so can the king if he pleases; for one wrong shall not be excused by another wrong."[3]

THE SEPARATION OF CRIME AND TORT

So far, then, the story has been briefly this. Early in the thirteenth century the royal courts have a well-defined jurisdiction over felony, and a very large and varied assortment of torts which could be redressed by a *quare* action. Local courts, on the other hand, have a large jurisdiction over many sorts of minor offence which we may call misdemeanours (the word itself, however, is modern). In the middle of that century, trespass *contra pacem* puts the *quare* action to a new use, and begins to remedy certain violent offences by means of a civil action in the King's Court, which may also result in fine and imprisonment in some cases. Trespass *contra pacem* was thus double in its nature, but soon it began to lose its criminal characteristics, perhaps reflecting the overwhelmingly civil atmosphere of the Court of Common Pleas. At the beginning of the fourteenth century the justices of the peace were becoming the principal jurisdiction for criminal matters, and in their sessions the indictable trespass is as conspicuous as the civil trespass was in the Common Pleas; consequently, there was no gap in criminal law forcing litigants to use civil remedies for lack of criminal ones. The contrast between indictment and original writ thus corresponded nearly enough with the distinction between crime and tort. Parliament in the fourteenth century realised this. Instead of adding " punishments " to actions of trespass (as it had

---

[1] In post-mediaeval times the scope of indictable trespass was rather narrowed: Holdsworth, xii. 514.

[2] Sayles, *King's Bench*, ii. 134.

[3] Marowe, *De Pace*, in Putnam, *Early Treatises*, 375. By " trespass " Marowe evidently means " indictable trespass " (*i.e.* misdemeanour). For the relations of tort and felony, see Holdsworth. iii. 331.

done under Edward I), it created new offences less than felony by making them indictable as trespasses under Edward III and his successors—riot, forcible entry, maintenance and labour offences are typical examples. Early in the sixteenth century the word " misdemeanour " served to distinguish the indictable from the actionable trespass. It is, of course, characteristic that the distinction should be procedural rather than substantial.

THE STAR CHAMBER

The Star Chamber had equal influence with the legislature in developing the field of misdemeanour, largely, no doubt, because an old tradition (reinforced by many statutes) excluded the council, and all similar authorities, save the ancient courts of the Crown, from jurisdiction over felony, which involved judgment of life and loss of the sacred freehold. But just as the Common Pleas did not trouble to distinguish civil from criminal law when it appropriated a new field with the writ of trespass *contra pacem*, so the Star Chamber in turn administered civil and criminal justice simultaneously in dealing with its expanding list of " Star Chamber cases ". Forgery, perjury, riot, maintenance, fraud, libel and conspiracy were the principal heads of the Star Chamber's jurisdiction according to its clerk, Hudson. Even crimes which were treason or felony at common law might be punished in the Star Chamber as high misdemeanours, while it claimed the right to punish as crimes acts which escaped the existing classification. It also developed the principle that an unsuccessful attempt might itself be criminal.

This development took place at a fortunate moment, for the manipulation of rules relating to pardons and benefit of clergy was at the same time introducing more variety into the common law system. When the Star Chamber was abolished, the King's Bench realised that much of its work was of permanent value, and so a great deal of its law of misdemeanours finally passed into the common law.

THE FIELD OF TORT

The field of tort was by no means extensive until the last century, and consequently its development had not reached a very advanced stage. Much of it was also annexed to neighbouring provinces with the approach of modern times. Trespass *de clauso fracto* and *de ejectione* became part of the law of property, and deceit, with its derivative *assumpsit*, became one of the roots of the law of contract. The rapid prominence and growth of the law of tort in the last few generations is clearly associated with the sudden mechanisation of contemporary life, and with the growth of large and wealthy businesses (necessarily carried on through fallible servants and agents) engaged in finance, insurance, transport and an endless variety of enterprises which are productive of torts and tort litigation. There can be no doubt that the universal practice of insurance has provided the superior courts with thousands of cases which would probably have escaped the reports if parties had no other resources than their own in contesting them.

TORT AND THE FORMS OF ACTION

Although in our own day it has become possible to speak of tort as a homogeneous body of law, it is still useful at times to remember that this field is really the result of the enclosure of many different acres, and that the old boundaries between them are still visible. Some scores of torts were actionable early in the thirteenth century by means of special varieties of *quare* action. Many of these survived in the next century and later to form the unified action of case. The commonest type of tort was certainly assault and battery, and breach of close. These soon coalesced to form another group, trespass. By the end of the fourteenth century much of the law of tort was comprised under one or the other of these two heads, but it was only slowly that theory supplied a test to distinguish between them. A formal distinction grew up[1] since it had never been customary to allege *vi et armis* in some cases. Those cases became fixed upon no clear principle. Thus in the two chapters of Fitzherbert's *New Natura Brevium* (which is usually cited as *F.N.B.*) dealing respectively with trespass and case, it will be found that some of the writs he classifies as trespass do not allege force and arms,[2] while some of the writs which do contain this clause he describes as trespass on the case.[3] We can hardly say, therefore, that any distinction (other than tradition) served to distinguish the scope of trespass from that of case, even so late as Henry VIII's reign.[4] Even the test which later prevailed, namely, trespass for direct and case for indirect damage, would hardly apply to some of the cases discussed by Fitzherbert; thus if *A.* breaks his own pond in such wise that it causes *B.'s* pond to overflow, the remedy is trespass *vi et armis*.[5]

Gradually case acquires a few substantial characteristics. Thus case is appropriate when the defendant himself did not act, although his servants have caused damage for which he is liable. So, too, an old allegation of negligence becomes more prominent, until negligence finally became one of the most important features of the action. This does not mean that the notion of negligence was entirely absent from trespass; it was, however, concealed under another form. The defendant in trespass has long had the defence of inevitable accident. Any damage which he could have avoided will therefore charge him, although that which is " inevitable " will not. In case, on the other hand, the plaintiff

---

[1] Stated in Fitzherbert, *New Natura Brevium*, 86 H (but see Lord Hale's note).

[2] F.N.B., 90 A.

[3] *Ibid.*, 88 D and E.

[4] The first edition of Fitzherbert's *Natura Brevium* (not mentioned in Beale's *Bibliography*) was in either 1534 or 1537 (Putnam, *Early Treatises*, 34 n. 4); the author died in 1538.

[5] F.N.B., 87 L.

(who has to prove the defendant's negligence) in practice can only demand a moderate standard of care which undoubtedly fell short of that implied in trespass.

As a result of causes which have been skilfully traced by Professor Winfield and Professor Goodhart,[1] case (based on negligence) supplanted trespass (where negligence need not be proved) in the course of the nineteenth century. The reasons for this were procedural for the most part. An old statute[2] had the result that a verdict of nominal damages in trespass should carry with it nominal costs as well. In many cases there must also have been doubt whether the facts would show direct or only consequential damage, for the line between the two is necessarily vague. As a result, many cases which might have supported an action of trespass were framed in case, so that the idea of negligence implied in case has supplanted the older and stricter (though by no means absolute) liability which characterised the action of trespass. At the same time, this newer view of negligence has been now extended even to certain cases where the plaintiff has endeavoured to base his action on trespass and not on case—notably trespasses on or from the highway.[3]

THE TORT OF NEGLIGENCE

For many centuries it would have been impossible to state the common law otherwise than in the form of a list of various torts which have been remedied by various forms of action. As we have seen, the King's Courts were not anxious to entertain personal actions of any sort, and even in the sixteenth and seventeenth centuries there was legislation designed to keep actions not involving title to land in local courts.[4] Reluctantly more and more torts were admitted to the list of those actionable in the King's Courts, but still there was no theory which would draw all these details together into a coherent system. The forms of action stood in the way.

It was the action of case which first evolved a principle sufficiently wide to cover many of the constantly recurring forms of tort. This principle was negligence and its history will concern us in the next chapter. Here we are only concerned with the formal exterior of tort actions; for this purpose it will suffice to say that actions of case were very generally regarded from about 1800 onwards as being based on negligence. It became common to speak of " case for negligence ", " actions for negligence ", " actionable negligence ".[5] Such language was perhaps made more attractive because there still remained an older tradition about the nature of trespass with which " case for negligence "

---

[1] Winfield and Goodhart, *Trespass and Negligence*, Law Quarterly Review, xlix. 359–378.

[2] 22 & 23 Car. II, c. 9, s. 136 (1670); see above, p. 174.

[3] See Winfield and Goodhart, *u.s.*

[4] Above, p. 174.

[5] See the material collected by Winfield, *History of Negligence in Torts*, Law Quarterly Review, xlii. 184, and his App. A.

could be (rightly or wrongly) contrasted. By this time the emphasis on the general concept of negligence has become so steady and universal that it is possible to argue that we have outgrown the old method of " matching colours " whereby new cases were brought in under the cover of old ones, and that we now have created a distinct tort of negligence.[1]

[1] See now, however, Winfield's remark in Law Quarterly Review, lv. 450–451, where he preferred to regard the situation as still a tendency, rather than an established rule of law.

LIABILITY, CIVIL AND CRIMINAL

For reasons we have already mentioned, it is impracticable to speak of our early law in terms of a distinction between crime and tort. This observation becomes necessary once more in tracing the history of liability, for such few principles as there were had been derived from experience drawn indifferently from all parts of the law of wrongs. Nevertheless, some interplay between notions drawn from clearly criminal cases and those drawn from obviously civil ones may be expected, and in fact actually took place.

LIABILITY IN ANGLO-SAXON LAW

English writing on the subject generally goes back to a series of striking articles by Dean Wigmore which appeared in the *Harvard Law Review* in 1894. The author there set forth his theory that in early law (including Anglo-Saxon law) liability was absolute:[1]

> " The doer of a deed was responsible whether he acted innocently or inadvertently, because he was the doer; the owner of an instrument which caused harm was responsible, because he was the owner, though the instrument had been wielded by a thief; the owner of an animal, the master of a slave, was responsible because he was associated with it as owner, as master. . . ,"

and a great many similar propositions are advanced which do not all concern English law. In short, " a man acts at his peril ". This theory, even then, did not represent the unanimous opinion of common lawyers, for Mr Justice Holmes had already criticised it in 1881, doubting whether the common law had ever held such a rule in its best days.[2] Professor

[1] The articles were reprinted and revised for the *Select Essays in Anglo-American Legal History,* where this passage occurs at iii. 480.

[2] Holmes, *Common Law,* 89.

Winfield has more recently and more thoroughly examined the question, with the result that he declares it to be merely a myth.[1]

There was indeed a maxim *qui inscienter peccat, scienter emendet*, but there is no need to assume that maxims represented the state of the law with much more accuracy in 1100 than they do now. We may surmise, however, that there was a fatalistic attitude to life in earlier times which made men accept misfortune (in the shape of heavy liability for harm they did not mean to do) with more resignation than now.[2] We have also to bear in mind that " law in books " was itself a rarity in the four centuries preceding Glanvill, and so was much less in contact with " law in action " than it is to-day. The question of liability is frequently discussed by the author of the *Leges Henrici Primi*, but as Professor Winfield shows, he expressly warns us that his crude maxim is not the whole law, and frequently mentions the reduction of the compensation or penalty according to circumstances. Even the Anglo-Saxon laws themselves plainly discriminate between care and carelessness, and recommend clemency.

A passage appended to one of the laws of Aethelred (*c.* 1000) seems to represent the thought of his age in the determination of liability, and suggests that the Anglo-Saxon system of preordained payments was more flexible than would appear on the surface. It reads thus:

> " And always the greater a man's position in this present life or the higher the privileges of his rank, the more fully shall he make amends for his sins, and the more dearly shall he pay for all misdeeds; for the strong and the weak are not alike nor can they bear a like burden, any more than the sick can be treated like the sound. And therefore, in forming a judgement, careful discrimination must be made between age and youth, wealth and poverty, health and sickness, and the various ranks of life, both in the amends imposed by ecclesiastical authority, and in the penalties inflicted by the secular law.
>
> " And if it happens that a man commits a misdeed involuntarily or unintentionally, the case is different from that of one who offends of his own free will voluntarily and intentionally; and likewise he who is an involuntary agent in his misdeeds should always be entitled to clemency and better terms, owing to the fact that he acted as an involuntary agent."[3]

No doubt this is homiletic in tone, and perhaps even in origin, but the mere fact that it insists on principles seems to show that practice had already admitted the possibility of discretion in assessing liability, and was feeling the need of principles in exercising it. A few years later, the passage we have just quoted was embodied in the laws of Canute,[4] almost *verbatim*, and so we may conclude that it was certainly more than mere moralising by an unpractical cleric. As we have just seen, the author of the *Leges Henrici Primi* is equally emphatic, a century later, on the possibility of discretion. Moreover, the Church had long ago

---

[1] *The Myth of Absolute Liability*, Law Quarterly Review, xlii. 37.

[2] Huebner, *History of Germanic Private Law* (tr. Philbrick), 528.

[3] VI Aethelred, 52 1, (tr. A. J. Robertson).

[4] II Canute, 68, 3.

prepared the way, and the *Penitentials* of the seventh and eighth centuries were already abandoning the idea of fixed tariffs as a measure of human responsibility.[1]

This view of Anglo-Saxon practice in fixing liability is all the more attractive since it coincides with the results obtained from investigating German as well as English legal history.[2]

It may very well be that the history of tort liability has run the same course as the history of homicide which we have outlined in a previous chapter,[3] that is to say, a simple and severe legal rule, to which discretionary exceptions could be made by competent authorities, is typical of the first stage; the second stage is represented by the recognition by the law itself of those exceptions. Looking merely at the history of the formal rules, we thus gain the impression of an absolute liability which is in course of reduction to more rational limits; if, on the other hand, we take into account the discretionary tempering of strict law with mercy which the sources frequently allude to, the change seems to be one of form rather than of substance.

TRESPASS IN THE EARLY PLEA ROLLS

It is naturally to trespass that we first look for the later history of the onerous standard of liability just discussed. Here we have to recognise that the scope of trespass has considerably changed in the course of the centuries. Our earliest examples seem all to be cases of undoubted violence with a strong criminal element. The plaintiff has been beaten, wounded, chained, imprisoned, starved, carried away to a foreign country, and has suffered many " enormities ".[4] In later times it is agreed that many of these expressions are just traditional forms without much meaning; but there clearly was a time when they accurately represented the plaintiff's case. Defences to trespass in its earliest form therefore take one of two lines, a denial of the facts by a plea of not guilty, or a plea in justification such as self-defence, lawful authority, or the like.

LIABILITY IN TRESPASS

This was certainly the original nature of trespass, and as long as it was confined to cases which involved acts which must have been deliberate, there was little room for questions of liability to arise. A momentous departure was made when the common law began to admit what we may call constructive trespasses, and to remedy them by an action which hitherto had been confined to deliberate acts of violence in breach of the

[1] F. Cimetier, *Les Sources du droit ecclésiastique* (Paris, 1930), 32.

[2] Huebner, *op. cit.*, 527.

[3] Above, p. 445.

[4] Like tales of violence may occur in an assize of novel disseisin: *Eyre Rolls* (Selden Society, vol. lix), no. 232 (1221).

peace. The date of this revolution has not been ascertained, but it is very desirable that it should be, for we are clearly in the presence of a turning-point in the history of tort liability. The use of traditional formulae naturally tends to obscure the change. The beating, wounding, evil entreating, and other enormities continue to be alleged, but as words of court with purely artificial meanings. The persistence of the pleading rule that a defence of " not guilty " puts the facts in issue (and nothing else), and its corollary that proof of the facts is sufficient to condemn the defendant, must finally have raised the whole problem of liability. Such a change would hardly have been sudden, nor would purely technical trespasses have appeared immediately; we should expect, on the contrary, a gradual transition from the deliberate assault, through the accidental injury, and thence to the merely technical assault. Consequently, the problem of liability would only present itself gradually and in fragmentary fashion. Such cases become prominent when firearms are in general use;[1] how much earlier they are to be found seems at present unknown.

If we turn to trespass to land, the same stages of development are discernible. The action of trespass in its original form was concerned with violent invasions by marauders, accompanied in most cases by serious assaults on the owner and his servants, and the forcible removal of cattle and stock. Such a state of affairs was common enough in the time of the barons' wars, the period of the ordainers, and the Wars of the Roses. The admission of the plea that the close was not the plaintiff's freehold but the defendant's, introduced a technical element, however, by laying emphasis on the right of the plaintiff rather than on the tort of the defendant. Considerations of title thus became closely associated with trespass *quare clausum fregit*, and may be the explanation for the growth of highly technical trespasses to land. An early and very important example is the case in 1466 which is frequently cited all through the later discussions of liability.[2] The defendant clipped a thorn hedge, the clippings fell on the land of an adjoining landowner, and the defendant entered and removed them. The question was, whether this entry was an actionable trespass (the falling of the clippings was not laid as a trespass in the pleadings, it seems, although it was discussed in the argument). Upon demurrer, a remarkable debate took place.

For the plaintiff it was urged that " if a man does something, even something lawful, and in doing it tort and damage are caused against his will to another, yet he shall be punished if by any means he could have prevented the damage ", or, as another serjeant put it, " if a man does something, he is bound to do it in such wise that no prejudice or damage thereby ensues to others ". The defendant seems to have set up the view that the trespass was justifiable, and that he could enter to remove the clippings, just as he could enter if his cattle had strayed from

---

[1] Winfield, *Trespass and Negligence*, Law Quarterly Review, xlix. 360–361.
[2] Y.B. 6 Edward IV, Michs. no. 18, f. 7; Holmes, *Common Law*, 85–87; Holdsworth, iii. 375.

the highway to drive them out. This proposition was denied by Littleton, J., who declared that " the law is the same in small matters as in great ", only the damages might be slight in some cases. Choke, J., suggested that if the defendant had pleaded that the wind blew the clippings on to the plaintiff's land, then the defendant would have been justified in entering to remove them. Among other points touched upon, a clear distinction was drawn between criminal and civil liability. Malice prepense was essential to felony, it was said, and an accidental wounding could be trespass, even if it were not felony.

Such was the discussion; Mr Justice Holmes said that judgment was given for the plaintiff, but the Year Book says nothing of judgment either way. The case is hardly authority for any view of liability for it contains no decision; the preponderance of opinion seemed to be on the side of those who urged that the defendant was liable, but the most significant thing of all is the way in which it was argued. It seems clearly to have been a new point, and although imaginary cases were put (and disputed) there seems no confident appeal to any settled rule. However, the numerous *dicta* in this case were repeated some years later and gained force in the repetition. Particularly, the remark about an accidental wounding while shooting at butts was repeated with approval[1] and stands at the head of a long line of cases arising out of shooting accidents. A later age, therefore, concluded from this case of 1466 that the better opinion was that put forward for the plaintiff, and that liability attached for all harm done in the nature of a trespass, however involuntary, if it was " in any way " avoidable.

NEGLIGENCE AND TRESPASS

It is largely a matter of terminology how this standard of liability is described. It may be called " absolute " in that it is unconnected with the defendant's intention, and it might be argued that the exception of inevitable happenings is tantamount to saying that the defendant did not act voluntarily. On the other hand, it has appeared possible to some to regard this exception as the source from which the idea of negligence entered into these discussions, especially since in modern times the test of inevitability has varied. Thus, if we regard results as inevitable if no reasonable care would have prevented them, then the " absolute " liability will be reduced to liability for negligence only. It is quite conceivable that such a transition took place, although the case of 1466 is perfectly clear in describing the plaintiff's demand that liability attached if the defendant " by any means could have prevented the damage ". There is language in cases around the year 1800 which lends colour to this view;[2] it may be that it helped, together with the procedural changes

---

[1] By Rede, J., in Y.B. 21 Henry VII, Trin. no. 5, f. 27 (1506). This was not an accident case, but one where a defendant was held liable for a technical trespass to chattels by putting them into the plaintiff's barn: his kind intention did not justify him.

[2] Wigmore in *Select Essays in Anglo-American Legal History*, iii. 506–507.

which Professor Winfield regards as being primarily responsible, in spreading the idea of negligence throughout the field of trespass.[1]

It seems, however, rather too high an estimate of this possible transition in the measure of inevitability to say that " there has never been a time in English law, since (say) the early 1500's, when the defendant in an action of trespass was not allowed to appeal to some test or standard of moral blame or fault in addition to and beyond the mere question of his act having been voluntary ".[2] Professor Winfield has collected a line of cases from the early seventeenth century where the defence of accident or misadventure was rejected as inadmissible.[3] These seem to indicate clearly that the fifteenth-century standard of inevitability was still maintained.

If we look back we shall see that the flexibility of Anglo-Saxon law seems to have vanished with the advent of the common law. The early Year-Book period apparently contains no authority on liability for accident in trespass (although it was settled that no criminal liability attached). When we do find *dicta*, late in the fifteenth century, they state a rule which seems severe and inflexible, and in the time of Coke this is embodied in emphatic decisions. (At that very moment, as we shall see later, the liability of bailees was also greatly augmented.) The early seventeenth century seems therefore the age of greatest severity—and it is well to recall Holmes' remark that if there ever was a period of " absolute " liability it was " in that period of dry precedent which is so often to be found midway between a creative epoch and a period of solvent philosophical reaction ".[4]

If we look forward, we see no great development in trespass until the early nineteenth century. The old principle, enshrined in rules of pleading, was maintained. As we have indicated, there may have been a tendency for a moment to reduce liability by changing the standard of inevitability; but much more important were certain fairly old rules about cattle trespassing from the highway into adjoining land, for they were used as a guide in the multitude of traffic cases which are so prominent at the present time. Equally crucial are the procedural considerations which have led plaintiffs to abandon an action of trespass and bring case instead. We must now turn to the action on the case, therefore, and trace the principles of liability applicable to it.

NEGLIGENCE AND CASE

We have already suggested that the violent trespasses were the first varieties of *quare* action to acquire an independent existence. Of the large and varied collection which remained, some seem to have fallen out

---

[1] Above, pp. 466–463.
[2] Wigmore, *op. cit.*, 506.
[3] Winfield, *Trespass and Negligence*, Law Quarterly Review, xlix. 360.
[4] Holmes, *The Common Law*, 89; below, p. 479.

of use, others became independent actions in their turn, and the rest survived and were classified eventually as " actions on the case ". For a long time, case must have been an immense " miscellanea " in the classification of forms of action, and particular topics must have been put there because they would not fit in anywhere else, rather than because they had any logical connection with one another. Repulsion from trespass is therefore the main test, as soon as tests are thought to be desirable, and so we get the positive principle that direct assault to the person, and violation of the possession of chattels or land, constitute trespass; damage less direct, or damage caused by means less personal, will therefore be classified perforce as " case ". This view helped considerably when the damage was caused by the defendant's omission. Thus if A " maliciously " breaks his own pool so that the water floods his neighbour's land, trespass lies,[1] but if A fails in his duty to clean his ditch or to repair his banks, and so his neighbour's land is flooded, case will lie.[2] Here we have an important admission that some sorts of inactivity which cause damage are actionable. There are, in fact, grounds for believing that the word " negligence " was first used in this sense: the defendant " neglected " to do something, and thus caused the damage.[3]

The primitive conditions which are seen in violent trespasses and thefts were perpetuated in the principle that trespass, like larceny, was a violation of possession; consequently a bailee could not " steal " the chattels delivered to him,[4] and if he damaged them trespass would not lie either.[5] He had not violated the plaintiff's possession. The only remedy (apart from detinue) was case.[6] Closely connected with this notion was the feeling that if I ask someone to do work on my chattel, or even to operate surgically or medically upon my person, trespass will not lie if ill betides. Indeed, it would seem that no action lay of any sort, for the plaintiff himself invited trouble. This position was turned by the development of *assumpsit*; the defendant will not be liable unless he " undertook " to produce a particular result. If he gave this undertaking and failed to

---

[1] F.N.B., 87 L.

[2] *Ibid.*, 93 G; case for damage to realty which did not amount to an entry upon it seems to be derived from the twelfth-century assize of nuisance, whose history is very obscure.

[3] " Nonfeasance or negligence," said Coke in *Earl of Shrewsbury's Case* (1610), 9 Rep. 50 b. The criticism by Holdsworth, viii. 469 n. 3, of Blackstone, *Commentaries*, iii. 211, for basing liability for fire and cattle-trespass upon " negligent keeping " would be unnecessary if that phrase had retained its older sense of " neglecting to keep ". Cf. Y.BB. Edward II (Selden Society), xxiv. 98, for a termor who might have a fee, by the " negligence " of the mortgagor to redeem.

[4] Above, p. 449; Glanvill, x. 13.

[5] If the chattel were merely in the defendant's hand for a moment, in circumstances which did not amount to a bailment, then he is liable in trespass: Y.BB. Edward II (Selden Society), xxii. 290, when the defendant defaced a charter handed to him for his inspection.

[6] Y.B. 13 Richard II (Ames Foundation), 103–104 (1390). The general proposition as above stated, is implicit in the argument of Persay in Y.B. 46 Edward III, 19 (no. 19), that a declaration in case ought to allege a bailment expressly and omit *vi et armis*, and that if there were no bailment, then *vi et armis* must be alleged. Apparently the court inferred from the facts that a farrier was a bailee of the horse.

carry it out, then the plaintiff can frame his case in the nature of deceit. The earliest example was one in 1348. The report is brief:

> " J. de B. complained by bill that G. de F. on a certain day and year at B. on Humber undertook to carry his mare safe and sound in his boat across the water of Humber; whereas the said G. overloaded his boat with other horses, by reason of which overloading the mare perished, to his tort and damage.
>
> " *Richmond.* Judgment of the bill which does not suppose that we have done any tort, but rather proves that he would have an action by writ of covenant or[1] trespass.
>
> " BAUKWELL, J., K.B. It seems that you did him a trespass when you over-loaded your boat so that the mare perished; and so answer.
>
> " *Richmond.* Not guilty, and [the others said] we are ready to aver our bill."[2]

The case has some of the features of a new experiment. It was heard by bill while the King's Bench happened to be at York, and so the record is less technical than it would have been on an original writ. The nature of the action is obscure. The bill seems merely to have stated the facts. Richmond's objection seems to be that those facts *prima facie* might sustain an action of covenant, or an action of trespass; but since it alleges no covenant under seal, nor any use of force and arms, it does neither, and so the bill must fail as disclosing no cause of action. This dilemma between tort and contract henceforth appears with monotonous regularity in later cases, but its effectiveness as a dialectic device depends on the assumptions (which Richmond evidently had in his mind) that " tort " means only those wrongs which were actionable by trespass *vi et armis*, and covenant means only a covenant under seal. Baukwell was prepared to regard the facts as constituting a " trespass "—whether *vi et armis* or not, we are not told. According to the report the plaintiff alleged an *assumpsit*, but as we have seen, the judge declared that the action really was trespass.

The record, on the other hand, does not contain the word *assumpsit* although it does say that the defendant " ferryman " had " received the mare to carry safely in his ship ". The verdict further says that the boat was loaded " against the will of the plaintiff ". This seems to foreshadow the action of case against bailees, while the omission from the record of an express *assumpsit*, coupled with the description of the defendant as a ferryman, resembles the form used against those in common callings. All these indications of case are difficult to reconcile with the Year Book's statement that Baukwell, J., held that it was trespass. Luckily the report is amply confirmed on this point by the record which shows that *capias* issued against the vanquished defendant. Now *capias* (which may lead

---

[1] In the Vulgate text, *ou*; in MS. Bodley 364, f. 90 *b*, *plus que*, " rather than "; in Exeter College, Oxford, MS. 134, f. 37 *b*, *et nemye*, " and not ". (I owe these readings to the kindness of Mr Derek Hall.)

[2] 22 Ass. 94 (no. 41); record in *Bulletin of Institute of Historical Research* (1935), xiii. 36; C. H. S. Fifoot, *History and Sources: Tort and Contract* (1949), 330; A. K. Kiralfy, *Action on the Case* (1951), 154; A. K. Kiralfy, *The Humber Ferryman and the Action on the Case*, Cambridge Law Journal (1953), xi. 421.

to outlawry) was possible in trespass, but impossible in case.[1] The report is therefore correct, and the bill was treated by the court as a bill of trespass, although from the point of view of later lawyers, it seemed an example of case on *assumpsit*.[2]

In the farrier's case[3] we get a stage further. The writ was brought " on the case " and did not allege force and arms, nor that the defendant acted maliciously but was upheld in spite of these objections. There was, however, no mention of an *assumpsit*, for the farrier's is a common calling.

Other cases might also be considered, but their general effect seems to be that just after the middle of the fourteenth century it was not considered vital to distinguish the three forms of trespass, case, and *assumpsit*. That task was left for the reign of Richard II, and more particularly to the fifteenth century, which seems to have felt a special vocation for establishing logical distinctions. As a result of that development, *assumpsit* became in effect contractual;[4] and so we are left with trespass on the case.

Assumpsit left its mark, even on some of those types of trespass on the case which did not continue to allege it. When brought against physicians and horse-doctors, in particular, there was a tendency to insert in the writ and the declaration an allegation that the defendant had acted " negligently and recklessly " or similar words.[5] At first these words seem to be merely an example of that solemn abuse of the defendant which we expect in mediaeval pleadings,[6] but gradually they acquire a meaning; moreover, they seem to profit by an ambiguity, for by this time case was available where the defendant had " neglected " to do a duty (such as enclose, or repair, his property). Hence the combination of negligent action and passive inaction covers a fairly large part of the ground included in " case ". The trees were familiar to English lawyers long before they formed an idea of the wood, and not until 1762 did it occur to the compiler of an abridgment to collect material under the heading " action on the case for negligence ". As Professor Winfield remarks, " Comyns was not writing the law of torts; he was trying to classify remedies ".[7]

By 1800 " case for negligence " was a common expression, and it began to be said that the action was actually based upon negligence.[8]

---

[1] Until 1504; 19 Hen. VII, c. 9. It was possibly forbidden by 18 Edw. III, st. 2, c. 5 (1344). It has been stated, however, that outlawry had been possible in actions on the case throughout the reign of Edward IV: Margaret Hastings, *Common Pleas in the Fifteenth Century*, 170.

[2] Dr Kiralfy, Cambridge Law Journal, xi. 424, would regard it as in direct line with certain actions on the case.

[3] Y.B. 46 Edward III, 19 no. 19 (1372); above, p. 469, n. 6; Ames, *Lectures on Legal History*, 130; Holdsworth, iii. 430.

[4] The contractual implications of *assumpsit* will be considered later: below, pp. 637 ff.

[5] Y.B. 11 Richard II (ed. Thornley, Ames Foundation), 227.

[6] As Winfield has pointed out, Law Quarterly Review, xlii. 198.

[7] Winfield, in Law Quarterly Review, xlii. 195.

[8] *Ibid.*, 199.

Thenceforward it became possible to argue that negligence was an independent tort.

VICARIOUS LIABILITY

So far, we have been concerned with the liability of a man for his own acts, intentional or unintentional. We now have to consider the liability which he may incur for the acts of others.

Even criminal law occasionally visited the sins of the fathers upon the children. The traitor's and the felon's issue were disinherited, and the wife and children of a juryman convicted by attaint were to be thrust out of their homes. Indeed, the converse has also been maintained, and Dean Wigmore has argued that parents and masters were liable for the crimes of their children and servants. There certainly was some liability for the crimes of a slave, one passage suggesting that it could be discharged by the noxal surrender of the slave or his redemption at a fixed price.[1] The institution of slavery, however, has left little mark on our law, and most of what we find in earlier sources on masters' liability is rather of a police nature; the master must produce any members of his household in court if they are wanted. If he fails, the master may be pecuniarily liable.[2]

The liability of husband for wife, parent for child, and master for servant is a broader question, and needs a little comment. Dean Wigmore has collected a typical sample of the material.[3] From it he concludes that " there certainly was a time when the master bore full responsibility for the harmful acts of his serf or his domestic ",[4] although by the Norman period there was an " idea that it made a difference whether the master consented to or commanded the harm done by the servant or other member of his household ".[5] It made so much difference that it seems more natural to state the law in the converse, *i.e.* the master (like everyone else) is liable for acts he commanded, or subsequently ratified. If he proves that he did neither the one nor the other, he is quit. But (and this is important) he is very frequently put to his proof, for the thirteenth century in its wordly wisdom gravely suspected the master of complicity in the servant's misdeeds; so gravely, in fact, that it often imposed upon him the burden of proving his innocence. Such a suspicion, based upon a shrewd knowledge of contemporary society, is quite different, however, from a rule of law making the master criminally or civilly liable. Such cases are fairly common in local courts, but are hardly to be found in the King's Court. Indictment before the King's justices was a more serious and risky proceeding than a presentment or a plaint in a leet, and so we

---

[1] Ine, 74.

[2] Above, p. 97; Bracton, 124 *b*.

[3] *Select Essays in Anglo-American Legal History*, iii. 498–501.

[4] *Ibid.*, 495; cf. *Court Baron* (Selden Society), 79.

[5] *Ibid.*, 497. For an example of ratification, see *Rot. Parl.*, i. 74 *a*, and for command, *Eyre Rolls* (Selden Society, vol. lix), no. 85.

need not expect to find the King's Court systematically applying a presumption of the master's complicity whenever a servant is before the court.
If the master is to be reached, it must be on a clear charge of being a
principal or an accessory, and this later became the view even in local
courts.

The attitude of the King's Court is well illustrated by the picturesque
case of Bogo de Clare in Parliament in 1290. Having a suit in an ecclesiastical court against the Earl of Cornwall, Bogo obtained a citation which
was served on the earl as he was walking up Westminster Hall to Council.
This was to the manifest contempt of the King, who laid his damages at
ten thousand pounds.[1] Bogo had hardly got out of this dangerous
situation when one of his own adversaries tried to serve a citation in
Bogo's own house. Bogo had just learned that citations were distasteful
to the King, and his lackeys promptly made the apparitor eat his process,
parchment, wax and all.[2] Bogo had not realised that circumstances alter
cases, and found himself defending an action of trespass in Parliament.[3]
His defence is an important text for our purpose, for he took the line
that he was not liable for a wrong that his servants had done, and
demurred. The plaintiff was examined and admitted that Bogo himself
neither committed nor ordered the trespass, and so Bogo had judgment.
He still had to answer the King for the breach of Parliament's and the
King's peace by men in his mainpast. He mustered all his retinue, but
the authors of the outrage had fled, and the others swore that Bogo
knew nothing of it and never commanded it, and so the affair died down,
as nothing could be done to Bogo criminally until the principals had been
convicted.[4]

One who had others in his mainpast was under an obligation to secure
their attendance if a charge was brought against them. In some places
it certainly was a custom to exact a payment from the mainpast if there
was a conviction.[5] But it is equally clear that the mainpast could defend
a criminal charge by proving that he neither commanded nor condoned
the offence.[6] The King's Court did not tolerate these notions. In 1302
it held that fining the mainpast was illegal,[7] and in 1313 Staunton, J.,
declared " let those who have done wrong come and answer for their
own misdeeds ".[8]

---

[1] *Rot. Parl.,* i. 17.

[2] A favourite joke among the peerage. Clifford nearly lost his life through trying it on a
royal messenger in 1250: Pollock and Maitland, ii. 507–508.

[3] *Rot. Parl.,* i. 24.

[4] Cf. Bulletin of the Institute of Historical Research, v. 132; Sayles, *King's Bench*, ii. 19.
For an alleged conviction on similar facts, see Pollock and Maitland, ii. 485 n. 5.

[5] This amercement is clearly of a police, rather than a penal, character and need not imply
criminal liability (cf. the *murdrum*). For a suggested origin, see *Eyre of Kent* (Selden Society),
i. 95.

[6] *Court Baron* (Selden Society), nos. 13, 34.

[7] Y.B. 30 & 31 Edward I (Rolls Series), 202 (1302).

[8] *Eyre of Kent* (Selden Society), i. 90 (1313). For a different interpretation of these cases,
see 3 Holdsworth, 383.

We therefore do not feel justified in saying that a master was criminally liable for his servant's acts, save in the obvious case where he commanded them or approved them. Was he civilly liable? There is only one passage in the borough custumals on the point, and that comes from Waterford, where there was a rule that a citizen was liable for damage done by his apprentice, just as for his son who is of age (*i.e.* able to count twelve pence).[1] This is very meagre evidence for the proposition that mercantile custom held masters liable for their servants' torts. Hardly more illuminating is an oft-quoted passage in the statute of staples, which according to one view " states the general principle applicable to the master's liability for the torts of his servants ", by abolishing liability formerly imposed by mercantile custom.[2] The statute says:

> " No merchant or other person, of what condition soever he be, shall lose or forfeit his goods or merchandise for any trespass or forfeiture incurred by his servant, unless his act is by the command and consent of his master, or he has offended in the office in which his master put him, or unless the master is in some other way bound to answer for the servant's act by law merchant as has been used heretofore."[3]

The master's liability here mentioned can only mean such liability as that of the master of a ship for the acts of his crew, which was being laid down at this moment in maritime jurisdictions.[4] But the most common case of the loss of goods which the statute remedies is of quite a different nature. The Crown was constantly straining the law of forfeiture, and had obtained decisions that if a bailee incurs a forfeiture, the goods bailed to him are liable to it and the merchandise in his hands goes to the Crown.[5] So, too, a thief on conviction forfeited the stolen goods to the Crown.[6] Some boroughs had succeeded in maintaining a custom that the rule should not apply to them, and others got charters exempting them from its operation.[7] It was this indefensible rule which the statute finally abrogated for the whole country. As often happens,[8] the statute did not deal with the whole question, but only with one particular case—that of a servant. The Cinque Ports alone at this time had a general rule that bailed goods are not forfeit by the felony of the bailee.[9] One thing is clear, and that is that the object of the statute was

---

[1] *Borough Customs* (Selden Society), i. 222.

[2] Holdsworth, iii. 387.

[3] 27 Edw. III, st. 2, c. 19 (1353).

[4] *Select Cases in Law Merchant* (Selden Society), ii. pp. xcv–xcvi (1349), which is discussed by E. G. M. Fletcher, *History of Carrier's Liability*, 58–59.

[5] Fitz., *Corone*, 334 (1329); contrast Y.B. 12 Richard II (Ames Foundation), 4 (1388).

[6] *Ibid.*, 317, 318, 319 (1329); the writ of restitution was created by statute 21 Henry VIII, c. 11 (1529).

[7] Haverfordwest, *c.* 1200 (Bateson, *Borough Customs*, i. 221–222); Cork, 1242 (Ballard and Tait, *Borough Charters*, ii. 192).

[8] The queerest example is surely 5 Edward III, c. 10 (1331), which provides imprisonment for jurors who take bribes from *both* parties.

[9] *Borough Customs* (Selden Society), i. 71–72. For the forfeiture of the stolen goods, see above, p. 452.

not to change the law of liability (mercantile or common law), but to relieve merchants from a strained application of the law of forfeiture.[1]

Down to the close of the middle ages, therefore, the common law had stuck to its simple principle. A man is liable for his own voluntary acts, but he is not liable for his servant's acts unless they have become his own, by reason of his previous command or subsequent ratification. There were few exceptions. The innkeeper was liable for the harm done by his servants, but that is only incident to a still wider liability; so too, there was the liability of a householder for a fire started by his servant; the liability of a shipmaster for his crew belongs, on the other hand, to a completely different line of history.

RESPONDEAT SUPERIOR

In its best days, the common law has always been willing to moderate its rules where public policy requires, and the establishment of the principle of *respondeat superior* is a good example. A long line of statutes deals with the problem of the oppressive official—sheriff, under-sheriff, escheator, gaoler, bailiff, etc. The sheriffs themselves were not above reproach, but their underlings bore a thoroughly bad reputation in the middle ages. It was useless to make them civilly liable to injured members of the public because in many cases the underlings were themselves men of little substance, and if a defendant had no considerable land within the county there was little prospect of enforcing a judgment for damages against him. The legislature therefore set up the rule that if the underling of certain public officials was insufficient to satisfy a judgment, then his superior should answer.[2] This liability is therefore only applicable to public officials[3] and not to employers generally, and it is only a secondary liability which comes into play when the original defendant is unable to satisfy judgment.

GROWTH OF THE MODERN RULE OF EMPLOYER'S LIABILITY

As late as 1685 the courts were clinging to the mediaeval rule that if a master orders his servant to do something that is lawful, and the servant " misbehave himself, or do more ", the master is not liable in trespass.[4] With the advent of Lord Holt, the mercantile law (with which he was specially familiar) began to exert through him a considerable amount of influence on the common law's doctrine. In a shipping case, Holt took

[1] For another view, see Wigmore in *Select Essays in Anglo-American Legal History*, iii. 522.

[2] Westminster II, cc. 2, 11, 43 (1285), and other statutes collected in Pollock and Maitland, ii. 533 n. 1. The superior is sometimes referred to by the ecclesiastical term " sovereign ": Y.BB. Edward II (Selden Society), xxii. 266 (1318).

[3] There is one case where it is applied to the bailiff of a lord: Westminster I c. 17 (1275). Cf. Constitutions of Clarendon, c. 13 (above, p. 17).

[4] *Kingston* v. *Booth*, Skinner, 228; for the whole of this paragraph, see Holdsworth viii. 472 ff.

the opportunity of laying down a general rule—" whoever employs another is answerable for him, and undertakes for his care to all that make use of him ".[1] As a principle, the rule was clearly maritime (and eventually Roman); but the introduction of a strange rule can hardly take place unless plausible arguments can be produced tending to show that it is conformable to some things already established in the common law, and fortunately those excuses were easily found in certain rules about common callings, liability for fire, the *respondeat superior* rule, and the ratification which could be inferred if the master profited by the servant's tort.   Holt was willing to place the development on the broadest basis of convenience and public policy; others took refuge in various technicalities according to their taste or learning, and even Blackstone preferred to base an employer's liability on a variety of separate considerations rather than on the general policy of social duty.[2]

Even in the middle ages there were a few special situations in which the general rules of liability were modified, and a few words about them will illustrate the policy of the common law.

THE BAILEE'S LIABILITY

This subject has been much controverted, and has several features of special interest.[3]   Before the time of Bracton it is difficult to deduce any settled rule out of the few cases available.[4]   It is clear that a bailee could bring the appeal of larceny against a thief; this is a natural development, for, as we have seen, the appeal was a procedure which grew up as a result of the normal actions of persons who have lost chattels.   The bailee who discovers that the chattels bailed are missing, will, of course, begin to look for them, follow the trail, raise the neighbours, and consequently challenge the thief and claim the chattels.   Similarly, if need be, he can replevy them.   This perfectly natural procedure has been translated into terms of legal theory by saying that " the bailee, because he was possessor, had the rights of an owner as against all the world except his bailor ".[5]   This is certainly true, but confusion crept in at an early date, for some of the cases show the bailee supporting his appeal (perhaps unnecessarily) by the further statement that he had paid (or ought to pay) compensation to his bailor for the loss.[6]   It seems a little hazardous, however, to make the further deduction that " the bailor, by

---

[1] *Boson* v. *Sandford*, 2 Salk. 440 (1691).

[2] Bl. Comm., i. 430 ff.; Holt's view has been accepted as the real basis of the liability since the last hundred years.

[3] Pollock and Maitland, ii. 170; Holdsworth, iii. 340 ff.; Holdsworth, vii. 450 ff.; Holmes, *Common Law*, 164 ff.; E. G. M. Fletcher, *Carrier's Liability*, 1–35.

[4] See, however, Alfred, 20, Alfred, Einleitung 28 (in Liebermann, i. 36) and Stenton, *English Feudalism*, App. 46, for a deed limiting a bailee's liability, *c.* 1150.

[5] Holdsworth, vii. 450.

[6] *Select Pleas of the Crown* (Selden Society), no. 126; *Eyre Rolls* (Selden Society, vol. lix), no. 977 (1221).

reason of the bailment, had lost his real right to the chattel, and could only assert his better right by a personal action [*sc.* detinue] against the bailee ",[1] for we find a case[2] where the bailor seems to bring the appeal against the thief, offering to prove by the body of the bailee from whom the goods were stolen, and who was bound to repay them to the owner.

It has likewise been maintained that the liability of the bailee was absolute, both before and after the time of Bracton. There is singularly little evidence for this proposition,[3] which must be regarded at present as conjectural.

When we come to Bracton we find a difficulty which is so typical that it deserves mention, not only as part of the history of bailees' liability, but also as illustrating the Bractonian problem in general. Bracton has an elaborate classification of bailments and says that in some cases the bailee is liable for fraud and negligence only.[4] What are we to conclude from this? Is Bracton stating Roman law on a point where English law had not yet reached a decision, or is Bracton stating real English law, although in Roman terms? No amount of study of Bracton will settle this, for until we have independent evidence of the English law of Bracton's day, we must remain uncertain of how far we can take Bracton as stating current law and not merely his own Romanesque speculations. The principal situation which would raise the question is when the goods have been stolen from the bailee without his connivance and without his negligence. There is one early case where the bailee's defence was that the goods had been stolen when his house was burnt, but unfortunately judgment was given on default without discussing the point.[5]

The pre-Bracton law of bailment is very obscure. It is easier to speak of the two centuries following Bracton, and they seem to contain clear evidence that the bailee's liability was not absolute. Britton states as law that the borrower of a chattel is not liable for fire, flood or theft unless they were due to his fault or negligence.[6] Such a defence was actually allowed[7] in 1299. Another case in 1315, once obscure, but now clarified by the printing of the record by the Selden Society,[8] shows conclusively that theft without the default of the bailee was a good defence.

---

[1] Holdsworth, vii. 450; the doubt we have raised only applies to the earliest period of the common law. See in general, Bordwell, *Property in Chattels*, Harvard Law Review, xxix. 374. The bailor's action against strangers dates from the later fourteenth century.

[2] *Curia Regis Rolls*, ii. 181–182 (1203).

[3] Glanvill, x. 13, is uncorroborated.

[4] Bracton, f. 62 *b*, 99.

[5] *Select Civil Pleas* (Selden Society), no. 8 (1200).

[6] Britton (ed. Nichols), i. 157; adding that if he borrows money, and foolishly shows it among thieves, and they rob him, he is still liable to the creditor, for he ought to have been more careful. The line between debt and detinue was still rather thin. For an indenture of 1309 relieving an apprentice of liability for loss of his master's goods by fire, water, or robbers, see Y.BB. Edward II (Selden Society), xxii. 127 (1317).

[7] *Brinkburn Cartulary* (Surtees Society), 105.

[8] Fitz., *Detinue*, 59; Y.BB. Edward II (Selden Society), xvii. 136; Beale, in Harvard Law Review, xi. 158.

Further cases in 1339,[1] 1355[2] and 1431[3] confirm this, and in view of such a line of authority it seems difficult to maintain that " these attempts thus to modify the liability of the bailee never materialised ".[4] The evidence seems rather to support the view that the attempts were successful for nearly two centuries after Bracton.

Unfortunately, the peculiar nature of the Bractonian problem prevents us from saying whether there is clear continuity from the pre-Bracton period, for there is still, perhaps, the unanswered question whether Bracton was truthfully stating the law of his own day. If this was not the case, then there might be the possibility that the post-Bracton cases were in fact decided on the strength of his Romanesque exposition of the subject. A further element of ambiguity is suggested in the Harvard manuscript of *Brevia Placitata*, where it is alleged that a distrainor may be legally liable for accident, and yet escape by taking the general issue and trusting the jury to be lenient in the matter of damages.[5] It is, of course, very rarely that an experienced and crafty practitioner affords us so fascinating a glimpse of mediaeval law in action.

Be this as it may, it seems clear that from Britton down to 1431 it was familiar doctrine that a bailee was liable for fraud and negligence only. Just after the middle of the fifteenth century the discussion took a different turn. It had been settled for centuries that a bailee could sue a thief or a trespasser, and from time to time it had been suggested that this right to sue was perhaps based, not on his possession, but on the fact that he was liable to the bailor.[6] This view was argued in the famous *Marshal's Case*[7] in 1455. It was agreed that the marshal of a prison was in the position of a bailee, and was liable as a bailee to the party on whose process the prisoner had been committed. In this case, the plaintiff sued the marshal of the King's Bench prison for damages on the escape of a prisoner. The defence was that a multitude of the King's enemies[8] broke the prison and allowed the prisoners to escape. The argument which is reported shows one point clearly—that the bailee is not liable for the act of God or of the King's foreign enemies. Apart from that everything is obscure; the debate is fragmentarily reported, the Year Book gives no decision, and the record shows that none was reached, although the case was several times adjourned. The *Marshal's Case*, therefore, contains few *dicta*, and no judgment, and consequently is historically worthless. The one *dictum* of interest was a converse form

---

[1] Y.B. 12 & 13 Edward III (Rolls Series), 246.

[2] 29 Ass. 28 (a pledge stolen).

[3] Y.B. 10 Henry VI, 21 no. 69.

[4] Holdsworth, iii. 342.

[5] *Brevia Placitata* (Selden Society), 207.

[6] As early as 1317 there is a suggestion that a bailee, who is answerable to another, can replevy the cattle if they are distrained: Y.BB. Edward II (Selden Society), xxii. 49.

[7] 33 Henry VI, 1 no. 3; for an abstract of the record, see Fletcher, *Carrier's Liability*, 253.

[8] As this was in 1450, the allusion must be to Cade's rebellion.

of the liability-over theory. As Danby put it, the bailee was liable because he had a right of action against a thief or trespasser, and therefore he was liable for everything except act of God or the King's enemies, in both of which cases he obviously had no action and therefore no liability.

The stream of *dicta* continues during the reign of Henry VII and through the sixteenth century until *Southcote's Case* in 1601. As Dr Fletcher remarks,[1] " it is significant that before that case there is no actual decision holding an ordinary bailee liable for loss, such as theft, occasioned without any fault or negligence on his part ". There are several reports,[2] which is fortunate, for Coke's seems to have been somewhat embroidered. It seems that the only authority relied on was the *Marshal's Case*, which the court apparently regarded as having been decided for the plaintiff. The facts were simple. To detinue, the defendant pleaded that the goods had been stolen. The plaintiff replied that the thief was in fact the defendant's servant, but no stress seems to have been placed on that aspect of the case, and in fact the replication alleging it was held by the court to be " idle and vain ". Judgment was given on the plea, and for the plaintiff. Absolute liability was at last recognised in unequivocal terms by the court of King's Bench, and at a moment (as we have seen) when liability in other directions was being increased.[3]

The classifications of bailments attempted by Glanvill and Bracton did not commend themselves to the common law courts, and so for a long time we had but one rule applicable to all bailments. One apparent exception—servants and factors, who were excluded from the category of bailees—was due to a procedural accident, for in the action of account those who were accountable were not liable if the goods entrusted to them were stolen without their default.[4]

As a result of the rule in *Southcote's Case*, prudent bailees made express stipulations limiting their liability, as Coke in his note appended to the case recommended them. This in itself compelled some rough classification of bailments such as was familiar to the learned from Bracton, and to all from *Doctor and Student*,[5] whose author went even to the *Summa Rosella* for neat examples. This ferment of new ideas and new practices soon began to unsettle the law of *Southcote's Case*; the replacement of detinue by *assumpsit*, moreover, threw emphasis on negligence (and later on contract). Consequently, in spite of the apparent finality of *Southcote's Case*, Lord Holt had the opportunity in the case of *Coggs* v. *Bernard*[6] of

[1] Fletcher, *op. cit.*, 26; confirming Beale, *Carrier's Liability*, Select Essays in Anglo-American Legal History, iii. 152. The cases are collected and discussed, Fletcher, 24 ff.

[2] Cro. Eliz. 815; 4 Rep. 83 *b*; a MS. report at Harvard is printed in Harvard Law Review, xiii. 46.

[3] Above, p. 468.

[4] Fletcher, *Carrier's Liability*, 19.

[5] Extracts in Holdsworth, vii. 453 n. 3.

[6] 2 Ld. Raym. 909 (1703); for strictures upon Holt's handling of Roman Law, see Holmes, *Misunderstandings of the Civil Law*, Harvard Law Review, xlvii. 759 at 767.

treating the entire question as open, and of mapping out the whole field of bailment in the light of Bracton's learning, which was thus tardily received into the common law. His historical investigation showed that there was no authority for the decision in *Southcote's Case*, and for its single rigid rule of absolute liability he substituted several rules requiring standards of care suitable to the different sorts of bailment.

It having been now made clear that there was no absolute liability of bailee to bailor, the suggestion which was frequently made, especially in the seventeenth century, that the bailee's right to sue was based on that liability over, presented difficulties. That doctrine was still adhered to in 1892, but in 1902 the Court of Appeal held that the ultimate historical basis was the bailee's possession, as Holmes had long ago demonstrated, and abandoned the alternative which had tempted lawyers for over six hundred years.[1]

COMMON CALLINGS

It is characteristic of our mediaeval law that although it did not classify bailments, it did classify bailees, and imposed special liabilities upon people who had a special status by reason of their occupation. Carriers, innkeepers and farriers are well-known examples. The legal explanation of their onerous liability has exercised many minds, and one of the greatest of modern common lawyers urged that it was merely a survival of the absolute liability which once lay upon all bailees.[2] Simple and attractive, this theory has nevertheless been criticised by several scholars, notably Professor Beale.[3] One branch of this argument we have already examined, with the results that we gravely doubt whether absolute liability was a part of our earliest law, that we are fairly sure that it did not prevail in the fourteenth and fifteenth centuries, and that its first absolutely clear appearance is in 1601.

Now the special liability of those engaged in common callings begins to appear at a time when our evidence is clearest that the bailee's liability was only for fraud and negligence.[4] We have already mentioned the action of *assumpsit* which lay against one who was entrusted with a chattel to do work on it, and whose faulty workmanship resulted in loss or damage.[5] This action was available against all bailees, whether professionally or only casually engaged in work of that kind. As we have seen, it was based on the *assumpsit*—the express undertaking to employ proper skill and care and to obtain a particular result. Gradually a

---

[1] *Claridge* v. *South Staffs. Tramway Co.*, [1892] 1 Q.B. 422; *The Winkfield*, [1902] P. 42; Holdsworth, vii. 454, 461–462.

[2] Holmes, *The Common Law*, 188 ff.

[3] *History of Carrier's Liability*, Harvard Law Review, xi. 198, reprinted in Select Essays in Anglo-American Legal History, iii. 148. The latest and fullest discussion is that by Dr E. G. M. Fletcher, *Carrier's Liability* (London, 1932).

[4] Above, pp. 477–478.

[5] Above, pp. 469–470.

modification in the form of the writ indicated a somewhat different attitude. Instead of counting on an *assumpsit*, the plaintiff counts on " the custom of the realm " which he chooses as the basis of his action. The defendant's undertaking (or the absence of an undertaking) is therefore immaterial, and it is to the " custom of the realm " that we must look for his liability. A very early case[1] was against an innkeeper, thus:

> " Trespass was brought by *W*. against *T*., an innkeepér and his servant, counting that whereas it is accustomed and used throughout the realm of England that where there is a common inn, the innkeeper and his servants ought to guard the goods and things which their guests have in their chambers within the inn for as long as they are lodged there, the said *W*. came on a certain day in the town of Canterbury to the said *T*. and lodged with him, he and his horse, his goods and chattels (to wit, cloth) and twenty marks of silver counted in a purse, and took his room and put the goods, chattels and money in the room, and then went into the town about his business; while he was in the town the same goods, chattels and money were taken out of his said room by wicked folk by default of the innkeeper's keeping and of his servants, wrongfully and against the peace, to his damage, etc. (And he had a writ on all the matter according to his case.)
>
> " The innkeeper demanded judgement since he had not said in his writ nor in his count that he delivered the goods to him to keep, etc., nor that the goods were taken away by them [? the defendants] and so he has not supposed any manner of guilt [*culp'*] in them; and also he gave him a key to his room to keep the goods in the room; judgement whether action lies. And on this matter both sides demurred in judgement.
>
> " And it was adjudged by KNIVET, J. that the plaintiff recover against them, and the court taxed the damages, and he will not get the damages just as he counted them. . . . But there has been no guilt in them, for no manner of tort is supposed in their persons; for although they were charged in the law, that will not be a reason to put them into prison. . . .
>
> " And so he had an *elegit*."[2]

It will be noticed that it is a writ of trespass, but " he had a writ on all the matter according to his case ". In short, it comes at the moment when case is being distinguished from trespass. The discussion as to whether *capias* should issue shows the anomalous use of the words " guilt " and " tort " at this moment. It will also be noticed that the count alleges negligence in the form of " default of keeping ". In time it becomes clear that the allegation of negligence means less than it would seem. The early distinction is clearly that one in a common calling is liable without an *assumpsit*. Later there was the question of the extent of his liability. In the case of the innkeeper it was early established that his liability exceeded that of the contemporary bailee, but the similar case of the common carrier was not settled until much later. It may be doubted whether transport by land was a regular trade in the middle ages. Surviving family names indicate the commonest trades of the middle ages, but although we have numerous families of Bakers, Taylors

---

[1] Y.B. 42 Edward III, 11 no. 13 (1368); 42 Ass. 17. Cf. Y.B. 46 Edward III, 19 (1372); above, p. 471.

[2] For *elegit*, see above, p. 390.

and the like, we seem to have no Carriers.[1]   The Carter was a manorial tenant, and the Porter probably had an even narrower range of activity. As for carriage by sea, merchants still generally travelled with their cargo and supervised the handling of it.

The first mention of the common carrier as being in a peculiar legal position seems to be in *Doctor and Student*, where his liability is equated with that of other tradesmen who are liable for negligence.[2]   In the seventeenth century the cases show that his liability is stricter, and that he must answer for theft even if he has not been negligent.[3]   The influence of *Southcote's Case* may well be suspected here.   In admiralty, the carrier was not liable for theft except by the crew,[4] but the common law was capturing admiralty jurisdiction and soon treated sea carriers as common carriers subject to the custom of the realm.[5]

It was in *Coggs* v. *Bernard* that the carrier's liability received fullest and most reasoned treatment.   The negligence alleged in the count was now clearly otiose and had lost its original meaning; the limits set by Lord Holt are the mercantile exceptions " act of God and the King's enemies ".   In Holt's day these exceptions were construed liberally, and seem to have meant " inevitable accident ".   Nearly a century later, a serious change was made in the interpretation of the ancient, but unfortunate phrase " act of God ", by Lord Mansfield.   In *Forward* v. *Pittard*[6] he treated the words literally (as he conceived it), confined them to a few rare meteorological phenomena, and held a carrier liable for what was certainly an inevitable accident.   More than that, he used a striking phrase which has ever since been quoted as marking this, the high-water mark, of carrier's liability: " a carrier is in the nature of an insurer ".

[1] The earliest example I have found is a family called " Carryer " in 1563: G. J. Turner, *Hunts Feet of Fines* (Cambridge Antiquarian Society, vol. xxxvii), 153 no. 29.   For " common carrier " as an occupation, see Fifoot, *Sources: Tort and Contract*, 158 n. 25 (a deed of 1459), and Bayne, *Council of Henry VII* (Selden Society), 151 (a case of 1505).   The only earlier mention of a carrier I have found is in 1392: Putnam, *Justices of the Peace*, 440.

[2] The examples given are driving at night, or by dangerous ways, or overloading a boat, *Doctor and Student*, ii. c. 38.   Cf. Fifoot, *Sources: Tort and Contract*, 157.

[3] Fletcher, *Carrier's Liability*, 117.

[4] *Ibid.*, 119.

[5] *Morse* v. *Slue*, 3 Keb. 135 (1671), discussed at length by Fletcher, 134 ff.

[6] 1 Term Rep. 27 (1785).

CHAPTER 5

DEFAMATION

There are few chapters in our legal history which illustrate so many different aspects of historical development as does the history of defamation. Germanic elements, Roman elements, the rise and fall of courts, constitutional conflicts, mechanised printing, and later still mechanised distribution of printed matter, have all played their part in producing the body of law which historical accident has divided into the two categories of libel and slander.

SLANDER IN ANGLO-SAXON LAW

In common with most of the Germanic systems, Anglo-Saxon law was particularly concerned with insulting words addressed by one person to another. This was an offence which it punished with severity, sometimes with the excision of the tongue.[1] *Bot* and *wite* were due for certain terms of abuse before the Conquest, and long after the Conquest local courts frequently entertained cases of insult; such jurisdiction was naturally left to the local courts, for they alone could secure amends before the same community that had witnessed the affront. Such amends were a fine, and sometimes a humiliating confession. Thus at Preston, in England, as well as in Normandy, the offender must hold his nose and call himself a liar.[2]

[1] III Edgar, 4 (*c*. 946–*c*. 961); II Canute, 16 (*c*. 1027–*c*. 1034).

[2] *Borough Customs* (Selden Society), i. 78; Pollock and Maitland, ii. 537.

SLANDER IN CHURCH COURTS

The Church exercised criminal jurisdiction over many matters which modern law has relinquished to the *forum internum*. A great deal of scandalous gossip about the private life of one's neighbours, and a good many obscene and abusive expressions, were therefore in a special category, for they might have the effect of putting a person upon his trial before an ecclesiastical court.[1] The Church no doubt regarded defamation of this character as dangerous, mainly because it led inevitably to the abuse of her criminal procedure.[2] Indeed, the very word " defamation " is a technical term in church law, signifying that evil reputation which is sufficiently notorious to put a man on his trial. Mere rumour is not sufficient.[3] The *diffamatus* is thus a person whose reputation is so bad that it serves as an accusation; but if as a result of the trial he is acquitted, then clearly his ill-fame was unfounded, and those who spread the calumny have themselves committed a crime: " furthermore, we excommunicate all those who for lucre, hate, favour, or any other cause maliciously impute a crime whereby anyone is defamed among good and grave persons in such wise that he has been put to his purgation at least, or otherwise aggrieved "[4]—thus Stephen Langton enacted in 1222 at the council of Oxford, and we have already seen traces of the application by the Church of this principle to members of a grand jury whose indictments were not followed by conviction.[5]

SLANDER IN LOCAL COURTS

Gradually it becomes apparent that local courts are giving remedy for words which are not merely insults addressed to the plaintiff, but rather statements to his prejudice addressed to other persons. The remedy also takes the form of a civil action for damages rather than that of a prosecution for a petty misdemeanour.[6] Thus in the manorial court of King's Ripton, a plaintiff alleged that the defendant uttered defamatory words about him to a third party, and also sent a defamatory letter concerning him to another, with the result that he suffered general damage of 20*s.* and special damage of 30*s.* in respect of a lease which was not renewed.[7] Still more interesting is a case in 1333 where the county

---

[1] Indeed, mere ill-repute was enough to put him on trial not only in church courts, but also before royal justices: *Eyre Rolls* (Selden Society, vol. lix), no. 1239 (1221).

[2] The Church also punished insults (not within this class) as *contumelia*.

[3] Lyndwood, *Provinciale* (ed. 1679), 117 *diffamati*, distinguishes " fame " from " rumour ".

[4] Gibson, *Codex Juris Ecclesiastici* (ed. 1761), ii. 1252; Lyndwood, *Provinciale* (ed. 1679), 346. For a case of 1306 in a hundred court clearly illustrating the point of Stephen Langton's constitution, see Pollock and Maitland, ii. 538 n. 5.

[5] Above, p. 127 n. 1. So, too, one who brought an appeal of felony which ended in acquittal was liable to imprisonment and to pay damages for the defamation of the appellee: stat. Westminster II, c. 12 (1285).

[6] For what may be a mingling of the two (c. 1340) see Page, *Estates of Crowland Abbey*, 141.

[7] *Select Pleas in Manorial Courts* (Selden Society), 116 (1294). Slander of goods appears in 1320; Alice Batte " defamed the lord's corn, whereby other purchasers forebore to buy it "; *Court Baron* (Selden Society), 130.

court of Bedford tried an action in which the plaintiff alleged that the defendant called him a false and faithless fellow, whereby he was prevented from raising a loan which was being negotiated.[1]

SLANDER IN THE KING'S COURT

For serious matters, the church courts were the most practicable jurisdiction.[2] The King's courts were prepared to admit this—up to a point. In 1285 the writ called *Circumspecte Agatis* (which soon was reputed a statute) confirmed the principle that the punishment of defamation as a sin (*i.e.* by the Church's criminal procedure) was not subject to prohibition from the temporal courts; an exception was made, however, if " money is demanded " (*i.e.* in the civil proceedings for damages), and in that case prohibition presumably would lie.[3]

Ten years later a lively dispute in the King's Court in Ireland which (against all the rules of pleading) finally developed into an appeal of treason was called to England and the process quashed because it had begun as a complaint of defamation, " and in this realm it is not the practice to plead pleas of defamation in the King's Court ".[4] This statement in fact needs qualification. No doubt it is true that the King's Court would not follow the example of local courts, and when *A*. and *B*. have exchanged abuse, settle the damages due for each epithet, and determine the balance on account which remained to be paid.[5] But the King, like other lords, could not stand by while someone was saying that " there is no justice in the lord's court ",[6] nor could he tolerate similar statements about his principal officers. In 1275 we therefore find the beginning of a line of statutes creating the offence of *scandalum magnatum*, the slander of magnates.[7]

THE SLANDER OF MAGNATES: *SCANDALUM MAGNATUM*

The course of a statutory remedy or offence may sometimes be quite unexpected. Thus *scandalum magnatum* begins with a statute of 1275 which enacted that one who publishes false news or scandal tending to

[1] Text and translation in Plucknett, *The County Court*, Harvard Law Review, xlii. 639 at 668; the whole roll is now edited by Dr. G. H. Fowler, in Quarto Memoirs of the Bedfordshire Historical Record Society, iii. 66 no. 270, 74 no. 270.

[2] But, of course, not the only one. In 1273 a Christian sought remedy against a Jew for defamation: *Jewish Exchequer* (Selden Society), 70–71; in 1279 there was a plea of defamation in the King's Bench: Sayles, *King's Bench* (Selden Society), ii. p. cxxii; cf. *Exchequer of Pleas* (Selden Society), 103 (1280); a man falsely denounced as a " wild Irishman " released in 1401: *Cases before the King's Council* (Selden Society), 85–86; *Select Cases in Chancery* (Selden Society), no. 113 (1413–1417).

[3] Graves, *Circumspecte Agatis*, English Historical Review, xliii. 1.

[4] *Rotuli Parliamentorum*, i. 132–134.

[5] *E.g.* above, p. 98.

[6] *Ibid.*

[7] Case for slander is a later development; below, p. 491.

produce discord between the King and his people or the magnates shall be kept in prison until he produces in court the originator of the tale.[1] The statute was therefore essentially political in its nature, and succeeding legislation retained this characteristic. In 1378 the hundred-year-old statute was re-enacted, the word " magnates " being glossed as peers, prelates, justices and various named officials.[2] The moment was one of restless intrigue, much of it centring round John of Gaunt, and three years later came the Peasants' Revolt (1381), in the course of which (it is said) a demand was made for the repeal of the statute.[3] This would suggest that the statute was not a dead letter; it was in fact re-enacted shortly afterwards, in 1388,[4] with a very important additional clause that offenders may be punished " by the advice of the council ".

The statutes, therefore, are still political in scope, and criminal in nature. There is very little evidence of the working of these statutes during the middle ages, but cases begin to appear in the common law courts under Elizabeth. This is perhaps connected with the fact that the statutes on *scandalum magnatum* were once more re-enacted[5] in 1554 and again[6] in 1559, but with additional clauses on " seditious words "; justices of the peace were given jurisdiction, and the punishment was loss of ears for words, and of the right hand for writings. Towards the middle of the sixteenth century *scandalum magnatum* came under the influence of the doctrine that if a statute prescribes a punishment for acts which cause harm to others, then the injured party can have a civil action for damages in respect of breaches of the statute, even though the statute makes no provision for a civil remedy. It was the civil side of *scandalum magnatum* which the common law courts developed, and in doing so they established several harsh rules. Thus, words which were too vague and general to support an action for slander at common law would support an action on the statute; consequently vague criticisms or expressions of dislike or disrespect, although they did not make any definite imputation, were actionable if spoken of a " magnate ". More-over, the defendant could not justify by pleading that the words were true, in spite of the fact that the statute only penalises " false news and horrible lies ". The young Mr Coke, a few months after his call, did indeed hold a brief—his first in the King's Bench—for a neighbour in which he succeeded in getting the court to allow a sort of explanation to be put in, tending to show that the words were susceptible of another

---

[1] Westminster I (1275), c. 34.

[2] 2 Richard II, stat. 1, c. 5. For a case on this statute, see *Rot. Parl.* iii. 169 no. 15 (1382).

[3] For the connection of John of Gaunt with this statute, see Barrington, *Observations on the Statutes* (1775), 314.

[4] 12 Richard II, c. 11.

[5] 1 & 2 Philip and Mary, c. 3. The same Parliament (c. 9) declared it treason to have prayed, or to pray in the future, that God would shorten the queen's life, but with a curious clause modifying this retrospective operation.

[6] 1 Elizabeth, c. 6.

meaning,[1] but the position of defendants was very little strengthened by the concession.

The common law courts were therefore slow to apply the statutes relating to *scandalum magnatum*, and when they did do so they were most interested in the civil action based upon it.[2] The criminal aspect of the matter, as the statute of 1388 makes clear, was pre-eminently the province of the council, and it is unlikely that the justices of the peace would be allowed much scope for the independent exercise of their statutory powers under the act of 1559. The throne of Elizabeth was too unsteady, and the political situation much too dangerous for the council to resign the trial of political offences into the hand of the country justices. The council, therefore, and more particularly the Star Chamber, employed themselves in dealing with the slander of peers and seditious words and writings. It is well known that the Star Chamber made frequent use of the cruel punishments of mutilation for these offences, but it should be remembered that there was some statutory sanction for them. If this fact is often forgotten, it is because the Star Chamber itself was loth to rely upon legislation. This policy was particularly evident under James I and Charles I, when on several occasions an exercise of the prerogative which was quite defensible on strictly legal grounds was in fact defended on the much more debatable grounds of " absolute power ". *Bate's Case* is a well-known example;[3] another is the case *De Libellis Famosis*,[4] which Coke prosecuted as Attorney-General and subsequently reported. It was clearly within the definition of *scandalum magnatum*, yet this offence is not expressly mentioned; the court also referred to the possibility of mutilation, but avoided mentioning the statutes of 1554 and 1559. Instead, the Star Chamber laid down some general propositions on libel, private and public, which were evidently based on civilian learning. Rather than rely on statute, the court laid it down that " libelling and calumniation is an offence against the law of God ", and sought their legal basis in Exodus and Leviticus. Roman law had distinguished between the defamation which could be remedied by a civil action, and the *libellus famosus* which it visited with extraordinary punishment. The Star Chamber apparently used this latter conception to extend, far beyond the bounds of the statutes, our native *scandalum magnatum*.

---

[1] *Lord Cromwell's Case* (1578–1581), 4 Rep. 12 *b*.

[2] The criminal cases were apt to be either seditious, or in the nature of contempt of court. The common law courts, like the Star Chamber, were at pains to avoid using the statutes, and so created the impression that seditious words were a common-law misdemeanour; cf. Holdsworth, viii. 340.

[3] *Bate's Case* (1606), 2 St. Tr. 371. See extracts in Prothero, *Constitutional Documents*, 340; Tanner, *Constitutional Documents of James I*, 337–345; Holdsworth, vi. 43 ff.; G. D. G. Hall, *Bate's Case and " Lane's " Reports: the Authenticity of a Seventeenth-Century Legal Text*, Bulletin of the John Rylands Library, xxxv. 405, and *Impositions and the Courts, 1554–1606*, Law Quarterly Review, lxix. 200.

[4] *De Libellis Famosis* (1605), 5 Rep. 125.

THE BEGINNINGS OF LIBEL

Coke himself is credited with the rapid increase of libel cases in the Star Chamber while he was Attorney-General,[1] and it is clear that he was deeply interested in both branches of defamation.[2]

Looking back from the year 1605 we can see that the law has not yet advanced very far. The distinction between libel and slander has not yet settled at the place where it now rests, and it is hardly clear where it will ultimately lie. At this moment, libel is obviously a crime, and, as we shall see a little later, slander was obviously a tort. The crime was punished principally in the Star Chamber; the tort was actionable mainly in the courts of common law. For the origins of libel we have to go to the obscure mediaeval offence of *scandalum magnatum* which had definitely political origins. The events of the Barons' Wars left a sufficient crop of rumours and scandals (of which we have a surviving example[3]) to make the first statute of 1275 desirable. The feverish years of Richard II, with their mischievous tales of financial corruption, called for the re-enactment and extension of the offence and its association with the council—which is perhaps the reason why the ordinary sources for legal history tell us so little of *scandalum magnatum* during the middle ages. The troubles of the Reformation made it necessary for Mary to reaffirm the old legislation with the significant addition of a clause dealing with seditious words. Elizabeth, immediately on her accession, re-enacted Mary's statute, but later in her reign there took place a rapid development of a curious sort: the common law courts gave a civil action for damages on *scandalum magnatum*, but the Star Chamber concentrated mainly on the crime, preserved the spirit of the statutes (although abandoning the letter), and borrowed the name, and some of the principles, of Roman law, thus creating the crime of libel, which it henceforward will develop in a logical fashion.

THE SOURCES OF THE LAW OF LIBEL

The sources from which libel sprang are therefore very diverse. On the one hand we have the ancient Germanic insistence upon personal prestige, which gives us the punishment of insults in local courts, and which, in the crime of *scandalum magnatum*, left a very definite mark in the fact that words derogatory or disrespectful were actionable (or criminal) if spoken of a peer, although they were not otherwise defamatory. This irresistibly reminds us of the fact that there was once a tendency for ordinary persons to treat almost any tort as a personal affront: the abbot of Bury will complain in the King's Court that the bishop of Ely infringed his liberty " so that the abbot would not have the shame which

---

[1] Hudson, " Star Chamber " in *Collectanea Juridica*, ii. 100.

[2] See the cases collected in 4 Rep. 12–20.

[3] *Rot. Parl.*, i. 132 *a* (mentioned above, p. 485 n. 4).

the bishop did him for £100, nor the damage for 100 marks ",[1] and in local courts such allegations of shame are very common.[2]

The ecclesiastical element is discernible in the early law of libel, but its influence was greatest (as we shall see) in the law of slander. The Star Chamber pleadings in print show that as early as 1493 that court entertained complaints of defamation of private persons,[3] and it is curious to note how constantly defendants plead that the plaintiff's bill is " seditious and slanderous ";[4] malicious prosecutions and complaints before the prerogative courts were very frequently alleged as an argument against the jurisdiction which they exercised, and it may be that these courts were led to take notice of defamation of private persons in consequence of their suspicions that their procedure was particularly liable to be misused. As we have seen, malicious prosecution and defamation were closely connected in the church courts.

The greatest element in the formation of libel law, however, was political. Down to 1605 the main thread is the obscure history of *scandalum magnatum*. The statutory changes in this crime were apt to occur at moments when treason also was being extended, and the statutes of Mary and Elizabeth treated the crimes of " public libel " (*scandalum magnatum*), " private libel " and sedition as being substantially the same, or at least closely related.

The Roman element appeared at a critical moment. Libel having become primarily a political offence, it immediately became involved in the early Stuart mysticism of the Crown, and for centuries there had been a temptation to turn to Roman law when the *arcana* of government were under discussion. Naturally it was in the Star Chamber that the experimental work took place, but the eagerness of the common law courts to share in it is worthy of notice. In 1606 Coke asserted that libel could be prosecuted on indictment as well as in the Star Chamber, and already the common lawyers had extracted from the statute a civil remedy for the slander of nobles.

THE LAW OF LIBEL, 1605–1641

The generation between *De Libellis Famosis* and the abolition of the Star Chamber was the period during which the foundations of the modern law were laid down. The old distinction between public and private libels, even more than the distinction drawn in the statutes, helped to separate seditious from other libels. The vague authority of

---

[1] *Select Civil Pleas* (Selden Society), no. 183 (*post* 1205).

[2] *Select Pleas in Manorial Courts* (Selden Society), *passim*. Even in debt the plaintiff might recover for " shame " as well as damages: *Court Baron* (Selden Society), 47. In *Select Cases without Writ* (Selden Society), cviii ff., the editors would regard the notion as a Romanism. There is no ground for this.

[3] *Select Cases in Star Chamber* (Selden Society), i. 38 ff.

[4] *Select Cases in Star Chamber*, 20, 101, 109 163, 166, 182 *et passim*.

the law of God is gradually replaced by the alternative theory that libels are punishable because they disturb the State (if directed against magnates and magistrates), or because they provoke a breach of the peace (if directed against private individuals). This was by no means a fictitious or merely technical justification; the great vogue of the fashion of duelling at this moment seems to have given cause for great concern to the government. Already, too, it was settled that truth was not a defence. This was a break with Roman authority, and also with the construction which would seem required by the English statutes; the excuse given for the rule is that a grievance should be redressed by law, and not by the party himself using force, or circulating extra-judicial accusations. As this period progresses, there are signs of the modifications of this rule. Hudson (writing before 1635) states that spoken words (even against a magnate) can be justified by showing their truth, but written words are punishable in respect of the very fact that they were written.[1] Here we seem to see the influence of certain ordinances against writings and printed books which we shall mention later. The theory seems to regard writing as so deliberate an act that writing defamatory matter was criminal; words, on the other hand, were felt to be more spontaneous and irresponsible, and so justification could be pleaded. The rule as stated by Hudson is, of course, chiefly noteworthy as being an early sign of the different treatment of spoken and written defamation.

We are not yet at the point when libel and slander were distinguished along modern lines. Words still could be treated as libels,[2] and writings were actionable at common law as slander.[3] The distinction as yet is primarily one of courts and procedure. Action on the case for slander was clear and definite; it was in the Star Chamber that the newer and vaguer body of law was developed under the heads of *seandalum magnatum*, libel and seditious libel, which in the end coalesced into the law of libel. Hudson's distinction is certainly one indication that the rules of libel apply particularly to written defamation, and it may be that the distinction is itself a reflection of the fact that slander at common law had a different rule which in practice was generally (although not always) concerned with spoken words. Hudson's distinction may therefore be the result of common law example influencing the Star Chamber.

One other point calls for notice. The Star Chamber was not confined altogether to its criminal jurisdiction, and in cases of libel the court sometimes gave damages to the injured party as well as imposing a fine on the offender.

---

[1] Hudson, " Star Chamber " in Hargrave's *Collectanea Juridica*, ii. 104. He even applies this rule to *scandalum magnatum*, which Coke said could not be justified.

[2] Hudson, " Star Chamber " in Hargrave's *Collectanea Juridica*, ii. 104, and cases cited in Holdsworth, v. 211, n. 2.

[3] See the cases cited in Holdsworth, v. 207, n. 4.

ACTION ON THE CASE FOR WORDS

So far, we have traced those elements which contributed to the formation of a law of libel. It is now time to examine the other line of development which culminated in slander.

At the beginning of this chapter we gave some examples from local courts. They are of two distinct orders. In some of the cases the plaintiff is complaining of words which he regards as affronts and insults; in others, the plaintiff asserts that he has suffered in loss of money rather than loss of pride. Hence we find that defamatory statements which result in the breaking-off of business negotiations could be made the subject of an action for damages in the manorial or the county court. When the common law courts began to entertain actions for slander, they made provision for both types, but only slowly did they devise special rules for each.

The early cases are all of them interesting from different points of view. Thus, the first reported case[1] on defamation in the Year Books arose because one Lucy called Seton, J., a justice of the common pleas, who was entering the exchequer for a council, " traitor, felon and robber ". Seton proceeded against her by bill demanding £1000 damages. A jury of attorneys found her guilty but reduced the damages to 100 marks. The court, however, reserved the question whether the damages should be arrested. Several cases late in the fifteenth century allege that the defendant defamed the plaintiff by calling him his villein. In 1462, for example, a plaintiff counted that the defendant " contriving to prejudice the plaintiff's name and fame and to get his goods and lands, published and affirmed that he was the defendant's villein " and lay in wait to catch him, whereby the plaintiff was prevented from going about his business.[2] It seems to have been agreed by all that the action would not have been good unless the plaintiff said that he had been impeded in his business. Whether this means that the defamation is only actionable if special damage is pleaded, or that the defamation is not itself actionable unless accompanied by another tort, was left conveniently obscure.

Later in the reign the matter was raised again in a case which lasted several years. In 1475 a plaintiff[3] used exactly the same sort of count as we saw in 1462. The defendant had difficulty in framing a plea,[4] but

---

[1] 30 Ass. 19 (1356). For the record, see Sayles, *King's Bench*, iii, p. cxxxvi. The incident took place on 15 November, 1357, and so the report in 30 Ass. is misplaced. The case seems clearly an action for damages brought by bill by the injured party, rather than proceedings for contempt of court. Lucy aggravated matters by producing a papal bull excommunicating the justice; bulls were not evidence in English courts, and she was reminded that she had risked her neck in using it. Dr Kiralfy, *Action on the Case*, 115, has found other proceedings from which it would appear that Lucy had been Seton's wife whom he married for her property; she later got a divorce from Rome.

[2] Y.B. 2 Edward IV, 5 (10).

[3] Y.B. 15 Edward IV, 32 (15).

[4] There was great danger that the defendant might plead to the action, with the result that the plaintiff, although a villein, would then be enfranchised since the defendant had treated him as a free man.

eventually issue was joined on the plaintiff's status, and a jury found that he was free. Judgment for damages therefore followed. Two years later the case came up to the King's Bench on a writ of error.[1] After long debate, Billing, C.J., and Needham, J., both agreed that " there are divers cases in our law where one may have *damnum sine injuria*; thus the defamation by calling a man thief or traitor is a damage to him in our law, but no tort ". Even so, the court reserved its judgment, " for as much as this is the first time this matter has been argued ". Nothing further is reported. The general trend of the argument in the King's Bench seems to be that the defamation may aggravate a trespass, but is not a cause of action in itself; in this particular case, the principal trespass alleged consisted merely of threats, preparation and intention. Even admitting that the plaintiff was consequently unwilling to go out of doors, there was great doubt whether an action lay.[2]

Meanwhile, the common law courts looked with jealous eyes upon the jurisdiction of the church courts over defamation. Prohibitions were issued freely in the reign of Edward IV, and in one case[3] we have the interesting remark that " if a man has robbed me, and I afterwards tell it in the hearing of other people, and he then would sue me [for defamation] in court christian, I shall have a prohibition, for I might have had an appeal ". This seems to be the first indication that the King's Court will prohibit defamation suits in church courts where the imputation was a crime cognisable in common law courts. If once this position was established, then it would soon become necessary for the common law courts to give remedy for those defamations which they forbade the church to deal with. The development therefore follows the line that (*a*) an imputation of a crime cognisable in the common law courts ought not to be treated by the church as defamatory, for the church might thereby impede the right of prosecuting at common law;[4] it was soon afterwards observed (*b*) that even in cases which did not involve defamation a defendant might try to justify a trespass, for example, by alleging matter of a spiritual nature,[5] and cases of this sort gave a

---

[1] Y.B. 17 Edward IV, 3 (2).

[2] For this point, see Y.B. 9 Henry VII (1493), 7 (4).

[3] Y.B. 22 Edward IV (1482), 20 (47), continued *ibid.*, 29 (9). It seems that the court took advantage of a very curious state of facts in reaching this notion. An abbot of St. Albans is alleged to have enticed a married woman to his room and endeavoured to seduce her, whereupon her husband brought an action of false imprisonment. To this the abbot countered with a citation for defamation, and it was this suit that the Common Pleas prohibited. The further proceedings are equally curious; the abbot excommunicated the woman for getting the prohibition, the Court of Common Pleas ordered him to absolve her, and as he did not do so, he was attached for contempt. The truth of the allegations was apparently never tried.

[4] As in the *Abbot of St. Alban's Case* in the preceding footnote.

[5] Thus, in 1486, a constable would have justified imprisoning a man by a London custom which allowed him to enter houses and arrest adulterers, though adultery was not a crime at common law and the fact was therefore not triable; Y.B. 1 Henry VII, 6 (3). That case was undecided, but a later case escaped the difficulty of adultery, for the custom pleaded in justification was merely to arrest suspicious persons found in disorderly houses; Y.B. 13 Henry VII (1497), 10 (10).

great deal of trouble, but their ultimate effect was to make it clear (for a time at least) that a court could not usefully meddle with matters if it had no jurisdiction to try those issues which must inevitably be raised; it was therefore admitted (*c*) that an imputation of purely spiritual crimes was clearly outside the jurisdiction of the royal courts, and was not subject to prohibition.

The stages by which the common law finally overcame these difficulties are no longer ascertainable, but a case of 1497 contains an emphatic dictum[1] that " defamation is a purely spiritual offence which can only be punished there ", although by 1535 it seems assumed that if the imputation is one of an offence triable at common law, then the common law courts will treat it as an actionable defamation.[2] From that date onwards, slander has a continuous history in the common law courts, and little more than a century later it was possible to write a little book on the subject.[3]

It will be noticed that the first type of slander to be actionable in the common law courts was the sort which imputed a common law crime (as distinguished from an ecclesiastical crime). The royal courts were probably forced to assume this jurisdiction because they had already prevented the church from exercising it. At the same time, they were well aware that this type of slander was commonly associated with acts which constituted a trespass to the person—indeed, it was almost common form when counting on an assault and battery to add allegations of insult too. Hence slanders of this type retained as a relic of their early association with trespass the rule that the damages were at large, and this in spite of the fact that actions on the case were normally actions for special damages. As the law became more closely classified, such slanders were said to be actionable *per se*.

The list of slanders actionable *per se* was steadily lengthened during the seventeenth century, sometimes for reasons of policy frankly stated, and sometimes as a result of argumentation of an artificial kind. An immense chapter was added when imputations against holders of offices and members of professions and trades were treated as actionable *per se*; the number of cases brought by justices of the peace and clergymen would almost suggest that the innovation was due to the fact that they needed the same protection as *scandalum magnatum* afforded to the highest ranks of the church and the law.

SPIRITUAL SLANDER AND SPECIAL DAMAGE

As we have seen, a slander may be regarded either as an insult, or as a cause of pecuniary damage. Both aspects were known in the local courts during the middle ages, and as we have just seen, the former type

---

[1] Y.B. 12 Henry VII, 24.

[2] Y.B. 27 Henry VIII, 14 (4).

[3] John March, *Actions for Slander: or, Collection of what Words are actionable in the Law, and what not?* 1647.

was recognised in the royal courts in the sixteenth century and onwards. The latter type seems first to appear in a case[1] of 1593. Here words were used which the court chose to regard as not imputing any offence cognisable in the lay courts.[2] Nevertheless, the plaintiff recovered her special damage, viz. the loss of a marriage which was prevented as a result of the scandalous statements. Originally it was felt necessary to defend this innovation against the church. It was still the theory that general jurisdiction over defamation belonged to the church (subject to prohibition in certain cases). The new rule annexed the whole of the church's remaining jurisdiction if the plaintiff proved special damage; as the lay courts put it, defamation may be a " spiritual " crime, but the damage it causes is temporal.

The old dilemma between spiritual and temporal crimes which used to decide whether the action should be brought in a church court or in a lay court, henceforward will decide in many cases whether special damage need or need not be pleaded before the lay court. The results were far from satisfactory.

THE LAW OF SLANDER DOWN TO 1641

Having already surveyed the progress made by the law of libel down to the date of the abolition of the Court of Star Chamber, it now remains to ascertain the content of the law of slander at the same date.

The continued existence of the ecclesiastical courts on the one hand, and of the Star Chamber on the other, was sufficient reason for the failure of the common law to develop the criminal side of defamation which was more adequately dealt with elsewhere. They therefore concentrated upon the action for damages, and had already distinguished the two familiar categories of the modern law. Slanders actionable *per se* were originally imputations of temporal crimes, but by the close of this period reflections on fitness for office, skill in trade or profession, and imputations of certain diseases were added to the list.[3] These exceptions from the general nature of actions on the case show a clear understanding of the problem, and leave no doubt that the common law had the will and the skill to create a saisfactory law of defamation as long as it had a clear field before it. The fact that it did not complete the scheme is due to the difficulties created by the ecclesiastical jurisdiction. There is every reason to believe that those difficulties were real at this moment; the church courts were still powerful, and the Reformation and the royal supremacy had surprisingly little effect on the relation of church and state judicatures. For a time there must have been great force in the argument that it was useless to entertain an action where a " spiritual "

[1] *Davis* v. *Gardiner* (1593), 4 Rep. 16 *b*.

[2] The words (that a woman had a bastard child) could also have come under the older rule, for this was an offence punishable under the poor law of 18 Eliz., c. 3.

[3] Leprosy, syphilis and perhaps plague; no satisfactory explanation for this curious list seems available. See Holdsworth, viii. 349.

offence was imputed, unless the court had the means of trying the truth of the imputation, which would most commonly be put in issue by the defence.

Real as this difficulty was, the common law courts were ready to circumvent it. They had by this time resolved to entertain actions where the imputation was one of merely spiritual offences,[1] if special damage was proved, and were apparently ready to deal in their own way with an issue on a plea of justification. The formal reason for the distinction between the two classes of slander therefore became fictitious rather than real. The distinction unfortunately persisted, and we may well ask why the common law, which was making such energetic advances in the law of slander, should have stopped short at this point.

The answer most probably lies in the fact that the common law courts were dismayed at the mass of slander cases which came before it. This almost certainly was a new phenomenon; lawyers do not generally complain of too much business, and as a rule we have seen courts competing keenly for business. They realised, however, that there was some sort of social problem involved in defamation. The Star Chamber seems to have felt that severity was the proper remedy; the common law preferred to discourage such litigation, hoping, perhaps, that the effervescence of the Shakespearean age would soon subside.[2] Now the requirement of special damage was an admirable means of excluding a large class of cases which might plausibly be regarded as frivolous, and so the retention, and indeed the increased emphasis on this distinction, may well be attributed to the policy of discouraging actions for defamation.

They even went further, and deliberately debased the quality of the law in order to stem the demand. In this period, and in the eighteenth century also, much ingenuity was spent in arguing that words be taken *in mitiori sensu*, and should not be construed as defamatory unless no other meaning could be read into them. Great pains were necessary in pleading to escape this rule. Thus, in one well-known case, it was held not actionable to say that " Sir Thomas Holt struck his cook on the head with a cleaver and cleaved his head; the one part lay on one shoulder and another part on the other ", for it does not appear that the cook was dead, and so the imputation may be only of a trespass; as the court observed, a little ambiguously, " slander ought to be direct ".[3] So too if a married woman says: " *A*. stole my turkeys ", the words are not actionable, for a married woman could have no property in chattels;[4] a few years earlier, however, this rather fine point had been rejected.[5]

[1] *Davis* v. *Gardiner*, above, p. 494 n. 1.

[2] The legislature also took steps to discourage frivolous actions of slander by enacting that if the jury in actions on slander find the damages less than forty shillings, then the plaintiff shall not be awarded more than forty shillings costs: 21 James I, c. 16 (1624); cf. p. 174, above.

[3] *Holt* v. *Astrigg* (1607), Cro. Jac. 184.

[4] *Anon.* (1613), 1 Roll. Abr. 74 b, pl. 1.

[5] *Charnel's Case* (1592), Cro. Eliz. 279.

The law regarding publication was already receiving attention, although it had not yet reached a satisfactory position. Publication to a third party was clearly necessary, for in no other way could damage result; but a curious doctrine—perhaps imitated from the statute *De Scandalis Magnatum*—was sanctioned by the *dicta* in the *Earl of Northampton Case*[1] that one can justify a slander if it is merely a repetition of what someone else said. Thus if *A.* says that *B.* said something defamatory of *C.*, then *A.* could justify by proving that *B.* did in fact use those words.

Somewhat in a class by itself was slander of title. This consisted in false statements by a third party to an intending purchaser of land throwing doubt upon the vendor's title, in consequence of which the negotiations for the sale are broken off. Examples occur from 1585 onwards, and one of the earliest cases[2] had already made it clear that the action would not lie where the third person himself pretended, rightly or wrongly, to be entitled.

The state of the law of slander at this period is quickly seen from an examination of any old abridgment, when it will be clear that a vast mass of case law was accumulating at such a pace that lawyers had to compile dictionaries, as it were, of abusive and obscene expressions (including slang) in order to ascertain how particular language had been treated in previous cases. It will also be apparent that many highly damaging expressions were held to be not defamatory at all, or only with special damage, while others, seemingly less serious, fell under the ban. As Sir William Holdsworth remarked,[3] perhaps the worst kind of case law is that which grows up around the interpretation of words, deeds, wills—and we may add, statutes.

THE RESULTS OF THE FALL OF THE STAR CHAMBER

With the abolition of the Star Chamber as from August 1, 1641, a new situation was created. For twenty years confusion was inevitable. Cromwell's Council of State had to continue the more questionable practices of the Star Chamber, and at the Restoration it was clear that much useful work done by the Star Chamber would have to be continued by constitutional means. It was therefore tacitly assumed that the Court of King's Bench succeeded to as much of the Star Chamber's jurisdiction as was consistent with current constitutional thought. Consequently the Star Chamber's law of libel was henceforth to be administered by the same court as had developed the common law of slander; inevitably the two bodies of law were bound to influence each other, and tended to become more coherently combined into something approaching a systematic law of defamation.

As we have seen, the law of slander operated very capriciously, and

---

[1] (1612) 12 Rep. 132. This rule was finally abandoned two hundred years later.

[2] Gerrard *v.* Dickenson (1590) 4 Rep. 18; see the references in Holdsworth, viii. 351.

[3] Holdsworth, v. 358–359.

it is natural that more enlightened judges should try to amend it, or, failing that, to use their new jurisdiction in " libel " to mitigate its defects. Holt, Hale and Twisden tried to establish a rational rule that " words should stand on their own feet " and be deemed to have the meaning which bystanders would naturally give them, but were unsuccessful.[1] Partial relief came from the fact that the law of libel was not encumbered with the *mitior sensus* rule, and was also free from the requirement of special damage. It therefore only remained to find some way which would bring cases out of the category of common law slander into the category of libel. As early as 1670 Hale allowed an action on words which were too vague to be a common law slander, because in this case the words were written.[2] He took the view that many defamatory words spoken in heat could be safely ignored, but if they were written, then the obvious presence of malice would make them actionable, and actionable without special damage. The law of libel was thus used to supplement the law of slander. But as in so many other cases, the law was ready to admit a novelty, but reluctant to abolish an anachronism. The newer and more rational law of libel was welcomed gladly in cases of written defamation, but the *mitior sensus* rule and the rules about words actionable *per se*, and words actionable on special damage, remained in force if the defamation was by speech only. The distinction between spoken and written defamation therefore became vital, and has proved to be permanent.

The Star Chamber generally treated libel as a crime, although occasionally the award of damages shows that it might be considered also as a tort. But it is clear that the Star Chamber did not take any pains to distinguish the criminal from the tortious aspect of defamation, for there was no particular need for it. In the common law courts, however, the line between crime and tort was fairly clear, and highly important. Hence the Star Chamber rule that truth is no defence had to be reconsidered when libel came into the common law courts. They naturally retained their own rule about justification when dealing with libel as a tort (thus keeping it parallel with slander), and followed the Star Chamber rule for criminal libels.

The Star Chamber had little law on privilege as a defence, although there is some indication that it recognised statements made in the course of judicial proceedings as being to some extent privileged. The common law began to recognise privilege[3] as early as 1569, and by 1606 held that the privilege could be lost if malice was present.[4] These beginnings, however, did not develop to any great extent until the time of Lord Mansfield.

---

[1] *Somers* v. *House* (1693), Holt, K.B. 39; *Baker* v. *Pierce* (1703), 6 Mod. 24; *Harrison* v. *Thornborough* (1714), 10 Mod. 198.

[2] *King* v. *Lake* (1670), Hardres, 470; Skinner, 124.

[3] *Lord Beauchamp* v. *Croft* (1569), Dyer, 285 *a*.

[4] *Brook* v. *Montague* (1606), Cro. Jac. 90.

The law of slander has undergone very little substantial change in England since the close of the seventeenth century. The distinction between slanders actionable *per se* and those actionable only for special damage has undergone very little change. One exceptionally hard case, however, has been remedied by the legislature. The imputation of unchastity in a woman was not generally an imputation of a temporal crime, and so was not actionable *per se*. A few local jurisdictions, notably London, claimed a custom of carting " whores ". The city courts, therefore, treated the use of this expression as actionable *per se*, and after some hesitation extended the rule to a few other terms of similar import, but it is doubtful whether the common law courts would recognise the custom.[1] Not until 1891 did the Slander of Women Act make imputations of unchastity actionable *per se*.[2] In America, many states have enlarged the class of slanders actionable *per se*, and some states have gone so far as to abolish the requirement of special damage.

LIBEL AND THE PRESS

The invention of printing was not at first put to the ephemeral although dangerous use of political controversy, but as soon as the reduction of costs permitted this new development, governments throughout Europe had to deal with the problem of the press.

A long line of proclamations and statutes dealt with the new menace. According to one enactment, printing might constitute a statutory treason,[3] and succeeding statutes settled a policy of treating printing as an overt action of treason.[4] Still more numerous were the proclamations which regulated the book trade. As early as 1538 a proclamation required a licence from the Privy Council or a bishop before any English book could be printed,[5] and for a century and a half there is a steady stream of proclamations directed against unlicensed printing, and heretical and seditious literature. The system of licensing plays was regulated by proclamation[6] in 1661, although it was in fact a century old by this time, and many statutes from 1543 onwards[7] punished profane interludes and plays. Statutory in its origin, the control of the stage was finally appropriated as part of the prerogative after the Restoration. A proclamation of 1668 tried to prevent the hawking of newspapers in the streets,[8] and in 1688 the peddling of books was forbidden,[9] after a vain attempt to

---

[1] *Treyer* v. *Eastwick* (1767), 4 Burr. 2032.

[2] 54 & 55 Vict., c. 51.

[3] 25 Hen. VIII, c. 22, s. 5 (1534); Tanner, *Tudor Constitutional Documents*, 386.

[4] 1 Edw. VI, c. 12, s. 6 (1547); Tanner, *op. cit.*, 403. Compare 13 Eliz., c. 1 (1571); Tanner, *op. cit.*, 414.

[5] Steele, *Tudor and Stuart Proclamations*, i. no. 176.

[6] *Ibid.*, no. 3316.

[7] 34 & 35 Hen. VIII, c. 1 (1543).

[8] Steele, *op. cit.*, no. 3516.

[9] *Ibid.*, no. 3859.

license the pedlars.[1] Meanwhile the legitimate book trade, like other trades in the middle ages, was put under the regulation of a city company, the stationers,[2] while enforcement lay with the Privy Council, the Star Chamber, and (for theological matters) the High Commission, who took the view that all printing, however innocent, was a crime unless the work had been previously licensed. Conversely, the government would sometimes give monopoly rights of printing works which it considered meritorious or useful, and in this way the beginnings of copyright appear.

Amid such a vast mass of regulation, there was little need for the law of libel, as far as the press was concerned. The abolition of the Star Chamber and the Court of High Commission, however, left a void which the common law was later called upon to fill. The fall of these courts, moreover, removed the notion that press offences were peculiarly matters of the royal prerogative, and so legislation became increasingly important. Now as long as the Star Chamber and High Commission lasted, legislation on the press had been almost entirely by proclamation.[3] The events of 1641, therefore, created the utmost confusion, and the stationers' company put in a powerful memorial to the victorious Parliament showing that public safety depended on the continued control of the press, that the economic position of printers, publishers and authors had come to depend on the existence of copyright, and that the practical working of copyright depended on the company, which in effect kept a register of copyrights. They further argued that copyrights were property, that they ought to be as assignable as other forms of property, and that their destruction was unthinkable.[4]

The Parliaments of the interregnum, therefore, maintained the system and set up boards of licensers. At the Restoration the system was continued intermittently by statute until 1692, when the current act came to an end. A pamphlet controversy ensued, the act was renewed until 1694, when it was finally allowed to expire.

Once again a large mass of press law came to a sudden end. After a prolonged controversy, the Copyright Act[5] of 1709 retrieved the results of nearly two centuries of effort to establish literary property, while the common law courts had to rely on the law of treason, sedition and libel to carry out whatever control of the press might be needed.

It was no longer possible to say that printing was criminal merely because it was unauthorised, and so some positive ingredients of press

---

[1] Steele, *Tudor and Stuart Proclamations*, no. 3832.

[2] Holdsworth, vi. 362 ff., sketches their history, and the origin of copyright.

[3] See the Order in Council of 1566 in Tanner, *Tudor Constitutional Documents*, 245 (and in Prothero, *Select Statutes and Constitutional Documents*, 168), and the Star Chamber ordinance of 1586 in Tanner, *op. cit.*, 279 (and in Prothero, *op. cit.*, 169).

[4] From the earliest days of English printing, the Crown had issued its " privilege ": A. W. Reed, *Early Tudor Drama*, 176–186, 205.

[5] 8 Anne, c. 19; for the great question whether copyright exists at common law or is merely statutory, see Holdsworth, vi. 377–379.

offences had to be sought. Holt thought that " it is very necessary for all governments that the people should have a good opinion of it "[1] and from this it seemed to follow that any publication which reflected upon the Government was criminal. The same idea was applied to libels against private persons which brought them into hatred, ridicule or contempt. The Star Chamber, moreover, had permitted much strong language by plaintiffs against defendants, of which " maliciously " in the description of publication was characteristic. As long as libels were normally the outcome of reckless sedition and factiousness the term was appropriate, but under changed conditions it caused much trouble later on.

LIBEL AND JURY TRIAL

The law of libel had little contact with juries in its early days, and when that contact finally occurred, there was much controversy as to the position of the jury. The earliest cases seem to run on the principle that the jury should find the facts, and that the court should determine whether the matter published constituted a libel. A remarkable exception was the trial of the Seven Bishops, which, as several writers have observed, was altogether so anomalous that no argument, legal or historical, can be based on it.[2] In the eighteenth century the absence of a licensing system thrust the whole burden of surveillance over the press upon the courts, and trials for seditious libel grew steadily more frequent. The nature of malice and the question of intent were much discussed, and there arose an opinion that the jury were entitled to give a general verdict of guilty or not guilty according to their own opinion whether the writing constituted a libel. It required all Erskine's eloquence to make this look plausible in the face of the mass of authority which was against him; indeed, the basis of his view was not legal, but political, and his famous argument in the *Dean of St. Asaph's Case*[3] was delivered more in the hope of stimulating Parliament to change the law, than of convincing Mansfield that the law was in his favour. He failed in the latter, but succeeded in the former object, and in 1792 Fox's Libel Act[4] was passed, in spite of the unanimous opinion given by the judges at the demand of the House of Lords.[5] In form declaratory, it was in substance a momentous change in the law of libel. Until 1792 the strict legal theory has been accurately summed up in these words: " a seditious libel means written censure upon any public man whatever for any conduct whatever, or upon any law or institution whatever ".[6] The crime consisted in the publication of matter of a particular sort, and not in the publisher's

---

[1] *R.* v. *Tutchin* (1704), 14 S.T. 1095, at 1128.

[2] 12 S.T. 183 (1688); Stephen, ii. 315; Holdsworth, vi. 344. Similar causes produced a like result in the case of Peter Zenger in New York (1734).

[3] *R.* v. *Shipey* (1783), 21 S.T. 847, at 971, discussed at length in Stephen, ii. 330–343.

[4] 32 Geo. III, c. 60.

[5] 22 S.T. 296.

[6] Stephen, ii. 350.

intention. The obscurity of a proviso robbed the act for a time of some of its effect,[1] but inevitably there followed the result that juries would not regard the expression of reasonable political dissent as being criminal; criminality therefore shifted from the nature of the words to the intention of the writer. It is a curious reflection that the unnecessarily picturesque language of indictments, even before the act, loaded the defendant with abuse which was technically superfluous, although it had the effect of seeming to put the defendant's intention in issue. Thus the Dean of St. Asaph was indicted as " being a person of wicked and turbulent disposition, and maliciously designing and intending to excite and diffuse among the subjects of this realm discontents, jealousies and suspicions of our lord the King and his Government, and disaffection and disloyalty . . . and to raise very dangerous seditions and tumults "— with much more irrelevant matter as to the defendant's intent.[2]

Before the act, criticism, because it was criticism, rendered those who published it guilty of libel. After the act the application of this rule of law was left to the jury, and they quite naturally would not regard as criminal expressions whose offensiveness consisted merely in being distasteful to the authorities. It took many years, however, before a new definition of seditious libel was reached. This was probably due to the fact that the revolutionary wars soon began, and for some time juries found themselves on the side of the government rather than of its critics; they certainly felt, too, that expressions might become dangerous at moments of intense political excitement although in normal circumstances they would do no harm. The likelihood that the publication would produce tumult or disorder was, therefore, frequently considered as the principal factor in deciding whether a publication was criminal or not.

LIBEL AND NEWSPAPERS

Seditious libel became rarer after the Reform Act of 1832 and the cessation of the war had relieved some, at least, of the tension in political affairs. The rise of newspapers, however, created special problems in connection with libels on private persons.

In the course of the eighteenth century it was gradually being settled that although truth was not an absolute defence in libel, yet it could be proved in order to reduce damages or mitigate punishment.[3] Lord Campbell's Act[4] introduced another mitigating circumstance, namely that a prompt and suitable apology had been published, while in civil cases a newspaper owner might further show that the libel was inserted without malice and without negligence. In criminal cases the act made

[1] As to this curious point, see Stephen, ii. 246.

[2] Stephen ii. 353 n.

[3] The authorities (which are very obscure and conflicting) are collected in 5 Bac. Abr. 203–205.

[4] 6 & 7 Vict. (1843), c. 96.

truth a defence (thus reversing an age-old doctrine) if it could be shown that publication was for the public benefit. In 1881 elaborate arrangements were made for the registration of newspapers with the object of enabling the public to ascertain whom to sue,[1] and in 1888 the legislature dealt with the common difficulty when a newspaper published a report of a public meeting in the course of which defamatory matter was spoken and reported. In such cases the act conferred a qualified privilege, which may be lost if there was malice, or if the report was unfair or inaccurate.[2]

[1] 44 & 45 Vict. (1881), c. 60.

[2] 51 & 52 Vict. (1888), c. 64. The great constitutional case of *Stockdale* v. *Hansard* (1839), 9 Ad. & E. 1, raised the question whether privilege attached to publications authorised by the House of Commons. The Parliamentary Papers Act, 1840 (3 & 4 Vict. c. 9), conferred absolute privilege on such publications. The courts by decision accorded qualified privilege on reports of parliamentary debates in *Wason* v. *Walter* (1868), L.R., 4 Q.B. 73, which thus established the principle which was extended to public meetings by the act of 1888; documents strictly connected with legal or parliamentary proceedings, and not otherwise published, were privileged since the sixteenth and seventeenth centuries.

PART 3

REAL PROPERTY

SUMMARY

REAL PROPERTY

Real property law has been the battle-ground in most of the great struggles in our history. One of the bitterest conflicts between Church and State arose out of Henry II's determination that patronage was "lay fee", that is to say, real property amenable to the jurisdiction of the royal courts. Even earlier, the great social revolution which created feudalism, created thereby the foundations of the law of real property, and when the equally great revolution, late in the middle ages, replaced feudalism by the beginnings of modern society, we find corresponding changes in the law of land. Public law, too, owes much to the principles first worked out in connection with land. The barons won a notable victory against King John when they established the inviolability of the freeholder's land, and the law of freehold served the cause of freedom centuries later.

It is in terms of real property law that such social factors as the rise, and still stranger decline, of serfdom must be expressed, while the emergence of a mercantile community had important results which even went so far (as we have already seen) as the creation of peculiar mercantile estates in land. The long and obscure story of settlements and disentailing devices reflects not only social problems and the difficulty of expressing the family itself in terms of real property law, but also illustrates the growth of land as a commodity with a market value, and shows that land (especially in the eighteenth century) was now the object of intensive exploitation which required the sinking of considerable capital sums—and often this could only be achieved by selling or charging settled land. Corresponding difficulties existed even on the purely physical side, and so there came the enclosure movement which rapidly changed the face of the countryside. An economic history of the law of real property has not yet been written, and this is not the place to attempt so difficult a task; nevertheless, some reference to economic and social factors must be made in the pages that follow, even if they fail to receive all the weight to which they would be entitled in a fuller discussion.

CHAPTER 1

FEUDALISM

It is universally admitted that the great historical feature of our law of real property is its feudal character, and that in order to understand the reasons which brought about a good many doctrines of real property law it is necessary to regard the matter from the feudal point of view. Something, therefore, must be said as to the origin and characteristics of feudalism.[1]

If we had to sum up the social characteristics of the present age in one word, that word would probably be " capitalism ". If, on the other hand, we wish to describe the early middle ages in a similar way, we shall have to say that they were feudal. " Feudalism ", in fact, is merely a vague and general word describing the social structure of Western Europe from the tenth century onwards. It is beyond doubt that the word " feudalism " is just as vague and occasionally inaccurate as is the word " capitalism ". Society at the present day contains a number of different characteristics, some of them being inconsistent with a complete capitalism. When we speak of the present age as capitalistic it is perfectly easy to make all the obvious exceptions which are necessary in order to make the statement approximately true. There is no difficulty in doing this because we are perfectly familiar with the conditions of our own age. When we come to mediaeval times, however, the same problem arises in

[1] Two great classics have illuminated this subject: (1) F. L. Ganshof, *Qu'est-ce que la Féodalité?* (1944, 1947), translated by Philip Grierson as *Feudalism* (1952), and (2) Marc Bloch, *La Société féodale*, 2 vols., 1939, 1940). The *Cambridge Economic History* and the *Cambridge Medieval History* contain several valuable chapters.

a more difficult form. At no time were the middle ages completely and consistently feudal, any more than our own age is thoroughly capitalistic. The difficulty, of course, is to trace the exceptions to the more general feudalism in view of our unfamiliarity with mediaeval conditions. It must be constantly remembered, therefore, that " feudalism " is a vague word of modern origin which was completely unknown in the ages to which we apply it, and that it is nothing more than a rough generalisation upon the character of mediaeval society. It must likewise be remembered that mediaeval society varied considerably in different years and in different places, and that it is very difficult to find a state which continued for an appreciable length of time under strictly feudal conditions.

FEUDALISM: LORD AND MAN

There are a few characteristics which remain fairly constant through the feudal age, and which may be regarded as typically feudal. In the first place a prominent feature of it is the relationship of the lord and man. In its personal aspect this was felt to be a solemn and sacred bond; it was accompanied by an impressive ceremony called homage, and once that ceremony was performed it was hardly possible to dissolve the relationship. The obligations of mutual aid and support which grew out of it may perhaps owe their sacred character to the fact that they were so absolutely necessary to the preservation of society at the time when the institution arose. With a small and scattered populace, organisation became difficult, especially with the absence of all the modern mechanical devices which have made the power of the State paramount. Where a modern nation in a week or two can mobilise an army of millions of conscripts, the feudal age had to rely upon the relationship of homage to secure the attendance of its military forces. Society depended to a very great degree upon the fulfilment of the obligations arising out of homage, and therefore surrounded the ceremony with every available religious and social sanction. Even then, under some circumstances, a vassal could dissolve the relationship binding him to his lord if he gave proper notice in a form which was technically called " defiance ". The feudal relation of lord and man was therefore on its practical side decidedly weak; it was only while the religious and social sanctity attaching to homage endured that a lord could have any reasonable dependence upon the armed assistance of his vassals. Where so much hung upon the good faith of undertenants it is only natural that the power of the State should be very weak.

FEUDALISM AND LAND

The relationship of lord and man was most usually accompanied by a peculiarity in the law of land. In the days when feudalism was at its height, the vassal held his land of the lord. Originally the vassal's interest was not large. He might forfeit his land for any great breach

of the homage-relationship such as was described by the shameful word
" felony "; in any case his interest was only for life, and whether the
lord regranted the land after the tenant's death to any of his descendants
or kindred was a matter which rested in the lord's discretion. It will
therefore be seen that feudalism implied land holding rather than land
owning, save in the case of those few great lords and princes who had
no superior, and therefore owned their lands, both those they retained
and those which they granted out, by absolute right.

FEUDALISM AS A MILITARY SYSTEM

A third characteristic of feudalism was the fact that to the combination
of these two relationships of lord and man, landlord and tenant, was
added a system of military organisation. The vassal who held land of
his lord was bound by his tenure to provide a certain amount of military
assistance, and for this purpose the land was organised into units, each
one of which was charged with the provision of a certain number of
knights armed and mounted and attended by the requisite number of
subsidiary arms in squires and sergeants. This system of military service
lasted as long as the knight himself continued to be the basis of military
organisation. As time went on, the knight, who at first had been
an extremely mobile unit, gradually became more cumbersome. His
growing social importance necessitated measures for his protection, and
these took the form of heavy armament both for the horse and his rider.
This reduced his mobility, and when in the end the long bow was invented
the knight ceased to be of practical importance in warfare. Nevertheless,
the organisation of the land into knight's fees and the exaction of military
service still survived, together with many other elements of feudalism.
Consequently we have in the later middle ages the perpetuation for legal
and fiscal purposes of a feudalism which had long since ceased to represent
current conditions. In England the fiscal side of knight-service was in
fairly frequent operation until it was abolished in 1660, four hundred
years after it had ceased to be the working foundation of the military
system. Other aspects of feudalism, such as dependent tenure, have
never been abolished in England, and are presumed to exist still in some
jurisdictions even in America.

Feudalism arose largely out of military necessity and was a measure
to cope with a grave military situation—the invasion of Europe by the
Norse. Consequently in all fields of life the military expert was pre-
dominant, and for a time even overshadowed his great mediaeval rival,
the religious expert. Between the two of them, the military and the
clergy, there was little room for anything else. So grave was the crisis
that populations willingly (and wisely) accepted the domination of the
knights and the clergy as the only means of saving Europe and its culture
from barbarian invaders, and both of them did their duty. But the
social consequences of this were serious and showed how high a price

had to be paid for such precarious security as feudalism could afford. Towns and city life were hard put to it to find a place in the feudal system, while the peasantry had no alternative but to accept serfdom.

FEUDALISM AS A CONSTITUTION

Finally, all these elements so combined that they served the place of public law and a constitution. The defence of Europe had to be carried out throughout the length of its coast line at very widely scattered points; there were no railways and no telegraphs. It would therefore have been impossible for a government in Paris, for example, to defend France from attacks which might take place at any point upon the Channel, the Atlantic or the Mediterranean. It was therefore necessary to go to extreme lengths of decentralisation, and so we find another element of feudalism which consists in allowing each lord to assume governmental powers over his tenants. Whatever military defence is undertaken must be carried out by local forces organised and led by local leaders, and consequently it is necessary that those leaders should exercise powers of government within their locality. The tenant, therefore, owes to his lord fidelity, military service and counsel (which is expressed as an obligation to attend his lord whenever summoned, whether it be for services in the field or at the council table), and is subject to his lord's jurisdiction. And so the dogma will arise that every lord can hold a court for his tenants, compel their presence in it, and do justice to them in matters arising within the fee.

It will therefore be seen that the feudal age denied a good many things which in our own day are taken for granted. Feudalism implies the absence of anything corresponding to the State; each lord has jurisdiction over his tenants, and they in turn over their undertenants, and allegiance is owed to the lord to whom homage has been done. So, too, property in land as we know it to-day is inconsistent with thoroughly feudal conditions; while even the waging of war was not a national concern but was left to be the occupation of those whose tenure obliged them to undertake it.

All these characteristics of feudalism which we have described in general terms are subject to infinite variation in every quarter of Europe, and although we, at a distance of nearly a thousand years, can survey them all together as aspects of one social structure which we call feudalism, yet it must be remembered that to contemporaries it may very well have been the diversity rather than the unity which seemed most striking. The word "feudalism", once again, is merely a modern generalisation about mediaeval society.

CONTINENTAL ORIGINS OF FEUDALISM

A few indications may be given concerning the origins of feudalism, especially on the continent, for English conditions were apt to reproduce,

and even to imitate, society abroad.   Although some of the main lines
of development which finally produced feudalism have now become
fairly established, there still remains a great deal of controversy upon
innumerable points, and upon the relative influence which different
institutions had in the development of the final product.   Feudalism, in
fact, is not only the sum-total of a number of different institutions existing
at the same time, all of which contributed to promote the same end,
namely, the government and defence of the land, but is also the product
of many different lines of development, some of them coming from widely
separated places, which have converged and finally given rise to the state
of society called feudalism.

THE COMITATUS

There is, for example, the *comitatus*, of which we first hear in Caesar
and in Tacitus, both of whom describe the Germanic tribes as having a
social custom whereby a great chief would surround himself with a band
of chosen warriors and enter into a close personal bond with them.
They formed a fraternity for military adventure and seem to have lived
upon the spoils of war.   The *comitatus* steadily increased in importance,
and when finally many of the barbarians peacefully settled within the
Roman Empire, they found there a Roman institution of somewhat
similar character whereby a general or an Emperor would engage a
band of soldiers (often barbarians) for his personal service, such soldiers
being called *bucellarii*; it seems that the general provided a military outfit
for each of the men, which reverted to him after their death.   In the
history of the fifth and sixth centuries we find a great deal about the
doings of such bands of warriors.   The points of contact with later
feudalism seem to be the performance of a ceremonial oath of fidelity,
and the obligation, upon the man's death, to give or return to his lord
a varying amount of military equipment.   It is fairly clear that a similar
institution existed in England, where we read of thegns and gesiths.
With the gradual settlement of society both the chief and his train became
more fixed; the chief became something like a provincial governor and
his followers then settled down with him and became his household
and official staff.   In France there was such a class of court officials
called *sejones*, and in England, especially under the Danish kings, we find
a group of " huscarls " who not only fought around King Harold as his
bodyguard, but could also be sent around the country as administrative
officials to collect taxes.   Later still these officials tended to leave the
court and settled in the country, supporting themselves upon grants of
land from the King, who, however, still obliged them to serve him upon
demand.

THE PATROCINIUM

Another line of development which finally mingled with the former
was that of patronage—and here we have not a Germanic, but a Roman

institution.[1] Its general outline somewhat resembled the *comitatus*, except that it never had the marked military character of the Germanic institution. Patronage had a long history under the Republic and later under the Empire. As early as the year 122 it had become in some cases hereditary, but this, of course, was merely a matter of custom; patronage was no part of Roman law and was not an element of the political constitution, although it was a most powerful social institution. Many patrons had hundreds of clients, and here again we find the word " faith " closely connected with the relationship. Quite frequently a whole town would put itself in the faith of one person, such clients being described as commending themselves to their patron, the significance of which seems to have been that the client delivered himself over to the patron relying upon the patron's faith.[2] There were several ranks among clients and their principal obligation seems to have been to give service and counsel to their chief—in plainer words, they acted very much like a political " machine " as the expression is understood in America. The patron in turn defended his clients in litigation, and we may easily imagine that the support of a powerful patron was a great advantage.

In the Theodosian code (438) we find an attempt to prevent clients commending their lands as well as themselves; but it is equally clear that this attempt was unsuccessful and that nothing could prevent the spread of the practice of patrons getting control over the land as well as the persons of their clients. It would seem that this development was prompted by the rigours of the taxation system. The one sphere of government in which Rome was inefficient was that of taxation, and this defect contributed very largely to the distintegration of Roman society. The taxation fell heaviest on the smaller propertied class and their inability to support the burden eventually depressed that class into the condition of dependent tenants. The practice of commending land, as well as oneself, to a patron was an important step in this direction. At first it was merely a device whereby the patron assumed responsibility towards the State for taxes due, in return spreading the burden of taxation more evenly for the client. We also find patronage transferred to France, where it is clear that the French patronage is a direct descendant from the Roman. In France it sometimes took the name of a " trust ".[3] By this time the Church had acquired extremely wide property in land, and bishops and abbots were among the most powerful people in the country, and consequently we find a good deal of commendation to great ecclesiastics.

[1] See F. de Zulueta, *Patronage in the Later Empire* (Oxford Studies in Social and Legal History, vol. i), 1909.

[2] Note the contrast between the *comitatus* and feudal custom, where the lord demanded faith from the man.

[3] See Du Cange, *Glossarium* (1887), s.v. " Trustis ".

THE PRECARIA

An important part in this development was played by a legal institution called the *precarium*, which we must now consider. The *precarium* has a very long history in Rome, where it was closely associated with patronage, although for a long time the law took no notice of it save to attempt to abolish it. Roman lawyers had made certain categories into which property interests could be divided; there were ownership, possession, and usufruct. But the *precarium* could not be placed under any of these heads. Our first legal definition of it is by Ulpian at the beginning of the third century, who says that "a *precarium* is granted to a petitioner in answer to his prayers, for his use and for as long as the grantor pleases ".[1] It is the prayer or petition which is the characteristic of the *precarium*. The recipient gets the land as an outcome of his urgent petition. The characteristics of the *precarium* were, therefore, that it conveyed only the enjoyment of the property. The arrangement was terminated by the death of either party, the grantor (*rogatus*) or grantee (*rogans*). More than that, it was technically an act of charity and could therefore be revoked at any moment. Its legal position was anomalous; in one respect it was superior to the lease, for it conferred possession, but in others it was inferior, since it was not based upon contract. Gradually the praetor protected the *precarium* against third parties, although, of course, not against the *rogatus*. This arrangement was frequently used by embarrassed debtors, who would surrender their lands to their creditor and receive them back as a *precarium*, for in this way the debtor was assured of his immediate future while the creditor in the end received a good deal more than the original debt.

The combination of patronage and the system of *precaria* was inevitable, and the two together played a large part in the establishment of the *latifundia* or immense landed estates worked finally by slave labour, if at all. The *precarium* continued in use with increasing influence; late in the fifth century we find it described by Salvianus, who observes that it is revocable at will, that it confers a tenancy and not ownership, that the tenant owes gratitude to the donor, being bound to him in good faith, and that the breach of this faith will make him *ingratissimus* and *infidelissimus*—two of the most serious reproaches which could be made.

In the sixth century and onwards it is clear that the Church is a lavish grantor of *precaria*, and so the *precarium* passes to France and mingles with the general stream of influences which were finally to create feudal society. At the same time a number of changes take place. The *precarium* may be for life, or even for a number of generations; on the other hand, it may be merely for five years, although renewable on paying a very moderate rent, and this latter was generally called a *precaria*

---

[1] Dig. 43.26.1.

instead of a *precarium*.[1] Its origin seems to lie in a different quarter from the true *precarium*.[2]

GRANTS BY THE CROWN

This brings us to the deliberate attempt made by the French monarchs to remodel these institutions. The sixth and seventh centuries are occupied in French history by the Merovingian dynasty, which made a great attempt to establish a national government under almost impossible conditions. Their main difficulty was that of finance, for the Roman system of taxation was now unworkable and the Crown domain was fast becoming exhausted by the number of grants which the Crown had to make to reward its faithful servants. The solution which the Merovingians found was only partially successful. They seem to have rewarded their public servants by grants of land which in form were unqualified, but in practice were subject to vague conditions. The succession of the donee's heirs was a matter of favour rather than right; the donee could not alienate, and the grant was revoked if the donee incurred the grave displeasure of the King. The grant might also be conditional upon continued service, as well as a reward for past services.

THE CAROLINGIAN POLICY

This policy was not drastic enough to rescue the Merovingian kings from their financial difficulties, and their increasing powerlessness finally prepared the way for a new royal house, the Carolingians, which sprang from their own Mayors of the Palace. Under these vigorous statesmen the problem was attacked anew and at its centre, the Church. At first it was proposed to confiscate ecclesiastical lands outright and grant them to royal nominees; or as an alternative wealthy monasteries might be compelled to support a certain number of soldiers, while we occasionally find that some lay official will be provided for by appointing him abbot of a monastery. These unseemly[3] measures in the end gave way to a compromise reached by Pepin the Short in 743, according to which the Church granted lands to royal nominees to be held as *precariae*, owing services to the Crown and a very moderate rent to the Church.

There were other forces, too, which were making the Church the overlord of land. A great deal of its wealth came not from the great nobles but from the much smaller landowners who hoped to atone for their crimes and win spiritual favours by surrendering to the Church

---

[1] The Church had so much more land than she could use, that when she took an estate and gave it back as a *precaria* she usually added to it from her own estates; the *rogans* thus generally got twice as much as he had surrendered.

[2] There has been much controversy over this (and most other matters connected with the early history of feudalism). See Esmein, *Histoire du droit fran ais* (ed. Génestal), 122, for a summary.

[3] In the view of some historians the Crown had a legal right to mobilise the wealth of the Church in grave national emergencies. See Esmein, *Histoire du droit français* (ed. Génestal), 126.

free land and receiving it back by precarious tenure. It will be noticed that by this time the *precaria*, instead of being sought, is rather offered, and so we get an institution whose name is really a contradiction in terms —the *precaria oblata*. Churches would frequently have scattered estates, some of them quite remote from the bulk of the Church's interests, and in order to secure a revenue from these outlying lands the *precaria* was used once again as a means of letting them to tenants who would work them and pay a moderate rent. All these different types of *precariae*, together with the various forms of royal grant, had one element in common—the good will of the grantor; it is not surprising, therefore, that in time they are classified together, whatever their origin, under the name " benefices ". The word " benefice " has in fact been traced back to the particular sort of " benefit " whereby a *precaria* was granted for life, and gratuitously.[1]

MILITARY SERVICE

To these developments was soon to be added the factor of military service. It would seem that before the middle of the eighth century military service had become an obligation of those precarious tenures which had been instituted in response to the King's request. Charles the Great at the beginning of the ninth century had established the rule that all were liable to military service and not merely those who held of the Crown in chief, and consequently he had to make arrangements whereby the poorer men could join together in meeting the expenses of one of their number. By the end of the Carolingian period military service was becoming systematised, and early in the eleventh century the knight's fee appeared as a definite institution in Normandy. Indeed, the division of land into districts, each with an allotted quota of men and material, is a simple and obvious device; we find, for example, in 1679 that an act in Virginia required each district to provide one man armed and mounted for service in the Indian wars.[2]

JURISDICTION

We have now to consider the connection between land holding and jurisdiction. The factors which made for this development were to be found in both German and Roman institutions. Under Germanic custom every freeman had jurisdiction over his household, and this jurisdiction frequently took the form of holding him responsible for certain police measures. At the same time there was a tendency for large landed estates to be organised as separate concerns by their owners with little or no reference to the ordinary public jurisdiction; a striking example of this is the persistence of the ancient demesne of the Crown in England, which for some centuries held a position outside of the common law. On the

---

[1] Esmein, *Histoire du droit français* (ed. Génestal), 127 n. 302.

[2] Virginia Statutes at Large, ii. 434, 435.

Roman side there were even stronger tendencies in this direction. In the fifth and sixth centuries we find immunities granted to landowners, sometimes including an exemption from the visits of imperial justices, while at the same time the frequent grants of the profit of jurisdiction naturally led to the exercise of that jurisdiction by the grantee in an endeavour to make the most of his profits.

THE FEUDAL COURT

In Germany it seems clear that there were two different types of feudal court, each of which had its special history. Of these one was based directly upon the relationship between lord and vassal, while the other seems to have been originally a communal court which later fell under the control of some neighbouring landowner. It has recently been suggested[1] that the rise of feudal jurisdiction in France followed rather different lines, and that these two types of feudal court are not at first distinguished. The question therefore arises as to whether the origin of French feudal jurisdiction must be sought in the relationship of lord and vassal or in the appropriation of once public courts by private owners. There is reason to believe that French feudal jurisdiction did in fact derive from the old public courts, and in some cases it has been possible to trace the stages by which the transition was made. The Frankish equivalent for the county court was the *mallus*, in which, as in our own communal courts, judgment was given by suitors (often called *échevins*) who very frequently were obliged to fulfil this office because they were the holders of particular pieces of land. The office of these *échevins*, therefore, became hereditary in many cases. It has been shown, however, that the *mallus* at times begins to consider cases which are really feudal in character while simultaneously the *échevins* become rarer and finally disappear, for their duties must have been very burdensome and their attendance at court difficult to enforce. The count, on the other hand, had his band of vassals who were bound to attend him on demand, and so it is only natural that when the count discovered that it was difficult to secure *échevins* he should use his feudal connections and compel his vassals to take their place. In this way an old public court will become a private feudal jurisdiction.

[1] Ganshof, *Contribution à l'étude des origines des cours féodales*, Revue historique de droit (1928), 644.

FEUDALISM IN ENGLAND

These, then, were the general features of feudal development on the continent, subject, it will be understood, to an infinite variety in detail as one passes from district to district. Life was as varied then as now, perhaps even more so, and every local territory pursued its own history and followed its own destiny in accordance with conditions which in many cases must have been local and peculiar, although in the end the result was apt to be roughly analogous to that which had been reached by many other communities in different parts of Europe. In raising the question how far all this history of European feudalism applies to England there are many difficulties. Our sources seem somewhat less informative than those on the continent, and although the general outlines of feudal development in England can be traced, much of the detail must be left to conjecture. A good deal can be ascribed to conscious imitation, for English kings were naturally tempted to look for their model to the continent, where the new type of organisation was undoubtedly more advanced.

ANGLO-SAXON FEUDALISM

In general terms it may be confidently stated that the Anglo-Saxon period had already developed before the Norman Conquest the principal features of feudalism, although the means by which this development took place are not always apparent.[1] On the eve of the Conquest we find a good deal of dependent land tenure which was subject to rents and services, and even to military service as well. The Anglo-Saxon book-land may in its earlier days have been a grant of full ownership, but in

---

[1] On Anglo-Saxon feudalism there has been considerable controversy; see especially Maitland, *Domesday Book and Beyond*, 80–107, 150–172, 258–292, and notably 293–318; Adams, *Origin of the English Constitution*, 44–54; the criticism of Maitland's views by Stenton, *English Feudalism*, 122 ff., is based on a very special definition of feudalism as embodied in the knight and the castle, and so cannot have much effect on the wider question (see, however, the comment of Douglas, *Feudal Documents*, civ. n. 2); Jolliffe, *Constitutional History*; Goebel, *Felony and Misdemeanour*; Stenton, *Anglo-Saxon England*. Note especially the summary of the controversy by D. C. Douglas, *The Norman Conquest and English Feudalism*, Economic History Review, ix. 128.

the later period it resembles more closely the continental benefice in spite of the fact that its history was somewhat different. The Anglo-Saxon sources also tell us about " laen land ", which seems half-way between the benefice and a lease for three lives. Private and personal jurisdiction played a prominent part in the police system; lordless men were compelled to find a lord. At the same time immunities of varying extent were lavished upon the Church and later upon laymen, and by the end of the period it seems to be assumed that landowning involves some elements of lordship. The old hundred court not infrequently fell into private hands and it is to be presumed (at least in law) that this was in consequence of a royal grant. The origins of the greater jurisdictions can in many cases be traced, but the great mystery in Anglo-Saxon institutions is the development of the small private franchise. Upon this we have very little light at all.[1]

THE RESULTS OF THE CONQUEST

The effect of the Norman Conquest in England[2] was to introduce a body of administrators who were familiar with the more highly organised type of feudal society existing on the continent, and the result of their presence must have been to give a definite form to institutions which in England were thus far somewhat vague. From this point of view *Domesday Book* must be regarded as an attempt by those administrators to express English conditions in the technical terminology of continental feudalism. It may be said, perhaps, that although the Norman Conquest did not introduce feudalism into England, yet it may very well have largely contributed to the development of a feudal system in England, for there can be no doubt that, as far as the law of land is concerned, England became the most thoroughly and consistently feudal of all the European states. In particular, it has recently been shown that William the Conqueror exercised a degree of control over subinfeudation which would certainly not have been any longer possible on the continent, and the Salisbury oath, already mentioned, may be taken as a further illustration.[3] In assessing the Norman contribution to English feudalism the unique opportunity of a complete conquest must be allowed to account for many things; it permitted much more rapid development, the importation of a technical terminology, and the more precise definition of relationships. The Norman introduction of the knight's fee is a well-known example. But the general outlines of feudal society with its seignories, services and franchises cannot have been so very novel to eleventh-century England.

---

[1] See Corbett in *Cambridge Medieval History*, iii. 405–408.

[2] Douglas, *Norman Conquest and English Feudalism*, Economic History Review, ix. 128, sums up recent work.

[3] Douglas, *Feudal Documents*, xcix–c; c, n. 1; above, p. 13.

BOOKLAND

When we come to examine the Anglo-Saxon law of land we find three terms in use, " bookland ", " folkland " and " laen land ". Of these bookland is by far the most frequently mentioned in the sources, and necessarily so, for bookland is peculiar in being held by a written document.[1] Many documents constituting bookland are to be found in the large collections of Anglo-Saxon charters which still survive. Even in the form of the document we can see continental and papal influence; the wording of the charters is frequently florid and full of religious and moral commonplaces, which seems to show that these documents were not yet in ordinary everyday use; it is upon exceptional and solemn occasions that a charter has to be drawn up, and the grantee (who normally seems to have been the draftsman) lavished his literary skill upon a charter which was to be the symbol of exceptional privileges. During most of the Anglo-Saxon age the grantees of these charters are almost always churches, and it is therefore to be expected that continental influences should play their part. In spite of their length it is not always clear exactly what an Anglo-Saxon charter purports to convey. It will say, with a great deal of precise Roman terminology, that it conveys the ownership of land, but this very term is not free from ambiguity. In many cases it is clear that what passes under the charter is not land but rather rights and privileges over land which is, in fact, occupied by others. Such rights consist of tributes or farms payable to the lord; then, too, there are various immunities which will exempt the grantee from nearly all public burdens (especially a heavy liability to purveyance)—and it seems that these rights over freemen were numerous and profitable; to them must be added forest and hunting rights, together with the profits of jurisdiction—and as Anglo-Saxon law exacted money payments for all sorts of faults, trivial or grave, the profits of jurisdiction must have been considerable. This does not mean that property in land (as distinguished from jurisdiction over other people's land) could not be conveyed by charter; no doubt it was, but the significant feature is that the same form serves for both purposes. This feature long survived, and even in the classical common law the same form of words will pass a piece of land, or a manor, which is not entirely land, or an honour, which is not land at all but merely feudal jurisdiction over land.

When we come to the later bookland we find that it is no longer peculiarly ecclesiastical. Laymen seem pleased to obtain it on account of certain legal advantages, notably devisability, which seems to have been a characteristic which the Church at first valued highly, since bookland could be left by will, and so one bishop was able to provide for his successor, for as yet prelates did not have perpetual succession. Another advantage which undoubtedly contributed to its popularity was

---

[1] For a brief survey of the controversy on this subject, see Plucknett, *Bookland and Folkland*, Economic History Review, vi. 64–72.

the fact that litigation concerning bookland took place before the king and the witan; the folk courts of the hundred and the shire had no jurisdiction over it. In addition to this, we can see in the procedure of such cases that the holder by book or the claimant by book, was in a very privileged position.[1] Then, as for a thousand years to come, no oath could be given against a charter—just as no wager of law lay against a deed. Finally, bookland, besides being devisable, was also alienable (unless, as sometimes happened, the grantor set up a sort of entail in the book), and so was free from the family restrictions which lay upon ordinary land.

FOLKLAND

A word must be said about folkland. The word only occurs three times in the whole of Anglo-Saxon legal literature, but nevertheless a vast edifice of supposition and conjecture has been built upon it. It has been alleged that folkland was the public property of the State, and so the Anglo-Saxon nation has been credited with vast possessions in its own right, completely distinct from the property of the kings. This theory was demolished by Sir Paul Vinogradoff, who established that the meaning of folkland is simply land which is held according to customary law by folk right, which therefore constitutes its great contrast to bookland.[2] As Maitland has said:

> " Land, it would seem, is either bookland or folkland. Bookland is land held by book, by a royal and ecclesiastical *privilegium*. Folkland is land held without book, by unwritten title, by the folk-law. ' Folkland ' is the term which modern historians have [erroneously] rejected in favour of the outlandish *alod*. The holder of folkland is a free landowner, though at an early date the King discovers that over him and his land there exists an alienable superiority. Partly by alienations of this superiority, partly perhaps by gifts of land of which the King is himself the owner, bookland is created."[3]

LAEN LAND

As for laen land, we have here perhaps the closest English analogy to the continental *precaria*. We even find some curiously close parallels between the position of the Church in England and its position on the continent; thus, we find the Church being called upon by the English kings to grant laen land to royal nominees.[4] One of the great difficulties in studying this laen land is the confusion which often exists between the laen (which strictly should be nothing more than a loan) and an

---

[1] These two points are made by Jolliffe, *English Book-Right*, English Historical Review, l. 1–21.

[2] Vinogradoff, *Collected Papers*, i. 91, 92. The recent attempt by Turner, " Bookland and Folkland ", *Historical Essays in Honour of James Tait*, 357–386, to reinstate folkland as State property has not been supported by other scholars; see the summary in Economic History Review, vi. 64–72.

[3] Maitland, *Domesday Book and Beyond*, 257.

[4] Maitland, *op. cit.*, 302; Douglas, *Feudal Documents*, xcix.

absolute gift; " the loan is a gift for a time ".[1]   Then, again, although laen land is sometimes constituted by written charter yet it is perfectly clear that a good many grants must have been made without charter. In a few cases where we find the incidents of laen land set out the similarities with later feudalism are most striking.   Thus we find that the tenants are bound to ride upon the lord's errands, transport his goods, pay rent, and perhaps fight.   Then, too, laen land is within limits inheritable.   The limit seems to have been for three lives,[2] each of the two inheritors paying relief.   Under normal circumstances the three generations would cover a period of about eighty years, but it is not at all clear how the Church proposed to secure its reversion after so long a period.   Indeed, it is known that the Church of Worcester had a good deal of trouble in this matter, and there is certainly a very strong tendency for such land to become perpetually inheritable, although subject to relief.   We even find in the year 983 an indication that the widow of a tenant of laen land might be under pressure to marry one of the lord's subjects, and in the days of Edward the Confessor this has grown into the right of granting an heiress and her lands to the nominee of the lord.[3]   If laen land were at all common in England it would seem that we had in it the most remarkable link between English and continental feudalism;   but unfortunately the chances of time have only left us documents in any considerable quantity from one church, the Cathedral of Worcester, and it is uncertain how far they represent conditions generally throughout the country, and how much they owe to the originality of the great Bishop Oswald, who ruled the see towards the close of the tenth century.

[1] Maitland, *Domesday Book and Beyond*, 299.   It is also worth noting that the Anglo-Saxon *laen* is cognate with the German *Lehn*, a fief.

[2] This may be a reminiscence of Justinian, Nov. vii. 3.

[3] Maitland, *Domesday Book and Beyond*, 310.

INHERITANCE AND ALIENABILITY

Numerous attempts have been made to discover the origin of property in land, but unfortunately they have in many cases been prompted by political or economic prepossessions, with the result that the discussions upon this subject are by no means always good examples of scientific research. The age-long instinct of the human race which would imagine an ideal state of perfection in some remote age of the past has been very influential in directing men's studies to the early history of property.

THE MARK THEORY

Early in the nineteenth century a school of German historians, of whom von Maurer was one of the greatest, discovered something like an earthly paradise in the condition of the Germanic tribes in the days of Caesar. They were even prepared to assert that as late as the seventh century the Germanic peoples practised communism in land, and that the idea of private property in land did not prevail among them until they had been corrupted by the influence of Roman law. The ancient Germanic village community from this point of view consisted of a highly socialistic state, very small, but very compact, which held the title to all the land in the community, allowing individuals only a right of user. This hypothesis is known as the mark system.[1] In 1887 a brilliant and searching criticism of this theory was made by one of the greatest of modern historians, Fustel de Coulanges, who demonstrated the falseness of this position. For some strange reason there has been great reluctance to accept the results of Fustel; by an unfortunate fate

---

[1] The theory is stated briefly in Stubbs, *Constitutional History* (1875), i. 49.

his disinterested scholarship became entangled both with party politics in France, and with national historical tradition in Germany, with the result that it is only at the present moment that his work is beginning to receive the attention which it deserves.[1] The results, however, are beginning to be silently adopted even in Germany, where historians have long resisted his influence.

AGRARIAN ORIGINS IN ENGLAND

The older English historians, notably Stubbs, accepted the mark system in its entirety until Maitland demonstrated in 1897 that it was inconsistent with the English documents. The results he reached are similar to those of Fustel de Coulanges although he differed from him on points of detail. Into the complicated controversy surrounding the village community we cannot enter.[2] The most we will say is that the English sources show us individual ownership which as time goes on steadily becomes more intense. There was, however, a great deal of co-operation between neighbouring villagers, and then as now they would combine their resources in order to secure some particularly costly piece of agricultural equipment—the team of oxen which drew the heavy plough, for example—to arrange the rotation of crops and fallow, and other matters where united action was an advantage. This does not mean, of course, that there never was any communism in land at some remote period in England; but it does mean that we have no evidence of such a condition, and that as far as history is concerned the sources indicate individual ownership. The organisation of the village community in prehistoric times is an investigation which cannot be handled by the methods of the historian, and the theories which have been suggested on the subject must be taken subject to the reservations necessarily applicable to speculations in prehistory.

FAMILY OWNERSHIP

There is some historical reason for believing that in early times land was owned by families rather than by individuals, but the antiquity of this arrangement, its origins and its significance, have been much disputed; indeed, it has been suggested by Ficker and Maitland that this apparent family ownership is in fact only the product of the working of various rules of individual inheritance. This may very well be, for a similar process can be observed in other periods of legal history. The results produced by a strict settlement in the eighteenth century, for example, might easily produce the impression upon an historian of a thousand

---

[1] Fustel de Coulanges, *Les Origines du système féodale* (1900); *Recherches sur quelques problèmes d'histoire* (1913).   For his life see Pierre Gaxotte in the *Criterion* (1928), 258, and for his work see Professor de Blécourt's article in *Tijdschrift voor Rechtsgeschiedenis* (1929) 150.   Cf. Dopsch, *European Civilisation* (London, 1937), 20–26.

[2] For a summary, see Vinogradoff's article, " Village Communities ", in the *Encyclopaedia Britannica* (1911) and Peake, " Village Community " in *Encyclopaedia of Social Sciences*.

years in the future, who had no access to the deeds, that land was held by the family, and yet a history of real property law would show clearly that such a settlement was in fact the outcome of an ingenious arrangement of very individualistic rules of property and inheritance. Then, again, good reasons have recently been shown for believing that another body of rules, in themselves individualistic, combined to produce in France the system of community property between husband and wife.[1] These considerations will serve as a warning that there is no absolute necessity in the nature of things why property should first have been ascribed either to the community or the family before it became individual. Generalisations of this sort cannot be used as aids to research; they are in fact useless for all purposes, until independent research has established their truth.

HERITABILITY OF MILITARY LAND

In tracing the history of the heritability of land we are faced by two problems. The first is comparatively easy; the practice, and later the law, relating to the descent of great military fiefs, are fairly clear. A number of documents have survived relating to these matters, for they were of great political importance. But, as we have seen, the vast properties which were granted as benefices to nobles and rulers consisted only in part of land for use and occupation; the major portion of these immense holdings certainly consisted of superiorities and fiscal rights superimposed upon the humbler orders of society who occupied and worked the land according to customs which in all probability were considerably older. Moreover, vast as they were, these holdings consisted almost always in an accumulation of scattered units, and the difference between a great landed magnate and a small one was simply the difference in the number of these units held by each. Whatever law was developed for the succession of great estates must therefore necessarily apply to small ones too, for the great estate was but a congeries of small units such as any minor landowner enjoyed. The result was of great importance. Socially, it meant that there was not a special law relating to nobles and great landowners, and a different one for the rest of the free landed classes. Legally, it meant that the developments of the law which took place primarily with reference to great tenants in chief, came to be applied to all free tenancies.

It is therefore the law relating to fiefs which we must consider. By the time of Bracton it is settled law that the word " fee " connotes inheritability and indeed the maximum of legal ownership. At the time of the Conquest this was certainly not the case. We have already seen that the feudal benefice on the continent assured little beyond a life tenure in its early days, and so it is not surprising to find the same state

---

[1] See Lemaire, *Les Origines de la communauté de biens entre époux*, Revue historique de droit français et étranger (1928), 584–643. Cf. Y.BB. Edward II (Selden Society), x. 240, for a wife's will of half the total chattels of husband and wife.

of affairs in England when the Conqueror repeated history in his grants
of fiefs to his followers, and they in turn subinfeudated.[1] More often,
English charters immediately after the Conquest seem careful to avoid
saying whether the donee is to take an estate for life, or whether his heir
is to have any rights.[2] Indeed, at this very moment in France itself
(which was generally in the front rank of feudal development) the question
of the quantum of a feudal tenant's interest was uncertain. There is
abundant English evidence after the Conquest of lords refusing to regrant
on any terms to a deceased tenant's heir.[3]

We have already mentioned the fact that the heir of a military tenant
who wished to obtain a regrant of his ancestor's lands had to treat with
the feudal lord, who might or might not decide to admit the heir. The
decisive argument was generally a sum of money, and it is possible to
trace the gradual changes of attitude towards this payment. At first it is
clearly no more than a payment to persuade the lord to make a grant of
a benefice. Later it came to be an arbitrary due payable when an heir
succeeded his ancestor, *i.e.* the succession of the heir has become normal,
although the " relief " may be so heavy that it was equivalent to " buying
back " the fief; hence a tenant might hesitate whether he would pay, or
forgo the lands. In 1100 the charter of Henry I contained this clause:

> " If any of my earls, barons or other tenants in chief die, his heir shall not
> redeem his land as he did in the time of my brother (*i.e.* William II), but shall take
> it up with a just and lawful relief.
> " The men of my barons shall likewise take up (*relevabunt*) their lands from their
> lords with a just and lawful relief."[4]

By 1100 it therefore appears that the hereditary principle was admitted
by the king in favour of his tenants in chief, and by them in favour of
their sub-tenants. Having gone that far, it must rapidly have spread all
through the feudal network.

HERITABILITY OF NON-MILITARY LAND

The second problem, and one of much greater difficulty, is the
question of what law governed the descent of land in the middle and
lower classes. These people were of no great political importance;
their pedigrees are almost always lost. The succession of owners of the
more modest estates is difficult to establish and the records of their
litigation only begin at dates much later than the critical period which
we should like to examine. Only occasionally do we find surviving
collections of deeds which throw some light upon the law under which
they held their land. This is particularly true of the Anglo-Saxon age.

---

[1] Galbraith, *An Episcopal Land Grant of 1085*, English Historical Review, xliv. 355.

[2] Douglas, *Feudal Documents from the Abbey of Bury St. Edmunds*, ciii, where the matter is
admirably illustrated.

[3] Chew, *Ecclesiastical Tenants-in-Chief* (1932), 118.

[4] Printed in Stubbs, *Select Charters*, and annotated in Robertson, *Laws of the Kings of England*,
276, 370. Relief was fixed at a rate per fee by *Magna Carta* (1215), c. 2.

We have, of course, a good deal of evidence (although it is by no means easy to interpret) relating to bookland, but it is obvious that bookland was a luxury for the wealthy; much of it was held by churches and monasteries and so the question of inheritance does not arise. There is good ground for believing, however, that bookland was alienable and devisable. It would seem from a passage in the Laws of Alfred that it was possible to insert in the charter constituting bookland limitations upon its descent, and that those limitations would be upheld in law.[1] In this way Anglo-Saxon society of the ninth century acquired a device very closely resembling the entail of the late thirteenth century. Judging from surviving sources, however, no very great use was made of these powers. It is when we come to folkland that we reach the difficult problem of how land descended by common custom among the mass of the middle-class population, and here it is extremely difficult to reach a conclusion.

THE RELATION OF HERITABILITY TO ALIENABILITY

It may be helpful to consider the problem of inheritance in connection with that of alienation. Land was certainly not yet a commodity of commerce. The buying and selling of land on a large scale can hardly have existed. The population was very small and there was enough land to meet its requirements many times over, and it would seem that the land worked by a family in those days, as now, was worked by the labour of every member of the family. One of the striking features of peasant life is that every member of the family works, from the oldest to the youngest. The death of the head of the family can hardly have made very much difference beyond the substitution of a new head to control the general working of the estate; the other members of the family must surely have continued their old tasks. Under such circumstances there was little room for inquiry as to the exact canon of descent, as to where precisely the legal title was, or as to the exact nature of the interests enjoyed by junior or collateral members of the family. Under the new head as under the old, the whole family was supported by the whole of the land, living most probably together at one table. While such conditions lasted, even quite a vague custom would have been sufficient to regulate the family patrimony. Questions as to ownership and restraints upon alienation and the nature of heritable rights would begin to arise in only a few situations. The most important of these, no doubt, was created when one member of the family attempted to alienate a substantial portion of the property to a church. It is in this situation that family rights are brought to the fore on the continent, and we find the Church taking every possible precaution in order to secure its title. How far these precautions were absolutely necessary and how far they were merely politic, it is impossible to say. In any case, it is clear that on the continent

[1] Alfred, 41.

an alienation to a church was accompanied by a confirmation by several members of the family who were deemed to have an interest in the land. This does not mean that the land was owned by all the family and that all must join in a conveyance. It seems rather that the Church felt it necessary or prudent to obtain the ratification of those who had expectations in the land. We find, for example, that when a gift was made to a church the donor would be required by ecclesiastical discipline to obtain the consent of his kinsmen, if necessary, by paying them a substantial sum of money. In England we find presumptive heirs joining in a conveyance in the eleventh and twelfth centuries but how much older this requirement is can hardly be stated—evidence discussed by Sir Paul Vinogradoff from the tenth century leaves us in doubt whether such consent was absolutely necessary.[1]

FAMILY RESTRAINTS IN GLANVILL

After the Norman Conquest, by means unknown, it became the regular form in conveyances to mention the consent of expectant heirs, while when we come to Glanvill we find this statement:[2]

" Every freeman, therefore, who holds land can give a certain part of it in marriage with his daughter or any other woman whether he has an heir or not, and whether the heir is willing or not, and even against the opposition and claim of such an heir. Every man, moreover, can give a certain part of his free tenement to whomsoever he will as a reward for his service, or in charity to a religious place, in such wise that if seisin has followed upon the gift it shall remain perpetually to the donee and his heirs if it were granted by hereditary right. But if seisin did not follow upon the gift it cannot be maintained after the donor's death against the will of the heir, for it is to be construed according to the accustomed interpretation of the realm as a bare promise rather than a true promise or gift. It is, moreover, generally lawful for a man to give during his lifetime a reasonable part of his land to whomsoever he will according to his fancy, but this does not apply to deathbed gifts, for the donor might then (if such gifts were allowed) make an improvident distribution of his patrimony as a result of a sudden passion or failing reason, as frequently happens. . . . However, a gift made to anyone in a last will can be sustained if it was made with the consent of the heir and confirmed by him.

" Moreover, when anyone alienates his land in marriage or otherwise, he has either inherited land only, or acquired land only, or some of both sorts. If he has only inherited land he can give a certain part of it, as we said before, to whomsoever he will. If, however, he has several legitimate sons, it is not at all easy without the consent of the heir to give any part of the inheritance to a younger son, because if this were allowed the disinheritance of elder sons would often occur, on account of the greater affection which fathers most frequently have for their younger sons. But can a man who has a son and heir give a portion of his inheritance to his bastard son? If this were true then a bastard is in a better condition than a legitimate son— and nevertheless this is the case.

" If, however, a man has nothing but acquired property then he can alienate it, but not all of it because he cannot disinherit his son and heir."

[1] Vinogradoff, *The Transfer of Land*, Collected Papers, i. 157. The transactions there discussed come from a district where there was Danish influence, which had a leaning towards freedom of alienation, see above, p. 10.

[2] Glanvill, vii, 1.

Glanvill continues to give several more pages to the same effect.   It would seem that he is anxious to frame general and reasonable rules, but that English law had not yet reached the concrete and definite provisions such as are to be found in various continental systems.   Glanvill is unable to tell us plainly that a man can alienate one-third or one-half of his patrimony or his conquest; such rules existed on the continent and Glanvill would surely have told us if there were similar rules in England; but all he says is that a man must be " reasonable ", that he must not disinherit his heirs, and that he can only alienate " a certain part ". Glanvill also distinguished between patrimony and conquest, but this soon dropped out of English law.[1]   It would almost seem that the vague rules which Glanvill mentions were only insecurely established, for not only were they indefinite on the vital question of how much land could be alienated, but also, when we come to Bracton two generations later, we find no trace of them left.

Still, there can be no doubt that Glanvill is good evidence of a feeling that alienation ought to be restricted and that expectant heirs should not be disappointed.   Starting from this fact we may say that the situation was probably something like this.   Under ordinary circumstances, just after the Conquest, land was equally divided among all the sons, and it was considered improper—Glanvill would say illegal as well—for a father to alienate during his lifetime more than a reasonable portion of his patrimony, and particularly reprehensible if he advanced one son to the disadvantage of another.[2]   The policy of the rule seems to be to maintain absolute equality among all the sons, and Glanvill even asserts that the rule was pushed to such an extremity that a man could advance a bastard son (who, not being in the family, is not limited as to the amount which he can take) although he cannot show the same favour to a legitimate son.   In short, the restrictions upon alienation have as one of their principal objects the maintenance of equality among the legitimate sons.

PRIMOGENITURE

We now come to the development of another rule which was to cause considerable difficulty, the rule of primogeniture.   Under this system the whole inheritance descends entire to the eldest son, his younger brothers receiving nothing.

This form of descent first appears in military fiefs, where there was obvious justification for the policy of keeping the fief entire.   It was long an opinion that primogeniture was introduced into England at the Norman Conquest, but Maitland felt uncertain whether primogeniture in Normandy had in fact proceeded any further than in England, and therefore concluded that we could not blame the Normans for " our amazing law of inheritance ".   It would seem that in the eleventh century

[1] It is to be seen in the king's court as late as 1203, however: *Select Civil Pleas*, no. 167.
[2] But see the case cited above, n. 1.

there were two tendencies in Normandy struggling for supremacy, the first being primogeniture and the maintenance intact of the whole patrimony, and the second being an attempt to compromise between this and equal partition through the device of *parage*, whereby each brother had his share but held it feudally of the eldest, who represented the whole inheritance.   It has been suggested that—

" it is the will of the father which first of all determined how his property should descend, and the practice of primogeniture grew into a custom of primogeniture.

" As for the date, it seems that of our two Norman systems, the one of absolute primogeniture, and the other of partition and parage, the former is the more ancient.   It was already dominant, if not in exclusive use, in the eleventh century.   The second system which in the end was to become the general custom only began to prevail at a more recent date."[1]

It may well be that Norman example played a considerable part in imposing primogeniture upon English military fiefs.

Although in England and Normandy primogeniture grew up as a matter of custom, that was not the case everywhere.   It was imposed upon Brittany in 1185 by an assize of Count Geoffrey,[2] and upon the town of Leicester by its lord, Simon de Montfort, at the request of the inhabitants who preferred it to their custom of borough-English (ultimogeniture).[3]

PRIMOGENITURE AND FREE ALIENATION

It will be evident that, with the spread of primogeniture to land which was originally partible, some modification will have to be introduced into the rule, which Glanvill mentions, restraining alienation.   Glanvill tells us that a father has no right to alienate his land unreasonably, or in any way which would benefit one son more than another.   But could these restrictions be maintained after the advent of primogeniture?   Would it be reasonable to maintain the restrictions upon alienation whose original object was to maintain equality among the sons, now that recent changes have abolished that equality and the whole inheritance goes to the eldest?   The force of these objections seems to have been felt, and the rise of primogeniture inevitably brought with it freedom of alienation. Henceforward the eldest son will inherit the whole of the father's property existing at his decease, but during his lifetime the father can make any provision which he sees fit for the younger sons without requiring the consent of his heir.   These great changes occurred just about the year

---

[1] Génestal, *La Formation du droit d'aînesse*, Normannia, i. 157, 174.

[2] Planiol, *L'Assise au comte Geoffroy*, Nouvelle revue historique de droit [1887], 117, 652 (it remained in force from 1185 until 1791); cf. Émile Chénon, *L'Ancien Droit dans le Morbihan* (Vannes, 1894), 10 ff.

[3] Mary Bateson, *Records of Leicester*, 49.   A French chronicler, on the other hand, asserted (*Grandes Chroniques de la France*, ed. Paulin, iv. 380) that an English parliament about 1263 wanted to abolish primogeniture.   As to this compare Pollock and Maitland, ii. 274 n. 1, with Bémont, *Simon de Montfort*, 201 n. 6 (tr. E. F. Jacob, 202 n. 1).

1200, but how they were carried out is a mystery. It may perhaps have been a few decisions of the King's Court which sufficed to enforce the new rule—or rather to turn the balance definitely in favour of one of the two competing systems of succession. Perhaps freedom of alienation was partly achieved through the doctrine of warranty. It began to be the custom for an alienor to bind himself and his heirs to warrant the alienee against all men. An obvious result of this obligation is that no person who is bound to warrant can claim the land; he is barred by his warranty. As soon as the rule is established that a man's heir is his eldest son, then that eldest son will inherit the burden of warranty and be barred by it. In this way a deed with warranty will be sufficient to bar whatever claim the grantor's eldest son might have. In 1225 the King's Court refused its help to an heir who had been completely disinherited[1] and left, it would seem, with the burden of military service but with no land to support it.

SOME ILLUSTRATIVE CASES

Lest the passage quoted above from Glanvill should seem too vague, it will be prudent to look at some cases on the early plea rolls, which date from shortly after Glanvill's day.

Thus we find the distinction between conquest and heritage clearly made in a case of 1200 in which Robert Fitz Nigel demanded a house and land against his brother Richard Battle.[2] Robert claims as " eldest brother to whom that land ought by law to descend ". The demandant is setting up the rule of primogeniture, but the tenant takes a more conservative position. True, he relies upon a gift by their common father to him, the younger son, but he does not state the full rule of freedom of alienation; he is content to rest on the older principle— " Richard comes and says that their father . . . of his conquest gave him that land during his lifetime ". So far, then, Richard only claims freedom of alienation in respect of conquests, but his case was in fact even stronger, for he adds that in the court of the chief lord of the fee Richard did homage to his eldest brother, the demandant. Here, then, we have the situation which was soon to develop into the rule that warranty will operate as a bar, for the fact that Richard did homage to Robert will soon be regarded as bringing into their relationship the obligation of warranty. That moment has not yet come (or rather, Richard has not yet heard of the new development) for instead of confidently pleading the homage as a bar, he concludes by praying the grand assize to recognise " whether he has more right to hold that land of Robert, by the gift of their father, and by the consent of Robert, than Robert has to hold it in demesne ". The case neatly illustrates the points which we have mentioned.

---

[1] *Bracton's Note Book*, no. 1054.
[2] *Select Civil Pleas* (ed. Maitland, Selden Society), no. 56.

PRIMOGENITURE BECOMES GENERAL

Besides appearing in the highest classes of society among the nobles and military tenants, impartible succession also appears among the villeins. The economic basis of this practice is clearly the endeavour to maintain the villein's holding intact and therefore sufficient to sustain the whole of his family and to meet the heavy burden which it owes to the lord. The rest of the freeholders in England continued what is assumed to be their former practice of equal partition among sons. For a time this was the general rule in all free non-military tenures (which are compendiously referred to as socage). It was inevitable, however, that the steady pressure of the royal courts should tend to eliminate exceptions and peculiarities, and as time goes on primogeniture gradually spreads to socage as well. The exceptions were the boroughs, which held to their custom of burgage, the county of Kent, which retained its ancient practices under the name of gavelkind, and numerous small landowners in villages where partibility persisted as a custom.[1]

TENURE AND ALIENABILITY

So far we have only discussed freedom of alienation from the point of view of the family. Fresh problems were created by the systematisation of feudal tenures, services and incidents, and the result was the imposition of a new type of restraint upon alienation in the interests of the lord of the fee. The history of their rise and abolition will form part of the next chapter, when tenures and incidents will be discussed.

[1] Homans, *Partible Inheritance*, Economic History Review, viii. 48.

CHAPTER 4

TENURES AND INCIDENTS

As feudalism progressed, attempts were made to introduce some sort
of order into the immense variety which had so far prevailed, and so a
large number of different characteristics which owed their rise to local or
peculiar circumstances were finally classified, with the result that there
were established a few categories which covered the greater number of
tenures.

KNIGHT SERVICE

Knight service was clearly the principal feudal tenure, and its history
in England, according to Maitland, falls into three periods.[1]   In the
first, from the Conquest in 1066 to about the year 1166, it was a living
institution.   The tenant did military service in the King's host accompanied by the number of knights required by his tenure.   In theory he
was only bound to serve forty days and never outside of the kingdom.
Great lords were usually assessed in multiples of five or ten knights,

---

[1] The following passages are based on Pollock and Maitland, i. 252–253, modified in the
light of the later work mentioned in the footnotes.

since ten knights formed a military unit called a *constabularia*; the lord in turn secured himself the services of the requisite number of knights by subinfeudating to other tenants who assumed the burden.

Military service of a sort had been attached to land even under the Anglo-Saxon régime, but it was of a different character, and designed to fit in with a different style of warfare. The Conqueror was one of the greatest military experts of the day, and he insisted on highly trained knights who were adept in the latest developments of military science. When St Anselm sent his old-fashioned " drengs " in answer to a feudal levy, William II threatened him with the judgment of the King's Court.[1] Heavy assessments of knight service were therefore made against the tenants in chief, but it is clear that they bore no relation to pre-Conquest dues, and that they were in no sense proportional to the size or value of the tenant's lands.[2] Political and personal considerations seem to have been uppermost.

The tenant in chief could take whatever measures he saw fit for providing himself with the requisite number of knights. Some simply kept the necessary number of knights in their household, like other domestic servants;[3] an alternative was to settle them on pieces of land, which they would thus hold as a knight's fee from the grantor.[4] And, of course, a combination of the two was possible. The obligations of the tenants in chief to the Crown were fixed by the Conqueror in or very near the year 1070,[5] but almost a century later it was found that by no means all the service due had been assured by subinfeudating knights.[6]

SCUTAGE

The first known occurrence of the word is in 1100,[7] and for a while it only seems to have applied to the knight service owed by the great ecclesiastical fiefs.[8] Later in the century it became an important question affecting all sorts of tenants, and in 1159 and again in 1166 we find prominent mention of scutage; this introduces the second stage in the history of knight service. The knight is becoming less important and professional mercenaries (as King John discovered) are more effective in the field. And so the lord paid to the king a sum of money instead of bringing his knights with him; this payment was called scutage, and the lord, of course, was allowed to recover the sum from those of his under-tenants who otherwise would have been liable to serve in person.

[1] Stenton, *First Century of English Feudalism*, 148.

[2] Chew, *Ecclesiastical Tenants in Chief*, 6.

[3] Stenton, *op. cit.*, 135 ff.

[4] *Ibid.*, 153.

[5] Chew, *op. cit.*, 3.

[6] Some had enfeoffed more knights than they owed; see the tables in Chew, 19–20; a few figures for lay tenants will be found in Stenton, 138.

[7] Stenton, *op. cit.*, 178.

[8] Chew, *op. cit.*, 38.

At the same time, it is clear that some tenants, instead of paying scutage at the normal rate, made a composition with the Crown which cost them even more than the scutage; why this should be is still a debatable question.[1] That the system was breaking down there can be no doubt. Even the Crown realised that the increased cost of equipping knights made the burden impossible for many tenants, and so only exacted a fraction of their due service. On the other hand, scutage having become a fixed rate, steadily declined in value. It is not surprising, therefore, that many tenants preferred to send for personal service the reduced number of knights which the Crown was now willing to take instead of the heavy assessments fixed in 1070. Hence in the reign of Henry III there is a marked increase in the number of tenants who actually sent knights.[2] Under Edward I it became a purely fiscal device.[3]

THE DECLINE OF KNIGHT SERVICE

The third stage is marked by the decline of scutage in or about 1266, and from this date for four hundred years (1266–1660) knight service remained as only a troublesome but lucrative anachronism. It was a very heavy burden upon certain of the landowners, and when it was finally abolished at the Restoration the landed interest succeeded in shifting it on to the nation at large by giving to the Crown instead of its feudal dues an excise on beer—an example of " the self-interest which so unhappily predominated even in representative assemblies ", as Hallam indignantly expressed it.

HOMAGE

The incidents of knight service were numerous and important. In the first place there was homage, an ancient and very solemn ceremony which established a strong and intimate relationship between lord and tenant.

> " He who has to do homage . . . ought to go to his lord anywhere he can find him within the realm or even elsewhere if he can conveniently get there; for the lord is not bound to seek out his tenant. And he ought to do his homage thus. The tenant ought to put both of his hands between the hands of his lord, by which is signified on the lord's side protection, defence and warranty, and on the tenant's side, reverence and subjection. And he ought to say these words: I become your man for the tenement which I hold of you, and I will bear you faith in life and member and earthly honour against all men, saving the faith due to the lord King."[4]

In the *Leges Henrici* we find the highest expression of homage. The tenant is to be faithful to his lord even under trying circumstances; if the lord seizes the tenant's land or deserts his tenant in mortal peril he

---

[1] Chew, *Ecclesiastical Tenants in Chief*, 46 ff.
[2] *Ibid.*, 52.
[3] *Ibid.*, 57.
[4] Bracton, f. 80.

ought to lose his lordship,[1] but the tenant must be longsuffering and must support the lord's ill-treatment for thirty days in war time, and for a year and a day in time of peace;[2] the lord must warrant and defend his man, while if the man kills his lord he is guilty of blasphemy against the Holy Ghost, and will be skinned alive, so it seems. Later still, Glanvill will observe that difficult situations may arise when a tenant has done homage to two lords and those two lords declare war upon each other. Homage was abolished in 1660,[3] but the simple oath of fealty which accompanied it is still in existence. In the thirteenth century clerks, narrators, champions, serjeants and others took oaths of fealty to their lords (*i.e.* employers), but it was necessary to make it clear that such an oath of fealty did not bind the employee to do suit of court.[4]

RELIEF

Another incident of knight service is relief, which was originally the price paid in order to secure a regrant of one's ancestor's land in times when the hereditary principle was hardly established in military tenures. At first it was arbitrary, but a series of charters and statutes regulated it in proportion to the number of knight's fiefs.[5] If the tenant held of the King in chief, the King had prerogative rights and had the *primer seisin* of all the tenant's lands, not only those held of the Crown but also those held of other lords—and it is in these intenser forms of feudal right claimed by the Crown that we first find the word " prerogative ".

WARDSHIP

Wardship means two things, wardship of the land, and wardship of the body; for the lord has the custody of the tenant's land until the tenant comes of age, and retains the profits, subject to a liability to educate the ward in a manner befitting his station, and this wardship of the land may be separated from wardship of the body. It was, in fact, a very important example of what was later called a " chattel real ".

It is tempting to conjecture that its origin lies in the time when hereditary succession in military fiefs was subject to the discretion of the lord, who might as a favour act as, or appoint, a guardian, until the heir came of age, instead of granting the fief to a stranger. Thus, the ancient custumal of Normandy defends the institution on the grounds that homage is a more sacred bond than merely blood relationship:

[1] For an interesting judgment in which a lord who had used undue influence over a ward, and by collusion with a prior had deprived her of her land, was condemned to lose the seignory, see *Bracton's Note Book*, no. 1840.

[2] For a tenant who surrendered his fee and his homage to a harsh lord, see *Eyre Rolls* (Selden Society, vol. lix), no. 1450 (1222).

[3] Stat. 12 Car. II, c. 24; Pound and Plucknett, *Readings*, 653–65 5.

[4] *Brevia Placitata* (Selden Society), 135–136.

[5] Above, p. 524.

" A fatherless heir must be in ward to someone. Who shall be his guardian? His mother? No. Why not? She will take another husband and have sons by him, and they, greedy of the heritage, will slay their first-born brother, or the stepfather will slay his stepson. Who then shall be the guardian? The child's blood kinsmen? No. Why not? Lest, thirsting for his heritage, they destroy him. For the prevention of such faithless cruelty, it is established that the boy be in ward to one who is bound to his father by the tie of homage. And who is such an one? The lord of the land who never can inherit that land in demesne; for heirs of a noble race always have many heirs. Besides they should be brought up in good houses and honourably educated. Those who are brought up in their lords' houses are the apter to serve their lords faithfully and love them in truth; and the lords cannot look with hatred on those whom they have reared, but will love them and faithfully guard their woods and tenements and apply the profits of their land to their advancement."[1]

Its early history is not, in fact, so simple as that. In the days of high feudalism, the charter of Henry I (1100) shows that " the widow or other kinsman . . . shall be guardian of the land and of the children " of a deceased baron, " and I order that my barons conduct themselves similarly towards the sons or daughters or widows of their men ".[2] We first hear of the general principle of the lord's right of wardship in 1176.[3]

MARRIAGE

Even in the tenth century, we find Bishop Oswald of Worcester taking an interest in the re-marriage of the widows of his tenants, and in the Confessor's day, apparently, another bishop of Worcester gave the daughter of his tenant and her land to one of his knights.[4] By 1100 the King requires his barons to consult him (without fee) when marrying their daughters; if the baron is dead, the King may marry his daughters and dispose of their lands.[5] The same rule is stated under Henry II.[6] A vast extension of this practice took place soon after Glanvill's day (c. 1188–1189), for in 1193 we find the King selling the marriage of male heirs.[7] So marriages were added to wardships and terms of years in the category of " chattels real ". Since this particular example was an interest in young people who might elope, and were often " ravished " (i.e. kidnapped), the attempts of the law to deal with the problem produced some interesting results.

---

[1] Pollock and Maitland, i. 326 (translating from the Très ancien coutumier (ed. Tardif); the date of composition is c. 1200—a little later than our Glanvill). Génestal, La Tutelle (Caen, 1930). For some lurid light on feudal family life which seems to confirm the custumal's argument, see Marc Bloch, Société féodale, i. 208 ff.

[2] Henry I, coronation charter (1100), c. 4 (in Subbs, Select Charters). This was the general Anglo-Saxon practice: D. Whitelock, Beginnings of English Society, 94.

[3] Assize of Northampton (1176), c. 4 (in Stubbs, Select Charters).

[4] Above, p. 520.

[5] Henry I, coronation charter (1100), c. 3.

[6] Glanvill (ed. Woodbine), vii. 9, 10 and ix. 4; he only mentions the marriage of daughters, not of sons.

[7] Pollock and Maitland, i. 324.

AIDS

Then, too, the tenant in knight service owed aid to his lord. The emergencies under which a lord could call for aid were at first numerous; it might be to pay his debts,[1] to stock his land, to help him pay a fine to the King. But in the end aids are only due (unless by voluntary consent) to ransom the lord's person, to knight his eldest son, and to marry his eldest daughter. Scutage, aids and similar payments were passed on from tenant to sub-tenant, until ultimately even the agricultural tenant was brought under contribution.[2] The long struggle for the principle that taxation must be by consent was finally fought out in connection with the parliamentary taxation of personal property, but all the same it has a very early counterpart in the struggle to make aids limited in extent and occasion, unless freely voted by the consent of the tenants.

ESCHEAT AND FORFEITURE

Finally, we come to the incidents of escheat and forfeiture. Escheat is due to the lord of the fee on the death of a tenant without an heir, or upon his committing felony. It is important to note that escheat is not necessarily to the Crown; even in very recent times, if a mesne lordship be proved, an escheat might go to the lord and not to the Crown.[3] The value of escheat to lords has depended a great deal upon the meaning of the word " felony ". In early times the felonies were few, but among them was the important one of deliberately refusing to do the services due to one's lord; this being a felony, escheat followed upon conviction and the lord resumed the land. Soon, however, cesser of services ceased to be a felony, and the lord in many cases had no remedy against a tenant who wilfully withheld services until the Statute of Gloucester (1278). Moreover, in cases of felony the Crown established its right to year, day and waste, holding the land for a year and a day and wasting it before it went to the lord as an escheat. In the case of treason the whole of the traitor's lands, of whomsoever they were held, were forfeited to the Crown and the lord got nothing unless the Crown granted the escheated land away; in that case the mesne tenancies revived.[4]

SERJEANTY

Another species of tenure is described as serjeanty and may be either grand or petty; in the former case it will resemble knight service. It is of little historical importance, although several serjeanties still survive in connection with coronation services.[5]

[1] See e.g. Law Quarterly Review, xlviii. 423.

[2] Stenton, *Feudalism*, 182–183.

[3] Escheat is now abolished, and real property left without an heir goes to the Crown as *bona vacantia* (Administration of Estates Act, 1925, ss. 45, 46).

[4] Pollock and Maitland, ii. 500.

[5] Much interesting material is to be found in J. H. Round, *The King's Serjeants and Officers of State*, E. G. Kimball, *Serjeanty Tenure in Mediaeval England*, and A. L. Poole, *Obligations of Society*.

SOCAGE

We now come to the tenure of socage, which really consists of a great variety of tenancies whose only common factor is that they are not servile nor military; sometimes homage may be due but not scutage, wardship[1] or marriage. The services are sometimes purely nominal, being the result of gifts to younger members of the family or to servants, or of a sale effected by subinfeudation. Sometimes we find a moderate rent, especially where a church is the lord; sometimes labour services are due, some of them so numerous and heavy that it is not easily distinguishable from villeinage. It is clear that socage is gradually becoming more free and of higher social status, until in the end it becomes the one free non-military tenure, for the statute abolishing chivalry in 1660 converted it into free and common socage. As we have already mentioned, the rule of primogeniture was soon applied to socage land.

The guardian in socage was a near relative, and he was accountable to the heir for all the profits (less the heir's expenses); he might indeed sell the heir's marriage, but the price had to be accounted for to the heir.[2] Nevertheless, lords sometimes tried to assert a right of guardianship even over socage tenants, but generally failed in the end.[3]

BURGAGE

Tenure in burgage was peculiar to towns, although it varied considerably from place to place. A study of burgage will soon make it clear that a borough in the middle ages was still an agricultural unit, being in fact a village or a manor which has acquired a certain measure of self-government. Burgage tenure was not subject to aids, marriage or homage and only rarely to relief. Wardship, however, had been developed in the course of a different history from that of military tenures, and usually pertained to the kinsmen of the ward or to town officials. Frequently land was devisable by local custom, and if a tenant wished to alienate, his relatives often had the right to the first option (*retrait lignager*) while a second option may go to the lord (*retrait féodal*).[4] Boroughs were liable to a form of taxation called tallage and to a variety of money rents.

Of tenure in free alms, or frankalmoign, it is only necessary to say that it was for the most part peculiar to the Church and that it owed

---

[1] Sometimes the heir is in ward to a near relative, who is accountable on the ward's coming of age.

[2] Statute of Marlborough (1267), c. 17.

[3] See the royal declaration, for use in Ireland, printed in Sayles, *King's Bench*, iii. p. xxx n. 5; in effect it applies the Statute of Marlborough, c. 17, to Ireland.

[4] There is nothing particularly " mercantile " in burgage tenure; it is best regarded as a survival of early forms of socage which (owing to the borough's customary status, or its charter) did not undergo the changes which the common law wrought in other unprivileged places; on this, see Tait, *The Medieval English Borough*, 100 ff.

feudal services unless it were of that sort which is called " free, pure and perpetual ", in which case it only owed spiritual services.[1]

VILLEINAGE

Finally, a word must be said about villeinage, for we shall not obtain a true picture of the common law in the middle ages if we neglect the large mass of population which was excluded from many of its benefits. As we have already remarked, in the early thirteenth century the common law was hesitating whether to take cognisance of unfree land. It soon decided not to, and we have already mentioned the results which this had upon the villein's legal position. It was not until the close of the fifteenth century that courts of equity and prerogative were prepared to give protection, cautiously and timidly, to villeins, principally in cases where intervention could be justified as sustaining a manorial custom, and not until the sixteenth century can we be sure that the common law would follow this example, while it remained for Coke at the beginning of the seventeenth century to establish the villein's rights on the common law itself, under the name of copyhold. As for his personal status, Bracton assures us that a serf is free against all men except his lord, against whom the only protection he receives is that of life and limb. The law was never consistent in dealing with the villein's personal property; in theory all a villein's chattels were deemed to belong to his lord, but in practice we find the villein doing business, being fined, and paying taxes exactly like other men. His unfree status was hereditary, but a villein who ran away and was *de facto* free was spoken of as being " seised of his liberty ", and this seisin might become the basis of a reasonably good title to freedom, subject only to the condition that he keep away from the manor to which he belonged, for if ever he returned to his " villein nest " the lord can seize him and put him in irons to prevent him leaving the manor again (as many of them must have discovered).

TENURE AND ALIENABILITY

Moreover, it must be remembered that the existence of tenure of any sort added another complication to the question of freedom of alienation. We have already mentioned this subject from the aspect of the family, and now it must be considered from the point of view of feudal law. Alienation may be effected in two ways. The grantor may substitute the grantee in his own place in the feudal pyramid; or else he may subinfeudate by creating a new tenure between himself as lord and the grantee as tenant. By the time the feudal formula had been applied to all land, it became clear that either of these two methods of alienation might work hardship to the grantor's lord. In the case of substitution the incoming tenant might be poor, dishonest, or unfriendly, and in either case the lord might find it more difficult to exact his services. In

---

[1] Above, p. 17; *Bracton's Note Book*, no. 21 (1219).

the case of subinfeudation the situation is different. Although the grantor may have disposed of the whole of his holding to the grantee, yet the feudal relationship between the grantor and his lord still continues, the only change being that the grantor, instead of being tenant of the land in demesne, is now only tenant in service, and instead of an estate in possession in land he has an incorporeal hereditament. Whatever services he owes to his lord are still due, and the lord can exact them by distraining any tenant who holds the land—in the present case, the grantee, the law allowing the grantee a remedy over against the grantor who must " acquit " or reimburse him. In the case we have put, the lord's principal loss through his tenant's subinfeudation is in respect of wardships, relief, marriage and escheat.

Let us call the lord A. and his tenant B. and suppose that B. holds of A. by substantial services, and that the tenement is large and productive of a good revenue. As long as this relationship lasts the lord A. derives a regular income from the services and has the expectation of important profits at irregular intervals. Upon B.'s death he may have the wardship and marriage of his heir, and if the heir is young the profits will be considerable; if the heir is already of age he can expect a substantial relief; if there is no heir at all, B.'s tenement will escheat, and the lord will therefore enjoy a very considerable windfall; so, too, if the tenant commits felony. Let us now suppose that B. sells his land. He receives a large sum of money from the purchaser, which, of course, is quite beyond the lord's reach. B. then enfeoffs C., the purchaser, to hold of him by the nominal service of a rose at midsummer. As a result of this arrangement B. only retains a seignory of which the nominal service is the symbol. We have now to consider how this arrangement will affect A. The regular services due from B. to A. are still secure, but the occasional profits of A.'s lordship are seriously impaired. Relief which is based upon the value of the tenement will no longer be considerable, for B.'s tenement produces nothing but a rose at midsummer. The wardship and the marriage of B.'s heir are likewise worthless, for the tenement is actually of negative value and under the most favourable circumstances the guardian could only collect a few roses in the course of a minority of twenty-one years; if B. commits felony the lord's escheat once again will only consist of the nominal services which B. reserved. It is clear that we have here a very difficult situation, which, moreover, must have very frequently arisen. The lord's position is even worse when B. alienates to a church, for then the seignory which B. reserved would merely be a lordship over a corporation which never dies, never marries, and never commits felony.

FEUDAL RESTRAINTS ON ALIENATION

In Normandy this difficulty was met by the regular requirement of a confirmation of any tenant's alienation by his lord and by all superior

lords up to the duke himself; this enabled a lord to safeguard his interests.[1]
In England, however, this fairly simple requirement was not much
developed, and for a long time there was doubt as to the extent to which
a feudal lord could restrain alienation by his tenants.   Glanvill makes no
mention whatever of any feudal restrictions, which may be interpreted
as meaning only that the King's Court will not enforce them; there was
a very remarkable case in 1203, however, when a plaintiff summoned his
tenant to the King's Court to show why he had sold his tenement to
the plaintiff's overlord (thus destroying the effectiveness of the plaintiff's
seignory).   Unfortunately no result is enrolled.[2]   It is quite probable
that such restrictions existed in some form and that they were enforceable
through the lord's feudal court.   In the third Great Charter (1217) we
find that a complaint by the barons evoked the following provision (c. 39):

" No freeman henceforward shall give or sell so much of his land that the
residue shall be insufficient to support the service due in respect thereof to the lord
of the fee."

This is the first express limitation of a feudal character upon alienation
in English legal history.   When we come to Bracton he assures us that
the arrangements we have just described may very well work to the
financial loss of the lord, but nevertheless he has suffered no injury which
can be remedied at law; if Bracton is reduced to this paradox we may be
sure that it is because under contemporary law the lord was completely
helpless in such a case, and that the provision in the Great Charter was
nothing more than the expression of an unenforceable principle.

It was not until 1290 that the Statute *Quia Emptores* afforded a solution.[3]
By this statute subinfeudation was absolutely forbidden in the case of
fee simple;[4] alienation was henceforth to be by substitution with an
equitable apportionment of the services.   The statute expressly stated
that alienation was to be free,[5] and consequently the Crown had everything to gain through the enactment of the statute.   No new tenures
could be created, although in the inevitable course of events many old
tenures became extinct, escheated to the lord above, or were forfeited to
the Crown.   The Crown was therefore gradually becoming less separated
by intermediate tenures from the tenant in demesne.   The reasons for the
statute are clearly set out in the preamble, and there are no grounds for

[1] Possible examples of this sort of transaction occur in *Eyre Rolls* (Selden Society, vol. lix),
no. 1459, Y.B. 30 & 31 Edward I (Rolls Series), 378 (1303) and in Y.BB. Edward II (Selden
Society), x. 281.

[2] *Select Civil Pleas* (Selden Society), no. 148; cf. *Eyre Rolls* (Selden Society, vol. lix), no. 173;
Flower, *Introduction to the Curia Regis Rolls* (Selden Society, vol. lxii), 195, 216–217; for the
effect of a purchase by a lord from his immediate tenant, see Y.BB. Edward II (Selden Society),
xi. 85.   Sayles, *King's Bench*, i. 45; Y.BB. Edward II (Selden Society), i. 119.

[3] Text in Stubbs, *Charters*.

[4] The hazardous suggestion of [Ellesmere], *Discourse upon Statutes* (ed. S. E. Thorne),
168 n. 204, that a new tenure can be created by the consent of the parties, even after *Quia
Emptores*, is not supported by F.N.B. 210 D.

[5] For a lord who exacted 1000 marks from his tenant's alienee " to have his good-will ",
see Y.B. 21 & 22 Edward I (Rolls Series), 274.

believing that the King had a deep-laid or far-seeing motive;[1] on the contrary, it is expressly stated that the statute was made " at the prayer of the magnates ". Nor could its operation increase the amount of land subject to the special burdens of tenure in chief. Indeed, the great charter contained elaborate provisions to prevent that happening in any case,[2] and the common law developed rules to protect mesne tenancies against the Crown as far as possible.[3]

MORTMAIN

During the reign of Henry III the grant of land to churches was becoming very frequent; more than that, tenants practised collusion with churches in order to defeat feudal services. The Great Charter of 1217 contains the first direct provision against this practice also:

" It shall not be lawful for anyone henceforward to give his land to any religious house in order to resume it again to hold of the house; nor shall it be lawful for any religious house to accept anyone's land and to return it to him from whom they received it. If anyone for the future shall give his land in this way to any religious house and be convicted thereof, the gift shall be quashed and the land forfeit to the lord of the fee."[4]

Here we have the serious sanction of forfeiture provided, and yet it was ineffectual to prevent these practices. At the very moment when Bracton was writing, the barons in their petition of 1258 gave as one of their grievances " that religious persons ought not to enter the fees of earls and barons and others against their will, whereby they lose forever wardships, marriages, reliefs and escheats ". As long as the barons were in the ascendancy they were able to secure legislation in this direction by c. 14 of the Provisions of Westminster (1259). At the final settlement after the Barons' War embodied in the Statute of Marlborough this provision, however, was omitted—perhaps we may see here an effect of Henry III's conspicuous favour to the Church which characterised the whole of his reign. It was under his son and successor, Edward I, that the problem was finally settled by the Statute of Mortmain (1279) which re-enacted in broader terms the provision of the Great Charter of 1217, again imposing forfeiture to the lord as a penalty for unauthorised alienations in mortmain.[5] The most remarkable feature of this statute,

---

[1] For the contrary view, see Pollock and Maitland, i. 337 n. 5.

[2] Magna Carta (1225), c. 31.

[3] Cf. the effect of forfeiture for treason on mesne tenancies, above, p. 536.

[4] Cf. the case of 1227 in *Bracton's Note Book*, no. 1840, *Pleas of the Crown for Gloucester*, no. 50 (1221), and *Eyre Rolls* (Selden Society, vol. lix), no. 1450. The exceptional position of the king enabled him to forbid his own tenants to alienate churches held of him " *in perpetuum* " (into mortmain, apparently) without his assent: Constitutions of Clarendon (1164), c. 2. Cf. Sayles, *King's Bench* (Selden Society), iii. pp. xxxix, 125.

[5] All these documents are in Stubbs, *Charters*. For some observations on the working of the law, and some curious attempts to evade it, see Wood-Legh, *Church Life under Edward III*, 60–88. For the long conflict on the relation of the statute to the customs of the city of London, see H. M. Chew, *Mortmain in medieval London*, English Historical Review, lx. 1, and Sayles, *King's Bench*, iii. pp. xxxix, 125.

however, is one which does not appear in the text. There is no provision in the statute for licences to alienate in mortmain; nevertheless, immediately after the statute was passed, such licences were lavishly granted by the Crown. It will be observed that the Crown dispensed from the statute and received fines for doing so without any statutory authority, and even in cases where the loss occasioned by the alienation fell not upon the Crown but upon a mesne lord.

TENANTS IN CHIEF

Tenants in chief of the Crown, on the other hand, were being subjected to increasing restrictions. Before they could alienate they had to satisfy the Crown that it would suffer no less thereby, and from 1256 onwards[1] we find an increasing number of restrictions upon tenants in chief; which were soon set forth in an unofficial tract called *Prerogativa Regis*, which later ages sometimes mistook for a statute.[2] As for the freedom of alienation granted by the Statute *Quia Emptores*, it was held that this could not be construed as restraining the Crown in the absence of express words to that effect.

In this and the preceding chapters we have therefore traced the development of the freedom of alienation (except into mortmain), and the removal of the somewhat vague restrictions based on ideas of family interest and the interests of the feudal lord. Even the Statute of Mortmain was easily dispensed with, and we may therefore assume that by the close of the thirteenth century land was freely alienable by all except tenants in chief of the Crown.

THE ALIENABILITY OF SEIGNORIES

There remains to consider the point where the alienation is not that of a tenement held in demesne but of one held in service. How far can a lord alienate his seignory and compel his tenant to accept the new lord? It would seem that in general he can do so, the sole difficulty arising where the bond of homage exists between the old lord and the tenant. In such a case the tenant is entitled to object if the incoming lord is his mortal enemy or too poor to be able to sustain the burden of warranty which is such a valuable outcome of homage. Consequently we find that the King's Court will compel a tenant to attourn all services

---

[1] For the text of an important legislative writ of this year, see G. J. Turner, *A newly discovered ordinance*, Law Quarterly Review, xii. 299.

[2] *Statutes of the Realm*, i. 226. It is ascribed to the early years of Edward I by Maitland, *Collected Papers*, ii. 180, and " before 1279 " by Sayles, *King's Bench* (Selden Society), iii. p. lii n. 5. There is printed in Sayles, *King's Bench*, iii. p. cxxii, a cutting letter from the king to Chief Justice Brabazon (which can be dated 1314) which accompanied a memorandum of prerogatives used in the chancery, for his information, since he had confessed his ignorance of the matter. If this memorandum was the tract *De Prerogativa Regis*—a tempting conjecture —then the tract may have had an official origin.

to a new lord save only homage, and as to this it seems to have hesitated.[1]

THE EFFECTS OF TENURE

Occasionally attempts have been made to estimate the effects of tenure upon English law, but it is curious that the subject has been so little explored.[2] A comparison between English and continental law in this respect should be fruitful, for on the continent the feudal lawyers admitted that tenure divided the ownership of the land between the lord and the tenant.[3] English law refused to admit this proposition. Instead of regarding lord and tenant as dividing between them the ownership of one thing, it looked upon each of them as a complete owner of two different things, the tenant being the owner of the land in demesne and the lord being owner of a seignory, which, although incorporeal, was treated in every way as property. One result, therefore, of the doctrine of tenure as it was developed in England, was not to divide ownership between lord and tenant but to add the lord's seignory to the growing list of incorporeal hereditaments which mediaeval law was particularly fond of handling on exactly the same lines as real property.

The Statute *Quia Emptores* did much to create a great gulf between the fee simple and the lesser estates; a fee simple could not be subinfeudated, but the lesser estates were expressly removed from the operation of the statute. Tenure continues to be created, therefore, by means of subinfeudation in a case of life estates and estates tail;[4] particular tenants all hold feudally of the reversioner or the remainderman in fee. It is important to remember that English law treated these two types of tenure in different ways. The tenant of a fee simple by virtue of a subinfeudation (which must have dated from a time earlier than 1290) was regarded as an unrestricted owner and the interest of his lord was no limitation upon his own; the tenant held the land and the lord held the seignory, both of them in complete ownership.

When we come to the tenure of estates less than a fee, we find a very different scheme of things. The tenants in this case are consistently treated in the mediaeval cases as something less than owners, and it soon becomes the theory that the total of the interests of all the tenants, together with that of their lord (the reversioner or remainderman in fee), constitutes the ownership of the land in question. Moreover, since

---

[1] This is perhaps the explanation of a transaction which is noticed in Stenton, *Feudalism*, 220, wherein a sub-tenant paid a sum to the King, asking him to ensure that the tenant's lord should not alienate the lordship without the tenant's consent.

[2] See F. Joüon des Longrais, *La tenure en Angleterre au moyen age*, Recueils de la Société Bodin, iii. 165; cf. Hogg, *The Effect of Tenure on Real Property Law*, Law Quarterly Review, xxv. 178–187.

[3] From this arose the theory of *dominium directum* and *dominium utile*, the history of which is elucidated by E. Meynial in *Mélanges Fitting*, ii. 409–461. Cf. Armand Piret, *La Rencontre chez Pothier des conceptions romaine et féodale de la propriété foncière* (Paris, 1937).

[4] An entail by substitution caused trouble: Y.BB. Edward II (Selden Society), ii. 21, and cf. *ibid.*, p. 5.

reversions (and sometimes remainders) in fee were seignories, the law could treat them as vested estates, and not merely as expectations. We therefore find that in the case of the entail, ownership is very successfully divided between the parties, while in the case of the fee simple, lord and tenant both have the fullest interest recognised by the law, the one in the land and the other in the seignory. This division of ownership in the case of the entail is certainly the origin of the common law system of estates and has therefore played an enormously important part in shaping the law of real property, but there is no reason to believe that this division of ownership is the result of tenure; if tenure involved divided *dominium*, then we ought to find ownership divided between a lord and his tenant in fee simple, but, as we have seen, this is not the case. It is less easy to see how the existence of horizontal hereditaments can be regarded as a result of tenure, as has been suggested by Mr Hogg.[1]

Direct results of tenure are hardly to be expected, therefore; as the system was worked out by the courts the seignory was regarded as an incorporeal hereditament which was " real property " in the person who held it. There was the curious rule that one cannot be both lord and heir, but the immense complications it engendered could be fairly well avoided by refraining from taking homage, and (later) by making a gift in tail instead of in fee; after *Quia Emptores* the rule could not be extended.[2]

The indirect results were more serious. The burden of the feudal incidents bore so heavily on tenants that the history of real property law is largely concerned with attempts to evade them. On the one hand lay the possibility of separating the enjoyment of land from the legal title to it—hence the long history of the use. On the other lay various devices to ensure that he who was really the heir should take not as heir but as purchaser, so avoiding the relief; this gave us the contingent remainder and the *Rule in Shelley's Case*. In short, the persistence of a system which had long ceased to correspond with the real social structure of the country, although it continued to be an important source of revenue to large numbers of landowners as well as to the Crown, inevitably drove tenants to devise evasions, with the result that the law was warped beyond endurance.

WARDSHIP AND THE FAMILY

The complete feudalisation of the common law is well illustrated by the law of wardship. Henry I in 1100 had indeed recognised the right of the widow or relatives to have the wardship of the land and children

---

[1] Much historical material is collected by S. S. Ball, *Division into Horizontal Strata of the Landspace above the Surface*, Yale Law Journal, xxxix. 616–658. Horizontal hereditaments were common in mediaeval Oxford (H. E. Salter, *City of Oxford in the Middle Ages*, History, xv. 101) and in Tudor London in the Temple (Ball, *u.s.*). On the maxim *Cujus est solum ejus est a coelo usque ad inferos* see H. Goudy in *Essays in Legal History* (ed. Vinogradoff), 229 ff., and F. Ashe Lincoln in *Starrs and Jewish Charters* (Jewish Historical Society), ii. pp. lxxii ff.

[2] The rule is discussed in Pollock and Maitland, ii. 289–294.

of a deceased tenant.[1] Very soon, however, feudal interests prevailed over family ties. The orphaned infant was treated as an adjunct to his lands: if he had lands held of several lords, the wardship of his body went to the lord of the oldest tenure, the lands being in the wardship of their respective lords.[2] The feudal guardian, however, was in no sense a Roman *curator* and there is nothing in the common law corresponding to that institution. A guardian did not represent an infant in court or out of court, and his concurrence added nothing to the validity of an infant's acts. Infants litigated freely and needed no formal intervention of guardians or even of " best friends ".[3] For feudal heirs the courts were sufficient protection, with their rules on the demurrer of the parole (suspending most important actions during minority), and the writ of entry *dum fuit infra aetatem* (enabling him to recall gifts made during infancy). It was the infant burgess who really needed legal help, but the common law was not concerned with him, for the city of London and other jurisdictions were accustomed to manage infants' businesses and watch their investments—matters in which local knowledge and constant attention were essential.

Even family solidarity made little resistance to the feudal conception of wardship. The feudal lord regularly took an infant from his mother (we often see her buying him back), but a lord cannot take an infant from his father.[4] The father's right to his own heir is protected by law, and by an action which is typically feudal.[5] Indeed, not infrequently a father will " sell " his own heir,[6] and as late as 1558 a statute against abducting children from their parents will only apply to heirs or heiresses.[7] Such other rights as parents may acquire over children not their heirs seem to be based on the singular fiction that they are " servants " within the scope of the old labour law.

[1] Coronation Charter of Henry I (1100), c. 4.

[2] Westminster II, c. 16.

[3] Westminster I, c. 48; II, c. 15.

[4] Y.BB. Edward II (Selden Society), i. 137 and xxii. 146; Littleton, *Tenures*, s. 114.

[5] Y.BB. Edward II (Selden Society), xix. 28; Y.B. 12 Richard II (Ames Foundation), 71 (1388).

[6] Wm. Salt Society, *Collections* [1921], 13-14. *Bracton's Note Book*, i. p. xvi, correcting ii. p. 534 n. 8 (case no. 695).

[7] 4 & 5 Phil. & Mar., c. 8.

THE RISE OF THE ENTAIL

As we have seen,[1] it was possible under Anglo-Saxon law to impose limitations upon bookland which resemble the entail rather closely. There is no evidence, however, that this practice survived much later than the Conquest, or that it was used to any considerable degree even in Anglo-Saxon times. We have also remarked that one of the most frequent occasions for alienating land was the establishment of a younger branch of the family, and particularly the endowment of a daughter. It is in this latter that the origin of the entail must be sought.

THE MARITAGIUM

The *maritagium* or " marriage " was a post-Conquest institution which in the course of time took fairly definite form as the result of many years of custom.[2] The terms and incidents of a *maritagium* were perfectly well known and in many cases were not embodied in any written document. We do find a few examples, however, of deeds from the twelfth century which show us the principal characteristics of the gift in free marriage, and confirm Glanvill's words. In the twelfth century the gift in *maritagium* seems regularly to declare that the donor gives the lands in question together with his daughter to the donee in frank marriage—it is worth noting that the earliest forms are gifts to the husband alone and not to the wife nor the two jointly.[3] From Glanvill we learn the conditions attaching to such a gift. He tells us[4] that if the marriage is " free ", the

---

[1] Above, p. 525.

[2] For the earliest known examples, see Pollock and Maitland, ii. 16 n. 2, and cf. Coronation Charter of Henry I (1100), c. 3.

[3] Round, *Ancient Charters* (Pipe Roll Society), no. 6; Madox, *Formulare Anglicanum*, cxlv, cxlvi, cxlviii.

[4] Glanvill, vii. 18.

feudal services will not be due (for it is clear that he contemplates the establishment of frank marriage by means of subinfeudation). Feudal services, however, will revive at the moment the third heir enters. The descent of frank marriage seems already in Glanvill's day to have followed the same canon as the thirteenth century would have expressed in the formula " to *A*. and *B*. and the heirs of their bodies ". As soon as the third heir enters feudal services revive—and clearly the presumption is that by this time (three generations average one hundred years) the new family will become established and perfectly capable of performing feudal services.

THE EFFECT OF HOMAGE ON MARITAGIUM

Glanvill also tells us that the third heir is the first one who shall do homage (whether the marriage is free or not) which henceforth shall be due from all his heirs. The reason for this is that while homage has not been done there will always be the possibility of the land reverting to the donor upon the extinction of the donee's line. When, however, homage has been taken upon the entry of the third heir the lord becomes bound to warrant and his reversion is therefore destroyed.[1] The evidence all goes to show that these feudal technicalities were imposed upon an older institution[2] whose characteristics apparently were heritability by a limited class of heirs, failing which there would be a reversion to the donor unless three heirs in succession had entered; in the latter case the gift became unrestricted and the reversion was destroyed. Glanvill does not say so, but it would rather seem that until the third heir had entered the *maritagium* could not be alienated;[3] it is only by supposing some such rule as this that the provisions concerning feudal service and the reversion take a consistent shape. Glanvill furthermore assures us that until homage has been taken the tenants are in a particularly weak position, since the donor and his heirs are not yet bound to warrant. This seems to be a difficulty created by applying feudal rules to an institution which was really more ancient. In order to circumvent it the constitution of a *maritagium* was accompanied by a pledge of faith binding the donor and his heirs to maintain the arrangement. Now the pledge of faith was a purely ecclesiastical affair—a ceremony whereby the promisor put into pledge or pawn his hopes of future salvation as security for the

---

[1] *Bracton's Note Book*, no. 241 (1227) is a good illustration of some of these rules. Cf. S. J. Bailey, *Warranties of Land in the Thirteenth Century*, Cambridge Law Journal, ix. 82 at 88 ff. On the absolute failure of heirs, the lord could still take by escheat, but on the failure of the heirs of the body of the donee the lord's reversion (while it lasted) would exclude the heirs general.

[2] For the additional complication caused by discussing this situation in terms of Roman law, see the controversy between Bulgarus and Martinus over *dos profectitia*: H. Kantorowicz and W. W. Buckland, *Studies in the Glossators*, 98.

[3] Cf. *Bracton's Note Book*, no. 566; Pollock and Maitland, ii. 16. The *maritagium* in Normandy became inalienable as a result of Roman influence; see its history in Génestal, *L'Inaliénabilité dotale normande*, Nouvelle revue historique de droit, 1925.

performance of his obligations.   Over such matters the Church courts had
competence, and so litigation concerning a *maritagium* which involved
the relationship between the donor and the donee could take place in
ecclesiastical as well as in royal courts.   It may be remarked that here as
at many other points the Church exercised a powerful influence in
insuring the stability of the family by securing an adequate economic
foundation for each new family.   As we shall see later on, the Church
also used its influence to secure proper dower rights for the sustenance of
widows.   Finally, Glanvill informs us that " when a man has received
lands with his wife in marriage " they shall revert to the donor after the
death of the wife unless issue has been born alive; it is not necessary
that it should have survived.   This rule bears an obvious resemblance
to the more general rule of " curtesy", but for our purpose its importance
lies in the fact that until the birth of issue the husband's estate is very
slender; it would be quite easy for a husband to get the impression that
as far as he was concerned the gift only became a really valuable one
upon the birth of issue.   From this it would be a very short step to the
theory that such a gift was really conditional upon the birth of issue—
and this idea was to play an important part in the future.

EVOLUTION OF THE ENTAIL

In the period between Glanvill and Bracton we get an increase in the
use of written documents and considerable variety in their forms.   Instead
of conveying an interest which is described simply as a *maritagium*,
donors set out in detail the principal points of the arrangement.   We
therefore find gifts to the man alone, or to the woman alone, or to both
of them jointly, and the descent limited to the heirs or to the heirs of
the body of either or both, according to the fancy of the donor.   It is
during the same period, moreover, that we find the appearance of some
other forms of gifts which we believe must be regarded as derived, or
imitated, from the *maritagium*.   The *maritagium* was the first institution
(other than life estates) in which a reversion was saved, and it may very
well be that donors would wish to devise some other means whereby a
reversion could be saved, which could be used in other circumstances
than those under which the *maritagium* was normally constituted.   This
is the explanation for the rise and early history of the entail.   The most
striking feature of the *maritagium* was the reversion to the donor upon
the failure of the descendants of those whom he wished to benefit,[1] and
the entail was an attempt to extend this characteristic to gifts which were
not to be confined within the traditional bounds of the *maritagium*, and,
indeed, which might be entirely unconnected with any marriage.

[1] The reversion after a *maritagium* was imposed by common law even although the deed
does not provide for it; but the reversion after a fee tail is not effective unless expressly saved
in the deed: Y.B. 30 & 31 Edward I (Rolls Series), 250 (1302), 384 (1303); *contra*, Bracton,
f. 47; Holdsworth, iii. 113 n. 2.   A gift in *maritagium* which limits a remainder will be construed
as a fee tail: Y.B. 17 & 18 Edward III (Rolls Series), 342 (1343).   For an early example of a
remainder after a *maritagium*, see *Bracton's Note Book*, no. 86 (1220).

CONDITIONAL FEES

Numerous difficulties arose. The only body of rules then in existence had been developed in connection with the *maritagium*. They were admirably devised for the purpose of governing property given to a new household in the expectation that it would become a permanent family, but when they were applied to these other situations they worked confusion and mischief. In the midst of this confusion Bracton was writing, and it must be said that he did nothing to make it clearer. He begins by stating an excellent principle; all the limitations expressed in the gift (which taken together he calls the *modus*) must govern the gift, " for the *modus* will override common law because a *modus* and a covenant restrain the law ".[1] If this principle had been observed, then the newer forms of gifts which we have described would have presented little difficulty. A gift to *A.* and the heirs of his body would have been construed along simple and fairly obvious lines. But Bracton immediately vitiates his principle by introducing implied conditions, and consequently the *modus* will not prevail in actual practice, for the law will presume a number of implied conditions which the donor did not express and probably did not contemplate.

There is no doubt that in this passage Bracton has had in mind certain portions of Roman law on the matter of conditional gifts. It would be unfair, however, to accuse Bracton, personally, of using his Roman learning in a place where it did not belong. If Bracton treated these gifts as conditional it is because he had some grounds for doing so in contemporary opinion, and there is no evidence that Bracton was the originator of the doctrine.[2] We have already suggested that such an opinion might easily arise in connection with the *maritagium*, for the husband's estate under this arrangement depended to a very large degree upon the birth of issue, and he might very naturally have regarded it as being conditional upon that event. So, too, the donor might likewise have imagined that his gift was in a sense conditional, for it is natural that he should intend the gift to be the foundation of a new family, and if that family did not become established, then the gift should revert to the donor. To him, also, the *maritagium* may therefore have looked very much like a gift conditional upon the birth of issue. Then, too, it must be remembered that in practice the donor may often have remained in possession, so that the donees did not get seisin until later. This was convenient, no doubt, but risky;[3] but once again, donors might easily get the impression that a *maritagium* was not a complete gift unless the donees founded a family. In view of all this Bracton not unnaturally

---

[1] Modus enim legem dat donationi, et modus tenendus est contra jus commune et contra legem, quia modus et conventio vincunt legem: Bracton, f. 17 *b*.

[2] There are a score of cases listed under " Fee, conditional " in Maitland's index to *Bracton's Note Book*.

[3] Cf. Glanvill, vii. 1 (ed. Woodbine, p. 97), who says that in such a case there is no gift, but only the promise of a gift.

looked to his Roman books for light upon the treatment of conditional gifts, for in Bracton's day the English law was evidently very unsettled; the traditional *maritagium* was undergoing numerous variations and donors were devising all sorts of fancy limitations, while many gifts containing limitations of this sort could hardly be described as *maritagia* at all.

BRACTON ON CONDITIONAL FEES

Bracton begins his discussion by the somewhat fruitless classification of practically every sort of gift which is not in fee simple as a conditional gift, throwing together in one category the *maritagium*, gifts to religious houses, to bastards, gifts for life, for years and fee farm.[1] This, of course, is not very helpful. He then proceeds to say that the *modus* will control the line of descent and exclude heirs of any class except those named in the *modus*, while upon the failure of the prescribed class of heirs there will be a reversion to the donor, which if it is not expressed in the deed will be based upon an implied condition—which is Bracton's way of saying in Roman terms that as a matter of custom there always has been a reversion in such cases, and that it is part of the legal institution of the *maritagium* and need not be set forth specially in the deed. He then proceeds to develop this curious theory: a gift to *A.* and the heirs of his body by a particular wife (an example of a *maritagium*) gives to *A.* a life estate only until the birth of an heir; upon that event the life estate swells to a fee simple; if the heir predeceases the donee that fee simple will shrink to a life estate. On the other hand, a gift to " *A.* and his heirs if he have heirs of his body ", once it has become a fee simple upon the birth of an heir,[2] will never shrink to a life estate again on the failure of that heir; the reason for this, it seems, lies in the fact that the former gift must be construed as a *maritagium* whose aim is to endow an enduring family, while the second is expressly conditional. Consequently, the eventual failure of issue in the case of a *maritagium* reduces the donee's estate to a life interest, thereby assuring the reversion after the death of the wife and of the husband (who will be entitled to a sort of curtesy even although the issue has failed).

MARITAGIA BECOME ALIENABLE

Bracton's most striking remarks are on the subject of the alienability of the *maritagium*. The donee has only a life estate until issue is born; but then—

" if heirs of the prescribed class are born, they only are called to the succession; and if the feoffee has alienated to someone else, that alienation is good and his

---

[1] Bracton, f. 17 (c. vi. § 1). Selections (with translation) will be found in Digby, *History of the Law of Real Property* (5th edn., 1897), 164 ff.

[2] Note that there is so far no dogma saying that one cannot be heir of a living person; cf. Plucknett, *Statutes and their Interpretation*, 45; Pollock and Maitland, ii. 44; Y.BB. Edward II (Selden Society), ix. 28, where the point was contested.

heirs will be bound to warrant, since they can claim nothing save by succession and descent from their parents—although some people think that they were enfeoffed at the same time as their parents, which is not true."[1]

It certainly seems that Bracton here lets technical rules defeat the *modus* whose power he so highly praised on this very page, for he uses the rule that "heirs" is a word of limitation to enable the donee to alienate so as to disinherit the heirs. This clearly defeats the intention of the donor and flouts the *modus*. Bracton's Romanism is not to blame, for it is clear that his learned language is merely expressing the state of contemporary English law.[2] At the moment he was writing, the insurgent barons had drawn up a list of grievances (called the Petition of the Barons, 1258), c. 27, in which we have this complaint:

> "The barons pray remedy concerning the alienation of *maritagia* in such cases as this: If one give a carucate of land with his daughter or sister in marriage to have and to hold to them and the heirs issuing of the said daughter or sister in such wise that if the said daughter or sister die without heir of her body the land shall wholly revert to the donor or his heirs, although the said gift is not absolute but conditional, yet women after the death of their husbands give or sell the said *maritagium* during their widowhood and make feoffments thereof at their will although they have no heirs of their body, nor have such feoffments so far been in any way revocable (by the donor). Wherefore the barons pray remedy that out of the equity of the law there be provided a remedy to recall such feoffments by reason of the said condition either by a writ of entry or in some other competent manner and that in such cases there should be judgment for the demandant."[3]

From this it will be seen that the barons' protest was against the rule which allows the donee (who by this time was often the woman as well as the man) to alienate in spite of the failure of issue. Their suggestion of a writ of entry clearly refers to the writ of entry at common law whereby a reversioner could recover land against the alienee of a tenant for life. The barons had to wait nearly a generation before they got a remedy.

THE STATUTE DE DONIS

The Statute *De Donis*, which is the first chapter of the Statute of Westminster II (1285), examines the whole situation and enacts:

> "Concerning tenements which are often given on condition, *viz.* when one gives his land to a man and his wife and the heirs begotten of that man and woman, with an express condition added that if the man and woman die without heir begotten of that man and woman the land thus given shall revert to the donor or his heir; in the case moreover when one gives a tenement in free marriage (which gift has a condition annexed although not expressed in the charter of gift, to the effect that if the man and woman die without an heir begotten of the man and woman the tenement thus given shall revert to the donor or his heir); in the case

---

[1] Bracton, f. 17 *b*. For a great lady who under Henry II alienated some of her *maritagium*, see S. J. Bailey, *The Countess Gundred's Lands*, Cambridge Law Journal, x. 89.

[2] A *maritagium* seems to be alienated by fine in *Eyre Rolls* (Selden Society, vol. lix), no. 100 a (1221). The pleadings in a case of the next year (*ibid.* no. 1479) on the other hand imply that a *maritagium* is properly inalienable.

[3] Text in Stubbs, *Charters*.

moreover when one gives a tenement to one and the heirs of his body issuing, it seemed (and still seems) hard to donors and their heirs that the intention expressed in the gift so far has not been (and still is not) observed for in all such cases after the birth of issue to the donees of such a conditional gift, the feoffees have so far had the power of alienating the tenement so given and disinheriting thereof their issue against the will of the donors and against the express form of the gift; and moreover whereas on the failure of issue of such feoffees a tenement so given ought to revert to the donor or his heir according to the expressed form in the charter of the gift, nevertheless donors have been thus far excluded from the reversion of their tenements on account of the deed and feoffment of the donees of the conditional gift, although the issue(if there were such) had died—which was manifestly against the form of the gift.

" Wherefore our lord the King perceiving how necessary and useful it is to appoint a remedy in the aforesaid case, has established that the will of the donor according to the form manifestly expressed in the charter shall henceforth be observed, in such wise that those to whom a tenement is thus given upon condition shall not have power of alienating it and preventing it from remaining to their issue after their death, or else to the donor or his heir if issue shall fail, either by reason that there was no issue at all or if there were, that the heir of such issue had failed."[1]

The preamble mentions the three cases of a gift (a) to husband and wife and the heirs of their bodies, with a reversion expressly reserved, (b) in " free marriage " (which will be construed in law as containing by implication analogous provisions), and (c) a gift in the form merely of " to X. and the heirs of his body ". It states the mischief of the existing rules to be that on the birth of issue the donees can alienate and so (a) disinherit their issue and (b) destroy the reversion, and (c) when there has been issue which has failed, the donee can defeat the reversion. For remedy, the statute enacts the general rule that the form of the gift is to be observed so that a donee cannot prevent the tenement either descending to his issue if such there be, or reverting to the donor, if there be no issue. As the machinery for its application, the statute gives the forms for a writ of formedon in the descender (" because in a new case, a new remedy must be provided "): it remarks that formedon in the reverter is already sufficiently common. It neither mentions nor implies any remedy for remaindermen.[2]

THE DURATION OF AN ENTAIL

An examination of the use of the word " issue " in the statute will show that its meaning was not an indefinitely long line of descendants of the prescribed class, but only the first generation; this is clear, for the statute speaks of " issue or the heir of such issue ".[3] It therefore follows that the statute only assures the inheritance to the issue of the donee,

---

[1] Stat. Westminster II, c. 1; Pound and Plucknett, *Readings*, 658–660.

[2] On the question whether these remedies existed even before the statute, see below p. 561, and for *De Donis* generally, see Plucknett, *Legislation of Edward I*, 125 ff.

[3] See Updegraff, *The Interpretation of " Issue " in De Donis*, Harvard Law Review, xxxix. 200–220. With this compare the curious rule that a bond binding " *A.* and his heirs " binds the son only, and not the son's heir: *Davy* v. *Pepys* (1573) Plowd. 441, and p. 720, below.

that is to say, his heir in the first generation. The statute imposes no restraint upon an alienation by the issue. This point was raised in 1311 when the famous Chief Justice Bereford admitted that this was the literal meaning of the statute, " but ", he said—

" he that made the statute meant to bind the issue in fee tail as well as the feoffees until the tail had reached the fourth degree, and it was only through negligence that he omitted to insert express words to that effect in the statute; therefore we shall not abate this writ."[1]

According to another reporter Bereford's words were these:

" *Herle.* That case was one of free marriage and in naught similar to the present one.
" BEREFORD, C.J. I take the law to be the same in both cases, for in both cases the tail continueth until after the fourth degree; and you are to know that we will not abate the writ in these circumstances."

From this passage we can clearly see the state of affairs in 1311. The Statute *De Donis* had been in operation for a quarter of a century and it is not surprising to find that so distinguished a lawyer as Herle (who afterwards became Chief Justice of the Common Pleas) should venture the opinion that there were now two forms of gift less than a fee simple, the *maritagium* and the fee tail. It is just as significant, however, that Bereford indicates the historical relationship between the two. So strong does he feel that connection to be that he applies to the estate tail (which by now is beginning to be regarded as the creation of the Statute *De Donis*) a characteristic which was once peculiar to the *maritagium*. Back in Glanvill's day a gift in free marriage remained free until the third heir had entered, and this in the canonical way of counting was the fourth degree.[2] Bereford applies and extends this rule; the fee tail like the *maritagium* is to retain its peculiar characteristics until the third heir (or the fourth degree) enters. (As we have already observed, Glanvill does not tell us expressly that the *maritagium* in his day was inalienable,[3] but we may well believe that until the end of the twelfth century it was rarely, if ever, disposed of.) True, the statute did not say this, but Bereford had a ready explanation. Chief Justice Hengham who drew the statute had done it carelessly; as he worded it the entail only lasted two degrees, but his intention was to make it last for four. This infor-

---

[1] Y.BB. Edward II (Selden Society), xi. 177; xii. 226.

[2] Four degrees (or thereabout) are a common limit for all sorts of purposes. Writs of entry in the *per* and *cui* comprise four degrees, after which only writs in the *post* will serve. The peculiarities of parcenry ceased after four degrees, and the third warrantor of the title to goods could vouch no further in Anglo-Saxon law. At the fourth generation Anglo-Saxon rank became hereditary (J. E. A. Jolliffe, *Constitutional History*, 2); so too, four degrees may be the limit of a family settlement in Malta, thus carrying us back to Code of Rohan (1784) and ultimately to Justinian's Novel 159 (as to which see D. T. Oliver, *Roman Law in Modern Cases*, in Cambridge Legal Essays, 255).

[3] For alienations of *maritagia* in the time of Glanvill and Henry II, see *Sir Christopher Hatton's Book of Seals*, nos. 68, 146, and cf. S. J. Bailey, *The Countess Gundred's Lands*, Cambridge Law Journal, x. 89.

mation Bereford, no doubt, derived from tradition, and there was no rule at that time to prevent him from setting aside the clear words of a statute when he had private information that the draftsman really meant something else.   It is curious to observe that one of the greatest pillars of real property law had been erected so carelessly.

Bereford's exposition of the statute, like many others of his striking contributions to the law, was not followed, and in the middle of the fourteenth century it was still an open question how long an entail was inalienable—the real test of Bereford's doctrine could not, of course, be made for some time, for four degrees would normally last nearly a century. Indeed, in 1344 it was not certain that an entail would last even as long as four degrees—a very long discussion on this point was inconclusive.[1] As to what happened after the fourth degree we have no indication until the year 1410 when we are told[2] that " after the fourth degree frank marriage becomes formedon "—in other words, it is already the doctrine that an entail will endure as long as there are heirs of the prescribed class, and this doctrine is now transferred to the *maritagium* so that the *maritagium* now becomes of indefinite duration.

THE NATURE OF THE HEIR'S INTEREST

In discussing Bracton, we have seen that his difficulty was due to the application to entails of the doctrine that the word " heirs " is a word of limitation and not of purchase.   This doctrine left no basis for the expectation of the heir in tail until the Statute *De Donis* gave him a legal estate and a form of action for its protection.   This statutory reform, however, made it difficult to retain Bracton's dogma; as things stood after the statute a gift to *A.* and the heirs of his body gave to the heir an interest which was protected by the writ of formedon in the descender;   how, then, could it be said that the heir takes nothing by purchase?   An examination of the attempts to resolve this difficulty would yield interesting results which we can only briefly indicate here.[3] Shortly after the statute a case of formedon in the descender arose in which the demandant was under age.[4]   On principle the infant heir of an ancestor who died seised could sue at once for his inheritance, but as the ancestor had alienated this rule did not apply.   The demandant therefore turned to the rule that an infant can sue as to his own purchase, and argued thus:

" After the gift was made to John our father and Alice our mother and the heirs of their two bodies, John and Alice had only a freehold before they had issue, for the fee and the right remained in the donor until they had issue;   immediately

[1] Y.B. 18 & 19 Edward III (Rolls Series), 201.   Cf. *Rot. Parl. Inediti*, 227, 230 (1333); *Rot. Parl.*, ii. 142 no. 47 (1343);   149, 150 no. 10 (1344);   Sayles, *King's Bench*, iii. pp. xxxv, cxx.

[2] Y.B. 12 Henry IV, 9.

[3] Since the above was written, some interesting matter has been collected by A. D. Hargreaves, *Shelley's Ghost*, Law Quarterly Review, liv. 73.

[4] Y.B. 20 & 21 Edward I (Rolls Series), 58 (1292).

thereafter the fee and right began to be in the person of the issue, and was out of the person of the donor, and then for the first time the issue became purchaser together with the others. Since he became a purchaser under age, judgement whether he ought not to be answered although still under age."

This ingenious point was open to much criticism; the demandant had counted upon his descent, not upon his purchase, and Howard pursued the theory until it became an absurdity:

" If his father and mother were now alive and were impleaded in respect of the tenements and were to say that the tenements were given to them and the heirs of their bodies, and that they had a son named William begotten between them who was a purchaser equally with them who were in possession, and were to pray aid of him—would they delay the plea until their issue should come of age? No, by God."[1]

Bewildered by these arguments the court took refuge in the fact that the demandant was nearly twenty-one, anyhow, and so he might as well be allowed to sue. The question of the heir's interest continued to arise, however, and the proposition which Howard had regarded as absurd was soon put forward in all seriousness. The machinery of aid-prayer worked in this way: when a tenant for life was defendant in an action where the title to the fee simple was in dispute, he was unable to proceed alone. The proper thing for him to do was to " pray aid of the reversioner in whom the fee resides " in order that the reversioner could come and defend his own title. It sometimes happened, however, that there was collusion between the plaintiff and the tenant for life, in consequence of which the tenant for life omitted to pray aid of the reversioner and instead defaulted or " pleaded faintly " so as to allow the plaintiff to recover by judgment. In order to prevent the reversioner losing his rights through the dishonesty of his tenant for life in refusing to pray aid of him, a number of rules were evolved, many of them statutory,[2] which allowed the reversioner to intervene and " pray to be received to defend his right ". Thus in 1307 Agnes, widow of Thomas Picot, was the surviving donee in tail, and upon her default in a real action her son and heir prayed receipt on the ground that his mother had only a freehold. His prayer for receipt was granted.[3] In 1308 Bereford, J., recognised that the issue (" in whom the fee and right repose ") might have to be joined with the tenant in frank marriage for some purposes,[4] and about 1311 we have a case on these facts: tenements were given in frank marriage, and the husband (who had survived his wife) attempted to alienate them fraudulently by having his alienee bring an action against him which he suffered to go by default. The heir intervened and prayed to be received, and his prayer was granted.[5]

[1] Cf. Y.BB. Edward II (Selden Society), x. 269.

[2] The peculiar wording of Westminster II, c. 3, was a disturbing factor.

[3] Y.B. 33 & 35 Edward I (Rolls Series), 496.

[4] Y.BB. Edward II (Selden Society), i. 117.

[5] Y.BB. Edward II (Selden Society), i. 70 (1308), s.c. xi. 160. For a new-born child who came to court in his cradle, and successfully prayed to be received on the default of both his parents (purchasers in tail), see *ibid*. i. 72 *per* Toudeby.

Two of these cases, it will be noticed, involve what was later called a " tenant in tail after possibility of issue extinct " and clearly this situation directed attention to the peculiarities of such an estate.[1] The doctrine we are concerned with was not to be confined, however, to the receipt of an heir in tail on the default of a tenant in tail after possibility, for in 1314 we get a formal theory of the entail announced by Serjeant Toudeby in these words: " In the case where tenements are granted in fee tail and the grantee has issue, the fee is severed from the freehold, and the fee is in the issue while the freehold only is in the father."[2] This time the court rejected the theory that the fee was in the issue. If this remarkable theory had prevailed long enough to combine with the development of the idea that an entail endured indefinitely as long as there were heirs, the law would have reached a very different result, for a tenant in tail in possession would always be a life tenant only, while his heir apparent held a fee—the books do not venture to say, however, that this would be a fee simple. By the middle of the fourteenth century this doctrine is extinct. Perhaps it was felt that if even the issue in tail had a fee, it would be difficult to describe what the reversioner had.[3] As late as Richard II, we occasionally find hints of uncertainty, even among the learned. Thus in 1387 Holt, J., suggested that if land is given to *A.* and the heirs of his body, it will descend to such heirs born after the gift, and not to issue already in existence when the gift was made. The serjeants ventured to dissent from this view.[4] From the middle of the fourteenth century onwards we can clearly see the growth of the dogmas which are to be fixed in the middle of the fifteenth century in the great treatise of Littleton where we find the classical doctrine, and can appreciate the length of time which separates it from the desperate attempt of Bracton to maintain that the *maritagium* and similar so-called conditional gifts were no more than fees simple subject to a peculiar line of descent or to a condition as to the birth of issue. Attempts to identify the fee tail and the fee simple had failed, whether they be Bracton's attempt to place the fee in the donee or Toudeby's attempt to place it in the issue, and the inevitable conclusion was at last reached that an entail in fact divides the fee among different people. The use of the word " tail " curiously illustrates this. Coke and all the old books are correct when they say that it is derived from the French verb *tailler* which means " to carve ". But this word " carve " has two senses. In the first place it may mean to give a particular shape to a thing as an artist does to marble; illustrations of this sense are common. Thus, when counsel indulged in some wishful thinking about law, Bereford, C.J., remarked, " *Vous taillez la lei*

---

[1] There was naturally an increasing desire to equate it with the life estate; attempts dating from 1348 (*Rot. Parl.,* ii. 170 no. 46) to make the tenant in tail after possibility impeachable for waste were unsuccessful.

[2] *Eyre of Kent* (Selden Soc.), iii. 44.

[3] The point is well made in *Willion* v. *Berkley* (1562), Plowden, 223 at 247 ff.

[4] Y.B. 11 Richard II (Ames Foundation), 71–72.

auxicom vous le volez "—" You fashion the law as you like it ".[1] This was the original meaning of the fee tail, for the descent of the fee was limited—*taillé*—to preordained lines. But in the view of Coke, *tailler* takes the second sense of the word " carve ", for to him a fee tail consists of a fee which is cut up and partitioned among the various parties to the entail;[2] in Coke's thought to carve an entail was analogous to carving a joint—a certain amount is cut off and a certain amount is left; adding them together we have exactly one fee simple.

[1] Y.BB. Edward II (Selden Series), x. 114. Littleton, *Tenures*, s. 18, seems to take this view.
[2] So, too, even earlier, *Willion* v. *Berkley* (1562), Plowden, 225 at 251.

THE COMMON LAW ESTATES DOWN TO 1540

In the preceding chapters we have seen that a fee simple was inheritable by primogeniture since about 1200; that it was alienable without the consent of presumptive heirs since about the same date; and that nearly a century later it became freely alienable without the lord's consent as a result of the Statute *Quia Emptores* of 1290. The first two of these advances had already been made by the time of Bracton, and from his day, too, we have a large number of surviving charters which attest the frequency with which land was transferred.[1]

THE FEE SIMPLE

Bracton has some interesting observations upon the nature of a fee simple, and one of the most remarkable things about them is the fact that he approaches the subject from the point of view of current conveyancing forms. This is somewhat unfortunate, for those forms grew up as a matter of convention and were not settled by men who were particularly concerned in defining the nature of a fee simple, their main care being only to use a form of words which had a conventional meaning, whether that form, literally interpreted, would have expressed the exact nature of the operation involved was of less importance. The thing that mattered was to use a form of words which had a recognised legal effect. However, when Bracton discusses the nature of a fee simple he does so by means of a commentary upon the conventional charter of

---

[1] On the subject of this chapter see the articles by Percy Bordwell in the Iowa Law Review, volumes xxxiii, xxxiv, xxxvi and xxxvii, and by G. L. Haskins in Harvard Law Review, lxii, Boston University Law Review, xxix, University of Pennsylvania Law Review, xcvii. 6.

feoffment.[1] In his day a fee simple could be granted by a deed which said that the donor gave and granted and by his charter confirmed to the donee and his heirs the land in question, to have and to hold by specified services either of the lord of the fee or of the donor, and that the donor bound himself and his heirs to warrant the donee and his heirs against all men. Bracton's discussion centres around the word " heirs ". A gift to A. and his heirs was the conventional form for conveying the maximum legal interest, a fee simple, and Bracton first of all has to explain that in spite of the words such a charter conveys the whole estate to A. and nothing at all to his heirs; as we should say to-day, " heirs " is a word of limitation, but not of purchase. As the discussion proceeds more difficulties appear. A gift to A. and his heirs gives the full estate to A. and nothing to his heirs, but neither does it give anything to the assigns of A. If the donee A. alienates over, can this alienee claim the benefit of the warranty which the donor bound himself to give only to A. and his heirs? Bracton thinks not, and apparently this opinion was widespread, for we find about this time numerous charters in favour of the donee, his heirs and assigns, evidently drawn to meet this situation. Under such a charter the donor would be bound to warrant A., his heirs and his alienee. By the time we get to the beginning of the fourteenth century the word " assigns " ceases to be necessary—at least such was Maitland's opinion, adding that " on the whole we cannot doubt that the use of this term played a large part in the obscure process which destroyed the old rules by which alienation was fettered ".[2]

REVERSIONS

In Coke's words " a reversion is where the residue of the estate doth always continue in him that made the particular estate ". Applying to ancient cases the doctrines of his own time, Coke, and following him Challis, set forth the proposition that there could be no reversion after a conditional fee.[3] This is completely erroneous. De Donis expressly tells us that there was already a writ to secure reversions, and there are cases on the Plea Rolls to confirm this. The result of the statute was, however, to strengthen the position of the reversioner very considerably by providing that the donee's alienation should no longer be a bar to such

[1] Bracton, f. 17.

[2] Pollock and Maitland, ii. 14 n. 4. As an alternative to his deduction from Y.B. 33 & 35 Edward I (Rolls Series), 362, it may be suggested that all that Bereford meant when he said that " there is no force in that word ' assigns ', but simply in the word ' heirs of Agnes ' ", was that the word " assigns " was indeed repugnant in a deed establishing a *maritagium*; wherefore he would construe the deed as if the word " assigns " were absent and the gift were in the common form establishing a *maritagium*. The necessity of mentioning assigns in a conveyance of a fee simple is not discussed in the case (but see Percy Bordwell, *The Running of Covenants—II*, Iowa Law Review, xxxvi. 484, n. 2). The point did arise, however, in Y.B. 20 & 21 Edward I (Rolls Series), 232-233 (1292).

[3] Challis, *Real Property*, 83. The idea goes back to the late fifteenth century. For the thirteenth-century view see the case reported in *Casus Placitorum* (Selden Society), 121, 124.

an action, while at the same moment that *De Donis* was passed, another portion of the Statute of Westminster II clarified the law of receipt in favour of the reversioner (c. 3). Consequently there are two great characteristics of reversions during the middle ages. In the first place, they are not future estates, but present estates of which the reversioner is " seised "—not in demesne, certainly, but in service. Expressed in other terms, a reversion is a seignory over the tenants for life and the tenants in tail, and like other seignories in the middle ages was regarded with a good deal of concreteness. Secondly, there resulted from this attitude that liberal measure of legal protection which was due to " him in whom reside the fee and the right ", as the Year Books constantly put it. Hence the elaboration of the law of aid, receipt and voucher which had the object, and the result, of protecting the reversion against any machinations by the tenants of inferior estates. In the classical common law the reversion was, therefore, indestructible.

REMAINDERS

Estates in remainder were much longer in acquiring a definite legal standing. Here, again, the modern student must beware of the deduction on theoretical grounds by Challis that there could be no remainder after a conditional fee. This deduction is based upon the view that a conditional fee before the Statute *De Donis* was in fact a fee simple conditional; this is taking Bracton's dogma too seriously, and Maitland easily showed from surviving documents that about one-half of the conditional fees of which we have record contain remainders limited after them.[1] It is, of course, to the *maritagium* that we must look for our earliest indications. In the year 1220 we find a case involving a *maritagium* where this defence was pleaded: Geoffrey had two sisters, Beatrice and Matilda, and gave land in *maritagium* with Beatrice to Reginald fitz Ursy with this covenant, that if the said Beatrice should die without heir of her body, or if her heirs should die without heir of their body, the land should revert (*sic*) to the said Matilda and her heirs.[2] Unfortunately, the decision in this case was made upon a point of pleading and so we do not get a full discussion of this " covenant ". It will be seen, however, that it is a clear example of a gift in *maritagium* to one sister with remainder in fee to the other. The fact that the word " revert " is used instead of " remain " is of little consequence, for the use of these words was far from settled.[3]

Bracton tells us that there is a writ for the use of remaindermen (or

---

[1] The following articles deserve careful study: Elphinstone, *Notes on the Alienation of Estates Tail*, Law Quarterly Review, vi. 280; Maitland, *Remainders after Conditional Fees*, ibid. vi. 22; Challis, *Real Property* (ed. Sweet), 428; cf. Percy Bordwell, *The Common Law Scheme of Estates and the " English Justinian* ", Iowa Law Review, xxxiii. 449, 466 n. 96.

[2] *Bracton's Note Book*, no. 86.

[3] As late as 1472 a remainder was referred to as a " reversion ": Y.B. Pasch. 12 Edward IV, no. 7, f. 2 (which contains some highly speculative matter on the nature of a fee tail).

" substitutes " as he calls them) and that he will give us its form;[1] but he does not do so. The frequent occurrence of remainders in thirteenth-century conveyancing seemed very strange when it was noted that no writ of formedon in the remainder was in existence for their protection, until after the statute. The inconclusive debate between Maitland and Challis was settled just fifty years later, when (in 1940) a writ of formedon in the remainder was discovered in a manuscript register of writs which can be dated 1282—a few years, that is to say, before the statute *De Donis*.[2]

As we have already noticed, the Statute *De Donis* itself does not say anything about remainders although it uses the word " remain " in the senses of " descend " and " revert ". The position of the remainderman was always less secure than that of the reversioner, particularly because he was unable to use the writ of right; this grave disability resulted from the fact that a remainderman could not say that he himself, or his ancestors, had ever been seised. Consequently, there were obvious advantages in creating remainders by fine instead of by deed.[3] In 1311 a remainderman in fee successfully prayed receipt upon the default of a tenant for life.[4] A generation later the point was argued afresh, and the same decision reached, in 1345; in this case a long discussion, no doubt heated, concluded with the oft-quoted words:

> " *R. Thorpe*: I think you will do as others have done in the same case, or else we do not know what the law is.
> " HILARY, J.: It is the will of the justices.
> " STONORE, J.: No, law is reason."

In this case it was again held by the court that the remainderman was receivable, but it is significant how vigorously this opinion was contested, considering that it is the simplest possible case in which the question could be raised.[5] Indeed, as late as 1472 it was possible to put forward some speculative doubts as to the possibility of even a vested remainder after a fee tail.[6]

---

[1] Bracton, f. 68 *b*, who treats the remainderman as a " quasi-heir who takes by substitution according to the form of the gift ". For a short outline of the *substitution*, see Viollet, *Histoire du droit français*, 757 ff. The language of " substitution " may even occur in early private deeds: *Cartulary of St. Mary Clerkenwell* (ed. W. O. Hassall), 46 no. 66 (before 1182), at least in an ecclesiastical context.

[2] W. H. Humphreys, *Formedon en Remainder at Common Law*, Cambridge Law Journal, vii. 238. But see now S. J. Bailey, *Warranties of Land in the Thirteenth Century*, Cambridge Law Journal, viii. 275 n. 9, where point (ii) seems cogent; the initials in mediaeval registers, however, are rarely right.

[3] Cf. Y.BB. Edward II (Selden Society), x. p. xl; Y.B. 18 & 19 Edward III (Rolls Series), 374–378 (1345).

[4] Y.BB. Edward II (Selden Society), x. 98. Here the remainder was limited by indenture.

[5] Y.B. 18 & 19 Edward III (Rolls Series), 378. It was strongly contended that the old doctrine laid down by Bereford and Herle was that a remainder could entitle to receipt only if it were created by fine. This tradition was inaccurate, for the case in 1311 shows Bereford granting receipt to a remainderman by deed. The tenant's attornment made a reversion a fact ascertainable by a jury, but a remainder was " mere words ".

[6] Y.B. 12 Edward IV, Pasch. no. 7.

EARLY CONTINGENT REMAINDERS

A still more difficult problem was the contingent remainder.[1] The very earliest examples seem to have aroused little comment; for example, a fine (a particularly solemn form of conveyance) was drawn in this form according to a Year Book of 1304:[2]

> " He granted and rendered the same tenements to the aforesaid man and his wife, to have and to hold to them, and to the heirs of their bodies begotten, and if they died without such heirs the tenements should remain to the right heirs of the man.—This, however, is strange seeing that the remainder was not granted to any certain person."

In 1309 we get another fine which the Year Book reports thus:[3]

> " B grants the tenements to Robert and renders them to him in this court, to have and to hold to Robert for his whole life of the chief lord of the fee; and after the decease of Robert the tenements are to remain to C and the heirs of his body begotten, to hold of the chief lord of the fee; and if C die without heir of his body, the tenements are to remain to the right heirs of Robert to hold of the chief lord of the fee.
>
> " BEREFORD, J., asked who was to do homage."[4]

In both of these cases it must be remembered that the rule in *Shelley's Case* had not yet been formulated, and so we have in both cases a feudal difficulty which will weigh heavily upon contingent remainders in the beginning of the fourteenth century: when the remainder in fee is contingent, who is the person to do the feudal services pertaining to a fee simple? Whatever arrangement the tenant may make, it must not destroy the right of the lord to have some certain tenant all the time who will be responsible to him for the feudal services. A very curious case occurred in 1336.[5] Lands were granted by fine to Osbern and Florence his wife for life, remainder to Geoffrey his son in tail, remainder to Austin the brother of Geoffrey in tail, remainder to the right heirs of Osbern. In a real action brought against her, Florence made default after default, whereupon one John prayed to be received, as right heir of Osbern. When it was objected that there were still in existence the two remainders in tail to Geoffrey and Austin, prior to his own remainder in fee, John urged that they were void on the ground that at the time the fine was levied neither Geoffrey nor Austin was in existence,[6] and that

---

[1] On this, see generally, Percy Bordwell, *The Common Law Scheme of Estates and the Remainder*, Iowa Law Review, xxxiv. 401, 413 ff.

[2] Y.B. 32 & 33 Edward I (Rolls Series), 328.

[3] Y.BB. Edward II (Selden Society), ii. 4.

[4] For a somewhat similar argument suggesting the abeyance of the fee, see Y.BB. Edward II (Selden Society), xx. 142 (1316).

[5] Y.B. 10 Edward III, Michs. no. 8.

[6] Professor A. D. Hargreaves has suggested to me that the parents gave to their third and fourth sons (born after the fine) the names of the original remaindermen who had died without issue. For a case in 1373 of a fine to " Robert and William his son ", where it appears that Robert had two sons both called William, see Y.B. 47 Edward III, Michs. no. 16, and the comment in *Lord Cheyney's Case* (1591), 5 Rep. 68 *b*.

it was only after the fine that Osbern and Florence achieved the requisite two sons to take the names assigned to them in the fine. The court held that the remainders to Geoffrey and Austin were bad but allowed John to be received as right heir of Osbern. It thus appears that although these remainders to named persons not *in esse* at the time of the gift were bad,[1] yet as early as 1336 the court supported a remainder, contingent at first, which had subsequently vested.

Later still in 1388 a party brought detinue to obtain possession of a charter, alleging that he was entitled to the land to which the charter referred. It appeared that one *W.* gave the land to *A. C.* in tail, the remainder to the right heirs of *A. S.*; *A. C.* enfeoffed one *B.* with warranty and his executor (after his death without heir) gave *W.*'s charter to *B.* as a document of title. *A. S.* is also dead, and the plaintiff is suing as his right heir. Cherlton, C.J., observed: " You think that although *A. S.* was alive when the remainder was limited, yet since he was dead when the remainder fell in and had a right heir, that therefore the remainder is good." The plaintiff was successful.[2] The case is therefore consistent with the view which is to be found in other cases from 1336 onwards that if a contingent remainder in the course of circumstances subsequently becomes vested, then it is good enough. These decisions, however, were not reached without a good deal of discussion. In 1410 a determined attack on such a remainder was made, but it was finally held good.[3] In 1431 Martin, J., upheld such a remainder, although Paston, J., remarked that it could not be proved by reason, *i.e.* was not defensible on principle; counsel added that the point had been argued in the moots.[4]

Littleton does not seem to discuss the question, but he does make it clear that in his opinion there were other sorts of contingent remainder of which he personally did not approve. Thus, in discussing the settlement alleged to have been made by Rickhill, J., in the reign of Richard II, Littleton argues against the validity of the remainders limited in it.[5] According to what Littleton had heard, there were successive entails to the judge's sons, with a proviso that if one of the sons should attempt to break the entail his estate should cease and the land should pass to the one next entitled. Such a proviso, in Littleton's view, was a condition,

---

[1] Cf. 39 Ass. 20 (1365).

[2] *Detinue*, 46. This case admirably illustrates the need for combining all available sources in the study of Year Book material. In the first edition of this work we stated (as the text in Fitzherbert's *Abridgement* expressly says) that the plaintiff was unsuccessful, and hazarded the opinion that nevertheless the case might not be inconsistent with those already discussed. The case has now been re-edited in Y.B. 11 Richard II (ed. Thornley, Ames Foundation), 283–288. It now appears that the best MS. has a blank where the others state that the defendant had judgment, and the plea roll records judgment in the plaintiff's favour. In consequence of the discovery of the correct decision of this case, and a re-examination of the other cases, it would seem that the recognition of this type of remainder took place a century earlier than the date suggested in Holdsworth, iii. 135.

[3] Y.B. 11 Henry IV, 74 no. 14.

[4] Y.B. 9 Henry VI, 23 no. 19 at p. 23.

[5] Littleton, s. 720.

and while he agreed that a reversioner could enter for the breach of a condition, a remainderman could not. Whether Littleton's views represent what a court would have decided either in Littleton's day or (seventy years earlier) in Rickhill's day, it is impossible to say; nor is there any satisfactory proof that Rickhill ever made such a settlement. Even the enthusiastic Coke places it no higher than " those things that one hath by credible hearsay " which " are worthy of observation ".[1]

We may conclude from this evidence that, during most of the fourteenth and fifteenth centuries, the courts were willing to recognise remainders to the right heirs of a living person, in cases where that person died before the remainder fell in. Other types of contingent remainder seem hardly to have arisen in litigation.

It is noteworthy, however, that as early as 1431 it was recognised that there was a difference between grants by deed and devises.[2] There were places (particularly boroughs) where land was devisable by local custom, and it was recognised that remainders (and other dispositions) which would be void in a deed might be good in a devise. It is therefore clear that the differences between dispositions by deed and those in a devise are at least a century older than the statutes of wills made by Henry VIII, and that the common law was considering these problems as they were presented by local customs long before those statutes permitted the devise of lands held by common law tenures. It is likewise clear that the peculiarities permitted in a devise do not derive from the freedom associated with the use, but were part of the tradition of local customs.

The difficulties connected with seisin in limiting remainders we have already mentioned. In part they were avoided by the device of giving seisin to the particular tenant, which seisin was held to enure to the benefit of the remainderman. This doctrine, however, had the important corollary that the remainder was dependent upon the life estate, and that the destruction of the life estate would involve the destruction of the remainder too. This doctrine was worked out in connection with vested remainders by Littleton, and was destined to have important results in later law.

THE RULE IN SHELLEY'S CASE

In spite of Bracton's doctrine, attempts were still made from time to time to use the word " heirs " as a word of purchase. We have seen this in the history of the contingent remainder, while here we may note a series of cases which anticipate by two hundred years the famous rule in *Shelley's Case*.[3] In the reign of Edward II a few obscure references

---

[1] Co. Lit. 377 b. Cf. below, p. 590.

[2] Y.B. 9 Henry VI, 23 no. 19, where Babington observed that a devise is " marvellous ".

[3] 1 Rep. 88 b (1581). For discussions, see Challis, *Real Property* (ed. Sweet), 154; Holdsworth, iii. 107; Hargreaves, *Shelley's Ghost*, Law Quarterly Review, liv. 75, casts doubt on the view expressed above.

occur, and in the reign of Edward III we find some clear discussions of the problem involved. Thus in 1350 we find that lands were conveyed by fine to *D.* for life, remainder to *K.* for life if she survived *D.*, remainder to the right heirs of *D.* The question was whether *D.* by his deed could have permitted *K.* (who was to succeed him as life tenant) to commit waste. As a mere life tenant he could not, but in the course of the discussion, Willoughby, J., observed that " according to some people, when the fee is limited to the right heirs of a certain person then the fee is in the ancestor ". To this proposition Serjeant Seton agreed, and the court held that the deed ought to be answered, whereupon issue of *non est factum* was joined.[1] Again, in 1366 a case arose upon the following facts:[2] land was given to *J.* for life, remainder in tail to his eldest son, remainder in fee to the right heirs of *J.* After the death of the life tenant and the extinction of the entail, Richard Sutton, second son of *J.*, entered as the right heir. Thereupon the provost of Beverley distrained Richard for relief which would be due if Richard entered as heir, but not if he entered as purchaser. This discussion took place:

" *Cavendish.* If the lease was made to your father for life with remainder to his right heirs then the father had the fee . . . and if you were under age the lord would have wardship and consequently relief.

" *Finchden.* He cannot avow upon us for relief as heir of the tenant in special tail, because we are not in as his heir.

" Thorpe, C.J. I know very well what you want to say. You have pleaded that you ought not to have to pay relief since you are in as purchaser, being the first in whom the remainder takes effect according to the words of the deed; but you are in as heir to your father . . . and the remainder was not entailed to you by your proper name but under the description of heir; and so it was awarded by all the justices that the lord should have return of the distress."

From this it is clear that there is very strong mediaeval precedent for the rule in *Shelley's Case,* and that the foundation of it was the hardship to lords if their tenants were allowed to limit remainders to their heirs, and thus make them purchasers.[3] This rule, therefore, like many others, once had a perfectly rational basis (while feudalism lasted) in protecting lords against serious loss through conveyances of this kind, which in those days would have seemed almost fraudulent. As with so many other troublesome rules, confusion was increased by the attempts which have been made by the courts to restrict its operation, and especially by the endeavours of Lord Mansfield to lessen its importance.[4] As a result,

---

[1] Y.B. 24 Edward III, 70 no. 79. An interesting case in 1353 shows a gift to husband and wife in special tail, remainder to the right heirs of the husband; they had no issue, and the husband devised the fee simple. Held, that the devisee has sufficient title to bring the assize: 27 Ass. 60.

[2] Y.B. 40 Edward III, f. 9 no. 18. Unhappily the text of the black-letter edition leaves the precise state of the pedigree in doubt.

[3] In the previous century tenants pursued the same object by simply enfeoffing their eldest sons, until 52 Hen. III, c. 6, made the device ineffective.

[4] Fifoot, *Mansfield,* 167–180.

doubt was thrown upon it, and a vast mass of litigation was needed to establish it anew.

DOWER

We now come to dower, whose early history is singularly obscure.[1] Ancient forms insist that it is a voluntary gift of a portion of his property made by the husband to the wife. Such seems to have been the law as late as Bracton's day, although as early as Glanvill it was thought that church and lay law compelled the husband to make the gift. The gift might take place at the time of the marriage, although in some cases on the continent we find dower constituted many years after the marriage. In England the royal courts only recognised dower which was constituted at the church door, that is to say, at the moment of the solemnisation of the marriage; it naturally followed, therefore, that a husband could only grant dower out of land which he actually held at the time of the marriage. Informal or clandestine marriages did not confer legal protection upon dower constituted on such irregular occasions, for the marriage must be " solemnised "—although it would seem there was no need for the nuptial Mass. In this we see very clearly the hand of the Church, which was fighting a hard battle to make marriage a precise, definite and public ceremony, although it is curious to observe that the common law was (for a moment) ready to move faster in this direction than the Church.[2] The common law also showed especial distrust of death-bed endowments —as also of death-bed marriages hastily contracted in the hope of legitimising the offspring. In England, the King's Court refused to recognise dower constituted at any moment save at the marriage ceremony.

This is, generally speaking, the position of dower down to the time of Bracton. Shortly afterwards, very important changes took place whose progress has not been traced in detail. Under the new order dower consists of one-third of the land held by the husband at the time the marriage was made, unless he has specified less. By the time of Edward I dower also attached to land acquired by the husband subsequent to the marriage,[3] while an endowment of less than one-third soon ceased to be a bar to a widow's demand of a full third. On the other hand, an endowment of more than one-third would be reduced by the court at the instance of the heir. In this way dower ceases to be a gift and becomes

[1] In Anglo-Saxon times a husband covenanted with his wife's family to make her a satisfactory " morning-gift ". His widow would forfeit this if she remarried (Canute II, 73 a); cf. the Kentish " Free-bench ", Pollock and Maitland, ii. 418. That seems also to have been the common law rule at the opening of the twelfth century: Henry I's Coronation Charter (1100), c. 4. The fullest history of dower in the middle ages is in F. Joüon des Longrais, La Saisine, 315–441.

[2] The policy of requiring an unmistakable public ceremony for a marriage conflicted with the policy of freeing marriage from complicated formalities, and with the desire to construe relationships as matrimonial whenever possible.

[3] This rule seems implied in the pleadings of a case as early as 1221: Eyre Rolls (Selden Society, vol. lix), no. 1080, and was later regarded as the result of the language of Magna Carta (1217), c. 7.

an estate arising by operation of law.   Britton expressed the change very clearly: " Since the usage of dower is become law, a wife is sufficiently endowed although her husband say nothing."[1]   If the husband alienated after the marriage the widow could recover one-third—and this is protected by statute[2] against the husband's warranty and against a collusive recovery, although it had long been possible to convey free of dower by fine, if the wife came into court and expressed her assent to it.

The forfeiture or escheat incurred by the husband's treason or felony (which may be regarded as involuntary alienation) raised interesting problems.   At the time of the Conquest at least one local custom held that forfeiture did not always exclude dower.[3]   By the thirteenth century, however, we find that the felon's widow loses her dower.[4]

In England the widow's interest has always been for her life only, but in some continental customs it was absolute, and so it sometimes played a part in the development of community.

It will be seen that dower is likely to interfere considerably with strict feudal notions; it reduces the resources of the incoming heir by one-third, and if that heir is a minor, it reduces the quantity of land which will be in the lord's wardship by the same proportion.   It is significant that the widow of a military tenant is endowed less liberally than the Kentish free-bencher; boroughs, too, often gave dower of one-half, and villein widows so frequently had the whole tenement in dower that there arose a sort of presumption that if a tenement was subject to dower of the whole, it was a villein tenement.

There were, however, mitigations in the strict rule.   Dower obviously could not attach to joint estates (and for centuries this rule was a boon to joint feoffees to uses and to trustees).   The relation of dower to entailed estates caused some difficulty for a time, until it was settled that the widow was endowable of an entail if, under the limitations, any issue of hers could have inherited.   Thus a widow will have dower of lands which her husband held to himself and the heirs of his body: but a second wife is not endowable of lands held by the husband to himself and his heirs by the first wife.[5]   The greatest difficulty of all was naturally the risk to purchasers, who after the vendor's death might have to answer an action of dower by his widow.   At a comparatively early date, therefore, it became possible to avoid this situation by taking a conveyance by fine.

[1] Britton, ii. 236 ff., Harvard Law Review, xl. 925 at n. 13.

[2] Exposition of the Statute of Gloucester, 6 Edw. I (1278), c. 3; Westminster II, 12 Edw. I (1285), cc. 3 and 4.   For an earlier case in which dower was defeated by alienation, see *Eyre Rolls* (Selden Society, vol. lix.), no. 257 (1221).   In no. 1159 (also dated 1221) a claim was bought out, and in no. 1433 (1222) a doweress got judgment against an alienee.

[3] *Domesday Book*, i. 154 *b*; Pollock and Maitland, ii. 457.

[4] *Bracton's Note Book*, no. 1334 (1217); *Eyre Rolls* (Selden Society, vol. lix), no. 1023 (1221). So, too, the escheat on the death of a bastard deprives his widow of her dower: Y.BB. Edward II (Selden Society), x. 12.

[5] The history of this has recently been explained by Sir William Holdsworth in his introduction to Y.B. 10 Edw. II, 1316–1317 (52 Selden Society), xvii.   Cf. *Casus Placitorum* (Selden Society), 26 no. 68; Y.B. 11 Richard II (Ames Foundation), 158; Y.B. 13 Richard II (*ibid.*), 52.

In order to bar dower effectually, the wife was brought into court and examined, whereupon she could of her own free will resign her dower rights.[1]

With the close of the middle ages the increasing efficiency of settlements made dower less important and the rule appears in the Statute of Uses that a jointure will bar dower;[2] at the same time equity refused dower out of a use, and the eighteenth-century Chancellors would not allow dower out of a trust. Since the Dower Act[3] in England, dower ceased to be of practical importance, but that policy has not been adopted universally in America. The later distrust of dower is reflected in the fact that there was a tendency among some of the American colonies to enable a husband to defeat dower simply by deed or will, but later the stricter rule of the common law was received.

CURTESY

Tenancy by the curtesy of England is the husband's right to hold his wife's lands for the remainder of his life after her decease, if issue has been born alive,[4] although it is not necessary that it should survive. Glanvill[5] tells us this curious rule but gives it no special name; Bracton[6] calls it " tenancy by the law of England ", while in the earliest Year Book[7] it is described as " the curtesy of England ", which, as Maitland[8] suggests, may be a name applied to it by appreciative husbands. In Normandy such a right only lasted until remarriage,[9] but in England curtesy was for life, and even went so far as to allow a second husband's curtesy to postpone the entry of an heir by the first husband, and thus to defeat the lord's wardship.[10] There is an old tradition, so far unconfirmed, that curtesy owed its origin, or at least its more striking features, to a

---

[1] This appears in Bracton, f. 95 b, who includes a recovery also.

[2] Statute of Uses, 27 Hen. VIII, c. 10, s. 6. If the whole of the husband's property was in uses, the wife was unprotected, for there could be no dower out of a use, but it was customary to make her a jointure of part of the property. As the statute executed all the uses, dower would arise out of the husband's separate uses which had become legal estates; the statute foresaw this and enacted that the jointure should be a bar to dower.

[3] 3 & 4 Will. IV, c. 105 (1833).

[4] The child must have been heardt o cry, according to a decision of the king and council: Sayles, King's Bench, i. 32–33 (1277).

[5] Glanvill, vii. 18; it should be noted that Glanvill only mentions the rule in connection with the maritagium, and gives no indication whether it applied to the wife's fees simple. (See, however, Pollock and Maitland, ii. 420 n. 1.)

[6] Bracton, f. 438.

[7] Y.B. 20 & 21 Edward I (Rolls Series), 39, 55 (1292).

[8] Pollock and Maitland, ii. 417.

[9] Summa de Legibus Normannie (ed. Tardif), cxix. 1. It was there called viduitas, or veufté. Remarriage was immaterial in England (except in Kent). See, however, Eyre Rolls (Selden Society, vol. lix), no. 1090 (1221).

[10] It was also settled in 1226 that a second husband's curtesy would take priority over the entry of an heir of full age to the previous husband. Patent Rolls (1225–1232), 96; cf. the case in the previous footnote. By De Donis a second husband had no curtesy in land entailed to the wife.

royal concession.[1] According to more modern views it seems to have developed from a wardship, first over the wife and next over the children.[2]

" To this, so we think, points the requirement that a child capable of inheriting from the wife shall be born—born and heard to cry within the four walls. This quaint demand for a cry within the four walls is explained to us in Edward I's day as a demand for the testimony of males—the males who are not permitted to enter the chamber where the wife lies, but stand outside listening for the wail which will give the husband his curtesy. In many systems of marital law the birth of a child, even though its speedy death follows, has important consequences for husband and wife; sometimes, for example, the ' community of goods ' between husband and wife begins, not with the marriage, but with the birth of the first-born. These rules will send back our thoughts to a time when the sterile wife may be divorced, and no marriage is stable until a child is born."[3]

A good deal of legislation from Edward I's reign[4] was necessary to prevent the abuse of curtesy rights, and the Year Books contain many cases where husbands attempted to exceed their powers in dealing with their wives' lands. In equity a husband could have curtesy out of his wife's separate uses, which, however, she could easily defeat, and modern legislation giving married women control over their separate property reduced curtesy to a minimum, long before it was finally abolished.

THE LIFE ESTATE

The tenant by curtesy owed his estate to the operation of law, and soon the doweress also acquired a legal right independent of her husband's act. Both of them, moreover, were asserting rights in the land of some-one else—the heir. Both of those estates were for life, destined to assure the economic independence of their owners within the framework of the family fortune. Naturally they were regarded as freeholders, as seised of a free tenement, and as protected by the petty assizes. With the new system of primogeniture and free alienation, however, such provision became necessary for others besides widows and widowers, and so we find life estates created by act of the parties, and following in general the same pattern. This development (if our hypothesis is true) is closely paralleled by the development of the entail from the old *maritagium*.

The implications of the life tenant's seisin were numerous and important. Its earlier sense included wide discretion in the use, and

---

[1] *Mirror of Justices* (Selden Society), 14. The object of the concession, according to an old, but plausible tradition, was to ease the lot of poor Normans who married English heiresses, and lost their fortunes when the wife died. " There are a number of cases, few but significant, in which there is reason to think that one of the Conqueror's barons has acquired his fief by marriage with the heiress of an Old English family ": Stenton, *English Families and the Norman Conquest*, Transactions of the Royal Historical Society [1944], 5.

[2] For a reference to this " wardship " see *Eyre Rolls* (Selden Society, vol. liii), no. 908 1219); vol. lix no. 559 (1221).

[3] Pollock and Maitland, ii. 418. In 1277 the issue was to be " seen, heard and baptised ": Sayles, *King's Bench*, i. 32.

[4] Statute of Gloucester (1278 ,c. 3; Westminster II, c. 3.

indeed, the abuse of the tenement. Thus Bracton[1] describes an elaborate law of waste by doweresses, but the tenant for life can use the land as his own within reason; indeed, he has a case to show that the court will not take notice of his waste unless it was considerable.[2] The guardian in chivalry, like the doweress, is clearly dealing with someone else's land, and is heavily penalised if he commits waste.[3] In Bracton's day the remedy was still of a discretionary nature. The reversioner obtained from the king a prohibition, and if the tenant still continued to waste, he could be attached for breach of the prohibition. In 1267 there was a statute[4] prohibiting waste generally, but the proceedings were still based upon the prohibition (now general instead of individual), until in 1285 summons was made to replace the prohibition; the reason given for abolishing the prohibition was that many people mistakenly thought that waste was not actionable unless it was committed after a prohibition.[5]

A further result of the life tenant's seisin was the capacity to deal with the land in ways which were admitted to be wrongful. Out of his seisin he could enfeoff a stranger and create a tortious fee simple,[6] nor could the reversioner have any remedy until after the life tenant's death, when he could bring entry *ad communem legem* against the alienee. By statute[7] in 1278, however, a doweress who acted thus forfeited her dower and the heir recovered immediately by entry *in casu proviso*, and the warranty of a tenant by curtesy was made less effectual. Alienations in fee by tenants by curtesy and tenants for life did not incur forfeiture until 1310.[8] Besides a tortious feoffment, a collusive recovery against a tenant for life would also create a fee simple in the alienee, and a complicated mass of rules, largely statutory, endeavoured to minimise the mischief.[9]

THE TERM OF YEARS

The term of years has a long and peculiar history. In the early days of the common law the position of the termor was remarkably weak. In the early thirteenth century his only remedy was an action of covenant against the lessor, which was in effect an action for specific performance.[10]

---

[1] Bracton, ff. 315, 316.

[2] *Ibid.* 316 *b*; *Bracton's Note Book*, no. 607 (1231).

[3] Bracton, f. 317; Magna Carta (1225), c. 4; 3 Edw. I (1275), c. 21; 6 Edw. I (1278), c. 5.

[4] 52 Hen. III, c. 23.

[5] 13 Edw. I, c. 14.

[6] So, too, could a guardian in chivalry; 3 Edw. I (1275), c. 48.

[7] 6 Edw. I, c. 7.

[8] Y.B. 3 Edward II, 16; for entry *in consimili casu*, see above, p. 362.

[9] The reversioner may " pray to be received to defend his right " if the tenant omits to " pray aid " of him. Receipt existed in Bracton's day on the default of a doweress (Bracton, f. 393 *b*) and was extended by Westminster II, c. 3 (1285), to reversioners after a tenant by curtesy, in dower, for life, or in tail. The procedure was amended by the Statute *De Defensione Juris* (20 Edw. I), 1292.

[10] The judgment on a writ of covenant will be " that the covenant be held "; *Bracton's Note Book*, no. 1739 (1226).

As against strangers the termor had no protection, and so had to content himself with enforcing an express warranty (if he had one) of quiet possession against his lessor.[1] Later, such a covenant will be implied. The disadvantages of a term of years were numerous; if the lessor died leaving an infant heir the term was suspended until the heir came of age, when the term was resumed;[2] the lessor's widow was entitled to one-third of the tenement for life as dower, and so the term had to be lengthened to compensate;[3] again, if the lessor alienated he could (for a time) convey free of the term.[4]

About the year 1235 the great judge Raleigh invented a new form of action called *quare ejecit infra terminum* which Bracton assures us was meant to protect the termor against all disturbers and to give him the recovery of his term.[5] This action would therefore be equivalent to an assize of *novel disseisin*. Such a remedy, however, was too drastic, and seems almost immediately to have been reduced to an action against those only who claimed under the feoffment from the original lessor.[6] Although the lessor's feoffment would not henceforth defeat a term, there were still other methods available, and until the Statute of Gloucester, c. 11 (1278), it was possible by means of a collusive recovery to convey free of the term; under the statute the termor was now allowed receipt.[7] Meanwhile the termor acquired another remedy. This was an action of trespass *de ejectione firmae* which by the time of Edward II was available against all disturbers, but this time the termor only got damages and not the recovery of his term.

THE ECONOMIC ROLE OF THE TERM

In order to explain this curious history we shall have to examine the function which the term of years performed in the thirteenth-century economic system. The great problem, of course, is why the termor was not protected by the petty assizes. It is certainly not because the term of years was only held by unimportant people: bishops, monasteries and

---

[1] To eject a lessee was a disseisin to the lessor, however: *Eyre Rolls* (Selden Society, vol. lix), no. 102 (1221).

[2] Bracton, f. 30. For a termor's defence to an assize of *mort d'ancestor* see Y.B. 20 & 21 Edward I (Rolls Series), 228–230 (1292).

[3] Bracton, f. 312 (citing two cases not in the *Note Book*). For doubts on the rule, see *Casus et Judicia*, no. 50 and (in the same volume) *Casus Placitorum*, 28-81; *Brevia Placitata*, 117.

[4] See, however, the curious passage in Bracton, f. 30 *b*.

[5] Bracton, f. 220 (who does not mention Raleigh's name); the attribution is found in certain manuscript registers: Pollock and Maitland, ii. 108 n. 2. It is important to remember that terms of years in the thirteenth century fulfilled the same functions as feudal wardships and marriages, *i.e.* they were bought and sold as investments. The action of *quare ejecit infra terminum* is therefore closely related to various forms of *quare ejecit* for holders of wardships.

[6] The writ as finally settled is directed against a purchaser from the lessor. There were some doubts for a while, however, as to whether the writ went even this far: Pollock and Maitland, ii. 108 n. 3. Cf. the note in Y.BB. Edward II (Selden Society), xiv (pt. 1), xv.

[7] In 1529 he was allowed to "falsify" a recovery: statute 21 Henry VIII, c. 15.

great lords are to be found holding terms of years. Nor can it be said that a term of years was non-feudal, for there was little appreciable difference between a life estate which did fealty only and a term of years which also involved fealty in many cases. Indeed, as a result of the real remedies devised by Raleigh and extended by the Statute of Gloucester, it was clear that the lessee had a tenement,[1] and in Raleigh's own day it was said that he was seised.[2] For centuries it remained the law that if the lessor makes a release of the fee to a termor in possession, then the termor is seised of the fee without receiving a livery of seisin—indeed, the common assurance of a Lease and Release is only explicable on the ground that a termor was seised. But the great distinction was that although the termor was seised of a tenement, yet he was not seised of a *free* tenement, which alone would entitle him to protection by the petty assizes. Why, then, is a term of years not treated as a free tenement? Maitland's solution ascribed this to the influence of Roman law which would reduce the term of years to an usufruct.

> " In an evil hour the English judges, who were controlling a new possessory action, which had been suggested by foreign models, adopted this theory at the expense of the termor. He must be the *conductor* who does not possess, or he must be the usufructuary who does not possess the land but has ' *quasi*-possession ' of a servitude. But they cannot go through with their theory. In less than a century it has broken down. The termor gets his possessory action; but it is a new action. He is ' seised ', but he is not ' seised of free tenement ', for he cannot bring an assize. At a somewhat later time he is not ' seised ' but is ' possessed '. English law for six centuries and more will rue this youthful flirtation with Romanism."[3]

Against this theory must be placed the important criticisms of Joüon des Longrais, who first of all establishes the economic history of the term of years.[4] The term of years was used for purposes which were immoral and speculative, largely to avoid the Church's prohibition of usury. It seems that the principal object of the term of years was to enable money to be lent on the security of land at considerable profit to the lender. A capitalist would give to an embarrassed landowner a sum of money down; in return he took a term of years sufficiently long to enable him to recover the capital, together with his profits, out of the revenues of the land. On the face of it this transaction was merely the sale of a lease in return for a lump sum, and technically it would seem to avoid the objection of usury. The termor, therefore, is not unnaturally placed

---

[1] See *contra* Challis, *Are Leaseholds Tenements?* Law Quarterly Review, vi. 69 (reprinted in his *Real Property*, ed. Sweet, 424).

[2] Thus Bracton, f. 268, describes a plea that " if *A.* had seisin, it was only for a term ", and as late as 1389 the Year Books will speak of a termor's seisin, *e.g.* Y.B. 13 Richard II (ed. Plucknett, Ames Foundation), 89. The suggestion in Pollock and Maitland, ii. 109, that a termor could sue for the breach of " his close " is not supported by mediaeval authority; the writs available for termors carefully avoided this expression for some time; the termor begins to talk about " his close " in the time of the Commonwealth: Bacon, *Abridgement* (1832), viii. 657.

[3] Pollock and Maitland, ii. 115.

[4] F. Joüon des Longrais, *La Conception anglaise de la saisine*, 141–148.

in popular literature in very bad company among usurers and other scoundrels who prey upon society.[1] A termor was no doubt seised in Bracton's day, but there was every reason for not calling his tenement a free tenement. Joüon des Longrais has shown that the free tenement of which the estates for life, in dower, by curtesy, in tail, or in fee simple are examples, is a very different thing. The free tenement which the petty assizes protected consists of " family property which is up to a point permanent, productive of revenue ". The essence of the free tenement is that it should be the permanent and normal economic basis of the family. Herein lies the importance of giving it full and speedy protection, and for this purpose the petty assizes were invented. Contrasted with the free tenements the estate of the termor is merely a speculative arrangement, calculated to evade the law against usury, made between a grasping money-lender on the one hand, and on the other a man whose difficulties temporarily compel him to part with his patrimony —and it must be remembered that during the middle ages a very wealthy landowner would usually find it difficult to produce a comparatively small sum of money at short notice. There was, therefore, no reason whatever for protecting the termor by those assizes whose object was to fortify the family and its means of subsistence against wrongdoers of another type. Viewed in this light there is ample explanation for the refusal of the common law to allow the termor to use the assizes.

" The object of the assizes is to protect the real property of the family which is the source of a constant revenue assuring the maintenance of a person at least for his whole life, all of which is implied in the words ' seisin of a free tenement '; but the tenure of land by lease for a few years has none of these characteristics."[2]

The law could not continue indefinitely to be governed by the social policy of a bygone age, and under Edward I it became necessary to give the lender of money a security in land much more solid than the term of years; of the statutory freeholds by which this was effected we have already spoken.[3]

THE HUSBANDRY LEASE

The term of years was not exclusively concerned with providing a form of financial security. Already in the late twelfth century land was granted for a term of years, sometimes with the accompanying agricultural stock, to tenants who farmed the land.[4] Here, as in a number of other cases, we have to take account of the results of the Black Death and the

---

[1] See the extracts from songs and sermons in Joüon des Longrais, 120, and in Harvard Law Review, xl. 924. Cf. Page, *Estates of Crowland Abbey*, 112 ff., who shows that lessors were generally poor or improvident.

[2] Joüon des Longrais, 143.

[3] Above, pp. 390 ff.

[4] See the examples in H. G. Richardson, *Oxford Law School under John*, Law Quarterly Review, lvii. 319 at 327 n. 35. Early thirteenth-century rolls also mention the " loan " or " bailment " of land; the true nature of these transactions is rarely ascertainable: *Eyre Rolls* (Selden Society, vol. lix), nos. 127, 272 (1221); in no. 1018 it seems to mean a royal grant during pleasure; cf. Plucknett, *The Mediaeval Bailiff*, 16 ff.

economic revolution which followed it.[1] One of these results was a slow increase in the number of people who took their lands under leases for terms of years, and so during the fourteenth century we find the rise of the husbandry lease as it exists to-day in England. At the same time, other and more effective methods were devised for rendering land a security for debt, and so the termor was no longer associated with the worst aspects of money-lending. For the future the termor will be regularly a freeman whose capital is insufficient to purchase much land, although he is active and enterprising enough to work the land of other owners. At the same time there was a tendency for the quantity of land under cultivation to increase somewhat since a good deal of waste was being reclaimed; such reclaimed land was frequently let out on lease. Small landowners of the yeoman class also seem to have found it often desirable to take an additional quantity of land under lease. The termor is, therefore, in every way deserving of the law's protection. As early as 1383 it was clearly stated that the unexpired term could not be recovered when an attempt was made to use trespass *de ejectione* for this purpose.[2] In 1454 it was again stated that this was impossible and that damages only were obtainable.[3] In 1467 and again in 1481 we find the opinion (although not a decision) that this action might give recovery of the term;[4] in 1498 or 1499 we get the first clear decision to that effect.[5] The termor was very slow in getting a real action, but in the end he got the most useful and practical of all the real actions. While freeholders had to be content with assizes and writs of entry, the termor could recover his term by the swift and simple action of trespass. So great a convenience was this that freeholders began to try to secure the same advantage. Finally they succeeded by means of the device called the action of ejectment.[6] In this way a good deal could be done without resorting to the older forms of action. This development took place during the sixteenth century and the finishing touches to the edifice of fiction were the work of Lord Chief Justice Rolle during the Commonwealth, but already at the beginning of the seventeenth century the action was so commonly used that Coke lamented the fact that the old real actions were becoming very rare. And so by a curious twist of history, the freeholder was glad in the end to avail himself of remedies originally designed for the protection of the humble termor.

---

[1] The changes were not everywhere immediate or catastrophic: Page, *op. cit.*, 120–129; Levett, *The Black Death* (Oxford Studies, vol. 5).

[2] It was further suggested that the damages were limited to the past, and did not extend to the future of the term: Fitz. *Ejectione Firme*, 2. This action was in fact appropriated at first to cases brought after the lease had expired; *quare ejecit*, on the other hand, could only be brought during the term.

[3] Y.B. 33 Henry VI, Michs. no. 19. The passage is merely a note of uncertain origin; there is no trace of any decision to this effect.

[4] Y.B. 7 Edward IV, Pasch. no. 16, fo. 6; 21 Edward IV, Michs. no. 2, fo. 11.

[5] There is no year book report, and so the sole authority for the statement is F.N.B. 220 H.

[6] Above, p. 373.

USES AND THE STATUTE

English lawyers are apt to believe that the use, and later the trust, are the peculiar inventions of English law. It is perfectly true that they were developed independently and along original lines, but it is interesting to observe that other legal systems have reached something like the same result by a different road. As early as the Salic Law in the fifth century we find the *salman*, whose position partly resembles that of a trustee and partly that of an executor, but it is in Mohammedan law of the present day that we find a most striking resemblance to the trust in an alien system.

> " In the wakf they invented a legal concept which equals if not excels in originality and practical utility the Anglican trust; it combines the ideas of trust, family entail, and charitable foundation. The grantor transfers the bare legal title to God and appoints an administrator to manage the property for the beneficiary; thus there are four parties to the transaction. This expedient has proved so flexible and so popular that in the Ottoman Empire three fourths of the city lands were held by this tenure."[1]

THE HISTORY OF THE WORD " USE "

As for the origins of the English use, several suggestions have been made, and for a long time the favourite was to seek it in some aspect of Roman law, either the *usufructus* or the *fideicommissum*. It is now possible to state with some certainty that neither of these two institutions has any practical bearing upon the development of the English use. As Mr Justice Holmes observes, the existence of the *salman* in the Salic Law is

[1] Wigmore, *Panorama of Legal History*, ii. 565.

proof enough that Germanic law was capable of developing from its own resources the idea of a feoffee to use.[1]

The English word " use " in this connection is in fact derived not from the Latin *usus* but from *opus*, the phrase being *A. tenet ad opus B.—A.* holds for the benefit of *B*. The use first occurs, as might be expected, in connections which are informal and non-technical.[2] The Latin phrase *ad opus* occurs as early as Merovingian times in France and appears in England in the ninth century, where it is used to express the purpose of a gift or the object to which it is to be devoted. The phrase *ad opus* is to be found on the continent in much the same context as in England.[3] In this connection it must be observed that chattels as well as land could be held by one person to the use of another, and that in some cases the beneficiary had a remedy at common law by detinue or debt, and in the case of money by the action of account.[4] These, however, were personal actions and we had no analogous actions for land; consequently, in enforcing uses of land the common law did not have the necessary machinery for acting *in personam*.[5] Besides this the common law seems to have adopted the policy of discouraging attempts to separate the enjoyment of land from the legal title, and for this attitude there was some justification; land was the basis of numerous public burdens as well as the source of those varied and valuable feudal incidents which we have had occasion to mention so often. The interposition of feoffees to uses between the beneficiary and his feudal lord would introduce endless complications into the feudal incidents and might, indeed, completely destroy them—and as we have seen on more than one occasion the common law was determined to maintain these incidents to the best of its ability.

EARLY HISTORY OF USES

Nevertheless, circumstances combined to promote the development of the use. The Crusades drew a large number of landowners from their homes to distant parts leaving their affairs in the greatest uncertainty, and

[1] Holmes, *Collected Legal Papers*, 4 (reprinted from Law Quarterly Review, i. 162). Cf. Ames, *Lectures on Legal History*, 235.

[2] Numerous examples will be found in Pollock and Maitland, ii. 233–239. The beneficiary was *cestui a que use le feoffment fuit fait*; when shortened to *cestui que use* it seemed that *use* was a verb, hence the plural *cestuis que usent* and, later, the forms *cestui[s] que trust[ent]*. Maitland, *Collected Papers*, iii. 343. The phrase might later take such bizarre shapes as *Setikki*.

[3] See, for example, Philippe Godding, *Actes relatifs an droit régissant la propriété foncière à Bruxelles au Moyen Age* (Bulletin de la Commission Royale des Anciennes Lois et Ordonnances de Belgique), xvii. 88–164, nos. 2 (1303), 4 (1358), 6 (1397), 13 (1289), etc.

[4] Some examples are collected in Ames, 238.

[5] For what seems to be the enforcement of a use of land through common law forms, see Y.B. 11 Richard II (ed. Thornley, Ames Foundation), 119 (1387). The question has been asked why uses were not enforceable by *assumpsit*: Pollock, *The Land Laws*, app. E; Maitland, *Equity*, 115. The principal reason must have been that *assumpsit* can only afford damages and not specific performance. So, too, the cetique could have account (a personal action only) against a feoffee: Fitzherbert, *New Natura Brevium*, 117. For another guess see O. W Holmes, *Collected Papers*, 11–12.

we find frequent examples of crusaders and others, before their departure for the Holy Land or some other hazardous journey, conveying their lands to a friend upon various conditions which are sometimes cast in the form of a use.[1] So, too, religious houses, following a practice which was common in every type of financial administration, would appropriate regular sources of revenue to specific purposes. When we come to the time of Bracton we find that he regards several of these questions as open to discussion. He even suggests that by means of a " condition " land could be made devisable.[2] The problem of the use reappeared in connection with the controversy whether the Franciscan Friars were entitled to hold property by the rule of their order,[3] while sokemen and villeins can only convey by surrendering their land to the lord " to the use of " the purchaser. As early as 1279 the papacy decided that it was lawful for friars to be the beneficiaries of property held by others to their use, and in other ways which upon the continent effected a similar result. In 1275 a statute ordained that when a guardian has proved to be fraudulent, the wardship shall be committed to a friend " to hold to the use of " the infant.[4]

FEOFFMENT AND RE-ENFEOFFMENT

A further element, which has not received sufficient emphasis, is the fact that a landowner could not change his estate without the intervention of strangers. For example, if he wished to make his wife a joint-tenant with himself, the only method available was to convey the land to a feoffee (or, more prudently, to several feoffees), who would then reconvey to the husband and wife jointly. A tenant in fee simple could create an entail for himself and a particular class of heirs and limit remainders only by first of all conveying to feoffees, who would then reconvey on the limitations agreed upon.[5] Nor was the estate of these feoffees a mere

[1] Sometimes this was expressed in terms of guardianship, as in *Eyre Rolls* (Selden Society, vol. lix), no. 257 (1221). Cf. below, n. 4.

[2] The case in the previous footnote was decided upon a condition. Soo, too, was the case of 1409 discussed by Professor Hargreaves, *Equity and the Latin Side of Chancery*, Law Quarterly Review, lxviii. 487–488. The rule was that only the reversioner could enter for breach of condition, and so it was rarely of any help to beneficiaries.

[3] Pollock and Maitland, ii. 237–239. There have been misunderstandings here. Friars could, and did, own their convents; but they could not hold revenue-producing investments: A. G. Little, *Franciscan Papers*, 56–57; no " uses " appear in the documents printed by Little in *Essays in Honour of James Tait*, 179. For a use held by Franciscans which they construed as a tenancy at will, see Y.BB. Edward II (Selden Series), ii. 76 (1308) where the plea seems closely modelled on that of a villein " who has nothing save at the will of his lord ".

[4] Westm. I, c. 48. From this the conclusion was drawn that since the friend entered to the use of the infant, therefore the freehold was in the infant and he could bring novel disseisin: 8 Ass. 28 (1334). For the close similarity of the ideas of wardship and use, see *Eyre Rolls* (Selden Society, vol. lix), nos. 200, 257, 1013 (1221); *Bracton's Note Book*, 754 (1233); Y.BB. Edward II (Selden Society), iii. 185 (1310).

[5] See the entertaining arguments in Y.B. 41 Edward III, Michs. no. 2 ff. 17–19. Licences to alienate were needed if the land was held in chief: cf. Nicolas, *Proceedings of the Privy Council*, iv. 336 (1436).

fiction; the validity of the settlement depended upon their having a real and effective seisin, and if the settlor remained on the land, the settlement could be subsequently upset. He was, therefore, very much at the mercy of his feoffees during the interval between the two transactions.[1] Much depended on their good faith, which will explain why clergy were often entrusted with these dangerous powers. It will be seen that the distinction between such feoffees and the feoffee to uses is very fine, and it seems highly probable that the connection between the two is close. The later feoffee to uses may easily have developed from feoffees of this sort when their duty to reconvey was postponed for a long interval, and in later times it would be easy to describe such feoffees as feoffees to uses.[2]

EARLY LEGISLATIVE INTERVENTION

By the close of the fourteenth century the use of lands must have been somewhat common. In 1377 the lands of fraudulent debtors, held by others for their benefit, are made liable to execution[3]—and so begins the long association of the use with fraud. In 1391 a statute declared that uses in favour of corporations fell within the statute of mortmain,[4] and in 1398 uses were declared forfeitable for treason.[5] So far, the *cestui que use* had no legal protection—indeed, all these statutes were directed against him; but at length he also appealed to the legislator, and so we find in 1402 the Commons in Parliament praying for a remedy—

" Since rent charges and also feoffments of tenements in demesne are made to dishonest persons by way of confidence to perform the wishes of the grantors and feoffors, which dishonest persons fraudulently grant the said rents to other persons in respect whereof the tenants attorn and such feoffees also charge the tenements in demesne without the assent of their grantors and feoffors, who have no remedy in such case unless one be ordained by this Parliament.
" Let this petition be committed to the King's council, for their consideration until the next parliament."[6]

Already, however, the Council had begun to intervene in such cases; in 1350 we find the first case concerning a use before the " chancellor, treasurer, and others of the king's council, being then in the chancery ". From this case it appears that a tax collector, who by virtue of his office was deeply indebted to the Crown, on his death-bed granted his lands, goods and chattels to one Thomas for the purpose of selling them in order to pay his debts to the Crown. Unfortunately the records of the case are extremely incomplete and all we have is a deposition containing these facts. From other sources it would appear that the matter may

---

[1] In some cases re-entry was a sufficient remedy: Y.B. 21 Edw. III. Pasch. no. 2 (1347).

[2] From *Chichele's Register* ii. (ed. E. F. Jacob) it is clear that testators usually ordered their feoffees to convey legal estates rather than declaring new uses.

[3] 51 Edw. III, c. 6, several times re-enacted.

[4] 15 Rich. II, c. 5.

[5] 21 Rich. II, c. 3.

[6] *Rot. Parl.*, iii. 511; no legislation resulted.

have got into the Council as the result of an attempt by his widow to compel the feoffee to hand over the balance of the proceeds after the payment of the debts.[1]

We may therefore conclude that although the *cestui que use* was often suspected of fraud and collusion, yet it was recognised that there was a legitimate place for the use. The case of 1350 possibly illustrates this; the petition of 1402 clearly argues this point of view, and during the fifteenth century cases become steadily more numerous.

It must be remembered that the earliest evidence, such as the statutes noted above, shows us a situation rather than an institution. As we have already suggested, the situation might be created in different ways and for different objects;[2] it is only in the fifteenth century that these situations are for the first time grouped together under the one legal concept of the use.

THE GROWTH OF A STATUTORY POLICY

Time only added to the possibilities of fraud when unscrupulous persons employed the use, and we can trace the gradual development by the legislature of a policy. For example, it was long ago discovered that a wrongful tenant of lands could prevent the rightful owner from bringing his action, or greatly delay him, by conveying the land to feoffees to his own use, and so a statute of 1485 gave a remedy by allowing the writ of formedon to be brought against anyone who was receiving the profits of the land[3]—it will be noticed that this statute adopts the momentous principle, already implied in the statutes of Edward III and Richard II, of treating the *cestui que use* as though he were the legal owner. All uses were not fraudulent, however, and Parliament recognised the fact by trying to remove one grave disadvantage which weighed upon *cestuis que use*, namely, that they could not convey a legal estate; and so another statute, in 1484, conferred this power upon them.[4] This statute, too, treated the *cestui que use* as a legal owner, and so foreshadowed the policy of Henry VIII in the great Statute of Uses. This time the policy was not so fortunate. The feoffee still had the power to make a legal estate,

---

[1] *Select Cases in Council* (Selden Society), 33–34.

[2] This attitude is neatly expressed by Montague in an argument in 1536: " to prove that uses were at common law, there is a writ in the *Register* called *causa matrimonii prelocuti* which lies when a woman enfeoffs a man with a view to a marriage between them, and the man then refuses to marry her, and she demands the land back; that writ is founded solely on the confidence which the woman placed in the man, and so it is clearly proved that confidence (and therefore the use) existed at common law ". How nearly common lawyers came to accepting the use can be seen from another remark of Montague (who next year became C.J., K.B.) in the same case: " the common law is nothing else than common reason, and common reason demands that one can put one's trust in others, and a use is a trust between feoffor and feoffee " (Y.B. 27 Henry VIII, Pasch. 22, fo. 10).

[3] 1 Hen. VII, c. 1 (repeating the policy of 1 Rich. II, c. 9, and 4 Hen IV, c. 7). For a petition on this subject *temp.* Edward III, see Sayles, *King's Bench*, iii. p. cxxi (*o*)—in line 5 reading *covyn* for *comyn* and in line 15 *averer per paiis* for *aver par pairs*.

[4] 1 Rich. III, c. 1.

and the grant of this power to the *cestui que use* concurrently could only add to the confusion since there were now two persons entitled to convey.

Under the Tudors the stream of legislation gathered speed and boldness. All trusts and uses of chattels to the use of the settlor were declared void[1] in 1487; still more significant was an act of 1489 enacting that wardship and relief shall be due from heirs who are *cestuis que usent* of military lands;[2] and in 1504 it was enacted that execution should lie against lands held in use, and that the *cestui que use* should enjoy all rights and defences in such proceedings as if he had the legal estate.[3] Clearly, there was a policy steadily pursued for over a century and a half before the great statute of uses, the main object of which was to treat the *cestui que use* as having the legal estate. The most significant of all the acts, however, was one which dealt with a personal problem created by Richard III's accession. As Duke of Gloucester he had several times been enfeoffed to uses by his friends; now that he was King it was evidently anomalous for this situation to continue. A statute therefore enacted " that such lands whereof he was sole seised for the use of others shall vest in the *cestui que use* ". For the first time Parliament ventured to transfer seisin from one person to another by its mere *fiat*.[4]

THE ESTABLISHMENT OF THE USE

By the end of the fifteenth century a fair body of law had been settled which gave a definite form to the use.

The commonest way of creating a use was by conveying the land to a number of joint-tenants; the advantage of this was greater security, since it was less likely that several feoffees would all turn out to be dishonest, while at the same time the rule of survivorship was a great convenience since neither dower nor feudal incidents attached upon the death of a joint-tenant—indeed, in the present day, the only reason for retaining the rule is its usefulness as between trustees. At the same time a joint feoffment eliminated complications due to dower. The uses might be declared at the time of the feoffment by writing or verbally, or it might be agreed that the uses should be those to be declared in the feoffor's will. The fact that the uses might not be declared fully, or even at all, at the time of the feoffment, gave rise to the rule that a gratuitous feoffment of land of which the feoffor continued in possession presumed a use in favour of the feoffor, and from the reign of Edward IV we find a formal doctrine of " resulting " uses.[5] Then, too, a bargain

---

[1] 3 Hen. VII, c. 4.

[2] 4 Hen. VII, c. 17. For a curious argument that this statute takes away prerogative wardship, see Y.B. Michs. 13 Henry VII, f. 4 or *Cases in Exchequer Chamber* (Selden Society) ii. 161 (1497); the case explains the failure of the statute, and gives a long and informative debate on uses, conscience, prerogative and the like.

[3] 19 Hen. VII, c. 15.

[4] 1 Rich. III, c. 5.

[5] Littleton, ss. 463, 464.

and sale from the reign of Henry VII onwards was taken as implying that the vendor who has received the purchase money, but who still remains in possession, will hold to the use of the purchaser;[1] and this rule played a large part in the later development of conveyancing.

It was decided fairly soon that a corporation could not be a feoffee to the use of any other person,[2] largely because the sanction which applied to relationships arising out of uses was the personal process of the Court of Chancery, and this was hardly effective against a corporation which had no body which could be coerced and no soul to be damned in consequence of a breach of confidence. It is clear, however, that a corporation could be a *cestui que use*.[3] The interest of the *cestui que use* at this time strictly followed the corresponding legal estates—a married woman, for example, until the seventeenth century, had no separate use, her interest under a use being exactly the same as it would have been in land at common law, save that neither dower nor curtesy attached to uses.[4] It was also a rule at this time that the feoffee must have a fee simple. The reasons for this were in a sense feudal, for it was stated in the form that tenure was so solemn a fact that the law would not allow even an expressed declaration of use to override it.[5] Thus if *A*. enfeoffs *B*. in fee-tail, *B*. will hold of *A*. (for the Statute *Quia Emptores* does not apply to fees tail); the existence of this tenure between *A*. and *B*. is so solemn a matter that the law will prevent *A*. from imposing upon *B*. any further use. As the older books put it, *A*. has enfeoffed *B*. to hold to the use of *B*. and any subsequent declaration of use is " repugnant " and void. A little later we shall see the importance of this rule.

The effects of a feoffment to use were to place the legal title in the feoffees, and, consequently, they may, and indeed must, defend that legal title. Moreover, the heirs[6] of the feoffees are bound by the use, but not purchasers for value without notice of the use, disseisors, abators, lords taking by escheat, or those who take by a title paramount. The law of forfeiture for treason had to be specially modified in particular cases (*e.g.* the rebel Earl of Northumberland in 1404) to ensure that the traitor lost lands settled to his use, and to prevent the forfeiture of legal estates held by him to the use of other persons.[7]

---

[1] Y.B. 21 Henry VII, Hill. 30 (1506), where sale is distinguished from covenant.

[2] Bro. *Feoffment al uses*, 40 (1532).

[3] Subject, of course, to having a licence in mortmain; 15 Rich. II, c. 5.

[4] The absence of these complications was much valued; early in the eighteenth century, however, curtesy was allowed out of a trust; Holdsworth, iii. 188.

[5] Bro. *Feoffment al uses*, 40 (1532); Co. Lit. 19 b; *Lord Cromwell's Case*, 2 Rep. 78 note 51. For the same reason, a term of years would not support a use according to the common lawyers, although the Chancery later allowed them; Holdsworth, iv. 471, 472. (For a clear early example of a use upon a term, see Y.B. 11 Richard II (1388), 240–242.)

[6] See the interesting recollections of Hussey, C.J., in Y.B. Pasch. 22 Edward IV, f. 4 no. 18 (1482) and cf. *Cases in Exchequer Chamber* (Selden Society), ii. 13.

[7] Titles depending on the earl were still obscure as late as 1439; see the documents in *Rot. Parl.*, v. 11–12.

The interest of the *cestui que use* is best described as being at first just one more of a large variety of titles, weak or defective in varying ways and to various extents. The complication of the common law of real property by the early days of the sixteenth century must have familiarised people with the fact that a good many held by titles which fell short of perfection, and were not so very much the worse for it.

ADVANTAGES OF USES

There were, indeed, numerous countervailing advantages enjoyed by the *cestui que use*. In the first place he had the valuable privilege of being able to dispose of his land after his death by will, which was impossible in common law except in the case of certain lands (often burgages) which had been subject to the custom of devisability from of old. Then, too, settlements could be drawn with much greater freedom by handling uses than by handling common law estates, which by this time had hardened into an inflexible system. So, too, feoffees could be directed to sell portions of the land to pay the debts of a testator, which was impossible at common law. Then, also, there was the advantage of not having to use technical forms, for so long as the intention of the settlor was clear it was unnecessary to be as precise as in defining common law estates. It was soon discovered, also, that the use could be employed in order to secure the benefits of ownership to unincorporated bodies such as guilds, parishes and so on.[1] And so by the beginning of the sixteenth century—

" it was a wholly unique form of ownership which the Chancellor had thus developed from a conscientious obligation of a very personal kind. It was not a true *jus in rem* because it was not available against the whole world. There were or might be many persons as against whom it could not be asserted. Then although it rested on the Chancellor's power to proceed against the person whose conscience was affected by notice of the use, it was far more than a mere *jus in personam*."[2]

There were, however, on the other hand, some good reasons for interference by the legislature, for in no other way was there much likelihood of removing several abuses attendant upon the development of the use; we have seen already that even in the fourteenth century the use was employed to defraud creditors, on whose behalf Parliament several times intervened.[3] At the same time since unincorporated bodies could take as *cestuis que use* it was possible to place land into mortmain in spite of the statute. Then, also, during the disorders of the fifteenth century lands were frequently given to great lords to the use of the donor, who thereby secured the support of a great magnate in defending the title—thus raising the old problem of maintenance.

[1] By 23 Henry VIII, c. 12 (1532) such uses hereafter to be made, whether active or passive, are declared void unless they are limited to endure twenty years or less.

[2] Holdsworth, iv. 433–434.

[3] Above, pp. 578–580.

USES AND FEUDAL REVENUE

Finally, from the standpoint of national finance and politics, the most important aspect of uses was the impossibility of fitting them into the feudal system. Their effect was usually to defraud the lord of the incidents of wardship, marriage and relief. This was not so serious a matter for the great nobility, for to some extent they could obtain the same advantage by the same means against the Crown. But it will be observed that whoever gains by the arrangement the Crown is sure to lose, and this aspect of the situation was already apparent to Henry VII. In the next reign the matter became still more urgent. The great Reformation Parliament had accomplished a tremendous amount of epoch-making legislation, especially in carrying out the religious settlement. This settlement was viewed without enthusiasm by a large part of the populace, and Parliament itself was none too well disposed towards the Crown. Henry VIII felt that it would be unwise and perhaps unavailing to seek from Parliament a further grant of taxes, and was therefore left to depend upon the hereditary revenues of the Crown. Of these only the feudal incidents seemed capable of any great expansion,[1] and here the situation was complicated by the existence of uses. Having just carried out the Reformation settlement and assumed the headship of the Church, it is not surprising that Henry VIII was ready to apply heroic remedies. He contemplated nothing short of a drastic revision of the common law along lines which would suit the interests of the Crown. In 1529 a proposal was drawn up in the form of a draft bill based on a treaty between the Crown and the peerage with this end in view.[2] The King and the lords proposed this arrangement: there was to be only one estate in land and that a fee simple, except that peers of the realm were to have the privilege of entailing their lands; uses were only to be valid if registered in the Court of Common Pleas, and elaborate provisions were drafted to ensure the utmost publicity; the lands of peers were to be subject to feudal dues in respect to equitable as well as legal estates; they could also be entailed, devised and settled, but elaborate provisions ensured that none of these devices should defeat the feudal rights of the Crown; and finally, in return for the heavy burden of feudal duties it was proposed that the land of peers of the realm should be inalienable save by royal licence. This bargain, if it could have been carried out, was eminently satisfactory to the King and to the peers, for the latter in return for their liability to inescapable feudal duties acquired

---

[1] It will be remembered that Henry VII's ministers, Empson and Dudley, earned their ill-fame by their enforcement of these dues through the common law side of Chancery. Brodie, *Edmund Dudley*, (1932) Trans. R. Hist. Soc., 149, 157.

[2] Stubbs first drew attention to these documents, and Maitland, *English Law and the Renaissance*, 45 note 11, printed an extract from *Starkey's England* in which similar views are ascribed to Cardinal Pole. The documents were first printed and fully discussed in Holdsworth, iv. 572 ff., 449 ff.

the privilege of having their fortunes assured to them by inalienable rights.[1]

THE KING'S DEFEAT

It has always been a feature of English society that there was no deep line drawn between the peerage and other classes. There were plenty of great landowners as wealthy and as influential as the peers, who were in fact untitled, and it was this large and powerful class which, combined with the common lawyers, defeated the 1529 compromise. The large landowners who did not happen to be peers found themselves deprived by these proposals of the right to entail or to make secret settlements or alienations; all the details of their family arrangements were to be proclaimed in the parish church, confirmed by the parish priest, and sealed by the mayor of the county town. Feudal incidents were to be rigorously exacted from them as from the peers, only the commoners got nothing in return. As for the common lawyers they saw in this arrangement the ruin of their profession; it left them no more interesting topic of study than a fee simple, save in the very few cases of peers, and at this moment there were but fifty peers of the realm. The use still remained and was to be the means of effecting settlements, and the common lawyers secured a provision for registering them in the common pleas instead of in Chancery, but the capture was of little value after the publicity clauses had robbed the use of its chief attraction. A combination of great landowners and common lawyers, therefore, defeated these proposals in the House of Commons and convinced the King that an alliance with the peerage had no chance of success. He therefore had to seek support elsewhere and that support would have to be in the House of Commons.

THE KING'S NEW TACTICS

It seemed clear that the common lawyers might very well turn out to be the key to the situation; in any case whatever settlement was eventually made would depend for its working upon the machinery of the law. And so, first of all, the lawyers had to be reduced to a tractable frame of mind, and to this end Henry VIII received with marked sympathy a petition complaining of the delays of the common law, its expense and its failure to do justice. This gesture gave the common lawyers to understand that the Crown might demand from them some very radical reforms, and once again the profession felt that its existence was at stake. At the same time numerous commissioners were conducting searching examinations into the affairs of the landed gentry, suspecting that the King's rights were being defeated by the common lawyers' allies. Various

---

[1] The idea of peerage becomes prominent in this reign; cf. 31 Hen. VIII, c. 10 (1539), which is the first act to settle precedency among the nobility and official classes. Attempts were made to include similar provisions in the Act of Settlement, and in Stanhope's Peerage Bill of 1719.

proposals were made in the course of the next few years, and gradually the attack now centred against the use.

" The list of grievances suffered by the realm from uses is long and detailed. It is written in two hands and there is a certain amount of repetition. In some cases it gives particular instances of inconveniences suffered, and at the end there is a summary statement of the various fraudulent purposes which uses had been made to serve. The writers insist much on the disadvantages of uses from the point of view of the *cestui que use*, of the public at large, of the King and lords, and of the law. The *cestui que use* is at the mercy of a fraudulent bailiff or feoffee; nor can he take action against a trespasser. He loses his curtesy, and his wife her dower. The King loses his forfeitures, and King and lords lose their incidents of tenure. The public at large is defrauded because no man can tell against whom to bring his action, nor is anyone secure in his purchase. The law is wholly uncertain —' the openyons of the Justices do chaunge dely apon the suertyez for landes in use '. The use is ' but the shadowe of the thyng and not the thyng indeyd '. It causes the law to be double, and to sever the real from the apparent ownership, ' which is a grett disseytt '. ' Where per case some one man takyth esyngler welth their be a hundrioth against one that takyth hurt and losse theirby, is yt a good law ? ' the writer asks. He thinks that it would be a good thing if uses were ' clene put out the lawe '. The document is an able statement of the case against uses; and it may well have been the raw material upon which those who drew the preamble to the statute worked."[1]

THE STATUTE OF USES

Of these various schemes, one finally became the famous Statute of Uses (1536).[2] Under this arrangement the King secured his feudal dues, but the price he paid was to the common lawyers instead of to the nobility and Chancery. Indeed, it was the common lawyers who gained most by the Statute of Uses. After a great deal of difficulty and some concessions from the Crown the statute finally passed.

" Maitland[3] has truly said that the Statute of Uses ' was forced upon an extremely unwilling Parliament by an extremely strong-willed King '. But I think that the evidence shows that this strong-willed King was obliged first to frighten and then to conciliate the common lawyers in order to get the statute through the House of Commons; and that probably their opposition caused the failure of his well-considered scheme for the registration of conveyances. If this be so the action of the common lawyers has had a large effect upon the form which the Statute of Uses and the Statute of Enrolments finally assumed, and consequently upon the whole of the future history of the law of real property."[4]

The statute carried to its logical conclusion the policy begun by Richard III, whose statutes had allowed the *cestui que use* to be treated for certain purposes as though he were the legal owner. Under the Statute of Uses the *cestui que use* becomes the legal owner for all purposes, and is

---

[1] Holdsworth, iv. 455, 456; the text of the memorandum on uses is printed in Holdsworth, iv. 577–580.

[2] 27 Hen. VIII, c. 10. The text is in Digby, *History of the Law of Real Property*, 347–354. (His history must be taken subject to correction by Holdsworth.)

[3] Maitland, *Equity*, 35.

[4] Holdsworth, iv. 461.

invested by the statute with the benefits of the mysterious seisin which
is the essence of a common law estate. This transformation operated
by the statute converting a use into a legal estate is described in the Act
itself (s. 10) as " executing the use ". It is clear that professional opinion
was ready for this transformation, for even before the statute we find
common layers loosely describing the *cestui que use* as being " seised " of
the uses.[1] As for the King, he was to receive all his feudal dues unimpaired, for the uses will be executed and feudal incidents will attach
to the legal estates created by the statute.

As for the common lawyers, they won a great victory over Chancery;
under the statute they not only retained the entail but obtained jurisdiction
over all matters arising out of uses, since under the statute they were
executed and became common law estates. The landowners had less
cause for satisfaction. They retained the entail and the use, but after the
statute, uses could no longer be employed as a machinery for the devise
of land,[2] while at the same time the Statute of Enrolments[3] (which was a
part of the scheme) enacted that a bargain and sale of freeholds and fees
must be by deed enrolled. The bargain and sale was a very popular
form of conveyance depending upon the use for its operation, and so the
statute in substance compelled publicity of conveyance—until a way
was found to evade it by means of the lease and the release. Finally, if
we are to consider the nation at large, it was they who paid the heaviest
price, for the complicated diplomacy which ensured the passage of the
statute depended upon the understanding that there should be no more
talk of reforming the common law.

After a long and argumentative preamble—" the sixteenth-century
equivalent of a leading article in a government newspaper upon a government measure "[4]—the statute proceeds to enact that *cestuis que usent* shall
be seised of legal estates corresponding to the estates they had in use.
Then we come to the provision that a jointure shall be a bar to dower.[5]
It must be remembered that the statute did not propose to abolish uses,
for in more than one place it contemplated the creation of uses in the
future. Its object was to avoid the inconveniences which were caused by
having two forms of ownership, one legal and the other equitable, by
declaring that the beneficiary shall have a complete legal estate and that
the feoffee to use shall have none at all. This altered the character of the
use, but did not destroy it. The statute did not apply to active uses, nor

---

[1] Y.B. 21 Henry VII, Hill. 30 (1506).

[2] The exercise of a power of appointment in certain circumstances has been suggested as
a possibility which survived the statute: R. E. Megarry, *The Statute of Uses and the power to
devise*, Cambridge Law Journal, vii. 354.

[3] 27 Hen. VIII, c. 16. Text in Digby, *op. cit.* 368.

[4] Holdsworth, iv. 460, who adds, " it is far from being a sober statement of historical
fact ". The language is certainly colourful, but the substance of the preamble is undoubtedly
true.

[5] Above, p. 568 n. 2. Originally the jointure was (as its name implies) an estate for life
jointly with the husband, but it soon came to mean also a sole life interest.

to uses out of chattels real or personal. The great merit of the arrangement was that the greater freedom in conveyancing by means of the use was preserved and made available to common lawyers.

COMPLETION OF THE STATUTORY SETTLEMENT

To the landed gentry the Statute of Uses seemed a calamity, and in the rebellion of 1536, which described itself as the " Pilgrimage of Grace ", we find among numerous other grievances—the dissolution of the monasteries, the religious changes, the divorce question—a demand for the repeal of the Statute of Uses, particularly because it abolished the powers of devise hitherto enjoyed by landowners. Henry VIII was well aware of the seriousness of opposition when it came from so important a class as the country gentry. By this time the enforcement of any government policy (and Henry VIII's revolutionary policies needed a good deal of enforcement) depended very largely upon the co-operation of the local gentry, who as justices of the peace were responsible for local government. He felt that the time had come for a concession to the landed gentry, and this took the form of the Statute of Wills[1] (1540), which conferred complete powers of devise over socage lands, and over two-thirds of land held by knight-service, accompanied by the usual provisions (based on the principle that a devisee was to be deemed as in by inheritance) to safeguard feudal dues. Three years later the statute was amended in numerous points of detail.[2] In 1540, following the usual Tudor policy of erecting administrative courts for special business, Henry VIII established the Court of Wards, whose duties were to be the supervision of the King's feudal revenue especially as it was affected by the Statutes of Uses and Wills.[3]

[1] 32 Hen. VIII, c. 1.
[2] 34 & 35 Hen. VIII, c. 5 (1543).
[3] Above, p. 174.

CHAPTER 8

THE LATER LAW OF REAL PROPERTY

AFTER THE STATUTE OF USES

Bacon, in a well-known passage, declared that the Statute of Uses was " the most perfectly and exactly conceived and penned of any law in the book . . . the best pondered in all the words and clauses of it of any statute that I find ". Anyone who reads the statute will be led to the same conclusion. An act of wide-sweeping scope, it is worded with care; after the fashion of the time, it contains a clear *exposé de motifs* in the preamble indicating its general objects; the first section enacts a clear and general rule, based on a tendency long apparent in legislation; this rule is unencumbered with exceptions and provisos, and (unlike previous acts) extends to all uses possible at that time, and executes them for all purposes; succeeding clauses foresee, and provide for, the situations arising under the operation of clause one. No statute before 1536 shows such evident signs of thoughtful care, and such clear and logical arrangement.

The objects of the act were obvious. First, it aimed at combining equitable and legal ownership and abolishing the screen of feoffees to use. In this it succeeded. No use, at this time, could subsist save upon the seisin of feoffees, and the statute successfully executed all uses. Secondly, it aimed at restoring publicity in dealings with land. The Statute of Enrolments[1] was passed because it was realised that the use on a bargain and sale in favour of the bargainee who had paid the purchase money would be executed by the statute; to prevent this being employed as a secret conveyance, such bargains and sales were to be enrolled. Other conveyances were at common law and required livery of seisin. It is

[1] 27 Hen. VIII, c. 16 (1536).

true that under the statute it was possible for legal estates to spring and
shift in various ways but the general aim of publicity was attained, for it
was no longer possible for a person in apparent enjoyment of land to
escape the legal consequences of ownership by saying that the legal title
was elsewhere. Once again, the statute attained its object. Two other
aims were also realised, although later legislation decided that they were
in fact undesirable. The virtual prevention of the devise of land was in
fact an attempt to put the clock back a century or more, and the statute
of wills soon recognised that this was impossible. The preservation of
the incidents of tenure, achieved by the statute, had over a century of
extended life; they, too, were abandoned in 1660.[1]

THE ATTITUDE OF THE COMMON LAWYERS

The common lawyers had a difficult situation before them, but one
rich with possibilities. For something like a century after the statutes
of uses and wills they could draw upon several bodies of law, and had
the opportunity of welding them into a coherent and reasonable system.
It was the great disaster of the sixteenth century that they failed to do so.
The long reign of Elizabeth was occupied by a succession of judges who
had great gifts of dialectic, and a taste for artificial refinement. The
sweeping victory of the profession, as exemplified in the Statute of Uses,
put them above the reach of criticism. The flood of new wealth released
by the dissolution of the monasteries created a new and prosperous
landed class, closely attached to the Crown, which could afford to tolerate
a mass of real property law which steadily grew more fantastic. The
legal profession became even more deeply entrenched in the House of
Commons, and the excitement of religious and political controversy
seems to have left no desire to raise the issue of law reform.

The materials available were, first of all, the common law itself.
Littleton's immortal work shows clearly that the mediaeval law of land
was comparatively simple, reasonable and capable of expression in concise
and orderly form. The one disturbing factor was the feudal incidents
and the attempts to escape them. The law of estates was, apart from
this, clear and simple. Secondly, there was the law of uses. The
creation of uses was perfectly simple in 1536; its chief defect was the
possibility of creating a use by words only—a difficulty which reappeared
later in connection with trusts, and was easily removed by requiring all
declarations of trust relating to land to be in writing.[2] There was as
yet very little law to decide whether any particular scheme of uses was
valid or invalid. Thirdly, there was the institution of the devise. The
Statute of Wills required that this should take effect as a legal estate,
and at the moment it seems that there was little law to restrain testators
in the disposition of their lands as they pleased.[3]

[1] 12 Car. II, c. 24.

[2] Statute of Frauds (1677), 29 Car. II, c. 3, s. 7.

[3] Cf. p. 564, above

The common lawyers, therefore, had in their hands a vastly augmented mass of law, much of it comparatively new, and much of it in an amorphous condition. No doubt it was too vague in some places; no doubt, too, the fancy of settlors and testators needed restraint at times; but did the situation demand all the subtleties and complications which the sixteenth and early seventeenth centuries imposed?

LEGAL CONTINGENT REMAINDERS

As we have seen, the common law at the close of the middle ages recognised only one type of contingent remainder as valid.[1] The doctrine was often stated in the form that there must be no interruption of seisin, but the real reason at first was the difficulty which ensued in the matter of feudal services, particularly if the contingent remainder is in fee, thereby leaving the lord without a tenant, and an interest without an owner.

To the middle ages, a lord deprived of a tenant seemed the greater difficulty. In the sixteenth century, however, the interest without an owner appeared more remarkable. Fortunately, the middle ages had refused to be troubled by this point,[2] and so sixteenth-century lawyers were able to take comfort from the fact that all through history the law had tolerated the gap in ownership between the death of one parson and the appointment of his successor. Relying on this curious circumstance, they ventured to admit the possibility of such a gap between the moment when the grantor parts with his fee, and the moment when the contingent fee is ready to take effect.

Colthirst v. *Bejushin* (1550)[3] is a sign of the changing view. Littleton's discussion of Rickhill's settlement[4] was cited to the court in support of the traditional view that the death of a living person was the only contingency recognised by the law, but Montague, C.J., brushed it aside and stated that it was now settled law that a remainder may commence upon a condition, provided that the condition was not illegal or " repugnant "; the remainders limited by Rickhill he regarded as bad, not because they were conditions, but because they were " repugnant " conditions.[5] The result of this case was, therefore, the recognition of an increasing variety of contingent remainders.

Even if a contingent remainder was valid, however, it might be destroyed in a number of ways. There was a rule, to which the common law courts clung tightly, that a contingent remainder must be supported

---

[1] Above, pp. 562–564.

[2] Littleton, *Tenures*, s. 646.

[3] Plowden, 21. Two " conditions " were discussed—a remainder to *C.* if *B.* die living *A.*; and to *C.* for life if he reside at Barton.

[4] Littleton, *Tenures*, s. 720; above, p. 563.

[5] The discontinuance put the fee in the alienee; this is " repugnant " to the proviso that the next remainderman should take.

by a precedent estate of freehold or by a right of entry.[1]   A contingent
remainder to a posthumous son will therefore fail,[2] for there is an interval
between the death of the father and the birth of the son during which
there is no freehold to support the remainder.   This common difficulty
was often avoided by limiting a freehold to the mother, but was still more
satisfactorily removed by statute.[3]   Similarly, destruction might result
from a tortious alienation by the tenant for life, or if he were disseised.[4]
Furthermore, if the estate of the tenant for life became merged with a
subsequent vested estate, the result will be the destruction of any intervening contingent remainder.   Such merger might take place owing to
conveyance between the parties, or by descent, or by the operation of
the rule in *Shelley's Case*.   During the Commonwealth a device was
invented by Sir Orlando Bridgman and Sir Geoffrey Palmer (if tradition
is correct) which consisted in limiting a remainder to trustees for the life
of the life tenant.   If the life tenant were to make a tortious feoffment,
there would still be this vested remainder ready to support subsequent
contingent remainders.   This solution was generally accepted, in spite of
theoretical objections.[5]   Meanwhile, the doctrine of merger created so
many difficulties that some of it had to be abandoned.   So a distinction
was drawn between merger effected by means of conveyances between
the parties, and merger resulting from the disposition of estates in the
settlement.   The latter type was so common in practice that the public
had to be relieved of the results which flowed from a strict application
of legal doctrine, and so it was held that the merged estates might " open
and let in " the intervening contingent remainder.[6]

From the middle of the sixteenth century, therefore, the tendency was
to enlarge the class of contingent remainders which the law would
recognise, although still emphasising their destructibility.   It has been
suggested that there was a conscious policy behind this—the prevention
of " perpetuities ".   By the close of the middle ages the common law
had, in fact, come to the conclusion that an entail could be barred;[7]
soon it proceeded to the further proposition that all entails ought to
be barrable, and that this characteristic was inseparable from entails.
Whether this paradox was maintained out of a deliberate policy of further-
ing freedom of alienation (as is often suggested), or merely out of reluctance to abandon the supposed logical results flowing from a particular
combination of technicalities, it is difficult to determine.   In any case,
the courts seem conscious of the fact that if contingent remainders were

---

[1] *Butler* v. *Bray* (1561), Dyer, 189 *b*, at 190 *b*; *Archer's Case* (1597), 1 Rep. 66 *b*.

[2] *Reeve* v. *Long* (1695), 3 Lev. 408; 1 Salk. 227; 4 Mod. 282.   The reversal of this decision
by the Lords carried little weight at this time with the profession.

[3] 10 Will. III, c. 22 (1699); cf. the comment in Challis, *Real Property* (ed. Sweet), 140.

[4] This point is put forward as early as 1317 in the very interesting discussion in Y.BB.
Edward II (Selden Society), xxii. 15.

[5] See the discussion in Holdsworth, vii. 112.

[6] *Archer's Case* (1597), 1 Rep. 66 *b*; *Purefoy* v. *Rogers* (1669), 2 Wms. Saunders, 380 at 387.

[7] Below, p. 620.

allowed to become indestructible, the result would be to impede the alienation of land. In fact, entails could be devised which would be unbarrable for a considerable period.

The rules on the validity and destructibility of contingent remainders were drastic, and modifications had to be made, but the swing-back of the pendulum was assisted by the fact that the problem of perpetuities was now to be attacked from a more reasonable standpoint. With the establishment of a rule against perpetuities[1] the danger was removed, and contingent remainders began to be viewed with less suspicion. The use of trustees to preserve them was sanctioned by the courts by the beginning of the eighteenth century,[2] and no legislation became necessary until the nineteenth century. The abolition of large masses of technicalities then gave parliament the opportunity of restating the law in simpler and less artificial language.[3]

USES EXECUTED AND EXECUTORY

Besides the traditional common law, however, the courts now controlled a second system of property law, namely, that which had been transferred to them by the Statute of Uses. Before the statute, considerable latitude was permitted in the limitation of uses; certainly Chancery did not insist upon the observance of the common law rules on the derivation of estates. After the statute, there immediately arose the question as to how far the common law courts would continue this policy now that the uses were executed (or in the future might be executed) by the statute. There was, moreover, a further question. Besides the various *cestuis que usent* there were the feoffees to uses, and their position since the statute was at first uncertain, and later was expressed in very metaphysical terms. At first sight, this second question would seem settled by the statute: the feoffees have nothing, for the policy of the act was clearly to eliminate them from the situation. This was certainly the case in the simplest possible situation, where *A.* holds to the use of *B.* and his heirs. Under the statute *A.*'s seisin passes wholly to *B.* More complicated limitations, however, raised a difficulty which the sixteenth-century lawyers felt to be acute. If the feoffee had only a life estate, it was held that any uses limited would cease at his death;[4] soon afterwards, in a case of a use for life, followed by a contingent use, a dilemma was discovered. The seisin of the feoffees passed by the statute to the *cestui que use* for life; was there anything left which could support the contingent use? The court felt that whatever the statute said, if there is a use, then there must be someone who is seised to that use. It therefore followed

---

[1] Below, p. 596.

[2] *Duncomb* v. *Duncomb* (1697), 3 Lev. 437; *Dormer* v. *Parkhurst* (1740), 6 Bro. P.C. 351.

[3] See, in general, Challis, 138–141, and Holdsworth, vii. 114–115; Contingent Remainders Act, 1877.

[4] *Anon.* (1561), Dyer, 186 *a* (note that the old rule that the feoffee must have a fee simple is already disappearing).

that the feoffees, although their seisin was already exhausted, still had something which would support the subsequent use. This something Dyer christened with the picturesque name of *scintilla juris*.[1]

Before the statute, no doubt, a use did require a feoffee for its creation and for its continuance, but the statute clearly aimed at eliminating the feoffee altogether. There were some lawyers who had a trust in legislation sufficiently strong to accept this drastic change as a mystery to be received in faith; others felt the need of rationalising the seeming miracle, and so attributed this *scintilla juris* to the feoffee.[2] For three hundred years the controversy lasted; Coke against Bacon, Booth against Fearne, Sanders against Sugden, the House of Commons (it seems) against the House of Lords. Not until 1860 was the *scintilla* at last extinguished after a stubborn legislative struggle.[3]

It was, however, the prevailing theory, and so for practical purposes the position of the feoffees was material to the question whether any particular contingent use was or was not good. A most important result was the rule that " if the estate of the feoffees, which is the root of the uses, be destroyed by the alienation of the land before the uses have their being, no use can afterwards rise ";[4] but, conversely, there were circumstances in which the feoffees could enter in order to preserve contingent uses from destruction by those who had vested estates.[5]

A further question was whether the derivation of estates by way of use should or should not be bound by common law rules. Before the statute, uses were the most flexible means of effecting settlements, and hardly any restrictions were imposed in Chancery. Thus, even a shifting fee was possible by means of a use. The statute gives no hint of any dissatisfaction with this state of affairs, and so we may conclude that the framers of it were ready to tolerate this liberty in limiting uses, however shocking the results might be to common lawyers. The courts were not so sure, however, and sometimes went so far as to suggest that no limitations by way of use were valid unless they would have been valid in a deed at common law. This would have prevented springing and shifting uses and most types of " contingency ", and is hardly distinguishable from the proposition that the statute abolished uses.[6] This extreme doctrine was slowly abandoned, but only in part. A most important relic of it is the rule which became firmly settled that if an executory use (or devise) could be construed as a contingent remainder, then it must be

---

[1] *Brent's Case* (1575), Dyer, 339 *b* at 340. The expression occurs in Bracton, f. 160, 183 *b* (last line).

[2] In spite of vigorous opposition the *scintilla* was recognised by a majority in *Chudleigh's Case* (1595), 1 Rep. 113 *b*, after an entertaining controversy.

[3] 23 & 24 Vict. (1860), c. 38, s. 7; see the references in Holdsworth, vii. 140.

[4] *Brent's Case* (1575), 2 Leo. 14 at 18; Dyer, 339 *b*.

[5] *Chudleigh's Case* (1595), 1 Rep. 113 *b* at 137. The feoffee's entry might also serve to revive vested uses: *Delamere* v. *Burnard* (1568), Plowden, 346.

[6] Coke's argument and the judgment of Popham, C.J., in *Chudleigh's Case* are examples.

so construed.[1] Fear of " perpetuities " probably made for the acceptance of this doctrine, which, of course, resulted in making many types of contingent use as destructible as contingent remainders.

EXECUTORY DEVISES

The Statute of Wills allowed land to be devised, and the devise operated under the statute as a new means of conveying land. This therefore constitutes the third body of property law at the disposal of the common law courts. At the same time, some testators, remembering pre-statute days, preferred the old method of the use, and so we find devises of land to persons who were to hold to various uses; the devisees therefore took under the Statute of Wills, and the beneficiaries took under the Statute of Uses.[2] At first there was a feeling among some judges that devises, as well as uses, ought to be subjected to the common law of estates; this movement proceeded no further with devises than it did with uses, and so was checked as soon as it was established that executory devises, like executory uses, which were capable of being construed as contingent remainders, must be so construed.[3] This left a remarkable class of executory devises which did not fall under the rule, but they, too, were somewhat precarious until the last years of Elizabeth, when opinion began to change as a result of recent developments both in common law and Chancery.

These novelties were concerned with terms of years. As we have seen, the term of years was always viewed with some suspicion, particularly when it was employed merely as a conveyancing device. It was old doctrine that uses could not be declared on a term—there had to be feoffees seised of a fee. If uses were declared upon a term, they were certainly not executed by the statute, and for a long time they received little sympathy from the Chancellor, on the ground that they constituted a device to evade feudal incidents. It was equally certain in the sixteenth century that a remainder could not be created in a term by deed. Whether it could be so created by devise, however, was a question on which opinion fluctuated. In 1536 it was held that if a term was devised to A. in tail, remainder to B., the remainder was bad.[4] In 1542 the view was that such a remainder after a life interest only, was good[5] but destructible by the first taker; and to the end of the century cases sometimes assert

---

[1] The classical statement of the rule is in *Purefoy* v. *Rogers* (1669), 2 Wms. Saund. 380 at 388, by which time the rule was about eighty years old (Holdsworth, vii. 127); cf. below, n. 3.

[2] Examples are collected in Holdsworth, vii. 120–121.

[3] There are hints of the rule in *Chudleigh's Case* (1595), and it was applied to an executory devise even earlier in *Challoner and Bowyer's Case* (1587), 2 Leo. 70; cf. above, n. 1.

[4] *Anon.* (1536), Dyer, 7 a.

[5] *Anon.* (1542), Br. *Chattels* 23; Bro. N.C. 33. Sometimes the gift was not expressed simply as for life (which might have swallowed up the whole term, to the detriment of the remainderman) but as " to A. for as many years as she shall live ": *Weleden* v. *Elkington* (1578), Plowden, 516.

and at other times repudiate these principles.[1] The question was not settled until *Manning's Case*[2] and *Lampet's Case*[3] decided that an executory devise in a term after a life interest was not only good, but indestructible, " and although these decisions have been grumbled at, they have never been overruled ".[4] The common law attitude was the old dogma that a term of years, however long, was of less consideration than an estate for life, but Lord Nottingham many years later claimed that Chancery had helped the common lawyers to reach " the true reason of the thing " instead of " the vulgar reason of the books " by allowing the remainder-man to compel the devisee for life to give security in Chancery not to destroy the remainder, and that the change of view of the law courts was largely due to their desire not to send litigants to Chancery.[5]

By the end of the sixteenth century, therefore, executory devises of terms in remainder after a life interest were in substance indestructible as Chancery would take measures to preserve them: shortly afterwards, the common law itself adopted this changed view in *Manning's Case*. Why then should destructibility continue to attach to executory devises of freeholds? The logic of the situation was certainly felt, and the common law courts began to retreat cautiously from their extreme position. Already in 1600 (even before *Manning's Case*) they held in a case of an executory devise of a freehold in the form " to *A.* in fee, but if *A.* fails to pay certain annuities, then to *B.*," that the executory devise to *B.* was indestructible if it was to an ascertained person.[6] This decision helped a great deal in the frequent cases where the enjoyment of land was made conditional on paying annuities to junior members of the family. Twenty years later a slightly different type of conditional limitation was sanctioned. In *Pells* v. *Brown*[7] a fee was devised to *A.* and his heirs, but if *A.* died without issue in the lifetime of *B.*, then to *B.* It was held that *B.* is not barred by a recovery suffered by *A.* As an eminent writer has said, it is difficult to over-estimate the influence of this decision on the subsequent history of conveyancing.[8]

THE RULE AGAINST PERPETUITIES

By this time, therefore, executory interests in freeholds or in terms were indestructible unless they could be construed as contingent

---

[1] The cases are listed in Gray, *Rule against Perpetuities*, 120–121.

[2] (1609), 8 Rep. 94 *b.*

[3] (1612), 10 Rep. 46 *b.*

[4] Gray, *op. cit.*, 122.

[5] *Duke of Norfolk's Case* (1681), 2 Swanst. 454 at 464; quoted in Holdsworth, vii. 131.

[6] *Purslowe* v. *Parker* (1600), 2 Rolle, *Abridgement*, 253 no. 2, 793 no. 2; cited in *Pells* v. *Brown* (1620), 2 Rolle Rep. 216 at 218–219.

[7] (1620), Cro. Jac. 590. 2 Rolle Rep. 216.

[8] Gray, *Rule against Perpetuities*, 128.

remainders, or were limited after an entailed interest.[1] This result represented a considerable change from the doctrine prevalent in the early days of Elizabeth, and it has been very plausibly suggested that competition from Chancery had much to do with the change: *Pells* v. *Brown* certainly came at a moment—1620—when the common law had most to fear from the rival system. But Chancery and the common law courts were in consequence both faced by the problem of perpetuities, and so combined their forces in devising a solution, for it must be remembered that chancellors frequently consulted the common law judges in difficult cases.

The word perpetuity was for a long time vaguely used: it first becomes precise when it is used to designate attempts to produce an unbarrable entail, of which Rickhill's settlement is an early example.[2] A bill against " perpetuities " which passed its first reading in the Lords on 19 January, 1598, was directed against uses arising in one person when another person attempts to alienate.[3] The term was then extended to analogous situations where the employment of contingent remainders, springing and shifting uses, and executory devises resulted in making the fee inalienable for a considerable length of time. An early instance of the word is in *Chudleigh's Case*,[4] but the problem itself may be regarded in one sense as very much older, and indeed as being a continuation of the history of freedom of alienation which we have treated in earlier pages. Old rules thus came to be justified on newer grounds. Thus the rule in *Shelley's Case* was devised in mediaeval times for a feudal purpose,[5] but its continuance was assured because it rendered the creation of perpetuities more difficult. The rule in *Purefoy* v. *Rogers*,[6] whatever its technical justification, likewise owed its survival to similar considerations.

The first attempts to prevent perpetuities took the form of the complicated rules which we have briefly described. It was hoped that rules limiting the creation and derivation of interests, coupled with rules permitting their destruction, would make undesirable settlements impossible. They probably did; but at the cost of upsetting many others which were perfectly harmless and even convenient. The ponderous machinery was, therefore, reversed and soon gathered alarming speed in the opposite direction. An acute dilemma presented itself between the two dangers of permitting perpetuities and upsetting reasonable arrangements, and slowly it was being realised that the sort of rules then being developed would inevitably cut both ways. The first gleam of light appears in an

---

[1] *Child* v. *Baylie* (1623), Cro. Jac. 459, confirmed previous opinions that such limitations were void.

[2] Above, p. 563.

[3] Printed in Holdsworth, vii. 546.

[4] (1595), 1 Rep. 120, " commonly called the *Case of Perpetuities* " (1 Rep. was published in 1602).

[5] Above, p. 564.

[6] Above, pp. 593–594.

argument by Davenport (later C.B.) when *Child* v. *Baylie*[1] came into the Exchequer chamber. He argued that since in this case the contingency must be determined in the lifetime of a living person, then there could be no fear of a perpetuity. The argument was unsuccessful, but slowly attention began to fasten on the life in being, helped at first by the settlement of the rule that an executory devise of a term after an entailed interest was bad, although it would be good after a life interest.[2]

A line of hesitating decisions culminated in the *Duke of Norfolk's Case*[3] in which Lord Nottingham laid the foundations of the rule against perpetuities, not so much by defining its content, as by settling the lines upon which it was subsequently to develop. In that case, the Earl of Arundel had conveyed a long term in trust for *B.*, his second son in tail male; but if his eldest son, *A.*, should die without male issue in *B.*'s lifetime, or if the title should descend to *B.*, then in trust for the third son, *C.* In fact, *A.* died without issue during *B.*'s lifetime, and the validity of the executory trust for *C.* was the principal point of the case.[4] Lord Nottingham, the Chancellor, called into consultation Pemberton, C.J., K.B., North, C.J., C.P., and Montagu, C.B. All three heads of the common law courts advised against the settlement, but Nottingham was not bound to accept their view, and decreed in its favour. On Nottingham's death, his old friend North succeeded him on the woolsack,[5] and in view of his dissent, it is not surprising that a bill of review was brought before him whereupon he reversed Nottingham's decree. A further appeal to the House of Lords resulted in another reversal and the restoration of Nottingham's decree (1685). In the course of his decision, Nottingham went fully into the history of the subject, and poured scorn on the mass of artificialities with which the common lawyers had encumbered it. The suggestion that the settlement could be better effected by means of a trust on a new term to *C.* instead of a new trust on the original term drew from him the famous words:[6]

" Pray let us so resolve cases here, that they may stand with the reason of mankind when they are debated abroad. Shall that be reason here that is not reason in any part of the world besides? I would fain know the difference why I may not raise a new springing trust upon the same term, as well as a new springing term upon the same trust; that is such a chicanery of law as will be laughed at all over the Christian world."

---

[1] (1618–1623), Cro. Jac. 459; 2 Roll. R. 129; Palmer, 334; it was a devise of a term to *A.* and his assigns, but if *A.* die without issue living at his death, then to *B.* Both courts held that the devise over to *B.* was bad. Note, however, that while this was pending it was held in *Pells* v. *Brown* that corresponding limitations in a devise of a freehold were good. As Gray, *Perpetuities*, 119, remarks, the courts were especially suspicious of settlements of terms, and it was in connection with terms that the rule against perpetuities was first developed.

[2] Above, p. 595.

[3] (1681), 3 Cas. in Ch. 1; 2 Swanst. 454.

[4] As the law stood after *Child* v. *Baylie* it was invalid.

[5] Later becoming Lord Guilford.

[6] 3 Cas. in Ch. at 33.

Such language must have been profoundly shocking to the common lawyers, and the House of Lords no doubt relished the opportunity of restoring Nottingham's decree. The basis of his decision was that since the trust to *C*. must arise, if at all, within the lifetime of a person then in being it could in no wise be properly called a perpetuity. It was true that *B*. had a fee-tail, but it was likewise true that his interest was determinable on one or the other of two events which could only happen in his lifetime. For two centuries the rule has continued to develop on that broad and reasonable basis, although Nottingham himself refused to be enticed into the discussion of hypothetical difficulties; to the question where would he stop in such cases he retorted:[1]

> " I will tell you where I will stop: I will stop where-ever any visible inconvenience doth appear; for the just bounds of a fee simple upon a fee simple are not yet determined, but the first inconvenience that ariseth upon it will regulate it."

Inconveniences have arisen, and the growing rule received its due measure of complexities and difficulties, but it is thanks to Lord Nottingham's courage and perception that the rule has as its basis a reasonable and simple proposition, instead of the artificial complications which the common law courts had been devising in order to meet the problem.

Such is the history, in brief outline, of the three systems of real property law controlled by the common law courts in the sixteenth and seventeenth centuries—the common law itself, uses executed under the Statute of Uses, and devises of freeholds and of terms under the Statute of Wills. Obviously they were faced with a bewildering situation, but it is difficult to show that they did anything to clarify it. All three systems raised the problem of perpetuities, but the common lawyers seemed to lack the courage, if not the penetration, to state a general solution. The rule was first adumbrated in Chancery, and to Chancery we must now turn for the fourth system of real property law in force during our period—the trust.

THE RISE OF THE TRUST

The Statute of Uses deals with the situation where *A*. is seised to the " use, confidence or trust " of *B*. It is clear that the statute operates wherever that situation exists, irrespective of the terms in which it is expressed, neither use, confidence nor trust being technical terms. Indeed, even a use implied in law (as on a bargain and sale) is equally within the statute, although none of these words is employed, and indeed no words at all. Nevertheless, a convention soon arose of confining the word " use " to those relationships which fell within the statute, and of describing those outside of it as " trusts ". The word " trust " had a more general meaning, however, and this vaguer sense has had great influence in the establishment of the modern trust; this broader sense seems to apply to any case where one person was under a moral

[1] 3 Cas. in Ch. 49.

duty to deal with property for another's benefit. We have already mentioned the fact that feoffees to uses could re-enter in order to preserve certain executory uses. In *Brent's Case*[1] Dyer and Manwood state this fact, and give as the reason that the feoffees " were the persons put in trust by the feoffor ". The uses involved in that case were, of course, executed by the statute, but there still remained a " trust "—a duty to take certain steps in order to further the intentions of the settlor.

The origin of the modern passive trust seems to lie in the regular enforcement by Chancery of a duty to convey arising in a few situations of common occurrence; as time goes on it becomes evident that the duty will be enforced with such mechanical regularity that there is no need to pursue the remedy, and the person entitled came to be treated as though he had already received a conveyance. It was in fact a repetition of a process which had already taken place much earlier in the history of the use. It is well known that a purchaser of land who had paid the price could compel the vendor to convey by a suit in Chancery. This rule became so well established that it could be expressed in the now familiar form that a vendor who has been paid, but who remains in seisin of the land, is seised to the use of the purchaser. The purchaser's right to be put into seisin thus became a " use "—something very like a property right—and after the statute, became a true legal title. The same process was repeated in the history of the trust. There were circumstances, often involving fraud or mistake, in which Chancery would compel a conveyance to the party who in conscience was entitled; this right to have a conveyance, we suspect, gradually acquired the character of a trust.

THE USE UPON A USE

Unfortunately there is very little material available in print from which to construct a history of equity, more especially for the critical reign of Elizabeth. Such scraps as have survived are therefore apt to stand out in undue prominence. This is certainly true of the famous " use upon a use ". The common belief that this was originally, as well as ultimately, a device to evade the Statute of Uses and to create a purely passive trust in spite of the statute, seems unlikely. The origin of the situation, we suspect, was a misunderstanding of the effect of the Statute of Uses upon a bargain and sale, which by now had become so common a conveyance that the true mechanism of it was sometimes forgotten by careless attorneys, with the result that even before the statute we find cases, such as arose in 1532, where it was stated[2] that land cannot be given to the use of *A*. where the rent is reserved to *B*. and that one cannot bargain and sell to *A*. for valuable consideration moving from *A*. to the use of *B*. Both the first and the second of these propositions turn upon the rule (already discussed)[3] that uses must be clear, and not

---

[1] (1575), 3 Dyer, 339 *b* at 340.

[2] *Anon.*, Bro. *Feoffement al Uses*, 40, 54.

[3] Above, p. 581.

conflicting with other uses or with other duties. Thus, uses cannot be declared upon terms or fees tail, for they would be repugnant to the duty owed to the reversioners; and in the second proposition, the use expressed is void, for it is repugnant to the implied use raised by the consideration. Such was the law even before the statute.[1] After the statute, some people seem to have thought that the implied use having been executed by the statute, a bargain and sale was henceforth merely a device for transferring legal seisin from vendor to purchaser, and that it was therefore equivalent, for these purposes, to a feoffment. Attempts were therefore made to bargain and sell to *A.* to the use of *B.* hoping that the use to *B.* would be executed by the statute, just as it would have been if there had been a feoffment of *A.* to the use of *B.*[2]

TYRREL'S CASE

That seems to have been the situation in *Tyrrel's Case*.[3] Jane Tyrrel bargained and sold her lands to George her son and his heirs for ever, in consideration of £400 paid by him to have and to hold to him and his heirs for ever, to the use of Jane for life with divers limitations over. An attempt to support the limitation of uses by reference to the Statute of Enrolments seems to indicate that some people were under the impression that bargains and sales were now equivalent (for these purposes) to a feoffment. The whole bench of the Common Pleas (sitting in the Court of Wards) held that the Statute of Enrolments did nothing to change the nature of a bargain and sale, and that the uses limited were void. The reason for their invalidity is clearly stated to be the same as that expressed in the case before the statute—the bargain for money implies one use, and the limitation of a further is " merely contrary ". Several cases contain the same decision.

This was the view not only of the common law courts, but of Chancery as well; *A.* bargained and sold to *B.* to the use of *A.*—Chancery just as firmly declined to help *A.*[4] Again, *A.* enfeoffed his sons to the use of himself for life, and after to the use of the sons and their heirs for the performance of his last will. Here also the uses to the last will are repugnant to the use in fee to the sons.[5] These decisions were no doubt harsh, defeating the manifest intentions of the parties, who had to suffer for the unskilfulness of their advisers. Those old rules about repugnant

---

[1] Hence a bargain and sale (of the fee) before the statute was followed in practice by a feoffment. Similarly, a *cestui que use* in the late fifteenth century would give notice of his intention to the feoffee to uses, who would thereupon make a legal estate accordingly: *Cases in Exchequer Chamber* (Selden Society), ii. 12 no. 7.

[2] In this and the succeeding cases it is clear that the parties hoped that the second use was executed by the statute, and that they had no thought of evading it, still less of creating a trust. They only turned to Chancery when they discovered their failure to come within the statute.

[3] (1557), Dyer, 155 (and in Digby, *Real Property*, 375); 1 And. 37.

[4] *Anon.*, Cary, 14 (undated).

[5] *Girland* v. *Sharp* (1595), Cro. Eliz. 382 (and in Digby, *Real Property*, 375).

uses were clearly working mischief when applied to deeds drawn by unlearned attorneys. Could the old rules be abandoned in view of this tendency to mistake them? Clearly we need not ask such a question of the common lawyers. Even Chancery was stubborn, until in the last years of Elizabeth and during the reign of James I, the idea of enforcing trusts of various sorts began to expand. Here there seemed a way out of the difficulty. Not that the Chancery was tempted to restore the passive use—there was no thought of that, but at least it might be possible to compel the parties to carry out the intention of the settlors, which had only failed through imperfect draftsmanship. Particularly, favour was now being shown to charitable trusts and trusts to convey. The former were favoured no doubt on grounds of public policy; the latter could be regarded as active trusts and so not within the Statute of Uses. To give effect to them the trustee had actually to convey and Chancery would compel him to do so. In *Sir Moyle Finch's Case*[1] it is implied that a bargain and sale of lands by *A.* to *B.* on trust for the payment of *A.*'s debts might be enforceable in equity. A trust for the payment of debts was regarded as a charitable trust, and although technically a bargain and sale was not the correct form of conveyance in such a case, yet Chancery seemed ready to overlook the use upon a use, and to compel the bargainee to carry out the trust.

SAMBACH *v.* DALSTON

Chancery was therefore prepared to tolerate a charitable trust limited upon a use in spite of the technical repugnancy. A generation later *Sambach* v. *Dalston*[2] seems to have revived the old difficulty of a bargain and sale by *A.* to *B.* to the use of *C. Tyrrel's Case* had held that since *B.* had a use, the further use to *C.* was void. By 1634 the influence of Chancery's care for charitable trusts and trusts to convey is now evident. It is felt to be unconscionable for *B.* to retain land which he well knows was meant for *C.* and it was doubtless on these grounds that Chancery decreed that *B.* must convey to *C.* The decision was not an attempt to settle the nature of *C.*'s interest, and it said nothing of trusts; its sole concern was to order *B.* to convey to *C.* who, he knew perfectly well, was the intended beneficiary.

It must not be imagined that this case created the modern trust. Active trusts have a continuous history from modern times back to the middle ages, for they were not affected by the Statute of Uses. The passive trust, on the other hand, makes no appearance in *Sambach* v. *Dalston*, nor for some years afterwards. That case merely decided that a bargain and sale by *A.* to *B.* to the use of *C.* should no longer have the curious effect of giving all to *B.* and nothing to *C.*; in other words, that *B.*, having the legal title of land which ought to be *C.*'s, can be compelled

---

[1] (1600) 4 Inst. 86; for an analysis, see Holdsworth, v. 307.

[2] (1634). " Because one use cannot be raised out of another, yet ordered and the defendant ordered to pass according to the intent " (Tothill, 188).

to convey it to *C*. This is a long way from the trust of modern times in which *B*. retains legal ownership and *C*. has equitable ownership. Although this case did not create the modern passive trust, however, it did provide a curious, but convenient, way of creating it when later on passive trusts were recognised. The practice of deliberately limiting a use upon a use in order to create a trust seems to have been established early in the eighteenth century; it is referred to as something of a novelty as late as 1715.[1]

The line of development from *Tyrrel's Case* to *Sambach* v. *Dalston* is, therefore, only a minor factor in the history of the trust. More significant elements in that history seem to be the development of Chancery's policy to compel conveyance by legal owners who were put under an express trust to convey (such as the trust which appears in *Sir Moyle Finch's Case* and was voluntarily carried out by the trustees making a conveyance), and secondly, by compelling legal owners to convey to those who in conscience were better entitled. It has often been remarked that the right in equity to receive a conveyance only needs a slight change of emphasis to become equitable ownership, thus growing imperceptibly into a passive trust.

Trusts of personal chattels were undoubtedly recognised in Chancery as they had been for a century and more. Terms of years presented a difficult problem. Chancery finally took steps to preserve executory interests in terms, at least in those normal cases where a testator was making limitations in a term which was already in existence; the creation of terms merely as a conveyancing device was a different matter, and for some time Chancery refused to give any assistance, especially where they concerned lands held in chief of the Crown. With the abolition of knight-service in 1660 this objection was removed, and so Chancery was free to consider terms as capable of supporting trusts, as well as of being limited in remainder.

[1] Ames, *op. cit.* 247 n. 2; *Daw* v. *Newborough*, Comyns, 242.

THE MORTGAGE

EARLY FORMS OF GAGE

The development of the mortgage is an interesting example of the interplay between legal doctrine and conveyancing custom. The gage, which is the root idea of the transaction, is really a relic of the days when credit was not yet in existence.[1] It has been conjectured that in its oldest form the gage (in Latin *vadium*, and in modern English pledge[2]) was payment, subject only to the option of the purchaser to substitute at a later time payment in a different kind. Under this arrangement the handing over of the gage settled the debt; the creditor could not demand the substitution of a different kind of payment, and the debtor had no way of recovering any excess value in the gage over the price which he could substitute later. According to this hypothesis, the primitive gage was capable of development in two directions: first, the gage may become a slight object whose transfer is treated as a binding form in a contract for future payment; or, the transaction may take its modern aspect of security only for the future payment of the principal debt. Procedure, judicial and extra-judicial, probably assisted this transformation. The royal courts soon make a practice of taking gages of litigants and security for their obedience, and the long history of the law of distress is really concerned with the compulsory taking of gages.[3]

Here we are particularly concerned with the gage of land, which appears in England as early as *Domesday Book*. A century later Glanvill describes it,[4] first of all stating that if the king's court is to take notice

---

[1] See Wigmore, *The Pledge-Idea*, Harvard Law Review, x. 321, 389, *ibid.*, xi. 18; and Hazeltine, *Geschichte des englischen Pfandrechts*; Hazeltine, *The Gage of Land*, Essays in Anglo-American Legal History, iii. 636.

[2] Remember that the mediaeval " pledge " (*plegius*) is almost always a person, not a thing. The Teutonic *wed* has come down to us by various routes as " gage ", " engagement ", " wage ", " wager ", and " wedding ".

[3] Distress is at least as old as II Cnut, 19 (1027–1034), and the distrainor held as a gagee only; the right of selling a distress to satisfy a debt occurs in a few late local customs, but did not enter the common law until 2 Will. & Mary, sess. 1, c. 5 (1690).

[4] Glanvill, x. 6–12.

of a gage it is essential that the gagee be in possession; otherwise, he says, the same land might be engaged to successive creditors, creating a situation much too complicated for royal justice to unravel.[1] The gagee may hold in several different ways. For example, the land may be given for a term of years with a covenant that at the end of the term the debt must be paid; on default the gagee will be entitled to hold the property henceforth as his own. Or, on the other hand, the gift may be for a term of years without containing a covenant releasing the title to the creditor on default; in such a case it will apparently be necessary to obtain the judgment of the court before the creditor's title becomes complete. Another possibility was a charter accompanied by an indenture which imposed conditions upon its effectiveness.[2] As we have seen, the gagee is always in possession and receiving the profits of the land. If those profits are applied to the reduction of the debt, Glanvill tells us the transaction is just and lawful; if, however, the profits do not reduce the debt but are taken by the gagee, then the proceeding is usurious, dishonest and sinful, and is therefore called *mortuum vadium*, a mortgage.[3] The mortgage is, nevertheless, legal as far as the king's court is concerned, but if the mortgagee dies, his property will be forfeit, like that of other usurers.

This type of gage as described by Glanvill finally fell into disuse. Its obvious disadvantages were that the debtor was always out of possession; that although the gagee was in possession yet he was not protected by the petty assizes, and so if he were ejected he had no means of recovering his security; and worse still, the debtor himself might eject the gagee and thereby reduce him to the position of an unsecured creditor.[4]

THE GAGE IN BRACTON'S DAY

When we come to Bracton we see attempts to fit the gage into the scheme of estates. Gages may therefore be effected by selling a term of years for a sum down; the advantage of this is that there is no debt at all, and, therefore, no usury, and no gage, while the termor is now protected against the lessor.[5] An alternative arrangement was a true gage for a term of years with the condition that if the debt is not paid at the end the lessee shall hold over in fee. This shifting fee for a time raised no technical difficulties.[6] It is obvious that several forms were

---

[1] Glanvill, x. 8.

[2] For an example of the difficulty caused by this sort of transaction, see Y.BB. Edward II Selden Society), xviii. 36, 46. Cf. below, p. 605 n. 1.

[3] The corresponding *vifgage* is a term of Norman law, but does not appear in English documents; Pollock and Maitland, ii. 119 n. 2.

[4] Glanvill, x. 11.

[5] Above, p. 572.

[6] Bracton, f. 268 *b*; it will be remembered that such springing and shifting fees were common in connection with the fee conditional, already mentioned.

used, and sometimes in combination. Thus the Year Book of 1314 tells of a lease for five years " by way of mortgage " whereof indentures were made, but accompanied by a deed of feoffment in fee simple with warranty in common form. Bereford, C.J., compelled the tenant (who relied on the feoffment) to answer to the indenture.[1] The very next case was one of a mortgage by feoffment, with a covenant in a separate deed for the defeasance of the feoffment and the " reversion " of the land.[2] One early case even allowed a charter of feoffment to be governed by a parol condition.[3]

Britton makes the significant remark that there is no equity of redemption although some people think there ought to be.[4] Furthermore, a common law judge in 1314 used these remarkable words: " When a man pledges tenements his intention is not to grant an estate of inheritance, but to secure the payment of the money which he borrowed promptly, and to get back the tenements when he had paid the money."[5] If the common law had kept to this doctrine it would have anticipated by several centuries the achievements of Chancery; very soon, however, the common law courts lost the equitable spirit which distinguished them in the reign of Edward II, and construed the terms of a mortgage strictly according to the letter.

JEWISH MORTGAGES

While the Jews were in England matters were in a much more satisfactory state. They had their own law and customs and the Crown maintained a special court (a division of the Exchequer) for their enforcement. Among these customs was the possibility of a gage in which the gagee was not bound to take possession; gages to Jews were, however, subject to a system of registration established by Richard I.

" Very early in the thirteenth century we may see an abbot searching the register, or rather the chest, of Jewish mortgages at York in quite modern fashion. A little later an abbot of the same house, when buying land, has to buy up many encumbrances that had been given to Jews, but has difficulty in doing so because some of them have been transferred. The debts due to Israelites were by the King's licence freely bought and sold when as yet there was no other traffic in obligations. We

---

[1] Y.BB. Edward II (Selden Society), xviii. 35 (1314). The charter was delivered to the neutral custody of a friar. Bereford's practice in his private investments seems to reflect the equitable spirit of his judgment. See *Sir Christopher Hatton's Book of Seals* (ed. D. M. Stenton), no. 251.

[2] Y.BB. Edward II (Selden Society), xviii. 36, 50 (1314).

[3] Y.B. 30 & 31 Edw. I (Rolls Series), 210 (1302). The case has many interesting features. The mortgagee refused the money when tendered, so the mortgagor paid it into the county court, re-entered the land, and was seised for a day and a night. This slight seisin, aided by her good title, enabled her to succeed in novel disseisin against the mortgagor who had ejected her and pleaded the charter of feoffment. For lengthy arguments in a similar but more complicated case (where also the mortgagee refused a tender) see Y.BB. Edward II (Selden Society), xi. 169–181 (1318).

[4] Britton (ed. Nichols), ii. 128; the hope came from the heirs of improvident ancestors, but Britton replies that alienation is free, and so the heirs have suffered no wrong.

[5] *Eyre of Kent* (Selden Society), iii. 85; below, p. 607.

may guess that, if the Jews had not been expelled from England, the clumsy mortgage by way of conditional conveyance would have given way before a simpler method of securing debts, and would not still be encumbering our modern law."[1]

From the fourteenth century onwards we therefore find the common law courts construing mortgages strictly—so strictly, that for practical purposes other and more convenient devices had to be invented under statutory authority, such as the *elegit* and obligations under the statutes of merchants and staples.[2] The great advantage of these forms was that they were statutory, enacted with a careful explanation of their real nature as securities, and with an express repeal of such common law principles as would have impeded their operation. The old common law mortgages, on the other hand, suffered from the incurable defect that they employed formulas which contradicted the true nature of the operation—they spoke of feoffments in fee, and leases for years, when the transaction was really neither—and such forms inevitably attracted several doctrines of seisin and the derivation of estates, which tended to defeat their purpose.

LITTLETON ON MORTGAGES

The fifteenth-century type of mortgage is described by Littleton, who incidentally gives a novel reason for the word:

" If a feoffment be made upon such a condition that if the feoffor pay to the feoffee at a certain day forty pounds of money, that then the feoffor may re-enter; then the feoffee is called tenant in mortgage, which is as much as to say in French *mort gage* and in Latin *mortuum vadium*. And it seemeth that the reason why it is called mortgage is that it is doubtful whether the feoffor will pay at the day limited such sum; and if he doth not pay, then the land which is put in pledge upon condition for the payment of the money is taken from him for ever, and so dead to him on condition. And if he doth pay the money, then the pledge is dead as to the tenant."[3]

He goes on to state that the feoffee may take for years, for life or in tail, instead of in fee; that if no date is limited, that then the redemption can only be made by the feoffor, and that his heir cannot redeem; if a date is fixed, however, and the feoffor die before it, then his heir can redeem on the day. He states in rather less confident tones his view that if the feoffee die within the term, tender should be made to his executors although his heir will have the land; if the feoffor die, his executors should render.[4]

The general scheme is therefore a feoffment in fee, with a provision

---

[1] Pollock and Maitland, ii. 124. Much detail is available in *Select Pleas of the Jewish Exchequer* (ed. Rigg, Selden Society); *Calendar of Plea Rolls in the Exchequer of Jews* (ed. Rigg and Jenkinson, Jewish Historical Society); *Starrs and Jewish Charters* (ed. Loewe, Jewish Historical Society).

[2] Above, pp. 390–394. *Elegit* may also have Jewish affiliations; Pollock and Maitland, i. 475.

[3] Littleton, s. 332. For a charter in fee simple, with livery " to hold until payment ", see Y.B. 21 Edward III, Pasch. no. 2 (1347).

[4] Littleton, ss. 333, 337, 339.

for re-entry upon a condition subsequent. Such an arrangement in the early fourteenth century was certainly invalid;[1] attempts to express the situation in terms of reversions or remainders after a fee simple, or in defeasance of a fee simple, were no more satisfactory,[2] and so Littleton had no alternative but to classify it as an " estate upon condition ". The courts certainly had a long-standing distrust of such devices. Littleton assumes that in his day the forms he gives were valid, but the scanty annotations suggest that there was little authority for his statement, and it may be conjectured that the common law mortgage was not much used; it is clear, on the other hand, that the statutory forms of security were popular, and very widely employed.

THE CLASSICAL COMMON LAW MORTGAGE

There is great obscurity over the history of mortgages in the fifteenth and sixteenth centuries. At what date it became usual to effect them by the newer device of a feoffment with a covenant for re-conveyance (instead of a condition of defeasance or of re-entry) it seems impossible to say.[3] The law of conditions, defeasance and entry was certainly growing steadily more unsatisfactory, and this may account for the preference for a covenant to re-convey which would be actionable by a writ of covenant. Perhaps the greatest factor of the change was the growing strength of equity, which concurrently with common law would compel re-conveyance on payment (which many creditors were loth to do), and was already drawing the whole transaction, and not merely certain aspects of it, within its jurisdiction. The covenant, however, would be enforced by the common law courts strictly as it stood. In this respect it closely resembled the widely used bond for £10 defeasible on payment of £5 on a certain date. In both cases it was the mission of Chancery to give relief against penalties which were enforceable at law.[4] In the present state of knowledge, it seems that the classical form of mortgage was actually established subsequent to equity's entry into the field, and with a definite recognition that mortgages were to come before Chancery rather than the common law courts.[5]

A further obscure point is the slow change in practice by which the mortgagor was allowed to remain in possession. This is certainly post-mediaeval, and, indeed, as late as the middle of the seventeenth century

[1] *Eyre of Kent* (Selden Society), iii. 85, 132 (1314), where the rule about livery of seisin on different terms from those in the deed is the opposite of that in Littleton, s. 359.

[2] On this, see H. D. Hazeltine's valuable introduction to R. W. Turner, *Equity of Redemption*, xxxviii.

[3] Exceptionally, there is an early example in *Bracton's Note Book*, no. 458 (1230).

[4] Some lurid examples of the unconscionable use of these instruments by a man whom even Chancery and Star Chamber failed to reach, in consequence of his influence at the court of Elizabeth, will be found in the valuable documents appended to Leslie Hotson, *Shakespeare and Shallow*.

[5] This is the conclusion of Professor Hazeltine, *loc. cit.* xli.

it seems that mortgagors generally gave up possession to the mortgagee.[1] It is significant that some curious forms of mortgage, devised by the eminent conveyancer, Sir Orlando Bridgman, were effected by giving the mortgagee a long term of years (to which conditions and provisos were more easily attached than to fees), and that among the provisos was a clause permitting the mortgagor to retain possession.[2]

In the sixteenth century Chancery began to give relief against penalties and it may be that it was partly on this basis that Chancery also intervened in mortgage transactions at the close of the sixteenth century, and developed its doctrine of the equity of redemption. Another factor, possibly of equal importance, may well have been Chancery's insistence that man, who ought in conscience to convey land to another, could be compelled to do so. This principle, applied to one type of situation, made possible the development of the later trust;[3] applied to the mortgage, it made possible the equity of redemption. It is, however, from the close of the seventeenth century, when Sir Orlando Bridgman was Lord Keeper, and after him Lord Nottingham, that equity began to elaborate a considerable body of law,[4] some of which modified the common law mortgage, while the rest applied to types of mortgages which were peculiar to equity, such as second and subsequent mortgages, and the remarkable equitable mortgage effected by merely depositing title deeds— which was clearly contrary to the words and the policy of the Statute of Frauds.[5] Conveyancers themselves made the valuable addition (which the legislature subsequently developed) of the power of sale which has made the modern mortgage so effective an instrument, originally prompted, it seems, by a desire to avoid the slow and costly foreclosure proceedings in Chancery.

STATUTES MERCHANT, STATUTES STAPLE, ELEGIT

The fact that the mortgage was not a very satisfactory institution is shown by the continued use of the mediaeval statutes merchant and staple. There was much legislation[6] and both merchants and landowners made much use of them. By means of a " statute " a debtor could voluntarily make his land a security for debt. If judgment was given against him, the judgment creditor could reach his land by the writ of *elegit*.

---

[1] Turner, *Equity of Redemption*, 90.

[2] Holdsworth, vii. 365.

[3] Above, p. 602.

[4] For a valuable history of this period in considerable detail, see Turner, *op. cit.* The *Prolegomena of Chancery and Equity*, by Lord Nottingham, will appear in the " Cambridge Studies in Legal History ", and his own notes of his decisions will come from the Selden Society; both works are edited by D. E. C. Yale.

[5] *Fitzjames* v. *Fitzjames* (1673), Finch, 10, is the earliest example (and is a little earlier than the statute); *Russel* v. *Russel* (1783), 1 Bro. C.C. 269, stated the subtle reasons for taking the case out of the Statute of Frauds.

[6] See Hubert Hall, *Select Cases in Law Merchant* (Selden Society) for a list of the statutes (iii. 126), and the whole of vol. iii for illustrative cases.

A creditor in possession by either method had a " freehold " and (by statute) was protected by the assize of novel disseisin. Thus a great breach was made in the ancient principle that the sacred freehold was not liable to creditors—but at the expense of much complication in the law of land.

CHAPTER 10

CONVEYANCES

ANGLO-SAXON CHARTERS

The Anglo-Saxon form of conveyance was at first extremely elaborate and was imitated from continental models.[1] Whether, like them, it acted as a conveyance, that is to say, transferred the complete title without the requirement of any further ceremonies, it is very difficult to say.[2] Of the transfer of folkland it is even less possible to speak with confidence, since in the ordinary course of events it seems to have been effected without charter or written document. Such traces as we have seem to indicate a ceremonial transfer accompanied by great publicity, sometimes in the county court and more frequently in the hundred court. At the same time we find the appearance of *festermen*, whose function is particularly obscure.[3] If we may venture a guess, it would be that they partly represent the *borh* or surety whose presence so frequently rendered an Anglo-Saxon contract a three-cornered affair.

Towards the end of the Anglo-Saxon period the elaborate charter is replaced by a simpler form which modern historians call a " writ-charter ". This is derived from the administrative writ and was originally merely a letter of instructions sent by the king to some official. This brief and convenient form was soon used for all sorts of purposes. From this single ancestor are derived the charter and letters patent which are the

---

[1] For a brief collection of typical forms, see Holdsworth, iii. 666–673, iv. 568–572, vii. 547–559; the classical repertory is still Madox, *Formulare Anglicanum* (1702). The diplomatic (or formal) aspect is stressed in Hubert Hall, *Studies in Official Historical Documents*, and *Formula Book* (2 vols.); the best brief account is the introduction of F. M. Stenton, *Gilbertine Charters* (Lincoln Record Society) and his recent *Latin Charters of the Anglo-Saxon Period* (1955).

[2] Plucknett, *Bookland and Folkland*, Economic History Review, vi. 64–72.

[3] Vinogradoff, *Transfer of Land*, Harvard Law Review, xx. 532; *Collected Papers*, i. 149.

form of a good many grants of property and privileges, including the Great Charter; so, also, the letters close which were the great administrative instrument in the middle ages; likewise the original writs on which the forms of action were based; and so, too, the conventional forms of conveyance used by private persons.

POST-NORMAN CHARTERS

When we come to the Anglo-Norman age we find that already the law had made a great decision. It is clearly recognised that a deed does not operate as a conveyance, but is simply evidence. With the decline of the Anglo-Saxon charter, according to one view,[1] we therefore reach the end of a brief period during which a document was capable of transferring rights, and a return to the more ancient native practice which insisted upon an actual delivery of chattels or livery of seisin of land. We have already remarked, however, that the existence of this momentary aberration has not yet been clearly established.[2] In any case, the importance of the deed is much reduced, and in the Anglo-Norman age there can be no doubt that a great deal of land was transferred without deed. The essence of the transaction was a complete and public change of the occupancy of the land in question; even the symbolic transfers of the previous age are no longer effective (if, indeed, they ever were); instead, we find the purchaser entering upon the land and expelling from it the previous owner and his family, his servants, beasts and chattels, all of which is done in the most public way. The deed is at first a sort of memorandum in the form of a writ-charter recounting the transaction in the past tense. The document usually begins in the name of the vendor in such words as these, in the thirteenth and later centuries:

> " Know all men present and to come, that I, *A. B.*, have given and granted and by my present charter confirmed to *C. D.*, his heirs and assigns forever, all that land of mine . . ."

—and here the boundaries are set out with some particularity. Then comes the following clause:

> " To have and to hold to *C. D.*, his heirs and assigns, of me and my heirs rendering therefor annually. . . ."

At this point (called the *habendum*) the nature of the donee's interest is stated, and if the gift is in fee-tail the limitations will be specified. In deeds executed after the Statute *Quia Emptores* the *tenendum* will have to be in the form " to hold to *C. D.*, his heirs and assigns, of the chief lord of the fee by the services rightfully and customarily due ", and if the grantor reserves any rights (such as rent on a lease) a clause beginning *reddendo* will specify them. We then come to the very important clause of warranty in this form:

[1] Pollock and Maitland, ii. 87.

[2] See the impressive criticism by Galbraith, *Foundation Charters*, Cambridge Historical Journal, iv. 205.

"And I, my heirs and assigns will warrant the said land to *C. D.* and his heirs
and assigns against all men forever. . . ."

This warranty clause[1] was a great protection to the purchaser, for if
his title was subsequently attacked he could call upon his warrantor to
come into court and defend it, and, if he lost, the warrantor was bound
to recompense him with land of equal value in the same county; at the
same time the warranty acted as a bar to any claim by the donor and
those whom he bound. As we have already said, at the beginning of
the thirteenth century the clause of warranty served to bar the claims
of heirs who might otherwise try to recall their ancestor's gift.[2] The
clause of warranty was followed by a clause announcing that the deed
was sealed, in forms that varied considerably; it is not infrequent to
find even something like this:

"And in order that this gift, grant and confirmation may remain forever good
and valid, I have appended to this present writing my seal (*or* the seal of *E. F.*
because I have not one of my own). In the presence of these witnesses . . ."[3]

In the fourteenth century the charter frequently omits to mention the
seal, although it remained the law that no deed was valid without a seal.
Before the reign of Edward I it is unusual to find the deed dated, but
from the fourteenth century onwards the sealing and witness clauses are
replaced by a dating clause announcing the time and place. In the
fifteenth century livery of seisin degenerates into a ceremony, and frequently the vendor and purchaser made attorneys to give and receive
livery of seisin; a memorandum of the due performance of this was
endorsed upon the deed. We do not commonly find signatures on
deeds before the sixteenth century, and they did not become generally
necessary until the Statute of Frauds. Sometimes as a greater security
the deed was written in duplicate (particularly if it were a lease containing
elaborate covenants) upon the same piece of parchment, and the two
deeds were then separated by an indented cut passing through the word
CHYROGRAPHUM. Such a deed was called an indenture or a "writing
indented", although it is only later that we find the appearance of the
modern form beginning, "This indenture made at such a date witnesses
that . . ." At first the form of an indenture was merely a precaution,[4]

---

[1] In early charters the warranty may be secured by a pledge of faith: Stenton, *Gilbertine
Charters* (Lincoln Record Society), xxix.

[2] If the donee in fee was to hold of the donor by homage, then he was entitled to warranty
as an incident of homage; tenants in tail are likewise entitled to warranty by the reversioner
as an incident of tenure. Where there was substitution instead of subinfeudation and no
express warranty, the Statute of Bigamists, 1276 (4 Edw. I), c. 6, imposed certain implied
warranties. For a rich collection of material and a very valuable discussion, see S. J. Bailey,
Warranties of Land in the Reign of Richard I, Cambridge Law Journal, ix. 192, and *Warranties
of Land in the Thirteenth Century, ibid.,* viii. 274, ix. 82.

[3] Even the royal acts of the infant Henry III were sealed with William Marshall's seal
"because we have no seal".

[4] For the Anglo-Saxon and remoter origins, see Hazeltine, introduction to Whitelock,
Anglo-Saxon Wills, xxiv n. 2.

the middle ages. In its early days, after a short period of limitation a fine operated as a bar to all the world. The period was at first twelve months, and the only exceptions were in favour of minors, lunatics, prisoners and people beyond the seas. A fine, like other judicial proceedings, could be set aside by a writ of error and, in general, was not effective unless the conusee took seisin under it[1]—herein resembling the charter, which was useless unless the grantee was given livery of seisin. The statutory changes which were made were chiefly important as affecting the efficacy of the fine as a disentailing device, and of this we shall speak later.[2]

Collusive recoveries were also used in a variety of forms during the middle ages, but in almost every case they seem to be tainted with fraud. It can hardly be said that a recovery becomes a common assurance and a strictly legitimate proceeding until the sixteenth century. In the middle ages it was used to convey land free of a term, to bar dower, by a husband to alienate his wife's land and to defeat her heirs, and to alienate into mortmain. A stream of legislation checks first one and then another of these practices.

All the forms which we have so far considered were typically mediaeval in the sense that they were not operative in themselves, but depended upon an actual change of seisin. A charter was accompanied by livery of seisin effected by the parties themselves or their attorneys; fines and recoveries were both incomplete until seisin had been given to the conusee or the recoveror by the sheriff under a writ from the court.

BARGAIN AND SALE

In the fifteenth century Chancery held that a vendor of land who had received the purchase price, but who remained in seisin of the land, was seised thenceforward to the use of the purchaser. Already, it would seem, sixteenth-century purchasers had such confidence in this rule that they were content with this equitable title, especially since it was a secret one. The Statue of Uses, however, executed this implied use and made it a legal estate, and the Statute of Enrolments was immediately passed to prevent legal estates being conveyed with the same secrecy. The act only applied to bargains and sales for an estate of freehold or

---

[1] The fine *sur conusance de droit come ceo q'il ad de son done* contains an implication that the conusee is already seised; this may or may not have been true, but as it is matter of record it thus is practically equivalent to seisin, and the whole operation resembles a disseisee's release to his disseisor. In other fines the sheriff delivers seisin. Since the statute *de finibus levatis*, 1299 (27 Edw. I), parties and their heirs were forbidden to deny the seisin, but strangers could continue to do so. For an early discussion of theory, see Sayles, *King's Bench*, iii. 167. For the necessity of seisin even after a judgment, see Pollock and Maitland, ii. 101–102, and the cases collected in Holdsworth, iii. 241 n. 2. The procedure and technicalities of fines are elaborately explored in the introductions of G. J. Turner, *Huntingdon Feet of Fines* (Cambridge Antiquarian Society, octavo publications, vol. xxxvii) and C. A. F. Meekings, *Surrey Feet of Fines* (Surrey Record Society, nos. xlv, xlvi). For an important discussion of theory, see Y.BB. 21 & 22 Edward I (Rolls Series), 404.

[2] Below, p. 619.

inheritance, but upon them it imposed the condition that the bargain must be " in writing indented,[1] sealed, and enrolled " within six months. The statute contains words which seem to imply that no use shall arise on the bargain if it is not enrolled. The object apparently was to prevent Chancery finding equitable estates arising from bargains which did not comply with the act. If so, the act was successful; but the words had also the effect of obscuring the nature of a bargain and sale, for some people were led to believe that the act had somehow abolished the implied use altogether, and so were tempted to limit further uses on a bargain and sale. As we have seen,[2] confusion lasted for a long time, until finally the profession came to the conclusion that a bargain and sale was a dangerous instrument if it was used to effect settlements.[3]

LEASE AND RELEASE

The Statute of Enrolments did not affect bargains for a term, and so these were left to the combined operation of the Chancery rule and the Statute of Uses; the bargainor is therefore seised to the use of the termor, and the termor acquires the legal term under the statute, without having to enter. Hence it was possible to convey secretly by using two deeds— a bargain and sale for a term, followed by a release of the fee to the termor. Neither had to be enrolled, and neither needed actual entry for its completion. This ingenious device is ascribed to Sir Francis Moore, and was sanctioned[4] by the courts in 1621. By the end of the century, in spite of some doubts, it was in general use, for besides its secrecy it had the additional advantage over the bargain and sale enrolled, that uses could be limited in the deed of release.

WILLS

Since the Statute of Wills these documents must be considered as conveyances, and until a century ago they were treated on strictly conveyancing lines. For example, a will would only pass such lands as the testator was seised of both at the time of making the will and at the time of his death, which perpetuates the situation existing before the Statute of Uses when land was devised by conveying it to feoffees to the uses of the feoffor's will. The rule is therefore older than the statute of 1540, although certainly consistent with it; Coke delighted to attribute the rule to the words of the act which authorise a testator to devise such land as he " has ".[5] Henry VIII's statutes made no requirements as to the form of a will save that it be in writing, and it was not until the

---

[1] Hitherto even a parol bargain and sale would raise the use.

[2] Above, p. 600.

[3] Sheppard, *Touchstone* (ed. Atherley), 225 n.

[4] *Lutwich* v. *Mitton*, Cro. Jac. 604. Common law leases followed by releases occur as early as 1260: R. Stewart-Brown, *Chester County Court Rolls*, 5.

[5] *Butler and Baker's Case* (1591), 3 Rep. 25 at 30 *b*.

Statute of Frauds that this and a good many other matters were required
to be expressed in writing, signed, and in the case of wills witnessed.
The Statute of Frauds also required written documents for the creation of
trusts of land, and for the assignment of all sorts of trusts, and therefore
contributed a great deal towards the treatment of these equitable interests
as though they were property. A mass of very unsatisfactory law,
mainly the work of the seventeenth and eighteenth centuries, was swept
away by the Wills Act, 1837.[1]

DISENTAILING DEVICES: WARRANTIES

We have already seen[2] that when a tenant in fee simple alienated,
binding himself and his heirs to warrant the alienee and his heirs, the
warranty operated as a bar which peremptorily excluded the donor and
his heirs from any claim to the land in question. This principle probably
played a part in establishing the alienability of fees simple, free from
family restraints.

It now remains to consider the effect of warranties created by those
who were not tenants in fee simple. The problem first became acute
when doweresses and tenants by the curtesy resorted to tortious feoffments coupled with warranties. When there was issue of the marriage
it would normally happen that the issue would be heir to both parents;
hence as heir to his father's warranty he would be barred from claiming
lands to which he was entitled as his mother's heir, and as heir to his
mother's warranty (created while she was doweress) he would be barred
from claiming lands which were his paternal inheritance.[3] Such practices
struck at the root of the common law scheme of family relationships, and
in 1278 the legislature intervened. The Statute of Gloucester, c. 3,
enacted that an heir, who has inherited nothing from his father, shall
not be barred from demanding lands inherited from his mother, although
the father had alienated them with warranty. If he has inherited from
his father, but not enough (*assetz*) to fulfil the warranty completely, then
he is barred to the extent that " assets " had descended to him. The
statute only deals with warranties created by tenants by curtesy.[4]

What of warranties by a tenant in tail? A simple feoffment (without
warranty) by a tenant in tail will give a fee simple to the alienee, but will
not bar actions by the heir in tail, remaindermen or reversioners; *De*

---

[1] 7 Will. IV & 1 Vict., c. 26.

[2] Above, p. 529.

[3] For the denial of these propositions by Bracton, ff. 349*b*–350, see the comments by Lady
Stenton in *Yorkshire Eyre Rolls* (Selden Society, 56), xvi.

[4] It says nothing of the parallel situation of warranties by a doweress. There were petitions
for a similar enactment to cover these also in 1315 (*Rot. Parl.*, i. 336 no. 3, which arose out
of a case in 1313, Y.BB. Edward II (Selden Society), xv. 118 ff.) and again a few years later
(Sayles, *King's Bench*, iii. p. cxvi g), but no remedy was given until the statute 11 Henry VII,
c. 20 (1495). Another aspect of collateral warranty was raised in parliament in 1376, but
again without result: *Rot. Parl.*, ii. 334 no. 77. For the pre-statutory rules of assets by
descent (which affected the *excambium* only, and not the duty to warrant), see J. S. Bailey, in
Cambridge Law Journal, viii. 293.

Donis itself provides that even a fine by the donee in tail will not bar his issue or the reversioner. Experiments were therefore made with the deed with warranty and some very curious results followed, for the Statute *De Donis* made no provision for this case. The simplest case was when a father, being a tenant in tail, alienated with warranty and the warranty descended together with the entail to his heir. This warranty, it would seem, barred the heir from his recovery, and so in this way an entail might be effectively barred as against the heirs in tail: of course it did not affect remainders or reversions. This did not last very long, for the Statute of Gloucester, c. 3 (which, as we have seen, expressly applied only to warranties created by tenants by curtesy) was extended by judicial interpretation to warranties created by tenants in tail, in a case of 1306.[1] The result was that if the issue in tail had inherited from his ancestor " assets by descent "[2] he was barred to the extent of those assets, otherwise not. Consequently from 1306 onwards it is a growing opinion that a deed with warranty might not be a bar if there were no assets by descent.

By the time of Littleton, an attempt had been made to generalise these rules and to classify warranties. Some were described as *lineal* warranties because the burden of the warranty and the title both descended by the same line; but this was not always the case, for a warranty might be *collateral*, and it was held that collateral warranties were always a bar.[3] Normally, a warranty was created by one who was seised of the land, and was about to enfeoff an alienee. Soon, however, it was admitted that anyone could bind himself and his heirs to warranty, whether he had any interest in the land or not.[4] This afforded opportunities for a good deal of ingenuity. It was not always easy to use collateral warranties, for it needed the co-operation of other members of the family and also depended upon relatives dying in the proper order, conditions which were not always available. When they were, a collateral warranty was a very effective bar to the issue in tail:

> " If land be given to a man and the heirs of his body begotten, who taketh a wife and have issue a son between them, and the husband discontinues the tail in fee and dieth, and after the wife releaseth to the discontinuee in fee with warranty, and dieth, and the warranty descends to the son, this is a collateral warranty."[5]

[1] Y.B. 33–35 Edward I (Rolls Series), 388 (by this time the rule was so well established that the court frustrated the father's attempt to evade it by conveying assets to his heir in such wise that they did not " descend ": cf. *Bracton's Note Book*, no. 1683 (1225)). In 1292 (Y.B. 20 & 21 Edward I (Rolls Series), 302) the bar was pleaded unsuccessfully—if one can trust the very obscure report. The principle of assets by descent was admitted in Y.BB. Edward II (Selden Society), x. 36 (1311), and *ibid.* xii. 133 (1312).

[2] The old books use the French expression *assetz par descent*—which seems to be the origin of the modern English " assets ".

[3] These words were ill-chosen, and do not in themselves assist in the classification of warranties. The clearest exposition of this very tangled subject is Charles Butler's note to Co. Lit. 373 *b*, n. 2 (1823).

[4] For very early attempts, see Richardson, Law Quarterly Review, xlviii. 422 (1181), and *Bracton's Note Book*, no. 77 (1219); the point is clearly decided in 1316 in Y.BB. Edward II (Selden Society), xx. 99 ff.; Littleton, s. 712.

[5] Littleton, s. 713.

Sometimes even remainders could be barred. Thus suppose that the eldest of several sons is a tenant in tail, with successive remainders to his brothers in tail. If the eldest discontinue with warranty and die without issue, then the second son will be heir to the warranty; the remainder, however, is his by purchase and not by inheritance from his elder brother. The warranty is therefore collateral to him, and he is barred.[1] Protests were made in Parliament against the collateral warranty rule[2] during the reign of Edward III, but it was not until the reign of Queen Anne that the bar by collateral warranty was abolished; curiously enough the statute did not abolish the bar by lineal warranty with assets descended.[3] The effect of both of these warranties upon remainders and reversions was very much dependent upon circumstances and in order to bar these estates more effective devices had to be invented.[4]

DISENTAILING BY FINE

Among these was the fine. By *De Donis* a fine was no bar to the issue in tail.[5] Fines of fees simple, however, were a bar to all the world after a year and a day. In 1361 this old principle was completely reversed by statute,[6] and for over a century fines ceased to be a bar to any claimants except the parties themselves. This, however, introduced so much uncertainty and permitted the assertion of so many remote and dormant titles that Richard III by a statute which was re-enacted by Henry VII[7] (who usually got the credit for Richard III's reforms) enacted that a fine should be a bar after certain proclamations and the lapse of five years, while remaindermen and reversioners were to be barred by a fine with proclamations unless they claimed within five years of the time when their estates accrued. Once again the fine becomes " a piece of firm ground in the midst of shifting quicksands ".[8] A case, and later a statute,[9] made it clear that a fine with proclamations was a complete bar to the issue in tail since they are deemed to be privy to it. A fine, consequently, after the statute will bar the issue, but not remainders or reversions save in the unlikely case where they let their rights go by default.

[1] Littleton, s. 716. But see Y.BB. Edward II (Selden Society), xx. 280 (1318), where issue is taken on the descent of assets; Littleton's rule was not yet in existence.

[2] *Rot. Parl.*, ii. 334 no. 77 (1376). London had already taken the matter into its own hands by abolishing the rule in 1365 (*Liber Albus*, 496; *Letter Book G*, f. 154) in terms closely resembling the act of 1706.

[3] 4 & 5 Anne, c. 3, s. 21 (1706).

[4] For a reversion barred by a collateral warranty, see *Rot. Parl.*, ii. 195, no. 81 (1347).

[5] It was suggested (but not seriously maintained) that since *De Donis* exempts the issue from the effects of a fine, but says nothing of remainders, that therefore a fine would bar remainders: Y.BB. Edward II (Selden Society), xxii. 18 (1318).

[6] 34 Edw. III, c. 16.

[7] 1 Rich. III, c. 7 (1484); 4 Hen. VII, c. 24 (1490).

[8] Pollock and Maitland, ii. 102.

[9] *Anon.* (1527), Dyer, 2 *b*; 28 Hen. VIII, c. 36 (1536).

THE COMMON RECOVERY

The problem of barring remainders and reversions was finally settled by means of the recovery. Of the earlier history of recoveries we have already spoken; in the fifteenth century a number of forms were tried with the evident object of barring entails,[1] but it seems always assumed that the recovery could be " falsified " if fraud or collusion were proved.

In Littleton's day their effect was restricted. Thus if a tenant in tail suffered a recovery (without voucher, and therefore not a " common " recovery), and the recoveror was duly put in seisin by the court, it would nevertheless be possible to destroy its effects, for if the erstwhile tenant in tail disseised the recoveror, died seised, and his issue inherited, then the issue is remitted to the entail.[2] It was perfectly clear that a recovery by a tenant for life could have little effect; remaindermen and the reversioner after him could intervene, and even if they did not, they might treat his suffering a recovery as a forfeiture; at the most, failing any entry on their part, it seems that remainders and reversions were only thereby discontinued, and not barred.[3]

A statute of Henry VIII cleared up this situation by making the recovery absolutely void unless it was made with the consent of the remainderman or reversioner.[4] It seems, however, that the statute was evaded by tenants for life alienating to a stranger who then suffered a recovery in which he vouched the tenant for life, " to the great prejudice " of those in remainder or reversion: hence an act of Elizabeth[5] avoided all recoveries by a tenant for life, including those where the tenant for life came in as vouchee, unless the consent of the remainderman or reversioner appeared on the record. Clearly, then, the statute preserves the situation (long since established) of a recovery by a tenant for life who vouches the remainderman or the reversioner in fee.

A tenant for life in possession is therefore powerless unless the tenant in tail will join him. So we must now consider the powers of a tenant in tail in possession. If he suffered a collusive recovery (not a " common " recovery) the reversioner could intervene immediately,[6] or could recover by action of formedon when his estate fell in. There was therefore little to be done by any mechanism whereby the tenant in tail actually lost the land. Eventually this difficulty was met by a very ingenious device whereby the tenant in tail could part with the land without suffering any technical loss. On being impleaded, he vouched to warranty a stranger, a man of straw, who then defaulted. The recoveror had judgment against the tenant in tail (and so got the land), but the tenant in tail had judgment against the " common vouchee " (who in later times was the

---

[1] Much historical matter on recoveries is collected in *Pelham's Case* (1590), 1 Rep. 14.

[2] Littleton, s. 689.

[3] Co. Lit., 362 a.

[4] 32 Hen. VIII, c. 31 (1540).

[5] 14 Eliz., c. 8 (1572).

[6] Westminster II, c. 3 (1285), and *De Defensione Juris*, 20 Edw. I, c. 1 (1292); the right was later lost, *Registrum Brevium*, f. 235; 2 Inst. 345.

crier of the court) for recompense in land to the value of that which had been lost. The success of this device depended on the rule that subsequent remaindermen and the reversioner have still their rights and remedies, but that they are available only against the land which the tenant in tail received as recompense—and as the common vouchee carefully refrained from landownership, there was never any possibility of recompense being actually enforced. The right to it subsisted, however, and so remaindermen and reversioners suffered loss but no injury. And, of course, the device could not have worked unless the courts were determined to close their ears to the obvious charge that the whole proceeding was a barefaced fraud. As we have seen, the courts had long tolerated the creation of collateral warranties by deed by persons who had no interest in the land, and it was but a step further to allow the voucher to warranty of persons who likewise had no real interest in the proceedings, and who had no means of fulfilling the heavy obligations which they undertook.

In its classical form, the common recovery was suffered, not by the tenant in tail, but by a " tenant to the *precipe* " to whom an estate had been made, either by bargain and sale or by fine, for the express purpose of suffering the recovery. The *precipe* or original writ issues against this person, who vouches the tenant in tail to warranty: the tenant in tail then vouches the common vouchee, who enters into the warranty and then defaults. The recoveror then has judgment against the tenant, the tenant has judgment to the value against the tenant in tail, and he against the common vouchee. The proceedings were always surrounded with a certain amount of mystery, and the precise reason for their effectiveness was not always clearly apprehended. The author of the *Touchstone*[1] could think of nothing better than that *communis error facit jus*; one of his annotators convicts Hale of misunderstanding the nature of a recovery; another speculator thought that the entail would continue (by a fiction) for ever and ever in the recoveror, his heirs and assigns, and consequently remainders and reversions would never fall in;[3] Willes, C.J., thought it best not to inquire.[4]

If the theory of the recovery is obscure, its history is even more so. Under the common law system, everything ought to have a history, and so a singularly obscure case came to be conventionally regarded as the historical foundation for common recoveries. This was *Taltarum's Case*,[5]

---

[1] Sheppard, *Touchstone*, 40. The first edition was in 1641; there is a general opinion that so good a book could not have been written by Sheppard, and a late tradition ascribes it to Dodderidge, J., K.B., 1612–1628; Holdsworth, v. 391–392.

[2] *Touchstone* (ed. Atherley), 38 n. *b*; *Hudson* v. *Benson* (1671), 2 Lev. 28.

[3] Pigott, *Common Recoveries* (1739), 13 ff.

[4] Adding, " Mr Pigott has confounded himself and everybody else who reads his book "; *Martin* d. *Tregonwell* v. *Strachan* (1744), 1 Wils. 73.

[5] Y.B. 12 Edward IV, 19 (translated in Digby, *Real Property*, 255–258). For comments see Elphinstone, *Alienation of Estates Tail*, Law Quarterly Review, vi. 280; Maitland, *Taltarum's Case*, *ibid.*, ix. 1; G. J. Turner, *Taltarum's Case*, *ibid.*, xii. 301; Challis, *Real Property* (ed. Sweet), 309; Holdsworth, iii. 119, 137.

1472. Within the succeeding century there can be no doubt that the common recovery rapidly became a regular part of the law, and of the law of entails—it thus became part of the nature of an entail that it could be barred.

STATUTORY DEVICES

Out of the depths of the eighteenth century, whose tortuous learning on this subject is assembled in Cruise on *Fines and Recoveries* (1783–1786), comes the prophetic voice of Blackstone.[1] Having first given a very lucid exposition of these devices, Blackstone proceeds to call for the abolition of " such awkward shifts, such subtle refinements, and such strange reasoning ". He examines several possible methods. The repeal of *De Donis* might cause trouble by reviving the conditional fee; it might be enacted that every tenant in tail of full age should be deemed to be tenant in fee simple absolute (but this might seem hard on reversioners); or better still, a tenant in tail might be empowered to bar the entail by a solemn deed enrolled, " which is . . . warranted by the usage of our American colonies ". To have suggested the abolition of fines and recoveries in 1766 was an achievement; to have cited American example for it in the years of the Stamp Act is surely notable, too; nor should Blackstone's remarks on vested interests be overlooked. Fines and recoveries brought handsome revenues by way of fees to numbers of court officials, and there is no doubt that this circumstance made reform difficult. Blackstone was ready to suggest a higher necessity, at least in a protasis:

" And if, in so national a concern, the emoluments of the officers concerned in passing recoveries are thought to be worthy of attention, those might be provided for in the fees to be paid upon each enrolment."

In fact, Blackstone lived in the early stages of an historical movement which he discerned and appreciated. He remarks that for a century and a half bankrupt tenants in tail had been empowered to bar their entails by deed enrolled, so that their commissioners in bankruptcy could sell them.[2] Moreover, Elizabeth's statute of charitable uses[3] was construed as " supplying all defects of conveyances " so that a tenant in tail could devise, and even settle, entailed land to charitable uses, without fine or recovery.[4] Already, then, some cases needed no fine and recovery, but merely a deed. Blackstone's suggestion was carried out by the Fines and Recoveries Act, 1833, which enabled a tenant in tail who is of full age, with the consent of the tenant for life, to bar the entail by his deed enrolled.

In the common form of settlements, however, a considerable period

[1] 2 Bl. Comm., 358–361.
[2] 21 James I, c. 19, s. 12 (1624).
[3] 43 Eliz., c. 4 (1601).
[4] 2 Bl. Comm., 376.

might elapse before there was a tenant in tail of full age, and during this period the tenant for life could not deal with the land to any great extent. In the middle of the eighteenth century it became a common, though costly, practice to secure a private act of Parliament to disentail in such cases; the close of the century saw the great outburst of canal construction, to be followed soon by railway and dock undertakings, and in the acts authorising the compulsory purchase of land for these purposes, tenants for life of settled land were given powers to sell without having recourse to separate private estate acts. As such enterprises became more frequent, these powers were made permanently available by various acts, but were still confined to sales to certain types of public undertakings, until the Settled Land Act, 1882, placed them at the disposal of tenants for life generally, transferring the limitations of the settlement to the proceeds of the sale.

PART 4

CONTRACT

SUMMARY

CONTRACT

It is remarkable that, in spite of the numerous foreign influences which were at work in the field of contract, the common law was so little affected by them. The Church very early took a strong view of the sanctity of contractual relationships, insisting that in conscience the obligation of a contract was completely independent of writings, forms and ceremonies, and tried as far as she could to translate this moral theory into terms of law. Then, too, there were the mercantile courts which were endeavouring to enforce the practice of the best merchants and to express that practice in terms acceptable to either or both of the two conflicting schools of legal experts whose approbation was necessary —the civilians and the canonists. In England all these influences were at work. Glanvill knew just enough of the Roman classification of contracts to be able to describe—and then misapply—it, while Bracton endeavoured to express common law in Romanesque language. In the later middle ages ecclesiastical Chancellors in England were acting on canonical ideas—and yet in spite of all this the English law of contract is neither Roman nor canonical. If we are to seek the reasons for this we shall have to examine a good deal of procedural detail. The various forms of action had come into existence, and had taken definite shape, long before English law regarded the field of contract as a whole. By the time these foreign influences became strong the common law had already developed an inflexible system of procedure which did not easily permit the introduction of new ideas. In consequence, the common law courts were left to develop a law of contract as best they could out of the stubborn materials of the forms of action, and so, after many years of uncertainty and long conflicts with the technical and procedural difficulties which by that time were inherent in the common law system, we finally arrived at a systematic law of contract about three centuries later than the rest of the world. This Part will therefore be devoted to a brief summary of the lines along which the common law of contract developed.

CHAPTER 1

ORIGINS

In the Anglo-Saxon period a law of contract would have been a luxury. The enforcement of public order and the elementary protection of life and property were as much as the Anglo-Saxon states could undertake with any hope of success. We therefore find that the Anglo-Saxon law regarded contract as somewhat exceptional and only undertook to enforce it under particular circumstances.

CONTRACT IN ANGLO-SAXON LAW

In order to conclude a contract Anglo-Saxon law required numerous external acts, and several of these survived for many centuries. First of all there was the *wed*, which after the Norman Conquest was called a *gage*, and consisted of a valuable object which was delivered by the promisor either to the promisee himself or to a third party as security for carrying out the contract. Then, too, there was the *borh*, who after the Norman Conquest was called a " pledge ", and consisted of personal sureties. It must always be remembered that during the middle ages the word " pledge " means a person and not a thing. In the course of time the valuable gage is frequently replaced by a trifling object of slight value or even by a small sum of money; the gage consequently becomes merely a symbol instead of a valuable security, and the contract is then said to be formal. The Statute of Frauds and later legislation sanctioned the continuance of this type of contract concluded by earnest money.

The occasions upon which it became necessary to contract during the Anglo-Saxon age were mainly of two types. In the first place the solemn ceremonies by which a betrothal was effected were essentially contractual, for the betrothal was in effect a contract for a sale. The Anglo-Saxon marriage on its civil side (which was independent of the Church's sacramental views) still consisted of the sale by the woman's kinsfolk of the jurisdiction or guardianship over her (which they called *mund*) to the prospective husband.[1] Even after this ceased to be a

---

[1] For marriage as a sale, see Ine, 31. There is a short Anglo-Saxon tract on marriage in Liebermann, *Gesetze*, i. 442; it is translated in *Essays in Anglo-Saxon Law*, 171–172.

strictly commercial transaction, betrothal and marriage ceremonies retained a good many survivals of the older order—Maitland has described the marriage forms of the Church of England as " a remarkable cabinet of legal antiquities ", and the Episcopal Church of America has also retained most of them.[1] The betrothal was effected by the delivery of a *wed* and thus became a " wedding ", that is to say, the conclusion of a contract for a future marriage.

The other great situation in which contract played a part was the conclusion of a treaty subsequent to a homicide. The Anglo-Saxon texts tell us with great particularity the procedure to be followed in order to exact the payment of *wer* by the slayer to the kinsmen of the victim.[2] The sum involved was considerable, and then, as throughout the middle ages, it was difficult to liquidate a large debt in cash at short notice. It therefore became necessary to allow the slayer credit and this was done by assembling every contractual engine known to the law. Spokesmen were appointed, and they negotiated until it seemed prudent to allow the parties to come face to face. Then the treaty was made, the slayer promising to pay and the kinsmen of the slain calling off the feud; until finally the transaction was completed by giving *wed* and finding *borh*.

Buying and selling there undoubtedly was, but sale seems always to have been an executed contract, and the Anglo-Saxon law of sale is really little more than a set of police regulations to prevent dealings in stolen goods.[3] It is a matter of conjecture whether there was a law of debt; there were, however, a few rules on the vendor's warranty of title[4] and quality[5] of goods sold.

A possible third occasion when the Anglo-Saxons made executory contracts was the remarkable procedure to secure the presence of a defendant before the courts; in Anglo-Saxon law this was effected by means which were clearly contractual.[6]

THE THREE-PARTY CONTRACT

Gradually other matters came to be treated in the same manner and with the same machinery, that is to say, the valuable security of *wed* and the surety of *borh*. This *borh* becomes, in effect, a third party to the proceedings and in many cases the Anglo-Saxon contract is clearly a three-party arrangement.[7] Thus we find a party contracting by *wed* and

---

[1] There is a valuable collection of old English wedding rituals in Freisen, *Eheschliessungsrecht Grossbritanniens* (Görresgesellschaft, 1919).

[2] Liebermann, *Gesetze*, i. 392.

[3] IV Edgar, 6–11 (962–963), is typical.

[4] II Æthelred, 8–9 (991).

[5] Oaths, 7 (Liebermann, i. 399).

[6] Above, p. 384.

[7] The system was not confined to England—cf. *Lex Salica*, 46; Vinogradoff, *Collected Papers*, i. 150. It may be that espousal was a three-party contract; if so, this might explain the mysterious *foresprecher* of the Anglo-Saxon text (for whom, see Esmein, *Mariage en droit canonique* (2nd edn.), i. 201).

borh to appear in court, which in those days was regarded in much the same light as a modern submission to arbitration. As Sir William Holdsworth observes:

" The furnishing of the sureties was no mere form; it was a substantial sanction. These sureties were bound primarily to the creditor; and it was to the sureties that he looked for the carrying out of the undertaking. The debtor, according to the Lombard law, gave the *wed* to the creditor, who handed it to the surety as the sign and proof of his primary liability. There is thus some ground for the view that the institution of suretyship is the base upon which liability for the fulfilment of procedural and eventually other undertakings was founded. Probably these sureties were regarded somewhat in the light of hostages; and English law still retains a trace of this primitive conception in the fact that the bail of our modern criminal law are bound ' body for body '. As Holmes says, modern books still find it necessary to explain that this undertaking does not now render them liable to the punishment of the principal offender, if the accused is not produced."[1]

As we have said, the *wed* in many cases became a form, very often consisting of a rod or stick which was handed over, or held, as a symbol of the transaction.[2] Another form, the hand grasp, seems to have been originally Roman[3] and may have been brought to England from the continent by the Church; in the marriage ceremony, for example, both forms are employed (the hand grasp and the gift of a ring), while the ceremony of homage is likewise done by a peculiar form of hand grasp. Typically mercantile forms were earnest money, and a drink.[4]

PLEDGE OF FAITH

Under the influence of the Church another form appears, the pledge of faith. It is perhaps hardly accurate to regard this as a form, for the object involved was intensely real to the mediaeval mind. The *wed* in this case was the promisor's hope of salvation, and it was characteristic of mediaeval thought that this could be treated as a material object, and handed over to a third person as security for a debt or for the performance of a promise. Owing to its sacred character the faith was usually pledged to an ecclesiastic—in important cases to a bishop—but examples are to be found where this holy thing was committed to the strong hands of the sheriff. Later still, less solemn objects could be pledged, such as the promisor's " honour " or his " word ". The Church always maintained that when faith was pledged she had jurisdiction over all the circumstances of the case, including the contract itself as well as the pledge. If this claim had been established England might very soon have received

[1] Holdsworth, ii. 83, 84. With this compare H. F. Jolowicz, *Historical Introduction to Roman Law* (2nd edn.), 163. It has also been suggested that the joinder of several debtors in one debt was due to the difficulties which arose if the debtor died before discharge: A. Esmein, *L'Intransmissibilité première des créances et des dettes*, Nouvelle Revue historique de droit (1887), 48.

[2] Pollock and Maitland, ii. 187.

[3] To other writers it seems Germanic; it is easy to exaggerate the antithesis between Roman and Germanic elements in early law.

[4] Cf. A. Esmein, *Le Vin d'appointement*, Nouvelle Revue historique de droit (1887), 61 where a commentary is given on Rabelais, *Pantagruel*, iii. 41.

the canon law of contract, but Henry II, and later Edward I, firmly held out against it; by the Constitutions of Clarendon[1] the Church's jurisdiction over the contract was denied, although the Crown did not object to the Church punishing breach of faith by spiritual censures as a sin. In other words, the Church was permitted to treat breach of faith as a crime, but was forbidden to give a civil remedy.[2]

CONTRACTS UNDER SEAL

We have said nothing of written contracts in Anglo-Saxon law, and indeed it seems that they were not in general use. When they do appear after the Conquest the contract under seal is treated as a form of the most solemn and binding kind.[3] It has even been suggested that there may be a connection between the delivery by the promisor of a sealed document to the promisee, and the older method of delivering a *wed*. This may be, but still there can be no doubt that the written contract (which after the Conquest, and throughout the year-book period, was called an " obligation ") was mainly of continental origin.

GLANVILL ON DEBT

When we come to Glanvill, we find that the common law of contract is still slight and that the King's court is not anxious to enlarge it. There was now an action of debt about which he gives a fair amount of seemingly settled law. A new procedure appears, moreover, which will long remain important. This consisted in bringing an action of debt in the King's court which the defendant declined to contest. Judgment was therefore entered for the plaintiff, who thus acquired the advantage of the royal machinery in enforcing judgment. There can be no doubt that many of these actions were collusive, one might almost say fictitious, and brought for the sole purpose of giving the creditor the benefit of a debt of record.[4] This becomes common soon after Glanvill's day. Glanvill enumerates various sorts of contracts in Roman terms, and correctly defines them, but later on he does not hold himself bound by these definitions.[5] He expressly warns us that the King's court cannot

[1] Constitutions of Clarendon, c. 15 (1164); Glanvill, x. 12; *Circumspecte Agatis* (1285; the text, authenticity and date of this document have been established by E. B. Graves, English Historical Review, xliii. 1).

[2] The Church continued to encroach on contract, *e.g. Rot. Parl.*, ii. 319 (1373), in spite of the settled common law that all suits in ecclesiastical courts for chattels could be prohibited unless they arose out of matrimonial or testamentary matters.

[3] For some speculations from the thirteenth century about the theory of the deed under seal, see *Brevia Placitata* (Selden Society), 111, 202–203; cf. *Casus Placitorum* (Selden Society), lxxxvii, no. 35.

[4] Compare the use of the fine as a conveyance; a later practice was simply to confess the debt without any litigation and have it enrolled on the back of the close roll in Chancery. This was called a recognisance. The Statutes of Merchants and Staples set up special machinery for the recording of debts of this sort, and even allowed land to be taken in execution upon them; above, p. 392.

[5] Glanvill, x. 3.

be troubled with " private conventions ". He leaves us a clear impression that the writ of debt is as far as the *curia regis* will go in the direction of a law of contract.[1] In Glanvill's time, and later, it is clear that the writ of debt is rather a costly luxury; it is certainly framed upon an expensive model, for it is a *praecipe quod reddat* like the writ of right and demands a sum of money of which the defendant deforces[2] the creditor; the King may also demand a handsome commission[3] for he is still apt to think rather of the business side of debt-collecting than of his duty to administer public justice, and for a time the action of debt, like other *praecipe* actions, might perhaps lead to trial by battle.[4]

BRACTON ON COVENANT

When we come to Bracton we find that he mentions an action which was unknown to Glanvill, namely, the action of covenant. By Bracton's day it was quite certain that the King's court had decided not to enforce those contracts which were concluded merely by such forms as the delivery of sticks and other trifling objects; the only form which the King's courts recognised henceforward being the deed under seal and the recognisance of record. Whereas Glanvill would exclude all " private covenants " from the King's court, Bracton, on the other hand, assures us that they are justiciable there, provided that they comply with this rule. Bracton has a good many Romanesque generalisations on the matter of contract, but it is clear, at least in this case, that his statements of substantive law accurately represent the practice of the King's courts, which insisted that to be actionable a contract should be either real, that is to say, money or chattels must have passed, or formal, and here Bracton identifies the deed under seal with the *stipulatio*. A curious survival from Anglo-Saxon times, however, was the rule that the contract of suretyship, though made verbally (like the Anglo-Saxon *borh*), was yet enforceable; on the other hand, contracts effected by pledge of faith could not be enforced in the King's court, nor would the Crown allow them to be enforced in the Church courts—at least in theory. " Although these courts, in spite of royal prohibitions, long continue to exercise much jurisdiction of this kind, it is clear that according to the common law as laid down in the royal courts the real and the formal principles were fast coming to be the only two recognised. . . . Bracton practically admits that there is no such thing as a consensual contract in English law."[5]

---

[1] Glanvill, x. 8, and 18.

[2] For the significance of this word, see Pollock and Maitland, ii. 205. For its use as late as 1367, see Page, *Crowland Abbey*, 172. As to whether debt was " real " or " personal ", see above, p. 362.

[3] In John's day, a register of writs regarded one-third as the proper proportion: Pollock and Maitland, i. 554.

[4] Glanvill's assertion (x. 12) is not supported by the rolls; see Woodbine's note in his edition, 256–257.

[5] Holdsworth, iii, 416.

THE FOURTEENTH CENTURY

In this chapter we shall describe the forms of action which might be used in contractual matters from the days of Bracton until the general use of the action of assumpsit, which only becomes common at the beginning of the fifteenth century.

THE ACTION OF DEBT

The oldest and most important was the action of debt[1] which lay for formal contracts (" obligations ") under seal if they specified a sum certain, and for a number of real contracts, that is to say, contracts where a *res* has passed between the parties. Debt could thus be used to recover the price of goods sold and delivered, to recover money lent, and to recover the rent on a lease even although the lease was not written.[2] It could also be used for certain special purposes such as the recovery of statutory penalties and for the enforcement of obligations arising out of suretyship. On the other hand there were grave defects attaching to the action of debt. The most notable of these was the form of trial by wager of law;[3] early in the fifteenth century, petitioners would go to Chancery alleging that their debtor either intends to or actually has waged his law in defence of the debt, and Chancery openly treated this as amounting to the absence of remedy at common law.[4] Then, too, as the middle ages proceeded the method of pleading in the action of debt became remarkably complicated, and, as we shall see, the law of contract was influenced considerably by various procedural devices which were designed to avoid having to bring an action of debt. It will be noticed that in all

---

[1] Of debt as a " real " action we have already spoken; above, p. 362.

[2] The lessee would have to be in possession, apparently.

[3] Except in actions on specialty, for the courts soon refused to allow wager of law against a seal. The wooden tally was a favourite proof of debt, but it did not become a true specialty unless it was also sealed. Cf. the curious case in Y.B. 21 & 22 Edward I (Rolls Series), 1 (1293).

[4] Cases from 1413 onwards are collected in Barbour, *Contract in Equity*, 99, and 111 (detinue; petition and decree, 187). On the other hand, it is necessary to weigh carefully such statutes as 5 Henry IV, c. 8 (1404) which extends wager of law to debt upon account stated, since the practice has arisen of alleging fictitiously that an account had been taken. The preamble implies that compurgation is more likely to discover the truth than jury trial.

the real contracts which are actionable by debt the defendant has received something—money, goods, a lease—from the plaintiff; in the language of the fifteenth century, there has been a *quid pro quo*, which is in fact a generalisation from those real contracts which were actionable by a writ of debt.

COVENANT

Of the general nature of covenant in royal and local courts we have already spoken.[1] By the close of Edward I's reign it becomes a rule that covenant cannot be used in cases where debt would lie,[2] and also that it is best to support an action of covenant by a writing of some sort, and very soon this becomes a strict requirement for an enforceable covenant to be under seal.[3] From this it has been conjectured that the covenant under seal changed its character; originally merely " a promise well-proved ", as Holmes neatly expressed it, we now find that it has become a promise " of a distinct nature for which a distinct form of action was provided ".[4] In the middle of the sixteenth century it begins to be said that a " seal imports a consideration ". This was merely a loose way of saying that just as a simple contract was enforceable because there was consideration, so a contract under seal was enforceable in debt or covenant because there was a seal—because it was made in a binding form. The expression must not be allowed to obscure the fact that sealed contracts did not need a consideration, and were enforceable solely on the ground that they were formal. Nor was there any presumption of consideration, for sealed contracts were enforceable centuries before the doctrine of consideration came into existence.

It was more convenient, however, to sue on a debt than a covenant in the royal courts in the fourteenth century, and hence there arose a very common device of a bond under seal in a sum of money with a " defeasance " endorsed upon it saying that the bond shall be null and void upon the performance of certain acts. This was a practical method, for the courts by now refused to allow wager of law against a deed, and so we find manuscript collections containing a great variety of " defeasances ". For those who were prepared to risk a judgment on the bond if they failed to fulfil the contract (there was no relief against penalties in either law or equity in this century), and whose affairs were considerable enough to warrant so formal a deed, the bond and defeasance provided many possibilities.

---

[1] Above, p. 365.

[2] It seemed generally understood that this was the case. Attempts to use covenant instead of debt appear again in the sixteenth century, and in the seventeenth were successful. Ames, *Lectures on Legal History*, 152–153.

[3] The rule was applied as early as 1235, but a long period of hesitation followed. The cases are collected in Pollock and Maitland, ii. 220 n. 1.

[4] Holmes, *The Common Law*, 272–273. This hypothesis seems to place the formal contract at too late a stage of our legal history.

ACCOUNT

In some of its aspects the action of account has a bearing upon our subject, but during the fourteenth century its scope was very limited. In its origin it lay between lord and bailiff and was based upon a personal relationship. In view of this the procedure upon the writ of account was made exceptionally stringent—for example, a lord could appoint auditors, and if they found the account unsatisfactory they could commit the bailiff to the King's prison without any trial whatever.[1] Soon we find that account could also be used between partners, but here again the basis of the action is a particular relationship. If one were not the lord of a bailiff (or receiver), nor a partner, the action of account was little good. Its fate was finally settled when it was held that one could not contract to become liable to an action of account; the action only applied to certain relationships.[2] This very factor, however, afforded an opportunity for development in cases which could not be brought within the sphere of contract. If A. gives money to B. for the benefit of C., there was no contract between B. and C. Since 1367, however, it was held that B. was accountable to C.[3] From this significant beginning important developments in the field of quasi-contract took place in the late sixteenth century.

CONTRACT IN THE FOURTEENTH CENTURY

We therefore see that in the fourteenth century the only contracts which are actionable are those which Bracton had enumerated—those in fact which were enforceable by an action of debt, either because they are formal and supported by a deed under seal, or real, in which case the fact that the defendant has received a substantial thing will establish his liability. Some explanation is obviously needed for the extreme poverty and narrowness of the field of contract in our mediaeval common law. Westminster Hall had no monopoly as yet of English legal thought, and such records as the Littleport rolls[4] show clearly that in towns and villages there were petty tribunals which gave remedies in cases which would have met a *non possumus* in the common pleas. There is no need to suppose that country stewards and bailiffs had analysed the conception of a contract; they had, however, developed a reasonable mass of settled practice in such cases, and the real cause for the backwardness of the common law is perhaps the fact that theorising began before practice nad accumulated a sufficiently large mass of data.

---

[1] Statute of Westminster II (1285), c. 11. Lords would gladly have committed defaulting accountants to their own private prisons; but the statute is explicit that it must be the king's prison only.

[2] The non-contractual nature of account is very well illustrated by Langdell, *Equity Jurisdiction*, 75; cf. Jackson, *History of Quasi-Contract*, 32.

[3] Y.B. 41 Edward III. Pasch. no. 5.

[4] Above, p. 98.

As for mercantile affairs, there was special custom to govern them. Edward I by his charter to the merchants[1] expressly saved to them their old custom of making binding contracts by more simple forms, such as earnest money, instead of by deed under seal, and such mercantile contracts were actionable in the local commercial courts. It may be said with some fairness that the existence on the one hand of mercantile jurisdictions, and on the other of the spiritual courts which could bring moral pressure to bear, together with the remedies available locally, afford some explanation for the common law courts declining to expend their law of contract. Debt, account and covenant covered the cases which usually arose in a jurisdiction which consisted so far of landlords; where extension was needed for the protection of this particular class a parliament of landlords was ready to give it—the statutory process on the action of account is an extreme example. For the rest, the common law apparently felt that it could abstain with a clear conscience, knowing that the matter was already in the expert hands of the Church and the merchants, and that the bond with defeasance was flexible enough to serve for a large variety of executory contracts, as its very frequent use abundantly proves. It is only in the fifteenth century that the common law was compelled to face the problem of the simple contract, and this will form the subject of the next chapter.

[1] *Carta Mercatoria* (1303), printed in *Munimenta Gildhallae*, II. i. 205–211, at 206–207.

ASSUMPSIT TO SLADE'S CASE

The King's court was not very fond of contract, but it showed some interest in tort, and it is in the action of trespass that the quickest progress was made. In a number of cases it is possible to regard a particular situation from either point of view, and it was the treatment of such cases which served to introduce the idea of contract into actions of trespass.

We have already traced briefly the development of the action of trespass on the case,[1] and we have seen that, in spite of some talk about an " undertaking ", the famous *Humber Ferry Case* was, procedurally at least, a bill of trespass. After all, the defendant had, in effect, drowned the plaintiff's mare.[2]

A different line of approach is seen when the breach of a promise is treated as a " deceit " of the promisee—as a tort, in other words. Hence we find the allegation that the defendant " undertook " to do something as the necessary preliminary to the deception of the plaintiff when the undertaking was not fulfilled. Soon this situation is reconciled with the existing scheme of forms of action, by allowing trespass on the case to be brought for deceit caused by failure to perform an undertaking.

THE BEGINNINGS OF ASSUMPSIT

This was a long step, and it was not taken all at once. An important halt was made half-way. The first stage, in fact, was concerned with a special group of cases where the resulting loss was the damage or destruction of chattels. Such cases were the first to be admitted, for it was possible to construe them as quasi-trespasses (as we have seen, Baukwell, J., argued that the *Humber Ferry Case*, in spite of the assumpsit, was substantially a case of trespass). Again, in 1369, *Waldon* v. *Marshall*[3] is brought on a writ (not a bill) which mentions an assumpsit to cure a

---

[1] Above, p. 372.

[2] Above, p. 470.

[3] Y.B. 43 Edward III, Michs. no. 38.

horse, and "negligent" treatment of it so that it died. Both bench and bar seem to have thought that the writ said *contra pacem* as if it were purely trespass; in time it occurred to someone to read the writ, whereupon it was found that *contra pacem* was not alleged, and so we have an example of trespass on the case. As in most of these cases, the defence urged that the matter was contractual, and that the plaintiff's remedy was in covenant:

> "*Belknap.* We cannot bring covenant without a deed; and this action is brought because you did your cure 'so negligently' that the horse died. So it is more reasonable to maintain this special writ according to the case, than to abate it, for other writ we cannot have.
> "*Kirton.* You can have a writ of trespass by simply saying that he killed your horse.
> "*Belknap.* We could not have brought a simple writ of trespass because he did not kill the horse with force, for it died for lack of cure. . . . (And then the writ was adjudged good, and THORPE, C.J., said that he had seen one *M.* indicted for that he undertook to cure a man of a malady and killed him for default of cure.)
> "*Kirton.* . . . He did his cure as well as he could, without this that the horse died by default of his cure; ready. And the others said the contrary."

This debate makes it clear that all parties recognised that the situation was fundamentally contractual, and that it was being forced into the form of tort simply because the action of covenant could only be brought upon a deed under seal. In this particular instance the contrast with trespass is well made, and the case is left, procedurally at least, as a case of negligent damage to a chattel. But it must not be imagined that this is the story of the slow dawn of the idea of contract in the minds of common lawyers. They knew quite well what a covenant was, but they deliberately resorted to this juggling with trespass because they felt unable to sustain an action of covenant without a deed.

THE MEANING OF ASSUMPSIT

Why then should it need an allegation and a proof of assumpsit to support an action in tort? Ames[1] has suggested with great plausibility that the insistence upon an express assumpsit is derived from the mediaeval notion of liability. If I voluntarily hand over my horse to the care of a horse-doctor, he treats the animal at my invitation and therefore at my risk. If, however, he undertakes to cure it, and I on the faith of that undertaking allow him to treat the horse, then the risk falls upon him and I have suffered a wrong if my horse is the worse for his treatment.[2] When this is understood it will be seen that the assumpsit is not treated as basing the action upon contract, but as one of the elements leading up to damage to the plaintiff's person or property; the defendant undertook to do something, and did it so badly that the plaintiff, who had relied upon the undertaking, suffered damage at the hands of the defendant.

---

[1] Ames, *Lectures on Legal History*, 131.

[2] The idea comes out clearly in Y.B. 19 Henry VI, Hil. no. 5 (1441).

In the course of the fifteenth century assumpsit becomes quite common but the theory of it remains the same, as may be seen from the remarks of Newton (who shortly afterwards became Chief Justice) in 1436:

" I quite agree that it is the law that if a carpenter makes a covenant with me to make me a house good and strong and of a certain form, and he makes me a house which is weak and bad and of another form, I shall have an action of trespass on my case. So if a smith makes a covenant with me to shoe my horse well and properly, and he shoes him and lames him, I shall have a good action. So if a leech takes upon himself to cure me of my diseases, and he gives me medicines, but does not cure me, I shall have an action on my case. So if a man makes a covenant with me to plough my land in seasonable time, and he ploughs in a time which is not seasonable, I shall have action on my case. And the cause is in all these cases that there is an undertaking and a matter in fact besides that which sounds merely in covenant. . . . In these cases the plaintiffs have suffered a wrong."[1]

It is clear from this passage that although strict theory is being maintained, it is very difficult to keep contract out of the picture. The assumpsit can hardly be described by any other word unless that word be " covenant ". One of the earliest cases (1388) already shows a strong tendency in this direction, and the declaration even asserts that the assumpsit was " in return for a sum of money paid ".[2] As theory hardened, the question of consideration was seen to be irrelevant;[3] nevertheless, the ambiguity of the word " assumpsit " was ineradicable— and fortunately so, for it helped us through a very difficult stage in the history of contract.

ASSUMPSIT FOR NON-FEASANCE

Thus far we have been concerned with damage to the person or to chattels, which was treated as akin to trespass.[4] The assumpsit, although it suggested covenant, was primarily meant to fix a tortious liability on the defendant. If, however, the defendant failed to act at all, then the idea of trespass or quasi-trespass was no longer helpful. Non-feasance, therefore, raised a different problem.

At the beginning of the fifteenth century we find assumpsit brought on certain cases of non-feasance—and for a time unsuccessfully. As the fifteenth century proceeds, however, it becomes more clear that a remedy for non-feasance is desirable.

The question was first raised in connection with building contracts. Thus *Watton* v. *Brinth*[5] was brought on an assumpsit to build a house within a certain time. The suggestion was made that if the work had

[1] Y.B. 14 Henry VI, no. 58.

[2] Y.B. 11 Richard II (ed. Thornley), 223, 227.

[3] Ames, 130–131. With newer views on tort liability the allegation of an assumpsit was no longer felt necessary and the action in such cases of damage to the person or chattels was brought simply as " case ".

[4] The extract above from the case of 1436 shows how physical damage to the person or to chattels began to be silently abandoned.

[5] Y.B. 2 Henry IV, Michs. no. 9 (1400).

been begun but not finished, then the action might lie for " negligence ", but there was no discussion of this;[1] the action was dismissed because the matter was covenant, and no deed was shown. Several similar cases met the same fate. In 1424 an inconclusive discussion[2] ranged over several points. It was suggested that the non-performance of a promise to roof a house would be actionable if the interior of the house was damaged by rain, on the analogy of trespass; an obscure allusion to the price paid to the contractor produced a comment based on the action of deceit—an omen whose significance will soon be appreciated. In 1436 arose the case from which we have already printed an extract.[3] It concerned a sale of land, the defendant having promised to secure certain releases to the plaintiff purchaser. It was argued that misfeasance and non-feasance were not necessarily distinct, " for it all depends from the covenant ". No franker statement that contract is the root of the matter could be desired; but these expressions do not go so far as actually to give judgment in favour of the plaintiff.[4]

ASSUMPSIT COUPLED WITH DECEIT

These cases show the impossibility of bringing cases of non-feasance under the old type of assumpsit—the defendant had done nothing which could by any stretch of logic be construed as a trespass to the plaintiff's person or goods. A new principle was needed, and it was finally found in the notion that the breach of an undertaking constitutes a deceit.[5]

The earlier instances seem to indicate that this action was often begun by bill, because it was primarily designed for use against officers of a court, or against persons already within its jurisdiction. There was also an original writ for deceit, which, like the bill, was concerned with the abuse of legal procedure, and could be brought by the Crown if the injured party did not do so, for its nature was essentially penal.[6] The writ is as old as 1201,[7] and a bill of deceit for what was in substance a breach of contract[8] was proffered in 1293, while a writ of deceit, on facts which were seemingly contractual,[9] occurs in 1311. By the fifteenth

---

[1] The idea reappears several times, e.g. Y.BB. 11 Henry IV, Michs. no. 80 (1409); 2 Henry VII, Hil. no. 9 (1487).

[2] Y.B. 3 Henry VI, Hil. no. 33.

[3] Y.B. 14 Henry VI, no. 58; above, p. 639.

[4] Ames, Lectures on Legal History, 140, assumes that judgment went (against all authority) for the plaintiff, but without influencing subsequent decisions. Apparently there was no decision.

[5] For Italian parallels, see Pollock and Maitland, ii. 196.

[6] F.N.B., 95 E.

[7] Pollock and Maitland, ii. 534.

[8] Plaintiff paid defendant for a plot of land; defendant sold the land to another, and retained the money (note that there is no question of deceiving the court): Select Bills in Eyre (Selden Society), 62 no. 92. There is no decision known. (Compare Doige's Case, below, p. 642).

[9] Defendant agreed to compromise a case in the king's court, but later pursued the case to judgment: Y.BB. Edward II (Selden Society), x. 11. There is no decision enrolled.

century it had been classified as trespass on the case for deceit, and considerably extended in scope. Late in the fourteenth century it entered upon a useful career by enforcing express warranties of the quality of goods sold. Such warranties, to be actionable, had to be made in words which showed that the seller meant to undertake a legal obligation: mere " selling talk ", even assertions, were not sufficient, without the word " warrant " or something equally technical and precise.[1]

There is an obvious similarity between the express warranty and the express assumpsit. If an express warranty could be coupled with a deceit in order to found an action, might not the breach of an express assumpsit be laid as a deceit, and so become actionable?

This provided the eventual solution of the problem of non-feasance. In 1428 we find this idea carried out.[2] The plaintiff brought " a writ on his case in the nature of a writ of deceit ", and counted that he had agreed to marry the defendant's daughter, and the defendant agreed to enfeoff the pair of certain land. The defendant later married his daughter to someone else. The answer was short and significant: he had not shown that the defendant had received a *quid pro quo*, and so there was no bargain. Already the contractual element was clearly recognised. The next example is *Somerton's Case*.[3] The plaintiff had retained the defendant (for a fee) as his legal adviser in connection with his proposed purchaser or lease of a manor. The defendant undertook (*assumpsit*) these duties, but " falsely and in deceit of the plaintiff " he revealed the plaintiff's counsel, allied himself with a stranger and negotiated a lease to that stranger. There were long discussions on pleading points, and the usual argument that the matter was one of covenant provoked the reply that matters of covenant may be transformed by subsequent events into deceits. Attempts to plead to the action were abandoned, and the parties eventually pleaded to an issue.

In *Somerton's Case*, therefore, we are very near to a remedy for non-feasance. The peculiar facts, however, seem to have left their mark for some years in the distinction between such a case and a pure case of non-feasance. In *Somerton's Case* the defendant not only failed to perform his undertaking, but had done something which " disabled " him from ever performing it, for he had arranged a lease to another. *Doige's Case*,[4] shortly afterwards, was a bill of deceit in the King's Bench, but it raised

---

[1] Ames, *op. cit.*, 136–138; for a case in a local court a century earlier than Ames cited, see Sayles, *King's Bench*, i. 34, iii. p. xcix.

[2] Y.B. 7 Henry VI, Michs. no. 3.

[3] (1433). The reports in the Year Book have been misplaced; the true order seems to be as follows. The original writ is appended to Y.B. 11 Henry VI, Pasch. no. 1 at f. 25; the arguments begin in the passage printed as Y.B. 11 Henry VI Trin. no. 26, are continued *ibid.*, Hil. no. 10, and conclude to an issue *ibid.*, Pasch. no. 1. The case is discussed at length in Holdsworth, iii. 431–434.

[4] (1442). Y.B. 20 Henry VI, Trin. no. 4; *Select Cases in Exchequer Chamber* (ed. Hemmant, Selden Society), 97 (but the first line on p. 98 is mis-translated; omit " to be "). The record has now been found: A. K. Kiralfy, *Action on the Case*, 227 (the lady in the case is " Dogge " not " Doige "). For a full analysis of the case, see Holdsworth, iii. 435–439.

the same questions. The plaintiff paid Doige £100 for some land. Instead of enfeoffing the plaintiff, Doige enfeoffed someone else. Doige demurred to the bill and the case was argued in the Exchequer Chamber. To some it seemed important that Doige had " disabled " himself from ever performing the undertaking; to others this seemed immaterial. The general question whether the only remedy would be a writ of covenant was argued at length, but the roll, of course, only contains the formal pleadings. They consist of a declaration and a plea that the remedy should have been covenant, and not deceit. Judgment was enrolled for the plaintiff.[1]

These two lengthy arguments seem to have created a hopeful impression, if nothing more, and a generation later we find the action clearly upheld. In 1476 " deceit on the case " was successfully brought against a defendant who had received the purchase price of some land, and had enfeoffed another.[2] In 1487 the strength of the " disablement " idea was shown when it was held that the action could not be brought unless it was counted and proved that the defendant enfeoffed another,[3] but in 1504 this old distinction is abandoned, and we have a broad general statement of the nature of the remedy for non-feasance:

" FROWYKE, C.J. If I sell you my land and covenant to enfeoff you and do not, you shall have a good action on the case, and this is adjudged. . . . And if I covenant with a carpenter to build a house, and pay him £20 for the house to be built by a certain time, now I shall have a good action on my case because of the payment of money. . . ."[4]

This result was not achieved merely through the enterprise of the common lawyers; on the contrary, it is clear that for some time the chancellors had been giving relief, certainly from the reign of Henry V onwards, to purchasers who had paid their money and had not got their land or goods. Indeed, they were even enforcing purely consensual contracts for the sale of land.[5]

The cases just discussed show deceits of an aggravated sort: the plaintiff has parted with money, and that money is in the defendant's pocket. Cases might easily arise, however, where the plaintiff's loss did not in fact enrich the defendant. Here, as in other instances, Chancery may have shown the way. As early as 1378 it heard a petition from a disappointed purchaser whose loss consisted in travelling and legal expenses connected with a sale of land which the defendant refused to

---

[1] Kiralfy, *loc. cit.* Compare the curiously similar bill in eyre, above, p. 640 **n. 8**. The idea of " disablement " was part of the law of covenants: Lit. s. 355; Holdsworth, ii. 594 n. 5.

[2] Y.B. 16 Edw. IV, Pasch. no. 7.

[3] Y.B. 2 Henry VII, Hil. no. 15. When it was argued in a similar case the same year that no action lies for such a " non-feasance " the court replied that the sale to a stranger was " a great misfeasance "; Y.B. 3 Henry VII, Michs. no. 20 (1487).

[4] Keilway, 77; Y.B. 20 Henry VII, Michs. no. 18.

[5] Barbour, *Contract in Early English Equity*, 118–119; case 98 (*ibid.*, p. 173) can hardly be later than 1424.

complete.[1] The common law over a century later slowly reached the same position. In 1520 a plaintiff succeeded on a declaration that he sold goods to *A.* in reliance upon *B.*'s (the defendant's) assurance that he would be duly paid. The defendant derived no benefit from the arrangement, nor did he profit by the breach of it, but the plaintiff suffered loss through the deceit.[2] Shortly afterwards, St Germain[3] regarded it as settled that " if he to whom the promise is made have a charge by reason of the promise . . . he shall have an action . . . though he that made the promise had no worldly profit by it ".

MUTUAL PROMISES

That seems to have helped forward the next development, which lay in the solution of the problem created by mutual promises. As we have already seen, the mediaeval English law of sale rested where Glanvill left it: the sale was effected by delivery.[4] If the price was paid, the buyer could bring detinue for the goods; if the goods were delivered, the seller could bring debt for the price. If neither party had performed, neither could have an action. This rule was not relaxed until the close of the middle ages, as a result of a process beginning, it seems,[5] in 1442, although the first steps in that direction had been taken a century earlier. Its implication was not at first recognised. It was certainly not regarded as showing the enforceability of mutual promises, still less was there any discussion of consent. When an explanation was needed, recourse was had to a theory that each party " granted " (not promised) to the other— a theory derived from what the fifteenth-century lawyers took to be the true nature of the action of detinue.[6]

At the close of the middle ages, when the problem of mutual promises was being attacked, this peculiarity of the law of sale was constantly cited, and there can be no doubt that the basis of assumpsit was gradually shifted; at first the emphasis was on the final result of the parties' acts— the deception of the plaintiff, but as time goes on attention is fixed upon the beginning of their story—the assumpsit, and concurrently the habit grows of discussing these matters in terms of promises rather than deceits, of contract rather than tort. When this stage is reached, it becomes necessary to decide the effect of an exchange of promises. In 1558 we find the famous words " every contract executory is an assumpsit in

[1] 2 Calendar of Proceedings in Chancery (Record Commission), ii; Ames, *Lectures* 143–144.

[2] Y.B. 12 Henry VIII, Michs. no. 3.

[3] *Doctor and Student*, ii. c. 24.

[4] Above, p. 629; Glanvill, x. 14; Bracton, f. 62; *Fleta*, ii. 58, § 8.

[5] *Doig's Case*, Y.B. 20 Henry VI, Trin. no. 4; *Select Cases in Exchequer Chamber* (Selden Society), 97 at 101. The example of Chancery is a possible source (above, p. 642 n. 5). A suggestive discussion of the transition from the " real " to the " consensual " contract is in C. H. S. Fifoot, *History and Sources: Contract and Tort*, 227 ff.

[6] Upon this, see further Holdsworth, iii. 355–357.

itself ", which suggest that the mediaeval " contract " (of which sale and loan are typical) is now being interpreted as an exchange of promises.[1] In 1589 the process is complete and the result clear: " a promise against a promise will maintain an action upon the case ".[2]

INDEBITATUS ASSUMPSIT

The idea of deceit was carried a step further. If a defendant is indebted to a creditor, the latter has an action of debt, not because the one has promised to pay the other, but because the parties are in a relationship which has been covered by the action of debt ever since the twelfth century at least, and certainly before there was any theory of contract. But suppose that a promisor, being already in a situation which renders him liable to an action of debt, subsequently expressly undertakes to pay the debt by a certain date. In this situation it was possible to say that besides being liable in debt, the promisor by his undertaking had now rendered himself liable to an action of assumpsit if he did not fulfil that undertaking, for he has deceived the plaintiff. Consequently we find a new variety of assumpsit appearing in the middle of the sixteenth century called *indebitatus assumpsit*, in which the plaintiff declares that the defendant, being already indebted (*indebitatus*), undertook (*assumpsit*) to pay a particular sum.[3] The earliest example seems to be in 1542, and a few years afterwards we find the statement (apparently a comment or generalisation by Sir Robert Brooke) that " where a man is indebted to me and promises to pay before Michaelmas, I can have an action of debt on the contract or an action on the case [*assumpsit*] on the promise; for on the promise no action of debt will lie ".[4] In all the early cases the distinction between debt and *indebitatus assumpsit* is strictly maintained. The subsequent *assumpsit* must be alleged, and, if traversed, must be proved.[5]

At this point there enters a factor of much importance in the legal history of the sixteenth and seventeenth centuries—the competition between the courts for jurisdiction. *Assumpsit*, being a form of trespass, could be brought either in the King's Bench or Common Pleas: debt, on the other hand, could only be brought in the Common Pleas. The King's Bench could therefore not resist the temptation to use *indebitatus assumpsit* as an equivalent to debt. This was easily done by holding that where a debt existed, a subsequent *assumpsit* would be presumed in law,

[1] *Norwood* v. *Reed* (1558), Plowd. 180.

[2] *Strangborough* v. *Warner* (1589), 4 Leo. 3. " Have you ever found any *logical* reason why mutual promises are sufficient consideration of one another? . . . I have not ", wrote Pollock, and Holmes agreed: *The Pollock-Holmes Letters*, i. 146, 177.

[3] It has been observed (Pollock and Maitland, ii. 196) that this curious notion has a mediaeval counterpart in Italy, when a subsequent promise might be a *vestimentum* for a pre-existing *nudum pactum*; the results are similar but the theories are different.

[4] Brooke, Abr. *Action sur le Cas*, 105; *ibid.*, 5.

[5] *Anon.* (1572), Dalison, 84, no. 35.

and need not be proved as a fact.[1]   This device captured much business
(for litigants in King's Bench were glad to employ barristers instead of
the costly serjeants, and appreciated the swifter process, and the absence
of compurgation), but at the expense of confounding legal theory.   The
Common Pleas carefully distinguished " contract " (situations in which
debt would lie without a specialty)[2] from *assumpsit* or " promise " (which
was actionable as a deceit).   The justices of the Common Pleas had a
chance of checking this audacious manœuvre, however, for under
Elizabeth's statute error lay from King's Bench as a court of first instance
to the Exchequer Chamber, and that Chamber contained all the Common
Pleas judges and the barons of the Exchequer, but none of the King's
Bench justices.[3]   The Exchequer Chamber therefore promptly reversed
such cases when they were brought up from the King's Bench.   This
unseemly situation lasted for almost a generation, until the question was
finally referred to that other assembly, also called the Exchequer Chamber,
consisting of all the judges of all three courts assembled for discussion,
in *Slade's Case* (1602).

SLADE'S CASE, 1602

The whole matter was thoroughly examined in this memorable case.[4]
The facts were the simplest possible.   The plaintiff's bill of Middlesex
declared that the defendant, Humphrey Morley, " in consideration that
the said John [Slade], . . . at the special instance and request of the said
Humphrey Morley had bargained and sold[5] unto the said Humphrey . . .
all the ears of wheat and corn which then did grow upon the said close
called Rack Park . . ., did assume, and then and there faithfully
promised " to pay a sum of money at a future fixed date.   Upon the
general issue, the jury found the bargain and sale, but said that there was
no subsequent *assumpsit*.   The objections raised in the course of the ensuing
argument were : (*a*) since an action of debt lay on the facts, that therefore
case (*i.e. indebitatus assumpsit*) could not lie; and (*b*) that this new form
of action deprives the defendant of his right to wage his law.
   The King's Bench, realising the scandal caused by the difference
between their rule and that in the Common Pleas, adjourned the case
into the Exchequer Chamber of all the judges of England (not the
chamber set up by Elizabeth), and then to the conference at Serjeants'
Inn, where Coke, Attorney-General, argued for the plaintiff and Bacon
for the defendant.   It was finally resolved that *indebitatus assumpsit* was
an alternative to debt, at the plaintiff's choice; that by *assumpsit* the

---

[1] *Edwards* v. *Burre* (1573), Dalison, 104 no. 45.

[2] The regular mediaeval sense of the word—" loan or the like " (Y.B. 41 Edward III,
Pasch. no. 5).

[3] Above, p. 171.

[4] 4 Rep. 92 *b*.

[5] For references upon the meaning of " bargain and sale " see S. J. Stoljar, *Substantial
Performance in Contracts of Sale*, Canadian Bar Review, xxxii. 272 n. 98.

plaintiff should recover not only damages but the original debt; that recovery in *assumpsit* should be a bar to an action of debt; that in the case of instalment debts, *assumpsit* can be brought on the first default, but debt only after all the days of payment have passed; and (most important of all) that a subsequent *assumpsit* need not be proved, but will be presumed:

" Every contract executory imports in itself an assumpsit, for when one agrees to pay money or to deliver anything, thereby he assumes or promises to pay or deliver it; and therefore when one sells any goods to another and agrees to deliver them at a day to come, and the other in consideration thereof agrees to pay so much money at such a day, both parties may have an action of debt or an action of the case on assumpsit, for the mutual executory agreement of both parties imports in itself actions upon the case as well as actions of debt."

CONTRACT AFTER SLADE'S CASE

THE RESULTS OF SLADE'S CASE

It is not surprising that the results of this momentous decision appeared more and more important as the years passed. From a strict point of view, it was merely the settlement of a pleading point upon which two courts had differed. To settle the matter that an *assumpsit* need not be proved, however, was in effect to make *indebitatus assumpsit* equivalent to debt; already, then, the larger matter of the relations between the forms of action was involved, and this in itself was sufficient to alarm conservative minds. Two generations later we still find the learned Vaughan, C.J., lamenting that *Slade's Case* was " a false gloss " designed to substitute *assumpsit* for debt.[1] So it was; on principle, the decision is indefensible, for it obliterates the distinction between debt and deceit, between contract and tort. It therefore introduced much confusion into the scheme of forms of action. In doing this, it infringed the procedural rights of defendants in a way which seemed almost as alarming. Defendants might henceforth find themselves charged with debts merely because a jury thought that such debts existed, and could no longer relieve themselves by compurgatory oaths. Here there was a real problem. There was little law of evidence; lawyers had as yet but short experience of the delicate art of jury trials in such matters; written memoranda of simple contracts were not often to be had; parties were not competent witnesses; there was a deep feeling that the old procedure, of which wager of law was a part, was a sort of constitutional right of Englishmen;[2] executors, particularly, feared that they would be charged with piles of alleged debts of which they knew, and could know, nothing.[3]

---

[1] *Edgcomb* v. *Dee* (1670), Vaughan, 101.

[2] Cf. above, pp. 115, 380, 633; trial by battle had a similar sanctity in eighteenth-century thought, above, p. 117.

[3] This point was forcibly put in *Norwood* v. *Read* (1558), Plowd. 180, 181, but did not arise in *Slade's Case*; in *Pinchon's Case* (1612), 9 Rep. 86 *b*, it was decided that *assumpsit* lay against executors, confirming *Norwood* v. *Read*. To succeed in simple debt against executors, the older cases allow the plaintiff to have his suit (*secta*) examined, or to " prove " his tally: Y.B. 21 & 22 Edward I (Rolls Series), 456 (1294); in detinue on bailment brought by executors, Bereford, J., refused to allow defence by wager of law: Y.BB. Edward II (Selden Society), ii. 16 (1308–1309).

Indeed, one vital factor in the popularity of *indebitatus assumpsit* was the fact that a creditor who had a right against a testator's executors in debt, might nevertheless have no effectual remedy; this was due to the rule that executors could not wage their law in the name of their testator, and consequently were not answerable.[1] This common situation was neatly met by *indebitatus assumpsit*, for the executors were undoubtedly " indebted ", and by presuming an *assumpsit*, they could be made to pay. A large proportion of the early examples of this form was therefore brought against executors.

Many people had reason to feel that they had lost a valuable safeguard. Chancery, indeed, affected to scorn wager of law; but Chancery did at least put the defendant on his oath and hear (or read) what he had to say, but in a court of common law the defendant's mouth was closed. Misgivings were therefore well founded, and the Statute of Frauds[2] was a direct result of the difficulties in matter of proof caused by *Slade's Case*.

More profound and less obvious results were also to flow from this decision. Forms were unchanged, it is true, and declarations will continue to allege the subsequent *assumpsit*, and that the defendant, " his assumption and promise aforesaid little regarding, but endeavouring and intending subtilly and craftily to deceive and defraud " the plaintiff, refused to pay, but it is now clear that the deceit element has been eliminated, and the contractual element, long latent as we have seen, became the sole basis of the action, which now rested on the " mutual executory agreement of both parties ". The stages in this progress are clear. At first *assumpsit* is brought upon explicit undertakings, and *indebitatus assumpsit* likewise lay upon a subsequent promise which was as necessary as the express words of warranty of quality in a sale of chattels. The second stage is marked by *Slade's Case*, where the action is based on the original contract instead of upon the subsequent *assumpsit*. A third stage was almost bound to follow, and in the course of the succeeding generations there is a strong movement to hasten the process. If the subsequent *assumpsit* could become a legal presumption where there had been in fact a pre-existing contract, could not the contract itself be some-times presumed? If an *assumpsit* could be implied, might not a contract be implied? This step was quickly taken, and in 1610 an innkeeper recovered the value of goods and services rendered to a guest who had not agreed upon a price.[3] Soon a large variety of implied contracts, and eventually of quasi-contracts, were remedied by *indebitatus assumpsit*. This development over a wide and hitherto untouched field was only rendered possible by the bold decision in *Slade's Case*.

---

[1] Above, p. 377.

[2] 29 Charles II, c. 3.

[3] *Warbrook* v. *Griffin* (1610), 2 Brownl. 254; debt, in such a case, had failed in *Young* v. *Ashburnham* (1587), 3 Leo. 161.

CONSIDERATION

From the reign of Henry VIII onwards,[1] the declaration in *indebitatus assumpsit* took the form which we have briefly summarised from *Slade's Case*. This consists of a preamble introduced by the words " in consideration that . . ." and setting out the precedent indebtedness which the defendant subsequently undertook to discharge. The matters set out in it could therefore be shortly referred to as " the considerations ".[2] This statement of facts in the consideration clause was necessary, because without it the defendant's promise would be only a " nude pact "—a continental expression[3] which became current in England, meaning a bare promise which would not support an action. On the continent, in jurisdictions (and particularly in class-rooms) where contract could be treated as a whole, a good deal of theorising took the picturesque form of deciding what " vestments " were sufficient for a pact to appear with propriety in a court of law. The canonists, on the other hand, held it sufficient if there was a reasonable and lawful " cause " for making the promise, and our Chancery in the fifteenth century was inclined to agree with them.[4]

The English common lawyers, however, hardly felt the need for either theory. Their formulary system was too rigid to take in the whole field, and the only contracts which were furnished with appropriate forms of action were of such a simple nature that speculation was unnecessary. It is true that down to the end of the fourteenth century, as long as we had several contractual actions such as debt, covenant, account and special *assumpsit* (to which must be added in the fifteenth century the peculiar treatment of contract in equity), there was a possibility that each one of these actions would develop a body of contract law peculiar to itself. If this had happened we should have had four or five different types of contract, every one of which would be governed by its own peculiar law. Events so happened that this did not occur; as we read in *Doctor and Student*:

> " It is not much argued in the laws of England what diversity is between a contract, a concord, a promise, a gift, a loan or a pledge, a bargain, a covenant or such other. For the intent of the law is to have the effect of the matter argued and not the terms."[5]

[1] Ames, *Lectures on Legal History*, 147.

[2] As in *Manwood* v. *Burston* (1587), 2 Leo. 203. In later ages this case could be looked to for a " definition of consideration " (cf. Fifoot, *Sources: Contract and Tort*, 401), but Manwood himself described his remarks as " three manners of considerations ", i.e. a list, not a doctrine.

[3] See Pollock and Maitland, ii. 196, for the Italian view that " an additional express promise (*pactum geminatum* or *duplex*) was a sufficient 'clothing' of the natural obligation of a *nudum pactum* to make it actionable ".

[4] This theory was widely adopted on the continent; see the valuable comparison drawn by Lorenzen, *Cause and Consideration*, Yale Law Journal, xxviii. 621. For an early case on failure of consideration where it was said that *la cause est cesse*, see Y.B. 21 Edward III, Pasch. no. 2.

[5] Christopher St Germain, *Doctor and Student*, dialogue II, c. 24.

This happy result was due to several causes. In the first place the different courts were, in fact, on intimate terms. It did not matter so much that they were usually terms of rivalry, for even then they kept close watch upon developments in other institutions, and competed in providing the best remedy. Then, again, since development took the form of modifying the different forms of action, it was inevitable that there should be a good deal of overlapping, and consequently the boundaries between forms of action became obscure. Hence it was all the more easy to emphasise substance above form. Finally, one of those forms of action supplanted all the rest for practical purposes, and from the seventeenth century onwards the law relating to *assumpsit* is the law of contract, and, historically speaking, that consideration which makes a contract enforceable was principally the conditions which were necessary to maintain an action of *assumpsit*. This was indeed the situation by 1602, but St Germain was certainly rather optimistic in stating the law in such general terms in 1530.

It was the unification of the law of contract under the single head of *assumpsit* which first created the desire for a general theory. The immediate origins of consideration must be carefully distinguished from the ultimate sources from which it was drawn. The only doctrine of contract which common lawyers were accustomed to state in foreign terms was the rule that a " nude pact " would not support an action. A bare *assumpsit*, therefore, could not be actionable (from the time when *assumpsit* was regarded as a contractual factor and not merely as a circumstance forming part of a tort). To make it actionable it was necessary to show the circumstances which were the " consideration " which moved the party to promise. Then came *Slade's Case*. The *assumpsit* thenceforward is presumed. The defendant is now charged upon an obligation which the law fixes upon him as a result of the matter shown in the " consideration " clause, irrespective of whether he subsequently acknowledged the obligation. The " consideration " clause in the count will therefore become much more important, for its consequences are more serious. It is no longer merely a matter of showing enough grounds to make a deliberate promise actionable, but must for the future set forth the very basis of the defendant's liability, even in cases where he made no promise whatever.

THE SOURCES OF CONSIDERATION

Slade's Case, therefore, compelled a more careful scrutiny for the future of the matters alleged in the consideration clause, and so we find a narrowing of grounds of action in some cases, although great extension in others. It was not immediately possible to state a general rule of consideration in one sentence, but some elements were already settled and served as the nucleus of the new doctrine.

Of these sources, the original nature of the action of *assumpsit* was one. From it was derived the emphasis upon the loss caused to the promisee by the promisor's failure to perform. In its origin this was the basis of the plaintiff's case, which was founded upon the " deceit " which he suffered at the hands of the defendant; it appears in modern theory as " detriment to the promisee ". Another source was the action of debt. Here some confusion was introduced, for the action of debt was primarily concerned with older forms of contract whose nature was settled long before any theory of contract was attempted. However, since assumpsit took over the field of debt, it became desirable to bring the debt-situations within the general scheme of contract, and to express them in terms of consideration. Debt on a loan, and debt for rent on a lease, and debt for the price of goods delivered were all exmples of real contracts which the common lawyers described by the home-made expression of *quid pro quo*. In such cases a declaration in *assumpsit* will therefore set out this *quid pro quo* as the consideration for the defendant's promise. Historically there are thus two branches of the theory of consideration, one of which is native to the action of *assumpsit*, and the other an importation from the action of debt. With the development of the consensual sale, and later still the recognition of other consensual contracts, a further modification became necessary, for in such cases one promise had to be laid as the consideration for a counter-promise. Still another element which had finally to be fitted in was provided by the deed under seal. This ancient example of the formal contract stood completely outside of the newer family of contracts, for its force depended entirely upon the delivery of a suitably inscribed piece of parchment and wax. The much more modern tag that " a seal imports consideration " is merely another way of saying that deeds under seal had no place in the common law scheme of consideration.

The foregoing paragraph represents the state of doctrine in the seventeenth and early eighteenth centuries. It is hardly a coherent whole, but all the same it served as an enumeration of those considerations which were approved, and which were sufficient for the ordinary run of cases. As it became more and more evident that *assumpsit* could extend over an ever wider field, and as an ever-increasing variety of transactions came before the courts, it naturally followed that attempts were made to create out of these fragments a general theory which could be applied to all new cases.

OUTSIDE INFLUENCES

Late in the fifteenth century it would seem that Chancery had been developing a law of contract on completely independent lines, and that the ecclesiastical Chancellors tried to apply the canon law doctrine of *cause*.[1] By means of a long and curious history the *causa* of Roman law

---

[1] On this, see the valuable researches of W. T. Barbour, *The Early History of Contract* (Oxford Studies in Social and Legal History, ed. Vinogradoff, vol. iv, 1914).

assumed a completely different aspect in the thought of the canonists.[1] In their view *cause* might consist in any definite object which the promisor at the time proposed to attain; if his promise was deliberately made with some definite aim in view there was sufficient *cause* to sustain an action. The end in view need not necessarily be of a business character; peace, charity and moral obligation were all sufficient *cause* to make a promise actionable.

It has been suggested that there may have been a certain amount of influence by Chancery upon the common law courts during those last years of the fifteenth century and the beginning of the sixteenth when the chancellors and the common law judges are so frequently found conferring together. But this possibility must not be over-estimated, especially in the formation of the doctrine of consideration. It is certainly true that Chancery during that period gave remedies for breach of contract which were not for the moment available in the common law. It may perhaps be true that the Chancery's theory of contract was some form of *causa*. Feeling the effects of this competition, the common law courts undoubtedly set to work to devise equivalent remedies in some cases, but this is no proof that they borrowed any legal dogmas from Chancery. Indeed, it would have been almost impossible to graft a theory of *causa* upon the common law until *Slade's Case* had changed the express *assumpsit* into a legal obligation imposed by the law itself upon parties to executory contracts. Only then was the field sufficiently free from procedural technicalities for contract to be regarded as a whole. Now this great act of self-liberation took place at the moment when relations between the common lawyers and Chancery were at their worst. The philosophical idea of conscience, and the political idea of prerogative upon which Chancery took its stand, were alike anathema to the common lawyers. There was ample explanation, therefore, for the fact that common lawyers were eager to afford rival remedies to those of Chancery, but equally stubborn in evolving those remedies from their own common law heritage, without borrowing Chancery's theories.

It was not until the eighteenth century that a serious search for a general theory of contract was undertaken. Thus, Blackstone[2] felt the need of a broad view of contract, and found it in a writer who is little known to modern common lawyers, Giovanni Vincenzo Gravina (1664–1718), an Italian professor of civil and canon law, who promptly sent him to the Digest. Even so, Blackstone's treatment of contract does not quite fill one chapter, and even that chapter is hidden away in a volume devoted to property, conveyancing, administration and the like. Moreover, at the very moment when Blackstone was writing,

---

[1] Briefly summarised by Le Bras in *Legacy of the Middle Ages*, 354, and in Holdsworth, viii. 42. This doctrine of *causa* (which was Roman before it became canonical) has survived in modern French law as *cause*. See generally, Chevrier, *Histoire de la causa dans les obligations* (1929).

[2] 2 Bl. Comm. 444.

Robert Joseph Pothier[1] (1699–1772) was publishing in rapid succession his monumental series of works on contract, which were eagerly studied by thoughtful lawyers in England.

LORD MANSFIELD ON CONTRACT

Among these was Mansfield, who was able to refer, in support of foreign theories, to some practices of Chancery, as well as to certain mercantile practices and to natural law, which indeed was often latent in English legal thinking.[2]

The new point of view regarded moral obligation as the primary factor which made promises actionable, while the mass of common law rules concerning consideration were to be treated as merely affording evidence. The process begins even before his day with *indebitatus assumpsit* brought on a preceding debt where that debt for one reason or another, although actually incurred, was not enforceable. For example, in 1697 a defendant who promised to pay debts incurred during his minority was held bound in assumpsit;[3] so, too, one who promised to pay debts barred by the Statute of Limitation.[4] Lord Mansfield carried this idea still further when he applied it to a promise by a discharged bankrupt, declaring that in conscience a discharge from bankruptcy does not relieve the debtor of his debts, and that a promise to fulfil this moral obligation is actionable.[5] He made his most drastic innovation, however, when he expressed the view that consideration was, and historically always had been, in the nature of a rule of evidence; hence lack of consideration was merely a lack of evidence. Now the Statute of Frauds had met this problem by its requirement of a written memorandum; therefore, he argued, the writing required by the statute took the place of the older requirement of consideration.[6]

The difficulties of proof were certainly a factor in the history of contract before the statute, but as we have seen, there were many complexities and divagations in that history which Mansfield brushed aside— and it was precisely these which had produced the doctrine of consideration. Mansfield's historical equipment, though respectable, was not entirely adequate; in his day the detailed history of contract was still unexplored. But his attitude towards history was sound. If (as he could believe in the contemporary state of learning) consideration was

---

[1] There is a useful article on Pothier by J. E. G. de Montmorency in *Great Jurists of the World* (ed. Macdonell), 447.

[2] The matter is fully discussed in Fifoot, *Lord Mansfield*, 118–140; Holdsworth, viii. 26–48, xii. 517–521.

[3] *Ball* v. *Hesketh* (1697), Comb. 381.

[4] *Hyleing* v. *Hastings* (1699), 1 Ld. Raym. 389.

[5] *Trueman* v. *Fenton* (1777), 2 Cowper, 544.

[6] *Pillans* v. *Van Mierop* (1765), 3 Burr. 1663 at 1669. See the analysis in C. H. S. Fifoot, *Lord Mansfield*, 129–134, J. M. Holden, *History of Negotiable Instruments*, 134 ff.

historically a set of restrictions due to the difficulty of proving contracts in olden days, and if those difficulties had now been removed by the Statute of Frauds and by more methodical business methods, was it reasonable that those restrictions should continue to fetter the law of contract? If the actual state of the law was unsatisfactory judged by contemporary moral sentiment, was it a defence to say that there were remote ages when it did conform to a situation which has now ceased to exist? Mansfield would use history itself to liberate law from its historical fetters, and we can imagine him reading with delight the words of Maitland, referring to another branch of law:

> " It seems to me to be full of rules which no one would enact nowadays unless he were in a lunatic asylum. And surely that should be the test. Would you enact that rule nowadays? Can you conceive that any sane man would enact that rule nowadays?
>
> " To say that a rule is historically interesting is not to the point. For myself, I happen to think that legal history is a fascinating matter for study. It is pleasant, and I even believe that it is profitable, to trace the origins of legal rules in the social and economic conditions of a bygone age. But anyone who really possesses what has been called the historic sense must, so it seems to me, dislike to see a rule or an idea unfitly surviving in a changed environment. An anachronism should offend not only his reason, but his taste. Roman law was all very well at Rome; mediaeval law in the middle ages. But the modern man in a toga, or a coat of mail, or a chasuble, is not only uncomfortable but unlovely. The Germans have been deeply interested in legal history; they were the pioneers; they were the masters. That has not prevented them from bringing their own law up to date. Rather I should say that it encouraged them to believe that every age should be the mistress of its own law."[1]

Although the extreme doctrine of *Pillans* v. *Van Mierop* was overruled by the House of Lords some years later[2] in 1778, it was still possible to hold (and indeed such was the prevailing opinion) that the requirements of consideration were fulfilled if there existed a moral obligation. This point of view prevailed during the rest of the eighteenth century[3] and was not abandoned until just a hundred years ago.[4] Among the influences which made for this last change of policy was the stricter observance of the Statute of Frauds, which defeated Lord Mansfield's attempt to make any informal writing enforceable, even although it did not comply with the statute;[5] and then, too, the real history of consideration began to be studied, with the result that it was discovered that there was no historical basis for Lord Mansfield's view. A learned note inserted in a law report of 1802 argued that " moral consideration "

---

[1] Maitland, *Collected Papers*, iii. 486–487 (on the German Civil Code of 1900).

[2] *Rann* v. *Hughes* (1778), 7 T.R. 350 n.

[3] For a discussion of those cases, see Holdsworth, viii. 26 ff.

[4] *Eastwood* v. *Kenyon* (1840), 11 Ad. & E., 438.

[5] Holdsworth, viii. 35; it had been settled that writing conferred enforceability, not validity; thus an unwritten agreement might become enforceable by being embodied in a subsequent memorandum.

could not be reconciled with old cases, and was widely cited thereafter.[1] Finally, the Hilary Rules of 1834 abolished the general issue in *assumpsit* and therefore compelled plaintiffs to plead specially all those matters which they considered necessary to their action. Consideration, therefore, as a result of these Rules tended to become what it had been originally, namely, all those requirements which were necessary in seventeenth-century special pleading.[2] This accelerated a revival of black-letter learning which was already taking place, and consequently the development of consideration has been brought back to common law principles, save in those cases where the influence of equity in Chancery (or the imitation of equitable doctrines by the common law courts) has introduced rules which still remain and which refuse to fit in with any general theory of consideration.[3]

The result has been a body of doctrine which, " roughly stated, seems plain and sensible; the court will hold people to their bargains but will not enforce gratuitous promises unless they are made in solemn form ". But it is inevitable that situations should arise at times in which the doctrine of consideration produces unsatisfactory results, and there is a good deal of criticism in consequence. Holdsworth suggests that " there is good sense in Lord Mansfield's view that consideration should be treated not as the sole test as to the validity of a simple contract, but simply as a piece of evidence which proved its conclusion ".[4] The very changes which the doctrine of consideration has undergone are a warning that there is nothing in it more peculiarly fundamental than in many other legal doctrines, and that a theory which has changed so much in the past may very well change once again in the future.

> " A legal history is not perhaps the place to make suggestions as to the law of the future. It is concerned with the past. But if history is to be something more than mere antiquarianism, it should be able to originate suggestions as to the best way in which reforms in the law might be carried out so as to make it conform with present needs."[5]

Since this chapter was first written, it has become possible to carry the matter a stage further. The whole question of consideration (especially as raised in the cases of *Dunlop Pneumatic Tyre Co., Ltd.* v. *Selfridge & Co., Ltd.*,[6] *Pillans* v. *Van Mierop*, and *Rann* v. *Hughes*) was referred by Lord Sankey to the committee on law reform presided over by Lord Wright. To a historian this small group of judges and lawyers is strangely reminiscent of the little group of experts which must have gathered round the great Chancellor Burnell in the far-off days of Edward I

---

[1] Note to *Wennall* v. *Adney* (1802), 3 B. & P. 249; Holdsworth, viii. 36.

[2] Holdsworth, *The Hilary Rules*, Cambridge Law Journal, i. 274.

[3] See Pound, *Consideration in Chancery*, Wigmore Celebration Essays, 435–460.

[4] Holdsworth, viii. 47; Lorenzen, *Causa and Consideration in Contracts*, Yale Law Journal, xxviii. 621–646.

[5] Holdsworth, viii. 48.

[6] [1915] A.C. 847.

when Parliament's first care was the strengthening and reform of the law. The report[1] which they have made is almost Edwardian in its recommendations of fundamental changes in several portions of the law of contract.

[1] Law Revision Committee, Sixth Interim Report [1937] Cmd. 5449.

LAW MERCHANT AND ADMIRALTY

We have several times mentioned the law merchant, particularly in connection with the history of contract, and so a brief account of its origin and progress must be included here, in spite of the great difficulty of dealing with an international subject with many bewildering ramifications. Its history is the subject of much learned controversy, and the literature in English, and for its history in England, is very scanty.[1]

SOURCES OF MARITIME AND MERCANTILE LAW

It is natural that the sources of European mercantile law should be found in the lands adjoining the Mediterranean Sea. From very early times there was much sea-borne commerce there, and business practices were based upon very old traditions. Two or three centuries before Christ there was a body of law known as the *Lex Rhodia*[2] which grew up in the great maritime centre in the island of Rhodes. The Roman law also contained a great deal of commercial matter which may have been originally evolved by the mercantile community. When the *Corpus Juris* of Justinian became out of date, the eastern Emperors, Basil I (867–886) and Leo VI (886–912), published the *Basilica* near the end of the ninth century, which contained a collection of maritime rules, while a new

---

[1] For an excellent general survey, see Wigmore, *Panorama of the World's Legal Systems*, ii. 875–929; for more detail, see Holdsworth, v. 60–154: the most complete work in English is Sanborn, *Origins of the Early English Maritime and Commercial Law*, which is a good introduction to the continental literature; cf. Sanborn, " Maritime Law ", *Encyclopedia of Social Sciences*, x. 122.

[2] Only a slight fragment has survived, in Dig. xiv. 2, 1.

collection had probably already become current under the name of the *Rhodian Sea Law*.[1]

The decline of the empires, east and west, defeated these efforts to compile collections of wide applicability, and so commercial law during the middle ages became mainly a matter of local customs. From the eleventh century onwards, therefore, the sources will consist of the custumals of numerous commercial and maritime towns, and diversity inevitably increased as the law became localised. In some cases we have collections of decisions—for customary law is very prone to seek its sources in decisions as well as in texts. At the same time, local legislation adds to the bulk of each local stock and to the diversity of the whole. Thus we find ordinances at Trani purporting to come[2] from the year 1063; Amalfi claims to have published its laws as early as 954, and a manuscript claims 1010 as their date; Pisa had a *constitutum* between 1156 and 1160, and in the thirteenth century such mercantile local custumals become increasingly common. Three of them were particularly famous and influential. Of these, the *Consulato del Mare* dates from about 1340 and was compiled, unofficially it seems, from the custom of Barcelona. The *Rolls of Oléron* are based on decisions of the merchant court of the little island of Oléron. They seem to date from the twelfth century, but now exist in the form of several later redactions. For some time Oléron (being part of Guienne) was under the English crown, and this, together with the fact that the great wine trade from Bordeaux to England passed close by, may explain why the laws of Oléron enjoyed special prestige in this country, and were copied into the Black Book of the Admiralty,[3] the Oak Book of Southampton[4] and the Little Red Book of Bristol.[5] Much later, and remoter, was the third great code, that of Wisby, which was current in parts of the Baltic. Even Wisby, however, came under the influence of the laws of Oléron through the channel of a Flemish version.[6]

The above are mainly maritime laws; the mobility of sea-borne trade easily accounts for the spread of particular customs along shipping routes. The custom of merchants on land seems to have been more varied. Every town tended to develop a more or less comprehensive body of merchant custom,[7] and hundreds of these custumals are still extant. Divergences in detail are very numerous, but even here attempts were made to secure some sort of uniformity.

[1] Edited, with a long introduction, by Ashburner, *Rhodian Sea Law*; it is possibly a century earlier than the *Basilica*. Cf. F. H. Lawson, *The Basilica*, Law Quarterly Review, xlvi. 486, xlvii. 536.

[2] Modern historians put them three centuries later.

[3] Edited by Sir H. Travers Twiss (Rolls Series).

[4] Edited by P. Studer (1910).

[5] Edited by F. B. Bickley (1900).

[6] Descriptions and extracts of all these will be found in Sanborn, *op. cit.*

[7] In England this mercantile custom is easily traced in the *Borough Customs*, edited by Mary Bateson for the Selden Society.

There was a movement from local law towards a cosmopolitan law, and this process was not completed until after the close of the middle ages. The factor which promoted the change was, of course, the international character of commerce, which necessarily brought merchants of different countries into contact with one another in the great fairs and seaports. Then, too, the smallness and weakness of many of the states had given rise to the formation of guilds of merchants who acquired considerable privileges. These privileges naturally grew in extent as commerce increased and spread over a wide area. Unification was further assisted by the dominant position in Mediterranean trade acquired by certain Italian cities, and consequently the spread of their particular customs. Many towns actually organised research in comparative legislation, and entrusted to officials called *emendatori* or *statutarii* the task of examining the laws and customs of other communities and recommending the adoption of those features which seemed to them desirable. There was, therefore, a deliberate attempt to promote uniform legislation. We have already noticed the tendency in England for towns to acquire the customs of some great city such as London. The Church, too, was exerting a growing influence upon mercantile practice. Particularly in the law of contract the Church asserted the principle of keeping faith— a principle which must lie at the root of commercial life.[1] And finally, there came the great Reception of Roman law which provided a scientific apparatus for the development of mercantile law, which, however, remained in substance deeply tinged with canonist doctrine.

THE ENGLISH SOURCES

The specifically English sources during the middle ages are of the sort already described. The borough charters and custumals are the most accessible, and to them may be added the volumes of black, white, red and other books which contained the memoranda of many city jurisdictions. London had several such volumes,[2] and the officers of the Crown themselves kept a " black book of the admiralty ".[3] In some cases it is possible to add actual records of mercantile jurisdictions, such as London possesses in abundance;[4] we have already mentioned some surviving rolls of fair and market courts.[5]

The systematic treatment of law merchant in formal text-books does not appear in England until after the middle ages, and even then it was merchants rather than lawyers who undertook the task. We had several writers of eminence on international law, and Professor Welwod of St Andrews published an *Abridgement of All the Sea Lawes* in 1613, but

[1] Cf. above, pp. 304–305.
[2] Printed as *Munimenta Gildhallae* (ed. Ryley, Rolls Series).
[3] Edited by Sir Travers Twiss in the Rolls Series.
[4] Edited by Dr A. H. Thomas, *Plea and Memoranda Rolls*.
[5] *Select Cases in Law Merchant* (ed. Gross, Selden Society).

academic writers were chiefly interested in the polemics over admiralty, the freedom of the seas and the Church courts in which they were professionally interested. A notary, John Marius, gave some *Advice concerning Bils of Exchange* in 1651, but the merchant Gerard Malynes wrote the first general English treatise on commercial law, *Consuetudo, vel Lex Mercatoria*, in 1622. The law is put in the midst of all the other matters which interested merchants—weights and measures, geodesy, theory of numbers, economics—and although he was not a lawyer, he had a wide and accurate knowledge of the principal civilian works on his subject. In the eighteenth century the principal work was Beawes' *Lex Mercatoria Rediviva*, which appeared in 1758 and had a successful career until about 1789, when a flood of new works in the modern style finally separated commercial law from the practice and theory of trade.

COMMERCIAL JURISDICTIONS

The institutions which administered commercial and maritime law were the civic authorities in numerous continental towns, who frequently had the title of consuls. They appear in Milan as early as 1154 and seem first to have been the officials of a gild merchant, although their importance soon made it necessary for the cities to associate themselves with the work. Markets and fairs had their own machinery for applying commercial law; most famous of them are the courts of piepowder, which were specially concerned with wandering merchants who travelled from market to market. The word seems to have been at first a nickname referring to the " dusty feet " of its clients, but was later accepted as the official style of the court. The English courts of piepowder closely resembled similar courts on the continent,[1] but just as the royal Admiralty superseded the local maritime courts, so a system of royal courts was set up by statute at various times in the fourteenth century which competed seriously with the local mercantile courts. These were called courts of the staple.[2]

MARITIME JURISDICTIONS

For a long time the administration of maritime as well as commercial law rested in the hands of local jurisdictions. Seaport towns had their own maritime courts sitting on the seashore from tide to tide, but the only ones which survived in active working in England into modern times was the jurisdiction of the group of five towns called the Cinque Ports, which is the oldest existing maritime jurisdiction in England.[3] The

[1] Markets and fairs were franchises, operated primarily for the profit of the owners. For specimen proceedings of English fairs and piepowder courts, see *Select Cases in Law Merchant* (ed. Gross, Selden Society).

[2] Statute of Staples (1353), 27 Edw. III, st. 2, consolidating earlier enactments; the policy was to force all foreign trade to pass through these monopolistic organisations, largely to simplify customs control.

[3] For a thorough study of this remarkable league of ports see K. M. E. Murray, *Constitutional History of the Cinque Ports* (Manchester, 1935).

other local maritime courts in the end were largely superseded by a newer and more centralised jurisdiction, the courts of Admiralty, held in the name of the Lord High Admiral who was appointed by the Crown.

The office of admiral[1] resembled those of the chancellor, steward, constable and marshal in that it gradually developed a judicial side. At times there were several admirals, each with duties confined to particular seas, but eventually it became the practice to appoint a single admiral with powers varying according to his commission. The earliest distinct reference to a court of Admiralty in England is in 1357, and in 1361 we have the first known record of such a case[2] which was heard before Sir Robert Herle, " admiral of all the fleets ". The case is interesting, for the defendant having pleaded several defences, the plaintiffs demurred; but the court overruled them, " since this court, which is the office of the admiral, will not be so strictly ruled as the other courts of the realm which are ruled by the common law of the land, but is ruled by equity and marine law, whereby every man will be received to tell his facts . . . and to say the best he can " for his defence.

In 1301 we find English and foreign merchants endeavouring to use the court of the steward and marshal for commercial causes, both because of its speed, and also because it took cognisance of contracts made out of the realm; their prayer for its further recognition failed: *non potest fieri quia contra magnam cartam*.[3]

In the meanwhile, however, it was the council which had most influence. All through the middle ages the council had made itself the protector of foreign merchants for the obvious reason that dealings with them frequently raised matters of international politics. The council developed this position, and in the later sixteenth century acquired a considerable commercial jurisdiction both original and also of a supervisory character over other courts, such as Admiralty, sometimes exercising it in the Star Chamber. Civilians were regularly called in to assist the council, for the commercial and maritime matters in the Digest were taken as forming part of the custom of merchants, while common law judges upon occasion would be consulted too. This jurisdiction of the council in the later sixteenth century was matched by that of the Star Chamber in the earlier part of the century and for obvious reasons.

The court of Admiralty has left us regular records from the year 1524, and it is clear that in the Tudor period it exercised a steady and direct influence upon both commercial and maritime law. Its procedure, however, was of the slower civilian type, and not that of the continental jurisdictions which operated under the decretal *Saepe*.[4] Nevertheless,

---

[1] Holdsworth, i. 544 ff.

[2] This case was discovered by Mr Charles Johnson and printed in the *Camden Miscellany*, vol. xv (1929). For a collection of early material, see *Select Cases in Admiralty* (ed. Marsden), 2 vols., Selden Society.

[3] Sayles, *King's Bench*, iii. pp. lxxxvii, cxxv; Magna Carta (1225), c. 11; cf. Articuli super Cartas (1300), 28 Edward I, c. 3.

[4] Above, p. 305.

the English court of Admiralty acquired a familiarity with negotiable instruments, insurance, charter-parties, bills of lading and other commercial business of which the common law as yet knew nothing. The other prerogative courts were less important in this connection, although the accident that most of the judges of the court of Requests were also Admiralty lawyers temporarily gave the court of Requests a certain amount of Admiralty jurisdiction by delegation from the Council. Chancery was principally concerned with partnership (for it had facilities for investigating accounts) and bankruptcy.

STATUTORY JURISDICTIONS

In the middle ages opinion was not altogether satisfied with Admiralty. In 1390 and 1391 statutes used strong language in criticism of it and restricted its powers;[1] in 1450 and 1453 portions of its work were transferred to Chancery;[2] not until the Tudors did Admiralty, like the navy itself, come into its own. From Henry VIII's reign onwards the admiral's commission empowered him to hear matters of shipping contracts, and of contracts to be performed beyond the seas, or made beyond the seas, the statutes notwithstanding.[3] A remarkable act of 1536 inaugurated the new policy of strengthening Admiralty by confirming its jurisdiction over crime committed on the seas, and permitting trial by jury; the reason given is that the civil law of proof by confession or witnesses is practically impossible under the circumstances without torture, for witnesses are unobtainable.[4] Shortly afterwards, another statute confirmed and enlarged its civil jurisdiction.[5] There was also a tendency, however, to place a few mercantile matters under the jurisdiction of a special statutory court; thus the recorder of London, two civilians, two common lawyers and eight merchants were set up as a summary court for insurance matters[6] in 1601.

ATTACKS BY THE COMMON LAWYERS

As soon as mercantile and maritime jurisdiction seemed desirable, the common lawyers began to covet it. The local courts felt the attack first. Fair courts were being hampered both by statute and by decision even in the fifteenth century;[7] in the sixteenth, the local maritime courts waged

[1] 13 Rich. II, st. 1, c. 5; 15 Rich. II, c. 3.

[2] 29 Hen. VI, c. 2; 31 Hen. VI, c. 4.

[3] Holdsworth, i. 549 n. 7; cf. the commission of 1618 in Prothero, *Statutes and Documents*, 388 at 391.

[4] 28 Hen. VIII, c. 15. The act was followed by a sharp rise in the number of convictions. But if witnesses were unobtainable, how did the juries reach their verdicts? The trials were to be before commissioners, of whom the admiral might be one. Later on, the commission was filled by common lawyers.

[5] 32 Hen. VIII, c. 14.

[6] 43 Eliz. c. 12.

[7] Holdsworth, i. 539.

a losing fight with Admiralty,[1] and in the late sixteenth century Admiralty itself came into conflict with the courts of common law.

At the close of the fifteenth and the beginning of the sixteenth centuries we had in England a Reception of the Italian mercantile law; and yet, a century later, in the first years of the seventeenth century, Coke asserted that " the law merchant is part of the law of this realm ".[2] This Reception was effected largely through the prerogative courts. Italian influence had always been strong in English finance, and when the revival of Roman law spread over Europe in the sixteenth century the Mediterranean mercantile customs, together with their civilian and canonist aspects, accompanied it. This Reception was general in northern Europe, and it was obviously prudent that England should follow suit, if, as the Tudors always maintained, England was to develop its pace in European trade. The prerogative courts, therefore, contained a strong element of foreign-taught civilians, whose activities were never welcomed by practitioners of the native system. The common law judges were frequently present at conferences, and this may have tempted the common lawyers to try to acquire this jurisdiction for themselves; when Coke came to the bench he deliberately set himself to cripple the court of Admiralty and to capture mercantile law for the common lawyers. Prohibitions were constantly issued to the Admiralty and other mercantile courts, while by a daring fiction which begins to appear frequently in the sixteenth century the common law courts assumed jurisdiction over acts which took place abroad, by the simple device of describing the place as being " in the parish of St Mary-le-Bow in the ward of Cheap ". This allegation was not traversable. In this way the common law began to capture the field of mercantile affairs, but for a long time it regarded itself as administering a strange and foreign law. It viewed the matter from the standpoint of custom; it was prepared to apply mercantile custom when that custom had been proved. Each case, therefore, had to allege the existence of a mercantile custom and then establish it by a jury of merchants.[3]

Admiralty did not submit without a struggle. They secured a conference with the common law judges in which the position was defined and a few concessions made to Admiralty,[4] in 1575. When Coke came to the bench in 1606 he denied that the agreement was ever ratified, and renewed the conflict with much bitterness. It was, of course, the mercantile community which suffered through the attachments, contempts, prohibitions, writs of *corpus cum causa* and the rest; whichever court he sued in the other was powerful enough to frustrate him and prevent its rival from doing justice; and the common law courts were clearly incapable of doing anything in a large proportion of

[1] Holdsworth, i. 531.

[2] Co. Lit., 182.

[3] For an early example (1292) see Sayles, *King's Bench*, ii. 69–72.

[4] The documents are printed in Prynne, *Animadversions on Coke's Fourth Institute.*

mercantile cases.[1]   Ambassadors protested, and finally another conference
and another settlement (also in favour of the Admiralty) was effected in
1632.   Like that of 1575 it was not observed, and the conflict continued
through the Commonwealth, was renewed at the Restoration, and dragged
on until the nineteenth century reconstituted Admiralty jurisdiction.

Meanwhile, the claim of the common law courts to rival some at
least of the law of the Admiralty was being made good.   What was
merely a claim when Coke made it, became something more in the hands
of Holt a century later, for by the close of the seventeenth century the
constant repetition of finding mercantile custom in each case that arose
was seen to be unnecessary, and the courts began to take notice of some
of the more notable mercantile customs without requiring proof of
them, and this policy was finally adopted as a general practice by Lord
Mansfield.[2]   In this way the common law set out to rediscover principles
of commercial law which were known to the Admiralty judges several
generations earlier, and to fit them into its framework of historical forms—
which fortunately was a little more flexible in the eighteenth than in the
seventeenth century.

THE CONTENT OF EARLY LAW MERCHANT

We must now consider the law which these local mercantile authorities
administered.   They exercised a very wide power of regulation—and the
middle ages thoroughly believed in the public regulation of every sort of
activity.   The only restrictions imposed upon them were the law of the
city authorities which must not be contravened, a general requirement
of reasonableness, and a restriction to purely mercantile matters.

Besides developing law and applying discipline to members of the
estate of merchants, there were also matters of a diplomatic character
which the consuls undertook.   Treaties and commercial conventions
with other communities were frequently negotiated, while down to the
fourteenth century they were frequently engaged in reprisals.   This
meant that if a merchant was unable to obtain justice against a foreigner
in the foreigner's court, then his own government would authorise him
to recoup himself out of the property of any merchant of the foreign
jurisdiction in question whom he could find.   The foreigner was then
left to take the matter up with his own government if he could.   This
system was, of course, extremely inconvenient.   Nevertheless it was
widespread; even in England we find different cities taking reprisals
against one another, justifying it on the custom of merchants.[3]   By the
fourteenth century reprisals became much more rare.

---

[1] See the examples in Holdsworth, i. 555.

[2] See generally, L. S. Sutherland, [1934] Trans. R. Hist. Soc., 149–176; in detail, Fifoot,
Mansfield, 82–117.

[3] For the abolition of this rule in Kent, save merchant towns, in 1259, see the remarkable
example of county legislation in E. F. Jacob, *Baronial Rebellion*, 351, 352, and in Law Quarterly
Review, xli. 232.

If we turn to the development of mercantile law in England, we find that by the end of the fifteenth century the English mercantile courts had developed a few principles, and from the occasional records which survive we can see how they worked in practice. The courts of the fairs in England show us numerous actions upon contracts of sale which had been concluded by the typically mercantile form of the payment of earnest money or God's penny.[1] Warranties of quality were enforced if express (as at common law);[2] and warranties of title were not yet presumed. The defence of innocent purchase for value in an open market was certainly good against a criminal charge of theft, but it was only at the close of the fifteenth century that it gave a good title to the purchaser against the original owner; this rule was virtually reached by 1473 and was settled a century later.[3] *Caveat emptor* had already become a policy of the law.[4] We also find that impeding a sale gave rise to an action in tort; some simple cases on partnership appear; brokers figure prominently both as binding their principals in contract and also as suing for their fees and commission—and in this last connection lawyers are on the same footing. And finally the merchant courts imposed a heavier liability both in contract and in tort than did the common law upon masters in respect of their servants' acts.

BONDS AND PROMISES TO PAY

A few brief words may now be said upon the content of this Italian law merchant which the English courts received, and first as to bills of exchange. All through the middle ages attempts were being made to make debts assignable and if possible payable to anyone who was the bearer of a document.[5] The principle was widespread; in the year 771 a monk gave to a church, " or the bearer of this document ", the right of avenging his death and collecting the *wer* if he were murdered; in 1036 a man left by his will the guardianship of his wife to two relatives

---

[1] This was preserved as a formal contract by the Statute of Frauds. The extent of law merchant in London can be seen in A. H. Thomas, *Plea and Memoranda Rolls, 1381–1412*, Intro.

[2] Goods not up to sample might be forfeit to the crown by law merchant: Gross, *Law Merchant* (Selden Society), i. 91 (1312).

[3] *Case of Market Overt* (1596), 5 Rep. 83 *b*. The privilege was subject to several statutory restrictions in this and the next century. On the continent the privilege was wider. Cf. Holdsworth, ii. 561, iv. 522, v. 104, 110.

[4] On the history of this, see W. H. Hamilton, *The Ancient Maxim Caveat Emptor*, Yale Law Journal, xl. 1133, and S. J. Stoljar, *Specific Performance in Contracts of Sale*, Canadian Bar Journal, xxxii. 251 at 273 n. 99.

[5] See, in general, Bailey, *Assignment of Debts*, Law Quarterly Review, xlvii. 516; Postan, *Private Financial Instruments*, Vierteljahrsschrift für Sozial- und Wirtschaftsgeschichte, xxiii. 26; Holdsworth, viii. 115 ff.; Sayles, *A Dealer in Wardrobe Bills*, Economic History Review, iii. 268; Tout, *Administrative History*, ii. 101 n. 4; Bigwood, *Commerce de l'Argent* (Académie royale de Belgique, 1921); Esmein, *L'Intransmissibilité première des créances et des dettes*, Nouvelle Revue historique de droit (1887), 48. For an inter-departmental bill payable to bearer (*temp.* Edward II), see J. Conway Davies, *Edward II*, 596 no. 130. For a vivid impression of international trade in the middle ages, see Y. Renouard, *Les Hommes d'affaires italiens*.

" or to whoever shall bear this writing ". In mercantile affairs this device became a common feature of sealed promises to pay. They were first drawn in favour of a named payee " or his attorney ", and in such cases a formal deed of attorney would be necessary to entitle anyone except the payee to sue upon the instrument. Documents of this type were common in the thirteenth and fourteenth centuries, for in fact they were simply the bond under seal which figures in countless actions of debt. Debtors were careful not to pay even an attorney except in return for the original bond, for payment was no defence if the creditor still held the sacred document.[1] It therefore naturally followed that a debtor was safe in paying anyone who returned him his deed. Later still, therefore, the mere production of the document was accepted as sufficient authority entitling the bearer to sue, at first in the name of the payee, and later in his own name. In the fifteenth century the validity of written promises to pay made out in this form was questioned, save in the single instance where the bearer was the properly constituted attorney of the payee. We therefore find the appearance of a new, brief and unsealed " bill ", written and signed by the debtor, payable to the creditor or bearer. This was a substitute for the bond under seal, and for centuries had no standing in the common law.

> " Probably this difficulty was especially keenly felt by the French lawyers, because the Renaissance school of jurists, which was especially influential in France, endeavoured to get back as far as possible to the classical texts. They therefore rejected many of those modifications of pure classical doctrine which the influence of the older customary law, and commercial convenience and practice, had caused the school of the glossators to accept. But the difficulty was not confined to the French lawyers. It was felt in Italy, and indeed in all countries in which Roman law was received, in proportion to the extent to which the doctrines of that law gained supremacy. The lawyers were at once learned in the classical texts of Justinian's *Corpus Juris*, and ignorant of the modern mechanism of commerce. They did not hesitate, therefore, to sacrifice commercial convenience on the shrine of legal orthodoxy—even suggesting that the merchants purposely adopted obscure forms in order that illegal transactions might pass unnoticed. On the other hand, the technical difficulty was not felt so keenly in Northern Europe, nor, as we shall see, in England. It is probable that in these places the older ideas lived on and saved the lawyers the trouble of finding a new speculative basis, consonant with the doctrines of Roman law, upon which the peculiar characteristics of negotiable instruments could be based."[2]

BILLS OF EXCHANGE

The future lay rather in the development of " exchange " than in the promise to pay or the " writing obligatory ".[3] " Exchange " was at first the simple process of changing coins of one currency against those of another, but there soon grew up an organisation of international bankers having agents or correspondents in the principal commercial

---

[1] Hence the court might deface a bond: Y.BB. Edward II (Selden Society), xxiv. 86 (1319).

[2] Holdsworth, viii. 122, 123.

[3] See, in general, Holdsworth, viii. 113–176.

centres, and these firms, instead of actually delivering coins of one type in exchange for coins of another, would write a letter of exchange to their correspondents, effecting the transfer purely on paper. With an international organisation they quickly realised that the transfer of money between various countries could be effected by merely transferring balances, setting off a credit balance in one country against a debit balance in another. A merchant who wished to remit money abroad would therefore address himself most usually to one of these bankers. The remitter A. therefore secures from his banker B. (in exchange for money paid to him) a bill drawn in foreign currency by B. upon C., payable to D. B. and C. are very often partners or agents of the same international bank. Under the ordinary form this arrangement would be embodied in a formal deed. Already in the fourteenth century, however, the formal deed began to be replaced by the informal letter of advice which accompanied it; it is this letter of advice which eventually grew into the modern bill of exchange.[1]

So far we have a document which enables A. to effect a payment to D. in a foreign country without transporting money, but this document is payable to D. only, and is in no sense transferable. Late in the sixteenth century the habit grew up in Italy of drawing bills of exchange in favour of a payee or order, whereupon the payee would endorse the bill with an order to pay X. as agent of the payee. This was one step further in the development of transferability, but X. was still unable to transfer further. The payee's order was X., and not any other person whom X. might name.

In the middle of the seventeenth century it became established that one endorsee can endorse over, and so bills become assignable by successive endorsement; but the theory still prevailed that an endorsee was agent of the payee. However, the fact that the endorsement and delivery served instead of a power of attorney, and gave the endorsee the right to sue, made it look as though the endorsee sued in his own name—and so the lawyers compromised by calling him an agent although in respect of his own property (*procurator in rem suam*).

At the same time—in the middle of the seventeenth century—lawyers began to make certain presumptions in connection with bills of exchange, notably that an acceptance was for value. Having once begun to make presumptions it was easy to carry the process further; a further presumption was made that the bill was in good order (*omnia rite acta*), and this presumption could not be rebutted so long as the holder took in good faith, the result being that a *bona fide* holder for value was protected against prior irregularities. By this time the wave of academic enthusiasm for the letter of classical Roman law had spent its force, and the bill of exchange became finally established in substantially its modern form, and with the modern characteristic of negotiability.[2]

---

[1] The process was still incomplete even in the sixteenth century: Postan, *loc. cit.*, 63. The later bill of exchange also was often accompanied by a " letter of advice ".

[2] See generally R. de Roover, *L'Evolution de la lettre de change, 14e à 18e siècles* (Paris, 1953).

BILLS OF EXCHANGE IN ENGLAND

The history of bills of exchange in English law is the history first of the reception of Italian practice among English merchants in the fifteenth and sixteenth centuries. As Professor Postan suggests, there is no need to assume that England was deeply touched by the juridical controversies which Brunner[1] stressed. The reception of the bill of exchange in English mercantile practice is easiest explained by more practical considerations. The bill was *par excellence* a device for international exchange, and that was the service which Italian international banks were rendering to the English wool trade. Hence the early familiarity of the bill of exchange. The progress of this reception can be traced by noting the changes which appear upon comparing the treatise of Marius (1651) with that of Malynes which appeared in 1622. In the interval between these two works it is clear that great developments took place in English mercantile practice, which now follows closely the stages of continental development. In England, as on the continent, we see the sixteenth-century writing obligatory drawn to bearer—and it was often the custom to draw it in blank, leaving the payee's name to be inserted later. This was superseded in the middle of the century[2] by the true bill of exchange, and upon this we have a fair amount of information in the records of the court of Admiralty, which concerned itself with these documents. Malynes shows us the old four-party bill which we have described, which was not yet payable to order or bearer. Marius shows us the three-party bill in its modern form which was transferable, and also available for internal as well as in foreign trade—for there had long been doubts whether a bill of exchange could be used in domestic commerce.

By the middle of the sixteenth century, therefore, English merchants were accustomed to the use of the continental bill of exchange[3] as it then existed, and if litigation arose there was the court of Admiralty in which to sue. From time to time, however, attempts were made to sue at common law upon bills of exchange, using the action of *assumpsit*. The books of entries of the second half of the sixteenth century contain pleadings for this purpose, and in 1602 we find the first reported case of *assumpsit* being brought on a bill.[4] The early forms show that there was some difficulty in pleading a bill of exchange in terms of the common law. Matters were soon greatly simplified by merely stating the facts of acceptance, endorsement and so on, and then resting the case upon the custom of merchants. In this way there was no need to express in terms known to the common law the rights and liabilities of all parties to a bill. This practice becomes general from 1612 onwards.[5] The next step

---

[1] Whose view is adopted by Holdsworth; cf. p. 666 above.

[2] In 1532 there had been complaints that Flemish bills were not actionable in England: *Letters and Papers of Henry VIII*, v. no. 843.

[3] See generally, J. Milnes Holden, *The History of Negotiable Instruments in English Law* (1955).

[4] *Martin* v. *Boure*, Cro. Jac. 6.

[5] *Oaste* v. *Taylor*, Cro. Jac. 306.

logically followed; once the common law courts were familiar with the nature of a bill of exchange, it was no longer necessary to plead specially the custom of merchants. This great change was largely due to Lord Holt. During the period when he sat as Chief Justice of the King's Bench we find that the negotiability of bills of exchange was recognised at common law. His decisions laid it down that a bill drawn to order could be transferred by endorsement, that the title of a *bona fide* holder was not invalidated by defects in the title of his transferor, and that consideration will be presumed.

PROMISSORY NOTES

In the seventeenth century merchants did not draw a very sharp distinction between bills of exchange and the old informal and unsealed writing obligatory,[1] which now became simplified in form as a promissory note. In mercantile practice they negotiated notes in the same way as bills, but, as we have seen, the " writing " was a very old form, and therefore associated in men's minds with very old law, and the common lawyers, like the civilians, had technical reasons for holding that promises to pay were not transferable save to attorneys. Lord Holt refused to recognise the promissory note as being on the same footing as a bill of exchange in the famous case of *Buller* v. *Crips*.[2] Holt's view was that these promissory notes were a novelty invented by the goldsmiths, whose practice was to accept money from their customers on deposit, giving in return a promissory note which they thought was negotiable.[3] The goldsmiths were doing, in a less convenient way, what a modern bank does in accepting a customer's money, only to-day, instead of always issuing notes, the bank undertakes to honour its customer's cheques. In so far as promissory notes were used in this operation Holt maintained that they represented an attempt by Lombard Street to dictate law to Westminster Hall. There was also a good deal of technical force in Holt's argument that the same result could be obtained through a bill, and that while the bill of exchange had a proper place in the common law, the promissory note had not. He therefore refused to allow an endorsee to sue on a promissory note. Nevertheless mercantile opinion in favour of notes was so strong that a statute was passed expressly making them negotiable.[4]

At this point we reach the beginning rather than the end of the story. Future development lay in the direction of elaborating the idea of negotiability and applying it to a great variety of documents, some of them of very recent origin. Although a number of negotiable instruments have

---

[1] Above, p. 666.

[2] 6 Mod. 29 (1704); Pound and Plucknett, *Readings*, 219–221.

[3] On these matters, see R. D. Richards, *Early History of Banking in England*, and R. H. Tawney, introduction to Wilson, *Discourse on Usury*.

[4] 3 & 4 Anne, c. 8 (1705).

arisen in modern times, yet the really fundamental idea of negotiability was established in the seventeenth century, and the greatness of that achievement can only be appreciated with reference to the vast modern developments which it made possible.

Space forbids more than mention of the many other contributions which the custom of merchants made. Insurance has a long and interesting history,[1] at first maritime and then general; so, too, has the law of partnership,[2] of which many varieties were known during the middle ages, enabling large international banks and financial houses to conduct their operations, while in the seventeenth century the partnership or company is expanded into the trading corporation.[3] The law of agency is especially interesting for its mingling of common law, ecclesiastical ideas on the management of monasteries, and mercantile practice.[4]

[1] Holdsworth, viii. 294; Trenerry, *Early History of Insurance, including Bottomry*.

[2] Holdsworth, viii. 192–222.

[3] Sir Cecil Carr, *Select Charters of Trading Companies* (Selden Society); W. R. Scott, *Joint Stock Companies*.

[4] Holdsworth, viii. 222–229; Holmes, *Collected Papers*, 49–116; H. Würdinger, *Geschichte der Stellvertretung in England*; Fegan, *Undisclosed Principal*, University of Pennsylvania Law Review, lxxx. 858; W. Müller-Freienfels, *The Undisclosed Principal*, Modern Law Review, xvi. 299; T. F. T. Plucknett, *The Mediaeval Bailiff*, 30.

PART 5

EQUITY

SUMMARY

EQUITY

Equity is often spoken of as a supplement or an appendix to the common law; a mediaeval lawyer would perhaps have caught our meaning better if we were to say that it is a sort of gloss written by later hands around an ancient and venerable text. Law books were particularly apt to accumulate such glosses (Coke's gloss on Littleton is the latest English example). In a sense, the gloss and the text are a unity, an expanded version of the original, and the two must be read together. This does not mean, however, that there may not be conflict and contradiction between text and gloss; still less does it mean that there will be a logical and systematic distribution of material between the text and the gloss. It is commonly observed, however, that the gloss tends to grow in importance. It may corrupt the text at points; it will often be clearer, representing a later state of learning with new facts, and more elaborate thought. It often happened in the end that the gloss was of more practical importance than the original.

The simile we have just suggested is more than a mere figure of speech, for it is in fact a deduction from the mediaeval habits of study. Reverence for authority made it necessary to preserve ancient texts, such as the *Corpus Juris*, but the practical demands of daily life made it equally necessary to have the gloss which alone made the system workable. This reconciliation between two divergent instincts seems to lie at the root of the scheme of law and equity as it existed, say, in the reign of Henry VII, when the relations between them were fairly friendly. But there were seeds of dissension. When the text is the sacred book of one profession and the gloss the work of another, the unity of the two may be in peril. This happened when canonists wrote a gloss, so to speak (and a distinctly " equitable " one), on the texts of the civilians; and to some extent it happened, too, when chancellors glossed the common law.

Neither theory nor practice required the administration of law and equity to be assigned to different institutions; in practice, courts of law could administer equity whenever the need arose. Thus Beaumanoir[1] at the end of his book discusses some situations when law should be tempered with equity. In England (but not in Scotland) equity became the special concern of the chancery which administered equity, while the historical courts continued to administer law.[2] Institutional history has therefore had a confusing effect upon the result. More especially, the accidents of history made equity a fragmentary thing. First one point, then another, was developed, but at no time was it the theory or the fact that equity would supplement the law at all places where it was unsatis-

---

[1] Beaumanoir (ed. Salmon), ss. 1939 ff.

[2] For the view of Bacon, *Aphorism 45*, upon the desirability of this, see below, p. 687 n. 2.

factory; consequently it has never been possible to erect a general theory of equity. In the last resort, we are always reduced to a more or less disguised enumeration of the historical heads of equity jurisdiction.

Finally, just as we have spoken of the common law as the custom and practice of the common law courts, so we might, with equal truth, describe equity as the custom of the Chancery. The decisive test for the existence or not of an equitable rule or remedy is to be found in a search of the records and decisions of the court of Chancery and its modern successors. There are indeed a number of maxims which have almost attained the dignity of principles; but deduction alone will not reveal the content of our system of equity. The only authoritative source is the custom of the court, and that must be gathered from an examination of the cases.

THE EARLY HISTORY OF EQUITY

THE RISE OF COURTS OF EQUITY

Of the institutional aspects of equity we have already spoken. Thus we have seen fourteenth-century parliaments occasionally dispensing remedies which later were typical of equity;[1] the council, moreover, was so flooded with petitions of every sort that it was there that these new practices inevitably became settled, and, as the council was finally overwhelmed, the task was shifted to the chancellor, who had ampler resources in the way of office staff.[2] The need for a supplement to common law procedure was very evident in the fourteenth century,[3] and even its doctrine was not above criticism. We have remarked upon the abandonment by the common law judges of their ancient powers of discretion,[4] and the feeling among contemporaries that the old institutions were no longer entirely adequate—even the seignorial courts felt the same difficulty, and met it in the same way by erecting councils (often of civilians and canonists) which became courts of equity.[5] A long struggle in Parliament failed to check this development either at Westminster or in many seignorial jurisdictions, and in the end the situation was accepted.[6] Equity was henceforth tolerated and even strengthened by statute, and the movement continued with increasing vigour. Late in the fifteenth century there was a search for a theory and there was some talk of "absolute power", "conscience" and "natural law".[7] A century later the spread of equity is still evident: municipal courts of equity

[1] Above, p. 179 n. 2.
[2] Above, pp. 178–180.
[3] Above, p. 177.
[4] Above, p. 158.
[5] Above, p. 186.
[6] Above, pp. 187–188.
[7] Above, p. 194.

begin to appear, such as the Mayor's court in London[1] and the court of equity in the cinque ports,[2] while a similar process in the great feudal liberties produced the court of chancery in the palatinate of Durham,[3] a court of chancery in Lancashire, and the court of Duchy Chamber which sat in London or Westminster.[4] Indeed, it is already clear that one royal court of equity is not enough. So we find such institutions as the court of requests,[5] and subsidiary councils with equitable powers for the marches and the north.[6] Moreover, this intense activity in the courts of equity affected the common law itself. It was the competition of equity which stimulated the growth of a common law of contract;[7] in 1566 a disappointed litigant declared that Catlin, C.J., had made the Queen's Bench a court of conscience (and was indicted for it);[8] that same bench was now beginning to develop such writs as *mandamus*[9] (which might well have become equitable), and in the next century it inherited a wide jurisdiction from the Star Chamber, which was, in a sense, criminal equity.[10]

Until later in the middle ages it was not yet apparent to contemporaries that there were, or could be, two different and sometimes conflicting systems in England, one of them common law and the other equity. They were, however, well aware of conflicting courts, and on numerous occasions complaints were heard that the chancellor, the council, the steward, the constable, the admiral and other authorities had exceeded their jurisdiction. Moreover, it seems that the council and chancellor were at first concerned principally with the *de facto* failings of the common law, rather than with its doctrinal shortcomings. It was the over-mighty subject who broke through the net of procedure and controlled juries through his local influence who first taxed the powers of the council. As late as 1618 a decree of Lord Bacon was thwarted by a force of two hundred armed men.[11] A later stage is marked when the council and the chancellor apply different rules from those prevailing in the common law courts, and herein lies the principal theme in the history of equity.

[1] For the court of equity before the mayor, see 4 Inst. 248, and R. B. Morris, *Mayor's Court of New York City*, 35, for much MS. material for London. For the London Inner Chamber, see A. H. Thomas, *Pleas and Memoranda, 1381–1412*, xix, who notes that equity here means law merchant.

[2] K. M. E. Murray, *Cinque Ports*, 106.

[3] G. T. Lapsley, *Durham*, 189.

[4] On these, see R. Somerville, *The Duchy of Lancaster Council and Court of Duchy Chamber*, Transactions of the Royal Historical Society (1941), 159; *Case of the Duchy of Lancaster* (1561), Plowden, 212.

[5] Above, p. 184. The statutory Courts of Great Sessions which existed from 1542 to 1830 exercised an equitable jurisdiction, the origin of which is obscure: W. H. D. Winder, in Law Quarterly Review, lv. 106.

[6] Above, pp. 184–185.

[7] Above, p. 642.

[8] Foss, *Judges*, 159.

[9] Above, p. 173.

[10] Above, pp. 459, 497, 499.

[11] *Cases decided by Lord Bacon* (ed. Ritchie), 122.

We have already noticed the fragmentary character of equity, and in fact its history is even more fragmentary. This is partly due to the fact that the rules were a product of the institution, and so partook of the external accidents which often mould the history of institutions. History would have been very different if the idea of equity had been the cause, instead of the result, of the chancellor's powers.

EQUITABLE FEATURES IN THE COMMON LAW

In fact, many rules which have since become distinctive of chancery make their first appearance in the common law courts. The application of these principles does not, therefore, imply anything in itself alien to the spirit of the common law, for the common law courts had themselves exercised these powers.

This has been admirably demonstrated by Professor Hazeltine, who observes numerous points upon which equity was anticipated by the common law courts.[1] There was a moment when it seemed likely that uses in land might be enforced by the action of covenant[2] and uses in chattels by account and detinue.[3] In Henry II's reign we find something like an equity of redemption recognised by the King's Court, which had vanished, however, by the reign of Edward I.[4] Then, too, in a famous case[5] Chief Justice Bereford proposed to give relief against a penalty as late as 1309: " What equity would it be to award you the debt when the document is tendered and when you cannot show that you have been damaged by the detention? " he asked. And again: " Moreover this is not properly a debt but a penalty; and with what equity (look you) can you demand this penalty? " And so Bereford told the plaintiff that if he wanted judgment he would have to wait seven years for it. It is true that this case is almost unique, and that Bereford was a judge of remarkable originality and courage;[6] but it is still apparent that there is nothing inconsistent with the common law in the idea of limiting recovery of penalties to the measure of damages actually sustained, if such there were. Indeed, in 1307 the court of exchequer (in which Bereford was in fact present) reduced a statute merchant on the ground that it was " only security ".[7] Twice in one roll we find the defence that the maker

[1] The following remarks are based on his paper, *The Early History of English Equity* (in Essays in Legal History, ed. Vinogradoff), 261–285, with some additional references. Cf. Holdsworth, ii. 241–249.

[2] Above, p. 576; for an extreme form of this view, see Holmes, *Early English Equity*, Collected Papers, 1; the common law idea of conditional feoffments certainly permitted some uses to be litigated at common law (*Rot. Parl.*, ii. 79; Y.B. 11 Rich. II (Ames Foundation), 119; above, p. 576, n. 5), and the idea of wardship also looked promising. *Bracton's Note Book*, nos. 754, 999, 1683, 1851, are earlier examples of the tendency.

[3] Y.B. 20 Hen. VI, Hil. 2; Ames, *Lectures*, 118, 238.

[4] It took the form of delay, Glanvill, x. 8; cf. above, p. 604.

[5] Y.BB. Edward II (Selden Society), ii. pp. xiii, 59.

[6] Above, p. 240; see further, p. 605, above.

[7] The case is *Folyot* v. *Walter Langton*, recorded in J.I. 1. 1344 m. 20, and E13/31 m. 30. I am grateful to Miss Alice Beardwood for these valuable references. Cf. Y.BB. Edward II (Selden Society), xxiv. p. lxxxviii.

of a charter was " deceived " in doing so;[1] the King's court will not allow the requirements of a form of action to be used as part of a fraud;[2] it will order the cancellation of a deed;[3] it will not entertain matters which have been unreasonably delayed;[4] the court of exchequer would give to a litigant copies of documents he needed which were in the hands of his adversary.[5]

When we come to the question of specific performance it is important to observe that some of the oldest common law actions were of this character.[6] The action of covenant will give specific restitution to a lessee whose lessor has broken the agreement; so, too, covenants to convey land, the provisions of final concords, the obligations of warranty, and obligations to perform or to acquit " foreign service " (a matter of great complication in feudal law) were enforceable at common law by actions which went much further than giving damages, for they concluded with judgments that the defendant was to perform the obligations to which he had been proved liable.[7] Once again, then, it is clear that there is no very great reason in the nature of things why common law should confine itself to an action for damages—save that in all these matters the great difficulty of the common law lay in the ancient rule which only allowed it to enforce its judgments by distress, and not by imprisonment on the ground of contempt of court.

Then, too, there were occasions upon which the common law would issue what is really an injunction under the name of a writ of prohibition restraining a party from committing waste in a variety of circumstances;[8] upon breach of his prohibition the party is attached to show cause; even in the seventeenth century this aspect of the common law was highly praised by Coke,[9] who says of prohibitions of waste, " this was the remedy that the law appointed before the waste done by the tenant in dower, tenant by the curtesy or the guardian, to prevent the same, and this was an excellent law—and this remedy may be used in this day ". The famous Luffield register (c. 1282) contains a writ *De Minis* which is partly a grant of the king's peace, and partly an injunction against attacks which had been threatened against him.[10] Then in 1308 we find an interesting

---

[1] *Curia Regis Rolls*, vii. 136, 179 (1214).

[2] *Eyre Rolls* (Selden Society, vol. lix), no. 474 (1221); cf. no. 1073.

[3] *Ibid.*, no. 1073 (1221).

[4] No attaint of a jury after nineteen years, *ibid.*, no. 77 (1221), nor an appeal of homicide after nine years, *Select Pleas of the Crown*, no. 28 (1202).

[5] *Select Cases in Exchequer of Pleas*, 114–115 (1286); they were rolls of accounts. But account was not described in the middle ages as an equitable action (R. M. Jackson, *History of Quasi-Contract*, 36); in the Year Book passages there cited ' 'account " means the accounting (which is governed by equity and good faith and not by rigour of law), not the action. Cf. Y.BB. Edward II (Selden Society), xxiv. 147 (1319).

[6] Details in Hazeltine, *Early History of Specific Performance*, Festgabe für Kohler, 67–87.

[7] Such as the action of mesne, as to which see Westminster II, c. 5 (1285).

[8] Bracton, f. 315 *b*; *Bracton's Note Book*, nos. 27, 56.

[9] 2 Inst. 299.

[10] *Registers of Writs* (Selden Society), 65 no. 107.

case where a lord secured a judgment forbidding his tenants from selling their goods elsewhere than in his market;[1] and similar judgments could be given on questions arising out of suit of mill, whereby tenants could be compelled to grind at the lord's mill. As Maitland has remarked, " if this is not an injunction, and a perpetual injunction, we hardly know what to call it ". Professor Hazeltine has observed:

" The early common law jurisdiction *in personam* by means of prohibitions was not narrow. . . . Parties were not only ordered not to commit waste, not to commit nuisance, not to sell land, not to distrain the plaintiff to do suit of court, not to destroy the wood in which the plaintiff has housebote and haybote, not to expose wares for sale elsewhere than in the plaintiff's market, not to sue in the ecclesiastical courts; but parties were ordered to repair walls and buildings, to erect houses, to place property in the same condition in which it had been, and to remove existing nuisances."[2]

Closely connected with the writs of prohibition were the writs *quia timet*, which, like the Chancery bills of the same name, aim at preventing a wrong which is threatened before it occurs.[3] So also, in the exchequer in 1284, a Christian could plead (and prove by a jury) against a Jew, that he had paid a debt but had lost the acquittance.[4]

From all this it is clear that many of those features which were later characteristic of equity were once a part to a greater or less degree of the earlier common law. There was, therefore, no fundamental inconsistency between equity and common law: the one was not alien to the other. Professor Hazeltine summarises these results as follows:

" Enough has already been said, I hope, to indicate that not all the ideas which we associate with English Equity were either borrowed from the Roman system by the Chancellors or original with them. The advent of the Chancellor as a judicial officer of the Crown was at a time when the older tribunals, although expanding their own system to meet the needs of a growing society, were nevertheless fettered in their powers by statute and precedent as well as by the conservatism and technicality of the legal profession. The Chancellor's court, exercising very wide discretionary powers, gradually developed the elaborate and effective system of rules and principles which we of the twentieth century know as English Equity. But, while fully recognising the achievements of the Chancery, let us not forget that the new tribunal built partly upon the older practice of the common law and other courts whose equitable jurisdiction it supplanted. The new tribunal did not originate English Equity, for it simply carried on the work of the older courts by developing in greater fullness and with a different machinery the equity inherent in royal justice."[5]

That " equity inherent in royal justice " is frequently mentioned, not only by mediaeval political scientists but also in the course of practical affairs. Thus a statute[6] asserts that " the king, who is sovereign lord,

---

[1] Y.BB. Edward II (Selden Society), ii. pp. xiii, 74.

[2] Hazeltine, *Early Equity*, Essays in Legal History (ed. Vinogradoff), 282. Cf. the examples given by Bordwell, *Running of Covenants*, Iowa Law Review, xxxvi. 504.

[3] Hazeltine, *op. cit.*, 284; Co. Lit. 100 *a* (but see Holdsworth, ii. 344 n. 6).

[4] *Cases in Law Merchant* (ed. Hall, Selden Society), iii. 93.

[5] Hazeltine, *op. cit.*, 285.

[6] Westminster I, c. 17 (1275).

shall do right unto all such as will complain "—in spite of procedural and feudal complications, and plea rolls assert the same duty of an over-riding equity in the king.[1]

Indeed, even in the middle of the fourteenth century the common lawyers still occasionally appealed to " conscience "—not merely to those more liberal practical features which we have just described, but to equity in the abstract, apart from any question of its having been embodied in one of their own established rules or procedures.[2]

THE STRICTER SCHOOL OF LEGAL THOUGHT

It is here that the problem was raised most clearly, and it is here that we can see the fatal hesitation of the common lawyers. They were of two minds. If we cite these references to conscience and equity in the abstract which some of them made, we must also cite other expressions in the opposite sense. The lawyers had a maxim that they would tolerate a " mischief " (a failure of substantial justice in a particular case) rather than an " inconvenience " (a breach of legal principle). To a bishop who brought an unconscionable action, Bereford, C.J., declared " it is a dishonest thing for an honourable man to demand what his predecessor released "; but the bishop's claim nevertheless succeeded. " Once in the name of good faith he urged the defendant's counsel to admit a fact that had not been proved. Back came the retort: ' You must not allow conscience to prevent your doing law.' "[3] Our common lawyers in fact were beginning to feel the attraction of the " legal mind ",[4] the delight of pushing a principle as far as it will go and even further, and were enthusiastic over their first lessons in the *rigor juris*. This was no doubt the first step in legal wisdom (though certainly not the last); the real question which they had to face was how the future of the law should be developed. Was it to be a system of strict rule, mainly procedural, or was there to be a broader principle of conscience, reason, natural justice, equity? Plainly there were two points of view on this matter in the reign of Edward II, but it must have been fairly evident by the middle of the century that the stricter party had won. The law no doubt grew in content, but its growth was within a framework of technical doctrine and procedure instead of being the outcome of a broad principle of general equity; " logic yields to life, protesting all the while that it is only be-coming more logical ".[5]

---

[1] Sayles, *King's Bench* (Selden Society), iii. 58 (1298).

[2] Y.B. 13 & 14 Edward III (Rolls Series), 96; 18 & 19 Edward III (*ibid.*), 58, 60; 27 Edward III, Michs. no. 20; Holdsworth, ii. 344.

[3] Maitland, Introduction to Y.BB. Edward II (Selden Society), i. p. xix, now printed, *ibid.* xxiv. 84.

[4] Amos, *The Legal Mind*, Law Quarterly Review, xlix. 27, 39.

[5] Maitland, *loc. cit.*

EQUITY SEPARATES FROM LAW

The triumph of the stricter school of legal thought was in part the cause, and in part the effect, of the institutional changes which we have already mentioned.[1] As a result of those changes the common law courts lost much of their discretion and explicitly abandoned any thought of tempering law with equity, but on the other hand they gained in independence of the Crown.

It must be remembered that just as there were several courts of common law, so there were several bodies capable of administering law modified with discretion or equity. The exchequer may have done so, and the council certainly did. The decline of discretion in the common law courts, therefore, had the effect of throwing increased emphasis upon the discretion which had always been exercised in the council, and so we reached the position, so full of possible dangers, in which justice was partitioned between two bodies, neither of which could completely deal with a matter. Council and Chancery no longer could manage the complicated machinery of writs and pleadings and process; common law courts no longer exercised discretion. This profound schism in the administration of justice had the most momentous effects. Adjudication, like most other questions of human conduct, depends upon a nice balance between law and equity, rule and exception, tradition and innovation. Each of these different principles became exaggerated when it became the badge of an institution, with the result that law and equity instead of being complementary, became rivals in a political upheaval.

THE CONTINUITY OF EQUITY

Such was the general outline of the process. There has been some controversy about one aspect of it, however. The suggestion (which has been made in very guarded language by Professor Hazeltine[2]) that the chancellors drew some ideas, at least, from the pre-existing practices of the common law courts, has been disputed. Sir William Holdsworth has maintained that the chancellor's equity was " a new, a distinct, and an independent development ".[3] In discussing this contention, Professor Adams[4] has remarked upon the different appearance of history when viewed from the different standpoints of institutions and of legal doctrine. He is surely right in urging that, in one sense at least, equity is inseparable from the duty of the king to do justice and his power to exercise discretion, and that this duty and power is at least as old as the conquest. The characteristic of our classical equity is the idea of conscience; but are we

[1] Above, p. 158.

[2] Quoted above, pp. 677–679.

[3] Holdsworth, *The Relation of the Equity administered by the Common Law Judges to the Equity administered by the Chancellor*, Yale Law Journal, xxvi. 1.

[4] Adams, *Continuity of English Equity*, Yale Law Journal, xxvi. 550–563 (and in his *Council and Courts*, 195 ff.).

entitled to say that this idea was so novel that it resulted in a complete break with the past? It is hardly likely. Such scanty material as we have, seems to show that in the early period of chancery the use of " conscience " was no more definite than it had been in the common law courts. Conscience as a juristic theory (such as St Germain propounded) is apparently a late-fifteenth-century growth; and consequently the gulf between the chancery and common law traditions was not a deliberate breach with the past, but rather the slow drifting apart of two institutions.

CHANCERY BILLS AND BILLS IN EYRE

There has been the further suggestion that the justices in eyre exercised an equitable jurisdiction when they heard bills in eyre, and that here also we have a common law origin for equity.[1]

The greatest difficulty here is to find evidence of the justices in eyre overstepping the bounds of the common law. A good many bills in eyre have survived,[2] and so far as we can judge, they neither ask for nor receive any remedy which was not available in the common law. It is moreover clear that the jurisdiction of the justices in eyre was on a par with that of the Common Pleas, and, if anything, inferior to that of the King's Bench; there is no possibility, therefore, of them using extraordinary powers.[3]

Nor must the word " bill " receive too much emphasis. Any brief document or memoranda was a bill, and the word seems to imply brevity as its principal characteristic. We have already spoken of bills in the King's Bench and other courts,[4] and bills in eyre seem to have been essentially of the same nature, that is to say, brief written statements initiating proceedings which otherwise would begin with the formal and costly original writ.[5] The bill in eyre has an especially interesting history because the reforming barons in the middle of the thirteenth century encouraged the public to make complaints (*querelae*) to the justices wherever they felt there had been oppression by local officers or magnates.[6] The complaint, as a procedure, is very old, as we have seen,[7] and a particular class of complaints formed the nucleus of the action of trespass; but this development did not exhaust the possibilities of the *querela* and

[1] Vinogradoff, introduction to E. F. Jacob, *Baronial Reform*, vi; Pollock, *Transformation of Equity*, Essays in Legal History (ed. Vinogradoff), 291.

[2] *Select Bills in Eyre* (ed. Bolland, Selden Society). Like the King's Bench (above, p. 470), the justices in eyre could deal with bills on matters arising within the county in which they happened to be sitting.

[3] Holdsworth, i. 267 (dissenting from Bolland). (But see Putnam, *Sir William Shareshull*, 131 at n. 350.)

[4] Above, p. 386; for bills in the exchequer, see Hilary Jenkinson, *Select Cases in the Exchequer of Pleas* (Selden Society), cxxviii ff.

[5] Jenkinson, *loc. cit.*, suggests that most bills were substituted for writs.

[6] Above, p. 370.

[7] Above, p. 371; Adams, *Council and Courts*, 349.

the complaints in eyre often covered matter which formal procedure would have expressed as a demand (*e.g.* debt, detinue). It is difficult to say whether the complaints heard by Hugh le Bigod were oral or written, but during the reigns of Edward I and his two successors we have written complaints still surviving, and it is clear that these were sometimes very informal documents, ill-spelt and ill-drafted, although occasionally there is one which was undoubtedly drawn by a lawyer in the strict form of a common law declaration.

It is true that the eyre expires (and bills in eyre with it) at the crucial moment in the fourteenth century when the common law courts relinquished their discretionary powers, and when the first signs of the chancellor's jurisdiction appear. But we cannot conclude that the chancellor's equity came from the eyre; first, because it is very doubtful whether the eyre really administered equity of any sort; and secondly, because the origin of the chancery bill must surely lie close at hand in those thousands of petitions or " bills " which, in the normal course of administration, passed through the hands of the council and the chancellor rather than in the practice of justices in the country, who by now were commissioned only rarely and at long intervals.[1]

THE SUB POENA AND COUNCIL PROCESS

Just as the bill or petition was originally a prayer for administrative intervention,[2] so the next step in the process, the *sub poena*, was also drawn from administrative origins. This threat of a penalty had been used by the government to stimulate the activity of officials[3] as early as 1232; even the common law courts occasionally used a *sub poena* clause; in 1302 Justice Berrewyk ordered a party to bring an infant before the court " under the pain of one hundred pounds ".[4] In the middle of the fourteenth century the Council produced an effective writ by adding the clause of *sub poena* to the somewhat older writ of *certis de causis*, which was in effect a simple summons to appear before the Council " for certain reasons ". *Quibusdam certis de causis* is at least as old as 1346,[5] and closely resembles the summons sent to a peer on the calling of a parliament.[6] The great objection which common lawyers made to writs in this form was their failure to mention the cause of the summons. It was a principle of the common law that a party should not be brought into court without

---

[1] It must be remembered that most of the business of the eyre was conducted by writ on the usual common law lines.

[2] Above, pp. 177–179.

[3] *Close Rolls* (1231–1234), 161.

[4] Y.B. 30 & 31 Edward I, 195 (Rolls Series); above, p. 187.

[5] Baldwin, *Select Cases in Council* (Selden Society), xxxviii. Professor Sayles has shown me a very striking example earlier still on Coram Rege Roll 280, m. 38 (1330).

[6] Magna Carta (1215), c. 14, required that the cause of the summons be expressed in the writ, and it generally was.

due notice of the matters which he would have to answer,[1] and there is
no doubt that the *sub poena* gave no such warning. Protests in parliament
became frequent.[2] On the other hand, it must be remembered that in
most cases the party must have known the real reason for his summons,
for litigation as a rule is preceded by private negotiations, and in any
case, having appeared, he was given ample time to prepare his defence.
The best justification, however, for the Chancery's practice, must no doubt
be sought in the fact that the common law was a warning example of the
mischief which might result if a plaintiff were compelled to state in detail
his cause of action in the originating writ, with the almost inevitable
consequence that he was unable to make any change once the writ was
issued. It was, no doubt, the deliberate policy of the Chancery to avoid
this situation, and this policy is constantly adhered to, as witness the
freedom with which Chancery pleadings could be amended.

THE FIRST PHASE OF EQUITY

So far, the early history of equity has followed very much the same
lines as the history of the common law three hundred years earlier. The
common law gradually made a place for itself, although the country was
already well provided with an ancient system of law courts; its intervention was at first political and administrative, being designed to safeguard the feudal supremacy of the Crown and even to exploit that situation; its process, the original writ, was of administrative origin, and in
its oldest form, the *praecipe quod reddat*, undoubtedly encroached upon the
sphere of already existing institutions. And so it was with equity. It
imposed itself in spite of the existence of a well-ordered common law
system: the basis of its intervention was at first the enforcement problem
of the later fourteenth and fifteenth centuries, the preservation of order
and the defence of the weak against the strong, together with the correction of the real or supposed defects of the common law; its process by
bill and *sub poena* was not in its origin judicial, but part of the administrative machinery of the Council; and there was no doubt that the
common lawyers had grounds for regarding equity as encroaching upon
their province.

---

[1] Whereupon the following tale was told by Bereford in 1312. The countess of Aumale
was summoned as defendant to proceedings in Parliament by a writ which disclosed no reasons,
and when she appeared some thirty articles were exhibited against her. She tried to abate
the writ, but two judges who were present were ready to rule it good. Hengham, C.J., made
some personal remarks (to the effect that one of those judges had hanged the receiver of stolen
goods although the thief had been acquitted, and the other had hanged a man outlawed on
civil process), and then laid down the principle that " the law willeth that none be taken by
surprise in the king's court ". " Then rose the king, who was very wise, and said, ' I care
nothing for your disputations, but by God's Blood you shall give me a good writ ere you rise
hence ' " (Y.BB. Edward II (Selden Society), xii. 44). Note, however, the odd custom of
one manor " that a party shall never be informed of what he is to answer until he comes into
court ": Y.B. 11 & 12 Edward III (Rolls Series), 328 (1337).

[2] *E.g. Rot. Parl.*, iii. 471 no. 69 (1401). Other examples are given at p. 187 above.

THE FORMATIVE PERIOD

THE IDEA OF EQUITY

During the middle ages we do not hear very much of " equity ", although chancery and council are constantly mentioned. It can hardly be said that the modern idea of equity appears at all commonly in the sources until the sixteenth century, when we find a formal theory in *Doctor and Student* upon the relation of equity to law.[1] It remains to be seen whether the legal theory expressed in that remarkable treatise was not in large part the origin of the English idea of equity, rather than a mere historical description of already existing thought.[2] In the fifteenth century, when the chancellors were regularly ecclesiastics, it may well have been that they wielded the royal prerogative through the machinery of the council in accordance with canonical ideas. This does not necessarily mean that the chancellors were deeply learned in the technicalities of canon law; it may very well mean, however, that they acted in the spirit of the canon law, which, as we have seen, was impatient of pedantry and inclined to place substance before form. In any case, the ecclesiastical chancellors were certainly not common lawyers, and it must have been a perfectly natural instinct, then as now, for a bishop, when faced by a conflict between law and morals, to decide upon lines of morality rather than technical law. As a chancellor (Cardinal Morton) said in 1489: " every law should be in accordance with the law of God; and I know well that an executor who fraudulently misapplies the goods and does not make restitution will be damned in Hell, and to remedy this

---

[1] Above, p. 279. For an excellent introduction to this work see Vinogradoff, *Reason and Conscience in Sixteenth Century Jurisprudence*, Law Quarterly Review, xxiv. 373, and Collected Papers, ii. 190.

[2] It is noteworthy that the student converses with a theologian, not a canonist; St Germain's main interest was theology and his principal source was Gerson, a theologian and not a canonist.

is in accordance with conscience, as I understand it ".[1]   By this time—the middle of the fifteenth century—the chancellors clearly pass beyond the stage of purely administrative and political intervention, and begin to meddle with highly technical matters of legal doctrine.   As they were not lawyers, they naturally summoned the common law judges into conference and called upon them to explain the state of the law on a given point.   In return, the judges got the views of an intelligent non-lawyer, and doubtless discovered that outsiders do not regard " technical reasons " as an excuse for reaching obviously wrong results.   The judges had to admit in several cases that their rules actually favoured iniquity at the expense of the righteous, and themselves advised the chancellor to give equitable relief.[2]

This voluntary acceptance of equity by the judges was all the more easy in the fifteenth century when, under the Yorkist kings, the increased power of the Crown was largely accepted by the nation voluntarily as a sort of dictatorship which alone could be effective in restoring law and order.   It was perhaps this attitude which made possible Catesby's remark in 1464 that " the law of Chancery is the common law of the land ".[3]   It will be seen that we are in the presence of a transition between an earlier type of jurisdiction which was more administrative than judicial, and based merely upon the elementary duty of governments to maintain order through administrative forms, and the more developed jurisdiction of classical equity based on the idea of conscience.   The transition from one to the other, which is especially noticeable in the early and obscure years of Henry VII's reign, was doubtless facilitated by the old canonist idea of good faith which easily became transformed into conscience and thence into a formal system of legal philosophy.

EQUITY AND LAW MERCHANT

There is another factor in this transition which deserves particular attention—the circumstance that the council and the chancellor received a good deal of mercantile business.   This had to be despatched with an eye to treaty obligations, and according to law merchant.   Now that law was regarded at this time as being " equitable " in the sense that neither forms of transactions nor technicalities of law should prevent substantial justice being done according to conscience.   Our chancellors may have heard more about conscience and equity from mercantile litigants than they did from lectures on canon law (if indeed any of them had ever received formal instruction in that system).

We have already noticed that mercantile influences were so strong in London that the city courts administered equity as well as law.[4]   If our

---

[1] Y.B. 4 Hen. VII, Hil. no. 8.

[2] Several examples are given in Holdsworth, v. 220-222.

[3] Above, p. 189.

[4] Above, p. 676.

common law courts had acquired mercantile jurisdiction in the middle ages, they too might have been driven to the same result; it is certainly significant that when Lord Mansfield finally achieved a reception of mercantile law, he had to import some equity with it. It has recently been suggested that the American colonists were more partial to borough law than to common law,[1] and if that is so, then it is clear why so many of their common law courts administered equity concurrently with the traditional system.[2]

THE BEGINNING OF FRICTION

In the fifteenth century the chancellors therefore made every endeavour to conciliate the common law courts, and we frequently find them consulting with common law judges. The same attitude persisted into the sixteenth century. Wolsey's exercise of his judicial powers aroused some antagonism, but his successor was of different temper, and we find that Sir Thomas More, when he heard complaints against the Chancery, entertained the judges at dinner:

"And after dinner when he had broken with them what complaints he had heard of his injunctions, and moreover showed them both the number and causes of every one of them in order so plainly, that upon full debating of those matters, they were all enforced to confess, that they in like case could have done no otherwise themselves, then offered he this unto them, that if the justices of every court (unto whom the reformation of rigour of the law, by reason of their office, most specially appertained) would upon reasonable considerations, by their own discretions (as they were, as he thought, in conscience bound) mitigate and reform the rigour of the law themselves, there should from thenceforth by him no more injunctions be granted. Whereupon, when they refused to condescend, then said he unto them: 'Forasmuch as yourselves, my lords, drive me to that necessity for awarding out injunctions to relieve the people's injury, you cannot hereafter any more justly blame me.' And after that he said secretly unto me [his son-in-law, William Roper], 'I perceive, son, why they like not so to do, for they see that they may by the verdict of the jury cast off all quarrels from themselves upon them, which they account their chief defence; and therefore am I compelled to abide the adventure of all such reports.'"[3]

It is very unfortunate that Roper, a lawyer, should have treated the incident so succinctly, for we would gladly know more of the reasons

[1] Goebel, *King's Law and Local Custom in Seventeenth Century New England*, 31 Columbia Law Review, xxxi. 416.

[2] Wilson, *Courts of Chancery in the American Colonies*, Select Essays, ii. 779; Fisher, *Administration of Equity through Common Law Forms in Pennsylvania*, ibid., 810; Woodruff, *Chancery n Massachusetts*, Law Quarterly Review, v. 370; Z. Chafee, introduction to Colonial Society of Massachusetts, *Collections*, xxix. pp. l–lvi. There were other reasons, too: their memories of English judicial history may have prejudiced them against equity as being part of the prerogative, and it has been suggested that they restricted the activity of common law judges in view of the oppressive conduct of several of our Restoration judges (Pound, *Spirit of the Common Law*, 51). Incidentally, the American development was soon to show that there was no basis for Bacon's view (*Aphorism 45*, quoted in Holdsworth, v. 486 n. 3) that equity and law ought always to be administered by separate courts.

[3] Roper, *Life of More* (ed. Hitchcock), 44–45; quoted in R. W. Chambers, *Thomas More*, 272–273.

why the common lawyers refused at this opportune moment to receive some equitable principles into their system. It seems that the judges in some way took shelter behind the jury, but this is certainly not the whole story, nor even the principal reason, probably, for their obduracy. However that may be, in this incident the contrast between law and equity is dramatically expressed; when the chancellor invited the judges to reform the common law by introducing into it the element of discretion and conscience, all the judges could do was to reply with a *non possumus*. More made it clear that in his view the jurisdiction of Chancery was a moral necessity based upon the duty of government to give not merely law but justice to its subjects. Although, no doubt, a character of More's idealism found this a sufficient justification for equity, the more practical minded could adduce additional reasons from the political situation. The undercurrent of grave discontent which never ceased from the Peasants' Revolt in 1381 down to the Pilgrimage of Grace in 1536 had a good deal of its origin in the inefficiency of legal enforcement and the inadequacy of the law itself,[1] so that, although an idealist such as More was ready to make conscience the philosophic basis of equity, it was at the same time, no doubt, possible for the statesmen to regard it from the ancient standpoint of the Crown as the fountain of justice, which was compelled to act in this way in consequence of the stubbornness of the common law courts. In Henry VIII's reign laymen begin to appear again as chancellors and they become the constant rule from Elizabeth's accession.[2] It is more significant that these chancellors were in many cases not merely laymen but also common lawyers, such as Thomas More (1529–1532), Nicholas Bacon (1558–1579) and Thomas Bromley (1579–1587). It is to this fact that we owe, no doubt, the cordial relations which existed during Elizabeth's reign between common law and equity.

It is in the seventeenth century that we find a conflict forced between them owing to the identification of the Chancery with the other prerogative courts and with a theory of royal absolutism.[3] The falseness of this issue is clearly shown in the fact that even the Commonwealth found it necessary to retain the Court of Chancery and to increase its efficiency by procedural reforms.

THE CONDITION OF TUDOR EQUITY

In the fifteenth and early sixteenth centuries we therefore find the development of the rules of equity determined, for the most part, by the

---

[1] They did not object to injunctions after mature deliberation in Chancery, but did protest against their issuing indiscriminately before there had been a real examination of the case; Holdsworth, iv. 39 n. 2. The standard work is Dodds, *Pilgrimage of Grace* (2 vols., 1915); a full treatment will be found in Pickthorn, *Henry VIII*, 304–371.

[2] The first lay chancellor was Sir Robert Bourchier in 1340; his immediate successors were both laymen and common lawyers (Parving 1341, Sadington, 1343). The two chief justices (Thorpe, C.P., 1371, Knyvet, K.B., 1372) succeeded one another as chancellors. The best list is in the *Handbook of British Chronology*, ed. Powicke. The last clerical chancellor was bishop John Williams (1621–1625) who succeeded Lord Bacon.

[3] Above, pp. 191–196.

procedural or substantive defects of the common law system—its slowness, its expense, its inefficiency, its technicality, its abuse by the mighty, its antiquated methods of proof (for it refused to allow parties or any interested persons to testify, and stubbornly maintained wager of law), its suspicions of volunteer witnesses, and its inability to compel one party to an action to discover evidence useful to his adversary. Among the defects of the common law which were most frequently supplied in Chancery was its inability at this date to give specific relief in actions on contract and tort, and so we find in Chancery bills to secure specific chattels, to compel a conveyance in accordance with a contract of sale, to obtain the cancellation of deeds, and for injunctions against a variety of wrongful acts, especially waste.[1] The Chancery's powers of examining parties and witnesses and of joining all interested persons enabled it to act efficiently in matters of accounting and the administration of assets. Then the complete refusal of the common law courts to consider cases of uses and trusts left a very wide field exclusively to equity. The common law relating to fraud, mistake, accident and forgery was extremely meagre, while in Chancery alone could relief be obtained against penalties.[2] In the matter of contract the common law in the fifteenth century consisted largely of the uncertain results of a tangle of procedure, but Chancery was inclined to view the matter from a somewhat different angle and had already developed the additional remedy in certain cases of decreeing specific performance. Chancery jurisdiction, therefore, was based upon the defects of the common law, and even a chancery lawyer such as Lord Bacon at the end of the sixteenth century could look upon the popularity of Chancery as a bad sign;[3] the more people resorted to equity, the more obvious it was that law was defective. Some of these defects in the common law were remedied in the course of the sixteenth century, Westminster Hall quietly adopting rules which had originated in Chancery. But this improvement in common law was accompanied by a certain degree of degeneration in equity. Chancery procedure became slower, more technical and more expensive, and ceased to be available to the poor. Some of this, no doubt, was due to a defect which equity never cured—the theory that Chancery was a one-man court, which soon came to mean that a single Chancellor was unable to keep up with the business of the court.[4] Not until 1813 do we find the appointment of a Vice-Chancellor.

[1] Examples of these are given in Barbour, *Contract in Equity* (Oxford Studies, ed. Vinogradoff).

[2] Until the statutes 8 & 9 William III, c. 11, s. 8, and 4 Anne c. 16, ss. 12, 13.

[3] See the passage quoted in Holdsworth, v. 486.

[4] From the time of Wolsey in Henry VIII's reign the Master of the Rolls acted as an auxiliary judge, without affording any appreciable relief, however. His powers were much contested until a statute settled them in 1730 (3 Geo. II, c. 30). His acts were always subject to an appeal to the Chancellor. Common law judges were frequently given temporary commissions to assist in clearing off Chancery business.

THE EXTENT OF STUART EQUITY

James I having established equity's right to exist unhampered by the attacks of the common lawyers, the question henceforward takes the more useful form of ascertaining the proper boundaries between the two jurisdictions.[1] The growth of a disposition for common law and equity to settle their respective spheres amicably, produced the natural result that equity should begin to introduce some order into the very miscellaneous mass of rules which it had developed. Bacon himself seems to have effected a great deal, and it is clear from his decisions that he made a practice of co-operating with the courts of law, took notice of precedents in his own court, and achieved some degree of consistency.[2] In the later seventeenth century the Restoration chancellors were less inclined to exercise the vague and formless equity which had prevailed a century before; the movement in favour of defining the external limits of equity as against the common law naturally inclined equity lawyers to define the content of equity by expressing its principles in clear and precise form. Consequently equity becomes at last a system, although even here the fact that equity began by supplementing the casual deficiencies of the common law left its mark, and for a long time equity looked less like a single system than several systems upon unrelated topics.

The greatest subject of equity jurisdiction is, of course, the trust and its predecessor, the use. Of these we have already spoken in discussing real property. As for mortgages, equity had begun to intervene at the very beginning of the seventeenth century, apparently on the ground of relieving against a penalty or preventing usury. Already in 1612 we find the equity of redemption[3] and a tendency to view the transaction as being designed to give security for a debt instead of construing the legal documents strictly according to their tenor. At the same time Chancery was prepared to decree foreclosure in suitable circumstances. By the end of the seventeenth century this new conception of the mortgage had become established, and a long line of cases begins, some defending it against attempts to " clog the equity ", and others settling the rights of successive mortgagees—a complication which now became possible under the new view of the mortgage. We already find early seventeenth-century cases on consolidation and tacking—subjects whose elaboration was the special mission of the eighteenth-century Chancellors. The Restoration chancellors also developed the family settlement, particularly in the direction of securing the married woman's property to her separate use, and in enforcing separation agreements and separate maintenance. The court also exercised a wide jurisdiction over infants, which it based upon the

---

[1] Above, p. 194.

[2] *Cases decided by Lord Bacon* (ed. Ritchie); see the very useful comments by Sir William Holdsworth, *Francis Bacon's Decisions*, Law Quarterly Review, xlix. 61–69.

[3] *Hanmer* v. *Lochard*, Tothill 132; Turner, *Equity of Redemption*, 26.

royal prerogative and the duty of the Crown as "*parens patriae*"; in point of fact, however, Chancery was really carrying on the principles of the common law (which gave wide protection to infants), and the practice of the Court of Wards which had been erected by Henry VIII for the control of feudal wardships.

Equity supervision over matters of account[1] by this time had grown to a considerable mercantile jurisdiction, including bankruptcy, partnership, the chartering and ownership of ships, and the relations between merchants and factors, principals and sureties, although the commercial community was not entirely satisfied, owing to the delays of Chancery procedure which were already beginning to arouse comment. Much of this power was doubtless exercised by the Chancery as successor to the mediaeval Council. In the administration of estates Chancery captured a good deal of ecclesiastical jurisdiction, and basing itself upon the rules already laid down by the common law courts it developed a very valuable body of law, which, however, was complicated in form as a result of its dual origin. Specific relief continued to be developed and the equitable treatment of contract was less dominated by the Statute of Frauds than that of the common law courts, the principle of part performance being used effectively.

When we come to the close of the seventeenth century, we see the extension of equitable relief against accident, mistake and fraud to include cases of undue influence—a matter which frequently could not be raised at common law. In the law of evidence equity maintained its advantage in having longer experience of handling oral testimony, which it treated with great freedom. We find some cases, for example, in which parole evidence was admitted to prove that the author of a document meant something different from what he had expressed, this step being justified on the ground that it was not admitted as evidence to a jury, but only as evidence to the court, " being to inform the conscience of the court who cannot be biased or prejudiced by it ".[2] From this period, too, we find the beginnings of one of equity's original contributions to the law of property. In the *Duke of Norfolk's Case* (1681) originates the modern rule against perpetuities; while by using the trust the newer forms of personal property which became prominent after the Restoration, especially stocks and shares, could be brought into settlement. "Equity treated them as property and allowed them to be assigned as property; and it can hardly be doubted that this divergence between law and equity is the reason why it is so difficult to define a chose in action."[3]

---

[1] Legal historians interested in this matter will find much interesting material collected by writers on the history of the stage; theatre owners were frequently engaged in litigation, and the literary historians have recently printed a good many Chancery proceedings involving them.

[2] Holdsworth, vi. 662; Spence, *Equity Jurisdiction*, i. 380. A civilian origin is suggested.

[3] Holdsworth, vi. 667.

EQUITY AFTER THE RESTORATION

It is in the period from the Restoration in 1660 down to the beginning of the eighteenth century that equity finally achieves its new form of a consistent and definite body of rules, and the chancellors accept the conclusion that equity has no place for a vague and formless discretion; in short, equity is now, for practical purposes, a body of law which can only be defined as the law which was administered by the chancellors. The relations of law and equity were now amicable, and even cordial. Hale once said that he regarded equity as part of the common law—a sentiment with a characteristic mediaeval cast[1]—but the growing bulk and consistency of equitable rules emphasised the difference of its point of view. The change occurs soon after the Restoration, and we can see it in watching the growth of the principle of precedent in Chancery. As we have seen, Bacon was already moving in that direction, but as late as 1670 Chief Justice Vaughan was surprised that precedents should be cited in Chancery, " for if there be equity in a case, that equity is an universal truth, and there can be no precedent in it ". To this Lord Keeper[2] Bridgman replied that " in them we may find the reasons of the equity to guide us; and, besides, the authority of those who made them is much to be regarded. . . . It would be very strange and very ill if we should distrust and set aside what has been the course for a long series of times and ages."[3] And soon afterwards Lord Nottingham declared that the conscience of the Chancellor is not his natural and private conscience but a civil and official one.[4] However, the growth of precedent was slow, for the early equity reports are far from satisfactory, and it is not until the eighteenth century is well advanced that they become continuous.

THE EARLY SOURCES

Indeed, the history of equity throughout its course, until late in the eighteenth century, is rendered difficult by reason of the peculiar state of the sources. The early activities of the council, the Star Chamber and Chancery can only be traced through the masses of petitions which still survive in the Public Record Office. There have been great losses, but those which remain are a forbidding mass of material. In many cases they are undated, and it is often uncertain which of these institutions was concerned with a particular case. Selections have been published by the

[1] Burnet, *Life of Hale*, 176, quoted in Holdsworth, vi. 547.

[2] The Great Seal was sometimes entrusted to a Lord Keeper instead of to a Chancellor; for our purposes the distinction is immaterial, the judicial powers of a Lord Keeper being the same as those of a Chancellor. It was probably economy, for a keeper's fee was less than a chancellor's, and the fear of the political power of the Chancellor which led the Crown on many occasions to confer only the less dignified title of Lord Keeper, and sometimes even to appoint only commissioners. Below, p. 697 n. 1.

[3] *Fry* v. *Porter* (1670), 1 Mod. 300, at 307.

[4] *Cook* v. *Fountain* (1672), 3 Swanst. 585, at 600.

Record Commission,[1] the Selden Society[2] and others[3] from the principal types of this material.

In the sixteenth century Chancery became much more methodical and began to register its decrees in rolls and its orders in books,[4] while a system of dockets provides a slender clue through the masses of documents; but in the meanwhile the bulk of the collections easily counterbalances these facilities, while the pleadings themselves are vast in number and verbiage. It must have required immense labour to produce such a calendar (in the form of a modern report) as Mr John Ritchie has published of Bacon's decisions.[5] It is much to be desired that similar volumes should deal with the material from the chancellorships of Cardinal Wolsey, Sir Thomas More and Sir Nicholas Bacon. On the procedural side we fortunately possess a collection of rules,[6] owing to the fact that the chancellors had more control over the details of procedure than had the judges of the common law courts.

EQUITY REPORTS

The year books of the later fifteenth century and those of Henry VII and Henry VIII occasionally give us incidental chancery cases, and so do the common law reporters of the sixteenth and seventeenth centuries, but exclusively Chancery reports begin with Tothill, whose brief notes of cases from 1559 to 1646, arranged alphabetically, were posthumously published in 1649. The following year came Cary's reports[7] based on notes taken by Lambarde, covering the period 1557–1604. Shortly afterwards came the anonymous *Choyce Cases in Chancery* (1652) covering the years 1557–1606. An anonymous volume of reports appeared in 1693, with a second part the next year, and a third in 1716; subsequent editions published the three parts together, which are commonly cited as *Reports in Chancery*. They cover the years 1625–1710. A similar collection of separate parts resulted in the *Cases in Chancery* covering 1660–1687.

The chancellorship of Lord Nottingham naturally attracted the attention of reporters, but the only early publications were *Cases tempore Finch*, and the reports of Nelson and Vernon. Some valuable material drawn from Nottingham's own notes was published a century ago as an

[1] *Calendar of Proceedings in Chancery* (3 vols., 1827–1832). The calendar deals with Elizabeth, but the introduction has material going back to Richard II.

[2] *Select Cases in Chancery, 1364–1471*, ed. Baildon (cf. *Select Cases before the King's Council, 1243–1482*, ed. Baldwin, and *Select Cases in Star Chamber, 1477–1509*, ed. Leadham); *Acta Cancellaria* (1558–1624), ed. Cecil Monro, 1847.

[3] Several local societies have dealt with Chancery and Star Chamber cases concerning particular counties, *e.g.* Somerset Record Society and the William Salt Society (Staffordshire); cf. the University of Wales: Board of Celtic Studies, for the equity side of the exchequer relating to Wales.

[4] Decree rolls begin in 1534 and order books in 1544.

[5] Above, p. 690 n. 2.

[6] *Orders of the Court of Chancery*, ed. Sanders (1845). They extend from 1388.

[7] His name is also spelt Carey, or Carew.

appendix to Swanston's reports; Nottingham's manuscripts are in the British Museum and a further selection from them has long been desired.[1] It is significant how long chancery lawyers waited before producing a sound and accurate reporter who gave enough facts and reasoning to make the study of his work really profitable. He at last appeared in Peere Williams, whose reports covering the period 1695–1736 were published in 1740 and were subsequently re-edited and annotated. That was an important period, but it was followed by the still more brilliant term of Lord Hardwicke, which Peere Williams did not live to see. The contemporary reports (Vesey, senior, and others) are only of moderate reputation, but Martin John West began the publication of Hardwicke's cases from the chancellor's own notes in 1827—the year in which Swanston's third volume did the same service for Nottingham. Unfortunately, he only covered three years.

THE LATER LITERATURE OF EQUITY

Of *Doctor and Student* we have several times spoken. In the main, the literature of equity was jejune and fragmentary. The organisation of Chancery, its clerks, their rights and privileges, the position of the master of the rolls, and little works on practice form the bulk of it, while the obscurities of its history left room for much polemical erudition. An attempt to collect materials was made in 1732 when the work generally referred to as *Equity Cases Abridged* began to appear, and in 1741 Viner began publishing his *General Abridgement of Law and Equity*. Not until the close of the eighteenth century do we find systematic works on equity, apart from its practice and pleading (on which there is a large literature). A *Treatise on Equity* by Henry Ballow (or Bellewe) had indeed been published as early as 1737, but it had little success until Fonblanque relaunched it in 1793 for a successful career. With the new century several writers exercised their skill on the subject, but none of their works equalled in renown and longevity the *Commentaries on Equity Jurisprudence* of Judge Story, which first appeared at Boston in 1836 and was re-edited many times, the last being in London as late as 1920.[2]

---

[1] Nottingham's own notes are being published by the Selden Society, and some of his treatises will appear in the Cambridge Studies in Legal History; the editor is Mr. D. E. C, Yale. Roger North, *Lives of the Norths* (Francis, Lord Guilford who succeeded Nottingham. Sir Dudley North, merchant, and Dr John North, Master of Trinity College, Cambridge) is a contemporary account from a high-Tory standpoint.

[2] The literature has now been described in Holdsworth, xii. 179–193.

THE WORK OF THE CHANCELLORS

Some reference to the early history of the office of chancellor is essential if the later development of the office is to appear in its full significance.

Originally a strictly household office, it separated much slower than the exchequer.[1] Some of the twelfth-century holders became powerful enough to withstand the King, but their power was not yet derived from the office; on the contrary, it seems that it was they who conferred dignity upon the Chancery. In the hands of a Becket or a Longchamp, the office of chancellor threatened to become a menace to the Crown, and it is not surprising that Henry II kept it vacant for eleven years. On the continent the papacy suppressed the office altogether; in France it was left vacant for generations at a time; in other realms it became attached as an *ex officio* dignity to certain sees (which at least prevented it becoming hereditary). In England it was common to give the office to clerks who had risen from the lower ranks of the civil service, but early in the thirteenth century there appears the practice of selling the office, the holder repaying himself out of the profits. Henry III stubbornly maintained the tradition tha the headship of the Chancery was a household position, to be occupied by professional administrators, and to be shorn of political significance; above all, the chancellor was the King's man, responsible to him alone.[2] His office was therefore partly the headship of an administrative department, and partly that of an informal confidential adviser of the King.

---

[1] Above, pp. 163–165.

[2] The place of the Chancery in the thirteenth century is still the subject of debate among historians; see the various interpretations by Tout, *A ministrative History*, i, and his *Edward II*, 58; Treharne, *Baronial Plan of Reform*, 14–21; Wilkinson, *Chancery under Edward III*.

ROBERT BURNELL

Edward I allowed the chancellorship to take on a new importance
with the appointment of Robert Burnell. He was the trusted personal
friend and chancellor of Edward even before he came to the throne, and
was made Chancellor of England as soon as the new King came home
from the Crusade in 1274. For eighteen years he held the Great Seal,
and for eighteen years there flowed the vast stream of reforming legislation
which extends from the Statute of Westminster the First to *Quia Emptores*.
Burnell (who soon became bishop of Bath and Wells) must have had a
large part in the preparation of these statutes, and must be regarded as
legally the most eminent of our mediaeval chancellors.[1]

THE LATER MEDIAEVAL CHANCELLORS

After Burnell's day the office of chancellor steadily increases in
importance. It was not yet a judicial office, and his successors, like
Burnell himself, took a prominent part in politics. It soon became
clear that the office of chancellor generally implied that its holder was
the King's principal adviser, and since that advice came from the head
of the chief government department the chancellors appear as a sort of
mediaeval prime minister. This duty of counselling the King involved
the chancellor, like the judges, in several political crises, one of which
we have already mentioned,[2] and as the demands of the baronial opposition to the official class become more clearly defined, they sometimes
include a demand that laymen should be appointed chancellors—possibly
with the hope that members of the baronial class would be appointed
instead of clerical civil servants. This made no difference to the general
nature of the office, which continued to be political, whether it was held
by a bishop, a knight or a common lawyer. It is only when the equitable
jurisdiction of the office made the work of it too arduous that we find
the character of the chancellorship changing. Even in modern times the
chancellors have frequently had an extremely important influence upon
politics, which is a relic of their mediaeval position; at the present day
in England the Lord Chancellor is a member of the Cabinet and comes
in and goes out with the Government. Henry VIII's reign contains two
notable examples of political chancellors. Cardinal Wolsey (1515–1529)
achieved fame as a statesman, although it is also clear that he was deeply
interested in equity jurisdiction, for it was he, perhaps, who accentuated
the separation between Chancery, Council and Star Chamber, and
insisted that Chancery was a court of conscience. Of his activities as
chancellor we know nothing save by indirect evidence, but the protests
of the common lawyers clearly indicate that he was vigorously extending
the jurisdiction of his court, and this, together with his overbearing

---

[1] Lord Campbell, *Lives of the Chancellors*, c. 10, seems the first to realise this; his estimate is
confirmed by Tout's article in the *Dictionary of National Biography*.

[2] Above, p. 240.

manner, made him enemies among them and increased his political difficulties.[1]

SIR THOMAS MORE

Sir William Holdsworth has made the attractive suggestion that the appointment of Sir Thomas More (1529–1532) to succeed Wolsey was dictated by the necessity of conciliating the common lawyers in Parliament,[2] for Sir Thomas More was himself a common lawyer and his father (still living) was a common law judge. This may have had some influence, but the King hesitated for a time between Archbishop Warham (an ex-chancellor), the Duke of Suffolk (courtier and soldier) and More. It must have been political considerations which finally prevailed. We therefore have the unusual spectacle for those days of a common lawyer becoming chancellor. More's saintly character fitted him admirably for the chancellorship at this moment, for equity was still for practical purposes very largely the conscience of the Chancellor, and Lord Nottingham's distinction, which we have already quoted, was still a century and a half in the future. Moreover, Wolsey's frequent absences had resulted in heavy arrears, and More chose the judicial side of the office as the more important. He liked judicial work better, and had long administered mingled law and equity as Under-Sheriff of London. As we have seen,[3] More made every endeavour to live at peace with the common law courts,[4] and the relations he established seem to have lasted for two generations until the days of Coke.

The succeeding chancellors were men of lesser importance. The next distinguished name is that of Sir Nicholas Bacon, who was Lord Keeper for the first twenty-one years (1558–1579) of Queen Elizabeth's reign. At Cambridge he acquired a love of learning, and in later years endowed a school and provided it with scholarships tenable at Cambridge. As a statesman he won the confidence of Queen Elizabeth; as a judge he strengthened the position of his court both against the common law courts and against the peers, establishing that the latter, like commoners, could be committed for contempt. He reorganised the establishment of the court, which was now large and complicated, and has left us the earliest surviving rules of Chancery procedure.

LORD ELLESMERE

Of his successors during the same reign the most important was Sir Thomas Egerton, successively Baron Ellesmere (1603) and Viscount

---

[1] See A. F. Pollard, *Wolsey* (1929). For Wolsey's anomalous patent for life, and the distinction between Lord Keepers and Lord Chancellors, see Pollard, *Wolsey and the Great Seal*, Bulletin of the Institute of Historical Research, vii. 85–97.

[2] Holdsworth, v. 222–223.

[3] Above, p. 687.

[4] Much new material, and a fresh evaluation of *Utopia*, will be found in R. W. Chambers, *Thomas More* (1935).

Brackley (1616) who held the Seal from 1596 to 1617.[1] Egerton was called to the bar in 1572 and enjoyed a large Chancery practice, until Queen Elizabeth (so the story goes) heard him argue in a case against the Crown and was so impressed by his ability that she determined he should never appear again against her, and so made him Solicitor-General in 1581, Master of the Rolls in 1594, and Lord Keeper in 1596; he only became Lord Chancellor in 1603 under James I. His political influence seems to have been considerable, especially with Queen Elizabeth, who had great confidence in him. As with most other prominent people, the accession of James I compelled him to take a side in those controversies which the old Queen had succeeded in repressing, and Ellesmere attached himself to the party of prerogative. In the early years of James I he was obviously trying to treat the new King as a Tudor and to enable him to carry on Elizabeth's policy. In Chancery he issued numerous orders on the procedure and organisation of the court, especially with a view to shortening pleadings and preventing delay. Rather curiously, he discouraged the taking of accounts in Chancery—which was afterwards to become a notable part of equity jurisdiction. He refused to allow the court's process to be abused, and even ordered that pauper plaintiffs who sued without cause should be whipped, since it was useless to condemn them to fines or costs. Contempt of the court's decrees was visited with imprisonment and irons, and when Richard Mylward, an equity pleader, drew a replication in a hundred and twenty pages, when sixteen would have been sufficient, Ellesmere ordered—

> " That the Warden of the Fleet shall take the said Richard Mylward . . . into his custody, and shall bring him unto Westminster Hall . . . and there and then shall cut a hole in the midst of the same engrossed replication . . . and put the said Richard's head through the same hole and so let the same replication hang about his shoulders with the written side outward; and then the same so hanging shall lead the same Richard bareheaded and barefaced round about Westminster Hall whilst the courts are sitting and shall show him at the bar of every of the three courts within the Hall."[2]

Ellesmere himself, however, was capable of delivering very lengthy opinions; in *Calvin's Case* we are told that " he argued very profoundly and was exceeding long, but read much in his book and had taken infinite pains, for he had wrote a great volume and was almost four hours in his arguments "—which judgment for long constituted his only published work.[3] Several small tracts have been attributed to him on insufficient evidence, especially certain *Observations on Coke's Reports.* The lack of adequate equity reports at this time makes it difficult to trace his activities save in those cases where emulation with Coke prompted

[1] He was at the same time Master of the Rolls from 1594 to 1603.

[2] Monro, *Acta Cancellaria*, cited in Holdsworth, v. 233.

[3] An able and very interesting essay dating from his student days has now been excellently edited by S. E. Thorne, *A Discourse upon Statutes* (1942). For his authorship of this tract, see Plucknett, *Ellesmere on Statutes*, Law Quarterly Review, lx. 242.

him to preserve his decisions. From such evidence it is clear that the principles expressed in *Doctor and Student* were regarded, at least by Ellesmere, as the foundation of the court's jurisdiction; but already he is careful to declare that equity is law and not merely discretion, and to maintain that Chancery, like the other courts, had " usages and customs " to guide its proceedings.

It was during Lord Ellesmere's tenure of the Seal that the independence of Chancery was finally asserted—for such was the outcome of the great struggle between him and Coke. With two such headstrong antagonists the quarrel soon became vigorous. Coke prohibited suitors from going into equity; Ellesmere enjoined them from pursuing common law judgments. The result was a deadlock, and James I appointed a committee which included Sir Francis Bacon, the Attorney-General, to advise him, and after due consideration decreed in favour of the Chancery. Dissension occasionally broke out between Chancery and the common law courts at various later moments during the seventeenth century, but the position of Chancery could not be seriously assailed after Ellesmere's victory.

LORD BACON

Ellesmere was succeeded in 1617 by Sir Francis Bacon, Lord Verulam (1618), Viscount St Albans (1621), commonly called Lord Bacon.[1] It is hardly possible for any one person to form an adequate estimate of Bacon's achievements, so great and so varied were they. As a man of letters, historian, statesman, lawyer, philosopher, he has many separate titles to fame. In politics in his early days under Queen Elizabeth he had held liberal opinions and had even suggested that the royal prerogative was subject to the control of law, but in her closing years he drew nearer to the court, and by the accession of James I he was recognised as a royalist. His political progress was thus exactly the reverse of Coke's. Such indeed seemed the only way to office and influence, and it may well be that Bacon had other reasons for desiring office than merely the advancement of his personal fortunes, for he had in mind vast schemes of legal and political reform—the union with Scotland, the civilisation of Ireland, the colonisation of America, the abolition of feudalism, and far-reaching measures for the improvement of the law—and at that time the only possible means of carrying them out was through the active participation of the Crown. Like many others during the early days of James I, he thought that the Tudor idea of government by Crown and Council, with Parliament registering their decisions, was still practical politics, but even Elizabeth was finding this difficult in her later years, and for James it was obviously impossible. Bacon therefore found himself

[1] He was the son of the Lord Keeper, Sir Nicholas Bacon, mentioned above, p. 697, and his mother was the sister of Lady Burleigh. A grand-daughter of Burleigh was suggested as a possible alliance for Bacon, but she eventually married his rival, Coke.

attached to a cause which was hardly worthy of him, and which in the end gave no help in the furtherance of his schemes.[1]

His early career began at Trinity College, Cambridge, Gray's Inn, and the British Embassy at Paris. In 1584 he entered Parliament and soon learned that opposing the Queen would block his prospects. His letters are full of attempts to obtain office, which in those days could hardly be got without a good deal of court influence. Bacon at first was not very successful, for his uncle, Lord Burleigh, declined to use his influence on behalf of his nephew, and it was only in 1607 that he became Solicitor-General, and in 1613 Attorney-General, and in that capacity he took a leading part in the victory which Ellesmere had just won for the Chancery. In 1617 he succeeded Ellesmere as Lord Keeper and in 1618 he received the title of Chancellor and a peerage as Baron Verulam. His life at court seems at first sight something unnatural for a man of his temperament, but he was clear-sighted enough to realise that the influence required to carry out his schemes could only be obtained by engaging himself in the welter of intrigue which surrounded James I, and so we find this matchless philosopher taking careful notes in order to train himself in the miserable business of a seventeenth-century courtier. In the midst of all this he found time to lay the foundations of modern scientific thought in a work which the learned James I likened to the peace of God because it passed all understanding (that is to say his own), and which Coke inscribed with a satirical couplet.

Lord Bacon naturally followed the extravagant mode of life fashionable among courtiers and could hardly help adopting the courtier's morality. Indeed, the only unity running through his life seems to be his genuine belief in the prerogative view of kingship and of the State. Hence state office is to him the highest of all duties, and in the pursuit of power (and therefore of wealth) he conformed to the standards of the new ruling class which dated from Henry VIII. He seems to have permitted the Earl of Buckingham to exercise undue influence in the conduct of Chancery proceedings, if not in the formation of his decisions. In the end, the common lawyers were able to bring and to sustain grave charges against the corruption of Chancery, and when one of the officials of the court was found guilty of forging court orders and dismissed, he took his revenge by accusing the chancellor himself of corruption. He was impeached on twenty-eight charges and pleaded guilty.[2] The facts alleged against him he admitted, but maintained that the presents and

[1] The standard biography is Spedding, *Letters and Life of Bacon* (7 vols., 1861–1874), who also edited his *Works* (14 vols.). A useful estimate of Bacon's character is Charles Williams, *Bacon* (1933). To read this after Chambers' *Thomas More*, will bring out the contrast between the mediaeval and the renaissance view.

[2] A later chancellor, Lord Macclesfield, was impeached under somewhat similar circumstances. On the regular practice of sending presents to chancellors, cf. Chambers, *Thomas More*, 267–270. The public long persisted in regarding chancellors not as judges, but as court officials who could only be approached in that way.

influence brought to bear upon him had never once perverted his judgment. He was removed in 1621, and died in 1626.

The tragedy of Bacon's life was that he first sought power for the noble end of carrying out his reforms, but in the endeavour to obtain that power his ideal became clouded and he employed means unworthy of the object he had in view. Worst of all—and this is a point which a clearer-sighted politician might have seen—however much power he attained in the court of James I, there was little probability of his being able to use it for the great purposes he had in mind. The foundation of the courtier's art is a sound judgment of human character, and Lord Bacon suffered two deceptions. He may perhaps have had no illusions as to the court favourites whose support he sought, but he misjudged Sir Edward Coke, underestimated the strength of the common lawyer's position, and failed to realise that Coke's bitter enmity was sufficient to frustrate his designs. Then, too, he misjudged James I. When most men soon discovered that James did not possess the greatness of the Tudor monarchs, Bacon still continued to hope that the King's influence could be used to further his ideals.

Although Lord Bacon's public life can hardly be regarded as anything but a failure, the other aspects of his work entitle him to the highest fame. Of his labours in literature and philosophy we cannot speak here, but his work as a jurist deserves careful attention. As a common lawyer he achieved great distinction, which was only the more remarkable for its contrast with his great rival, Sir Edward Coke. His *Reading on the Statute of Uses* and his *Argument* in *Chudleigh's Case* show his mastery of real property law. Contemporaries are unanimous in praising his eloquence, the masterly manner in which he grasped legal principles, and the clearness with which he presented his arguments. This broad view on legal questions he himself attributed to the results of studying Roman law, which also enabled him to estimate the value of the common law with more accuracy than Coke. His observations upon the defects of the common law are very penetrating. Among the remedies which he suggested were two digests, one of case law and one of statute law, to be followed by works of an institutional character—it is clear that he is thinking of the sort of reforms which Justinian carried out in Roman law.[1]

Very little was known of Bacon's decrees as Chancellor until Mr Ritchie published a selection[2] of them in 1932. He seems to have imitated the practice of Sir Thomas More in trying to establish better personal relations with the common law judges, and he did his part in establishing goodwill by making orders to prevent the abuse of injunctions. In all this he seems to have been successful. The policy which he outlined when he took his seat in Chancery shows that he intended to keep as far as possible important matters in his own hands; he disapproved

---

[1] His proposals are described in Holdsworth, v. 486 ff.

[2] Noticed above, p. 693.

of the growing weight given to the reports of the Masters in Chancery, and of the freedom with which orders were made on *ex parte* applications. The hundred and one orders which he issued in 1619 were the basis of Chancery practice until the nineteenth century, and constitute the one piece of codification which he was able to carry out. And finally, he had that rare merit in a chancellor of keeping level with his work.

" It may be fairly said, therefore, that Bacon left his mark upon the Court of Chancery. As attorney-general he had been largely instrumental in vindicating the independence of the court, and in thus securing the free development of equity. As Chancellor he helped to restore harmony between the Chancery and the courts of common law; and he created from the scattered orders of his predecessors a code of procedure, the formation of which was a condition precedent to the development of a system of equity. Thus he consolidated and completed the work of that school of lawyer Chancellors which had come with the chancellorship of Sir Thomas More. That the development of a system of equity did not make rapid way till after the Restoration was due wholly to political causes."[1]

LORD NOTTINGHAM

Of the chancellors who succeeded Bacon it is not easy to speak in the absence of adequate reports of their decrees; some of them achieved fame in other fields than that of the law, Lord Clarendon for example. Equity suffered an eclipse during the Commonwealth but it quickly recovered at the Restoration. The chancellors of Charles II after Lord Clarendon (1658–1667) were, first, Sir Orlando Bridgman (Lord Keeper, 1667–1672), an eminent conveyancer who is credited with having contributed to the invention of trustees to preserve contingent remainders[2] and the rule against perpetuities.[3] Bridgman's judicial work in equity was undistinguished. He was succeeded for a year by the Earl of Shaftesbury, a courtier and a wit who was prominent in the Cabal ministry, and who was made chancellor in order to deal with the *Bankers' Cases* which followed the Stop of the Exchequer; he in turn was succeeded by Sir Heneage Finch (1673–1682) who later became Lord Finch (1674) and Earl of Nottingham (1681). The Finch family had already achieved legal eminence[4] and the future Lord Nottingham, after his call to the bar by the Inner Temple in 1645, rapidly acquired a good practice under the Commonwealth. At the Restoration in 1660 he became Solicitor-General, in 1670 Attorney-General, Lord Keeper in 1673 and Chancellor in 1675, holding the Seal until his death in 1682. In politics he was a strong, but not an extreme, royalist. To immense legal learning he

[1] Holdsworth, v. 254.

[2] Holdsworth, vii. 112.

[3] The settlement involved in the *Duke of Norfolk's Case* was drawn by Sir Orlando Bridgman; Holdsworth, vii. 222 nn. 2 and 5.

[4] His cousin was the Speaker, Sir John Finch, who was held in the chair (1629), becoming later C.J., C.P., Baron Finch and Lord Keeper (1640–1641); the Lord Keeper's father, Sir Henry Finch, was the author of *Law: or a Discourse thereof*, which was almost the only students' book of the time. His father was Recorder of London, and his grandfather the Sir Moyle Finch whose case has been mentioned earlier.

added a broad general culture which served as the basis for his policy of conservative reform; as Solicitor-General he introduced the bill abolishing military tenure, and as Chancellor he drafted the Statute of Frauds.[1] In spite of his mastery of legal technicalities, he would deliberately place himself in the position of a layman in order to test the reasonableness and fairness of the decisions he was to make in the name of equity; indeed, his attitude both in law and in politics was substantially the same, namely, a determination to keep State policy and legal practice in harmony with contemporary thought and conditions.[2]

Among his decisions are some notable contributions to international law, but his greatest title to fame is his work in the development of equity. His greatest decision was in the *Duke of Norfolk's Case* (1682–1685)[3] on the rule against perpetuities. In *Cook* v. *Fountain*[4] he undertook a logical classification of trusts; in *Thornborough* v. *Baker*[5] he decided that the executor and not the heir of a mortgagee is entitled to the debt secured by the mortgage, and of this rule he said: " This has long been a controverted point and was never fully settled until my time. . . . Therefore it is not fit to look too far backwards or to give occasion for multiplying suits." He was well aware of the fact that he was establishing new principles and abrogating old ones which would make the former precedents useless. We have already mentioned his dictum that a Chancellor's conscience is politic and civil rather than internal and natural, and that therefore equity was a matter of rule and not of discretion; as he said in *Cook* v. *Fountain*, " it is infinitely better for the public that a trust, security or agreement which is wholly secret should miscarry, than that men should lose their estates by the mere fancy and imagination of a Chancellor ". Already during the seventeenth century several Chancellors had reached the Woolsack by way of the bench, and so naturally brought with them some of the ideas of the common law, and it was this influence which Lord Nottingham strengthened in making the first serious attempt to fix the doctrines of equity—a process which was not completed until the close of the next century.

" He deserves a place by the side of such Chancellors as Ellesmere and Bacon. His work was different from, and yet a continuation of, theirs. They had organised and systematised the court of Chancery, its practice, and its procedure. He began the work of organising and systematising the principles upon which the court acted; and, as a result of his work, equity began to assume its final form. His success was due partly to his own industry and genius, partly to the fact that the time was ripe for the beginning of such a settlement. The man and the opportunity happily coincided; and so, whether we look at his influence upon the principles of equity, or upon the character of equity itself, we must admit that he deserves his traditional title of the Father of Modern Equity."[6]

[1] Above, p. 55.
[2] For his writings and notes of cases, see above, pp. 693–694.
[3] Above, pp. 597–598.
[4] 3 Swanst. 585 (1672).
[5] 3 Swanst. 628 (1675).
[6] Holdsworth, vi. 547, 548.

POST-REVOLUTION CHANCELLORS

Of the successors of Lord Nottingham mention must be made of Francis North, Lord Guilford (1682–1685), during the reign of Charles II, and of Lord Somers (1692–1700), the first Chancellor after the Revolution.[1] Somers has left the reputation of a very great lawyer; his political career is best known, however, and many of his decisions are upon the important points of constitutional law arising out of the Revolution. The most important case he decided was the *Bankers' Case* (1695–1696),[2] which he treated from a sound historical point of view, his attitude being in striking contrast to the more practical judgment of Lord Holt. Nevertheless, to both of these two judges we are indebted for the decision reached by different reasoning, that a petition of right can be used to obtain damages for breach of contract against the Crown.

The reigns of Queen Anne (1702–1714) and George I (1714–1727) saw several chancellors whose names are still held in respect for their work in the formation of equity; we may mention Lord Cowper (1705–1708, 1714–1718), Lord Harcourt (1708–1714), and the Earl of Macclesfield (1718–1725), while under George II there were Lord King (1725–1733) and the short term of Lord Talbot (1733–1737).

LORD HARDWICKE

The greatest legal figure in the reign, however, was Sir Philip Yorke, first Earl of Hardwicke. He was born in 1690 and left school for an attorney's office. He then entered the Middle Temple and was called in 1715, entering Parliament in 1719 as a protégé of Lord Macclesfield. His political career was that of a Whig supporting the Revolution settlement and the House of Hanover. In 1720 he was Solicitor-General, and in 1724 Attorney-General, where his first official case was to have been the impeachment of his old friend and patron, Lord Macclesfield— a duty which he was allowed to delegate to the Solicitor-General. He was a consistent supporter in the House of Sir Robert Walpole. In 1733 he succeeded Lord Raymond as Lord Chief Justice of the King's Bench and became Baron Hardwicke. In 1737 he succeeded Lord Talbot on the Woolsack, becoming one of the most influential members of the government and interesting himself greatly in foreign politics. In 1751 he supported the reform of the calendar, and in 1753 he secured the enactment of the Marriage Act,[3] usually called Lord Hardwicke's Act. Contemporaries gave him the reputation of being a conservative and of being conspicuous even in those days for securing rich sinecures for his numerous children; as one of his enemies said: " Touch but a cobweb of Westminster Hall, and the old spider of the law is out upon you with

---

[1] From 1689 to 1693 the Great Seal was in commission.

[2] 14 S. T. 1.

[3] 26 Geo. II, c. 33.

all his younger vermin at his heels."[1] In truth his temperament seems to be fitted rather for gradual judicial reform by way of decision than for the speedier methods of the legislature. As Attorney-General in 1727 he successfully argued in *Curl's Case*[2] that an obscene libel was a misdemeanour at common law, and that the exclusive power of punishing it was not in the ecclesiastical courts. His decisions as Lord Chief Justice present no special interest, save perhaps one in 1737 which involved a clandestine marriage; this case, it seems, directed his attention to the unsatisfactory state of the law of marriage and prompted him to reform it in later years by statute. As Chancellor he had the great advantage of twenty years' uninterrupted tenure which enabled him to carry out a systematic policy.

" His restatement of the basic principles of equity, harmonising the precedents with the philosophic notions of his age, almost completed the system. After his day it was possible to advise with some confidence on the probable result of a Chancery suit. He was accustomed to ascertain what questions arose in the cases before him, and then to examine whether the principles to be drawn from the precedents afforded a solution. Often the precedents consisted merely of the record of the proceedings, with no clue as to the reasons which had led to the decree. Sometimes a report was available, and then the reasoning could be followed, though too often in those days the report was inaccurate. Where no guidance could be had from precedent, there was always the Roman law and the modern systems based on that law. The reports diligently gathered these decisions and made them accessible to practitioners. Not all Hardwicke's judgments have survived subsequent judicial examination, but it is a noteworthy fact that even now the last edition of White and Tudor's *Leading Cases in Equity* still retains ten of Lord Hardwicke's decisions to illustrate the leading principles of equity. Apart from these ten, hundreds of his judgments have become embodied in the very structure of equity and are followed every day in confident reliance upon their inherent justice."[3]

Among his decisions was one which allowed a husband to have curtesy in an equity of redemption;[4] in another he held that the compromise of a doubtful right is good consideration for an agreement[5]—the case had turned upon a family's effort to conceal the fact that one of its members was illegitimate, and Lord Hardwicke here and on other occasions held that equity was particularly interested in the protection of family honour, which indeed was a logical deduction from a century and a half of history during which equity had busied itself with composing family difficulties. In 1747 he found a way around a recording statute which at first sight looks very much like frustrating it in the name of

[1] The hostile treatment accorded him in Lord Campbell's *Lives of the Chancellors* prompted a fuller biography by his kinsman, P. C. Yorke (1913).

[2] 2 Stra. 788 (1727).

[3] Birkenhead, *Fourteen English Judges*, 158. Hardwicke's work has now been fully treated in Holdsworth, xii. 237–297.

[4] *Casborne* v. *Scarfe* (1737), 1 Atk. 603.

[5] *Stapilton* v. *Stapilton* (1739), 1 Atk. 2.

equity.[1] In 1750 we have the great case of *Penn* v. *Baltimore*[2] involving the boundaries of Pennsylvania and Maryland; as the defendant at the moment happened to be in England, Lord Hardwicke held that the Court of Chancery had jurisdiction by acting *in personam* to compel him to do equity.

LORD ELDON

Of Hardwicke's successors there were many who achieved distinction, but we must now pass to the chancellorships of John Scott, Lord Eldon (1801–1806, 1807–1827), nearly fifty years later. He was the son of a prosperous tradesman of Newcastle. He was educated at Oxford and persuaded his older brother (who afterwards was to become Lord Stowell) to take the same course. His plans were temporarily interrupted by his elopement with a banker's daughter, which at first brought him into difficulty, although upon regularising the marriage the banker made a settlement upon the couple. For a small salary he undertook to read the lectures prepared by the Vinerian Professor at Oxford,[3] and in the meantime studied law and devoted himself to an equity practice. In 1780 his opportunity came. He was given a brief to consent to an order, but perceived that his client had a case which was worth arguing. He argued it and won, and the decision was upheld on appeal by the House of Lords. There is a story that shortly afterwards he was engaged in a case where he was to argue against the point which he had thus established, to which the judge said, " Mr. Scott, I have read your argument in *Ackroyd* v. *Smithson*[4] and I defy you or any other man to answer it. Sit down, I beg you." He immediately obtained a large and important practice, and three years later he took silk and entered Parliament. At first unsuccessful, he gradually made his way in politics and tn 1788 he became Solicitor-General and had to deal with the constitutional difficulties caused by the King's malady. In 1793 the outbreak of the French Revolution caused him to promote a stringent series of statutes for the prevention of sedition, and to conduct numerous prosecutions based upon them. In 1799 he became Lord Chief Justice of the Court of Common Pleas and was raised to the peerage as Baron Eldon. Two years later he succeeded Lord Loughborough as Chancellor. Among other troubles, he had the delicate duty of composing the difficulties in the royal family, attaching himself to Caroline, Princess of Wales. In 1806 he was succeeded by Lord Erskine, but was restored in 1807 and continued to sit for another twenty years. He was now a conservative of the most uncompromising type, and during those twenty critical years the whole of his immense influence was employed

[1] *Le Neve* v. *Le Neve* (1747), 1 Amb. 436.

[2] 1 Ves. Sen. 444 (1750).

[3] It is said that he found the first of the professor's lectures somewhat embarrassing—it concerned the statutory crimes of eloping with heiresses.

[4] 1 Bro. C.C. 503.

in frustrating every possible reform. The same policy was pursued simultaneously by the Chief Justice of the King's Bench, Lord Ellenborough. Only on one or two occasions did he lend his name to reforming legislation, such as the abolition by statute[1] in 1819 of trial by battle, which had been practically obsolete for many hundreds of years—an obvious reform which most curiously was opposed by the radicals, who believed that the liberty of the subject was being thereby attacked—while in 1815 trial by jury in civil cases was introduced into Scotland.[2] In 1819 Lord Eldon actively promoted the drastic series of six acts which were calculated to repress political discussion after the Peterloo incident.

In 1820 George IV came to the throne. Lord Eldon received an earldom and abandoned his support of Caroline (whom the King refused to recognise as Queen), and had to undertake the proceedings upon a bill of pains and penalties. Political changes had brought the liberal Canning into the ministry, and when he finally became Prime Minister in 1827 Lord Eldon resigned. Although he was now seventy-six he gathered his strength for his last great fight, and lived to see the enactment of all the measures which he feared most. In 1828 the religious disabilities of Protestant non-conformists were removed;[3] in 1829 the Catholic Emancipation Act was passed,[4] and in 1832 the Great Reform Act[5] laid the foundation of modern democracy.

His work as Chancellor had great merits and great defects. His mind was particularly fitted for drawing fine distinctions and discussing subtleties and niceties, while his scrupulous character would not permit him to decide a case until he had exhausted all its possibilities and examined it from every angle. As a result his decrees, although excellent, became increasingly slow, and the accumulation of business was steadily reducing Chancery to the position which Dickens has described in *Bleak House*.[6] His legal work was to complete the process whereby equity hardened into law, and for work of this type he was admirably fitted. It was his success in this direction which enabled the Judicature Act within fifty years of his death to amalgamate law and equity, and to authorise the administration of both systems by the same court. Of the vast number of his decisions, many are leading cases of present as well as historical importance, and will be encountered by the student in his studies.

[1] 59 Geo. III, c. 46; E. A. Kendall's *Argument . . . on Trial by Battle* had three editions in 1818.

[2] 55 Geo. III, c. 42.

[3] 9 Geo. IV, c. 17.

[4] 10 Geo. IV, c. 7.

[5] 2 & 3 Will. IV, c. 45.

[6] See Sir William Holdsworth's learned and entertaining study, *Dickens as a Legal Historian* (Yale University Press).

PART 6

SUCCESSION

SUMMARY

SUCCESSION

The law of succession is an attempt to express the family in terms of property. To historians of early societies this branch of law has always been of exceptional interest and importance, for it states in precise terms the structure of the most significant of early institutions. Other branches of law shared this characteristic in earlier times: thus our own civil and criminal procedure, as we have already seen, was once largely a matter between families rather than individuals. The rise of the crown eventually withdrew these topics from family influences and placed them upon a strictly individual basis, but succession to property lay at the very heart of the problem, for families and their members derived their subsistence from land—and this statement was equally true of the king, the magnates, the country gentry, the copyholders and the villeins.

It was but natural, therefore, that property and succession should be the points at which the family sought most eagerly to preserve its stability and safety. As individuals or as members of other groups, mediaeval men filled our history with political turbulence, economic adventure and intellectual questionings. Conquests, the clash of races, and the forces of economic change are the most obvious of the factors which shaped the later history of the family. Less violent, but not less powerful, are the conflicts of ideas—the feudal view of life, the pressure of the crown, the doctrine of the Church which derived the family itself from the sacrament of marriage. In England the rival forces of local custom and common law, the conflicts of church and state, law and equity, succeeded in dividing our law of succession into fragments which have only just been reunited. The tenacity of English family law in withstanding all these assaults without making wholesale recourse to the splendid unity of the civilians' system is well worth remembering; it may even temper somewhat the harshness of Maitland's judgment:

"It is in the province of inheritance that our mediaeval law made its worst mistakes. They were natural mistakes. There was much to be said for the simple plan of giving all the land to the eldest son. There was much to be said for allowing the courts of the church to assume a jurisdiction, even an exclusive jurisdiction, in testamentary causes. We can hardly blame our ancestors for their dread of intestacy without attacking their religious beliefs. But the consequences have been evil. We rue them at the present day, and shall rue them so long as there is talk of real and personal property."[1]

[1] Pollock and Maitland, ii. 363.

CHAPTER 1

INHERITANCE

During most of the Anglo-Saxon period the law of succession must have been customary. Surviving written sources give us only occasional glimpses, and the lack of genealogical material prevents us drawing any safe conclusions from its actual results in family history. Holders of folkland can hardly have been able to modify the devolution of their property to any great extent, and even the privileged bookland owner (as we shall see in dealing with the early history of wills) had only imperfect means at his disposal when he tried to direct the future course of his fortune. In the absence of precise information, even fundamental questions can receive but conjectural answers. The most striking example is the revival from time to time of the view that the Anglo-Saxons had a family community as a land-owning entity.[1] English legal historians in general are inclined to reject this view, but the fact that it is still maintained will remind us how inconclusive the evidence is on Anglo-Saxon inheritance law.

INHERITANCE IN THE NORMAN PERIOD

Our material begins to be abundant in the Norman age, when it shows us that the family groups, if such there were, have already dissolved, leaving a true system of inheritance by individuals from individuals. The sanctity of inheritance as the great safeguard of family security is a theme which runs continually through the history of property. It would

[1] It is maintained by Lodge in *Essays in Anglo-Saxon Law* (1876); cf. Braude, *Familien-gemeinschaften der Angelsachsen* (Leipzig, 1932). Above, p. 522. The same proposition has been applied to French law of this period, but has not been substiantiated (save perhaps for Burgundy); C. Lefebvre, *Ancien Droit des successions*, i. 17.

be hard to find a more striking illustration than the charter of 1066: the Conqueror's message of reassurance to the nation was in terms which all could appreciate: " I will that every child be his father's heir."[1]

We may doubt whether that promise was kept any more faithfully than most political promises. William, like others in his position, might argue with some fairness that circumstances were changing so rapidly that the best endeavours to provide stability could only have partial success. In fact, the reorganisation of the country upon feudal lines soon produced drastic changes upon the old system of inheritance. The crown made exacting demands of forfeitures from traitors which were a most serious breach in the old idea of inheritance,[2] and mesne lords secured corresponding escheats when their tenants committed felony. " Father to the bough, son to the plough " was a rule of law in Kent, and a deep-rooted sentiment everywhere else. The principle of forfeiture was designed to weaken the power of opposition to the Crown at the expense of possibly innocent members of the rebel's family. To some extent it succeeded, but very often a traitor's lands were later restored to his family; later, adventurous politicians or turbulent gentry resorted to entails[3] or uses[4] in order to protect their families. In the end the power of parliament (either by statute or by acts of attainder) over-rode all these devices.

These losses were balanced by gains in other directions. The Conquest had settled many families which looked for their economic foundation to purely feudal holdings. As we have seen, the Crown and other lords regarded these grants as being for life only, but a long and persistent struggle ended with the recognition of the heritability of these fiefs[5]— indeed, the word fee finally became a term of art for a heritable interest in land, so thorough was the victory of the family principle over political feudalism. In other ranks of the feudal hierarchy a somewhat similar struggle was in progress, lesser tenants finally achieving the same terms against their lords as the tenants in chief had won from the king.

[1] Above, p. 13.

[2] For much interesting material on disinheritance as a punishment both in France and England, see Goebel, *Felony and Misdemeanour*, i. 248–279.

[3] The notion has been discussed above, p. 554, that a tenant in tail had only an interest for his life, together with the principle that successive tenants in tail take as heirs in turn of the donee and not of one another. This important although subtle point seems involved in the case in Dyer, 2 *b*–3 *b* which is discussed in the introduction by C. A. F. Meekings to *Surrey Feet of Fines*, pp. xxxiii ff. It is to be seen whether it finally produced the rule that a traitor's or felon's entail is forfeited for his life only, the heir in tail taking after his death. Entails were forfeited absolutely after 26 Hen. VIII, c. 13 (1534). Forfeiture defeated dower in spite of parliamentary protests (*Rot. Parl.* ii. 8 no. 13) until 1 Edw. VI, c. 2 (1547), preserved dower in all cases; but this was soon repealed as to treason by 5 & 6 Edw. VI, c. 11 (1552). Escheat for felony defeated dower: *Bracton's Note Book*, no. 1334 (1217), *Eyre Rolls* (Selden Society, vol. lix), no. 1023 (1221); so did escheat for lack of issue of a bastard, Y.BB. Edw. II (Selden Series, vol. x), 12 (1311). On the forfeiture of joint-estates, see *Rot. Parl.*, i. 76 *b*.

[4] Uses were forfeitable by 1 & 2 Philip & Mary, c. 10 (1554).

[5] Above, pp. 523–524. The assize of *mort d'ancestor* is an important landmark in the conflict between the family and feudalism.

THE HEIR IN THE TWELFTH CENTURY

These alternations of success and failure, however, were comparatively minor matters compared with the great revolution of the twelfth century which produced primogeniture and freedom of alienation. The story has already been briefly told;[1] here we are concerned with the profound change it wrought in the conception of inheritance. The heir acquired a newer significance with his new right to the whole of the land. So great a disturbance of ancient rules made free alienation a necessity, as we have seen; but free alienation in turn placed immense new powers in the hands of landowners. They secured the stability of their gifts by burdening their heirs with warranties, and these warranties were not only duties to defend the title, but also disabilities which barred the warrantor from recalling the gift.[2] The makers of deeds soon proceeded further to make their heirs liable for their debts, and if this practice had ever become permanent, the heir would have become in a large measure the representative of his ancestor.[3] To this point we shall have to return later.

THE RULES OF DESCENT

Above all, these changes induced a complete revision of the canons of descent in order to fit them into the primogenitary system. The old Anglo-Saxon rules determined the persons among whom the heritage was to be divided; the rules of Glanvill's day determined who was to become the " heir " entitled to take the whole.

These new rules, it is clear, were worked out within the general framework of the parentelic system. How old that system may have been, in England and elsewhere, is a question which has been lengthily debated, and in any case it is a question which can only be discussed by comparing several systems of old law. Its essence is to be found in the rules of descent set forth in Blackstone,[4] who wrote while the system, in its most developed form, was still in force. Those rules are of two sorts, first, to determine the group (*parentela*) in which the heir must be sought, and secondly, to identify the heir within the proper group. The choice of the *parentela* is comparatively easy. The decedent's own descendants obviously come first. If there is no heir among them, " the right resorts " (as the Year Books put it) to the descendants of the decedent's father (thus leaving us the choice between brothers, sisters, nephews, nieces and their issue); if this *parentela* provides no heir, the right resorts again to the next senior *parentela*, that is to say, the descendants

[1] Above, pp. 525–530.

[2] Above, pp. 529, 617.

[3] Above, p. 377.

[4] Blackstone, *Law of Descents* (1759); Comm. ii. 202–240. Pollock and Maitland, ii. 240–313, will place the subject in the setting of general legal history. The classical work on the subject is H. Brunner, *Das anglo-normannische Erbfolge-system*, 1869.

of the decedent's grandfather (and here we have to choose among his uncles, aunts, cousins); and so on, until an heir is found.

The choice of the heir within a given *parentela* is a more complicated matter, and was governed by principles, some of which are obvious, and others the result of obscure historical forces. Thus it is obvious that the decedent's descendants should first be called, and it is not unnatural that a living person should exclude his own descendants. Some momentous decisions seem to have been reached in quite early times. Thus the rule that males exclude females of equal degree is certainly very old—much older than primogeniture.[1] As everyone knows, the Salic law absolutely excluded females from the inheritance of ancestral land,[2] but there is no trace of so rigid a rule in England, where they were merely postponed.

ASCENDANTS

At the head of each *parentela* stands a lineal ancestor of the decedent—his father, grandfather, etc. Will they become heirs if the decedent has left no issue? The Salic law was explicit on the point: in such a case the father and mother will inherit.[3] This rule seems simple and natural, but by the time of Glanvill our law had excluded all ascendants. The *Libri Feodorum* give no reason for the rule that a fief cannot ascend,[4] and there is no visible connection between this Italian exposition and our own law, which seems to have reached the same result independently. Our rule, moreover, did not prevail in Normandy and so is almost certainly of native growth. Maitland has sought the origin of our exclusion of ascendants in the old rule, stated by Glanvill, that one cannot be lord and heir, *i.e.* a lord cannot be the heir of a tenant who has done homage to him.[5] Glanvill's discussion comes at the moment when the law was trying to make the necessary adjustments after the acceptance of the new rule of primogeniture. Families were used to the old scheme of partition among sons, and felt the need of curbing the excessive rights of the first-born with his new claim to the whole inheritance. Fathers redressed the balance by making *inter vivos* grants to younger sons (by subinfeudation), and Glanvill's rule is designed to prevent such land coming back, on the death without issue of a younger son, (*a*) to the father, or (*b*) to the eldest son. The feeling seems to have been that the eldest son has enough already, and so should not inherit from a younger brother, either directly or through his father; it would be more equitable that such a gift should go to the next youngest son rather than enrich the

[1] Pollock and Maitland, ii. 261; cf. Lefebvre, *Ancien Droit des successions*, i. 26–33.

[2] *Lex Salica*, lix. 5.

[3] *Ibid.*, lix. 1.

[4] *Libri Feodorum*, ii. 50.

[5] Pollock and Maitland, ii. 286–295; Glanvill, ed. Woodbine, vii. 1, and cases on pp. 224–225.

line of the heir to the main part of the fortune.[1] It needed but a slight
change for this maxim that a lord cannot be heir, to become a rule that
a father cannot inherit, because at this moment the father was very
generally the lord. The rule, even in England, is therefore the outcome
of feudal conditions.

Quia Emptores[2] naturally prevented the creation of such a situation in
the future, since it forbade subinfeudation, but by this time the mischief
was done.[3] Moreover, the rule only applied when the tenant had done
homage,[4] and (on the analogy of the *maritagium*[5]) lords might omit this
important formality. If they did, the result was not unlike an entail
with a reversion, and in practice the entail solved the difficulty, for the
reversioner did not inherit from the previous tenant.

COLLATERALS

In fact, the situation is not so simple. At the head of a *parentela*
there stands not only a father, but also a mother, and sometimes a choice
must be made between them. Our law naturally returned to the mother's
kin those lands which had descended from her side of the family.[6] If
the decedent was a purchaser, however, this principle gives no guidance,
and we are left with a preference for the male line.[7]

REPRESENTATION: THE *CASUS REGIS*

Suppose a decedent is survived by his second son, and also by the
son of his predeceased eldest son: which will inherit, the grandson or
the son? Under the oldest Frankish law surviving sons would exclude
the grandsons. Very slowly this rule was abandoned. In France
Childebert II legislated in 596 in favour of the grandson and the repre-

---

[1] The point is neatly illustrated in *Eyre Rolls* (Selden Society, vol. lix), no. 560 (1221).
Forms of action were a disturbing feature, however, and on a writ of error it was held that
the eldest brother would succeed in *mort d'ancestor* (although he is also lord), but the younger
brother would succeed in a writ of right: *Bracton's Note Book*, no. 564 (1231).

[2] 18 Edw. I (1290).

[3] The argument, summarised above, is put forward by Maitland with the warning that it
is largely conjecture. It is an essential part of it that the exclusion of ascendants should have
been established before *Quia Emptores*. Now Britton's express statement to the contrary
raised great difficulties which Maitland explains away with persuasive skill. For a criticism
of Brunner's application of the lord and heir rule to Normandy, see R. Besnier, *Représentation
successorale*, 111.

[4] Bracton, f. 65 *b*.

[5] Above, p. 547.

[6] But our books do not seem to employ the maxim, *paterna pa ernis, materna maternis*, which
was current on the continent.

[7] Maitland's rejection of the evidence of Glanvill, Bracton, Fleta and Britton (*History of
English Law*, ii. 301 n. 1) can now be supported by a case in Y.BB. Edward II (Selden Series),
x. 276 (1311); cf. the introduction, pp. xlii–xlv. Cf. *Clere* v. *Brook* (1573), Plowd. 442. It is
curious that, having rejected the evidence of the text-writers on this point, Maitland followed
them on the related point of the half-blood: below, p. 721 nn. 6–8; Pollock and Maitland,
ii. 304.

sentative principle,[1] and in Germany a judicial duel in the presence of Otto I in 938 established the same result.[2] The great solemnity of these solutions shows how difficult the problem was felt to be; another aspect of the matter is the long succession of wicked uncles which it is customary to mention in this connection, from Clothar in the sixth century, to King John and Richard III. The fact that these tragedies were felt to be necessary seems to indicate a growing sense that the grandchild rightfully ought to represent his deceased parent for the purposes of inheritance.

Some sort of representation is logically implied in the parentelic system as soon as an elder *parentela* is called to the succession,[3] but it was only gradually that this fact was recognised. The assize of *mort d'ancestor* was not open to a grandson who claimed that his grandfather had died seised. But if this seems to deny the principle of representation, the acceptance of the principle may be argued from the fact that *mort d'ancestor* lies for a nephew on the death of his uncle. In Glanvill's day the king's court was hesitating whether to admit the son of a predeceased elder son or the younger son of the decedent.[4] Here, as in many other cases, the voluntary dispositions of parties finally became rules of law. In England the head of a family would often persuade his lord to take the homage of his eldest son in order to make the inheritance doubly sure. If this had been done, the issue of the eldest son would represent him if he predeceased his father.[5] A similar process is observable on the continent.[6] This tendency was interrupted by the famous *casus regis*, the accession of King John in 1199. Henry II had four sons, Henry, Richard, Geoffrey and John. Henry died without issue in his father's lifetime; Richard I therefore succeeded Henry II. On the death without issue of Richard I, the claimants were Arthur (son of Geoffrey who had previously died), and John. Richard I himself seems to have finally designated John as his successor, and in any case John promptly snatched the inheritance. This incident was regarded for a time as settling the principle both in England and Normandy (where it soon earned the name of *la mauvaise coutume*).[7] Judged even from the immediate political standpoint, the rule was unfortunate; John was not a model king, and the principle actually provided Louis VIII with some sort of claim to

---

[1] MGH., Legum sect. II, *Capitularia*, i. 15.

[2] Widukind, *Res Gestae Saxonicae*, in MGH., *Scriptores*, iii. 440. Arbitration had been proposed, but the king took " the wiser course " of trial by battle.

[3] Besnier, *Représentation successorale en droit normand*, 118 ff.; later lawyers in France explained it as reposing upon a fiction, Lefebvre, i. 97.

[4] In Poitou there was the curious custom of the fief passing from the eldest son to his brothers successively for life; on the death of the youngest son, it returned to the eldest son's son: Marcel Garaud, *Le Viage ou le retour du vieux " Coustumier de Poictou*," Société des Antiquaires de l'Ouest, Bulletin (1921), 747.

[5] Glanvill, vii. 3 (ed. Woodbine), p. 104.

[6] Lefebvre, *Ancient Droit des successions*, i. 42, 95, 172, describes letters of *rappe à succession*.

[7] On the abandonment of representation in Normandy by decision in 1235, see R. Besnier, *Représentation successorale*, 122.

the English throne.[1]   The murder of Arthur in 1203 added little to John's title, for Arthur had a sister, Eleanor, who thereupon became the representative of John's elder brother Geoffrey.   After John's death, his son and successor, Henry III (1216), lived for many years with the knowledge that Eleanor's claim was senior to his, and took the precaution of keeping her in captivity until her death without issue in 1241.

From John's accession in 1199, therefore, until Eleanor's death in 1241, an English court could hardly apply the representative principle in favour of a nephew against an uncle without thereby denying the title of the reigning monarch.

What to do in such cases was more than the court would undertake to decide.   As early as 1201 a nephew who sued his uncle was told that the judgment depended on the wish of the king.[2]   As soon as a policy appears, it seems to be that which Glanvill suggested while the question was still open (although as yet uncomplicated by the *casus regis*), namely, whichever got there first, nephew or uncle, was to succeed.   Glanvill justifies this on the principle that *melior est condicio possidentis*;[3] his rule may be a distant echo of an old notion which favoured the claimant who was at the dead man's hearth when he died[4]—as late as 1304 the Year Books may speak occasionally of the *astrier*, the hearth-child.[5]   By the end of Edward I's reign this compromise is being abandoned; perhaps another royal case had now established the principle of representation when Balliol succeeded against Bruce in the great plea for the Scottish crown before the English king as overlord.[6]

THE PROBLEM OF THE DISTANT HEIR

If the parentelic system had been enforced to its logical limits there would have been nothing to prevent the succession of an heir, however distant, provided there were proof of his relationship.   In point of fact, however, the course of history does not show us a series of attempts to apply a preconceived theory of descent.   The parentelic system itself was only evolved gradually, beginning no doubt with those fairly close relationships which commonly occur in the normal family pedigree.

[1] Details in Pollock and Maitland, ii. 284 n. 4.   For other instances of uncle supplanting nephew, see J. M. Potter, *Salic Law*, English Historical Review, lii. 239 n. 1.

[2] *Select Civil Pleas* (Selden Society), no. 194; the facts in this case are exactly the same as those of John's accession.

[3] Glanvill, vii. 2 (*in fine*).

[4] A good illustration is *Eyre Rolls* (Selden Society, vol. lix), no. 232 (1221).

[5] Y.B. 32 & 33 Edward I, 264–271: here a nephew demanded against one claiming through the uncle.   There is no decision, but a later Year Book has an undated note to the effect that a descent cast on the uncle's side will extinguish the nephew's right—Y.B. 33 & 35 Edward I, 154 (possibly referring to that case).   For a slightly different sense of *astrier* see Y.BB. Edward II, xxi. 79 (1317); the footnote there is erroneous.   The *astrier* appears on several occasions in *Bracton's Note Book*: see nos. 230, 892, 951, 982, 988, 1830.   Cf. Sayles, *King's Bench*, II, clvii (1239).

[6] Pedigree and discussion in Pollock and Maitland, ii. 298.   The *mauvaise coutume* lasted longer in Normandy and caused a great deal of trouble; Besnier, 157 ff.

The old laws set limits: the Salic law apparently would not go beyond the sixth *parentela*; the neighbouring Ripuarian law stopped at the fifth; the Lombardic law admitted the seventh. We seem to have had no such rules in England,[1] but instead we had a characteristic procedural limitation. The would-be heir, if he is too distant to use the summary action of *mort d'ancestor* or the more solemn actions of *aiel, besaiel* or *cosinage*, will be put to his ultimate remedy of the writ of right. Now a demandant in a writ of right must prove (*a*) that an ancestor of his was seised, and (*b*) that he is that ancestor's heir. In other words, his count and his writ must select one *parentela* (the most ancient one of which there are still surviving members) and show that he is the best representative of that line. It would have been perfectly consistent with this style of pleading if there had been a rule that demandants could not claim on the seisin of an ancestor more than so many generations removed from the demandant. It so happened, however, that English courts were more interested in the presumed possibility of proof than in the remoteness of the heir. Our oldest date of limitation was the death of Henry I on 1 December 1135; no claim could be founded on a seisin earlier than that day.[2] That limitation was felt to be too long when it passed the century, and so a statute of 1236 fixed a new date—construed as being Henry II's coronation on 19 December 1154 (a period of over eighty years).[3] By 1275 this period had grown to a hundred and twenty years, and so a new date was fixed, the coronation of Richard I on 3 September 1189.[4] Our legislature seems to have felt that, roughly, a century was a suitable limit. As things stood in 1275, therefore, claims rooted only three or four generations back might be barred. Unfortunately, no further changes were made[5] until 1540, when it was noticed that three and a half centuries were a severe tax on the memory, with resulting peril to men's consciences; it was therefore enacted that no seisin could found a claim in a writ of right unless it was within sixty years of the date of the writ.[6] Late in the middle ages and until 1540, therefore, extremely remote claims could be made, but in England the objection to them was based upon difficulty of proof and the unsettling of respectably old titles, rather than upon any conceptions of inheritance as such.

THE HALF-BLOOD

Upon this there has been much controversy. " In all the literature which enshrines the pretended philosophy of law, there is nothing more

---

[1] Bracton, f. 67, proposes to stop at the sixth degree of ascendants, since anything further back would be out of memory.

[2] *Bracton's Note Book*, no. 280 (1228).

[3] Statute of Merton, 20 Hen. III, c. 8.

[4] Westminster I, c. 39. It was extended to crown proceedings by a writ of 1293: *Placita de Quo Waranto*, 352 *b*. Cf. above, p. 312 n. 2.

[5] In spite of several attempts: J. Conway Davies, *Baronial Opposition*, 583 (1322); *Rot. Parl.*, ii. 300 no. 16 (1369); *ibid.*, ii . 341 no. 119 (1376)

[6] 32 Henry VIII, c. 2.

curious than the pages of elaborate sophistry in which Blackstone attempts to explain and justify the exclusion of the half-blood." So wrote Sir Henry Maine.[1] Maitland also rejected Blackstone's neo-feudalism, merely mentioned Maine's " agnatic family " explanation, and noted that Maine had mis-read Norman law. In Maitland's view,[2] our rule excluding the half-blood was neither old nor particularly interesting, and its origin lay in nothing more profound than " a few precedents " reaching a " capricious " solution.

The early cases, such as those in *Bracton's Note Book*, only deal with part of the problem. For the most part they are merely concerned to show that female representatives of the whole-blood will take before males of the half-blood. Whether this means that the half-blood is totally excluded, or only postponed, is not so clear. Inone case[3] judgment was given for representatives of the whole-blood of a purchaser against the representative of the half-blood, the successful parties basing their claim, and the court its judgment, on the fact that this land had not descended from the common father of the half-brothers. This seems to hint that half-brothers might succeed one another as heirs to land coming from their common parent.

At first sight this might seem plausible, but examination will show that it is counter to common law principles, and especially to the rule *seisina facit stipitem*—in other words, successive heirs do not take because each in turn is the heir of some more or less remote ancestor, but because each is the heir of his immediate predecessor.[4] Thus either of two half-brothers may become the heir of his father, but once a half-brother has been seised a new line of descent begins. The sources of our exclusion of the half-blood seem to be twofold. In the first place, the requirement that the heir must be the heir of the person last seised (*seisina facit stipitem*) is not, on the face of it, obvious. Its origin possibly lies in the assize of *mort d'ancestor* where the demandant necessarily made himself the heir of the one last seised.[5] In a writ of right, on the other hand, the demandant made himself heir of some ancestor of his, and for some time lawyers suspected that these different methods might possibly produce different results.[6] There is no evidence that they ever did, and it seems that the

---

[1] Maine, *Ancient Law* (ed. Pollock), 16 .

[2] Pollock and Maitland, ii. 302–305.

[3] *Bracton's Note Book*, no. 44 (1219).

[4] This distinction becomes clear when the entail is considered. Every heir in tail takes because he is the heir (of the prescribed class) of the donee. Thus, under a gift to *A*. and the heirs male of his body, an elder son may be succeeded by his half-brother because the latter has become the heir male of the donee's body, although not heir of the previous tenant. This point is well made in Y.BB. Edward II (Selden Society), vi. 58 (1311). Thus the burden of a bond binding *X*. and his heirs may not descend to the same person as the lands of *X*.: see this curious point discussed in *Davy* v. *Pepys* (1573), Plowd. 441, and above, p. 552.

[5] The action *nuper obiit* shared this peculiarity with *mort d'ancestor*: Y.BB. Edward II (Selden Series), x. 285 (*c.* 1311).

[6] For an illuminating argument on this point see Y.BB. Edward II (Selden Society) xvii.215 (1315; other reports *ibid.*, xv. 74, and in the Vulgate at f. 147).

principle of *seisina facit stipitem* was soon accepted as applying to writs of right as well. The second source of the rule excluding the half-blood must be found in the new rule of primogeniture. Where equal partition prevailed it was natural to ignore the distinction between issue of different marriages, for all the issue were equally the heirs, at least of their common parent.[1] Even in England, all the daughters become parceners in their mother's inheritance although they have different fathers.[2] Had it not been for primogeniture the same might have become the rule for sons. Moreover, for a time our early rule seems to have been that parceners are " one heir ". Hence if two half-sisters are parceners and one dies without issue, the other gets the whole—not because she has inherited from her half-sister, but because there is a right of accruer between the people composing the parcenary which is itself one heir.[3]

All our cases, from 1200 onwards,[4] run on the principle that *possessio fratris facit sororem heredem*; no case has been found in which the half-blood succeeded. The rule of exclusion is therefore as old as the revolution which imposed primogeniture upon the common law.

This conclusion is very different from Maitland's view that the rule of exclusion is post-Bractonian, and still uncertain in the early fourteenth century. The causes for this divergence are instructive, for they bring us back to the problem of Bracton. It is only in the pages of Bracton,[5] *Fleta*[6] and Britton[7] that we find the inheritance of the half-blood. To maintain such a doctrine Bracton has to deny expressly the rule that *seisina facit stipitem*,[8] and Britton even allows a half-brother to inherit a stepfather's land—a proposition which the courts expressly denied.[9] Litigants joined the text writers in trying to get recognition for the half-blood. The bench sometimes spoke emphatically in favour of admitting the half-blood, and at least once the half-blood was admitted— but in spite of his brave words, Spigurnel, J., carefully based his decision on other grounds.[10] When Inge, J., said, " we do not find that the heir by the second wife should be barred either by usage or by law," Bereford, C.J., characteristically replied, " *Nom de Dieu!* you will find it in the law of England ".[11] All the cases support Bereford's claim. Where, then,

---

[1] So it was in gavelkind: *Placitorum Abbreviatio*, 279 *a* (1286).

[2] As in Y.BB. Edward II (Selden Series), x. 284 (c. 1311).

[3] At least in the opinion of Britton, ii. 73—a view very soon obsolete; cf. Y.BB. Edward II (Selden Series), ii. 153 (1318), and Y.B. 19 Edward II, f. 628 (1325).

[4] *Select Civil Pleas* (Selden Society), 1.

[5] Bracton, ff. 65–66 *b*, 279 *b*–280.

[6] *Fleta*, 371.

[7] Britton, ii. 319.

[8] Bracton, f. 65 *b*.

[9] *Bracton's Note Book*, no. 1128 (1234–1235).

[10] This remarkable case is in Y.BB. Edward II (Selden Society), x. 286 (c. 1311).

[11] Y.BB. Edward II (Selden Society), xv. 75–76. A manorial court was fined in 1234 for not appreciating this: *Bracton's Note Book*, no. 834. It was admitted that they might have been justified if they could have appealed to a local custom, but they failed to do so.

did Bracton get his notion? Not in " the law of England " assuredly;
but there is a passage in his master Azo where the half-blood is admitted,[1]
and many continental customs were taking that shape. It may be no
coincidence that Inge, too, had also been looking at foreign books.[2]

The commons petitioned in parliament for legislation in favour of
the half-blood, but in vain.[3]

THE CREATION OF HEIRS

As a result of the sanctity attaching to the idea of inheritance, there
was naturally a feeling that the system with its growing mass of rigid
rules was beyond human control. " God alone can make an heir ",
said Glanvill,[4] and earlier still in France it was said that " heirs are born,
not made by writings "—*gignuntur heredes, non scribuntur*. For all that,
attempts were constantly being made to direct the course of an inheritance.
We have seen that a father might persuade the lord to take his eldest
son's homage, and thus ensure the sucession of the grandchildren.[5] So
too the Anglo-Saxon charter sometimes professed to make an heir.[6]
In the Norman period tenants of church estates occasionally talk of
instituting heirs[7] and still later examples sometimes turn up.[8] With the
firm refusal of the king's court to hear anything resembling a devise of
land, it therefore followed logically that the institution of heirs, calls to
succession, adoption[9] and the like devices must also fail. The one
possible method was the entail, and this was confined as yet within a very
narrow pattern of possible dispositions, and above all, it was irrevocable.
It is not surprising that landowners turned to the use, precarious as it
was, in order to obtain testamentary powers over their land.

THE POSITION OF THE HEIR

If a stranger " abates " or " intrudes " upon land whose owner has
just died seised, he has committed no disseisin. The lawful heir cannot

---

[1] Azo, *Summa*, col. 721, § 6 (the passage is not in Maitland's *Bracton and Azo*).

[2] The point of Bereford's outburst was an earlier remark by Inge in the same case, to
the effect that *possessio fratris* was " an imperial law on which the law of the land is founded ".

[3] *Rot. Parl.*, ii. 314 no. 42 (1372).

[4] Glanvill, vii. 1.

[5] Above, p. 717. In 1221 a father did the like for his second son: *Eyre Rolls* (Selden
Society, vol. lix), no. 232.

[6] Pollock and Maitland, ii. 254.

[7] *Ibid.*, 328. Cf. F. M. Stenton, *English Feudalism*, 51–53, 262, for a man who made his
brother his heir, to the exclusion of his own son; other examples are *Registrum Antiquissimum*
(ed. C. W. Foster and K. Major, Lincoln Record Society), iv. no. 1299, iv. no. 1439.

[8] An endowment *ex assensu patris* could be expressed in 1200 as the father constituting his
son heir: *Se ect Civil Pleas* (Selden Society), no. 65. There is an original deed, *temp*. Edward I,
in the Harvard Law Library (Ms. Doc. o. 014), purporting to constitute an heir.

[9] For a " son by purchase " (apparently a bastard acknowledged and adopted by his father),
see *Eyre Rolls* (Selden Society, vol. lix), no. 187 (1221); he did not contest the claim of the
legitimate heiress.

say that he was disseised unless he had in fact been previously seised. In other words, the heir does not inherit his ancestor's seisin.[1] Like everyone else, an heir cannot acquire the privileges of seisin unless he enters, stays in, and conducts himself like the peaceful holder of a free tenement. Until then he has, for a short time, a right of entry and thenceforward only a right of action in which he must prove the seisin of the decedent and his own " right " descending to him from the person last seised. While seisin was still of this simple character—we might almost say, a state of facts rather than a legal abstraction—it was quite impossible to speak of seisin being hereditary. Some steps in that direction were taken, however. We never went so far as those French and German custumals which held that *le mort saisit le vif*,[2] *der Todte erbt den Lebendigen*. The common law solution began by recognising that an heir might obtain a legally recognised seisin somewhat easily; merely to place his foot upon his inheritance sufficed in 1305.[3] By Littleton's day this doctrine has expanded considerably. The conception of an " estate " in land enabled theorists to say that an heir, even though he has not entered, nevertheless has a " freehold in law which is cast upon him by force of the descent ", of which he is seised in law (Littleton even goes so far as to say that if he dies without entering, his widow is still dowable).[4] The common law had therefore travelled far from the early physical conception of seisin and was conferring upon an absent heir a seisin as rarefied and artificial as that seisin which was later the creature of the statute of uses.

The rights of an heir to land were thus gradually being intensified. On the other hand, the heir was soon relieved of his liability (apart from specialty) for the decedent's debts, and the final recognition under Edward I of the representative character of executors completed the process. The age of Glanvill and Bracton felt Romanist influences sufficiently to play with the idea that our feudal heir might be turned into a true representative of the decedent. The temporary success of this movement was possibly won at the expense of the Church, and it was certainly to the Church that the ground was finally lost.[5] By the reign of Henry VIII it had to be explained that in England *haeres* is called executor—a doctrine long familiar to mediaeval canonists and civilians.[6]

---

[1] See the discussions in Pollock and Maitland, ii. 59–60, and Joüon des Longrais, *La Saisine*, 71 n. 2. Trespass (which followed the law of novel disseisin very closely) was similarly inadequate for the protection of chattels before the executors had obtained actual possession of them: J. Conway Davies, *Baronial Opposition*, 583 (1322).

[2] The maxim *Le roi est mort: vive le roi* is the constitutional aspect of the same principle. The history of *le mort saisit le vif* is discussed in detail by Lefebvre, *L'Ancien Droit des successions*, ii. 281–304.

[3] Y.B. 33 & 35 Edward I, 54.

[4] Littleton, *Tenures*, sec. 448.

[5] Above, p. 377.

[6] St Germain, *Doctor and Student*, i. 19; cf. Holdsworth, iii. 537, 563 n. 1.

THE HEIR IN THE NINETEENTH CENTURY

Confined within the limits of real property law, the position of the heir became an historical curiosity.[1] The heavy feudal burdens on heirship incited conveyancers to find means of disguising heirs under the form of purchasers,[2] and the combined effects of this and of the devisability of land since 1540 deprived the more recondite portions of the law of inheritance of much of their practical importance. Consequently Blackstone's chapter on descent is purely mediaeval in substance, and there was little legislation to consider until the nineteenth century. In 1833 the Inheritance Act made important changes, although retaining the fundamental conception of an heir at common law. The ancient principle of *seisina facit stipitem* was abolished, and instead of it the last purchaser became the root of descent; ascendants and the half-blood were admitted.[3]

More serious were the changes which slowly began to undermine the whole mediaeval conception of inheritance. The strong contrast between an heir and a personal representative had been maintained ever since its establishment early in the fourteenth century. The rule stated by *Fleta*[4] that an heir was not liable for the decedent's debts unless specially bound by deed, still represented the law with fair accuracy[5] until 1833. In that year the land of a decedent was made assets for the payment of debts of all descriptions.[6] At long last, therefore, land came to be treated as merely one form of wealth among many, which were to be equally available for the discharge of the decedent's debts. By the time this had become familiar, the heir's position began to look anomalous, as well as causing inconvenience. Although shorn of his mediaeval prerogatives, he still inherited the land, subject to the equitable rights accorded to creditors by statute. By 1897 it was felt simpler to abolish the mysterious process of inheritance, and by statute land was made to devolve upon the decedent's personal representatives as trustees for the heir.[7] This greatly facilitated the payment of debts, and possibly for the first time in our history gave us a single representative for all purposes. Having reached that stage, it was only logical to extend the scheme for the distribution of chattels to land also,[8] and with it to extinguish the most ancient institution of English private law.

[1] Cf. Maitland's brilliant invective of 1879 reprinted in Collected Papers, i. 162–201.

[2] They begin as early as 1267, statute of Marlborough, c. 6. Thus, " he cannot purchase his own heritage "—Berewyke, J., in Y.B. 20 & 21 Edward I (Rolls Series), 266 (1292); but contrast *ibid.*, 212, and Y.B. 21 & 22 Edward I (Rolls Series), 446 (1294).

[3] 3 & 4 William IV, c. 106; the relation of this act to the older law is set out in Challis (ed. Sweet), 237–250.

[4] *Fleta*, ii. 62, 10; above, p. 377.

[5] Creditors of a deceased trader could reach his land by Chancery proceedings against his heir, under 47 Geo. III, session 2, c. 74 (1807).

[6] 3 & 4 William IV, c. 104.

[7] Land Transfer Act, 1897, 60 & 61 Vict. ,c. 65.

[8] Administration of Estates Act, 1925.

CHAPTER 2

INTESTACY

As we have seen, our mediaeval law expected that the devolution of land would be left to follow the course laid down for it in the common law. Deep suspicion was felt of those attempts to direct the destination of decedents' land which nevertheless were made from time to time. Against the devise of real property the law steadily maintained an intransigeant attitude for centuries. The precisely opposite policy came to be applied to personalty. Chattels not only could, but ought to be disposed of by will; intestacy came to be regarded as a sin, and very nearly a crime. Moreover, the elaborate and precise rules governing the inheritance of land have no counterpart in the succession to chattels. Instead, we find vague customs, and an equally vague discretion exercisable, in the later period, by ecclesiastical officers.

THE SEPARATION OF LAND AND CHATTELS

Most striking of all is the fact that a decedent's estate will not devolve as a whole. Even his lands may take divergent paths as a result of tenures, customs and the state of the family tree—Maitland constructed a case where a decedent's land might go twelve different ways.[1] If such things were possible of land, we need not expect succession to chattels to bear any relation to the law of inheritance.

It is customary to say that the differing successions to land and chattels are the result of the church's jurisdiction over the latter. The perpetuation of these differences was evidently caused by the common law's recognition that the succession to chattels was an ecclesiastical matter, but the cause of the original divergence must be sought further back. For example, it is obvious that the acceptance of primogeniture as the common law scheme for land would make it quite impossible to send the chattels along with the land; but much earlier even than primogeniture, there is a strong tendency in the Germanic laws to separate land from chattels—this is already visible in the Salic law, which has a

---

[1] Pollock and Maitland, ii. 256.

725

different scheme of devolution for each. It must be remembered that the unification of succession in modern systems of law is due to the economic fact, increasingly clear since the eighteenth century, that modern conditions require that all forms of wealth should be equally available for economic activities; that necessity did not exist in the middle ages save in the case of a small and very distinctive class of merchants. Nor was there the religious factor of hereditary cults, which produced the universal succession of Roman law.

THE EFFECT OF INTESTACY

Our earliest sources give only slight hints of what happened to the goods of a decedent, but the general impression is that there was a customary scheme for their distribution. Thus at the opening of the seventh century, we are told, in the earliest of our Anglo-Saxon laws, that if a woman bears a living child she shall have half her husband's goods if he dies first,[1] and that there was already a " child's share ".[2] About a century later we hear of the wife's share of the household goods,[3] and in the tenth century the wife, even of a thief, was guaranteed her third if she were not an accomplice.[4] All this seems to indicate a customary mode of distribution. When we come to Canute there is a marked change. We hear for the first time of " intestacy " (although nothing about wills), and, also for the first time, of lords' claims based upon it. The law of Canute seems to be maintaining an old order against innovation:[5]

> " If a man departs this life intestate, whether through negligence or through sudden death, his lord shall take no more from his property than his legal heriot;[6] but according to his direction the property shall be very strictly divided among his wife and children and near kinsmen, each according to the share that belongs to him."

The passage comes early in a long list of abuses which the king denounced, and seems to be in substance a compromise.[7] The lord's claim to intestates' goods is rejected, but his right to direct the administration of them is admitted. The traditional scheme of distribution, moreover, extends to kinsmen as well as to wife and children.

INTESTACY AFTER THE CONQUEST

The reign of the Conqueror did not produce any immediate change. His charter to London at once proclaimed his policy of maintaining the old order of inheritance,[8] and the compiler of the " Laws of William "

[1] Aethelbert, 78.
[2] *Ibid.*, 80.
[3] Ine, 57.
[4] VI Aethelstan, 1, § 1.
[5] II Canute, 70.
[6] For the heriot, see Pollock and Maitland, i. 312.
[7] For the effect of William the Conqueror's charter on this, see above, p. 13 n. 5.
[8] Above, pp. 13, 713.

attributes to him the rule that " if a man dies without a will, his children shall divide the heritage equally between them ".[1] It will be noticed that there is no mention of the lord here, nor is there in Henry I's coronation charter which promises that the chattels (*pecunia*) of a suddenly deceased tenant in chief shall remain where he has " given " them, and that if he has not disposed of them, then " his wife, or children, or kinsmen, or his lawful men shall divide them as seems to them fittest for the good of his soul ".[2] This very interesting text seems to show that the king resigns any claim to receive or control the distribution of his tenants' goods, and seems to imply that lords in general have no such claim either, at least in cases where sudden death provided a reasonable excuse for intestacy. Indeed, it is the decedent's tenants who are mentioned in this connection, not his lord. Like all our earlier texts, it presupposes a scheme of distributing between wife, children and near kinsmen, but adds a new element when it says that the motive is the good of the decedent's soul. This brings us to the crucial, and difficult, question of the church's attitude towards intestacy.

THE CHURCH AND INTESTACY

In the twelfth and thirteenth centuries, especially in the age of Glanvill and Bracton, a number of different, but closely related views come into prominence connecting the church with the law of succession to chattels. The church was naturally concerned with those of her clergy who had accumulated fortunes—presumably out of the profits of their benefices. Such a fortune was itself unseemly, and, in addition, clergy were not burdened with dependants. It was therefore expected that clergy would make wills disposing of the bulk of their chattels to charitable and pious purposes. Further, the expression of some charitable intentions was naturally associated with the dying Christian's last confession. So close was this association that to die intestate raised a strong presumption that the decedent had refused the ministrations of the church and had in fact died " desperate ". Illustrations of the point of view are common,[3] and its results were serious: intestacy became a very grave sin, and there were some to say that it was also a crime.

COMPETITION FOR FORFEITURES

The result was a spectacle quite common in the middle ages. The king, feudal lords, civic communes, the bishops, and the popes entered

---

[1] Leis Willelme, 34. It is pointed out in Pollock and Maitland, i. 103 n., that this passage is in Romanesque company, and that " unless *enfans* means ' sons ', can hardly be English or Norman law ". This seems questionable. A " heritage " which the decedent omitted to " divide " is more likely to be land than chattels at this date, and so its distribution to " children " is perfectly consonant with the earlier laws already cited.

[2] Henry I, Coronation Charter, c. 7. Cf. Stephen's Second Charter, c. 4 (1136), on wills of the clergy, and on their intestacies.

[3] Examples will be found in Pollock and Maitland, ii. 357.

into competition for the possible forfeitures resulting from intestacy.[1]
Glanvill puts the matter succinctly: " when anyone dies intestate, all his
chattels are deemed to be his lord's ".[2] By 1215 this had to be modified;
the barons prayed that an intestate's goods should be distributed by his
kin and friends under the supervision of the church,[3] and their prayer
was granted in the Great Charter.[4] We may guess that this represented
the barons' rather than the church's wishes, and that their mention of the
church was merely politic; we must also conclude that by this time the
crown had been claiming forfeitures on intestacy as a general principle
in order to explain the presence of this clause; but in any case the later
charters omit this clause, no doubt in order not to diminish the patrimony
of an infant king. The royal claim was therefore restored and undoubtedly enforced. Bracton, like Glanvill, however, still speaks of the
claim of lords rather than of the king, and explains that it is unfair to
treat sudden death intestate as a crime to be punished—in such a case
the church and his friends should distribute his goods.[5]

It seems that a distinction ought to be made between the intestacies
of feudal tenants (in which case the lord was entitled, as Glanvill and
Bracton assert) and the special case of the burgess. The bulk of a
wealthy burgess's fortune might often be in chattels, and so a forfeiture
would be well worth having. It is in the towns that we first hear of
claims by the crown, and it is in the towns that competition for forfeitures
was keenest. As early as Domesday Book (1086) the king had intestates'
goods in Hereford and the surviving charters[6] and custumals[7] suggest
that exemption from this due was highly valued. The clause in the
Great Charter mentioned above may well have been the result of an
attempt to extend this royal claim outside boroughs to the public at large.[8]

Meanwhile, the papacy entered into competition with both lords and
king. Innocent IV laid a claim to the goods of all intestate clergy as a
forfeiture in 1246, but soon withdrew the claim;[9] a generation later,
Edward I (who was not the man to admit an adverse right if it could
be helped) petitioned Martin IV for a grant of all intestates' goods to

---

[1] Other examples of this sort of competition are treason (the king had to compromise
with the lords, above, p. 443); felony (lords got the land, and the king the chattels, holding
them free of any liability for the felon's debts—Baldwin, in *English Government at Work* (ed.
J. F. Willard), 136 n. 2; usury (the king got the chattels—Glanvill, vii. 16); and heresy
(inconclusive contest of king and pope—cf. Plucknett, *Case of the Miscreant Cardinal*,
American Historical Review, xxx. 1). See also Gaston Baril, *Droit de l'évêque aux meubles des
intestats en Normandie*, Caen, 1911.

[2] Glanvill, vii. 16.

[3] Articles of the Barons, c. 16.

[4] Magna Carta (1215), c. 27.

[5] Bracton, f. 60 *b*.

[6] Ballard, *Borough Charters*, 75–76; Ballard and Tait, *Borough Charters*, 95.

[7] Collected in Bateson, *Borough Customs* (Selden Society), ii. 75–78, 200–201.

[8] Henry I's charter only concerned tenants in chief; hence the claim he resigned was feudal
rather than royal. The crown was also the feudal lord of many (though not all) boroughs.

[9] Matthew Paris, *Chronica Majora* (R.S.), iv. 552, 604; above, p. 727 n. 2.

meet the expenses of his proposed crusade, and was refused.[1] These extreme papal claims were not long maintained, and it soon became clear that the suppressed clause of the Great Charter of 1215 was the most that could reasonably be expected by the church.

THE CHURCH AND ADMINISTRATION

The one permanent factor was the recognition that the church could supervise the distribution of intestates' chattels. This was done by the ordinary (normally the bishop), who at first seems to have acted personally, and it was the bishop whom our earliest legislation touched. Henry II had prohibited John of Belmeis, bishop of Poitiers, from distributing the goods of intestates in 1163.[2] Edward I, however, enacted in 1285 that whereas the goods of an intestate come to the ordinary, he must answer for the decedent's debts up to the limit of the estate, in the same way as executors would.[3] As we have seen, however, Magna Carta had contemplated an administration by the deceased's family and friends which was merely supervised by the church, and this soon became the common practice; by a statute of 1357 the ordinary is required to appoint administrators, and they (as his deputies) were made capable of suing and being sued in the king's courts as if they were executors.[4] Henceforth the position of administrators was assimilated to that of executors as far as possible. A statute of Henry VIII required the ordinary to commit the administration to the widow or the next-of-kin, or both[5]—an interesting variant from the act of 1357, which only mentioned the " next and most lawful friends ".

ADMINISTRATION, CUSTOMARY AND STATUTORY

The laws of Canute, the *Leis Willelme*, the charter of Henry I, all bear witness to the existence of customary modes of distribution. For a time this mass of custom was seriously threatened by the claims of various authorities to forfeitures, but slowly, and by stages which seem never to have been traced in detail, those claims were abandoned. An early exception was doubtless made in cases of sudden death; then, as early as the Great Charter of 1215 it was recognised that intestacy ought not to prejudice the deceased's creditors; the " pious uses " to which the whole estate was to be devoted may well have been construed as including provision for the deceased's dependants. An old and very common scheme gave a third each to the widow, the children, and the " dead man's part "—this last being available for the provision of religious

[1] *Calendar of Papal Letters*, i. 474.

[2] *Materials for the history of Thomas Becket* (Rolls Series), v. 38.

[3] Westminster II, c. 19. An attempt to base upon this act a claim against the ordinary's executors apparently failed in (?) 1337: Y.B. 11 & 12 Edward III, 142.

[4] 31 Edw. III, st. 1, c. 11.

[5] 21 Hen. VIII, c. 5 (1529).

offices, distributions to the poor, and, it would seem, the relief of poor relations. The earliest surviving example of letters of administration[1] is dated 1313 and gives a valuable glimpse of the state of law and practice before the statute of 1357: by these letters the widow and others are made administrators, they are to make an inventory, pay debts, carry out the tripartite division " according to the custom of the realm ", apply the dead man's part to pious uses at their discretion, act as curators and guardians of the bairns' part until they are of age, defend actions and indemnify the bishop if he is impleaded by creditors of the estate, and account to the bishop or his commissaries. Already, then, the administrators were in effect deputies of the bishop, who was doubtless glad to transfer to them the laborious details of the work. The form shows the effect of the statute of 1285, for it is the bishop and not the administrators who is legally liable for the debts of the deceased. That statute made no provision, however, for recovering debts due to the estate, and the form of the letters is likewise silent. The matter was obscure. In 1343 the Commons prayed that administrators should have the same actions as the decedent, to which the king replied that he was willing for the ordinary to have the action.[2] No formal legislation followed until the statute of 1357 equated administrators with executors.

The position after 1357 was for a time satisfactory. The goods of an intestate passed on his death to the ordinary, and by the statute the ordinary had to appoint administrators who thereby acquired the goods and the right of suing and being sued, their conduct in other respects being subject to the supervision of the ordinary. With the deterioration of the church courts there was bound to arise a good deal of difficulty, and from the late fifteenth century onwards the common law courts pursued a reckless policy of impeding the ordinary's control over administrators. Creditors of an intestate estate continued to enjoy their statutory rights, but distributees had no remedy save through the ordinary, and in the seventeenth century the common law courts succeeded in rendering him powerless. As a result, once the debts were paid the administrator appropriated all that remained.

This appalling state of affairs lasted from early in Elizabeth's reign until the Restoration. A particularly scandalous case in 1666 brought matters to a head; Bridgman, C.J., alone of all the judges was in favour of compelling the administrator to distribute, and Charles II personally urged him to secure a reform in the law. Legislation was prepared, and after some parliamentary adventures,[3] finally became the Statute of Distributions, 1670.[4]

---

[1] Text in *Registrum Palatinum Dunelmense* (ed. Hardy, Rolls Series), i. 369; Pollock and Maitland, ii. 362.

[2] *Rot. Parl.*, ii. 142 (49).

[3] For the state of the law before the statute, and its parliamentary history, see Holdsworth, iii. 556–563.

[4] 22 & 23 Charles II, c. 10.

The act grew out of a resolve to reassert and strengthen the jurisdiction of the ordinary to compel administrators to distribute. This object was not attained, for the common law courts continued to obstruct the ecclesiastical courts, without themselves offering any alternative remedy. In fact, since the beginning of the seventeenth century it was becoming clear that the only hope lay in chancery, where the equitable views of accountability and trusteeship were being applied to executors and administrators. In the course of its passage through parliament, however, a clause was added to the statute which prescribed a scheme of distribution, and this clause was to serve for over two centuries to come. In two respects it seems to have abolished very old rules—first, by allowing the heir at law to be also a distributee, and second, by allowing a deceased child to be represented by its descendants. The ancient dead man's part disappeared finally, and so the scheme gave one-third to the widow and two-thirds to the children. If there were no children then the widow took one-half, and the other half went to the next of kin; if there were no widow, the children took the whole; if there were neither widow nor children, then all went to the next of kin.

In order to maintain equality among the children, the statute incorporated the ancient principle of hotch-pot which formed part of the mediaeval custom of London.[1] The determination of the " next of kin " is only partly settled by the statute; the canonists' version of the gradualistic mode was continued by the statute,[2] and a number of cases and a few slight amendments were needed. The most important were cases admitting half-brothers[3] and half-sisters,[4] and a statute[5] allowing the intestate's mother to share with his brothers and sisters.

---

[1] See Co. Lit. 176–177.

[2] Jekyll, M.R., chose to regard the statute as the work of a civilian: W. H. D. Winder, *Sir Joseph Jekyll*, Law Quarterly Review, lvii. 535.

[3] *Smith* v. *Tracy* (1677), 1 Mod. 209; 2 Mod. 204.

[4] *Brown* v. *Farndell* (1689), Carth. 51.

[5] 1 James II, c. 17 (1685).

WILLS

The history of the will as an institution of English law is a long and very complicated story.[1] A number of different expedients were used at different dates by persons who wished to direct the future enjoyment of their property after their own day: some of them left marks which long survived on the law of wills. It was only very slowly that the characteristic features of the modern will came to be combined in a single document, and those features were difficult to reconcile with the traditional modes of legal thought—indeed, the very nature and purpose of a will were inconsistent with the traditional reverence for the mystery of inheritance, and a will could hardly be carried into effect without defeating the legitimate hopes, perhaps even the legal rights, of the testator's family. It is not surprising, then, that the history of wills seems tortuous. It might have been much more so, had it not been for the example of Roman law. In Italy and southern France the history of the will was continuous from Roman times, although of course influenced by intervening social and legal changes. In England no such continuity existed. Instead, the English development took place in an atmosphere slowly but increasingly charged with Romanist ideas, which only became dominant, however, when most of the law of wills came under the jurisdiction of the church's courts.

[1] The earlier period is briefly dealt with in Pollock and Maitland, ii. 314–341, and Hazeltine, introduction to D. Whitelock, *Anglo-Saxon Wills*. Valuable continental material is to be found in R. Caillemer, *Exécution testamen aire*.

ANGLO-SAXON WILLS

The Anglo-Saxon charter was normally in Latin, often quite florid Latin; the wills, on the other hand, are almost all in the vernacular, and it has been argued that the few examples which survive in Latin are not originals but translations.[1]   Naturally, a vernacular document was less formal than the artificial Latin charter.   There is little trace of the elaborate " diplomatic " style which to experts reveals so much of the date, provenance and authenticity of the *landboc*.   In fact there is much to indicate that the documents before us were in theory as well as practice merely memoranda of what the author said.   They often relate that the author *cwaeth his cwide*—says his say, and these words still survived into middle English as " quoth ", and into modern English as " bequeath " and " bequest ".   This oral element at once distinguishes the Anglo-Saxon will from the charter which is of necessity a *boc*, a " book " or writing.   The structure of the Anglo-Saxon will is therefore variable. Sometimes it is in narrative form relating that " this is the *quide* that Aelfric bequoth ere he fared over sea . . ." the substance following in the first person.   Sometimes the whole document may be in the third person; frequently it is in the form of an address, and sometimes reads almost like a letter.

THE OPERATION OF ANGLO-SAXON WILLS

So informal and untechnical are these documents that it is impossible to draw any certain conclusions as to their mode of operation.   Frequently they merely say, " I give " this and that—without further qualification, although it is clear that the donor is not in fact immediately divesting himself of his property.   Often a donor will use the expression " I give after my death . . ."; and sometimes he explains that he reserves the gift to himself for his lifetime.   Occasionally he undertakes to pay a nominal rent to the grantee in order to make the situation perfectly clear.

Some of the wills contain language which suggests contractual notions, and so assume a promissory character,[2] while others (as we have just seen) take the form of a gift becoming effective only at death.   Others resemble more a settlement effected *inter vivos*.   Occasionally the document which has come down to us claims to be not merely the saying of the donor, but his last saying—and so we must include the *novissima verba* as well as the gift *post obitum*, the settlement, and the promise, among the elements comprising the Anglo-Saxon testamentary devices.   To inquire how such varied documents operated would lead us into a region of great obscurity, and lively controversy.

Testators themselves were somewhat apprehensive.   They invoke the good offices of a lord or of the king with earnest prayers that the

---

[1] Most of them are edited and translated by D. Whitelock, *Anglo-Saxon Wills*, to which Professor Hazeltine has prefixed a valuable introduction.

[2] Hazeltine, *loc. cit.*, stresses this aspect.

will may be carried out, and conclude with hearty curses against all
who obstruct its operation. Not infrequently a testator asks some
great man to be his *Mund* or protector; sometimes this may be merely
the guardian of his child, but at other times it clearly implies the duty of
carrying out the provisions of the will. Language of that sort seems to
indicate that the testator's wishes are to be carried out by his friends
after his death: on the other hand, there are documents which imply
that the beneficiaries acquire their rights immediately. This latter type
would necessarily be irrevocable, and it seems that the majority of
Anglo-Saxon wills were irrevocable whatever their form. Alfred indeed
burnt his earlier wills—but he was a king; occasionally a subject expressly
reserves the right to vary his will. We must likewise assume that the
Anglo-Saxon will was not in its nature ambulatory, and it is very rarely
that a testator attempts to make it so.[1]

In one respect, the Anglo-Saxon will must be placed beside the
Anglo-Saxon charter: both were privileges, outside and above the
ordinary law. Both enabled the grantor to dispose of his property to an
extent which was not permitted under ordinary circumstances. Both,
apparently, depended in the end for their efficacy upon the king's co-
operation.

THE ANGLO-SAXON ACHIEVEMENT

Many problems will be raised if we try to assess the Anglo-Saxon
achievement in the development of a law of wills. According to the
well-known dictum of Tacitus, the testament was unknown to the
Germans, and that may be equally true of the Germanic tribes in general.
It is thus highly probable that the Anglo-Saxon wills were an innovation
derived from abroad, and that they, like the charters, are due ultimately
to the church's influence. In very general terms, this is true; but it is
important to remember that this connection must not be exaggerated.
The eagerness of converts to endow the clergy of the new religion
certainly induced them to seek for testamentary machinery, but it seems
quite clear that they did not in fact import that machinery from abroad.
They could have done so if they had wished, for the testament in its
Roman form was still common down to the ninth century on the continent.
Instead, we see the Anglo-Saxons experimenting with institutions already
familiar to them, such as the contract, the grant of a reversion, and the
post obit gift. Even then, these native forms take a somewhat peculiar
twist, for, as we have seen, they insist upon their oral origin; their very
name, *cwide*, is a warning that whatever forms may clothe them, it is an
oral institution which lies beneath. Hence there is a great deal to be
said for the view that the Anglo-Saxon will was the outcome of the
novissima verba, nihsta cwide, the last will or words.

A Germanic origin has been suggested. Even in pagan times it was
apparently a custom for a decedent's widow to take one-third, his children

---

[1] Whitelock, 2–3, is an example.

another third, and his soul the remaining third of his goods. The " soul's part " seems to have been either burnt or buried with him for use in the after-world.[1] With the advent of Christianity this practice took a new significance. The old " soul's part " was already free from family claims and in the absolute disposition of the owner; it was natural that the church should recommend the dying Christian to devote this share to works of piety and charity, and that the church should attach special sanctity to the " last words " in which the dispositions were declared. It has been conjectured that such a gift was in fact complete in many cases—the goods were handed over then and there. From this simple beginning, the Anglo-Saxon will developed, first, by the testator stating while in health what he considered his last words should be, and secondly, by disposing of property which originally was not subject to testamentary disposition, notably land; for this latter purpose the *cwide*, like the *landboc*, needed royal approbation.

WILLS IN THE NORMAN PERIOD

It is plausible to suppose that the purely oral *novissima verba* served the purpose of ordinary folk, while the magnate would seek royal permission to use the written *cwide*. The effect of the conquest seems to have been the rapid disappearance of the written will. At first sight it would seem that the conquest had produced a drastic legal change, and that in some way the devise of land was abolished. The fact that it also disappeared in Normandy raises the tempting thought that there might be something peculiarly Norman in this rule. In point of fact, however, the indevisability of land was not an established rule in Normandy until some centuries after its establishment in England.[2]

The English situation is therefore independent of the Norman and must be the outcome of local conditions in England. The principal factors seem to have been these: in the first place, the will of lands was never a matter of common practice under the Anglo-Saxon reigns. It was an exceptional privilege which the crown could grant or withhold; nor need we suppose that it was greatly sought after by the generality of people, for it defeated the expectations of heirs in an age when freedom of alienation was directly contrary to prevailing sentiment. If the Conqueror declined to enforce wills for the future, very few persons would be disappointed, and probably a great many would be thankful. This feeling is clearly apparent in the deep suspicion which the common law felt over the death-bed gift of land. Secondly, the Conqueror himself must have seen the problem from a different angle. The year 1066 was the beginning, not the end, of the conquest; for twenty years the success

[1] Some historians see in the " soul's part " the first appearance of strictly individual property. Cf. E. F. Bruck, *Kirchlich-sociales Erbrecht in Byzanz*, Studi in onore di Salvatore Riccobono, iii. 377 ff.

[2] Génestal, *L'Interdiction du legs d'immeuble* (Semaine de droit normand, XIV), [1928] Revue historique de droit français.

of the great adventure hung in the balance.[1]　The main preoccupation of William's reign was to keep his faithful followers on a war-footing.　His concern was knight-service, and the moulding of feudal institutions to suit his purpose.　There could never have been any thought of the devisability of military land in his day—indeed, his tenants were none too sure that even their sons would succeed them.　A sharp struggle eventually ended by the crown acknowledging the heritability of military fiefs, and much later, their free alienability; but it was too late to entertain thoughts of their devisability, for the memory of the time when they were merely precarious life interests was too recent.[2]

As for the devisability of non-military land, we have already suggested that few people could ever have aspired to the royal privilege of making a will, and many of the great Saxon houses were ruined by the conquest. When, in the twelfth century, the common law was imposed upon all land of free tenure, the indevisability of military fees was extended to the whole country.　After the conquest a feudal lord might occasionally permit his tenant to make a *post obit* gift (as he might also acquiesce in an alienation *inter vivos*), and on rare occasions a favoured magnate might make a devise of land in the presence of the king—but even then the devisee had to pay the crown a heavy price to get possession.[3]　When we get to Glanvill, even such exceptional attempts to grant *post obit* are now formally invalidated, and it was laid down as a rule of law that land is not devisable.[4]　In Bracton's day hope seemed to come from gifts " to *A.*, his heirs, assigns or legatees ", but Bracton's own words show his doubts whether legatees could ever acquire land by such a gift.[5]　Glanvill's discussion[6] is directed not against wills of land generally, nor even against *post obit* gifts, but against death-bed gifts.　His argument is that the grantor is not in a condition to deal wisely with his property, and that such a gift cannot stand unless confirmed by the heir.　It is soon clear, moreover, that the old *post obit* gift is no longer effective.　The king ceased to lend his authority to the act, and without it there is the insuperable difficulty of seisin: such a gift between subjects cannot take effect (and, particularly, cannot be known to a jury) unless there has been a real change of seisin.　Hence the nearest possible equivalent was to enfeoff the beneficiary, who would then give back a life estate—and all that was necessarily a transaction *inter vivos* far removed from any form of testament.

[1] This point is well made by D. C. Douglas, *The Norman Conquest and English Feudalism*, Economic History Review, ix. 128.

[2] The charter of Henry I, c. 7, of 1100 accords freedom of testation of chattels only; so it would seem that land was already indevisable by that date.

[3] Eudo the Dapifer is an example, Pollock and Maitland, ii. 327.

[4] A chronicler alleges a decree of about 1189 by Geoffrey Fitz Peter, instigated by the servants of Satan; *ibid.*

[5] Maitland, *Bracton's Note Book*, i. 36.　For a case of 1252, showing that the device could have a limited effectiveness, see the *Casus et Judicia* printed in *Casus Placitorum* (Selden Society), lxxvii no. 22.　Cf. above, p. 722.

[6] Glanvill, VII, 1.

DEVISABLE BURGAGES

There remains the problem of the boroughs where land was devisable by custom. Although this came to be the most striking feature of burgage tenure, its history has never been investigated, and its origin is unknown. Some historians place great emphasis upon Norman influence over English municipal history; but in Normandy burgages were never devisable.[1] The much more probable alternative is that borough law was in general a survival of older law which had not been submerged by the common law; but this will not explain the devisable burgage unless we assume that devise of land was common and widespread in the Anglo-Saxon period. Of that there is no evidence. Moreover, even in England devisability was not equally allowed in all boroughs.[2] The tentative suggestion may be made that the devisability of burgages was not in fact so very old, and that it may have been due to the late twelfth-century[3] revival of the testament (of which we shall speak later). Boroughs were much concerned with mercantile law, which in turn was much influenced by the church and the canonists. In the thirteenth century the common law courts were content to let the boroughs develop all sorts of curious rules about land without any hindrance, and devisability may have been among them.

The church's growing jurisdiction over testamentary chattels, led some people to describe devisable burgages as " chattels ",[4] and in at least one case an attempt was made to enlist the aid of the church in devising land (which apparently was not in truth devisable) by litigating in the church court about a legacy of money which was in reality its market value.[5] The general rule of the indevisability of land may well be part of the policy to exclude the church from any sort of jurisdiction whatever over " lay fee ".[6]

THE RISE OF THE EXECUTOR

The renascence of Roman law studies in the twelfth century brought with it the re-discovery of the Roman testament; this, combined with the institution of the executor, produced the later mediaeval English will.

The early history of the executor passes on the continent, and is of particular interest. It was not a Roman institution, but the product of

---

[1] Tait, *The Medieval English Borough*, 111.

[2] Newcastle upon Tyne is an example; Sayles, *King's Bench*, ii. 52. Here and in some other towns only purchases were devisable. Cf. Hemmeon, *Burgage Tenure*, 135, and Y.B. 20 & 21 Edward I (Rolls Series), 264 (1292). Bracton is confused on the subject; Pollock and Maitland, ii. 330.

[3] The ambiguous passage in Pollock and Maitland, ii. 330, line 4, must not be read as meaning that Glanvill mentions the devisability of burgages (as Hemmeon, 130).

[4] *Eyre Rolls* (Selden Society, vol. lix), no. 290 (1221).

[5] Flower, *Introduction to Curia Regis Rolls* (Selden Society), 110–111.

[6] The question arises not only in testamentary but also in matrimonial causes. Here again the church was excluded, and the common law courts developed their own writ of entry *causa matrimonii prelocuti*. Even jurisdiction over the *maritagium* had once been claimed by the church.

typically mediaeval conditions which produced similar institutions both in Byzantine and Mohammedan law. The old soul's part, as we have seen, became the portion which the church encouraged her subjects to bequeath by their *novissima verba*. Such gifts were generally of a charitable nature, and it was necessary to have an intermediary, partly to choose and supervise the charity, and partly in order to deal legally with the property. These earlier bequests seem to have been given at the very moment when they were made by the testator to a third party, who then carried out the will after the testator's death. Such a third party is described by many different names, according as one or another aspect of his functions is emphasised. Thus he may be called an " almoner " because it is he who distributes the alms; or a *vadiator* because he is at first appointed by pledge; the words *salman* and *treuhand* take us back to the old three-party contract already mentioned;[1] *tutor* seems a rough parallel to our own Anglo-Saxon *mund* with its connotations of protection and guardianship. Like the much later (and unrelated) feoffee to uses in England, these persons were fiduciaries with moral duties to carry out the deceased's wishes, but they were also legal owners. Another fact which made the appointment of some sort of executor necessary was the fear of the heir, who, according to common experience, was the person least likely to dissipate the fortune in charity. Failure to appoint an executor might thus mean in practice that the dispositions of the testator would be ineffectual, unless the church was powerful enough to coerce the heir by spiritual censures. The church therefore insisted that failure to appoint an executor who was able and willing to act was almost equivalent to intestacy.

The executor was therefore of the highest importance throughout the middle ages, and his position steadily grew. He became the representative of the deceased, paid his debts and enforced his actions. In England the victory of the executor over the heir proved to be permanent, but on the continent a new wave of Romanism in the sixteenth and following centuries gradually reduced his importance.

This institution was attached to the revived testament. The study of Roman law at last convinced the lawyers of the twelfth and thirteenth centuries that there could be a testament which was merely a unilateral document, neither contract nor grant, which was revocable, and which disposed of property without the necessity of the testator handing it over in his lifetime. The word " heir " had already been appropriated to a very different sense, and so the attributes of the Roman *haeres* were transferred, as far as they were applicable, to the executor. The executor thus became the channel through which the property devolved.

THE MEDIAEVAL ENGLISH WILL

From the thirteenth century onwards, the history of testation in England is the history of the reception of the new concepts of the will

[1] Above, pp. 629–630.

and the executor which reached us no doubt through ecclesiastical channels. The Norman period, as we have seen, made an end of the old written *cwide* and its protector the *mund*. There survived, of course, the *novissima verba* which the priest (prudently accompanied by one or two laymen) received. Just as the end of the twelfth century is the period when we find the revival of the written charter of land, so at the same moment we find once again the written will—not the old *cwide*, however, but the newly imported testament with its accompanying executors.

The form and contents of the typical mediaeval will in England can be seen from the numerous examples available in print[1] which throw light not only on the law but also on the manners, customs, mode of life, literary tastes and many other details of everyday life.

FORMAL REQUIREMENTS

In conformity with the general policy of canon law, the church was loth to insist upon formalities in wills, especially as technical defects would have the effect of producing intestacy. The nuncupative will was recognised, although not common among the upper classes of society. The written will might be in Latin, French or English. The higher clergy often had it drawn in notarial form, or at least attested by a notary, but this seems to have been in no way necessary. Signatures are, of course, very rare in the middle ages, and the usual mode of authentication was by the testator's seal, sometimes accompanied by the seals of the executors or witnesses. Although there were no necessary formal clauses, most wills run on the same lines—the testator bequeaths his soul to God and the saints, his body to a particular church; there follow details of the funeral arrangements (often very elaborate); in many places custom requires the bequest of the best beast as a mortuary (the mediaeval ghost was frequently seen astride the mortuary[2] which was a heavy charge upon small estates); there was often an express direction for the payment of debts, sometimes with provisions as to how this was to be done; long lists of chattels bestowed on friends and relatives, and sometimes attempts to prevent their alienation (Bankes, B., left his year books, acquired from Plessington, C.B., " to be kept for the use of his sons and of the longest living of them, and after their death, if they have no issue who can profit by the books, they are to be sold at the best price obtainable and the proceeds given to the poor "[3]); gifts of the residue of the estate

---

[1] *Testamenta Eboracensia*, and *Wills and Inventories from the Registry of Durham* (both in the Surtees Society); *Fifty English Wills* (Early English Text Society); Nicolas, *Testamenta Vetusta*; *Register of Henry Chichele*, vol. II (ed. E. F. Jacob), contains a valuable introduction. Cf. the general description of old wills in Pollock and Maitland, ii. 337 ff. There are some typical examples from various dates in Holdsworth, iii. 670

[2] James, *Medieval Ghost Stories*, English Historical Review, xxxvii. 413. If the lord took the best beast as heriot, the parson would have to be content with the second best as mortuary: Y.B. 21 & 22 Edward I (Rolls Series), 590 (1294).

[3] *Chichele's Register*, ii. 68 (1415); cf. Nicolas, *Testamenta Vetusta*, 553 (1517).

only become frequent in the fifteenth century, when they are commonly made to the executors with vague directions for their charitable disposal.

The Statute of Wills, 1540, merely required that a will of land should be " in writing ";[1] the Statute of Frauds, 1677, required as an essential form that a devise of lands be in writing, signed, and witnessed " by three or four credible witnesses ",[2] but the requirement of signing and witnessing of wills generally dates from 1837.[3] The word " credible " caused much trouble. By taking as a model the common law rules about witnesses, it was at once apparent that a person interested in the subject-matter could not be a witness; from this it followed that if a witness to a will devising land was a beneficiary under it, then he was not a " credible " witness, since he could not give his evidence in a court, with the result that (unless there was a sufficient number of other witnesses who were qualified) the will was void under the Statute of Frauds.[4] This disastrous conclusion was remedied in 1752 when it was enacted that a legatee could be a witness, but that the legacy to him should be void.[5]

PROBATE JURISDICTION

The jurisdiction of the church over testamentary matters was more extensive in England than in other countries, and indeed exceeded the claims made by the church herself. Those claims were naturally to supervise the pious purposes which testators might indicate in their wills, but in the twelfth century the royal courts were still to be reckoned with— both the Anglo-Saxon *cwide* and the few Anglo-Norman wills looked to the king or a great lord for their enforcement. Thus Glanvill states in one place that there is a writ *precipe quod facias stare* ordering the sheriff to cause the reasonable division of the testator's goods to be carried out; but if the will is disputed, then the plea must go to the court christian, for " a testamentary plea ought to be before the ecclesiastical judge ".[6] Just half a century after Glanvill, a legatee was told by the king's court to sue in court christian.[7] Quietly and without a struggle, therefore, the common law had abandoned to the church an important part of its jurisdiction over testamentary matters.

This right to decide upon a disputed will if the question was brought before the ecclesiastical court, seems to have given rise to the further right to require the production and proof of the will as a matter of course as soon as the testator dies. This jurisdiction first appears in the early thirteenth century, and its origin is a very obscure problem of continental legal history.

[1] 32 Henry VIII, c. 1.
[2] 29 Charles II, c. 3.
[3] 7 William IV & 1 Victoria, c. 26.
[4] *Hilliard* v. *Jennings* (1700) Comyns, 91; 1 Ld. Raym. 505.
[5] 25 Geo. II, c. 6.
[6] Glanvill, vii. 6, 7; xii. 17.
[7] *Bracton's Note Book*, no. 381 (1230).

The jurisdiction was pre-eminently that of the bishop of the diocese, as " ordinary ", but during the middle ages many dignitaries acquired " ordinary " jurisdiction besides bishops, and so we find numerous deans, chapters, prebendaries, archdeacons and others who had probate jurisdiction.   Quite a number of lords of manors also exercised it, but until the local history of each jurisdiction has been investigated it is impossible to say whether this is a relic of a very old manorial jurisdiction, or merely the result of privileged ecclesiastical estates passing into lay hands (generally at the Reformation).[1]   The territory even of a bishop was comparatively small, however, and after a long struggle the archbishop of Canterbury established his " prerogative " to grant probate when there were " notable goods " in more than one diocese; the wills of the well-to-do are therefore to be sought in the registers of the prerogative court of Canterbury.   Much of the church's testamentary jurisdiction fell into desuetude at the Reformation, largely as a result of the persistent attacks of the common law courts; probate, however, remained until the erection of the new and lay Court of Probate[2] in 1857.

THE COMMON LAW AND EXECUTORS

We have already remarked upon the special emphasis placed upon inheritance in the common law system.   At first it was only the right to land which passed to the heir, but by Bracton's day the heir is liable for the ancestor's debts and can also enforce his credits—the common lawyers seem to have thought of making the heir a personal representative, at least for some purposes.   Meanwhile, the church courts were busy equating the executor with the Roman *haeres*; consequently the heir was representative at common law, and the executors in ecclesiastical law. This confused situation was cleared up under Edward I, when the common law courts allowed executors to sue and be sued, and relieved the heir of the representation unless it was specially cast upon him by his ancestor's deed.[3]   Executors did not easily fit in with common law procedure, however.   For a generation they took advantage of the common law rule requiring all defendants in an action of debt to be present together, until " fourcher " between executors was abolished;[4] for centuries they escaped liability on their testator's simple contract debts, because they could not wage law in his name.[5]   Indeed, if they did pay such a debt, it would be considered as a *devastaverunt*.[6]   Another

---

[1] Compare Pollock and Maitland, ii. 341, with Holdsworth, i. 625.

[2] 20 & 21 Victoria, c. 77.

[3] Above, p. 377.

[4] Above, pp. 647 n. 3, 377 n. 6.

[5] 9 Edw. III, stat. 1, c. 3 (1335).

[6] Y.B. 20 Henry VII, Michs. no. 5 (1504).   Eventually, however, the exchequer of pleas would compel executors to answer.

statute continued the representation by the executors of a deceased executor.[1]

The common law courts seem to have borrowed some of their law from the church[2]—the right of retainer is an example, apparently accepted as early as 1346, but not settled beyond dispute until the fifteenth century.[3] On the other hand, there was much argument whether the debt of an executor to the testator was extinguished;[4] this time theory was satisfied by denying that it was actionable, and practical necessity was recognised by regarding such a debt as assets.[5] A similar compromise is seen in the form of judgment against executors. Normally it recognised their representative character by going against the goods of the testator, but occasions were multiplied when judgment went against the executors personally on grounds of misconduct or even of fairly slight procedural faults. The result was that the common law placed a heavy burden on executors which nineteenth-century legislation has lightened somewhat.

ECCLESIASTICAL COURTS AND CHANCERY

There remained to the church a large body of law in spite of the encroachments of the common law actions of debt, detinue, account and *assumpsit*. Besides all the questions of validity of the will, and matters arising out of legacies, the church at one time exercised a strict supervision over executors, calling for accounts, examining them, and directing the work of administration generally. Such a jurisdiction was never popular in the middle ages, and there was some talk of indicting ordinaries for the " extortion " of high fees.[6] The common law courts, as a result of attacks by prohibition, soon succeeded in crippling the church's work, but without providing an equivalent remedy themselves. Early in the fifteenth century, however, chancery already competed with the church courts,[7] and as time went on the necessity for chancery's intervention became abundantly clear. Particularly in the sixteenth and seventeenth centuries, the inadequacy for all practical purposes of the ecclesiastical courts drove litigants into chancery. Thus, an ordinary could only

---

[1] 25 Edw. III, stat. 5, c. 5 (1352); this had already been established by case law, Y.B. 11 & 12 Edward III, 186 (1337), Y.B. 13 & 14 Edward III, 328 (1340), the object of the statute being merely to remove doubts and to state the position in more general terms.

[2] See Holdsworth, iii. 585 ff.

[3] Y.B. 20 Edward III, ii. 422 (1346); details in Holdsworth, iii. 588. See *Woodward* v. *Lord Darcy* (1557), Plowd. 184, where the point was discussed at length.

[4] Y.B. 11 Richard II, 187, Y.B. 12 Richard II, 1 (1388); Holdsworth, iii. 589. For the suggestion that a common law account was sometimes preferable to the canonical remedy, see Y.B. 12 & 13 Edward III (Rolls Series), 82–84.

[5] For the equitable extension of the doctrine in the seventeenth century, see Spence, *Equitable Jurisdiction*, i. 584.

[6] 25 Edw. III, stat. 6, c. 9 (1352).

[7] For an interesting example, see *Select Cases in Chancery*, no. 140 (1456); the petitioner's case against a bishop's executors rested on the common clause in the will directing them to compensate those whom the testator had wronged—seemingly a very " spiritual" matter.

accept an executor's account as presented, nor could a creditor question the account in a church court. The same seems to have been true of an inventory. The executor's bond, like the administrator's, was a nullity since the common lawyers held that by the grant of administration the ordinary lost all his interest in the goods—and the bond was the only practical means of coercion which the church courts could use. It will not be surprising that in the course of the conflict some useful things were lost (progress is not inevitable). A particularly striking example is the fact that in the time of Edward I it was possible to advertise for creditors and to announce that claims not lodged within six weeks would fail, unless good cause for the delay was shown.[1]

Legacies were slower to appear in chancery litigation. It has been conjectured that the earliest examples were where legatees were compelled to give security to refund if further debts should be discovered,[2] and where chancery took steps to protect the legacies of married women from their husbands—sometimes restraining the husband from suing for them in the ecclesiastical courts until he had made a suitable settlement. The church courts had adopted many Roman principles relating to legacies, and chancery in turn developed its law of legacies upon Roman lines, having practically superseded the church's jurisdiction in the matter by the time of Charles I.[3]

THE FAMILY RESERVE

In introducing the topic of succession, we observed that one possible approach would be to regard the law as the expression of the family in terms of property. If we adopt that point of view for a moment, we shall be led to some interesting conclusions. Down to the rise of the common law, the ancient custom of the land certainly did reflect the structure of the family: the equal inheritance of sons, the wife's dower, the husband's curtesy and the *maritagium* of daughters all combined to make a secure economic basis for family life. With the opening of the thirteenth century, however, no English family could rely upon the operation of law to secure the equitable treatment of all its members. Primogeniture upset everything. It is true that freedom of alienation accompanied it and gave landowners the power to make their own dispositions, and that most of them no doubt used those powers reasonably; but nevertheless it is obvious that the law henceforth disclaimed any responsibility for seeing that those dispositions were equitable. The rise of the use was certainly prompted in a large measure by the desire of settlors to exercise a wider discretion in making provision for

[1] Pollock and Maitland, ii. 343.

[2] Alternatively, " it may be that the cases in which the Chancery first interfered were cases in which the legatee was not a mere legatee but was also a *cestui que trust* ": Maitland, *Equity*, 193.

[3] Valuable references to printed and unprinted sources in support of the above summary are collected in Spence, *Equitable Jurisdiction*, i. 578 ff.

their families than was possible at common law, and since the Statute of Wills, 1540, most landowners had the absolute disposition of their estates in their hands.   Henceforth little was left to the operation of law.   The general scheme of a seventeenth-century settlement with recurring re-settlements as occasion arose left little place for inheritance, dower and all the old machinery of the law.   All those safeguards of the family which occur on the continent—the community, the inalienable family reserve, the *retrait lignager* and similar institutions are conspicuously absent.[1]   In the boroughs alone do we find devices of this sort.

The law of succession to chattels for a time ran along different lines and retained for a while the ancient tripartite division, the theory being that the testator disposed only of the dead man's part.[2]   The scheme must be old, but difficulties arose when it became necessary to determine its place in the new common law.   An extraordinary situation arose, for the king's court would not whole-heartedly accept the principle of " legitim ".   Nevertheless, the public seems to have been convinced that it was universal throughout the land.   They brought actions alleging " the custom of the realm " and were generally told that there may be local customs, but there is no custom of the realm save common law.[3] So it gradually became clear that if a custom is pleaded, it must be a local custom, and cases of detinue *de rationabili parte* against the executors of a testator who had transgressed the principle of legitim occasionally occur.[4]   An alternative was to base the action upon the Great Charter,[5] but here too there were difficulties of statutory construction.[6]   These difficulties were purely technical, but they show that the common law courts were not sympathetic to legitim as a principle.[7]

Eventually, as we have seen, the church assumed control over executors, and so it is likely that claims against them for legitim would have come most frequently before the church courts.   A provincial con-stitution of 1342 certainly condemned testators who made insufficient provision for wife and children,[8] which suggests that the rule was weaken-ing.   That impression is confirmed by a case of 1366 where the defence to an action of *rationabili parte* admitted the action but pleaded that the

---

[1] The Norman scheme can be studied in (1923) Travaux de la Semaine d'histoire du droit normand (Astoul, *Les Propres de mariage*; Bridrey, *La Réserve héréditaire*; Génestal, *Le Retrait lignager*).

[2] Glanvill, vii. 5.   So too Bracton and *Fleta*.

[3] 3 Y.B. 17 Edward II, f. 536 (1324); Y.B. 40 Edward III, Michs. 12 (1366); the writ on " the custom of the realm " against those in common callings is anomalous.

[4] To the list in Pollock and Maitland, ii. 351 n. 4, may be added Y.B. 13 Richard II (Ames Foundation), 9 (1389).

[5] Great Charter (1225), c. 18.

[6] Bereford, C.J., was firmly for free testation, and restricted the Charter to " *propres* ": Y.B. 17 Edward II, f. 536 (1324).

[7] The classical Romanists, on the other hand, were sympathetic to rules which they associated with " nature ".   Jean de Laplanche, *La " Soutenance " on " Pourvéance " dans le droit coutumier français*, 5.

[8] Wilkins, *Concilia*, II, 706.

plaintiff had been advanced, the court, however, remarking " how can we give judgment when you have admitted an action which is against the law? " Mowbray, J., even stated that " the lords in parliament will not admit that this action is maintainable by any common custom or by the law of this realm ".[1]

For practical purposes the preservation of legitim, therefore, rested upon the firmness of the ecclesiastical courts, and at some time before Elizabeth's reign the provinces of Canterbury and York drifted apart. Legitim was retained throughout the northern province; in the southern it survived only in some local customs. It is very difficult to account for this radical change of law upon so important a subject.[2] The survival of restrictions upon testation in the boroughs is natural enough, and the disappearance of them among the landed class is not surprising, for landowners would naturally want to treat their family arrangements as a whole. Neither consideration, however, explains the survival of the restrictions in the province of York.

Soon after the Revolution these remaining survivals were removed by statute. In 1692 the inhabitants of the northern province (except citizens of York and Chester) were given freedom of testation because the widow could claim her reasonable part even although she had a jointure; this necessarily reduced the provision that could be made for children.[3] That seems a good reason for excepting the classes who habitually made jointures from the operation of the old rules. Similar reasons were given for abolishing the old rule in Wales, but this time with a saving of the rights of women then married and children then in existence—a considerable delay which was not accorded to the northern province.[4] It would seem that the Welsh were not so very eager for the change. The city of York procured legislation giving them immediate freedom of testation (for reasons unstated),[5] and later still a repeal of the rule was very curiously interjected into an act regulating elections in London, since persons of ability and substance were discouraged from becoming freemen.[6] As far as this legislation is concerned, it seems clear that the objections to the old rule were that it obstructed the making of settlements in the form usually employed by the landed classes: but, as so often happened in our legal history, it was the law of the wealthy which became the common law of the land.

Freedom of testation could work little harm where the bulk of the family's resources consisted of settled land: in other circumstances it might sometimes produce bizarre results. In the eighteenth century some testators (or their solicitors) seem to have thought that a will

---

[1] Y.B. 40 Edward III, Michs. 12.

[2] See the remarks in Holdsworth, iii. 554.

[3] 4 William & Mary, c. 2.

[4] 7 & 8 William III, c. 38 (1696).

[5] 2 & 3 Anne, c. 5 (1704).

[6] 11 George I, c. 18 (1724).

making no provision for wife or children was in peril of being upset as a *testamentum inofficiosum*, and so " cut off with a shilling " the unfortunate relatives they disliked. We seem never to have had any formal doctrine of inofficious wills, and so this " vulgar error ", as Blackstone calls it,[1] is all the more curious. Subterfuges there were, for a harsh law always invites evasion by litigants and by sympathetic courts, but theory remained untouched: a testator who is competent to make a will at all, is competent to make it as inofficious as he likes.

That state of affairs was at variance with the legal sense of most countries—even common law countries, and at length the legislature has intervened.[2] It did not revive legitim (although the ancient tripartite division does appear in the Act); nor does it introduce the Roman learning of inofficious wills, or the lists of reasons preserved in some continental customs which justify disinheritance (although the court is directed to consider the reasons where the testator has expressed them). Nor in general does the Act authorise more than maintenance grants, and then only in a few carefully restricted cases. Extremely timid as the new Act is, there can be no denial that it reverses the attitude adopted just over two centuries ago, and that once more it recognises the family as being of paramount importance in the law of succession.

[1] 2 Blackstone, Comm., 503.

[2] See the comments of J. Unger, *The Inheritance Act and the Family*, 6 Modern Law Review 215; 1 & 2 Geo. VI, c. 45, Inheritance (Family Provision) Act, 1938.

INDEX

A

[1]

K

L

S